The Cambridge Edition of the Poets

SPENSER

EDITED BY

R. E. NEIL DODGE

The Cambridge Poets

The
Complete Poetical Works
of
SPENSER

Buckingham Palace

HOUGHTON MIFFLIN COMPANY BOSTON

Cambridge Edition

The Riverside Press Cambridge

The Riverside Press

CAMBRIDGE · MASSACHUSETTS

PRINTED IN THE U.S.A.

PREFACE

THE text of Spenser given in this volume is the result of a double collation. First, the copy to be sent to the printer was collated throughout with the original editions in the British Museum; then the proof-sheets of the greater part, as they came from the press, were collated with other copies of the same editions obtained in this country. The *Faery Queen* (except for a few pages), *Complaints*, *Colin Clout's Come Home Again*, *Astrophel*, and the *Four Hymns* were thus collated a second time, and, in effect, the *Shepherd's Calendar*, too, though, for that, recourse was had not to the original itself, but to the photographic facsimile of Dr. Sommer. *Daphnaïda*, the *Amoretti and Epithalamion*, the *Prothalamion*, the four *Commendatory Sonnets*, and the matter in the Appendix could not be collated twice, because copies of the original editions were not in this country accessible.

For most of these separate volumes or single pieces there could be no dispute about the text to be adopted as standard, for they were published but once during the poet's lifetime, and the collected folios of 1609 and 1611, issued ten years after his death, could pretend to no superior authoritativeness. For them the standard text was manifestly that of the first edition. Three, however, were published during his lifetime more than once: the *Shepherd's Calendar* in 1579, 1581, 1586, 1591, and 1597; *Daphnaïda* in 1591 and 1596; the first three books of the *Faery Queen* in 1590 and 1596. Concerning these there might be doubt. As to the *Shepherd's Calendar*, whoever will study the long list of variants of all kinds in the successive editions of that volume will probably note (1) that the first edition contains several perfectly obvious misprints or blunders corrected in the later; (2) that of those changes in the later editions which are not the mere correction of obvious blunders in the first, a considerable proportion are changes which mar the style; (3) that most others are changes which are neither for the better nor for the worse, which are mere changes; (4) that not more than one or two could fairly be called improvements. A poet, for instance, who has written

'Up, then, Melpomene ! thou mournefulst Muse of nyne !'

does not deliberately change *thou* to *the ;* and if a poet has written of Abel

'So lowted he unto his Lord,
Such favour couth he fynd,
That sithens never was abhord
The simple shepheards kynd,'

he does not take the trouble to change *sithens never* to *never sithens*. When one notes, too, that these changes are mostly such as might result from careless reading of copy, and that those which cannot be misreadings merely reduce archaic irregularities to the level of academic evenness, one inclines to attribute them to the printer. When one notes, finally, that the first edition contains fewer obvious blunders and misprints than the later, these later will hardly seem more trustworthy. The same is true of *Daphnaïda :* the two or three changes found in the second edition by no means bear the mark of authenticity. If, indeed, we had any fair reason to suppose that Spenser, like Ronsard and Tasso, was given to the revision of his work, that after he had once completed a poem and seen it in print, he would study it anew with an eye to perfecting it in detail, we might give more credit to the variants of these later editions. Such revision as we know him to have undertaken, however, was confined to bringing unpublished manuscript, as the phrase goes, 'up to date,' for printing. We have no reason to suppose that, if the printed poem were reissued, he at all concerned himself with revision of its text. For the *Shepherd's Calendar* and *Daphnaïda*, therefore, the text adopted is in each case that of the first edition.

For the first three books of the *Faery Queen* the problem is somewhat different. Since these were not an independent poem, but merely the first installment of his *magnum opus*, Spenser found occasion, when he republished them in 1596 along with the first issue of the second three books, to make certain changes. He altered the original conclusion of Book III, that it might lead up more directly to Book IV. Certain inconsistencies of detail having perhaps been pointed out to him, he got rid of them with as little effort as might suffice — somewhat clumsily. He rewrote a line or two which did not please him. In one place he inserted a new stanza. These changes, not more than a dozen or so in all, are unmistakably his work. Unfortunately, there are many others in this second edition which resemble only too closely the variants in later editions of the *Shepherd's Calendar*. They bear every mark, that is, of being mere blunders of the printer due to hasty reading of copy: they do not spoil the sense, but they are too trivial and purposeless to be ascribed to the poet himself; sometimes they spoil the poetry. Under these circumstances the problem of the editor was not simple. He could not follow the first edition and ignore the authentic changes of the poet; nor did he wish to follow the second into all the changes that were mere printer's blunders; nor, of course, was there any certain test by which the changes of the poet might be distinguished from those of the printer. In the end, it seemed best to adopt the readings of the second edition as generally authoritative, but occasionally to retain those of the first when they were beyond fair question more characteristic, when, that is, one could not believe that Spenser would deliberately change from the earlier to the later.

It is not only in verbal readings, however, that the two editions differ; they differ also in spelling. The spelling of 1590 is somewhat like that of the *Shepherd's Calendar*, markedly archaic; that of 1596 is like that of the second three books of the poem, published at the same time, very much more modern. The difference extends to the forms of words: *hether* usually becomes *hither; lenger, longer; then, than,* etc. Now, it may be that the poet, having adopted for his second three books more modern spelling, and, in some cases, more modern forms of words, authorized his printer to reprint the first books in that style. Nobody who knows his work will for one minute suppose that he went through the first books himself and made all the changes necessary, together with hundreds of others absolutely unnecessary — for a good quarter of the differences in spelling are altogether without significance. In any case, the first edition of these books is printed much more correctly than the second; it represents a definite stage in Spenser's spelling and use of archaic word-forms; and there appears to be no compelling reason why, when an editor adopts the changes in phrasing, not more than two or three to the canto, which appear in the later edition, he should also adopt extensive changes in spelling which are of altogether doubtful authenticity and which serve no other purpose than to give a kind of external uniformity of appearance to the first and the second three books. The spelling of 1590 has therefore been retained.

The cantos on Mutability first appeared in the folio of 1609. In general, however, that and the folio of 1611 do no more than emend for the first time (without known authority) certain readings of the earlier texts which are untenable. Some of these emendations have been adopted — for want of better. Another set, adopted or suggested at random by various modern editors, calls for particular notice. Here and there in the *Faery Queen*, in perhaps twenty cases, the system of the stanza is shattered by an impossible rhyme, by a rhyme-word which does not even make assonance with its fellows. In some instances the blunder is beyond all correction; in most the correction lies open to every eye. *Play* is set down where the rhyme calls for *sport; enclose* where the rhyme calls for *contain, spyde* for *saw, place* for *stead*, etc. Some editors have treated these cases capriciously, now correcting, now leaving uncorrected; some have systematically refrained from correction, on the ground that the carelessness was probably of the poet's own commission. And so it may have been: in copying his manuscript fair he may have set down one word for another of the same meaning, or if he worked his stanza out in his mind before committing it to paper, he may have blundered in the mere writing. To maintain, however, that when he set down *play* as a rhyme to *support, resort, port*, he did not really intend to set down *sport*, is to credit him with singular obtuseness, and to print *play*, when there is at least an even chance that the blunder was the printer's, is surely to push fidelity to one's text beyond the bounds of reason. In these cases, therefore, the word demanded by rhyme and declared by sense is in this edition unhesitatingly adopted. All such emendations, and others, are noted, of course, in the List of Rejected Readings.

For the spelling, it is that of the original texts, but with three modifications: (1) the old use of capitals is made to conform to modern practice; (2) contractions are commonly expanded (e. g. *Lo.* to *Lord*); and (3) in some few cases, when the old division of words might puzzle the reader, it is disregarded — e. g. *for thy* (therefore) is uniformly printed *forthy*. The punctuation is modernized — with care not to falsify the sense.

The Glossary was built up on the principle of recording all words and phrases which in modern poetry would be obsolete or markedly archaic. Later, some of this material was transferred to the Notes. The scheme of division is that all words obsolete in form will be found in the Glossary, and such words, modern in form but obsolete in sense, as are of frequent occurrence. Rarer examples of modern words in obsolete senses will be found in the Notes, with due machinery of cross references. It is hoped that without much difficulty the 'general reader' may be able to acquaint himself with the exact meaning of any word or phrase which puzzles him. If he is annoyed by the inclusion of much that he could understand unaided, he is begged to remember that one purpose of Notes and Glossary is to furnish an approximately complete list of Spenser archaisms.

The debt of the editor of any classic to his predecessors must necessarily be great. That of the present editor was too great to be acknowledged in detail. To indicate in the Notes and elsewhere the source of every explanation or idea would have been to load them with the names of most who have labored in this field: all that could be done was to mark direct quotations. For some of the matter here offered for the first time he is furthermore indebted to various learned colleagues and friends, who helped him to what he could not find unaided; to others he owes much in the way of criticism and direct assistance. His thanks are particularly due to the Principal Librarian of the British Museum and to the Librarian of Harvard College for the use of those early editions of Spenser without which he could never have undertaken the most important part of his work.

R. E. N. D.

MADISON, WISCONSIN, March 1, 1908.

TABLE OF CONTENTS

BIOGRAPHICAL SKETCH

WHEN we read, toward the close of *Hesperides*,

> 'A wearied pilgrim, I have wandered here
> Twice five-and-twenty, bate me but one year,'

we are sure that at the time of so writing Robert Herrick was forty-nine years old. If we could put equal trust in the similar record of sonnet LX of the *Amoretti*, we should know the exact year of the birth of Edmund Spenser, for beyond reasonable doubt that sonnet dates from the closing months of 1593. The record is, that

> 'since the winged god his planet cleare
> Began in me to move, one yeare is spent:
> The which doth longer unto me appeare,
> Then al those fourty which my life outwent.'

In prose: it is now a year since I fell in love; that twelvemonth seems longer to me than all the forty of my previous life. To deduct 41 from 1593 is to get 1552, which has accordingly found general acceptance as the poet's birth-year, and indeed is not in any respect improbable. One need only note that 'al those fourty' is a phrase somewhat too conveniently round to inspire confidence, that it might serve equally well for thirty-nine or forty-one, and thereby spoil the foregoing calculation.

The place of his birth is recorded in the classic passage of the *Prothalamion*: —

> 'At length they all to mery London came,
> To mery London, my most kyndly nurse,
> That to me gave this lifes first native sourse;
> Though from another place I take my name,
> An house of auncient fame.'

That is, though he was born, and presumably bred, in the capital, his paternal forbears were not Londoners. What was their native seat he nowhere tells us, but his most assiduous biographer, Dr. Grosart, has collected sufficient evidence to place them in eastern Lancashire, where, among many families of the name, were the Spensers of Hurstwood, lesser gentry of that region. These might well enough stand for the 'house of auncient fame.' It is likely, though, that this phrase includes a more distinguished family, the Spencers of Althorpe, with whom the poet frequently claims kinship. To the three daughters of that house are dedicated 'The Tears of the Muses,' 'Mother Hubberd's Tale,' and 'Muiopotmos,' and they are the 'Phyllis, Charillis, and sweet Amaryllis' of *Colin Clout's Come Home Again*,

> 'the sisters three,
> The honor of the noble familie
> Of which I meanest boast my selfe to be,
> And most that unto them I am so nie.'

In any case, it is obvious that Spenser held himself to be of gentle birth. He never felt the need of establishing his gentility after the manner of Shakespeare.

That the name of his mother was Elizabeth [1] is all he tells us about either parent. We know, however, that his father most probably belonged to the guild of the Merchant

---

[1] See *Amoretti* LXXIV.

Tailors, and Dr. Grosart seeks to identify him with a John Spenser mentioned in the guild records, October, 1566, as 'a free journeyman' in the 'arte or mysterie of cloth-makynge.' Whoever he may have been, the poet's father was not well-to-do, for as late as the early months of 1569, the name of his son is entered among the 'poore scholers' in the 'scholls about London' who were presented with gowns from the estate of Robert Nowell; and in the accounts of the same fund, for the same year, is a second charitable item: '28 Aprill. To Edmond Spensore, scholler of the M'chante Tayler Schoole, at his gowinge to Penbrocke Hall in Chambridge, Xs.' At the university, too, in November, 1570, and in April, 1571, we find the poet still receiving aid from this fund.

Narrowness of means, however, did not harm the boy's education. The school of the Merchant Tailors, founded in 1560, was taught by Richard Mulcaster, and under his charge was becoming as good as any in London. Mulcaster, indeed, was in every way a remarkable teacher — a man of system, strict, even harsh, a believer in the educative powers of the rod, master, too, of wide and thorough learning. He certainly could train efficient scholars and men, and if he did not do well by Edmund Spenser, his pupil's later achievement does not declare the failure. It was while still under his training, that the youthful poet first appeared in print. The verse translations in Van der Noot's *Theatre* [1] cannot claim the dignity of an independent volume of juvenilia; they were quite possibly paid for at the classic rate of a penny a line; they cannot be said to bear witness to even the most ordinary knowledge of French; yet they do make evident that the boy's schooling, formal or informal, had brought him a very pretty command of his mother tongue and the faculty of turning out good verse to order.

On May 20, 1569, a short while before the *Theatre* was put on the market, Spenser matriculated at Pembroke Hall, Cambridge, as a sizar. There he remained for seven years. In January, 1573, he proceeded B. A., in June, 1576, he commenced M. A.; then, whether that a fellowship was denied him, or that he did not care for one, he left the university for good. His life there cannot have been always pleasant. As a sizar, or 'poor scholar,' his circumstances, if not painfully narrow, were at any rate far from easy. His health, too, was apparently uncertain, for at intervals we find his name on the sick list, once for seven weeks. On one occasion he seems to have been in trouble with the authorities for neglect of curriculum work or other such offence. That, in his own way, he nevertheless studied and read effectively is obvious from the varied learning which he later made manifest.

It was at Cambridge that Spenser first met Gabriel Harvey, the Hobbinol of his pastoral verse. Harvey was older than he by at least a year or two and much his senior in academic rank, for he came to Pembroke as fellow in November, 1570, when Spenser was still very far from his B. A. How early they became friends we cannot tell; it is sufficiently curious that they ever became friends at all. For Harvey was one of those exorbitantly superior people who make enemies right and left without knowing why, and, in spite of all that can be said for him, a 'ferocious pedant;' about the last man, one would think, to win the regard of Spenser. Yet he seems to have been kindly enough at bottom, and perhaps his serene self-conceit was offensive chiefly to the commonplace. As for his pedantry (which is nowadays being denied), one must bear in mind Spenser's own predilection for learning, which in those early years, before his genius had humanized his knowledge, may well have been somewhat undiscriminating. The course of their friendship was long. For a period, while Spenser was feeling his way to full self-possession, Harvey played the part of counsellor and guide, a part which found half-jesting,

[1] See Appendix I.

half-serious acceptance. Then, at about the time when their fundamental differences were becoming too seriously apparent, Spenser went to Ireland, and thereafter there could be no occasion for breach.

From Harvey's letters of 1573 we learn of a singular war at Pembroke. It was brought on, to his own wondering dismay, by Harvey himself, who, in the normal and unconscious exercise of his self-conceit, had contrived to exasperate some of his colleagues beyond all measure. When the time came for him to commence M. A., these men suddenly broke out, and for three months succeeded in blocking his path; then, having been discomfited, avenged themselves by shabby persecution. Nor did their enmity subside, for when, in 1578, his tenure of the fellowship expired, not even the influence of Leicester could secure its extension for a year. Such open animosities as these can hardly have failed to involve or affect Spenser. They and his supposed conflict with the authorities may serve to explain why, instead of taking a fellowship, the natural goal of such a career as his, he left the university on obtaining his second degree.

In any case, it was apparently not to a regular occupation that he retired, but to a sojourn of several months among his kinsfolk of eastern Lancashire. In that out-of-the-way and unpromising corner of the country there could of course be no settled career for a man of his gifts; there could at best be leisure for infinite verse-making, and, as auxiliary interest, leisure to fall in love. He seems to have found both. Who Rosalind was and what befell him at her hands are topics that belong rather to the history of the *Shepherd's Calendar* than to the concrete life of the poet: at all events, she furnished him matter for verses a plenty. In the end, 'for speciall occasion of private affayres,' says E. K. in the gloss to 'June,' 'and for his more preferment, removing out of the North-parts, [he] came into the South, as Hobbinoll indeede advised him privately.' Hobbinol, that is Harvey, might well think it time that his friend should begin life in earnest.

To do that it was not sufficient that he should compose poems and put them on the market. In those days the reading public was almost ludicrously small; even pamphleteering and playwriting were not yet recognized occupations, and pure poetry, however popular, would not keep a man in bread. All the poets of that day were first men of another calling, then poets. For any impecunious young bard who could claim gentility and whose tastes were aristocratic, the natural course was to attach himself to the service of some nobleman, and to use his poetry, as best he might, for the furthering of his personal claims. To barter it for money was moreover in some degree to discredit his gentility.

When, therefore, Spenser came south again, perhaps in 1577, it was to obtain preferment with the great. We have evidence, not altogether conclusive, that in that year he was with Sir Henry Sidney in Ireland, acting as one of his secretaries; in any case, by 1578 we get a glimpse of him as secretary to Bishop Young of Rochester (the Roffynn of the September eclogue), who, as Master of Pembroke, had known him from the outset of his university days. Then, in the autumn of 1579, when the first of his extant letters is sent to Cambridge, we find him 'in some use of familiarity' with 'the twoo worthy gentlemen,' Philip Sidney and Edward Dyer, admitted to audience with the Queen, and employed as confidential emissary by the Earl of Leicester. There is reference in that letter to a coming mission to France; he is on the point of setting out; and in the Epistle of E. K., prefixed to the *Shepherd's Calendar* and dated in the preceding April, he is said to be 'for long time furre estraunged,' that is, far away from home, or out of the country, and not soon to return. It is evident that he was cultivating aristocratic connections to some purpose.

He was also cultivating the Muse, and with assiduity. These years are the period of his most multifarious poetizing. They are marked not only by the publication of the *Shepherd's Calendar*, but by the beginnings of the *Faery Queen*, by the first two *Hymns*, by 'Virgil's Gnat,' 'Mother Hubberd's Tale,' and the 'Tears of the Muses' (all five not to be published till long years later), and by a notable array of 'lost works,' recorded here and there in the Harvey letters, in the commentary of E. K., and in Ponsonby's preface to *Complaints*. Many of these last, indeed, presumably belong to other periods of his life, but a number may fairly be set down to the years from 1577 to 1580. Some may possibly have survived under the disguise of other titles; one, at least, the *Pageants*, of which E. K. quotes a line,[1] would seem to have been used for the building up of the *Faery Queen*.[2] Another, *Dreams* (of which *My Slumber*[3] may be no more than an earlier title), is mentioned in the postscript of the second letter to Harvey as equipped with commentary and illustrations, all ready for the press. Then there are *Legends* and the *Court of Cupid*,[4] the latter title suggestive of a well-known episode in the *Faery Queen*,[5] and the *Dying Pelican*.[6] *A Sennight's Slumber*, *The Hell of Lovers*, and *Purgatory*, mentioned by Ponsonby,[7] would seem, by evident subject matter, to belong also to this early period; the others on Ponsonby's list, except the *Dying Pelican*, already noted, may be later. Harvey has not a little to say[8] about nine comedies named after the Muses, which he likens, somewhat ambiguously, to those of Ariosto. Finally, there are *Stemmata Dudleiana*,[9] which may have been utilized in 1590 for the 'Ruins of Time,' though it was probably composed in neo-classical metre; *Epithalamion Thamesis*,[10] also in that metre, a work projected, but probably cut off by the departure, within a brief space, for Ireland; and a treatise entitled *The English Poet*,[11] which, together with the nine comedies, may be regarded as the most serious loss of all. Even if we attribute most of these works to an earlier period, it is evident that, once embarked upon his career in London, Spenser plied his various faculties with keen enthusiasm.

That with so much poetry on hand he should have given so little to the press, was due apparently to discretion. In the circle to which he was now beginning to be admitted on terms of some familiarity, publication in print would probably be regarded as not quite 'the thing,' if it were made the deliberate means of earning money. A passage in the first letter to Harvey[12] is suggestive. The poet hesitates to publish his *Calendar* because, among other considerations, 'I was minded for a while to have intermitted the uttering [i. e. giving out] of my writings; leaste, by over-much cloying their [his patrons'] noble eares, I should gather a contempt of my self, or else seeme rather for gaine and commoditie to doe it, for some sweetnesse that I have already tasted.' The 'uttering' referred to is probably not by means of the press, but by more or less public presentation to the patron; yet if such could by too great frequency win a poor gentleman contempt, much more would the other. Except, then, for the *Calendar*, Spenser contented himself with seeing his poems circulate in manuscript among the literary coteries at court; even *Dreams*, reported as ready for the press, was apparently, in the end, withheld.

The letters to and from Harvey, which tell us so much about Spenser's literary activities, tell us also of a certain club, founded, it would appear, by Philip Sidney and Edward Dyer, and named the Areopagus. Just what it stood for is not altogether clear; perhaps

---

[1] See p. 31, l. 77.
[4] See p. 7, l. 263.
[7] See p. 57.
[10] See p. 772, l. 77 ff.

[2] Bk. II, c. iii, st. 22–31, especially st. 25, l. 1.
[5] Bk. VI, c. viii, st. 19 ff.
[8] See p. 773.
[11] See p. 44.

[3] See p. 769, l. 76.
[6] See p. 772, l. 99.
[9] See p. 772, l. 127.
[12] See p. 768, l. 16 ff.

its founders, inspired by the recent work of the Pléiade in France, aimed at a general reformation of English poetry, then, beyond doubt, in very debatable plight. If so, they soon became involved, to the exclusion of almost all other topics, in the problem of prosody. England had produced but one really eminent poet, Chaucer, and his metres could no longer be perfectly understood; the great bulk of contemporary verse was metrically thin or slipshod. Might it not be true, then, as Roger Ascham had maintained in his *Schoolmaster* a few years before, that English poetry could never hope to rival that of Greece and Rome till it had discarded barbarous rhyme and equipped itself with genuine quantitative measures ? These young men were poets, but they had not yet found themselves in poetry. They were also good scholars. To them, therefore, the doctrine of Ascham seemed worth putting to the proof. What should determine English quantities, whether, as Archdeacon Drant maintained, the law of Rome, or, as Harvey would have it, the natural accent of words, was matter for excellent debate. In the mean time experiment in various metres went on apace, the results of which now chiefly survive in the pages of Sidney's *Arcadia*.

What may have been the membership of the Areopagus we have now small means of determining. Fulke Greville was probably of the number, and almost all accounts of the club reckon in Spenser, too, perhaps with reason. He was certainly much interested in the proceedings, avowed himself a convert to its main doctrine, composed and projected works in the new style, and discussed quantitative standards with Harvey — all as if he were considerably more than half in earnest. Yet when he refers to this foundation of Sidney and Dyer he speaks of it as 'their' club;[1] and though he writes that they have 'drawen mee to their faction,'[2] he apparently means no more than that they have converted him to their views; and the total impression left by the letters is that he was an interested outsider, admitted to a kind of indirect participation in the debates, by favor of the two leaders. They had him, he says, 'in some use of familiarity.' Perhaps, however, in the interval between the first of these epistles and his departure for Ireland, he may have been received into formal membership. It may be, too, that in the same period his relations with Sidney became more intimate, though to speak, as some biographers do, of 'friendship' (in the sense in which Fulke Greville styled himself 'the friend of Sir Philip Sidney') is surely to exaggerate. Sidney was his especial patron in letters, had possibly been the means of his finding employment with Leicester; but if there had been any substantial friendship between them, Spenser would hardly have waited till 1590 to commemorate that chivalric death which in 1586 so stirred all England.

At the time of his second letter to Harvey, Spenser might seem, to all appearances, in very prosperous trim. The *Shepherd's Calendar*, recently given out, had been accorded a veritable triumph, and had moreover brought him in enough money to make Harvey almost jealous. He was under the direct patronage of Sidney, in confidential employment by the powerful Earl of Leicester, on good terms at the court, and able, if we are to trust the gallant messages of Harvey, to live only too agreeably in private. Yet in the later passages of the letters there are signs of disquietude, if not disappointment. His project for an *Epithalamion Thamesis* in neo-classic measures, 'a worke, beleeve me, of much labour,' ends

> ' O Tite, siquid ego,
> Ecquid erit pretij ? '

which might be taken for motto to the melancholy October eclogue of the *Calendar ;* and in Harvey's reply the note is unmistakable: 'I have little joy to animate and encourage

---

[1] See p. 769, l. 61. [2] See p. 769, l. 67.

. . . you . . . to goe forward, unlesse ye might make account of some certaine ordinarie wages, or at the leastwise have your meate and drinke for your dayes workes.'
'Certaine ordinarie wages' were just what Spenser lacked. His verse had brought him
reputation and some money; but he could not expect to live by it, and it was apparently
not helping him to preferment in active service, to a really settled career. Work as confidential emissary for Leicester might be very pleasant, but it was precarious, and unless
the earl secured for him some regular office, his future would be very doubtful. When next
we hear of him, accordingly, he has left England, as secretary to Arthur Lord Grey of
Wilton, the Queen's new Deputy to Ireland. Thenceforth his life is one of virtual exile.

It was on August 12, 1580, that Grey, with his numerous viceregal suite, landed at Dublin. The sword of state was in the south, with his predecessor Pelham, who was ravag-
ing Munster in hopes of starving out the great Desmond rebellion; and till Pelham's
return there could be no formal investiture. But between them lay the rebel Baltinglas,
newly revolted, and Grey was not the man to wait upon a ceremony, when he had the
power to act. By virtue of his patent, he at once assumed control, and gathering such
forces as were at hand, marched into Wicklow. There in the savage valley of Glendalough, or Glenmalure, he came upon the rebel forces. Against the advice of his oldest
captains, he rashly attacked in front. His men, partly raw recruits, were disconcerted
by the roughness of the ground and the fire of hidden enemies; in the end, ' through God's
appointment,' they were completely routed. The loss of life was not great, but several distinguished officers fell, shot down in the action or captured and killed in cold blood. Returning to Dublin, he had barely time to be formally installed in office, when news arrived
that a body of Spaniards had landed on the coast of Kerry, for the support of the Desmond rebels. Here was a danger far more serious than any temporary check by the
Irish. In slow and painful marches, impeded by the autumn floods, he made his way
across the island toward the southwest, to find, upon arrival, that the foreigners were
blockaded by an English fleet in a little fort on the shores of Smerwick Bay, the so-called
Fort del Oro. The sequel was short and stern. Two days of regular siege and bombard-
ment reduced the garrison to extremities. They surrendered at discretion. Their leaders came out and were held for ransom; the remainder, some six hundred in all, mostly
Italians (for the expedition had been set afoot by the Pope), were simply massacred. A
number of non-combatants, including women, were hanged. Three special victims, a
renegade Englishman, an Irishman of some note, and a Catholic friar, before hanging
had their arms and legs broken.

From the account which Spenser gives of this affair in his treatise on Ireland, it has
been inferred that he was present in person. Since he was not the official secretary,
who might be expected to remain chiefly at the capital, but secretary by private appointment, he would be likely enough to follow his patron about. If he did, he must have
seen rapid and rough service in most quarters of the island, for Grey went to and fro
like a shuttle. The hanging of rebels, the pressing of men to death, the cutting off of
the ears of rascally purveyors, the burning of crops in Munster, and the horrible desolation of that region, where those who had escaped the sword were barely able to drag
themselves about, for famine, — sights like these must have become as familiar to the poet
as the dense forest valleys, the bogs, and the innumerable streams of his new home. His
picture of the famine in the south is evidently that of an eyewitness: 'Out of every
corner of the woodes and glinnes they came creeping foorthe upon theyr handes, for theyr
legges could not beare them; they looked like anatomyes of death; they spake like ghostes
crying out of theyr graves; they did eate of the dead carrions; happy were they yf they

could finde them; yea, and one another soone after, insoemuch as the very carcasses they spared not to scrape out of theyr graves; and yf they founde a plotte of water-cresses or sham-rokes, there they flocked as to a feast for the time, yet not able long to continue therewithall; that in shorte space there were none allmost left, and a most populous and plentifull countrey suddaynly made voyde of man or beast.' At the capital itself he might witness conditions not altogether different, for there the streets were full of Irish 'poor souls,' so famished that once, when a horse was burned in its stable, a crowd of them set upon the half-roasted carcass and devoured it whole. Barnaby Googe, the eclogue writer, who reports this scene in August, 1582, remarks that Dublin is so changed for the worse (since 1574) that he hardly knows it.

This general misery Spenser saw only through the eyes of Grey, whose policy was that there could be no talk of building up 'before force have planed the ground for the foundation.' Years later, when he came to elaborate a scheme of his own for the reformation of the island, he could conceive of no other beginning than the absolute and final putting down of rebellion by the sword and by famine. That done, there would be opportunity to reform with some effect, upon a settled and orderly plan. What the Irish thought of Grey there can be no need to ask. Burghley and the Queen called his severity mere violence and his rule 'a gulf of consuming treasure,' — ignorant that, in their day, the gulf was not to be closed, though they sent into it Curtius after Curtius. To the poet, this 'bloudy man' was one 'whom, who that well knewe, knewe him to be most gentell, affable, loving, and temperate, but that the necessitye of that present state of thinges enforced him to that violence, and allmost chaunged his very naturall disposition.' The stern Puritan Deputy, who could not away with the Queen's desire to be lenient in matters of religion, he transfigured, years later, into Arthegall, the champion of Justice, the real, though not the titular, hero of the *Faery Queen*.

When Grey left Ireland in August, 1582, Spenser remained behind. His service had brought him various grants of lands and houses forfeited by rebels, and he had been appointed, in March, 1581, Registrar or Clerk of the Faculties in the Court of Chancery, a position of honor and profit. In Ireland he might now look to a career: if he returned to England, he could have no serious prospects at all. Much, therefore, as he must have regretted his exile, he found resolution to bear with it for at least some years longer. How he might fare for intellectual companionship may be guessed from the account of the gathering at Lodowick Bryskett's cottage near Dublin, (probably of this same year,) quoted at length in all the longer biographies. There we see a party of English officers and civilians, among them the poet himself, listening to a three-day discourse on moral philosophy and discussing the same with the zest of amateurs temporarily unoccupied. They are all very respectful to Spenser, who is recognized as a professional. He, one suspects, must have been thinking the while of his former intercourse with Sidney and Dyer. He was, of course, not the only man of letters at the Irish capital, but in that raw and provincial atmosphere he must often have felt himself very much alone. Luckily, he could have the new books sent over to him from London without great difficulty.

Spenser was not dependent altogether upon the proceeds of his office: grants had been made him, as aforesaid, from time to time, out of various forfeited estates of rebels, which he must have had opportunity enough to profit by. Finally, in June, 1586, his name appears among those of the English 'undertakers' who were to colonize the attainted Desmond lands in Munster. Just two years from then, in June, 1588, he resigned his Dublin clerkship, which he had originally obtained by 'purchase' from his friend Lodowick Bryskett, and obtained, again by 'purchase' from the same friend, the office of

Clerk of the Council of Munster. It is perhaps from this time that he began to reside regularly upon his new estate, at the castle of Kilcolman.

It was a 'seignory' of a little over three thousand acres. To the north stood the western end of the Ballahoura hills, the 'Old Father Mole' of his verse, from which the river Awbeg, his 'Mulla,' flowed in a great half-circle to the west and south. To the east another stream, the Bregog, ran down from the same hills, to meet the Awbeg, their united waters then flowing off southeast for a few miles to the great river of the district, the Blackwater. Toward the centre of this rough circle of hills and streams stood the castle, on a rise of ground. Thirty miles to the southeast, near Youghal, lay the twelve-thousand-acre seignory of Sir Walter Raleigh, also an undertaker, and beyond him the eleven thousand acres allotted to Sir Christopher Hatton. Twenty-five miles to the south lay the city of Cork, the fairest of those parts; to the north, at an equal distance, the city of Limerick, the capital of the Munster presidency and therefore the place of his official duties as Clerk of the Council. To the west and northeast lay wilder country.

These seignories were held upon a rental proportioned to their size, and upon condition that the land be colonized by English households, also in proportion. Great pains were taken that the 'mere Irish' should not find means to get a fresh foothold. The undertakers were to furnish their quota of armed men to the regular forces, but, in the early years, if need be, they were also to be protected by garrisons. They were to pay no taxes for a time, and were to be allowed, for a time, the free importation of goods from England. Some, of course, like Hatton and Raleigh, were absentees, but the great majority were supposed to be in residence, and perhaps did mainly reside.

The situation of the latter was not altogether pleasant. About them on every side were native gentry who, having come through the storm of the late rebellion without attainder, were disposed to defend as they best might what little power was left them. These men saw land to which they had claims, real or imaginary, absorbed into this seignory or that, and when they protested, were asked by the commissioners for their title deeds, or other proof of ownership, as little to be expected in that country as Irish glibs in England. Hence hard words, jealousies, and fears on both sides. The special antagonist of Spenser was Lord Roche. They were at law more than once. Roche accused the poet of trying to steal land from him by false representations of title, of occupying the said land, of threatening his tenants and taking away their cattle, and of beating the servants and bailiffs who resisted. On his side, the poet filed countercharges: they are interesting. 'He [Roche] relieved one Kedagh O'Kelley, his foster brother, a proclaimed traitor; has imprisoned men of Mr. Verdons, Mr. Edmund Spenser, and others. He speaks ill of Her Majesty's government and hath uttered words of contempt of Her Majesty's laws, calling them unjust. He killed a fat beef of Teig O'Lyne's, because Mr. Spenser lay in his house one night as he came from the sessions at Limerick. He also killed a beef of his smith's for mending Mr. Piers' plough iron. He has forbidden his people to have any trade or conference with Mr. Spenser or Mr. Piers or their tenants.' To seek for the right and the wrong in such quarrels is to find a hopeless mixture. Roche, no doubt, was a violent man; yet it was surely hard dealing to bring against him as a crime that he had protected his own foster brother. In any case, with feuds like this on their hands, with outlaws in every recess of that thickly forested region, with native discontent and sense of injury awaiting another chance to rebel, the undertakers can hardly have expected a life of settled peace.

It was after a year of this colonizing that, in the summer of 1589, Spenser was visited by Sir Walter Raleigh. The two had probably met before in service under Lord Grey,

perhaps at the gloomy Fort del Oro, where Raleigh was one of the two captains ' put in '
for the work of general slaughter. A twelvemonth afterward, the brilliant officer had
gone to court, where he had quickly made himself the leading favorite of the Queen.
Now, being driven from court, as the gossips said, by the new favorite, Essex, he was back
for a time in Ireland, on a visit to the estates recently granted him there as undertaker.
He found his old acquaintance at Kilcolman near by, and his old acquaintance showed
him the manuscript of the *Faery Queen.*

Spenser had begun this poem ten years back, in England; since coming over with Grey
he had worked at no other poetry or prose that we know of, except perhaps a casual sonnet or two; yet he had been able to complete only three books of the projected twelve.
Probably he had found the early years of his service in Ireland too distracting for sustained poetical effort. Parts of the work he had shown long before this to various friends
of his exile, perhaps even to Raleigh, but the three books as a whole Raleigh must now
have seen for the first time. Their effect upon his imaginative and sanguine mind can
easily be guessed. Here was a poet, once famous, with a new magnificent poem, hidden
away in a God-forsaken corner among savages. He must be taken to court, he must present his work to the Queen; she could not fail to find room in her service for the author
of Gloriana. In any case, he must make himself known again at the capital, where
by this time he and the old fame of his *Shepherd's Calendar* were ' quite forgot.' But
Raleigh's visit and the sequel are best read between the lines of *Colin Clout's Come Home
Again.*

Spenser and his new friend crossed the seas together in the autumn. On December 1
the *Faery Queen* was registered with the Stationers' Company for publication, and about
that time, or earlier, the poet was doubtless being accorded those audiences with Elizabeth of which *Colin Clout* informs us, audiences for the reading of his poem, which she
was graciously pleased to applaud. With her graciousness to cheer him, and with the
backing of Raleigh, he is not likely to have missed very much his old patrons, Sidney
and Leicester, by this time dead. In their place was the Countess of Pembroke (for
whom he now commemorated them in belated panegyric, at the suggestion of friends),
and besides her, there were his noble relatives, the three daughters of Sir John Spencer
of Althorpe — and others. The list of distinguished personages, indeed, whose names
appear in his verse, or in the inscriptions of his longer poems and sonnets, makes clear
that he was now at the very centre of courtly life. Meanwhile he was working with a
will. There was his *Faery Queen* to see through the press, and he was also revising old
poems and composing new, as means of commending himself. He probably hoped for a
substantial reward.

What he hoped for chiefly was perhaps some place in the government service at the
capital. For this, however, he had to reckon with Burghley, and Burghley did not believe
in poets. The great lord treasurer might recollect him, too, as a former *protégé* of
his old enemy, Leicester; possibly he had, ten years earlier, set a precedent for deny-
ing him office — when the poet had been obliged to content himself with a private
secretaryship in Ireland. An uncompromising biographer might also note the later complaint of Bacon (himself a disappointed suitor for office) that ' in the times of the Cecils
able men were, of purpose, suppressed.' In any case, whatever the cause, there can be
no doubt that Burghley showed himself unfavorable to Spenser. An apocryphal story
relates that when the Queen ordered the payment of a hundred pounds, in recognition of
the poet's genius, the treasurer objected to the amount; whereupon she replied, ' Then
give him what is reason; ' whereupon the treasurer let the matter rest altogether, till the

poet, by a rhymed appeal to his sovereign, secured the hundred pounds and a censure for his enemy. The truth, as far as we know it, is, that in February, 1591, some sixteen months after his arrival in London and nearly, if not quite, a year after the appearance of his poem, Spenser received the grant of a pension of £50, and that he received no other substantial recognition of his genius. Fifty pounds a year and the doubtful profits of a small Munster seignory would not support him suitably in London. He was no more inclined than he had been ten years earlier to attempt literature as a profession. If he had hoped to get footing at the capital, therefore, he bore the disappointment as he might, and set out for home. His opinion of Burghley he left behind him in 'Mother Hubberd's Tale.'

This poem appeared in the volume entitled *Complaints*, which was entered upon the Stationers' register, as approved by the official censors, December 29, 1590. Since Ponsonby, in his opening address, speaks of the poet's 'departure over sea,' and since the volume bears the date of 1591, which would not be given it till the official beginning of the new year on March 25, it may be supposed that Spenser went home in the late winter or early spring, before the volume was ready for sale. On the preceding New Year's[1] he had signed the dedication of *Daphnaïda* at London; on the following 27th of December, he signed the dedication of *Colin Clout's Come Home Again* at Kilcolman. This poetic acknowledgment of Raleigh's patronage was presumably sent over to his friend in manuscript at once, though it was not to be published till 1595.

Back at Kilcolman again, Spenser fell into the old round of official duties (executed in part, no doubt, by deputy) and of seignorial cares. By this time he could probably command more leisure, much of which he would give to pushing on with his *Faery Queen*. But a new adventure now befell him: he met the woman whom he was to marry. She was a certain gentlewoman, Elizabeth Boyle, of kin to that Richard Boyle who later became the first Earl of Cork. Her home seems to have been at Kilcoran, near Youghal, on the coast to the southeast of Spenser's domain. If we are to believe the story of the *Amoretti*, which is altogether consistent, he began his wooing late in 1592; the marriage was of June 11, 1594. These are the bare facts. Those who wish the romance, which rests upon well-documented facts of its own, must turn to the *Amoretti* and *Epithalamion* themselves and read with the inward eye.

Before his marriage Spenser had contrived, with commendable foresight, to finish the second three books of his *Faery Queen*. These he kept by him till he could take them to London himself. The *Amoretti* and *Epithalamion* he sent over to Ponsonby without delay, and Ponsonby published them in the spring of 1595. In the same year, or early in 1596 (for according to the old style the computation was from March 25 to March 24), Ponsonby also brought out *Colin Clout's Come Home Again* and *Astrophel*. By January 20 (old style 1595, new style 1596) the poet himself was in London, for on that date there was registered with the Stationers' Company the second part of the *Faery Queen*. Since one of the main objects of his coming over would be the publication of this work, it is not likely that he had arrived much earlier.

Another object was undoubtedly the furtherance of his material welfare. Not content with what had been done for him in 1591, he was set upon urging his claims a second time. On that former occasion he had appeared under the patronage of Raleigh, which not only had not helped him to full success, but had prevented his wooing the apparently greater influence of Essex; for the two favorites were bitter rivals. Except, then, for a very flattering sonnet to the young earl, he seems at that time to have paid him no court.

[1] For this date see the introduction to *Daphnaïda*.

Perhaps it is to exaggerate to say that he paid him court now, or that Essex was the patron of his second venture. In the *Prothalamion*, his first thought concerning Essex House is that it was once the abode of Leicester,

> ' Whose want too well now feeles my freendles case ; '

and his following panegyric upon Leicester's successor contains no hint of patronage. Yet it was Essex who, a little over two years later, was to pay his funeral expenses. In any case, Spenser gained no further reward. The second part of the *Faery Queen* did not heighten the wonder of the first, and therefore did not move Elizabeth to fresh bounty. As for her lord treasurer, the poet could hope for nothing from him after ' Mother Hubberd's Tale.' The references to his ill humor, set at the beginning and the end of this part, read, in fact, like a challenge.

Spenser was not a lucky courtier. One could wish, indeed, that he had never tried courting, for its influence upon his spirit was malign. Naturally high-minded, he reveals here and there in his verse, under the sting of disappointment, a petulance, somewhat unmanly, that his most radical admirers would fain argue away. Others would fain forget the adulation, sometimes offensive, into which the pursuit of reward too often tempted him. Loitering about the court, in hopes of preferment, was surely no fit business for the poet of the *Faery Queen*. Happily, his experiences there stirred him less often to petulance or gross flattery than to manly disdain.

The dedication of the *Four Hymns* is dated from Greenwich (where the court often lay), September 1, 1596; the *Prothalamion* is probably of the early autumn. Not long afterward Spenser may be thought to have given up his suit and gone home. If he had written less poetry during this second visit than in 1590, one cause may have been that he was busied in prose, for it is probably to 1596 that one must assign his *View of the Present State of Ireland*.[1] This elaborate survey and plan of reform would explain, if further explanation were needed, why the poet was so ill content with his lot. Fifteen years of life in Ireland had not reconciled him in the slightest to Irish manners and customs, or taught him the smallest sympathy with the Irish temperament. Not to speak of his plan for the systematic starving out and strangling of rebellion and for systematic colonizing, he would carry reform even to the point of cutting off the glibs of the natives and taking away their long mantles, because both were convenient to thieves. Even their easy-minded laziness was offence to him. In his general contempt for the Irish and in his advocacy of the sternest measures of repression, he was, of course, not alone among the English of his day; but one judges that he also lacked that faculty of compromise which might have moved him to make the most of disagreeable neighbors.

In 1593, or thereabouts, Spenser had disposed of his clerkship of the Munster Council. On September 30, 1598, not quite two years after his return from England, he was appointed Sheriff of Cork. Within a week the revolt broke out which was to ruin the undertakers of Munster.

The original grants had provided that every undertaker should people his estate with English. A seignory of twelve thousand acres called for the establishment of ninety-two families; smaller seignories, of a number proportionately less. Whether by negligence or sheer inability, however, the undertakers had failed to observe this condition of their tenure. After bringing over a few families, often anything but respectable and sober, they had commonly let their remaining land to natives, just the folk whom the government aimed to supplant, or had allowed it to lie idle. Most of them, perhaps, had not the means

---

[1] Not included in this volume. It was first printed, long after his death, in 1633.

of financing their venture properly. They had almost all counted on peace and neglected to make provision against attack. When, therefore, the victory of Tyrone in the north inflamed the Irish of Munster to rebellion, the undertakers, who lived far apart, were helpless. The Lord President, Sir Thomas Norris, might have organized them for defence, but the storm came on so rapidly that he lost heart, they thought of nothing but escape to Cork and Waterford with their families, and the whole province, outside the walled towns, was left open to pillage. Here and there an undertaker defended himself as he best might, but the majority simply ran away, if they could. The Irish tenants whom they had admitted upon their estates commonly joined the rebels in the general work of pillage, burning, mutilation, and murder.

With his wife and four children Spenser escaped to Cork. Whether or not he attempted to defend his castle we do not know; we hear only of a certain Edmund M'Shee 'killed by an Englishman at the spoil of Kilcolman.' The story told by Ben Jonson, that an infant child of the poet perished in the flames, is probably apocryphal. At Cork he found time and composure to prepare a review of the situation, for the Queen; then he was sent to London with despatches, which he delivered the day before Christmas. On the 16th of the following January (in modern style, 1599) he died at Westminster. The Earl of Essex took charge of his funeral. Poets attended him to his grave in the Abbey, near Chaucer, and threw in elegies, with the pens that had written them. Queen Elizabeth ordered him a monument — which was never erected.

Spenser's reputation among his contemporaries was of the highest. No other English poet ever won more immediate and abiding recognition than he. The *Shepherd's Calendar* was at once accepted as a masterpiece, and when the *Faery Queen* appeared, there was no one to dispute his right to the heritage of Chaucer. Between 1590 and his death he was held, by general consent, the supreme poet of his time in England. This unanimity of acceptance was due, perhaps, in some measure, to the fact that he was not of that quarrelsome community which praised him, the turbulent literary world of London, but an exile. He had left England at a time when most of the men now seeking fame for themselves were mere youths, and when he returned to their world, at intervals, with fresh poetry, their feeling was in part enthusiasm for its magic, and in part reverence for their senior, who had no share in their quarrels, and whose art was not of their schools, though it instantly made disciples. To speculate how far his remoteness from the growing world of letters may have been favorable to his originality would be futile: it most certainly was favorable to his immediate fame.

What his fame may be to-day is a topic more engaging, but less tangible, and not to be discussed *in extenso* here. One aspect of it, however, may be glanced at. There are some who go to him, as they go to Keats, for the 'life of sensations' which they prefer to the 'life of ideas,' who appreciate nothing but his sensuous delightsomeness. Others, who feel also his grave moral charm, are, like Lowell, impatient of his too overt moralizing. Others yet, like Dowden, accept the moralizing and all. In the main, the trend of unofficial contemporary opinion seems to be against that element in Spenser's poetry which he himself took for the chief of all. He had run the length of the full university curriculum of his day. If one had talked to him of the cultivation of the sensibilities, he would have stared: he had been feeding his brain. To be able to think in poetry, that, he would have said, was the chief end of the poet; and it would grieve him now in Elysium, could he know what moderns have thought about his thinking. Perhaps these moderns are, after all, wrong. It is well enough to say that his thinking too often protrudes through his art, like ill-covered wire framework, — but why then, in Dante, call the same phenomenon 'a residuum of prose in the depths of his poetry'? The failing is all but inevitable to poetic dogmatists. In Spenser, too, as in others, it is merely one manifestation of the faculty that directs his noblest work, that informs the superb energy of the conflict between the Redcross Knight and Despair, and the serenities of the *Hymn in Honor of Beauty*.

THE

SHEPHEARDES CALENDER

CONTEYNING TWELVE ÆGLOGUES PROPORTIONABLE TO THE TWELVE MONETHES

ENTITLED

TO THE NOBLE AND VERTUOUS GENTLEMAN MOST WORTHY OF ALL TITLES BOTH OF LEARNING AND CHEVALRIE MAISTER PHILIP SIDNEY

AT LONDON

PRINTED BY HUGH SINGLETON, DWELLING IN CREEDE LANE NEERE UNTO LUDGATE
AT THE SIGNE OF THE GYLDEN TUNNE, AND ARE THERE TO BE SOLDE

1579

[*The Shepherd's Calender* was entered on the books of the Stationers' Company December 5, 1579, and was probably published before the end of the following March, when the old year officially expired. The little volume must have had a certain attraction of mysteriousness. It was full of veiled allusions and the secret of its authorship was enticingly dangled before the eyes of readers. The author of the eclogues signed himself 'Immeritô' and was styled by the author of the commentary 'the new poet.' This other signed himself E. K. Yet though the book thus challenged curiosity, the secret seems to have been well enough kept. At court, perhaps, or at Cambridge, it would be penetrated in time by a few, but generally, and at least as a matter of form, the anonymity was acknowledged for a full decade to come. Spenser's main share in the work was confessed when the *Faery Queen* came out in 1590.

For E. K., his initials seem to have been left, even then, to explain themselves — or perhaps real explanation was not greatly heeded. In either case, who he may have been is now beyond absolute proof. Some recent scholars, arguing from a few special passages and from the apparent intimacy of his knowledge, an intimacy in no way contradicted by occasional rather arch professions of ignorance, have maintained that he was Spenser himself, acting as his own commentator. Their theory is plausible — but only at first sight. It cannot meet the fact that E. K. has in several places plainly misunderstood his text, and it implies that Spenser could write about the men he imitated and about his own work in the tone of such slurs as those, in the beginning of the 'January' gloss and in the argument of 'November,' on the genial Marot. Most critics, therefore, abide by the older opinion that E. K. was Edward Kirke, a contemporary of Spenser and Harvey at Cambridge (sizar, for a time, in their own hall, Pembroke) and of kin, perhaps, to the 'Mistresse Kerke' of Spenser's first letter. This opinion, though but conjectural, clashes with neither fact nor sentiment.

The main riddle of the eclogues themselves is, of course, Rosalinde. Who she was, and how seriously the tale of which she is the faithless heroine must be taken, have busied, it may be thought, only too many minds. For her identity, the evidence comprises three points: that, according to the gloss on 'January,' her poetic name is an anagram of her real; that, according to the gloss on 'April,' she was 'a gentlewoman of no meane house;' and that, to judge by the general tenor of the narrative, her home was in that northeast corner of Lancashire which is unmistakably the scene of the love-eclogues. Yet after much patient work, the most recent of investigators has produced no one but a quite supposititious Rose Dineley, of a surname common in those parts, — and there the matter may rest. Nor need the love-story itself be discussed, or the depth of the poet's passion. Concerning this last, however, one point may be noted. That Rosalinde is celebrated as late as *Colin Clout's Come Home Again*, in 1591, need mean no more than that she was then still, in a sense, the poet's official mistress, remembered with kindly appreciation and not yet displaced by the woman whom shortly afterwards he wooed to good purpose.

Though we do not know her name or the real facts of her story, and though the pastoral

disguise of the eclogues is quite baffling, Rosalinde is none the less a curiously distinct personage. E. K. and Harvey have both recorded
her qualities. 'Shee is a gentlewoman of no
meane house,' says E. K. in his gloss for
'April,' 'nor endewed with anye vulgare and
common gifts both of nature and manners.'
Harvey speaks more intimately — in a letter to
Spenser of April, 1580. In one part of this, ex-
tolling the charms of that mysterious beauty
with whom the poet was then solacing his
wounded heart, he declares her to be ' another
little Rosalinde' (altera Rosalindula — the
diminutive suggests that the true Rosalinde
was of more native dignity) ; and in another
part, upon a matter of literary interest, he appeals to ' his conceite whom gentle Mistresse
Rosalinde once reported to have all the intelligences at commaundement, and at another time
christened her Segnior Pegaso.' That last frag-
ment tells us more about the real qualities of
this ' gentlewoman of no meane house,' and
suggests more about her probable dealings
with the poet, than all the tuneful lamentations
of the eclogues.

The love-story of Rosalinde and Colin Clout
is the central theme of the Calendar. It gives
to what might else have been a collection
of independent eclogues the appearance of
dramatic continuity, and at the end, in ' December,' it broadens into a kind of tragic allegory of life which closes the round of the
months with philosophic dignity. For purposes
of artistic centralization, indeed, it was undoubtedly the fittest theme that Spenser could
have selected, and it had the special appeal to
him of a fresh and perhaps poignant experience.
It is not the only theme, however, to be developed with recurrent emphasis. That of the
central eclogues, ' May,' ' July,' and ' September,' is elaborated with almost equal ampli-
tude, and with such apparent earnestness that
these eclogues have very generally been held
to express sincere personal convictions. If that
opinion be true (and there is certainly some
truth in it), Spenser was, at this stage of his
life, more or less a Puritan.

Nothing, indeed, would be more natural
than that, in 1579, when the Elizabethan Church
was but just emerging from its earlier days of
uncertainty, a young man of generous moral
instincts, a seeker of the ideal, should sympathize with the main attitude of the Puritans.
Among the several parties of the composite and
still rather incoherent Anglican communion,
they stood most typically for moral earnestness. This temper might sometimes run to
extremes ; the more violent of them, Cart-
wright and such, might be root and branch re-
formers, hewers of Agag in pieces before the

Lord ; but the greater part were men whose
zeal showed itself chiefly in diligent preaching
and urging of their convictions — the need of
simplicity in the worship and of earnestness in
the service of God. Compared with these men,
those higher ecclesiastics who had the difficult
task of maintaining the Queen's policy of compromise, and of preserving what could be preserved of the older ceremonies and dignities of
religion, might conceivably seem lukewarm and
worldly-minded. And among the lower clergy,
especially in the rural districts, there were still
but too many like the priest in 'Mother Hubberd's Tale,' who had been Catholic and were
now half Protestant, ignorant, lazy, worthless.
The energy of vital religion might at this
time seem to be with the Puritans. The objects
of their denunciation were, moreover, not all
mere matters of ritual and form, but, many of
them, very real abuses.

To what extent Spenser may have held with
the Puritans is nevertheless a somewhat perplexed question. One could wish that the
allegory of the three eclogues were clearer. A
few specific allusions, to be sure, give it an air
of actuality, but they do not carry us very far.
' Old Algrind,' the type of the pious and ven-
erable shepherd, is beyond fair question Grindal, Archbishop of Canterbury, then in utter
disgrace with the Queen for having refused
to put down Puritan ' prophesyings.' Morrell,
the ' goteheard prowde,' is quite probably
Aylmer, Bishop of London, one of those who
helped to do the work that Grindal declined.
When we look for definite ideas, however, we
find ourselves continually at a balance between
the Puritan and the more broadly Protestant.
If the sentiment of the first part of ' May ' is
distinctly Puritan, the remainder of that eclogue, which inveighs against the wiles of the
Papists, conveys little more than the general
sentiment of the English Reformation. As for
the main burden of the eclogues, against the
pride, luxury, and corruption of a worldly
priesthood, one is perpetually in doubt whether
it be directed against the orthodox clergy
of the Church of England or against the clergy
of the Church of Rome. This ambiguity, to
be sure, may be the poet's safeguard against
possible ill-consequences : it suggests, however,
that he was not a thorough-going partisan.
With those who held Anglicanism to be mere
Popery he of course had no ties at all, or he
would not have admitted E. K.'s comment in
' May ' upon Some gan, etc. On the whole, then,
beyond strong disapproval of abuses in church
patronage, such as those described in ' Mother
Hubberd's Tale,' and of high living and laziness
and spiritual dullness among the clergy, Spenser's Puritan sympathies do not seem to have

extended far. Except for a brief passage upon the intercession of saints, the thought of which is broadly Protestant, there is hardly a glance at dogma.

In two out of the three eclogues, in 'July' and 'September,' Spenser borrows themes and even whole passages from his pastoral forerunner, Mantuan, the satirist of the Roman clergy. How far this borrowing may make against his sincerity is matter for individual judgment. In any case, it exemplifies one of the fundamental characteristics of the *Calendar*. When young Alexander Pope, in the days of his ardent reading among the classics, undertook to compose a set of pastorals, he first fixed his attention on ' the only undisputed authors ' of that *genre*, Theocritus and Virgil, then, from a study of their eclogues, derived four absolute types, comprehensive of ' all the subjects which the criticks upon Theocritus and Virgil will allow to be fit for pastoral.' Young Spenser, equally ardent with his books and living in a less formally critical age, proceeded on quite another principle. Since the days of the Greek and Latin fathers of the pastoral there had been a goodly line of successors, under whom the *genre* had developed in many directions. Petrarch, Mantuan, Sannazaro, Marot, to mention but a few of the chief, had each contributed his share of themes and methods. The main development had been in allegory, the use of the pastoral form, that is, for the discussion of contemporary or personal affairs and the introduction of real people. By the time Spenser came to write, then, the literature of the pastoral was immense and surpassingly diverse ; it had, moreover, quite lost the peculiar quality of its earliest days, when an idyll was a direct poetic rendering of real life, and had crystallized into a system of conventional symbols, which might still be used by a master with living imaginative effect, but which, without a radical reversion, could hardly again render real life. Out of this literature Spenser adopted types and definite themes, and imitated special passages, with studied care for variety. The types need not here be particularized, but of definite themes, elaborated in part by direct translation or paraphrase, we have, for instance, the religious satire of ' July ' and 'September,' out of Mantuan, the complaint of the hard lot of poets, in ' October,' also out of Mantuan, the dirge in ' November ' and parts of ' December,' in imitation of Marot, ' March ' after Bion. For the general scheme of stringing the loose eclogues on a slight thread of romance, that, too, though perhaps mainly original, had been, in a way, anticipated by Boccaccio and Sannazaro. Of real contributions to the *genre* we find few beyond the use of the

fable and the idea of making an eclogue-series a calendar.

This imitativeness, the eagerness to appropriate interesting or otherwise attractive themes by which to give his work variety, to experiment in various acknowledged styles, is, indeed, the most distinguishing characteristic of the *Calendar*. It is one manifestation of what may be called the voracity of taste in youth. Spenser was doing what Stevenson, in a well-known essay, has told us that he, in his time, did, and that every active young follower of letters must inevitably do, what, in the various performances of his early period, Pope did himself. And as imitation goes hand in hand with experiment, the impulse toward variety in his work shows itself not merely in themes and styles appropriated from earlier pastoral poets, but in the very measures and stanza-forms of his verse. These are strikingly various. There is the irregular accentual verse of ' February ' and other eclogues, side by side with the even, finely modulated ten-syllable iambic. There is the ballad measure and stanza of ' July,' side by side with the elaborate and musical eight-line stanza of ' June.' Formal quatrains, now separate, now linked by rhyme ; the stanzas, equal in length but vitally different in harmonic effect, of ' January ' and ' October ; ' a lively roundelay, a starched sestina — one could hardly be more varied. Then there are the hymn-strophes of ' April ' and ' November.' The strophe of this last, opening sonorously with an alexandrine, sinking through melodious decasyllables to the plaintive shorter verses, and rising at the close into another decasyllable, to fall away in a brief refrain, is as noble a prophecy of the larger stanzaic art of the *Epithalamion* as a young poet could conceivably give. Spenser, indeed, won his supreme mastery of the stanza by long and honest experiment.

The youthfulness of the art is finally evident in the mere arrangement of the eclogues. This reminds one of nothing so much as of that almost mathematical balance with which, as Professor Norton has pointed out, Dante disposed the poems of his *Vita Nuova*. Formality of structure is of course one of the most common characteristics of youthful art. In the *Calendar*, this formality, though less exact than in the *Vita Nuova*, is rather more obvious. The series of eclogues, being in number twelve, has naturally, if one may use the phrase, two centres, ' June ' and ' July : ' Spenser's plan of arrangement is to place, approximately at a balance on either of these centres, such eclogues as stand in contrast or are supplementary to each other. The eclogues, for instance, in which Colin Clout laments his wretched case are three : two must round out the series in 'January' and 'December ;' the third is placed at one of the centres, 'June.' The two at the extremes are monologues and both in the crude six-line stanza of even iambics that is used nowhere else : the third, at the centre, is a dialogue in an elaborate eight-line stanza that is also used only here. The three religious eclogues, two in accentual couplets, one in ballad measure, balance in like manner upon 'July.' One may note, too, the hymn of praise in 'April' over against the dirge in 'November,' and may feel, perhaps, a balance in the complaint for poets, of ' October,' and the two main tributes, in ' February ' and ' June,' to Chaucer. But one might easily push the analysis too far.

It is with Chaucer, the Tityrus of the eclogues, that any survey of them most naturally concludes. Barring a certain mysterious Wrenock, he is the one master whom Colin Clout acknowledges.

> 'The god of shepheards, Tityrus, is dead,
> Who taught me, homely as I can, to make.'

So says Colin in ' June,' and in ' December ' it is said of him that ' he of Tityrus his songs did lere.' How far, then, we inevitably ask ourselves, is Spenser really the disciple of his one great English forerunner ? In two prominent characteristics, more or less external, Chaucer's influence upon the *Calendar* is, of course, generally admitted. The irregular accentual verse, which is managed so well in ' February ' and often so poorly in other eclogues and incidental passages, though in general of the decadent Chaucerian school, seems to owe much to direct study of the master himself. And for the diction, in its varying degrees of strangeness, if Spenser, to the discontent of Sidney, 'framed his style to an old rustic language,' it was in the main by authority of Chaucer, whose English, now rustic to the modern Elizabethans, was yet their greatest literary tradition. So much can hardly be disputed, and so much does not carry us very far : those who stop there, indeed, must view the professed discipleship as more or less a sentiment. Yet one may fairly believe that

Chaucer's influence is wider and deeper than that. We doubt its extent, perhaps, chiefly when we consider the *Calendar* too much by itself. As, in the *Faery Queen*, the strongest immediate influence might be thought to be that of Ariosto, so, in the *Calendar*, it is unquestionably that of the great pastoral school. If, however, we look, not to themes and methods and merely occasional characteristics of style in this one poem, but to the persistent characteristics of style in Spenser's total achievement, may we not fairly see the influence of Chaucer dominating all others ? That archaism which is held to be the chief note of his influence on the *Calendar* is not a garb assumed for the time as appropriate : it is the very body of Spenser's speech. E. K., early in the epistle to Harvey, has suggested its natural growth, which indeed is clear. Reading and rereading the ' auncient poetes' of his own tongue, in chief the master of them all, Spenser's imagination and native sense for language were so saturated with the charm of that older speech that to him it became in the end more real than the speech of his contemporaries, and attracting to itself, by force of sympathetic likeness, provincialisms from a dozen sources, grew to be the living language of his genius. To this, the largest artistic contribution would be Chaucer's. And for that other element of poetry, verse, we can hardly think that Spenser derived from his great forerunner nothing but models for the measures of 'February' and ' August.' It is frequently said that, when the final *e* died out and was forgotten, Chaucer's verse could be read only by accent and with a kind of popular lilt. Yet there were long passages that would still preserve almost their full metrical flow and beauty. If Spenser, then, became master of a verse ideally flowing and musical, he assuredly learned the art of it in no small measure from the golden cadences of Chaucer. From foreign poets, in brief, he might learn and borrow much in a hundred ways, but the one master who can teach a native style is a native artist, and the one great artist of England, prior to ' the new poet,' was Chaucer.]

TO HIS BOOKE

Goe, little booke: thy selfe present,
As child whose parent is unkent,
To him that is the president
Of noblesse and of chevalree:
And if that Envie barke at thee,
As sure it will, for succoure flee
Under the shadow of his wing;
And asked, who thee forth did bring,

A shepheards swaine, saye, did thee sing,
All as his straying flocke he fedde:
And when his honor has thee redde,
Crave pardon for my hardyhedde.
But if that any aske thy name,
Say thou wert base begot with blame:
Forthy thereof thou takest shame.
And when thou art past jeopardee,
Come tell me what was sayd of mee:
And I will send more after thee.

IMMERITÔ.

TO THE MOST EXCELLENT AND LEARNED BOTH ORATOR AND POETE, MAYSTER GABRIELL HARVEY,

HIS VERIE SPECIAL AND SINGULAR GOOD FREND E. K. COMMENDETH THE GOOD LYKING OF THIS HIS LABOUR, AND THE PATRONAGE OF THE NEW POETE

Uncouthe, unkiste, sayde the olde famous poete Chaucer: whom for his excellencie and wonderfull skil in making, his scholler Lidgate, a worthy scholler of so excellent a maister, calleth the loadestarre of our language: and whom our Colin Clout in his æglogue calleth Tityrus the god of shepheards, comparing hym to the worthines of the Roman Tityrus, Virgile. Which proverbe, myne owne good friend Maister 10 Harvey, as in that good old poete it served well Pandares purpose, for the bolstering of his baudy brocage, so very well taketh place in this our new poete, who for that he is uncouthe (as said Chaucer) is unkist, and unknown to most men, is regarded but of few. But I dout not, so soone as his name shall come into the knowledg of men, and his worthines be sounded in the tromp of Fame, but that he shall be not 20 onely kiste, but also beloved of all, embraced of the most, and wondred at of the best. No lesse, I thinke, deserveth his wittinesse in devising, his pithinesse in uttering, his complaints of love so lovely, his discourses of pleasure so pleasantly, his pastorall rudenesse, his morall wisenesse, his dewe observing of decorum everye where, in personages, in seasons, in matter, in speach, and generally in al seemely sim- 30 plycitie of handeling his matter, and framing his words: the which, of many thinges which in him be straunge, I know will seeme the straungest, the words them selves being so auncient, the knitting of them so short and intricate, and the whole periode and compasse of speache so delightsome for the roundnesse, and so grave for the straungenesse. And firste of the wordes to speake, I graunt they be something hard, 40 and of most men unused, yet both English, and also used of most excellent authors and most famous poetes. In whom whenas this our poet hath bene much traveiled and

throughly redd, how could it be, (as that worthy oratour sayde,) but that walking in the sonne, although for other cause he walked, yet needes he mought be sunburnt; and, having the sound of those auncient poetes still ringing in his eares, he mought needes 50 in singing hit out some of theyr tunes. But whether he useth them by such casualtye and custome, or of set purpose and choyse, as thinking them fittest for such rusticall rudenesse of shepheards, eyther for that theyr rough sounde would make his rymes more ragged and rustical, or els because such olde and obsolete wordes are most used of country folke, sure I think, and think I think not amisse, that they bring great 60 grace and, as one would say, auctoritie to the verse. For albe amongst many other faultes it specially be objected of Valla against Livie, and of other against Saluste, that with over much studie they affect antiquitie, as coveting thereby credence and honor of elder yeeres, yet I am of opinion, and eke the best learned are of the lyke, that those auncient solemne wordes are a great ornament both in the one and in the 70 other; the one labouring to set forth in hys worke an eternall image of antiquitie, and the other carefully discoursing matters of gravitie and importaunce. For if my memory fayle not, Tullie, in that booke wherein he endevoureth to set forth the paterne of a perfect oratour, sayth that ofttimes an auncient worde maketh the style seeme grave, and as it were reverend: no otherwise then we honour and reverence gray 80 heares, for a certein religious regard which we have of old age. Yet nether every where must old words be stuffed in, nor the commen dialecte and maner of speaking so corrupted therby, that, as in old buildings, it seme disorderly and ruinous. But all as in most exquisite pictures they use to blaze and portraict not onely the daintie lineaments of beautye, but also rounde about it to shadow the rude thickets and craggy 90 clifts, that, by the basenesse of such parts, more excellency may accrew to the principall (for oftimes we fynde our selves, I knowe not how, singularly delighted with the shewe of such naturall rudenesse, and take great pleasure in that disorderly order) even so doe those rough and harsh termes enlumine and make more clearly to appeare the brightnesse of brave and glorious words. So ofentimes a dischorde in 100 musick maketh a comely concordaunce: so great delight tooke the worthy poete Alceus to behold a blemish in the joynt of a wel shaped body. But if any will rashly blame such his purpose in choyse of old and unwonted words, him may I more justly blame and condemne, or of witlesse headinesse in judging, or of heedelesse hardinesse in condemning: for not marking the compasse of hys bent, he wil judge of the 110 length of his cast: for in my opinion it is one special prayse, of many whych are dew to this poete, that he hath laboured to restore, as to theyr rightfull heritage, such good and naturall English words as have ben long time out of use and almost cleare disherited. Which is the onely cause that our mother tonge, which truely of it self is both ful enough for prose and stately enough for verse, hath long time ben counted 120 most bare and barrein of both. Which default when as some endevoured to salve and recure, they patched up the holes with peces and rags of other languages, borrowing here of the French, there of the Italian, every where of the Latine; not weighing how il those tongues accorde with themselves, but much worse with ours: so now they have made our English tongue a gallimaufray or hodgepodge of al other speches. Other 130 some, not so wel seene in the English tonge as perhaps in other languages, if they happen to here an olde word, albeit very naturall and significant, crye out streight way that we speak no English, but gibbrish, or rather such as in old time Evanders mother spake. Whose first shame is, that they are not ashamed, in their own mother tonge straungers to be counted and alienes. The second shame no lesse then the first, that 140 what so they understand not, they streight way deeme to be sencelesse, and not at al to be understode. Much like to the mole in Æsopes fable, that, being blynd her selfe, would in no wise be perswaded that any beast could see. The last more shameful then both, that of their owne country and natural speach, which together with their nources milk they sucked, they have so base regard and bastard judgement, that 150 they will not onely themselves not labor to garnish and beautifie it, but also repine that of other it shold be embellished. Like to the dogge in the maunger, that him

selfe can eate no hay, and yet barketh at the hungry bullock, that so faine would feede: whose currish kinde, though it cannot be kept from barking, yet I conne them thanke that they refrain from byting. 160

Now, for the knitting of sentences, whych they call the joynts and members therof, and for al the compasse of the speach, it is round without roughnesse, and learned wythout hardnes, such indeede as may be perceived of the leaste, understoode of the moste, but judged onely of the learned. For what in most English wryters useth to be loose, and as it were ungyrt, in this authour is well grounded, finely framed, and strongly 170 trussed up together. In regard whereof, I scorne and spue out the rakehellye route of our ragged rymers (for so themselves use to hunt the letter) which without learning boste, without judgement jangle, without reason rage and fome, as if some instinct of poeticall spirite had newly ravished them above the meanenesse of commen capacitie. And being in the middest of all theyr bravery, sodenly eyther for want of matter, 180 or of ryme, or having forgotten theyr former conceipt, they seeme to be so pained and traveiled in theyr remembrance as it were a woman in childebirth, or as that same Pythia, when the traunce came upon her : '*Os rabidum fera corda domans,*' &c. Nethelesse, let them a Gods name feede on theyr owne folly, so they seeke not to darken the beames of others glory. As for Colin, under whose person the Authour selfe is 190 shadowed, how furre he is from such vaunted titles and glorious showes, both him selfe sheweth, where he sayth,

'Of Muses, Hobbin, I conne no skill,' and

'Enough is me to paint out my unrest,' &c.,

and also appeareth by the basenesse of the name, wherein, it semeth, he chose rather to unfold great matter of argument covertly then, professing it, not suffice thereto 200 accordingly. Which moved him rather in æglogues then other wise to write, doubting perhaps his habilitie, which he little needed, or mynding to furnish our tongue with this kinde, wherein it faulteth, or following the example of the best and most auncient poetes, which devised this kind of wryting, being both so base for the matter, and homely for the manner, at the first to trye theyr habilities, and, as young birdes 210 that be newly crept out of the nest, by little first to prove theyr tender wyngs, before they make a greater flyght. So flew Theocritus, as you may perceive he was all ready full fledged. So flew Virgile, as not yet well feeling his winges. So flew Mantuane, as being not full somd. So Petrarque. So Boccace. So Marot, Sanazarus, and also divers other excellent both Italian and French poetes, whose foting this author every 220 where followeth, yet so as few, but they be wel sented, can trace him out. So finally flyeth this our new poete, as a bird whose principals be scarce growen out, but yet as that in time shall be hable to keepe wing with the best.

Now, as touching the generall dryft and purpose of his Æglogues, I mind not to say much, him selfe labouring to conceale it. Onely this appeareth, that his unstayed 230 yougth had long wandred in the common labyrinth of Love; in which time, to mitigate and allay the heate of his passion, or els to warne (as he sayth) the young shepheards, sc. his equalls and companions, of his unfortunate folly, he compiled these xij Æglogues, which, for that they be proportioned to the state of the xij monethes, he termeth the *Shepheards Calendar*, applying an olde name to a new worke. Hereunto 240 have I added a certain glosse or scholion, for thexposition of old wordes and harder phrases: which maner of glosing and commenting, well I wote, wil seeme straunge and rare in our tongue: yet for somuch as I knew many excellent and proper devises, both in wordes and matter, would passe in the speedy course of reading, either as unknowen, or as not marked, and that in this kind, as in other, we might be equal to the 250 learned of other nations, I thought good to take the paines upon me, the rather for that, by meanes of some familiar acquaintaunce, I was made privie to his counsell and secret meaning in them, as also in sundry other works of his: which albeit I know he nothing so much hateth as to promulgate, yet thus much have I adventured upon his frendship, him selfe being for long time furre estraunged; hoping that this will the rather 260 occasion him to put forth divers other excellent works of his, which slepe in silence, as his *Dreames*, his *Legendes*, his *Court of Cupide*, and sondry others; whose commendations to set out were verye vayne, the thinges, though worthy of many, yet being knowen to few. These my present paynes if to any they be pleasurable or profitable, be you judge, mine own good Maister Harvey, to whom I have, both in respect of 270 your worthinesse generally, and otherwyse upon some particular and special considerations, voued this my labour, and the maydenhead of this our commen frends poetrie, himselfe having already in the beginning dedicated it to the noble and worthy gentleman, the right worshipfull Maister Philip Sidney, a special favourer and maintainer of all kind of learning. Whose cause, I pray you sir, yf envie shall stur up any wrongful 280 accusasion, defend with your mighty rhetorick and other your rare gifts of learning, as you can, and shield with your good wil, as you ought, against the malice and outrage of so many enemies as I know wilbe set on fire with the sparks of his kindled glory. And thus recommending the Author unto you, as unto his most special good frend, and my selfe unto you both, as one making singuler account of two so very good and 290 so choise frends, I bid you both most hartely farwel, and commit you and your most commendable studies to the tuicion of the Greatest.

Your owne assuredly to be commaunded,
E. K.

POST SCR.

Now I trust, Maister Harvey, that upon sight of your speciall frends and fellow poets doings, or els for envie of so many 300 unworthy quidams, which catch at the garlond which to you alone is dewe, you will be perswaded to pluck out of the hatefull darknesse those so many excellent English poemes of yours which lye hid, and bring them forth to eternall light. Trust me, you doe both them great wrong, in depriving them of the desired sonne, and also your selfe, in smoothering your deserved prayses; and all men generally, in withholding 310 from them so divine pleasures which they might conceive of your gallant English verses, as they have already doen of your Latine poemes, which, in my opinion, both for invention and elocution are very delicate and superexcellent. And thus againe I take my leave of my good Mayster Harvey. From my lodging at London, thys 10 of Aprill, 1579.

THE GENERALL ARGUMENT OF THE WHOLE BOOKE

LITTLE, I hope, needeth me at large to discourse the first originall of Æglogues, having alreadie touched the same. But, for the word Æglogues, I know, is unknowen to most, and also mistaken of some the best learned (as they think) I wyll say somewhat thereof, being not at all impertinent to my present purpose.

They were first of the Greekes, the inventours of them, called *Æglogai*, as it were 10 αἰγῶν, or αἰγονόμων, λόγοι, that is, Goteheards tales. For although in Virgile and others the speakers be more shepherds then goatheards, yet Theocritus, in whom is more ground of authoritie then in Virgile, this specially from that deriving, as from the first head and welspring, the whole invencion of his Æglogues, maketh goteheards the persons and authors of his tales. This being, who seeth not the grossenesse 20 of such as by colour of learning would make us beleeve that they are more rightly termed *Eclogai*; as they would say, extraordinary discourses of unnecessarie matter? which difinition, albe in substaunce and meaning it agree with the nature of the thing, yet no whit answereth with the ἀνάλυσις and interpretation of the word. For they be not termed *Eclogues*, but *Æglogues* : which sentence this authour very well observ- 30 ing, upon good judgement, though indeede few goteheards have to doe herein, nethelesse doubteth not to cal them by the used and best knowen name. Other curious discourses hereof I reserve to greater occasion.

These xij Æglogues, every where answering to the seasons of the twelve monthes, may be well devided into three formes or ranckes. For eyther they be plaintive, as 40 the first, the sixt, the eleventh, and the twelfth; or recreative, such as al those be which containe matter of love, or commendation of special personages; or moral, which for the most part be mixed with some satyrical bitternesse: namely the second, of reverence dewe to old age, the fift, of coloured deceipt, the seventh and ninth, of dissolute shepheards and pastours, the tenth, of contempt of poetrie and pleasaunt wits. And to this division may every thing 50 herein be reasonably applyed: a few onely

except, whose speciall purpose and meaning I am not privie to. And thus much generally of these xij Æglogues. Now will we speake particularly of all, and first of the first, which he calleth by the first monethes name, Januarie: wherein to some he may seeme fowly to have faulted, in that he erroniously beginneth with that moneth which beginneth not the yeare. For it 60 is wel known, and stoutely mainteyned with stronge reasons of the learned, that the yeare beginneth in March; for then the sonne reneweth his finished course, and the seasonable spring refresheth the earth, and the plesaunce thereof, being buried in the sadnesse of the dead winter now worne away, reliveth. This opinion maynteine the olde astrologers and philosophers, namely the reverend Andalo, and Macrobius in 70 his holydayes of Saturne; which accompt also was generally observed both of Grecians and Romans. But saving the leave of such learned heads, we mayntaine a custome of coumpting the seasons from the moneth January, upon a more speciall cause then the heathen philosophers ever coulde conceive, that is, for the incarnation of our mighty Saviour and eternall Redeemer, the Lord Christ, who, as then renewing the 80 state of the decayed world, and returning the compasse of expired yeres to theyr former date and first commencement, left to us his heires a memoriall of his birth in the ende of the last yeere and beginning of the next: which reckoning, beside that eternall monument of our salvation, leaneth also uppon good proofe of special judgement. For albeit that in elder times, when as yet the coumpt of the yere was not perfected, 90 as afterwarde it was by Julius Cæsar, they began to tel the monethes from Marches beginning, and according to the same, God (as is sayd in Scripture) comaunded the people of the Jewes to count the moneth *Abib*, that which we call March, for the first moneth, in remembraunce that in that moneth he brought them out of the land of Ægipt, yet according to tradition of latter times it hath bene otherwise observed, 100 both in government of the Church and rule of mightiest realmes. For from Julius Cæsar, who first observed the leape yeere, which he called *Bissextilem Annum*, and brought into a more certain course the odde wandring dayes which of the Greekes were called ὑπερβαίνοντες, of the Romanes *intercalares* (for in such matter of learning I am forced to use the termes of the learned) the monethes have bene nombred xij, which in the first [110] ordinaunce of Romulus were but tenne, counting but ccciiij dayes in every yeare, and beginning with March. But Numa Pompilius, who was the father of al the Romain ceremonies and religion, seeing that reckoning to agree neither with the course of the sonne, nor of the moone, thereunto added two monethes, January and February: wherin it seemeth, that wise king minded upon good reason to begin the yeare at [120] Januarie, of him therefore so called *tanquam janua anni*, the gate and entraunce of the yere, or of the name of the god *Janus*, to which god for that the old Paynims attributed the byrth and beginning of all creatures new comming into the worlde, it seemeth that he therfore to him assigned the beginning and first entraunce of the yeare. Which account for the most part hath hetherto continued: notwithstanding that [130] the Ægiptians beginne theyr yeare at September, for that, according to the opinion of the best rabbins and very purpose of the Scripture selfe, God made the worlde in that moneth, that is called of them *Tisri*. And therefore he commaunded them to keepe the feast of Pavilions in the end of the yeare, in the xv. day of the seventh moneth, which before that time was the first.

But our authour, respecting nether the [140] subtiltie of thone parte, nor the antiquitie of thother, thinketh it fittest, according to the simplicitie of commen understanding, to begin with Januarie, wening it perhaps no decorum that shepheard should be seene in matter of so deepe insight, or canvase a case of so doubtful judgment. So therefore beginneth he, and so continueth he throughout.

JANUARYE

ÆGLOGA PRIMA

ARGUMENT

IN this fyrst Æglogue Colin Cloute, a shepheardes boy, complaineth him of his unfortunate love, being but newly (as semeth) enamoured of a countrie lasse called Rosalinde: with which strong affection being very sore traveled, he compareth his carefull case to the sadde season of the yeare, to the frostie ground, to the frosen trees, and to his owne winterbeaten flocke. And lastlye, fynding himselfe robbed of all former pleasaunce and delights, hee breaketh his pipe in peeces, and casteth him selfe to the ground.

COLIN CLOUTE.

A SHEPEHEARDS boye (no better doe him call)
When winters wastful spight was almost spent,
All in a sunneshine day, as did befall,
Led forth his flock, that had bene long ypent.
So faynt they woxe, and feeble in the folde,
That now unnethes their feete could them uphold.

All as the sheepe, such was the shepheards looke,
For pale and wanne he was, (alas the while!)
May seeme he lovd, or els some care he tooke:
Well couth he tune his pipe, and frame his stile. [10]
Tho to a hill his faynting flocke he ledde,
And thus him playnd, the while his shepe there fedde.

'Ye gods of love, that pitie lovers payne,
(If any gods the paine of lovers pitie,)
Looke from above, where you in joyes remaine,
And bowe your eares unto my dolefull dittie.
And Pan, thou shepheards god, that once didst love,
Pitie the paines that thou thy selfe didst prove.

'Thou barrein ground, whome winters wrath hath wasted,
Art made a myrrhour to behold my plight:
Whilome thy fresh spring flowrd, and after hasted [21]
Thy sommer prowde with daffadillies dight,
And now is come thy wynters stormy state,
Thy mantle mard wherein thou maskedst late.

'Such rage as winters reigneth in my heart,
My life bloud friesing with unkindly cold:

Such stormy stoures do breede my balefull
　　smart,
As if my yeare were wast and woxen old.
And yet, alas! but now my spring be-
　　gonne,
And yet, alas! yt is already donne.　　30

'You naked trees, whose shady leaves are
　　lost,
Wherein the byrds were wont to build their
　　bowre,
And now are clothd with mosse and hoary
　　frost,
Instede of bloosmes, wherwith your buds
　　did flowre:
I see your teares, that from your boughes
　　doe raine,
Whose drops in drery ysicles remaine.

'All so my lustfull leafe is drye and sere,
My timely buds with wayling all are wasted;
The blossome which my braunch of youth
　　did beare
With breathed sighes is blowne away and
　　blasted;　　40
And from mine eyes the drizling teares
　　descend,
As on your boughes the ysicles depend.

'Thou feeble flocke, whose fleece is rough
　　and rent,
Whose knees are weake through fast and
　　evill fare,
Mayst witnesse well by thy ill governement,
Thy maysters mind is overcome with
　　care.
Thou weake, I wanne; thou leane, I quite
　　forlorne:
With mourning pyne I; you with pyning
　　mourne.

'A thousand sithes I curse that carefull
　　hower
Wherein I longd the neighbour towne to
　　see:　　50
And eke tenne thousand sithes I blesse the
　　stoure
Wherein I sawe so fayre a sight as shee.
Yet all for naught: such sight hath bred
　　my bane.
Ah, God! that love should breede both joy
　　and payne!

'It is not Hobbinol wherefore I plaine,
Albee my love he seeke with dayly suit:

His clownish gifts and curtsies I disdaine,
His kiddes, his cracknelles, and his early
　　fruit.
Ah, foolish Hobbinol! thy gyfts bene
　　vayne:
Colin them gives to Rosalind againe.　　60

'I love thilke lasse, (alas! why doe I love?)
And am forlorne, (alas! why am I lorne?)
Shee deignes not my good will, but doth
　　reprove,
And of my rurall musick holdeth scorne.
Shepheards devise she hateth as the
　　snake,
And laughes the songes that Colin Clout
　　doth make.

'Wherefore, my pype, albee rude Pan thou
　　please,
Yet for thou pleasest not where most I
　　would:
And thou, unlucky Muse, that wontst to
　　ease
My musing mynd, yet canst not, when thou
　　should:　　70
Both pype and Muse shall sore the while
　　abye.'
So broke his oaten pype, and downe dyd
　　lye.

By that, the welked Phœbus gan availe
His weary waine, and nowe the frosty
　　Night
Her mantle black through heaven gan over-
　　haile.
Which seene, the pensife boy, halfe in des-
　　pight,
Arose, and homeward drove his sonned
　　sheepe,
Whose hanging heads did seeme his care-
　　full case to weepe.

COLINS EMBLEME.

Anchôra speme.

GLOSSE

Colin Cloute is a name not greatly used, and
yet have I sene a poesie of Maister Skeltons
under that title. But indeede the word Colin
is Frenche, and used of the French poete Marot
(if he be worthy of the name of a poete) in a
certein æglogue. Under which name this poete
secretly shadoweth himself, as sometime did
Virgil under the name of Tityrus, thinking it

much fitter then such Latine names, for the great unlikelyhoode of the language.   10

Unnethes, scarcely.

Couthe commeth of the verbe *Conne*, that is, to know or to have skill. As well interpreteth the same the worthy Sir Tho. Smitth, in his booke of government : wherof I have a perfect copie in wryting, lent me by his kinseman, and my verye singular good freend, Maister Gabriel Harvey : as also of some other his most grave and excellent wrytings.

Sythe, time.   20

Neighbour towne, the next towne : expressing the Latine *vicina*.

Stoure, a fitt.

Sere, withered.

His clownish gyfts imitateth Virgils verse,

'Rusticus es Corydon, nec munera curat Alexis.'

Hobbinol is a fained country name, whereby, it being so commune and usuall, seemeth to be hidden the person of some his very speciall and most familiar freend, whom he entirely and   30 extraordinarily beloved, as peradventure shall be more largely declared hereafter. In thys place seemeth to be some savour of disorderly love, which the learned call *pæderastice* : but it is gathered beside his meaning. For who that hath red Plato his dialogue called *Alcybiades*, Xenophon, and Maximus Tyrius, of Socrates opinions, may easily perceive that such love is muche to be alowed and liked of, specially so meant as Socrates used it : who sayth, that   40 in deede he loved Alcybiades extremely, yet not Alcybiades person, but hys soule, which is Alcybiades owne selfe. And so is *pæderastice* much to be præferred before *gynerastice*, that is, the love whiche enflameth men with lust toward womankind. But yet let no man thinke, that herein I stand with Lucian, or his develish disciple Unico Aretino, in defence of execrable and horrible sinnes of forbidden and unlawful fleshlinesse. Whose abominable errour is   50 fully confuted of Perionius, and others.

I love, a prety epanorthosis in these two verses, and withall a paronomasia or playing with the word, where he sayth, *I love thilke lasse* (alas, &c.

Rosalinde is also a feigned name, which, being wel ordered, wil bewray the very name of hys love and mistresse, whom by that name he coloureth. So as Ovide shadoweth hys love under the name of Corynna, which of some   60 is supposed to be Julia, themperor Augustus his daughter, and wyfe to Agryppa. So doth Aruntius Stella every where call his lady Asteris and Ianthis, albe it is wel knowen that her right name was Violantilla : as witnesseth Statius in his *Epithalamium*. And so the famous paragone of Italy, Madonna Cœlia, in her letters envelopeth her selfe under the name of

Zima : and Petrona under the name of Bell-ochia. And this generally hath bene a com-   70 mon custome of counterfeicting the names of secret personages.

Avail, bring downe.

Overhaile, drawe over.

His *Embleme* or *poesye* is here under added in Italian, *Anchôra speme :* the meaning wherof is, that notwithstandeing his extreme passion and lucklesse love, yet, leaning on hope, he is some what recomforted.

FEBRUARIE

ÆGLOGA SECUNDA

ARGUMENT

THIS Æglogue is rather morall and generall then bent to any secrete or particular purpose. It specially conteyneth a discourse of old age, in the persone of Thenot, an olde shepheard, who, for his crookednesse and unlustinesse, is scorned of Cuddie, an unhappy heardmans boye. The matter very well accordeth with the season of the moneth, the yeare now drouping, and, as it were, drawing to his last age. For as in this time of yeare, so then in our bodies, there is a dry and withering cold, which congealeth the crudled blood, and frieseth the wether-beaten flesh, with stormes of fortune and hoare frosts of care. To which purpose the olde man telleth a tale of the Oake and the Bryer, so lively and so feelingly, as, if the thing were set forth in some picture before our eyes, more plainly could not appeare.

CUDDIE. THENOT.

Cud. Ah for pittie ! wil rancke winters rage
These bitter blasts never ginne tasswage ?
The kene cold blowes through my beaten hyde,
All as I were through the body gryde.
My ragged rontes all shiver and shake,
As doen high towers in an earthquake:
They wont in the wind wagge their wrigle tailes,
Perke as peacock: but nowe it avales.
    The. Lewdly complainest thou, laesie ladde,
Of winters wracke, for making thee sadde.
Must not the world wend in his commun course,   11
From good to badd, and from badde to worse,

From worse unto that is worst of all,
And then returne to his former fall?
Who will not suffer the stormy time,
Where will he live tyll the lusty prime?
Selfe have I worne out thrise threttie
    yeares,
Some in much joy, many in many teares;
Yet never complained of cold nor heate,
Of sommers flame, nor of winters threat; 20
Ne ever was to fortune foeman,
But gently tooke that ungently came:
And ever my flocke was my chiefe care;
Winter or sommer they mought well fare.
    Cud. No marveile, Thenot, if thou can
    beare
Cherefully the winters wrathfull cheare:
For age and winter accord full nie,
This chill, that cold, this crooked, that
    wrye;
And as the lowring wether lookes downe,
So semest thou like Good Fryday to
    frowne.   30
But my flowring youth is foe to frost,
My shippe unwont in stormes to be tost.
    The. The soveraigne of seas he blames
    in vaine,
That, once seabeate, will to sea againe.
So loytring live you little heardgroomes,
Keeping your beastes in the budded
    broomes:
And when the shining sunne laugheth once,
You deemen the spring is come attonce.
Tho gynne you, fond flyes, the cold to scorne,
And, crowing in pypes made of greene
    corne,   40
You thinken to be lords of the yeare.
But eft, when ye count you freed from feare,
Comes the breme winter with chamfred
    browes,
Full of wrinckles and frostie furrowes,
Drerily shooting his stormy darte,
Which cruddles the blood, and pricks the
    harte.
Then is your carelesse corage accoied,
Your carefull heards with cold bene an-
    noied:
Then paye you the price of your surquedrie,
With weeping, and wayling, and misery. 50
    Cud. Ah, foolish old man! I scorne thy
    skill,
That wouldest me my springing youngth to
    spil.
I deeme thy braine emperished bee
Through rusty elde, that hath rotted thee:
Or sicker thy head veray tottie is,

So on thy corbe shoulder it leanes amisse.
Now thy selfe hast lost both lopp and topp,
Als my budding braunch thou wouldest
    cropp:
But were thy yeares greene, as now bene
    myne,
To other delights they would encline.   60
Tho wouldest thou learne to caroll of love,
And hery with hymnes thy lasses glove:
Tho wouldest thou pype of Phyllis prayse:
But Phyllis is myne for many dayes:
I wonne her with a gyrdle of gelt,
Embost with buegle about the belt:
Such an one shepeheards woulde make full
    faine,
Such an one would make thee younge
    againe.
    The. Thou art a fon, of thy love to
    boste;
All that is lent to love wyll be lost.   70
    Cud. Seest howe brag yond bullocke
    beares,
So smirke, so smoothe, his pricked eares?
His hornes bene as broade as rainebowe
    bent,
His dewelap as lythe as lasse of Kent.
See howe he venteth into the wynd.
Weenest of love is not his mynd?
Seemeth thy flocke thy counsell can,
So lustlesse bene they, so weake, so wan,
Clothed with cold, and hoary wyth frost.
Thy flocks father his corage hath lost: 80
Thy ewes, that wont to have blowen bags,
Like wailefull widdowes hangen their crags:
The rather lambes bene starved with cold,
All for their maister is lustlesse and old.
    The. Cuddie, I wote thou kenst little
    good,
So vainely tadvaunce thy headlessehood.
For youngth is a bubble blown up with
    breath,
Whose witt is weakenesse, whose wage is
    death,
Whose way is wildernesse, whose ynne
    penaunce,
And stoopegallaunt age, the hoste of gree-
    vaunce.   90
But shall I tel thee a tale of truth,
Which I cond of Tityrus in my youth,
Keeping his sheepe on the hils of Kent?
    Cud. To nought more, Thenot, my mind
    is bent,
Then to heare novells of his devise:
They bene so well thewed, and so wise,
What ever that good old man bespake.

The. Many meete tales of youth did he
    make,
And some of love, and some of chevalrie:
But none fitter then this to applie.   100
Now listen a while, and hearken the end.
    There grewe an aged tree on the greene,
A goodly Oake sometime had it bene,
With armes full strong and largely dis-
    playd,
But of their leaves they were disarayde:
The bodie bigge, and mightely pight,
Throughly rooted, and of wonderous hight:
Whilome had bene the king of the field,
And mochell mast to the husband did yielde,
And with his nuts larded many swine.   110
But now the gray mosse marred his rine,
His bared boughes were beaten with
    stormes,
His toppe was bald, and wasted with
    wormes,
His honor decayed, his braunches sere.
    Hard by his side grewe a bragging Brere,
Which proudly thrust into thelement,
And seemed to threat the firmament.
Yt was embellisht with blossomes fayre,
And thereto aye wonned to repayre   119
The shepheards daughters, to gather flowres,
To peinct their girlonds with his colowres:
And in his small bushes used to shrowde
The sweete nightingale singing so lowde:
Which made this foolish Brere wexe so
    bold,
That on a time he cast him to scold
And snebbe the good Oake, for he was old.
    'Why standst there,' quoth he, 'thou
    brutish blocke?
Nor for fruict nor for shadowe serves thy
    stocke.
Seest how fresh my flowers bene spredde,
Dyed in lilly white and cremsin redde,   130
With leaves engrained in lusty greene,
Colours meete to clothe a mayden queene?
Thy wast bignes but combers the grownd,
And dirks the beauty of my blossomes
    round.
The mouldie mosse, which thee accloieth,
My sinamon smell too much annoieth.
Wherefore soone, I rede thee, hence remove,
Least thou the price of my displeasure
    prove.'
So spake this bold Brere with great dis-
    daine:
Little him answered the Oake againe,   140
But yielded, with shame and greefe adawed,
That of a weede he was overawed.

    Yt chaunced after upon a day,
The husbandman selfe to come that way,
Of custome for to survewe his grownd,
And his trees of state in compasse rownd.
Him when the spitefull Brere had espyed,
Causlesse complained, and lowdly cryed
Unto his lord, stirring up sterne strife:
    'O my liege lord, the god of my life,   150
Pleaseth you ponder your suppliants plaint,
Caused of wrong, and cruell constraint,
Which I your poore vassall dayly endure:
And but your goodnes the same recure,
Am like for desperate doole to dye,
Through felonous force of mine enemie.'
    Greatly aghast with this piteous plea,
Him rested the goodman on the lea,
And badde the Brere in his plaint proceede.
With painted words tho gan this proude
    weede   160
(As most usen ambitious folke)
His coloured crime with craft to cloke.
    ' Ah my soveraigne, lord of creatures all,
Thou placer of plants both humble and tall,
Was not I planted of thine owne hand,
To be the primrose of all thy land,
With flowring blossomes to furnish the
    prime,
And scarlot berries in sommer time?
How falls it then, that this faded Oake,
Whose bodie is sere, whose braunches
    broke,   170
Whose naked armes stretch unto the fyre,
Unto such tyrannie doth aspire;
Hindering with his shade my lovely light,
And robbing me of the swete sonnes sight?
So beate his old boughes my tender side,
That oft the bloud springeth from wounds
    wyde:
Untimely my flowres forced to fall,
That bene the honor of your coronall.
And oft he lets his cancker wormes light
Upon my braunches, to worke me more
    spight: 180
And oft his hoarie locks downe doth cast,
Where with my fresh flowretts bene defast.
For this, and many more such outrage,
Craving your goodlihead to aswage
The ranckorous rigour of his might,
Nought aske I, but onely to hold my right;
Submitting me to your good sufferance,
And praying to be garded from greevance.'
    To this the Oake cast him to replie
Well as he couth: but his enemie   190
Had kindled such coles of displeasure,
That the good man noulde stay his leasure,

But home him hasted with furious heate,
Encreasing his wrath with many a threate.
His harmefull hatchet he hent in hand,
(Alas, that it so ready should stand !)
And to the field alone he speedeth,
(Ay little helpe to harme there needeth.)
Anger nould let him speake to the tree,
Enaunter his rage mought cooled bee;   200
But to the roote bent his sturdy stroke,
And made many wounds in the wast Oake.
The axes edge did oft turne againe,
As halfe unwilling to cutte the graine:
Semed, the sencelesse yron dyd feare,
Or to wrong holy eld did forbeare.
For it had bene an auncient tree,
Sacred with many a mysteree,
And often crost with the priestes crewe,
And often halowed with holy water dewe.
But sike fancies weren foolerie,   211
And broughten this Oake to this miserye.
For nought mought they quitten him from
      decay:
For fiercely the goodman at him did laye.
The blocke oft groned under the blow,
And sighed to see his neare overthrow.
In fine, the steele had pierced his pitth:
Tho downe to the earth he fell forthwith:
His wonderous weight made the grounde
      to quake,
Thearth shronke under him, and seemed to
      shake.   220
There lyeth the Oake, pitied of none.
Now stands the Brere like a lord alone,
Puffed up with pryde and vaine pleasaunce:
But all this glee had no continuaunce.
For eftsones winter gan to approche,
The blustring Boreas did encroche,
And beate upon the solitarie Brere:
For nowe no succoure was seene him nere.
Now gan he repent his pryde to late:
For naked left and disconsolate,   230
The byting frost nipt his stalke dead,
The watrie wette weighed downe his head,
And heaped snowe burdned him so sore,
That nowe upright he can stand no more:
And being downe, is trodde in the durt
Of cattell, and brouzed, and sorely hurt.
Such was thend of this ambitious Brere,
For scorning eld —
  Cud. Now I pray thee, shepheard, tel it
      not forth:
Here is a long tale, and little worth.   240
So longe have I listened to thy speche,
That graffed to the ground is my breche:
My hartblood is welnigh frorne, I feele,

And my galage growne fast to my heele:
But little ease of thy lewd tale I tasted.
Hye thee home, shepheard, the day is nigh
      wasted.

THENOTS EMBLEME.

Iddio, perchè è vecchio,
Fa suoi al suo essempio.

CUDDIES EMBLEME.

Niuno vecchio
Spaventa Iddio.

GLOSSE

Kene, sharpe.
Gride, perced : an olde word much used of
Lidgate, but not found (that I know of) in
Chaucer.
Ronts, young bullockes.
Wracke, ruine or violence, whence commeth
shipwracke : and not *wreake*, that is vengeaunce
or wrath.
Foeman, a foe.
Thenot, the name of a shepheard in Marot
his Æglogues.   11
The soveraigne of seas is Neptune the god
of the seas. The saying is borowed of Mimus
Publianus, which used this proverb in a verse,
'Improbè Neptunum accusat, qui iterum naufragium
      facit.'

Heardgromes, Chaucers verse almost whole.
Fond Flyes: He compareth carelesse slug-
gardes, or ill husbandmen, to flyes, that so
soone as the sunne shineth, or yt wexeth any
thing warme, begin to flye abroade, when
sodeinly they be overtaken with cold.   21
But eft when, a verye excellent and lively
description of winter, so as may bee indiffer-
ently taken, eyther for old age, or for winter
season.
Breme, chill, bitter.
Chamfred, chapt, or wrinckled.
Accoied, plucked downe and daunted.
Surquedrie, pryde.
Elde, olde age.   30
Sicker, sure.
Tottie, wavering.
Corbe, crooked.
Herie, worshippe.
Phyllis, the name of some mayde unknowen,
whom Cuddie, whose person is secrete, loved.
The name is usuall in Theocritus, Virgile, and
Mantuane.
Belte, a girdle or wast band.
A fon, a foole.   40
Lythe, soft and gentile.
Venteth, snuffeth in the wind.
Thy flocks father, the ramme.

Crags, neckes.

Rather lambes, that be ewed early in the beginning of the yeare.

Youth is, a verye moral and pitthy allegorie of youth, and the lustes thereof, compared to a wearie wayfaring man.

Tityrus: I suppose he meanes Chaucer, 50 whose prayse for pleasaunt tales cannot dye, so long as the memorie of hys name shal live, and the name of poetrie shal endure.

Well thewed, that is, *bene moratæ,* full of morall wisenesse.

There grew: This tale of the Oake and the Brere he telleth as learned of Chaucer, but it is cleane in another kind, and rather like to Æsopes fables. It is very excellente for pleasaunt descriptions, being altogether a 60 certaine icon or hypotyposis of disdainfull younkers.

Embellisht, beautified and adorned.

To wonne, to haunt or frequent.

Sneb, checke.

Why standst: The speach is scorneful and very presumptuous.

Engrained, dyed in grain.

Accloieth, encombreth.

Adawed, daunted and confounded. 70

Trees of state, taller trees, fitte for timber wood.

Sterne strife, said Chaucer, sc. fell and sturdy.

O my liege, a maner of supplication, wherein is kindly coloured the affection and speache of ambitious men.

Coronall, garlande.

Flourets, young blossomes.

The Primrose, the chiefe and worthiest.

Naked armes, metaphorically ment of the 80 bare boughes, spoyled of leaves. This colourably he speaketh, as adjudging hym to the fyre.

The blood, spoken of a blocke, as it were of a living creature, figuratively, and (as they say) κατ᾽ εἰκασμόν.

Hoarie lockes, metaphorically for withered leaves.

Hent, caught.

Nould, for would not. 90

Ay, evermore.

Wounds, gashes.

Enaunter, least that.

The priestes crewe, holy water pott, wherewith the popishe priest used to sprinckle and hallowe the trees from mischaunce. Such blindnesse was in those times, which the poete supposeth to have bene the finall decay of this auncient Oake.

The blocke oft groned, a livelye figure, 100 whiche geveth sence and feeling to unsensible creatures, as Virgile also sayeth: 'Saxa gemunt gravido,' &c.

Boreas, the northerne wynd, that bringeth the moste stormie weather.

Glee, chere and jollitie.

For scorning eld: And minding (as shoulde seme) to have made ryme to the former verse, he is conningly cutte of by Cuddye, as disdayning to here any more. 110

Galage, a startuppe or clownish shoe.

EMBLEME.

This embleme is spoken of Thenot, as a moral of his former tale: namelye, that God, which is himselfe most aged, being before al ages, and without beginninge, maketh those whom he loveth like to himselfe, in heaping yeares unto theyre dayes, and blessing them wyth longe lyfe. For the blessing of age is not given to all, but unto those whome God will so blesse: and albeit that many evil men 120 reache unto such fulnesse of yeares, and some also wexe olde in myserie and thraldome, yet therefore is not age ever the lesse blessing. For even to such evill men such number of yeares is added, that they may in their last dayes repent, and come to their first home. So the old man checketh the rashheaded boy for despysing his gray and frostye heares. Whom Cuddye doth counterbuff with a byting and bitter proverbe, spoken indeede at 130 the first in contempt of old age generally. For it was an old opinion, and yet is continued in some mens conceipt, that men of yeares have no feare of god at al, or not so much as younger folke. For that being rypened with long experience, and having passed many bitter brunts and blastes of vengeaunce, they dread no stormes of Fortune, nor wrathe of gods, nor daunger of menne, as being eyther by longe and ripe wisedome armed against all mis- 140 chaunces and adversitie, or with much trouble hardened against all troublesome tydes: lyke unto the Ape, of which is sayd in Æsops fables, that oftentimes meeting the Lyon, he was at first sore aghast and dismayed at the grimnes and austeritie of hys countenance, but at last being acquainted with his lookes, he was so furre from fearing him, that he would familiarly gybe and jest with him: suche longe experience breedeth in some men securitie. Although 150 it please Erasmus, a great clerke and good old father, more fatherly and favourablye to construe it, in his Adages, for his own behoofe, that by the proverbe, 'Nemo senex metuit Jovem,' is not meant, that old men have no feare of God at al, but that they be furre from superstition and idolatrous regard of false gods, as is Jupiter. But his greate learning notwithstanding, it is to plaine to be gainsayd, that olde men are muche more enclined to such fond fooleries, then younger heades.

MARCH

ÆGLOGA TERTIA

ARGUMENT

IN this Æglogue two shepheards boyes, taking occasion of the season, beginne to make purpose of love, and other pleasaunce which to springtime is most agreeable. The speciall meaning hereof is to give certaine markes and tokens to know Cupide, the poets god of love. But more particularlye, I thinke, in the person of Thomalin is meant some secrete freend, who scorned Love and his knights so long, till at length him selfe was entangled, and unwares wounded with the dart of some beautifull regard, which is Cupides arrow.

WILLYE. THOMALIN.

Wil. Thomalin, why sytten we soe,
As weren overwent with woe,
  Upon so fayre a morow ?
The joyous time now nigheth fast,
That shall alegge this bitter blast,
  And slake the winters sorowe.
Tho. Sicker, Willye, thou warnest well:
For winters wrath beginnes to quell,
  And pleasant spring appeareth.
The grasse nowe ginnes to be refresht,   10
The swallow peepes out of her nest,
  And clowdie welkin cleareth.
Wil. Seest not thilke same hawthorne studde,
How bragly it beginnes to budde,
  And utter his tender head ?
Flora now calleth forth eche flower,
And bids make ready Maias bowre,
  That newe is upryst from bedde.
Tho shall we sporten in delight,
And learne with Lettice to wexe light,   20
  That scornefully lookes askaunce;
Tho will we little Love awake,
That nowe sleepeth in Lethe lake,
  And pray him leaden our daunce.
Tho. Willye, I wene thou bee assott:
For lustie Love still sleepeth not,
  But is abroad at his game.
Wil. How kenst thou that he is awoke ?
Or hast thy selfe his slomber broke ?
  Or made previe to the same ?   30
Tho. No, but happely I hym spyde,
Where in a bush he did him hide,
  With winges of purple and blewe.
And were not that my sheepe would stray,
The previe marks I would bewray,
  Whereby by chaunce I him knewe

Wil. Thomalin, have no care forthy;
My selfe will have a double eye,
  Ylike to my flocke and thine:
For als at home I have a syre,   40
A stepdame eke, as whott as fyre,
  That dewly adayes counts mine.
Tho. Nay, but thy seeing will not serve,
My sheepe for that may chaunce to swerve,
  And fall into some mischiefe.
For sithens is but the third morowe
That I chaunst to fall a sleepe with sorowe,
  And waked againe with griefe:
The while thilke same unhappye ewe,
Whose clouted legge her hurt doth shewe,
  Fell headlong into a dell,   51
And there unjoynted both her bones:
Mought her necke bene joynted attones,
  She shoulde have neede no more spell.
Thelf was so wanton and so wood,
(But now I trowe can better good)
  She mought ne gang on the greene.
Wil. Let be, as may be, that is past:
That is to come, let be forecast.
  Now tell us what thou hast seene.   60
Tho. It was upon a holiday,
When shepheardes groomes han leave to
    play,
  I cast to goe a shooting.
Long wandring up and downe the land,
With bowe and bolts in either hand,
  For birds in bushes tooting,
At length within an yvie todde
(There shrouded was the little god)
  I heard a busie bustling.
I bent my bolt against the bush,   70
Listening if any thing did rushe,
  But then heard no more rustling.
Tho peeping close into the thicke,
Might see the moving of some quicke,
  Whose shape appeared not:
But were it faerie, feend, or snake,
My courage earnd it to awake,
  And manfully thereat shotte.
With that sprong forth a naked swayne,
With spotted winges like peacocks trayne,
  And laughing lope to a tree,   81
His gylden quiver at his backe,
And silver bowe, which was but slacke,
  Which lightly he bent at me.
That seeing I, levelde againe,
And shott at him with might and maine,
  As thicke as it had hayled.
So long I shott that al was spent:
Tho pumie stones I hastly hent,
  And threwe; but nought availed: 90

He was so wimble and so wight,
From bough to bough he lepped light,
  And oft the pumies latched.
Therewith affrayd I ranne away:
But he, that earst seemd but to playe,
  A shaft in earnest snatched,
And hit me running in the heele:
For then, I little smart did feele;
  But soone it sore encreased.
And now itranckleth more and more,   100
And inwardly it festreth sore,
  Ne wote I how to cease it.
Wil. Thomalin, I pittie thy plight.
Perdie, with Love thou diddest fight:
  I know him by a token.
For once I heard my father say,
How he him caught upon a day,
  (Whereof he wilbe wroken)
Entangled in a fowling net,
Which he for carrion crowes had set,   110
  That in our peeretree haunted.
Tho sayd, he was a winged lad,
But bowe and shafts as then none had,
  Els had he sore be daunted.
But see, the welkin thicks apace,
And stouping Phebus steepes his face:
  Yts time to hast us homeward.

WILLYES EMBLEME.

To be wise and eke to love,
Is graunted scarce to god above.

THOMALINS EMBLEME.

Of hony and of gaule in love there is store:
The honye is much, but the gaule is more.

GLOSS

This Æglogue seemeth somewhat to resemble
that same of Theocritus, wherein the boy likewise telling the old man, that he had shot at a
winged boy in a tree, was by hym warned to
beware of mischiefe to come.

Overwent, overgone.

Alegge, to lessen or aswage.

To quell, to abate.

Welkin, the skie.

The swallow, which bird useth to be 10
counted the messenger, and as it were, the forerunner, of springe.

Flora, the goddesse of flowres, but indede
(as saith Tacitus) a famous harlot, which, with
the abuse of her body having gotten great
riches, made the people of Rome her heyre:
who, in remembraunce of so great beneficence,
appointed a yearely feste for the memoriall of
her, calling her, not as she was, nor as some
doe think, *Andronico.* but *Flora:* making 20
her the goddesse of all floures, and doing yerely
to her solemne sacrifice.

Maias bower, that is, the pleasaunt field, or
rather the Maye bushes. Maia is a goddes and
the mother of Mercurie, in honour of whome
the moneth of Maye is of her name so called,
as sayth Macrobius.

Lettice, the name of some country lasse.

Ascaunce, askewe or asquint.

Forthy, therefore.   30

Lethe is a lake in hell, which the poetes call
the lake of forgetfulnes. For *Lethe* signifieth
forgetfulnes. Wherein the soules being dipped,
did forget the cares of their former lyfe. So
that by Love sleeping in Lethe lake, he meaneth
he was almost forgotten, and out of knowledge,
by reason of winters hardnesse, when al pleasures, as it were, sleepe and weare oute of
mynde.

Assotte, to dote.   40

His slomber: To breake Loves slomber is to
exercise the delightes of love and wanton pleasures.

Winges of purple, so is he feyned of the
poetes.

For als: He imitateth Virgils verse,

' Est mihi namque domi pater, est injusta noverca, &c. '

A dell, a hole in the ground.

Spell is a kinde of verse or charme, that in
elder tymes they used often to say over every 50
thing that they would have preserved, as the
nightspel for theeves, and the woodspell. And
herehence, I thinke, is named the gospell, as it
were Gods spell or worde. And so sayth Chaucer, ' Listeneth Lordings to my spell.'

Gange, goe.

An yvie todde, a thicke bush.

Swaine, a boye: for so is he described of
the poetes to be a boye, sc. alwayes freshe and
lustie: blindfolded, because he maketh no 60
difference of personages: wyth divers coloured
winges, sc. ful of flying fancies: with bowe and
arrow, that is, with glaunce of beautye, which
prycketh as a forked arrowe. He is sayd also
to have shafts, some leaden, some golden: that
is, both pleasure for the gracious and loved,
and sorow for the lover that is disdayned or
forsaken. But who liste more at large to behold Cupids colours and furniture, let him reade
ether Propertius, or Moschus his Idyllion 70
of *wandring Love,* being now most excellently
translated into Latine, by the singuler learned
man Angelus Politianus: whych worke I have
seene, amongst other of thys poets doings, very
wel translated also into Englishe rymes.

Wimble and wighte, quicke and deliver.

In the heele is very poetically spoken, and
not without speciall judgement. For I remember that in Homer it is sayd of Thetis, that shee
tooke her young babe Achilles, being newly 80

borne, and, holding him by the heele, dipped him in the River of Styx. The vertue whereof is, to defend and keepe the bodyes washed therein from any mortall wound. So Achilles being washed al over, save onely his hele, by which his mother held, was in the rest invulnerable : therfore by Paris was feyned to bee shotte with a poysoned arrowe in the heele, whiles he was busie about the marying of Polyxena in the temple of Apollo : which mysticall 90 fable Eustathius unfolding sayth : that by wounding in the hele is meant lustfull love. For from the heele (as say the best phisitions) to the previe partes there passe certaine veines and slender synnewes, as also the like come from the head, and are carryed lyke little pypes behynd the eares : so that (as sayth Hipocrates) yf those veynes there be cut asonder, the partie straighte becometh cold and unfruiteful. Which reason our poete wel weighing, mak- 100 eth this shepheards boye of purpose to be wounded by Love in the heele.

Latched, caught.

Wroken, revenged.

For once: In this tale is sette out the simplicitye of shepheards opinion of Love.

Stouping Phœbus is a periphrasis of the sunne setting.

EMBLEME.

Hereby is meant, that all the delights of love, wherein wanton youth walloweth, be but 110 follye mixt with bitternesse, and sorow sawced with repentaunce. For besides that the very affection of love it selfe tormenteth the mynde, and vexeth the body many wayes, with unrestfulnesse all night, and wearines all day, seeking for that we can not have, and fynding that we would not have : even the selfe things which best before us lyked, in course of time and chaung of ryper yeares, whiche also therewithall chaungeth our wonted lyking and 120 former fantasies, will then seeme lothsome and breede us annoyaunce, when yougthes flowre is withered, and we fynde our bodyes and wits aunswere not to suche vayne jollitie and lustfull pleasaunce.

APRILL

ÆGLOGA QUARTA

ARGUMENT

THIS Æglogue is purposely intended to the honor and prayse of our most gracious sovereigne, Queene Elizabeth. The speakers herein be Hobbinoll and Thenott, two shepheardes : the which Hobbinoll, being before mentioned greatly to have loved Colin, is here set forth more largely, complayning him of that boyes great misadventure in love, whereby his mynd was alienate and withdrawen not onely from him, who moste loved him, but also from all former delightes and studies, aswell in pleasaunt pyping as conning ryming and singing, and other his laudable exercises. Whereby he taketh occasion, for proofe of his more excellencie and skill in poetrie, to recorde a songe which the sayd Colin sometime made in honor of her Majestie, whom abruptely he termeth Elysa.

THENOT. HOBBINOLL.

The. Tell me, good Hobbinoll, what garres thee greete ?
    What ! hath some wolfe thy tender lambes ytorne ?
Or is thy bagpype broke, that soundes so sweete ?
    Or art thou of thy loved lasse forlorne ?

Or bene thine eyes attempred to the yeare,
    Quenching the gasping furrowes thirst with rayne ?
Like April shoure, so stremes the trickling teares
    Adowne thy cheeke, to quenche thy thristye payne.

Hob. Nor thys, nor that, so muche doeth make me mourne,
    But for the ladde whome long I lovd so deare 10
Nowe loves a lasse that all his love doth scorne :
    He, plongd in payne, his tressed locks dooth teare.

Shepheards delights he dooth them all forsweare,
    Hys pleasaunt pipe, whych made us meriment,
He wylfully hath broke, and doth forbeare
    His wonted songs, wherein he all outwent.

The. What is he for a ladde you so lament ?
    Ys love such pinching payne to them that prove ?
And hath he skill to make so excellent,
    Yet hath so little skill to brydle love ? 20

Hob. Colin thou kenst, the southerne shepheardes boye :
    Him Love hath wounded with a deadly darte.

Whilome on him was all my care and joye,
  Forcing with gyfts to winne his wanton
    heart.

But now from me hys madding mynd is
    starte,
  And woes the widdowes daughter of the
    glenne:
So nowe fayre Rosalind hath bredde hys
    smart,
  So now his frend is chaunged for a frenne.

The. But if hys ditties bene so trimly dight,
  I pray thee, Hobbinoll, recorde some
    one,   30
The whiles our flockes doe graze about in
    sight,
  And we close shrowded in thys shade
    alone.

Hob. Contented I: then will I singe his
    laye
Of fayre Elisa, queene of shepheardes all;
Which once he made, as by a spring he laye,
  And tuned it unto the waters fall.

'Ye dayntye Nymphs, that in this blessed
    brooke
  Doe bathe your brest,
Forsake your watry bowres, and hether
    looke,
  At my request.   40
And eke you Virgins that on Parnasse dwell,
Whence floweth Helicon, the learned well,
  Helpe me to blaze
  Her worthy praise
Which in her sexe doth all excell.

'Of fayre Elisa be your silver song,
  That blessed wight:
The flowre of virgins, may shee florish long
  In princely plight.
For shee is Syrinx daughter without spotte,
Which Pan, the shepheards god, of her
    begot: 51
  So sprong her grace
  Of heavenly race,
No mortall blemishe may her blotte.

'See, where she sits upon the grassie greene,
  (O seemely sight!)
Yclad in scarlot, like a mayden queene
  And ermines white.
Upon her head a cremosin coronet,
With damaske roses and daffadillies set: 60

Bayleaves betweene,
And primroses greene,
Embellish the sweete violet.

'Tell me, have ye seene her angelick face,
  Like Phœbe fayre?
Her heavenly haveour, her princely grace,
  Can you well compare?
The redde rose medled with the white yfere,
In either cheeke depeincten lively chere.
  Her modest eye,   70
  Her majestie,
Where have you seene the like, but there?

'I sawe Phœbus thrust out his golden hedde,
  Upon her to gaze:
But when he sawe how broade her beames
    did spredde,
  It did him amaze.
He blusht to see another sunne belowe,
Ne durst againe his fyrye face out showe:
  Let him, if he dare,
  His brightnesse compare   80
With hers, to have the overthrowe.

'Shewe thy selfe, Cynthia, with thy silver
    rayes,
  And be not abasht:
When shee the beames of her beauty dis-
    playes,
  O how art thou dasht!
But I will not match her with Latonaes
    seede;
Such follie great sorow to Niobe did breede:
  Now she is a stone,
  And makes dayly mone,
Warning all other to take heede.   90

'Pan may be proud, that ever he begot
  Such a bellibone,
And Syrinx rejoyse, that ever was her lot
  To beare such an one.
Soone as my younglings cryen for the dam,
To her will I offer a milkwhite lamb:
  Shee is my goddesse plaine,
  And I her shepherds swayne,
Albee forswonck and forswatt I am.

'I see Calliope speede her to the place, 100
  Where my goddesse shines,
And after her the other Muses trace,
  With their violines.
Bene they not bay braunches which they
    doe beare,
All for Elisa in her hand to weare?

So sweetely they play,
And sing all the way,
That it a heaven is to heare.

'Lo, how finely the Graces can it foote
    To the instrument: 110
They dauncen deffly, and singen soote,
    In their meriment.
Wants not a fourth Grace, to make the
    daunce even ?
Let that rowme to my Lady be yeven:
    She shalbe a Grace,
    To fyll the fourth place,
And reigne with the rest in heaven.

'And whither rennes this bevie of ladies
    bright,
    Raunged in a rowe ?
They bene all Ladyes of the Lake behight,
    That unto her goe.   121
Chloris, that is the chiefest nymph of al,
Of olive braunches beares a coronall:
    Olives bene for peace,
    When wars doe surcease:
Such for a princesse bene principall.

'Ye shepheards daughters, that dwell on
    the greene,
    Hye you there apace:
Let none come there, but that virgins bene,
    To adorne her grace.   130
And when you come whereas shee is in place,
See that your rudenesse doe not you dis-
    grace:
    Binde your fillets faste,
    And gird in your waste,
For more finesse, with a tawdrie lace.

'Bring hether the pincke and purple cul-
    lambine,
    With gelliflowres;
Bring coronations, and sops in wine,
    Worne of paramoures;
Strowe me the ground with daffadowndil-
    lies,   140
And cowslips, and kingcups, and loved lil-
    lies:
    The pretie pawnce,
    And the chevisaunce,
Shall match with the fayre flowre delice.

'Now ryse up, Elisa, decked as thou art,
    In royall aray;
And now ye daintie damsells may depart
    Echeone her way.

I feare I have troubled your troupes to
    longe:
Let Dame Eliza thanke you for her song:
    And if you come hether   151
    When damsines I gether,
I will part them all you among.'

The. And was thilk same song of Colins
    owne making ?
Ah, foolish boy, that is with love yblent !
Great pittie is, he be in such taking,
    For naught caren, that bene so lewdly
    bent.

Hob. Sicker, I hold him for a greater
    fon,
    That loves the thing he cannot purchase.
But let us homeward, for night draweth
    on,   160
    And twincling starres the daylight hence
    chase.

THENOTS EMBLEME.

O quam te memorem, virgo ?

HOBBINOLS EMBLEME.

O dea certe !

GLOSSE

Gars thee greete, causeth thee weepe and
complain.
Forlorne, left and forsaken.
Attempred to the yeare, agreeable to the season of the yeare, that is April, which moneth
is most bent to shoures and seasonable rayne :
to quench, that is, to delaye the drought, caused
through drynesse of March wyndes.
The Ladde, Colin Clout.
The Lasse, Rosalinda.   10
Tressed locks, wrethed and curled.
Is he for a ladde ? A straunge manner of
speaking, sc. what maner of ladde is he ?
To make, to rime and versifye. For in this
word, *making*, our olde Englishe poetes were
wont to comprehend all the skil of poetrye, according to the Greeke woorde ποιεῖν, to make,
whence commeth the name of poetes.
Colin thou kenst, knowest. Seemeth hereby
that Colin perteyneth to some Southern noble 20
man, and perhaps in Surrye or Kent, the rather
bicause he so often nameth the Kentish downes,
and before, *As lythe as lasse of Kent.*
The widowes: He calleth Rosalind the
widowes daughter of the glenne, that is, of a
country hamlet or borough, which I thinke is
rather sayde to coloure and conceIe the person,
then simply spoken. For it is well knowen,

even in spighte of Colin and Hobbinoll, that shee is a gentlewoman of no meane house, nor endewed with anye vulgare and common gifts both of nature and manners : but suche indeede, as neede nether Colin be ashamed to have her made knowne by his verses, nor Hobbinol be greved, that so she should be commended to immortalitie for her rare and singular vertues : specially deserving it no lesse then eyther Myrto, the most excellent poete Theocritus his dearling, or Lauretta, the divine Petrarches goddesse, or Himera, the worthye poete Stesichorus hys idole : upon whom he is sayd so much to have doted, that, in regard of her excellencie, he scorned and wrote against the beauty of Helena. For which his præsumptuous and unheedie hardinesse, he is sayde by vengeaunce of the gods, thereat being offended, to have lost both his eyes.

Frenne, a straunger. The word, I thinke, was first poetically put, and afterwarde used in commen custome of speach for *forenne*.

Dight adorned.

Laye, a songe, as roundelayes and virelayes. In all this songe is not to be respected, what the worthinesse of her Majestie deserveth, nor what to the highnes of a prince is agreeable, but what is moste comely for the meanesse of a shepheards witte, or to conceive, or to utter. And therefore he calleth her Elysa, as through rudenesse tripping in her name : and a shepheards daughter, it being very unfit that a shepheards boy, brought up in the shepefold, should know, or ever seme to have heard of a queenes roialty.

Ye daintie is, as it were, an exordium *ad preparandos animos.*

Virgins, the nine Muses, daughters of Apollo and Memorie, whose abode the poets faine to be on Parnassus, a hill in Grece, for that in that countrye specially florished the honor of all excellent studies.

Helicon is both the name of a fountaine at the foote of Parnassus, and also of a mounteine in Bæotia, out of which floweth the famous spring Castalius, dedicate also to the Muses : of which spring it is sayd that, when Pegasus, the winged horse of Perseus, (whereby is meant fame and flying renowme) strooke the grownde with his hoofe, sodenly thereout sprange a wel of moste cleare and pleasaunte water, which fro thence forth was consecrate to the Muses and ladies of learning.

Your silver song seemeth to imitate the lyke in Hesiodus ἀργύρεον μέλος.

Syrinx is the name of a nymphe of Arcadie, whom when Pan being in love pursued, she, flying from him, of the gods was turned into a reede. So that Pan, catching at the reedes in stede of the damosell, and puffing hard, (for he was almost out of wind) with hys breath made the reedes to pype : which he seeing, tooke of them, and, in remembraunce of his lost love, made him a pype thereof. But here by Pan and Syrinx is not to bee thoughte, that the shephearde simplye meante those poeticall gods : but rather supposing (as seemeth) her graces progenie to be divine and immortall (so as the paynims were wont to judge of all kinges and princes, according to Homeres saying,

' Θυμὸς δὲ μέγας ἐστὶ διοτρεφέος βασιλῆος
Τιμὴ δ' ἐκ Διός ἐστι, φιλεῖ δέ ἑ μητίετα Ζεύς,') 100

could devise no parents in his judgement so worthy for her, as Pan the shepeheards god, and his best beloved Syrinx. So that by Pan is here meant the most famous and victorious king, her highnesse father, late of worthy memorye, King Henry the Eyght. And by that name, oftymes (as hereafter appeareth) be noted kings and mighty potentates ; and in some place Christ himselfe, who is the verye Pan and god of shepheardes.

Cremosin coronet : He deviseth her crowne to be of the finest and most delicate flowers, instede of perles and precious stones, wherewith princes diademes use to bee adorned and embost.

Embellish, beautifye and set out.

Phebe, the moone, whom the poets faine to be sister unto Phæbus, that is, the sunne.

Medled, mingled.

Yfere, together. By the mingling of the redde rose and the white is meant the uniting of the two principall houses of Lancaster and of Yorke : by whose longe discord and deadly debate this realm many yeares was sore traveiled, and almost cleane decayed. Til the famous Henry the Seventh, of the line of Lancaster, taking to wife the most vertuous Princesse Elisabeth, daughter to the fourth Edward of the house of Yorke, begat the most royal Henry the Eyght aforesayde, in whom was the firste union of the whyte rose and the redde.

Calliope, one of the nine Muses ; to whome they assigne the honor of all poetical invention, and the firste glorye of the heroicall verse. Other say that shee is the goddesse of rhetorick : but by Virgile it is manifeste, that they mystake the thyng. For there, in hys Epigrams, that arte semeth to be attributed to Polymnia, saying,

' Signat cuncta manu loquiturque Polymnia gestu : ' 140

which seemeth specially to be meant of action and elocution, both special partes of rhetorick : besyde that her name, which (as some construe it) importeth great remembraunce, conteineth another part ; but I holde rather with them, which call her Polymnia, or Polyhymnia, of her good singing.

Bay branches be the signe of honor and victory, and therfore of myghty conquerors worn in theyr triumphes, and eke of famous 150 poets, as saith Petrarch in hys Sonets,

‘ Arbor vittoriosa triomphale,
Honor d’imperadori e di poeti,’ &c.

The Graces be three sisters, the daughters of Jupiter, (whose names are Aglaia, Thalia, Euphrosyne ; and Homer onely addeth a fourth, sc. Pasithea) otherwise called Charites, that is, thanks : whom the poetes feyned to be the goddesses of al bountie and comelines, which therefore (as sayth Theodontius) they make three, 160 to wete, that men first ought to be gracious and bountiful to other freely, then to receive benefits at other mens hands curteously, and thirdly, to requite them thankfully : which are three sundry actions in liberalitye. And Boccace saith, that they be painted naked (as they were indeede on the tombe of C. Julius Cæsar) the one having her backe toward us, and her face fromwarde, as proceeding from us : the other two toward us, noting double thanke 170 to be due to us for the benefit we have done.

Deaffly, finelye and nimbly.

Soote, sweete.

Meriment, mirth.

Bevie : A beavie of ladyes is spoken figuratively for a company or troupe : the terme is taken of larkes. For they say a bevie of larkes, even as a covey of partridge, or an eye of pheasaunts.

Ladyes of the Lake be Nymphes. For it 180 was an olde opinion amongste the auncient heathen, that of every spring and fountaine was a goddesse the soveraigne. Whiche opinion stucke in the myndes of men not manye yeares sithence, by meanes of certain fine fablers and lowd lyers, such as were the authors of King Arthure the Great, and such like, who tell many an unlawfull leasing of the Ladyes of the Lake, that is, the Nymphes. For the word Nymphe in Greeke signifieth well water, or 190 otherwise a spouse or bryde.

Behight, called or named.

Cloris, the name of a nymph, and signifieth greenesse ; of whome is sayd, that Zephyrus, the westerne wind, being in love with her, and coveting her to wyfe, gave her for a dowrie the chiefedome and soveraigntye of al flowres and greene herbes, growing on earth.

Olives bene : The olive was wont to be the ensigne of peace and quietnesse, eyther for 200 that it cannot be planted and pruned, and so carefully looked to as it ought, but in time of peace : or els for that the olive tree, they say, will not growe neare the firre tree, which is dedicate to Mars the god of battaile, and used most for speares and other instruments of warre. Whereupon is finely feigned, that

when Neptune and Minerva strove for the naming of the citie of Athens, Neptune striking the ground with his mace, caused a 210 horse to come forth, that importeth warre, but at Minervaes stroke sprong out an olive, to note that it should be a nurse of learning, and such peaceable studies.

Binde your : Spoken rudely, and according to shepheardes simplicitye.

Bring : All these be names of flowers. *Sops in wine,* a flowre in colour much like to a coronation, but differing in smel and quantitye. *Flowre delice,* that which they use to mis- 220 terme *Flowre de Luce,* being in Latine called *Flos delitiarum.*

A bellibone, or a bonibell, homely spoken for a fayre mayde or bonilasse.

Forswonck and forswatt, overlaboured and sunneburnt.

I saw Phœbus, the sunne. A sensible narration, and present view of the thing mentioned, which they call παρουσία.

Cynthia, the moone, so called of *Cynthus* a 231 hyll, where she was honoured.

Latonaes seede was Apollo and Diana. Whom when as Niobe the wife of Amphion scorned, in respect of the noble fruict of her wombe, namely her seven sonnes, and so many daughters, Latona, being therewith displeased, commaunded her sonne Phœbus to slea al the sonnes, and Diana all the daughters : whereat the unfortunate Niobe being sore dismayed, and lamenting out of measure, was feigned 240 of the poetes to be turned into a stone upon the sepulchre of her children : for which cause the shepheard sayth, he will not compare her to them, for feare of like mysfortune.

Now rise is the conclusion. For having so decked her with prayses and comparisons, he returneth all the thanck of hys laboure to the excellencie of her Majestie.

When damsins, a base reward of a clownisb giver. 250

Yblent, Y is a poeticall addition : *blent,* blinded.

EMBLEME.

This poesye is taken out of Virgile, and there of him used in the person of Æneas to his mother Venus, appearing to him in likenesse of one of Dianaes damosells : being there most divinely set forth. To which similitude of divinitie Hobbinoll comparing the excelency of Elisa, and being through the worthynes of Colins song, as it were, overcome with the huge- 260 nesse of his imagination, brusteth out in great admiration, (*O quam te memorem virgo ?*) being otherwise unhable, then by soddein silence, to expresse the worthinesse of his conceipt. Whom Thenot answereth with another part of the like verse, as confirming by his graunt and approvaunce, that Elisa is no whit inferiour to the majestie of her of whome that poete so boldly pronounced *O dea certe.*

MAYE

ÆGLOGA QUINTA

ARGUMENT

IN this fift Æglogue, under the persons of two shepheards, Piers and Palinodie, be represented two formes of pastoures or ministers, or the Protestant and the Catholique: whose chiefe talke standeth in reasoning whether the life of the one must be like the other. With whom having shewed that it is daungerous to mainteine any felowship, or give too much credit to their colourable and feyned goodwill, he telleth him a tale of the Foxe, that by such a counterpoynt of craftines deceived and devoured the credulous Kidde.

PALINODE. PIERS.

Pal. Is not thilke the mery moneth of May,
When love lads masken in fresh aray ?
How falles it then, we no merrier bene,
Ylike as others, girt in gawdy greene ?
Our bloncket liveryes bene all to sadde
For thilke same season, when all is ycladd
With pleasaunce: the grownd with grasse, the wods
With greene leaves, the bushes with bloomsing buds.
Yougthes folke now flocken in every where,
To gather may buskets and smelling brere:
And home they hasten the postes to dight, 11
And all the kirke pillours eare day light,
With hawthorne buds, and swete eglantine,
And girlonds of roses and sopps in wine.
Such merimake holy saints doth queme,
But we here sytten as drownd in a dreme.
Piers. For younkers, Palinode, such follies fitte,
But we tway bene men of elder witt.
Pal. Sicker, this morrowe, ne lenger agoe,
I sawe a shole of shepeheardes outgoe   20
With singing, and shouting, and jolly chere:
Before them yode a lusty tabrere,
That to the many a horne pype playd,
Whereto they dauncen eche one with his mayd.
To see those folkes make such jouysaunce,
Made my heart after the pype to daunce.

Tho to the greene wood they speeden hem all,
To fetchen home May with their musicall:
And home they bringen in a royall throne,
Crowned as king; and his queene attone   30
Was Lady Flora, on whom did attend
A fayre flocke of faeries, and a fresh bend
Of lovely nymphs. O that I were there,
To helpen the ladyes their maybush beare !
Ah, Piers ! bene not thy teeth on edge, to thinke
How great sport they gaynen with little swinck ?
Piers. Perdie, so farre am I from envie,
That their fondnesse inly I pitie.
Those faytours little regarden their charge,
While they, letting their sheepe runne at large,   40
Passen their time, that should be sparely spent,
In lustihede and wanton meryment.
Thilke same bene shepeheardes for the Devils stedde,
That playen while their flockes be unfedde.
Well is it seene, theyr sheepe bene not their owne,
That letten them runne at randon alone.
But they bene hyred for little pay
Of other, that caren as little as they
What fallen the flocke, so they han the fleece,   49
And get all the gayne, paying but a peece.
I muse what account both these will make,
The one for the hire which he doth take,
And thother for leaving his lords taske,
When great Pan account of shepeherdes shall aske.
Pal. Sicker, now I see thou speakest of spight,
All for thou lackest somedele their delight.
I (as I am) had rather be envied,
All were it of my foe, then fonly pitied:
And yet, if neede were, pitied would be,
Rather then other should scorne at me: 60
For pittied is mishappe that nas remedie,
But scorned bene dedes of fond foolerie.
What shoulden shepheards other things tend,
Then, sith their God his good does them send,
Reapen the fruite thereof, that is pleasure,
The while they here liven, at ease and leasure ?
For when they bene dead, their good is ygoe,
They sleepen in rest, well as other moe.

Tho with them wends what they spent in
cost,
But what they left behind them is lost.　70
Good is no good, but if it be spend:
God giveth good for none other end.
　　Piers. Ah, Palinodie ! thou art a worldes
child:
Who touches pitch mought needes be de-
filde.
But shepheards (as Algrind used to say)
Mought not live ylike as men of the laye:
With them it sits to care for their heire,
Enaunter their heritage doe impaire:
They must provide for meanes of mainte-
naunce,
And to continue their wont countenaunce. 80
But shepheard must walke another way,
Sike worldly sovenance he must foresay.
The sonne of his loines why should he regard
To leave enriched with that he hath spard ?
Should not thilke God that gave him that
good
Eke cherish his child, if in his wayes he
stood ?
For if he mislive in leudnes and lust,
Little bootes all the welth and the trust
That his father left by inheritaunce:
All will be soone wasted with misgovern-
aunce.　90
But through this, and other their miscre-
aunce,
They maken many a wrong chevisaunce,
Heaping up waves of welth and woe,
The floddes whereof shall them overflowe.
Sike mens follie I cannot compare
Better then to the apes folish care,
That is so enamoured of her young one,
(And yet, God wote, such cause hath she
none)
That with her hard hold, and straight em-
bracing,
She stoppeth the breath of her young-
ling.　100
So often times, when as good is meant,
Evil ensueth of wrong entent.
　　The time was once, and may againe re-
torne,
(For ought may happen, that hath bene be-
forne)
When shepheards had none inheritaunce,
Ne of land, nor fee in sufferaunce,
But what might arise of the bare sheepe,
(Were it more or lesse) which they did
keepe.
Well ywis was it with shepheards thoe:

Nought having, nought feared they to for-
goe.　110
For Pan himselfe was their inheritaunce,
And little them served for their maynte-
naunce.
The shepheards God so wel them guided,
That of nought they were unprovided,
Butter enough, honye, milke, and whay,
And their flockes fleeces, them to araye.
But tract of time, and long prosperitie,
(That nource of vice, this of insolencie,)
Lulled the shepheards in such securitie,
That not content with loyall obeysaunce,　120
Some gan to gape for greedie governaunce,
And match them selfe with mighty poten-
tates,
Lovers of lordship and troublers of states.
Tho gan shepheards swaines to looke a loft,
And leave to live hard, and learne to ligge
soft:
Tho, under colour of shepeheards, some-
while
There crept in wolves, ful of fraude and
guile,
That often devoured their owne sheepe,
And often the shepheards that did hem
keepe.
This was the first sourse of shepheards
sorowe,　130
That now nill be quitt with baile nor bor-
rowe.
　　Pal. Three thinges to beare bene very
burdenous,
But the fourth to forbeare is outragious:
Wemen that of loves longing once lust,
Hardly forbearen, but have it they must:
So when choler is inflamed with rage,
Wanting revenge, is hard to asswage:
And who can counsell a thristie soule,
With patience to forbeare the offred bowle ?
But of all burdens that a man can beare, 140
Moste is, a fooles talke to beare and to
heare.
I wene the geaunt has not such a weight,
That beares on his shoulders the heavens
height.
Thou findest faulte where nys to be found,
And buildest strong warke upon a weake
ground:
Thou raylest on right withouten reason,
And blamest hem ·much, for small en-
cheason.
How shoulden shepheardes live, if not so ?
What ! should they pynen in payne and
woe ?

Nay saye I thereto, by my deare bor-
rowe,   150
If I may rest, I nill live in sorrowe.
  Sorrowe ne neede be hastened on:
For he will come, without calling, anone.
While times enduren of tranquillitie,
Usen we freely our felicitie.
For when approchen the stormie stowres,
We mought with our shoulders beare of the
   sharpe showres.
And sooth to sayne, nought seemeth sike
   strife,
That shepheardes so witen ech others life,
And layen her faults the world beforne, 160
The while their foes done eache of hem
   scorne.
Let none mislike of that may not be mended:
So conteck soone by concord mought be
   ended.
  Piers. Shepheard, I list none accordaunce
   make
With shepheard that does the right way
   forsake.
And of the twaine, if choice were to me,
Had lever my foe then my freend he be.
For what concord han light and darke sam ?
Or what peace has the lion with the lambe ?
Such faitors, when their false harts bene
   hidde,   170
Will doe as did the Foxe by the Kidde.
  Pal. Now Piers, of felowship, tell us that
   saying:
For the ladde can keepe both our flocks
   from straying.
  Piers. Thilke same Kidde (as I can well
   devise)
Was too very foolish and unwise.
For on a tyme in sommer season,
The Gate her dame, that had good reason,
Yode forth abroade unto the greene wood,
To brouze, or play, or what shee thought
   good.
But, for she had a motherly care   180
Of her young sonne, and wit to beware,
Shee set her youngling before her knee,
That was both fresh and lovely to see,
And full of favour as kidde mought be.
His vellet head began to shoote out,
And his wreathed horns gan newly sprout;
The blossomes of lust to bud did beginne,
And spring forth ranckly under his chinne.
'My sonne,' quoth she, (and with that gan
   weepe;
For carefull thoughts in her heart did
   creepe)   190

'God blesse thee, poore orphane, as he
   mought me,
And send thee joy of thy jollitee.
Thy father,' (that word she spake with
   payne;
For a sigh had nigh rent her heart in twaine)
'Thy father, had he lived this day,
To see the braunche of his body displaie,
How would he have joyed at this sweete
   sight !
But ah ! false Fortune such joy did him
   spight,
And cutte of hys dayes with untimely woe,
Betraying him into the traines of hys foe.
Now I, a wayfull widdowe behight,   201
Of my old age have this one delight,
To see thee succeede in thy fathers steade,
And florish in flowres of lustyhead:
For even so thy father his head upheld,
And so his haucy hornes did he weld.'
  Tho marking him with melting eyes,
A thrilling throbbe from her hart did aryse,
And interrupted all her other speache
With some old sorowe that made a newe
   breache: 210
Seemed shee sawe in the younglings face
The old lineaments of his fathers grace.
At last her solein silence she broke,
And gan his newe budded beard to stroke.
'Kiddie,' quoth shee, 'thou kenst the great
   care
I have of thy health and thy welfare,
Which many wyld beastes liggen in waite
For to entrap in thy tender state:
But most the Foxe, maister of collusion;
For he has voued thy last confusion.   220
Forthy, my Kiddie, be ruld by mee,
And never give trust to his trecheree.
And if he chaunce come when I am abroade,
Sperre the yate fast, for feare of fraude;
Ne for all his worst, nor for his best,
Open the dore at his request.'
  So schooled the Gate her wanton sonne,
That answerd his mother, all should be done.
Tho went the pensife damme out of dore,
And chaunst to stomble at the threshold
   flore: 230
Her stombling steppe some what her
   amazed,
(For such as signes of ill luck bene dis-
   praised)
Yet forth shee yode, thereat halfe aghast:
And Kiddie the dore sperred after her fast.
It was not long after shee was gone,
But the false Foxe came to the dore anone:

Not as a foxe, for then he had be kend,
But all as a poore pedler he did wend,
Bearing a trusse of tryfles at hys backe,
As bells, and babes, and glasses, in hys
    packe.   240
A biggen he had got about his brayne,
For in his headpeace he felt a sore payne:
His hinder heele was wrapt in a clout,
For with great cold he had gotte the gout.
There at the dore he cast me downe hys
    pack,
And layd him downe, and groned, ' Alack !
    alack !
Ah, deare Lord ! and sweete Saint Chari-
    tee !
That some good body woulde once pitie
    mee ! '
  Well heard Kiddie al this sore constraint,
And lengd to know the cause of his com-
    plaint: 250
Tho, creeping close behind the wickets
    clinck,
Prevelie he peeped out through a chinck:
Yet not so previlie but the Foxe him spyed:
For deceitfull meaning is double eyed.
  ' Ah, good young maister ! ' then gan he
    crye,
' Jesus blesse that sweete face I espye,
And keepe your corpse from the carefull
    stounds
That in my carrion carcas abounds.'
  The Kidd, pittying hys heavinesse,
Asked the cause of his great distresse, 260
And also who and whence that he were.
  Tho he, that had well ycond his lere,
Thus medled his talke with many a teare:
' Sicke, sicke, alas ! and little lack of dead,
But I be relieved by your beastlyhead.
I am a poore sheepe, albe my coloure donne:
For with long traveile I am brent in the
    sonne.
And if that my grandsire me sayd be true,
Sicker, I am very sybbe to you:
So be your goodlihead doe not disdayne 270
The base kinred of so simple swaine.
Of mercye and favour then I you pray,
With your ayd to forstall my neere decay.'
  Tho out of his packe a glasse he tooke,
Wherein while Kiddie unwares did looke,
He was so enamored with the newell,
That nought he deemed deare for the jewell.
Tho opened he the dore, and in came
The false Foxe, as he were starke lame. 279
His tayle he clapt betwixt his legs twayne,
Lest he should be descried by his trayne.

Being within, the Kidde made him good
    glee,
All for the love of the glasse he did see.
After his chere, the pedler can chat,
And tell many lesings of this and that,
And how he could shewe many a fine knack.
Tho shewed his ware and opened his packe,
All save a bell, which he left behind
In the basket for the Kidde to fynd.
Which when the Kidde stooped downe to
    catch,   290
He popt him in, and his basket did latch;
Ne stayed he once, the dore to make fast,
But ranne awaye with him in all hast.
  Home when the doubtfull damme had her
    hyde,
She mought see the dore stand open wyde.
All agast, lowdly she gan to call
Her Kidde; but he nould answere at all.
Tho on the flore she sawe the merchandise
Of which her sonne had sette to dere a prise.
What helpe ? her Kidde shee knewe well
    was gone: 300
Shee weeped, and wayled, and made great
    mone.
Such end had the Kidde, for he nould
    warned be
Of craft coloured with simplicitie:
And such end, perdie, does all hem remayne
That of such falsers freendship bene fayne.
  Pal. Truly, Piers, thou art beside thy wit,
Furthest fro the marke, weening it to hit.
Now I pray thee, lette me thy tale borrowe
For our Sir John to say to morrowe
At the kerke, when it is holliday: 310
For well he meanes, but little can say.
But and if foxes bene so crafty as so,
Much needeth all shepheards hem to knowe.
  Piers. Of their falshode more could I re-
    count:
But now the bright sunne gynneth to dis-
    mount;
And, for the deawie night now doth nye,
I hold it best for us home to hye.

PALINODES EMBLEME.

Πᾶς μὲν ἄπιστος ἀπιστεῖ.

PIERS HIS EMBLEME.

Τίς δ' ἄρα πίστις ἀπίστῳ;

GLOSSE

Thilke, this same moneth. It is applyed to
the season of the moneth, when all menne de-

light them selves with pleasaunce of fieldes, and gardens, and garments.

Bloncket liveries, gray coates.

Yclad, arrayed. Y redoundeth, as before.

In every where, a straunge, yet proper kind of speaking.

Buskets, a diminutive, sc. little bushes of hauthorne. 10

Kirke, church.

Queme, please.

A shole, a multitude; taken of fishe, whereof some going in great companies, are sayde to swimme in a shole.

Yode, went.

Jouyssance, joye.

Swinck, labour.

Inly, entirely.

Faytours, vagabonds. 20

Great Pan is Christ, the very God of all shepheards, which calleth himselfe the greate and good shepherd. The name is most rightly (me thinkes) applyed to him, for Pan signifieth all, or omnipotent, which is onely the Lord Jesus. And by that name (as I remember) he is called of Eusebius, in his fifte booke *De Preparat. Evang.;* who thereof telleth a proper storye to that purpose. Which story is first recorded of Plutarch, in his booke of the ceas- 30 ing of oracles, and of Lavetere translated, in his booke of walking sprightes. Who sayth, that about the same time that our Lord suffered his most bitter passion for the redemtion of man, certein passengers, sayling from Italy to Cyprus and passing by certain iles called Paxæ, heard a voyce calling alowde 'Thamus, Thamus!' (now Thamus was the name of an Ægyptian, which was pilote of the ship) who, giving eare to the cry, was bidden, when he 40 came to Palodes, to tel that the great Pan was dead: which he doubting to doe, yet for that when he came to Palodes, there sodeinly was such a calme of winde, that the shippe stoode still in the sea unmoved, he was forced to cry alowd, that Pan was dead: wherewithall there was heard suche piteous outcryes and dreadfull shriking, as hath not bene the like. By whych Pan, though of some be understoode the great Satanas, whose kingdome at that time 50 was by Christ conquered, the gates of hell broken up, and death by death delivered to eternall death, (for at that time, as he sayth, all oracles surceased, and enchaunted spirits, that were wont to delude the people, thenceforth held theyr peace) and also at the demaund of the Emperoure Tiberius, who that Pan should be, answere was made him by the wisest and best learned, that it was the sonne of Mercurie and Penelope, yet I think it 60 more properly meant of the death of Christ, the onely and very Pan, then suffering for his flock.

I as I am seemeth to imitate the commen proverb, *Malim invidere mihi omnes, quam miserescere.*

Nas is a syncope, for *ne has,* or *has not:* as *nould* for *would not.*

Tho with them doth imitate the epitaphe of the ryotous king Sardanapalus, whych he caused to be written on his tombe in Greeke: which 70 verses be thus translated by Tullie.

'Hæc habui quæ edi, quæque exaturata libido
Hausit, at illa manent multa ac præclara relicta.'

Which may thus be turned into English.

'All that I eate did I joye, and all that I greedily gorged:
As for those many goodly matters left I for others.'

Much like the epitaph of a good olde Erle of Devonshire, which, though much more wisedome bewraieth then Sardanapalus, yet hath a smacke of his sensuall delights and beastli- 80 nesse. The rhymes be these:

'Ho, ho! who lies here?
I the good Erle of Devonshere,
And Maulde my wife, that was ful deare:
We lived together lv. yeare.
That we spent, we had:
That we gave, we have:
That we lefte, we lost.'

Algrind, the name of a shepheard.

Men of the lay, lay men. 90

Enaunter, least that.

Sovenaunce, remembraunce.

Miscreaunce, despeire, or misbeliefe.

Chevisaunce, sometime of Chaucer used for gaine: sometime of other for spoyle, or bootie, or enterprise, and sometime for chiefdome.

Pan himselfe, God: according as is sayd in Deuteronomie, that, in division of the lande of Canaan, to the tribe of Levie no portion of heritage should bee allotted, for GOD him- 100 selfe was their inheritaunce.

Some gan, meant of the Pope, and his Antichristian prelates, which usurpe a tyrannical dominion in the Churche, and with Peters counterfet keyes open a wide gate to al wickednesse and insolent government. Nought here spoken, as of purpose to deny fatherly rule and godly governaunce (as some malitiously of late have done, to the great unreste and hinderaunce of the Churche) but to displaye the pride and 110 disorder of such as, in steede of feeding their sheepe, indeede feede of theyr sheepe.

Sourse, welspring and originall.

Borrowe, pledge or suertie.

The geaunte is the greate Atlas, whom the poetes feign to be a huge geaunt, that beareth Heaven on his shoulders: being in deede a merveilous highe mountaine in Mauritania, that now is Barbarie, which, to mans seeming, perceth the cloudes, and seemeth to touch the 120 heavens. Other thinke, and they not amisse.

that this fable was meant of one Atlas, king of the same countrye, (of whome may bee, that that hil had his denomination) brother to Prometheus, who (as the Grekes say) did first fynd out the hidden courses of the starres, by an excellent imagination: wherefore the poetes feigned, that he susteyned the firmament on hys shoulders. Many other conjectures needelesse be told hereof.   130

Warke, worke.

Encheason, cause, occasion.

Deare borow, that is our Saviour, the commen pledge of all mens debts to death.

Wyten, blame.

Nought seemeth, is unseemely.

Conteck, strife, contention.

Her, theyr, as useth Chaucer.

Han, for have.

Sam, together.   140

This tale is much like to that in Æsops fables, but the catastrophe and end is farre different. By the Kidde may be understoode the simple sorte of the faythfull and true Christians. By hys dame, Christe, that hath alreadie with carefull watchewords (as heere doth the gote) warned his little ones, to beware of such doubling deceit. By the Foxe, the false and faithlesse Papistes, to whom is no credit to be given, nor felowshippe to be used.   150

The Gate, the Gote: northernely spoken, to turne O into A.

Yode, went: afforesayd.

She set, a figure called *Fictio*, which useth to attribute reasonable actions and speaches to unreasonable creatures.

The bloosmes of lust be the young and mossie heares, which then beginne to sproute and shoote foorth, when lustfull heate beginneth to kindle.

And with, a very poetical πάθος.   160

Orphane, a youngling or pupill, that needeth a tutour and governour.

That word, a patheticall parenthesis, to encrease a carefull hyperbaton.

The braunch of the fathers body is the child.

For even so alluded to the saying of Andromache to Ascanius in Virgile.

‘ Sic oculos, sic ille manus, sic ora ferebat.’

A thrilling throb, a percing sighe.

Liggen, lye.   170

Maister of collusion, sc. coloured guile, because the Foxe, of al beasts, is most wily and crafty.

Sperre the yate, shut the dore.

For such: The gotes stombling is here noted as an evill signe. The like to be marked in all histories: and that not the leaste of the Lorde Hastingues in King Rycharde the Third his dayes. For beside his daungerous dreame (whiche was a shrewde prophecie of his mishap that folowed) it is sayd that in the morning, 180

ryding toward the Tower of London, there to sitte uppon matters of counsell, his horse stombled twise or thrise by the way : which of some, that, ryding with hym in his company, were privie to his neere destenie, was secretly marked, and afterward noted for memorie of his great mishap that ensewed. For being then as merye as man might be, and least doubting any mortall daunger, he was, within two howres after, of the tyranne put to a shamefull deathe. 190

As belles: By such trifles are noted, the reliques and ragges of popish superstition, which put no smal ,religion in belles, and babies, sc. idoles, and glasses, sc. paxes, and such lyke trumperies.

Great cold : For they boast much of their outward patience, and voluntarye sufferaunce, as a worke of merite and holy humblenesse.

Sweete S. Charitie, the Catholiques comen othe, and onely speache, to have charitye 200 alwayes in their mouth, and sometime in their outward actions, but never inwardly in fayth and godly zeale.

Clincke, a key hole. Whose diminutive is clicket, used of Chaucer for a key.

Stoundes, fittes: aforesayde.

His lere, his lesson.

Medled, mingled.

Bestlihead, agreeing to the person of a beast.

Sibbe, of kynne.   210

Newell, a newe thing.

To forestall, to prævent.

Glee, chere : afforesayde.

Deare a price, his lyfe, which he lost for those toyes.

Such ende is an epiphonema, or rather the morall of the whole tale, whose purpose is to warne the Protestaunt beware, howe he geveth credit to the unfaythfull Catholique : whereof we have dayly proofes sufficient, but one 220 moste famous of all, practised of late yeares in Fraunce, by Charles the Nynth.

Fayne, gladde or desyrous.

Our Sir John, a Popishe priest. A saying fit for the grosenesse of a shepheard, but spoken to taunte unlearned priestes.

Dismount, descende or set.

Nye, draweth nere.

EMBLEME.

Both these emblemes make one whole hexametre. The first spoken of Palinodie, as in 230 reproche of them that be distrustfull, is a peece of Theognis verse, intending, that who doth most mistrust is most false. For such experience in falshod breedeth mistrust in the mynd, thinking no lesse guile to lurke in others then in hymselfe. But Piers thereto strongly replyeth with another peece of the same verse, saying, as in his former fable, what fayth then is there in the faythlesse? For if fayth be the ground of religion, which fayth they dayly 240 false, what hold then is there of theyr religion? And thys is all that they saye.

JUNE

ÆGLOGA SEXTA

ARGUMENT

THIS Æglogue is wholly vowed to the complayning of Colins ill successe in his love. For being (as is aforesaid) enamoured of a country lasse, Rosalind, and having (as seemeth) founde place in her heart, he lamenteth to his deare frend Hobbinoll, that he is nowe forsaken unfaithfully, and in his steede Menalcas, another shepheard, received disloyally. And this is the whole argument of this Æglogue.

HOBBINOL. COLIN CLOUTE.

Hob. Lo, Collin, here the place whose pleasaunt syte
From other shades hath weand my wan-
    dring mynde.
Tell me, what wants me here to worke de-
    lyte?
The simple ayre, the gentle warbling wynde,
So calme, so coole, as no where else I fynde,
The grassye ground with daintye daysies
    dight,
The bramble bush, where byrds of every
    kynde
To the waters fall their tunes attemper
    right.

Col. O happy Hobbinoll! I blesse thy
    state,
That Paradise hast found, whych Adam
    lost. 10
Here wander may thy flock, early or late,
Withouten dreade of wolves to bene ytost:
Thy lovely layes here mayst thou freely
    boste.
But I, unhappy man, whom cruell Fate
And angry gods pursue from coste to coste,
Can nowhere fynd to shroude my lucklesse
    pate.

Hob. Then if by me thou list advised be,
Forsake the soyle that so doth the bewitch;
Leave me those hilles, where harbrough nis
    to see,
Nor holybush, nor brere, nor winding
    witche. 20

And to the dales resort, where shepheards
    ritch,
And fruictfull flocks, bene every where to
    see.
Here no night ravens lodge, more black
    then pitche,
Nor elvish ghosts, nor gastly owles doe
    flee.

But frendly Faeries, met with many Graces,
And lightfote Nymphes, can chace the lin-
    gring night
With heydeguyes and trimly trodden traces,
Whilst systers nyne, which dwell on Par-
    nasse hight,
Doe make them musick for their more de-
    light;
And Pan himselfe, to kisse their christall
    faces,
Will pype and daunce, when Phœbe shineth 30
    bright:
Such pierlesse pleasures have we in these
    places.

Col. And I, whylst youth and course of
    carelesse yeeres
Did let me walke withouten lincks of love,
In such delights did joy amongst my peeres:
But ryper age such pleasures doth reprove;
My fancye eke from former follies move
To stayed steps: for time in passing weares,
(As garments doen, which wexen old
    above)
And draweth newe delightes with hoary
    heares. 40

Tho couth I sing of love, and tune my
    pype
Unto my plaintive pleas in verses made;
Tho would I seeke for queene apples un-
    rype,
To give my Rosalind, and in sommer shade
Dight gaudy girlonds was my comen trade,
To crowne her golden locks; but yeeres
    more rype,
And losse of her, whose love as lyfe I wayd,
Those weary wanton toyes away dyd wype.

Hob. Colin, to heare thy rymes and
    roundelayes,
Which thou were wont on wastfull hylls to
    singe, 50
I more delight then larke in sommer dayes:
Whose echo made the neyghbour groves to
    ring,

And taught the byrds, which in the lower
        spring
Did shroude in shady leaves from sonny
        rayes,
Frame to thy songe their chereful cherip-
        ing,
Or hold theyr peace, for shame of thy swete
        layes.

I sawe Calliope wyth Muses moe,
Soone as thy oaten pype began to sound,
Theyr yvory luyts and tamburins forgoe,
And from the fountaine, where they sat
        around,   60
Renne after hastely thy silver sound.
But when they came where thou thy skill
        didst showe,
They drewe abacke, as halfe with shame
        confound,
Shepheard to see, them in theyr art outgoe.

   Col. Of Muses, Hobbinol, I conne no
        skill:
For they bene daughters of the hyghest
        Jove,
And holden scorne of homely shepheards
        quill.
For sith I heard that Pan with Phœbus
        strove,
Which him to much rebuke and daunger
        drove,
I never lyst presume to Parnasse hyll,   70
But, pyping lowe in shade of lowly grove,
I play to please my selfe, all be it ill.

Nought weigh I, who my song doth prayse
        or blame,
Ne strive to winne renowne, or passe the
        rest:
With shepheard sittes not followe flying
        fame,
But feede his flocke in fields where falls
        hem best.
I wote my rymes bene rough, and rudely
        drest:
The fytter they my carefull case to frame:
Enough is me to paint out my unrest,
And poore my piteous plaints out in the
        same.   80

The god of shepheards, Tityrus, is dead,
Who taught me, homely as I can, to make.
He, whilst he lived, was the soveraigne
        head
Of shepheards all that bene with love ytake:

Well couth he wayle his woes, and lightly
        slake
The flames which love within his heart had
        bredd,
And tell us mery tales, to keepe us wake,
The while our sheepe about us safely fedde.

Nowe dead he is, and lyeth wrapt in lead,
(O why should Death on hym such outrage
        showe ?)   90
And all hys passing skil with him is fledde,
The fame whereof doth dayly greater growe.
But if on me some little drops would
        flowe
Of that the spring was in his learned hedde,
I soone would learne these woods to wayle
        my woe,
And teache the trees their trickling teares
        to shedde.

Then should my plaints, causd of discurte-
        see,
As messengers of all my painfull plight,
Flye to my love, where ever that she bee,
And pierce her heart with poynt of worthy
        wight,   100
As shee deserves, that wrought so deadly
        spight.
And thou, Menalcas, that by trecheree
Didst underfong my lasse to wexe so light
Shouldest well be knowne for such thy vil-
        lanee.

But since I am not as I wish I were,
Ye gentle shepheards, which your flocks do
        feede,
Whether on hylls, or dales, or other where,
Beare witnesse all of thys so wicked deede;
And tell the lasse, whose flowre is woxe a
        weede,
And faultlesse fayth is turned to faithlesse
        fere,   110
That she the truest shepheards hart made
        bleede
That lyves on earth, and loved her most
        dere.

   Hob. O carefull Colin ! I lament thy case:
Thy teares would make the hardest flint to
        flowe.
Ah, faithlesse Rosalind, and voide of grace,
That art the roote of all this ruthfull woe !
But now is time, I gesse, homeward to goe:
Then ryse, ye blessed flocks, and home
        apace,

Least night with stealing steppes doe you
   forsloe,
And wett your tender lambes that by you
   trace.   120

COLINS EMBLEME.

Già speme spenta.

GLOSSE

Syte, situation and place.

Paradise. A Paradise in Greeke signifieth a
garden of pleasure, or place of delights. So
he compareth the soile wherin Hobbinoll made
his abode, to that earthly Paradise, in Scripture called Eden, wherein Adam in his first
creation was placed: which, of the most
learned, is thought to be in Mesopotamia, the
most fertile and pleasaunte country in the
world (as may appeare by Diodorus Sycu- 10
lus description of it, in the hystorie of Alexan-
ders conquest thereof :) lying betweene the two
famous ryvers, (which are sayd in Scripture to
flowe out of Paradise) Tygris and Euphrates,
whereof it is so denominate.

Forsake the soyle. This is no poetical fiction,
but unfeynedly spoken of the poete selfe, who
for speciall occasion of private affayres, (as I
have bene partly of himselfe informed) and
for his more preferment, removing out of the 20
Northparts, came into the South, as Hobbinoll
indeede advised him privately.

Those hylles, that is the North countrye,
where he dwelt.

Nis, is not.

The dales, the Southpartes, where he nowe
abydeth, which thoughe they be full of hylles
and woodes (for Kent is very hyllye and
woodye; and therefore so called: for *Kantsh*
in the Saxons tongue signifieth woodie,) yet 30
in respecte of the Northpartes they be called
dales. For indede the North is counted the
higher countrye.

Night ravens, &c. By such hatefull byrdes,
hee meaneth all misfortunes (whereof they be
tokens) flying every where.

Frendly faeries. The opinion of faeries and
elfes is very old, and yet sticketh very religiously in the myndes of some. But to roote
that rancke opinion of elfes oute of mens 40
hearts, the truth is, that there be no such
thinges, nor yet the shadowes of the things,
but onely by a sort of bald friers and knavish
shavelings so feigned ; which, as in all other
things, so in that, soughte to nousell the comen
people in ignoraunce, least, being once acquainted with the truth of things, they woulde
in tyme smell out the untruth of theyr packed
pelfe and massepenie religion. But the sooth
is, that when all Italy was distraicte into the 50

factions of the Guelfes and the Gibelins, being
two famous houses in Florence, the name began, through their great mischiefes and many
outrages, to be so odious, or rather dreadfull,
in the peoples eares, that if theyr children at
any time were frowarde and wanton, they
would say to them that the Guelfe or the Gibe-
line came. Which words nowe from them (as
many thinge els) be come into our usage, and,
for Guelfes and Gibelines, we say elfes and 60
goblins. No otherwise then the Frenchmen
used to say of that valiaunt captain, the very
scourge of Fraunce, the Lord Thalbot, afterward Erle of Shrewsbury ; whose noblesse
bred such a terrour in the hearts of the French,
that oft times even great armies were defaicted
and put to flyght at the onely hearing of hys
name. In somuch that the French wemen, to
affray theyr chyldren, would tell them that
the Talbot commeth.   70

Many Graces. Though there be indeede but
three Graces or Charites (as afore is sayd) or
at the utmost but foure, yet in respect of many
gyftes of bounty, there may be sayde more.
And so Musæus sayth, that in Heroes eyther
eye there satte a hundred Graces. And by
that authoritye, thys same poete, in his Pageaunts, saith ' An hundred Graces on her eye-
ledde satte,' &c.

Haydeguies, a country daunce or rownd. 80
The conceipt is, that the Graces and Nymphes
doe daunce unto the Muses and Pan his musicke all night by moonelight. To signifie the
pleasauntnesse of the soyle.

Peeres, equalles and felow shepheards.

Queneapples unripe, imitating Virgils verse,

' Ipse ego cana legam tenera lanugine mala.'

Neighbour groves, a straunge phrase in English, but word for word expressing the Latine
vicina nemora.   90

Spring, not of water, but of young trees
springing.

Calliope, afforesayde. Thys staffe is full of
verie poetical invention.

Tamburines, an olde kind of instrument,
which of some is supposed to be the clarion.

Pan with Phœbus. The tale is well knowne,
howe that Pan and Apollo, striving for excellencye in musicke, chose Midas for their judge
Who, being corrupted wyth partiall affec- 100
tion, gave the victorye to Pan undeserved : for
which Phœbus sette a payre of asses eares
upon hys head, &c.

Tityrus. That by Tityrus is meant Chaucer,
hath bene already sufficiently sayde, and by
thys more playne appeareth, that he sayth, he
tolde merye tales. Such as be hys Canterburie
Tales. Whom he calleth the god of poetes
for hys excellencie, so as Tullie calleth Lentulus, *Deum vitæ suæ,* sc. the god of hys lyfe. 110

To make, to versifie.

O why, a pretye epanorthosis or correction.

Discurtesie. He meaneth the falsenesse of his lover Rosalinde, who, forsaking hym, hadde chosen another.

Poynte of worthy wite, the pricke of deserved blame.

Menalcas, the name of a shephearde in Virgile; but here is meant a person unknowne and secrete, agaynst whome he often bit- 120 terly invayeth.

Underfonge, undermynde and deceive by false suggestion.

EMBLEME.

You remember that in the fyrst Æglogue, Colins poesie was *Anchora speme*: for that as then there was hope of favour to be found in tyme. But nowe being cleane forlorne and rejected of her, as whose hope, that was, is cleane extinguished and turned into despeyre, he renounceth all comfort, and hope of 130 goodnesse to come: which is all the meaning of thys embleme.

JULYE

ÆGLOGA SEPTIMA

ARGUMENT

THIS Æglogue is made in the honour and commendation of good shepeheardes, and to the shame and disprayse of proude and ambitious pastours: such as Morrell is here imagined to bee.

THOMALIN. MORRELL.

Thom. Is not thilke same a goteheard prowde,
   That sittes on yonder bancke,
Whose straying heard them selfe doth shrowde
   Emong the bushes rancke?
Mor. What ho! thou jollye shepheards swayne,
   Come up the hyll to me:
Better is then the lowly playne,
   Als for thy flocke and thee.
Thom. Ah, God shield, man, that I should clime,
   And learne to looke alofte;   10
This reede is ryfe, that oftentime
   Great clymbers fall unsoft.
In humble dales is footing fast,
   The trode is not so tickle,
And though one fall through heedlesse hast,
   Yet is his misse not mickle.

And now the Sonne hath reared up
   His fyriefooted teme,
Making his way betweene the Cuppe
   And golden Diademe: 20
The rampant Lyon hunts he fast,
   With Dogge of noysome breath,
Whose balefull barking bringes in hast
   Pyne, plagues, and dreery death.
Agaynst his cruell scortching heate
   Where hast thou coverture?
The wastefull hylls unto his threate
   Is a playne overture.
But if thee lust to holden chat
   With seely shepherds swayne,   30
Come downe, and learne the little what
   That Thomalin can sayne.
Mor. Syker, thous but a laesie loord,
   And rekes much of thy swinck,
That with fond termes, and weetlesse words,
   To blere myne eyes doest thinke.
In evill houre thou hentest in hond
   Thus holy hylles to blame,
For sacred unto saints they stond,
   And of them han theyr name.   40
St. Michels Mount who does not know,
   That wardes the westerne coste?
And of St. Brigets Bowre, I trow,
   All Kent can rightly boaste:
And they that con of Muses skill
   Sayne most-what, that they dwell
(As goteheards wont) upon a hill,
   Beside a learned well.
And wonned not the great god Pan
   Upon Mount Olivet,   50
Feeding the blessed flocke of Dan,
   Which dyd himselfe beget?
Thom. O blessed sheepe! O shepheard great,
   That bought his flocke so deare,
And them did save with bloudy sweat
   From wolves, that would them teare!
Mor. Besyde, as holy fathers sayne,
   There is a hyllye place,
Where Titan ryseth from the mayne,
   To renne hys dayly race: 60
Upon whose toppe the starres bene stayed,
   And all the skie doth leane;
There is the cave where Phebe layed
   The shepheard long to dreame.
Whilome there used shepheards all
   To feede theyr flocks at will,
Till by his foly one did fall,
   That all the rest did spill.
And sithens shepheardes bene foresayd
   From places of delight: 70

Forthy I weene thou be affrayd
  To clime this hilles height.
Of Synah can I tell thee more,
  And of Our Ladyes Bowre:
But little needes to strow my store,
  Suffice this hill of our.
Here han the holy Faunes recourse,
  And Sylvanes haunten rathe;
Here has the salt Medway his sourse,
  Wherein the Nymphes doe bathe;   80
The salt Medway, that trickling stremis
  Adowne the dales of Kent,
Till with his elder brother Themis
  His brackish waves be meynt.
Here growes melampode every where,
  And teribinth, good for gotes:
The one, my madding kiddes to smere,
  The next, to heale theyr throtes.
Hereto, the hills bene nigher heven,
  And thence the passage ethe: 90
As well can prove the piercing levin,
  That seeldome falls bynethe.
Thom. Syker, thou speakes lyke a lewde lorrell,
  Of heaven to demen so:
How be I am but rude and borrell,
  Yet nearer wayes I knowe.
To kerke the narre, from God more farre,
  Has bene an old sayd sawe,
And he that strives to touch the starres
  Oft stombles at a strawe.   100
Alsoone may shepheard clymbe to skye,
  That leades in lowly dales,
As goteherd prowd, that, sitting hye,
  Upon the mountaine sayles.
My seely sheepe like well belowe,
  They neede not melampode:
For they bene hale enough, I trowe,
  And liken theyr abode.
But, if they with thy gotes should yede,
  They soone myght be corrupted,   110
Or like not of the frowie fede,
  Or with the weedes be glutted.
The hylls where dwelled holy saints
  I reverence and adore:
Not for themselfe, but for the sayncts
  Which han be dead of yore.
And nowe they bene to heaven forewent,
  Theyr good is with them goe,
Theyr sample onely to us lent,
  That als we mought doe soe.   120
Shepheards they weren of the best,
  And lived in lowlye leas:
And sith theyr soules bene now at rest,
  Why done we them disease?

Such one he was (as I have heard
  Old Algrind often sayne)
That whilome was the first shepheard,
  And lived with little gayne:
As meeke he was as meeke mought be,
  Simple as simple sheepe,   130
Humble, and like in eche degree
  The flocke which he did keepe.
Often he used of hys keepe
  A sacrifice to bring,
Nowe with a kidde, now with a sheepe
  The altars hallowing.
So lowted he unto hys Lord,
  Such favour couth he fynd,
That sithens never was abhord
  The simple shepheards kynd.   140
And such, I weene, the brethren were
  That came from Canaan,
The brethren twelve, that kept yfere
  The flockes of mighty Pan.
But nothing such thilk shephearde was
  Whom Ida hyll dyd beare,
That left hys flocke to fetch a lasse,
  Whose love he bought to deare.
For he was proude, that ill was payd,
  (No such mought shepheards bee)   150
And with lewde lust was overlayd:
  Tway things doen ill agree:
But shepheard mought be meeke and mylde,
  Well eyed as Argus was,
With fleshly follyes undefyled,
  And stoute as steede of brasse.
Sike one (sayd Algrin) Moses was,
  That sawe hys Makers face,
His face, more cleare then christall glasse,
  And spake to him in place.   160
This had a brother, (his name I knewe)
  The first of all his cote,
A shepheard trewe, yet not so true
  As he that earst I hote.
Whilome all these were lowe and lief,
  And loved their flocks to feede,
They never stroven to be chiefe,
  And simple was theyr weede.
But now (thanked be God therefore)
  The world is well amend,   170
Their weedes bene not so nighly wore;
  Such simplesse mought them shend:
They bene yclad in purple and pall,
  So hath theyr God them blist,
They reigne and rulen over all.
  And lord it as they list·
Ygyrt with belts of glitterand gold,
  (Mought ther good sheepeheards bene)

Theyr Pan theyr sheepe to them has
   sold;
   I saye as some have seene.   180
For Palinode (if thou him ken)
   Yode late on pilgrimage
To Rome, (if such be Rome) and then
   He sawe thilke misusage.
For shepeheards, sayd he, there doen leade,
   As lordes done other where;
Theyr sheepe han crustes, and they the
   bread;
The chippes, and they the chere:
They han the fleece, and eke the flesh;
   (O seely sheepe the while !)   190
The corne is theyrs, let other thresh,
   Their hands they may not file.
They han great stores and thriftye stockes,
   Great freendes and feeble foes:
What neede hem caren for their flocks ?
   Theyr boyes can looke to those.
These wisards weltre in welths waves,
   Pampred in pleasures deepe;
They han fatte kernes, and leany knaves,
   Their fasting flockes to keepe.   200
Sike mister men bene all misgone,
   They heapen hylles of wrath:
Sike syrlye shepheards han we none,
   They keepen all the path.
Mor. Here is a great deale of good mat-
   ter
   Lost for lacke of telling.
Now sicker I see, thou doest but clatter:
   Harme may come of melling.
Thou medlest more then shall have cnanke,
   To wyten shepheards welth: 210
When folke bene fat, and riches rancke,
   It is a signe of helth.
But say me, what is Algrin, he
   That is so oft bynempt ?
Thom. He is a shepheard great in gree,
   But hath bene long ypent.
One daye he sat upon a hyll,
   As now thou wouldest me:
But I am taught, by Algrins ill,
   To love the lowe degree.   220
For sitting so with bared scalpe,
   An eagle sored hye,
That, weening hys whyte head was chalke,
   A shell fish downe let flye:
She weend the shell fishe to have broake,
   But therewith bruzd his brayne;
So now, astonied with the stroke,
   He lyes in lingring payne.
Mor. Ah, good Algrin ! his hap was ill,
   But shall be bett in time.   230

Now farwell, shepheard, sith thys hyll
   Thou hast such doubt to climbe.

THOMALINS EMBLEME.

In medio virtus.

MORRELLS EMBLEME.

In summo fœlicitas.

GLOSSE

A goteheard. By gotes, in scrypture, be re-
presented the wicked and reprobate, whose
pastour also must needes be such.
Banck is the seate of honor.
Straying heard, which wander out of the
waye of truth.
Als, for also.
Clymbe, spoken of ambition.
Great clymbers, according to Seneca his verse.

    ' Decidunt celsa, graviore lapsu.'   10

Mickle, much.
The sonne, a reason why he refuseth to
dwell on mountaines, because there is no shelter against the scortching sunne, according to
the time of the yeare, whiche is the whotest
moneth of all.
The Cupp and Diademe be two signes in the
firmament, through which the sonne maketh
his course in the moneth of July.
Lion. Thys is poetically spoken, as if the   20
Sunne did hunt a Lion with one dogge. The
meaning whereof is, that in July the sonne is
in Leo. At which tyme the Dogge starre,
which is called Syrius, or Canicula, reigneth
with immoderate heate, causing pestilence,
drough, and many diseases.
Overture, an open place. The word is borrowed of the French, and used in good writers.
To holden chatt, to talke and prate.
A loorde was wont among the old Britons   30
to signifie a lorde. And therefore the Danes,
that long time usurped theyr tyrannie here in
Brytanie, were called, for more dread and dignitie, Lurdanes, sc. *Lord Danes.* At which time
it is sayd, that the insolencie and pryde of
that nation was so outragious in thys realme,
that if it fortuned a Briton to be going over a
bridge, and sawe a Dane set foote upon the
same, he muste retorne back, till the Dane
were cleane over, or els abyde the pryce of   40
his displeasure, which was no lesse then present
death. But being afterwarde expelled, that
name of Lurdane became so odious unto the
people, whom they had long oppressed, that
even at this daye they use, for more reproche,
to call the quartane ague the Fever Lurdane.
Recks much of thy swinck, counts much of thy
paynes.

Weetelesse, not understoode.

St. Michels Mount is a promontorie in the west part of England. 51

A hill, Parnassus afforesayd.

Pan, Christ.

Dan. One trybe is put for the whole nation *per synecdochen.*

Where Titan, the sonne. Which story is to be redde in Diodorus Syculus of the hyl Ida ; from whence he sayth, all night time is to bee seene a mightye fire, as if the skye burned, which toward morning beginneth to gather into a 60 rownd forme, and thereof ryseth the sonne, whome the poetes call Titan.

The shepheard is Endymion, whom the poets fayne to have bene so beloved of Phœbe, sc. the moone, that he was by her kept a sleepe in a cave by the space of xxx yeares, for to enjoye his companye.

There, that is, in Paradise, where, through errour of shepheards understanding, he sayth, that all shepheards did use to feede theyr 70 flocks, till one, (that is Adam) by hys follye and disobedience, made all the rest of hys ofspring be debarred and shutte out from thence.

Synah, a hill in Arabia, where God appeared.

Our Ladyes Bowre, a place of pleasure so called.

Faunes or Sylvanes be of poetes feigned to be gods of the woode. 80

Medway, the name of a ryver in Kent, which, running by Rochester, meeteth with Thames ; whom he calleth his elder brother, both because he is greater, and also falleth sooner into the sea.

Meynt, mingled.

Melampode and terebinth be hearbes good to cure diseased gotes : of thone speaketh Mantuane, and of thother Theocritus.

Τερμίνθου τράγων ἔσχατον ἀκρέμονα. 90

Nigher heaven. Note the shepheards simplenesse, which supposeth that from the hylls is nearer waye to heaven.

Levin, lightning ; which he taketh for an argument to prove the nighnes to heaven, because the lightning doth comenly light on hygh mountaynes, according to the saying of the poete :

'Feriuntque summos fulmina montes.'

Lorrell, a losell. 100

A borrell, a playne fellowe.

Narre, nearer.

Hale, for hole.

Yede, goe.

Frowye, mustye or mossie.

Of yore, long agoe.

Forewente, gone afore.

The firste shepheard was Abell the righteous, who (as Scripture sayth) bent hys mind to keeping of sheepe, as did hys brother Cain 110 to tilling the grownde.

His keepe, hys charge, sc. his flocke.

Lowted, did honour and reverence.

The brethren, the twelve sonnes of Jacob, which were shepemaisters, and lyved onelye thereupon.

Whom Ida, Paris, which being the sonne of Priamus king of Troy, for his mother Hecubas dreame, which, being with child of hym, dreamed shee broughte forth a firebrand, 120 that set all the towre of Ilium on fire, was cast forth on the hyll Ida ; where being fostered of shepheards, he eke in time became a shepheard, and lastly came to knowledge of his parentage.

A lasse. Helena, the wyfe of Menelaus king of Lacedemonia, was by Venus, for the golden aple to her geven, then promised to Paris, who thereupon with a sorte of lustye Troyanes, stole her out of Lacedemonia, and kept her in 130 Troye : which was the cause of the tenne yeares warre in Troye, and the moste famous citye of all Asia most lamentably sacked and defaced.

Argus was of the poets devised to be full of eyes, and therefore to hym was committed the keeping of the transformed cow, Io : so called, because that, in the print of a cowes foote, there is figured an I in the middest of an O.

His name : he meaneth Aaron : whose name, for more decorum, the shephearde sayth he 140 hath forgot, lest his remembraunce and skill in antiquities of holy writ should seeme to exceede the meanenesse of the person.

Not so true, for Aaron, in the absence of Moses, started aside, and committed idolatry.

In purple, spoken of the popes and cardinalles, which use such tyrannical colours and pompous paynting.

Belts, girdles. 149

Glitterand, glittering, a participle used sometime in Chaucer, but altogether in J. Goore.

Theyr Pan, that is, the Pope, whom they count theyr god and greatest shepheard.

Palinode, a shephearde, of whose report he seemeth to speake all thys.

Wisards, greate learned heads.

Welter, wallowe.

Kerne, a churl or farmer.

Sike mister men, suche kinde of men.

Surly, stately and prowde. 160

Melling, medling.

Bett, better.

Bynempte, named.

Gree, for degree.

Algrin, the name of a shepheard afforesayde. whose myshap he alludeth to the chaunce that

happened to the poet Æschylus, that was
brayned with a shellfishe.

EMBLEME.

By thys poesye Thomalin confirmeth that
which in hys former speach by sondrye rea- 170
sons he had proved. For being both hymselfe
sequestred from all ambition, and also abhor-
ring it in others of hys cote, he taketh occasion
to prayse the meane and lowly state, as that
wherein is safetie without feare, and quiet
without danger ; according to the saying of
olde philosophers, that vertue dwelleth in the
middest, being environed with two contrary
vices : whereto Morrell replieth with continuaunce of the same philosophers opinion, 180
that albeit all bountye dwelleth in mediocritie,
yet perfect felicitye dwelleth in supremacie.
For they say, and most true it is, that happinesse is placed in the highest degree, so as if
any thing be higher or better, then that streight
way ceaseth to be perfect happines. Much like
to that which once I heard alleaged in defence
of humilitye, out of a great doctour, 'Suorum
Christus humillimus : ' which saying a gentle
man in the company taking at the rebownd, 190
beate backe again with lyke saying of another
doctoure, as he sayde, 'Suorum Deus altissi-
mus.'

AUGUST

ÆGLOGA OCTAVA

ARGUMENT

In this Æglogue is set forth a delectable
controversie, made in imitation of that in
Theocritus : whereto also Virgile fashioned his
third and seventh Æglogue. They choose for
umpere of their strife, Cuddie, a neatheards
boye, who, having ended their cause, reciteth
also himselfe a proper song, whereof Colin, he
sayth, was authour.

WILLYE. PERIGOT. CUDDIE.

Wil. Tell me, Perigot, what shalbe the
    game,
Wherefore with myne thou dare thy mu-
    sick matche ?
Or bene thy bagpypes renne farre out of
    frame ?
Or hath the crampe thy joynts benomd
    with ache ?
Per. Ah ! Willye, when the hart is ill
    assayde,
How can bagpipe or joynts be well apayd ?

Wil. What the foule evill hath thee so
    bestadde ?
Whilom thou was peregall to the best,
And wont to make the jolly shepeheards
    gladde
With pyping and dauncing, didst passe the
    rest.   10
Per. Ah ! Willye, now I have learnd a
    newe daunce :
My old musick mard by a newe mischaunce.

Wil. Mischiefe mought to that newe mis-
    chaunce befall,
That so hath raft us of our meriment !
But reede me, what payne doth thee so
    appall ?
Or lovest thou, or bene thy younglings
    miswent ?
Per. Love hath misled both my younglings
    and mee :
I pyne for payne, and they my payne to
    see.

Wil. Perdie and wellawaye ! ill may they
    thrive :
Never knewe I lovers sheepe in good
    plight.   20
But and if in rymes with me thou dare
    strive,
Such fond fantsies shall soone be put to
    flight.
Per. That shall I doe, though mochell worse
    I fared :
Never shall be sayde that Perigot was
    dared.

Wil. Then loe, Perigot, the pledge which
    I plight !
A mazer ywrought of the maple warre :
Wherein is enchased many a fayre sight
Of beres and tygres, that maken fiers
    warre ;
And over them spred a goodly wild
    vine,
Entrailed with a wanton yvie-twine.   30

Thereby is a lambe in the wolves jawes :
But see, how fast renneth the shepheard
    swayne,
To save the innocent from the beastes
    pawes ;
And here with his shepehooke hath him
    slayne.
Tell me, such a cup hast thou ever sene ?
Well mought it beseme any harvest queene

Per. Thereto will I pawne yonder spotted
    lambe;
Of all my flocke there nis sike another;
For I brought him up without the dambe.
But Colin Clout rafte me of his brother, 40
That he purchast of me in the playne field:
Sore against my will was I forst to yield.

Wil. Sicker, make like account of his
    brother.
But who shall judge the wager wonne or
    lost ?
Per. That shall yonder heardgrome, and
    none other,
Which over the pousse hetherward doth
    post.
Wil. But, for the sunnebeame so sore doth
    us beate,
Were not better to shunne the scortching
    heate ?

Per. Well agreed, Willy: then sitte thee
    downe, swayne:
Sike a song never heardest thou but Colin
    sing.   50
Cud. Gynne when ye lyst, ye jolly shep-
    heards twayne:
Sike a judge as Cuddie were for a king.

Per. It fell upon a holly eve,
Wil.   Hey ho, hollidaye !
Per. When holly fathers wont to shrieve:
Wil.   Now gynneth this roundelay.
Per. Sitting upon a hill so hye,
Wil.   Hey ho, the high hyll !
Per. The while my flocke did feede thereby,
Wil.   The while the shepheard selfe did
    spill ;   60
Per. I saw the bouncing Bellibone,
Wil.   Hey ho, bonibell !
Per. Tripping over the dale alone;
Wil.   She can trippe it very well:
Per. Well decked in a frocke of gray,
Wil.   Hey ho, gray is greete !
Per. And in a kirtle of greene saye;
Wil.   The greene is for maydens meete.
Per. A chapelet on her head she wore,
Wil.   Hey ho, chapelet !   70
Per. Of sweete violets therein was store,
Wil.   She sweeter then the violet.
Per. My sheepe did leave theyr wonted
    foode,
Wil.   Hey ho, seely sheepe !
Per. And gazd on her, as they were wood,
Wil.   Woode as he that did them keepe.

Per. As the bonilasse passed bye,
Wil.   Hey ho, bonilasse !
Per. She rovde at me with glauncing eye,
Wil.   As cleare as the christall glasse: 80
Per. All as the sunnye beame so bright,
Wil.   Hey ho, the sunne beame !
Per. Glaunceth from Phœbus face forth-
    right,
Wil.   So love into thy hart did streame:
Per. Or as the thonder cleaves the cloudes,
Wil.   Hey ho, the thonder !
Per. Wherein the lightsome levin shroudes,
Wil.   So cleaves thy soule a sonder:
Per. Or as Dame Cynthias silver raye,
Wil.   Hey ho, the moonelight !   90
Per. Upon the glyttering wave doth playe:
Wil.   Such play is a pitteous plight.
Per. The glaunce into my heart did glide,
Wil.   Hey ho, the glyder !
Per. Therewith my soule was sharply gryde:
Wil.   Such woundes soone wexen wider.
Per. Hasting to raunch the arrow out,
Wil.   Hey ho, Perigot !
Per. I left the head in my hart roote:
Wil.   It was a desperate shot.   100
Per. There it ranckleth ay more and
    more,
Wil.   Hey ho, the arrowe !
Per. Ne can I find salve for my sore:
Wil.   Love is a curelesse sorrowe.
Per. And though my bale with death I
    bought,
Wil.   Hey ho, heavie cheere !
Per. Yet should thilk lasse not from my
    thought:
Wil.   So you may buye gold to deare.
Per. But whether in paynefull love I
    pyne,
Wil.   Hey ho, pinching payne !   110
Per. Or thrive in welth, she shalbe mine:
Wil.   But if thou can her obteine.
Per. And if for gracelesse greefe I dye,
Wil.   Hey ho, gracelesse griefe!
Per. Witnesse, shee slewe me with her
    eye:
Wil.   Let thy follye be the priefe.
Per. And you, that sawe it, simple shepe,
Wil.   Hey ho, the fayre flocke!
Per. For priefe thereof, my death shall
    weepe,
Wil.   And mone with many a mocke. 120
Per. So learnd I love on a hollye eve,
Wil.   Hey ho, holidaye!
Per. That ever since my hart did greve.
Wil.   Now endeth our roundelay.

Cud. Sicker, sike a roundle never heard I
   none.
Little lacketh Perigot of the best,
And Willye is not greatly overgone,
So weren his undersongs well addrest.
Wil. Herdgrome, I fear me thou have a
   squint eye:
Areede uprightly, who has the victorye ? 130

Cud. Fayth of my soule, I deeme ech
   have gayned.
Forthy let the lambe be Willye his
   owne;
And for Perigot so well hath hym payned,
To him be the wroughten mazer alone.
Per. Perigot is well pleased with the
   doome,
Ne can Willye wite the witelesse herd-
   groome.

Wil. Never dempt more right of beautye,
   I weene,
The shepheard of Ida that judged beauties
   queene.

Cud. But tell me, shepherds, should it not
   yshend
Your roundels fresh to heare a doolefull
   verse   140
Of Rosalend, (who knowes not Rosalend?)
That Colin made, ylke can I you rehearse.
Per. Now say it, Cuddie, as thou art a
   ladde:
With mery thing its good to medle sadde.

Wil. Fayth of my soule, thou shalt ycrouned
   be
In Colins stede, if thou this song areede :
For never thing on earth so pleaseth me
As him to heare, or matter of his deede.
Cud. Then listneth ech unto my heavy
   laye,
And tune your pypes as ruthful as ye may.

' Ye wastefull woodes beare witnesse of my
   woe,   151
Wherein my plaints did oftentimes resound:
Ye carelesse byrds are privie to my cryes,
Which in your songs were wont to make a
   part:
Thou pleasaunt spring hast luld me oft
   a sleepe,
Whose streames my tricklinge teares did
   ofte augment.

' Resort of people doth my greefs augment,
The walled townes do worke my greater
   woe :
The forest wide is fitter to resound
The hollow echo of my carefull cryes: 160
I hate the house, since thence my love did
   part,
Whose waylefull want debarres myne eyes
   from sleepe.

' Let stremes of teares supply the place of
   sleepe:
Let all, that sweete is, voyd : and all that
   may augment
My doole drawe neare. More meete to
   wayle my woe
Bene the wild woddes, my sorrowes to resound,
Then bedde, or bowre, both which I fill
   with cryes,
When I them see so waist, and fynd no part

' Of pleasure past. Here will I dwell apart
In gastfull grove therefore, till my last
   sleepe   170
Doe close mine eyes: so shall I not aug-
   ment,
With sight of such a chaunge, my rest-
   lesse woe.
Helpe me, ye banefull byrds, whose shriek-
   ing sound
Ys signe of dreery death, my deadly cryes

' Most ruthfully to tune. And as my cryes
(Which of my woe cannot bewray least
   part)
You heare all night, when nature craveth
   sleepe,
Increase, so let your yrksome yells aug-
   ment.
Thus all the night in plaints, the daye in
   woe
I vowed have to wayst, till safe and sound

' She home returne, whose voyces silver
   sound   181
To cheerefull songs can chaunge my chere-
   lesse cryes.
Hence with the nightingale will I take part,
That blessed byrd, that spends her time of
   sleepe
In songs and plaintive pleas, the more taug-
   ment
The memory of hys misdeede, that bred
   her woe.

'And you that feele no woe, / when as the
 sound
Of these my nightly cryes / ye heare apart,
Let breake your sounder sleepe / and pitie
 augment.'   189

Per. O Colin, Colin, the shepheards joye,
 How I admire ech turning of thy verse !
And Cuddie, fresh Cuddie, the liefest boye,
 How dolefully his doole thou didst re-
 hearse !
Cud. Then blowe your pypes, shepheards,
 til you be at home:
The night nigheth fast, yts time to be gone.

PERIGOT HIS EMBLEME.

Vincenti gloria victi.

WILLYES EMBLEME.

Vinto non vitto.

CUDDIES EMBLEME.

Felice chi può.

GLOSSE

Bestadde, disposed, ordered.
Peregall, equall.
Whilome, once.
Rafte, bereft, deprived.
Miswent, gon a straye.
Ill may, according to Virgile.

  ' Infelix o semper ovis pecus.'

A mazer. So also do Theocritus and Virgile
feigne pledges of their strife.   9
Enchased, engraven. Such pretie descriptions
every where useth Theocritus to bring in his
Idyllia. For which speciall cause, indede, he
by that name termeth his Æglogues : for Idyllion in Greke signifieth the shape or picture of
any thyng, wherof his booke is ful. And not,
as I have heard some fondly guesse, that they
be called not Idyllia, but Hædilia, of the goteheards in them.
Entrailed, wrought betwene.   19
Harvest queene, the manner of country folke
in harvest tyme.
Pousse, pease.
It fell upon. Perigot maketh hys song in
prayse of his love, to whom Willy answereth
every under verse. By Perigot who is meant,
I can not uprightly say : but if it be who is
supposed, his love deserveth no lesse prayse
then he giveth her.
Greete, weeping and complaint.
Chaplet, a kind of garlond lyke a crowne. 30
Leven lightning.

Cynthia was sayd to be the moone.
Gryde, perced.
But if, not unlesse.
Squint eye, partiall judgement.
Ech have, so saith Virgile,
  ' Et vitula tu dignus, et hic,' &c.
So by enterchaunge of gyfts Cuddie pleaseth
both partes.
Doome, judgement.   40
Dempt, for deemed, judged.
Wite the witelesse, blame the blamelesse.
The shepherd of Ida was sayd to be Paris.
Beauties queene, Venus, to whome Paris ad-
judged the goldden apple, as the pryce of her
beautie.

EMBLEME.

The meaning hereof is very ambiguous : for
Perigot by his poesie claming the conquest,
and Willye not yeelding, Cuddie the arbiter of
theyr cause, and patron of his own, semeth 50
to chalenge it, as his dew, saying, that he is
happy which can, — so abruptly ending ; but
hee meaneth eyther him that can win the beste,
or moderate him selfe being best, and leave of
with the best.

SEPTEMBER

ÆGLOGA NONA

ARGUMENT

HEREIN Diggon Davie is devised to be a
shepheard that, in hope of more gayne, drove
his sheepe into a farre countrye. The abuses
whereof, and loose living of popish prelates,
by occasion of Hobbinols demaund, he discourseth at large.

HOBBINOL. DIGGON DAVIE.

Hob. Diggon Davie, I bidde her god
 day :
Or Diggon her is, or I missaye.
 Dig. Her was her while it was daye
 light,
But now her is a most wretched wight.
For day, that was, is wightly past,
And now at earst the dirke night doth
 hast.
 Hob. Diggon, areede, who has thee so
 dight ?
Never I wist thee in so poore a plight.
Where is the fayre flocke thou was wont
 to leade ?
Or bene they chaffred ? or at mischiefe
 dead ?   10

Dig. Ah! for love of that is to thee
moste leefe,
Hobbinol, I pray thee gall not my old griefe:
Sike question ripeth up cause of newe woe,
For one opened mote unfolde many moe.

Hob. Nay, but sorrow close shrouded in
hart,
I know, to kepe is a burdenous smart.
Eche thing imparted is more eath to beare:
When the rayne is faln, the cloudes wexen
cleare.
And nowe, sithence I sawe thy head last,
Thrise three moones bene fully spent and
past: 20
Since when thou hast measured much
grownd,
And wandred, I wene, about the world
rounde,
So as thou can many thinges relate:
But tell me first of thy flocks astate.

Dig. My sheepe bene wasted, (wae is me
therefore!)
The jolly shepheard that was of yore
Is nowe nor jollye, nor shepehearde more.
In forrein costes, men sayd, was plentye:
And so there is, but all of miserye.
I dempt there much to have eeked my
store,   30
But such eeking hath made my hart sore.
In tho countryes whereas I have bene,
No being for those that truely mene,
But for such as of guile maken gayne,
No such countrye as there to remaine.
They setten to sale their shops of shame,
And maken a mart of theyr good name.
The shepheards there robben one another,
And layen baytes to beguile her brother.
Or they will buy his sheepe out of the
cote,   40
Or they will carven the shepheards throte.
The shepheards swayne you cannot wel ken,
But it be by his pryde, from other men:
They looken bigge as bulls that bene bate,
And bearen the cragge so stiffe and so
state
As cocke on his dunghill crowing cranck.

Hob. Diggon, I am so stiffe and so stanck,
That uneth may I stand any more:
And nowe the westerne wind bloweth sore,
That nowe is in his chiefe sovereigntee,   50
Beating the withered leafe from the tree.
Sitte we downe here under the hill:
Tho may we talke and tellen our fill,
And make a mocke at the blustring blast.
Now say on, Diggon, what ever thou hast.

Dig. Hobbin, ah, Hobbin! I curse the
stounde
That ever I cast to have lorne this grounde.
Wel-away the while I was so fonde
To leave the good that I had in hande,
In hope of better, that was uncouth: 60
So lost the dogge the flesh in his mouth.
My seely sheepe (ah, seely sheepe!)
That here by there I whilome usd to keepe,
All were they lustye, as thou didst see,
Bene all sterved with pyne and penuree.
Hardly my selfe escaped thilke payne,
Driven for neede to come home agayne.

Hob. Ah, fon! now by thy losse art taught
That seeldome chaunge the better brought.
Content who lives with tryed state   70
Neede feare no chaunge of frowning fate;
But who will seeke for unknowne gayne,
Oft lives by losse, and leaves with payne.

Dig. I wote ne, Hobbin, how I was be-
witcht
With vayne desyre and hope to be enricht;
But, sicker, so it is as the bright starre
Seemeth ay greater when it is farre.
I thought the soyle would have made me
rich;
But nowe I wote it is nothing sich.
For eyther the shepeheards bene ydle and
still,   80
And ledde of theyr sheepe what way they
wyll,
Or they bene false, and full of covetise,
And casten to compasse many wrong em-
prise.
But the more bene fraight with fraud and
spight,
Ne in good nor goodnes taken delight,
But kindle coales of conteck and yre,
Wherewith they sette all the world on fire:
Which when they thinken agayne to quench,
With holy water they doen hem all drench.
They saye they con to heaven the high
way,   90
But, by my soule, I dare undersaye
They never sette foote in that same troade,
But balk the right way and strayen abroad.
They boast they han the devill at com-
maund,
But aske hem therefore what they han
paund:
Marrie! that great Pan bought with deare
borrow,
To quite it from the blacke bowre of sor-
rowe.
But they han sold thilk same long agoe:

Forthy woulden drawe with hem many moe.
But let hem gange alone a Gods name;   100
As they han brewed, so let hem beare blame.
  Hob. Diggon, I praye thee speake not so dirke.
Such myster saying me seemeth to mirke.
  Dig. Then, playnely to speake of shepheards most what,
Badde is the best (this English is flatt.)
Their ill haviour garres men missay
Both of their doctrine, and of their faye.
They sayne the world is much war then it wont,
All for her shepheards bene beastly and blont:
Other sayne, but how truely I note,   110
All for they holden shame of theyr cote.
Some sticke not to say, (whote cole on her tongue !)
That sike mischiefe graseth hem emong,
All for they casten too much of worlds care,
To deck her dame, and enrich her heyre:
For such encheason, if you goe nye,
Fewe chymneis reeking you shall espye:
The fatte oxe, that wont ligge in the stal,
Is nowe fast stalled in her crumenall.
Thus chatten the people in theyr steads,   120
Ylike as a monster of many heads:
But they that shooten neerest the pricke
Sayne, other the fat from their beards doen lick:
For bigge bulles of Basan brace hem about,
That with theyr hornes butten the more stoute;
But the leane soules treaden under foote.
And to seeke redresse mought little boote;
For liker bene they to pluck away more,
Then ought of the gotten good to restore:
For they bene like foule wagmoires overgrast,   130
That if thy galage once sticketh fast,
The more to wind it out thou doest swinck,
Thou mought ay deeper and deeper sinck.
Yet better leave of with a little losse,
Then by much wrestling to leese the grosse.
  Hob. Nowe, Diggon, I see thou speakest to plaine:
Better it were a little to feyne,
And cleanly cover that cannot be cured:
Such il as is forced mought nedes be endured.
But of sike pastoures howe done the flocks creepe ?   14c

  Dig. Sike as the shepheards, sike bene her sheepe:
For they nill listen to the shepheards voyce,
But if he call hem at theyr good choyce:
They wander at wil and stray at pleasure,
And to theyr foldes yeed at their owne leasure.
But they had be better come at their cal;
For many han into mischiefe fall,
And bene of ravenous wolves yrent,
All for they nould be buxome and bent.
  Hob. Fye on thee, Diggon, and all thy foule leasing !   150
Well is knowne that sith the Saxon king,
Never was woolfe seene, many nor some,
Nor in all Kent, nor in Christendome:
But the fewer woolves (the soth to sayne,)
The more bene the foxes that here remaine.
  Dig. Yes, but they gang in more secrete wise,
And with sheepes clothing doen hem disguise:
They walke not widely as they were wont,
For feare of raungers and the great hunt,
But prively prolling to and froe,   160
Enaunter they mought be inly knowe.
  Hob. Or prive or pert yf any bene,
We han great bandogs will teare their skinne.
  Dig. Indeede, thy Ball is a bold bigge curre,
And could make a jolly hole in theyr furre.
But not good dogges hem needeth to chace,
But heedy shepheards to discerne their face:
For all their craft is in their countenaunce,
They bene so grave and full of mayntenaunce.
But shall I tell thee what my selfe knowe   170
Chaunced to Roffynn not long ygoe?
  Hob. Say it out, Diggon, what ever it hight,
For not but well mought him betight:
He is so meeke, wise, and merciable,
And with his word his worke is convenable.
Colin Clout, I wene, be his selfe boye,
(Ah for Colin, he whilome my joye!)
Shepheards sich, God mought us many send,
That doen so carefully theyr flocks tend.
  Dig. Thilk same shepheard mought I well marke: 180
He has a dogge to byte or to barke;
Never had shepheard so kene a kurre,
That waketh and if but a leafe sturre.
Whilome there wonned a wicked wolfe,
That with many a lambe had glutted his gulfe.

And ever at night wont to repayre
Unto the flocke, when the welkin shone
faire,
Ycladde in clothing of seely sheepe,
When the good old man used to sleepe.
Tho at midnight he would barke and ball, 190
(For he had eft learned a curres call,)
As if a woolfe were emong the sheepe.
With that the shepheard would breake his
sleepe,
And send out Lowder (for so his dog hote)
To raunge the fields with wide open throte.
Tho, when as Lowder was farre awaye,
This wolvish sheepe would catchen his
pray,
A lambe, or a kidde, or a weanell wast:
With that to the wood would he speede
him fast.
Long time he used this slippery pranck, 200
Ere Roffy could for his laboure him thanck.
At end, the shepheard his practise spyed,
(For Roffy is wise, and as Argus eyed)
And when at even he came to the flocke,
Fast in theyr folds he did them locke,
And tooke out the woolfe in his counterfect
cote,
And let out the sheepes bloud at his throte.
  Hob. Marry, Diggon, what should him
affraye
To take his owne where ever it laye ?
For had his wesand bene a little widder, 210
He would have devoured both hidder and
shidder.
  Dig. Mischiefe light on him, and Gods
great curse !
Too good for him had bene a great deale
worse:
For it was a perilous beast above all,
And eke had he cond the shepherds call,
And oft in the night came to the shepecote,
And called Lowder, with a hollow throte,
As if it the old man selfe had bene.
The dog his maisters voice did it weene,
Yet halfe in doubt he opened the dore, 220
And ranne out, as he was wont of yore.
No sooner was out, but, swifter then
thought,
Fast by the hyde the wolfe Lowder caught:
And had not Roffy renne to the steven,
Lowder had be slaine thilke same even.
  Hob. God shield, man, he should so ill
have thrive,
All for he did his devoyre belive.
If sike bene wolves as thou hast told,
How mought we, Diggon, hem behold ?

  Dig. How, but with heede and watch-
fulnesse 230
Forstallen hem of their wilinesse ?
Forthy with shepheard sittes not playe,
Or sleepe, as some doen, all the long day:
But ever liggen in watch and ward,
From soddein force theyr flocks for to gard.
  Hob. Ah, Diggon ! thilke same rule were
too straight,
All the cold season to wach and waite:
We bene of fleshe, men as other bee:
Why should we be bound to such miseree ?
What ever thing lacketh chaungeable
rest, 240
Mought needes decay, when it is at best.
  Dig. Ah ! but Hobbinol, all this long tale
Nought easeth the care that doth me for-
haile.
What shall I doe ? what way shall I wend,
My piteous plight and losse to amend ?
Ah, good Hobbinol ! mought I thee praye
Of ayde or counsell in my decaye.
  Hob. Now by my soule, Diggon, I lament
The haplesse mischief that has thee hent.
Nethelesse thou seest my lowly saile, 250
That froward fortune doth ever availe.
But were Hobbinoll as God mought please,
Diggon should soone find favour and ease.
But if to my cotage thou wilt resort,
So as I can I wil thee comfort:
There mayst thou ligge in a vetchy bed,
Till fayrer fortune shewe forth her head.
  Dig. Ah, Hobbinol, God mought it thee
requite !
Diggon on fewe such freendes did ever lite.

DIGGONS EMBLEME.

Inopem me copia fecit.

GLOSSE

  The dialecte and phrase of speache, in this
dialogue, seemeth somewhat to differ from the
comen. The cause whereof is supposed to be,
by occasion of the party herein meant, who,
being very freend to the author hereof, had
bene long in forraine countryes, and there seene
many disorders, which he here recounteth to
Hobbinoll.
  Bidde her, bidde good morrow. For to
bidde, is to praye, whereof commeth *beades* 10
for prayers, and so they say, to bidde his
beades, sc. to saye his prayers.
  Wightly, quicklye, or sodenlye.
  Chaffred, solde.
  Dead at mischiefe, an unusuall speache, but

much usurped of Lidgate, and sometime of Chaucer.

Leefe, deare.
Ethe, easie.
Thrise thre moones, nine monethes.   20
Measured, for traveled.
Wae, woe, Northernly.
Eeked, encreased.
Carven, cutte.
Kenne, know.
Cragge, neck.
State, stoutely.
Stanck, wearie or fainte.
And nowe. He applieth it to the tyme of the yeare, which is in thend of harvest, which 30 they call the fall of the leafe : at which tyme the westerne wynde beareth most swaye.
A mocke, imitating Horace, ' *Debes ludibrium ventis.*'
Lorne, lefte.
Soote, swete.
Uncouthe, unknowen.
Here by there, here and there.
As the brighte, translated out of Mantuane.
Emprise, for enterprise. *Per syncopen.*   40
Contek, strife.
Trode, path.
Marrie that, that is, their soules, which by popish exorcismes and practices they damne to hell.
Blacke, hell.
Gange, goe.
Mister, maner.
Mirke, obscure.
Warre, worse.   50
Crumenall, purse.
Brace, compasse.
Encheson, occasion.
Overgrast, overgrowen with grasse.
Galage, shoe.
The grosse, the whole.
Buxome and bent, meeke and obedient.
Saxon king, King Edgare that reigned here in Brytanye in the yeare of our Lord [957–975] which king caused all the wolves, whereof 60 then was store in thys countrye, by a proper policie to be destroyed. So as never since that time there have ben wolves here founde, unlesse they were brought from other countryes. And therefore Hobbinoll rebuketh him of untruth, for saying there be wolves in England.
Nor in Christendome. This saying seemeth to be strange and unreasonable : but indede it was wont to be an olde proverbe and comen phrase. The original whereof was, for that 70 most part of England in the reigne of King Ethelbert was christened, Kent onely except, which remayned long after in mysbeliefe and unchristened : so that Kent was counted no part of Christendome.

Great hunt, executing of lawes and justice.
Enaunter, least that.
Inly, inwardly : afforesayde.
Prevely or pert, openly, sayth Chaucer.
Roffy, the name of a shepehearde in 80 Marot his Æglogue of Robin and the Kinge. Whome he here commendeth for greate care and wise governance of his flock.
Colin Cloute. Nowe I thinke no man doubteth but by Colin is ever meante the authour selfe : whose especiall good freend Hobbinoll sayth he is, or more rightly Mayster Gabriel Harvey : of whose speciall commendation, aswell in poetrye as rhetorike and other choyce learning, we have lately had a sufficient tryall in di- 90 verse his workes, but specially in his *Musarum Lachrymæ*, and his late *Gratulationum Valdinensium*, which boke, in the progresse at Audley in Essex, he dedicated in writing to her Majestie, afterward presenting the same in print unto her Highnesse at the worshipfull Maister Capells in Hertfordshire. Beside other his sundrye most rare and very notable writings, partely under unknown tytles, and partly under counterfayt names, as hys *Tyrannomastix*, 100 his *Ode Natalitia*, his *Rameidos*, and esspecially that parte of *Philomusus*, his divine *Anticosmopolita*, and divers other of lyke importance. As also, by the names of other shepheardes, he covereth the persons of divers other his familiar freendes and best acquayntaunce.

This tale of Roffy seemeth to coloure some particular action of his. But what, I certeinlye know not.

Wonned, haunted.   110
Welkin, skie : afforesaid.
A weanell waste, a weaned youngling.
Hidder and shidder, he and she, male and female.
Steven, noyse.
Belive, quickly.
What ever, Ovids verse translated.
' *Quod caret alterna requie durabile non est.*'
Forehaile, drawe or distresse.
Vetchie, of pease strawe.   120

EMBLEME.

This is the saying of Narcissus in Ovid. For when the foolishe boye, by beholding hys face in the brooke, fell in love with his owne likenesse : and not hable to content him selfe with much looking thereon, he cryed out, that plentye made him poore, meaning that much gazing had bereft him of sence. But our Diggon useth it to other purpose, as who that by tryall of many wayes had founde the worst, 130 and through greate plentye was fallen into great penurie. This poesie I knowe to have bene much used of the author, and to suche like effecte as fyrste Narcissus spake it.

OCTOBER

ÆGLOGA DECIMA

ARGUMENT

In Cuddie is set out the perfecte paterne of a poete, whiche, finding no maintenaunce of his state and studies, complayneth of the contempte of Poetrie, and the causes thereof: specially having bene in all ages, and even amongst the most barbarous, alwayes of singular accounpt and honor, and being indede so worthy and commendable an arte: or rather no arte, but a divine gift and heavenly instinct, not to bee gotten by laboure and learning, but adorned with both, and poured into the witte by a certain ἐνθουσιασμός and celestiall inspiration; as the author hereof els where at large discourseth in his booke called *The English Poete*, which booke being lately come to my hands, I mynde also by Gods grace, upon further advisement, to publish.

PIERCE. CUDDIE.

Piers. Cuddie, for shame! hold up thy
    heavye head,
And let us cast with what delight to chace
And weary thys long lingring Phœbus race.
Whilome thou wont the shepheards laddes
    to leade
In rymes, in ridles, and in bydding base:
Now they in thee, and thou in sleepe art
    dead.

Cud. Piers, I have pyped erst so long
    with payne,
That all mine oten reedes bene rent and
    wore:
And my poore Muse hath spent her spared
    store,
Yet little good hath got, and much lesse
    gayne.   10
Such pleasaunce makes the grashopper so
    poore,
And ligge so layd, when winter doth her
    straine.

The dapper ditties that I wont devise,
To feede youthes fancie and the flocking
    fry,
Delighten much: what I the bett forthy?
They han the pleasure, I a sclender prise:
I beate the bush, the byrds to them doe
    flye:
What good thereof to Cuddie can arise?

Piers. Cuddie, the prayse is better then
    the price,
The glory eke much greater then the gayne:
O what an honor is it, to restraine   21
The lust of lawlesse youth with good ad-
    vice,
Or pricke them forth with pleasaunce of
    thy vaine,
Whereto thou list their trayned willes
    entice!

Soone as thou gynst to sette thy notes in
    frame,
O how the rurall routes to thee doe cleave!
Seemeth thou doest their soule of sense
    bereave,
All as the shepheard, that did fetch his
    dame
From Plutoes balefull bowre withouten
    leave:
His musicks might the hellish hound did
    tame.   30

Cud. So praysen babes the peacoks
    spotted traine,
And wondren at bright Argus blazing
    eye;
But who rewards him ere the more forthy?
Or feedes him once the fuller by a graine?
Sike prayse is smoke, that sheddeth in the
    skye,
Sike words bene wynd, and wasten soone in
    vayne.

Piers. Abandon then the base and viler
    clowne:
Lyft up thy selfe out of the lowly dust,
And sing of bloody Mars, of wars, of
    giusts:
Turne thee to those that weld the awful
    crowne,   40
To doubted knights, whose woundlesse
    armour rusts,
And helmes unbruzed wexen dayly browne.

There may thy Muse display her fluttryng
    wing,
And stretch her selfe at large from east to
    west:
Whither thou list in fayre Elisa rest,
Or if thee please in bigger notes to sing,
Advaunce the worthy whome shee loveth
    best,
That first the white beare to the stake did
    bring.

And when the stubborne stroke of stronger
    stounds
Has somewhat slackt the tenor of thy
    string,   50
Of love and lustihead tho mayst thou sing,
And carrol lowde, and leade the myllers
    rownde,
All were Elisa one of thilke same ring.
So mought our Cuddies name to heaven
    sownde.

Cud. Indeede the Romish Tityrus, I
    heare,
Through his Mecœnas left his oaten reede,
Whereon he earst had taught his flocks to
    feede,
And laboured lands to yield the timely eare,
And eft did sing of warres and deadly drede,
So as the heavens did quake his verse to
    here.   60

But ah! Mecœnas is yclad in claye,
And great Augustus long ygoe is dead,
And all the worthies liggen wrapt in leade,
That matter made for poets on to play:
For, ever, who in derring doe were dreade,
The loftie verse of hem was loved aye.

But after vertue gan for age to stoupe,
And mighty manhode brought a bedde of
    ease,
The vaunting poets found nought worth a
    pease
To put in preace among the learned troupe.
Tho gan the streames of flowing wittes to
    cease,   71
And sonnebright honour pend in shamefull
    coupe.

And if that any buddes of poesie
Yet of the old stocke gan to shoote agayne,
Or it mens follies mote be forst to fayne,
And rolle with rest in rymes of rybaudrye,
Or, as it sprong, it wither must agayne:
Tom Piper makes us better melodie.

Piers. O pierlesse Poesye, where is then
    thy place?
If nor in princes pallace thou doe sitt,   80
(And yet is princes pallace the most fitt)
Ne brest of baser birth doth thee embrace.
Then make thee winges of thine aspyring
    wit,
And, whence thou camst, flye backe to
    heaven apace.

Cud. Ah, Percy! it is all to weake and
    wanne,
So high to sore, and make so large a
    flight;
Her peeced pyneons bene not so in plight:
For Colin fittes such famous flight to
    scanne:
He, were he not with love so ill bedight,
Would mount as high and sing as soote as
    swanne.   90

Piers. Ah, fon! for love does teach him
    climbe so hie,
And lyftes him up out of the loathsome
    myre:
Such immortall mirrhor as he doth ad-
    mire
Would rayse ones mynd above the starry
    skie,
And cause a caytive corage to aspire;
For lofty love doth loath a lowly eye.

Cud. All otherwise the state of poet
    stands:
For lordly Love is such a tyranne fell,
That, where he rules, all power he doth ex-
    pell.
The vaunted verse a vacant head de-
    maundes,   100
Ne wont with crabbed Care the Muses
    dwell:
Unwisely weaves, that takes two webbes in
    hand.

Who ever casts to compasse weightye
    prise,
And thinks to throwe out thondring words
    of threate,
Let powre in lavish cups and thriftie bitts
    of meate;
For Bacchus fruite is frend to Phœbus
    wise,
And when with wine the braine begins to
    sweate,
The nombers flowe as fast as spring doth
    ryse.

Thou kenst not, Percie, howe the ryme
    should rage.
O if my temples were distaind with wine,
And girt in girlonds of wild yvie twine,   110
How I could reare the Muse on stately
    stage,
And teache her tread aloft in buskin fine,
With queint Bellona in her equipage!

But ah! my corage cooles ere it be
  warme;
Forthy content us in thys humble shade,
Where no such troublous tydes han us
  assayde.
Here we our slender pipes may safely
  charme.
Piers. And when my gates shall han their
  bellies layd,
Cuddie shall have a kidde to store his
  farme.

CUDDIES EMBLEME.

A gitante calescimus illo, &c.

GLOSSE

This Æglogue is made in imitation of Theocritus his xvi. Idilion, wherein hee reproved the
tyranne Hiero of Syracuse for his nigardise
towarde poetes, in whome is the power to make
men immortall for theyr good dedes, or shameful for their naughty lyfe. And the lyke also
is in Mantuane. The style hereof, as also that
in Theocritus, is more loftye then the rest, and
applyed to the heighte of poeticall witte.
Cuddie. I doubte whether by Cuddie be 10
specified the authour selfe, or some other. For
in the eyght Æglogue the same person was
brought in, singing a cantion of Colins making,
as he sayth. So that some doubt that the persons be different.
Whilome, sometime.
Oaten reedes, Avena.
Ligge so layde, lye so faynt and unlustye.
Dapper, pretye.
Frye is a bold metaphore, forced from the 20
spawning fishes: for the multitude of young
fish be called the frye.
To restraine. This place seemeth to conspyre
with Plato, who in his first booke *de Legibus*
sayth, that the first invention of poetry was of
very vertuous intent. For at what time an infinite number of youth usually came to theyr
great solemne feastes called Panegyrica, which
they used every five yeere to hold, some learned
man, being more hable then the rest for spe- 30
ciall gyftes of wytte and musicke, would take
upon him to sing fine verses to the people, in
prayse eyther of vertue or of victory or of immortality, or such like. At whose wonderful
gyft al men being astonied and as it were
ravished with delight, thinking (as it was indeed) that he was inspired from above, called
him *vatem:* which kinde of men afterwarde
framing their verses to lighter musick (as of
musick be many kinds, some sadder, some 40
lighter, some martiall, some heroical: and so

diversely eke affect the mynds of men) found
out lighter matter of poesie also, some playing
wyth love, some scorning at mens fashions,
some powred out in pleasures: and so were
called poetes or makers.
Sence bereave. What the secrete working of
musick is in the myndes of men, aswell appeareth hereby, that some of the auncient
philosophers, and those the moste wise, as 50
Plato and Pythagoras, held for opinion, that
the mynd was made of a certaine harmonie
and musicall nombers, for the great compassion and likenes of affection in thone and in the
other, as also by that memorable history of
Alexander: to whom when as Timotheus the
great musitian playd the Phrygian melodie, it
is said that he was distraught with such unwonted fury, that streight way rysing from the
table in great rage, he caused himselfe to be 60
armed, as ready to goe to warre, (for that musick is very warlike:) and immediatly when
as the musitian chaunged his stroke into the
Lydian and Ionique harmony, he was so furr
from warring, that he sat as styl, as if he had
bene in matters of counsell. Such might is in
musick. Wherefore Plato and Aristotle forbid the Arcadian melodie from children and
youth. For that being altogither on the fyft
and vii. tone, it is of great force to molifie 70
and quench the kindly courage, which useth to
burne in yong brests. So that it is not incred-
ible which the poete here sayth, that musick
can bereave the soule of sence.
The shepheard that, Orpheus: of whom is
sayd, that by his excellent skil in musick and
poetry, he recovered his wife Eurydice from
hell.
Argus eyes. Of Argus is before said, that
Juno to him committed hir husband Jupiter 80
his paragon, Iô, bicause he had an hundred
eyes: but afterwarde Mercury, wyth hys musick
lulling Argus aslepe, slew him and brought
Iô away, whose eyes it is sayd that Juno, for
his eternall memory, placed in her byrd the
peacocks tayle: for those coloured spots indeede resemble eyes.
Woundlesse armour, unwounded in warre, doe
rust through long peace.
Display, a poeticall metaphore: whereof 90
the meaning is, that, if the poet list showe his
skill in matter of more dignitie then is the
homely Æglogue, good occasion is him offered
of higher veyne and more heroicall argument
in the person of our most gratious soveraign,
whom (as before) he calleth Elisa. Or if mater
of knighthoode and chevalrie please him better,
that there be many noble and valiaunt men,
that are both worthy of his payne in theyr deserved prayses, and also favourers of hys 100
skil and faculty.

The worthy. He meaneth (as I guesse) the most honorable and renowmed the Erle of Leycester, whom by his cognisance (although the same be also proper to other) rather then by his name he bewrayeth, being not likely that the names of noble princes be known to country clowne.

Slack, that is when thou chaungest thy verse from stately discourse, to matter of more 110 pleasaunce and delight.

The millers, a kind of daunce.

Ring, company of dauncers.

The Romish Tityrus, wel knowen to be Virgile, who by Mecænas means was brought into the favour of the Emperor Augustus, and by him moved to write in loftier kinde then he erst had doen.

Whereon. In these three verses are the three severall workes of Virgile intended. For 120 in teaching his flocks to feede, is meant his *Æglogues.* In labouring of lands, is hys *Bucoliques.* In singing of wars and deadly dreade, is his divine *Æneis* figured.

In derring doe, in manhoode and chevalrie.

For ever. He sheweth the cause why poetes were wont be had in such honor of noble men, that is, that by them their worthines and valor shold through theyr famous posies be commended to al posterities. Wherefore it is 130 sayd, that Achilles had never bene so famous, as he is, but for Homeres immortal verses: which is the only advantage which he had of Hector. And also that Alexander the Great, comming to his tombe in Sigeus, with naturall teares blessed him, that ever was his hap to be honoured with so excellent a poets work, as so renowned and ennobled onely by hys meanes. Which being declared in a most eloquent oration of Tullies, is of Petrarch no 140 lesse worthely sette forth in a sonet.

' Giunto Alexandro a la famosa tomba
Del fero Achille, sospirando disse :
O fortunato, che si chiara tromba Trovasti,' &c.

And that such account hath bene alwayes made of poetes, aswell sheweth this, that the worthy Scipio, in all his warres against Carthage and Numantia, had evermore in his company, and that in a most familiar sort, the good olde poet Ennius : as also that Alexander, destroy- 150 ing Thebes, when he was enformed, that the famous lyrick poet Pindarus was borne in that citie, not onely commaunded streightly, that no man should, upon payne of death, do any violence to that house, by fire or otherwise : but also specially spared most, and some highly rewarded, that were of hys kinne. So favoured he the only name of a poete. Whych prayse otherwise was in tne same man no lesse famous, that when he came to ransacking of King 160 Darius coffers, whom he lately had over-

throwen, he founde in a little coffer of silver the two bookes of Homers works, as layd up there for speciall jewels and richesse, which he, taking thence, put one of them dayly in his bosome, and thother every night layde under his pillowe. Such honor have poetes alwayes found in the sight of princes and noble men : which this author here very well sheweth, as els where more notably. 170

But after. He sheweth the cause of contempt of poetry to be idlenesse and basenesse of mynd.

Pent, shut up in slouth, as in a coope or cage.

Tom Piper, an ironicall sarcasmus, spoken in derision of these rude wits, whych make more account of a ryming rybaud, then of skill grounded upon learning and judgment.

Ne brest, the meaner sort of men.

Her peeced pineons, unperfect skil. Spoken wyth humble modestie. 181

As soote as swanne. The comparison seemeth to be strange : for the swanne hath ever wonne small commendation for his swete singing : but it is sayd of the learned that the swan, a little before hir death, singeth most pleasantly, as prophecying by a secrete instinct her neere destinie. As wel sayth the poete elsewhere in one of his sonetts.

' The silver swanne doth sing before her dying day,
As shee that feeles the deepe delight that is in
death,' &c. 191

Immortall myrrhour, Beauty, which is an excellent object of poeticall spirites, as appeareth by the worthy Petrarchs saying,

' Fiorir faceva il mio debile ingegno,
A la sua ombra, et crescer ne gli affanni.'

A caytive corage, a base and abject minde.

For lofty love. I think this playing with the letter to be rather a fault then a figure, aswel in our English tongue, as it hath bene al- 200 wayes in the Latine, called *Cacozelon.*

A vacant imitateth Mantuanes saying, ' vacuum curis divina cerebrum Poscit.'

Lavish cups resembleth that comen verse, ' Fæcundi calices quem non fecere disertum ? '

O if my. He seemeth here to be ravished with a poetical furie. For (if one rightly mark) the numbers rise so ful, and the verse groweth so big, that it seemeth he hath forgot the meanenesse of shepheards state and stile. 210

Wild yvie, for it is dedicated to Bacchus, and therefore it is sayd, that the Mænades (that is, Bacchus franticke priestes) used in theyr sacrifice to carry thyrsos, which were pointed staves or javelins, wrapped about with yvie.

In buskin. It was the maner of poetes and plaiers in tragedies to were buskins, as also in comedies to use stockes and light shoes. So that the buskin in poetry is used for tragical matter, as is said in Virgile, ' Sola Sophocleo 220

tua carmina digna cothurno.' And the like in Horace, ' Magnum loqui, nitique cothurno.'

Queint, strange. *Bellona ;* the goddesse of battaile, that is, Pallas, which may therefore wel be called queint, for that (as Lucian saith) when Jupiter hir father was in traveile of her, he caused his sonne Vulcane with his axe to hew his head. Out of which leaped forth lustely a valiant damsell armed at all poyntes, whom 230 seeing Vulcane so faire and comely, lightly leaping to her, preferred her some cortesie, which the lady disdeigning, shaked her speare at him, and threatned his saucinesse. Therefore such straungenesse is well applyed to her.

Æquipage, order.

Tydes, seasons.

Charme, temper and order : for charmes were wont to be made by verses, as Ovid sayth, ' Aut si carminibus.'

EMBLEME.

Hereby is meant, as also in the whole 240 course of this Æglogue, that poetry is a divine instinct and unnatural rage passing the reache of comen reason. Whom Piers answereth epiphonematicos, as admiring the excellency of the skyll, whereof in Cuddie hee hadde alreadye hadde a taste.

NOVEMBER

ÆGLOGA UNDECIMA

ARGUMENT

IN this xi. Æglogue he bewayleth the death of some mayden of greate bloud, whom he calleth Dido. The personage is secrete, and to me altogether unknowne, albe of him selfe I often required the same. This Æglogue is made in imitation of Marot his song, which he made upon the death of Loys the Frenche Queene : but farre passing his reache, and in myne opinion all other the Eglogues of this booke.

THENOT. COLIN.

The. Colin, my deare, when shall it please thee sing,
As thou were wont, songs of some jouisaunce ?
Thy Muse to long slombreth in sorrowing,
Lulled a sleepe through loves misgovernaunce:
Now somewhat sing whose endles sovenaunce
Emong the shepeheards swaines may aye remaine,

Whether thee list thy loved lasse advaunce,
Or honor Pan with hymnes of higher vaine.

Col. Thenot, now nis the time of merimake,   9
Nor Pan to herye, nor with love to playe:
Sike myrth in May is meetest for to make,
Or summer shade, under the cocked haye.
But nowe sadde winter welked hath the day,
And Phœbus, weary of his yerely taske,
Ystabled hath his steedes in lowlye laye,
And taken up his ynne in Fishes haske.
Thilke sollein season sadder plight doth aske,
And loatheth sike delightes as thou doest prayse:
The mornefull Muse in myrth now list ne maske,
As shee was wont in youngth and sommer dayes.   20
But if thou algate lust light virelayes,
And looser songs of love, to underfong,
Who but thy selfe deserves sike Poetes prayse ?
Relieve thy oaten pypes that sleepen long.

The. The nightingale is sovereigne of song,
Before him sits the titmose silent bee:
And I, unfitte to thrust in skilfull thronge,
Should Colin make judge of my fooleree.
Nay, better learne of hem that learned bee,
And han be watered at the Muses well: 30
The kindlye dewe drops from the higher tree,
And wets the little plants that lowly dwell
But if sadde winters wrathe, and season chill,
Accorde not with thy Muses meriment,
To sadder times thou mayst attune thy quill,
And sing of sorrowe and deathes dreeriment:
For deade is Dido, dead, alas ! and drent,
Dido, the great shepehearde his daughter sheene:
The fayrest may she was that ever went,
Her like shee has not left behinde I weene.
And if thou wilt bewayle my wofull tene,   41
I shall thee give yond cosset for thy payne:
And if thy rymes as rownd and rufull bene
As those that did thy Rosalind complayne,
Much greater gyfts for guerdon thou shalt gayne
Then kidde or cosset, which I thee bynempt.

Then up, I say, thou jolly shepeheard
  swayne,
Let not my small demaund be so contempt.
  Col. Thenot, to that I choose thou doest
    me tempt:
But ah! to well I wote my humble vaine,
And howe my rymes bene rugged and un-
    kempt: 51
Yet, as I conne, my conning I will strayne.

Up, then, Melpomene, thou mournefulst
  Muse of nyne!
Such cause of mourning never hadst afore:
Up, grieslie ghostes! and up my rufull
  ryme!
Matter of myrth now shalt thou have no
  more:
For dead shee is that myrth thee made of
  yore.
  Dido, my deare, alas! is dead,
  Dead, and lyeth wrapt in lead:
  O heavie herse!   60
Let streaming teares be poured out in store:
  O carefull verse!

Shepheards, that by your flocks on Kentish
  downes abyde,
Waile ye this wofull waste of Natures
  warke:
Waile we the wight whose presence was
  our pryde:
Waile we the wight whose absence is our
  carke.
The sonne of all the world is dimme and
  darke:
  The earth now lacks her wonted light,
  And all we dwell in deadly night:
  O heavie herse!   70
Breake we our pypes, that shrild as lowde
  as larke:
  O carefull verse!

Why doe we longer live, (ah, why live we
  so long?)
Whose better dayes death hath shut up in
  woe?
The fayrest floure our gyrlond all emong
Is faded quite, and into dust ygoe.
Sing now, ye shepheards daughters, sing no
  moe
  The songs that Colin made in her
    prayse,
  But into weeping turne your wanton
    layes:
  O heavie herse!   80

Now is time to die. Nay, time was long
  ygoe:
  O carefull verse!

Whence is it that the flouret of the field
  doth fade,
And lyeth buryed long in winters bale:
Yet soone as spring his mantle doth dis-
  playe,
It floureth fresh, as it should never fayle?
But thing on earth that is of most availe,
  As vertues braunch and beauties budde,
  Reliven not for any good.
  O heavie herse!   90
The braunch once dead, the budde eke
  needes must quaile:
  O carefull verse!

She, while she was, (that was, a woful word
  to sayne!)
For beauties prayse and plesaunce had no
  pere:
So well she couth the shepherds enter-
  tayne
With cakes and cracknells and such country
  chere.
Ne would she scorne the simple shepheards
  swaine,
  For she would cal hem often heame,
  And give hem curds and clouted creame.
  O heavie herse!   100
Als Colin Cloute she would not once dis-
  dayne.
  O carefull verse!

But nowe sike happy cheere is turnd to
  heavie chaunce,
Such pleasaunce now displast by dolors
  dint:
All musick sleepes where Death doth leade
  the daunce,
And shepherds wonted solace is extinct.
The blew in black, the greene in gray, is
  tinct;
  The gaudie girlonds deck her grave,
  The faded flowres her corse embrave.
  O heavie herse!   110
Morne nowe, my Muse, now morne with
  teares besprint.
  O carefull verse!

O thou greate shepheard, Lobbin, how great
  is thy griefe!
Where bene the nosegayes that she dight
  for thee?

The colourd chaplets, wrought with a
    chiefe,
The knotted rushringes, and gilte rose-
    maree ?
For shee deemed nothing too deere for thee.
    Ah ! they bene all yclad in clay,
    One bitter blast blewe all away.
    O heavie herse !   120
Thereof nought remaynes but the memoree.
    O carefull verse !

Ay me ! that dreerie Death should strike
    so mortall stroke,
That can undoe Dame Natures kindly
    course:
The faded lockes fall from the loftie oke,
The flouds do gaspe, for dryed is theyr
    sourse,
And flouds of teares flowe in theyr stead
    perforse.
    The mantled medowes mourne,
    Theyr sondry colours tourne.
    O heavie herse !   130
The heavens doe melt in teares without re-
    morse.
    O carefull verse !

The feeble flocks in field refuse their
    former foode,
And hang theyr heads, as they would learne
    to weepe:
The beastes in forest wayle as they were
    woode,
Except the wolves, that chase the wandring
    sheepe,
Now she is gon that safely did hem keepe.
    The turtle, on the bared braunch,
    Laments the wound that Death did
        launch.
    O heavie herse !   140
And Philomele her song with teares doth
    steepe.
    O carefull verse !

The water nymphs, that wont with her to
    sing and daunce,
And for her girlond olive braunches beare,
Now balefull boughes of cypres doen ad-
    vaunce:
The Muses, that were wont greene bayes
    to weare,
Now bringen bitter eldre braunches seare:
    The Fatall Sisters eke repent
    Her vitall threde so soone was spent
    O heavie herse !   150

Morne now, my Muse, now morne with
    heavie cheare.
    O carefull verse !

O trustlesse state of earthly things, and
    slipper hope
Of mortal men, that swincke and sweate for
    nought,
And shooting wide, doe misse the marked
    scope:
Now have I learnd, (a lesson derely
    bought)
That nys on earth assuraunce to be sought:
    For what might be in earthlie mould,
    That did her buried body hould.
    O heavie herse !   160
Yet saw I on the beare when it was brought.
    O carefull verse !

But maugre Death, and dreaded sisters
    deadly spight,
And gates of Hel, and fyrie furies forse,
She hath the bonds broke of eternall night,
Her soule unbodied of the burdenous corpse.
Why then weepes Lobbin so without re-
    morse ?
    O Lobb ! thy losse no longer lament;
    Dido nis dead, but into heaven hent.
    O happye herse !   170
Cease now, my Muse, now cease thy sor-
    rowes sourse:
    O joyfull verse !

Why wayle we then ? why weary we the
    gods with playnts,
As if some evill were to her betight ?
She raignes a goddesse now emong the
    saintes,
That whilome was the saynt of shepheards
    light:
And is enstalled nowe in heavens hight.
    I see thee, blessed soule, I see,
    Walke in Elisian fieldes so free.
    O happy herse !   180
Might I once come to thee ! O that I
    might !
    O joyfull verse !

Unwise and wretched men, to weete whats
    good or ill,
Wee deeme of death as doome of ill de-
    sert:
But knewe we, fooles, what it us bringes
    until,
Dye would we dayly, once it to expert.

No daunger there the shepheard can astert:
Fayre fieldes and pleasaunt layes there
    bene,
The fieldes ay fresh, the grasse ay greene:
O happy herse !   190
Make hast, ye shepheards, thether to revert:
O joyfull verse !

Dido is gone afore (whose turne shall be
    the next ?)
There lives shee with the blessed gods in
    blisse,
There drincks she nectar with ambrosia
    mixt,
And joyes enjoyes that mortall men doe
    misse.
The honor now of highest gods she is,
    That whilome was poore shepheards
        pryde,
    While here on earth she did abyde.
O happy herse !   200
Ceasse now, my song, my woe now wasted
    is.
O joyfull verse !

The. Ay, francke shepheard, how bene
    thy verses meint
With doolfull pleasaunce, so as I ne wotte
Whether rejoyce or weepe for great con-
    strainte !
Thyne be the cossette, well hast thow it
    gotte.
Up, Colin, up, ynough thou morned hast:
Now gynnes to mizzle, hye we homeward
    fast.

COLINS EMBLEME.

La mort ny mord.

GLOSSE

Jouisaunce, myrth.
Sovenaunce, remembraunce.
Herie, honour.
Welked, shortned, or empayred. As the
moone being in the waine is sayde of Lidgate
to welk.
In lowly lay, according to the season of the
moneth November, when the sonne draweth
low in the south toward his tropick or returne.
In Fishes haske. The sonne reigneth, that 10
is, in the signe Pisces all November. A *haske*
is a wicker pad, wherein they use to cary fish.
Virelaies, a light kind of song.
Bee watred. For it is a saying of poetes, that
they have dronk of the Muses well Castalias,
whereof was before sufficiently sayd.

Dreriment, dreery and heavy cheere.
The great shepheard is some man of high
degree, and not, as some vainely suppose, God
Pan. The person both of the shephearde and 20
of Dido is unknowen, and closely buried in the
authors conceipt. But out of doubt I am, that
it is not Rosalind, as some imagin : for he
speaketh soone after of her also.
Shene, fayre and shining.
May, for mayde.
Tene, sorrow.
Guerdon, reward.
Bynempt, bequethed.   29
Cosset, a lambe brought up without the dam.
Unkempt, incompti ; not comed, that is, rude
and unhansome.
Melpomene, the sadde and waylefull Muse,
used of poets in honor of tragedies : as saith
Virgile,

'Melpomene tragico proclamat mæsta boatu.'

Up griesly gosts, the maner of tragicall
poetes, to call for helpe of furies and damned
ghostes : so is Hecuba of Euripides, and Tantalus brought in of Seneca; and the rest of 40
the rest.
Herse is the solemne obsequie in funeralles.
Wast of, decay of so beautifull a peece.
Carke, care.
Ah why, an elegant epanorthosis, as also
soone after : *nay, time was long ago.*
Flouret, a diminutive for a little floure. This
is a notable and sententious comparison ' *A
minore ad majus.*'
Reliven not, live not againe, sc. not in theyr 50
earthly bodies : for in heaven they enjoy their
due reward.
The braunch. He meaneth Dido, who being,
as it were, the mayne braunch now withered,
the buddes, that is, beautie (as he sayd afore)
can no more flourish.
With cakes, fit for shepheards bankets.
Heame, for home : after the northerne pro-
nouncing.
Tinct, deyed or stayned.   60
The gaudie. The meaning is, that the things
which were the ornaments of her lyfe are made
the honor of her funerall, as is used in burialls.
Lobbin, the name of a shepherd, which seemeth to have bene the lover and deere frende of
Dido.
Rushrings, agreeable for such base gyftes.
Faded lockes, dryed leaves. As if Nature
her selfe bewayled the death of the mayde.
Sourse, spring.   70
Mantled medowes, for the sondry flowres are
like a mantle or coverlet wrought with many
colours.
Philomele, the nightingale : whome the poetes
faine once to have bene a ladye of great beauty,
till, being ravished by hir sisters husbande

she desired to be turned into a byrd of her name. Whose complaintes be very well set forth of Maister George Gaskin, a wittie gentleman, and the very chefe of our late rymers, 80 who, and if some partes of learning wanted not (albee it is well knowen he altogyther wanted not learning) no doubt would have attayned to the excellencye of those famous poets. For gifts of wit and naturall promptnesse appeare in hym abundantly.

Cypresse, used of the old paynims in the furnishing of their funerall pompe, and properly the signe of all sorow and heavinesse.

The fatall sisters, Clotho, Lachesis, and 90 Atropos, daughters of Herebus and the Nighte, whom the poetes fayne to spinne the life of man, as it were a long threde, which they drawe out in length, till his fatal howre and timely death be come; but if by other casualtie his dayes be abridged, then one of them, that is, Atropos, is sayde to have cut the threde in twain. Hereof commeth a common verse.

'Clotho colum bajulat, Lachesis trahit, Atropos occat.'

O trustlesse, a gallant exclamation, moral- 100 ized with great wisedom, and passionate wyth great affection.

Beare, a frame, wheron they use to lay the dead corse.

Furies, of poetes be feyned to be three, Persephone, Alecto, and Megera, which are sayd to be the authours of all evill and mischiefe.

Eternall night is death or darknesse of hell.

Betight, happened. 110

I see, a lively icon or representation, as if he saw her in heaven present.

Elysian fieldes be devised of poetes to be a place of pleasure like Paradise, where the happye soules doe rest in peace and eternal happynesse.

Dye would, the very expresse saying of Plato in Phædone.

Astert, befall unwares.

Nectar and ambrosia be feigned to be the 120 drink and foode of the gods: ambrosia they liken to manna in scripture, and nectar to be white like creme, whereof is a proper tale of Hebe, that spilt a cup of it, and stayned the heavens, as yet appeareth. But I have already discoursed that at large in my Commentarye upon the *Dreames* of the same authour.

Meynt, mingled.

EMBLEME.

Which is as much to say as, *death biteth not*. For although by course of nature we be 130 borne to dye, and being ripened with age, as with a timely harvest, we must be gathered in time, or els of our selves we fall like rotted ripe

fruite fro the tree: yet death is not to be counted for evill, nor (as the poete sayd a little before) as doome of ill desert. For though the trespasse of the first man brought death into the world, as the guerdon of sinne, yet being overcome by the death of one that dyed for al, it is now made (as Chaucer sayth) the 140 grene path way to life. So that it agreeth well with that was sayd, that Death byteth not (that is) hurteth not at all.

DECEMBER

ÆGLOGA DUODECIMA

ARGUMENT

This Æglogue (even as the first beganne) is ended with a complaynte of Colin to God Pan: wherein, as weary of his former wayes, he proportioneth his life to the foure seasons of the yeare, comparing hys youthe to the spring time, when he was fresh and free from loves follye; his manhoode to the sommer, which, he sayth, was consumed with greate heate and excessive drouth, caused throughe a comet or blasinge starre, by which hee meaneth love, which passion is comenly compared to such flames and immoderate heate; his riper yeares hee resembleth to an unseasonable harveste, wherein the fruites fall ere they be rype; his latter age to winters chyll and frostie season, now drawing neare to his last ende.

THE gentle shepheard satte beside a springe,
All in the shadowe of a bushye brere,
That Colin hight, which wel could pype and singe,
For he of Tityrus his songs did lere.
There as he satte in secreate shade alone,
Thus gan he make of love his piteous mone.

'O soveraigne Pan, thou god of shepheards all,
Which of our tender lambkins takest keepe,
And when our flocks into mischaunce mought fall,
Doest save from mischiefe the unwary sheepe, 10
Als of their maisters hast no lesse regard
Then of the flocks, which thou doest watch and ward:

'I thee besche (so be thou deigne to heare
Rude ditties, tund to shepheards oaten reede,

Or if I ever sonet song so cleare
As it with pleasaunce mought thy fancie
  feede)
Hearken awhile, from thy greene cabinet,
The rurall song of carefull Colinet.

' Whilome in youth, when flowrd my joyfull
  spring,
Like swallow swift I wandred here and
  there: 20
For heate of heedlesse lust me so did sting,
That I of doubted daunger had no feare.
I went the wastefull woodes and forest
  wyde,
Withouten dreade of wolves to bene espyed.

' I wont to raunge amydde the mazie
  thickette,
And gather nuttes to make me Christmas
  game;
And joyed oft to chace the trembling
  pricket,
Or hunt the hartlesse hare til shee were
  tame.
What recked I of wintrye ages waste ?
Tho deemed I, my spring would ever
  laste.   30

' How often have I scaled the craggie oke,
All to dislodge the raven of her nest !
Howe have I wearied, with many a stroke,
The stately walnut tree, the while the
  rest
Under the tree fell all for nuts at strife !
For ylike to me was libertee and lyfe.

' And for I was in thilke same looser yeares,
(Whether the Muse so wrought me from
  my birth,
Or I to much beleeved my shepherd peres,)
Somedele ybent to song and musicks
  mirth,   40
A good olde shephearde, Wrenock was his
  name,
Made me by arte more cunning in the
  same.

' Fro thence I durst in derring doe compare
With shepheards swayne what ever fedde
  in field:
And if that Hobbinol right judgement bare,
To Pan his owne selfe pype I neede not
  yield:
For if the flocking nymphes did folow Pan,
The wiser Muses after Colin ranne.

' But ah ! such pryde at length was ill re-
  payde:
The shepheards god (perdie, god was he
  none)   50
My hurtlesse pleasaunce did me ill up-
  braide;
My freedome lorne, my life he lefte to
  mone.
Love they him called that gave me check-
  mate,
But better mought they have behote him
  Hate.

' Tho gan my lovely spring bid me farewel,
And sommer season sped him to display
(For Love then in the Lyons house did
  dwell)
The raging fyre that kindled at his ray.
A comett stird up that unkindly heate,
That reigned (as men sayd) in Venus
  seate.   60

' Forth was I ledde, not as I wont afore,
When choise I had to choose my wandring
  waye,
But whether Luck and Loves unbridled lore
Would leade me forth on Fancies bitte to
  playe.
The bush my bedde, the bramble was my
  bowre,
The woodes can witnesse many a wofull
  stowre.

' Where I was wont to seeke the honey bee,
Working her formall rowmes in wexen
  frame,
The grieslie todestoole growne there
  mought I se,
And loathed paddocks lording on the
  same: 70
And where the chaunting birds luld me a
  sleepe,
The ghastlie owle her grievous ynne doth
  keepe.

' Then as the springe gives place to elder
  time,
And bringeth forth the fruite of sommers
  pryde,
Also my age, now passed youngthly pryme,
To thinges of ryper reason selfe applyed,
And learnd of lighter timber cotes to
  frame,
Such as might save my sheepe and me fro
  shame.

'To make fine cages for the nightingale,
And baskets of bulrushes, was my wont: 80
Who to entrappe the fish in winding sale
Was better seene, or hurtful beastes to
hont ?
I learned als the signes of heaven to ken,
How Phœbe fayles, where Venus sittes and
when.

'And tryed time yet taught me greater
thinges:
The sodain rysing of the raging seas,
The soothe of byrds by beating of their
wings,
The power of herbs, both which can hurt
and ease,
And which be wont tenrage the restlesse
sheepe,
And which be wont to worke eternall
sleepe.   90

'But ah, unwise and witlesse Colin Cloute !
That kydst the hidden kinds of many a
wede,
Yet kydst not ene to cure thy sore hart
roote,
Whoseranckling wound as yet does rifelye
bleede !
Why livest thou stil, and yet hast thy
deathes wound ?
Why dyest thou stil, and yet alive art
founde ?

'Thus is my sommer worne away and
wasted,
Thus is my harvest hastened all to rathe:
The eare that budded faire is burnt and
blasted,
And all my hoped gaine is turnd to scathe.
Of all the seede that in my youth was
sowne,   101
Was nought but brakes and brambles to be
mowne.

'My boughes with bloosmes that crowned
were at firste,
And promised of timely fruite such store,
Are left both bare and barrein now at
erst:
The flattring fruite is fallen to grownd
before,
And rotted ere they were halfe mellow
ripe:
My harvest, wast, my hope away dyd
wipe.

'The fragrant flowres that in my garden
grewe
Bene withered, as they had bene gathered
long: 110
Theyr rootes bene dryed up for lacke of
dewe,
Yet dewed with teares they han be ever
among.
Ah ! who has wrought my Rosalind this
spight,
To spil the flowres that should her girlond
dight ?

'And I, that whilome wont to frame my
pype
Unto the shifting of the shepheards foote,
Sike follies nowe have gathered as too
ripe,
And cast hem out as rotten and unsoote.
The loser lasse I cast to please nomore:
One if I please, enough is me therefore. 120

'And thus of all my harvest hope I have
Nought reaped but a weedye crop of care:
Which, when I thought have thresht in
swelling sheave,
Cockel for corne, and chaffe for barley,
bare.
Soone as the chaffe should in the fan be
fynd,
All was blowne away of the wavering wynd.

'So now my yeare drawes to his latter
terme,
My spring is spent, my sommer burnt up
quite,
My harveste hasts to stirre up Winter
sterne,
And bids him clayme with rigorous rage
hys right: 130
So nowe he stormes with many a sturdy
stoure,
So now his blustring blast eche coste doth
scoure.

'The carefull cold hath nypt my rugged
rynde,
And in my face deepe furrowes eld hath
pight:
My head besprent with hoary frost I fynd,
And by myne eie the crow his clawe dooth
wright.
Delight is layd abedde, and pleasure past;
No sonne now shines, cloudes han all over-
cast.

'Now leave, ye shepheards boyes, your
      merry glee;
My Muse is hoarse and weary of thys
      stounde: 140
Here will I hang my pype upon this tree;
Was never pype of reede did better sounde.
Winter is come, that blowes the bitter
      blaste,
And after winter dreerie death does hast.

'Gather ye together, my little flocke,
My little flock, that was to me so liefe:
Let me, ah ! lette me in your folds ye lock,
Ere the breme winter breede you greater
      griefe.
Winter is come, that blowes the balefull
      breath,   149
And after winter commeth timely death.

'Adieu, delightes, that lulled me asleepe;
Adieu, my deare, whose love I bought so
      deare;
Adieu, my little lambes and loved sheepe;
Adieu, ye woodes, that oft my witnesse
      were;
Adieu, good Hobbinol, that was so true:
Tell Rosalind her Colin bids her adieu.'

COLINS EMBLEME.

[*Vivitur ingenio : cœtera mortis erunt.*]

GLOSSE

Tityrus, Chaucer, as hath bene oft sayd.
Lambkins, young lambes.
Als of their semeth to expresse Virgils verse.
      ' Pan curat oves oviumque magistros.'
Deigne, voutchsafe.
Cabinet, Colinet, diminutives.
Mazie : For they be like to a maze whence it
is hard to get out agayne.
Peres. felowes and companions.
Musick, that is poetry, as Terence sayth, 10
' Qui artem tractant musicam,' speking of
poetes.
Derring doe, aforesayd.
Lions house. He imagineth simply that Cupid,
which is Love, had his abode in the whote signe
Leo, which is in middest of somer; a pretie
allegory, whereof the meaning is, that love in
him wrought an extraordinarie heate of lust.
His ray, which is Cupides beame or flames
of love.   20
A comete, a blasing starre, meant of beautie,
which was the cause of his whote love.
Venus, the goddesse of beauty or pleasure.
Also a signe in heaven, as it is here taken. So

he meaneth that beautie, which hath always
aspect to Venus, was the cause of all his un-
quietnes in love.
Where I was, a fine discription of the chaunge
of hys lyfe and liking; for all things nowe 30
seemed to hym to have altered their kindly
course.
Lording : spoken after the maner of paddocks and frogges sitting, which is indeed
lordly, not removing nor looking once a side,
unlesse they be sturred.
Then as : the second part. That is, his
manhoode.
Cotes, sheepecotes : for such be the exercises
of shepheards.
Sale, or salow, a kind of woodde like wyl- 40
low, fit to wreath and bynde in leapes to catch
fish withall.
Phœbe fayles, the eclipse of the moone,
which is always in Cauda or Capite Draconis,
signes in heaven.
Venus starre, sc. Venus starre, otherwise called
Hesperus, and Vesper, and Lucifer, both because he seemeth to be one of the brightest
starres, and also first ryseth, and setteth last.
All which skill in starres being convenient 50
for shepheardes to knowe, Theocritus and the
rest use.
Raging seas. The cause of the swelling and
ebbing of the sea commeth of the course of the
moone, sometime encreasing, sometime
wayning and decreasing.
Sooth of byrdes, a kind of sooth saying used
in elder tymes, which they gathered by the flying of byrds : first (as is sayd) invented by the
Thuscanes, and from them derived to the 60
Romanes, who, (as is sayd in Livie) were so
supersticiously rooted in the same, that they
agreed that every noble man should put his
sonne to the Thuscanes, by them to be brought
up in that knowledge.
Of herbes : That wonderous thinges be
wrought by herbes, aswell appeareth by the
common working of them in our bodies, as also
by the wonderful enchauntments and sorceries
that have bene wrought by them ; insomuch 70
that it is sayde that Circe. a famous sorceresse,
turned men into sondry kinds of beastes and
monsters, and onely by herbes : as the poete
sayth,
      ' Dea sæva potentibus herbis,' &c.

Kidst, knewest.
Eare, of corne.
Scathe, losse. hinderaunce.
Ever among, ever and anone.
Thus is my, the thyrde parte, wherein is set 80
forth his ripe yeres as an untimely harvest,
that bringeth little fruite.
The fragraunt flowres. sundry studies and
laudable partes of learning, wherein how our

poete is seene, be they witnesse, which are privie to his study.

So now my yeere, the last part, wherein is described his age, by comparison of wyntrye stormes.

Carefull cold, for care is sayd to coole the blood. 91

Glee, mirth.

Hoary frost, a metaphore of hoary heares scattred lyke to a gray frost.

Breeme, sharpe and bitter.

Adiew delights is a conclusion of all, where in sixe verses he comprehendeth briefly all that was touched in this booke. In the first verse his delights of youth generally : in the second, the love of Rosalind : in the thyrd, the keep- 100 ing of sheepe, which is the argument of all Æglogues : in the fourth, his complaints : and in the last two, his professed frendship and good will to his good friend Hobbinoll.

EMBLEME.

The meaning wherof is, that all thinges perish and come to theyr last end, but workes of learned wits and monuments of poetry abide for ever. And therefore Horace of his Odes, a work though ful indede of great wit and learn- 110 ing, yet of no so great weight and impor- taunce, boldly sayth,

'Exegi monimentum ære perennius,
   Quod nec imber [edax], nec aquilo vorax,' &c.

Therefore let not be envied, that this poete in his Epilogue sayth, he hath made a Calen-dar that shall endure as long as time, &c.,

folowing the ensample of Horace and Ovid in the like.

'Grande opus exegi, quod nee Jovis ira, nec ignis,
   Nec ferrum poterit nec edax abolere vetustas,' &c.

Loe ! I have made a Calender for every yeare,
That steele in strength, and time in durance, shall outweare:
And if I marked well the starres revolu-tion,
It shall continewe till the worlds dissolu-tion,
To teach the ruder shepheard how to feede his sheepe,
And from the falsers fraud his folded flocke to keepe.
   Goe, lyttle Calender ! thou hast a free passeporte:
Goe but a lowly gate emongste the meaner sorte:
Dare not to match thy pype with Tityrus hys style,
Nor with the Pilgrim that the Ploughman playde awhyle:
But followe them farre off, and their high steppes adore:
The better please, the worse despise ; I aske no more.

MERCE NON MERCEDE.

COMPLAINTS

CONTAINING SUNDRIE SMALL POEMES OF THE WORLDS VANITIE
WHEREOF THE NEXT PAGE MAKETH MENTION

BY ED. SP.

LONDON
IMPRINTED FOR WILLIAM PONSONBIE, DWELLING IN PAULES CHURCHYARD
AT THE SIGNE OF THE BISHOPS HEAD

1591

A NOTE OF THE SUNDRIE POEMES CONTAINED IN THIS VOLUME

THE PRINTER TO THE GENTLE READER

SINCE my late setting foorth of the *Faerie Queene*, finding that it hath found a favourable passage amongst you, I have sithence endevoured by all good meanes (for the better encrease and accomplishment of your delights,) to get into my handes such smale poemes of the same authors as I heard were disperst abroad in sundrie hands, and not easie to bee come by, by himselfe; some of them having bene diverslie imbeziled and purloyned from him, since his departure over sea. Of the which I have by good meanes gathered togeather these fewe parcels present, which I have caused to bee imprinted altogeather, for that they al seeme to containe like matter of argument in them, being all complaints and meditations of the worlds vanitie, verie grave and profitable. To which effect I understand that he besides wrote sundrie others, namelie, *Ecclesiastes* and *Canticum Canticorum* translated, *A Senights Slumber*, *The Hell of Lovers*, his *Purgatorie*, being all dedicated to ladies, so as it may seeme he ment them all to one volume: besides some other pamphlets looselie scattered abroad: as *The Dying Pellican*, *The Howers of the Lord*, *The Sacrifice of a Sinner*, *The Seven Psalmes*, &c., which when I can either by himselfe or otherwise attaine too, I meane likewise for your favour sake to set foorth. In the meane time, praying you gentlie to accept of these, and graciouslie to entertaine the 'new poet,' I take leave.

[Though *Complaints* was not published till 1591, a year after the first issue of the *Faery Queen*, the poems of which it is composed are more properly to be classed with the *Shepherd's Calendar*. Most of them might have been printed, though perhaps not exactly as they now stand, before 1580; the others are best understood in company with these. The *Calendar* and *Complaints*, indeed, taken together, are the record of Spenser's growth to maturity.

The circumstances of the publication are very oddly confused. In the opening address the credit for the whole enterprise is assumed by 'the Printer,' Ponsonby, who, we are told, hunted the poems out and made up and issued the volume by his own efforts. This work, we gather, was mainly prosecuted after the poet's 'departure over sea'—his return, that is, to Ireland early in 1591. And the volume certainly was published after his 'departure.' Yet we know that it had been made ready for printing while he was still in England. It appears on the Stationers' Register for December 29, 1590, as approved by one of the official censors : at that time, therefore, the copy must have been at least approximately complete. Three of the poems, moreover, 'The Tears of the Muses,' 'Mother Hubberd's Tale,' and 'Muiopotmos,' the central poems of the volume, bear signs of having been prepared for the press by himself and issued individually — 'Muiopotmos' in 1590. The plausible address of 'the Printer,' in fine, is not wholly to be trusted. What, then, is to be made of it ? According to Dr. Grosart, it was devised by the poet as a blind, in the manner of Swift. For such a device one seeks a reason. May this be that, as, in 1579 (by the first letter to Harvey), he was shy of 'seeming to utter his writings for gaine and commoditie,' so now, but a year after the issue of the Faery Queen, he was loth to accept the full responsibility of a second considerable volume ? Any account of the publication, however, must be very largely conjectural.

The chronology of the poems is less in doubt. Though two or three of them are somewhat hard to place, the majority can at least be grouped in certain main periods with reasonable probability. First of all is the group that belongs to his university days, 1570-1576, and his subsequent sojourn in Lancashire: 'The Visions of Petrarch,' 'The Visions of Bellay,' 'Ruins of Rome,' and, perhaps, 'Visions of the World's Vanity.' Following upon these days is what may loosely be called his first London period, during which, until it ended with his departure for Ireland in 1580, his headquarters were probably in the capital. These three years were of marked literary activity. To them belong most, if not all, of the Calendar, and presumably the greater number of his so-called 'lost works,' besides the beginnings of the Faery Queen; to them belong also some of the most important 'complaints,' 'Virgil's Gnat,' 'Mother Hubberd's Tale,' and, less certainly, 'The Tears of the Muses.' Then follow the years of service in Ireland, till Raleigh brought him back in 1589. During this period he would seem to have given his leisure for poetry almost exclusively to the Faery Queen. Of the two remaining 'complaints,' 'The Ruins of Time' was written shortly after his return to England, and 'Muiopotmos' perhaps at about the same time.

'The Ruins of Time' and 'Muiopotmos' were composed not long before publication and probably needed no retouching. 'Mother Hubberd's Tale' and 'The Tears of the Muses,' early poems, were to some extent revised for the press. The others, one may think, were allowed to appear as first finished, or were at most but casually retouched. For, from the general tenor of his output, one infers that Spenser was not very sedulous in the revision of work once

completed, and these poems were relatively unimportant — all but one, translations. They are not, like their companions, dedicated to people alive and influential in 1590 : their chief function, indeed, would seem to be to fill out the volume. If Ponsonby really had a share in the collecting of Complaints, it must have been these, or some of them, that he gathered.

To the reader of Complaints one name recurs more frequently than others, that of Joachim Du Bellay, who, from 1549 to his early death in 1560, was one of the leaders of the new school of poetry in France. From him Spenser translated 'The Visions of Bellay' and 'Ruins of Rome,' and from him chiefly he must have acquired those poetic theories of the Pléiade which are the staple of 'The Tears of the Muses.' Du Bellay is a personality of great attractiveness. Not so distinguished an artist as his colleague Ronsard, he had qualities of mind and character that win us more : dignity untouched by arrogance, guarded from it by native sense of fitness, the distinction of a finely congruous nature ; in especial, a singularly penetrating and human melancholy. On any Elizabethan author of a volume of 'complaints' his influence might be among the deepest of that day. It is noteworthy, however, that his really central work, the Regrets, does not seem to have touched Spenser at all. And indeed, the 'life-long vein of melancholy' which Dr. Grosart detects in 'the newe poete' must have been, at best, rather thin. His elegies are hardly convincing. When he strikes the note of personal disappointment, his verse occasionally betrays a feeling akin to sadness, but the bulk of his really characteristic and genuine work is anything but sad. In the Faery Queen one may search far and wide, in vain, for a touch of that peculiar feeling which pervades the romance-epic of the genuinely melancholy Tasso. His most constant mood would seem rather to have been a serenity neither sad nor cheerful. In any case, one will not infer his temperament from the professed melancholy of his earlier work. That much of the Calendar is gloomy, that he wrote a whole volume of 'complaints,' was to have been expected: work in that vein was a convention of the days into which he was born. The cosmopolitan pastoral invited, if it did not impose, a strain of lamentation, and in England, since the days of Sir Thomas Wyatt, love-poetry in the manner and tone of the plaintive Petrarch, meditations upon the vanity of life, elegies, stories of the falls of the mighty had formed, in good measure, the staple of serious poetry. Spenser's early work but continues a convention already well established.]

THE RUINES OF TIME

DEDICATED

TO THE RIGHT NOBLE AND BEAUTI-FULL LADIE, THE LADIE MARIE COUNTESSE OF PEMBROOKE

MOST honourable and bountifull Ladie, there bee long sithens deepe sowed in my brest the seede of most entire love and humble affection unto that most brave knight, your noble brother deceased; which taking roote began in his life time somewhat to bud forth, and to shew themselves to him, as then in the weakenes of their first spring: and would in their riper strength (had it pleased High God till then to drawe out his daies) spired forth fruit of more perfection. But since God hath disdeigned the world of that most noble spirit, which was the hope of all learned men, and the patron of my young Muses; togeather with him both their hope of anie further fruit was cut off, and also the tender delight of those their first blossoms nipped and quite dead. Yet sithens my late cumming into England, some frends of mine (which might much prevaile with me, and indeede commaund me) knowing with howe straight bandes of duetie I was tied to him, as also bound unto that noble house, (of which the chiefe hope then rested in him) have sought to revive them by upbraiding me, for that I have not shewed anie thankefull remembrance towards him or any of them, but suffer their names to sleep in silence and forgetfulnesse. Whome chieflie to satisfie, or els to avoide that fowle blot of unthankefulnesse, I have conceived this small poeme, intituled by a generall name of *The Worlds Ruines:* yet speciallie intended to the renowming of that noble race, from which both you and he sprong, and to the eternizing of some of the chiefe of them late deceased. The which I dedicate unto your Ladiship as whome it most speciallie concerneth, and to whome I acknowledge my selfe bounden, by manie singular favours and great graces. I pray for your honourable happinesse: and so humblie kisse your handes.

Your Ladiships ever
humblie at commaund,
É. S.

['The Ruins of Time' is mainly official verse, melodious and uninspired. It is the one poem of the volume confessedly written to order — confessedly, in the frank and dignified letter of dedication. Had Sidney alone been Spenser's theme, or Sidney and Leicester, both his early patrons, this poem might perhaps have been comparable with *Daphnaïda*, but the great house to which they belonged having recently lost other distinguished members besides, Spenser saw fit to undertake a sort of necrology of the Dudleys, and the issue was perfunctoriness. Perhaps he was busy with other matters. Perhaps, too, as some have inferred, he built his poem up in good part of earlier material. It certainly is composite and ill-digested, and the device of the 'visions' clearly harks back to the days of his artistic apprenticeship. If he did take recourse to his early manuscripts, he may possibly have helped himself with *Stemmata Dudleiana*, mentioned in the postscript of the second letter to Harvey. On these points, however, we have ground for nothing more definite than surmise.]

THE RUINES OF TIME

IT chaunced me on day beside the shore
Of silver streaming Thamesis to bee,
Nigh where the goodly Verlame stood of
    yore,
Of which there now remaines no memorie,
Nor anie little moniment to see,
By which the travailer that fares that way
This once was she may warned be to say.

There on the other side, I did behold
A woman sitting sorrowfullie wailing,   9
Rending her yeolow locks, like wyrie golde
About her shoulders careleslie downe trail-
    ing,
And streames of teares from her faire eyes
    forth railing.
In her right hand a broken rod she held,
Which towards heaven shee seemd on high
    to weld.

Whether she were one of that rivers
    nymphes,
Which did the losse of some dere love la-
    ment,
I doubt; or one of those three fatall impes
Which draw the dayes of men forth in ex-
    tent;
Or th' auncient genius of that citie brent;
But seeing her so piteouslie perplexed,   20
I (to her calling) askt what her so vexed.

'Ah! what delight,' quoth she, 'in earthlie
   thing,
Or comfort can I, wretched creature, have?
Whose happines the heavens envying,
From highest staire to lowest step me drave,
And have in mine owne bowels made my
   grave,
That of all nations now I am forlorne,
The worlds sad spectacle, and Fortunes
   scorne.'

Much was I mooved at her piteous plaint,
And felt my heart nigh riven in my brest 30
With tender ruth to see her sore constraint;
That shedding teares a while I still did rest,
And after did her name of her request.
'Name have I none,' quoth she, 'nor anie
   being,
Bereft of both by Fates unjust decreeing.

'I was that citie which the garland wore
Of Britaines pride, delivered unto me
By Romane victors, which it wonne of yore;
Though nought at all but ruines now I bee,
And lye in mine owne ashes, as ye see: 40
Verlame I was; what bootes it that I was,
Sith now I am but weedes and wastfull
   gras?

'O vaine worlds glorie, and unstedfast state
Of all that lives on face of sinfull earth!
Which from their first untill their utmost
   date
Tast no one hower of happines or merth,
But like as at the ingate of their berth
They crying creep out of their mothers
   woomb,
So wailing backe go to their wofull toomb.

'Why then dooth flesh, a bubble glas of
   breath,   50
Hunt after honour and advauncement vaine,
And reare a trophee for devouring death
With so great labour and long lasting paine,
As if his daies for ever should remaine?
Sith all that in this world is great or gaie
Doth as a vapour vanish, and decaie.

'Looke backe, who list, unto the former
   ages,
And call to count, what is of them become:
Where be those learned wits and antique
   sages,
Which of all wisedome knew the perfect
   somme?   60

Where those great warriors, which did over-
   comme
The world with conquest of their might and
   maine,
And made one meare of th' earth and of
   their raine?

'What nowe is of th' Assyrian Lyonesse,
Of whome no footing now on earth ap-
   peares?
What of the Persian Beares outragious-
   nesse,
Whose memorie is quite worne out with
   yeares?
Who of the Grecian Libbard now ought
   heares,
That overran the East with greedie powre,
And left his whelps their kingdomes to de-
   voure?   70

'And where is that same great seven head-
   ded beast,
That made all nations vassals of her pride,
To fall before her feete at her beheast,
And in the necke of all the world did
   ride?
Where doth she all that wondrous welth
   nowe hide?
With her own weight down pressed now
   shee lies,
And by her heaps her hugenesse testifies.

'O Rome, thy ruine I lament and rue,
And in thy fall my fatall overthrowe,
That whilom was, whilst heavens with
   equall vewe   80
Deignd to behold me, and their gifts
   bestowe,
The picture of thy pride in pompous shew:
And of the whole world as thou wast the
   empresse,
So I of this small Northerne world was
   princesse.

'To tell the beawtie of my buildings fayre,
Adornd with purest golde and precious
   stone,
To tell my riches, and endowments rare,
That by my foes are now all spent and
   gone,
To tell my forces, matchable to none,
Were but lost labour, that few would be-
   leeve,   90
And with rehearsing would me more
   agreeve.

'High towers, faire temples, goodly thea-
    ters,
Strong walls, rich porches, princelie pal-
    laces,
Large streetes, brave houses, sacred sepul-
    chers,
Sure gates, sweete gardens, stately galleries
Wrought with faire pillours, and fine
    imageries,
All those (O pitie!) now are turnd to dust,
And overgrowen with blacke oblivions rust.

'Theretoo, for warlike power and peoples
    store,
In Britannie was none to match with mee,
That manie often did abie full sore: 101
Ne Troynovant, though elder sister shee,
With my great forces might compared
    bee;
That stout Pendragon to his perill felt,
Who in a siege seaven yeres about me
    dwelt.

'But long ere this, Bunduca Britonnesse
Her mightie hoast against my bulwarkes
    brought,
Bunduca, that victorious conqueresse,
That, lifting up her brave heroïck thought
Bove womens weaknes, with the Romanes
    fought,   110
Fought, and in field against them thrice
    prevailed:
Yet was she foyld, when as she me as-
    sailed.

'And though at last by force I conquered
    were
Of hardie Saxons, and became their thrall,
Yet was I with much bloodshed bought
    full deere,
And prizde with slaughter of their gen-
    erall:
The moniment of whose sad funerall,
For wonder of the world, long in me
    lasted;
But now to nought, through spoyle of time,
    is wasted.

'Wasted it is, as if it never were,   120
And all the rest that me so honord made,
And of the world admired ev'rie where,
Is turnd to smoake, that doth to nothing
    fade,
And of that brightnes now appeares no
    shade,

But greislie shades, such as doo haunt in
    hell
With fearfull fiends, that in deep darknes
    dwell.

'Where my high steeples whilom usde to
    stand,
On which the lordly faulcon wont to towre,
There now is but an heap of lyme and sand,
For the shriche-owle to build her balefull
    bowre: 130
And where the nightingale wont forth to
    powre
Her restles plaints, to comfort wakefull
    lovers,
There now haunt yelling mewes and whin-
    ing plovers.

'And where the christall Thamis wont to
    slide
In silver channell, downe along the lee,
About whose flowrie bankes on either side
A thousand nymphes, with mirthfull jolli-
    tee,
Were wont to play, from all annoyance free,
There now no rivers course is to be seene,
But moorish fennes, and marshes ever
    greene.   140

'Seemes that that gentle river, for great
    griefe
Of my mishaps, which oft I to him plained,
Or for to shunne the horrible mischiefe,
With which he saw my cruell foes me
    pained,
And his pure streames with guiltles blood
    oft stained,
From my unhappie neighborhood farre fled,
And his sweete waters away with him led.

'There also where the winged ships were
    seene
In liquid waves to cut their fomie waie,
And thousand fishers numbred to have
    been,   150
In that wide lake looking for plenteous
    praie
Of fish, which they with baits usde to be-
    traie,
Is now no lake, nor anie fishers store,
Nor ever ship shall saile there anie more.

'They all are gone, and all with them is
    gone:
Ne ought to me remaines, but to lament

My long decay, which no man els doth
    mone,
And mourne my fall with dolefull dreri-
    ment.
Yet it is comfort in great languishment,
To be bemoned with compassion kinde, 160
And mitigates the anguish of the minde.

' But me no man bewaileth, but in game,
Ne sheddeth teares from lamentable eie:
Nor anie lives that mentioneth my name
To be remembred of posteritie,
Save one, that maugre Fortunes injurie,
And Times decay, and Envies cruell tort,
Hath writ my record in true-seeming sort.

' Cambden, the nourice of antiquitie,
And lanterne unto late succeeding age, 170
To see the light of simple veritie
Buried in ruines, through the great outrage
Of her owne people, led with warlike rage,
Cambden, though Time all moniments ob-
    scure,
Yet thy just labours ever shall endure.

' But whie (unhappie wight) doo I thus
    crie,
And grieve that my remembrance quite is
    raced
Out of the knowledge of posteritie,
And all my antique moniments defaced ?
Sith I doo dailie see things highest placed,
So soone as Fates their vitall thred have
    shorne,   181
Forgotten quite as they were never borne.

' It is not long, since these two eyes beheld
A mightie Prince, of most renowmed race,
Whom England high in count of honour
    held,
And greatest ones did sue to gaine his
    grace;
Of greatest ones he greatest in his place,
Sate in the bosome of his Soveraine,
And Right and loyall did his word main-
    taine.

' I saw him die, I saw him die, as one   190
Of the meane people, and brought foorth
    on beare;
I saw him die, and no man left to mone
His dolefull fate that late him loved deare:
Scarse anie left to close his eylids neare;
Scarse anie left upon his lips to laie
The sacred sod, or requiem to saie.

' O trustlesse state of miserable men,
That builde your blis on hope of earthly
    thing,
And vainly thinke your selves halfe happie
    then,
When painted faces with smooth flatter-
    ing   200
Doo fawne on you, and your wide praises
    sing,
And when the courting masker louteth
    lowe,
Him true in heart and trustie to you trow !

' All is but fained, and with oaker dide,
That everie shower will wash and wipe
    away,
All things doo change that under heaven
    abide,
And after death all friendship doth decaie.
Therefore, what ever man bearst worldlie
    sway,
Living, on God and on thy selfe relie;
For when thou diest, all shall with thee
    die.   210

' He now is dead, and all is with him dead,
Save what in heavens storehouse he up-
    laid:
His hope is faild, and come to passe his
    dread,
And evill men (now dead) his deeds up-
    braid:
Spite bites the dead, that living never baid.
He now is gone, the whiles the foxe is
    crept
Into the hole the which the badger swept.

' He now is dead, and all his glorie gone,
And all his greatnes vapoured to nought,
That as a glasse upon the water shone, 220
Which vanisht quite, so soone as it was
    sought:
His name is worne alreadie out of thought,
Ne anie poet seekes him to revive;
Yet manie poets honourd him alive.

' Ne doth his Colin, carelesse Colin Cloute,
Care now his idle bagpipe up to raise,
Ne tell his sorrow to the listning rout
Of shepherd groomes, which wont his songs
    to praise:
Praise who so list, yet I will him dispraise,
Untill he quite him of this guiltie blame: 230
Wake, shepheards boy, at length awake for
    shame !

'And who so els did goodnes by him gaine,
And who so els his bounteous minde did
trie,
Whether he shepheard be, or shepheards
swaine,
(For manie did, which doo it now denie)
Awake, and to his song a part applie:
And I, the whilest you mourne for his de-
cease,
Will with my mourning plaints your plaint
increase.

'He dyde, and after him his brother dyde,
His brother prince, his brother noble
peere,   240
That whilste he lived was of none envyde,
And dead is now, as living, counted deare,
Deare unto all that true affection beare,
But unto thee most deare, O dearest dame,
His noble spouse and paragon of fame.

'He, whilest he lived, happie was through
thee,
And, being dead, is happie now much more;
Living, that lincked chaunst with thee to
bee,
And dead, because him dead thou dost adore
As living, and thy lost deare love deplore. 250
So whilst that thou, faire flower of chastitie,
Dost live, by thee thy lord shall never die.

'Thy lord shall never die, the whiles this
verse
Shall live, and surely it shall live for ever:
For ever it shall live, and shall rehearse
His worthie praise, and vertues dying never,
Though death his soule doo from his bodie
sever.
And thou thy selfe herein shalt also live;
Such grace the heavens doo to my verses
give.

'Ne shall his sister, ne thy father die,   260
Thy father, that good earle of rare renowne,
And noble patrone of weake povertie;
Whose great good deeds, in countrey and in
towne,
Have purchast him in heaven an happie
crowne;
Where he now liveth in eternall blis,
And left his sonne t' ensue those steps of
his.

'He, noble bud, his grandsires livelie hayre,
Under the shadow of thy countenaunce

Now ginnes to shoote up fast, and flourish
fayre
In learned artes and goodlie governaunce,   270
That him to highest honour shall advaunce.
Brave impe of Bedford, grow apace in
bountie,
And count of wisedome more than of thy
countie.

'Ne may I let thy husbands sister die,
That goodly ladie, sith she eke did spring
Out of this stocke and famous familie,
Whose praises I to future age doo sing,
And foorth out of her happie womb did
bring
The sacred brood of learning and all
honour,
In whom the heavens powrde all their gifts
upon her.   280

'Most gentle spirite breathed from above,
Out of the bosome of the Makers blis,
In whom all bountie and all vertuous
love
Appeared in their native propertis,
And did enrich that noble breast of his
With treasure passing all this worldes
worth,
Worthie of heaven it selfe, which brought
it forth.

'His blessed spirite, full of power divine
And influence of all celestiall grace,
Loathing this sinfull earth and earthlie
slime,   290
Fled backe too soone unto his native place,
Too soone for all that did his love em-
brace,
Too soone for all this wretched world,
whom he
Robd of all right and true nobilitie.

'Yet ere his happie soule to heaven went
Out of this fleshlie goale, he did devise
Unto his heavenlie Maker to present
His bodie, as a spotles sacrifise;
And chose, that guiltie hands of enemies
Should powre forth th' offring of his guilt-
les blood: 300
So life exchanging for his countries good.

'O noble spirite, live there ever blessed,
The worlds late wonder, and the heavens
new joy,

Live ever there, and leave me here dis-
tressed
With mortall cares, and cumbrous worlds
anoy.
But where thou dost that happines enjoy,
Bid me, O bid me quicklie come to thee,
That happie there I maie thee alwaies
see.

'Yet, whilest the Fates affoord me vitall
breath,
I will it spend in speaking of thy praise, 310
And sing to thee, untill that timelie death
By heavens doome doo ende my earthlie
daies:
Thereto doo thou my humble spirite raise,
And into me that sacred breath inspire,
Which thou there breathest perfect and
entire.

'Then will I sing; but who can better
sing
Than thine owne sister, peerles ladie bright,
Which to thee sings with deep harts sorrow-
ing,
Sorrowing tempered with deare delight,
That her to heare I feele my feeble spright
Robbed of sense, and ravished with joy: 321
O sad joy, made of mourning and anoy!

'Yet will I sing; but who can better sing,
Than thou thy selfe, thine owne selfes
valiance,
That, whilest thou livedst, madest the for-
rests ring,
And fields resownd, and flockes to leap and
daunce,
And shepheards leave their lambs unto mis-
chaunce,
To runne thy shrill Arcadian pipe to heare:
O happie were those dayes, thrice happie
were!

'But now more happie thou, and wretched
wee,   330
Which want the wonted sweetnes of thy
voice,
Whiles thou now in Elisian fields so free,
With Orpheus, and with Linus, and the
choice
Of all that ever did in rimes rejoyce,
Conversest, and doost heare their heavenlie
layes,
And they heare thine, and thine doo better
praise.

'So there thou livest, singing evermore,
And here thou livest, being ever song
Of us, which living loved thee afore,
And now thee worship, mongst that blessed
throng   340
Of heavenlie poets and heroes strong.
So thou both here and there immortall
art,
And everie where through excellent desart.

'But such as neither of themselves can
sing,
Nor yet are sung of others for reward,
Die in obscure oblivion, as the thing
Which never was, ne ever with regard
Their names shall of the later age be heard,
But shall in rustie darknes ever lie,
Unles they mentiond be with infamie.   350

'What booteth it to have been rich alive?
What to be great? what to be gracious?
When after death no token doth survive
Of former being in this mortall hous,
But sleepes in dust dead and inglorious,
Like beast, whose breath but in his nos-
trels is,
And hath no hope of happinesse or blis.

'How manie great ones may remembred be,
Which in their daies most famouslie did
florish,
Of whome no word we heare, nor signe
now see,   360
But as things wipt out with a sponge to-
perishe,
Because they, living, cared not to cherishe
No gentle wits, through pride or covetize,
Which might their names for ever mem-
orize!

'Provide therefore (ye princes) whilst ye
live,
That of the Muses ye may friended bee,
Which unto men eternitie do give;
For they be daughters of Dame Memorie
And Jove, the father of Eternitie,
And do those men in golden thrones repose,
Whose merits they to glorifie do chose. 371

'The seven fold yron gates of grislie Hell,
And horrid house of sad Proserpina,
They able are with power of mightie spell
To breake, and thence the soules to bring
awaie
Out of dread darkenesse to eternall day,

And them immortall make, which els would
die
In foule forgetfulnesse, and nameles lie.

'So whilome raised they the puissant brood
Of golden girt Alcmena, for great merite,
Out of the dust to which the Oetæan wood
Had him consum'd, and spent his vitall
  spirite,   382
To highest heaven, where now he doth in-
herite
All happinesse in Hebes silver bowre,
Chosen to be her dearest paramoure.

'So raisde they eke faire Ledaes warlick
twinnes,
And interchanged life unto them lent,
That, when th' one dies, th' other then be-
ginnes
To shew in heaven his brightnes orient;
And they, for pittie of the sad wayment, 390
Which Orpheus for Eurydice did make,
Her back againe to life sent for his sake.

'So happie are they, and so fortunate,
Whom the Pierian sacred sisters love,
That freed from bands of impacable fate,
And power of death, they live for aye
  above,
Where mortall wreakes their blis may not
remove:
But with the gods, for former vertues
  meede,
On nectar and ambrosia do feede.

'For deeds doe die, how ever noblie donne,
And thoughts of men do as themselves
  decay,   401
But wise wordes taught in numbers for to
runne,
Recorded by the Muses, live for ay,
Ne may with storming showers be washt
away;
Ne bitter breathing windes with harmfull
blast,
Nor age, nor envie, shall them ever wast.

'In vaine doo earthly princes then, in vaine,
Seeke with pyramides, to heaven aspired,
Or huge colosses, built with costlie paine,
Or brasen pillours, never to be fired, 410
Or shrines, made of the mettall most de-
sired,
To make their memories for ever live:
For how can mortall immortalitie give?

'Such one Mausolus made, the worlds great
wonder,
But now no remnant doth thereof remaine:
Such one Marcellus, but was torne with
thunder:
Such one Lisippus, but is worne with raine:
Such one King Edmond, but was rent for
gaine.
All such vaine moniments of earthlie masse,
Devour'd of Time, in time to nought doo
  passe.   420

'But Fame with golden wings aloft doth
flie,
Above the reach of ruinous decay,
And with brave plumes doth beate the
azure skie,
Admir'd of base-borne men from farre
away:
Then who so will with vertuous deeds assay
To mount to heaven, on Pegasus must ride,
And with sweete poets verse be glorifide.

'For not to have been dipt in Lethe lake
Could save the sonne of Thetis from to die;
But that blinde bard did him immortall
  make   430
With verses, dipt in deaw of Castalie:
Which made the Easterne conquerour to
crie,
O fortunate yong-man, whose vertue found
So brave a trompe thy noble acts to sound !

'Therefore in this halfe happie I doo read
Good Melibæ, that hath a poet got
To sing his living praises being dead,
Deserving never here to be forgot,
In spight of envie, that his deeds would
spot:
Since whose decease, learning lies unre-
  garded,   440
And men of armes doo wander unrewarded.

'Those two be those two great calamities,
That long agoe did grieve the noble spright
Of Salomon with great indignities;
Who whilome was alive the wisest wight:
But now his wisedome is disprooved quite:
For he that now welds all things at his will
Scorns th' one and th' other in his deeper
skill.

'O griefe of griefes ! O gall of all good
heartes !
To see that vertue should dispised bee 450

Of him that first was raisde for vertuous
    parts,
And now, broad spreading like an aged
    tree,
Lets none shoot up, that nigh him planted
    bee.
O let the man of whom the Muse is scorned,
Nor alive nor dead, be of the Muse
    adorned !

' O vile worlds trust, that with such vaine
    illusion
Hath so wise men bewitcht and overkest,
That they see not the way of their confu-
    sion !
O vainesse to be added to the rest,
That do my soule with inward griefe in-
    fest !   460
Let them behold the piteous fall of mee,
And in my case their owne ensample see.

' And who so els that sits in highest seate
Of this worlds glorie, worshipped of all,
Ne feareth change of time, nor fortunes
    threate,
Let him behold the horror of my fall,
And his owne end unto remembrance call;
That of like ruine he may warned bee,
And in himselfe be moov'd to pittie mee.'

Thus having ended all her piteous plaint, 470
With dolefull shrikes shee vanished away,
That I, through inward sorrowe wexen
    faint,
And all astonished with deepe dismay
For her departure, had no word to say;
But sate long time in sencelesse sad af-
    fright,
Looking still, if I might of her have sight.

Which when I missed, having looked long,
My thought returned greeved home againe,
Renewing her complaint with passion
    strong,
For ruth of that same womans piteous
    paine;   480
Whose wordes recording in my troubled
    braine,
I felt such anguish wound my feeble heart,
That frosen horror ran through everie
    part.

So inlie greeving in my groning brest,
And deepelie muzing at her doubtfull
    speach,

Whose meaning much I labored foorth to
    wreste,
Being above my slender reasons reach,
At length, by demonstration me to teach,
Before mine eies strange sights presented
    were,
Like tragicke pageants seeming to appeare.

I

I saw an image, all of massie gold,   491
Placed on high upon an altare faire,
That all which did the same from farre
    beholde
Might worship it, and fall on lowest staire.
Not that great idoll might with this com-
    paire,
To which th' Assyrian tyrant would have
    made
The holie brethren falslie to have praid.

But th' altare on the which this image
    staid
Was (O great pitie!) built of brickle
    clay,
That shortly the foundation decaid,   500
With showres of heaven and tempests
    worne away:
Then downe it fell, and low in ashes lay,
Scorned of everie one which by it went;
That I, it seing, dearelie did lament.

II

Next unto this a statelie towre appeared,
Built all of richest stone that might bee
    found,
And nigh unto the heavens in height up-
    reared,
But placed on a plot of sandie ground:
Not that great towre which is so much re-
    nownd
For tongues confusion in Holie Writ,   510
King Ninus worke, might be compar'd to it.

But O vaine labours of terrestriall wit,
That buildes so stronglie on so frayle a
    soyle,
As with each storme does fall away and
    flit,
And gives the fruit of all your travailes
    toyle,
To be the pray of Tyme, and Fortunes
    spoyle,
I saw this towre fall sodainlie to dust,
That nigh with griefe thereof my heart
    was brust.

III

Then did I see a pleasant paradize,
Full of sweete flowres and daintiest de-
    lights,   520
Such as on earth man could not more devize,
With pleasures choyce to feed his cheerefull
    sprights:
Not that which Merlin by his magicke
    slights
Made for the gentle Squire, to entertaine
His fayre Belphœbe, could this gardine
    staine.

But O short pleasure bought with lasting
    paine!
Why will hereafter anie flesh delight
In earthlie blis, and joy in pleasures vaine,
Since that I sawe this gardine wasted quite,
That where it was scarce seemed anie
    sight?   530
That I, which once that beautie did beholde,
Could not from teares my melting eyes with-
    holde.

IV

Soone after this a giaunt came in place,
Of wondrous power, and of exceeding stat-
    ure,
That none durst vewe the horror of his face;
Yet was he milde of speach, and meeke of
    nature.
Not he, which in despight of his Creatour
With railing tearmes defied the Jewish
    hoast,
Might with this mightie one in hugenes
    boast.

For from the one he could to th' other
    coast   540
Stretch his strong thighes, and th' ocæan
    overstride,
And reatch his hand into his enemies hoast.
But see the end of pompe and fleshlie pride:
One of his feete unwares from him did
    slide,
That downe hee fell into the deepe abisse,
Where drownd with him is all his earthlie
    blisse.

V

Then did I see a bridge, made all of golde,
Over the sea from one to other side,
Withouten prop or pillour it t' upholde,
But like the coulored rainbowe arched
    wide: 550

Not that great arche which Trajan edi-
    fide,
To be a wonder to all age ensuing,
Was matchable to this in equall vewing.

But ah! what bootes it to see earthlie thing
In glorie or in greatnes to excell,
Sith time doth greatest things to ruine
    bring?
This goodlie bridge, one foote not fastned
    well,
Gan faile, and all the rest downe shortlie
    fall,
Ne of so brave a building ought remained,
That griefe thereof my spirite greatly
    pained.   560

VI

I saw two beares, as white as anie milke,
Lying together in a mightie cave,
Of milde aspect, and haire as soft as
    silke,
That salvage nature seemed not to have,
Nor after greedie spoyle of blood to crave:
Two fairer beasts might not elswhere be
    found,
Although the compast world were sought
    around.

But what can long abide above this ground
In state of blis, or stedfast happinesse?
The cave in which these beares lay sleeping
    sound   570
Was but earth, and with her owne weighti-
    nesse
Upon them fell, and did unwares oppresse;
That, for great sorrow of their sudden
    fate,
Henceforth all worlds felicitie I hate.

¶ Much was I troubled in my heavie
    spright,
At sight of these sad spectacles forepast,
That all my senses were bereaved quight,
And I in minde remained sore agast,
Distraught twixt feare and pitie; when at
    last
I heard a voyce, which loudly to me
    called,   580
That with the suddein shrill I was ap-
    palled.

'Behold,' said it, 'and by ensample see,
That all is vanitie and griefe of minde,

Ne other comfort in this world can be,
But hope of heaven, and heart to God in-
    clinde;
For all the rest must needs be left behinde.'
With that it bad me to the other side
To cast mine eye, where other sights I
    spide.

I

Upon that famous rivers further shore,
There stood a snowie swan, of heavenly
    hiew   590
And gentle kinde, as ever fowle afore;
A fairer one in all the goodlie criew
Of white Strimonian brood might no man
    view:
There he most sweetly sung the prophecie
Of his owne death in dolefull elegie.

At last, when all his mourning melodie
He ended had, that both the shores re-
    sounded,
Feeling the fit that him forewarnd to die,
With loftie flight above the earth he
    bounded,
And out of sight to highest heaven
    mounted,   600
Where now he is become an heavenly
    signe:
There now the joy is his, here sorrow mine.

II

Whilest thus I looked, loe! adowne the lee
I sawe an harpe, stroong all with silver
    twyne,
And made of golde and costlie yvorie,
Swimming, that whilome seemed to have
    been
The harpe on which Dan Orpheus was
    seene
Wylde beasts and forrests after him to
    lead,
But was th' harpe of Philisides now dead.

At length out of the river it was reard,   610
And borne above the cloudes to be divin'd,
Whilst all the way most heavenly noyse
    was heard
Of the strings, stirred with the warbling
    wind,
That wrought both joy and sorrow in my
    mind:
So now in heaven a signe it doth appeare,
The Harpe well knowne beside the North-
    ern Beare.

III

Soone after this I saw on th' other side
A curious coffer made of heben wood,
That in it did most precious treasure hide,
Exceeding all this baser worldes good: 620
Yet through the overflowing of the flood
It almost drowned was and done to nought,
That sight thereof much griev'd my pensive
    thought.

At length, when most in perill it was
    brought,
Two angels, downe descending with swift
    flight,
Out of the swelling streame it lightly caught,
And twixt their blessed armes it carried
    quight
Above the reach of anie living sight:
So now it is transform'd into that starre,
In which all heavenly treasures locked are.

IV

Looking aside I saw a stately bed,   631
Adorned all with costly cloth of gold,
That might for anie princes couche be red,
And deckt with daintie flowres, as if it
    shold
Be for some bride, her joyous night to hold:
Therein a goodly virgine sleeping lay;
A fairer wight saw never summers day.

I heard a voyce that called farre away,
And her awaking bad her quickly dight,
For lo! her bridegrome was in readie ray
To come to her, and seeke her loves de-
    light: 641
With that she started up with cherefull
    sight;
When suddeinly both bed and all was gone,
And I in languor left there all alone.

V

Still as I gazed, I beheld where stood
A knight all arm'd, upon a winged steed,
The same that was bred of Medusaes blood,
On which Dan Perseus, borne of heavenly
    seed,
The faire Andromeda from perill freed:
Full mortally this knight ywounded was,
That streames of blood foorth flowed on the
    gras.   651

Yet was he deckt (small joy to him,
    alas!)
With manie garlands for his victories,

And with rich spoyles, which late he did
    purchas
Through brave atcheivements from his ene-
    mies:
Fainting at last through long infirmities,
He smote his steed, that straight to heaven
    him bore,
And left me here his losse for to deplore.

VI

Lastly, I saw an arke of purest golde
Upon a brazen pillour standing hie,   660
Which th' ashes seem'd of some great
    prince to hold,
Enclosde therein for endles memorie
Of him whom all the world did glorifie:
Seemed the heavens with the earth did dis-
    agree,
Whether should of those ashes keeper bee.

At last me seem'd wing footed Mercurie,
From heaven descending to appease their
    strife,
The arke did beare with him above the
    skie,
And to those ashes gave a second life,   669
To live in heaven, where happines is rife:
At which the earth did grieve exceedingly,
And I for dole was almost like to die.

L'ENVOY

Immortall spirite of Philisides,
Which now art made the heavens orna-
    ment,
That whilome wast the worldes chiefst
    riches,
Give leave to him that lov'de thee to lament
His losse, by lacke of thee to heaven hent,
And with last duties of this broken verse,
Broken with sighes, to decke thy sable
    herse.

And ye, faire ladie, th' honor of your
    daies   680
And glorie of the world, your high thoughts
    scorne,
Vouchsafe this moniment of his last praise
With some few silver dropping teares t'
    adorne:
And as ye be of heavenlie off-spring borne,
So unto heaven let your high minde aspire,
And loath this drosse of sinfull worlds de-
    sire.

FINIS.

THE TEARES OF THE MUSES
BY ED. SP.

LONDON
IMPRINTED FOR WILLIAM
PONSONBIE, DWELLING IN PAULES
CHURCHYARD AT THE SIGNE OF
THE BISHOPS HEAD
1591

TO THE RIGHT HONORABLE
THE LADIE STRANGE

MOST brave and noble Ladie, the things
that make ye so much honored of the world
as ye bee, are such as (without my simple
lines testimonie) are throughlie knowen to
all men; namely, your excellent beautie,
your vertuous behavior, and your noble
match with that most honourable lord, the
verie paterne of right nobilitie: but the
causes for which ye have thus deserved of
me to be honoured (if honour it be at all)
are, both your particular bounties, and also
some private bands of affinitie, which it
hath pleased your Ladiship to acknowledge. Of which whenas I found my selfe
in no part worthie, I devised this last slender meanes, both to intimate my humble
affection to your Ladiship, and also to make
the same universallie knowen to the world;
that by honouring you they might know
me, and by knowing me they might honor
you. Vouchsafe, noble Lady, to accept this
simple remembrance, thogh not worthy of
your self, yet such as perhaps, by good acceptance therof, ye may hereafter cull out
a more meet and memorable evidence of
your own excellent deserts. So recommending the same to your Ladiships good
liking, I humbly take leave.
    Your Ladiships humbly ever
                Ed. Sp.

[To what period this poem may belong has
been somewhat disputed. On the whole, it
would seem, like 'Mother Hubberd's Tale,' to
be early work revised, for though the allusions
in the lament of Thalia refer that passage to
1589 or 1590, there are good grounds for be-
lieving that the poem first took form before
1580. Its doleful account of the state of
literature, for instance, is quite at odds with

that survey in *Colin Clout's Come Home Again* (of 1591) wherein Spenser deals so sympathetically with his fellow poets, and is not unlike in tone to various passages in the *Calendar*. One can hardly understand, moreover, how, in 1590, even as a matter of convention, he could take so dismal a view of English literature. In 1580, on the other hand, before Sidney, Greene, Marlowe, and their fellows of the first great generation had begun to write, when, Spenser himself excepted, Lyly with his *Euphues* was the one brilliant name in English letters, such a view is quite conceivable. The matter might be argued much further, to the same result.

The general tone of the poem, its mental attitude, cannot but impress a modern reader somewhat unpleasantly. The complaint that 'mightie peeres' no longer care for the immortality which only poets can confer, that poets and scholars, 'the learned,' are left without patronage, may be set down partly to a trying personal experience. The note of contempt, however, and of arrogance that one is glad to believe youthful, the complaint of universal vulgarity, the cry that Ignorance and Barbarism have quite laid waste the fair realm of the Muses — all this comes near, in the end, to seeming insufferable. If the Areopagus, the select literary club in which Sidney and Dyer and Fulke Greville, with perhaps Spenser himself, discussed the condition of English letters and planned great reforms, if this *cénacle* is fairly represented by 'The Tears of the Muses,' it must have been, one thinks, a more than usually supercilious clique of young radicals. Yet what may be distasteful in the poem is not so much the underlying opinions, which for 1579 or 1580 are quite intelligible, as the particular tone or mood. In this one almost suspects an echo of Ronsard. For in the great movement by which, thirty years before the Areopagus and in much the same way, the Pléiade endeavored to regenerate French literature, Ronsard is notably distinguished from his colleagues by an odd faculty for making their common views offensive or ridiculous. His rampant egotism and utter deficiency in the sense of humor lured him at times, like his greater descendant Victor Hugo, into strange extravagances. Now, the members of the Areopagus knew the poets of the Pléiade well, especially Ronsard and Du Bellay. They seem to have felt that their own problem in England was not unlike that which these men had met in France. In them they found ideals with which they sympathized, opinions which seemed to be of value for their own difficulties. That the poet was directly inspired of God (or

the gods), that great men could obtain immortality from the poets alone, that poetry must go hand in hand with learning, that the arch enemy of the Muses was Ignorance, that poetry in their day languished because the great were given over to luxury and the vulgar would listen only to a horde of unlearned and base rhymesters, — these theories of the Pléiade and various precepts for the elevation of their own mother tongue to a place beside the tongues of Greece and Rome were caught at by the youthful members of the Areopagus with very lively interest. In the work of Spenser they may be traced unmistakably, chiefly in 'October,' 'The Ruins of Time,' and 'The Tears of the Muses.' This last, unhappily, voices them in a tone which, as so often in Ronsard and rarely in Du Bellay, makes sympathy quite impossible.]

THE TEARES OF THE MUSES

REHEARSE to me, ye sacred sisters nine,
The golden brood of great Apolloes wit,
Those piteous plaints and sorowfull sad tine,
Which late ye powred forth as ye did sit
Beside the silver springs of Helicone,
Making your musick of hart-breaking mone.

For since the time that Phœbus foolish sonne,
Ythundered through Joves avengefull wrath,
For traversing the charret of the Sunne
Beyond the compasse of his pointed path,
Of you, his mournfull sisters, was lamented,   11
Such mournfull tunes were never since invented.

Nor since that faire Calliope did lose
Her loved twinnes, the dearlings of her joy,
Her Palici, whom her unkindly foes,
The Fatall Sisters, did for spight destroy,
Whom all the Muses did bewaile long space,
Was ever heard such wayling in this place.

For all their groves, which with the heavenly noyses
Of their sweete instruments were wont to sound,   20
And th' hollow hills, from which their silver voyces
Were wont redoubled echoes to rebound,

Did now rebound with nought but rufull
    cries,
And yelling shrieks throwne up into the
    skies.

The trembling streames which wont in
    chanels cleare
To romble gently downe with murmur soft,
And were by them right tunefull taught to
    beare
A bases part amongst their consorts oft,
Now forst to overflowe with brackish teares,
With troublous noyse did dull their daintie
    eares.   30

The joyous nymphes and lightfoote faeries
Which thether came to heare their musick
    sweet,
And to the measure of their melodies
Did learne to move their nimble shifting
    feete,
Now hearing them so heavily lament,
Like heavily lamenting from them went.

And all that els was wont to worke de-
    light
Through the divine infusion of their skill,
And all that els seemd faire and fresh in
    sight,
So made by nature for to serve their will,   40
Was turned now to dismall heavinesse,
Was turned now to dreadfull uglinesse.

Ay me! what thing on earth, that all thing
    breeds,
Might be the cause of so impatient plight?
What furie, or what feend with felon deeds
Hath stirred up so mischievous despight?
Can griefe then enter into heavenly harts,
And pierce immortall breasts with mortall
    smarts?

Vouchsafe ye then, whom onely it concernes,
To me those secret causes to display;   50
For none but you, or who of you it learnes,
Can rightfully aread so dolefull lay.
Begin, thou eldest sister of the crew,
And let the rest in order thee ensew.

CLIO.

Heare, thou great Father of the Gods on
    hie,
That most art dreaded for thy thunder
    darts:

And thou our syre, that raignst in Castalie
And Mount Parnasse, the god of goodly
    arts:
Heare and behold the miserable state
Of us thy daughters, dolefull desolate.   60

Behold the fowle reproach and open shame,
The which is day by day unto us wrought
By such as hate the honour of our name,
The foes of learning and each gentle
    thought;
They, not contented us themselves to scorne,
Doo seeke to make us of the world forlorne.

Ne onely they that dwell in lowly dust,
The sonnes of darknes and of ignoraunce,
But they whom thou, great Jove, by doome
    unjust   69
Didst to the type of honour earst advaunce;
They now, puft up with sdeignfull insolence,
Despise the brood of blessed Sapience.

The sectaries of my celestiall skill,
That wont to be the worlds chiefe orna-
    ment,
And learned impes that wont to shoote up
    still,
And grow to hight of kingdomes govern-
    ment,
They underkeep, and with their spredding
    armes
Doo beat their buds, that perish through
    their harmes.

It most behoves the honorable race
Of mightie peeres true wisedome to sus-
    taine,   80
And with their noble countenaunce to grace
The learned forheads, without gifts or
    gaine:
Or rather learnd themselves behoves to
    bee;
That is the girlond of nobilitie.

But ah! all otherwise they doo esteeme
Of th' heavenly gift of wisdomes influence,
And to be learned it a base thing deeme;
Base minded they that want intelligence:
For God himselfe for wisedome most is
    praised,
And men to God thereby are nighest raised.

But they doo onely strive themselves to
    raise   91
Through pompous pride, and foolish vanitie:

In th' eyes of people they put all their
    praise,
And onely boast of armes and auncestrie:
But vertuous deeds, which did those armes
    first give
To their grandsyres, they care not to atchive.

So I, that doo all noble feates professe
To register, and sound in trump of gold,
Through their bad dooings, or base sloth-
    fulnesse,
Finde nothing worthie to be writ, or told:
For better farre it were to hide their
    names,   101
Than telling them to blazon out their
    blames.

So shall succeeding ages have no light
Of things forepast, nor moniments of time,
And all that in this world is worthie hight
Shall die in darknesse, and lie hid in slime:
Therefore I mourne with deep harts sorrow-
    ing,
Because I nothing noble have to sing.

With that she raynd such store of stream-
    ing teares,
That could have made a stonie heart to
    weep,   110
And all her sisters rent their golden heares,
And their faire faces with salt humour
    steep.
So ended shee: and then the next anew
Began her grievous plaint, as doth ensew.

MELPOMENE.

O who shall powre into my swollen eyes
A sea of teares that never may be dryde,
A brasen voice that may with shrilling cryes
Pierce the dull heavens and fill the ayer
    wide,
And yron sides that sighing may endure,
To waile the wretchednes of world im-
    pure?   120

Ah, wretched world! the den of wicked-
    nesse,
Deformd with filth and fowle iniquitie;
Ah, wretched world! the house of heavi-
    nesse,
Fild with the wreaks of mortall miserie;
Ah, wretched world, and all that is therein!
The vassals of Gods wrath, and slaves of sin.

Most miserable creature under sky
Man without understanding doth appeare;
For all this worlds affliction he thereby,
And Fortunes freakes, is wisely taught to
    beare: 130
Of wretched life the onely joy shee is,
And th' only comfort in calamities.

She armes the brest with constant patience
Against the bitter throwes of dolours darts,
She solaceth with rules of sapience
The gentle minds, in midst of worldlie
    smarts:
When he is sad, shee seeks to make him
    merie,
And doth refresh his sprights when they be
    werie.

But he that is of reasons skill bereft,
And wants the staffe of wisedome him to
    stay,   140
Is like a ship in midst of tempest left
Withouten helme or pilot her to sway:
Full sad and dreadfull is that ships event:
So is the man that wants intendiment.

Whie then doo foolish men so much despize
The precious store of this celestiall riches?
Why doo they banish us, that patronize
The name of learning? Most unhappie
    wretches!
The which lie drowned in deep wretchednes,
Yet doo not see their owne unhappines.   150

My part it is and my professed skill
The stage with tragick buskin to adorne,
And fill the scene with plaint and outcries
    shrill
Of wretched persons, to misfortune borne:
But none more tragick matter I can finde
Than this, of men depriv'd of sense and
    minde.

For all mans life me seemes a tragedy,
Full of sad sights and sore catastrophees;
First comming to the world with weeping
    eye,
Where all his dayes, like dolorous tro-
    phees,   160
Are heapt with spoyles of fortune and of
    feare,
And he at last laid forth on balefull beare

So all with rufull spectacles is fild,
Fit for Megera or Persephone:

But I, that in true tragedies am skild,
The flowre of wit, finde nought to busie me:
Therefore I mourne, and pitifully mone,
Because that mourning matter I have none.

Then gan she wofully to waile, and wring
Her wretched hands in lamentable wise; 170
And all her sisters, thereto answering,
Threw forth lowd shrieks and drerie dole-
full cries.
So rested she: and then the next in rew
Began her grievous plaint, as doth ensew.

THALIA.

Where be the sweete delights of learnings
treasure,
That wont with comick sock to beautefie
The painted theaters, and fill with pleasure
The listners eyes, and eares with melodie;
In which I late was wont to raine as queene,
And maske in mirth with graces well be-
seene?   180

O, all is gone! and all that goodly glee,
Which wont to be the glorie of gay wits,
Is layd abed, and no where now to see;
And in her roome unseemly Sorrow sits,
With hollow browes and greisly counte-
naunce,
Marring my joyous gentle dalliaunce.

And him beside sits ugly Barbarisme,
And brutish Ignorance, ycrept of late
Out of dredd darknes of the deep abysme,
Where being bredd, he light and heaven
does hate: 190
They in the mindes of men now tyrannize,
And the faire scene with rudenes foule dis-
guize.

All places they with follie have possest,
And with vaine toyes the vulgare enter-
taine;
But me have banished, with all the rest
That whilome wont to wait upon my traine,
Fine Counterfesaunce and unhurtfull Sport,
Delight and Laughter deckt in seemly sort.

All these, and all that els the comick stage
With seasoned wit and goodly pleasance
graced,   200
By which mans life in his likest image
Was limned forth. are wholly now defaced;

And those sweete wits which wont the like
to frame
Are now despizd,and made a laughing game.

And he, the man whom Nature selfe had
made
To mock her selfe, and truth to imitate,
With kindly counter under mimick shade,
Our pleasant Willy, ah! is dead of late:
With whom all joy and jolly meriment
Is also deaded, and in dolour drent.   210

In stead thereof scoffing Scurrilitie,
And scornfull Follie with Contempt is crept,
Rolling in rymes of shameles ribaudrie
Without regard, or due decorum kept;
Each idle wit at will presumes to make,
And doth the learneds taske upon him take.

But that same gentle spirit, from whose pen
Large streames of honnie and sweete nectar
flowe,
Scorning the boldnes of such base-borne
men,
Which dare their follies forth so rashlie
throwe,   220
Doth rather choose to sit in idle cell,
Than so himselfe to mockerie to sell.

So am I made the servant of the manie,
And laughing stocke of all that list to
scorne,
Not honored nor cared for of anie;
But loath'd of losels as a thing forlorne:
Therefore I mourne and sorrow with the
rest,
Untill my cause of sorrow be redrest.

Therewith she lowdly did lament and shrike
Pouring forth streames of teares abun
dantly;   230
And all her sisters, with compassion like,
The breaches of her singulfs did supply.
So rested shee: and then the next in rew
Began her grievous plaint, as doth ensew.

EUTERPE.

Like as the dearling of the summers pryde,
Faire Philomele, when winters stormie
wrath
The goodly fields, that earst so gay were
dyde
In colours divers, quite despoyled hath,

All comfortlesse doth hide her chearlesse
　　head
During the time of that her widowhead: 240

So we, that earst were wont in sweet accord
All places with our pleasant notes to fill,
Whilest favourable times did us afford
Free libertie to chaunt our charmes at
　　will,
All comfortlesse upon the bared bow,
Like wofull culvers, doo sit wayling now.

For far more bitter storme than winters
　　stowre
The beautie of the world hath lately wasted,
And those fresh buds, which wont so faire
　　to flowre,
Hath marred quite, and all their blossoms
　　blasted: 250
And those yong plants, which wont with
　　fruit t' abound,
Now without fruite or leaves are to be
　　found.

A stonie coldnesse hath benumbd the sence
And livelie spirits of each living wight,
And dimd with darknesse their intelligence,
Darknesse more than Cymerians daylie
　　night:
And monstrous Error, flying in the ayre,
Hath mard the face of all that semed fayre.

Image of hellish horrour, Ignorance, 259
Borne in the bosome of the black abysse,
And fed with Furies milke, for sustenaunce
Of his weake infancie, begot amisse
By yawning Sloth on his owne mother
　　Night;
So hee his sonnes both syre and brother
　　hight:

He, armd with blindnesse and with boldnes
　　stout,
(For blind is bold) hath our fayre light
　　defaced;
And gathering unto him a ragged rout
Of faunes and satyres, hath our dwellings
　　raced,
And our chast bowers, in which all vertue
　　rained,
With brutishnesse and beastlie filth hath
　　stained. 270

The sacred springs of horsefoot Helicon,
So oft bedeawed with our learned layes,

And speaking streames of pure Castalion,
The famous witnesse of our wonted praise,
They trampled have with their fowle foot-
　　ings trade,
And like to troubled puddles have them made.

Our pleasant groves, which planted were
　　with paines,
That with our musick wont so oft to ring,
And arbors sweet, in which the shepheards
　　swaines
Were wont so oft their pastoralls to sing,
They have cut downe, and all their plea-
　　saunce mard, 281
That now no pastorall is to bee hard.

In stead of them, fowle goblins and shriek-
　　owles
With fearfull howling do all places fill;
And feeble Eccho now laments and howles,
The dreadfull accents of their outcries shrill.
So all is turned into wildernesse,
Whilest Ignorance the Muses doth oppresse.

And I, whose joy was earst with spirit full
To teach the warbling pipe to sound aloft,
My spirits now dismayd with sorrow dull,
Doo mone my miserie in silence soft. 292
Therefore I mourne and waile incessantly,
Till please the heavens affoord me remedy.

Therewith shee wayled with exceeding woe,
And pitious lamentation did make,
And all her sisters, seeing her doo soe,
With equall plaints her sorrowe did partake.
So rested shee: and then the next in rew
Began her grievous plaint, as doth ensew. 300

TERPSICHORE.

Who so hath in the lap of soft delight
Beene long time luld, and fed with pleasures
　　sweet,
Feareles through his own fault or Fortunes
　　spight,
To tumble into sorrow and regreet,
Yf chaunce him fall into calamitie,
Findes greater burthen of his miserie.

So wee, that earst in joyance did abound,
And in the bosome of all blis did sit,
Like virgin queenes with laurell garlands
　　cround,
For vertues meed and ornament of wit, 310

Sith Ignorance our kingdome did confound,
Bee now become most wretched wightes on
ground.

And in our royall thrones, which lately
stood
In th' hearts of men to rule them care-
fully,
He now hath placed his accursed brood,
By him begotten of fowle Infamy;
Blind Error, scornefull Follie, and base
Spight,
Who hold by wrong that wee should have
by right.

They to the vulgar sort now pipe and sing,
And make them merrie with their fooler-
ies; 320
They cherelie chaunt and rymes at randon
fling,
The fruitfull spawne of their ranke fan-
tasies;
They feede the eares of fooles with flat-
tery,
And good men blame, and losels magnify.

All places they doo with their toyes possesse,
And raigne in liking of the multitude;
The schooles they fill with fond newfanglenesse,
And sway in court with pride and rashnes
rude;
Mongst simple shepheards they do boast
their skill,
And say their musicke matcheth Phœbus
quill. 330

The noble hearts to pleasures they allure,
And tell their Prince that learning is but
vaine;
Faire ladies loves they spot with thoughts
impure,
And gentle mindes with lewd delights dis-
taine;
Clerks they to loathly idlenes entice,
And fill their bookes with discipline of
vice.

So every where they rule and tyrannize,
For their usurped kingdomes maintenaunce,
The whiles we silly maides, whom they dis-
pize
And with reprochfull scorne discounte-
naunce, 340

From our owne native heritage exilde,
Walk through the world of every one revilde.

Nor anie one doth care to call us in,
Or once vouchsafeth us to entertaine,
Unlesse some one perhaps of gentle kin,
For pitties sake, compassion our paine,
And yeeld us some reliefe in this distresse;
Yet to be so reliev'd is wretchednesse.

So wander we all carefull comfortlesse,
Yet none doth care to comfort us at all; 350
So seeke we helpe our sorrow to redresse,
Yet none vouchsafes to answere to our call:
Therefore we mourne and pittilesse com-
plaine,
Because none living pittieth our paine.

With that she wept and wofullie way-
mented,
That naught on earth her griefe might
pacifie;
And all the rest her dolefull din augmented
With shrikes and groanes and grievous
agonie.
So ended shee: and then the next in rew
Began her piteous plaint, as doth ensew. 360

ERATO.

Ye gentle spirits breathing from above,
Where ye in Venus silver bowre were bred,
Thoughts halfe devine, full of the fire of
love,
With beawtie kindled and with pleasure
fed,
Which ye now in securitie possesse,
Forgetfull of your former heavinesse:

Now change the tenor of your joyous layes,
With which ye use your loves to deifie,
And blazon foorth an earthlie beauties
praise
Above the compasse of the arched skie: 370
Now change your praises into piteous cries,
And eulogies turne into elegies.

Such as ye wont, whenas those bitter
stounds
Of raging love first gan you to torment,
And launch your hearts with lamentable
wounds
Of secret sorrow and sad languishment,

Before your loves did take you unto grace;
Those now renew, as fitter for this place.

For I that rule in measure moderate
The tempest of that stormie passion,   380
And use to paint in rimes the troublous state
Of lovers life in likest fashion,
Am put from practise of my kindlie skill,
Banisht by those that love with leawdnes fill.

Love wont to be schoolmaster of my skill,
And the devicefull matter of my song;
Sweete love devoyd of villanie or ill,
But pure and spotles, as at first he sprong
Out of th' Almighties bosome, where he nests;
From thence infused into mortall brests. 390

Such high conceipt of that celestiall fire,
The base-borne brood of Blindnes cannot gesse,
Ne ever dare their dunghill thoughts aspire
Unto so loftie pitch of perfectnesse,
But rime at riot, and doo rage in love;
Yet little wote what doth thereto behove.

Faire Cytheree, the mother of delight
And queene of beautie, now thou maist go pack;
For lo ! thy kingdome is defaced quight,
Thy scepter rent, and power put to wrack;
And thy gay sonne, that winged God of Love,   401
May now goe prune his plumes like ruffed dove.

And ye three twins, to light by Venus brought,
The sweete companions of the Muses late,
From whom what ever thing is goodly thought
Doth borrow grace, the fancie to aggrate,
Go beg with us, and be companions still,
As heretofore of good, so now of ill.

For neither you nor we shall anie more
Finde entertainment, or in court or schoole:
For that which was accounted heretofore   411
The learneds meed is now lent to the foole;
He sings of love, and maketh loving layes,
And they him heare, and they him highly prayse.

With that she powred foorth a brackish flood
Of bitter teares, and made exceeding mone;
And all her sisters, seeing her sad mood,
With lowd laments her answered all at one.
So ended she: and then the next in rew
Began her grievous plaint, as doth ensew. 420

CALLIOPE.

To whom shall I my evill case complaine,
Or tell the anguish of my inward smart,
Sith none is left to remedie my paine,
Or deignes to pitie a perplexed hart;
But rather seekes my sorrow to augment
With fowle reproach, and cruell banishment ?

For they to whom I used to applie
The faithfull service of my learned skill,
The goodly off-spring of Joves progenie,
That wont the world with famous acts to fill;   430
Whose living praises in heroïck style,
It is my chiefe profession to compyle;

They all corrupted through the rust of time,
That doth all fairest things on earth deface,
Or through unnoble sloth, or sinfull crime,
That doth degenerate the noble race,
Have both desire of worthie deeds forlorne,
And name of learning utterly doo scorne.

Ne doo they care to have the auncestrie
Of th' old heroës memorizde anew;   440
Ne doo they care that late posteritie
Should know their names, or speak their praises dew:
But die forgot from whence at first they sprong,
As they themselves shalbe forgot ere long.

What bootes it then to come from glorious
Forefathers, or to have been nobly bredd ?
What oddes twixt Irus and old Inachus,
Twixt best and worst, when both alike are dedd,
If none of neither mention should make,
Nor out of dust their memories awake ? 450

Or who would ever care to doo brave deed,
Or strive in vertue others to excell,
If none should yeeld him his deserved meed,
Due praise, that is the spur of dooing well ?

For if good were not praised more than ill,
None would choose goodnes of his owne
    freewill.

Therefore the nurse of vertue I am hight,
And golden trompet of eternitie,
That lowly thoughts lift up to heavens hight,
And mortall men have powre to deifie: 460
Bacchus and Hercules I raisd to heaven,
And Charlemaine, amongst the starris
    seaven.

But now I will my golden clarion rend,
And will henceforth immortalize no more,
Sith I no more finde worthie to commend
For prize of value, or for learned lore:
For noble peeres, whom I was wont to raise,
Now onely seeke for pleasure, nought for
    praise.

Their great revenues all in sumptuous pride
They spend, that nought to learning they
    may spare;   470
And the rich fee which poets wont divide
Now parasites and sycophants doo share:
Therefore I mourne and endlesse sorrow
    make,
Both for my selfe and for my sisters sake.

With that she lowdly gan to waile and
    shrike,
And from her eyes a sea of teares did powre,
And all her sisters, with compassion like,
Did more increase the sharpnes of her
    showre.
So ended she: and then the next in rew
Began her plaint, as doth herein ensew. 480

URANIA.

What wrath of gods, or wicked influence
Of starres conspiring wretched men t' afflict,
Hath powrd on earth this noyous pestilence,
That mortall mindes doth inwardly infect
With love of blindnesse and of ignorance,
To dwell in darkenesse without sovenance?

What difference twixt man and beast is left,
When th' heavenlie light of knowledge is
    put out,
And th' ornaments of wisdome are bereft?
Then wandreth he in error and in doubt, 490
Unweeting of the danger hee is in,
Through fleshes frailtie and deceipt of sin.

In this wide world in which they wretches
    stray,
It is the onelie comfort which they have,
It is their light, their loadstarre and their
    day;
But hell and darkenesse and the grislie grave
Is ignorance, the enemie of grace,
That mindes of men borne heavenlie doth
    debace.

Through knowledge we behold the worlds
    creation,
How in his cradle first he fostred was; 500
And judge of Natures cunning operation,
How things she formed of a formelesse mas:
By knowledge wee do learne our selves to
    knowe,
And what to man, and what to God, wee
    owe.

From hence wee mount aloft unto the skie,
And looke into the christall firmament;
There we behold the heavens great hier-
    archie,
The starres pure light, the spheres swift
    movement,
The spirites and intelligences fayre,
And angels waighting on th' Almighties
    chayre.   510

And there, with humble minde and high in-
    sight,
Th' eternall Makers majestie wee viewe,
His love, his truth, his glorie, and his might,
And mercie more than mortall men can vew.
O soveraigne Lord, O soveraigne happinesse,
To see thee, and thy mercie measurelesse!

Such happines have they that doo embrace
The precepts of my heavenlie discipline;
But shame and sorrow and accursed case
Have they that scorne the schoole of arts
    divine,   520
And banish me, which do professe the skill
To make men heavenly wise through hum-
    bled will.

How ever yet they mee despise and spight,
I feede on sweet contentment of my thought,
And please my selfe with mine owne selfe-
    delight,
In contemplation of things heavenlie
    wrought:
So loathing earth, I looke up to the sky,
And being driven hence, I thether fly.

Thence I behold the miserie of men,
Which want the blis that wisedom would
    them breed,   530
And like brute beasts doo lie in loathsome
    den
Of ghostly darkenes, and of gastlie dreed:
For whom I mourne, and for my selfe com-
    plaine,
And for my sisters eake, whom they dis-
    daine.

With that shee wept and waild so pityous-
    lie,
As if her eyes had beene two springing
    wells:
And all the rest, her sorrow to supplie,
Did throw forth shrieks and cries and dreery
    yells.
So ended shee: and then the next in rew
Began her mournfull plaint, as doth ensew.

POLYHYMNIA.

A dolefull case desires a dolefull song,   541
Without vaine art or curious complements,
And squallid fortune, into basenes flong,
Doth scorne the pride of wonted ornaments.
Then fittest are these ragged rimes for mee,
To tell my sorrowes that exceeding bee.

For the sweet numbers and melodious mea-
    sures,
With which I wont the winged words to tie,
And make a tunefull diapase of pleasures,
Now being let to runne at libertie   550
By those which have no skill to rule them
    right,
Have now quite lost their naturall delight.

Heapes of huge words uphoorded hideously,
With horrid sound, though having little
    sence,
They thinke to be chiefe praise of poëtry;
And thereby wanting due intelligence,
Have mard the face of goodly poësie,
And made a monster of their fantasie.

Whilom in ages past none might professe,
But princes and high priests, that secret
    skill;   560
The sacred lawes therein they wont ex-
    presse,
And with deepe oracles their verses fill:
Then was shee held in soveraigne dignitie,
And made the noursling of nobilitie.

But now nor prince nor priest doth her
    maintayne,
But suffer her prophaned for to bee
Of the base vulgar, that with hands un-
    cleane
Dares to pollute her hidden mysterie;
And treadeth under foote hir holie things,
Which was the care of kesars and of kings.

One onelie lives, her ages ornament,   571
And myrrour of her Makers majestie;
That with rich bountie and deare cherish-
    ment
Supports the praise of noble poësie:
Ne onelie favours them which it professe,
But is her selfe a peereles poëtresse.

Most peereles prince, most peereles poë-
    tresse,
The true Pandora of all heavenly graces,
Divine Elisa, sacred Emperesse:
Live she for ever, and her royall p'laces 580
Be fild with praises of divinest wits,
That her eternize with their heavenlie writs.

Some few beside this sacred skill esteme,
Admirers of her glorious excellence,
Which being lightned with her beawties
    beme,
Are thereby fild with happie influence,
And lifted up above the worldes gaze,
To sing with angels her immortall praize.

But all the rest, as borne of salvage brood,
And having beene with acorns alwaies
    fed,   590
Can no whit savour this celestiall food,
But with base thoughts are into blindnesse
    led,
And kept from looking on the lightsome
    day:
For whome I waile and weepe all that I
    may.

Eftsoones such store of teares shee forth
    did powre,
As if shee all to water would have gone;
And all her sisters, seeing her sad stowre,
Did weep and waile and made exceeding
    mone;
And all their learned instruments did
    breake:
The rest untold no living tongue can
    speake.   600
FINIS.

VIRGILS GNAT

LONG SINCE DEDICATED
TO THE MOST NOBLE AND EXCELLENT LORD,
THE EARLE OF LEICESTER, LATE
DECEASED

WRONG'D, yet not daring to expresse my
   paine,
To you (great Lord) the causer of my care,
In clowdie teares my case I thus complaine
Unto your selfe, that onely privie are:
But if that any Œdipus unware
Shall chaunce, through power of some di-
   vining spright,
To reade the secrete of this riddle rare,
And know the purporte of my evill plight,
Let him rest pleased with his owne insight,
Ne further seeke to glose upon the text:
For griefe enough it is to grieved wight
To feele his fault, and not be further
   vext.
But what so by my selfe may not be showen,
May by this Gnatts complaint be easily
   knowen.

[' Virgil's Gnat ' may be thought to follow
close upon the latest of the sonnet series. The
main period to which it belongs is, in any case,
certain, for in the title it is described as 'long
since dedicated' to the Earl of Leicester; it
deals with some mishap in the personal relations of the poet with that nobleman, and such
relations would seem to have been confined to
the years 1577–1580. What the mishap may
have been has remained, on the other hand,
obscure. The curious must divine it as they
best may from the sonnet of dedication and
from the main allegory, always remembering
that the poem is not an invention based upon
the circumstances, but a mere paraphrase of
the pseudo-Virgilian *Culex*. Of greater moment is the style, which, moving in a freer
course than is natural to the sonnet, wins
nearer than that of the ' Visions ' and ' Ruins
of Rome' to the cadences of the *Faery Queen*.
The use of *ottava rima*, the stanza of the great
Italian romances, points forward, too.]

VIRGILS GNAT

WE now have playde (Augustus) wantonly,
Tuning our song unto a tender Muse,
And like a cobweb weaving slenderly,
Have onely playde: let thus much then ex-
   cuse

This Gnats small poeme, that th' whole
   history
Is but a jest, though envie it abuse:
But who such sports and sweet delights
   doth blame,
Shall lighter seeme than this Gnats idle
   name.

Hereafter, when as season more secure
Shall bring forth fruit, this Muse shall
   speak to thee   10
In bigger notes, that may thy sense allure,
And for thy worth frame some fit poesie:
The golden ofspring of Latona pure,
And ornament of great Joves progenie,
Phœbus, shall be the author of my song,
Playing on yvorie harp with silver strong.

He shall inspire my verse with gentle mood,
Of poets prince, whether he woon beside
Faire Xanthus sprincled with Chimæras
   blood,
Or in the woods of Astery abide,   20
Or whereas Mount Parnasse, the Muses
   brood,
Doth his broad forhead like two hornes di-
   vide,
And the sweete waves of sounding Castaly
With liquid foote doth slide downe easily.

Wherefore ye sisters, which the glorie bee
Of the Pierian streames, fayre Naiades,
Go too, and dauncing all in companie,
Adorne that god: and thou holie Pales,
To whome the honest care of husbandrie
Returneth by continuall successe,   30
Have care for to pursue his footing light,
Throgh the wide woods and groves with
   green leaves dight.

Professing thee I lifted am aloft
Betwixt the forrest wide and starrie sky:
And thou most dread (Octavius) which oft
To learned wits givest courage worthily,
O come (thou sacred childe) come sliding
   soft,
And favour my beginnings graciously:
For not these leaves do sing that dreadfull
   stound,
When giants bloud did staine Phlegræan
   ground;   40

Nor how th' halfe horsy people, Centaures
   hight,
Fought with the bloudie Lapithaes at bord;

Nor how the East with tyranous despight
Burnt th' Attick towres, and people slew
    with sword;
Nor how Mount Athos through exceeding
    might
Was digged downe; nor yron bands abord
The Pontick sea by their huge navy cast,
My volume shall renowne, so long since past:

Nor Hellespont trampled with horses feete,
When flocking Persians did the Greeks
    affray;   50
But my soft Muse, as for her power more
    meete,
Delights (with Phœbus friendly leave) to
    play
An easie running verse with tender feete.
And thou (dread sacred child) to thee alway
Let everlasting lightsome glory strive,
Through the worlds endles ages to survive.

And let an happie roome remaine for thee
Mongst heavenly ranks, where blessed
    soules do rest;
And let long lasting life with joyous glee,
As thy due meede that thou deservest
    best,   60
Hereafter many yeares remembred be
Amongst good men, of whom thou oft are
    blest;
Live thou for ever in all happinesse:
But let us turne to our first businesse.

The fiery Sun was mounted now on hight
Up to the heavenly towers, and shot each
    where
Out of his golden charet glistering light;
And fayre Aurora with her rosie heare
The hatefull darknes now had put to flight;
When as the shepheard, seeing day ap-
    peare,   70
His little goats gan drive out of their stalls,
To feede abroad, where pasture best befalls.

To an high mountaines top he with them
    went,
Where thickest grasse did cloath the open
    hills:
They, now amongst the woods and thickets
    ment,
Now in the valleies wandring at their wills,
Spread themselves farre abroad through
    each descent:
Some on the soft greene grasse feeding their
    fills;

Some, clambring through the hollow cliffes
    on hy,
Nibble the bushie shrubs, which growe
    thereby.   80

Others the utmost boughs of trees doe crop,
And brouze the woodbine twigges, that
    freshly bud;
This with full bit doth catch the utmost top
Of some soft willow, or new growen stud;
This with sharpe teeth the bramble leaves
    doth lop,
And chaw the tender prickles in her cud;
The whiles another high doth overlooke
Her owne like image in a christall brooke.

O the great happines which shepheards have,
Who so loathes not too much the poore es-
    tate   90
With minde that ill use doth before deprave,
Ne measures all things by the costly rate
Of riotise, and semblants outward brave!
No such sad cares, as wont to macerate
And rend the greedie mindes of covetous
    men,
Do ever creepe into the shepheards den.

Ne cares he if the fleece which him arayes
Be not twice steeped in Assyrian dye;
Ne glistering of golde, which underlayes
The summer beames, doe blinde his gazing
    eye;   100
Ne pictures beautie, nor the glauncing rayes
Of precious stones, whence no good commeth
    by;
Ne yet his cup embost with imagery
Of Bætus or of Alcons vanity.

Ne ought the whelky pearles esteemeth hee,
Which are from Indian seas brought far
    away:
But with pure brest from carefull sorrow
    free,
On the soft grasse his limbs doth oft dis-
    play,
In sweete spring time, when flowres varietie
With sundrie colours paints the sprincled
    lay;   110
There, lying all at ease from guile or spight,
With pype of fennie reedes doth him delight.

There he, lord of himselfe, with palme be-
    dight,
His looser locks doth wrap in wreath of
    vine:

There his milk dropping goats be his delight,
And fruitefull Pales, and the forrest greene,
And darkesome caves in pleasaunt vallies
    pight,
Wheras continuall shade is to be seene,
And where fresh springing wells, as chris-
    tall neate,
Do alwayes flow, to quench his thirstie
    heate.   120

O who can lead then a more happie life
Than he, that with cleane minde and heart
    sincere,
No greedy riches knowes nor bloudie strife,
No deadly fight of warlick fleete doth
    feare,
Ne runs in perill of foes cruell knife,
That in the sacred temples he may reare
A trophee of his glittering spoyles and
    treasure,
Or may abound in riches above measure?

Of him his God is worshipt with his sythe,
And not with skill of craftsman pol-
    ished: 130
He joyes in groves, and makes himselfe
    full blythe
With sundrie flowers in wilde fieldes gath-
    ered;
Ne frankincens he from Panchæa buyth:
Sweete Quiet harbours in his harmeles
    head,
And perfect Pleasure buildes her joyous
    bowre,
Free from sad cares, that rich mens hearts
    devowre.

This all his care, this all his whole inde-
    vour,
To this his minde and senses he doth bend,
How he may flow in quiets matchles trea-
    sour,
Content with any food that God doth send;
And how his limbs, resolv'd through idle
    leisour,   141
Unto sweete sleepe he may securely lend,
In some coole shadow from the scorching
    heat,
The whiles his flock their chawed cuds do
    eate.

O flocks, O faunes, and O ye pleasaunt
    springs
Of Tempe, where the countrey nymphs are
    rife,

Through whose not costly care each shep-
    heard sings
As merrie notes upon his rusticke fife
As that Ascræan bard, whose fame now
    rings
Through the wide world, and leads as joy-
    full life,   150
Free from all troubles and from worldly
    toyle,
In which fond men doe all their dayes tur-
    moyle.

In such delights whilst thus his carelesse
    time
This shepheard drives, upleaning on his
    batt,
And on shrill reedes chaunting his rustick
    rime,
Hyperion, throwing foorth his beames full
    hott,
Into the highest top of heaven gan clime,
And the world parting by an equall lott,
Did shed his whirling flames on either side,
As the great Ocean doth himselfe divide. 160

Then gan the shepheard gather into one
His stragling goates, and drave them to a
    foord,
Whose cærule streame, rombling in pible
    stone,
Crept under mosse as greene as any goord
Now had the sun halfe heaven overgone,
When he his heard back from that water
    foord
Drave from the force of Phœbus boyling
    ray,
Into thick shadowes, there themselves to
    lay.

Soone as he them plac'd in thy sacred wood
(O Delian goddesse) saw, to which of
    yore   170
Came the bad daughter of old Cadmus
    brood,
Cruell Agave, flying vengeance sore
Of King Nictileus for the guiltie blood
Which she with cursed hands had shed be-
    fore;
There she halfe frantick having slaine her
    sonne,
Did shrowd her selfe like punishment to
    shonne.

Here also playing on the grassy greene,
Woodgods, and satyres, and swift dryades,

With many fairies oft were dauncing seene.
Not so much did Dan Orpheus represse 180
The streames of Hebrus with his songs, I
    weene,
As that faire troupe of woodie goddesses
Staied thee (O Peneus) powring foorth to
    thee,
From cheereful lookes, great mirth and
    gladsome glee.

The verie nature of the place, resounding
With gentle murmure of the breathing
    ayre,
A pleasant bowre with all delight abounding
In the fresh shadowe did for them prepayre,
To rest their limbs with wearines redound-
    ing.
For first the high palme trees, with
    braunches faire,   190
Out of the lowly vallies did arise,
And high shoote up their heads into the
    skyes.

And them amongst the wicked lotos grew,
Wicked, for holding guilefully away
Ulysses men, whom rapt with sweetenes
    new,
Taking to hoste, it quite from him did stay;
And eke those trees, in whose transformed
    hew
The Sunnes sad daughters waylde the rash
    decay
Of Phaeton, whose limbs with lightening
    rent
They gathering up, with sweete teares did
    lament.   200

And that same tree, in which Demophoon,
By his disloyalty lamented sore,
Eternall hurte left unto many one:
Whom als accompanied the oke, of yore
Through fatall charmes transformd to such
    an one:
The oke, whose acornes were our foode, be-
    fore
That Ceres seede of mortall men were
    knowne,
Which first Triptoleme taught how to be
    sowne.

Here also grew the rougher rinded pine,
The great Argoan ships brave ornament, 210
Whom golden fleece did make an heavenly
    signe;
Which coveting, with his high tops extent,

To make the mountaines touch the starres
    divine,
Decks all the forrest with embellishment;
And the blacke holme that loves the watrie
    vale;
And the sweete cypresse, signe of deadly
    bale.

Emongst the rest the clambring yvie grew,
Knitting his wanton armes with grasping
    hold,
Least that the poplar happely should rew
Her brothers strokes, whose boughes she
    doth enfold   220
With her lythe twigs, till they the top sur-
    vew,
And paint with pallid greene her buds of
    gold.
Next did the myrtle tree to her approach,
Not yet unmindfull of her olde reproach.

But the small birds, in their wide boughs
    embowring,
Chaunted their sundrie tunes with sweete
    consent;
And under them a silver spring, forth
    powring
His trickling streames, a gentle murmure
    sent;
Thereto the frogs, bred in the slimie scow-
    ring
Of the moist moores, their jarring voyces
    bent;   230
And shrill grashoppers chirped them
    around:
All which the ayrie echo did resound.

In this so pleasant place this shepheards
    flocke
Lay everie where, their wearie limbs to
    rest,
On everie bush, and everie hollow rocke,
Where breathe on them the whistling wind
    mote best;
The whiles the shepheard self, tending his
    stocke,
Sate by the fountaine side, in shade to
    rest,
Where gentle slumbring sleep oppressed
    him,
Displaid on ground, and seized everie lim.

Of trecherie or traines nought tooke he
    keep,   241
But, looslie on the grassie greene dispredd,

His dearest life did trust to careles sleep;
Which, weighing down his drouping drowsie
      hedd,
In quiet rest his molten heart did steep,
Devoid of care, and feare of all falshedd:
Had not inconstant Fortune, bent to ill,
Bid strange mischance his quietnes to spill.

For at his wonted time in that same place
An huge great serpent, all with speckles
      pide,   250
To drench himselfe in moorish slime did
      trace,
There from the boyling heate himselfe to
      hide:
He, passing by with rolling wreathed pace,
With brandisht tongue the emptie aire did
      gride,
And wrapt his scalie boughts with fell de-
      spight,
That all things seem'd appalled at his sight.

Now more and more having himselfe en-
      rolde,
His glittering breast he lifteth up on hie,
And with proud vaunt his head aloft doth
      holde;   259
His creste above, spotted with purple die,
On everie side did shine like scalie golde,
And his bright eyes, glauncing full dread-
      fullie,
Did seeme to flame out flakes of flashing
      fyre,
And with sterne lookes to threaten kindled
      yre.

Thus wise long time he did himselfe dispace
There round about, when as at last he spide,
Lying along before him in that place,
That flocks grand captaine and most trustie
      guide:
Eftsoones more fierce in visage and in pace,
Throwing his firie eyes on everie side,   270
He commeth on, and all things in his way
Full stearnly rends, that might his passage
      stay.

Much he disdaines, that anie one should
      dare
To come unto his haunt; for which intent
He inly burns, and gins straight to prepare
The weapons which Nature to him hath
      lent;
Fellie he hisseth, and doth fiercely stare,
And hath his jawes with angrie spirits rent,

That all his tract with bloudie drops is
      stained,
And all his foldes are now in length out-
      strained.   280

Whom, thus at point prepared, to prevent,
A litle noursling of the humid ayre,
A Gnat, unto the sleepie shepheard went,
And marking where his ey-lids, twinckling
      rare,
Shewd the two pearles which sight unto him
      lent,
Through their thin coverings appearing
      fayre,
His little needle there infixing deep,
Warnd him awake, from death himselfe to
      keep.

Wherewith enrag'd, he fiercely gan upstart,
And with his hand him rashly bruzing,
      slewe,   290
As in avengement of his heedles smart,
That streight the spirite out of his senses
      flew,
And life out of his members did depart:
When suddenly casting aside his vew,
He spide his foe with felonous intent,
And fervent eyes to his destruction bent.

All suddenly dismaid, and hartles quight,
He fled abacke, and, catching hastie holde
Of a yong alder hard beside him pight,
It rent, and streight about him gan be-
      holde   300
What god or fortune would assist his might.
But whether god or fortune made him bold
Its hard to read: yet hardie will he had
To overcome, that made him lesse adrad.

The scalie backe of that most hideous snake
Enwrapped round, oft faining to retire,
And oft him to assaile, he fiercely strake
Whereas his temples did his creast front
      tyre;
And, for he was but slowe, did slowth off
      shake,
And gazing ghastly on (for feare and yre 310
Had blent so much his sense, that lesse he
      feard;)
Yet, when he saw him slaine, himselfe he
      cheard.

By this the Night forth from the darksome
      bowre
Of Herebus her teemed steedes gan call,

And laesie Vesper in his timely howre
From golden Oeta gan proceede withall;
Whenas the shepheard after this sharpe
    stowre,
Seing the doubled shadowes low to fall,
Gathering his straying flocke, does home-
    ward fare,
And unto rest his wearie joynts prepare. 320

Into whose sense so soone as lighter sleepe
Was entered, and now loosing everie lim,
Sweete slumbring deaw in carelesnesse did
    steepe,
The image of that Gnat appeard to him,
And in sad tearmes gan sorrowfully weepe,
With greislie countenaunce and visage grim,
Wailing the wrong which he had done of
    late,
In steed of good, hastning his cruell fate.

Said he, 'What have I, wretch, deserv'd,
    that thus
Into this bitter bale I am outcast,   330
Whilest that thy life more deare and pre-
    cious
Was than mine owne, so long as it did last?
I now, in lieu of paines so gracious,
Am tost in th' ayre with everie windie blast:
Thou, safe delivered from sad decay,
Thy careles limbs in loose sleep dost dis-
    play.

'So livest thou; but my poore wretched
    ghost
Is forst to ferrie over Lethes river,   338
And, spoyld of Charon, too and fro am tost.
Seest thou, how all places quake and quiver,
Lightned with deadly lamps on everie post?
Tisiphone each where doth shake and shiver
Her flaming fire brond, encountring me,
Whose lockes uncombed cruell adders be.

'And Cerberus, whose many mouthes doo
    bay,
And barke out flames, as if on fire he fed;
Adowne whose necke, in terrible array,
Ten thousand snakes, cralling about his hed,
Doo hang in heapes, that horribly affray,
And bloodie eyes doo glister firie red;   350
He oftentimes me dreadfullie doth threaten,
With painfull torments to be sorely beaten.

'Ay me! that thankes so much should faile
    of meed!
For that I thee restor'd to life againe,

Even from the doore of death and deadlie
    dreed.
Where then is now the guerdon of my
    paine?
Where the reward of my so piteous deed?
The praise of pitie vanisht is in vaine,
And th' antique faith of justice long agone
Out of the land is fled away and gone.   360

'I saw anothers fate approaching fast,
And left mine owne his safetie to tender;
Into the same mishap I now am cast,
And shun'd destruction doth destruction
    render:
Not unto him that never hath trespast,
But punishment is due to the offender:
Yet let destruction be the punishment,
So long as thankfull will may it relent.

'I carried am into waste wildernesse,   369
Waste wildernes, amongst Cymerian shades,
Where endles paines and hideous heavinesse
Is round about me heapt in darksome glades.
For there huge Othos sits in sad distresse,
Fast bound with serpents that him oft in-
    vades,
Far of beholding Ephialtes tide,
Which once assai'd to burne this world so
    wide.

'And there is mournfull Tityus, mindefull
    yet
Of thy displeasure, O Latona faire;
Displeasure too implacable was it,
That made him meat for wild foules of the
    ayre: 380
Much do I feare among such fiends to sit;
Much do I feare back to them to repayre,
To the black shadowes of the Stygian shore,
Where wretched ghosts sit wailing ever-
    more.

'There next the utmost brinck doth he abide,
That did the bankets of the gods bewray,
Whose throat, through thirst, to nought
    nigh being dride,
His sense to seeke for ease turnes every
    way:
And he that in avengement of his pride,
For scorning to the sacred gods to pray,   390
Against a mountaine rolls a mightie stone,
Calling in vaine for rest, and can have none.

'Go ye with them, go, cursed damosells,
Whose bridale torches foule Erynnis tynde,

And Hymen, at your spousalls sad, foretells
Tydings of death and massacre unkinde:
With them that cruell Colchid mother
    dwells,
The which conceiv'd in her revengefull
    minde,
With bitter woundes her owne deere babes
    to slay,
And murdred troupes upon great heapes to
    lay.   400

' There also those two Pandionian maides,
Calling on Itis, Itis evermore,
Whom, wretched boy, they slew with guiltie
    blades;
For whome the Thracian king lamenting
    sore,
Turn'd to a lapwing, fowlie them upbraydes,
And fluttering round about them still does
    sore;
There now they all eternally complaine
Of others wrong, and suffer endles paine.

' But the two brethren borne of Cadmus
    blood,
Whilst each does for the soveraignty con-
    tend,   410
Blinde through ambition, and with ven-
    geance wood,
Each doth against the others bodie bend
His cursed steele, of neither well withstood,
And with wide wounds their carcases doth
    rend;
That yet they both doe mortall foes re-
    maine,
Sith each with brothers bloudie hand was
    slaine.

' Ah (waladay !) there is no end of paine,
Nor chaunge of labour may intreated bee:
Yet I beyond all these am carried faine,
Where other powers farre different I
    see,   420
And must passe over to th' Elisian plaine:
There grim Persephone, encountring mee,
Doth urge her fellow Furies earnestlie,
With their bright firebronds me to terrifie.

' There chast Alceste lives inviolate,
Free from all care, for that her husbands
    daies
She did prolong by changing fate for fate:
Lo ! there lives also the immortall praise
Of womankinde, most faithfull to her mate,
Penelope; and from her farre awayes   430

A rulesse rout of yongmen, which her woo'd,
All slaine with darts, lie wallowed in their
    blood.

' And sad Eurydice thence now no more
Must turne to life, but there detained bee,
For looking back, being forbid before:
Yet was the guilt thereof, Orpheus, in thee.
Bold sure he was, and worthie spirite bore,
That durst those lowest shadowes goe to
    see,
And could beleeve that anie thing could
    please   439
Fell Cerberus, or Stygian powres appease.

' Ne feard the burning waves of Phlegeton,
Nor those same mournfull kingdomes, com-
    passed
With rustie horrour and fowle fashion,
And deep digd vawtes, and Tartar covered
With bloodie night, and darke confusion,
And judgement seates, whose judge is
    deadlie dred,
A judge that, after death, doth punish sore
The faults which life hath trespassed be-
    fore.

' But valiant fortune made Dan Orpheus
    bolde:
For the swift running rivers still did stand,
And the wilde beasts their furie did with-
    hold,   451
To follow Orpheus musicke through the
    land:
And th' okes, deep grounded in the earthly
    molde,
Did move, as if they could him understand;
And the shrill woods, which were of sense
    bereav'd,
Through their hard barke his silver sound
    receav'd.

' And eke the Moone her hastie steedes did
    stay,
Drawing in teemes along the starrie skie;
And didst (O monthly virgin) thou delay
Thy nightly course, to heare his melodie ?
The same was able, with like lovely lay,
The Queene of Hell to move as easily,   462
To yeeld Eurydice unto her fere,
Backe to be borne, though it unlawfull
    were.

' She (ladie) having well before approoved,
The feends to be too cruell and severe.

Observ'd th' appointed way, as her be-
    hooved,
Ne ever did her ey-sight turne arere,
Ne ever spake, ne cause of speaking
    mooved:
But cruell Orpheus, thou much crueller,
Seeking to kisse her, brok'st the gods
    decree,   471
And thereby mad'st her ever damn'd to be.

'Ah! but sweete love of pardon worthie
    is,
And doth deserve to have small faults re-
    mitted;
If Hell at least things lightly done amis
Knew how to pardon, when ought is
    omitted:
Yet are ye both received into blis,
And to the seates of happie soules ad-
    mitted,
And you beside the honourable band
Of great heroës doo in order stand.   480

'There be the two stout sonnes of Aeacus,
Fierce Peleus, and the hardie Telamon,
Both seeming now full glad and joyeous
Through their syres dreadfull jurisdiction,
Being the judge of all that horrid hous:
And both of them, by strange occasion,
Renown'd in choyce of happie marriage
Through Venus grace, and vertues cariage.

'For th' one was ravisht of his owne bond-
    maide,
The faire Ixione, captiv'd from Troy: 490
But th' other was with Thetis love assaid,
Great Nereus his daughter and his joy.
On this side them there is a yongman layd,
Their match in glorie, mightie, fierce and
    coy,
That from th' Argolick ships, with furious
    yre,
Bett back the furie of the Trojan fyre.

'O who would not recount the strong di-
    vorces
Of that great warre, which Trojanes oft
    behelde,
And oft beheld the warlike Greekish
    forces,
When Teucrian soyle with bloodie rivers
    swelde,   500
And wide Sigæan shores were spred with
    corses,
And Simois and Xanthus blood outwelde,

Whilst Hector raged with outragious
    minde,
Flames, weapons, wounds in Greeks fleete
    to have tynde?

'For Ida selfe, in ayde of that fierce fight,
Out of her mountaines ministred supplies,
And like a kindly nourse, did yeeld (for
    spight)
Store of firebronds out of her nourseries
Unto her foster children, that they might
Inflame the navie of their enemies,   510
And all the Rhætean shore to ashes turne,
Where lay the ships which they did seeke
    to burne.

'Gainst which the noble sonne of Tela-
    mon
Opposd' himselfe, and thwarting his huge
    shield,
Them battell bad; gainst whom appeard
    anon
Hector, the glorie of the Trojan field:
Both fierce and furious in contention
Encountred, that their mightie strokes so
    shrild
As the great clap of thunder, which doth
    ryve
The ratling heavens, and cloudes asunder
    dryve.   520

'So th' one with fire and weapons did con-
    tend
To cut the ships from turning home againe
To Argos; th' other strove for to defend
The force of Vulcane with his might and
    maine.
Thus th' one Aeacide did his fame extend:
But th' other joy'd, that, on the Phrygian
    playne
Having the blood of vanquisht Hector
    shedd,
He compast Troy thrice with his bodie
    dedd.

'Againe great dole on either partie grewe,
That him to death unfaithfull Paris sent;
And also him that false Ulysses slewe,   531
Drawne into danger through close ambush-
    ment:
Therefore from him Laërtes sonne his
    vewe
Doth turne aside, and boasts his good event
In working of Strymonian Rhæsus fall,
And efte in Dolons slye surprysall.

'Againe the dreadfull Cycones him dis-
        may,
And blacke Læstrigones, a people stout:
Then greedie Scilla, under whom there bay
Manie great bandogs, which her gird
        about: 540
Then doo the Aetnean Cyclops him affray,
And deep Charybdis gulphing in and out:
Lastly the squalid lakes of Tartarie,
And griesly feends of hell him terrifie.

'There also goodly Agamemnon bosts,
The glorie of the stock of Tantalus,
And famous light of all the Greekish hosts,
Under whose conduct most victorious,
The Dorick flames consum'd the Iliack
        posts.
Ah! but the Greekes themselves more
        dolorous,   550
To thee, O Troy, paid penaunce for thy
        fall,
In th' Hellespont being nigh drowned all.

'Well may appeare, by proofe of their mis-
        chaunce,
The chaungfull turning of mens slipperie
        state,
That none, whom fortune freely doth ad-
        vaunce,
Himselfe therefore to heaven should ele-
        vate:
For loftie type of honour, through the
        glaunce
Of envies dart, is downe in dust prostrate;
And all that vaunts in worldly vanitie
Shall fall through fortunes mutabilitie.   560

'Th' Argolicke power returning home
        againe,
Enricht with spoyles of th' Ericthonian
        towre,
Did happie winde and weather entertaine,
And with good speed the fomie billowes
        scowre:
No signe of storme, no feare of future
        paine,
Which soone ensued them with heavie
        stowre.
Nereïs to the seas a token gave,
The whiles their crooked keeles the surges
        clave.

'Suddenly, whether through the gods de-
        cree,   569
Or haplesse rising of some froward starre,

The heavens on everie side enclowded bee:
Black stormes and fogs are blowen up from
        farre,
That now the pylote can no loadstarre see,
But skies and seas doo make most dread-
        full warre;
The billowes striving to the heavens to
        reach,
And th' heavens striving them for to im-
        peach.

'And, in avengement of their bold attempt,
Both sun and starres and all the heavenly
        powres
Conspire in one to wreake their rash con-
        tempt,
And downe on them to fall from highest
        towres: 580
The skie, in pieces seeming to be rent,
Throwes lightning forth, and haile, and
        harmful showres,
That death on everie side to them appeares,
In thousand formes, to worke more ghastly
        feares.

'Some in the greedie flouds are sunke and
        drent;
Some on the rocks of Caphareus are
        throwne;
Some on th' Euboick cliffs in pieces rent;
Some scattred on the Hercæan shores un-
        knowne;
And manie lost, of whom no moniment
Remaines, nor memorie is to be showne:
Whilst all the purchase of the Phrigian
        pray,   591
Tost on salt billowes, round about doth stray.

'Here manie other like heroës bee,
Equall in honour to the former crue,
Whom ye in goodly seates may placed see,
Descended all from Rome by linage due,
From Rome, that holds the world in sove-
        reigntie,
And doth all nations unto her subdue:
Here Fabii and Decii doo dwell,
Horatii that in vertue did excell.   600

'And here the antique fame of stout Camill
Doth ever live; and constant Curtius,
Who, stifly bent his vowed life to spill
For countreyes health, a gulph most hideous
Amidst the towne with his owne corps did
        fill,
T' appease the powers; and prudent Mutius,

Who in his flesh endur'd the scorching flame,
To daunt his foe by ensample of the same.

' And here wise Curius, companion
Of noble vertues, lives in endles rest;   610
And stout Flaminius, whose devotion
Taught him the fires scorn'd furie to detest;
And here the praise of either Scipion
Abides in highest place above the best,
To whom the ruin'd walls of Carthage
          vow'd,
Trembling their forces, sound their praises
          lowd.

' Live they for ever through their lasting
          praise:
But I, poore wretch, am forced to retourne
To the sad lakes, that Phœbus sunnie rayes
Doo never see, where soules doo alwaies
          mourne;   620
And by the wayling shores to waste my
          dayes,
Where Phlegeton with quenchles flames
          doth burne;
By which just Minos righteous soules doth
          sever
From wicked ones, to live in blisse for ever.

' Me therefore thus the cruell fiends of
          hell,
Girt with long snakes and thousand yron
          chaynes,
Through doome of that their cruell judge,
          compell,
With bitter torture and impatient paines,
Cause of my death and just complaint to
          tell.
For thou art he whom my poore ghost com-
          plaines   630
To be the author of her ill unwares,
That careles hear'st my intollerable cares.

' Them therefore as bequeathing to the
          winde,
I now depart, returning to thee never,
And leave this lamentable plaint behinde.
But doo thou haunt the soft downe rolling
          river,
And wilde greene woods, and fruitful pas-
          tures minde,
And let the flitting aire my vaine words
          sever.'
Thus having said, he heavily departed
With piteous crie, that anie would have
          smarted.   640

Now, when the sloathfull fit of lifes sweete
          rest
Had left the heavie shepheard, wondrous
          cares
His inly grieved minde full sore opprest;
That balefull sorrow he no longer beares
For that Gnats death, which deeply was
          imprest,
But bends what ever power his aged yeares
Him lent, yet being such as through their
          might
He lately slue his dreadfull foe in fight.

By that same river lurking under greene,
Eftsoones he gins to fashion forth a place,
And squaring it in compasse well beseene,
There plotteth out a tombe by measured
          space: 652
His yron headed spade tho making cleene,
To dig up sods out of the flowrie grasse,
His worke he shortly to good purpose
          brought,
Like as he had conceiv'd it in his thought.

An heape of earth he hoorded up on hie,
Enclosing it with banks on everie side,
And thereupon did raise full busily
A little mount, of greene turffs edifide;   660
And on the top of all, that passers by
Might it behold, the toomb he did provide
Of smoothest marble stone in order set,
That never might his luckie scape forget.

And round about he taught sweete flowres
          to growe,
The rose engrained in pure scarlet die,
The lilly fresh, and violet belowe,
The marigolde, and cherefull rosemarie,
The Spartan mirtle, whence sweet guml
          does flowe,
The purple hyacinthe, and fresh cost-
          marie,   670
And saffron, sought for in Cilician soyle,
And lawrell, th' ornament of Phœbus toyle:

Fresh rhododaphne, and the Sabine flowre,
Matching the wealth of th' auncient frank-
          incence,
And pallid yvie, building his owne bowre,
And box, yet mindfull of his olde offence,
Red amaranthus, lucklesse paramour.
Oxeye still greene, and bitter patience;
Ne wants there pale Narcisse, that, in a
          well
Seeing his beautie, in love with it fell.   680

And whatsoever other flowre of worth,
And whatso other hearb of lovely hew
The joyous Spring out of the ground brings
    forth,
To cloath her selfe in colours fresh and
    new,
He planted there, and reard a mount of
    earth,
In whose high front was writ as doth ensue:

To thee, small Gnat, in lieu of his life saved,
The Shepheard hath thy deaths record en-
    graved.

FINIS.

PROSOPOPOIA
OR
MOTHER HUBBERDS TALE
BY ED. SP.

DEDICATED TO THE RIGHT HONORABLE
THE LADIE COMPTON AND
MOUNTEGLE

LONDON

IMPRINTED FOR WILLIAM
PONSONBIE, DWELLING IN PAULES
CHURCHYARD AT THE SIGNE OF
THE BISHOPS HEAD
1591

TO THE RIGHT HONOURABLE, THE LADIE COMPTON AND MOUNTEGLE

MOST faire and vertuous Ladie : having
often sought opportunitie by some good
meanes to make knowen to your Ladiship
the humble affection and faithfull duetie
which I have alwaies professed, and am
bound to beare, to that house from whence
yee spring, I have at length found occasion
to remember the same, by making a simple
present to you of these my idle labours ;
which having long sithens composed in the
raw conceipt of my youth, I lately amongst
other papers lighted upon, and was by others,
which liked the same, mooved to set them
foorth. Simple is the device, and the composition meane, yet carrieth some delight,
even the rather because of the simplicitie
and meannesse thus personated. The same
I beseech your Ladiship take in good part,
as a pledge of that profession which I have

made to you, and keepe with you untill,
with some other more worthie labour, I do
redeeme it out of your hands, and discharge
my utmost dutie. Till then, wishing your
Ladiship all increase of honour and happinesse, I humblie take leave.

    Your Ladiships ever
        humbly,
           Ed. Sp.

['Mother Hubberd's Tale' is of the same
period with 'Virgil's Gnat.' In the dedicatory
letter of 1591 it is said to have been 'long sithens
composed in the raw conceipt of my youth,'
and 'long sithens' is limited by the satire on
court life to the years from 1577 to 1580. A
probable glance at the disgrace of Leicester in
1579 (l. 628) may limit it still more. Yet beside this very reference is one, equally probable, to events of ten years later, and other
such insertions may be found. It would appear, therefore, that when, during his second
sojourn at court, Spenser 'lighted upon' this
early poem and was 'mooved to set it foorth,'
he to some extent revised and enlarged it.

    The most obvious characteristic of 'Mother
Hubberd's Tale' is the range of its satire. The
career of the Ape and the Fox is a kind of
rogues' progress through the three estates to
the crown. They begin among the common
people, rise from thence to the clergy and from
thence to the court, among the nobility ; in
the end they cap the climax of their villainies
by making themselves king and prime minister. The satire is mainly concentrated, to be
sure, upon life at the court and the intrigues
of those in power, topics of direct personal
concern to Spenser, yet the poem as a whole
does survey, however imperfectly and unsym-
metrically, some of the main conditions of
life in the nation at large. In this it harks
back unmistakably to *Piers Plowman*. Though
the satiric scope is of Langland, however,
there is much in the style to suggest the vein
of Chaucer, and the *dramatis personæ* and
stage-setting are those of *Reynard the Fox*.
The combination results at times in curious
contrasts. In their first sojourn at court, the
Fox and the Ape are among lords and ladies,
suitors, a world of men, from the midst of
which emerges the figure of the 'brave courtier :' in their second sojourn there, this
world is suddenly transformed ; for lords and
ladies, suitors, men, we have the animals of
Caxton's book, the Wolf, the Sheep, the Ass,
and their like ; it is the court of King Lion.
Yet so spontaneous and creative are the acts
of the poet's imagination that at no point in
the long range of this satire are we checked

by the sense of incongruity. The strange succession of scenes and figures, all admirably alive, the variety of artistic effects ranging from grotesqueness to romantic beauty, the sudden eruptions of strong personal feeling from levels of cool satire, the fluctuations of the style from crudity to masterliness, produce, in a small way, the sense of a world almost as real as that of the *Faery Queen*. This is mediæval satire at its best. The Italians, with whom Spenser was at this time rapidly becoming familiar, had already, for at least two generations, been cultivating the classic Roman form, and their lead had been followed by the head of the new English school, Sir Thomas Wyatt: one might expect that Spenser, who from boyhood had been steeped in the classics, should also adopt this revived form. Nothing shows better the independence of his artistic eclecticism, his gift for taking here, there, and everywhere whatever appeals to his imagination, than the mediævalism of this his one satire.]

PROSOPOPOIA: OR MOTHER HUBBERDS TALE

It was the month in which the righteous
  Maide,
That, for disdaine of sinfull worlds up-
  braide,
Fled back to heaven, whence she was first
  conceived,
Into her silver bowre the Sunne received;
And the hot Syrian Dog on him awayting,
After the chafed Lyons cruell bayting,
Corrupted had th' ayre with his noysome
  breath,
And powr'd on th' earth plague, pestilence,
  and death.
Emongst the rest a wicked maladie
Raign'd emongst men, that manie did to
  die,   10
Depriv'd of sense and ordinarie reason;
That it to leaches seemed strange and
  geason.
My fortune was, mongst manie others moe,
To be partaker of their common woe;
And my weake bodie, set on fire with
  griefe,
Was rob'd of rest and naturall reliefe.
In this ill plight, there came to visite mee
Some friends, who, sorie my sad case to
  see,
Began to comfort me in chearfull wise,
And meanes of gladsome solace to devise.

But seeing kindly sleep refuse to doe   20
His office, and my feeble eyes forgoe,
They sought my troubled sense how to de-
  ceave
With talke, that might unquiet fancies
  reave;
And sitting all in seates about me round,
With pleasant tales (fit for that idle
  stound)
They cast in course to waste the wearie
  howres:
Some tolde of ladies, and their paramoures;
Some of brave knights, and their renowned
  squires;
Some of the faeries and their strange at-
  tires;   30
And some of giaunts hard to be beleeved;
That the delight thereof me much re-
  leeved.
Amongst the rest a good old woman was,
Hight Mother Hubberd, who did farre
  surpas
The rest in honest mirth, that seem'd her
  well:
She, when her turne was come her tale to
  tell,
Tolde of a strange adventure, that betided
Betwixt the Foxe and th' Ape by him mis-
  guided;
The which, for that my sense it greatly
  pleased,
All were my spirite heavie and diseased, 40
Ile write in termes, as she the same did
  say,
So well as I her words remember may.
No Muses aide me needes heretoo to call;
Base is the style, and matter meane withall.
  ¶ Whilome (said she) before the world
  was civill,
The Foxe and th' Ape, disliking of their
  evill
And hard estate, determined to seeke
Their fortunes farre abroad, lyeke with his
  lyeke:
For both were craftie and unhappie witted;
Two fellowes might no where be better
  fitted.   50
The Foxe, that first this cause of griefe did
  finde,
Gan first thus plaine his case with words
  unkinde:
'Neighbour Ape, and my goship eke be-
  side,
(Both two sure bands in friendship to be
  tide,)

To whom may I more trustely complaine
The evill plight that doth me sore con-
    straine,
And hope thereof to finde due remedie?
Heare then my paine and inward agonie.
Thus manie yeares I now have spent and
    worne,
In meane regard, and basest fortunes
    scorne,   60
Dooing my countrey service as I might,
No lesse I dare saie than the prowdest
    wight;
And still I hoped to be up advaunced,
For my good parts; but still it hath mis-
    chaunced.
Now therefore that no lenger hope I see,
But froward fortune still to follow mee,
And losels lifted up on high, where I did
    looke,
I meane to turne the next leafe of the
    booke.
Yet ere that anie way I doo betake,
I meane my gossip privie first to make.' 70
'Ah, my deare gossip!' answer'd then the
    Ape,
'Deeply doo your sad words my wits
    awhape,
Both for because your griefe doth great
    appeare,
And eke because my selfe am touched
    neare:
For I likewise have wasted much good time,
Still wayting to preferment up to clime,
Whilest others alwayes have before me
    stept,
And from my beard the fat away have
    swept;
That now unto despaire I gin to growe,
And meane for better winde about to
    throwe.   80
Therefore to me, my trustie friend, aread
Thy councell: two is better than one head.'
'Certes,' said he, 'I meane me to disguize
In some straunge habit, after uncouth wize,
Or like a pilgrime, or a lymiter,
Or like a gipsen, or a juggeler,
And so to wander to the worldes ende,
To seeke my fortune, where I may it mend:
For worse than that I have I cannot meete.
Wide is the world, I wote, and everie
    streete   90
Is full of fortunes and adventures straunge,
Continuallie subject unto chaunge.
Say, my faire brother, now, if this device
Doth like you, or may you to like entice.'

'Surely,' said th' Ape, 'it likes me wondrous
    well;
And would ye not poore fellowship expell,
My selfe would offer you t' accompanie
In this adventures chauncefull jeopardie.
For to wexe olde at home in idlenesse
Is disadventrous, and quite fortunelesse: 100
Abroad, where change is, good may gotten
    bee.'
The Foxe was glad, and quickly did agree:
So both resolv'd, the morrow next ensuing,
So soone as day appeard to peoples vewing,
On their intended journey to proceede;
And over night, whatso theretoo did neede
Each did prepare, in readines to bee.
The morrow next, so soone as one might
    see
Light out of heavens windowes forth to
    looke,
Both their habiliments unto them tooke, 110
And put themselves (a Gods name) on their
    way.
Whenas the Ape, beginning well to wey
This hard adventure, thus began t' advise:
'Now read, Sir Reynold, as ye be right
    wise,
What course ye weene is best for us to
    take,
That for our selves we may a living make.
Whether shall we professe some trade or
    skill?
Or shall we varie our device at will,
Even as new occasion appeares?
Or shall we tie our selves for certaine
    yeares   120
To anie service, or to anie place?
For it behoves, ere that into the race
We enter, to resolve first hereupon.'
'Now surely, brother,' said the Foxe anon,
'Ye have this matter motioned in season:
For everie thing that is begun with reason
Will come by readie meanes unto his end;
But things miscounselled must needs mis-
    wend.
Thus therefore I advize upon the case:
That not to anie certaine trade or place, 130
Nor anie man, we should our selves applie;
For why should he that is at libertie
Make himselfe bond? Sith then we are
    free borne,
Let us all servile base subjection scorne;
And as we bee sonnes of the world so wide,
Let us our fathers heritage divide,
And chalenge to our selves our portions dew
Of all the patrimonie, which a few   138

Now hold in hugger mugger in their hand,
And all the rest doo rob of good and land.
For now a few have all, and all have nought,
Yet all be brethren ylike dearly bought.
There is no right in this partition,
Ne was it so by institution
Ordained first, ne by the law of Nature,
But that she gave like blessing to each
    creture,
As well of worldly livelode as of life,
That there might be no difference nor strife,
Nor ought cald mine or thine: thrice happie
    then
Was the condition of mortall men.   150
That was the golden age of Saturne old,
But this might better be the world of gold:
For without golde now nothing wilbe got.
Therefore (if please you) this shalbe our
    plot:
We will not be of anie occupation;
Let such vile vassalls, borne to base voca-
    tion,
Drudge in the world, and for their living
    droyle,
Which have no wit to live withouten toyle.
But we will walke about the world at plea-
    sure,
Like two free men, and make our ease a
    treasure.   160
Free men some beggers call; but they be
    free,
And they which call them so more beggers
    bee:
For they doo swinke and sweate to feed the
    other,
Who live like lords of that which they doo
    gather,
And yet doo never thanke them for the
    same,
But as their due by nature doo it clame.
Such will we fashion both our selves to bee,
Lords of the world, and so will wander free
Where so us listeth, uncontrol'd of anie.
Hard is our hap, if we (emongst so manie)
Light not on some that may our state
    amend;   171
Sildome but some good commeth ere the
    end.'
Well seemd the Ape to like this ordinaunce:
Yet, well considering of the circumstaunce,
As pausing in great doubt, awhile he staid,
And afterwards with grave advizement
    said:
' I cannot, my lief brother, like but well
The purpose of the complot which ye tell:

For well I wot (compar'd to all the rest
Of each degree) that beggers life is best:
And they that thinke themselves the best
    of all   181
Oft-times to begging are content to fall.
But this I wot withall, that we shall ronne
Into great daunger, like to bee undonne,
Thus wildly to wander in the worlds eye,
Without pasport or good warrantie,
For feare least we like rogues should be re-
    puted,
And for eare marked beasts abroad be
    bruted.
Therefore I read that we our counsells
    call,
How to prevent this mischiefe ere it fall,
And how we may, with most securitie,   191
Beg amongst those that beggers doo defie.'
' Right well, deere gossip, ye advized
    have,'
Said then the Foxe, 'but I this doubt will
    save:
For ere we farther passe, I will devise
A pasport for us both in fittest wize,
And by the names of souldiers us protect;
That now is thought a civile begging
    sect.
Be you the souldier, for you likest are
For manly semblance, and small skill in
    warre: 200
I will but wayte on you, and, as occasion
Falls out, my selfe fit for the same will
    fashion.'
The pasport ended, both they forward
    went;
The Ape clad souldierlike, fit for th' in-
    tent,
In a blew jacket with a crosse of redd
And manie slits, as if that he had shedd
Much blood throgh many wounds therein
    receaved,
Which had the use of his right arme be-
    reaved.
Upon his head an old Scotch cap he wore,
With a plume feather all to peeces tore:
His breeches were made after the new
    cut,   211
Al Portugese, loose like an emptie gut;
And his hose broken high above the heel-
    ing,
And his shooes beaten out with traveling.
But neither sword nor dagger he did
    beare;
Seemes that no foes revengement he did
    feare:

In stead of them a handsome bat he held,
On which he leaned, as one farre in elde.
Shame light on him, that through so false illusion
Doth turne the name of souldiers to abu-
    sion,   220
And that, which is the noblest mysterie,
Brings to reproach and common infamie.
Long they thus travailed, yet never met
Adventure, which might them a working set:
Yet manie waies they sought, and manie tryed;
Yet for their purposes none fit espyed.
At last they chaunst to meete upon the way
A simple Husbandman in garments gray;
Yet, though his vesture were but meane and bace,
A good yeoman he was of honest place,   230
And more for thrift did care than for gay clothing:
Gay without good is good hearts greatest loathing.
The Foxe, him spying, bad the Ape him dight
To play his part, for loe! he was in sight
That (if he er'd not) should them enter-
    taine,
And yeeld them timely profite for their paine.
Eftsoones the Ape himselfe gan up to reare,
And on his shoulders high his bat to beare,
As if good service he were fit to doo;
But little thrift for him he did it too: 240
And stoutly forward he his steps did straine,
That like a handsome swaine it him be-
    came.
When as they nigh approached, that good man,
Seeing them wander loosly, first began
T' enquire, of custome, what and whence they were.
To whom the Ape: 'I am a souldiere,
That late in warres have spent my deerest blood,
And in long service lost both limbs and good;
And now, constrain'd that trade to over-
    give,
I driven am to seeke some meanes to live: 250
Which might it you in pitie please t' af-
    ford,
I would be readie, both in deed and word,

To doo you faithfull service all my dayes.
This yron world' (that same he weeping sayes)
'Brings downe the stowtest hearts to lowest state:
For miserie doth bravest mindes abate,
And make them seeke for that they wont to scorne,
Of fortune and of hope at once forlorne.'
The honest man, that heard him thus com-
    plaine,
Was griev'd, as he had felt part of his paine;   260
And, well disposd' him some reliefe to showe,
Askt if in husbandrie he ought did knowe,
To plough, to plant, to reap, to rake, to sowe,
To hedge, to ditch, to thrash, to thetch, to mowe;
Or to what labour els he was prepar'd:
For husbands life is labourous and hard.
Whenas the Ape him hard so much to talke
Of labour, that did from his liking balke,
He would have slipt the coller handsomly,
And to him said: 'Good sir, full glad am I   270
To take what paines may anie living wight:
But my late maymed limbs lack wonted might
To doo their kindly services, as needeth:
Scarce this right hand the mouth with diet feedeth;
So that it may no painfull worke endure,
Ne to strong labour can it selfe enure.
But if that anie other place you have,
Which askes small paines, but thriftines to save,
Or care to overlooke, or trust to gather,
Ye may me trust as your owne ghostly father.'   280
With that the Husbandman gan him avize,
That it for him were fittest exercise
Cattell to keep, or grounds to oversee;
And asked him, if he could willing bee
To keep his sheep, or to attend his swyne,
Or watch his mares, or take his charge of kyne.
'Gladly,' said he, 'what ever such like paine
Ye put on me, I will the same sustaine:
But gladliest I of your fleecie sheepe
(Might it you please) would take on me the keep.   290

For ere that unto armes I me betooke,
Unto my fathers sheepe I usde to looke,
That yet the skill thereof I have not loste:
Thereto right well this curdog by my coste '
(Meaning the Foxe) ' will serve, my sheepe
    to gather,
And drive to follow after their belwether.'
The Husbandman was meanly well con-
    tent,
Triall to make of his endevourment,
And home him leading, lent to him the
    charge
Of all his flocke, with libertie full large, 300
Giving accompt of th' annuall increce
Both of their lambes, and of their woolley
    fleece.
Thus is this Ape become a shepheard
    swaine,
And the false Foxe his dog: (God give
    them paine)
For ere the yeare have halfe his course
    out-run,
And doo returne from whence he first
    begun,
They shall him make an ill accompt of
    thrift.
Now whenas Time, flying with winges swift,
Expired had the terme, that these two
    javels
Should render up a reckning of their
    travels   310
Unto their master, which it of them sought,
Exceedingly they troubled were in thought,
Ne wist what answere unto him to frame,
Ne how to scape great punishment, or
    shame,
For their false treason and vile theeverie.
For not a lambe of all their flockes sup-
    ply
Had they to shew; but ever as they bred,
They slue them, and upon their fleshes
    fed:
For that disguised dog lov'd blood to spill,
And drew the wicked shepheard to his
    will.   320
So twixt them both they not a lambkin
    left,
And when lambes fail'd, the old sheepes
    lives they reft;
That how t' acquite themselves unto their
    lord
They were in doubt, and flatly set abord.
The Foxe then counsel'd th' Ape for to re-
    quire
Respite till morrow t' answere his desire:

For times delay new hope of helpe still
    breeds.
The goodman granted, doubting nought
    their deeds,
And bad, next day that all should readie be.
But they more subtill meaning had than
    he: 330
For the next morrowes meed they closely
    ment,
For feare of afterclaps, for to prevent:
And that same evening, when all shrowded
    were
In careles sleep, they, without care or
    feare,
Cruelly fell upon their flock in folde,
And of them slew at pleasure what they
    wolde:
Of which whenas they feasted had their
    fill,
For a full complement of all their ill,
They stole away, and tooke their hastie
    flight,   339
Carried in clowdes of all-concealing night.
So was the Husbandman left to his losse,
And they unto their fortunes change to
    tosse.
After which sort they wandered long
    while,
Abusing manie through their cloaked guile:
That at the last they gan to be descryed
Of everie one, and all their sleights es-
    pyed:
So as their begging now them failed quyte;
For none would give, but all men would
    them wyte.
Yet would they take no paines to get their
    living,
But seeke some other way to gaine by
    giving,   350
Much like to begging, but much better
    named;
For manie beg, which are thereof ashamed.
And now the Foxe had gotten him a gowne,
And th' Ape a cassocke sidelong hanging
    downe;
For they their occupation meant to change,
And now in other state abroad to range:
For since their souldiers pas no better
    spedd,
They forg'd another, as for clerkes booke-
    redd,
Who passing foorth, as their adventures
    fell,
Through manie haps, which needs not here
    to tell,   360

At length chaunst with a formall Priest to
    meete,
Whom they in civill manner first did greete,
And after askt an almes for Gods deare
    love.
The man straight way his choler up did
    move,
And with reproachfull tearmes gan them
    revile,
For following that trade so base and vile;
And askt what license or what pas they
    had.
' Ah ! ' said the Ape, as sighing wondrous
    sad,
' Its an hard case, when men of good de-
    serving
Must either driven be perforce to sterving,
Or asked for their pas by everie squib, 371
That list at will them to revile or snib:
And yet (God wote) small oddes I often
    see
Twixt them that aske, and them that asked
    bee.
Natheles because you shall not us mis-
    deeme,
But that we are as honest as we seeme,
Yee shall our pasport at your pleasure see,
And then ye will (I hope) well mooved bee.'
Which when the Priest beheld, he vew'd it
    nere,
As if therein some text he studying were,
But little els (God wote) could thereof
    skill: 381
For read he could not evidence nor will,
Ne tell a written word, ne write a letter,
Ne make one title worse, ne make one
    better.
Of such deep learning little had he neede,
Ne yet of Latine, ne of Greeke, that
    breede
Doubts mongst divines, and difference of
    texts,
From whence arise diversitie of sects,
And hatefull heresies, of God abhor'd.
But this good Sir did follow the plaine
    word,   390
Ne medled with their controversies vaine:
All his care was, his service well to saine,
And to read homelies upon holidayes;
When that was done, he might attend his
    playes:
An easie life, and fit High God to please.
He, having overlookt their pas at ease,
Gan at the length them to rebuke againe,
That no good trade of life did entertaine,

But lost their time in wandring loose
    abroad;
Seeing the world, in which they bootles
    boad,   400
Had wayes enough for all therein to live;
Such grace did God unto his creatures
    give.
Said then the Foxe: ' Who hath the world
    not tride
From the right way full eath may wander
    wide.
We are but novices, new come abroad,
We have not yet the tract of anie troad,
Nor on us taken anie state of life,
But readie are of anie to make preife.
Therefore might please you, which the
    world have proved,
Us to advise, which forth but lately moved,
Of some good course, that we might under-
    take,   411
Ye shall for ever us your bondmen make.'
The Priest gan wexe halfe proud to be so
    praide,
And thereby willing to affoord them aide;
' It seemes,' said he, ' right well that ye be
    clerks,
Both by your wittie words and by your
    werks.
Is not that name enough to make a living
To him that hath a whit of Natures giv-
    ing ?
How manie honest men see ye arize
Daylie thereby, and grow to goodly prize ?
To deanes, to archdeacons, to commissar-
    ies,   421
To lords, to principalls, to prebendaries;
All jolly prelates, worthie rule to beare,
Who ever them envie: yet spite bites neare.
Why should ye doubt, then, but that ye like-
    wise
Might unto some of those in time arise?
In the meane time to live in good estate,
Loving that love, and hating those that hate·
Being some honest curate, or some vicker,
Content with little in condition sicker.' 430
' Ah ! but,' said th' Ape, ' the charge is
    wondrous great,
To feed mens soules, and hath an heavie
    threat.'
' To feede mens soules,' quoth he, ' is not in
    man:
For they must feed themselves, doo what
    we can.
We are but charg'd to lay the meate before:
Eate they that list, we need to doo no more.

But God it is that feedes them with his
    grace,
The bread of life powr'd downe from hea-
    venly place.
Therefore said he, that with the budding rod
Did rule the Jewes, *All shalbe taught of
    God.*   440
That same hath Jesus Christ now to him
    raught,
By whom the flock is rightly fed and taught:
He is the shepheard, and the priest is hee;
We but his shepheard swaines ordain'd to
    bee.
Therefore herewith doo not your selfe dis-
    may;
Ne is the paines so great, but beare ye may;
For not so great, as it was wont of yore,
It 's now a dayes, ne halfe so streight and
    sore.
They whilome used duly everie day
Their service and their holie things to say,
At morne and even, besides their anthemes
    sweete,   451
Their penie masses, and their complynes
    meete,
Their dirges, their trentals, and their shrifts,
Their memories, their singings, and their
    gifts.
Now all those needlesse works are laid
    away;
Now once a weeke, upon the Sabbath day,
It is enough to doo our small devotion,
And then to follow any merrie motion.
Ne are we tyde to fast, but when we list,
Ne to weare garments base of wollen
    twist,   460
But with the finest silkes us to aray,
That before God we may appeare more gay,
Resembling Aarons glorie in his place:
For farre unfit it is, that person bace
Should with vile cloaths approach Gods
    majestie,
Whom no uncleannes may approachen nie:
Or that all men, which anie master serve,
Good garments for their service should de-
    serve,
But he that serves the Lord of Hoasts Most
    High,
And that in highest place, t' approach him
    nigh,   470
And all the peoples prayers to present
Before his throne, as on ambassage sent
Both too and fro, should not deserve to
    weare
A garment better than of wooll or heare.

Beside, we may have lying by our sides
Our lovely lasses, or bright shining brides:
We be not tyde to wilfull chastitie,
But have the gospell of free libertie.'
By that he ended had his ghostly sermon,
The Foxe was well induc'd to be a parson;
And of the Priest eftsoones gan to enquire,
How to a benefice he might aspire.   482
'Marie, there,' said the Priest, 'is arte in-
    deed:
Much good deep learning one thereout may
    reed;
For that the ground-worke is, and end of
    all,
How to obtaine a beneficiall.
First therefore, when ye have in handsome
    wise
Your selfe attyred, as you can devise,
Then to some noble man your selfe applye,
Or other great one in the worldes eye,   490
That hath a zealous disposition
To God, and so to his religion.
There must thou fashion eke a godly zeale,
Such as no carpers may contrayre reveale:
For each thing fained ought more warie
    bee.
There thou must walke in sober gravitee,
And seeme as saintlike as Saint Radegund:
Fast much, pray oft, looke lowly on the
    ground,
And unto everie one doo curtesie meeke:
These lookes (nought saying) doo a bene-
    fice seeke,   500
And be thou sure one not to lacke or long.
But if thee list unto the court to throng,
And there to hunt after the hoped pray,
Then must thou thee dispose another way:
For there thou needs must learne to laugh,
    to lie,
To face, to forge, to scoffe, to companie,
To crouche, to please, to be a beetle stock
Of thy great masters will, to scorne, or
    mock:
So maist thou chaunce mock out a benefice,
Unlesse thou canst one conjure by device,
Or cast a figure for a bishoprick: 511
And if one could, it were but a schoole
    trick.
These be the wayes, by which without re-
    ward
Livings in court be gotten, though full hard.
For nothing there is done without a fee:
The courtier needes must recompenced bee
With a benevolence, or have in gage
The primitias of your parsonage:

Scarse can a bishoprick forpas them by,
But that it must be gelt in privitie.   520
Doo not thou therefore seeke a living there,
But of more private persons seeke els-
     where,
Whereas thou maist compound a better
     penie,
Ne let thy learning question'd be of anie.
For some good gentleman, that hath the
     right
Unto his church for to present a wight,
Will cope with thee in reasonable wise;
That if the living yerely doo arise
To fortie pound, that then his yongest sonne
Shall twentie have, and twentie thou hast
     wonne: 530
Thou hast it wonne, for it is of franke gift,
And he will care for all the rest to shift;
Both that the bishop may admit of thee,
And that therein thou maist maintained bee.
This is the way for one that is unlern'd
Living to get, and not to be discern'd.
But they that are great clerkes have nearer
     wayes,
For learning sake to living them to raise:
Yet manie eke of them (God wote) are
     driven,
T' accept a benefice in peeces riven.   540
How saist thou (friend) have I not well dis-
     courst
Upon this common place (though plaine,
     not wourst)?
Better a short tale than a bad long shriving.
Needes anie more to learne to get a living?'
'Now sure, and by my hallidome,' quoth he,
'Ye a great master are in your degree:
Great thankes I yeeld you for your dis-
     cipline,
And doo not doubt, but duly to encline
My wits theretoo, as ye shall shortly heare.'
The Priest him wisht good speed, and well
     to fare.   550
So parted they, as eithers way them led.
But th' Ape and Foxe ere long so well them
     sped,
Through the Priests holesome counsell
     lately tought,
And throgh their own faire handling wisely
     wroght,
That they a benefice twixt them obtained;
And craftie Reynold was a priest ordained,
And th' Ape his parish clarke procur'd to
     bee.
Then made they reveil route and goodly
     glee.   558

But ere long time had passed, they so ill
Did order their affaires, that th' evill will
Of all their parishners they had constraind;
Who to the ordinarie of them complain'd,
How fowlie they their offices abusd',
And them of crimes and heresies accusd';
That pursivants he often for them sent:
But they neglected his commaundement.
So long persisted obstinate and bolde,
Till at the length he published to holde
A visitation, and them cyted thether:
Then was high time their wits about to
     geather.   570
What did they then, but made a composition
With their next neighbor priest, for light
     condition,
To whom their living they resigned quight
For a few pence, and ran away by night.
So passing through the countrey in disguize,
They fled farre off, where none might them
     surprize,
And after that long straied here and there,
Through everie field and forrest farre and
     nere;
Yet never found occasion for their tourne,
But, almost sterv'd, did much lament and
     mourne.   580
At last they chaunst to meete upon the way
The Mule, all deckt in goodly rich aray,
With bells and bosses, that full lowdly rung,
And costly trappings, that to ground downe
     hung.
Lowly they him saluted in meeke wise;
But he through pride and fatnes gan despise
Their meanesse; scarce vouchsafte them to
     requite.
Whereat the Foxe deep groning in his sprite,
Said: 'Ah, Sir Mule! now blessed be the
     day,
That I see you so goodly and so gay   590
In your attyres, and eke your silken hyde
Fil'd with round flesh, that everie bone
     doth hide.
Seemes that in fruitfull pastures ye doo live,
Or Fortune doth you secret favour give.'
'Foolish Foxe!' said the Mule, 'thy
     wretched need
Praiseth the thing that doth thy sorrow
     breed.
For well I weene, thou canst not but envie
My wealth, compar'd to thine owne mis-
     erie,
That art so leane and meagre waxen late,
That scarse thy legs uphold thy feeble
     gate.'   600

' Ay me ! ' said then the Foxe, ' whom evill
     hap
Unworthy in such wretchednes doth wrap,
And makes the scorne of other beasts to
     bee.
But read (faire sir, of grace) from whence
     come yee ?
Or what of tidings you abroad doo heare ?
Newes may perhaps some good unweeting
     beare.'
' From royall court I lately came,' said
     he,
' Where all the braverie that eye may see,
And all the happinesse that heart desire,
Is to be found; he nothing can admire,   610
That hath not seene that heavens portrac-
     ture:
But tidings there is none, I you assure,
Save that which common is, and knowne to
     all,
That courtiers as the tide doo rise and fall.'
' But tell us,' said the Ape, ' we doo you
     pray,
Who now in court doth beare the greatest
     sway:
That, if such fortune doo to us befall,
We may seeke favour of the best of all.'
' Marie,' said he, ' the highest now in grace,
Be the wilde beasts, that swiftest are in
     chase;   620
For in their speedie course and nimble
     flight
The Lyon now doth take the most delight:
But chieflie joyes on foote them to beholde,
Enchaste with chaine and circulet of golde.
So wilde a beast so tame ytaught to bee,
And buxome to his bands, is joy to see;
So well his golden circlet him beseemeth:
But his late chayne his Liege unmeete es-
     teemeth;
For so brave beasts she loveth best to see
In the wilde forrest raunging fresh and
     free.   630
Therefore if fortune thee in court to live,
In case thou ever there wilt hope to thrive,
To some of these thou must thy selfe
     apply:
Els as a thistle-downe in th' ayre doth flie,
So vainly shalt thou too and fro be tost,
And loose thy labour and thy fruitles cost.
And yet full few which follow them, I see,
For vertues bare regard advaunced bee,
But either for some gainfull benefit,
Or that they may for their owne turnes be
     fit.   640

Nath'les, perhaps ye things may handle soe,
That ye may better thrive than thousands
     moe.'
' But,' said the Ape, ' how shall we first
     come in,
That after we may favour seeke to win ? '
' How els,' said he, ' but with a good bold
     face,
And with big words, and with a stately
     pace,
That men may thinke of you, in generall,
That to be in you, which is not at all:
For not by that which is, the world now
     deemeth,
(As it was wont) but by that same that
     seemeth.   650
Ne do I doubt, but that ye well can fashion
Your selves theretoo, according to occa-
     sion:
So fare ye well; good courtiers may ye
     bee.'
So, proudlie neighing, from them parted
     hee.
Then gan this craftie couple to devize,
How for the court themselves they might
     aguize:
For thither they themselves meant to ad-
     dresse,
In hope to finde there happier successe.
So well they shifted, that the Ape anon
Himselfe had cloathed like a gentleman,   660
And the slie Foxe, as like to be his groome;
That to the court in seemly sort they come.
Where the fond Ape, himselfe uprearing hy
Upon his tiptoes, stalketh stately by,
As if he were some great magnifico,
And boldlie doth amongst the boldest go;
And his man Reynold, with fine counterfe-
     saunce,
Supports his credite and his countenaunce.
Then gan the courtiers gaze on everie side,
And stare on him, with big lookes basen
     wide,   670
Wondring what mister wight he was, and
     whence:
For he was clad in strange accoustrements,
Fashion'd with queint devises never seene
In court before, yet there all fashions beene:
Yet he them in newfanglenesse did pas.
But his behaviour altogether was
Alla Turchesca, much the more admyr'd,
And his lookes loftie, as if he aspyr'd
To dignitie, and sdeign'd the low degree;
That all which did such strangenesse in
     him see   680

By secrete meanes gan of his state enquire,
And privily his servant thereto hire:
Who, throughly arm'd against such cover-
ture,
Reported unto all, that he was sure
A noble gentleman of high regard,
Which through the world had with long
travel far'd,
And seene the manners of all beasts on
ground;
Now here arriv'd, to see if like he found.
Thus did the Ape at first him credit gaine,
Which afterwards he wisely did maintaine
With gallant showe, and daylie more aug-
ment   691
Through his fine feates and courtly com-
plement;
For he could play, and daunce, and vaute,
and spring,
And all that els pertaines to reveling,
Onely through kindly aptnes of his joynts.
Besides he could doo manie other poynts,
The which in court him served to good
stead:
For he mongst ladies could their fortunes
read
Out of their hands, and merie leasings
tell,
And juggle finely, that became him well:
But he so light was at legier demaine,   701
That what he toucht came not to light
againe;
Yet would he laugh it out, and proudly
looke,
And tell them that they greatly him mis-
tooke.
So would he scoffe them out with mockerie,
For he therein had great felicitie;
And with sharp quips joy'd others to deface,
Thinking that their disgracing did him
grace:
So whilst that other like vaine wits he
pleased
And made to laugh, his heart was greatly
eased.
But the right gentle minde would bite his   710
lip,
To heare the javell so good men to nip:
For though the vulgar yeeld an open eare,
And common courtiers love to gybe and
fleare
At everie thing, which they heare spoken
ill,
And the best speaches with ill meaning
spill;

Yet the brave courtier, in whose beauteous
thought
Regard of honour harbours more than
ought,
Doth loath such base condition, to backbite
Anies good name for envie or despite.   720
He stands on tearmes of honourable minde,
Ne will be carried with the common winde
Of courts inconstant mutabilitie,
Ne after everie tattling fable flie;
But heares and sees the follies of the rest,
And thereof gathers for himselfe the best.
He will not creepe, nor crouche with
fained face,
But walkes upright with comely stedfast
pace,
And unto all doth yeeld due curtesie;
But not with kissed hand belowe the
knee,   730
As that same apish crue is wont to doo:
For he disdaines himselfe t' embase there-
too.
He hates fowle leasings, and vile flatterie,
Two filthie blots in noble gentrie;
And lothefull idlenes he doth detest,
The canker worme of everie gentle brest;
The which to banish with faire exercise
Of knightly feates, he daylie doth devise:
Now menaging the mouthes of stubborne
steedes,
Now practising the proofe of warlike
deedes,
Now his bright armes assaying, now his   740
speare,
Now the nigh aymed ring away to beare:
At other times he casts to sew the chace
Of swift wilde beasts, or runne on foote a
race,
T' enlarge his breath (large breath in
armes most needfull)
Or els by wrestling to wex strong and
heedfull,
Or his stiffe armes to stretch with eughen
bowe,
And manly legs, still passing too and fro,
Without a gowned beast him fast beside;
A vaine ensample of the Persian pride,   750
Who after he had wonne th' Assyrian foe,
Did ever after scorne on foote to goe.
Thus when this courtly gentleman with
toyle
Himselfe hath wearied, he doth recoyle
Unto his rest, and there with sweete de-
light
Of musicks skill revives his toyled spright;

Or els with loves and ladies gentle sports,
The joy of youth, himselfe he recomforts:
Or lastly, when the bodie list to pause,
His minde unto the Muses he withdrawes;
Sweete Ladie Muses, ladies of delight,   761
Delights of life, and ornaments of light:
With whom he close confers, with wise
    discourse,
Of Natures workes, of heavens continuall
    course,
Of forreine lands, of people different,
Of kingdomes change, of divers govern-
    ment,
Of dreadfull battailes of renowmed knights;
With which he kindleth his ambitious
    sprights
To like desire and praise of noble fame,
The onely upshot whereto he doth ayme.
For all his minde on honour fixed is,   771
To which he levels all his purposis,
And in his princes service spends his dayes,
Not so much for to gaine, or for to raise
Himselfe to high degree, as for his grace,
And in his liking to winne worthie place,
Through due deserts and comely carriage,
In whatso please employ his personage,
That may be matter meete to gaine him
    praise;
For he is fit to use in all assayes,   780
Whether for armes and warlike amenaunce,
Or else for wise and civill governaunce.
For he is practiz'd well in policie,
And thereto doth his courting most applie:
To learne the enterdeale of princes strange,
To marke th' intent of counsells, and the
    change
Of states, and eke of private men some-
    while,
Supplanted by fine falshood and faire guile;
Of all the which he gathereth what is fit
T' enrich the storehouse of his powerfull
    wit,   790
Which through wise speaches and grave
    conference
He daylie eekes, and brings to excellence.
Such is the rightfull courtier in his kinde:
But unto such the Ape lent not his minde;
Such were for him no fit companions,
Such would descrie his lewd conditions:
But the yong lustie gallants he did chose
To follow, meete to whom he might dis-
    close
His witlesse pleasance and ill pleasing vaine.
A thousand wayes he them could enter-
    taine,   800

With all the thriftles games that may be
    found;
With mumming and with masking all
    around,
With dice, with cards, with balliards farre
    unfit,
With shuttelcocks, misseeming manlie wit,
With courtizans, and costly riotize,
Whereof still somewhat to his share did
    rize:
Ne, them to pleasure, would he sometimes
    scorne
A pandares coate (so basely was he borne);
Thereto he could fine loving verses frame,
And play the poet oft. But ah! for shame,
Let not sweete poets praise, whose onely
    pride   811
Is vertue to advaunce, and vice deride,
Be with the worke of losels wit defamed,
Ne let such verses poetrie be named.
Yet he the name on him would rashly take,
Maugre the sacred Muses, and it make
A servant to the vile affection
Of such as he depended most upon,
And with the sugrie sweete thereof allure
Chast ladies eares to fantasies impure.   820
To such delights the noble wits he led
Which him reliev'd, and their vaine humours
    fed
With fruitles follies and unsound delights.
But if perhaps into their noble sprights
Desire of honor or brave thought of armes
Did ever creepe, then with his wicked
    charmes
And strong conceipts he would it drive
    away,
Ne suffer it to house there halfe a day.
And whenso love of letters did inspire
Their gentle wits, and kindly wise desire,   830
That chieflie doth each noble minde adorne,
Then he would scoffe at learning, and eke
    scorne
The sectaries thereof, as people base
And simple men, which never came in
    place
Of worlds affaires, but, in darke corners
    mewd,
Muttred of matters, as their bookes them
    shewd,
Ne other knowledge ever did attaine,
But with their gownes their gravitie main-
    taine.
From them he would his impudent lewde
    speach
Against Gods holie ministers oft reach,   840

And mocke divines and their profession:
What else then did he by progression,
But mocke High God himselfe, whom they
   professe ?
But what car'd he for God, or godlinesse ?
All his care was himselfe how to advaunce,
And to uphold his courtly countenaunce
By all the cunning meanes he could devise;
Were it by honest wayes, or otherwise,
He made small choyce: yet sure his honestie
Got him small gaines, but shameles flat-
   terie,   850
And filthie brocage, and unseemly shifts,
And borowe base, and some good ladies gifts:
But the best helpe, which chiefly him sus-
   tain'd,
Was his man Raynolds purchase which he
   gain'd.
For he was school'd by kinde in all the skill
Of close conveyance, and each practise ill
Of coosinage and cleanly knaverie,
Which oft maintain'd his masters braverie.
Besides, he usde another slipprie slight,
In taking on himselfe, in common sight, 860
False personages fit for everie sted,
With which he thousands cleanly coosined:
Now like a merchant, merchants to deceave,
With whom his credite he did often leave
In gage, for his gay masters hopelesse dett:
Now like a lawyer, when he land would lett,
Or sell fee-simples in his masters name,
Which he had never, nor ought like the same:
Then would he be a broker, and draw in
Both wares and money, by exchange to
   win: 870
Then would he seeme a farmer, that would
   sell
Bargaines of woods, which he did lately fell,
Or corne, or cattle, or such other ware,
Thereby to coosin men not well aware;
Of all the which there came a secret fee
To th' Ape, that he his countenaunce might
   bee.
Besides all this, he usd' oft to beguile
Poore suters, that in court did haunt some
   while:
For he would learne their busines secretly,
And then informe his master hastely,   880
That he by meanes might cast them to pre-
   vent,
And beg the sute the which the other ment.
Or otherwise false Reynold would abuse
The simple suter, and wish him to chuse
His master, being one of great regard
In court, to compas anie sute not hard,

In case his paines were recompenst with
   reason:
So would he worke the silly man by trea-
   son
To buy his masters frivolous good will,
That had not power to doo him good or
   ill.   890
So pitifull a thing is suters state.
Most miserable man, whom wicked fate
Hath brought to court, to sue for had ywist,
That few have found, and manie one hath
   mist !
Full little knowest thou that hast not tride,
What hell it is, in suing long to bide:
To loose good dayes, that might be better
   spent;
To wast long nights in pensive discontent;
To speed to day, to be put back to morrow;
To feed on hope, to pine with feare and
   sorrow;   900
To have thy Princes grace, yet want her
   Peeres;
To have thy asking, yet waite manie yeeres;
To fret thy soule with crosses and with
   cares;
To eate thy heart through comfortlesse
   dispaires;
To fawne, to crowche, to waite, to ride, to
   ronne,
To spend, to give, to want, to be undonne.
Unhappie wight, borne to desastrous end,
That doth his life in so long tendance
   spend !
Who ever leaves sweete home, where meane
   estate
In safe assurance, without strife or hate, 910
Findes all things needfull for contentment
   meeke,
And will to court, for shadowes vaine to
   seeke,
Or hope to gaine, himselfe will a daw trie:
That curse God send unto mine enemie !
For none but such as this bold Ape unblest
Can ever thrive in that unluckie quest;
Or such as hath a Reynold to his man,
That by his shifts his master furnish can.
But yet this Foxe could not so closely hide
His craftie feates, but that they were de-
   scride   920
At length, by such as sate in justice seate,
Who for the same him fowlie did entreate;
And having worthily him punished,
Out of the court for ever banished.
And now the Ape, wanting his huckster man,
That wont provide his necessaries, gan

To growe into great lacke, ne could up-
   holde
His countenaunce in those his garments
   olde;
Ne new ones could he easily provide,
Though all men him unceased gan deride,
Like as a puppit placed in a play,   931
Whose part once past all men bid take away:
So that he driven was to great distresse,
And shortly brought to hopelesse wretch-
   ednesse.
Then, closely as he might, he cast to leave
The court, not asking any passe or leave;
But ran away in his rent rags by night,
Ne ever stayd in place, ne spake to wight,
Till that the Foxe, his copesmate, he had
   found;
To whome complayning his unhappy
   stound,   940
At last againe with him in travell joynd,
And with him far'd some better chaunce
   to fynde.
So in the world long time they wandered,
And mickle want and hardnesse suffered;
That them repented much so foolishly
To come so farre to seeke for misery,
And leave the sweetnes of contented home,
Though eating hipps and drinking watry
   fome.
Thus as they them complayned too and fro,
Whilst through the forest rechlesse they
   did goe,   950
Lo! where they spide, how in a gloomy
   glade
The Lyon sleeping lay in secret shade,
His crowne and scepter lying him beside,
And having doft for heate his dreadfull
   hide:
Which when they sawe, the Ape was sore
   afrayde,
And would have fled with terror all dis-
   mayde.
But him the Foxe with hardy words did
   stay,
And bad him put all cowardize away:
For now was time (if ever they would
   hope)
To ayme their counsels to the fairest
   scope,   960
And them for ever highly to advaunce,
In case the good, which their owne happie
   chaunce
Them freely offred, they would wisely take.
Scarse could the Ape yet speake, so did he
   quake:

Yet, as he could, he askt how good might
   growe,
Where nought but dread and death do
   seeme in show.
'Now,' sayd he, 'whiles the Lyon sleepeth
   sound,
May we his crowne and mace take from
   the ground,
And eke his skinne, the terror of the wood,
Wherewith we may our selves (if we thinke
   good)   970
Make kings of beasts, and lords of forests
   all,
Subject unto that powre imperiall.'
'Ah! but,' sayd the Ape, 'who is so bold a
   wretch,
That dare his hardy hand to those out-
   stretch,
When as he knowes his meede, if he be
   spide,
To be a thousand deathes, and shame be-
   side?'
'Fond Ape!' sayd then the Foxe, 'into
   whose brest
Never crept thought of honor nor brave
   gest,
Who will not venture life a king to be,
And rather rule and raigne in soveraign
   see,   980
Than dwell in dust inglorious and bace,
Where none shall name the number of his
   place?
One joyous houre in blisfull happines,
I chose before a life of wretchednes.
Be therefore counselled herein by me,
And shake off this vile harted cowardree.
If he awake, yet is not death the next,
For we may coulor it with some pretext
Of this or that, that may excuse the cryme:
Else we may flye; thou to a tree mayst
   clyme,   990
And I creepe under ground; both from his
   reach:
Therefore be rul'd to doo as I doo teach.'
The Ape, that earst did nought but chill
   and quake,
Now gan some courage unto him to take,
And was content to attempt that enterprise,
Tickled with glorie and rash covetise.
But first gan question, whither should as-
   say
Those royall ornaments to steale away.
'Marie, that shall your selfe,' quoth he
   theretoo,
'For ye be fine and nimble it to doo;   1000

Of all the beasts which in the forrests bee
Is not a fitter for this turne than yee:
Therefore, mine owne deare brother, take
    good hart,
And ever thinke a kingdome is your part.'
Loath was the Ape, though praised, to ad-
    venter,
Yet faintly gan into his worke to enter,
Afraid of everie leafe that stir'd him by,
And everie stick that underneath did ly:
Upon his tiptoes nicely he up went,   1009
For making noyse, and still his eare he lent
To everie sound that under heaven blew;
Now went, now stept, now crept, now back-
    ward drew,
That it good sport had been him to have
    eyde.
Yet at the last (so well he him applyde)
Through his fine handling and cleanly play
He all those royall signes had stolne away,
And with the Foxes helpe them borne aside
Into a secret corner unespide.
Whether whenas they came, they fell at
    words,
Whether of them should be the lord of
    lords: 1020
For th' Ape was stryfull and ambicious,
And the Foxe guilefull and most covetous;
That neither pleased was, to have the rayne
Twixt them divided into even twaine,
But either algates would be lord alone:
For love and lordship bide no paragone.
'I am most worthie,' said the Ape, 'sith I
For it did put my life in jeopardie:
Thereto I am in person and in stature
Most like a man, the lord of everie crea-
    ture;   1030
So that it seemeth I was made to raigne,
And borne to be a kingly soveraigne.'
'Nay,' said the Foxe, 'Sir Ape, you are
    astray;
For though to steale the diademe away
Were the worke of your nimble hand, yet I
Did first devise the plot by pollicie;
So that it wholly springeth from my wit:
For which also I claime my selfe more fit
Than you to rule: for government of state
Will without wisedome soone be ruinate.
And where ye claime your selfe for out-
    ward shape   1041
Most like a man, man is not like an ape
In his chiefe parts, that is, in wit and spirite;
But I therein most like to him doo merite,
For my slie wyles and subtill craftinesse,
The title of the kingdome to possesse.

Nath'les (my brother) since we passed
    are
Unto this point, we will appease our jarre;
And I with reason meete will rest content,
That ye shall have both crowne and gov-
    ernment,   1050
Upon condition that ye ruled bee
In all affaires, and counselled by mee;
And that ye let none other ever drawe
Your minde from me, but keepe this as a
    lawe:
And hereupon an oath unto me plight.'
The Ape was glad to end the strife so light,
And thereto swore: for who would not oft
    sweare,
And oft unsweare, a diademe to beare ?
Then freely up those royall spoyles he
    tooke:
Yet at the Lyons skin he inly quooke;   1060
But it dissembled; and upon his head
The crowne, and on his backe the skin, he
    did,
And the false Foxe him helped to array.
Then when he was all dight he tooke his
    way
Into the forest, that he might be seene
Of the wilde beasts in his new glory sheene.
There the two first whome he encountred
    were
The Sheepe and th' Asse, who, striken both
    with feare
At sight of him, gan fast away to flye;
But unto them the Foxe alowd did cry,   1070
And in the kings name bad them both to
    stay,
Upon the payne that thereof follow may.
Hardly naythles were they restrayned so,
Till that the Foxe forth toward them did
    goe,
And there disswaded them from needlesse
    feare,
For that the king did favour to them beare;
And therefore dreadles bad them come to
    corte:
For no wild beasts should do them any
    torte
There or abroad, ne would his Majestye
Use them but well, with gracious clemen-
    cye,   1080
As whome he knew to him both fast and
    true.
So he perswaded them, with homage due
Themselves to humble to the Ape pros-
    trate,
Who, gently to them bowing in his gate,

Receyved them with chearefull entertayne.
Thenceforth proceeding with his princely
	trayne,
He shortly met the Tygre, and the Bore,
Which with the simple Camell raged sore
In bitter words, seeking to take occasion,
Upon his fleshly corpse to make invasion: 1090
But soone as they this mock-king did espy,
Their troublous strife they stinted by and
	by,
Thinking indeed that it the Lyon was.
He then, to prove whether his powre would
	pas
As currant, sent the Foxe to them streight
	way,
Commaunding them their cause of strife
	bewray;
And, if that wrong on eyther side there
	were,
That he should warne the wrenger to ap-
	peare
The morrow next at court, it to defend; 1099
In the meane time upon the king t' attend.
The subtile Foxe so well his message sayd,
That the proud beasts him readily obayd:
Whereby the Ape in wondrous stomack
	woxe,
Strongly encorag'd by the crafty Foxe;
That king indeed himselfe he shortly
	thought,
And all the beasts him feared as they ought,
And followed unto his palaice hye;
Where taking conge, each one by and by
Departed to his home in dreadfull awe,
Full of the feared sight, which late they
	sawe.	1110
The Ape, thus seized of the regall throne,
Eftsones by counsell of the Foxe alone
Gan to provide for all things in assurance,
That so his rule might lenger have endur-
	ance.
First, to his gate he pointed a strong gard,
That none might enter but with issue hard:
Then, for the safegard of his personage,
He did appoint a warlike equipage
Of forreine beasts, not in the forest bred,
But part by land and part by water fed; 1120
For tyrannie is with strange ayde supported.
Then unto him all monstrous beasts resorted
Bred of two kindes, as Griffons, Minotaures,
Crocodiles, Dragons, Beavers, and Cen-
	taures:
With those himselfe he strengthned mighte-
	lie,
That feare he neede no force of enemie.

Then gan he rule and tyrannize at will,
Like as the Foxe did guide his graceles
	skill,
And all wylde beasts made vassals of his
	pleasures,
And with their spoyles enlarg'd his private
	treasures.	1130
No care of justice, nor no rule of reason,
No temperance, nor no regard of season,
Did thenceforth ever enter in his minde,
But crueltie, the signe of currish kinde,
And sdeignfull pride, and wilfull arro-
	gaunce;
Such followes those whom fortune doth ad-
	vaunce.
But the false Foxe most kindly plaid his
	part:
For whatsoever mother wit or arte
Could worke, he put in proofe: no practise
	slie,
No counterpoint of cunning policie,	1140
No reach, no breach, that might him profit
	bring,
But he the same did to his purpose wring.
Nought suffered he the Ape to give or
	graunt,
But through his hand must passe the fiaunt.
All offices, all leases by him lept,
And of them all whatso he likte he kept.
Justice he solde injustice for to buy,
And for to purchase for his progeny.
Ill might it prosper, that ill gotten was,
But, so he got it, little did he pas.	1150
He fed his cubs with fat of all the soyle,
And with the sweete of others sweating
	toyle;
He crammed them with crumbs of bene-
	fices,
And fild their mouthes with meeds of male-
	fices;
He cloathed them with all colours save
	white,
And loded them with lordships and with
	might,
So much as they were able well to beare,
That with the weight their backs nigh
	broken were.
He chaffred chayres in which churchmen
	were set,
And breach of lawes to privie ferme did
	let;	1160
No statute so established might bee,
Nor ordinaunce so needfull, but that hee
Would violate, though not with violence
Yet under colour of the confidence

The which the Ape reposd' in him alone,
And reckned him the kingdomes corner
stone.
And ever, when he ought would bring to
pas,
His long experience the platforme was:
And when he ought not pleasing would put
by,
The cloke was care of thrift, and hus-
bandry,   1170
For to encrease the common treasures store.
But his owne treasure he encreased more,
And lifted up his loftie towres thereby,
That they began to threat the neighbour
sky;
The whiles the princes pallaces fell fast
To ruine, (for what thing can ever last?)
And whilest the other peeres, for povertie,
Were forst their auncient houses to let
lie,
And their olde castles to the ground to fall,
Which their forefathers, famous over
all,   1180
Had founded for the kingdomes ornament,
And for their memories long moniment.
But he no count made of nobilitie,
Nor the wilde beasts whom armes did
glorifie,
The realmes chiefe strength and girlond of
the crowne.
All these through fained crimes he thrust
adowne,
Or made them dwell in darknes of dis-
grace:
For none but whom he list might come in
place.
Of men of armes he had but small regard,
But kept them lowe, and streigned verie
hard.   1190
For men of learning little he esteemed;
His wisedome he above their learning
deemed.
As for the rascall commons, least he cared;
Nor not so common was his bountie shared:
'Let God,' said he, 'if please, care for the
manie,
I for my selfe must care before els anie.'
So did he good to none, to manie ill,
So did he all the kingdome rob and pill,
Yet none durst speake, ne none durst of
him plaine;
So great he was in grace, and rich through
gaine.   1200
Ne would he anie let to have accesse
Unto the prince, but by his owne addresse:

For all that els did come were sure to
faile;
Yet would he further none but for availe.
For on a time the Sheepe, to whom of
yore
The Foxe had promised of friendship store,
What time the Ape the kingdome first did
gaine,
Came to the court, her case there to com-
plaine;
How that the Wolfe, her mortall enemie,
Had sithence slaine her lambe most cruel-
lie;   1210
And therefore crav'd to come unto the
king,
To let him knowe the order of the thing.
'Soft, Gooddie Sheepe!' then said the
Foxe, 'not soe:
Unto the king so rash ye may not goe;
He is with greater matter busied
Than a lambe, or the lambes owne mothers
hed.
Ne certes may I take it well in part,
That ye my cousin Wolfe so fowly thwart,
And seeke with slaunder his good name to
blot:
For there was cause, els doo it he would
not: 1220
Therefore surcease, good dame, and hence
depart.'
So went the Sheepe away with heavie hart;
So manie moe, so everie one was used,
That to give largely to the boxe refused.
Now when high Jove, in whose almightie
hand
The care of kings and power of empires
stand,
Sitting one day within his turret hye,
From whence he vewes with his blacklid-
ded eye
Whatso the heaven in his wide vawte con-
taines,
And all that in the deepest earth re-
maines,   1230
And troubled kingdome of wilde beasts be-
helde,
Whom not their kindly sovereigne did
welde,
But an usurping Ape, with guile suborn'd,
Had all subverst, he sdeignfully it scorn'd
In his great heart, and hardly did refraine
But that with thunder bolts he had him
slaine,
And driven downe to hell, his dewest meed.
But him avizing, he that dreadfull deed

Forbore, and rather chose with scornfull
    shame   1239
Him to avenge, and blot his brutish name
Unto the world, that never after anie
Should of his race be voyd of infamie:
And his false counsellor, the cause of all,
To damne to death, or dole perpetuall,
From whence he never should be quit nor
    stal'd.
Forthwith he Mercurie unto him cal'd,
And bad him flie with never resting speed
Unto the forrest, where wilde beasts doo
    breed,
And there enquiring privily, to learne
What did of late chaunce to the Lyon
    stearne,   1250
That he rul'd not the empire, as he ought;
And whence were all those plaints unto him
    brought
Of wrongs and spoyles by salvage beasts
    committed;
Which done, he bad the Lyon be remitted
Into his seate, and those same treachours
    vile
Be punished for their presumptuous guile.
The sonne of Maia, soone as he receiv'd
That word, streight with his azure wings he
    cleav'd
The liquid clowdes and lucid firmament;
Ne staid, till that he came with steep de-
    scent   1260
Unto the place, where his prescript did
    showe.
There stouping, like an arrowe from a
    bowe,
He soft arrived on the grassie plaine,
And fairly paced forth with easie paine,
Till that unto the pallace nigh he came.
Then gan he to himselfe new shape to frame,
And that faire face, and that ambrosiall
    hew,
Which wonts to decke the gods immortall
    crew,
And beautefie the shinie firmament,
He doft, unfit for that rude rabblement. 1270
So standing by the gates in strange disguize,
He gan enquire of some in secret wize,
Both of the king, and of his government,
And of the Foxe, and his false blandish-
    ment:
And evermore he heard each one complaine
Of foule abuses both in realme and raine:
Which yet to prove more true, he meant to
    see,
And an ey-witnes of each thing to bee.

Tho on his head his dreadfull hat he dight,
Which maketh him invisible in sight,   1280
And mocketh th' eyes of all the lookers on,
Making them thinke it but a vision.
Through power of that, he runnes through
    enemies swerds;
Through power of that, he passeth through
    the herds
Of ravenous wilde beasts, and doth beguile
Their greedie mouthes of the expected
    spoyle;
Through power of that, his cunning theev-
    eries
He wonts to worke, that none the same es-
    pies;
And through the power of that, he putteth
    on
What shape he list in apparition.   1290
That on his head he wore, and in his hand
He tooke Caduceus, his snakie wand,
With which the damned ghosts he gov-
    erneth,
And furies rules, and Tartare tempereth.
With that he causeth sleep to seize the eyes,
And feare the harts of all his enemyes;
And when him list, an universall night
Throughout the world he makes on everie
    wight,
As when his syre with Alcumena lay.
Thus dight, into the court he tooke his
    way,   1300
Both through the gard, which never him
    describe,
And through the watchmen, who him never
    spide:
Thenceforth he past into each secrete part,
Whereas he saw, that sorely griev'd his
    hart,
Each place abounding with fowle injuries,
And fild with treasure rackt with robberies:
Each place defilde with blood of guiltles
    beasts,
Which had been slaine, to serve the Apes
    beheasts;
Gluttonie, malice, pride, and covetize,
And lawlesnes raigning with riotize;   1310
Besides the infinite extortions,
Done through the Foxes great oppressions,
That the complaints thereof could not be
    tolde.
Which when he did with lothfull eyes be-
    holde,
He would no more endure, but came his
    way,
And cast to seeke the Lion, where he may,

That he might worke the avengement for
  this shame
On those two caytives, which had bred him
  blame;
And seeking all the forrest busily,
At last he found where sleeping he did ly.
The wicked weed, which there the Foxe did
  lay,   1321
From underneath his head he tooke away,
And then him waking, forced up to rize.
The Lion, looking up, gan him avize,
As one late in a traunce, what had of long
Become of him: for fantasie is strong.
' Arise,' said Mercurie, ' thou sluggish beast,
That here liest senseles, like the corpse de-
  ceast,
The whilste thy kingdome from thy head
  is rent,
And thy throne royall with dishonour
  blent: 1330
Arise, and doo thy selfe redeeme from
  shame,
And be aveng'd on those that breed thy
  blame.'
Thereat enraged, soone he gan upstart,
Grinding his teeth, and grating his great
  hart,
And, rouzing up himselfe, for his rough
  hide
He gan to reach; but no where it espide.
Therewith he gan full terribly to rore,
And chafte at that indignitie right sore.
But when his crowne and scepter both he
  wanted,
Lord ! how he fum'd, and sweld, and rag'd,
  and panted,   1340
And threatned death and thousand deadly
  dolours
To them that had purloyn'd his princely
  honours !
With that in hast, disroabed as he was,
He toward his owne pallace forth did
  pas;
And all the way he roared as he went,
That all the forrest with astonishment
Thereof did tremble, and the beasts therein
Fled fast away from that so dreadfull din.
At last he came unto his mansion,
Where all the gates he found fast lockt
  anon,   1350
And manie warders round about them stood:
With that he roar'd alowd, as he were
  wood,
That all the pallace quaked at the stound,
As if it quite were riven from the ground,

And all within were dead and hartles left;
And th' Ape himselfe, as one whose wits
  were reft,
Fled here and there, and everie corner
  sought,
To hide himselfe from his owne feared
  thought.
But the false Foxe, when he the Lion heard,
Fled closely forth, streightway of death
  afeard,
And to the Lion came, full lowly creeping, 1360
With fained face, and watrie eyne halfe
  weeping,
T' excuse his former treason and abusion,
And turning all unto the Apes confusion:
Nath'les the royall beast forbore beleeving,
But bad him stay at ease till further preev-
  ing.
Then when he saw no entrance to him
  graunted,
Roaring yet lowder, that all harts it
  daunted,
Upon those gates with force he fiercely
  flewe,
And, rending them in pieces, felly slewe
Those warders strange, and all that els he
  met.   1371
But th' Ape, still flying, he no where might
  get:
From rowme to rowme, from beame to
  beame he fled,
All breathles, and for feare now almost
  ded:
Yet him at last the Lyon spide, and caught,
And forth with shame unto his judgement
  brought.
Then all the beasts he causd' assembled
  bee,
To heare their doome, and sad ensample
  see:
The Foxe, first author of that treacherie,
He did uncase, and then away let flie.   1380
But th' Apes long taile (which then he
  had) he quight
Cut off, and both eares pared of their hight;
Since which, all apes but halfe their eares
  have left,
And of their tailes are utterlie bereft.
So Mother Hubberd her discourse did
  end:
Which pardon me, if I amisse have pend,
For weake was my remembrance it to hold,
And bad her tongue, that it so bluntly
  tolde.

FINIS.

RUINES OF ROME
BY BELLAY

[The *Songe* of Du Bellay, of which the 'Visions of Bellay' are a rendering, forms a kind of appendix to his *Antiquitez de Rome*. Spenser, having had his attention directed to the former, would naturally read also the latter: the result was this other translation, 'Ruins of Rome.' It is difficult to believe that this work is not also of his university days. In the 'Envoy,' to be sure, he refers to the *Sepmaine* of Du Bartas, first published in 1578, but the 'Envoy,' or that part of it, may very well be an afterthought. Both the weight of antecedent probability and the evidence of style would place the translation proper with the two earliest series of 'visions,' those of Bellay and of Petrarch. They are all three much of a piece. As translations in the larger sense, though often resourceful and apt, they can hardly be said to foretell the rare felicity of his later renderings from Tasso. As poetic exercises, however, they show at least the rudiments of that copious ease which is the mark of his maturer style.]

I

Ye heavenly spirites, whose ashie cinders lie
Under deep ruines, with huge walls opprest,
But not your praise, the which shall never die,
Through your faire verses, ne in ashes rest;
If so be shrilling voyce of wight alive
May reach from hence to depth of darkest hell,
Then let those deep abysses open rive,
That ye may understand my shreiking yell.
Thrice having seene, under the heavens veale,
Your toombs devoted compasse over all,
Thrice unto you with lowd voyce I appeale,
And for your antique furie here doo call,
    The whiles that I with sacred horror sing
    Your glorie, fairest of all earthly thing.

II

Great Babylon her haughtie walls will praise,
And sharped steeples high shot up in ayre;
Greece will the olde Ephesian buildings blaze;
And Nylus nurslings their pyramides faire;
The same yet vaunting Greece will tell the storie
Of Joves great image in Olympus placed;

Mausolus worke will be the Carians glorie;
And Crete will boast the Labyrinth, now raced;
The antique Rhodian will likewise set forth
The great colosse, erect to Memorie;
And what els in the world is of like worth,
Some greater learned wit will magnifie.
    But I will sing above all moniments
    Seven Romane hils, the worlds seven wonderments.

III

Thou stranger, which for Rome in Rome here seekest,
And nought of Rome in Rome perceiv'st at all,
These same olde walls, olde arches, which thou seest,
Olde palaces, is that which Rome men call.
Behold what wreake, what ruine, and what wast,
And how that she, which with her mightie powre
Tam'd all the world, hath tam'd herselfe at last,
The pray of Time, which all things doth devowre.
Rome now of Rome is th' onely funerall,
And onely Rome of Rome hath victorie;
Ne ought save Tyber hastning to his fall
Remaines of all: O worlds inconstancie!
    That which is firme doth flit and fall away,
    And that is flitting doth abide and stay.

IV

She, whose high top above the starres did sore,
One foote on Thetis, th' other on the Morning,
One hand on Scythia, th' other on the More,
Both heaven and earth in roundnesse compassing,
Jove, fearing least, if she should greater growe,
The old giants should once againe uprise,
Her whelm'd with hills, these seven hils, which be nowe
Tombes of her greatnes, which did threate the skies:
Upon her head he heapt Mount Saturnal,
Upon her bellie th' antique Palatine,
Upon her stomacke laid Mount Quirinal,
On her left hand the noysome Esquiline,
    And Cælian on the right; but both her feete
    Mount Viminal and Aventine doo meete.

V

Who lists to see what ever nature, arte,
And heaven could doo, O Rome, thee let
  him see,
In case thy greatnes he can gesse in harte
By that which but the picture is of thee.
Rome is no more: but if the shade of Rome
May of the bodie yeeld a seeming sight,
It 's like a corse drawne forth out of the
  tombe
By magicke skill out of eternall night:
The corpes of Rome in ashes is entombed,
And her great spirite, rejoyned to the
  spirite
Of this great masse, is in the same en-
  wombed;
But her brave writings, which her famous
  merite,
  In spight of Time, out of the dust doth
  reare,
  Doo make her idole through the world
  appeare.

VI

Such as the Berecynthian goddesse bright,
In her swift charret with high turrets
  crownde,
Proud that so manie gods she brought to
  light,
Such was this citie in her good daies fownd:
This citie, more than that great Phrygian
  mother
Renowm'd for fruite of famous progenie,
Whose greatnes by the greatnes of none
  other,
But by her selfe, her equall match could
  see:
Rome onely might to Rome compared
  bee,
And onely Rome could make great Rome
  to tremble:
So did the gods by heavenly doome decree,
That other earthlie power should not re-
  semble
  Her that did match the whole earths
  puissaunce,
  And did her courage to the heavens ad-
  vaunce.

VII

Ye sacred ruines, and ye tragick sights,
Which onely doo the name of Rome retaine,
Olde moniments, which of so famous
  sprights
The honour yet in ashes doo maintaine,

Triumphant arcks, spyres neighbours to
  the skie,
That you to see doth th' heaven it selfe
  appall,
Alas ! by little ye to nothing flie,
The peoples fable, and the spoyle of all:
And though your frames do for a time
  make warre
Gainst Time, yet Time in time shall ruin-
  ate
Your workes and names, and your last rel-
  iques marre.
  My sad desires, rest therefore moderate:
  For if that Time make ende of things so
  sure,
  It als will end the paine which I endure.

VIII

Through armes and vassals Rome the world
  subdu'd,
That one would weene that one sole cities
  strength
Both land and sea in roundnes had sur-
  vew'd,
To be the measure of her bredth and
  length:
This peoples vertue yet so fruitfull was
Of vertuous nephewes, that posteritie,
Striving in power their grandfathers to
  passe,
The lowest earth join'd to the heaven hie;
To th' end that, having all parts in their
  power,
Nought from the Romane Empire might
  be quight;
And that though Time doth commonwealths
  devowre,
Yet no time should so low embase their
  hight,
  That her head, earth'd in her foundations
  deep,
  Should not her name and endles honour
  keep.

IX

Ye cruell starres, and eke ye gods unkinde,
Heaven envious, and bitter stepdame Na-
  ture,
Be it by fortune, or by course of kinde,
That ye doo weld th' affaires of earthlie
  creature;
Why have your hands long sithence tra-
  veiled
To frame this world, that doth endure se
  long ?

Or why were not these Romane palaces
Made of some matter no lesse firme and
    strong?
I say not, as the common voyce doth say,
That all things which beneath the moone
    have being
Are temporall, and subject to decay:
But I say rather, though not all agreeing
  With some that weene the contrarie in
      thought,
  That all this whole shall one day come
      to nought.

X

As that brave sonne of Aeson, which by
    charmes
Atcheiv'd the golden fleece in Colchid land,
Out of the earth engendred men of armes
Of dragons teeth, sowne in the sacred sand;
So this brave towne, that in her youthlie
    daies
An hydra was of warriours glorious,
Did fill with her renowmed nourslings
    praise
The firie sunnes both one and other hous:
But they at last, there being then not living
An Hercules, so ranke seed to represse,
Emongst themselves with cruell furie striv-
    ing,
Mow'd downe themselves with slaughter
    mercilesse;
  Renewing in themselves that rage un-
      kinde,
  Which whilom did those earthborn bre-
      thren blinde.

XI

Mars, shaming to have given so great head
To his off-spring, that mortall puissaunce,
Puft up with pride of Romane hardie-
    head,
Seem'd above heavens powre it selfe to ad-
    vaunce,
Cooling againe his former kindled heate,
With which he had those Romane spirits
    fild,
Did blowe new fire, and with enflamed
    breath
Into the Gothicke colde hot rage instil'd:
Then gan that nation, th' earths new giant
    brood,
To dart abroad the thunder bolts of warre,
And, beating downe these walls with furious
    mood
Into her mothers bosome, all did marre;

To th' end that none, all were it Jove his
    sire,
Should boast himselfe of the Romane
    Empire.

XII

Like as whilome the children of the earth
Heapt hils on hils, to scale the starrie skie,
And fight against the gods of heavenly
    berth,
Whiles Jove at them his thunderbolts let
    flie;
All suddenly with lightning overthrowne,
The furious squadrons downe to ground did
    fall,
That th' earth under her childrens weight
    did grone,
And th' heavens in glorie triumpht over all:
So did that haughtie front, which heaped
    was
On these seven Romane hils, it selfe up-
    reare
Over the world, and lift her loftie face
Against the heaven, that gan her force to
    feare.
  But now these scorned fields bemone her
      fall,
  And gods secure feare not her force at
      all.

XIII

Nor the swift furie of the flames aspiring,
Nor the deep wounds of victours raging
    blade,
Nor ruthlesse spoyle of souldiers blood-
    desiring,
The which so oft thee (Rome) their con-
    quest made;
Ne stroke on stroke of fortune variable,
Ne rust of age hating continuance,
Nor wrath of gods, nor spight of men un-
    stable,
Nor thou opposd' against thine owne puis-
    sance;
Nor th' horrible uprore of windes high
    blowing,
Nor swelling streames of that god snakie-
    paced,
Which hath so often with his overflowing
Thee drenched, have thy pride so much
    abaced,
  But that this nothing, which they have
      thee left,
  Makes the world wonder what they from
      thee reft.

XIV

As men in summer fearles passe the foord,
Which is in winter lord of all the plaine,
And with his tumbling streames doth beare
    aboord
The ploughmans hope and shepheards la-
    bour vaine:
And as the coward beasts use to despise
The noble lion after his lives end,
Whetting their teeth, and with vaine fool-
    hardise
Daring the foe, that cannot him defend:
And as at Troy most dastards of the
    Greekes
Did brave about the corpes of Hector colde;
So those which whilome wont with pallid
    cheekes
The Romane triumphs glorie to behold,
  Now on these ashie tombes shew bold-
    nesse vaine,
  And, conquer'd, dare the conquerour dis-
    daine.

XV

Ye pallid spirits, and ye ashie ghoasts,
Which, joying in the brightnes of your
    day,
Brought foorth those signes of your pre-
    sumptuous boasts
Which now their dusty reliques do bewray;
Tell me, ye spirits (sith the darksome
    river
Of Styx, not passable to soules returning,
Enclosing you in thrice three wards for
    ever,
Doo not restraine your images still mourn-
    ing)
Tell me then (for perhaps some one of you
Yet here above him secretly doth hide)
Doo ye not feele your torments to ac-
    crewe,
When ye sometimes behold the ruin'd pride
  Of these old Romane works, built with
    your hands,
  To have become nought els but heaped
    sands ?

XVI

Like as ye see the wrathfull sea from farre,
In a great mountaine heap't with hideous
    noyse,
Eftsoones of thousand billowes shouldred
    narre,
Against a rocke to breake with dreadfull
    poyse:

Like as ye see fell Boreas with sharpe
    blast,
Tossing huge tempests through the troubled
    skie,
Eftsoones having his wide wings spent in
    wast,
To stop his wearie cariere suddenly:
And as ye see huge flames spred diverslie,
Gathered in one up to the heavens to spyre,
Eftsoones consum'd to fall downe feebily:
So whilom did this monarchie aspyre
  As waves, as winde, as fire spred over
    all,
  Till it by fatall doome adowne did fall.

XVII

So long as Joves great bird did make his
    flight,
Bearing the fire with which heaven doth us
    fray,
Heaven had not feare of that presumptuous
    might,
With which the giaunts did the gods assay.
But all so soone as scortching sunne had
    brent
His wings, which wont the earth to over-
    spredd,
The earth out of her massie wombe forth
    sent
That antique horror, which made heaven
    adredd.
Then was the Germane raven in disguise
That Romane eagle seene to cleave asunder,
And towards heaven freshly to arise
Out of these mountaines, now consum'd to
    pouder:
  In which the foule that serves to beare
    the lightning
  Is now no more seen flying, nor alighting.

XVIII

These heapes of stones, these old wals which
    ye see,
Were first enclosures but of salvage soyle;
And these brave pallaces, which maystred
    bee
Of Time, were shepheards cottages some-
    while.
Then tooke the shepheards kingly orna-
    ments,
And the stout hynde arm'd his right hand
    with steele:
Eftsoones their rule of yearely presidents
Grew great, and six months greater a great
    deele;

Which, made perpetuall, rose to so great
  might,
That thence th' imperiall eagle rooting
  tooke,
Till th' heaven it selfe, opposing gainst her
  might,
Her power to Peters successor betooke;
  Who, shepheardlike, (as Fates the same
    foreseeing)
  Doth shew that all things turne to their
    first being.

XIX

All that is perfect, which th' heaven beau-
  tefies;
All that 's imperfect, borne belowe the
  moone;
All that doth feede our spirits and our eies;
And all that doth consume our pleasures
  soone;
All the mishap, the which our daies out-
  weares;
All the good hap of th' oldest times afore,
Rome in the time of her great ancesters,
Like a Pandora, locked long in store.
But destinie this huge chaos turmoyling,
In which all good and evill was enclosed,
Their heavenly vertues from these woes
  assoyling,
Caried to heaven, from sinfull bondage
  losed:
  But their great sinnes, the causers of
    their paine,
  Under these antique ruines yet remaine.

XX

No otherwise than raynie cloud, first fed
With earthly vapours gathered in the ayre,
Eftsoones in compas arch't, to steepe his
  hed,
Doth plonge himselfe in Tethys bosome
  faire;
And mounting up againe, from whence he
  came,
With his great bellie spreds the dimmed
  world,
Till at the last, dissolving his moist frame,
In raine, or snowe, or haile he forth is
  hor'ld;
This citie, which was first but shepheards
  shade,
Uprising by degrees, grewe to such height,
That queene of land and sea her selfe she
  made.
At last, not able to beare so great weight,

Her power, disperst, through all the
  world did vade;
To shew that all in th' end to nought
  shall fade.

XXI

The same which Pyrrhus and the puis-
  saunce
Of Afrike could not tame, that same brave
  citie,
Which, with stout courage arm'd against
  mischaunce,
Sustein'd the shocke of common enmitie;
Long as her ship, tost with so manie
  freakes,
Had all the world in armes against her
  bent,
Was never seene that anie fortunes
  wreakes
Could breake her course begun with brave
  intent.
But when the object of her vertue failed,
Her power it selfe against it selfe did
  arme;
As he that having long in tempest sailed,
Faine would arive, but cannot for the
  storme,
  If too great winde against the port him
    drive,
  Doth in the port it selfe his vessell rive.

XXII

When that brave honour of the Latine
  name,
Which mear'd her rule with Africa and
  Byze,
With Thames inhabitants of noble fame,
And they which see the dawning day arize,
Her nourslings did with mutinous uprore
Harten against her selfe, her conquer'd
  spoile,
Which she had wonne from all the world
  afore,
Of all the world was spoyl'd within a while.
So, when the compast course of the uni-
  verse
In sixe and thirtie thousand yeares is
  ronne,
The bands of th' elements shall backe re-
  verse
To their first discord, and be quite un-
  donne:
  The seedes, of which all things at first
    were bred,
  Shall in great Chaos wombe againe be hid.

XXIII

O warie wisedome of the man that would
That Carthage towres from spoile should
    be forborne,
To th' end that his victorious people should
With cancring laisure not be overworne !
He well foresaw, how that the Romane
    courage,
Impatient of pleasures faint desires,
Through idlenes would turne to civill rage,
And be her selfe the matter of her fires.
For in a people given all to ease,
Ambition is engendred easily;
As in a vicious bodie, grose disease
Soone growes through humours super-
    fluitie.
    That came to passe, when, swolne with
      plenties pride,
    Nor prince, nor peere, nor kin, they
      would abide.

XXIV

If the blinde Furie, which warres breedeth
    oft,
Wonts not t' enrage the hearts of equall
    beasts,
Whether they fare on foote, or flie aloft,
Or armed be with clawes, or scalie creasts,
What fell Erynnis, with hot burning tongs,
Did grype your hearts, with noysome rage
    imbew'd,
That, each to other working cruell wrongs,
Your blades in your owne bowels you em-
    brew'd ?
Was this, ye Romanes, your hard destinie ?
Or some old sinne, whose unappeased guilt
Powr'd vengeance forth on you eternallie ?
Or brothers blood, the which at first was
    spilt
Upon your walls, that God might not en-
    dure
Upon the same to set foundation sure ?

XXV

O that I had the Thracian poets harpe,
For to awake out of th' infernall shade
Those antique Cæsars, sleeping long in
    darke,
The which this auncient citie whilome made!
Or that I had Amphions instrument,
To quicken with his vitall notes accord
The stonie joynts of these old walls now
    rent,
By which th' Ausonian light might be re-
    stor'd !

Or that at least I could with pencill fine
Fashion the pourtraicts of these palacis,
By paterne of great Virgils spirit divine !
I would assay with that which in me is
    To builde, with levell of my loftie style,
    That which no hands can evermore com-
      pyle.

XXVI

Who list the Romane greatnes forth to
    figure,
Him needeth not to seeke for usage right
Of line, or lead, or rule, or squaire, to mea-
    sure
Her length, her breadth, her deepnes, or
    her hight;
But him behooves to vew in compasse round
All that the ocean graspes in his long armes;
Be it where the yerely starre doth scortch
    the ground,
Or where colde Boreas blowes his bitter
    stormes.
Rome was th' whole world, and al the world
    was Rome,
And if things nam'd their names doo equal-
    ize,
When land and sea ye name, then name ye
    Rome,
And naming Rome, ye land and sea com-
    prize:
    For th' auncient plot of Rome, displayed
      plaine,
    The map of all the wide world doth con-
      taine.

XXVII

Thou that at Rome astonisht dost behold
The antique pride, which menaced the skie,
These haughtie heapes, these palaces of
    olde,
These wals, these arcks, these baths, these
    temples hie,
Judge, by these ample ruines vew, the rest
The which injurious time hath quite out-
    worne,
Since, of all workmen helde in reckning best,
Yet these olde fragments are for paternes
    borne:
Then also marke, how Rome, from day to
    day,
Repayring her decayed fashion,
Renewes herselfe with buildings rich and
    gay;
    That one would judge that the Romaine
      Dæmon

Doth yet himselfe with fatall hand enforce,
Againe on foote to reare her pouldred
corse.

XXVIII

He that hath seene a great oke drie and
dead,
Yet clad with reliques of some trophees
olde,
Lifting to heaven her aged hoarie head,
Whose foote in ground hath left but feeble
holde,
But halfe disbowel'd lies above the ground,
Shewing her wreathed rootes, and naked
armes,
And on her trunke, all rotten and unsound,
Onely supports herselfe for meate of
wormes,
And though she owe her fall to the first
winde,
Yet of the devout people is ador'd,
And manie yong plants spring out of her
rinde;
Who such an oke hath seene, let him re-
cord
That such this cities honour was of yore,
And mongst all cities florished much
more.

XXIX

All that which Aegypt whilome did de-
vise,
All that which Greece their temples to em-
brave,
After th' Ionicke, Atticke, Doricke guise,
Or Corinth skil'd in curious workes to
grave,
All that Lysippus practike arte could
forme,
Apelles wit, or Phidias his skill,
Was wont this auncient citie to adorne,
And the heaven it selfe with her wide
wonders fill.
All that which Athens ever brought forth
wise,
All that which Afrike ever brought forth
strange,
All that which Asie ever had of prise,
Was here to see. O mervelous great
change !
Rome, living, was the worlds sole orna-
ment,
And dead, is now the worlds sole moni-
ment.

XXX

Like as the seeded field greene grasse first
showes,
Then from greene grasse into a stalke doth
spring,
And from a stalke into an eare forth-
growes,
Which eare the frutefull graine doth shortly
bring;
And as in season due the husband mowes
The waving lockes of those faire yeallow
heares,
Which, bound in sheaves, and layd in
comely rowes,
Upon the naked fields in stackes he reares:
So grew the Romane Empire by degree,
Till that barbarian hands it quite did spill,
And left of it but these olde markes to see,
Of which all passers by doo somewhat pill,
As they which gleane, the reliques use to
gather,
Which th' husbandman behind him chanst
to scater.

XXXI

That same is now nought but a champian
wide,
Where all this worlds pride once was
situate.
No blame to thee, whosoever dost abide
By Nyle, or Gange, or Tygre, or Euphrate;
Ne Afrike thereof guiltie is, nor Spaine,
Nor the bolde people by the Thamis
brincks,
Nor the brave warlicke brood of Alemaine,
Nor the borne souldier which Rhine run-
ning drinks.
Thou onely cause, O Civill Furie, art:
Which, sowing in th' Aemathian fields thy
spight,
Didst arme thy hand against thy proper
hart;
To th' end that when thou wast in greatest
hight
To greatnes growne, through long pros-
peritie,
Thou then adowne might'st fall more
horriblie.

XXXII

Hope ye, my verses, that posteritie
Of age ensuing shall you ever read ?
Hope ye that ever immortalitie
So meane harpes worke may chalenge for
her meed ?

If under heaven anie endurance were,
These moniments, which not in paper writ,
But in porphyre and marble doo appeare,
Might well have hop'd to have obtained it.
Nath'les, my lute, whom Phœbus deigned
    to give,
Cease not to sound these olde antiquities:
For if that Time doo let thy glorie live,
Well maist thou boast, how ever base thou
    bee,
    That thou art first which of thy nation
        song
    Th' olde honour of the people gowned
        long.

L'ENVOY

Bellay, first garland of free poësie
That France brought forth, though fruit-
    full of brave wits,
Well worthie thou of immortalitie,
That long hast traveld by thy learned writs,
Olde Rome out of her ashes to revive,
And give a second life to dead decayes:
Needes must he all eternitie survive,
That can to other give eternall dayes.
Thy dayes therefore are endles, and thy
    prayse
Excelling all that ever went before;
And, after thee, gins Bartas hie to rayse
His heavenly Muse, th' Almightie to adore.
    Live happie spirits, th' honour of your
        name,
    And fill the world with never dying fame.

FINIS.

MUIOPOTMOS,
OR
THE FATE OF THE BUTTER-
FLIE

BY ED. SP.

DEDICATED TO THE MOST FAIRE AND
VERTUOUS LADIE: THE LADIE
CAREY

LONDON

IMPRINTED FOR WILLIAM
PONSONBIE, DWELLING IN PAULES
CHURCHYARD AT THE SIGNE OF
THE BISHOPS HEAD

1590

TO THE RIGHT WORTHY AND VERTUOUS LADIE; THE LADIE CAREY

MOST brave and bountifull Lady: for so excellent favours as I have received at your sweet handes, to offer these fewe leaves as in recompence, should be as to offer flowers to the gods for their divine benefites. Therefore I have determined to give my selfe wholy to you, as quite abandoned from my selfe, and absolutely vowed to your services: which in all right is ever held for full recompence of debt or damage to have the person yeelded. My person I wot wel how little worth it is. But the faithfull minde and humble zeale which I beare unto your Ladiship may perhaps be more of price, as may please you to account and use the poore service thereof; which taketh glory to advance your excellent partes and noble vertues, and to spend it selfe in honouring you: not so much for your great bounty to my self, which yet may not be unminded; nor for name or kindreds sake by you vouchsafed, beeing also regardable; as for that honorable name, which yee have by your brave deserts purchast to your self, and spred in the mouths of al men: with which I have also presumed to grace my verses, and under your name to commend to the world this smal poëme; the which beseeching your Ladiship to take in worth, and of all things therein according to your wonted graciousnes to make a milde construction, I humbly pray for your happines.

Your Ladiships ever
            humbly;
                    E. S.

['Muiopotmos' cannot be dated with certainty. In style it would seem to be more mature than the work of the *Calendar* period; it may have been written in Ireland; one rather associates it with that period of delight in London while the poet was seeing his *Faery Queen* through the press. If the date upon its separate title-page, 1590, is to be trusted, it must have been written, at latest, not long after his arrival in England.

By contrast to the motley and impressive mediævalism of 'Mother Hubberd's Tale,' this poem would seem to be conspicuously Renaissance Italian. Its subject is a mere nothing: it tells no story that could not be told in full in a stanza, it presents no situation for the delicate rhetoric of the emotions: it is a mere running frieze of images and scenes, linked in fanciful continuity. It is organized as a mock-heroic poem, but its appeal is essentially to the eye. Myths, invented or real, that seem to form themselves spontaneously into pictures, the landscape of the gardens, fantastic armor, the figured scenes of tapestry richly bordered, these are of a poetry akin to the plastic arts, such as one finds in the *Stanze* of Poliziano. Yet the temper of 'Muiopotmos' is not that of the *Stanze* and their like. It is rather of the air than of the earth. One might think it an emanation of the theme itself and fancy that the frail wings of the butterfly had been spread for the style, delicately colored, ethereal. The poet of the *Faery Queen* never more happily escaped into 'delight with liberty' than here.]

MUIOPOTMOS: OR
THE FATE OF THE BUTTERFLIE

I sing of deadly dolorous debate,
Stir'd up through wrathfull Nemesis despight,
Betwixt two mightie ones of great estate,
Drawne into armes, and proofe of mortall fight,
Through prowd ambition and hartswelling hate,
Whilest neither could the others greater might
And sdeignfull scorne endure; that from small jarre
Their wraths at length broke into open warre.

The roote whereof and tragicall effect,
Vouchsafe, O thou the mournfulst Muse of nyne,   10
That wontst the tragick stage for to direct,
In funerall complaints and waylfull tyne,
Reveale to me, and all the meanes detect
Through which sad Clarion did at last declyne
To lowest wretchednes: And is there then
Such rancour in the harts of mightie men?

Of all the race of silver-winged flies
Which doo possesse the empire of the aire,
Betwixt the centred earth and azure skies,
Was none more favourable, nor more faire,
Whilest heaven did favour his felicities,   21
Then Clarion, the eldest sonne and haire

Of Muscaroll, and in his fathers sight
Of all alive did seeme the fairest wight.

With fruitfull hope his aged breast he fed
Of future good, which his yong toward yeares,
Full of brave courage and bold hardyhed,
Above th' ensample of his equall peares,
Did largely promise, and to him forered
(Whilst oft his heart did melt in tender teares)   30
That he in time would sure prove such an one,
As should be worthie of his fathers throne.

The fresh yong flie, in whom the kindly fire
Of lustfull yongth began to kindle fast,
Did much disdaine to subject his desire
To loathsome sloth, or houres in ease to wast,
But joy'd to range abroad in fresh attire,
Through the wide compas of the ayrie coast,
And with unwearied wings each part t' inquire
Of the wide rule of his renowmed sire.   40

For he so swift and nimble was of flight,
That from this lower tract he dar'd to stie
Up to the clowdes, and thence, with pineons light,
To mount aloft unto the christall skie,
To vew the workmanship of heavens hight:
Whence downe descending he along would flie
Upon the streaming rivers, sport to finde;
And oft would dare to tempt the troublous winde.

So on a summers day, when season milde
With gentle calme the world had quieted,
And high in heaven Hyperions fierie childe   51
Ascending, did his beames abroad dispred,
Whiles all the heavens on lower creatures smilde,
Yong Clarion, with vauntfull lustiehead,
After his guize did cast abroad to fare,
And theretoo gan his furnitures prepare.

His breastplate first, that was of substance pure,
Before his noble heart he firmely bound,

That mought his life from yron death as-
sure,
And ward his gentle corpes from cruell
wound: 60
For it by arte was framed to endure
The bit of balefull steele and bitter
stownd,
No lesse than that which Vulcane made to
sheild
Achilles life from fate of Troyan field.

And then about his shoulders broad he
threw
An hairie hide of some wilde beast, whom
hee
In salvage forrest by adventure slew,
And reft the spoyle his ornament to bee:
Which, spredding all his backe with dread-
full vew,
Made all that him so horrible did see   70
Thinke him Alcides with the lyons skin,
When the Næmean conquest he did win.

Upon his head, his glistering burganet,
The which was wrought by wonderous
device,
And curiously engraven, he did set:
The mettall was of rare and passing
price;
Not Bilbo steele, nor brasse from Corinth
fet,
Nor costly oricalche from strange Phœnice;
But such as could both Phœbus arrowes
ward,
And th' hayling darts of heaven beating
hard.   80

Therein two deadly weapons fixt he bore,
Strongly outlaunced towards either side,
Like two sharpe speares, his enemies to
gore:
Like as a warlike brigandine, applyde
To fight, layes forth her threatfull pikes
afore,
The engines which in them sad death doo
hyde:
So did this flie outstretch his fearefull
hornes,
Yet so as him their terrour more adornes.

Lastly his shinie wings, as silver bright,
Painted with thousand colours, passing
farre   90
All painters skill, he did about him dight:
Not halfe so manie sundrie colours arre

In Iris bowe, ne heaven doth shine so bright,
Distinguished with manie a twinckling
starre,
Nor Junoes bird in her ey-spotted traine
So manie goodly colours doth containe.

Ne (may it be withouten perill spoken)
The Archer god, the sonne of Cytheree,
That joyes on wretched lovers to be wroken,
And heaped spoyles of bleeding harts to
see,   100
Beares in his wings so manie a changefull
token.

Ah! my liege lord, forgive it unto mee,
If ought against thine honour I have tolde;
Yet sure those wings were fairer manifolde.

Full manie a ladie faire, in court full oft
Beholding them, him secretly envide,
And wisht that two such fannes, so silken
soft
And golden faire, her love would her pro-
vide;
Or that, when them the gorgeous flie had
doft,
Some one, that would with grace be grati-
fide,   110
From him would steale them privily away,
And bring to her so precious a pray.

Report is that Dame Venus on a day,
In spring when flowres doo clothe the fruit-
ful ground,
Walking abroad with all her nymphes to
play,
Bad her faire damzels, flocking her arownd,
To gather flowres, her forhead to array.
Emongst the rest a gentle nymph was
found,
Hight Astery, excelling all the crewe
In curteous usage and unstained hewe.   120

Who, being nimbler joynted than the rest,
And more industrious, gathered more store
Of the fields honour than the others best;
Which they in secret harts envying sore,
Tolde Venus, when her as the worthiest
She praisd', that Cupide (as they heard be-
fore)
Did lend her secret aide in gathering
Into her lap the children of the Spring.

Whereof the goddesse gathering jealous
feare,
Not yet unmindfull how not long agoe   130

Her sonne to Psyche secrete love did beare,
And long it close conceal'd, till mickle woe
Thereof arose, and manie a rufull teare,
Reason with sudden rage did overgoe,
And giving hastie credit to th' accuser,
Was led away of them that did abuse her.

Eftsoones that damzel, by her heavenly
          might,
She turn'd into a winged butterflie,
In the wide aire to make her wandring
          flight;
And all those flowres, with which so plen-
          teouslie   140
Her lap she filled had, that bred her spight,
She placed in her wings, for memorie
Of her pretended crime, though crime none
          were:
Since which that flie them in her wings doth
          beare.

Thus the fresh Clarion, being readie dight,
Unto his journey did himselfe addresse,
And with good speed began to take his
          flight:
Over the fields, in his franke lustinesse,
And all the champion he soared light,   149
And all the countery wide he did possesse,
Feeding upon their pleasures bounteouslie,
That none gainsaid, nor none did him envie.

The woods, the rivers, and the medowes
          green,
With his aire-cutting wings he measured
          wide,
Ne did he leave the mountaines bare un-
          seene,
Nor the ranke grassie fennes delights un-
          tride.
But none of these, how ever sweete they
          beene,
Mote please his fancie, nor him cause t'
          abide:
His choicefull sense with everie change doth
          flit;
No common things may please a wavering
          wit.   160

To the gay gardins his unstaid desire
Him wholly caried, to refresh his sprights:
There lavish Nature, in her best attire,
Powres forth sweete odors, and alluring
          sights;
And Arte, with her contending, doth aspire
T' excell the naturall with made delights:

And all that faire or pleasant may be found
In riotous excesse doth there abound.

There he arriving, round about doth flie,
From bed to bed, from one to other bor-
          der,   170
And takes survey, with curious busie eye,
Of everie flowre and herbe there set in
          order;
Now this, now that, he tasteth tenderly,
Yet none of them he rudely doth disorder,
Ne with his feete their silken leaves de-
          face;
But pastures on the pleasures of each place.

And evermore with most varietie,
And change of sweetnesse (for all change
          is sweete)
He casts his glutton sense to satisfie;
Now sucking of the sap of herbe most
          meete,   180
Or of the deaw, which yet on them does lie,
Now in the same bathing his tender feete:
And then he pearcheth on some braunch
          thereby,
To weather him, and his moyst wings to
          dry.

And then againe he turneth to his play,
To spoyle the pleasures of that paradise:
The wholsome saulge, and lavender still
          gray,
Ranke smelling rue, and cummin good for
          eyes,
The roses raigning in the pride of May,
Sharpe isope, good for greene wounds reme-
          dies,   190
Faire marigoldes, and bees-alluring thime,
Sweete marjoram, and daysies decking
          prime:

Coole violets, and orpine growing still,
Embathed balme, and chearfull galingale,
Fresh costmarie, and breathfull camomill,
Dull poppie, and drink-quickning setuale,
Veyne-healing verven, and hed-purging dill,
Sound savorie, and bazill hartie-hale,
Fat colworts, and comforting perseline,
Colde lettuce, and refreshing rosmarine. 200

And whatso else of vertue good or ill
Grewe in this gardin, fetcht from farre
          away,
Of everie one he takes, and tastes at will,
And on their pleasures greedily doth pray

Then, when he hath both plaid, and fed his
fill,
In the warme sunne he doth himselfe em-
bay,
And there him rests in riotous suffisaunce
Of all his gladfulnes and kingly joyaunce.

What more felicitie can fall to creature
Than to enjoy delight with libertie,   210
And to be lord of all the workes of
Nature,
To raine in th' aire from earth to highest
skie,
To feed on flowres and weeds of glorious
feature,
To take what ever thing doth please the
eie ?
Who rests not pleased with such happines,
Well worthie he to taste of wretchednes.

But what on earth can long abide in state,
Or who can him assure of happie day;
Sith morning faire may bring fowle evening
late,
And least mishap the most blisse alter
may ?   220
For thousand perills lie in close awaite
About us daylie, to worke our decay;
That none, except a God, or God him
guide,
May them avoyde, or remedie provide.

And whatso heavens in their secret doome
Ordained have, how can fraile fleshly wight
Forecast, but it must needs to issue come ?
The sea, the aire, the fire, the day, the
night,
And th' armies of their creatures all and
some
Do serve to them, and with importune
might   230
Warre against us, the vassals of their will.
Who then can save what they dispose to
spill ?

Not thou, O Clarion, though fairest thou
Of all thy kinde, unhappie happie flie,
Whose cruell fate is woven even now
Of Joves owne hand, to worke thy miserie:
Ne may thee helpe the manie hartie vow,
Which thy olde sire with sacred pietie
Hath powred forth for thee, and th' altars
sprent:
Nought may thee save from heavens
avengement.   240

It fortuned (as heavens had behight)
That in this gardin, where yong Clarion
Was wont to solace him, a wicked wight,
The foe of faire things, th' author of con-
fusion,
The shame of Nature, the bondslave of
spight,
Had lately built his hatefull mansion,
And, lurking closely, in awayte now lay,
How he might anie in his trap betray.

But when he spide the joyous butterflie
In this faire plot dispacing too and fro,   250
Fearles of foes and hidden jeopardie,
Lord ! how he gan for to bestirre him tho,
And to his wicked worke each part applie !
His heart did earne against his hated foe,
And bowels so with ranckling poyson swelde,
That scarce the skin the strong contagior
helde.

The cause why he this flie so maliced
Was (as in stories it is written found)
For that his mother which him bore and
bred,
The most fine-fingred workwoman on
ground,   260
Arachne, by his meanes was vanquished
Of Pallas, and in her owne skill confound,
When she with her for excellence con-
tended,
That wrought her shame, and sorrow never
ended.

For the Tritonian goddesse, having hard
Her blazed fame, which all the world had
fil'd,
Came downe to prove the truth, and due
reward
For her prais-worthie workmanship to
yeild:
But the presumptuous damzel rashly dar'd
The goddesse selfe to chalenge to the
field,   270
And to compare with her in curious skill
Of workes with loome, with needle, and
with quill.

Minerva did the chalenge not refuse,
But deign'd with her the paragon to make:
So to their worke they sit, and each doth
chuse
What storie she will for her tapet take.
Arachne figur'd how Jove did abuse
Europa like a bull, and on his backe

Her through the sea did beare; so lively
    seene,
That it true sea and true bull ye would
    weene.   280

She seem'd still backe unto the land to
    looke,
And her play-fellowes aide to call, and
    feare
The dashing of the waves, that up she
    tooke
Her daintie feete, and garments gathered
    neare:
But (Lord!) how she in everie member
    shooke,
When as the land she saw no more ap-
    peare,
But a wilde wildernes of waters deepe!
Then gan she greatly to lament and weepe.

Before the bull she pictur'd winged Love,
With his yong brother Sport, light flutter-
    ing   290
Upon the waves, as each had been a dove;
The one his bowe and shafts, the other
    spring
A burning teade about his head did move,
As in their syres new love both triumph-
    ing:
And manie Nymphes about them flocking
    round,
And manie Tritons, which their hornes did
    sound.

And round about, her worke she did em-
    pale
With a faire border wrought of sundrie
    flowres,
Enwoven with an yvie winding trayle: 299
A goodly worke, full fit for kingly bowres,
Such as Dame Pallas, such as Envie pale,
That al good things with venemous tooth
    devowres,
Could not accuse. Then gan the goddesse
    bright
Her selfe likewise unto her worke to dight.

She made the storie of the olde debate,
Which she with Neptune did for Athens
    trie:
Twelve gods doo sit around in royall state,
And Jove in midst with awfull majestie,
To judge the strife betweene them stirred
    late:
Each of the gods by his like visnomie   310

Eathe to be knowen; but Jove above them
    all,
By his great lookes and power imperiall.

Before them stands the god of seas in place,
Clayming that sea-coast citie as his right,
And strikes the rockes with his three-forked
    mace;
Whenceforth issues a warlike steed in sight,
The signe by which he chalengeth the place;
That all the gods, which saw his wondrous
    might,
Did surely deeme the victorie his due:
But seldome seene, forejudgement proveth
    true.   320

Then to her selfe she gives her Aegide
    shield,
And steelhed speare, and morion on her
    hedd,
Such as she oft is seene in warlicke field:
Then sets she forth, how with her weapon
    dredd
She smote the ground, the which streight
    foorth did yield
A fruitfull olyve tree, with berries spredd,
That all the gods admir'd; then all the
    storie
She compast with a wreathe of olyves
    hoarie.

Emongst those leaves she made a butterflie,
With excellent device and wondrous slight,
Fluttring among the olives wantonly,   331
That seem'd to live, so like it was in sight:
The velvet nap which on his wings doth lie,
The silken downe with which his backe is
    dight,
His broad outstretched hornes, his hayrie
    thies,
His glorious colours, and his glistering eies.

Which when Arachne saw, as overlaid
And mastered with workmanship so rare,
She stood astonied long, ne ought gaine-
    said,   339
And with fast fixed eyes on her did stare,
And by her silence, signe of one dismaid,
The victorie did yeeld her as her share:
Yet did she inly fret, and felly burne,
And all her blood to poysonous rancor
    turne:

That shortly from the shape of womanhed,
Such as she was, when Pallas she attempted,

She grew to hideous shape of dryrihed,
Pined with griefe of follie late repented:
Eftsoones her white streight legs were
    altered
To crooked crawling shankes, of marrowe
    empted,   350
And her faire face to fowle and loathsome
    hewe,
And her fine corpes to a bag of venim grewe.

This cursed creature, mindfull of that olde
Enfested grudge, the which his mother
    felt,
So soone as Clarion he did beholde,
His heart with vengefull malice inly swelt;
And weaving straight a net with manie a
    folde
About the cave in which he lurking dwelt,
With fine small cords about it stretched
    wide,
So finely sponne that scarce they could be
    spide.   360

Not anie damzell, which her vaunteth most
In skilfull knitting of soft silken twyne;
Nor anie weaver, which his worke doth boast
In dieper, in damaske, or in lyne;
Nor anie skil'd in workmanship embost;
Nor anie skil'd in loupes of fingring fine,
Might in their divers cunning ever dare,
With this so curious networke to compare.

Ne doo I thinke that that same subtil gin,
The which the Lemnian god framde craf-
    tilie,   370
Mars sleeping with his wife to compasse in,
That all the gods with common mockerie
Might laugh at them, and scorne their
    shamefull sin,
Was like to this. This same he did applie
For to entrap the careles Clarion,
That rang'd each where without suspition.

Suspition of friend, nor feare of foe,
That hazarded his health, had he at all,
But walkt at will, and wandred too and
    fro,
In the pride of his freedome principall: 380
Litle wist he his fatall future woe,
But was secure; the liker he to fall.
He likest is to fall into mischaunce,
That is regardles of his governaunce.

Yet still Aragnoll (so his foe was hight)
Lay lurking covertly him to surprise,

And all his gins, that him entangle might,
Drest in good order as he could devise.
At length the foolish flie, without foresight,
As he that did all daunger quite despise, 390
Toward those parts came flying careleslie,
Where hidden was his hatefull enemie.

Who, seeing him, with secrete joy therefore
Did tickle inwardly in everie vaine,
And his false hart, fraught with all treasons
    store,
Was fil'd with hope his purpose to obtaine:
Himselfe he close upgathered more and
    more
Into his den, that his deceiptfull traine
By his there being might not be bewraid,
Ne anie noyse, ne anie motion made.   400

Like as a wily foxe, that, having spide
Where on a sunnie banke the lambes doo
    play,
Full closely creeping by the hinder side,
Lyes in ambushment of his hoped pray,
Ne stirreth limbe, till, seeing readie tide,
He rusheth forth, and snatcheth quite away
One of the litle yonglings unawares:
So to his worke Aragnoll him prepares.

Who now shall give unto my heavie eyes
A well of teares, that all may overflow? 410
Or where shall I finde lamentable cryes,
And mournfull tunes enough my griefe to
    show?
Helpe, O thou Tragick Muse, me to devise
Notes sad enough, t' expresse this bitter
    throw:
For loe! the drerie stownd is now arrived,
That of all happines hath us deprived.

The luckles Clarion, whether cruell Fate
Or wicked Fortune faultles him misled,
Or some ungracious blast out of the gate
Of Aeoles raine perforce him drove on
    hed,
Was (O sad hap and howre unfortunate!)
With violent swift flight forth caried   422
Into the cursed cobweb, which his foe
Had framed for his finall overthroe.

There the fond flie, entangled, strugled
    long,
Himselfe to free thereout; but all in vaine.
For, striving more, the more in laces strong
Himselfe he tide, and wrapt his winges
    twaine

In lymie snares the subtill loupes among;
That in the ende he breathelesse did re-
      maine,   430
And all his yougthly forces idly spent
Him to the mercie of th' avenger lent.

Which when the greisly tyrant did espie,
Like a grimme lyon rushing with fierce
      might
Out of his den, he seized greedelie
On the resistles pray, and with fell spight,
Under the left wing stroke his weapon slie
Into his heart, that his deepe groning spright
In bloodie streames foorth fled into the aire,
His bodie left the spectacle of care.   440

FINIS.

VISIONS OF THE WORLDS
VANITIE

[This series of original 'visions' is manifestly of kin to those translated from Petrarch
and Du Bellay and, more distantly, to 'Ruins
of Rome.' It is unquestionably of later composition, but how much later has been disputed.
Some critics, observing that, whereas the sonnets of the three earlier series are in the common Elizabethan form, the sonnets of this are
in the special form that Spenser devised for
himself, have argued that the interval of time
must be considerable. In the first place, however, we have no proof that Spenser may not
have devised his own sonnet-form early (we
meet it in the dedication to 'Virgil's Gnat,' of
Calendar days) ; in the second place, for the
three series that were translations he might
naturally choose the looser and therefore easier
Elizabethan form, when, for original sonnets, he
would adopt his own more complicated scheme.
This point set aside, there is nothing in the
series to denote a much later period : the style
is, indeed, distinctly immature. One may plau-
sibly conclude that 'Visions of the World's
Vanity' was suggested by the earlier 'Visions'
and executed not long after them.
   The noteworthy fact about these various
early poems is that they show Spenser, at the
outset of his career, driving full on allegory.
Partly by accident and partly by choice, he has
committed himself to a special form of the art,
from which he later progresses to others more
comprehensive. This form is the literary coun-
terpart of a mixed type, in which poetry and
the graphic arts are combined, the so-called
'emblem.' The essence of both consists in the
expression of an idea by means of a complete
image or picture. Thus Du Bellay, having

composed in his *Antiquitez de Rome* (' Ruins of
Rome ') a series of meditations upon the tran-
sitoriness of human grandeur, went on, in his
supplementary *Songe* (' Visions of Bellay '), to
express those same ideas in a series of poetic
pictures. These, when borrowed by Van der
Noot for the *Théâtre* of 1568, were made into
emblems proper by the addition of engravings
that rendered them to the eye. Such emblem
books, of engravings and poetry combined,
were enormously popular through most of the
sixteenth century. They affected the imagination of that period incalculably. Book followed book, edition edition. Mythology, fable,
natural history, history were ransacked for
themes and illustrations, which were repeated
in a dozen forms. Poetry, which, as the
' Visions of Petrarch ' show, had long since
practised a variety of this art, was stimulated
to it afresh. Spenser, in his turn, wrote ' Visions
of the World's Vanity,' among which the sonnets on the Scarabee and the Remora, adapted
from the first great emblem-writer Alciati,
sufficiently declare his indebtedness. The influence may be thought to extend even to the
allegory of the *Faery Queen ;* for the figures
in the procession at the House of Pride and
in the Masque of Cupid, with others of their
kind, are in a way but figures from the
emblem books glorified by a larger art. At
this point, however, the emblem as a special
type merges in the more common forms of
allegory.]

I

ONE day, whiles that my daylie cares did
      sleepe,
My spirit, shaking off her earthly prison,
Began to enter into meditation deepe
Of things exceeding reach of common rea-
      son;
Such as this age, in which all good is geason,
And all that humble is and meane debaced,
Hath brought forth in her last declining
      season,
Griefe of good mindes, to see goodnesse
      disgraced.
On which when as my thought was throghly
      placed,
Unto my eyes strange showes presented
      were,
Picturing that which I in minde embraced,
That yet those sights empassion me full
      nere.
   Such as they were (faire Ladie) take in
      worth,
   That when time serves, may bring things
      better forth.

II

In summers day, when Phœbus fairly shone,
I saw a bull as white as driven snowe,
With gilden hornes embowed like the
    moone,
In a fresh flowring meadow lying lowe:
Up to his eares the verdant grasse did
    growe,
And the gay floures did offer to be eaten;
But he with fatnes so did overflowe,
That he all wallowed in the weedes downe
    beaten,
Ne car'd with them his daintie lips to
    sweeten:
Till that a brize, a scorned little creature,
Through his faire hide his angrie sting did
    threaten,
And vext so sore, that all his goodly feature
    And all his plenteous pasture nought him
        pleased:
    So by the small the great is oft diseased.

III

Beside the fruitfull shore of muddie Nile,
Upon a sunnie banke outstretched lay,
In monstrous length, a mightie crocodile,
That, cram'd with guiltles blood and greedie
    pray
Of wretched people travailing that way,
Thought all things lesse than his disdain-
    full pride.
I saw a little bird, cal'd Tedula,
The least of thousands which on earth abide,
That forst this hideous beast to open wide
The greisly gates of his devouring hell,
And let him feede, as Nature doth provide,
Upon his jawes, that with blacke venime
    swell.
    Why then should greatest things the
        least disdaine,
    Sith that so small so mightie can con-
        straine?

IV

The kingly bird, that beares Joves thunder-
    clap,
One day did scorne the simple scarabee,
Proud of his highest service and good hap,
That made all other foules his thralls to
    bee:
The silly flie, that no redresse did see,
Spide where the eagle built his towring nest,
And kindling fire within the hollow tree,
Burnt up his yong ones, and himselfe dis-
    trest;

Ne suffred him in anie place to rest,
But drove in Joves owne lap his egs to
    lay;
Where gathering also filth him to infest,
Forst with the filth his egs to fling away:
    For which when as the foule was wroth,
        said Jove,
    'Lo! how the least the greatest may re-
        prove.'

V

Toward the sea turning my troubled eye,
I saw the fish (if fish I may it cleepe)
That makes the sea before his face to flye,
And with his flaggie finnes doth seeme to
    sweepe
The fomie waves out of the dreadfull deep,
The huge Leviathan, Dame Natures wonder,
Making his sport, that manie makes to weep:
A sword-fish small him from the rest did
    sunder,
That, in his throat him pricking softly
    under,
His wide abysse him forced forth to spewe,
That all the sea did roare like heavens
    thunder,
And all the waves were stain'd with filthie
    hewe.
    Hereby I learned have, not to despise
    What ever thing seemes small in com-
        mon eyes.

VI

An hideous dragon, dreadfull to behold,
Whose backe was arm'd against the dint of
    speare
With shields of brasse, that shone like
    burnisht golde,
And forkhed sting, that death in it did
    beare,
Strove with a spider, his unequall peare,
And bad defiance to his enemie.
The subtill vermin, creeping closely neare,
Did in his drinke shed poyson privilie;
Which, through his entrailes spreddin
    diversly,
Made him to swell, that nigh his bowells
    brust,
And him enforst to yeeld the victorie,
That did so much in his owne greatnesse
    trust.
    O how great vainnesse is it then to
        scorne
    The weake, that hath the strong so oft
        forlorne!

VII

High on a hill a goodly cedar grewe,
Of wondrous length and streight proportion,
That farre abroad her daintie odours
    threwe;
Mongst all the daughters of proud Libanon,
Her match in beautie was not anie one.
Shortly within her inmost pith there bred
A litle wicked worme, perceiv'd of none,
That on her sap and vitall moysture fed:
Thenceforth her garland so much honoured
Began to die, (O great ruth for the same!)
And her faire lockes fell from her loftie
    head,
That shortly balde and bared she became.
    I, which this sight beheld, was much
        dismayed,
    To see so goodly thing so soone decayed.

VIII

Soone after this I saw an elephant,
Adorn'd with bells and bosses gorgeouslie,
That on his backe did beare (as batteilant)
A gilden towre, which shone exceedinglie;
That he himselfe through foolish vanitie,
Both for his rich attire and goodly forme,
Was puffed up with passing surquedrie,
And shortly gan all other beasts to scorne:
Till that a little ant, a silly worme,
Into his nosthrils creeping, so him pained,
That, casting downe his towres, he did de-
    forme
Both borrowed pride, and native beautie
    stained.
    Let therefore nought, that great is,
        therein glorie,
    Sith so small thing his happines may
        varie.

IX

Looking far foorth into the ocean wide,
A goodly ship with banners bravely dight,
And flag in her top-gallant, I espide,
Through the maine sea making her merry
    flight:
Faire blew the winde into her bosome right,
And th' heavens looked lovely all the while,
That she did seeme to daunce, as in delight,
And at her owne felicitie did smile.
All sodainely there clove unto her keele
A little fish, that men call Remora,
Which stopt her course, and held her by
    the heele,
That winde nor tide could move her thence
    away.

Straunge thing me seemeth, that so small
    a thing
Should able be so great an one to wring.

X

A mighty lyon, lord of all the wood,
Having his hunger throughly satisfide
With pray of beasts and spoyle of living
    blood,
Safe in his dreadles den him thought to
    hide:
His sternesse was his prayse, his strength
    his pride,
And all his glory in his cruell clawes.
I saw a wasp, that fiercely him defide,
And bad him battaile even to his jawes;
Sore he him stong, that it the blood forth
    drawes,
And his proude heart is fild with fretting
    ire:
In vaine he threats his teeth, his tayle, his
    pawes,
And from his bloodie eyes doth sparkle fire;
    That dead himselfe he wisheth for de-
        spight.
    So weakest may anoy the most of might.

XI

What time the Romaine Empire bore the
    raine
Of all the world, and florisht most in might,
The nations gan their soveraigntie disdaine,
And cast to quitt them from their bondage
    quight:
So, when all shrouded were in silent night,
The Galles were, by corrupting of a mayde,
Possest nigh of the Capitol through slight,
Had not a goose the treachery bewrayde.
If then a goose great Rome from ruine
    stayde,
And Jove himselfe, the patron of the place,
Preservd from being to his foes betrayde,
Why do vaine men mean things so much
    deface,
    And in their might repose their most
        assurance,
    Sith nought on earth can chalenge long
        endurance?

XII

When these sad sights were overpast and
    gone,
My spright was greatly moved in her rest,
With inward ruth and deare affection,
To see so great things by so small distrest:

Thenceforth I gan in my engrieved brest
To scorne all difference of great and small,
Sith that the greatest often are opprest,
And unawares doe into daunger fall.
And ye, that read these ruines tragicall,
Learne by their losse to love the low de-
  gree,
And if that Fortune chaunce you up to call
To honours seat, forget not what you be:
For he that of himselfe is most secure
Shall finde his state most fickle and unsure.

FINIS.

THE VISIONS OF BELLAY

['The Visions of Bellay' and 'The Visions
of Petrarch,' which belong together, are presumably the earliest poems of the volume.
They are but a remodelling of Spenser's first
known literary work, the translation done in
1569 for Van der Noot's *Théâtre*: it is more
than likely, therefore, that they were executed
while that work was still of interest to him,
during his early days at Cambridge. The object of the youthful poet in these *rifacimenti*
was apparently not to better his translation,
but, for merely artistic effect, to turn the
irregular stanzas of the Petrarch group and
the blank verse poems of the Bellay group into
formal sonnets. He does not seem to have con-
sulted his foreign originals afresh, except that
he here renders for the first time four sonnets
out of Du Bellay which Van der Noot, in trans-
ferring the Frenchman's series to his book, had
dropped. The version of 1569 will be found
in the Appendix.]

I

It was the time when rest, soft sliding
  downe
From heavens hight into mens heavy eyes,
In the forgetfulnes of sleepe doth drowne
The carefull thoughts of mortall miseries.
Then did a ghost before mine eyes appeare,
On that great rivers banck, that runnes by
  Rome,
Which, calling me by name, bad me to reare
My lookes to heaven, whence all good gifts
  do come,
And crying lowd, 'Loe now, beholde,'
  quoth hee,
'What under this great temple placed is:
Lo, all is nought but flying vanitee!'
So I, that know this worlds inconstancies.

Sith onely God surmounts all times decay,
In God alone my confidence do stay.

II

On high hills top I saw a stately frame,
An hundred cubits high by just assize,
With hundreth pillours fronting faire the
  same,
All wrought with diamond after Dorick
  wize:
Nor brick, nor marble was the wall in
  view,
But shining christall, which from top to
  base
Out of her womb a thousand rayons threw
On hundred steps of Afrike golds enchase:
Golde was the parget, and the seeling bright
Did shine all scaly with great plates of
  golde;
The floore of jasp and emeraude was dight.
O worlds vainesse! Whiles thus I did be-
  hold,
  An earthquake shooke the hill from lowest
    seat,
  And overthrew this frame with ruine
    great.

III

Then did a sharped spyre of diamond
  bright,
Ten feete each way in square, appeare to
  mee,
Justly proportion'd up unto his hight,
So far as archer might his level see:
The top thereof a pot did seeme to beare,
Made of the mettall which we most do
  honour,
And in this golden vessell couched weare
The ashes of a mightie emperour:
Upon foure corners of the base were pight,
To beare the frame, foure great lyons of
  gold;
A worthy tombe for such a worthy wight.
Alas! this world doth nought but grievance
  hold.
  I saw a tempest from the heaven descend,
  Which this brave monument with flash
    did rend.

IV

I saw raysde up on yvorie pillours tall,
Whose bases were of richest mettalls warke,
The chapters alablaster, the fryses christall,
The double front of a triumphall arke:

On each side purtraid was a Victorie,
Clad like a nimph, that wings of silver weares,
And in triumphant chayre was set on hie
The auncient glory of the Romaine peares.
No worke it seem'd of earthly craftsmans wit,
But rather wrought by his owne industry,
That thunder-dartes for Jove his syre doth fit.
Let me no more see faire thing under sky,
  Sith that mine eyes have seene so faire a sight
  With sodain fall to dust consumed quight.

V

Then was the faire Dodonian tree far seene
Upon seaven hills to spread his gladsome gleame,
And conquerours bedecked with his greene,
Along the banckes of the Ausonian streame:
There many an auncient trophee was addrest,
And many a spoyle, and many a goodly show,
Which that brave races greatnes did attest,
That whilome from the Troyan blood did flow.
Ravisht I was so rare a thing to vew;
When lo! a barbarous troupe of clownish fone
The honour of these noble boughs down threw:
Under the wedge I heard the tronck to grone;
  And since, I saw the roote in great disdaine
  A twinne of forked trees send forth againe.

VI

I saw a wolfe under a rockie cave
Noursing two whelpes; I saw her litle ones
In wanton dalliance the teate to crave,
While she her neck wreath'd from them for the nones.
I saw her raunge abroad to seeke her food,
And roming through the field with greedie rage
T' embrew her teeth and clawes with lukewarm blood
Of the small heards, her thirst for to asswage.
I saw a thousand huntsmen, which descended
Downe from the mountaines bordring Lombardie,

That with an hundred speares her flank wide rended:
I saw her on the plaine outstretched lie,
  Throwing out thousand throbs in her owne soyle:
  Soone on a tree uphang'd I saw her spoyle.

VII

I saw the bird that can the sun endure
With feeble wings assay to mount on hight;
By more and more she gan her wings t' assure,
Following th' ensample of her mothers sight:
I saw her rise, and with a larger flight
To pierce the cloudes, and with wide pinneons
To measure the most haughtie mountaines hight,
Untill she raught the gods owne mansions:
There was she lost; when suddaine I behelde,
Where, tumbling through the ayre in firie fold,
All flaming downe she on the plaine was felde,
And soone her bodie turn'd to ashes colde.
  I saw the foule that doth the light dispise
  Out of her dust like to a worme arise.

VIII

I saw a river swift, whose fomy billowes
Did wash the ground work of an old great wall;
I saw it cover'd all with griesly shadowes,
That with black horror did the ayre appall:
Thereout a strange beast with seven heads arose,
That townes and castles under her brest did coure,
And seem'd both milder beasts and fiercer foes
Alike with equall ravine to devoure.
Much was I mazde, to see this monsters kinde
In hundred formes to change his fearefull hew;
When as at length I saw the wrathfull winde,
Which blows cold storms, burst out of Scithian mew,
  That sperst these cloudes, and in so short as thought,
  This dreadfull shape was vanished to nought.

IX

Then all astoined with this mighty ghoast,
An hideous bodie, big and strong, I sawe,
With side long beard, and locks down
    hanging loast,
Sterne face, and front full of Saturnlike
    awe;
Who, leaning on the belly of a pot,
Pourd foorth a water, whose out gushing
    flood
Ran bathing all the creakie shore aflot,
Whereon the Troyan prince spilt Turnus
    blood;
And at his feete a bitch wolfe suck did
    yeeld
To two young babes: his left the palme
    tree stout,
His right hand did the peacefull olive
    wield,
And head with lawrell garnisht was about.
    Sudden both palme and olive fell away,
    And faire greene lawrell branch did quite
        decay.

X

Hard by a rivers side a virgin faire,
Folding her armes to heaven with thousand
    throbs,
And outraging her cheekes and golden
    haire,
To falling rivers sound thus tun'd her
    sobs.
'Where is,' quoth she, 'this whilom hon-
    oured face?
Where the great glorie and the auncient
    praise,
In which all worlds felicitie had place,
When gods and men my honour up did
    raise?
Suffisd' it not that civill warres me made
The whole worlds spoile, but that this
    Hydra new,
Of hundred Hercules to be assaide,
With seven heads, budding monstrous
    crimes anew,
    So many Neroes and Caligulaes
    Out of these crooked shores must dayly
        rayse?'

XI

Upon an hill a bright flame I did see,
Waving aloft with triple point to skie,
Which, like incense of precious cedar tree,
With balmie odours fil'd th' ayre farre and
    nie.

A bird all white, well feathered on each
    wing,
Hereout up to the throne of gods did flie,
And all the way most pleasant notes did
    sing,
Whilst in the smoake she unto heaven did
    stie.
Of this faire fire the scattered rayes forth
    threw
On everie side a thousand shining beames:
When sudden dropping of a silver dew
(O grievous chance!) gan quench those
    precious flames;
    That it, which earst so pleasant sent did
        yeld,
    Of nothing now but noyous sulphure
        smeld.

XII

I saw a spring out of a rocke forth rayle,
As cleare as christall gainst the sunnie
    beames,
The bottome yeallow, like the golden grayle
That bright Pactolus washeth with his
    streames:
It seem'd that Art and Nature had assem-
    bled
All pleasure there, for which mans hart
    could long;
And there a noyse alluring sleepe soft
    trembled,
Of manie accords, more sweete than mer-
    maids song:
The seates and benches shone as yvorie,
And hundred nymphes sate side by side
    about:
When from nigh hills, with hideous outcrie,
A troupe of satyres in the place did rout,
    Which with their villeine feete the
        streame did ray,
    Threw down the seats, and drove the
        nymphs away.

XIII

Much richer then that vessell seem'd to bee,
Which did to that sad Florentine appeare,
Casting mine eyes farre off, I chaunst to
    see
Upon the Latine coast herselfe to reare.
But suddenly arose a tempest great,
Bearing close envie to these riches rare,
Which gan assaile this ship with dreadfull
    threat,
This ship, to which none other might com-
    pare.

And finally the storme impetuous
Sunke up these riches, second unto none,
Within the gulfe of greedie Nereus.
I saw both ship and mariners each one,
    And all that treasure, drowned in the maine:
    But I the ship saw after raisd' againe.

XIV

Long having deeply gron'd these visions sad,
I saw a citie like unto that same,
Which saw the messenger of tidings glad,
But that on sand was built the goodly frame:
It seem'd her top the firmament did rayse,
And no lesse rich than faire, right worthie sure
(If ought here worthie) of immortall dayes,
Or if ought under heaven might firme endure.
Much wondred I to see so faire a wall:
When from the Northerne coast a storme arose,
Which, breathing furie from his inward gall
On all which did against his course oppose,
    Into a clowde of dust sperst in the aire
    The weake foundations of this citie faire.

XV

At length, even at the time when Morpheus
Most trulie doth unto our eyes appeare,
Wearie to see the heavens still wavering thus,
I saw Typhæus sister comming neare;
Whose head, full bravely with a morion hidd,
Did seeme to match the gods in majestie.
She, by a rivers bancke that swift downe slidd,
Over all the world did raise a trophee hie;
An hundred vanquisht kings under her lay,
With armes bound at their backs in shamefull wize.
Whilst I thus mazed was with great affray,
I saw the heavens in warre against her rize:
    Then downe she stricken fell with clap of thonder,
    That with great noyse I wakte in sudden wonder.

FINIS.

THE VISIONS OF PETRARCH
FORMERLY TRANSLATED

I

BEING one day at my window all alone,
So manie strange things happened me to see,
As much it grieveth me to thinke thereon.
At my right hand a hynde appear'd to mee,
So faire as mote the greatest god delite;
Two eager dogs did her pursue in chace,
Of which the one was blacke, the other white:
With deadly force so in their cruell race
They pincht the haunches of that gentle beast,
That at the last, and in short time, I spide,
Under a rocke, where she, alas! opprest,
Fell to the ground, and there untimely dide.
    Cruell death vanquishing so noble beautie
    Oft makes me wayle so hard a destenie.

II

After, at sea a tall ship did appeare,
Made all of heben and white yvorie;
The sailes of golde, of silke the tackle were:
Milde was the winde, calme seem'd the sea to bee,
The skie eachwhere did show full bright and faire:
With rich treasures this gay ship fraighted was:
But sudden storme did so turmoyle the aire,
And tumbled up the sea, that she (alas!)
Strake on a rock, that under water lay,
And perished past all recoverie.
O how great ruth, and sorrowfull assay,
Doth vex my spirite with perplexitie,
    Thus in a moment to see lost and drown'd
    So great riches as like cannot be found!

III

Then heavenly branches did I see arise
Out of the fresh and lustie lawrell tree,
Amidst the yong greene wood: of Paradise
Some noble plant I thought my selfe to see.
Such store of birds therein yshrowded were,
Chaunting in shade their sundrie melodie,
That with their sweetnes I was ravish't nere.
While on this lawrell fixed was mine eie,

The skie gan everie where to overcast,
And darkned was the welkin all about:
When sudden flash of heavens fire out brast,
And rent this royall tree quite by the
    roote;
    Which makes me much and ever to com-
        plaine;
    For no such shadow shalbe had againe.

IV

Within this wood, out of a rocke did rise
A spring of water, mildly rumbling downe,
Whereto approched not in anie wise
The homely shepheard, nor the ruder
    clowne;
But manie Muses, and the nymphes with-
    all,
That sweetly in accord did tune their voyce
To the soft sounding of the waters fall,
That my glad hart thereat did much re-
    joyce.
But while herein I tooke my chiefe delight,
I saw (alas!) the gaping earth devoure
The spring, the place, and all cleane out of
    sight:
Which yet aggreeves my hart even to this
    houre,
    And wounds my soule with rufull me-
        morie,
    To see such pleasures gon so suddenly.

V

I saw a phœnix in the wood alone,
With purple wings, and crest of golden hewe;
Strange bird he was, whereby I thought
    anone,
That of some heavenly wight I had the
    vewe;
Untill he came unto the broken tree,
And to the spring, that late devoured was.
What say I more? Each thing at last we
    see
Doth passe away: the phœnix there, alas!
Spying the tree destroid, the water dride,
Himselfe smote with his beake, as in dis-
    daine,
And so foorthwith in great despight he
    dide:
That yet my heart burnes in exceeding
    paine,

For ruth and pitie of so haples plight.
O, let mine eyes no more see such a
    sight!

VI

At last, so faire a ladie did I spie,
That thinking yet on her I burne and
    quake:
On hearbs and flowres she walked pen-
    sively,
Milde, but yet love she proudly did for-
    sake:
White seem'd her robes, yet woven so they
    were
As snow and golde together had been
    wrought:
Above the wast a darke clowde shrouded
    her,
A stinging serpent by the heele her caught;
Wherewith she languisht as the gathered
    floure,
And well assur'd she mounted up to joy.
Alas! on earth so nothing doth endure,
But bitter griefe and sorrowfull annoy:
    Which make this life wretched and mis-
        erable,
    Tossed with stormes of fortune variable.

VII

When I behold this tickle trustles state
Of vaine worlds glorie, flitting too and fro,
And mortall men tossed by troublous fate
In restles seas of wretchednes and woe,
I wish I might this wearie life forgoe,
And shortly turne unto my happie rest,
Where my free spirite might not anie moe
Be vext with sights, that doo her peace
    molest.
And ye, faire Ladie, in whose bounteous
    brest
All heavenly grace and vertue shrined is,
When ye these rythmes doo read, and vew
    the rest,
Loath this base world, and thinke of hea-
    vens blis:
    And though ye be the fairest of Gods
        creatures,
    Yet thinke, that death shall spoyle your
        goodly features.
                    FINIS.

THE FAERIE QUEENE

DISPOSED INTO TWELVE BOOKS, FASHIONING

XII MORALL VERTUES

LONDON
PRINTED FOR WILLIAM PONSONBIE
1590

TO THE
MOST MIGHTIE
AND
MAGNIFICENT EMPRESSE
ELIZABETH,
BY THE
GRACE OF GOD
QUEENE OF ENGLAND,
FRANCE AND
IRELAND
DEFENDER OF THE FAITH &C.
HER MOST HUMBLE
SERVANT:
ED. SPENSER

[Dedication of the edition of 1590.]

TO THE MOST HIGH
MIGHTIE AND MAGNIFICENT EMPRESSE
RENOWMED FOR PIETIE, VERTUE,
AND ALL GRATIOUS GOVERNMENT
ELIZABETH
BY THE GRACE OF GOD QUEENE OF
ENGLAND FRAUNCE AND IRELAND
AND OF VIRGINIA,
DEFENDOUR OF THE FAITH, &C.
HER MOST HUMBLE SERVAUNT
EDMUND SPENSER
DOTH IN ALL HUMILITIE
DEDICATE, PRESENT AND CONSECRATE
THESE HIS LABOURS
TO LIVE WITH THE ETERNITIE
OF HER FAME

[Dedication of the edition of 1596.]

[When the first three books of the *Faery Queen* were published in 1590, Spenser had been at work upon the poem for at least ten years. The earliest records of its existence are worth transcribing. In the letter to Harvey of April 2, 1580, he writes: 'Nowe, my *Dreames* and *Dying Pellicane* being fully finished . . . and presentlye to bee imprinted, I wil in hande forthwith with my *Faery Queene*, whyche I praye you hartily send me with al expedition, and your frendly letters and long expected judgement wythal, whyche let not be shorte, but in all pointes suche as you ordinarilye use and I extraordinarily desire.' That was in the days just following the publication of the *Calendar*, some three months and a half before he went with Lord Grey to Ireland. There, probably in the year 1582, occurred that gathering in the little cottage near Dublin so memorably recounted by his friend Lodowick Bryskett. Being invited to speak of moral philosophy, its benefits and its nature, Spenser declined: 'For,' said he, 'sure I am that it is not unknowne

unto you that I have already undertaken a work tending to the same effect, which is in heroical verse, under the title of a *Faerie Queene*, to represent all the moral vertues, assigning to every virtue a knight to be the patron and defender of the same: in whose actions and feates of armes and chivalry the operations of that virtue whereof he is the protector are to be expressed, and the vices and unruly appetites that oppose themselves against the same to be beaten downe and overcome. Which work . . . I have already well entred into.' The company were content to await its conclusion.

Eight years passed, completing a decade, with but a quarter of the whole work done, and still this conclusion seemed to the poet within easy reach. The Letter to Raleigh shows him quite confident of achieving his hundred and forty-fourth canto, shows him even planning another hundred and forty-four in sequel. Mortality, that favorite theme of his generation, the theme of *Complaints*, was assuredly not in his mind when he thought of his *Faery Queen*

And, indeed, the second three books were executed much more rapidly than the first, at the rate, it seems, of about a book a year; for they can hardly have been taken up in earnest before his return to Ireland in 1591, and they were completed in the spring of 1594, under the pressure, one may think, of his approaching marriage. How he progressed with them is partly recorded in the thirty-third and the eightieth sonnets of the *Amoretti*. They were not published till 1596, apparently because he could not take them to London earlier.

This eightieth sonnet of the *Amoretti*, which announces the completion of thus much of his poem, declares that, 'being halfe fordonne' (i. e. exhausted), the poet will rest, 'and gather to himself new breath awhile.' That is the last we hear about the further progress of the *Faery Queen* until the publication in 1609, ten years after his death, of the cantos on Mutability. These have been regarded by some as an independent poem (not unlike the *Cinque Canti* of Ariosto) — for the reason, it seems, that they are competent to stand alone. Yet the mere fact that they were numbered VI, VII, and VIII (surely not by the printer) indicates that they are part of a larger whole, and stanza 37 of the first of them gives the clearest possible evidence that they belong to the great romance. Were these cantos, then, all that Spenser found time during four years to compose for the remaining books of his poem, or did he write others, which may have perished in the disaster of 1598? Again, their being numbered as they are is suggestive: Spenser may be thought, at least to have planned this one book in outline, possibly to have executed other parts of it. A generation after his death, Sir James Ware asserted that the *Faery Queen* had been finished, and that the unpublished books had been lost in 1598 'by the disorder and abuse of his servant, whom he had sent before him into England.' The story is, of course, apocryphal (that Spenser could have composed six books in four years is a manifest impossibility; nor would any so extensive a loss have failed to be recorded earlier); yet it may well be that the sack of Kilcolman deprived the world of not a few such fragments as this.

In that letter of April 2, 1580, from which our first knowledge of the *Faery Queen* is derived, Spenser, we have seen, called for the judgment of Harvey upon his new venture. Harvey, never loath to express an opinion, sent back one of those misguided verdicts to which men of his stamp are unluckily prone: it would be a mere curiosity of criticism, did it not by chance record the views of the poet himself. 'To be plaine,' is the summing up, 'I am voyde of al judgement, if your *Nine Comœdies* . . . come not neerer Ariostoes comœdies . . . than that *Elvish Queene* doth to his *Orlando Furioso*, which, notwithstanding, you wil needes seeme to emulate, and hope to overgo, as you flatly professed your self in one of your last letters.' In undertaking what he must have meant to be the grand work of his life, Spenser, then, was deliberately setting himself to rival Ariosto.

This avowed rivalry is involved in the very origins of his plan. For, first and most obviously, he must build up an extended poem of action: the material in which his didactic purpose was to be worked out, was epic. In this field all the many influences that would control his choice drew him irresistibly to one quarter, the romance. The poetry in which the traditions of his native literature were embodied gave him, for epics, romances. The great legendary hero of his race, the ancestor of his Queen, Arthur, was at the very heart of romance. The highest embodiment of his own spiritual ideals was in chivalry, and chivalry implied romance. Romance, too, satisfied to the full his native delight in color and warmth and magic of beauty. The epics of antiquity, on the other hand, dealt with alien matter, in an alien, though noble, spirit. Such imitations of them as had been made by Trissino, Ronsard, and others, were too utterly dreary to encourage a like attempt, and the *Gerusalemme Liberata* of Tasso, in which the native glamour of romance was to be informed by their more spacious and simpler art, had not yet been given to the world. Nothing could be more natural, then, more inevitable, than that Spenser should set himself to rival the *Orlando Furioso*. In 1580 it still stood as the one really great poem of epic scope that sixteenth-century Europe had produced, the accepted masterpiece, moreover, of that variety of the epic to which he was irresistibly drawn, the romance poem.

But this was not all. Ariosto was furthermore accounted a grave and moral poet, a master in the art of poetic edification. He had come by this repute through the clearest of critical necessities. His fertility and delightfulness, which seemed to revive the lost epical spirit of Homer, had captivated at once all lovers of poetry; but poetry could not in those days be its own *raison d'être*, it must make for moral edification: the inevitable concern of his admirers, therefore, had for generations been to expound the ultimate seriousness of his purpose. His easy-going scepticism, his irreverence, his delight in life and action, moral and immoral, for their own sake, without ethical prepossessions, these qualities they ignored or explained away: his seriousness (sometimes, by force of imaginative sympathy, very genuine, but more often conventional or factitious) they exalted to a level with the high seriousness of Virgil. The chief engine of their work was allegory. Ariosto, who made free use of whatever might enrich his poem, had adorned it here and there with frankly allegorical episodes : successive commentators had forced a like interpretation upon other passages, till, by 1580, the whole poem was expounded as a many-colored, comprehensive allegory of life, and all its admirers were agreed on its fundamental morality.

'Our sage and serious Spenser,' then, could find even in the moral aspects of the *Orlando* matter for sincere emulation : in particular, of course, that allegory which had been so thoroughly read into it by commentators. This was, at best, somewhat irregular : it illustrated the moral problems of life, efficiently perhaps, but rather at random : it left room for a more philosophic method. He must have felt that, in this regard, he might safely 'hope to overgo' the Italian. For, with a genuine fervor for allegory, impossible to the more worldly and modern Ariosto, impossible even to those commentators on the *Orlando* who had pushed allegorical interpretation so far, he had conceived a plan of vastly greater scope and more thorough method. His poem was to expound a complete system of Christian ethics, modelled upon the Aristotelian scheme of the virtues and vices, and this main allegory was to be enriched by another, to deal with notable contemporary events and personages.

It is one thing, however, to compose a great poem of action which commentators may find means to interpret allegorically, and quite another to develop a set of ideas allegorically in a great poem of action. For, given the action, it will go hard but some definite spiritual parrallel may be found for it (as Tasso, having composed his romance-epic, safeguarded the most seductive passages by *ex post facto* allegorizing) : given the set of ideas, however, action, free, self-sustaining, moving of its own impulse in a plain path, is by no means easy to invent. And Spenser's material was unusually stubborn. He had twelve 'private morall vertues,' each to be embodied in a knight, whose 'feates of armes and chivalry' were to show the workings of that virtue with regard to 'the vices and unruly appetites that oppose themselves against the same.' To devise twelve appropriate courses of action was manifestly but to begin : these must furthermore be held together ; and how ? If he carried them all forward simultaneously, by interweaving, after the manner of the *Orlando Furioso*, he might indeed achieve unity, but he would also confuse the philosophic development of each separate virtue : if he developed the action of each virtue separately and continuously, the second not begun until the first was ended, he would be composing not one poem but twelve. The alternative was certainly hard. In the philosophic scheme, however, after which his own was planned, Aristotle's, Spenser found the rudiments of a solution. Concerning Magnanimity he read that 'it seems to be a kind of ornament of all the other virtues, in that it makes them better and cannot be without them.' From this hint he developed means of unification. The twelve virtues were to be treated separately, but at the same time brought into relation to the master virtue Magnanimity, — or, as he chose, Magnificence. In narrative terms, there was to be a hero, who, by playing an important, though it might be a brief, part in the enterprise of each knight, should be gradually developed as the central agent of the poem. Epical dignity would be furthered if this hero were historic, and romance pointed to the British Arthur. Then there must be a heroine — who could hardly be Guenevere. At this point the allegory gave an opening to loyalty — or, if one pleases, adulation. For according to Aristotle, the object-matter of Magnanimity is honor, or 'Glory,' and who could better stand for this than Spenser's sovereign, Elizabeth ? This choice determined the rest. She could not be introduced *in propria persona*, still less as another historic character. The poet, therefore, invented for her the disguise of Gloriana, Queen of Faery Land. For narrative function he gave her the initiation of the twelve enterprises.

This general outline of action once conceived, the separate parts could be planned as the poem progressed. There was no need that the matter of each book should be determined at the outset ; even the conclusion might be left for a time undecided. The one problem to be solved immediately was the beginning The various enterprises were to start from the court of Gloriana on successive days of her great annual feast. Should this feast be described at the outset in a sort of proem, or should each separate book begin with an account of that particular day of the feast on which the knight of the book was sent forth ? One or other of these methods would unquestionably have been the choice of Ariosto, who, as a genuine romance poet, believed in beginning at the beginning. To begin there, however, would not be epic (Ariosto himself had been blamed for just that); the genuine epic poet plunged at once *in medias res ;* and the *Faery Queen*, though not epic in formal structure, ought none the less to acknowledge classical law. Spenser, therefore, determined to keep his beginnings, the feast, for retrospective presentment. Since he evidently felt also, however, that this feast was one great pageant, to be preserved entire and not distributed among the several books, it must manifestly, in default of first place, come last. So far his plan might seem to be clear. Yet the account given in the prefatory letter is oddly perplexing. According to one passage, the twelfth and last book is to be devoted entire to the beginnings; according to another, it would seem to be intended for the enterprise of the twelfth knight; and surely, one might expect from it some termination to the quest of Magnificence for Glory, of Arthur for his Faery Queen. One inclines to doubt if Spenser really knew just where his plan was taking him.

So organized, the *Faery Queen* must manifestly be at a disadvantage with other great poems of action. Despite the ingenious device for linking the separate enterprises to the quest of Arthur and the rule of Gloriana, the poem could not have that unity, that centralization of forces, which distinguishes the epics of antiquity. In the six books composed, Arthur does not really become a controlling and guiding power in the action, nor is it likely that all the twelve could have made him that. Gloriana could never have become much more than a kind of presiding divinity, a transcendent looker-on. Nor, in lieu of centralization, could the poem attain the forward energy of the *Orlando Furioso.* Ariosto's romance moves like a broad river, in a dozen currents, now mingling, now separating, ever on, leisurely, irresistibly. In the *Faery Queen,* one enterprise must run its course uninterrupted to the end, and then disappear forever; a fresh start must be made, another enterprise, with new characters, set in motion and followed through; and then a third. That these enterprises succeed each other in time, that certain episodes are carried over from book to book, and certain characters, can hardly create the impression of forward energy. As it progresses, indeed, the poem takes on more and more the external aspect of the *Orlando,* but the ground plan of separate enterprises keeps its action fundamentally different. It moves without clearly perceptible goal.

This peculiarity of organization, however, is hardly the cause that so many have found the *Faery Queen* tedious. They might complain, rather, that the poem is not grounded in action, that in those simple human energies which alone could sustain an epic or a romance at such length it is sadly wanting. And they would complain with some reason. Spenser's knights pass from chivalric feat to chivalric feat with due enterprise, but the eye of their creator is less often upon the doing than the deed. Scene follows scene in the narrative, less often an encounter of active forces than a picture

of spiritual conditions. Spenser, indeed, had not that delight in the realities of living action, that native sense for the situations that lurk in the conflict of living energies, which were the gift of the poet he particularly emulated. The combats of his knights, for example, how often they seem to be repetitions of a set ceremony! To Ariosto each combat is a new and quite peculiar act of life; it is the outbreak of forces that meet in a fresh combination or under fresh conditions; simple or intricate, it has a spirit and growth of its own. That unending recurrence of encounters, therefore, which is the special infirmity of romance, becomes in his poem a manifestation of exuberant vitality. In the *Faery Queen,* on the other hand, spirited as some few of the combats are, particularly those of the second book, one recognizes only too clearly that Spenser's heart is not in this eager work. Nor is it in that active conflict of will with will, of purpose with circumstance, which is the life of the poetry of action. Even in those scenes which are most truly dynamic, not merely picturesque or expository, scenes like the meeting of the Redcross Knight with Despair, the action, the power, is mainly embodied in one personage; there is little interplay of forces. For situations his sense is at times curiously fallible; as when Britomart at the close of her combat with Arthegall, and during and after the negotiations for truce, is left standing, like an image, with her sword uplifted to strike.

It would seem sufficiently clear that such failings as these, in so far as they are failings, spring from a native inaptitude for the poetry of action. Yet how often we hear them and others ascribed to the allegorical design! If, in any passage, the poet's imagination seems to flag, the blame is always on the allegory. The combat of the Redcross Knight with the Dragon is conventional and lifeless — because the allegory obliges Spenser to draw the fighting out to the third day. Medina and her two sisters are desperately uninteresting, the domestic organization of the House of Alma is described in rather ridiculous detail — again because of the allegory. The allegory, in short, is mainly a check or drag upon the poet's naturally spontaneous and fresh imagination. That many of the leading characters, for instance, are too shadow-like, not living men and women in whom one can take a living interest, is what might have been expected; as embodiments of abstractions they could not be other. Bunyan, to be sure, has shown that allegory can be made vital at length, but the length of the *Pilgrim's Progress* is as nothing to that of the *Faery Queen,* and its plan is the perfection of simplicity. To an allegorical scheme, on the other hand, so vast and so complicated as that devised by Spenser, no poet could have given full imaginative life. Hence, in the end, the poem's peculiar tediousness.

In criticism such as this there is just enough truth to be misleading. The combat of the Redcross Knight with the Dragon, Medina and her sisters, the House of Alma — it cannot be denied that these must be charged on the allegory. Yet when we survey the poem from end to end, how many such staring failures do we find, how many failures that can clearly be laid to allegorical pressure ? It is true also that, if many of the leading characters are somewhat shadow-like and unreal, the fault may partly be that they personate abstractions. But has Spenser, anywhere in his work at large, shown signs of the power to create substantial men and women ? If the *Faery Queen* had been designed as pure romance, would its leading characters have been more human ? Is not their remoteness due quite as much to his absorption in the ideal as to his love of mere allegory ? Indeed, this supposed domination of the poem by allegory, the allegory of abstractions, will hardly bear the test of simple reading. In the first two books, of course, those with which everybody is familiar, it is indisputable. The Redcross Knight and Una, Sir Guyon and his Palmer, and the long array of personages among whom these two champions execute their 'feates of armes and chivalry' very manifestly stand for qualities, ideas, and the like, and the 'feates of armes and chivalry' for successive 'operations' of the spirit. With Book III, however, there comes a sudden and most curious change. Britomart, the heroine, is still nominally of the old order, the formal embodiment of chastity, and she is accompanied by a few figures like Malecasta, also of the old order ; but other figures appear, and in the greater number, who can be reduced to abstractions by nothing short of violence. Florimel is no more than a beautiful maiden of romance, faithful to her love amid disasters ; Hellenore is but a frail wife, Malbecco, up to the time of his transformation, but an old and jealous husband ; and their actions are equally unsymbolic. In a word, barring personal and historic allusions, most of the characters in Book III are no more than men and women of certain general types engaged in actions which are typically moral. One may, of course, with Spenser, call such work allegory, but it is manifestly not that kind of allegory which can hamper free movement of the imagination ; and when one notices that it prevails throughout the better part of the remaining books, one wonders at the persistence of the old cry.

Yet after this much-abused allegory of abstractions has ceased to dominate the romance, it still remains a mode of the poet's rarest creative power — among the minor figures. Throughout the poem, indeed, these figures are, on the whole, more vivid than those which lead the action, and when they are particularly vivid it is often because of their allegorical intensity. The main characters draw but little life from the allegory ; when they impress us, it is rather as types of ideal humanity ; but those others, among whom they move, how often their life is the very quintessence of an emotion or an idea ! It is not the procession at the House of Pride, or the Masque of Cupid, that one need cite anew. Splendid as these pageants are, they are mainly ornamental, and the value of allegory as ornament has always been recognized. But those strange figures that play a small but real part in the action, one succeeding another in brief stages, how much of the power of the poem issues from them ! We may be indifferent to Arthur, to Belphœbe, to Duessa, to Cambell and Triamond ; but Despair and Atin and Guile and the blacksmith Care and Talus (if he be a minor figure), these are unforgettable. They are not human beings ; their very life of feature and action is rooted in the immaterialities they embody. If ever abstractions took flesh and walked, it is these. And beside them are half-human creatures, such as Ignaro, to link them with wholly human and delightful creatures such as Phædria, whose charm is forever at odds with her allegorical duty. Surely, had the *Faery Queen* been pure romance, it would have been a much less exquisite creation.

For, in fine, the world of the *Faery Queen* is not altogether the world of romance ; it is, if possible, more remote, more strange, more diverse. By its forest fountains meet Venus and Diana, almost within the ken of Christian knights and ladies, and in its castles or upon its open hillsides and heaths, among gentry and retainers and shepherds and very rabble, side by side with giants and monsters, move sheer incarnations of the immaterial. It is a world of jarring elements gathered from antiquity and the Middle Ages and the Renaissance, and harmonized by the serenest of poetic imaginations. In such a world as this, if we can breathe its atmosphere, we shall not crave the vigor and sparkle of movement that are at such full tide in the *Orlando Furioso*, nor even the graver human energies of the great epics : it has a life to which these are not essential. For, externally a poem of action, meant to rival Ariosto's, the *Faery Queen* is at heart but the vision of a contemplative mind to which the main realities of life are beauty and the law of the spirit. If it quickens at rare intervals into action full and vigorous, the quickening is but for a moment, and when it subsides we are not regretful. Faint in passion, faint even in pathos, the poem appeals most intimately to that 'inward eye' which can read forms and hues of beauty, and feature and bearing as they reveal the spirit, and to the mind that can read the spirit in speech. And this world that Spenser has created can never be to us a mere Kubla Khan paradise of romance. Amid its throng of ideal creatures, though we may not feel the force of the express moral doctrine they enact, we shall feel the force of the poet's own bent. His temper of grave and sweet spirituality, always human, that tone of the mind which is ever the chief spring of moral influence, this will be unescapable, and, in the end, it will be this as much as the pure magic of his imagination that will seem to impart to the poem its peculiar and imperturbable atmosphere.

Spenser was long ago called 'the Rubens of our poets,' and the phrase is still passed about. The vision which it evokes of large, plump, pink-and-white women and of big-limbed, tawny men, of superb physical vigor and of bright magnificence of color, will hardly appeal to the judicious as Spenserian. If one must have a phrase, let it be Charles Lamb's 'the poet of poets,' since that, despite its apparent vagueness, has a meaning. For what finally impresses us in the *Faery Queen* is its triumph over a dozen capital defects by the power of a very few, and those the essential, poetic qualities. Its narrative plan is fundamentally vicious, the narrative execution of the various episodes is weakened again and again by the most singular blunders, it is neither consistent allegory nor consistent romance, it gives over one canto to rhymed genealogy, another to rhymed chronicle, another to a merely ingenious transmogrification of the human body almost as crude as that at the conclusion of the *Roman de la Rose:* one might continue the story of its defects, general and particular, for pages. And yet, as unmistakably as the *Divina Commedia*, it has the imaginative and spiritual tone of high poetry. Perhaps just because of these defects, moreover, no poem makes us feel more keenly the mere virtue of style. Spenser's almost unerring sense for language and his apparently inexhaustible power of welling out the most limpid and exquisitely modulated verse, these make poetry of material that his imagination cannot vivify. It is these, too, that have made him master to so many poetic spirits of alien temper. He has taught more poets than almost any other poet in our literature.

The most patent, though not the most inti-

mate, mode of his influence has been his great stanza. Much has been written about its qualities of form, which have been illustrated by a long line of masterpieces; a word, therefore, about its origins may be better worth while, especially since critics have not always remembered that, if he invented this stanza, it was, in part, of necessity. When he began the *Faery Queen*, indeed, the forms among which he might have chosen were few and not all good. Blank verse had not yet been suppled to free movement by generations of dramatic artists; it was a yet new and strange invention. The ten-syllable couplet labored under the name of 'riding rimes' and was associated chiefly with the more humorous passages of the *Canterbury Tales*. Spenser might well have disregarded this prejudice, but it was of weight. In stanzas, the accredited form for high poetry was the rhyme royal, the stanza of his own *Hymns*. This was capable of sweetness and grace, even of vigor: seven lines, however, was rather narrow compass for the more extended harmonies of verse, and the arrangement of the rhymes at the close restricted free movement. Finally, there was the Italian *ottava rima*, the stanza of Ariosto's romance and of his own 'Virgil's Gnat.' For such a poem as he was about to undertake it might seem to have been the most natural form. Yet, admirably adapted to a rapid and flexible style and to the ready interchange of pathos, humor, and lively action, as also to facile sweetness, it was hardly capable of graver modulations, of such higher harmonies as Spenser was then dreaming. The first six lines were too fluent, the distinct couplet at the close was too epigrammatic. In defect, then, of satisfactory models, he was driven to invention. He knew, in Chaucer and Lyndesay, a fine, sonorous old stanza in eight verses, built of two quatrains linked by rhyme. Such linking by rhyme was familiar to him from Marot as well, and he had practised the art in the *Calendar*. He had also there experimented with the alexandrine, had learned to moderate and vary its pendulum movement, and had found that, in combination with other measures, it was capable of the most unexpected sonorities. For his *Faery Queen*, therefore, he merely added to the old stanza that he knew a final alexandrine, and by that simplest combination transfigured them both.

'Beauty making beautiful old rime,
  In praise of ladies dead and lovely knights.'

Those verses of Shakespeare might seem to have been meant for motto to the *Faery Queen*. Read somewhat fantastically, they might also fit the stanza to which the *Faery Queen* owes so much of its abiding charm.]

A LETTER OF THE AUTHORS
EXPOUNDING HIS WHOLE INTENTION IN
THE COURSE OF THIS WORKE: WHICH
FOR THAT IT GIVETH GREAT LIGHT
TO THE READER, FOR THE BETTER
UNDERSTANDING IS HEREUNTO
ANNEXED

TO THE RIGHT NOBLE, AND VALOROUS,
SIR WALTER RALEIGH KNIGHT, LORD
WARDEIN OF THE STANNERYES,
AND HER MAJESTIES LIEFE-
TENAUNT OF THE COUNTY
OF CORNEWAYLL

SIR, knowing how doubtfully all allegories may be construed, and this booke of mine, which I have entituled the *Faery Queene*, being a continued allegory, or darke conceit, I have thought good, aswell for avoyding of gealous opinions and misconstructions, as also for your better light in reading therof, (being so by you commanded,) to discover unto you the general intention and meaning, which in the whole course thereof I have fashioned, without expressing of any particular purposes or by accidents therein occasioned. The generall end therefore of all the booke is to fashion a gentleman or noble person in vertuous and gentle discipline : which for that I conceived shoulde be most plausible and pleasing, being coloured with an historicall fiction, the which the most part of men delight to read, rather for variety of matter then for profite of the ensample, I chose the historye of King Arthure, as most fitte for the excellency of his person, being made famous by many mens former workes, and also furthest from the daunger of envy, and suspition of present time. In which I have followed all the antique poets historicall : first Homere, who in the persons of Agamemnon and Ulysses hath ensampled a good governour and a vertuous man, the one in his Ilias, the other in his Odysseis ; then Virgil, whose like intention was to doe in the person of Æneas ; after him Ariosto comprised them both in his Orlando ; and lately Tasso dissevered them againe, and formed both parts in two persons. namely that part which they in philosophy call Ethice, or vertues of a private man, coloured in his Rinaldo ; the other

named Politice in his Godfredo. By ensample of which excellente poets, I labour to pourtraict in Arthure, before he was king, the image of a brave knight, perfected in the twelve private morall vertues, as Aristotle hath devised, the which is the purpose of these first twelve bookes : which if I finde to be well accepted, I may be perhaps encoraged to frame the other part of polliticke vertues in his person, after that hee came to be king. To some, I know, this methode will seeme displeasaunt, which had rather have good discipline delivered plainly in way of precepts, or sermoned at large, as they use, then thus clowdily enwrapped in allegoricall devises. But such, me seeme, should be satisfide with the use of these dayes, seeing all things accounted by their showes, and nothing esteemed of, that is not delightfull and pleasing to commune sence. For this cause is Xenophon preferred before Plato, for that the one, in the exquisite depth of his judgement, formed a commune welth such as it should be, but the other in the person of Cyrus and the Persians fashioned a governement, such as might best be : so much more profitable and gratious is doctrine by ensample, then by rule. So have I laboured to doe in the person of Arthure : whome I conceive, after his long education by Timon, to whom he was by Merlin delivered to be brought up, so soone as he was borne of the Lady Igrayne, to have seene in a dream or vision the Faery Queen, with whose excellent beauty ravished, he awaking resolved to seeke her out, and so being by Merlin armed, and by Timon throughly instructed, he went to seeke her forth in Faerye Land. In that Faery Queene I meane glory in my generall intention, but in my particular I conceive the most excellent and glorious person of our soveraine the Queene, and her kingdome in Faery Land. And yet, in some places els, I doe otherwise shadow her. For considering she beareth two persons, the one of a most royall queene or empresse, the other of a most vertuous and beautifull lady, this latter part in some places I doe expresse in Belphœbe, fashioning her name according to your owne excellent conceipt of Cynthia, (Phœbe and Cynthia being both names of Diana.) So in the person of Prince Arthure I sette forth magnificence in particular, which vertue, for that (according to Aristotle and the rest) it is the perfection of all the rest, and conteineth in it them all, therefore in the whole course I mention the deedes of Arthure applyable to that vertue which I write of in that booke. But of the xii. other vertues I make xii. other knights the patrones, for the more variety of the history : of which these three bookes contayn three. The first of the Knight of the Redcrosse, in whome I expresse holynes : The seconde of Sir Guyon, in whome I sette forth temperaunce : The third of Britomartis, a lady knight, in whome I picture chastity. But because the beginning of the whole worke seemeth abrupte and as depending upon other antecedents, it needs that ye know the occasion of these three knights severall adventures. For the methode of a poet historical is not such as of an historiographer. For an historiographer discourseth of affayres orderly as they were donne, accounting as well the times as the actions ; but a poet thrusteth into the middest, even where it most concerneth him, and there recoursing to the thinges forepaste, and divining of thinges to come, maketh a pleasing analysis of all. The beginning therefore of my history, if it were to be told by an historiographer, should be the twelfth booke, which is the last; where I devise that the Faery Queene kept her annuall feaste xii. dayes, uppon which xii. severall dayes, the occasions of the xii. severall adventures hapned, which being undertaken by xii. severall knights, are in these xii. books severally handled and discoursed. The first was this. In the beginning of the feast, there presented him selfe a tall clownish younge man, who, falling before the Queen of Faries, desired a boone (as the manner then was) which during that feast she might not refuse : which was that hee might have the achievement of any adventure, which during that feaste should happen : that being graunted, he rested him on the floore, unfitte through his rusticity for a better place. Soone after entred a faire ladye in mourning weedes, riding on a white asse, with a dwarfe behind her leading a warlike steed, that bore the armes of a knight, and his speare in the dwarfes hand. Shee, falling before the Queene of Faeries, complayned that her father and mother, an ancient king and queene, had bene by an huge dragon many years shut up in a brasen castle, who thence suffred them not to yssew : and therefore besought the Faery Queene to assygne her some one of her knights to take on him that exployt. Presently that clownish person, upstarting, desired that adventure : whereat the Queene much wondering, and the lady much gainesaying, yet he earnestly importuned his desire. In the end the lady told him, that unlesse that armour which she brought would serve him (that is, the armour of a Christian man specified by Saint Paul, vi. Ephes.), that he could not succeed in that enterprise : which being forthwith put upon him with dewe furnitures thereunto, he seemed the goodliest man in al that company, and was well liked of the lady. And eftesoones taking on him knighthood, and mounting on that straunge courser, he went forth with her on that adventure : where beginneth the first booke, vz.

A gentle knight was pricking on the playne, &c.

The second day ther came in a palmer bearing an infant with bloody hands, whose parents he complained to have bene slayn by an enchaunteresse called Acrasia : and therfore craved of the Faery Queene, to appoint him some knight to performe that adventure; which being assigned to Sir Guyon, he presently went forth with that same palmer: which is the beginning of the second booke and the whole subject thereof. The third day there came in a groome, who complained before the Faery Queene, that a vile enchaunter, called Busirane, had in hand a most faire lady, called Amoretta, whom he kept in most grievous torment, because she would not yield him the pleasure of her body. Whereupon Sir Scudamour, the lover of that lady, presently tooke on him that adventure. But being unable to performe it by reason of the hard enchauntments, after long sorrow, in the end met with Britomartis, who succoured him, and reskewed his love.

But by occasion hereof, many other adventures are intermedled, but rather as accidents then intendments : as the love of Britomart, the overthrow of Marinell, the misery of Florimell, the vertuousnes of Belphœbe, the lasciviousnes of Hellenora, and many the like.

Thus much, Sir, I have briefly overronne, to direct your understanding to the wel-head of the history, that from thence gathering the whole intention of the conceit, ye may, as in a handfull, gripe al the discourse, which otherwise may happily seeme tedious and confused. So humbly craving the continuaunce of your honourable favour towards me, and th' eternall establishment of your happines, I humbly take leave.   211

23. January, 1589.
Yours most humbly affectionate,
Ed. Spenser.

A VISION UPON THIS CONCEIT OF THE FAERY QUEENE

ME thought I saw the grave where Laura lay,
Within that temple where the vestall flame
Was wont to burne; and passing by that way,
To see that buried dust of living fame,
Whose tumbe faire Love, and fairer Vertue kept,
All suddeinly I saw the Faery Queene:
At whose approch the soule of Petrarke wept,
And from thenceforth those graces were not seene.
For they this Queene attended; in whose steed
Oblivion laid him downe on Lauras herse:
Hereat the hardest stones were seene to bleed,
And grones of buried ghostes the hevens did perse:
Where Homers spright did tremble all for griefe,
And curst th' accesse of that celestiall theife.

ANOTHER OF THE SAME

THE prayse of meaner wits this worke like profit brings,
As doth the Cuckoes song delight when Philumena sings.
If thou hast formed right true Vertues face herein,
Vertue her selfe can best discerne, to whom they written bin.
If thou hast Beauty praysd, let her sole lookes divine
Judge if ought therein be amis, and mend it by her eine.

If Chastitie want ought, or Temperaunce her dew,
Behold her princely mind aright, and write thy Queene anew.
Meane while she shall perceive, how far her vertues sore
Above the reach of all that live, or such as wrote of yore:
And thereby will excuse and favour thy good will:
Whose vertue can not be exprest, but by an angels quill.
Of me no lines are lov'd, nor letters are of price,
Of all which speak our English tongue, but those of thy device.   W. R.

TO THE LEARNED SHEPEHEARD

COLLYN, I see by thy new taken taske,
Some sacred fury hath enricht thy braynes,
That leades thy Muse in haughty verse to maske,
And loath the layes that longs to lowly swaynes;
That lifts thy notes from shepheardes unto kinges,
So like the lively Larke that mounting singes.

Thy lovely Rosolinde seemes now forlorne,
And all thy gentle flockes forgotten quight;
Thy chaunged hart now holdes thy pypes in scorne,
Those prety pypes that did thy mates delight,
Those trusty mates, that loved thee so well,
Whom thou gav'st mirth, as they gave thee the bell.

Yet, as thou earst, with thy sweete roundelayes,
Didst stirre to glee our laddes in homely bowers,
So moughtst thou now in these refyned layes
Delight the daintie eares of higher powers:
And so mought they, in their deepe skanning skill,
Alow and grace our Collyns flowing quyll.

And faire befall that Faery Queene of thine,
  In whose faire eyes Love linckt with Ver-
    tue sittes:
Enfusing, by those bewties fyers devyne,
  Such high conceites into thy humble
    wittes,
As raised hath poore pastors oaten reede,
From rustick tunes, to chaunt heroique
    deedes.

So mought thy Redcrosse Knight with
    happy hand
  Victorious be in that faire Ilands right,
Which thou dost vayle in type of Faery
    Land,
  Elizas blessed field, that Albion hight:
That shieldes her friendes, and warres her
    mightie foes,
Yet still with people, peace, and plentie
    flowes.

But (jolly shepheard) though with pleasing
    style
  Thou feast the humour of the courtly
    trayne,
Let not conceipt thy setled sence beguile,
  Ne daunted be through envy or disdaine.
Subject thy dome to her empyring spright,
From whence thy Muse, and all the world,
    takes light.   HOBYNOLL.

FAYRE Thamis streame, that from Ludds
    stately towne
Runst paying tribute to the ocean seas,
Let all thy nymphes and syrens of renowne
Be silent, whyle this Bryttane Orpheus
    playes:
Nere thy sweet bankes, there lives that sa-
    cred Crowne,
Whose hand strowes palme and never-dying
    bayes:
Let all at once, with thy soft murmuring
    sowne,
Present her with this worthy poets prayes:
For he hath taught hye drifts in shepe-
    herdes weedes,
And deepe conceites now singes in Faeries
    deedes.   R. S.

GRAVE Muses, march in triumph and with
    prayses;
Our Goddesse here hath given you leave to
    land,

And biddes this rare dispenser of your graces
Bow downe his brow unto her sacred hand.
Desertes findes dew in that most princely
    doome,
In whose sweete brest are all the Muses
    bredde:
So did that great Augustus erst in Roome
With leaves of fame adorne his poets hedde.
Faire be the guerdon of your *Faery Queene*,
Even of the fairest that the world hath
    seene.   H. B.

WHEN stout Achilles heard of Helens rape
And what revenge the states of Greece de-
    visd:
Thinking by sleight the fatall warres to scape,
In womans weedes him selfe he then dis-
    guisde:
But this devise Ulysses soone did spy,
And brought him forth, the chaunce of
    warre to try.

When Spencer saw the fame was spredd so
    large,
Through Faery Land, of their renowned
    Queene,
Loth that his Muse should take so great a
    charge,
As in such haughty matter to be seene,
To seeme a shepeheard then he made his
    choice;
But Sydney heard him sing, and knew his
    voice.

And as Ulysses brought faire Thetis sonne
From his retyred life to menage armes,
So Spencer was by Sidneys speaches wonne
To blaze her fame, not fearing future
    harmes:
For well he knew, his Muse would soone
    be tyred
In her high praise, that all the world ad-
    mired.

Yet as Achilles, in those warlike frayes,
Did win the palme from all the Grecian
    peeres,
So Spencer now, to his immortall prayse,
Hath wonne the laurell quite from all his
    feres.
What though his taske exceed a humaine
    witt ?
He is excus'd, sith Sidney thought it fitt.
                                W. L.

To looke upon a worke of rare devise
The which a workman setteth out to view,
And not to yield it the deserved prise
That unto such a workmanship is dew,
  Doth either prove the judgement to be
    naught,
  Or els doth shew a mind with envy
    fraught.

To labour to commend a peece of worke
Which no man goes about to discommend,
Would raise a jealous doubt, that there did
    lurke
Some secret doubt, whereto the prayse did
    tend:
  For when men know the goodnes of the
    wyne,
  'Tis needlesse for the hoast to have a
    sygne.

Thus then, to shew my judgement to be such
As can discerne of colours blacke and white,
As alls to free my minde from envies tuch,
That never gives to any man his right,
  I here pronounce this workmanship is
    such,
  As that no pen can set it forth too much.

And thus I hang a garland at the dore,
Not for to shew the goodnes of the ware,
But such hath beene the custome hereto-
    fore,
And customes very hardly broken are.
  And when your tast shall tell you this is
    trew,
  Then looke you give your hoast his ut-
    most dew.   Ignoto.

TO THE RIGHT HONOURABLE SIR CHRIS-
TOPHER HATTON, LORD HIGH CHAUN-
CELOR OF ENGLAND, &c.

Those prudent heads, that with theire coun-
    sels wise
  Whylom the pillours of th' earth did sus-
    taine,
  And taught ambitious Rome to tyrannise,
  And in the neck of all the world to rayne,
Oft from those grave affaires were wont
    abstaine,
  With the sweet Lady Muses for to play:
  So Ennius the elder Africane,
  So Maro oft did Cæsars cares allay.

So you, great Lord, that with your counsell
    sway
  The burdeine of this kingdom mightily,
  With like delightes sometimes may eke
    delay
  The rugged brow of carefull Policy;
And to these ydle rymes lend litle space,
Which for their titles sake may find more
    grace.

TO THE MOST HONOURABLE AND EXCEL-
LENT LORD THE EARLE OF ESSEX.
GREAT MAISTER OF THE HORSE
TO HER HIGHNESSE, AND
KNIGHT OF THE NOBLE
ORDER OF THE GAR-
TER, &c.

Magnificke Lord, whose vertues excellent
  Doe merit a most famous poets witt,
  To be thy living praises instrument,
  Yet doe not sdeigne to let thy name be
    writt
In this base poeme, for thee far unfitt:
  Nought is thy worth disparaged thereby.
  But when my Muse, whose fethers, no-
    thing flitt,
  Doe yet but flagg, and lowly learne to
    fly,
With bolder wing shall dare alofte to sty
  To the last praises of this Faery Queene,
  Then shall it make more famous memory
  Of thine heroicke parts, such as they
    beene.
Till then vouchsafe thy noble countenaunce,
To these first labours needed furtheraunce.

TO THE RIGHT HONOURABLE THE EARLE
OF OXENFORD, LORD HIGH CHAM-
BERLAYNE OF ENGLAND, &c.

Receive, most noble Lord, in gentle gree
  The unripe fruit of an unready wit,
  Which by thy countenaunce doth crave
    to bee
  Defended from foule Envies poisnous
    bit:
Which so to doe may thee right well
    befit,
  Sith th' antique glory of thine auncestry
  Under a shady vele is therein writ,
  And eke thine owne long living memory,
Succeeding them in true nobility;
  And also for the love which thou doest
    beare

To th' Heliconian ymps, and they to
  thee,
They unto thee, and thou to them, most
  deare.
Deare as thou art unto thy selfe, so love
That loves and honours thee, as doth behove.

TO THE RIGHT HONOURABLE THE EARLE
OF NORTHUMBERLAND

The sacred Muses have made alwaies clame
  To be the nourses of nobility,
  And registres of everlasting fame,
  To all that armes professe and chev-
    alry.
Then, by like right, the noble progeny,
  Which them succeed in fame and worth,
    are tyde
T'embrace the service of sweete poetry,
  By whose endevours they are glorifide;
And eke from all of whom it is envide
  To patronize the authour of their praise,
  Which gives them life, that els would
    soone have dide,
  And crownes their ashes with immortall
    baies.
To thee, therefore, right noble Lord, I
  send
This present of my paines, it to defend.

TO THE RIGHT HONOURABLE THE EARLE
OF ORMOND AND OSSORY

Receive, most noble Lord, a simple taste
  Of the wilde fruit which salvage soyl hath
    bred,
  Which, being through long wars left al-
    most waste,
  With brutish barbarisme is overspredd:
And in so faire a land as may be redd,
  Not one Parnassus nor one Helicone
  Left for sweete Muses to be harboured,
  But where thy selfe hast thy brave man-
    sione:
There in deede dwel faire Graces many
  one,
  And gentle nymphes, delights of learned
    wits,
  And in thy person without paragone
  All goodly bountie and true honour
    sits.
Such, therefore, as that wasted soyl doth
  yield,
Receive, dear Lord, in worth, the fruit of
  barren field.

TO THE RIGHT HONOURABLE THE LORD
CH. HOWARD, LORD HIGH ADMIRAL
OF ENGLAND, KNIGHT OF THE
NOBLE ORDER OF THE GAR-
TER, AND ONE OF HER
MAJESTIES PRIVIE
COUNSEL, &c.

And ye, brave Lord, whose goodly person-
  age
  And noble deeds, each other garnishing,
  Make you ensample to the present age
  Of th' old heroes, whose famous ofspring
The antique poets wont so much to sing,
  In this same pageaunt have a worthy
    place,
  Sith those huge castles of Castilian king,
  That vainly threatned kingdomes to dis-
    place,
Like flying doves ye did before you chace,
  And that proud people, woxen insolent
  Through many victories, didst first de-
    face:
  Thy praises everlasting monument
Is in this verse engraven semblably,
That it may live to all posterity.

TO THE MOST RENOWMED AND VALIANT
LORD, THE LORD GREY OF WILTON,
KNIGHT OF THE NOBLE ORDER
OF THE GARTER, &c.

Most noble Lord, the pillor of my life,
  And patrone of my Muses pupillage,
  Through whose large bountie, poured on
    me rife,
  In the first season of my feeble age,
I now doe live, bound yours by vassalage:
  Sith nothing ever may redeeme, nor
    reave
  Out of your endlesse debt so sure a gage,
  Vouchsafe in worth this small guift to
    receave,
Which in your noble hands for pledge I
  leave
  Of all the rest that I am tyde t' ac-
    count:
  Rude rymes, the which a rustick Muse
    did weave
  In savadge soyle, far from Parnasso
    mount,
And roughly wrought in an unlearned
  loome:
The which vouchsafe, dear Lord, your fa-
  vorable doome.

TO THE RIGHT NOBLE AND VALOROUS
KNIGHT,   SIR   WALTER   RALEIGH,
LORD WARDEIN OF THE STAN-
NERYES, AND LIEFTENAUNT
OF CORNEWAILE

To thee that art the sommers Nightingale,
Thy soveraine Goddesses most deare de-
light,
Why doe I send this rusticke madrigale,
That may thy tunefull eare unseason
quite ?
Thou onely fit this argument to write,
In whose high thoughts Pleasure hath
built her bowre,
And dainty Love learnd sweetly to en-
dite.
My rimes I know unsavory and sowre,
To tast the streames, that like a golden
showre
Flow from thy fruitfull head, of thy loves
praise;
Fitter perhaps to thonder martiall stowre,
When so thee list thy lofty Muse to
raise:
Yet till that thou thy poeme wilt make
knowne,
Let thy faire Cinthias praises bee thus
rudely showne.

TO THE RIGHT HONOURABLE THE LORD
BURLEIGH, LORD HIGH THREA-
SURER OF ENGLAND

To you, right noble Lord, whose carefull
brest
To menage of most grave affaires is
bent,
And on whose mightie shoulders most
doth rest
The burdein of this kingdomes governe-
ment,
As the wide compasse of the firmament
On Atlas mighty shoulders is upstayd,
Unfitly I these ydle rimes present,
The labor of lost time, and wit unstayd:
Yet if their deeper sence be inly wayd,
And the dim vele, with which from
comune vew
Their fairer parts are hid, aside be layd,
Perhaps not vaine they may appeare to
you.
Such as they be, vouchsafe them to receave,
And wipe their faults out of your censure
grave.   E. S.

TO THE RIGHT HONOURABLE THE EARLE
OF CUMBERLAND

REDOUBTED Lord, in whose corageous mind
The flowre of chevalry, now bloosming
faire,
Doth promise fruite worthy the noble kind
Which of their praises have left you the
haire;
To you this humble present I prepare,
For love of vertue and of martiall praise;
To which though nobly ye inclined are,
As goodlie well ye shew'd in late assaies,
Yet brave ensample of long passed daies,
In which trew honor yee may fashioned
see,
To like desire of honor may ye raise,
And fill your mind with magnanimitee.
Receive it, Lord, therefore, as it was ment,
For honor of your name and high descent.
E. S.

TO THE RIGHT HONOURABLE THE LORD
OF HUNSDON, HIGH CHAMBER-
LAINE TO HER MAJESTY

RENOWMED Lord, that for your worthinesse
And noble deeds, have your deserved
place
High in the favour of that Emperesse,
The worlds sole glory and her sexes grace;
Here eke of right have you a worthie place,
Both for your nearnes to that Faerie
Queene,
And for your owne high merit in like cace,
Of which apparaunt proofe was to be
seene,
When that tumultuous rage and fearfull
deene
Of Northerne rebels ye did pacify,
And their disloiall powre defaced clene,
The record of enduring memory.
Live, Lord, for ever in this lasting verse,
That all posteritie thy honor may reherse.
E. S.

TO THE RIGHT HONOURABLE THE LORD
OF BUCKHURST, ONE OF HER MA-
JESTIES PRIVIE COUNSELL

IN vain I thinke, right honourable Lord,
By this rude rime to memorize thy name,
Whose learned Muse hath writ her owne
record
In golden verse, worthy immortal fame:

Thou much more fit (were leasure to the
  same)
  Thy gracious Soverains praises to com-
  pile,
  And her imperiall majestie to frame
  In loftie numbers and heroicke stile.
But sith thou maist not so, give leave a
  while
  To baser wit his power therein to spend,
  Whose grosse defaults thy daintie pen
  may file,
  And unadvised oversights amend.
But evermore vouchsafe it to maintaine
Against vile Zoilus backbitings vaine.

TO THE RIGHT HONOURABLE SIR FR.
  WALSINGHAM, KNIGHT, PRINCIPALL
  SECRETARY TO HER MAJESTY
  AND OF HER HONOURABLE
  PRIVY COUNSELL

THAT Mantuane poetes incompared spirit,
  Whose girland now is set in highest
  place,
  Had not Mecænas, for his worthy merit,
  It first advaunst to great Augustus
  grace,
Might long, perhaps, have lien in silence
  bace,
  Ne bene so much admir'd of later age.
This lowly Muse, that learns like steps
  to trace,
  Flies for like aide unto your patronage;
That are the great Mecenas of this age,
  As wel to al that civil artes professe,
  As those that are inspir'd with martial
  rage,
  And craves protection of her feeblenesse:
Which if ye yield, perhaps ye may her
  rayse
In bigger tunes to sound your living prayse.
                                        E. S.

TO THE RIGHT NOBLE LORD AND MOST
  VALIAUNT CAPTAINE, SIR JOHN
  NORRIS, KNIGHT, LORD PRE-
  SIDENT OF MOUNSTER

WHO ever gave more honourable prize
  To the sweet Muse then did the martiall
  crew,
  That their brave deeds she might immortalize
  In her shril tromp, and sound their
  praises dew ?

Who then ought more to favour her then
  you,
  Moste noble Lord, the honor of this age,
  And precedent of all that armes ensue ?
  Whose warlike prowesse and manly cour-
  age,
Tempred with reason and advizement sage,
  Hath fild sad Belgicke with victorious
  spoile,
  In Fraunce and Ireland left a famous
  gage,
  And lately shakt the Lusitanian soile.
Sith, then, each where thou hast dispredd
  thy fame,
Love him that hath eternized your name.
                                        E. S.

TO THE RIGHT HONOURABLE AND MOST
  VERTUOUS LADY, THE COUNTESSE
  OF PENBROKE

REMEMBRAUNCE of that most heroicke
  spirit,
  The hevens pride, the glory of our daies,
  Which now triumpheth through immor-
  tall merit
  Of his brave vertues, crownd with last-
  ing baies
Of hevenlie blis and everlasting praies;
  Who first my Muse did lift out of the flore,
  To sing his sweet delights in lowlie laies;
  Bids me, most noble Lady, to adore
His goodly image living evermore
  In the divine resemblaunce of your face;
  Which with your vertues ye embellish
  more,
  And native beauty deck with hevenlie
  grace:
For his, and for your owne especial sake,
Vouchsafe from him this token in good
  worth to take.   E. S.

TO THE MOST VERTUOUS AND BEAUTI-
  FULL LADY, THE LADY CAREW

NE may I, without blot of endlesse blame,
  You, fairest Lady, leave out of this place,
  But with remembraunce of your gracious
  name,
  Wherewith that courtly garlond most ye
  grace,
And deck the world, adorne these verses
  base.
  Not that these few lines can in them
  comprise

Those glorious ornaments of hevenly
grace,
Wherewith ye triumph over feeble eyes,
And in subdued harts do tyranyse;
For thereunto doth need a golden quill
And silver leaves, them rightly to devise;
But to make humble present of good
will:
Which, whenas timely meanes it purchase
may,
In ampler wise it selfe will forth display.
E. S.

TO ALL THE GRATIOUS AND BEAUTIFULL
LADIES IN THE COURT

THE Chian peincter, when he was requirde
To pourtraict Venus in her perfect hew,
To make his worke more absolute, de-
sird
Of all the fairest maides to have the vew.
Much more me needs, to draw the sem-
blant trew
Of Beauties Queene, the worlds sole
wenderment,
To sharpe my sence with sundry beauties
vew,
And steale from each some part of orna-
ment.
If all the world to seeke I overwent,
A fairer crew yet no where could I see
Then that brave court doth to mine eie
present,
That the worlds pride seemes gathered
there to bee.
Of each a part I stole by cunning thefte:
Forgive it me, faire Dames, sith lesse ye
have not lefte. E. S.

THE FIRST BOOKE
OF THE FAERIE QUEENE
CONTAYNING
THE LEGEND OF THE KNIGHT
OF THE RED CROSSE
OR
OF HOLINESSE

I

Lo! I the man, whose Muse whylome did
maske,
As time her taught, in lowly shephards
weeds.

Am now enforst, a farre unfitter taske,
For trumpets sterne to chaunge mine oaten
reeds,
And sing of knights and ladies gentle deeds;
Whose praises having slept in silence long,
Me, all too meane, the sacred Muse areeds
To blazon broade emongst her learned
throng:
Fierce warres and faithfull loves shall
moralize my song.

II

Helpe then, O holy virgin, chiefe of nyne,
Thy weaker novice to performe thy will;
Lay forth out of thine everlasting scryne
The antique rolles, which there lye hidden
still,
Of Faerie knights, and fayrest Tanaquill,
Whom that most noble Briton Prince so long
Sought through the world, and suffered so
much ill,
That I must rue his undeserved wrong:
O helpe thou my weake wit, and sharpen
my dull tong.

III

And thou, most dreaded impe of highest
Jove,
Faire Venus sonne, that with thy cruell
dart
At that good knight so cunningly didst rove,
That glorious fire it kindled in his hart,
Lay now thy deadly heben bowe apart,
And with thy mother mylde come to mine
ayde:
Come both, and with you bring triumphant
Mart,
In loves and gentle jollities arraid,
After his murdrous spoyles and bloudie
rage allayd.

IV

And with them eke, O Goddesse heavenly
bright,
Mirrour of grace and majestie divine,
Great Ladie of the greatest Isle, whose light
Like Phœbus lampe throughout the world
doth shine,
Shed thy faire beames into my feeble eyne,
And raise my thoughtes, too humble and
too vile,
To thinke of that true glorious type of thine,
The argument of mine afflicted stile:
The which to heare vouchsafe, O dearest
dread, a while.

CANTO I

The patrone of true Holinesse
Foule Errour doth defeate:
Hypocrisie, him to entrappe,
Doth to his home entreate.

I

A GENTLE knight was pricking on the
    plaine,
Ycladd in mightie armes and silver shielde,
Wherein old dints of deepe woundes did
    remaine,
The cruell markes of many' a bloody fielde;
Yet armes till that time did he never wield:
His angry steede did chide his foming
    bitt,
As much disdayning to the curbe to yield:
Full jolly knight he seemd, and faire did
    sitt,
As one for knightly giusts and fierce en-
    counters fitt.

II

But on his brest a bloodie crosse he bore,
The deare remembrance of his dying Lord,
For whose sweete sake that glorious badge
    he wore,
And dead as living ever him ador'd:
Upon his shield the like was also scor'd,
For soveraine hope, which in his helpe he
    had:
Right faithfull true he was in deede and
    word,
But of his cheere did seeme too solemne
    sad;
Yet nothing did he dread, but ever was
    ydrad.

III

Upon a great adventure he was bond,
That greatest Gloriana to him gave,
That greatest glorious queene of Faery
    Lond,
To winne him worshippe, and her grace to
    have,
Which of all earthly thinges he most did
    crave;
And ever as he rode his hart did earne
To prove his puissance in battell brave
Upon his foe, and his new force to learne;
Upon his foe, a dragon horrible and stearne.

IV

A lovely ladie rode him faire beside,
Upon a lowly asse more white then snow,

Yet she much whiter, but the same did hide
Under a vele, that wimpled was full low,
And over all a blacke stole shee did throw:
As one that inly mournd, so was she sad,
And heavie sate upon her palfrey slow:
Seemed in heart some hidden care she had;
And by her in a line a milkewhite lambe
    she lad.

V

So pure and innocent, as that same lambe,
She was in life and every vertuous lore,
And by descent from royall lynage came
Of ancient kinges and queenes, that had of
    yore
Their scepters stretcht from east to west-
    erne shore,
And all the world in their subjection held,
Till that infernall feend with foule uprore
Forwasted all their land, and them expeld:
Whom to avenge, she had this knight from
    far compeld.

VI

Behind her farre away a dwarfe did lag,
That lasie seemd, in being ever last,
Or wearied with bearing of her bag
Of needments at his backe. Thus as they
    past,
The day with cloudes was suddeine overcast,
And angry Jove an hideous storme of raine
Did poure into his lemans lap so fast,
That everie wight to shrowd it did constrain,
And this faire couple eke to shroud them-
    selves were fain.

VII

Enforst to seeke some covert nigh at hand,
A shadie grove not farr away they spide,
That promist ayde the tempest to withstand:
Whose loftie trees, yclad with sommers
    pride,
Did spred so broad, that heavens light did
    hide,
Not perceable with power of any starr:
And all within were pathes and alleies wide,
With footing worne, and leading inward
    farr:
Faire harbour that them seemes, so in they
    entred ar.

VIII

And foorth they passe, with pleasure for-
    ward led,
Joying to heare the birdes sweete harmony,

Which, therein shrouded from the tempest
dred,
Seemd in their song to scorne the cruell sky.
Much can they praise the trees so straight
and hy,
The sayling pine, the cedar proud and tall,
The vine-propp elme, the poplar never dry,
The builder oake, sole king of forrests all,
The aspine good for staves, the cypresse
funerall,

IX

The laurell, meed of mightie conquerours
And poets sage, the firre that weepeth still,
The willow worne of forlorne paramours,
The eugh obedient to the benders will,
The birch for shaftes, the sallow for the mill,
The mirrhe sweete bleeding in the bitter
wound,
The warlike beech, the ash for nothing ill,
The fruitfull olive, and the platane round,
The carver holme, the maple seeldom in-
ward sound.

X

Led with delight, they thus beguile the way,
Untill the blustring storme is overblowne;
When, weening to returne whence they did
stray,
They cannot finde that path, which first was
showne,
But wander too and fro in waies unknowne,
Furthest from end then, when they neerest
weene,
That makes them doubt, their wits be not
their owne:
So many pathes, so many turnings seene,
That which of them to take, in diverse
doubt they been.

XI

At last resolving forward still to fare,
Till that some end they finde, or in or out,
That path they take, that beaten seemd most
bare,
And like to lead the labyrinth about;
Which when by tract they hunted had
throughout,
At length it brought them to a hollowe cave,
Amid the thickest woods. The champion
stout
Eftsoones dismounted from his courser
brave,
And to the dwarfe a while his needlesse
spere he gave.

XII

'Be well aware,' quoth then that ladie milde,
'Least suddaine mischiefe ye too rash pro-
voke:
The danger hid, the place unknowne and
wilde,
Breedes dreadfull doubts: oft fire is with-
out smoke,
And perill without show: therefore your
stroke,
Sir knight, with-hold, till further tryall
made.'
'Ah, ladie,' sayd he, 'shame were to revoke
The forward footing for an hidden shade:
Vertue gives her selfe light, through darke-
nesse for to wade.'

XIII

'Yea, but,' quoth she, 'the perill of this
place
I better wot then you; though nowe too late
To wish you backe returne with foule dis-
grace,
Yet wisedome warnes, whilest foot is in the
gate,
To stay the steppe, ere forced to retrate.
This is the wandring wood, this Errours den,
A monster vile, whom God and man does
hate:
Therefore I read beware.' 'Fly, fly!' quoth
then
The fearefull dwarfe: 'this is no place for
living men.'

XIV

But full of fire and greedy hardiment,
The youthfull knight could not for ought
be staide,
But forth unto the darksom hole he went,
And looked in: his glistring armor made
A litle glooming light, much like a shade,
By which he saw the ugly monster plaine,
Halfe like a serpent horribly displaide,
But th' other halfe did womans shape re-
taine,
Most lothsom, filthie, foule, and full of vile
disdaine.

XV

And as she lay upon the durtie ground,
Her huge long taile her den all overspred,
Yet was in knots and many boughtes up-
wound,
Pointed with mortall sting. Of her there
bred

A thousand yong ones, which she dayly fed,
Sucking upon her poisnous dugs, eachone
Of sundrie shapes, yet all ill favored:
Soone as that uncouth light upon them shone,
Into her mouth they crept, and suddain all
    were gone.

XVI

Their dam upstart, out of her den effraide,
And rushed forth, hurling her hideous taile
About her cursed head, whose folds dis-
    plaid
Were stretcht now forth at length with-
    out entraile.
She lookt about, and seeing one in mayle,
Armed to point, sought backe to turne
    againe;
For light she hated as the deadly bale,
Ay wont in desert darknes to remaine,
Where plain none might her see, nor she
    see any plaine.

XVII

Which when the valiant Elfe perceiv'd, he
    lept
As lyon fierce upon the flying pray,
And with his trenchand blade her boldly
    kept
From turning backe, and forced her to stay:
Therewith enrag'd she loudly gan to bray,
And turning fierce, her speckled taile ad-
    vaunst,
Threatning her angrie sting, him to dis-
    may:
Who, nought aghast, his mightie hand en-
    haunst:
The stroke down from her head unto her
    shoulder glaunst.

XVIII

Much daunted with that dint, her sence was
    dazd,
Yet kindling rage her selfe she gathered
    round,
And all attonce her beastly bodie raizd
With doubled forces high above the ground:
Tho, wrapping up her wrethed sterne
    arownd,
Lept fierce upon his shield, and her huge
    traine
All suddenly about his body wound,
That hand or foot to stirr he strove in
    vaine:
God helpe the man so wrapt in Errours
    endlesse traine.

XIX

His lady, sad to see his sore constraint,
Cride out, 'Now, now, sir knight, shew
    what ye bee:
Add faith unto your force, and be not faint:
Strangle her, els she sure will strangle
    thee.'
That when he heard, in great perplexitie,
His gall did grate for griefe and high dis-
    daine;
And knitting all his force, got one hand free,
Wherewith he grypt her gorge with so great
    paine,
That soone to loose her wicked bands did
    her constraine.

XX

Therewith she spewd out of her filthie maw
A floud of poyson horrible and blacke,
Full of great lumps of flesh and gobbets
    raw,
Which stunck so vildly, that it forst him
    slacke
His grasping hold, and from her turne him
    backe:
Her vomit full of bookes and papers was,
With loathly frogs and toades, which eyes
    did lacke,
And creeping sought way in the weedy gras:
Her filthie parbreake all the place defiled
    has.

XXI

As when old father Nilus gins to swell
With timely pride above the Aegyptian vale,
His fattie waves doe fertile slime outwell,
And overflow each plaine and lowly dale:
But when his later spring gins to avale,
Huge heapes of mudd he leaves, wherin
    there breed
Ten thousand kindes of creatures, partly
    male
And partly femall, of his fruitful seed;
Such ugly monstrous shapes elswher may
    no man reed.

XXII

The same so sore annoyed has the knight,
That, welnigh choked with the deadly stinke,
His forces faile, ne can no lenger fight.
Whose corage when the feend perceivd to
    shrinke,
She poured forth out of her hellish sinke
Her fruitfull cursed spawne of serpents
    small,

Deformed monsters, fowle, and blacke as
  inke,
Which swarming all about his legs did crall,
And him encombred sore, but could not
  hurt at all.

XXIII

As gentle shepheard in sweete eventide,
When ruddy Phebus gins to welke in west,
High on an hill, his flocke to vewen wide,
Markes which doe byte their hasty supper
  best;
A cloud of cumbrous gnattes doe him mo-
  lest,
All striving to infixe their feeble stinges,
That from their noyance he no where can
  rest,
But with his clownish hands their tender
  wings
He brusheth oft, and oft doth mar their
  murmurings.

XXIV

Thus ill bestedd, and fearefull more of
  shame
Then of the certeine perill he stood in,
Halfe furious unto his foe he came,
Resolvd in minde all suddenly to win,
Or soone to lose, before he once would lin;
And stroke at her with more then manly
  force,
That from her body, full of filthie sin,
He raft her hatefull heade without remorse:
A streame of cole black blood forth gushed
  from her corse.

XXV

Her scattred brood, soone as their parent
  deare
They saw so rudely falling to the ground,
Groning full deadly, all with troublous feare,
Gathred themselves about her body round,
Weening their wonted entrance to have
  found
At her wide mouth: but being there with-
  stood,
They flocked all about her bleeding wound,
And sucked up their dying mothers bloud,
Making her death their life, and eke her
  hurt their good.

XXVI

That detestable sight him much amazde,
To see th' unkindly impes, of heaven accurst,

Devoure their dam; on whom while so he
  gazd,
Having all satisfide their bloudy thurst,
Their bellies swolne he saw with fulnesse
  burst,
And bowels gushing forth: well worthy
  end
Of such as drunke her life, the which them
  nurst !
Now needeth him no lenger labour spend;
His foes have slaine themselves, with whom
  he should contend.

XXVII

His lady, seeing all that chaunst, from
  farre,
Approcht in hast to greet his victorie,
And saide, ' Faire knight, borne under hap-
  pie starre,
Who see your vanquisht foes before you lye,
Well worthie be you of that armory,
Wherein ye have great glory wonne this
  day,
And proov'd your strength on a strong eni-
  mie,
Your first adventure: many such I pray,
And henceforth ever wish that like succeed
  it may.'

XXVIII

Then mounted he upon his steede againe,
And with the lady backward sought to wend;
That path he kept which beaten was most
  plaine,
Ne ever would to any by way bend,
But still did follow one unto the end,
The which at last out of the wood them
  brought.
So forward on his way (with God to frend)
He passed forth, and new adventure sought:
Long way he traveiled, before he heard of
  ought.

XXIX

At length they chaunst to meet upon the
  way
An aged sire, in long blacke weedes yclad,
His feete all bare, his beard all hoarie gray,
And by his belt his booke he hanging had;
Sober he seemde, and very sagely sad,
And to the ground his eyes were lowly bent,
Simple in shew, and voide of malice bad,
And all the way he prayed as he went,
And often knockt his brest, as one that did
  repent.

XXX

He faire the knight saluted, louting low,
Who faire him quited, as that courteous
    was;
And after asked him, if he did know
Of straunge adventures, which abroad did
    pas.
'Ah! my dear sonne,' quoth he, 'how should,
    alas!
Silly old man, that lives in hidden cell,
Bidding his beades all day for his trespas,
Tydings of warre and worldly trouble tell?
With holy father sits not with such thinges
    to mell.

XXXI

'But if of daunger, which hereby doth dwell,
And homebredd evil ye desire to heare,
Of a straunge man I can you tidings tell,
That wasteth all this countrie farre and
    neare.'
'Of such,' saide he, 'I chiefly doe inquere,
And shall you well rewarde to shew the
    place,
In which that wicked wight his dayes doth
    weare:
For to all knighthood it is foule disgrace,
That such a cursed creature lives so long a
    space.'

XXXII

'Far hence,' quoth he, 'in wastfull wilder-
    nesse,
His dwelling is, by which no living wight
May ever passe, but thorough great dis-
    tresse.'
'Now,' saide the ladie, 'draweth toward
    night,
And well I wote, that of your later fight
Ye all forwearied be: for what so strong,
But, wanting rest, will also want of might?
The Sunne, that measures heaven all day
    long,
At night doth baite his steedes the ocean
    waves emong.

XXXIII

'Then with the Sunne take, sir, your timely
    rest,
And with new day new worke at once begin:
Untroubled night, they say, gives counsell
    best.'
'Right well, sir knight, ye have advised
    bin,'
Quoth then that aged man; 'the way to win

Is wisely to advise: now day is spent;
Therefore with me ye may take up your in
For this same night.' The knight was well
    content:
So with that godly father to his home they
    went.

XXXIV

A litle lowly hermitage it was,
Downe in a dale, hard by a forests side,
Far from resort of people, that did pas
In traveill to and froe: a litle wyde
There was an holy chappell edifyde,
Wherein the hermite dewly wont to say
His holy thinges each morne and even-tyde:
Thereby a christall streame did gently play,
Which from a sacred fountaine welled
    forth alway.

XXXV

Arrived there, the litle house they fill,
Ne looke for entertainment, where none
    was:
Rest is their feast, and all thinges at their
    will;
The noblest mind the best contentment has.
With faire discourse the evening so they pas:
For that olde man of pleasing wordes had
    store,
And well could file his tongue as smooth
    as glas:
He told of saintes and popes, and evermore
He strowd an Ave-Mary after and before.

XXXVI

The drouping night thus creepeth on them
    fast,
And the sad humor loading their eye liddes,
As messenger of Morpheus, on them cast
Sweet slombring deaw, the which to sleep
    them biddes:
Unto their lodgings then his guestes he
    riddes:
Where when all drownd in deadly sleepe
    he findes,
He to his studie goes, and there amiddes
His magick bookes and artes of sundrie
    kindes,
He seekes out mighty charmes, to trouble
    sleepy minds.

XXXVII

Then choosing out few words most horrible,
(Let none them read) thereof did verses
    frame;

With which and other spelles like terrible,
He bad awake blacke Plutoes griesly dame,
And cursed heven, and spake reprochful
    shame
Of highest God, the Lord of life and light:
A bold bad man, that dar'd to call by name
Great Gorgon, prince of darknes and dead
    night,
At which Cocytus quakes, and Styx is put
    to flight.

XXXVIII

And forth he cald out of deepe darknes
    dredd
Legions of sprights, the which, like litle
    flyes
Fluttring about his ever damned hedd,
Awaite whereto their service he applyes,
To aide his friendes, or fray his enimies:
Of those he chose out two, the falsest twoo,
And fittest for to forge true-seeming lyes;
The one of them he gave a message too,
The other by him selfe staide, other worke
    to doo.

XXXIX

He, making speedy way through spersed
    ayre,
And through the world of waters wide and
    deepe,
To Morpheus house doth hastily repaire.
Amid the bowels of the earth full steepe,
And low, where dawning day doth never
    peepe,
His dwelling is; there Tethys his wet
    bed
Doth ever wash, and Cynthia still doth
    steepe
In silver deaw his ever-drouping hed,
Whiles sad Night over him her mantle
    black doth spred.

XL

Whose double gates he findeth locked fast,
The one faire fram'd of burnisht yvory,
The other all with silver overcast;
And wakeful dogges before them farre doe
    lye,
Watching to banish Care their enimy,
Who oft is wont to trouble gentle Sleepe.
By them the sprite doth passe in quietly,
And unto Morpheus comes, whom drowned
    deepe
In drowsie fit he findes: of nothing he
    takes keepe.

XLI

And more, to lulle him in his slumber soft,
A trickling streame from high rock tum-
    bling downe,
And ever drizling raine upon the loft,
Mixt with a murmuring winde, much like
    the sowne
Of swarming bees, did cast him in a swowne:
No other noyse, nor peoples troublous cryes,
As still are wont t' annoy the walled towne,
Might there be heard: but carelesse Quiet
    lyes,
Wrapt in eternall silence farre from eni-
    myes.

XLII

The messenger approching to him spake,
But his waste wordes retournd to him in
    vaine:
So sound he slept, that nought mought him
    awake.
Then rudely he him thrust, and pusht with
    paine,
Whereat he gan to stretch: but he againe
Shooke him so hard, that forced him to
    speake.
As one then in a dreame, whose dryer braine
Is tost with troubled sights and fancies
    weake,
He mumbled soft, but would not all his
    silence breake.

XLIII

The sprite then gan more boldly him to
    wake,
And threatned unto him the dreaded name
Of Hecate: whereat he gan to quake,
And, lifting up his lompish head, with blame
Halfe angrie asked him, for what he came.
'Hether,' quoth he, ' me Archimago sent,
He that the stubborne sprites can wisely
    tame;
He bids thee to him send for his intent
A fit false dreame, that can delude the
    sleepers sent.'

XLIV

The god obayde, and calling forth straight
    way
A diverse dreame out of his prison darke,
Delivered it to him, and downe did lay
His heavie head, devoide of careful carke;
Whose sences all were straight benumbd
    and starke.
He, backe returning by the yvorie dore,

Remounted up as light as chearefull larke,
And on his litle winges the dreame he bore
In hast unto his lord, where he him left afore.

XLV

Who all this while, with charmes and hidden artes,
Had made a lady of that other spright,
And fram'd of liquid ayre her tender partes,
So lively and so like in all mens sight,
That weaker sence it could have ravisht quight:
The maker selfe, for all his wondrous witt,
Was nigh beguiled with so goodly sight:
Her all in white he clad, and over it
Cast a black stole, most like to seeme for Una fit.

XLVI

Now when that ydle dreame was to him brought,
Unto that Elfin knight he bad him fly,
Where he slept soundly, void of evil thought,
And with false shewes abuse his fantasy,
In sort as he him schooled privily:
And that new creature, borne without her dew,
Full of the makers guyle, with usage sly
He taught to imitate that lady trew,
Whose semblance she did carrie under feigned hew.

XLVII

Thus well instructed, to their worke they haste,
And comming where the knight in slomber lay,
The one upon his hardie head him plaste,
And made him dreame of loves and lustfull play,
That nigh his manly hart did melt away,
Bathed in wanton blis and wicked joy.
Then seemed him his lady by him lay,
And to him playnd, how that false winged boy
Her chaste hart had subdewd to learne Dame Pleasures toy.

XLVIII

And she her selfe, of beautie soveraigne queene,
Fayre Venus, seemde unto his bed to bring
Her, whom he, waking, evermore did weene
To bee the chastest flowre that aye did spring

On earthly braunch, the dæughter of a king,
Now a loose leman to vile service bound:
And eke the Graces seemed all to sing
Hymen iö Hymen, dauncing all around,
Whylst freshest Flora her with yvie girlond crownd.

XLIX

In this great passion of unwonted lust,
Or wonted feare of doing ought amis,
He started up, as seeming to mistrust
Some secret ill, or hidden foe of his:
Lo ! there before his face his ladie is,
Under blacke stole hyding her bayted hooke,
And as halfe blushing offred him to kis,
With gentle blandishment and lovely looke,
Most like that virgin true, which for her knight him took.

L

All cleane dismayd to see so uncouth sight,
And halfe enraged at her shamelesse guise,
He thought have slaine her in his fierce despight:
But hastie heat tempring with sufferance wise,
He stayde his hand, and gan himselfe advise
To prove his sense, and tempt her faigned truth.
Wringing her hands in wemens pitteous wise,
Tho can she weepe, to stirre up gentle ruth,
Both for her noble blood, and for her tender youth.

LI

And sayd, ' Ah sir, my liege lord and my love,
Shall I accuse the hidden cruell fate,
And mightie causes wrought in heaven above,
Or the blind god, that doth me thus amate,
For hoped love to winne me certaine hate ?
Yet thus perforce he bids me do, or die.
Die is my dew: yet rew my wretched state
You, whom my hard avenging destinie
Hath made judge of my life or death indifferently.

LII

' Your owne deare sake forst me at first to leave
My fathers kingdom ' — There she stopt with teares;

Her swollen hart her speech seemd to be-
reave;
And then againe begonne: 'My weaker
yeares,
Captiv'd to fortune and frayle worldly
feares,
Fly to your fayth for succour and sure ayde:
Let me not die in languor and long teares.'
'Why, dame,' quoth he, 'what hath ye thus
dismayd?
What frayes ye, that were wont to comfort
me affrayd?'

LIII

'Love of your selfe,' she saide, 'and deare
constraint,
Lets me not sleepe, but waste the wearie
night
In secret anguish and unpittied plaint,
Whiles you in carelesse sleepe are drowned
quight.'
Her doubtfull words made that redoubted
knight
Suspect her truth: yet since no' untruth he
knew,
Her fawning love with foule disdainefull
spight
He would not shend, but said, 'Deare dame,
I rew,
That for my sake unknowne such griefe
unto you grew.

LIV

'Assure your selfe, it fell not all to ground;
For all so deare as life is to my hart,
I deeme your love, and hold me to you bound;
Ne let vaine feares procure your needlesse
smart,
Where cause is none, but to your rest de-
part.'
Not all content, yet seemd she to appease
Her mournefull plaintes, beguiled of her
art,
And fed with words, that could not chose
but please;
So slyding softly forth, she turnd as to her
ease.

LV

Long after lay he musing at her mood,
Much griev'd to thinke that gentle dame so
light,
For whose defence he was to shed his blood.
At last dull wearines of former fight
Having yrockt a sleepe his irkesome spright,

That troublous dreame gan freshly tosse
his braine
With bowres, and beds, and ladies deare
delight:
But when he saw his labour all was vaine,
With that misformed spright he backe returnd againe.

CANTO II

The guilefull great enchaunter parts
The Redcrosse Knight from Truth:
Into whose stead faire Falshood steps,
And workes him woefull ruth.

I

By this the northerne wagoner had set
His sevenfold teme behind the stedfast
starre,
That was in ocean waves yet never wet,
But firme is fixt, and sendeth light from
farre
To al that in the wide deepe wandring arre:
And chearefull Chaunticlere with his note
shrill
Had warned once, that Phoebus fiery carre
In hast was climbing up the easterne hill,
Full envious that night so long his roome
did fill:

II

When those accursed messengers of hell,
That feigning dreame, and that faire-forged
spright,
Came to their wicked maister, and gan tel
Their bootelesse paines, and ill succeed-
ing night:
Who, all in rage to see his skilfull might
Deluded so, gan threaten hellish paine
And sad Proserpines wrath, them to af-
fright.
But when he saw his threatning was but
vaine,
He cast about, and searcht his baleful
bokes againe.

III

Eftsoones he tooke that miscreated faire,
And that false other spright, on whom he
spred
A seeming body of the subtile aire,
Like a young squire, in loves and lustyhed
His wanton daies that ever loosely led,
Without regard of armes and dreaded fight:
Those twoo he tooke, and in a secrete bed,

Covered with darkenes and misdeeming
    night,
Them both together laid, to joy in vaine
    delight.

IV

Forthwith he runnes with feigned faithfull
    hast
Unto his guest, who, after troublous sights
And dreames, gan now to take more sound
    repast;
Whom suddenly he wakes with fearful
    frights,
As one aghast with feends or damned
    sprights,
And to him cals: 'Rise, rise, unhappy
    swaine,
That here wex old in sleepe, whiles wicked
    wights
Have knit themselves in Venus shameful
    chaine;
Come see, where your false lady doth her
    honor staine.'

V

All in amaze he suddenly up start
With sword in hand, and with the old man
    went;
Who soone him brought into a secret part,
Where that false couple were full closely
    ment
In wanton lust and leud enbracement:
Which when he saw, he burnt with gealous
    fire,
The eie of reason was with rage yblent,
And would have slaine them in his furious
    ire,
But hardly was restreined of that aged
    sire.

VI

Retourning to his bed in torment great,
And bitter anguish of his guilty sight,
He could not rest, but did his stout heart
    eat,
And wast his inward gall with deepe de-
    spight,
Yrkesome of life, and too long lingring
    night.
At last faire Hesperus in highest skie
Had spent his lampe, and brought forth
    dawning light;
Then up he rose, and clad him hastily;
The dwarfe him brought his steed: so both
    away do fly.

VII

Now when the rosy fingred Morning faire,
Weary of aged Tithones saffron bed,
Had spred her purple robe through deawy
    aire,
And the high hils Titan discovered,
The royall virgin shooke of drousyhed,
And rising forth out of her baser bowre,
Lookt for her knight, who far away was
    fled,
And for her dwarfe, that wont to wait each
    howre:
Then gan she wail and weepe, to see that
    woeful stowre.

VIII

And after him she rode with so much
    speede,
As her slowe beast could make; but all in
    vaine:
For him so far had borne his light-foot
    steede,
Pricked with wrath and fiery fierce dis-
    daine,
That him to follow was but fruitlesse paine;
Yet she her weary limbes would never rest,
But every hil and dale, each wood and
    plaine,
Did search, sore grieved in her gentle brest,
He so ungently left her, whome she loved
    best.

IX

But subtill Archimago, when his guests
He saw divided into double parts,
And Una wandring in woods and forrests,
Th' end of his drift, he praisd his divelish
    arts,
That had such might over true meaning
    harts:
Yet rests not so, but other meanes doth
    make,
How he may worke unto her further smarts:
For her he hated as the hissing snake,
And in her many troubles did most pleasure
    take.

X

He then devisde himselfe how to disguise;
For by his mighty science he could take
As many formes and shapes in seeming
    wise,
As ever Proteus to himselfe could make:
Sometime a fowle, sometime a fish in lake,
Now like a foxe, now like a dragon fell,

That of himselfe he ofte for feare would
  quake,
And oft would flie away. O who can tell
The hidden powre of herbes, and might of
  magick spel ?

XI

But now seemde best, the person to put on
Of that good knight, his late beguiled guest:
In mighty armes he was yclad anon,
And silver shield; upon his coward brest
A bloody crosse, and on his craven crest
A bounch of heares discolourd diversly:
Full jolly knight he seemde, and wel ad-
  drest,
And when he sate uppon his courser free,
Saint George himselfe ye would have
  deemed him to be.

XII

But he, the knight whose semblaunt he did
  beare,
The true Saint George, was wandred far
  away,
Still flying from his thoughts and gealous
  feare;
Will was his guide, and griefe led him
  astray.
At last him chaunst to meete upon the way
A faithlesse Sarazin, all armde to point,
In whose great shield was writ with letters
  gay
Sans foy : full large of limbe and every joint
He was, and cared not for God or man a
  point.

XIII

Hee had a faire companion of his way,
A goodly lady clad in scarlot red,
Purfled with gold and pearle of rich assay;
And like a Persian mitre on her hed
Shee wore, with crowns and owches gar-
  nished,
The which her lavish lovers to her gave:
Her wanton palfrey all was overspred
With tinsell trappings, woven like a wave,
Whose bridle rung with golden bels and
  bosses brave.

XIV

With faire disport and courting dalliaunce
She intertainde her lover all the way:
But when she saw the knight his speare
  advaunce,
Shee soone left of her mirth and wanton play,

And bad her knight addresse him to the
  fray :
His foe was nigh at hand. He, prickte with
  pride
And hope to winne his ladies hearte that
  day,
Forth spurred fast: adowne his coursers
  side
The red bloud trickling staind the way, as
  he did ride.

XV

The Knight of the Redcrosse, when him he
  spide
Spurring so hote with rage dispiteous,
Gan fairely couch his speare, and towards
  ride :
Soone meete they both, both fell and furi-
  ous,
That, daunted with theyr forces hideous,
Their steeds doe stagger, and amazed stand,
And eke themselves, too rudely rigorous,
Astonied with the stroke of their owne
  hand,
Doe backe rebutte, and ech to other yealdeth
  land.

XVI

As when two rams, stird with ambitious
  pride,
Fight for the rule of the rich fleeced flocke,
Their horned fronts so fierce on either side
Doe meete, that, with the terror of the
  shocke
Astonied, both stand senceless as a blocke,
Forgetfull of the hanging victory:
So stood these twaine, unmoved as a rocke,
Both staring fierce, and holding idely
The broken reliques of their former cruelty.

XVII

The Sarazin, sore daunted with the buffe,
Snatcheth his sword, and fiercely to him
  flies;
Who well it wards, and quyteth cuff with
  cuff :
Each others equall puissaunce envies,
And through their iron sides with cruell
  spies
Does seeke to perce: repining courage yields
No foote to foe. The flashing fier flies,
As from a forge, out of their burning
  shields,
And streams of purple bloud new dies the
  verdant fields.

XVIII

'Curse on that Crosse,' quoth then the Sara-
    zin,
'That keepes thy body from the bitter fitt !
Dead long ygoe, I wote, thou haddest bin,
Had not that charme from thee forwarned
    itt.·
But yet I warne thee now assured sitt,
And hide thy head.' Therewith upon his
    crest
With rigor so outrageous he smitt,
That a large share it hewd out of the rest,
And glauncing downe his shield, from blame
    him fairely blest.

XIX

Who thereat wondrous wroth, the sleeping
    spark
Of native vertue gan eftsoones revive,
And at his haughty helmet making mark,
So hugely stroke, that it the steele did rive,
And cleft his head. He, tumbling downe
    alive,
With bloudy mouth his mother earth did
    kis,
Greeting his grave: his grudging ghost did
    strive
With the fraile flesh; at last it flitted is,
Whether the soules doe fly of men that live
    amis.

XX

The lady, when she saw her champion fall,
Like the old ruines of a broken towre,
Staid not to waile his woefull funerall,
But from him fled away with all her powre;
Who after her as hastily gan scowre,
Bidding the dwarfe with him to bring away
The Sarazins shield, signe of the conquer-
    oure.
Her soone he overtooke, and bad to stay,
For present cause was none of dread her to
    dismay.

XXI

Shee, turning backe with ruefull counte-
    naunce,
Cride, 'Mercy, mercy, sir, vouchsafe to
    showe
On silly dame, subject to hard mischaunce,
And to your mighty wil !' Her humblesse
    low,
In so ritch weedes and seeming glorious
    show,
Did much emmove his stout heroïcke heart,

And said, 'Deare dame, your suddein over-
    throw
Much rueth me; but now put feare apart,
And tel, both who ye be, and who that tooke
    your part.'

XXII

Melting in teares, then gan shee thus la-
    ment:
'The wreched woman, whom unhappy howre
Hath now made thrall to your commande-
    ment,
Before that angry heavens list to lowre,
And Fortune false betraide me to your
    powre,
Was, (O what now availeth that I was ?)
Borne the sole daughter of an emperour,
He that the wide west under his rule has,
And high hath set his throne where Tiberis
    doth pas.

XXIII

'He, in the first flowre of my freshest age,
Betrothed me unto the onely haire
Of a most mighty king, most rich and sage;
Was never prince so faithfull and so faire,
Was never prince so meeke and debonaire;
But ere my hoped day of spousall shone,
My dearest lord fell from high honors staire,
Into the hands of hys accursed fone,
And cruelly was slaine, that shall I ever
    mone.

XXIV

'His blessed body, spoild of lively breath,
Was afterward, I know not how, convaid
And fro me hid: of whose most innocent
    death
When tidings came to mee, unhappy maid,
O how great sorrow my sad soule assaid !
Then forth I went his woefull corse to find,
And many yeares throughout the world I
    straid,
A virgin widow, whose deepe wounded mind
With love, long time did languish as the
    striken hind.

XXV

'At last it chaunced this proud Sarazin
To meete me wandring; who perforce me
    led
With him away, but yet could never win
The fort, that ladies hold in soveraigne
    dread.
There lies he now with foule dishonor dead,

Who, whiles he livde, was called proud
    Sansfoy:
The eldest of three brethren, all three bred
Of one bad sire, whose youngest is Sansjoy,
And twixt them both was born the bloudy
    bold Sansloy.

XXVI

' In this sad plight, friendlesse, unfortunate,
Now miserable I Fidessa dwell,
Craving of you, in pitty of my state,
To doe none ill, if please ye not doe well.'
He in great passion al this while did dwell,
More busying his quicke eies, her face to
    view,
Then his dull eares, to heare what shee did
    tell;
And said, 'Faire lady, hart of flint would rew
The undeserved woes and sorrowes which
    ye shew.

XXVII

' Henceforth in safe assuraunce may ye rest,
Having both found a new friend you to aid,
And lost an old foe, that did you molest:
Better new friend then an old foe is said.'
With chaunge of chear the seeming simple
    maid
Let fal her eien, as shamefast, to the earth,
And yeelding soft, in that she nought gain-
    said,
So forth they rode, he feining seemely merth,
And shee coy lookes: so dainty, they say,
    maketh derth.

XXVIII

Long time they thus together traveiled,
Til, weary of their way, they came at last
Where grew two goodly trees, that faire
    did spred
Their armes abroad, with gray mosse over-
    cast,
And their greene leaves, trembling with
    every blast,
Made a calme shadowe far in compasse
    round:
The fearefull shepheard, often there aghast,
Under them never sat, ne wont there sound
His mery oaten pipe, but shund th' unlucky
    ground.

XXIX

But this good knight, soone as he them can
    spie,
For the coole shade him thither hastly got:
For golden Phoebus, now ymounted hie,
From fiery wheeles of his faire chariot
Hurled his beame so scorching cruell hot,
That living creature mote it not abide;
And his new lady it endured not.
There they alight, in hope themselves to
    hide
From the fierce heat, and rest their weary
    limbs a tide.

XXX

Faire seemely pleasaunce each to other
    makes,
With goodly purposes, there as they sit:
And in his falsed fancy he her takes
To be the fairest wight that lived yit;
Which to expresse, he bends his gentle wit,
And thinking of those braunches greene to
    frame
A girlond for her dainty forehead fit,
He pluckt a bough; out of whose rifte there
    came
Smal drops of gory bloud, that trickled
    down the same.

XXXI

Therewith a piteous yelling voice was heard,
Crying, ' O spare with guilty hands to teare
My tender sides in this rough rynd embard;
But fly, ah! fly far hence away, for feare
Least to you hap that happened to me
    heare,
And to this wretched lady, my deare love;
O too deare love, love bought with death
    too deare ! '
Astond he stood, and up his heare did
    hove,
And with that suddein horror could no
    member move.

XXXII

At last, whenas the dreadfull passion
Was overpast, and manhood well awake,
Yet musing at the straunge occasion,
And doubting much his sence, he thus be-
    spake:
' What voice of damned ghost from Limbo
    lake,
Or guilefull spright wandring in empty aire,
Both which fraile men doe oftentimes mis-
    take,
Sends to my doubtful eares these speaches
    rare,
And ruefull plaints, me bidding guiltlesse
    blood to spare? '

XXXIII

Then groning deep: 'Nor damned ghost,'
  quoth he,
'Nor guileful sprite to thee these words
  doth speake,
But once a man, Fradubio, now a tree;
Wretched man, wretched tree! whose na-
  ture weake
A cruell witch, her cursed will to wreake,
Hath thus transformd, and plast in open
  plaines,
Where Boreas doth blow full bitter bleake,
And scorching sunne does dry my secret
  vaines:
For though a tree I seme, yet cold and heat
  me paines.'

XXXIV

'Say on, Fradubio, then, or man or tree,'
Quoth then the knight; 'by whose mis-
  chievous arts
Art thou misshaped thus, as now I see?
He oft finds med'cine who his griefe im-
  parts;
But double griefs afflict concealing harts,
As raging flames who striveth to suppresse.'
'The author then,' said he, 'of all my smarts,
Is one Duessa, a false sorceresse,
That many errant knights hath broght to
  wretchednesse.

XXXV

'In prime of youthly yeares, when corage
  hott
The fire of love and joy of chevalree
First kindled in my brest, it was my lott
To love this gentle lady, whome ye see
Now not a lady, but a seeming tree;
With whome as once I rode accompanyde,
Me chaunced of a knight encountred bee,
That had a like faire lady by his syde;
Lyke a faire lady, but did fowle Duessa hyde.

XXXVI

'Whose forged beauty he did take in hand
All other dames to have exceded farre;
I in defence of mine did likewise stand,
Mine, that did then shine as the morning
  starre:
So both to batteill fierce arraunged arre;
In which his harder fortune was to fall
Under my speare: such is the dye of warre:
His lady, left as a prise martiall,
Did yield her comely person, to be at my
  call.

XXXVII

'So doubly lov'd of ladies unlike faire,
Th' one seeming such, the other such in-
  deede,
One day in doubt I cast for to compare,
Whether in beauties glorie did exceede;
A rosy girlond was the victors meede.
Both seemde to win, and both seemde won
  to bee,
So hard the discord was to be agreede:
Frælissa was as faire as faire mote bee,
And ever false Duessa seemde as faire as
  shee.

XXXVIII

'The wicked witch, now seeing all this while
The doubtfull ballaunce equally to sway,
What not by right, she cast to win by guile;
And by her hellish science raisd streight
  way
A foggy mist, that overcast the day,
And a dull blast, that, breathing on her face,
Dimmed her former beauties shining ray,
And with foule ugly forme did her dis-
  grace:
Then was she fayre alone, when none was
  faire in place.

XXXIX

'Then cride she out, "Fye, fye! deformed
  wight,
Whose borrowed beautie now appeareth
  plaine
To have before bewitched all mens sight;
O leave her soone, or let her soone be
  slaine."
Her loathly visage viewing with disdaine,
Eftsoones I thought her such as she me
  told,
And would have kild her; but with faigned
  paine
The false witch did my wrathfull hand
  with-hold:
So left her, where she now is turnd to
  treen mould.

XL

'Thensforth I tooke Duessa for my dame,
And in the witch unweeting joyd long time,
Ne ever wist but that she was the same:
Till on a day (that day is everie prime,
When witches wont do penance for their
  crime)
I chaunst to see her in her proper hew,
Bathing her selfe in origane and thyme:

A filthy foule old woman I did vew,
That ever to have toucht her I did deadly
rew.

XLI

'Her neather partes misshapen, monstruous,
Were hidd in water, that I could not see,
But they did seeme more foule and hide-
ous,
Then womans shape man would beleeve to
bee.
Thensforth from her most beastly com-
panie
I gan refraine, in minde to slipp away,
Soone as appeard safe opportunitie:
For danger great, if not assurd decay,
I saw before mine eyes, if I were knowne
to stray.

XLII

'The divelish hag, by chaunges of my cheare,
Perceiv'd my thought; and drownd in sleepie
night,
With wicked herbes and oyntments did be-
smeare
My body all, through charmes and magicke
might,
That all my senses were bereaved quight:
Then brought she me into this desert waste,
And by my wretched lovers side me pight,
Where now enclosd in wooden wals full
faste,
Banisht from living wights, our wearie
daies we waste.'

XLIII

'But how long time,' said then the Elfin
knight,
'Are you in this misformed hous to dwell?'
'We may not chaunge,' quoth he, 'this evill
plight
Till we be bathed in a living well;
That is the terme prescribed by the spell.'
'O how,' sayd he, 'mote I that well out find,
That may restore you to your wonted well?'
'Time and suffised fates to former kynd
Shall us restore; none else from hence may
us unbynd.'

XLIV

The false Duessa, now Fidessa hight,
Heard how in vaine Fradubio did lament,
And knew well all was true. But the good
knight
Full of sad feare and ghastly dreriment,

When all this speech the living tree had
spent,
The bleeding bough did thrust into the
ground,
That from the blood he might be innocent,
And with fresh clay did close the wooden
wound:
Then turning to his lady, dead with feare
her fownd.

XLV

Her seeming dead he fownd with feigned
feare,
As all unweeting of that well she knew,
And paynd himselfe with busie care to reare
Her out of carelesse swowne. Her eylids
blew,
And dimmed sight, with pale and deadly hew,
At last she up gan lift: with trembling
cheare
Her up he tooke, too simple and too trew,
And oft her kist. At length, all passed feare,
He set her on her steede, and forward
forth did beare.

CANTO III

Forsaken Truth long seekes her love,
And makes the lyon mylde,
Marres Blind Devotions mart, and fals
In hand of leachour vylde.

I

NOUGHT is there under heav'ns wide hol-
lownesse,
That moves more deare compassion of mind,
Then beautie brought t'unworthie wretch-
ednesse
Through envies snares, or fortunes freakes
unkind:
I, whether lately through her brightnes
blynd,
Or through alleageance and fast fealty,
Which I do owe unto all womankynd,
Feele my hart perst with so great agony,
When such I see, that all for pitty I could
dy.

II

And now it is empassioned so deepe,
For fairest Unaes sake, of whom I sing,
That my frayle eies these lines with teares
do steepe,
To thinke how she through guyleful hande-
ling,

Though true as touch, though daughter of
    a king,
Though faire as ever living wight was fayre,
Though nor in word nor deede ill meriting,
Is from her knight divorced in despayre,
And her dew loves deryv'd to that vile
    witches shayre.

III

Yet she, most faithfull ladie, all this while
Forsaken, wofull, solitarie mayd,
Far from all peoples preace, as in exile,
In wildernesse and wastfull deserts strayd,
To seeke her knight; who, subtily betrayd
Through that late vision which th' en-
    chaunter wrought,
Had her abandond. She, of nought affrayd,
Through woods and wastnes wide him daily
    sought;
Yet wished tydinges none of him unto her
    brought.

IV

One day, nigh wearie of the yrkesome way,
From her unhastie beast she did alight,
And on the grasse her dainty limbs did lay
In secrete shadow, far from all mens sight:
From her fayre head her fillet she undight,
And layd her stole aside. Her angels face
As the great eye of heaven shyned bright,
And made a sunshine in the shady place;
Did never mortall eye behold such heavenly
    grace.

V

It fortuned, out of the thickest wood
A ramping lyon rushed suddeinly,
Hunting full greedy after salvage blood:
Soone as the royall virgin he did spy,
With gaping mouth at her ran greedily,
To have attonce devourd her tender corse;
But to the pray when as he drew more ny,
His bloody rage aswaged with remorse,
And with the sight amazd, forgat his furi-
    ous forse.

VI

In stead thereof he kist her wearie feet,
And lickt her lilly hands with fawning tong,
As he her wronged innocence did weet.
O how can beautie maister the most strong,
And simple truth subdue avenging wrong!
Whose yielded pryde and proud submission,
Still dreading death, when she had marked
    long,

Her hart gan melt in great compassion,
And drizling teares did shed for pure affec-
    tion.

VII

'The lyon, lord of everie beast in field,'
Quoth she, 'his princely puissance doth
    abate,
And mightie proud to humble weake does
    yield,
Forgetfull of the hungry rage, which late
Him prickt, in pittie of my sad estate:
But he, my lyon, and my noble lord,
How does he find in cruell hart to hate
Her that him lov'd, and ever most adord
As the god of my life? why hath he me
    abhord?'

VIII

Redounding teares did choke th' end of her
    plaint,
Which softly ecchoed from the neighbour
    wood;
And sad to see her sorrowfull constraint,
The kingly beast upon her gazing stood;
With pittie calmd, downe fell his angry
    mood.
At last, in close hart shutting up her payne,
Arose the virgin borne of heavenly brood,
And to her snowy palfrey got agayne,
To seeke her strayed champion if she might
    attayne.

IX

The lyon would not leave her desolate,
But with her went along, as a strong gard
Of her chast person, and a faythfull mate
Of her sad troubles and misfortunes hard:
Still, when she slept, he kept both watch
    and ward,
And when she wakt, he wayted diligent,
With humble service to her will prepard:
From her fayre eyes he tooke commande-
    ment,
And ever by her lookes conceived her in-
    tent.

X

Long she thus traveiled through deserts
    wyde,
By which she thought her wandring knight
    shold pas,
Yet never shew of living wight espyde;
Till that at length she found the troden gras
In which the tract of peoples footing was,

Under the steepe foot of a mountaine hore:
The same she followes, till at last she has
A damzell spyde slow footing her before,
That on her shoulders sad a pot of water
    bore.

XI

To whom approching, she to her gan call,
To weet if dwelling place were nigh at hand;
But the rude wench her answerd nought
    at all;
She could not heare, nor speake, nor under-
    stand;
Till, seeing by her side the lyon stand,
With suddeine feare her pitcher downe she
    threw,
And fled away: for never in that land
Face of fayre lady she before did vew,
And that dredd lyons looke her cast in
    deadly hew.

XII

Full fast she fled, ne ever lookt behynd,
As if her life upon the wager lay,
And home she came, whereas her mother
    blynd
Sate in eternall night: nought could she say,
But, suddeine catching hold, did her dis-
    may
With quaking hands, and other signes of
    feare:
Who, full of ghastly fright and cold affray,
Gan shut the dore. By this arrived there
Dame Una, weary dame, and entrance did
    requere.

XIII

Which when none yielded, her unruly page
With his rude clawes the wicket open rent,
And let her in; where, of his cruell rage
Nigh dead with feare, and faint astonish-
    ment,
Shee found them both in darkesome corner
    pent;
Where that old woman day and night did
    pray
Upon her beads, devoutly penitent:
Nine hundred *Pater nosters* every day,
And thrise nine hundred *Aves*, she was wont
    to say.

XIV

And to augment her painefull penaunce
    more,
Thrise every weeke in ashes shee did sitt,

And next her wrinkled skin rough sacke-
    cloth wore,
And thrise three times did fast from any bitt:
But now for feare her beads she did for-
    gett.
Whose needelesse dread for to remove away,
Faire Una framed words and count'naunce
    fitt:
Which hardly doen, at length she gan them
    pray
That in their cotage small that night she
    rest her may.

XV

The day is spent, and commeth drowsie
    night,
When every creature shrowded is in sleepe:
Sad Una downe her laies in weary plight,
And at her feete the lyon watch doth keepe:
In stead of rest, she does lament, and weepe
For the late losse of her deare loved knight,
And sighes, and grones, and evermore does
    steepe
Her tender brest in bitter teares all night;
All night she thinks too long, and often
    lookes for light.

XVI

Now when Aldeboran was mounted hye
Above the shinie Cassiopeias chaire,
And all in deadly sleepe did drowned lye,
One knocked at the dore, and in would fare;
He knocked fast, and often curst, and sware,
That ready entraunce was not at his call:
For on his backe a heavy load he bare
Of nightly stelths and pillage severall,
Which he had got abroad by purchas
    criminall.

XVII

He was, to weete, a stout and sturdy thiefe,
Wont to robbe churches of their ornaments,
And poore mens boxes of their due reliefe,
Which given was to them for good intents;
The holy saints of their rich vestiments
He did disrobe, when all men carelesse slept,
And spoild the priests of their habiliments;
Whiles none the holy things in safety kept,
Then he by conning sleights in at the win-
    dow crept.

XVIII

And all that he by right or wrong could
    find
Unto this house he brought, and did bestow

Upon the daughter of this woman blind,
Abessa, daughter of Corceca slow,
With whom he whoredome usd, that few
    did know,
And fed her fatt with feast of offerings,
And plenty, which in all the land did grow;
Ne spared he to give her gold and rings:
And now he to her brought part of his
    stolen things.

XIX

Thus, long the dore with rage and threats
    he bett,
Yet of those fearfull women none durst rize,
(The lyon frayed them,) him in to lett:
He would no lenger stay him to advize,
But open breakes the dore in furious wize,
And entring is; when that disdainfull beast,
Encountring fierce, him suddein doth sur-
    prize,
And seizing cruell clawes on trembling
    brest,
Under his lordly foot him proudly hath sup-
    prest.

XX

Him booteth not resist, nor succour call,
His bleeding hart is in the vengers hand;
Who streight him rent in thousand peeces
    small,
And quite dismembred hath: the thirsty
    land
Dronke up his life; his corse left on the
    strand.
His fearefull freends weare out the wofull
    night,
Ne dare to weepe, nor seeme to understand
The heavie hap which on them is alight;
Affraid, least to themselves the like mis-
    happen might.

XXI

Now when broad day the world discovered
    has,
Up Una rose, up rose the lyon eke,
And on their former journey forward pas,
In waies unknowne, her wandring knight to
    seeke,
With paines far passing that long wandring
    Greeke,
That for his love refused deitye;
Such were the labours of this lady meeke,
Still seeking him, that from her still did flye;
Then furthest from her hope, when most
    she weened nye.

XXII

Soone as she parted thence, the fearfull
    twayne,
That blind old woman and her daughter dear,
Came forth, and finding Kirkrapine there
    slayne,
For anguish great they gan to rend their
    heare,
And beat their brests, and naked flesh to
    teare.
And when they both had wept and wayld
    their fill,
Then forth they ran like two amazed deare,
Halfe mad through malice and revenging
    will,
To follow her, that was the causer of their
    ill.

XXIII

Whome overtaking, they gan loudly bray,
With hollow houling and lamenting cry,
Shamefully at her rayling all the way,
And her accusing of dishonesty,
That was the flowre of faith and chastity;
And still, amidst her rayling, she did pray
That plagues, and mischiefes, and long mis-
    ery
Might fall on her, and follow all the way,
And that in endlesse error she might ever
    stray.

XXIV

But when she saw her prayers nought pre-
    vaile,
Shee backe retourned with some labour lost;
And in the way, as shee did weepe and waile,
A knight her mett in mighty armes embost,
Yet knight was not for all his bragging
    bost,
But subtill Archimag, that Una sought
By traynes into new troubles to have toste:
Of that old woman tidings he besought,
If that of such a lady shee could tellen
    ought.

XXV

Therewith she gan her passion to renew,
And cry, and curse, and raile, and rend her
    heare,
Saying, that harlott she too lately knew,
That causd her shed so many a bitter teare,
And so forth told the story of her feare.
Much seemed he to mone her haplesse
    chaunce,
And after for that lady did inquere;

Which being taught, he forward gan advaunce
His fair enchaunted steed, and eke his charmed launce.

XXVI

Ere long he came where Una traveild slow,
And that wilde champion wayting her beside:
Whome seeing such, for dread hee durst not show
Him selfe too nigh at hand, but turned wyde
Unto an hil; from whence when she him spyde,
By his like seeming shield her knight by name
Shee weend it was, and towards him gan ride:
Approching nigh, she wist it was the same,
And with faire fearefull humblesse towards him shee came;

XXVII

And weeping said, ' Ah! my long lacked lord,
Where have ye bene thus long out of my sight?
Much feared I to have bene quite abhord,
Or ought have done, that ye displeasen might,
That should as death unto my deare heart light:
For since mine eie your joyous sight did mis,
My chearefull day is turnd to chearelesse night,
And eke my night of death the shadow is;
But welcome now, my light, and shining lampe of blis.'

XXVIII

He thereto meeting said, 'My dearest dame,
Far be it from your thought, and fro my wil,
To thinke that knighthood I so much should shame,
As you to leave, that have me loved stil,
And chose in Faery court, of meere goodwil,
Where noblest knights were to be found on earth:
The earth shall sooner leave her kindly skil

To bring forth fruit, and make eternall derth,
Then I leave you, my liefe, yborn of hevenly berth.

XXIX

' And sooth to say, why I lefte you so long,
Was for to seeke adventure in straunge place,
Where Archimago said a felon strong
To many knights did daily worke disgrace;
But knight he now shall never more deface:
Good cause of mine excuse, that mote ye please
Well to accept, and ever more embrace
My faithfull service, that by land and seas
Have vowd you to defend. Now then your plaint appease.'

XXX

His lovely words her seemd due recompence
Of all her passed paines: one loving howre
For many yeares of sorrow can dispence:
A dram of sweete is worth a pound of sowre:
Shee has forgott how many a woeful stowre
For him she late endurd; she speakes no more
Of past: true is, that true love hath no powre
To looken backe; his eies be fixt before.
Before her stands her knight, for whom she toyld so sore.

XXXI

Much like as when the beaten marinere,
That long hath wandred in the ocean wide,
Ofte soust in swelling Tethys saltish teare,
And long time having tand his tawney hide
With blustring breath of heaven, that none can bide,
And scorching flames of fierce Orions hound,
Soone as the port from far he has espide,
His chearfull whistle merily doth sound,
And Nereus crownes with cups; his mates him pledg around.

XXXII

Such joy made Una, when her knight she found;
And eke th' enchaunter joyous seemde no lesse

Then the glad marchant, that does vew
from ground
His ship far come from watrie wildernesse;
He hurles out vowes, and Neptune oft doth
blesse.
So forth they past, and all the way they
spent
Discoursing of her dreadfull late distresse,
In which he askt her, what the lyon ment:
Who told her all that fell in journey, as she
went.

XXXIII

They had not ridden far, when they might
see
One pricking towards them with hastie heat,
Full strongly armd, and on a courser free,
That through his fiersnesse fomed all with
sweat,
And the sharpe yron did for anger eat,
When his hot ryder spurd his chauffed side;
His looke was sterne, and seemed still to
threat
Cruell revenge, which he in hart did hyde;
And on his shield *Sans loy* in bloody lines
was dyde.

XXXIV

When nigh he drew unto this gentle payre,
And saw the red-crosse, which the knight
did beare,
He burnt in fire, and gan eftsoones prepare
Himselfe to batteill with his couched speare.
Loth was that other, and did faint through
feare,
To taste th' untryed dint of deadly steele;
But yet his lady did so well him cheare,
That hope of new good hap he gan to feele;
So bent his speare, and spurd his horse
with yron heele.

XXXV

But that proud Paynim forward came so
ferce
And full of wrath, that with his sharphead
speare
Through vainly crossed shield he quite did
perce;
And had his staggering steed not shronke
for feare,
Through shield and body eke he should him
beare:
Yet so great was the puissance of his push,
That from his sadle quite he did him
beare:

He, tombling rudely downe, to ground did
rush,
And from his gored wound a well of bloud
did gush.

XXXVI

Dismounting lightly from his loftie steed,
He to him lept, in minde to reave his life,
And proudly said: ' Lo there the worthie
meed
Of him that slew Sansfoy with bloody knife !
Henceforth his ghost, freed from repining
strife,
In peace may passen over Lethe lake,
When mourning altars, purgd with enimies
life,
The black infernall Furies doen aslake:
Life from Sansfoy thou tookst, Sansloy
shall from thee take.'

XXXVII

Therewith in haste his helmet gan unlace,
Till Una cride, ' O hold that heavie hand,
Deare sir, what ever that thou be in place !
Enough is, that thy foe doth vanquisht stand
Now at thy mercy: mercy not withstand:
For he is one the truest knight alive,
Though conquered now he lye on lowly
land,
And whilest him fortune favourd, fayre did
thrive
In bloudy field: therefore of life him not
deprive.'

XXXVIII

Her piteous wordes might notabate his rage,
But, rudely rending up his helmet, would
Have slayne him streight: but when he sees
his age,
And hoarie head of Archimago old,
His hasty hand he doth amased hold,
And, halfe ashamed, wondred at the sight:
For that old man well knew he, though un-
told,
In charmes and magick to have wondrous
might;
Ne ever wont in field, ne in round lists, to
fight.

XXXIX

And said, ' Why, Archimago, lucklesse syre,
What doe I see ? what hard mishap is this,
That hath thee hether brought to taste mine
yre ?
Or thine the fault, or mine the error is,

In stead of foe to wound my friend amis?'
He answered nought, but in a traunce still
    lay,
And on those guilefull dazed eyes of his
The cloude of death did sit. Which doen
    away,
He left him lying so, ne would no lenger
    stay;

XL

But to the virgin comes; who all this while
Amased stands, her selfe so mockt to see
By him, who has the guerdon of his guile,
For so misfeigning her true knight to bee:
Yet is she now in more perplexitie,
Left in the hand of that same Paynim bold,
From whom her booteth not at all to flie;
Who, by her cleanly garment catching hold,
Her from her palfrey pluckt, her visage to
    behold.

XLI

But her fiers servant, full of kingly aw
And high disdaine, whenas his soveraine
    dame
So rudely handled by her foe he saw,
With gaping jawes full greedy at him came,
And, ramping on his shield, did weene the
    same
Have reft away with his sharp rending
    clawes:
But he was stout, and lust did now inflame
His corage more, that from his griping
    pawes
He hath his shield redeemd, and forth his
    swerd he drawes.

XLII

O then too weake and feeble was the forse
Of salvage beast, his puissance to with-
    stand:
For he was strong, and of so mightie corse,
As ever wielded speare in warlike hand,
And feates of armes did wisely understand.
Eftsoones he perced through his chaufed
    chest
With thrilling point of deadly yron brand,
And launcht his lordly hart: with death
    opprest
He ror'd aloud, whiles life forsooke his
    stubborne brest.

XLIII

Who now is left to keepe the forlorne maid
From raging spoile of lawlesse victors will?

Her faithfull gard remov'd, her hope dis-
    maid,
Her selfe a yielded pray to save or spill.
He now, lord of the field, his pride to fill,
With foule reproches and disdaineful spight
Her vildly entertaines, and, will or nill,
Beares her away upon his courser light:
Her prayers nought prevaile; his rage is
    more of might.

XLIV

And all the way, with great lamenting paine,
And piteous plaintes, she filleth his dull
    eares,
That stony hart could riven have in twaine,
And all the way she wetts with flowing
    teares:
But he, enrag'd with rancor, nothing heares:
Her servile beast yet would not leave her
    so,
But followes her far of, ne ought he feares,
To be partaker of her wandring woe.
More mild, in beastly kind, then that her
    beastly foe.

CANTO IV

To sinfull Hous of Pryde Duessa
Guydes the faithfull knight,
Where, brothers death to wreak, Sansjoy
Doth chaleng him to fight

I

YOUNG knight what ever, that dost armes
    professe,
And through long labours huntest after
    fame,
Beware of fraud, beware of ficklenesse,
In choice, and chaunge, of thy deare loved
    dame,
Least thou of her believe too lightly blame,
And rash misweening doe thy hart remove:
For unto knight there is no greater shame,
Then lightnesse and inconstancie in love:
That doth this Redcrosse Knights ensample
    plainly prove.

II

Who, after that he had faire Una lorne,
Through light misdeeming of her loialtie,
And false Duessa in her sted had borne,
Called Fidess', and so supposd to be,
Long with her traveild, till at last they see
A goodly building, bravely garnished;
The house of mightie prince it seemd to be;

And towards it a broad high way that led,
All bare through peoples feet, which thether
traveiled.

III

Great troupes of people traveild thether-
ward
Both day and night, of each degree and
place;
But few returned, having scaped hard,
With balefull beggery, or foule disgrace;
Which ever after in most wretched case,
Like loathsome lazars, by the hedges lay.
Thether Duessa badd him bend his pace:
For she is wearie of the toilsom way,
And also nigh consumed is the lingring day.

IV

A stately pallace built of squared bricke,
Which cunningly was without morter laid,
Whose wals were high, but nothing strong
nor thick,
And golden foile all over them displaid,
That purest skye with brightnesse they dis-
maid:
High lifted up were many loftie towres,
And goodly galleries far over laid,
Full of faire windowes and delightful
bowres;
And on the top a diall told the timely
howres.

V

It was a goodly heape for to behould,
And spake the praises of the workmans witt;
But full great pittie, that so faire a mould
Did on so weake foundation ever sitt:
For on a sandie hill, that still did flitt
And fall away, it mounted was full hie,
That every breath of heaven shaked itt;
And all the hinder partes, that few could spie,
Were ruinous and old, but painted cun-
ningly.

VI

Arrived there, they passed in forth right;
For still to all the gates stood open wide:
Yet charge of them was to a porter hight,
Cald Malvenù, who entrance none denide:
Thence to the hall, which was on every side
With rich array and costly arras dight:
Infinite sortes of people did abide
There waiting long, to win the wished sight
Of her, that was the lady of that pallace
bright.

VII

By them they passe, all gazing on them
round,
And to the presence mount; whose glorious
vew
Their frayle amazed senses did confound:
In living princes court none ever knew
Such endlesse richesse, and so sumpteous
shew;
Ne Persia selfe, the nourse of pompous
pride,
Like ever saw. And there a noble crew
Of lords and ladies stood on every side,
Which, with their presence fayre the place
much beautifide.

VIII

High above all a cloth of state was spred,
And a rich throne, as bright as sunny day,
On which there sate, most brave embel-
lished
With royall robes and gorgeous array,
A mayden queene, that shone as Titans ray,
In glistring gold and perelesse pretious
stone;
Yet her bright blazing beautie did assay
To dim the brightnesse of her glorious
throne,
As envying her selfe, that too exceeding
shone:

IX

Exceeding shone, like Phœbus fayrest childe,
That did presume his fathers fyrie wayne,
And flaming mouthes of steedes unwonted
wilde,
Through highest heaven with weaker hand
to rayne:
Proud of such glory and advancement vayne,
While flashing beames do daze his feeble
eyen,
He leaves the welkin way most beaten
playne,
And, rapt with whirling wheeles, inflames
the skyen
With fire not made to burne, but fayrely
for to shyne.

X

So proud she shyned in her princely state,
Looking to heaven, for earth she did dis-
dayne,
And sitting high, for lowly she did hate:
Lo! underneath her scornefull feete, was
layne

A dreadfull dragon with an hideous trayne,
And in her hand she held a mirrhour
　　bright,
Wherein her face she often vewed fayne,
And in her selfe-lov'd semblance tooke de-
　　light;
For she was wondrous faire, as any living
　　wight.

XI

Of griesly Pluto she the daughter was,
And sad Proserpina, the queene of hell;
Yet did she thinke her pearelesse worth to
　　pas
That parentage, with pride so did she swell,
And thundring Jove, that high in heaven
　　doth dwell,
And wield the world, she claymed for her
　　syre,
Or if that any else did Jove excell:
For to the highest she did still aspyre,
Or, if ought higher were then that, did it
　　desyre.

XII

And proud Lucifera men did her call,
That made her selfe a queene, and crownd
　　to be;
Yet rightfull kingdome she had none at all,
Ne heritage of native soveraintie,
But did usurpe with wrong and tyrannie
Upon the scepter, which she now did hold:
Ne ruld her realme with lawes, but pol-
　　licie,
And strong advizement of six wisards old,
That with their counsels bad her kingdome
　　did uphold.

XIII

Soone as the Elfin knight in presence came,
And false Duessa, seeming lady fayre,
A gentle husher, Vanitie by name,
Made rowme, and passage for them did pre-
　　paire:
So goodly brought them to the lowest stayre
Of her high throne, where they, on humble
　　knee
Making obeysaunce, did the cause declare,
Why they were come, her roiall state to see,
To prove the wide report of her great
　　majestee.

XIV

With loftie eyes, halfe loth to looke so lowe,
She thancked them in her disdainefull wise,

Ne other grace vouchsafed them to showe
Of princesse worthy; scarse them bad arise.
Her lordes and ladies all this while devise
Themselves to setten forth to straungers
　　sight:
Some frounce their curled heare in courtly
　　guise,
Some prancke their ruffes, and others trimly
　　dight
Their gay attyre: each others greater pride
　　does spight.

XV

Goodly they all that knight doe entertayne,
Right glad with him to have increast their
　　crew;
But to Duess' each one himselfe did payne
All kindnesse and faire courtesie to shew;
For in that court whylome her well they
　　knew:
Yet the stout Faery mongst the middest
　　crowd
Thought all their glorie vaine in knightly
　　vew,
And that great princesse too exceeding
　　prowd,
That to strange knight no better counte-
　　nance allowd.

XVI

Suddein upriseth from her stately place
The roiall dame, and for her coche doth call:
All hurtlen forth, and she, with princely
　　pace,
As faire Aurora, in her purple pall,
Out of the east the dawning day doth call,
So forth she comes: her brightnes brode
　　doth blaze:
The heapes of people, thronging in the hall,
Doe ride each other, upon her to gaze:
Her glorious glitterand light doth all mens
　　eies amaze.

XVII

So forth she comes, and to her coche does
　　clyme,
Adorned all with gold and girlonds gay,
That seemd as fresh as Flora in her prime,
And strove to match, in roiall rich array,
Great Junoes golden chayre, the which, they
　　say,
The gods stand gazing on, when she does
　　ride
To Joves high hous through heavens bras-
　　paved way,

Drawne of fayre pecocks, that excell in
pride,
And full of Argus eyes their tayles dispredden wide.

XVIII

But this was drawne of six unequall beasts,
On which her six sage counsellours did ryde,
Taught to obay their bestiall beheasts,
With like conditions to their kindes ap-
plyde:
Of which the first, that all the rest did
guyde,
Was sluggish Idlenesse, the nourse of sin;
Upon a slouthfull asse he chose to ryde,
Arayd in habit blacke, and amis thin,
Like to an holy monck, the service to begin.

XIX

And in his hand his portesse still he bare,
That much was worne, but therein little
redd,
For of devotion he had little care,
Still drownd in sleepe, and most of his
daies dedd:
Scarse could he once uphold his heavie hedd,
To looken whether it were night or day:
May seeme the wayne was very evill ledd,
When such an one had guiding of the way,
That knew not whether right he went, or
else astray.

XX

From worldly cares himselfe he did es-
loyne,
And greatly shunned manly exercise;
From everie worke he chalenged essoyne,
For contemplation sake: yet otherwise
His life he led in lawlesse riotise;
By which he grew to grievous malady;
For in his lustlesse limbs, through evill
guise,
A shaking fever raignd continually.
Such one was Idlenesse, first of this com-
pany.

XXI

And by his side rode loathsome Gluttony,
Deformed creature, on a filthie swyne:
His belly was upblowne with luxury,
And eke with fatnesse swollen were his eyne;
And like a crane his necke was long and
fyne,
With which he swallowd up excessive feast,
For want whereof poore people oft did pyne:

And all the way, most like a brutish beast,
He spued up his gorge, that all did him
deteast.

XXII

In greene vine leaves he was right fitly
clad;
For other clothes he could not weare for
heat;
And on his head an yvie girland had,
From under which fast trickled downe the
sweat:
Still as he rode, he somewhat still did
eat,
And in his hand did beare a bouzing can,
Of which he supt so oft, that on his seat
His dronken corse he scarse upholden can:
In shape and life more like a monster then
a man.

XXIII

Unfit he was for any worldly thing,
And eke unhable once to stirre or go;
Not meet to be of counsell to a king,
Whose mind in meat and drinke was
drowned so,
That from his frend he seeldome knew his
fo:
Full of diseases was his carcas blew,
And a dry dropsie through his flesh did
flow,
Which by misdiet daily greater grew.
Such one was Gluttony, the second of that
crew.

XXIV

And next to him rode lustfull Lechery
Upon a bearded gote, whose rugged heare,
And whally eies (the signe of gelosy,)
Was like the person selfe, whom he did
beare:
Who rough, and blacke, and filthy, did ap-
peare,
Unseemely man to please faire ladies eye;
Yet he of ladies oft was loved deare,
When fairer faces were bid standen by:
O who does know the bent of womens fan-
tasy?

XXV

In a greene gowne he clothed was full
faire,
Which underneath did hide his filthinesse;
And in his hand a burning hart he bare,
Full of vaine follies and new fanglenesse:

For he was false, and fraught with fickle-
nesse,
And learned had to love with secret lookes,
And well could daunce, and sing with rue-
fulnesse,
And fortunes tell, and read in loving bookes,
And thousand other waies, to bait his
fleshly hookes.

XXVI

Inconstant man, that loved all he saw,
And lusted after all that he did love;
Ne would his looser life be tide to law,
But joyd weake wemens hearts to tempt,
and prove
If from their loyall loves he might them
move;
Which lewdnes fild him with reprochfull pain
Of that foule evill, which all men reprove,
That rotts the marrow, and consumes the
braine.
Such one was Lechery, the third of all this
traine.

XXVII

And greedy Avarice by him did ride,
Uppon a camell loaden all with gold:
Two iron coffers hong on either side,
With precious metall full as they might hold,
And in his lap an heap of coine he told;
For of his wicked pelfe his god he made,
And unto hell him selfe for money sold:
Accursed usury was all his trade;
And right and wrong ylike in equall bal-
launce waide.

XXVIII

His life was nigh unto deaths dore yplaste;
And thred-bare cote, and cobled shoes, hee
ware,
Ne scarse good morsell all his life did taste,
But both from backe and belly still did
spare,
To fill his bags, and richesse to compare;
Yet childe ne kinsman living had he none
To leave them to; but thorough daily care
To get, and nightly feare to lose his owne,
He led a wretched life, unto him selfe un-
knowne.

XXIX

Most wretched wight, whom nothing might
suffise,
Whose greedy lust did lacke in greatest
store,

Whose need had end, but no end covetise,
Whose welth was want, whose plenty made
him pore,
Who had enough, yett wished ever more,
A vile disease; and eke in foote and hand
A grievous gout tormented him full sore,
That well he could not touch, nor goe, nor
stand.
Such one was Avarice, the forth of this
faire band.

XXX

And next to him malicious Envy rode
Upon a ravenous wolfe, and still did chaw
Betweene his cankred teeth a venemous
tode,
That all the poison ran about his chaw;
But inwardly he chawed his owne maw
At neibors welth, that made him ever sad;
For death it was, when any good he saw;
And wept, that cause of weeping none he
had;
But when he heard of harme, he wexed
wondrous glad.

XXXI

All in a kirtle of discolourd say
He clothed was, ypaynted full of eies;
And in his bosome secretly there lay
An hatefull snake, the which his taile uptyes
In many folds, and mortall sting implyes.
Still as he rode, he gnasht his teeth, to see
Those heapes of gold with griple Covetyse;
And grudged at the great felicitee
Of proud Lucifera, and his owne companee.

XXXII

He hated all good workes and vertuous
deeds,
And him no lesse, that any like did use;
And who with gratious bread the hungry
feeds,
His almes for want of faith he doth accuse;
So every good to bad he doth abuse:
And eke the verse of famous poets witt
He does backebite, and spightfull poison
spues
From leprous mouth on all that ever writt:
Such one vile Envy was, that fifte in row
did sitt.

XXXIII

And him beside rides fierce revenging
Wrath,
Upon a lion, loth for to be led;

And in his hand a burning brond he hath,
The which he brandisheth about his hed:
His eies did hurle forth sparcles fiery red,
And stared sterne on all that him beheld:
As ashes pale of hew, and seeming ded;
And on his dagger still his hand he held,
Trembling through hasty rage, when choler
    in him sweld.

XXXIV

His ruffin raiment all was staind with blood,
Which he had spilt, and all to rags yrent,
Through unadvized rashnes woxen wood;
For of his hands he had no governement,
Ne car'd for blood in his avengement:
But when the furious fitt was overpast,
His cruell facts he often would repent;
Yet, wilfull man, he never would forecast,
How many mischieves should ensue his
    heedlesse hast.

XXXV

Full many mischiefes follow cruell Wrath;
Abhorred bloodshed, and tumultuous strife,
Unmanly murder, and unthrifty scath,
Bitter despight, with rancours rusty knife,
And fretting griefe, the enemy of life:
All these, and many evils moe haunt Ire;
The swelling splene, and frenzy raging rife,
The shaking palsey, and Saint Fraunces fire.
Such one was Wrath, the last of this un-
    godly tire.

XXXVI

And after all, upon the wagon beame,
Rode Sathan, with a smarting whip in hand,
With which he forward lasht the laesy
    teme,
So oft as Slowth still in the mire did stand.
Huge routs of people did about them band,
Showting for joy; and still before their
    way
A foggy mist had covered all the land;
And underneath their feet, all scattered lay
Dead sculls and bones of men, whose life
    had gone astray.

XXXVII

So forth they marchen in this goodly sort,
To take the solace of the open aire,
And in fresh flowring fields themselves to
    sport.
Emongst the rest rode that false lady faire,
The foule Duessa, next unto the chaire
Of proud Lucifer', as one of the traine·

But that good knight would not so nigh re-
    paire,
Him selfe estraunging from their joyaunce
    vaine,
Whose fellowship seemd far unfitt for war-
    like swaine.

XXXVIII

So having solaced themselves a space,
With pleasaunce of the breathing fields
    yfed,
They backe retourned to the princely place;
Whereas an errant knight, in armes ycled,
And heathnish shield, wherein with letters
    red
Was writt Sans joy, they new arrived find:
Enflam'd with fury and fiers hardyhed,
He seemd in hart to harbour thoughts un-
    kind,
And nourish bloody vengeaunce in his bit-
    ter mind.

XXXIX

Who, when the shamed shield of slaine
    Sansfoy
He spide with that same Fary champions
    page,
Bewraying him that did of late destroy
His eldest brother, burning all with rage,
He to him lept, and that same envious gage
Of victors glory from him snacht away:
But th' Elfin knight, which ought that war-
    like wage,
Disdaind to loose the meed he wonne in fray,
And him rencountring fierce, reskewd the
    noble pray.

XL

Therewith they gan to hurtlen greedily,
Redoubted battaile ready to darrayne,
And clash their shields, and shake their
    swerds on hy,
That with their sturre they troubled all the
    traine;
Till that great queene, upon eternall paine
Of high displeasure, that ensewen might,
Commaunded them their fury to refraine,
And if that either to that shield had right,
In equall lists they should the morrow next
    it fight.

XLI

'Ah! dearest dame,' quoth then the Paynim
    bold,
'Pardon the error of enraged wight,

Whome great griefe made forgett the raines
to hold
Of reasons rule, to see this recreaunt knight,
No knight, but treachour full of false de-
spight
And shameful treason, who through guile
hath slayn
The prowest knight that ever field did fight,
Even stout Sansfoy, (O who can then re-
frayn ?)
Whose shield he beares renverst, the more
to heap disdayn.

XLII

' And to augment the glorie of his guile,
His dearest love, the faire Fidessa, loe!
Is there possessed of the traytour vile,
Who reapes the harvest sowen by his foe,
Sowen in bloodie field, and bought with
woe:
That brothers hand shall dearely well re-
quight,
So be, O Queene, you equall favour showe.'
Him litle answerd th' angry Elfin knight;
He never meant with words, but swords, to
plead his right:

XLIII

But threw his gauntlet as a sacred pledg,
His cause in combat the next day to try:
So been they parted both, with harts on edg
To be aveng'd each on his enimy.
That night they pas in joy and jollity,
Feasting and courting both in bowre and
hall;
For steward was excessive Gluttony,
That of his plenty poured forth to all;
Which doen, the chamberlain Slowth did to
rest them call.

XLIV

Now whenas darkesome Night had all dis-
playd
Her coleblacke curtein over brightest skye,
The warlike youthes, on dayntie couches
layd,
Did chace away sweet sleepe from slug-
gish eye,
To muse on meanes of hoped victory.
But whenas Morpheus had with leaden
mace
Arrested all that courtly company,
Uprose Duessa from her resting place,
And to the Paynims lodging comes with
silent pace.

XLV

Whom broad awake she findes, in trou-
blous fitt,
Forecasting, how his foe he might annoy,
And him amoves with speaches seeming fitt:
' Ah deare Sansjoy, next dearest to Sansfoy,
Cause of my new griefe, cause of my new
joy,
Joyous, to see his ymage in mine eye,
And greevd, to thinke how foe did him de-
stroy,
That was the flowre of grace and cheval-
rye;
Lo! his Fidessa, to thy secret faith I flye.'

XLVI

With gentle wordes he can her fayrely
greet,
And bad say on the secrete of her hart.
Then, sighing soft, ' I learne that litle sweet
Oft tempred is,' quoth she, ' with muchell
smart:
For since my brest was launcht with lovely
dart
Of deare Sansfoy, I never joyed howre,
But in eternall woes my weaker hart
Have wasted, loving him with all my powre,
And for his sake have felt full many an
heavie stowre.

XLVII

' At last, when perils all I weened past,
And hop'd to reape the crop of all my care,
Into new woes unweeting I was cast
By this false faytor, who unworthie ware
His worthie shield, whom he with guilefull
snare
Entrapped slew, and brought to shamefull
grave.
Me, silly maid, away with him he bare,
And ever since hath kept in darksom cave,
For that I would not yeeld that to Sansfoy
I gave.

XLVIII

'But since faire sunne hath sperst that
lowring clowd,
And to my loathed life now shewes some
light,
Under your beames I will me safely shrowd
From dreaded storme of his disdainfull
spight:
To you th' inheritance belonges by right
Of brothers prayse, to you eke longes his
love.

Let not his love, let not his restlesse spright,
Be unreveng'd, that calles to you above
From wandring Stygian shores, where it
doth endlesse move.'

XLIX

Thereto said he, 'Faire dame, be nought
dismaid
For sorrowes past; their griefe is with them
gone:
Ne yet of present perill be affraid:
For needlesse feare did never vantage none,
And helplesse hap it booteth not to mone.
Dead is Sansfoy, his vitall paines are past,
Though greeved ghost for vengeance deep
do grone:
He lives, that shall him pay his dewties
last,
And guiltie Elfin blood shall sacrifice in
hast.'

L

' O ! but I feare the fickle freakes,' quoth
shee,
' Of Fortune false, and oddes of armes in
field.'
' Why, dame,' quoth he, ' what oddes can
ever bee,
Where both doe fight alike, to win or
yield ? '
' Yea, but,' quoth she, ' he beares a charmed
shield,
And eke enchaunted armes, that none can
perce,
Ne none can wound the man, that does
them wield.'
' Charmd or enchaunted,' answerd he then
ferce,
' I no whitt reck, ne you the like need to
reherce.

LI

' But, faire Fidessa, sithens Fortunes guile,
Or enimies powre, hath now captived you,
Returne from whence ye came, and rest a
while,
Till morrow next, that I the Elfe subdew,
And with Sansfoyes dead dowry you en-
dew.'
' Ay me ! that is a double death,' she said,
' With proud foes sight my sorrow to re-
new:
Where ever yet I be, my secrete aide
Shall follow you.' So, passing forth, she
him obaid.

CANTO V

The faithfull knight in equall field
Subdewes his faithlesse foe,
Whom false Duessa saves, and for
His cure to hell does goe.

I

THE noble hart, that harbours vertuous
thought,
And is with childe of glorious great intent
Can never rest, untill it forth have brought
Th' eternall brood of glorie excellent:
Such restlesse passion did all night tor-
ment
The flaming corage of that Faery knight,
Devizing how that doughtie turnament
With greatest honour he atchieven might:
Still did he wake, and still did watch for
dawning light.

II

At last, the golden orientall gate
Of greatest heaven gan to open fayre,
And Phoebus, fresh as brydegrome to his
mate,
Came dauncing forth, shaking his deawie
hayre,
And hurld his glistring beams through
gloomy ayre.
Which when the wakeful Elfe perceivd,
streight way
He started up, and did him selfe prepayre
In sunbright armes, and battailous array:
For with that Pagan proud he combatt will
that day.

III

And forth he comes into the commune hall,
Where earely waite him many a gazing eye,
To weet what end to straunger knights may
fall.
There many minstrales maken melody,
To drive away the dull melancholy,
And many bardes, that to the trembling
chord
Can tune their timely voices cunningly,
And many chroniclers, that can record
Old loves, and warres for ladies doen by
many a lord.

IV

Soone after comes the cruell Sarazin,
In woven maile all armed warily,
And sternly lookes at him, who not a pin
Does care for looke of living creatures eye.

They bring them wines of Greece and Araby
And daintie spices fetcht from furthest
    Ynd,
To kindle heat of corage privily:
And in the wine a solemne oth they bynd
T' observe the sacred lawes of armes, that
    are assynd.

V

At last forth comes that far renowmed
    queene,
With royall pomp and princely majestie:
She is ybrought unto a paled greene,
And placed under stately canapee,
The warlike feates of both those knights
    to see.
On th' other side, in all mens open vew,
Duessa placed is, and on a tree
Sansfoy his shield is hangd with bloody
    hew:
Both those, the lawrell girlonds to the vic-
    tor dew.

VI

A shrilling trompett sownded from on
    hye,
And unto battaill bad them selves addresse:
Their shining shieldes about their wrestes
    they tye,
And burning blades about their heades doe
    blesse,
The instruments of wrath and heavinesse:
With greedy force each other doth assayle,
And strike so fiercely, that they doe im-
    presse
Deepe dinted furrowes in the battred mayle:
The yron walles to ward their blowes are
    weak and fraile.

VII

The Sarazin was stout, and wondrous strong,
And heaped blowes like yron hammers
    great:
For after blood and vengeance he did long.
The knight was fiers, and full of youthly
    heat,
And doubled strokes, like dreaded thun-
    ders threat:
For all for praise and honour he did fight.
Both stricken stryke, and beaten both doe
    beat,
That from their shields forth flyeth firie
    light,
And helmets, hewen deepe, shew marks of
    eithers might.

VIII

So th' one for wrong, the other strives for
    right:
As when a gryfon, seized of his pray,
A dragon fiers encountreth in his flight,
Through widest ayre making his ydle way,
That would his rightfull ravine rend away:
With hideous horror both together smight,
And souce so sore, that they the heavens
    affray:
The wise southsayer, seeing so sad sight,
Th' amazed vulgar telles of warres and
    mortall fight.

IX

So th' one for wrong, the other strives for
    right,
And each to deadly shame would drive his
    foe:
The cruell steele so greedily doth bight
In tender flesh, that streames of blood down
    flow,
With which the armes, that earst so bright
    did show,
Into a pure vermillion now are dyde.
Great ruth in all the gazers harts did grow,
Seeing the gored woundes to gape so wyde,
That victory they dare not wish to either
    side.

X

At last the Paynim chaunst to cast his eye,
His suddein eye, flaming with wrathfull
    fyre,
Upon his brothers shield, which hong
    thereby:
Therewith redoubled was his raging yre,
And said: 'Ah, wretched sonne of wofull
    syre !
Doest thou sit wayling by blacke Stygian
    lake,
Whylest here thy shield is hangd for vic-
    tors hyre ?
And, sluggish german, doest thy forces slake
To after-send his foe, that him may over-
    take ?

XI

' Goe, caytive Elfe, him quickly overtake,
And soone redeeme from his long wandring
    woe:
Goe, guiltie ghost, to him my message make,
That I his shield have quit from dying foe.'
Therewith upon his crest he stroke him so,
That twise he reeled, readie twise to fall:

End of the doubtfull battaile deemed tho
The lookers on, and lowd to him gan call
The false Duessa, 'Thine the shield, and I,
    and all!'

XII

Soone as the Faerie heard his ladie speake,
Out of his swowning dreame he gan awake,
And quickning faith, that earst was woxen
    weake,
The creeping deadly cold away did shake:
Tho, mov'd with wrath, and shame, and
    ladies sake,
Of all attonce he cast avengd to be,
And with so' exceeding furie at him strake,
That forced him to stoupe upon his knee:
Had he not stouped so, he should have
    cloven bee.

XIII

And to him said: 'Goe now, proud mis-
    creant,
Thy selfe thy message do to german deare;
Alone he, wandring, thee too long doth want:
Goe say, his foe thy shield with his doth
    beare.'
Therewith his heavie hand he high gan
    reare,
Him to have slaine; when lo! a darke-
    some clowd
Upon him fell: he no where doth appeare,
But vanisht is. The Elfe him calls alowd,
But answer none receives: the darknes him
    does shrowd.

XIV

In haste Duessa from her place arose,
And to him running sayd: 'O prowest
    knight,
That ever ladie to her love did chose,
Let now abate the terrour of your might,
And quench the flame of furious despight
And bloodie vengeance; lo! th' infernall
    powres,
Covering your foe with cloud of deadly
    night,
Have borne him hence to Plutoes balefull
    bowres.
The conquest yours, I yours, the shield and
    glory yours!'

XV

Not all so satisfide, with greedy eye
He sought all round about, his thristy blade
To bathe in blood of faithlesse enimy;

Who all that while lay hid in secret shade:
He standes amazed, how he thence should
    fade.
At last the trumpets triumph sound on hie,
And running heralds humble homage made,
Greeting him goodly with new victorie,
And to him brought the shield, the cause
    of enmitie.

XVI

Wherewith he goeth to that soveraine
    queene,
And falling her before on lowly knee,
To her makes present of his service seene:
Which she accepts, with thankes and goodly
    gree,
Greatly advauncing his gay chevalree:
So marcheth home, and by her takes the
    knight,
Whom all the people followe with great
    glee,
Shouting, and clapping all their hands on
    hight,
That all the ayre it fils, and flyes to heaven
    bright.

XVII

Home is he brought, and layd in sump-
    tuous bed:
Where many skilfull leaches him abide,
To salve his hurts, that yet still freshly
    bled.
In wine and oyle they wash his woundes
    wide,
And softly can embalme on everie side.
And all the while, most heavenly melody
About the bed sweet musicke did divide,
Him to beguile of griefe and agony:
And all the while Duessa wept full bitterly.

XVIII

As when a wearie traveiler, that strayes
By muddy shore of broad seven-mouthed
    Nile,
Unweeting of the perillous wandring wayes,
Doth meete a cruell craftie crocodile,
Which, in false griefe hyding his harmefull
    guile,
Doth weepe full sore, and sheddeth tender
    teares:
The foolish man, that pitties all this while
His mournefull plight, is swallowd up un-
    wares,
Forgetfull of his owne, that mindes an
    others cares.

XIX

So wept Duessa untill eventyde,
That shyning lampes in Joves high house
            were light:
Then forth she rose, ne lenger would abide,
But comes unto the place, where th' he-
            then knight,
In slombring swownd, nigh voyd of vitall
            spright,
Lay cover'd with inchaunted cloud all day:
Whom when she found, as she him left in
            plight,
To wayle his wofull case she would not stay,
But to the easterne coast of heaven makes
            speedy way:

XX

Where griesly Night, with visage deadly
            sad,
That Phœbus chearefull face durst never
            vew,
And in a foule blacke pitchy mantle clad,
She findes forth comming from her dark-
            some mew,
Where she all day did hide her hated hew.
Before the dore her yron charet stood,
Already harnessed for journey new;
And coleblacke steedes yborne of hellish
            brood,
That on their rusty bits did champ, as they
            were wood.

XXI

Who when she saw Duessa sunny bright,
Adornd with gold and jewels shining cleare,
She greatly grew amazed at the sight,
And th' unacquainted light began to feare;
For never did such brightnes there appeare;
And would have backe retyred to her cave,
Untill the witches speach she gan to heare,
Saying : 'Yet, O thou dreaded dame, I
            crave
Abyde, till I have told the message which
            I have.'

XXII

She stayd, and foorth Duessa gan proceede:
'O thou most auncient grandmother of all,
More old then Jove, whom thou at first
            didst breede,
Or that great house of gods cælestiall,
Which wast begot in Dæmogorgons hall,
And sawst the secrets of the world unmade,
Why suffredst thou thy nephewes deare to
            fall

With Elfin sword, most shamefully betrade ?
Lo where the stout Sansjoy doth sleepe in
            deadly shade !

XXIII

'And him before, I saw with bitter eyes
The bold Sansfoy shrinck underneath his
            speare;
And now the pray of fowles in field he lyes,
Nor wayld of friends, nor layd on groning
            beare,
That whylome was to me too dearely deare.
O what of gods then boots it to be borne,
If old Aveugles sonnes so evill heare ?
Or who shall not great Nightes children
            scorne,
When two of three her nephews are so
            fowle forlorne ?

XXIV

'Up, then ! up, dreary dame, of darknes
            queene !
Go gather up the reliques of thy race,
Or else goe them avenge, and let be seene
That dreaded Night in brightest day hath
            place,
And can the children of fayre Light de-
            face.'
Her feeling speaches some compassion
            mov'd
In hart, and chaunge in that great mothers
            face:
Yet pitty in her hart was never prov'd
Till then: for evermore she hated, never
            lov'd:

XXV

And said, 'Deare daughter, rightly may I
            rew
The fall of famous children borne of mee,
And good successes, which their foes en-
            sew:
But who can turne the streame of destinee,
Or breake the chayne of strong necessitee,
Which fast is tyde to Joves eternall seat ?
The sonnes of Day he favoureth, I see,
And by my ruines thinkes to make them
            great:
To make one great by others losse is bad
            excheat.

XXVI

'Yet shall they not escape so freely all;
For some shall pay the price of others guilt:
And he, the man that made Sansfoy to fall,

Shall with his owne blood price that he
     hath spilt.
But what art thou, that telst of nephews
     kilt ? '
' I, that do seeme not I, Duessa ame,'
Quoth she, ' how ever now, in garments
     gilt
And gorgeous gold arayd, I to thee came;
Duessa I, the daughter of Deceipt and
     Shame.'

XXVII

Then bowing downe her aged backe, she
     kist
The wicked witch, saying: ' In that fayre
     face
The false resemblaunce of Deceipt, I wist,
Did closely lurke; yet so true-seeming grace
It carried, that I scarse in darksome place
Could it discerne, though I the mother bee
Of Falshood, and roote of Duessaes race.
O welcome, child, whom I have longd to
     see,
And now have seene unwares ! Lo, now I
     goe with thee.'

XXVIII

Then to her yron wagon she betakes,
And with her beares the fowle welfavourd
     witch:
Through mirkesome aire her ready way
     she makes.
Her twyfold teme, of which two blacke as
     pitch,
And two were browne, yet each to each
     unlich,
Did softly swim away, ne ever stamp,
Unlesse she chaunst their stubborne mouths
     to twitch;
Then foming tarre, their bridles they would
     champ,
And trampling the fine element, would
     fiercely ramp.

XXIX

So well they sped, that they be come at
     length
Unto the place, whereas the Paynim lay,
Devoid of outward sence and native strength,
Coverd with charmed cloud from vew of day
And sight of men, since his late luckelesse
     fray.
His cruell wounds, with cruddy bloud con-
     geald,
They binden up so wisely as they may,

And handle softly, till they can be heald:
So lay him in her charett, close in night
     conceald.

XXX

And all the while she stood upon the ground,
The wakefull dogs did never cease to bay,
As giving warning of th' unwonted sound,
With which her yron wheeles did them
     affray,
And her darke griesly looke them much
     dismay:
The messenger of death, the ghastly owle,
With drery shriekes did also her bewray;
And hungry wolves continually did howle
At her abhorred face, so filthy and so fowle.

XXXI

Thence turning backe in silence softe they
     stole,
And brought the heavy corse with easy pace
To yawning gulfe of deepe Avernus hole.
By that same hole an entraunce, darke and
     bace,
With smoake and sulphur hiding all the
     place,
Descends to hell: there creature never past,
That backe retourned without heavenly
     grace;
But dreadfull Furies, which their chaines
     have brast,
And damned sprights sent forth to make
     ill men aghast.

XXXII

By that same way the direfull dames doe
     drive
Their mournefull charett, fild with rusty
     blood,
And downe to Plutoes house are come
     bilive:
Which passing through, on every side them
     stood
The trembling ghosts with sad amazed
     mood,
Chattring their iron teeth, and staring wide
With stony eies; and all the hellish brood
Of feends infernall flockt on every side,
To gaze on erthly wight, that with the
     Night durst ride.

XXXIII

They pas the bitter waves of Acheron,
Where many soules sit wailing woefully,
And come to fiery flood of Phlegeton,

Whereas the damned ghosts in torments fry,
And with sharp shrilling shriekes doe bootlesse cry,
Cursing high Jove, the which them thither sent.
The house of endlesse paine is built thereby,
In which ten thousand sorts of punishment
The cursed creatures doe eternally torment.

XXXIV

Before the threshold dreadfull Cerberus
His three deformed heads did lay along,
Curled with thousand adders venemous,
And lilled forth his bloody flaming tong:
At them he gan to reare his bristles strong,
And felly gnarre, untill Dayes enemy
Did him appease; then downe his taile he hong,
And suffered them to passen quietly:
For she in hell and heaven had power equally.

XXXV

There was Ixion turned on a wheele,
For daring tempt the queene of heaven to sin;
And Sisyphus an huge round stone did reele
Against an hill, ne might from labour lin;
There thristy Tantalus hong by the chin;
And Tityus fed a vultur on his maw;
Typhœus joynts were stretched on a gin;
Theseus condemned to endlesse slouth by law;
And fifty sisters water in leke vessels draw.

XXXVI

They all, beholding worldly wights in place,
Leave off their worke, unmindfull of their smart,
To gaze on them; who forth by them doe pace,
Till they be come unto the furthest part:
Where was a cave ywrought by wondrous art,
Deepe, darke, uneasy, dolefull, comfortlesse,
In which sad Aesculapius far apart
Emprisond was in chaines remedilesse,
For that Hippolytus rent corse he did redresse.

XXXVII

Hippolytus a jolly huntsman was,
That wont in charett chace the foming bore;

He all his peeres in beauty did surpas,
But ladies love, as losse of time, forbore:
His wanton stepdame loved him the more;
But when she saw her offred sweets refusd,
Her love she turnd to hate, and him before
His father fierce of treason false accusd,
And with her gealous termes his open eares abusd.

XXXVIII

Who, all in rage, his sea-god syre besought,
Some cursed vengeaunce on his sonne to cast:
From surging gulf two monsters streight were brought,
With dread whereof his chacing steedes aghast
Both charett swifte and huntsman overcast.
His goodly corps, on ragged cliffs yrent,
Was quite dismembred, and his members chast
Scattered on every mountaine as he went,
That of Hippolytus was lefte no moniment.

XXXIX

His cruell stepdame, seeing what was donne,
Her wicked daies with wretched knife did end,
In death avowing th' innocence of her sonne.
Which hearing, his rash syre began to rend
His heare, and hasty tong, that did offend:
Tho, gathering up the relicks of his smart,
By Dianes meanes, who was Hippolyts frend,
Them brought to Aesculape, that by his art
Did heale them all againe, and joyned every part.

XL

Such wondrous science in mans witt to rain
When Jove avizd, that could the dead revive,
And fates expired could renew again,
Of endlesse life he might him not deprive,
But unto hell did thrust him downe alive,
With flashing thunderbolt ywounded sore:
Where long remaining, he did alwaies strive
Him selfe with salves to health for to restore,
And slake the heavenly fire, that raged evermore.

XLI

There auncient Night arriving, did alight
From her nigh weary wayne, and in her armes

To Æsculapius brought the wounded knight:
Whome having softly disaraid of armes,
Tho gan to him discover all his harmes,
Beseeching him with prayer, and with
    praise,
If either salves, or oyles, or herbes, or
    charmes
A fordonne wight from dore of death mote
    raise,
He would at her request prolong her
    nephews daies.

XLII

'Ah! dame,' quoth he, 'thou temptest me
    in vaine
To dare the thing, which daily yet I rew,
And the old cause of my continued paine
With like attempt to like end to renew.
Is not enough, that, thrust from heaven
    dew,
Here endlesse penaunce for one fault I pay,
But that redoubled crime with vengeaunce
    new
Thou biddest me to eeke? Can Night de-
    fray
The wrath of thundring Jove, that rules
    both Night and Day?'

XLIII

'Not so,' quoth she; 'but sith that heavens
    king
From hope of heaven hath thee excluded
    quight,
Why fearest thou, that canst not hope for
    thing,
And fearest not that more thee hurten
    might,
Now in the powre of everlasting Night?
Goe to then, O thou far renowmed sonne
Of great Apollo, shew thy famous might
In medicine, that els hath to thee wonne
Great pains, and greater praise, both never
    to be donne.'

XLIV

Her words prevaild: and then the learned
    leach
His cunning hand gan to his wounds to lay,
And all things els, the which his art did
    teach:
Which having seene, from thence arose
    away
The mother of dredd darkenesse, and let
    stay
Aveugles sonne there in the leaches cure,

And backe retourning, tooke her wonted
    way
To ronne her timely race, whilst Phoebus
    pure
In westerne waves his weary wagon did
    recure.

XLV

The false Duessa, leaving noyous Night,
Returnd to stately pallace of Dame Pryde;
Where when she came, she found the Faery
    knight
Departed thence, albee his woundes wyde,
Not throughly heald, unready were to ryde.
Good cause he had to hasten thence away;
For on a day his wary dwarfe had spyde
Where, in a dungeon deepe, huge nombers
    lay
Of caytive wretched thralls, that waylad
    night and day:

XLVI

A ruefull sight as could be seene with eie:
Of whom he learned had in secret wise
The hidden cause of their captivitie;
How mortgaging their lives to Covetise,
Through wastfull pride and wanton riotise,
They were by law of that proud tyran-
    nesse,
Provokt with Wrath, and Envyes false sur-
    mise,
Condemned to that dongeon mercilesse,
Where they should live in wo, and dye in
    wretchednesse.

XLVII

There was that great proud king of Baby-
    lon,
That would compell all nations to adore,
And him as onely God to call upon,
Till, through celestiall doome thrown out
    of dore,
Into an oxe he was transformd of yore:
There also was King Crœsus, that enhaunst
His hart too high through his great richesse
    store;
And proud Antiochus, the which advaunst
His cursed hand gainst God, and on his
    altares daunst.

XLVIII

And them long time before, great Nimrod
    was,
That first the world with sword and fire
    warrayd;

And after him old Ninus far did pas
In princely pomp, of all the world obayd;
There also was that mightie monarch layd
Low under all, yet above all in pride,
That name of native syre did fowle up-
    brayd,
And would as Ammons sonne be magnifide,
Till, scornd of God and man, a shamefull
    death he dide.

XLIX

All these together in one heape were
    throwne,
Like carkases of beastes in butchers stall.
And, in another corner, wide were strowne
The antique ruins of the Romanes fall:
Great Romulus, the grandsyre of them
    all,
Proud Tarquin, and too lordly Lentulus,
Stout Scipio, and stubborne Hanniball,
Ambitious Sylla, and sterne Marius,
High Caesar, great Pompey, and fiers An-
    tonius.

L

Amongst these mightie men were wemen
    mixt,
Proud wemen, vaine, forgetfull of their
    yoke:
The bold Semiramis, whose sides, transfixt
With sonnes own blade, her fowle reproches
    spoke;
Fayre Sthenobœa, that her selfe did choke
With wilfull chord, for wanting of her
    will;
High minded Cleopatra, that with stroke
Of aspes sting her selfe did stoutly kill:
And thousands moe the like, that did that
    dongeon fill.

LI

Besides the endlesse routes of wretched
    thralles,
Which thether were assembled day by day,
From all the world, after their wofull falles
Through wicked pride and wasted welthes
    decay.
But most, of all which in that dongeon lay,
Fell from high princes courtes, or ladies
    bowres,
Where they in ydle pomp, or wanton play,
Consumed had their goods, and thriftlesse
    howres,
And lastly thrown themselves into these
    heavy stowres.

LII

Whose case whenas the carefull dwarfe had
    tould,
And made ensample of their mournfull
    sight
Unto his maister, he no lenger would
There dwell in perill of like painefull plight,
But earely rose, and ere that dawning light
Discovered had the world to heaven wyde,
He by a privy posterne tooke his flight,
That of no envious eyes he mote be spyde:
For doubtlesse death ensewed, if any him
    descryde.

LIII

Scarse could he footing find in that fowle
    way,
For many corses, like a great lay-stall,
Of murdred men, which therein strowed
    lay,
Without remorse or decent funerall:
Which al through that great princesse pride
    did fall
And came to shamefull end. And them
    besyde,
Forth ryding underneath the castell wall,
A donghill of dead carcases he spyde,
The dreadfull spectacle of that sad House
    of Pryde.

CANTO VI

From lawlesse lust by wondrous grace
    Fayre Una is releast :
Whom salvage nation does adore,
    And learnes her wise beheast.

I

As when a ship, that flyes fayre under sayle,
An hidden rocke escaped hath unwares,
That lay in waite her wrack for to bewaile,
The marriner, yet halfe amazed, stares
At perill past, and yet in doubt ne dares
To joy at his foolhappie oversight:
So doubly is distrest twixt joy and cares
The dreadlesse corage of this Elfin knight,
Having escapt so sad ensamples in his sight.

II

Yet sad he was, that his too hastie speed
The fayre Duess' had forst him leave be-
    hind;
And yet more sad, that Una, his deare dreed,
Her truth had staynd with treason so un-
    kind:
Yet cryme in her could never creature find.

But for his love, and for her own selfe sake,
She wandred had from one to other Ynd,
Him for to seeke, ne ever would forsake,
Till her unwares the fiers Sansloy did over-
    take.

III

Who, after Archimagoes fowle defeat,
Led her away into a forest wilde,
And turning wrathfull fyre to lustfull heat,
With beastly sin thought her to have de-
    filde,
And made the vassall of his pleasures vilde.
Yet first he cast by treatie, and by traynes,
Her to persuade that stubborne fort to yilde:
For greater conquest of hard love he gaynes,
That workes it to his will, then he that it
    constraines.

IV

With fawning wordes he courted her a
    while,
And, looking lovely and oft sighing sore,
Her constant hart did tempt with diverse
    guile:
But wordes, and lookes, and sighes she
    did abhore,
As rock of diamond stedfast evermore.
Yet for to feed his fyrie lustfull eye,
He snatcht the vele that hong her face be-
    fore:
Then gan her beautie shyne as brightest
    skye,
And burnt his beastly hart t' efforce her
    chastitye.

V

So when he saw his flatt'ring artes to fayle,
And subtile engines bett from batteree,
With greedy force he gan the fort assayle,
Whereof he weend possessed soone to bee,
And win rich spoile of ransackt chastitee.
Ah! heavens, that doe this hideous act be-
    hold,
And heavenly virgin thus outraged see,
How can ye vengeance just so long with-
    hold,
And hurle not flashing flames upon that
    Paynim bold?

VI

The pitteous mayden, carefull comfort-
    lesse,
Does throw out thrilling shriekes, and
    shrieking cryes,

The last vaine helpe of wemens great dis-
    tresse,
And with loud plaintes importuneth the
    skyes;
That molten starres doe drop like weeping
    eyes,
And Phœbus, flying so most shamefull sight,
His blushing face in foggy cloud implyes,
And hydes for shame. What witt of mortall
    wight
Can now devise to quitt a thrall from such
    a plight?

VII

Eternall Providence, exceeding thought,
Where none appeares can make her selfe a
    way:
A wondrous way it for this lady wrought,
From lyons clawes to pluck the gryped
    pray.
Her shrill outcryes and shrieks so loud did
    bray,
That all the woodes and forestes did re-
    sownd;
A troupe of Faunes and Satyres far a way
Within the wood were dauncing in a rownd,
Whiles old Sylvanus slept in shady arber
    sownd.

VIII

Who, when they heard that pitteous strained
    voice,
In haste forsooke their rurall meriment,
And ran towardes the far rebownded noyce
To weet what wight so loudly did lament.
Unto the place they come incontinent:
Whom when the raging Sarazin espyde,
A rude, mishapen, monstrous rablement,
Whose like he never saw, he durst not byde,
But got his ready steed, and fast away gan
    ryde.

IX

The wyld woodgods, arrived in the place,
There find the virgin doolfull desolate,
With ruffled rayments, and fayre blubbred
    face,
As her outrageous foe had left her late,
And trembling yet through feare of former
    hate.
All stand amazed at so uncouth sight,
And gin to pittie her unhappie state;
All stand astonied at her beautie bright,
In their rude eyes unworthy of so wofull
    plight.

X

She, more amazd, in double dread doth
    dwell;
And every tender part for feare does shake:
As when a greedy wolfe, through honger
    fell,
A seely lamb far from the flock does take,
Of whom he meanes his bloody feast to
    make,
A lyon spyes fast running towards him,
The innocent pray in hast he does forsake,
Which, quitt from death, yet quakes in
    every lim
With chaunge of feare, to see the lyon
    looke so grim.

XI

Such fearefull fitt assaid her trembling hart,
Ne word to speake, ne joynt to move, she
    had:
The salvage nation feele her secret smart,
And read her sorrow in her count'nance sad:
Their frowning forheades, with rough hornes
    yclad,
And rustick horror, all a syde doe lay,
And, gently grenning, shew a semblance
    glad
To comfort her, and, feare to put away,
Their backward bent knees teach her hum-
    bly to obay.

XII

The doubtfull damzell dare not yet com-
    mitt
Her single person to their barbarous truth,
But still twixt feare and hope amazd does
    sitt,
Late learnd what harme to hasty trust en-
    su'th:
They, in compassion of her tender youth,
And wonder of her beautie soverayne,
Are wonne with pitty and unwonted ruth,
And all prostrate upon the lowly playne,
Doe kisse her feete, and fawne on her with
    count'nance fayne.

XIII

Their harts she ghesseth by their humble
    guise,
And yieldes her to extremitie of time;
So from the ground she fearelesse doth arise,
And walketh forth without suspect of crime:
They all as glad as birdes of joyous pryme,
Thence lead her forth, about her dauncing
    round,

Shouting, and singing all a shepheards ryme;
And, with greene braunches strowing all
    the ground,
Do worship her as queene with olive gir-
    lond cround.

XIV

And all the way their merry pipes they
    sound,
That all the woods with doubled eccho ring,
And with their horned feet doe weare the
    ground,
Leaping like wanton kids in pleasant spring.
So towards old Sylvanus they her bring;
Who with the noyse awaked, commeth out
To weet the cause, his weake steps govern-
    ing
And aged limbs on cypresse stadle stout;
And with an yvie twyne his waste is girt
    about.

XV

Far off he wonders what them makes so
    glad,
Or Bacchus merry fruit they did invent,
Or Cybeles franticke rites have made them
    mad.
They, drawing nigh, unto their god present
That flowre of fayth and beautie excellent:
The god himselfe, vewing that mirrhour
    rare,
Stood long amazd, and burnt in his intent:
His owne fayre Dryope now he thinkes not
    faire,
And Pholoe fowle, when her to this he doth
    compaire.

XVI

The woodborne people fall before her flat,
And worship her as goddesse of the wood;
And old Sylvanus selfe bethinkes not, what
To thinke of wight so fayre, but gazing
    stood,
In doubt to deeme her borne of earthly
    brood:
Sometimes Dame Venus selfe he seemes to
    see,
But Venus never had so sober mood;
Sometimes Diana he her takes to be,
But misseth bow, and shaftes, and buskins
    to her knee.

XVII

By vew of her he ginneth to revive
His ancient love, and dearest Cyparisse;

And calles to mind his pourtraiture alive,
How fayre he was, and yet not fayre to this;
And how he slew with glauncing dart amisse
A gentle hynd, the which the lovely boy
Did love as life, above all worldly blisse;
For griefe whereof the lad n'ould after joy,
But pynd away in anguish and selfewild
  annoy.

XVIII

The wooddy nymphes, faire Hamadryades,
Her to behold do thether runne apace,
And all the troupe of light-foot Naiades
Flocke all about to see her lovely face:
But when they vewed have her heavenly
  grace,
They envy her in their malitious mind,
And fly away for feare of fowle disgrace:
But all the Satyres scorne their woody kind,
And henceforth nothing faire, but her, on
  earth they find.

XIX

Glad of such lucke, the luckelesse lucky
  mayd
Did her content to please their feeble eyes,
And long time with that salvage people
  stayd,
To gather breath in many miseryes.
During which time her gentle wit she plyes,
To teach them truth, which worshipt her in
  vaine,
And made her th' image of idolatryes;
But when their bootlesse zeale she did re-
  strayne
From her own worship, they her asse
  would worship fayn.

XX

It fortuned, a noble warlike knight
By just occasion to that forrest came,
To seeke his kindred, and the lignage right,
From whence he tooke his weldeserved
  name:
He had in armes abroad wonne muchell
  fame,
And fild far landes with glorie of his might;
Plaine, faithfull, true, and enimy of shame,
And ever lov'd to fight for ladies right,
But in vaine glorious frayes he litle did
  delight.

XXI

A Satyres sonne yborne in forrest wyld,
By straunge adventure as it did betyde,
And there begotten of a lady myld,
Fayre Thyamis the daughter of Labryde,
That was in sacred bandes of wedlocke
  tyde
To Therion, a loose unruly swayne,
Who had more joy to raunge the forrest
  wyde,
And chase the salvage beast with busie
  payne,
Then serve his ladies love, and waste in
  pleasures vayne.

XXII

The forlorne mayd did with loves longing
  burne,
And could not lacke her lovers company,
But to the wood she goes, to serve her
  turne,
And seeke her spouse, that from her still
  does fly,
And followes other game and venery.
A Satyre chaunst her wandring for to finde,
And kindling coles of lust in brutish eye,
The loyall linkes of wedlocke did unbinde,
And made her person thrall unto his
  beastly kind.

XXIII

So long in secret cabin there he held
Her captive to his sensuall desyre,
Till that with timely fruit her belly sweld,
And bore a boy unto that salvage syre:
Then home he suffred her for to retyre,
For ransome leaving him the late-borne
  childe;
Whom, till to ryper yeares he gan aspyre,
He nousled up in life and manners wilde,
Emongst wild beastes and woods, from
  lawes of men exilde.

XXIV

For all he taught the tender ymp was but
To banish cowardize and bastard feare:
His trembling hand he would him force to
  put
Upon the lyon and the rugged beare,
And from the she beares teats her whelps to
  teare;
And eke wyld roring buls he would him
  make
To tame, and ryde their backes not made
  to beare;
And the robuckes in flight to overtake:
That everie beast for feare of him did fly
  and quake.

XXV

Thereby so fearelesse and so fell he grew,
That his owne syre and maister of his guise
Did often tremble at his horrid vew,
And oft, for dread of hurt, would him advise
The angry beastes not rashly to despise,
Nor too much to provoke: for he would
    learne
The lyon stoup to him in lowly wise,
(A lesson hard) and make the libbard sterne
Leave roaring, when in rage he for revenge
    did earne.

XXVI

And for to make his powre approved more,
Wyld beastes in yron yokes he would com-
    pell;
The spotted panther, and the tusked bore,
The pardale swift, and the tigre cruell,
The antelope, and wolfe both fiers and fell;
And them constraine in equall teme to
    draw.
Such joy he had their stubborne harts to
    quell,
And sturdie courage tame with dreadfull aw,
That his beheast they feared, as a tyrans
    law.

XXVII

His loving mother came upon a day
Unto the woodes, to see her little sonne;
And chaunst unwares to meet him in the
    way,
After his sportes and cruell pastime donne,
When after him a lyonesse did runne,
That roaring all with rage, did lowd requere
Her children deare, whom he away had
    wonne:
The lyon whelpes she saw how he did beare,
And lull in rugged armes, withouten child-
    ish feare.

XXVIII

The fearefull dame all quaked at the sight,
And turning backe gan fast to fly away,
Untill, with love revokt from vaine affright,
She hardly yet perswaded was to stay,
And then to him these womanish words gan
    say:
'Ah! Satyrane, my dearling and my joy,
For love of me leave off this dreadfull
    play;
To dally thus with death is no fit toy:
Go find some other play-fellowes, mine own
    sweet boy.'

XXIX

In these and like delightes of bloody game
He trayned was, till ryper yeares he raught;
And there abode, whylst any beast of name
Walkt in that forrest, whom he had not taught
To feare his force: and then his courage
    haught
Desyrd of forreine foemen to be knowne,
And far abroad for straunge adventures
    sought:
In which his might was never overthrowne,
But through al Faery Lond his famous
    worth was blown.

XXX

Yet evermore it was his maner faire,
After long labours and adventures spent,
Unto those native woods for to repaire,
To see his syre and ofspring auncient.
And now he thether came for like intent;
Where he unwares the fairest Una found,
Straunge lady, in so straunge habiliment,
Teaching the Satyres, which her sat around,
Trew sacred lore, which from her sweet
    lips did redound.

XXXI

He wondred at her wisedome hevenly rare,
Whose like in womens witt he never knew;
And when her curteous deeds he did com-
    pare,
Gan her admire, and her sad sorrowes rew,
Blaming of Fortune, which such troubles
    threw,
And joyd to make proofe of her cruelty
On gentle dame, so hurtlesse and so trew:
Thenceforth he kept her goodly company,
And learnd her discipline of faith and verity.

XXXII

But she, all vowd unto the Redcrosse Knight,
His wandring perill closely did lament,
Ne in this new acquaintaunce could delight,
But her deare heart with anguish did tor-
    ment,
And all her witt in secret counsels spent,
How to escape. At last in privy wise
To Satyrane she shewed her intent;
Who, glad to gain such favour, gan devise,
How with that pensive maid he best might
    thence arise.

XXXIII

So on a day, when Satyres all were gone
To doe their service to Sylvanus old,

The gentle virgin, left behinde alone,
He led away with corage stout and bold.
Too late it was to Satyres to be told,
Or ever hope recover her againe:
In vaine he seekes that, having, cannot hold.
So fast he carried her with carefull paine,
That they the wods are past, and come
   now to the plaine.

XXXIV

The better part now of the lingring day
They traveild had, whenas they far espide
A weary wight forwandring by the way,
And towards him they gan in hast to ride,
To weete of newes that did abroad betide,
Or tidings of her Knight of the Redcrosse.
But he, them spying, gan to turne aside
For feare, as seemd, or for some feigned
   losse:
More greedy they of newes fast towards
   him do crosse.

XXXV

A silly man, in simple weeds forworne,
And soild with dust of the long dried way;
His sandales were with toilsome travell
   torne,
And face all tand with scorching sunny ray,
As he had traveild many a sommers day
Through boyling sands of Arabie and Ynde;
And in his hand a Jacobs staffe, to stay
His weary limbs upon; and eke behind
His scrip did hang, in which his needments
   he did bind.

XXXVI

The knight, approching nigh, of him inquerd
Tidings of warre, and of adventures new;
But warres, nor new adventures, none he
   herd.
Then Una gan to aske, if ought he knew
Or heard abroad of that her champion trew,
That in his armour bare a croslet red.
'Ay me! deare dame,' quoth he, 'well may
   I rew
To tell the sad sight which mine eies have
   red:
These eies did see that knight both living
   and eke ded.'

XXXVII

That cruell word her tender hart so thrild,
That suddein cold did ronne through every
   vaine,
And stony horrour all her sences fild

With dying fitt, that downe she fell for
   paine.
The knight her lightly reared up againe,
And comforted with curteous kind reliefe:
Then, wonne from death, she bad him tellen
   plaine
The further processe of her hidden griefe;
The lesser pangs can beare, who hath en-
   dur'd the chief.

XXXVIII

Then gan the pilgrim thus: 'I chaunst this
   day,
This fatall day, that shall I ever rew,
To see two knights in travell on my way
(A sory sight) arraung'd in batteill new,
Both breathing vengeaunce, both of wrath-
   full hew:
My feareful flesh did tremble at their strife,
To see their blades so greedily imbrew,
That, dronke with blood, yet thristed after
   life:
What more? the Redcrosse Knight was
   slain with Paynim knife.'

XXXIX

'Ah, dearest Lord!' quoth she, 'how might
   that bee,
And he the stoutest knight, that ever
   wonne?'
'Ah, dearest dame,' quoth hee, 'how might
   I see
The thing, that might not be, and yet was
   donne?'
'Where is,' said Satyrane, 'that Paynims
   sonne,
That him of life, and us of joy, hath refte?'
'Not far away,' quoth he, 'he hence doth
   wonne,
Foreby a fountaine, where I late him lefte
Washing his bloody wounds, that through
   the steele were cleft.'

XL

Therewith the knight thence marched forth
   in hast,
Whiles Una, with huge heavinesse opprest,
Could not for sorrow follow him so fast;
And soone he came, as he the place had
   ghest,
Whereas that Pagan proud him selfe did
   rest
In secret shadow by a fountaine side:
Even he it was, that earst would have sup-
   prest

Faire Una: whom when Satyrane espide,
With foule reprochfull words he boldly him
    defide;

XLI

And said: 'Arise, thou cursed miscreaunt,
That hast with knightlesse guile and trech-
    erous train
Faire knighthood fowly shamed, and doest
    vaunt
That good Knight of the Redcrosse to have
    slain:
Arise, and with like treason now maintain
Thy guilty wrong, or els thee guilty yield.'
The Sarazin, this hearing, rose amain,
And catching up in hast his three square
    shield
And shining helmet, soone him buckled to
    the field;

XLII

And, drawing nigh him, said: 'Ah, mis-
    born Elfe!
In evill houre thy foes thee hither sent,
Anothers wrongs to wreak upon thy selfe:
Yet ill thou blamest me, for having blent
My name with guile and traiterous intent:
That Redcrosse Knight, perdie, I never
    slew;
But had he beene where earst his armes
    were lent,
Th' enchaunter vaine his errour should not
    rew:
But thou his errour shalt, I hope, now
    proven trew.'

XLIII

Therewith they gan, both furious and fell,
To thunder blowes, and fiersly to assaile
Each other, bent his enimy to quell;
That with their force they perst both plate
    and maile,
And made wide furrowes in their fleshes
    fraile,
That it would pitty any living eie.
Large floods of blood adowne their sides did
    raile;
But floods of blood could not them satisfie:
Both hongred after death: both chose to
    win, or die.

XLIV

So long they fight, and fell revenge pursue,
That, fainting each, them selves to breathen
    lett,

And, ofte refreshed, battell oft renue:
As when two bores, with rancling malice
    mett,
Their gory sides fresh bleeding fiercely frett,
Til breathlesse both them selves aside retire,
Where, foming wrath, their cruell tuskes
    they whett,
And trample th' earth, the whiles they may
    respire;
Then backe to fight againe, new breathed
    and entire.

XLV

So fiersly, when these knights had breathed
    once,
They gan to fight retourne, increasing more
Their puissant force and cruell rage at-
    tonce,
With heaped strokes more hugely then be-
    fore,
That with their drery wounds and bloody
    gore
They both deformed, scarsely could bee
    known.
By this, sad Una fraught with anguish sore,
Led with their noise, which through the
    aire was thrown,
Arriv'd, wher they in erth their fruitles
    blood had sown.

XLVI

Whom all so soone as that proud Sarazin
Espide, he gan revive the memory
Of his leud lusts, and late attempted sin,
And lefte the doubtfull battell hastily,
To catch her, newly offred to his eie:
But Satyrane, with strokes him turning,
    staid,
And sternely bad him other businesse
    plie
Then hunt the steps of pure unspotted
    maid:
Wherewith he al enrag'd, these bitter
    speaches said:

XLVII

'O foolish Faeries sonne! what fury mad
Hath thee incenst to hast thy dolefull
    fate?
Were it not better I that lady had
Then that thou hadst repented it too late?
Most sencelesse man he, that himselfe doth
    hate,
To love another. Lo then, for thine ayd,
Here take thy lovers token on thy pate.'

So they two fight; the whiles the royall
  mayd
Fledd farre away, of that proud Paynim
  sore afrayd.

XLVIII

But that false pilgrim, which that leasing
  told,
Being in deed old Archimage, did stay
In secret shadow, all this to behold,
And much rejoyced in their bloody fray:
But when he saw the damsell passe away,
He left his stond, and her pursewd apace,
In hope to bring her to her last decay.
But for to tell her lamentable cace,
And eke this battels end, will need another
  place.

CANTO VII

The Redcrosse Knight is captive made,
  By gyaunt proud opprest:
Prince Arthure meets with Una great-
  ly with those newes distrest.

I

WHAT man so wise, what earthly witt so
  ware,
As to discry the crafty cunning traine,
By which Deceipt doth maske in visour
  faire,
And cast her coulours died deepe in graine,
To seeme like Truth, whose shape she well
  can faine,
And fitting gestures to her purpose frame,
The guiltlesse man with guile to entertaine?
Great maistresse of her art was that false
  dame,
The false Duessa, cloked with Fidessaes
  name.

II

Who when, returning from the drery Night,
She fownd not in that perilous Hous of
  Pryde,
Where she had left, the noble Redcross
  Knight,
Her hoped pray, she would no lenger byde,
But forth she went to seeke him far and
  wide.
Ere long she fownd, whereas he wearie
  sate
To rest him selfe, foreby a fountaine syde,
Disarmed all of yron-coted plate,
And by his side his steed the grassy forage
  ate.

III

Hee feedes upon the cooling shade, and
  bayes
His sweatie forehead in the breathing wynd,
Which through the trembling leaves full
  gently playes,
Wherein the chearefull birds of sundry
  kynd
Doe chaunt sweet musick, to delight his
  mynd.
The witch approching gan him fayrely
  greet,
And with reproch of carelesnes unkynd
Upbrayd, for leaving her in place unmeet,
With fowle words tempring faire, soure
  gall with hony sweet.

IV

Unkindnesse past, they gan of solace treat,
And bathe in pleasaunce of the joyous
  shade,
Which shielded them against the boyling
  heat,
And, with greene boughes decking a
  gloomy glade,
About the fountaine like a girlond made;
Whose bubbling wave did ever freshly well,
Ne ever would through fervent sommer
  fade:
The sacred nymph, which therein wont to
  dwell,
Was out of Dianes favor, as it then befell.

V

The cause was this: one day when Phœbe
  fayre
With all her band was following the chace,
This nymph, quite tyr'd with heat of
  scorching ayre,
Satt downe to rest in middest of the race:
The goddesse wroth gan fowly her disgrace,
And badd the waters, which from her did
  flow,
Be such as she her selfe was then in place.
Thenceforth her waters wexed dull and
  slow,
And all that drunke thereof did faint and
  feeble grow.

VI

Hereof this gentle knight unweeting was,
And lying downe upon the sandie graile,
Dronke of the streame, as cleare as christall
  glas:
Eftsoones his manly forces gan to fayle,

And mightie strong was turnd to feeble
frayle:
His chaunged powres at first them selves
not felt,
Till crudled cold his corage gan assayle,
And chearefull blood in fayntnes chill did
melt,
Which, like a fever fit, through all his body
swelt.

VII

Yet goodly court he made still to his dame,
Pourd out in loosnesse on the grassy
grownd,
Both carelesse of his health, and of his fame:
Till at the last he heard a dreadfull sownd,
Which through the wood loud bellowing
did rebownd,
That all the earth for terror seemd to
shake,
And trees did tremble. Th' Elfe, therewith
astownd,
Upstarted lightly from his looser make,
And his unready weapons gan in hand to
take.

VIII

But ere he could his armour on him dight,
Or gett his shield, his monstrous enimy
With sturdie steps came stalking in his
sight,
An hideous geaunt, horrible and hye,
That with his tallnesse seemd to threat the
skye;
The ground eke groned under him for dreed:
His living like saw never living eye,
Ne durst behold: his stature did exceed
The hight of three the tallest sonnes of
mortall seed.

IX

The greatest Earth his uncouth mother
was,
And blustring Æolus his boasted syre;
Who with his breath, which through the
world doth pas,
Her hollow womb did secretly inspyre,
And fild her hidden caves with stormie yre,
That she conceiv'd; and trebling the dew
time,
In which the wombes of wemen doe expyre,
Brought forth this monstrous masse of
earthly slyme,
Puft up with emptie wynd, and fild with
sinfull cryme.

X

So growen great, through arrogant delight
Of th' high descent whereof he was yborne,
And through presumption of his matchlesse
might,
All other powres and knighthood he did
scorne.
Such now he marcheth to this man forlorne,
And left to losse: his stalking steps are
stayde
Upon a snaggy oke, which he had torne
Out of his mothers bowelles, and it made
His mortall mace, wherewith his foemen
he dismayde.

XI

That when the knight he spyde, he gan ad-
vaunce
With huge force and insupportable mayne,
And towardes him with dreadfull fury
praunce;
Who haplesse, and eke hopelesse, all in
vaine
Did to him pace, sad battaile to darrayne,
Disarmd, disgraste, and inwardly dismayde,
And eke so faint in every joynt and vayne,
Through that fraile fountain, which him
feeble made,
That scarsely could he weeld his bootlesse
single blade.

XII

The geaunt strooke so maynly mercilesse,
That could have overthrowne a stony towre,
And were not hevenly grace, that him did
blesse,
He had beene pouldred all, as thin as flowre:
But he was wary of that deadly stowre,
And lightly lept from underneath the blow:
Yet so exceeding was the villeins powre
That with the winde it did him overthrow,
And all his sences stoond, that still he lay
full low.

XIII

As when that divelish yron engin, wrought
In deepest hell, and framd by furies skill,
With windy nitre and quick sulphur fraught,
And ramd with bollet rownd, ordaind to
kill,
Conceiveth fyre, the heavens it doth fill
With thundring noyse, and all the ayre doth
choke,
That none can breath, nor see, nor heare at
will,

Through smouldry cloud of duskish stinck-
      ing smok,
That th' onely breath him daunts, who hath
      escapt the stroke.

XIV

So daunted when the geaunt saw the knight,
His heavie hand he heaved up on hye,
And him to dust thought to have battred
      quight,
Untill Duessa loud to him gan crye,
' O great Orgoglio, greatest under skye,
O hold thy mortall hand for ladies sake !
Hold for my sake, and doe him not to dye,
But vanquisht thine eternall bondslave
      make,
And me, thy worthy meed, unto thy leman
      take.'

XV

He hearkned, and did stay from further
      harmes,
To gayne so goodly guerdon as she spake:
So willingly she came into his armes,
Who her as willingly to grace did take,
And was possessed of his newfound make.
Then up he tooke the slombred sencelesse
      corse,
And ere he could out of his swowne awake,
Him to his castle brought with hastie forse,
And in a dongeon deep him threw without
      remorse.

XVI

From that day forth Duessa was his deare,
And highly honourd in his haughtie eye;
He gave her gold and purple pall to weare,
And triple crowne set on her head full hye,
And her endowd with royall majestye:
Then, for to make her dreaded more of
      men,
And peoples hartes with awfull terror tye,
A monstrous beast ybredd in filthy fen
He chose, which he had kept long time in
      darksom den.

XVII

Such one it was, as that renowmed snake
Which great Alcides in Stremona slew,
Long fostred in the filth of Lerna lake,
Whose many heades out budding ever new
Did breed him endlesse labor to subdew:
But this same monster much more ugly
      was;
For seven great heads out of his body grew,

An yron brest, and back of scaly bras,
And all embrewd in blood, his eyes did
      shine as glas.

XVIII

His tayle was stretched out in wondrous
      length,
That to the hous of hevenly gods it raught,
And with extorted powre, and borrow'd
      strength,
The everburning lamps from thence it
      braught,
And prowdly threw to ground, as things of
      naught;
And underneath his filthy feet did tread
The sacred thinges, and holy heastes fore-
      taught.
Upon this dreadfull beast with sevenfold
      head
He sett the false Duessa, for more aw and
      dread.

XIX

The wofull dwarfe, which saw his maisters
      fall,
Whiles he had keeping of his grasing steed,
And valiant knight become a caytive thrall,
When all was past, tooke up his forlorne
      weed;
His mightie armour, missing most at need;
His silver shield, now idle maisterlesse;
His poynant speare, that many made to
      bleed;
The ruefull moniments of heavinesse;
And with them all departes, to tell his
      great distresse.

XX

He had not travaild long, when on the way
He wofull lady, wofull Una, met,
Fast flying from the Paynims greedy pray,
Whilest Satyrane him from pursuit did let:
Who when her eyes she on the dwarf had
      set,
And saw the signes, that deadly tydinges
      spake,
She fell to ground for sorrowfull regret,
And lively breath her sad brest did forsake,
Yet might her pitteous hart be seene to pant
      and quake.

XXI

The messenger of so unhappie newes
Would faine have dyde; dead was his hart
      within;

Yet outwardly some little comfort shewes:
At last recovering hart, he does begin
To rubb her temples, and to chaufe her
    chin,
And everie tender part does tosse and
    turne:
So hardly he the flitted life does win,
Unto her native prison to retourne:
Then gins her grieved ghost thus to lament
    and mourne:

XXII

'Ye dreary instruments of dolefull sight,
That doe this deadly spectacle behold,
Why do ye lenger feed on loathed light,
Or liking find to gaze on earthly mould,
Sith cruell fates the carefull threds un-
    fould,
The which my life and love together tyde?
Now let the stony dart of sencelesse cold
Perce to my hart, and pas through everie
    side,
And let eternall night so sad sight fro me
    hyde.

XXIII

'O lightsome day, the lampe of highest
    Jove,
First made by him, mens wandring wayes
    to guyde,
When darknesse he in deepest dongeon
    drove,
Henceforth thy hated face for ever hyde,
And shut up heavens windowes shyning
    wyde:
For earthly sight can nought but sorow
    breed,
And late repentance, which shall long abyde.
Mine eyes no more on vanitie shall feed,
But, seeled up with death, shall have their
    deadly meed.'

XXIV

Then downe againe she fell unto the ground;
But he her quickly reared up againe:
Thrise did she sinke adowne in deadly
    swownd,
And thrise he her reviv'd with busie paine:
At last, when life recover'd had the raine,
And over-wrestled his strong enimy,
With foltring tong, and trembling everie
    vaine,
'Tell on,' quoth she, 'the wofull tragedy,
The which these reliques sad present unto
    mine eye.

XXV

'Tempestuous Fortune hath spent all her
    spight,
And thrilling Sorrow throwne his utmost
    dart;
Thy sad tong cannot tell more heavy plight
Then that I feele, and harbour in mine hart:
Who hath endur'd the whole, can beare ech
    part.
If death it be, it is not the first wound,
That launched hath my brest with bleeding
    smart.
Begin, and end the bitter balefull stound;
If lesse then that I feare, more favour I
    have found.'

XXVI

Then gan the dwarfe the whole discourse
    declare:
The subtile traines of Archimago old;
The wanton loves of false Fidessa fayre,
Bought with the blood of vanquisht Paynim
    bold;
The wretched payre transformd to treen
    mould;
The House of Pryde, and perilles round
    about;
The combat, which he with Sansjoy did
    hould;
The lucklesse conflict with the gyaunt stout,
Wherein captiv'd, of life or death he stood
    in doubt.

XXVII

She heard with patience all unto the end,
And strove to maister sorrowfull assay,
Which greater grew, the more she did con-
    tend,
And almost rent her tender hart in tway;
And love fresh coles unto her fire did lay:
For greater love, the greater is the losse.
Was never lady loved dearer day,
Then she did love the Knight of the Red-
    crosse;
For whose deare sake so many troubles her
    did tosse.

XXVIII

At last, when fervent sorrow slaked was,
She up arose, resolving him to find,
Alive or dead; and forward forth doth pas,
All as the dwarfe the way to her assynd;
And ever more, in constant carefull mind,
She fedd her wound with fresh renewed
    bale:

Long tost with stormes, and bet with bitter
    wind,
High over hills, and lowe adowne the dale,
She wandred many a wood, and measurd
    many a vale.

XXIX

At last she chaunced by good hap to meet
A goodly knight, faire marching by the
    way,
Together with his squyre, arayed meet:
His glitterand armour shined far away,
Like glauncing light of Phœbus brightest
    ray;
From top to toe no place appeared bare,
That deadly dint of steele endanger may:
Athwart his brest a bauldrick brave he
    ware,
That shind, like twinkling stars, with stones
    most pretious rare.

XXX

And in the midst thereof, one pretious stone
Of wondrous worth, and eke of wondrous
    mights,
Shapt like a ladies head, exceeding shone,
Like Hesperus emongst the lesser lights,
And strove for to amaze the weaker sights:
Thereby his mortall blade full comely hong
In yvory sheath, ycarv'd with curious
    slights;
Whose hilts were burnisht gold, and handle
    strong
Of mother perle, and buckled with a golden
    tong.

XXXI

His haughtie helmet, horrid all with gold,
Both glorious brightnesse and great terrour
    bredd;
For all the crest a dragon did enfold
With greedie pawes, and over all did spredd
His golden winges: his dreadfull hideous
    hedd,
Close couched on the bever, seemd to throw
From flaming mouth bright sparckles fiery
    redd,
That suddeine horrour to faint hartes did
    show;
And scaly tayle was stretcht adowne his
    back full low.

XXXII

Upon the top of all his loftie crest,
A bounch of heares discolourd diversly,

With sprincled pearle and gold full richly
    drest,
Did shake, and seemd to daunce for jollity;
Like to an almond tree ymounted hye
On top of greene Selinis all alone,
With blossoms brave bedecked daintily;
Whose tender locks do tremble every one
At everie little breath, that under heaven
    is blowne.

XXXIII

His warlike shield all closely cover'd was,
Ne might of mortall eye be ever seene;
Not made of steele, nor of enduring bras;
Such earthly mettals soone consumed beene;
But all of diamond perfect pure and cleene
It framed was, one massy entire mould,
Hewen out of adamant rocke with engines
    keene,
That point of speare it never percen could,
Ne dint of direfull sword divide the sub-
    stance would.

XXXIV

The same to wight he never wont disclose,
But when as monsters huge he would dis-
    may,
Or daunt unequall armies of his foes,
Or when the flying heavens he would af-
    fray:
For so exceeding shone his glistring ray,
That Phœbus golden face it did attaint,
As when a cloud his beames doth over-lay;
And silver Cynthia wexed pale and faynt,
As when her face is staynd with magicke
    arts constraint.

XXXV

No magicke arts hereof had any might,
Nor bloody wordes of bold enchaunters
    call,
But all that was not such as seemd in
    sight
Before that shield did fade, and suddeine
    fall:
And when him list the raskall routes ap-
    pall,
Men into stones therewith he could trans-
    mew,
And stones to dust, and dust to nought at
    all;
And when him list the prouder lookes sub-
    dew,
He would them gazing blind, or turne to
    other hew.

XXXVI

Ne let it seeme that credence this exceedes;
For he that made the same was knowne
    right well
To have done much more admirable deedes.
It Merlin was, which whylome did excell
All living wightes in might of magicke
    spell:
Both shield, and sword, and armour all he
    wrought
For this young Prince, when first to armes
    he fell;
But when he dyde, the Faery Queene it
    brought
To Faerie Lond, where yet it may be seene,
    if sought.

XXXVII

A gentle youth, his dearely loved squire,
His speare of heben wood behind him bare,
Whose harmeful head, thrise heated in the
    fire,
Had riven many a brest with pikehead
    square;
A goodly person, and could menage faire
His stubborne steed with curbed canon bitt,
Who under him did trample as the aire,
And chaufft, that any on his backe should
    sitt;
The yron rowels into frothy fome he bitt.

XXXVIII

Whenas this knight nigh to the lady drew,
With lovely court he gan her entertaine;
But when he heard her aunswers loth, he
    knew
Some secret sorrow did her heart distraine:
Which to allay, and calme her storming
    paine,
Faire feeling words he wisely gan display,
And for her humor fitting purpose faine,
To tempt the cause it selfe for to bewray;
Wherewith enmovd, these bleeding words
    she gan to say:

XXXIX

'What worlds delight, or joy of living
    speach,
Can hart, so plungd in sea of sorrowes
    deep,
And heaped with so huge misfortunes,
    reach ?
The carefull cold beginneth for to creep,
And in my heart his yron arrow steep,
Soone as I thinke upon my bitter bale:

Such helplesse harmes yts better hidden
    keep,
Then rip up griefe, where it may not availe;
My last left comfort is, my woes to weepe
    and waile.'

XL

'Ah! lady deare,' quoth then the gentle
    knight,
'Well may I ween your grief is wondrous
    great;
For wondrous great griefe groneth in my
    spright,
Whiles thus I heare you of your sorrowes
    treat.
But, woefull lady, let me you intrete
For to unfold the anguish of your hart:
Mishaps are maistred by advice discrete,
And counsell mitigates the greatest smart;
Found never help, who never would his
    hurts impart.'

XLI

'O but,' quoth she, 'great griefe will not be
    tould,
And can more easily be thought then said.'
'Right so,' quoth he; 'but he, that never
    would,
Could never: will to might gives greatest
    aid.'
'But griefe,' quoth she, 'does greater grow
    displaid,
If then it find not helpe, and breeds de-
    spaire.'
'Despaire breeds not,' quoth he, 'where
    faith is staid.'
'No faith so fast,' quoth she, 'but flesh
    does paire.'
'Flesh may empaire,' quoth he, 'but reason
    can repaire.'

XLII

His goodly reason and well guided speach
So deepe did settle in her gracious thought,
That her perswaded to disclose the breach,
Which love and fortune in her heart had
    wrought,
And said: 'Faire sir, I hope good hap hath
    brought
You to inquere the secrets of my griefe,
Or that your wisedome will direct my
    thought,
Or that your prowesse can me yield reliefe:
Then heare the story sad, which I shall tell
    you briefe.

XLIII

'The forlorne maiden, whom your eies have
        seene
The laughing stocke of Fortunes mockeries,
Am th' onely daughter of a king and
        queene;
Whose parents deare, whiles equal destinies
Did ronne about, and their felicities
The favourable heavens did not envy,
Did spred their rule through all the terri-
        tories,
Which Phison and Euphrates floweth by,
And Gehons golden waves doe wash con-
        tinually.

XLIV

'Till that their cruell cursed enemy,
An huge great dragon, horrible in sight,
Bred in the loathly lakes of Tartary,
With murdrous ravine, and devouring might,
Their kingdome spoild, and countrey wasted
        quight:
Themselves, for feare into his jawes to fall,
He forst to castle strong to take their flight,
Where, fast embard in mighty brasen wall,
He has them now fowr years besiegd, to
        make them thrall.

XLV

'Full many knights, adventurous and stout,
Have enterprizd that monster to subdew;
From every coast, that heaven walks about,
Have thither come the noble martial crew,
That famous harde atchievements still pur-
        sew;
Yet never any could that girlond win,
But all still shronke, and still he greater
        grew:
All they for want of faith, or guilt of sin,
The pitteous pray of his fiers cruelty have
        bin.

XLVI

'At last, yled with far reported praise,
Which flying fame throughout the world
        had spred,
Of doughty knights, whom Fary Land did
        raise,
That noble order hight of Maidenhed,
Forthwith to court of Gloriane I sped,
Of Gloriane, great queene of glory bright,
Whose kingdomes seat Cleopolis is red,
There to obtaine some such redoubted knight,
That parents deare from tyrants powre de-
        liver might.

XLVII

'Yt was my chaunce (my chaunce was faire
        and good)
There for to find a fresh unproved knight,
Whose manly hands imbrewd in guilty
        blood
Had never beene, ne ever by his might
Had throwne to ground the unregarded
        right:
Yet of his prowesse proofe he since hath
        made
(I witnes am) in many a cruell fight;
The groning ghosts of many one dismaide
Have felt the bitter dint of his avenging
        blade.

XLVIII

'And ye, the forlorne reliques of his powre,
His biting sword, and his devouring speare,
Which have endured many a dreadfull
        stowre,
Can speake his prowesse, that did earst you
        beare,
And well could rule: now he hath left you
        heare,
To be the record of his ruefull losse,
And of my dolefull disaventurous deare:
O heavie record of the good Redcrosse,
Where have yee left your lord, that could
        so well you tosse ?

XLIX

'Well hoped I, and faire beginnings had,
That he my captive languor should re-
        deeme;
Till, all unweeting, an enchaunter bad
His sence abusd, and made him to mis-
        deeme
My loyalty, not such as it did seeme,
That rather death desire then such despight.
Be judge, ye heavens, that all things right
        esteeme,
How I him lov'd, and love with all my
        might !
So thought I eke of him, and think I
        thought aright.

L

'Thenceforth me desolate he quite for-
        sooke,
To wander where wilde fortune would me
        lead,
And other bywaies he himselfe betooke,
Where never foote of living wight did
        tread,

That brought not backe the balefull body
    dead;
In which him chaunced false Duessa meete,
Mine onely foe, mine onely deadly dread,
Who with her witchcraft, and misseeming
    sweete,
Inveigled him to follow her desires un-
    meete.

LI

'At last, by subtile sleights she him be-
    traid
Unto his foe, a gyaunt huge and tall;
Who him disarmed, dissolute, dismaid,
Unwares surprised, and with mighty mall
The monster mercilesse him made to fall,
Whose fall did never foe before behold;
And now in darkesome dungeon, wretched
    thrall,
Remedilesse, for aie he doth him hold;
This is my cause of griefe, more great then
    may be told.'

LII

Ere she had ended all, she gan to faint;
But he her comforted, and faire bespake:
'Certes, madame, ye have great cause of
    plaint,
That stoutest heart, I weene, could cause
    to quake.
But be of cheare, and comfort to you take:
For till I have acquitt your captive knight,
Assure your selfe, I will you not forsake.'
His chearefull words reviv'd her chearelesse
    spright:
So forth they went, the dwarfe them guid-
    ing ever right.

CANTO VIII

Faire virgin, to redeeme her deare,
    Brings Arthure to the fight :
Who slayes the gyaunt, wounds the beast,
    And strips Duessa quight.

I

Ay me! how many perils doe enfold
The righteous man, to make him daily
    fall,
Were not that Heavenly Grace doth him
    uphold,
And stedfast Truth acquite him out of all !
Her love is firme, her care continuall,
So oft as he, through his own foolish pride
Or weaknes, is to sinfull bands made thrall:

Els should this Redcrosse Knight in bands
    have dyde,
For whose deliverance she this Prince doth
    thether guyd.

II

They sadly traveild thus, untill they came
Nigh to a castle builded strong and hye:
Then cryde the dwarfe, 'Lo ! yonder is the
    same,
In which my lord, my liege, doth lucklesse ly,
Thrall to that gyaunts hatefull tyranny:
Therefore, deare sir, your mightie powres
    assay.'
The noble knight alighted by and by
From loftie steed, and badd the ladie stay,
To see what end of fight should him befall
    that day.

III

So with the squire, th' admirer of his might,
He marched forth towardes that castle
    wall;
Whose gates he fownd fast shutt, ne living
    wight
To warde the same, nor answere commers
    call.
Then tooke that squire an horne of bugle
    small,
Which hong adowne his side in twisted gold
And tasselles gay.   Wyde wonders over all
Of that same hornes great vertues weren
    told,
Which had approved bene in uses manifold.

IV

Was never wight that heard that shrilling
    sownd,
But trembling feare did feel in every vaine:
Three miles it might be easy heard arownd,
And ecchoes three aunswerd it selfe againe:
No false enchauntment, nor deceiptfull
    traine
Might once abide the terror of that blast,
But presently was void and wholly vaine:
No gate so strong, no locke so firme and
    fast,
But with that percing noise flew open quite,
    or brast.

V

The same before the geaunts gate he blew,
That all the castle quaked from the grownd,
And every dore of freewill open flew:
The gyaunt selfe dismaied with that sownd,

Where he with his Duessa dalliaunce
fownd,
In hast came rushing forth from inner
bowre,
With staring countenance sterne, as one astownd,
And staggering steps, to weet what suddein
stowre
Had wrought that horror strange, and
dar'd his dreaded powre.

VI

And after him the proud Duessa came,
High mounted on her many headed beast;
And every head with fyrie tongue did flame,
And every head was crowned on his creast,
And bloody mouthed with late cruell feast.
That when the knight beheld, his mightie
shild
Upon his manly arme he soone addrest,
And at him fiersly flew, with corage fild,
And eger greedinesse through every mem-
ber thrild.

VII

Therewith the gyant buckled him to fight,
Inflamd with scornefull wrath and high dis-
daine,
And lifting up his dreadfull club on hight,
All armd with ragged snubbes and knottie
graine,
Him thought at first encounter to have
slaine.
But wise and wary was that noble pere,
And lightly leaping from so monstrous
maine,
Did fayre avoide the violence him nere;
It booted nought to thinke such thunder-
bolts to beare.

VIII

Ne shame he thought to shonne so hideous
might.
The ydle stroke, enforcing furious way,
Missing the marke of his misaymed sight,
Did fall to ground, and with his heavy
sway
So deepely dinted in the driven clay,
That three yardes deepe a furrow up did
throw:
The sad earth, wounded with so sore assay,
Did grone full grievous underneath the
blow,
And trembling with strange feare, did like
an erthquake show.

IX

As when almightie Jove, in wrathfull mood,
To wreake the guilt of mortall sins is bent,
Hurles forth his thundring dart with deadly
food,
Enrold in flames, and smouldring dreri-
ment,
Through riven cloudes and molten firma-
ment;
The fiers threeforked engin, making way,
Both loftie towres and highest trees hath
rent,
And all that might his angry passage stay,
And shooting in the earth, castes up a
mount of clay.

X

His boystrous club, so buried in the grownd,
He could not rearen up againe so light,
But that the knight him at advantage fownd,
And whiles he strove his combred clubbe to
quight
Out of the earth, with blade all burning
bright
He smott of his left arme, which like a
block
Did fall to ground, depriv'd of native
might:
Large streames of blood out of the truncked
stock
Forth gushed, like fresh water streame
from riven rocke.

XI

Dismayed with so desperate deadly wound,
And eke impatient of unwonted payne,
He lowdly brayd with beastly yelling
sownd,
That all the fieldes rebellowed againe:
As great a noyse, as when in Cymbrian
plaine
An heard of bulles, whom kindly rage doth
sting,
Doe for the milky mothers want complaine,
And fill the fieldes with troublous bellow-
ing:
The neighbor woods arownd with hollow
murmur ring.

XII

That when his deare Duessa heard, and saw
The evill stownd that daungerd her estate,
Unto his aide she hastily did draw
Her dreadfull beast, who, swolne with
blood of late.

Came ramping forth with proud presump-
    teous gate,
And threatned all his heades like flaming
    brandes.
But him the squire made quickly to retrate,
Encountring fiers with single sword in
    hand,
And twixt him and his lord did like a bul-
    warke stand.

XIII

The proud Duessa, full of wrathfull spight
And fiers disdaine, to be affronted so,
Enforst her purple beast with all her might,
That stop out of the way to overthroe,
Scorning the let of so unequall foe:
But nathemore would that corageous
    swayne
To her yeeld passage, gainst his lord to goe,
But with outrageous strokes did him re-
    straine,
And with his body bard the way atwixt
    them twaine.

XIV

Then tooke the angrie witch her golden cup,
Which still she bore, replete with magick
    artes;
Death and despeyre did many thereof sup,
And secret poyson through their inner
    partes,
Th' eternall bale of heavie wounded harts;
Which, after charmes and some enchaunt-
    ments said,
She lightly sprinkled on his weaker partes;
Therewith his sturdie corage soone was
    quayd,
And all his sences were with suddein dread
    dismayd.

XV

So downe he fell before the cruell beast,
Who on his neck his bloody clawes did
    seize,
That life nigh crusht out of his panting
    brest:
No powre he had to stirre, nor will to rize.
That when the carefull knight gan well
    avise,
He lightly left the foe with whom he
    fought,
And to the beast gan turne his enterprise;
For wondrous anguish in his hart it wrought,
To see his loved squyre into such thraldom
    brought.

XVI

And high advauncing his blood-thirstie
    blade,
Stroke one of those deformed heades so
    sore,
That of his puissaunce proud ensample
    made;
His monstrous scalpe downe to his teeth it
    tore,
And that misformed shape misshaped more:
A sea of blood gusht from the gaping
    wownd,
That her gay garments staynd with filthy
    gore,
And overflowed all the field arownd;
That over shoes in blood he waded on the
    grownd.

XVII

Thereat he rored for exceeding paine,
That, to have heard, great horror would
    have bred,
And scourging th' emptie ayre with his
    long trayne,
Through great impatience of his grieved
    hed,
His gorgeous ryder from her loftie sted
Would have cast downe, and trodd in durty
    myre,
Had not the gyaunt soone her succoured;
Who, all enrag'd with smart and frantick
    yre,
Came hurtling in full fiers, and forst the
    knight retyre.

XVIII

The force, which wont in two to be dis-
    perst,
In one alone left hand he now unites,
Which is through rage more strong then
    both were erst;
With which his hideous club aloft he dites,
And at his foe with furious rigor smites,
That strongest oake might seeme to over-
    throw:
The stroke upon his shield so heavie lites,
That to the ground it doubleth him full
    low:
What mortall wight could ever beare so
    monstrous blow ?

XIX

And in his fall his shield, that covered was,
Did loose his vele by chaunce, and open
    flew:

The light whereof, that hevens light did pas,
Such blazing brightnesse through the ayer threw,
That eye mote not the same endure to vew.
Which when the gyaunt spyde with staring eye,
He downe let fall his arme, and soft withdrew
His weapon huge, that heaved was on hye,
For to have slain the man, that on the ground did lye.

XX

And eke the fruitfull-headed beast, amazd
At flashing beames of that sunshiny shield,
Became stark blind, and all his sences dazd,
That downe he tumbled on the durtie field,
And seemd himselfe as conquered to yield.
Whom when his maistresse proud perceiv'd to fall,
Whiles yet his feeble feet for faintnesse reeld,
Unto the gyaunt lowdly she gan call,
'O helpe, Orgoglio, helpe! or els we perish all.'

XXI

At her so pitteous cry was much amoov'd
Her champion stout, and for to ayde his frend,
Againe his wonted angry weapon proov'd:
But all in vaine: for he has redd his end
In that bright shield, and all his forces spend
Them selves in vaine: for since that glauncing sight,
He hath no poure to hurt, nor to defend;
As where th' Almighties lightning brond does light,
It dimmes the dazed eyen, and daunts the sences quight.

XXII

Whom when the Prince, to batteill new addrest
And threatning high his dreadfull stroke, did see,
His sparkling blade about his head he blest,
And smote off quite his right leg by the knee,
That downe he tombled; as an aged tree,
High growing on the top of rocky clift,
Whose hartstrings with keene steele nigh hewen be;

The mightie trunck halfe rent, with ragged rift
Doth roll adowne the rocks, and fall with fearefull drift.

XXIII

Or as a castle, reared high and round,
By subtile engins and malitious slight
Is undermined from the lowest ground,
And her foundation forst, and feebled quight,
At last downe falles, and with her heaped hight
Her hastie ruine does more heavie make,
And yields it selfe unto the victours might;
Such was this gyaunts fall, that seemd to shake
The stedfast globe of earth, as it for feare did quake.

XXIV

The knight then, lightly leaping to the pray,
With mortall steele him smot againe so sore,
That headlesse his unweldy bodie lay,
All wallowd in his owne fowle bloody gore,
Which flowed from his wounds in wondrous store.
But soone as breath out of his brest did pas,
That huge great body, which the gyaunt bore,
Was vanisht quite, and of that monstrous mas
Was nothing left, but like an emptie blader was.

XXV

Whose grievous fall when false Duessa spyde,
Her golden cup she cast unto the ground,
And crowned mitre rudely threw asyde;
Such percing griefe her stubborne hart did wound,
That she could not endure that dolefull stound,
But leaving all behind her, fled away:
The light-foot squyre her quickly turnd around,
And by hard meanes enforcing her to stay,
So brought unto his lord, as his deserved pray.

XXVI

The roiall virgin, which beheld from farre,
In pensive plight and sad perplexitie,

The whole atchievement of this doubtfull warre,
Came running fast to greet his victorie,
With sober gladnesse and myld modestie,
And with sweet joyous cheare him thus bespake:
'Fayre braunch of noblesse, flowre of chevalrie,
That with your worth the world amazed make,
How shall I quite the paynes, ye suffer for my sake?

XXVII

'And you, fresh budd of vertue springing fast,
Whom these sad eyes saw nigh unto deaths dore,
What hath poore virgin for such perill past
Wherewith you to reward? Accept therefore
My simple selfe, and service evermore:
And He that high does sit, and all things see
With equall eye, their merites to restore,
Behold what ye this day have done for mee,
And what I cannot quite, requite with usuree.

XXVIII

'But sith the heavens, and your faire handeling,
Have made you master of the field this day,
Your fortune maister eke with governing,
And well begonne end all so well, I pray.
Ne let that wicked woman scape away;
For she it is, that did my lord bethrall,
My dearest lord, and deepe in dongeon lay,
Where he his better dayes hath wasted all.
O heare, how piteous he to you for ayd does call.'

XXIX

Forthwith he gave in charge unto his squyre,
That scarlot whore to keepen carefully;
Whyles he himselfe with greedie great desyre
Into the castle entred forcibly;
Where living creature none he did espye.
Then gan he lowdly through the house to call:
But no man car'd to answere to his crye.
There raignd a solemne silence over all,
Nor voice was heard, nor wight was seene in bowre or hall.

XXX

At last, with creeping crooked pace forth came
An old old man, with beard as white as snow,
That on a staffe his feeble steps did frame,
And guyde his wearie gate both too and fro;
For his eye sight him fayled long ygo:
And on his arme a bounch of keyes he bore,
The which unused rust did overgrow:
Those were the keyes of every inner dore,
But he could not them use, but kept them still in store.

XXXI

But very uncouth sight was to behold,
How he did fashion his untoward pace,
For as he forward moovd his footing old,
So backward still was turnd his wrincled face,
Unlike to men, who ever as they trace,
Both feet and face one way are wont to lead.
This was the auncient keeper of that place,
And foster father of the gyaunt dead;
His name Ignaro did his nature right aread.

XXXII

His reverend heares and holy gravitee
The knight much honord, as beseemed well,
And gently askt, where all the people bee,
Which in that stately building wont to dwell:
Who answerd him full soft, *He could not tell*.
Againe he askt, where that same knight was layd,
Whom great Orgoglio with his puissaunce fell
Had made his caytive thrall: againe he sayde,
He could not tell: ne ever other answere made.

XXXIII

Then asked he, which way he in might pas:
He could not tell, againe he answered.
Thereat the courteous knight displeased was,
And said: 'Old syre, it seemes thou hast not red

How ill it fits with that same silver hed,
In vaine to mocke, or mockt in vaine to bee:
But if thou be, as thou art pourtrahed
With natures pen, in ages grave degree,
Aread in graver wise what I demaund of
thee.'

XXXIV

His answere likewise was, *He could not tell.*
Whose sencelesse speach and doted igno-
rance
When as the noble Prince had marked well,
He ghest his nature by his countenance,
And calmd his wrath with goodly temper-
ance.
Then to him stepping, from his arme did
reach
Those keyes, and made himselfe free
enterance.
Each dore he opened without any breach;
There was no barre to stop, nor foe him to
empeach.

XXXV

There all within full rich arayd he found,
With royall arras and resplendent gold,
And did with store of every thing abound,
That greatest princes presence might behold.
But all the floore (too filthy to be told)
With blood of guiltlesse babes, and inno-
cents trew,
Which there were slaine, as sheepe out of
the fold,
Defiled was, that dreadfull was to vew,
And sacred ashes over it was strowed new.

XXXVI

And there beside of marble stone was built
An altare, carv'd with cunning ymagery,
On which trew Christians blood was often
spilt,
And holy martyres often doen to dye,
With cruell malice and strong tyranny:
Whose blessed sprites from underneath the
stone
To God for vengeance cryde continually,
And with great griefe were often heard to
grone,
That hardest heart would bleede to heare
their piteous mone.

XXXVII

Through every rowme he sought, and
everie bowr,
But no where could he find that wofull thrall:

At last he came unto an yron doore,
That fast was lockt, but key found not at
all
Emongst that bounch to open it withall;
But in the same a little grate was pight,
Through which he sent his voyce, and lowd
did call
With all his powre, to weet if living wight
Were housed therewithin, whom he en-
largen might.

XXXVIII

Therewith an hollow, dreary, murmuring
voyce
These pitteous plaintes and dolours did resound:
' O who is that, which bringes me happy
choyce
Of death, that here lye dying every stound,
Yet live perforce in balefull darkenesse
bound ?
For now three moones have changed thrice
their hew,
And have beene thrice hid underneath the
ground,
Since I the heavens chearefull face did
vew.
O welcome, thou, that doest of death bring
tydings trew ! '

XXXIX

Which when that champion heard, with
percing point
Of pitty deare his hart was thrilled sore,
And trembling horrour ran through every
joynt,
For ruth of gentle knight so fowle forlore:
Which shaking off, he rent that yron
dore,
With furious force and indignation fell;
Where entred in, his foot could find no
flore,
But all a deepe descent, as darke as hell,
That breathed ever forth a filthie banefull
smell.

XL

But nether darkenesse fowle, nor filthy
bands,
Nor noyous smell his purpose could with-
hold,
(Entire affection hateth nicer hands)
But that with constant zele, and corage
bold,
After long paines and labors manifold,

He found the meanes that prisoner up to
    reare;
Whose feeble thighes, unhable to uphold
His pined corse, him scarse to light could
    beare,
A ruefull spectacle of death and ghastly
    drere.

XLI

His sad dull eies, deepe sunck in hollow
    pits,
Could not endure th' unwonted sunne to
    view;
His bare thin cheekes for want of better
    bits,
And empty sides deceived of their dew,
Could make a stony hart his hap to rew;
His rawbone armes, whose mighty brawned
    bowrs
Were wont to rive steele plates, and hel-
    mets hew,
Were clene consum'd, and all his vitall
    powres
Decayd, and al his flesh shronk up like
    withered flowres.

XLII

Whome when his lady saw, to him she ran
With hasty joy: to see him made her glad,
And sad to view his visage pale and wan,
Who earst in flowres of freshest youth was
    clad.
Tho, when her well of teares she wasted
    had,
She said: 'Ah, dearest lord! what evill
    starre
On you hath frownd, and pourd his influ-
    ence bad,
That of your selfe ye thus berobbed arre,
And this misseeming hew your manly looks
    doth marre?

XLIII

'But welcome now, my lord, in wele or
    woe,
Whose presence I have lackt too long a
    day;
And fye on Fortune, mine avowed foe,
Whose wrathful wreakes them selves doe
    now alay,
And for these wronges shall treble penaunce
    pay
Of treble good: good growes of evils priefe.'
The chearelesse man, whom sorow did
    dismay,

Had no delight to treaten of his griefe;
His long endured famine needed more re-
    liefe.

XLIV

'Faire lady,' then said that victorious
    knight,
'The things, that grievous were to doe, or
    beare,
Them to renew, I wote, breeds no delight;
Best musicke breeds dislike in loathing
    eare:
But th' only good, that growes of passed
    feare,
Is to be wise, and ware of like agein.
This daies ensample hath this lesson deare
Deepe written in my heart with yron
    pen,
That blisse may not abide in state of mor-
    tall men.

XLV

'Henceforth, sir knight, take to you wonted
    strength,
And maister these mishaps with patient
    might:
Loe wher your foe lies stretcht in monstrous
    length,
And loe that wicked woman in your sight,
The roote of all your care and wretched
    plight,
Now in your powre, to let her live, or die.'
'To doe her die,' quoth Una, 'were de-
    spight,
And shame t' avenge so weake an enimy;
But spoile her of her scarlot robe, and let
    her fly.'

XLVI

So, as she bad, that witch they disaraid,
And robd of roiall robes, and purple pall,
And ornaments that richly were displaid;
Ne spared they to strip her naked all.
Then, when they had despoyld her tire and
    call,
Such as she was, their eies might her be-
    hold,
That her misshaped parts did them appall,
A loathly, wrinckled hag, ill favoured, old,
Whose secret filth good manners biddeth
    not be told.

XLVII

Her crafty head was altogether bald,
And, as in hate of honorable eld,

Was overgrowne with scurfe and filthy scald;
Her teeth out of her rotten gummes were
    feld,
And her sowre breath abhominably smeld;
Her dried dugs, lyke bladders lacking wind,
Hong downe, and filthy matter from them
    weld;
Her wrizled skin, as rough as maple rind,
So scabby was, that would have loathd all
    womankind.

XLVIII

Her neather parts, the shame of all her
    kind,
My chaster Muse for shame doth blush to
    write:
But at her rompe she growing had behind
A foxes taile, with dong all fowly dight;
And eke her feete most monstrous were in
    sight;
For one of them was like an eagles claw,
With griping talaunts armd to greedy fight,
The other like a beares uneven paw:
More ugly shape yet never living creature
    saw.

XLIX

Which when the knights beheld, amazd
    they were,
And wondred at so fowle deformed wight.
'Such then,' said Una, 'as she seemeth here,
Such is the face of Falshood, such the sight
Of fowle Duessa, when her borrowed light
Is laid away, and counterfesaunce knowne.'
Thus when they had the witch disrobed
    quight,
And all her filthy feature open showne,
They let her goe at will, and wander waies
    unknowne.

L

Shee, flying fast from heavens hated face,
And from the world that her discovered
    wide,
Fled to the wastfull wildernesse apace,
From living eies her open shame to hide,
And lurkt in rocks and caves, long un-
    espide.
But that faire crew of knights, and Una
    faire,
Did in that castle afterwards abide,
To rest them selves, and weary powres re-
    paire;
Where store they fownd of al that dainty
    was and rare.

CANTO IX

His loves and lignage Arthure tells:
    The knights knitt friendly bands:
Sir Trevisan flies from Despeyre,
    Whom Redcros Knight withstands.

I

O GOODLY golden chayne! wherewith yfere
The vertues linked are in lovely wize,
And noble mindes of yore allyed were,
In brave poursuitt of chevalrous emprize,
That none did others safety despize,
Nor aid envy to him, in need that stands,
But friendly each did others praise devize
How to advaunce with favourable bands,
As this good Prince redeemd the Red-
    crosse Knight from bands.

II

Who when their powres, empayrd through
    labor long,
With dew repast they had recured well,
And that weake captive wight now wexed
    strong,
Them list no lenger there at leasure dwell,
But forward fare, as their adventures fell:
But ere they parted, Una faire besought
That straunger knight his name and nation
    tell;
Least so great good, as he for her had
    wrought,
Should die unknown, and buried be in
    thankles thought.

III

'Faire virgin,' said the Prince, 'yee me
    require
A thing without the compas of my witt:
For both the lignage and the certein sire,
From which I sprong, from mee are hidden
    yitt.
For all so soone as life did me admitt
Into this world, and shewed hevens light,
From mothers pap I taken was unfitt,
And streight deliver'd to a Fary knight,
To be upbrought in gentle thewes and mar-
    tiall might.

IV

'Unto old Timon he me brought bylive,
Old Timon, who in youthly yeares hath
    beene
In warlike feates th' expertest man alive,
And is the wisest now on earth I weene:
His dwelling is low in a valley greene,

Under the foot of Rauran mossy hore,
From whence the river Dee, as silver cleene,
His tombling billowes rolls with gentle rore:
There all my daies he traind mee up in
    vertuous lore.

V

'Thether the great magicien Merlin came,
As was his use, ofttimes to visitt mee;
For he had charge my discipline to frame,
And tutors nouriture to oversee.
Him oft and oft I askt in privity,
Of what loines and what lignage I did
    spring.
Whose aunswere bad me still assured bee,
That I was sonne and heire unto a king,
As time in her just term the truth to light
    should bring.'

VI

'Well worthy impe,' said then the lady gent,
'And pupill fitt for such a tutors hand!
But what adventure, or what high intent,
Hath brought you hether into Fary Land,
Aread, Prince Arthure, crowne of martiall
    band?'
'Full hard it is,' quoth he, 'to read aright
The course of heavenly cause, or under-
    stand
The secret meaning of th' Eternall Might,
That rules mens waies, and rules the
    thoughts of living wight.

VII

'For whether He through fatal deepe fore-
    sight
Me hither sent, for cause to me unghest,
Or that fresh bleeding wound, which day
    and night
Whilome doth rancle in my riven brest,
With forced fury following his behest,
Me hether brought by wayes yet never
    found,
You to have helpt I hold my selfe yet
    blest.'
'Ah! courteous knight,' quoth she, 'what
    secret wound
Could ever find to grieve the gentlest hart
    on ground?'

VIII

'Deare dame,' quoth he, 'you sleeping
    sparkes awake,
Which, troubled once, into huge flames will
    grow,
Ne ever will their fervent fury slake,
Till living moysture into smoke do flow,
And wasted life doe lye in ashes low.
Yet sithens silence lesseneth not my fire,
But, told, it flames, and, hidden, it does
    glow,
I will revele what ye so much desire:
Ah Love! lay down thy bow, the whiles I
    may respyre.

IX

'It was in freshest flowre of youthly
    yeares,
When corage first does creepe in manly
    chest;
Then first the cole of kindly heat appeares,
To kindle love in every living brest:
But me had warnd old Timons wise behest,
Those creeping flames by reason to subdew,
Before their rage grew to so great unrest,
As miserable lovers use to rew,
Which still wex old in woe, whiles wo stil
    wexeth new.

X

'That ydle name of love, and lovers life,
As losse of time, and vertues enimy,
I ever scornd, and joyd to stirre up strife
In middest of their mournfull tragedy,
Ay wont to laugh, when them I heard to cry,
And blow the fire, which them to ashes
    brent:
Their god himselfe, grievd at my libertie,
Shott many a dart at me with fiers intent,
But I them warded all with wary govern-
    ment.

XI

'But all in vaine: no fort can be so strong,
Ne fleshly brest can armed be so sownd,
But will at last be wonne with battrie long,
Or unawares at disavantage fownd:
Nothing is sure that growes on earthly
    grownd:
And who most trustes in arme of fleshly
    might,
And boastes, in beauties chaine not to be
    bownd,
Doth soonest fall in disaventrous fight,
And yeeldes his caytive neck to victours
    most despight.

XII

'Ensample make of him your haplesse joy
And of my selfe now mated, as ye see;

Whose prouder vaunt that proud avenging
boy
Did soone pluck downe, and curbd my lib-
ertee.
For on a day, prickt forth with jollitee
Of looser life, and heat of hardiment,
Raunging the forest wide on courser free,
The fields, the floods, the heavens, with one
consent,
Did seeme to laugh on me, and favour
mine intent.

XIII

' Forwearied with my sportes, I did alight
From loftie steed, and downe to sleepe me
layd;
The verdant gras my couch did goodly
dight,
And pillow was my helmett fayre displayd:
Whiles every sence the humour sweet em-
bayd,
And slombring soft my hart did steale
away,
Me seemed, by my side a royall mayd
Her daintie limbes full softly down did
lay:
So fayre a creature yet saw never sunny
day.

XIV

' Most goodly glee and lovely blandishment
She to me made, and badd me love her
deare;
For dearely sure her love was to me bent,
As, when just time expired, should appeare.
But whether dreames delude, or true it
were,
Was never hart so ravisht with delight,
Ne living man like wordes did ever heare,
As she to me delivered all that night;
And at her parting said, she Queene of
Faries hight.

XV

' When I awoke, and found her place de-
voyd,
And nought but pressed gras where she had
lyen,
I sorrowed all so much as earst I joyd,
And washed all her place with watry eyen.
From that day forth I lov'd that face di-
vyne;
From that day forth I cast in carefull
mynd,
To seeke her out with labor and long tyne,

And never vow to rest, till her I fynd:
Nyne monethes I seek in vain, yet ni'll
that vow unbynd.'

XVI

Thus as he spake, his visage wexed pale,
And chaunge of hew great passion did be-
wray;
Yett still he strove to cloke his inward bale,
And hide the smoke that did his fire display;
Till gentle Una thus to him gan say:
' O happy Queene of Faries, that hast
fownd,
Mongst many, one that with his prowesse
may
Defend thine honour, and thy foes con-
fownd !
True loves are often sown, but seldom
grow on grownd.'

XVII

' Thine, O then,' said the gentle Redcrosse
Knight,
' Next to that ladies love, shalbe the place,
O fayrest virgin, full of heavenly light,
Whose wondrous faith, exceeding earthly
race,
Was firmest fixt in myne extremest case.
And you, my lord, the patrone of my life,
Of that great Queene may well gaine
worthie grace:
For onely worthie you through prowes
priefe,
Yf living man mote worthie be, to be her
liefe.'

XVIII

So diversly discoursing of their loves,
The golden sunne his glistring head gan
shew,
And sad remembraunce now the Prince
amoves
With fresh desire his voyage to pursew:
Als Una earnd her traveill to renew.
Then those two knights, fast frendship for
to bynd,
And love establish each to other trew,
Gave goodly gifts, the signes of gratefull
mynd,
And eke, as pledges firme, right hands to-
gether joynd.

XIX

Prince Arthur gave a boxe of diamond sure,
Embowd with gold and gorgeous ornament,

Wherein were closd few drops of liquor
    pure,
Of wondrous worth, and vertue excellent,
That any wownd could heale incontinent:
Which to requite, the Redcrosse Knight
    him gave
A booke, wherein his Saveours Testament
Was writt with golden letters rich and
    brave;
A worke of wondrous grace, and hable
    soules to save.

XX

Thus beene they parted, Arthur on his way
To seeke his love, and th' other for to fight
With Unaes foe, that all her realme did
    pray.
But she, now weighing the decayed plight
And shrunken synewes of her chosen
    knight,
Would not a while her forward course pur-
    sew,
Ne bring him forth in face of dreadfull
    fight,
Till he recovered had his former hew:
For him to be yet weake and wearie well
    she knew.

XXI

So as they traveild, lo ! they gan espy
An armed knight towards them gallop
    fast,
That seemed from some feared foe to fly,
Or other griesly thing, that him aghast.
Still as he fledd, his eye was backward
    cast,
As if his feare still followed him behynd;
Als flew his steed, as he his bandes had
    brast,
And with his winged heeles did tread the
    wynd,
As he had beene a fole of Pegasus his kynd.

XXII

Nigh as he drew, they might perceive his
    head
To bee unarmd, and curld uncombed heares
Upstaring stiffe, dismaid with uncouth
    dread;
Nor drop of blood in all his face appeares,
Nor life in limbe: and to increase his
    feares,
In fowle reproch of knighthoodes fayre
    degree,
About his neck an hempen rope he weares,

That with his glistring armes does ill
    agree;
But he of rope, or armes, has now no
    memoree.

XXIII

The Redcrosse Knight toward him crossed
    fast,
To weet what mister wight was so dis-
    mayd:
There him he findes all sencelesse and
    aghast,
That of him selfe he seemd to be afrayd;
Whom hardly he from flying forward
    stayd,
Till he these wordes to him deliver might:
' Sir knight, aread who hath ye thus arayd,
And eke from whom make ye this hasty
    flight ?
For never knight I saw in such misseeming
    plight.'

XXIV

He answerd nought at all, but adding new
Feare to his first amazment, staring wyde
With stony eyes and hartlesse hollow hew,
Astonisht stood, as one that had aspyde
Infernall furies, with their chaines untyde.
Him yett againe, and yett againe bespake
The gentle knight; who nought to him re-
    plyde,
But, trembling every joynt, did inly quake,
And foltring tongue at last these words
    seemd forth to shake:

XXV

' For Gods deare love, sir knight, doe me
    not stay;
For loe! he comes, he comes fast after mee!'
Eft looking back, would faine have runne
    away;
But he him forst to stay, and tellen free
The secrete cause of his perplexitie:
Yet nathemore by his bold hartie speach
Could his blood frosen hart emboldened
    bee,
But through his boldnes rather feare did
    reach;
Yett, forst, at last he made through silence
    suddein breach.

XXVI

' And am I now in safetie sure,' quoth he,
' From him that would have forced me to
    dye ?

And is the point of death now turnd fro mee,
That I may tell this haplesse history ?'
'Feare nought,' quoth he, 'no daunger now
   is nye.'
'Then shall I you recount a ruefull cace,'
Said he, 'the which with this unlucky eye
I late beheld; and had not greater grace
Me reft from it, had bene partaker of the
   place.

XXVII

'I lately chaunst (would I had never
   chaunst !)
With a fayre knight to keepen companee,
Sir Terwin hight, that well himselfe ad-
   vaunst
In all affayres, and was both bold and free,
But not so happy as mote happy bee:
He lov'd, as was his lot, a lady gent,
That him againe lov'd in the least degree:
For she was proud, and of too high intent,
And joyd to see her lover languish and
   lament.

XXVIII

'From whom retourning sad and comfort-
   lesse,
As on the way together we did fare,
We met that villen, (God from him me
   blesse !)
That cursed wight, from whom I scapt
   whyleare,
A man of hell, that calls himselfe Despayre:
Who first us greets, and after fayre areedes
Of tydinges straunge, and of adventures
   rare:
So creeping close, as snake in hidden weedes,
Inquireth of our states, and of our knightly
   deedes.

XXIX

'Which when he knew, and felt our feeble
   harts
Embost with bale, and bitter byting griefe,
Which love had launched with his deadly
   darts,
With wounding words, and termes of foule
   repriefe,
He pluckt from us all hope of dew reliefe,
That earst us held in love of lingring life:
Then hopelesse hartlesse, gan the cunning
   thiefe
Perswade us dye, to stint all further strife:
To me he lent this rope, to him a rusty
   knife.

XXX

'With which sad instrument of hasty death,
That wofull lover, loathing lenger light,
A wyde way made to let forth living breath.
But I, more fearefull or more lucky wight,
Dismayd with that deformed dismall sight,
Fledd fast away, halfe dead with dying
   feare;
Ne yet assur'd of life by you, sir knight,
Whose like infirmity like chaunce may
   beare:
But God you never let his charmed speaches
   heare.'

XXXI

'How may a man,' said he, 'with idle speach
Be wonne to spoyle the castle of his health?'
'I wote,' quoth he, 'whom tryall late did
   teach,
That like would not for all this worldes
   wealth:
His subtile tong, like dropping honny,
   mealt'h
Into the heart, and searcheth every vaine,
That ere one be aware, by secret stealth
His powre is reft, and weaknes doth re-
   maine.
O never, sir, desire to try his guilefull
   traine.'

XXXII

'Certes,' sayd he, 'hence shall I never rest,
Till I that treachours art have heard and
   tryde;
And you, sir knight, whose name mote I
   request,
Of grace do me unto his cabin guyde.'
'I that hight Trevisan,' quoth he, 'will
   ryde
Against my liking backe, to doe you grace:
But nor for gold nor glee will I abyde
By you, when ye arrive in that same place;
For lever had I die, then see his deadly
   face.'

XXXIII

Ere long they come, where that same wicked
   wight
His dwelling has, low in an hollow cave,
Far underneath a craggy clift ypight,
Darke, dolefull, dreary, like a greedy grave,
That still for carrion carcases doth crave:
On top whereof ay dwelt the ghastly owle,
Shrieking his balefull note, which ever
   drave

Far from that haunt all other chearefull
    fowle;
And all about it wandring ghostes did wayle
    and howle.

XXXIV

And all about old stockes and stubs of trees,
Whereon nor fruite nor leafe was ever
    seene,
Did hang upon the ragged rocky knees;
On which had many wretches hanged
    beene,
Whose carcases were scattred on the
    greene,
And throwne about the cliffs. Arrived there,
That bare-head knight, for dread and
    dolefull teene,
Would faine have fled, ne durst approchen
    neare,
But th' other forst him staye, and com-
    forted in feare.

XXXV

That darkesome cave they enter, where they
    find
That cursed man, low sitting on the ground,
Musing full sadly in his sullein mind:
His griesie lockes, long growen and un-
    bound,
Disordred hong about his shoulders round,
And hid his face; through which his hol-
    low eyne
Lookt deadly dull, and stared as astound;
His raw-bone cheekes, through penurie and
    pine,
Were shronke into his jawes, as he did
    never dyne.

XXXVI

His garment nought but many ragged
    clouts,
With thornes together pind and patched
    was,
The which his naked sides he wrapt abouts;
And him beside there lay upon the gras
A dreary corse, whose life away did pas,
All wallowd in his own yet luke-warme blood,
That from his wound yet welled fresh, alas!
In which a rusty knife fast fixed stood,
And made an open passage for the gushing
    flood.

XXXVII

Which piteous spectacle, approving trew
The wofull tale that Trevisan had told,

When as the gentle Redcrosse Knight did
    vew,
With firie zeale he burnt in courage bold,
Him to avenge, before his blood were cold;
And to the villein sayd : 'Thou damned
    wight,
The authour of this fact we here behold,
What justice can but judge against thee
    right,
With thine owne blood to price his blood,
    here shed in sight ? '

XXXVIII

' What franticke fit,' quoth he, ' hath thus
    distraught
Thee, foolish man, so rash a doome to give ?
What justice ever other judgement taught,
But he should dye, who merites not to
    live ?
None els to death this man despayring
    drive,
But his owne guiltie mind deserving death.
Is then unjust to each his dew to give ?
Or let him dye, that loatheth living breath ?
Or let him die at ease, that liveth here un-
    eath ?

XXXIX

' Who travailes by the wearie wandring
    way,
To come unto his wished home in haste,
And meetes a flood, that doth his passage
    stay,
Is not great grace to helpe him over past,
Or free his feet, that in the myre sticke
    fast ?
Most envious man, that grieves at neigh-
    bours good,
And fond, that joyest in the woe thou hast !
Why wilt not let him passe, that long hath
    stood
Upon the bancke, yet wilt thy selfe not pas
    the flood ?

XL

' He there does now enjoy eternall rest
And happy ease, which thou doest want and
    crave,
And further from it daily wanderest:
What if some little payne the passage have,
That makes frayle flesh to feare the bitter
    wave ?
Is not short payne well borne, that bringes
    long ease,
And layes the soule to sleepe in quiet grave ?

Sleepe after toyle, port after stormie seas,
Ease after warre, death after life does
   greatly please.'

XLI

The knight much wondred at his suddeine
   wit,
And sayd: 'The terme of life is limited,
Ne may a man prolong, nor shorten it:
The souldier may not move from watchfull
   sted,
Nor leave his stand, untill his captaine bed.'
'Who life did limit by almightie doome,'
Quoth he, 'knowes best the termes estab-
   lished;
And he that points the centonell his roome,
Doth license him depart at sound of morn-
   ing droome.

XLII

'Is not His deed, what ever thing is donne
In heaven and earth? Did not He all
   create,
To die againe? All ends, that was begonne.
Their times in His eternall booke of fate
Are written sure, and have their certein date.
Who then can strive with strong necessitie,
That holds the world in his still chaunging
   state,
Or shunne the death ordaynd by destinie?
When houre of death is come, let none aske
   whence, nor why.

XLIII

'The lenger life, I wote, the greater sin,
The greater sin, the greater punishment:
All those great battels, which thou boasts
   to win,
Through strife, and blood-shed, and avenge-
   ment,
Now praysd, hereafter deare thou shalt re-
   pent:
For life must life, and blood must blood re-
   pay.
Is not enough thy evill life forespent?
For he that once hath missed the right way,
The further he doth goe, the further he
   doth stray.

XLIV

'Then doe no further goe, no further stray,
But here ly downe, and to thy rest betake,
Th' ill to prevent, that life ensewen may.
For what hath life, that may it loved make,
And gives not rather cause it to forsake?

Feare, sicknesse, age, losse, labour, sorrow,
   strife,
Payne, hunger, cold, that makes the hart to
   quake;
And ever fickle Fortune rageth rife;
All which, and thousands mo, do make a
   loathsome life.

XLV

'Thou, wretched man, of death hast great-
   est need,
If in true ballaunce thou wilt weigh thy state:
For never knight, that dared warlike deed,
More lucklesse dissaventures did amate:
Witnes the dungeon deepe, wherein of late
Thy life shutt up for death so oft did call;
And though good lucke prolonged hath thy
   date,
Yet death then would the like mishaps fore-
   stall,
Into the which heareafter thou maist happen
   fall.

XLVI

'Why then doest thou, O man of sin, desire
To draw thy dayes forth to their last de-
   gree?
Is not the measure of thy sinfull hire
High heaped up with huge iniquitee,
Against the day of wrath, to burden thee?
Is not enough, that to this lady mild
Thou falsed hast thy faith with perjuree,
And sold thy selfe to serve Duessa vild,
With whom in al abuse thou hast thy selfe
   defild?

XLVII

'Is not He just, that all this doth behold
From highest heven, and beares an equall
   eie?
Shall He thy sins up in His knowledge fold,
And guilty be of thine impietie?
Is not His lawe, Let every sinner die:
Die shall all flesh?   What then must
   needs be donne,
Is it not better to doe willinglie,
Then linger till the glas be all out ronne?
Death is the end of woes: die soone, O
   Faries sonne.'

XLVIII

The knight was much enmoved with his
   speach,
That as a swords poynt through his hart
   did perse,

And in his conscience made a secrete
    breach,
Well knowing trew all that he did re-
    herse;
And to his fresh remembraunce did reverse
The ugly vew of his deformed crimes,
That all his manly powres it did disperse,
As he were charmed with inchaunted rimes,
That oftentimes he quakt, and fainted
    oftentimes.

XLIX

In which amazement when the miscreaunt
Perceived him to waver, weake and fraile,
Whiles trembling horror did his conscience
    daunt,
And hellish anguish did his soule assaile,
To drive him to despaire, and quite to
    quaile,
Hee shewd him, painted in a table plaine,
The damned ghosts, that doe in torments
    waile,
And thousand feends, that doe them end-
    lesse paine
With fire and brimstone, which for ever
    shall remaine.

L

The sight whereof so throughly him dis-
    maid,
That nought but death before his eies he
    saw,
And ever burning wrath before him laid,
By righteous sentence of th' Almighties
    law:
Then gan the villein him to overcraw,
And brought unto him swords, ropes, poison,
    fire,
And all that might him to perdition draw;
And bad him choose, what death he would
    desire:
For death was dew to him, that had pro-
    vokt Gods ire.

LI

But whenas none of them he saw him take,
He to him raught a dagger sharpe and
    keene,
And gave it him in hand: his hand did
    quake,
And tremble like a leafe of aspin greene,
And troubled blood through his pale face
    was seene
To come and goe, with tidings from the
    heart,

As it a ronning messenger had beene.
At last, resolv'd to worke his finall smart,
He lifted up his hand, that backe againe
    did start.

LII

Which whenas Una saw, through every
    vaine
The crudled cold ran to her well of life,
As in a swowne: but soone reliv'd againe,
Out of his hand she snatcht the cursed
    knife,
And threw it to the ground, enraged rife,
And to him said: 'Fie, fie, faint hearted
    knight!
What meanest thou by this reprochfull
    strife?
Is this the battaile, which thou vauntst to
    fight
With that fire-mouthed dragon, horrible
    and bright?

LIII

'Come, come away, fraile, feeble, fleshly
    wight,
Ne let vaine words bewitch thy manly
    hart,
Ne divelish thoughts dismay thy constant
    spright.
In heavenly mercies hast thou not a part?
Why shouldst thou then despeire, that
    chosen art?
Where justice growes, there grows eke
    greter grace,
The which doth quench the brond of hellish
    smart,
And that accurst hand-writing doth deface.
Arise, sir knight, arise, and leave this
    cursed place.'

LIV

So up he rose, and thence amounted streight.
Which when the carle beheld, and saw his
    guest
Would safe depart, for all his subtile
    sleight,
He chose an halter from among the rest,
And with it hong him selfe, unbid unblest.
But death he could not worke himselfe
    thereby;
For thousand times he so him selfe had
    drest,
Yet nathelesse it could not doe him die,
Till he should die his last, that is, eter-
    nally.

CANTO X

Her faithfull knight faire Una brings
To House of Holinesse,
Where he is taught repentaunce, and
The way to hevenly blesse.

I

WHAT man is he, that boasts of fleshly
    might,
And vaine assuraunce of mortality,
Which, all so soone as it doth come to
    fight
Against spirituall foes, yields by and by,
Or from the fielde most cowardly doth
    fly ?
Ne let the man ascribe it to his skill,
That thorough grace hath gained victory.
If any strength we have, it is to ill,
But all the good is Gods, both power and
    eke will.

II

By that which lately hapned, Una saw
That this her knight was feeble, and too
    faint;
And all his sinewes woxen weake and
    raw,
Through long enprisonment, and hard con-
    straint,
Which he endured in his late restraint,
That yet he was unfitt for bloody fight:
Therefore to cherish him with diets daint,
She cast to bring him, where he chearen
    might,
Till he recovered had his late decayed
    plight.

III

There was an auncient house not far away,
Renowmd throughout the world for sacred
    lore
And pure unspotted life: so well, they say,
It governd was, and guided evermore,
Through wisedome of a matrone grave and
    hore;
Whose onely joy was to relieve the needes
Of wretched soules, and helpe the helpe-
    lesse pore:
All night she spent in bidding of her bedes,
And all the day in doing good and godly
    deedes.

IV

Dame Cælia men did her call, as thought
From heaven to come, or thether to arise;

The mother of three daughters, well up-
    brought
In goodly thewes, and godly exercise:
The eldest two, most sober, chast, and wise,
Fidelia and Speranza, virgins were,
Though spousd, yet wanting wedlocks sol-
    emnize;
But faire Charissa to a lovely fere
Was lincked, and by him had many pledges
    dere.

V

Arrived there, the dore they find fast
    lockt;
For it was warely watched night and day,
For feare of many foes: but when they
    knockt,
The porter opened unto them streight way.
He was an aged syre, all hory gray,
With lookes full lowly cast, and gate full
    slow,
Wont on a staffe his feeble steps to stay,
Hight Humiltá. They passe in, stouping
    low;
For streight and narrow was the way which
    he did shew.

VI

Each goodly thing is hardest to begin;
But entred in, a spatious court they see,
Both plaine and pleasaunt to be walked in,
Where them does meete a francklin faire
    and free,
And entertaines with comely courteous
    glee:
His name was Zele, that him right well
    became;
For in his speaches and behaveour hee
Did labour lively to expresse the same,
And gladly did them guide, till to the hall
    they came.

VII

There fayrely them receives a gentle squyre,
Of myld demeanure and rare courtesee,
Right cleanly clad in comely sad attyre;
In word and deede that shewd great mod-
    estee,
And knew his good to all of each degree;
Hight Reverence. He them with speaches
    meet
Does faire entreat; no courting nicetee,
But simple trew, and eke unfained sweet,
As might become a squyre so great persons
    to greet.

VIII

And afterwardes them to his dame he
    leades,
That aged dame, the lady of the place:
Who all this while was busy at her beades:
Which doen, she up arose with seemely
    grace,
And toward them full matronely did pace.
Where when that fairest Una she beheld,
Whom well she knew to spring from
    hevenly race,
Her heart with joy unwonted inly sweld,
As feeling wondrous comfort in her weaker
    eld:

IX

And her embracing, said: 'O happy earth,
Whereon thy innocent feet doe ever tread,
Most vertuous virgin, borne of hevenly
    berth,
That to redeeme thy woefull parents head
From tyrans rage, and ever-dying dread,
Hast wandred through the world now long
    a day,
Yett ceassest not thy weary soles to lead!
What grace hath thee now hether brought
    this way?
Or doen thy feeble feet unweeting hether
    stray?

X

'Straunge thing it is an errant knight to see
Here in this place, or any other wight,
That hether turnes his steps: so few there
    bee,
That chose the narrow path, or seeke the
    right:
All keepe the broad high way, and take de-
    light
With many rather for to goe astray,
And be partakers of their evill plight,
Then with a few to walke the rightest way.
O foolish men! why hast ye to your owne
    decay?'

XI

'Thy selfe to see, and tyred limbes to rest,
O matrone sage,' quoth she, 'I hether
    came,
And this good knight his way with me ad-
    drest,
Ledd with thy prayses and broad-blazed
    fame,
That up to heven is blowne.' The auncient
    dame

Him goodly greeted in her modest guyse,
And enterteynd them both, as best became,
With all the court'sies that she could de-
    vyse,
Ne wanted ought, to shew her bounteous
    or wise.

XII

Thus as they gan of sondrie thinges devise,
Loe! two most goodly virgins came in place,
Ylinked arme in arme in lovely wise;
With countenance demure, and modest
    grace,
They numbred even steps and equall pace:
Of which the eldest, that Fidelia hight,
Like sunny beames threw from her christall
    face,
That could have dazd the rash beholders
    sight,
And round about her head did shine like
    hevens light.

XIII

She was araied all in lilly white,
And in her right hand bore a cup of gold,
With wine and water fild up to the hight,
In which a serpent did himselfe enfold,
That horrour made to all that did behold;
But she no whitt did chaunge her constant
    mood:
And in her other hand she fast did hold
A booke that was both signd and seald with
    blood,
Wherin darke things were writt, hard to
    be understood.

XIV

Her younger sister, that Speranza hight,
Was clad in blew, that her beseemed well:
Not all so chearefull seemed she of sight,
As was her sister; whether dread did dwell,
Or anguish, in her hart, is hard to tell:
Upon her arme a silver anchor lay,
Whereon she leaned ever, as befell:
And ever up to heven, as she did pray,
Her stedfast eyes were bent, ne swarved
    other way.

XV

They, seeing Una, towardes her gan wend,
Who them encounters with like courtesee;
Many kind speeches they betweene them
    spend,
And greatly joy each other well to see:
Then to the knight with shamefast modestie

They turne themselves, at Unaes meeke request,
And him salute with well beseeming glee;
Who faire them quites, as him beseemed
best,
And goodly gan discourse of many a noble
gest.

XVI

Then Una thus: ' But she your sister deare,
The deare Charissa, where is she become ?
Or wants she health, or busie is elswhere ? '
' Ah no,' said they, ' but forth she may not
come:
For she of late is lightned of her wombe,
And hath encreast the world with one sonne
more,
That her to see should be but troublesome.'
' Indeed,' quoth she, ' that should her
trouble sore;
But thankt be God, and her encrease so
evermore.'

XVII

Then saide the aged Cœlia: ' Deare dame,
And you, good sir, I wote that of youre
toyle
And labors long, through which ye hether
came,
Ye both forwearied be: therefore a whyle
I read you rest, and to your bowres re-
coyle.'
Then called she a groome, that forth him
ledd
Into a goodly lodge, and gan despoile
Of puissant armes, and laid in easie bedd:
His name was meeke Obedience rightfully
aredd.

XVIII

Now when their wearie limbes with kindly
rest,
And bodies were refresht with dew repast,
Fayre Una gan Fidelia fayre request,
To have her knight into her schoolehous
plaste,
That of her heavenly learning he might
taste,
And heare the wisedom of her wordes di-
vine.
She graunted, and that knight so much
agraste,
That she him taught celestiall discipline,
And opened his dull eyes, that light mote
in them shine.

XIX

And that her sacred Booke, with blood
ywritt,
That none could reade, except she did them
teach,
She unto him disclosed every whitt,
And heavenly documents thereout did
preach,
That weaker witt of man could never reach,
Of God, of grace, of justice, of free will,
That wonder was to heare her goodly
speach:
For she was hable with her wordes to kill,
And rayse againe to life the hart that she
did thrill.

XX

And when she list poure out her larger
spright,
She would commaund the hasty sunne to
stay,
Or backward turne his course from hevens
hight:
Sometimes great hostes of men she could
dismay;
Dry-shod to passe, she parts the flouds in
tway;
And eke huge mountaines from their native
seat
She would commaund, themselves to beare
away,
And throw in raging sea with roaring threat:
Almightie God her gave such powre and
puissaunce great.

XXI

The faithfull knight now grew in litle
space,
By hearing her, and by her sisters lore,
To such perfection of all hevenly grace,
That wretched world he gan for to abhore,
And mortall life gan loath, as thing forlore,
Greevd with remembrance of his wicked
wayes,
And prickt with anguish of his sinnes so
sore,
That he desirde to end his wretched dayes:
So much the dart of sinfull guilt the soule
dismayes.

XXII

But wise Speranza gave him comfort sweet,
And taught him how to take assured hold
Upon her silver anchor, as was meet;
Els had his sinnes so great and manifold

Made him forget all that Fidelia told.
In this distressed doubtfull agony,
When him his dearest Una did behold,
Disdeining life, desiring leave to dye,
She found her selfe assayld with great per-
    plexity:

XXIII

And came to Cœlia to declare her smart;
Who, well acquainted with that commune
    plight,
Which sinfull horror workes in wounded
    hart,
Her wisely comforted all that she might,
With goodly counsell and advisement right;
And streightway sent with carefull dili-
    gence,
To fetch a leach, the which had great in-
    sight
In that disease of grieved conscience,
And well could cure the same: his name was
    Patience.

XXIV

Who, comming to that sowle-diseased
    knight,
Could hardly him intreat to tell his grief:
Which knowne, and all that noyd his heavie
    spright
Well searcht, eftsoones he gan apply relief
Of salves and med'cines, which had passing
    prief,
And there to added wordes of wondrous
    might:
By which to ease he him recured brief,
And much aswag'd the passion of his plight,
That he his paine endur'd, as seeming now
    more light.

XXV

But yet the cause and root of all his ill,
Inward corruption and infected sin,
Not purg'd nor heald, behind remained still,
And festring sore did ranckle yett within,
Close creeping twixt the marow and the
    skin.
Which to extirpe, he laid him privily
Downe in a darksome lowly place far in,
Whereas he meant his corrosives to apply,
And with streight diet tame his stubborne
    malady.

XXVI

In ashes and sackcloth he did array
His daintie corse, proud humors to abate,
And dieted with fasting every day,
The swelling of his woundes to mitigate,
And made him pray both earely and eke
    late:
And ever as superfluous flesh did rott,
Amendment readie still at hand did wayt,
To pluck it out with pincers fyrie whott,
That soone in him was lefte no one cor-
    rupted jott.

XXVII

And bitter Penaunce, with an yron whip,
Was wont him once to disple every day:
And sharpe Remorse his hart did prick
    and nip,
That drops of blood thence like a well did
    play:
And sad Repentance used to embay
His body in salt water smarting sore,
The filthy blottes of sin to wash away.
So in short space they did to health re-
    store
The man that would not live, but erst lay
    at deathes dore.

XXVIII

In which his torment often was so great,
That like a lyon he would cry and rore,
And rend his flesh, and his owne synewes
    eat.
His owne deare Una, hearing evermore
His ruefull shriekes and gronings, often
    tore
Her guiltlesse garments and her golden
    heare,
For pitty of his payne and anguish sore;
Yet all with patience wisely she did beare;
For well she wist, his cryme could els be
    never cleare.

XXIX

Whom, thus recover'd by wise Patience
And trew Repentaunce, they to Una
    brought;
Who, joyous of his cured conscience,
Him dearely kist, and fayrely eke be-
    sought
Himselfe to chearish, and consuming
    thought
To put away out of his carefull brest.
By this Charissa, late in child-bed brought,
Was woxen strong, and left her fruitfull
    nest;
To her fayre Una brought this unac-
    quainted guest.

XXX

She was a woman in her freshest age,
Of wondrous beauty, and of bounty rare,
With goodly grace and comely personage,
That was on earth not easie to compare;
Full of great love, but Cupids wanton snare
As hell she hated, chaste in worke and will;
Her necke and brests were ever open bare,
That ay thereof her babes might sucke their
    fill:
The rest was all in yellow robes arayed still.

XXXI

A multitude of babes about her hong,
Playing their sportes, that joyd her to be-
    hold;
Whom still she fed, whiles they were weak
    and young,
But thrust them forth still, as they wexed
    old:
And on her head she wore a tyre of gold,
Adornd with gemmes and owches won-
    drous fayre,
Whose passing price uneath was to be told;
And by her syde there sate a gentle payre
Of turtle doves, she sitting in an yvory
    chayre.

XXXII

The knight and Una, entring, fayre her
    greet,
And bid her joy of that her happy brood;
Who them requites with court'sies seeming
    meet,
And entertaynes with friendly chearefull
    mood.
Then Una her besought, to be so good
As in her vertuous rules to schoole her
    knight,
Now after all his torment well withstood,
In that sad house of Penaunce, where his
    spright
Had past the paines of hell and long endur-
    ing night.

XXXIII

She was right joyous of her just request,
And taking by the hand that Faeries sonne,
Gan him instruct in everie good behest,
Of love, and righteousnes, and well to
    donne,
And wrath and hatred warely to shonne,
That drew on men Gods hatred and his
    wrath,
And many soules in dolours had fordonne:

In which when him she well instructed
    hath,
From thence to heaven she teacheth him
    the ready path.

XXXIV

Wherein his weaker wandring steps to
    guyde,
An aunciernt matrone she to her does call,
Whose sober lookes her wisedome well
    descryde:
Her name was Mercy, well knowne over all
To be both gratious and eke liberall:
To whom the carefull charge of him she
    gave,
To leade aright, that he should never fall
In all his waies through this wide worldes
    wave,
That Mercy in the end his righteous soule
    might save.

XXXV

The godly matrone by the hand him beares
Forth from her presence, by a narrow way,
Scattred with bushy thornes and ragged
    breares,
Which still before him she remov'd away,
That nothing might his ready passage stay:
And ever when his feet encombred were,
Or gan to shrinke, or from the right to
    stray,
She held him fast, and firmely did upbeare,
As carefull nourse her child from falling
    oft does reare.

XXXVI

Eftsoones unto an holy hospitall,
That was foreby the way, she did him
    bring,
In which seven bead-men, that had vowed
    all
Their life to service of high heavens King,
Did spend their daies in doing godly thing:
Their gates to all were open evermore,
That by the wearie way were traveiling,
And one sate wayting ever them before,
To call in commers by, that needy were
    and pore.

XXXVII

The first of them, that eldest was and best,
Of all the house had charge and governe-
    ment,
As guardian and steward of the rest:
His office was to give entertainement

And lodging unto all that came and went:
Not unto such, as could him feast againe,
And double quite for that he on them spent,
But such as want of harbour did constraine:
Those for Gods sake his dewty was to
  entertaine.

XXXVIII

The second was as almner of the place:
His office was, the hungry for to feed,
And thristy give to drinke, a worke of grace:
He feard not once him selfe to be in need,
Ne car'd to hoord for those whom he did
  breede:
The grace of God he layd up still in store,
Which as a stocke he left unto his seede;
He had enough; what need him care for
  more?
And had he lesse, yet some he would give
  to the pore.

XXXIX

The third had of their wardrobe custody,
In which were not rich tyres, nor garments
  gay,
The plumes of pride, and winges of vanity,
But clothes meet to keepe keene cold away,
And naked nature seemely to aray;
With which bare wretched wights he dayly
  clad,
The images of God in earthly clay;
And if that no spare clothes to give he had,
His owne cote he would cut, and it dis-
  tribute glad.

XL

The fourth appointed by his office was,
Poore prisoners to relieve with gratious ayd,
And captives to redeeme with price of bras,
From Turkes and Sarazins, which them had
  stayd;
And though they faulty were, yet well he
  wayd,
That God to us forgiveth every howre
Much more then that, why they in bands
  were layd,
And He, that harrowd hell with heavie
  stowre,
The faulty soules from thence brought to
  his heavenly bowre.

XLI

The fift had charge sick persons to attend,
And comfort those, in point of death which
  lay;

For them most needeth comfort in the end,
When sin, and hell, and death doe most
  dismay
The feeble soule departing hence away.
All is but lost, that living we bestow,
If not well ended at our dying day.
O man, have mind of that last bitter throw;
For as the tree does fall, so lyes it ever
  low.

XLII

The sixt had charge of them now being
  dead,
In seemely sort their corses to engrave,
And deck with dainty flowres their brydall
  bed,
That to their heavenly spouse both sweet
  and brave
They might appeare, when he their soules
  shall save.
The wondrous workmanship of Gods owne
  mould,
Whose face He made, all beastes to feare,
  and gave
All in his hand, even dead we honour should.
Ah! dearest God me graunt, I dead be not
  defould.

XLIII

The seventh, now after death and buriall
  done,
Had charge the tender orphans of the dead
And wydowes ayd, least they should be un-
  done:
In face of judgement he their right would
  plead,
Ne ought the powre of mighty men did
  dread
In their defence, nor would for gold or fee
Be wonne their rightfull causes downe to
  tread:
And when they stood in most necessitee,
He did supply their want, and gave them
  ever free.

XLIV

There when the Elfin knight arrived was,
The first and chiefest of the seven, whose
  care
Was guests to welcome, towardes him did
  pas:
Where seeing Mercie, that his steps upbare
And alwaies led, to her with reverence rare
He humbly louted in meeke lowlinesse,
And seemely welcome for her did prepare:

For of their order she was patronesse,
Albe Charissa were their chiefest founder-
esse.

XLV

There she awhile him stayes, him selfe to
rest,
That to the rest more hable he might bee:
During which time, in every good behest
And godly worke of almes and charitee
Shee him instructed with great industree:
Shortly therein so perfect he became,
That, from the first unto the last degree,
His mortall life he learned had to frame
In holy righteousnesse, without rebuke or
blame.

XLVI

Thence forward by that painfull way they
pas,
Forth to an hill, that was both steepe and
hy;
On top whereof a sacred chappell was,
And eke a litle hermitage thereby,
Wherein an aged holy man did lie,
That day and night said his devotion,
Ne other worldly busines did apply:
His name was Hevenly Contemplation;
Of God and goodnes was his meditation.

XLVII

Great grace that old man to him given had;
For God he often saw from heavens hight,
All were his earthly eien both blunt and
bad,
And through great age had lost their kindly
sight,
Yet wondrous quick and persaunt was his
spright,
As eagles eie, that can behold the sunne.
That hill they scale with all their powre
and might,
That his fraile thighes, nigh weary and for-
donne,
Gan faile; but by her helpe the top at last
he wonne.

XLVIII

There they doe finde that godly aged sire,
With snowy lockes adowne his shoulders
shed,
As hoary frost with spangles doth attire
The mossy braunches of an oke halfe ded.
Each bone might through his body well be
red,

And every sinew seene, through his long
fast:
For nought he car'd his carcas long unfed;
His mind was full of spirituall repast,
And pyn'd his flesh, to keepe his body low
and chast.

XLIX

Who, when these two approching he aspide,
At their first presence grew agrieved sore,
That forst him lay his hevenly thoughts
aside;
And had he not that dame respected more,
Whom highly he did reverence and adore,
He would not once have moved for the
knight.
They him saluted, standing far afore;
Who, well them greeting, humbly did re-
quight,
And asked, to what end they clomb that
tedious hight.

L

'What end,' quoth she, 'should cause us
take such paine,
But that same end, which every living
wight
Should make his marke, high heaven to
attaine?
Is not from hence the way, that leadeth
right
To that most glorious house, that glistreth
bright
With burning starres and everliving fire,
Whereof the keies are to thy hand behight
By wise Fidelia? Shee doth thee require,
To shew it to this knight, according his
desire.'

LI

'Thrise happy man,' said then the father
grave,
'Whose staggering steps thy steady hand
doth lead,
And shewes the way, his sinfull soule to
save!
Who better can the way to heaven aread
Then thou thy selfe, that was both borne
and bred
In hevenly throne, where thousand angels
shine?
Thou doest the praiers of the righteous sead
Present before the Majesty Divine,
And His avenging wrath to clemency in-
cline.

LII

'Yet, since thou bidst, thy pleasure shalbe
    donne.
Then come, thou man of earth, and see the
    way,
That never yet was seene of Faries sonne,
That never leads the traveiler astray,
But, after labors long and sad delay,
Brings them to joyous rest and endlesse
    blis.
But first thou must a season fast and pray,
Till from her bands the spright assoiled is,
And have her strength recur'd from fraile
    infirmitis.'

LIII

That done, he leads him to the highest
    mount;
Such one, as that same mighty man of God,
That blood-red billowes like a walled front
On either side disparted with his rod,
Till that his army dry-foot through them
    yod,
Dwelt forty daies upon; where writt in
    stone
With bloody letters by the hand of God,
The bitter doome of death and balefull
    mone
He did receive, whiles flashing fire about
    him shone.

LIV

Or like that sacred hill, whose head full
    hie,
Adornd with fruitfull olives all arownd,
Is, as it were for endlesse memory
Of that deare Lord, who oft thereon was
    fownd,
For ever with a flowring girlond crownd:
Or like that pleasaunt mount, that is for ay
Through famous poets verse each where
    renownd,
On which the thrise three learned ladies
    play
Their hevenly notes, and make full many a
    lovely lay.

LV

From thence, far off he unto him did shew
A litle path, that was both steepe and long,
Which to a goodly citty led his vew;
Whose wals and towres were builded high
    and strong
Of perle and precious stone, that earthly
    tong

LVI

Cannot describe, nor wit of man can tell;
Too high a ditty for my simple song:
The Citty of the Greate King hight it well,
Wherein eternall peace and happinesse doth
    dwell.

LVI

As he thereon stood gazing, he might see
The blessed angels to and fro descend
From highest heven, in gladsome companee,
And with great joy into that citty wend,
As commonly as frend does with his frend.
Whereat he wondred much, and gan en-
    quere,
What stately building durst so high extend
Her lofty towres unto the starry sphere,
And what unknowen nation there empeopled
    were.

LVII

'Faire knight,' quoth he, 'Hierusalem that
    is,
The New Hierusalem, that God has built
For those to dwell in, that are chosen his,
His chosen people purg'd from sinful guilt,
With pretious blood, which cruelly was
    spilt
On cursed tree, of that unspotted Lam,
That for the sinnes of al the world was kilt:
Now are they saints all in that citty sam,
More dear unto their God, then younglings
    to their dam.'

LVIII

'Till now,' said then the knight, 'I weened
    well,
That great Cleopolis, where I have beene,
In which that fairest Fary Queene doth
    dwell,
The fairest citty was, that might be seene;
And that bright towre all built of christall
    clene,
Panthea, seemd the brightest thing that
    was:
But now by proofe all otherwise I weene;
For this great citty that does far surpas,
And this bright angels towre quite dims
    that towre of glas.'

LIX

'Most trew,' then said the holy aged man;
'Yet is Cleopolis, for earthly frame,
The fairest peece that eie beholden can:
And well beseemes all knights of noble
    name,

That covett in th' immortall booke of fame
To be eternized, that same to haunt,
And doen their service to that soveraigne
    dame,
That glory does to them for guerdon graunt:
For she is hevenly borne, and heaven may
    justly vaunt.

LX

'And thou, faire ymp, sprong out from
    English race,
How ever now accompted Elfins sonne,
Well worthy doest thy service for her grace,
To aide a virgin desolate foredonne.
But when thou famous victory hast wonne,
And high emongst all knights hast hong thy
    shield,
Thenceforth the suitt of earthly conquest
    shonne,
And wash thy hands from guilt of bloody
    field:
For blood can nought but sin, and wars but
    sorrows yield.

LXI

'Then seek this path, that I to thee presage,
Which after all to heaven shall thee send;
Then peaceably thy painefull pilgrimage
To yonder same Hierusalem doe bend,
Where is for thee ordaind a blessed end:
For thou, emongst those saints whom thou
    doest see,
Shalt be a saint, and thine owne nations
    frend
And patrone: thou *Saint George* shalt
    called bee,
Saint George of mery *England*, the signe
    of victoree.'

LXII

'Unworthy wretch,' quoth he, 'of so great
    grace,
How dare I thinke such glory to attaine?'
'These, that have it attaynd, were in like
    cace,'
Quoth he, 'as wretched, and liv'd in like
    paine.'
'But deeds of armes must I at last be faine
And ladies love to leave, so dearely bought?'
'What need of armes, where peace doth ay
    remaine,'
Said he, 'and battailes none are to be
    fought?
As for loose loves, they' are vaine, and
    vanish into nought.'

LXIII

'O let me not,' quoth he, 'then turne againe
Backe to the world, whose joyes so fruitlesse
    are,
But let me heare for aie in peace remaine,
Or streight way on that last long voiage
    fare,
That nothing may my present hope empare.'
'That may not be,' said he, 'ne maist thou
    yitt
Forgoe that royal maides bequeathed care,
Who did her cause into thy hand committ,
Till from her cursed foe thou have her
    freely quitt.'

LXIV

'Then shall I soone,' quoth he, 'so God me
    grace,
Abett that virgins cause disconsolate,
And shortly back returne unto this place,
To walke this way in pilgrims poore estate.
But now aread, old father, why of late
Didst thou behight me borne of English
    blood,
Whom all a Faeries sonne doen nominate?'
'That word shall I,' said he, 'avouchen
    good,
Sith to thee is unknowne the cradle of thy
    brood.

LXV

'For well I wote, thou springst from ancient
    race
Of Saxon kinges, that have with mightie
    hand
And many bloody battailes fought in place
High reard their royall throne in Britane
    land,
And vanquisht them, unable to withstand:
From thence a Faery thee unweeting reft,
There as thou slepst in tender swadling
    band,
And her base Elfin brood there for thee
    left:
Such men do chaungelings call, so chaungd
    by Faeries theft.

LXVI

'Thence she thee brought into this Faery
    lond,
And in an heaped furrow did thee hyde;
Where thee a ploughman all unweeting
    fond,
As he his toylesome teme that way did
    guyde,

And brought thee up in ploughmans state
        to byde,
Whereof Georgos he thee gave to name;
Till prickt with courage, and thy forces
        pryde,
To Fary court thou cam'st to seeke for
        fame,
And prove thy puissaunt armes, as seemes
        thee best became.'

LXVII

' O holy sire,' quoth he, ' how shall I quight
The many favours I with thee have fownd,
That hast my name and nation redd aright,
And taught the way that does to heaven
        bownd ? '
This saide, adowne he looked to the grownd,
To have returnd, but dazed were his eyne,
Through passing brightnes, which did quite
        confound
His feeble sence, and too exceeding shyne:
So darke are earthly thinges compard to
        things divine.

LXVIII

At last, whenas himselfe he gan to fynd,
To Una back he cast him to retyre;
Who him awaited still with pensive mynd.
Great thankes and goodly meed to that
        good syre
He thens departing gave, for his paynes
        hyre.
So came to Una, who him joyd to see,
And after litle rest, gan him desyre,
Of her adventure myndfull for to bee.
So leave they take of Cœlia and her daugh-
        ters three.

CANTO XI

The knight with that old Dragon fights
Two dayes incessantly :
The third, him overthrowes, and gayns
Most glorious victory.

I

HIGH time now gan it wex for Una fayre
To thinke of those her captive parents deare,
And their forwasted kingdom to repayre:
Whereto whenas they now approched neare,
With hartie wordes her knight she gan to
        cheare,
And in her modest maner thus bespake:
' Deare knight, as deare as ever knight was
        deare,

That all these sorrowes suffer for my sake,
High heven behold the tedious toyle, ye for
        me take.

II

' Now are we come unto my native soyle,
And to the place, where all our perilles
        dwell;
Here hauntes that feend, and does his dayly
        spoyle;
Therefore henceforth bee at your keeping
        well,
And ever ready for your foeman fell.
The sparke of noble corage now awake,
And strive your excellent selfe to excell;
That shall ye evermore renowmed make
Above all knights on earth, that batteill
        undertake.'

III

And pointing forth, ' Lo ! yonder is,' said
        she,
' The brasen towre, in which my parents
        deare
For dread of that huge feend emprisond be;
Whom I from far see on the walles appeare,
Whose sight my feeble soule doth greatly
        cheare:
And on the top of all I do espye
The watchman wayting tydings glad to
        heare;
That, O my parents, might I happily
Unto you bring, to ease you of your misery!'

IV

With that they heard a roaring hideous
        sownd,
That all the ayre with terror filled wyde,
And seemd uneath to shake the stedfast
        ground.
Eftsoones that dreadfull dragon they espyde,
Where stretcht he lay upon the sunny side
Of a great hill, himselfe like a great hill.
But all so soone as he from far descryde
Those glistring armes, that heven with
        light did fill,
He rousd himselfe full blyth, and hastned
        them untill.

V

Then badd the knight his lady yede aloof,
And to an hill her selfe withdraw asyde,
From whence she might behold that bat-
        tailles proof,
And eke be safe from daunger far descryde:

She him obayd, and turnd a litle wyde.
Now, O thou sacred Muse, most learned
    dame,
Fayre ympe of Phœbus, and his aged bryde,
The nourse of time and everlasting fame,
That warlike handes ennoblest with im-
    mortall name;

VI

O gently come into my feeble brest,
Come gently, but not with that mightie rage,
Wherewith the martiall troupes thou doest
    infest,
And hartes of great heroës doest enrage,
That nought their kindled corage may
    aswage:
Soone as thy dreadfull trompe begins to
    sownd,
The god of warre with his fiers equipage
Thou doest awake, sleepe never he so sownd,
And scared nations doest with horror sterne
    astownd.

VII

Fayre goddesse, lay that furious fitt asyde,
Till I of warres and bloody Mars doe sing,
And Bryton fieldes with Sarazin blood be-
    dyde,
Twixt that great Faery Queene and Paynim
    King,
That with their horror heven and earth did
    ring,
A worke of labour long, and endlesse
    prayse:
But now a while lett downe that haughtie
    string,
And to my tunes thy second tenor rayse,
That I this man of God his godly armes
    may blaze.

VIII

By this the dreadfull beast drew nigh to
    hand,
Halfe flying and halfe footing in his haste,
That with his largenesse measured much
    land,
And made wide shadow under his huge
    waste;
As mountaine doth the valley overcaste.
Approching nigh, he reared high afore
His body monstrous, horrible, and vaste,
Which, to increase his wondrous greatnes
    more,
Was swoln with wrath, and poyson, and with
    bloody gore.

IX

And over, all with brasen scales was armd,
Like plated cote of steele, so couched neare,
That nought mote perce, ne might his corse
    bee harmd
With dint of swerd, nor push of pointed
    speare:
Which as an eagle, seeing pray appeare,
His aery plumes doth rouze, full rudely
    dight,
So shaked he, that horror was to heare:
For as the clashing of an armor bright,
Such noyse his rouzed scales did send unto
    the knight.

X

His flaggy winges, when forth he did dis-
    play,
Were like two sayles, in which the hollow
    wynd
Is gathered full, and worketh speedy way:
And eke the pennes, that did his pineons
    bynd,
Were like mayne-yardes, with flying canvas
    lynd,
With which whenas him list the ayre to
    beat,
And there by force unwonted passage fynd,
The clowdes before him fledd for terror
    great,
And all the hevens stood still, amazed with
    his threat.

XI

His huge long tayle, wownd up in hundred
    foldes,
Does overspred his long bras-scaly back,
Whose wreathed boughtes when ever he
    unfoldes,
And thick entangled knots adown does
    slack,
Bespotted as with shieldes of red and blacke,
It sweepeth all the land behind him farre,
And of three furlongs does but litle lacke;
And at the point two stinges in fixed arre,
Both deadly sharp, that sharpest steele ex-
    ceeden farr.

XII

But stinges and sharpest steele did far ex-
    ceed
The sharpnesse of his cruel rending clawes:
Dead was it sure, as sure as death in deed,
What ever thing does touch his ravenous
    pawes.

Or what within his reach he ever drawes.
But his most hideous head my tongue to
　　tell
Does tremble; for his deepe devouring
　　jawes
Wyde gaped, like the griesly mouth of
　　hell,
Through which into his darke abysse all
　　ravin fell.

XIII

And, that more wondrous was, in either
　　jaw
Threeranckes of yron teeth enraunged
　　were,
In which yett trickling blood and gobbets
　　raw
Of late devoured bodies did appeare,
That sight thereof bredd cold congealed
　　feare:
Which to increase, and all atonce to kill,
A cloud of smoothering smoke and sulphure
　　seare
Out of his stinking gorge forth steemed
　　still,
That all the ayre about with smoke and
　　stench did fill.

XIV

His blazing eyes, like two bright shining
　　shieldes,
Did burne with wrath, and sparkled living
　　fyre;
As two broad beacons, sett in open fieldes,
Send forth their flames far of to every
　　shyre,
And warning give, that enimies conspyre
With fire and sword the region to invade;
So flam'd his eyne with rage and rancorous
　　yre:
But far within, as in a hollow glade,
Those glaring lampes were sett, that made
　　a dreadfull shade.

XV

So dreadfully he towardes him did pas,
Forelifting up a loft his speckled brest,
And often bounding on the brused gras,
As for great joyaunce of his newcome
　　guest.
Eftsoones he gan advaunce his haughty
　　crest,
As chauffed bore his bristles doth upreare,
And shoke his scales to battaile ready
　　drest,

That made the Redcrosse Knight nigh
　　quake for feare,
As bidding bold defyaunce to his foeman
　　neare.

XVI

The knight gan fayrely couch his steady
　　speare,
And fiersely ran at him with rigorous
　　might:
The pointed steele, arriving rudely theare,
His harder hyde would nether perce nor
　　bight,
But, glauncing by, foorth passed forward
　　right:
Yet, sore amoved with so puissant push,
The wrathfull beast about him turned light,
And him so rudely, passing by, did brush
With his long tayle, that horse and man to
　　ground did rush.

XVII

Both horse and man up lightly rose againe,
And fresh encounter towardes him addrest:
But th' ydle stroke yet backe recoyld in
　　vaine,
And found no place his deadly point to rest.
Exceeding rage enflam'd the furious beast,
To be avenged of so great despight;
For never felt his imperceable brest
So wondrous force from hand of living
　　wight;
Yet had he prov'd the powre of many a
　　puissant knight.

XVIII

Then, with his waving wings displayed
　　wyde,
Himselfe up high he lifted from the ground,
And with strong flight did forcibly divyde
The yielding ayre, which nigh too feeble
　　found
Her flitting parts, and element unsound,
To beare so great a weight: he, cutting
　　way
With his broad sayles, about him soared
　　round;
At last, low stouping with unweldy sway,
Snatcht up both horse and man, to beare
　　them quite away.

XIX

Long he them bore above the subject
　　plaine,
So far as ewghen bow a shaft may send,

Till struggling strong did him at last con-
    straine
To let them downe before his flightes end:
As hagard hauke, presuming to contend
With hardy fowle, above his hable might,
His wearie pounces all in vaine doth spend
To trusse the pray too heavy for his flight;
Which, comming down to ground, does free
    it selfe by fight.

XX

He so disseized of his gryping grosse,
The knight his thrillant speare againe
    assayd
In his bras-plated body to embosse,
And three mens strength unto the stroake
    he layd;
Wherewith the stiffe beame quaked, as
    affrayd,
And glauncing from his scaly necke, did
    glyde
Close under his left wing, then broad dis-
    playd.
The percing steele there wrought a wound
    full wyde,
That with the uncouth smart the monster
    lowdly cryde.

XXI

He cryde, as raging seas are wont to rore,
When wintry storme his wrathful wreck
    does threat;
The rolling billowes beat the ragged shore,
As they the earth would shoulder from her
    seat,
And greedy gulfe does gape, as he would
    eat
His neighbour element in his revenge:
Then gin the blustring brethren boldly threat,
To move the world from off his stedfast
    henge,
And boystrous battaile make, each other to
    avenge.

XXII

The steely head stuck fast still in his flesh,
Till with his cruell clawes he snatcht the
    wood,
And quite a sunder broke. Forth flowed
    fresh
A gushing river of blacke gory blood,
That drowned all the land, whereon he
    stood:
The streame thereof would drive a water-
    mill.

Trebly augmented was his furious mood
With bitter sence of his deepe rooted ill,
That flames of fire he threw forth from
    his large nosethril.

XXIII

His hideous tayle then hurled he about,
And therewith all enwrapt the nimble
    thyes
Of his froth-fomy steed, whose courage
    stout
Striving to loose the knott, that fast him
    tyes,
Himselfe in streighter bandes too rash im-
    plyes,
That to the ground he is perforce con-
    straynd
To throw his ryder: who can quickly ryse
From of the earth, with durty blood dis-
    taynd,
For that reprochfull fall right fowly he
    disdaynd.

XXIV

And fercely tooke his trenchand blade in
    hand,
With which he stroke so furious and so
    fell,
That nothing seemd the puissaunce could
    withstand:
Upon his crest the hardned yron fell;
But his more hardned crest was armd so
    well,
That deeper dint therein it would not make;
Yet so extremely did the buffe him quell;
That from thenceforth he shund the like to
    take,
But, when he saw them come, he did them
    still forsake.

XXV

The knight was wroth to see his stroke be-
    guyld,
And smot againe with more outrageous
    might;
But backe againe the sparcling steele re-
    coyld,
And left not any marke where it did light,
As if in adamant rocke it had beene pight.
The beast, impatient of his smarting wound,
And of so fierce and forcible despight,
Thought with his winges to stye above the
    ground;
But his late wounded wing unserviceable
    found.

XXVI

Then, full of griefe and anguish vehement,
He lowdly brayd, that like was never heard,
And from his wide devouring oven sent
A flake of fire, that, flashing in his beard,
Him all amazd, and almost made afeard:
The scorching flame sore swinged all his
    face,
And through his armour all his body seard,
That he could not endure so cruell cace,
But thought his armes to leave, and helmet
    to unlace.

XXVII

Not that great champion of the antique
    world,
Whom famous poetes verse so much doth
    vaunt,
And hath for twelve huge labours high ex-
    told,
So many furies and sharpe fits did haunt,
When him the poysoned garment did en-
    chaunt,
With Centaures blood and bloody verses
    charmd,
As did this knight twelve thousand dolours
    daunt,
Whom fyrie steele now burnt, that erst him
    armd,
That erst him goodly armd, now most of
    all him harmd.

XXVIII

Faynt, wearie, sore, emboyled, grieved,
    brent
With heat, toyle, wounds, armes, smart,
    and inward fire,
That never man such mischiefes did tor-
    ment;
Death better were, death did he oft desire,
But death will never come, when needes
    require.
Whom so dismayd when that his foe be-
    held,
He cast to suffer him no more respire,
But gan his sturdy sterne about to weld,
And him so strongly stroke, that to the
    ground him feld.

XXIX

It fortuned (as fayre it then befell,)
Behynd his backe, unweeting, where he
    stood,
Of auncient time there was a springing well,
From which fast trickled forth a silver flood,
Full of great vertues, and for med'cine
    good.
Whylome, before that cursed dragon got
That happy land, and all with innocent
    blood
Defyld those sacred waves, it rightly hot
The Well of Life, ne yet his vertues had
    forgot.

XXX

For unto life the dead it could restore,
And guilt of sinfull crimes cleane wash
    away;
Those that with sicknesse were infected
    sore
It could recure, and aged long decay
Renew, as one were borne that very day.
Both Silo this, and Jordan, did excell,
And th' English Bath, and eke the German
    Spau,
Ne can Cephise, nor Hebrus match this
    well:
Into the same the knight back overthrowen
    fell.

XXXI

Now gan the golden Phœbus for to steepe
His fierie face in billowes of the west,
And his faint steedes watred in ocean deepe,
Whiles from their journall labours they did
    rest,
When that infernall monster, having kest
His wearie foe into that living well,
Can high advaunce his broad discoloured
    brest
Above his wonted pitch, with countenance
    fell,
And clapt his yron wings, as victor he did
    dwell.

XXXII

Which when his pensive lady saw from
    farre,
Great woe and sorrow did her soule assay,
As weening that the sad end of the warre,
And gan to highest God entirely pray,
That feared chaunce from her to turne
    away:
With folded hands, and knees full lowly
    bent,
All night shee watcht, ne once adowne
    would lay
Her dainty limbs in her sad dreriment,
But praying still did wake, and waking did
    lament.

XXXIII

The morrow next gan earely to appeare,
That Titan rose to runne his daily race;
But earely, ere the morrow next gan reare
Out of the sea faire Titans deawy face,
Up rose the gentle virgin from her place,
And looked all about, if she might spy
Her loved knight to move his manly pace:
For she had great doubt of his safety,
Since late she saw him fall before his enimy.

XXXIV

At last she saw, where he upstarted brave
Out of the well, wherein he drenched lay:
As eagle fresh out of the ocean wave,
Where he hath lefte his plumes all hory
gray,
And deckt himselfe with fethers youthly
gay,
Like eyas hauke up mounts unto the skies,
His newly budded pineons to assay,
And merveiles at him selfe, stil as he flies:
So new this new-borne knight to battell new
did rise.

XXXV

Whom when the damned feend so fresh
did spy,
No wonder if he wondred at the sight,
And doubted, whether his late enimy
It were, or other new supplied knight.
He, now to prove his late renewed might,
High brandishing his bright deaw-burning
blade,
Upon his crested scalp so sore did smite,
That to the scull a yawning wound it made:
The deadly dint his dulled sences all dis-
maid.

XXXVI

I wote not whether the revenging steele
Were hardned with that holy water dew,
Wherein he fell, or sharper edge did feele,
Or his baptized hands now greater grew,
Or other secret vertue did ensew;
Els never could the force of fleshly arme,
Ne molten mettall, in his blood embrew:
For till that stownd could never wight him
harme,
By subtilty, nor slight, nor might, nor
mighty charme.

XXXVII

The cruell wound enraged him so sore,
That loud he yelled for exceeding paine;

As hundred ramping lions seemd to rore,
Whom ravenous hunger did thereto con-
straine:
Then gan he tosse aloft his stretched traine,
And therewith scourge the buxome aire so
sore,
That to his force to yielden it was faine;
Ne ought his sturdy strokes might stand
afore,
That high trees overthrew, and rocks in
peeces tore.

XXXVIII

The same advauncing high above his head,
With sharpe intended sting so rude him
smott,
That to the earth him drove, as stricken
dead,
Ne living wight would have him life behott:
The mortall sting his angry needle shott
Quite through his shield, and in his shoulder
seasd,
Where fast it stucke, ne would thereout be
gott:
The griefe thereof him wondrous sore dis-
easd,
Ne might his rancling paine with patience
be appeasd.

XXXIX

But yet more mindfull of his honour deare
Then of the grievous smart, which him did
wring,
From loathed soile he can him lightly reare,
And strove to loose the far in fixed sting:
Which when in vaine he tryde with strug-
geling,
Inflam'd with wrath, his raging blade he
hefte,
And strooke so strongly, that the knotty
string
Of his huge taile he quite a sonder clefte;
Five joints thereof he hewd, and but the
stump him lefte.

XL

Hart cannot thinke, what outrage and what
cries,
With fowle enfouldred smoake and flashing
fire,
The hell-bred beast threw forth unto the
skies,
That all was covered with darknesse dire:
Then fraught with rancour, and engorged
yre,

He cast at once him to avenge for all,
And gathering up himselfe out of the mire
With his uneven wings, did fiercely fall
Upon his sunne-bright shield, and grypt it
fast withall.

XLI

Much was the man encombred with his
hold,
In feare to lose his weapon in his paw,
Ne wist yett how his talaunts to unfold;
For harder was from Cerberus greedy jaw
To plucke a bone, then from his cruell claw
To reave by strength the griped gage away:
Thrise he assayd it from his foote to draw,
And thrise in vaine to draw it did assay;
It booted nought to thinke to robbe him of
his pray.

XLII

Tho, when he saw no power might prevaile,
His trusty sword he cald to his last aid,
Wherewith he fiersly did his foe assaile,
And double blowes about him stoutly laid,
That glauncing fire out of the yron plaid,
As sparckles from the andvile use to fly,
When heavy hammers on the wedg are
swaid;
Therewith at last he forst him to unty
One of his grasping feete, him to defend
thereby.

XLIII

The other foote, fast fixed on his shield,
Whenas no strength nor stroks mote him
constraine
To loose, ne yet the warlike pledg to yield,
He smott thereat with all his might and
maine,
That nought so wondrous puissaunce might
sustaine:
Upon the joint the lucky steele did light,
And made such way, that hewd it quite in
twaine:
The paw yett missed not his minisht might,
But hong still on the shield, as it at first
was pight.

XLIV

For griefe thereof, and divelish despight,
From his infernall fournace forth he threw
Huge flames, that dimmed all the hevens
light,
Enrold in duskish smoke and brimstone
blew;

As burning Aetna from his boyling stew
Doth belch out flames, and rockes in peeces
broke,
And ragged ribs of mountaines molten new,
Enwrapt in coleblacke clowds and filthy
smoke,
That al the land with stench, and heven
with horror choke.

XLV

The heate whereof, and harmefull pesti-
lence,
So sore him noyd, that forst him to retire
A litle backeward for his best defence,
To save his body from the scorching fire,
Which he from hellish entrailes did ex-
pire.
It chaunst (Eternall God that chaunce did
guide)
As he recoiled backeward, in the mire
His nigh foreweried feeble feet did slide,
And downe he fell, with dread of shame
sore terrifide.

XLVI

There grew a goodly tree him faire beside,
Loaden with fruit and apples rosy redd,
As they in pure vermilion had beene dide,
Whereof great vertues over all were redd:
For happy life to all which thereon fedd,
And life eke everlasting did befall:
Great God it planted in that blessed stedd
With his Almighty hand, and did it call
The Tree of Life, the crime of our first
fathers fall.

XLVII

In all the world like was not to be fownd,
Save in that soile, where all good things did
grow,
And freely sprong out of the fruitfull
grownd,
As incorrupted Nature did them sow,
Till that dredd dragon all did overthrow.
Another like faire tree eke grew thereby,
Whereof who so did eat, eftsoones did know
Both good and ill: O mournfull memory!
That tree through one mans fault hath doen
us all to dy.

XLVIII

From that first tree forth flowd, as from a
well,
A trickling streame of balme, most soveraine

And dainty deare, which on the ground still
  fell,
And overflowed all the fertile plaine,
As it had deawed bene with timely raine:
Life and long health that gracious ointment
  gave,
And deadly wounds could heale, and reare
  againe
The sencelesse corse appointed for the
  grave.
Into that same he fell: which did from
  death him save.

XLIX

For nigh thereto the ever damned beast
Durst not approch, for he was deadly
  made,
And al that life preserved did detest:
Yet he it oft adventur'd to invade.
By this the drouping day-light gan to fade,
And yield his rowme to sad succeeding
  night,
Who with her sable mantle gan to shade
The face of earth, and wayes of living
  wight,
And high her burning torch set up in
  heaven bright.

L

When gentle Una saw the second fall
Of her deare knight, who, weary of long
  fight,
And faint through losse of blood, moov'd
  not at all,
But lay as in a dreame of deepe delight,
Besmeard with pretious balme, whose vertu-
  ous might
Did heale his woundes, and scorching heat
  alay,
Againe she stricken was with sore affright,
And for his safetie gan devoutly pray,
And watch the noyous night, and wait for
  joyous day.

LI

The joyous day gan early to appeare,
And fayre Aurora from the deawy bed
Of aged Tithone gan her selfe to reare,
With rosy cheekes, for shame as blushing
  red;
Her golden locks for hast were loosely
  shed
About her eares, when Una her did marke
Clymbe to her charet, all with flowers
  spred,

From heven high to chace the chearelesse
  darke;
With mery note her lowd salutes the
  mounting larke.

LII

Then freshly up arose the doughty knight,
All healed of his hurts and woundes wide,
And did himselfe to battaile ready dight;
Whose early foe awaiting him beside
To have devourd, so soone as day he spyde,
When now he saw himselfe so freshly reare,
As if late fight had nought him damnifyde,
He woxe dismaid, and gan his fate to feare;
Nathlesse with wonted rage he him ad-
  vaunced neare.

LIII

And in his first encounter, gaping wyde,
He thought attonce him to have swallowd
  quight,
And rusht upon him with outragious pryde;
Who him rencountring fierce, as hauke in
  flight,
Perforce rebutted backe. The weapon
  bright,
Taking advantage of his open jaw,
Ran through his mouth with so importune
  might,
That deepe emperst his darksom hollow
  maw,
And, back retyrd, his life blood forth with
  all did draw.

LIV

So downe he fell, and forth his life did
  breath,
That vanisht into smoke and cloudes swift;
So downe he fell, that th' earth him under-
  neath
Did grone, as feeble so great load to lift;
So downe he fell, as an huge rocky clift,
Whose false foundacion waves have washt
  away,
With dreadfull poyse is from the mayne-
  land rift,
And, rolling downe, great Neptune doth
  dismay;
So downe he fell, and like an heaped moun-
  taine lay.

LV

The knight him selfe even trembled at his
  fall,
So huge and horrible a masse it seemd;

And his deare lady, that beheld it all,
Durst not approch for dread which she
    misdeemd;
But yet at last, whenas the direfull feend
She saw not stirre, of-shaking vaine affright,
She nigher drew, and saw that joyous end:
Then God she praysd, and thankt her faith-
    full knight,
That had atchievde so great a conquest by
    his might.

CANTO XII

Fayre Una to the Redcrosse Knight
Betrouthed is with joy:
Though false Duessa, it to barre,
Her false sleightes doe imploy.

I

BEHOLD! I see the haven nigh at hand,
To which I meane my wearie course to
    bend;
Vere the maine shete, and beare up with the
    land,
The which afore is fayrly to be kend,
And seemeth safe from storms that may
    offend:
There this fayre virgin, wearie of her way,
Must landed bee, now at her journeyes end;
There eke my feeble barke a while may
    stay,
Till mery wynd and weather call her thence
    away.

II

Scarsely had Phœbus in the glooming east
Yett harnessed his fyrie-footed teeme,
Ne reard above the earth his flaming
    creast,
When the last deadly smoke aloft did
    steeme,
That signe of last outbreathed life did
    seeme
Unto the watchman on the castle wall;
Who thereby dead that balefull beast did
    deeme,
And to his lord and lady lowd gan call,
To tell, how he had seene the dragons fatall
    fall.

III

Uprose with hasty joy, and feeble speed,
That aged syre, the lord of all that land,
And looked forth, to weet if trew indeed
Those tydinges were, as he did understand:

Which whenas trew by tryall he out fond,
He badd to open wyde his brasen gate,
Which long time had beene shut, and out
    of hond
Proclaymed joy and peace through all his
    state;
For dead now was their foe, which them
    forrayed late.

IV

Then gan triumphant trompets sownd on
    hye,
That sent to heven the ecchoed report
Of their new joy, and happie victory
Gainst him, that had them long opprest
    with tort,
And fast imprisoned in sieged fort.
Then all the people, as in solemne feast,
To him assembled with one full consort,
Rejoycing at the fall of that great beast,
From whose eternall bondage now they
    were releast.

V

Forth came that auncient lord and aged
    queene,
Arayd in antique robes downe to the
    grownd,
And sad habiliments right well beseene:
A noble crew about them waited rownd
Of sage and sober peres, all gravely gownd;
Whom far before did march a goodly band
Of tall young men, all hable armes to
    sownd;
But now they laurell braunches bore in
    hand,
Glad signe of victory and peace in all their
    land.

VI

Unto that doughtie conquerour they came,
And him before themselves prostrating low,
Their lord and patrone loud did him pro-
    clame,
And at his feet their lawrell boughes did
    throw.
Soone after them, all dauncing on a row,
The comely virgins came, with girlands
    dight,
As fresh as flowres in medow greene doe
    grow,
When morning deaw upon their leaves
    doth light:
And in their handes sweet timbrels all up-
    held on hight.

VII

And them before, the fry of children yong
Their wanton sportes and childish mirth
  did play,
And to the maydens sownding tymbrels
  song,
In well attuned notes, a joyous lay,
And made delightfull musick all the way,
Untill they came where that faire virgin
  stood.
As fayre Diana, in fresh sommers day,
Beholdes her nymphes enraung'd in shady
  wood,
Some wrestle, some do run, some bathe in
  christall flood;

VIII

So she beheld those maydens meriment
With chearefull vew; who, when to her
  they came,
Themselves to ground with gracious hum-
  blesse bent,
And her ador'd by honorable name,
Lifting to heven her everlasting fame:
Then on her head they sett a girlond
  greene,
And crowned her twixt earnest and twixt
  game;
Who, in her self-resemblance well beseene,
Did seeme, such as she was, a goodly
  maiden queene.

IX

And after all the raskall many ran,
Heaped together in rude rablement,
To see the face of that victorious man;
Whom all admired, as from heaven sent,
And gazd upon with gaping wonderment.
But when they came where that dead
  dragon lay,
Stretcht on the ground in monstrous large
  extent,
The sight with ydle feare did them dis-
  may,
Ne durst approch him nigh, to touch, or
  once assay.

X

Some feard and fledd; some feard, and
  well it faynd;
One, that would wiser seeme then all the
  rest,
Warnd him not touch, for yet perhaps remaynd
Some lingring life within his hollow brest,

Or in his wombe might lurke some hidden
  nest
Of many dragonettes, his fruitfull seede;
Another saide, that in his eyes did rest
Yet sparckling fyre, and badd thereof take
  heed;
Another said, he saw him move his eyes
  indeed.

XI

One mother, whenas her foolehardy chyld
Did come to neare, and with his talants
  play,
Halfe dead through feare, her litle babe
  revyld,
And to her gossibs gan in counsell say:
' How can I tell, but that his talants may
Yet scratch my sonne, or rend his tender
  hand ? '
So diversly them selves in vaine they
  fray;
Whiles some more bold, to measure him
  nigh stand,
To prove how many acres he did spred of
  land.

XII

Thus flocked all the folke him rownd
  about,
The whiles that hoarie king, with all his
  traine,
Being arrived where that champion stout
After his foes defeasaunce did remaine,
Him goodly greetes, and fayre does enter-
  tayne
With princely gifts of yvory and gold,
And thousand thankes him yeeldes for all
  his paine:
Then when his daughter deare he does be-
  hold,
Her dearely doth imbrace, and kisseth
  manifold.

XIII

And after to his pallace he them bringes,
With shaumes, and trompets, and with
  clarions sweet;
And all the way the joyous people singes,
And with their garments strowes the paved
  street;
Whence mounting up, they fynd purvey-
  aunce meet
Of all that royall princes court became,
And all the floore was underneath their
  feet

Bespredd with costly scarlott of great
name,
On which they lowly sitt, and fitting purpose frame.

XIV

What needes me tell their feast and goodly
guize,
In which was nothing riotous nor vaine?
What needes of dainty dishes to devize,
Of comely services, or courtly trayne?
My narrow leaves cannot in them contayne
The large discourse of roiall princes state.
Yet was their manner then but bare and
playne:
For th' antique world excesse and pryde
did hate;
Such proud luxurious pompe is swollen up
but late.

XV

Then, when with meates and drinkes of
every kinde
Their fervent appetites they quenched had,
That aunciant lord gan fit occasion finde,
Of straunge adventures, and of perils sad,
Which in his travell him befallen had,
For to demaund of his renowmed guest:
Who then with utt'rance grave, and coun-
t'nance sad,
From poynt to poynt, as is before exprest,
Discourst his voyage long, according his re-
quest.

XVI

Great pleasure, mixt with pittifull regard,
That godly king and queene did passion-
ate,
Whyles they his pittifull adventures heard,
That oft they did lament his lucklesse
state,
And often blame the too importune fate,
That heapd on him so many wrathfull
wreakes;
For never gentle knight, as he of late,
So tossed was in Fortunes cruell freakes;
And all the while salt teares bedeawd the
hearers cheaks.

XVII

Then sayd the royall pere in sober wise:
' Deare sonne, great beene the evils which
ye bore
From first to last in your late enterprise,
That I note whether praise or pitty more:

For never living man, I weene, so sore
In sea of deadly daungers was distrest;
But since now safe ye seised have the shore,
And well arrived are, (High God be blest!)
Let us devize of ease and everlasting rest.'

XVIII

' Ah! dearest lord,' said then that doughty
knight,
' Of ease or rest I may not yet devize;
For by the faith which I to armes have
plight,
I bownden am streight after this emprize,
As that your daughter can ye well advize,
Backe to retourne to that great Faery
Queene,
And her to serve six yeares in warlike wize,
Gainst that proud Paynim King that works
her teene:
Therefore I ought crave pardon, till I there
have beene.'

XIX

' Unhappy falls that hard necessity,'
Quoth he, ' the troubler of my happy peace,
And vowed foe of my felicity;
Ne I against the same can justly preace:
But since that band ye cannot now release,
Nor doen undoe, (for vowes may not be
vayne)
Soone as the terme of those six yeares shall
cease,
Ye then shall hether backe retourne agayne,
The marriage to accomplish vowd betwixt
you twayn.

XX

' Which, for my part, I covet to performe,
In sort as through the world I did pro-
clame,
That who so kild that monster most de-
forme,
And him in hardy battayle overcame,
Should have mine onely daughter to his
dame,
And of my kingdome heyre apparaunt bee:
Therefore since now to thee perteynes the
same,
By dew desert of noble chevalree,
Both daughter and eke kingdome, lo! I
yield to thee.'

XXI

Then forth he called that his daughter fayre,
The fairest Un', his onely daughter deare,

His onely daughter and his only hayre;
Who forth proceeding with sad sober
    cheare,
As bright as doth the morning starre ap-
    peare
Out of the east, with flaming lockes be-
    dight,
To tell that dawning day is drawing neare,
And to the world does bring long wished
    light;
So faire and fresh that lady shewd her selfe
    in sight:

XXII

So faire and fresh, as freshest flowre in
    May;
For she had layd her mournefull stole
    aside,
And widow-like sad wimple throwne away,
Wherewith her heavenly beautie she did
    hide,
Whiles on her wearie journey she did ride;
And on her now a garment she did weare
All lilly white, withoutten spot or pride,
That seemd like silke and silver woven
    neare,
But neither silke nor silver therein did
    appeare.

XXIII

The blazing brightnesse of her beauties
    beame,
And glorious light of her sunshyny face,
To tell, were as to strive against the
    streame:
My ragged rimes are all too rude and bace,
Her heavenly lineaments for to enchace.
Ne wonder; for her own deare loved knight,
All were she daily with himselfe in place,
Did wonder much at her celestiall sight:
Oft had he seene her faire, but never so
    faire dight.

XXIV

So fairely dight, when she in presence came,
She to her syre made humble reverence,
And bowed low, that her right well be-
    came,
And added grace unto her excellence:
Who with great wisedome and grave elo-
    quence
Thus gan to say — But eare he thus had
    sayd,
With flying speede, and seeming great
    pretence,

Came running in, much like a man dismayd,
A messenger with letters, which his message
    sayd.

XXV

All in the open hall amazed stood
At suddeinnesse of that unwary sight,
And wondred at his breathlesse hasty mood.
But he for nought would stay his passage
    right,
Till fast before the king he did alight;
Where falling flat, great humblesse he did
    make,
And kist the ground whereon his foot was
    pight;
Then to his handes that writt he did betake,
Which he disclosing, read thus, as the paper
    spake:

XXVI

'To thee, most mighty king of Eden fayre,
Her greeting sends in these sad lines ad-
    drest
The wofull daughter and forsaken heyre
Of that great Emperour of all the West;
And bids thee be advized for the best,
Ere thou thy daughter linck in holy band
Of wedlocke to that new unknowen guest:
For he already plighted his right hand
Unto another love, and to another land.

XXVII

'To me, sad mayd, or rather widow sad,
He was affyaunced long time before,
And sacred pledges he both gave, and had,
False erraunt knight, infamous, and for-
    swore !
Witnesse the burning altars, which he swore,
And guilty heavens of his bold perjury,
Which though he hath polluted oft of yore,
Yet I to them for judgement just doe fly,
And them conjure t' avenge this shamefull
    injury.

XXVIII

'Therefore since mine he is, or free or bond,
Or false or trew, or living or else dead,
Withhold, O soverayne prince, your hasty
    hond
From knitting league with him, I you aread;
Ne weene my right with strength adowne
    to tread,
Through weakenesse of my widowhed or woe:
For Truth is strong, her rightfull cause to
    plead,

And shall finde friends, if need requireth
  soe.
So bids thee well to fare, thy neither friend
  nor foe,   FIDESSA.'

XXIX

When he these bitter byting wordes had
  red,
The tydings straunge did him abashed
  make,
That still he sate long time astonished,
As in great muse, ne word to creature
  spake.
At last his solemne silence thus he brake,
With doubtfull eyes fast fixed on his
  guest:
'Redoubted knight, that for myne only
  sake
Thy life and honor late adventurest,
Let nought be hid from me, that ought to
  be exprest.

XXX

'What meane these bloody vowes and idle
  threats,
Throwne out from womanish impatient
  mynd?
What hevens? what altars? what enraged
  heates,
Here heaped up with termes of love un-
  kynd,
My conscience cleare with guilty bands
  would bynd?
High God be witnesse, that I guiltlesse
  ame!
But if your selfe, sir knight, ye faulty fynd,
Or wrapped be in loves of former dame,
With cryme doe not it cover, but disclose
  the same.'

XXXI

To whom the Redcrosse Knight this answere
  sent:
'My lord, my king, be nought hereat dis-
  mayd,
Till well ye wote by grave intendiment,
What woman, and wherefore, doth me up-
  brayd
With breach of love and loialty betrayd.
It was in my mishaps, as hitherward
I lately traveild, that unwares I strayd
Out of my way, through perils straunge
  and hard;
That day should faile me ere I had them
  all declard.

XXXII

'There did I find, or rather I was fownd
Of this false woman, that Fidessa hight;
Fidessa hight the falsest dame on grownd,
Most false Duessa, royall richly dight,
That easy was t' inveigle weaker sight:
Who by her wicked arts and wiely skill,
Too false and strong for earthly skill or
  might,
Unwares me wrought unto her wicked will,
And to my foe betrayd, when least I feared
  ill.'

XXXIII

Then stepped forth the goodly royall mayd,
And on the ground her selfe prostrating low,
With sober countenaunce thus to him sayd:
'O pardon me, my soveraine lord, to sheow
The secret treasons, which of late I know
To have bene wrought by that false sor-
  ceresse.
Shee, onely she, it is, that earst did throw
This gentle knight into so great distresse,
That death him did awaite in daily wretch-
  ednesse.

XXXIV

'And now it seemes, that she suborned hath
This crafty messenger with letters vaine,
To worke new woe and improvided scath,
By breaking of the band betwixt us twaine;
Wherein she used hath the practicke paine
Of this false footman, clokt with simple-
  nesse,
Whome if ye please for to discover plaine,
Ye shall him Archimago find, I ghesse,
The falsest man alive; who tries, shall
  find no lesse.'

XXXV

The king was greatly moved at her speach,
And, all with suddein indignation fraight,
Bad on that messenger rude hands to
  reach.
Eftsoones the gard, which on his state did
  wait,
Attacht that faytor false, and bound him
  strait:
Who, seeming sorely chauffed at his band,
As chained beare, whom cruell dogs doe
  bait,
With ydle force did faine them to with-
  stand,
And often semblaunce made to scape out of
  their hand.

XXXVI

But they him layd full low in dungeon
    deepe,
And bound him hand and foote with yron
    chains,
And with continual watch did warely keepe:
Who then would thinke, that by his subtile
    trains
He could escape fowle death or deadly
    pains?
Thus when that princes wrath was pacifide,
He gan renew the late forbidden bains,
And to the knight his daughter deare he
    tyde,
With sacred rites and vowes for ever to
    abyde.

XXXVII

His owne two hands the holy knotts did
    knitt,
That none but death for ever can divide;
His owne two hands, for such a turne most
    fitt,
The housling fire did kindle and provide,
And holy water thereon sprinckled wide;
At which the bushy teade a groome did
    light,
And sacred lamp in secret chamber hide,
Where it should not be quenched day nor
    night,
For feare of evill fates, but burnen ever
    bright.

XXXVIII

Then gan they sprinckle all the posts with
    wine,
And made great feast to solemnize that
    day:
They all perfumde with frankincense divine,
And precious odours fetcht from far away,
That all the house did sweat with great
    aray:
And all the while sweete musicke did
    apply
Her curious skill, the warbling notes to
    play,
To drive away the dull melancholy;
The whiles one sung a song of love and
    jollity.

XXXIX

During the which there was an heavenly
    noise
Heard sownd through all the pallace plea-
    santly,

Like as it had bene many an angels voice
Singing before th' Eternall Majesty,
In their trinall triplicities on hye;
Yett wist no creature, whence that hevenly
    sweet
Proceeded, yet each one felt secretly,
Himselfe thereby refte of his sences
    meet,
And ravished with rare impression in his
    sprite.

XL

Great joy was made that day of young and
    old,
And solemne feast proclaymd throughout
    the land,
That their exceeding merth may not be
    told:
Suffice it heare by signes to understand
The usuall joyes at knitting of loves band.
Thrise happy man the knight himselfe did
    hold,
Possessed of his ladies hart and hand,
And ever, when his eie did her behold,
His heart did seeme to melt in pleasures
    manifold.

XLI

Her joyous presence and sweet company
In full content he there did long enjoy,
Ne wicked envy, ne vile gealosy,
His deare delights were hable to annoy:
Yet, swimming in that sea of blisfull joy,
He nought forgott, how he whilome had
    sworne,
In case he could that monstrous beast de-
    stroy,
Unto his Faery Queene backe to retourne:
The which he shortly did, and Una left to
    mourne.

XLII

Now strike your sailes, yee jolly mari-
    ners,
For we be come unto a quiet rode,
Where we must land some of our passen-
    gers,
And light this weary vessell of her lode.
Here she a while may make her safe abode,
Till she repaired have her tackles spent,
And wants supplide; and then againe
    abroad
On the long voiage whereto she is bent:
Well may she speede, and fairely finish her
    intent.

THE SECOND BOOKE
OF THE FAERIE QUEENE
CONTAYNING
THE LEGEND OF SIR GUYON
OR
OF TEMPERAUNCE

I

RIGHT well I wote, most mighty Sover-
        aine,
That all this famous antique history
Of some th' aboundance of an ydle braine
Will judged be, and painted forgery,
Rather then matter of just memory;
Sith none that breatheth living aire does
        know,
Where is that happy land of Faery,
Which I so much doe vaunt, yet no where
        show,
But vouch antiquities, which no body can
        know.

II

But let that man with better sence advize,
That of the world least part to us is red:
And daily how through hardy enterprize
Many great regions are discovered,
Which to late age were never mentioned.
Who ever heard of th' Indian Peru?
Or who in venturous vessell measured
The Amazons huge river, now found trew?
Or fruitfullest Virginia who did ever vew?

III

Yet all these were when no man did them
        know,
Yet have from wisest ages hidden beene;
And later times thinges more unknowne
        shall show.
Why then should witlesse man so much
        misweene,
That nothing is, but that which he hath
        seene?
What if within the moones fayre shining
        spheare,
What if in every other starre unseene,
Of other worldes he happily should heare?
He wonder would much more; yet such to
        some appeare.

IV

Of Faery Lond yet if he more inquyre,
By certein signes, here sett in sondrie place,

He may it fynd; ne let him then admyre,
But yield his sence to bee too blunt and
        bace,
That no'te without an hound fine footing
        trace.
And thou, O fayrest Princesse under sky,
In this fayre mirrhour maist behold thy
        face,
And thine owne realmes in lond of Faery,
And in this antique ymage thy great aun-
        cestry.

V

The which O pardon me thus to enfold
In covert vele, and wrap in shadowes light,
That feeble eyes your glory may behold,
Which ells could not endure those beames
        bright,
But would bee dazled with exceeding light.
O pardon! and vouchsafe with patient eare
The brave adventures of this Faery knight,
The good Sir Guyon, gratiously to heare;
In whom great rule of Temp'raunce goodly
        doth appeare.

CANTO I

Guyon, by Archimage abusd,
    The Redcrosse Knight awaytes;
Fyndes Mordant and Amavia slaine
    With Pleasures poisoned baytes.

I

THAT conning architect of cancred guyle,
Whom princes late displeasure left in bands,
For falsed letters and suborned wyle,
Soone as the Redcrosse Knight he under-
        stands
To beene departed out of Eden landes,
To serve againe his soveraine Elfin Queene,
His artes he moves, and out of caytives
        handes
Himselfe he frees by secret meanes un-
        seene;
His shackles emptie lefte, him selfe escaped
        cleene.

II

And forth he fares full of malicious mynd,
To worken mischiefe and avenging woe,
Where ever he that godly knight may fynd,
His onely hart sore and his onely foe;
Sith Una now he algates must forgoe,
Whom his victorious handes did earst re-
        store

To native crowne and kingdom late ygoe:
Where she enjoyes sure peace for ever-
    more,
As wetherbeaten ship arryv'd on happie
    shore.

III

Him therefore now the object of his spight
And deadly food he makes: him to offend
By forged treason, or by open fight,
He seekes, of all his drifte the aymed end:
Thereto his subtile engins he does bend,
His practick witt, and his fayre fyled tonge,
With thousand other sleightes: for well he
    kend
His credit now in doubtfull ballaunce hong;
For hardly could bee hurt, who was already
    stong.

IV

Still as he went, he craftie stales did lay,
With cunning traynes him to entrap un-
    wares,
And privy spyals plast in all his way,
To weete what course he takes, and how
    he fares;
To ketch him at a vauntage in his snares.
But now so wise and wary was the knight
By tryall of his former harmes and cares,
That he descryde, and shonned still his
    slight:
The fish that once was caught, new bait
    wil hardly byte.

V

Nath'lesse th' enchaunter would not spare
    his payne,
In hope to win occasion to his will;
Which when he long awaited had in vayne,
He chaungd his mynd from one to other ill:
For to all good he enimy was still.
Upon the way him fortuned to meet,
Fayre marching underneath a shady hill,
A goodly knight, all armd in harnesse
    meete,
That from his head no place appeared to his
    feete.

VI

His carriage was full comely and upright,
His countenance demure and temperate,
But yett so sterne and terrible in sight,
That cheard his friendes, and did his foes
    amate:
He was an Elfin borne, of noble state

And mickle worship in his native land;
Well could he tourney and in lists debate,
And knighthood tooke of good Sir Huons
    hand,
When with King Oberon he came to Fary
    Land.

VII

Him als accompanyd upon the way
A comely palmer, clad in black attyre,
Of rypest yeares, and heares all hoarie gray,
That with a staffe his feeble steps did stire,
Least his long way his aged limbes should
    tire:
And if by lookes one may the mind aread,
He seemd to be a sage and sober syre,
And ever with slow pace the knight did lead,
Who taught his trampling steed with equall
    steps to tread.

VIII

Such whenas Archimago them did view,
He weened well to worke some uncouth wyle.
Eftsoones, untwisting his deceiptfull clew,
He gan to weave a web of wicked guyle;
And with faire countenance and flattring
    style
To them approching, thus the knight be-
    spake:
'Fayre sonne of Mars, that seeke with war-
    like spoyle,
And great atchiev'ments, great your selfe to
    make,
Vouchsafe to stay your steed for humble
    misers sake.'

IX

He stayd his steed for humble misers sake,
And badd tell on the tenor of his playnt;
Who feigning then in every limb to quake,
Through inward feare, and seeming pale
    and faynt,
With piteous mone his percing speach gan
    paynt:
'Deare lady, how shall I declare thy cace,
Whom late I left in languorous constraynt?
Would God, thy selfe now present were in
    place,
To tell this ruefull tale! Thy sight could
    win thee grace.

X

'Or rather would, O! would it so had
    chaunst,
That you, most noble sir, had present beene

When that lewd rybauld, with vyle lust ad-
        vaunst,
Laid first his filthie hands on virgin cleene,
To spoyle her dainty corps, so faire and
        sheene
As on the earth, great mother of us all,
With living eye more fayre was never seene,
Of chastity and honour virginall:
Witnes, ye heavens, whom she in vaine to
        help did call.'

XI

'How may it be,' sayd then the knight halfe
        wroth,
'That knight should knighthood ever so
        have shent?'
'None but that saw,' quoth he,'would weene
        for troth,
How shamefully that mayd he did tor-
        ment.
Her looser golden lockes he rudely rent,
And drew her on the ground, and his sharpe
        sword
Against her snowy brest he fiercely bent,
And threatned death with many a bloodie
        word;
Tounge hates to tell the rest, that eye to
        see abhord.'

XII

Therewith amoved from his sober mood,
'And lives he yet,' said he, 'that wrought
        this act,
And doen the heavens afford him vitall
        food?'
'He lives,' quoth he, 'and boasteth of the
        fact,
Ne yet hath any knight his courage crackt.'
'Where may that treachour then,' sayd he,
        'be found,
Or by what meanes may I his footing
        tract?'
'That shall I shew,' said he, 'as sure as
        hound
The stricken deare doth chaleng by the
        bleeding wound.'

XIII

He stayd not lenger talke, but with fierce
        yre
And zealous haste away is quickly gone,
To seeke that knight, where him that crafty
        squyre
Supposd to be. They do arrive anone,
Where sate a gentle lady all alone,

With garments rent, and heare dischev-
        eled,
Wringing her handes, and making piteous
        mone:
Her swollen eyes were much disfigured,
And her faire face with teares was fowly
        blubbered.

XIV

The knight, approching nigh, thus to her
        said:
'Fayre lady, through fowle sorrow ill be-
        dight,
Great pitty is to see you thus dismayd,
And marre the blossom of your beauty
        bright:
Forthy appease your griefe and heavy
        plight,
And tell the cause of your conceived payne:
For if he live that hath you doen despight,
He shall you doe dew recompence agayne,
Or els his wrong with greater puissance
        maintaine.'

XV

Which when she heard, as in despightfull
        wise,
She wilfully her sorrow did augment,
And offred hope of comfort did despise:
Her golden lockes most cruelly she rent,
And scratcht her face with ghastly dreri-
        ment;
Ne would she speake, ne see, ne yet be
        seene,
But hid her visage, and her head downe
        bent,
Either for grievous shame, or for great
        teene,
As if her hart with sorow had transfixed
        beene:

XVI

Till her that squyre bespake: 'Madame,
        my liefe,
For Gods deare love be not so wilfull
        bent,
But doe vouchsafe now to receive reliefe,
The which good fortune doth to you pre-
        sent.
For what bootes it to weepe and to way-
        ment,
When ill is chaunst, but doth the ill in-
        crease,
And the weake minde with double woe tor-
        ment?'

When she her squyre heard speake, she gan
   appease
Her voluntarie paine, and feele some secret
   ease.

XVII

Eftsoone she said: 'Ah! gentle trustie
   squyre,
What comfort can I, wofull wretch, con-
   ceave,
Or why should ever I henceforth desyre
To see faire heavens face, and life not
   leave,
Sith that false traytour did my honour
   reave?'
'False traytour certes,' saide the Faerie
   knight,
'I read the man, that ever would deceave
A gentle lady, or her wrong through might:
Death were too little paine for such a fowle
   despight.

XVIII

'But now, fayre lady, comfort to you make,
And read who hath ye wrought this sham-
   full plight,
That short revenge the man may overtake,
Where so he be, and soone upon him light.'
'Certes,' saide she, 'I wote not how he
   hight,
But under him a gray steede did he wield,
Whose sides with dapled circles weren
   dight;
Upright he rode, and in his silver shield
He bore a bloodie crosse, that quartred all
   the field.'

XIX

'Now by my head,' saide Guyon, 'much I
   muse,
How that same knight should do so fowle
   amis,
Or ever gentle damzell so abuse:
For may I boldly say, he surely is
A right good knight, and trew of word ywis:
I present was, and can it witnesse well,
When armes he swore, and streight did
   enterpris
Th' adventure of the Errant Damozell;
In which he hath great glory wonne, as I
   heare tell.

XX

'Nathlesse he shortly shall againe be tryde,
And fairely quit him of th' imputed blame,

Els be ye sure he dearely shall abyde,
Or make you good amendment for the same:
All wrongs have mendes, but no amendes of
   shame.
Now therefore, lady, rise out of your paine,
And see the salving of your blotted name.'
Full loth she seemd thereto, but yet did
   faine;
For she was inly glad her purpose so to
   gaine.

XXI

Her purpose was not such as she did faine,
Ne yet her person such as it was seene;
But under simple shew and semblant plaine
Lurkt false Duessa secretly unseene,
As a chaste virgin, that had wronged beene:
So had false Archimago her disguysd,
To cloke her guile with sorrow and sad
   teene;
And eke himselfe had craftily devisd
To be her squire, and do her service well
   aguisd.

XXII

Her late, forlorne and naked, he had found,
Where she did wander in waste wildernesse,
Lurking in rockes and caves far under
   ground,
And with greene mosse cov'ring her naked-
   nesse,
To hide her shame and loathly filthinesse,
Sith her Prince Arthur of proud ornaments
And borrowd beauty spoyld. Her nathelesse
Th' enchaunter finding fit for his intents
Did thus revest, and deckt with dew habili-
   ments.

XXIII

For all he did was to deceive good knights,
And draw them from pursuit of praise and
   fame,
To slug in slouth and sensuall delights,
And end their daies with irrenowmed shame.
And now exceeding griefe him overcame,
To see the Redcrosse thus advaunced hye;
Therefore this craftie engine he did frame,
Against his praise to stirre up enmitye
Of such, as vertues like mote unto him
   allye.

XXIV

So now he Guyon guydes an uncouth way
Through woods and mountaines, till they
   came at last

Into a pleasant dale, that lowly lay
Betwixt two hils, whose high heads, over-
    plast,
The valley did with coole shade overcast:
Through midst thereof a little river rold,
By which there sate a knight with helme
    unlaste,
Himselfe refreshing with the liquid cold,
After his travell long, and labours manifold.

XXV

' Lo ! yonder he,' cryde Archimage alowd,
' That wrought the shamefull fact, which I
    did shew,
And now he doth himselfe in secret shrowd,
To fly the vengeaunce for his outrage dew;
But vaine: for ye shall dearely do him rew,
So God ye speed and send you good suc-
    cesse;
Which we far off will here abide to vew.'
So they him left, inflam'd with wrathful-
    nesse,
That streight against that knight his speare
    he did addresse.

XXVI

Who, seeing him from far so fierce to
    pricke,
His warlike armes about him gan embrace,
And in the rest his ready speare did sticke;
Tho, when as still he saw him towards pace,
He gan rencounter him in equall race:
They bene ymett, both ready to affrap,
When suddeinly that warriour gan abace
His threatned speare, as if some new mis-
    hap
Had him betide, or hidden danger did en-
    trap:

XXVII

And cryde, ' Mercie, sir knight ! and mercie,
    lord,
For mine offence and heedelesse hardi-
    ment,
That had almost committed crime abhord,
And with reprochfull shame mine honour
    shent,
Whiles cursed steele against that badge I
    bent,
The sacred badge of my Redeemers death,
Which on your shield is set for ornament.'
But his fierce foe his steed could stay un-
    eath,
Who, prickt with courage kene, did cruell
    battell breath.

XXVIII

But when he heard him speake, streight
    way he knew
His errour, and himselfe inclyning sayd:
' Ah ! deare Sir Guyon, well becommeth
    you,
But me behoveth rather to upbrayd,
Whose hastie hand so far from reason
    strayd,
That almost it did haynous violence
On that fayre ymage of that heavenly
    mayd,
That decks and armes your shield with
    faire defence:
Your court'sie takes on you anothers dew
    offence.'

XXIX

So beene they both at one, and doen up-
    reare
Their bevers bright, each other for to
    greet;
Goodly comportaunce each to other beare,
And entertaine themselves with court'sies
    meet.
Then saide the Redcrosse Knight: ' Now
    mote I weet,
Sir Guyon, why with so fierce saliaunce,
And fell intent, ye did at earst me meet;
For sith I know your goodly governaunce,
Great cause, I weene, you guided, or some
    uncouth chaunce.'

XXX

' Certes,' said he, ' well mote I shame to tell
The fond encheason that me hether led.
A false infamous faitour late befell
Me for to meet, that seemed ill bested,
And playnd of grievous outrage, which he
    red
A knight had wrought against a ladie gent;
Which to avenge, he to this place me led,
Where you he made the marke of his in-
    tent,
And now is fled: foule shame him follow,
    wher he went ! '

XXXI

So can he turne his earnest unto game,
Through goodly handling and wise tem-
    peraunce.
By this his aged guide in presence came,
Who, soone as on that knight his eye did
    glaunce,
Eftsoones of him had perfect cognizaunce,

Sith him in Faery court he late avizd;
And sayd: 'Fayre sonne, God give you
    happy chaunce,
And that deare Crosse uppon your shield
    devizd,
Wherewith above all knights ye goodly
    seeme aguizd.

XXXII

'Joy may you have, and everlasting fame,
Of late most hard atchiev'ment by you
    donne,
For which enrolled is your glorious name
In heavenly regesters above the sunne,
Where you a saint with saints your seat
    have wonne:
But wretched we, where ye have left your
    marke,
Must now anew begin like race to ronne.
God guide thee, Guyon, well to end thy
    warke,
And to the wished haven bring thy weary
    barke.'

XXXIII

'Palmer,' him answered the Redcrosse
    Knight,
'His be the praise, that this atchiev'ment
    wrought,
Who made my hand the organ of His
    might:
More then goodwill to me attribute nought;
For all I did, I did but as I ought.
But you, faire sir, whose pageant next en-
    sewes,
Well mote yee thee, as well can wish your
    thought,
That home ye may report thrise happy
    newes;
For well ye worthy bene for worth and
    gentle thewes.'

XXXIV

So courteous conge both did give and
    take,
With right hands plighted, pledges of good
    will.
Then Guyon forward gan his voyage make
With his blacke palmer, that him guided
    still.
Still he him guided over dale and hill,
And with his steedy staffe did point his
    way:
His race with reason, and with words his
    will,

From fowle intemperaunce he ofte did stay,
And suffred not in wrath his hasty steps to
    stray.

XXXV

In this faire wize they traveild long yfere,
Through many hard assayes, which did be-
    tide,
Of which he honour still away did beare,
And spred his glory through all countryes
    wide.
At last, as chaunst them by a forest side
To passe, for succour from the scorching
    ray,
They heard a ruefull voice, that dearnly
    cride,
With percing shriekes, and many a dole-
    full lay;
Which to attend, awhile their forward steps
    they stay.

XXXVI

'But if that carelesse hevens,' quoth she,
    'despise
The doome of just revenge, and take de-
    light
To see sad pageaunts of mens miseries,
As bownd by them to live in lives de-
    spight,
Yet can they not warne Death from
    wretched wight.
Come then, come soone, come, sweetest
    Death, to me,
And take away this long lent loathed light:
Sharpe be thy wounds, but sweete the med-
    icines be,
That long captived soules from weary
    thraldome free.

XXXVII

'But thou, sweete babe, whom frowning
    froward fate
Hath made sad witnesse of thy fathers
    fall,
Sith heven thee deignes to hold in living
    state,
Long maist thou live, and better thrive
    withall,
Then to thy lucklesse parents did befall:
Live thou, and to thy mother dead attest,
That cleare she dide from blemish crimi-
    nall:
Thy litle hands embrewd in bleeding brest,
Loe! I for pledges leave. So give me leave
    to rest.'

XXXVIII

With that a deadly shrieke she forth did
    throw,
That through the wood reechoed againe,
And after gave a grone so deepe and low,
That seemd her tender heart was rent in
    twaine,
Or thrild with point of thorough piercing
    paine:
As gentle hynd, whose sides with cruell
    steele
Through launched, forth her bleeding life
    does raine,
Whiles the sad pang approching shee does
    feele,
Braies out her latest breath, and up her
    eies doth seele.

XXXIX

Which when that warriour heard, dismount-
    ing straict
From his tall steed, he rusht into the thick,
And soone arrived where that sad pour-
    traict
Of death and dolour lay, halfe dead, halfe
    quick;
In whose white alabaster brest did stick
A cruell knife, that made a griesly wownd,
From which forth gusht a stream of gore-
    blood thick,
That all her goodly garments staind arownd,
And into a deepe sanguine dide the grassy
    grownd.

XL

Pitifull spectacle of deadly smart,
Beside a bubling fountaine low she lay,
Which shee increased with her bleeding
    hart,
And the cleane waves with purple gore did
    ray;
Als in her lap a lovely babe did play
His cruell sport, in stead of sorrow dew;
For in her streaming blood he did embay
His litle hands, and tender joints embrew;
Pitifull spectacle, as ever eie did vew.

XLI

Besides them both, upon the soiled gras
The dead corse of an armed knight was spred,
Whose armour all with blood besprincled
    was;
His ruddy lips did smyle, and rosy red
Did paint his chearefull cheekes, yett being
    ded;

Seemd to have beene a goodly personage,
Now in his freshest flowre of lustyhed,
Fitt to inflame faire lady with loves rage,
But that fiers fate did crop the blossome of
    his age.

XLII

Whom when the good Sir Guyon did behold,
His hart gan wexe as starke as marble stone,
And his fresh blood did frieze with feare-
    full cold,
That all his sences seemd berefte attone.
At last his mighty ghost gan deepe to grone,
As lion, grudging in his great disdaine,
Mournes inwardly, and makes to him selfe
    mone,
Til ruth and fraile affection did constraine
His stout courage to stoupe, and shew his
    inward paine.

XLIII

Out of her gored wound the cruell steel
He lightly snatcht, and did the floodgate
    stop
With his faire garment: then gan softly feel
Her feeble pulse, to prove if any drop
Of living blood yet in her veynes did hop;
Which when he felt to move, he hoped faire
To call backe life to her forsaken shop:
So well he did her deadly wounds repaire,
That at the last shee gan to breath out
    living aire.

XLIV

Which he perceiving, greatly gan rejoice,
And goodest counsell, that for wounded hart
Is meetest med'cine, tempred with sweete
    voice:
'Ay me! deare lady, which the ymage art
Of ruefull pitty, and impatient smart,
What direfull chaunce, armd with avenging
    fate,
Or cursed hand, hath plaid this cruell part,
Thus fowle to hasten your untimely date?
Speake, O dear lady, speake: help never
    comes too late.'

XLV

Therewith her dim eie-lids she up gan
    reare,
On which the drery death did sitt, as sad
As lump of lead, and made darke clouds
    appeare:
But when as him, all in bright armour
    clad,

Before her standing she espied had,
As one out of a deadly dreame affright,
She weakely started, yet she nothing drad:
Streight downe againe her selfe in great
    despight
She groveling threw to ground, as hating
    life and light.

XLVI

The gentle knight her soone with carefull
    paine
Uplifted light, and softly did uphold:
Thrise he her reard, and thrise she sunck
    againe,
Till he his armes about her sides gan fold,
And to her said: 'Yet if the stony cold
Have not all seized on your frozen hart,
Let one word fall that may your griefe un-
    fold,
And tell the secrete of your mortall smart:
He oft finds present helpe, who does his
    griefe impart.'

XLVII

Then, casting up a deadly looke, full low
Shee sight from bottome of her wounded
    brest,
And after, many bitter throbs did throw:
With lips full pale and foltring tong opprest,
These words she breathed forth from riven
    chest:
'Leave, ah! leave of, what ever wight thou
    bee,
To lett a weary wretch from her dew rest,
And trouble dying soules tranquilitee.
Take not away now got, which none would
    give to me.'

XLVIII

'Ah! far be it,' said he, 'deare dame, fro
    mee,
To hinder soule from her desired rest,
Or hold sad life in long captivitee:
For all I seeke is but to have redrest
The bitter pangs that doth your heart infest.
Tell then, O lady, tell what fatall priefe
Hath with so huge misfortune you opprest:
That I may cast to compas your reliefe,
Or die with you in sorrow, and partake
    your griefe.'

XLIX

With feeble hands then stretched forth on
    hye,
As heven accusing guilty of her death,
And with dry drops congealed in her eye,
In these sad wordes she spent her utmost
    breath:
'Heare then, O man, the sorrowes that un-
    eath
My tong can tell, so far all sence they pas:
Loe! this dead corpse, that lies here under-
    neath,
The gentlest knight, that ever on greene
    gras
Gay steed with spurs did pricke, the good
    Sir Mortdant was.

L

'Was (ay the while, that he is not so now!)
My lord, my love, my deare lord, my deare
    love,
So long as hevens just with equall brow
Vouchsafed to behold us from above.
One day, when him high corage did em-
    move,
As wont ye knightes to seeke adventures
    wilde,
He pricked forth, his puissant force to
    prove.
Me then he left enwombed of this childe,
This luckles childe, whom thus ye see with
    blood defild.

LI

'Him fortuned (hard fortune ye may
    ghesse)
To come where vile Acrasia does wonne,
Acrasia, a false enchaunteresse,
That many errant knightes hath fowle for-
    donne:
Within a wandring island, that doth ronne
And stray in perilous gulfe, her dwelling
    is:
Fayre sir, if ever there ye travell, shonne
The cursed land where many wend amis,
And know it by the name; it hight the
    Bowre of Blis.

LII

'Her blis is all in pleasure and delight,
Wherewith she makes her lovers dronken
    mad,
And then with words and weedes of won-
    drous might,
On them she workes her will to uses bad:
My liefest lord she thus beguiled had;
For he was flesh (all flesh doth frayltie
    breed):
Whom when I heard to beene so ill bestad,

Weake wretch, I wrapt myselfe in palmers
  weed,
And cast to seek him forth through danger
  and great dreed.

LIII

'Now had fayre Cynthia by even tournes
Full measured three quarters of her yeare,
And thrise three tymes had fild her crooked
  hornes,
Whenas my wombe her burdein would for-
  beare,
And bad me call Lucina to me neare.
Lucina came: a manchild forth I brought:
The woods, the nymphes, my bowres, my
  midwives, weare:
Hard helpe at need! So deare thee, babe, I
  bought;
Yet nought to dear I deemd, while so my
  deare I sought.

LIV

'Him so I sought, and so at last I fownd,
Where him that witch had thralled to her will,
In chaines of lust and lewde desyres ybownd,
And so transformed from his former skill,
That me he knew not, nether his owne ill;
Till through wise handling and faire gov-
  ernaunce,
I him recured to a better will,
Purged from drugs of fowle intemperaunce:
Then meanes I gan devise for his deliver-
  ance.

LV

'Which when the vile enchaunteresse per-
  ceiv'd,
How that my lord from her I would reprive,
With cup thus charmd, him parting she
  deceivd:
*Sad verse, give death to him that death does
  give,*
And losse of love to her that loves to live,
*So soone as Bacchus with the Nymphe does
  lincke.*
So parted we, and on our journey drive,
Till, comming to this well, he stoupt to
  drincke:
The charme fulfild, dead suddeinly he
  downe did sincke.

LVI

'Which when I, wretch'—Not one word
  more she sayd,
But breaking of the end for want of breath,

And slyding soft, as downe to sleepe her
  layd,
And ended all her woe in quiet death.
That seeing good Sir Guyon, could uneath
From teares abstayne, for griefe his hart
  did grate,
And from so heavie sight his head did
  wreath,
Accusing fortune, and too cruell fate,
Which plonged had faire lady in so wretched
  state.

LVII

Then, turning to his palmer, said: 'Old
  syre,
Behold the ymage of mortalitie,
And feeble nature cloth'd with fleshly tyre.
When raging passion with fierce tyranny
Robs reason of her dew regalitie,
And makes it servaunt to her basest part,
The strong it weakens with infirmitie,
And with bold furie armes the weakest
  hart:
The strong through pleasure soonest falles,
  the weake through smart.'

LVIII

'But Temperaunce,' said he, 'with golden
  squire
Betwixt them both can measure out a
  meane,
Nether to melt in pleasures whott desyre,
Nor frye in hartlesse griefe and dolefull
  tene.
Thrise happy man, who fares them both
  atweene!
But sith this wretched woman overcome
Of anguish, rather then of crime, hath
  bene,
Reserve her cause to her eternall doome,
And, in the meane, vouchsafe her honorable
  toombe.'

LIX

'Palmer,' quoth he, 'death is an equall
  doome
To good and bad, the commen in of rest;
But after death the tryall is to come,
When best shall bee to them that lived
  best:
But both alike, when death hath both sup-
  prest,
Religious reverence doth buriall teene,
Which who so wants, wants so much of his
  rest:

For all so great shame after death I weene,
As selfe to dyen bad, unburied bad to beene.'

LX

So both agree their bodies to engrave:
The great earthes wombe they open to the
sky,
And with sad cypresse seemely it embrave;
Then, covering with a clod their closed
eye,
They lay therein those corses tenderly,
And bid them sleepe in everlasting peace.
But ere they did their utmost obsequy,
Sir Guyon, more affection to increace,
Bynempt a sacred vow, which none should
ay releace.

LXI

The dead knights sword out of his sheath
he drew,
With which he cutt a lock of all their
heare,
Which medling with their blood and earth,
he threw
Into the grave, and gan devoutly sweare:
' Such and such evil God on Guyon reare,
And worse and worse, young orphane, be
thy payne,
If I or thou dew vengeance doe forbeare,
Till guiltie blood her guerdon doe obtayne.'
So shedding many teares, they closd the
earth agayne.

CANTO II

Babes bloody handes may not be clensd :
    The face of Golden Meane :
Her sisters, two Extremities,
    Strive her to banish cleane.

I

THUS when Sir Guyon, with his faithful
guyde,
Had with dew rites and dolorous lament
The end of their sad tragedie uptyde,
The litle babe up in his armes he hent;
Who, with sweet pleasaunce and bold blan-
dishment,
Gan smyle on them, that rather ought to
weepe,
As carelesse of his woe, or innocent
Of that was doen; that ruth emperced
deepe
In that knightes hart, and wordes with bit-
ter teares did steepe:

II

' Ah ! lucklesse babe, borne under cruell
starre,
And in dead parents balefull ashes bred,
Full little weenest thou, what sorrowes are
Left thee for porcion of thy livelyhed:
Poore orphane ! in the wide world scat-
tered,
As budding braunch rent from the native
tree,
And throwen forth, till it be withered !
Such is the state of men ! Thus enter we
Into this life with woe, and end with
miseree !'

III

Then soft him selfe inclyning on his knee
Downe to that well, did in the water weene
(So love does loath disdainefull nicitee)
His guiltie handes from bloody gore to
cleene.
He washt them oft and oft, yet nought they
beene
For all his washing cleaner. Still he strove,
Yet still the litle hands were bloody seene:
The which him into great amaz'ment drove,
And into diverse doubt his wavering wonder
clove.

IV

He wist not whether blott of fowle offence
Might not be purgd with water nor with
bath;
Or that High God, in lieu of innocence,
Imprinted had that token of his wrath,
To shew how sore bloodguiltinesse he
hat'th;
Or that the charme and veneme, which they
dronck,
Their blood with secret filth infected hath,
Being diffused through the sencelesse tronck,
That, through the great contagion, direfull
deadly stonck.

V

Whom thus at gaze the palmer gan to bord
With goodly reason, and thus fayre be-
spake:
' Ye bene right hard amated, gratious lord,
And of your ignorance great merveill
make,
Whiles cause not well conceived ye mis-
take.
But know, that secret vertues are infusd
In every fountaine, and in everie lake,

Which who hath skill them rightly to have
　　chusd
To proofe of passing wonders hath full
　　often usd.

VI

'Of those some were so from their sourse
　　indewd
By great Dame Nature, from whose fruit-
　　full pap
Their welheads spring, and are with moist-
　　ure deawd;
Which feedes each living plant with liquid
　　sap,
And filles with flowres fayre Floraes painted
　　lap:
But other some by guifte of later grace,
Or by good prayers, or by other hap,
Had vertue pourd into their waters bace,
And thenceforth were renowmd, and sought
　　from place to place.

VII

Such is this well, wrought by occasion
　　straunge,
Which to her nymph befell. Upon a day,
As she the woodes with bow and shaftes
　　did raunge,
The hartlesse hynd and robucke to dismay,
Dan Faunus chaunst to meet her by the
　　way,
And kindling fire at her faire burning
　　eye,
Inflamed was to follow beauties pray,
And chaced her, that fast from him did
　　fly;
As hynd from her, so she fled from her
　　enimy.

VIII

'At last, when fayling breath began to
　　faint,
And saw no meanes to scape, of shame
　　affrayd,
She set her downe to weepe for sore con-
　　straint,
And to Diana calling lowd for ayde,
Her deare besought, to let her die a mayd.
The goddesse heard, and suddeine, where
　　she sate,
Welling out streames of teares, and quite
　　dismayd
With stony feare of that rude rustick mate,
Transformd her to a stone from stedfast
　　virgins state.

IX

'Lo! now she is that stone, from whose two
　　heads,
As from two weeping eyes, fresh streames
　　do flow,
Yet colde through feare and old conceived
　　dreads;
And yet the stone her semblance seemes to
　　show,
Shapt like a maide, that such ye may her
　　know;
And yet her vertues in her water byde;
For it is chaste and pure, as purest snow,
Ne lets her waves with any filth be dyde,
But ever like her selfe unstayned hath beene
　　tryde.

X

'From thence it comes, that this babes
　　bloody hand
May not be clensd with water of this
　　well:
Ne certes, sir, strive you it to withstand,
But let them still be bloody, as befell,
That they his mothers innocence may tell,
As she bequeathd in her last testament;
That as a sacred symbole it may dwell
In her sonnes flesh, to mind revengement,
And be for all chaste dames an endlesse
　　moniment.'

XI

He harkned to his reason, and the childe
Uptaking, to the palmer gave to beare;
But his sad fathers armes with blood de-
　　filde,
An heavie load, himselfe did lightly reare;
And turning to that place, in which whyl-
　　eare
He left his loftie steed with golden sell
And goodly gorgeous barbes, him found not
　　theare:
By other accident, that earst befell,
He is convaide; but how or where, here fits
　　not tell.

XII

Which when Sir Guyon saw, all were he
　　wroth,
Yet algates mote he soft himselfe appease,
And fairely fare on foot, how ever loth:
His double burden did him sore disease.
So long they traveiled with litle ease,
Till that at last they to a castle came,
Built on a rocke adjoyning to the seas:

It was an auncient worke of antique fame,
And wondrous strong by nature, and by
    skilfull frame.

XIII

Therein three sisters dwelt of sundry sort,
The children of one syre by mothers three;
Who dying whylome did divide this fort
To them by equall shares in equall fee:
But stryfull mind and diverse qualitee
Drew them in partes, and each made others
    foe:
Still they strive, and daily disagree;
The eldest did against the youngest goe,
And both against the middest meant to
    worken woe.

XIV

Where when the knight arriv'd, he was
    right well
Receiv'd, as knight of so much worth be-
    came,
Of second sister, who did far excell
The other two; Medina was her name,
A sober sad, and comely courteous dame;
Who, rich arayd, and yet in modest guize,
In goodly garments, that her well be-
    came,
Fayre marching forth in honorable wize,
Him at the threshold mett, and well did
    enterprize.

XV

She led him up into a goodly bowre,
And comely courted with meet modestie,
Ne in her speach, ne in her haviour,
Was lightnesse seene, or looser vanitie,
But gratious womanhood, and gravitie,
Above the reason of her youthly yeares:
Her golden lockes she roundly did uptye
In breaded tramels, that no looser heares
Did out of order stray about her daintie
    eares.

XVI

Whilest she her selfe thus busily did frame,
Seemely to entertaine her new-come guest,
Newes hereof to her other sisters came,
Who all this while were at their wanton
    rest,
Accourting each her frend with lavish
    fest:
They were two knights of perelesse puis-
    saunce,
And famous far abroad for warlike gest,

Which to these ladies love did counte-
    naunce,
And to his mistresse each himselfe strove
    to advaunce.

XVII

He that made love unto the eldest dame
Was hight Sir Huddibras, an hardy man;
Yet not so good of deedes as great of
    name,
Which he by many rash adventures wan,
Since errant armes to sew he first began:
More huge in strength then wise in workes
    he was,
And reason with foole-hardize over ran;
Sterne melancholy did his courage pas;
And was, for terrour more, all armd in
    shyning bras.

XVIII

But he that lov'd the youngest was Sans-
    loy,
He that faire Una late fowle outraged,
The most unruly and the boldest boy,
That ever warlike weapons menaged,
And to all lawlesse lust encouraged
Through strong opinion of his matchlesse
    might;
Ne ought he car'd, whom he endamaged
By tortious wrong, or whom bereav'd of
    right.
He now this ladies champion chose for love
    to fight.

XIX

These two gay knights, vowd to so diverse
    loves,
Each other does envy with deadly hate,
And daily warre against his foeman moves,
In hope to win more favour with his mate,
And th' others pleasing service to abate,
To magnifie his owne. But when they heard,
How in that place straunge knight arrived
    late,
Both knights and ladies forth right angry
    far'd,
And fercely unto battell sterne themselves
    prepar'd.

XX

But ere they could proceede unto the place
Where he abode, themselves at discord
    fell,
And cruell combat joynd in middle space:
With horrible assault, and fury fell,

They heapt huge strokes, the scorned life to
quell,
That all on uprore from her settled seat
The house was raysd, and all that in did
dwell;
Seemd that lowde thunder with amazement
great
Did rend the ratling skyes with flames of
fouldring heat.

XXI

The noyse thereof cald forth that straunger
knight,
To weet what dreadfull thing was there in
hand;
Where when as two brave knightes in bloody
fight
With deadly rancour he enraunged fond,
His sunbroad shield about his wrest he
bond,
And shyning blade unsheathd, with which
he ran
Unto that stead, their strife to understond;
And at his first arrivall, them began
With goodly meanes to pacifie, well as he
can.

XXII

But they him spying, both with greedy
forse
Attonce upon him ran, and him beset
With strokes of mortall steele without re-
morse,
And on his shield like yron sledges bet:
As when a beare and tygre, being met
In cruell fight on Lybicke ocean wide,
Espye a traveiler with feet surbet,
Whom they in equall pray hope to divide,
They stint their strife, and him assayle on
everie side.

XXIII

But he, not like a weary traveilere,
Their sharp assault right boldly did rebut,
And suffred not their blowes to byte him
nere,
But with redoubled buffes them backe did
put:
Whose grieved mindes, which choler did
englut,
Against themselves turning their wrathfull
spight,
Gan with new rage their shieldes to hew and
cut;

But still when Guyon came to part their
fight,
With heavie load on him they freshly gan
to smight.

XXIV

As a tall ship tossed in troublous seas,
Whom raging windes, threatning to make
the pray
Of the rough rockes, doe diversly disease,
Meetes two contrarie billowes by the way,
That her on either side doe sore assay,
And boast to swallow her in greedy grave;
Shee, scorning both their spights, does make
wide way,
And with her brest breaking the fomy
wave,
Does ride on both their backs, and faire her
self doth save:

XXV

So boldly he him beares, and rusheth forth
Betweene them both, by conduct of his
blade.
Wondrous great prowesse and heroick
worth
He shewd that day, and rare ensample
made,
When two so mighty warriours he dis-
made:
Attonce he wards and strikes, he takes and
paies,
Now forst to yield, now forcing to invade,
Before, behind, and round about him laies:
So double was his paines, so double be his
praise.

XXVI

Straunge sort of fight, three valiaunt
knights to see
Three combates joine in one, and to darraine
A triple warre with triple enmitee,
All for their ladies froward love to gaine,
Which gotten was but hate. So Love does
raine
In stoutest minds, and maketh monstrous
warre;
He maketh warre, he maketh peace againe,
And yett his peace is but continuall jarre:
O miserable men, that to him subject arre !

XXVII

Whilst thus they mingled were in furious
armes,
The faire Medina, with her tresses torne

And naked brest, in pitty of their harmes,
Emongst them ran, and, falling them be-
  forne,
Besought them by the womb, which them
  had born,
And by the loves, which were to them most
  deare,
And by the knighthood, which they sure had
  sworn,
Their deadly cruell discord to forbeare,
And to her just conditions of faire peace to
  heare.

XXVIII

But her two other sisters, standing by,
Her lowd gainsaid, and both their cham-
  pions bad
Pursew the end of their strong enmity,
As ever of their loves they would be glad.
Yet she with pitthy words and counsell sad
Still strove their stubborne rages to revoke,
That, at the last, suppressing fury mad,
They gan abstaine from dint of direfull
  stroke,
And hearken to the sober speaches which
  she spoke.

XXIX

'Ah! puissaunt lords, what cursed evill
  spright,
Or fell Erinnys, in your noble harts
Her hellish brond hath kindled with de-
  spight,
And stird you up to worke your wilfull
  smarts?
Is this the joy of armes? be these the parts
Of glorious knighthood, after blood to
  thrust,
And not regard dew right and just desarts?
Vaine is the vaunt, and victory unjust,
That more to mighty hands then rightfull
  cause doth trust.

XXX

'And were there rightfull cause of differ-
  ence,
Yet were not better, fayre it to accord,
Then with bloodguiltinesse to heape offence,
And mortal vengeaunce joyne to crime ab-
  hord?
O fly from wrath! fly, O my liefest lord!
Sad be the sights, and bitter fruites of
  warre,
And thousand furies wait on wrathfull
  sword;

Ne ought the praise of prowesse more doth
  marre
Then fowle revenging rage, and base contentious jarre.

XXXI

'But lovely concord, and most sacred peace,
Doth nourish vertue, and fast friendship
  breeds;
Weake she makes strong, and strong thing
  does increace,
Till it the pitch of highest praise exceeds;
Brave be her warres, and honorable deeds,
By which she triumphes over yre and pride,
And winnes an olive girlond for her meeds:
Be therefore, O my deare lords, pacifide,
And this misseeming discord meekely lay
  aside.'

XXXII

Her gracious words their rancour did appall,
And suncke so deepe into their boyling
  brests,
That downe they lett their cruell weapons
  fall,
And lowly did abase their lofty crests
To her faire presence and discrete behests.
Then she began a treaty to procure,
And stablish termes betwixt both their re-
  quests,
That as a law for ever should endure;
Which to observe, in word of knights they
  did assure.

XXXIII

Which to confirme, and fast to bind their
  league,
After their weary sweat and bloody toile,
She them besought, during their quiet
  treague,
Into her lodging to repaire a while,
To rest themselves, and grace to reconcile.
They soone consent: so forth with her they
  fare,
Where they are well receivd, and made to
  spoile
Themselves of soiled armes, and to prepare
Their minds to pleasure, and their mouths
  to dainty fare.

XXXIV

And those two froward sisters, their faire
  loves,
Came with them eke, all were they wondrous loth,

And fained cheare, as for the time behoves;
But could not colour yet so well the troth,
But that their natures bad appeard in both:
For both did at their second sister grutch,
And inly grieve, as doth an hidden moth
The inner garment frett, not th' utter touch;
One thought her cheare too litle, th' other
    thought too mutch.

XXXV

Elissa (so the eldest hight) did deeme
Such entertainment base, ne ought would
    eat,
Ne ought would speake, but evermore did
    seeme
As discontent for want of merth or meat;
No solace could her paramour intreat
Her once to show, ne court, nor dalliaunce;
But with bent lowring browes, as she would
    threat,
She scould, and frownd with froward
    countenaunce,
Unworthy of faire ladies comely govern-
    aunce.

XXXVI

But young Perissa was of other mynd,
Full of disport, still laughing, loosely light,
And quite contrary to her sisters kynd;
No measure in her mood, no rule of right,
But poured out in pleasure and delight;
In wine and meats she flowd above the banck,
And in excesse exceeded her owne might;
In sumptuous tire she joyd her selfe to
    pranck,
But of her love too lavish (litle have she
    thanck.)

XXXVII

Fast by her side did sitt the bold Sansloy,
Fitt mate for such a mincing mineon,
Who in her loosenesse tooke exceeding joy;
Might not be found a francker franion,
Of her leawd parts to make companion:
But Huddibras, more like a malecontent,
Did see and grieve at his bold fashion;
Hardly could he endure his hardiment,
Yett still he satt, and inly did him selfe
    torment.

XXXVIII

Betwixt them both the faire Medina sate
With sober grace and goodly carriage:
With equall measure she did moderate
The strong extremities of their outrage.

That forward paire she ever would as-
    swage,
When they would strive dew reason to ex-
    ceed;
But that same froward twaine would ac-
    corage,
And of her plenty adde unto their need:
So kept she them in order, and her selfe in
    heed.

XXXIX

Thus fairely shee attempered her feast,
And pleasd them all with meete satiety:
At last, when lust of meat and drinke was
    ceast,
She Guyon deare besought of curtesie,
To tell from whence he came through
    jeopardy,
And whether now on new adventure bownd:
Who with bold grace, and comely gravity,
Drawing to him the eies of all arownd,
From lofty siege began these words aloud
    to sownd.

XL

'This thy demaund, O lady, doth revive
Fresh memory in me of that great Queene,
Great and most glorious virgin Queene
    alive,
That with her soveraine powre, and scepter
    shene,
All Faery Lond does peaceably sustene,
In widest ocean she her throne does reare,
That over all the earth it may be seene;
As morning sunne her beames dispredden
    cleare,
And in her face faire peace and mercy doth
    appeare.

XLI

' In her the richesse of all heavenly grace
In chiefe degree are heaped up on hye:
And all, that els this worlds enclosure bace
Hath great or glorious in mortall eye,
Adornes the person of her Majestye;
That men beholding so great excellence,
And rare perfection in mortalitye,
Doe her adore with sacred reverence,
As th' idole of her Makers great magnifi-
    cence.

XLII

' To her I homage and my service owe,
In number of the noblest knightes on
    ground,

Mongst whom on me she deigned to bestowe
Order of Maydenhead, the most renownd,
That may this day in all the world be
    found.
An yearely solemne feast she wontes to
    hold,
The day that first doth lead the yeare
    around;
To which all knights of worth and courage
    bold
Resort, to heare of straunge adventures to
    be told.

XLIII

'There this old palmer shewd himselfe
    that day,
And to that mighty Princesse did complaine
Of grievous mischiefes, which a wicked
    Fay
Had wrought, and many whelmd in deadly
    paine,
Whereof he crav'd redresse. My sove-
    raine,
Whose glory is in gracious deeds, and joyes
Throughout the world her mercy to main-
    taine,
Eftsoones devisd redresse for such an-
    noyes:
Me, all unfitt for so great purpose, she em-
    ployes.

XLIV

'Now hath faire Phebe with her silver
    face
Thrise seene the shadowes of the neather
    world,
Sith last I left that honorable place,
In which her roiall presence is enrold;
Ne ever shall I rest in house nor hold,
Till I that false Acrasia have wonne;
Of whose fowle deedes, too hideous to bee
    told,
I witnesse am, and this their wretched
    sonne,
Whose wofull parents she hath wickedly
    fordonne.'

XLV

'Tell on, fayre sir,' said she, 'that dolefull
    tale,
From which sad ruth does seeme you to
    restraine,
That we may pitty such unhappie bale,
And learne from Pleasures poyson to ab-
    staine:

Ill by ensample good doth often gayne.'
Then forward he his purpose gan pursew,
And told the story of the mortall payne,
Which Mordant and Amavia did rew;
As with lamenting eyes him selfe did lately
    vew.

XLVI

Night was far spent, and now in ocean deep
Orion, flying fast from hissing Snake,
His flaming head did hasten for to steep,
When of his pitteous tale he end did make;
Whilst with delight of that he wisely spake
Those guestes beguyled did beguyle their
    eyes
Of kindly sleepe, that did them overtake.
At last, when they had markt the chaunged
    skyes,
They wist their houre was spent; then each
    to rest him hyes.

CANTO III

Vaine Braggadocchio, getting Guyons
    horse, is made the scorne
Of knighthood trew, and is of fayre
    Belphœbe fowle forlorne.

I

Soone as the morrow fayre with purple
    beames
Disperst the shadowes of the misty night,
And Titan, playing on the eastern streames,
Gan cleare the deawy ayre with springing
    light,
Sir Guyon, mindfull of his vow yplight,
Uprose from drowsie couch, and him ad-
    drest
Unto the journey which he had behight:
His puissaunt armes about his noble brest,
And many-folded shield he bound about his
    wrest.

II

Then taking congè of that virgin pure,
The bloody-handed babe unto her truth
Did earnestly committ, and her conjure,
In vertuous lore to traine his tender youth,
And all that gentle noriture ensueth:
And that, so soone as ryper yeares he
    raught,
He might, for memory of that dayes ruth,
Be called Ruddymane, and thereby taught
T' avenge his parents death on them that
    had it wrought.

III

So forth he far'd, as now befell, on foot,
Sith his good steed is lately from him
  gone;
Patience perforce: helplesse what may it
  boot
To frett for anger, or for griefe to mone?
His palmer now shall foot no more alone.
So fortune wrought, as under greene
  woodes syde
He lately hard that dying lady grone,
He left his steed without, and speare besyde,
And rushed in on foot to ayd her, ere she
  dyde.

IV

The whyles a losell wandring by the way,
One that to bountie never cast his mynd,
Ne thought of honour ever did assay
His baser brest, but in his kestrell kynd
A pleasing vaine of glory he did fynd,
To which his flowing toung and troublous
  spright
Gave him great ayd, and made him more
  inclynd:
He, that brave steed there finding ready
  dight,
Purloynd both steed and speare, and ran
  away full light.

V

Now gan his hart all swell in jollity,
And of him selfe great hope and help con-
  ceiv'd,
That puffed up with smoke of vanity,
And with selfe-loved personage deceiv'd,
He gan to hope of men to be receiv'd
For such as he him thought, or faine would
  bee:
But for in court gay portaunce he perceiv'd
And gallant shew to be in greatest gree,
Eftsoones to court he cast t' advaunce his
  first degree.

VI

And by the way he chaunced to espy
One sitting ydle on a sunny banck,
To whom avaunting in great bravery,
As peacocke, that his painted plumes doth
  pranck,
He smote his courser in the trembling
  flanck,
And to him threatned his hart-thrilling
  speare:
The seely man, seeing him ryde so ranck

And ayme at him, fell flatt to ground for
  feare,
And crying 'Mercy!' loud, his pitious
  handes gan reare.

VII

Thereat the scarcrow wexed wondrous
  prowd,
Through fortune of his first adventure
  fayre,
And with big thundring voice revyld him
  lowd:
'Vile caytive, vassall of dread and despayre,
Unworthie of the commune breathed ayre,
Why livest thou, dead dog, a lenger day,
And doest not unto death thy selfe pre-
  payre?
Dy, or thy selfe my captive yield for ay;
Great favour I thee graunt, for aunswere
  thus to stay.'

VIII

'Hold, O deare lord, hold your dead-doing
  hand!'
Then loud he cryde, 'I am your humble
  thrall.'
'Ah, wretch!' quoth he, 'thy destinies with
  stand
My wrathfull will, and doe for mercy
  call.
I give thee life: therefore prostrated fall,
And kisse my stirrup; that thy homage
  bee.'
The miser threw him selfe, as an offall,
Streight at his foot in base humilitee,
And cleeped him his liege, to hold of him
  in fee.

IX

So happy peace they made and faire ac
  cord.
Eftsoones this liegeman gan to wexe mor
  bold,
And when he felt the folly of his lord,
In his owne kind he gan him selfe unfold:
For he was wylie witted, and growne old
In cunning sleightes and practick knavery
From that day forth he cast for to uphold
His ydle humour with fine flattery,
And blow the bellowes to his swelling
  vanity.

X

Trompart, fitt man for Braggadochio,
To serve at court in view of vaunting eye

Vaineglorious man, when fluttring wind
    does blow
In his light winges, is lifted up to skye;
The scorne of knighthood and trew cheval-
    rye,
To thinke, without desert of gentle deed
And noble worth, to be advaunced hye:
Such prayse is shame; but honour, vertues
    meed,
Doth beare the fayrest flowre in honourable
    seed.

XI

So forth they pas, a well consorted payre,
Till that at length with Archimage they
    meet:
Who, seeing one that shone in armour fayre,
On goodly courser thondring with his feet,
Eftsoones supposed him a person meet
Of his revenge to make the instrument:
For since the Redcrosse Knight he erst did
    weet,
To beene with Guyon knitt in one con-
    sent,
The ill, which earst to him, he now to
    Guyon ment.

XII

And comming close to Trompart gan in-
    quere
Of him, what mightie warriour that mote
    bee,
That rode in golden sell with single spere,
But wanted sword to wreake his enmi-
    tee.
' He is a great adventurer,' said he,
' That hath his sword through hard assay
    forgone,
And now hath vowd, till he avenged bee
Of that despight, never to wearen none;
That speare is him enough to doen a thou-
    sand grone.'

XIII

Th' enchaunter greatly joyed in the vaunt,
And weened well ere long his will to win,
And both his foen with equall foyle to
    daunt.
Tho to him louting lowly did begin
To plaine of wronges, which had committed
    bin
By Guyon, and by that false Redcrosse
    Knight,
Which two, through treason and deceiptfull
    gin,

Had slayne Sir Mordant and his lady bright:
That mote him honour win, to wreak so
    foule despight.

XIV

Therewith all suddeinly he seemd enragd,
And threatned death with dreadfull coun-
    tenaunce,
As if their lives had in his hand beene gagd;
And with stiffe force shaking his mortall
    launce,
To let him weet his doughtie valiaunce,
Thus said: ' Old man, great sure shalbe thy
    meed,
If, where those knights for feare of dew
    vengeaunce
Doe lurke, thou certeinly to mee areed,
That I may wreake on them their hainous
    hateful deed.'

XV

' Certes, my lord,' said he, ' that shall I
    soone,
And give you eke good helpe to their decay.
But mote I wisely you advise to doon,
Give no ods to your foes, but doe purvay
Your selfe of sword before that bloody day:
For they be two the prowest knights on
    grownd,
And oft approv'd in many hard assay;
And eke of surest steele, that may be
    fownd,
Doe arme your self against that day, them
    to confownd.'

XVI

' Dotard,' saide he, ' let be thy deepe ad-
    vise;
Seemes that through many yeares thy wits
    thee faile,
And that weake eld hath left thee nothing
    wise,
Els never should thy judgement be so frayle,
To measure manhood by the sword or
    mayle.
Is not enough fowre quarters of a man,
Withouten sword or shield, an hoste to
    quayle ?
Thou litle wotest what this right-hand can:
Speake they, which have beheld the bat-
    tailes which it wan.'

XVII

The man was much abashed at his boast;
Yet well he wist, that who so would contend

With either of those knightes on even
  coast,
Should neede of all his armes, him to defend;
Yet feared least his boldnesse should offend:
When Braggadocchio saide: 'Once I did
  sweare,
When with one sword seven knightes I
  brought to end,
Thence forth in battaile never sword to
  beare,
But it were that which noblest knight on
  earth doth weare.'

XVIII

' Perdy, sir knight,' saide then th' enchaun-
  ter blive,
' That shall I shortly purchase to your hond:
For now the best and noblest knight alive
Prince Arthur is, that wonnes in Faerie
  Lond;
He hath a sword, that flames like burning
  brond.
The same, by my device, I undertake
Shall by to morrow by thy side be fond.'
At which bold word that boaster gan to
  quake,
And wondred in his minde what mote that
  monster make.

XIX

He stayd not for more bidding, but away
Was suddein vanished out of his sight:
The northerne winde his wings did broad
  display
At his commaund, and reared him up light
From of the earth to take his aerie flight.
They lookt about, but no where could espye
Tract of his foot: then dead through great
  affright
They both nigh were, and each bad other
  flye:
Both fled attonce, ne ever backe retourned
  eye:

XX

Till that they come unto a forrest greene,
In which they shrowd themselves from
  causeles feare;
Yet feare them followes still, where so they
  beene.
Each trembling leafe and whistling wind
  they heare,
As ghastly bug, their haire on end does
  reare:

Yet both doe strive their fearefulnesse to
  faine.
At last they heard a horne, that shrilled
  cleare
Throughout the wood, that ecchoed againe,
And made the forrest ring, as it would rive
  in twaine.

XXI

Eft through the thicke they heard one
  rudely rush;
With noyse whereof he from his loftie
  steed
Downe fell to ground, and crept into a
  bush,
To hide his coward head from dying dreed.
But Trompart stoutly stayd to taken heed
Of what might hap. Eftsoone there stepped
  foorth
A goodly ladie clad in hunters weed,
That seemd to be a woman of great
  worth,
And, by her stately portance, borne of
  heavenly birth.

XXII

Her face so faire as flesh it seemed not,
But hevenly pourtraict of bright angels
  hew,
Cleare as the skye, withouten blame or
  blot,
Through goodly mixture of complexions
  dew;
And in her cheekes the vermeill red did
  shew
Like roses in a bed of lillies shed,
The which ambrosiall odours from them
  threw,
And gazers sence with double pleasure fed,
Hable to heale the sicke, and to revive the
  ded.

XXIII

In her faire eyes two living lamps did
  flame,
Kindled above at th' Hevenly Makers light,
And darted fyrie beames out of the same,
So passing persant, and so wondrous bright,
That quite bereav'd the rash beholders
  sight:
In them the blinded god his lustfull fyre
To kindle oft assayd, but had no might;
For with dredd majestie and awfull yre
She broke his wanton darts, and quenched
  bace desyre.

XXIV

Her yvorie forhead, full of bountie brave,
Like a broad table did it selfe dispred,
For Love his loftie triumphes to engrave,
And write the battailes of his great god-
hed:
All good and honour might therein be red:
For there their dwelling was. And when
she spake,
Sweete wordes, like dropping honny, she
did shed,
And twixt the perles and rubins softly
brake
A silver sound, that heavenly musicke
seemd to make.

XXV

Upon her eyelids many Graces sate,
Under the shadow of her even browes,
Working belgardes and amorous retrate,
And everie one her with a grace endowes,
And everie one with meekenesse to her
bowes.
So glorious mirrhour of celestiall grace,
And soveraine moniment of mortall vowes,
How shall frayle pen descrive her heavenly
face,
For feare, through want of skill, her beauty
to disgrace ?

XXVI

So faire, and thousand thousand times more
faire,
She seemd, when she presented was to
sight;
And was yclad, for heat of scorching aire,
All in a silken camus lylly whight,
Purfled upon with many a folded plight,
Which all above besprinckled was through-
out
With golden aygulets, that glistred bright,
Like twinckling starres, and all the skirt
about
Was hemd with golden fringe.

XXVII

Below her ham her weed did somewhat
trayne,
And her streight legs most bravely were
embayld
In gilden buskins of costly cordwayne,
All bard with golden bendes, which were
entayld
With curious antickes, and full fayre
aumayld:

Before, they fastned were under her knee
In a rich jewell, and therein entrayld
The ends of all their knots, that none might
see
How they within their fouldings close en-
wrapped bee.

XXVIII

Like two faire marble pillours they were
seene,
Which doe the temple of the gods support,
Whom all the people decke with girlands
greene,
And honour in their festivall resort;
Those same with stately grace and princely
port
She taught to tread, when she her selfe
would grace,
But with the woody nymphes when she did
sport,
Or when the flying libbard she did chace,
She could them nimbly move, and after fly
apace.

XXIX

And in her hand a sharpe bore-speare she
held,
And at her backe a bow and quiver gay,
Stuft with steele-headed dartes, wherewith
she queld
The salvage beastes in her victorious play,
Knit with a golden bauldricke, which fore-
lay
Athwart her snowy brest, and did divide
Her daintie paps; which, like young fruit
in May,
Now little gan to swell, and being tide,
Through her thin weed their places only
signifide.

XXX

Her yellow lockes, crisped like golden wyre,
About her shoulders weren loosely shed,
And when the winde emongst them did in-
spyre,
They waved like a penon wyde dispred,
And low behinde her backe were scattered:
And whether art it were, or heedelesse
hap,
As through the flouring forrest rash she
fled,
In her rude heares sweet flowres themselves
did lap,
And flourishing fresh leaves and blossomes
did enwrap.

XXXI

Such as Diana by the sandy shore
Of swift Eurotas, or on Cynthus greene,
Where all the nymphes have her unwares
　　forlore,
Wandreth alone with bow and arrowes
　　keene,
To seeke her game: or as that famous
　　queene
Of Amazons, whom Pyrrhus did destroy,
The day that first of Priame she was seene,
Did shew her selfe in great triumphant
　　joy,
To succour the weake state of sad afflicted
　　Troy.

XXXII

Such when as hartlesse Trompart her did
　　vew,
He was dismayed in his coward minde,
And doubted, whether he himselfe should
　　shew,
Or fly away, or bide alone behinde:
Both feare and hope he in her face did
　　finde,
When she at last, him spying, thus bespake:
' Hayle, groome ! didst not thou see a bleed-
　　ing hynde,
Whose right haunch earst my stedfast
　　arrow strake ?
If thou didst, tell me, that I may her over-
　　take.'

XXXIII

Wherewith reviv'd, this answere forth he
　　threw:
' O goddesse, (for such I thee take to bee)
For nether doth thy face terrestriall shew,
Nor voyce sound mortall) I avow to thee,
Such wounded beast as that I did not see,
Sith earst into this forrest wild I came.
But mote thy goodlyhed forgive it mee,
To weete which of the gods I shall thee
　　name,
That unto thee dew worship I may rightly
　　frame.'

XXXIV

To whom she thus — But ere her words
　　ensewd,
Unto the bush her eye did suddein glaunce,
In which vaine Braggadocchio was mewd,
And saw it stirre: she lefte her percing
　　launce,
And towards gan a deadly shafte advaunce,

In mind to marke the beast. At which sad
　　stowre,
Trompart forth stept, to stay the mortall
　　chaunce,
Out crying: ' O, what ever hevenly powre,
Or earthly wight thou be, withhold this
　　deadly howre !

XXXV

' O stay thy hand ! for yonder is no game
For thy fiers arrowes, them to exercize,
But loe ! my lord, my liege, whose warlike
　　name
Is far renowmd through many bold em-
　　prize;
And now in shade he shrouded yonder
　　lies.'
She staid: with that he crauld out of his
　　nest,
Forth creeping on his caitive hands and
　　thies,
And standing stoutly up, his lofty crest
Did fiercely shake, and rowze, as comming
　　late from rest.

XXXVI

As fearfull fowle, that long in secret cave
For dread of soring hauke her selfe hath
　　hid,
Not caring how, her silly life to save,
She her gay painted plumes disorderid,
Seeing at last her selfe from daunger rid,
Peepes forth, and soone renews her native
　　pride;
She gins her feathers fowle disfigured
Prowdly to prune, and sett on every side;
So shakes off shame, ne thinks how erst she
　　did her hide.

XXXVII

So when her goodly visage he beheld,
He gan himselfe to vaunt; but when he
　　vewd
Those deadly tooles which in her hand she
　　held,
Soone into other fitts he was transmewd,
Till she to him her gracious speach renewd:
' All haile, sir knight, and well may thee
　　befall,
As all the like, which honor have pur-
　　sewd
Through deeds of armes and prowesse mar-
　　tiall !
All vertue merits praise, but such the most
　　of all.'

XXXVIII

To whom he thus: 'O fairest under skie,
Trew be thy words, and worthy of thy praise,
That warlike feats doest highest glorifie.
Therein have I spent all my youthly daies,
And many battailes fought and many fraies
Throughout the world, wher so they might
  be found,
Endevoring my dreaded name to raise
Above the moone, that Fame may it resound
In her eternall tromp, with laurell girlond
  cround.

XXXIX

' But what art thou, O lady, which doest
  raunge
In this wilde forest, where no pleasure is,
And doest not it for joyous court exchaunge,
Emongst thine equall peres, where happy
  blis
And all delight does raigne, much more
  then this ?
There thou maist love, and dearly loved be,
And swim in pleasure, which thou here
  doest mis;
There maist thou best be seene, and best
  maist see:
The wood is fit for beasts, the court is fitt
  for thee.'

XL

' Who so in pompe of prowd estate,' quoth
  she,
' Does swim, and bathes him selfe in courtly
  blis,
Does waste his dayes in darke obscuritee,
And in oblivion ever buried is:
Where ease abownds, yt's eath to doe amis:
But who his limbs with labours, and his
  mynd
Behaves with cares, cannot so easy mis.
Abroad in armes, at home in studious kynd,
Who seekes with painfull toile, shal Honor
  soonest fynd.

XLI

' In woods, in waves, in warres she wonts to
  dwell,
And wilbe found with perill and with paine;
Ne can the man, that moulds in ydle cell,
Unto her happy mansion attaine:
Before her gate High God did sweate or-
  daine,
And wakefull watches ever to abide:
But easy is the way, and passage plaine

To Pleasures pallace; it may soone be spide,
And day and night her dores to all stand
  open wide.

XLII

' In princes court — ' The rest she would
  have sayd,
But that the foolish man, fild with delight
Of her sweete words, that all his sence dis-
  mayd,
And with her wondrous beauty ravisht
  quight,
Gan burne in filthy lust, and, leaping light,
Thought in his bastard armes her to em-
  brace.
With that she, swarving backe, her javelin
  bright
Against him bent, and fiercely did menace:
So turned her about, and fled away apace.

XLIII

Which when the pesaunt saw, amazd he
  stood,
And grieved at her flight; yet durst he nott
Pursew her steps through wild unknowen
  wood;
Besides he feard her wrath, and threatned
  shott,
Whiles in the bush he lay, not yet forgott:
Ne car'd he greatly for her presence vayne,
But turning said to Trompart: ' What
  fowle blott
Is this to knight, that lady should agayne
Depart to woods untoucht, and leave so
  proud disdayne ! '

XLIV

' Perdy,' said Trompart, ' lett her pas at
  will,
Least by her presence daunger mote befall.
For who can tell (and sure I feare it ill)
But that shee is some powre celestiall ?
For whiles she spake, her great words did
  apall
My feeble corage, and my heart oppresse,
That yet I quake and tremble over all.'
' And I,' said Braggadocchio, ' thought no
  lesse,
When first I heard her horn sound with such
  ghastlinesse.

XLV

' For from my mothers wombe this grace I
  have
Me given by eternall destiny,

That earthly thing may not my corage
brave
Dismay with feare, or cause on foote to
flye,
But either hellish feends, or powres on hye:
Which was the cause, when earst that horne
I heard,
Weening it had beene thunder in the skye,
I hid my selfe from it, as one affeard;
But when I other knew, my selfe I boldly
reard.

XLVI

' But now, for feare of worse that may be-
tide,
Let us soone hence depart.' They soone
agree;
So to his steed he gott, and gan to ride,
As one unfitt therefore, that all might see
He had not trayned bene in chevalree.
Which well that valiaunt courser did dis-
cerne;
For he despisd to tread in dew degree,
But chaufd and fom'd, with corage fiers and
sterne,
And to be easd of that base burden still did
erne.

CANTO IV

Guyon does Furor bind in chaines,
And stops Occasion :
Delivers Phedon, and therefore
By Strife is rayld uppon.

I

In brave poursuitt of honorable deed,
There is I know not what great difference
Betweene the vulgar and the noble seed,
Which unto things of valorous pretence
Seemes to be borne by native influence;
As feates of armes, and love to entertaine;
But chiefly skill to ride seemes a science
Proper to gentle blood: some others faine
To menage steeds, as did this vaunter; but
in vaine.

II

But he, the rightfull owner of that steede,
Who well could menage and subdew his
pride,
The whiles on foot was forced for to yeed,
With that blacke palmer, his most trusty
guide,
Who suffred not his wandring feete to slide;

But when strong passion, or weake fleshlinesse,
Would from the right way seeke to draw
him wide,
He would, through temperaunce and stedfastnesse,
Teach him the weak to strengthen, and the
strong suppresse.

III

It fortuned, forth faring on his way,
He saw from far, or seemed for to see,
Some troublous uprore or contentious fray,
Whereto he drew in hast, it to agree.
A mad man, or that feigned mad to bee,
Drew by the heare along upon the grownd
A handsom stripling with great crueltee,
Whom sore he bett, and gor'd with many a
wownd,
That cheekes with teares, and sydes with
blood did all abownd.

IV

And him behynd, a wicked hag did stalke,
In ragged robes and filthy disaray:
Her other leg was lame, that she no'te
walke,
But on a staffe her feeble steps did stay:
Her lockes, that loathly were and hoarie
gray,
Grew all afore, and loosly hong unrold,
But all behinde was bald, and worne away,
That none thereof could ever taken hold,
And eke her face ill favourd, full of
wrinckles old.

V

And ever as she went, her toung did walke
In fowle reproch and termes of vile despight,
Provoking him, by her outrageous talke,
To heape more vengeance on that wretched
wight;
Somtimes she raught him stones, wherwith
to smite,
Sometimes her staffe, though it her one leg
were,
Withouten which she could not goe upright;
Ne any evill meanes she did forbeare,
That might him move to wrath, and indig-
nation reare.

VI

The noble Guyon, mov'd with great remorse,
Approching, first the hag did thrust away,

And after, adding more impetuous forse,
His mighty hands did on the madman lay,
And pluckt him backe; who, all on fire
    streight way,
Against him turning all his fell intent,
With beastly brutish rage gan him assay,
And smott, and bitt, and kickt, and scratcht,
    and rent,
And did he wist not what in his avengement.

VII

And sure he was a man of mickle might,
Had he had governaunce, it well to guyde:
But when the frantick fitt inflamd his
    spright,
His force was vaine, and strooke more often
    wyde
Then at the aymed marke which he had
    eyde:
And oft himselfe he chaunst to hurt un-
    wares,
Whylest reason, blent through passion,
    nought descryde,
But as a blindfold bull at randon fares,
And where he hits, nought knowes, and
    whom he hurts, nought cares.

VIII

His rude assault and rugged handeling
Straunge seemed to the knight, that aye
    with foe
In fayre defence and goodly menaging
Of armes was wont to fight; yet nathemoe
Was he abashed now, not fighting so,
But, more enfierced through his currish
    play,
Him sternly grypt, and, hailing to and
    fro,
To overthrow him strongly did assay,
But overthrew him selfe unwares, and lower
    lay.

IX

And being downe, the villein sore did beate
And bruze with clownish fistes his manly
    face;
And eke the hag, with many a bitter threat,
Still cald upon to kill him in the place.
With whose reproch and odious menace
The knight emboyling in his haughtie hart,
Knitt all his forces, and gan soone un-
    brace
His grasping hold: so lightly did upstart,
And drew his deadly weapon, to maintaine
    his part.

X

Which when the palmer saw, he loudly
    cryde,
' Not so, O Guyon, never thinke that so
That monster can be maistred or destroyd:
He is not, ah ! he is not such a foe,
As steele can wound, or strength can over-
    throe.
That same is Furor, cursed cruel wight,
That unto knighthood workes much shame
    and woe;
And that same hag, his aged mother, hight
Occasion, the roote of all wrath and de-
    spight.

XI

' With her, who so will raging Furor tame,
Must first begin, and well her amenage:
First her restraine from her reprochfull
    blame
And evill meanes, with which she doth en-
    rage
Her frantick sonne, and kindles his corage;
Then, when she is withdrawne, or strong
    withstood,
It 's eath his ydle fury to aswage,
And calme the tempest of his passion wood:
The bankes are overflowne, when stopped
    is the flood.'

XII

Therewith Sir Guyon left his first emprise,
And turning to that woman, fast her hent
By the hoare lockes that hong before her
    eyes,
And to the ground her threw: yet n' ould
    she stent
Her bitter rayling and foule revilement,
But still provokt her sonne to wreake her
    wrong;
But nathelesse he did her still torment,
And catching hold of her ungratious tonge,
Thereon an yron lock did fasten firme and
    strong.

XIII

Then whenas use of speach was from her
    reft,
With her two crooked handes she signes
    did make,
And becknd him, the last help she had
    left:
But he that last left helpe away did take,
And both her handes fast bound unto a
    stake.

That she note stirre. Then gan her sonne
    to flye
Full fast away, and did her quite forsake;
But Guyon after him in hast did hye,
And soone him overtooke in sad perplexitye.

XIV

In his strong armes he stifly him embraste,
Who, him gainstriving, nought at all pre-
    vaild:
For all his power was utterly defaste,
And furious fitts at earst quite weren
    quaild:
Oft he re'nforst, and oft his forces fayld,
Yet yield he would not, nor his rancor
    slack.
Then him to ground he cast, and rudely
    hayld,
And both his hands fast bound behind his
    backe,
And both his feet in fetters to an yron rack.

XV

With hundred yron chaines he did him bind,
And hundred knots, that did him sore con-
    straine:
Yet his great yron teeth he still did grind,
And grimly gnash, threatning revenge in
    vaine:
His burning eyen, whom bloody strakes did
    staine,
Stared full wide, and threw forth sparkes
    of fyre,
And more for ranck despight then for great
    paine,
Shakt his long locks, colourd like copper-
    wyre,
And bitt his tawny beard to shew his raging
    yre.

XVI

Thus whenas Guyon Furor had captivd,
Turning about he saw that wretched squyre,
Whom that mad man of life nigh late de-
    privd,
Lying on ground, all soild with blood and
    myre:
Whom whenas he perceived to respyre,
He gan to comfort, and his woundes to
    dresse.
Being at last recured, he gan inquyre,
What hard mishap him brought to such dis-
    tresse,
And made that caytives thrall, the thrall of
    wretchednesse.

XVII

With hart then throbbing, and with watry
    eyes,
'Fayre sir,' quoth he, 'what man can shun
    the hap,
That hidden lyes unwares him to surpryse?
Misfortune waites advantage to entrap
The man most wary in her whelming lap.
So me, weake wretch, of many weakest one,
Unweeting, and unware of such mishap,
She brought to mischiefe through occasion,
Where this same wicked villein did me light
    upon.

XVIII

'It was a faithlesse squire, that was the
    sourse
Of all my sorrow, and of these sad teares,
With whom from tender dug of commune
    nourse
Attonce I was upbrought, and eft, when
    yeares
More rype us reason lent to chose our
    peares,
Our selves in league of vowed love wee
    knitt:
In which we long time, without gealous
    feares
Or faultie thoughts, contynewd, as was fitt;
And, for my part I vow, dissembled not a
    whitt.

XIX

'It was my fortune, commune to that age,
To love a lady fayre of great degree,
The which was borne of noble parentage,
And set in highest seat of dignitee,
Yet seemd no lesse to love then loved to
    bee:
Long I her serv'd, and found her faithfull
    still,
Ne ever thing could cause us disagree:
Love, that two harts makes one, makes eke
    one will:
Each strove to please, and others pleasure
    to fulfill.

XX

'My friend, hight Philemon, I did partake
Of all my love and all my privitie;
Who greatly joyous seemed for my sake,
And gratious to that lady, as to mee;
Ne ever wight, that mote so welcome bee
As he to her, withouten blott or blame,
Ne ever thing, that she could thinke or see,

But unto him she would impart the same:
O wretched man, that would abuse so gentle
    dame !

XXI

' At last such grace I found, and meanes I
    wrought,
That I that lady to my spouse had wonne;
Accord of friendes, consent of parents
    sought,
Affyaunce made, my happinesse begonne,
There wanted nought but few rites to be
    donne,
Which mariage make: that day too farre
    did seeme:
Most joyous man on whom the shining
    sunne
Did shew his face, my selfe I did esteeme,
And that my falser friend did no lesse joy-
    ous deeme.

XXII

'But ear that wished day his beame dis-
    closd,
He, either envying my toward good,
Or of himselfe to treason ill disposd,
One day unto me came in friendly mood,
And told for secret, how he understood,
That lady, whom I had to me assynd,
Had both distaind her honorable blood,
And eke the faith which she to me did bynd;
And therfore wisht me stay, till I more
    truth should fynd.

XXIII

' The gnawing anguish and sharp gelosy,
Which his sad speach infixed in my brest,
Ranckled so sore, and festred inwardly,
That my engreeved mind could find no rest,
Till that the truth thereof I did out wrest;
And him besought, by that same sacred
    band
Betwixt us both, to counsell me the best.
He then with solemne oath and plighted hand
Assurd, ere long the truth to let me under-
    stand.

XXIV

' Ere long with like againe he boorded mee,
Saying, he now had boulted all the floure,
And that it was a groome of base degree,
Which of my love was partener paramoure:
Who used in a darkesome inner bowre
Her oft to meete: which better to approve,
He promised to bring me at that howre,

When I should see that would me nearer
    move,
And drive me to withdraw my blind abused
    love.

XXV

' This gracelesse man, for furtherance of
    his guile,
Did court the handmayd of my lady deare,
Who, glad t' embosome his affection vile,
Did all she might, more pleasing to appeare.
One day, to worke her to his will more
    neare,
He woo'd her thus: " Pryene," (so she
    hight)
" What great despight doth Fortune to thee
    beare,
Thus lowly to abase thy beautie bright,
That it should not deface all others lesser
    light ?

XXVI

' " But if she had her least helpe to thee lent,
T' adorne thy forme according thy desart,
Their blazing pride thou wouldest soone
    have blent,
And staynd their prayses with thy least
    good part;
Ne should faire Claribell with all her art,
Though she thy lady be, approch thee neare:
For proofe thereof, this evening, as thou art,
Aray thy selfe in her most gorgeous geare,
That I may more delight in thy embrace-
    ment deare."

XXVII

' The mayden, proud through praise and
    mad through love,
Him hearkned to, and soone her selfe
    arayd,
The whiles to me the treachour did re-
    move
His craftie engin, and, as he had sayd,
Me leading, in a secret corner layd,
The sad spectatour of my tragedie;
Where left, he went, and his owne false part
    playd,
Disguised like that groome of base degree,
Whom he had feignd th' abuser of my love
    to bee.

XXVIII

' Eftsoones he came unto th' appointed
    place,
And with him brought Pryene, rich arayd,

In Claribellaes clothes. Her proper face
I not descerned in that darkesome shade,
But weend it was my love with whom he
    playd.
Ah God! what horrour and tormenting
    griefe
My hart, my handes, mine eyes, and all
    assayd!
Me liefer were ten thousand deathes priefe,
Then wounde of gealous worme, and shame
    of such repriefe.

XXIX

I home retourning, fraught with fowle de-
    spight,
And chawing vengeaunce all the way I
    went,
Soone as my loathed love appeard in sight,
With wrathfull hand I slew her innocent;
That after soone I dearely did lament:
For when the cause of that outrageous
    deede
Demaunded, I made plaine and evident,
Her faultie handmayd, which that bale did
    breede,
Confest how Philemon her wrought to
    chaunge her weede.

XXX

'Which when I heard, with horrible affright
And hellish fury all enragd, I sought
Upon my selfe that vengeable despight
To punish: yet it better first I thought,
To wreake my wrath on him that first it
    wrought.
To Philemon, false faytour Philemon,
I cast to pay that I so dearely bought:
Of deadly drugs I gave him drinke anon,
And washt away his guilt with guilty potion.

XXXI

'Thus heaping crime on crime, and griefe
    on griefe,
To losse of love adjoyning losse of frend,
I meant to purge both with a third mis-
    chiefe,
And in my woes beginner it to end:
That was Pryene; she did first offend,
She last should smart: with which cruell
    intent,
When I at her my murdrous blade did
    bend,
She fled away with ghastly dreriment,
And I, poursewing my fell purpose, after
    went.

XXXII

'Feare gave her winges, and rage enforst
    my flight:
Through woods and plaines so long I did
    her chace,
Till this mad man, whom your victorious
    might
Hath now fast bound, me met in middle
    space:
As I her, so he me poursewd apace,
And shortly overtooke: I, breathing yre,
Sore chauffed at my stay in such a cace,
And with my heat kindled his cruell fyre;
Which kindled once, his mother did more
    rage inspyre.

XXXIII

'Betwixt them both, they have me doen to
    dye,
Through wounds, and strokes, and stub-
    borne handeling,
That death were better then such agony
As griefe and fury unto me did bring;
Of which in me yet stickes the mortall
    sting,
That during life will never be appeasd.'
When he thus ended had his sorrowing,
Said Guyon: 'Squyre, sore have ye beene
    diseasd;
But all your hurts may soone through tem-
    perance be easd.'

XXXIV

Then gan the palmer thus: 'Most wretched
    man,
That to affections does the bridle lend!
In their beginning they are weake and wan,
But soone through suff'rance growe to
    fearefull end.
Whiles they are weake, betimes with them
    contend:
For when they once to perfect strength do
    grow,
Strong warres they make, and cruell battry
    bend
Gainst fort of reason, it to overthrow:
Wrath, gelosy, griefe, love this squyre have
    laide thus low.

XXXV

'Wrath, gealosie, griefe, love do thus
    expell:
Wrath is a fire, and gealosie a weede,
Griefe is a flood, and love a monster fell;
The fire of sparkes, the weede of little seede,

The flood of drops, the monster filth did
    breede:
But sparks, seed, drops, and filth do thus
    delay;
The sparks soone quench, the springing
    seed outweed,
The drops dry up, and filth wipe cleane
    away:
So shall wrath, gealosy, griefe, love die and
    decay.'

XXXVI

'Unlucky squire,' saide Guyon, 'sith thou
    hast
Falne into mischiefe through intemper-
    aunce,
Henceforth take heede of that thou now
    hast past,
And guyde thy waies with warie govern-
    aunce,
Least worse betide thee by some later
    chaunce.
But read how art thou nam'd, and of what
    kin.'
' Phedon I hight,' quoth he, 'and do ad-
    vaunce
Mine auncestry from famous Coradin,
Who first to rayse our house to honour did
    begin.'

XXXVII

Thus as he spake, lo ! far away they spyde
A varlet ronning towardes hastily,
Whose flying feet so fast their way applyde,
That round about a cloud of dust did fly,
Which, mingled all with sweate, did dim
    his eye.
He soone approched, panting, breathlesse,
    whot,
And all so soyld, that none could him de-
    scry.
His countenaunce was bold, and bashed
    not
For Guyons lookes, but scornefull eyglaunce
    at him shot.

XXXVIII

Behind his backe he bore a brasen shield,
On which was drawen faire, in colours fit,
A flaming fire in midst of bloody field,
And round about the wreath this word was
    writ,
Burnt I doe burne. Right well beseemed it
To be the shield of some redoubted knight:
And in his hand two dartes exceeding flit

And deadly sharp he held, whose heads
    were dight
In poyson and in blood of malice and de-
    spight.

XXXIX

When he in presence came, to Guyon first
He boldly spake: 'Sir knight, if knight
    thou bee,
Abandon this forestalled place at erst,
For feare of further harme, I counsell thee;
Or bide the chaunce at thine owne jeopar-
    dee.'
The knight at his great boldnesse wondered,
And though he scornd his ydle vanitee,
Yet mildly him to purpose answered;
For not to grow of nought he it conjectured.

XL

'Varlet, this place most dew to me I
    deeme,
Yielded by him that held it forcibly.
But whence shold come that harme, which
    thou dost seeme
To threat to him that mindes his chaunce
    t' abye ?'
' Perdy,' sayd he, ' here comes, and is hard
    by,
A knight of wondrous powre and great
    assay,
That never yet encountred enemy,
But did him deadly daunt, or fowle dismay;
Ne thou for better hope, if thou his pre-
    sence stay.'

XLI

' How hight he then,' sayd Guyon, 'and
    from whence ?'
' Pyrochles is his name, renowmed farre
For his bold feates and hardy confidence,
Full oft approvd in many a cruell warre;
The brother of Cymochles, both which arre
The sonnes of old Acrates and Despight,
Acrates, sonne of Phlegeton and Jarre;
But Phlegeton is sonne of Herebus and
    Night:
But Herebus sonne of Aeternitie is hight.

XLII

' So from immortall race he does proceede,
That mortall hands may not withstand his
    might,
Drad for his derring doe and bloody deed:
For all in blood and spoile is his delight.
His am I Atin, his in wrong and right,

That matter make for him to worke upon,
And stirre him up to strife and cruell fight.
Fly therefore, fly this fearfull stead anon,
Least thy foolhardize worke thy sad confu-
      sion.'

XLIII

'His be that care, whom most it doth con-
      cerne,'
Sayd he: ' but whether with such hasty
      flight
Art thou now bownd? for well mote I dis-
      cerne
Great cause, that carries thee so swifte and
      light.'
'My lord,' quoth he, ' me sent, and streight
      behight
To seeke Occasion, where so she bee:
For he is all disposd to bloody fight,
And breathes out wrath and hainous cruel-
      tee:
Hard is his hap, that first fals in his jeo-
      pardee.'

XLIV

'Mad man,' said then the palmer, ' that
      does seeke
Occasion to wrath, and cause of strife!
Shee comes unsought, and shonned followes
      eke.
Happy who can abstaine, when Rancor rife
Kindles revenge, and threats his rusty
      knife:
Woe never wants, where every cause is
      caught,
And rash Occasion makes unquiet life.'
'Then loe! wher bound she sits, whom thou
      hast sought,'
Said Guyon: ' let that message to thy lord
      be brought.'

XLV

That when the varlett heard and saw,
      streight way
He wexed wondrous wroth, and said: ' Vile
      knight,
That knights and knighthood doest with
      shame upbray,
And shewst th' ensample of thy childishe
      might,
With silly weake old woman thus to fight!
Great glory and gay spoile sure hast thou
      gott,
And stoutly prov'd thy puissaunce here in
      sight.

That shall Pyrochles well requite, I wott,
And with thy blood abolish so reprochfull
      blott.'

XLVI

With that, one of his thrillant darts he
      threw,
Headed with yre and vengeable despight:
The quivering steele his aymed end wel
      knew,
And to his brest it selfe intended right:
But he was wary, and, ere it empight
In the meant marke, advaunst his shield
      atweene,
On which it seizing, no way enter might,
But backe rebownding left the forckhead
      keene:
Eftsoones he fled away, and might no where
      be seene.

CANTO V

Pyrochles does with Guyon fight,
      And Furors chayne unbinds;
Of whom sore hurt, for his revenge
      Attin Cymochles finds.

I

Who ever doth to temperaunce apply
His stedfast life, and all his actions frame,
Trust me, shal find no greater enimy,
Then stubborne perturbation, to the same;
To which right wel the wise doe give that
      name;
For it the goodly peace of staied mindes
Does overthrow, and troublous warre pro-
      clame:
His owne woes author, who so bound it
      findes,
As did Pyrochles, and it wilfully unbindes.

II

After that varlets flight, it was not long,
Ere on the plaine fast pricking Guyon
      spide
One in bright armes embatteiled full strong,
That as the sunny beames doe glaunce and
      glide
Upon the trembling wave, so shined bright,
And round about him threw forth sparkling
      fire,
That seemd him to enflame on every side:
His steed was bloody red, and fomed yre,
When with the maistring spur he did him
      roughly stire.

III

Approching nigh, he never staid to greete,
Ne chaffar words, prowd corage to pro-
voke,
But prickt so fiers, that underneath his
feete
The smouldring dust did rownd about him
smoke,
Both horse and man nigh able for to choke;
And fayrly couching his steeleheaded speare,
Him first saluted with a sturdy stroke:
It booted nought Sir Guyon, comming
neare,
To thincke such hideous puissaunce on foot
to beare;

IV

But lightly shunned it, and passing by,
With his bright blade did smite at him so
fell,
That the sharpe steele, arriving forcibly
On his broad shield, bitt not, but glauncing
fell
On his horse necke before the quilted sell,
And from the head the body sundred quight.
So him, dismounted low, he did compell
On foot with him to matchen equall fight;
The truncked beast, fast bleeding, did him
fowly dight.

V

Sore bruzed with the fall, he slow uprose,
And all enraged, thus him loudly shent:
'Disleall knight, whose coward corage chose
To wreake it selfe on beast all innocent,
And shund the marke at which it should be
ment !
Therby thine armes seem strong, but man-
hood frayl:
So hast thou oft with guile thine honor
blent;
But litle may such guile thee now avayl,
If wonted force and fortune doe not much
me fayl.'

VI

With that he drew his flaming sword, and
strooke
At him so fiercely, that the upper marge
Of his sevenfolded shield away it tooke,
And glauncing on his helmet, made a large
And open gash therein: were not his targe,
That broke the violence of his intent,
The weary sowle from thence it would dis-
charge:

Nathelesse so sore a buff to him it lent,
That made him reele, and to his brest his
bever bent.

VII

Exceeding wroth was Guyon at that blow,
And much ashamd that stroke of living
arme
Should him dismay, and make him stoup so
low,
Though otherwise it did him litle harme:
Tho, hurling high his yron braced arme,
He smote so manly on his shoulder plate,
That all his left side it did quite disarme;
Yet there the steele stayd not, but inly bate
Deepe in his flesh, and opened wide a red
floodgate.

VIII

Deadly dismayd with horror of that dint
Pyrochles was, and grieved eke entyre;
Yet nathemore did it his fury stint,
But added flame unto his former fire,
That welnigh molt his hart in raging yre;
Ne thenceforth his approved skill, to ward,
Or strike, or hurtle rownd in warlike gyre,
Remembred he, ne car'd for his saufgard,
But rudely rag'd, and like a cruel tygre
far'd.

IX

He hewd, and lasht, and foynd, and thondred
blowes,
And every way did seeke into his life;
Ne plate, ne male could ward so mighty
throwes,
But yeilded passage to his cruell knife.
But Guyon, in the heat of all his strife,
Was wary wise, and closely did awayt
Avauntage, whilest his foe did rage most
rife:
Sometimes a thwart, sometimes he strook
him strayt,
And falsed oft his blowes, t' illude him
with such bayt.

X

Like as a lyon, whose imperiall powre
A prowd rebellious unicorne defyes,
T' avoide the rash assault and wrathfull
stowre
Of his fiers foe, him to a tree applyes,
And when him ronning in full course he
spyes,
He slips aside; the whiles that furious beast

His precious horne, sought of his enimyes,
Strikes in the stocke, ne thence can be re-
    least,
But to the mighty victor yields a bounteous
    feast.

XI

With such faire sleight him Guyon often
    fayld,
Till at the last all breathlesse, weary, faint
Him spying, with fresh onsett he assayld,
And kindling new his corage seeming
    queint,
Strooke him so hugely, that through great
    constraint
He made him stoup perforce unto his knee,
And doe unwilling worship to the saint,
That on his shield depainted he did see:
Such homage till that instant never learned
    hee.

XII

Whom Guyon seeing stoup, poursewed fast
The present offer of faire victory,
And soone his dreadfull blade about he cast,
Wherewith he smote his haughty crest so
    hye,
That streight on grownd made him full
    low to lye;
Then on his brest his victor foote he thrust:
With that he cryde: 'Mercy! doe me not
    dye,
Ne deeme thy force by Fortunes doome un-
    just,
That hath (maugre her spight!) thus low
    me laid in dust.'

XIII

Eftsoones his cruel hand Sir Guyon stayd,
Tempring the passion with advizement
    slow,
And maistring might on enimy dismayd;
For th' equall die of warre he well did know:
Then to him said: 'Live, and alleagaunce
    owe
To him that gives thee life and liberty,
And henceforth by this daies ensample trow,
That hasty wroth, and heedlesse hazardry,
Doe breede repentaunce late, and lasting
    infamy.'

XIV

So up he let him rise; who, with grim looke
And count'naunce sterne upstanding, gan to
    grind

His grated teeth for great disdeigne, and
    shooke
His sandy lockes, long hanging downe be-
    hind,
Knotted in blood and dust, for griefe of
    mind,
That he in ods of armes was conquered;
Yet in himselfe some comfort he did find,
That him so noble knight had maystered,
Whose bounty more then might, yet both,
    he wondered.

XV

Which Guyon marking said: 'Be nought
    agriev'd,
Sir knight, that thus ye now subdewed
    arre:
Was never man, who most conquestes at-
    chiev'd,
But sometimes had the worse, and lost by
    warre,
Yet shortly gaynd that losse exceeded farre:
Losse is no shame, nor to bee lesse then
    foe,
But to bee lesser then himselfe doth marre
Both loosers lott, and victours prayse alsoe:
Vaine others overthrowes who selfe doth
    overthrow.

XVI

'Fly, O Pyrochles, fly the dreadfull warre,
That in thy selfe thy lesser partes doe move,
Outrageous anger, and woe working jarre,
Direfull impatience, and hartmurdring love;
Those, those thy foes, those warriours far
    remove,
Which thee to endlesse bale captived lead.
But sith in might thou didst my mercy
    prove,
Of courtesie to mee the cause aread,
That thee against me drew with so impetu-
    ous dread.'

XVII

'Dreadlesse,' said he, 'that shall I soone
    declare:
It was complaind that thou hadst done great
    tort
Unto an aged woman, poore and bare,
And thralled her in chaines with strong
    effort,
Voide of all succour and needfull comfort:
That ill beseemes thee, such as I thee see,
To worke such shame. Therefore I thee
    exhort

To chaunge thy will, and set Occasion free,
And to her captive sonne yield his first
   libertee.'

XVIII

Thereat Sir Guyon smylde: 'And is that
   all,'
Said he, 'that thee so sore displeased hath ?
Great mercy sure, for to enlarge a thrall,
Whose freedom shall thee turne to greatest
   scath !
Nath'lesse now quench thy whott emboyl-
   ing wrath:
Loe ! there they bee; to thee I yield them
   free.'
Thereat he wondrous glad, out of the
   path
Did lightly leape, where he them bound did
   see,
And gan to breake the bands of their cap-
   tivitee.

XIX

Soone as Occasion felt her selfe untyde,
Before her sonne could well assoyled bee,
She to her use returnd, and streight defyde
Both Guyon and Pyrochles: th' one (said
   shee)
Bycause he wonne; the other because hee
Was wonne: so matter did she make of
   nought,
To stirre up strife, and do them disagree:
But soone as Furor was enlargd, she sought
To kindle his quencht fyre, and thousand
   causes wrought.

XX

It was not long ere she inflam'd him so,
That he would algates with Pyrochles fight,
And his redeemer chalengd for his foe,
Because he had not well mainteind his right,
But yielded had to that same straunger
   knight:
Now gan Pyrochles wex as wood as hee,
And him affronted with impatient might:
So both together fiers engrasped bee,
Whyles Guyon, standing by, their uncouth
   strife does see.

XXI

Him all that while Occasion did provoke
Against Pyrochles, and new matter fram'd
Upon the old, him stirring to bee wroke
Of his late wronges, in which she oft him
   blam'd

For suffering such abuse as knighthood
   sham'd,
And him dishabled quyte. But he was wise,
Ne would with vaine occasions be inflam'd;
Yet others she more urgent did devise;
Yet nothing could him to impatience entise.

XXII

Their fell contention still increased more,
And more thereby increased Furors might,
That he his foe has hurt, and wounded
   sore,
And him in blood and durt deformed
   quight.
His mother eke, more to augment his
   spight,
Now brought to him a flaming fyer brond,
Which she in Stygian lake, ay burning
   bright,
Had kindled: that she gave into his hond,
That, armd with fire, more hardly he mote
   him withstond.

XXIII

Tho gan that villein wex so fiers and strong,
That nothing might sustaine his furious
   forse:
He cast him downe to ground, and all along
Drew him through durt and myre without
   remorse,
And fowly battered his comely corse,
That Guyon much disdeignd so loathly sight.
At last he was compeld to cry perforse,
'Help, O Sir Guyon ! helpe, most noble
   knight,
To ridd a wretched man from handes of hell-
   ish wight !'

XXIV

The knight was greatly moved at his playnt,
And gan him dight to succour his distresse,
Till that the palmer, by his grave restraynt,
Him stayd from yielding pitifull redresse,
And said: 'Deare sonne, thy causelesse
   ruth represse,
Ne let thy stout hart melt in pitty vayne:
He that his sorow sought through wilful-
   nesse,
And his foe fettred would release agayne,
Deserves to taste his follies fruit, repented
   payne.'

XXV

Guyon obayd: so him away he drew
From needlesse trouble of renewing fight

Already fought, his voyage to poursew.
But rash Pyrochles varlett, Atin hight,
When late he saw his lord in heavie plight,
Under Sir Guyons puissaunt stroke to
    fall,
Him deeming dead, as then he seemd in
    sight,
Fledd fast away, to tell his funerall
Unto his brother, whom Cymochles men did
    call.

XXVI

He was a man of rare redoubted might,
Famous throughout the world for warlike
    prayse,
And glorious spoiles, purchast in perilous
    fight:
Full many doughtie knightes he in his dayes
Had doen to death, subdewde in equall
    frayes,
Whose carkases, for terrour of his name,
Of fowles and beastes he made the piteous
    prayes,
And hong their conquerd armes for more
    defame
On gallow trees, in honour of his dearest
    dame.

XXVII

His dearest dame is that enchaunteresse,
The vyle Acrasia, that with vaine delightes,
And ydle pleasures in her Bowre of Blisse,
Does charme her lovers, and the feeble
    sprightes
Can call out of the bodies of fraile wightes;
Whom then she does trasforme to monstrous
    hewes,
And horribly misshapes with ugly sightes,
Captiv'd eternally in yron mewes,
And darksom dens, where Titan his face
    never shewes.

XXVIII

There Atin fownd Cymochles sojourning,
To serve his lemans love: for he by kynd
Was given all to lust and loose living,
When ever his fiers handes he free mote
    fynd:
And now he has pourd out his ydle mynd
In daintie delices and lavish joyes,
Having his warlike weapons cast behynd,
And flowes in pleasures and vaine pleasing
    toyes,
Mingled emongst loose ladies and lascivious
    boyes.

XXIX

And over him, Art, stryving to compayre
With Nature, did an arber greene dispred,
Framed of wanton yvie, flouring fayre,
Through which the fragrant eglantine did
    spred
His prickling armes, entrayld with roses
    red,
Which daintie odours round about them
    threw;
And all within with flowres was garnished,
That, when myld Zephyrus emongst them
    blew,
Did breath out bounteous smels, and painted
    colors shew.

XXX

And fast beside, there trickled softly downe
A gentle streame, whose murmuring wave
    did play
Emongst the pumy stones, and made a
    sowne,
To lull him soft a sleepe, that by it lay:
The wearie traveiler, wandring that way,
Therein did often quench his thristy heat,
And then by it his wearie limbes display,
Whiles creeping slomber made him to for-
    get
His former payne, and wypt away his toil-
    som sweat.

XXXI

And on the other syde a pleasaunt grove
Was shott up high, full of the stately tree
That dedicated is t' Olympick Jove,
And to his sonne Alcides, whenas hee
Gaynd in Nemea goodly victoree:
Therein the mery birdes of every sorte
Chaunted alowd their chearefull harmonee,
And made emongst them selves a sweete
    consort,
That quickned the dull spright with music-
    all comfort.

XXXII

There he him found all carelesly displaid,
In secrete shadow from the sunny ray,
On a sweet bed of lillies softly laid,
Amidst a flock of damzelles fresh and gay,
That rownd about him dissolute did play
Their wanton follies and light meriment;
Every of which did loosely disaray
Her upper partes of meet habiliments,
And shewd them naked, deckt with many
    ornaments.

XXXIII

And every of them strove, with most de-
lights
Him to aggrate, and greatest pleasures
shew;
Some framd faire lookes, glancing like even-
ing lights,
Others sweet wordes, dropping like honny
dew;
Some bathed kisses, and did soft embrew
The sugred licour through his melting lips:
One boastes her beautie, and does yield to
vew
Her dainty limbes above her tender hips;
Another her out boastes, and all for tryall
strips.

XXXIV

He, like an adder lurking in the weedes,
His wandring thought in deepe desire does
steepe,
And his frayle eye with spoyle of beauty
feedes:
Sometimes he falsely faines himselfe to
sleepe,
Whiles through their lids his wanton eies do
peepe,
To steale a snatch of amorous conceipt,
Whereby close fire into his heart does
creepe:
So' he them deceives, deceivd in his deceipt,
Made dronke with drugs of deare voluptu-
ous receipt.

XXXV

Attin, arriving there, when him he spyde
Thus in still waves of deepe delight to wade,
Fiercely approching, to him lowdly cryde,
' Cymochles ! oh ! no, but Cymochles shade,
In which that manly person late did fade !
What is become of great Acrates sonne ?
Or where hath he hong up his mortall
blade,
That hath so many haughty conquests
wonne ?
Is all his force forlorne, and all his glory
donne ? '

XXXVI

Then pricking him with his sharp-pointed
dart,
He saide: ' Up, up ! thou womanish weake
knight,
That here in ladies lap entombed art,
Unmindfull of thy praise and prowest might,

And weetlesse eke of lately wrought despight,
Whiles sad Pyrochles lies on sencelesse
ground,
And groneth out his utmost grudging
spright,
Through many a stroke, and many a streaming wound,
Calling thy help in vaine, that here in joyes
art dround.'

XXXVII

Suddeinly out of his delightfull dreame
The man awoke, and would have questiond
more;
But he would not endure that wofull
theame
For to dilate at large, but urged sore,
With percing wordes and pittifull implore,
Him hasty to arise. As one affright
With hellish feends, or Furies mad uprore,
He then uprose, inflamd with fell despight,
And called for his armes; for he would al-
gates fight.

XXXVIII

They bene ybrought; he quickly does him
dight,
And, lightly mounted, passeth on his way;
Ne ladies loves, ne sweete entreaties might
Appease his heat, or hastie passage stay;
For he has vowd to beene avengd that day
(That day it selfe him seemed all too
long)
On him that did Pyrochles deare dismay:
So proudly pricketh on his courser strong,
And Attin ay him pricks with spurs of
shame and wrong.

CANTO VI

Guyon is of Immodest Merth
Led into loose desyre ;
Fights with Cymochles, whiles his bro-
ther burnes in furious fyre.

I

A HARDER lesson to learne continence
In joyous pleasure then in grievous paine:
For sweetnesse doth allure the weaker
sence
So strongly, that uneathes it can refraine
From that which feeble nature covets faine;
But griefe and wrath, that be her enemies,
And foes of life, she better can restraine;

Yet Vertue vauntes in both her victories,
And Guyon in them all shewes goodly maysteries.

II

Whom bold Cymochles traveiling to finde,
With cruell purpose bent to wreake on him
The wrath which Atin kindled in his mind,
Came to a river, by whose utmost brim
Wayting to passe, he saw whereas did swim
Along the shore, as swift as glaunce of eye,
A litle gondelay, bedecked trim
With boughes and arbours woven cun-
   ningly,
That like a litle forrest seemed outwardly.

III

And therein sate a lady fresh and fayre,
Making sweete solace to herselfe alone;
Sometimes she song, as lowd as larke in
   ayre,
Sometimes she laught, that nigh her breth
   was gone,
Yet was there not with her else any one,
That might to her move cause of meriment:
Matter of merth enough, though there were
   none,
She could devise, and thousand waies in-
   vent,
To feede her foolish humour and vaine
   jolliment.

IV

Which when far of Cymochles heard and
   saw,
He lowdly cald to such as were abord,
The little barke unto the shore to draw,
And him to ferry over that deepe ford.
The merry mariner unto his word
Soone hearkned, and her painted bote
   streightway
Turnd to the shore, where that same war-
   like lord
She in receiv'd; but Atin by no way
She would admit, albe the knight her much
   did pray.

V

Eftsoones her shallow ship away did slide,
More swift then swallow sheres the liquid
   skye,
Withouten oare or pilot it to guide,
Or winged canvas with the wind to fly:
Onely she turnd a pin, and by and by
It cut away upon the yielding wave;

Ne cared she her course for to apply:
For it was taught the way which she would
   have,
And both from rocks and flats it selfe could
   wisely save.

VI

And all the way, the wanton damsell found
New merth, her passenger to entertaine:
For she in pleasaunt purpose did abound,
And greatly joyed merry tales to faine,
Of which a store-house did with her re-
   maine:
Yet seemed, nothing well they her became;
For all her wordes she drownd with laugh-
   ter vaine,
And wanted grace in utt'ring of the same,
That turned all her pleasaunce to a scoffing
   game.

VII

And other whiles vaine toyes she would
   devize,
As her fantasticke wit did most delight:
Sometimes her head she fondly would
   aguize
With gaudy girlonds, or fresh flowrets
   dight
About her necke, or rings of rushes plight;
Sometimes, to do him laugh, she would
   assay
To laugh at shaking of the leaves light,
Or to behold the water worke and play
About her little frigot, therein making
   way.

VIII

Her light behaviour and loose dalliaunce
Gave wondrous great contentment to the
   knight,
That of his way he had no sovenaunce,
Nor care of vow'd revenge and cruell fight,
But to weake wench did yield his martiall
   might:
So easie was, to quench his flamed minde
With one sweete drop of sensuall delight;
So easie is, t' appease the stormy winde
Of malice in the calme of pleasaunt woman-
   kind.

IX

Diverse discourses in their way they spent,
Mongst which Cymochles of her questioned,
Both what she was, and what that usage
   ment,

Which in her cott she daily practized.
' Vaine man ! ' saide she, ' that wouldest be
    reckoned
A straunger in thy home, and ignoraunt
Of Phædria (for so my name is red)
Of Phædria, thine owne fellow servaunt;
For thou to serve Acrasia thy selfe doest
    vaunt.

X

' In this wide inland sea, that hight by
    name
The Idle Lake, my wandring ship I row,
That knowes her port, and thether sayles
    by ayme;
Ne care, ne feare I, how the wind do blow,
Or whether swift I wend, or whether slow:
Both slow and swift a like do serve my
    tourne:
Ne swelling Neptune, ne lowd thundring
    Jove
Can chaunge my cheare, or make me ever
    mourne:
My little boat can safely passe this perilous
    bourne.'

XI

Whiles thus she talked, and whiles thus
    she toyd,
They were far past the passage which he
    spake,
And come unto an island, waste and voyd,
That floted in the midst of that great lake.
There her small gondelay her port did
    make,
And that gay payre issewing on the shore
Disburdned her. Their way they forward
    take
Into the land, that lay them faire before,
Whose pleasaunce she him shewd, and
    plentifull great store.

XII

It was a chosen plott of fertile land,
Emongst wide waves sett, like a litle nest,
As if it had by Natures cunning hand
Bene choycely picked out from all the rest,
And laid forth for ensample of the best:
No dainty flowre or herbe, that growes on
    grownd,
No arborett with painted blossomes drest,
And smelling sweete, but there it might be
    fownd
To bud out faire, and her sweete smels
    throwe al arownd.

XIII

No tree, whose braunches did not bravely
    spring;
No braunch, whereon a fine bird did not
    sitt;
No bird, but did her shrill notes sweetely
    sing;
No song, but did containe a lovely ditt:
Trees, braunches, birds, and songs were
    framed fitt
For to allure fraile mind to carelesse ease.
Carelesse the man soone woxe, and his weake
    witt
Was overcome of thing that did him please;
So pleased, did his wrathfull purpose faire
    appease.

XIV

Thus when shee had his eyes and sences
    fed
With false delights, and fild with pleasures
    vayn,
Into a shady dale she soft him led,
And laid him downe upon a grassy playn;
And her sweete selfe without dread or dis-
    dayn
She sett beside, laying his head disarmd
In her loose lap, it softly to sustayn,
Where soone he slumbred, fearing not be
    harmd,
The whiles with a love lay she thus him
    sweetly charmd:

XV

' Behold, O man, that toilesome paines doest
    take,
The flowrs, the fields, and all that pleasaunt
    growes,
How they them selves doe thine ensample
    make,
Whiles nothing envious Nature them forth
    throwes
Out of her fruitfull lap; how no man
    knowes,
They spring, they bud, they blossome fresh
    and faire,
And decke the world with their rich pomp-
    ous showes;
Yet no man for them taketh paines or care,
Yet no man to them can his carefull paines
    compare.

XVI

' The lilly, lady of the flowring field,
The flowre deluce, her lovely paramoure,

Bid thee to them thy fruitlesse labors yield,
And soone leave off this toylsome weary
  stoure:
Loe, loe, how brave she decks her bounteous
  boure,
With silkin curtens and gold coverletts,
Therein to shrowd her sumptuous bela-
  moure!
Yet nether spinnes nor cards, ne cares nor
  fretts,
But to her mother Nature all her care she
  letts.

XVII

'Why then doest thou, O man, that of them
  all
Art lord, and eke of Nature soveraine,
Wilfully make thy selfe a wretched thrall,
And waste thy joyous howres in needelesse
  paine,
Seeking for daunger and adventures vaine?
What bootes it al to have, and nothing use?
Who shall him rew, that swimming in the
  maine
Will die for thrist, and water doth refuse?
Refuse such fruitlesse toile, and present
  pleasures chuse.'

XVIII

By this she had him lulled fast a sleepe,
That of no worldly thing he care did take;
Then she with liquors strong his eies did
  steepe,
That nothing should him hastily awake:
So she him lefte, and did her selfe betake
Unto her boat again, with which she clefte
The slouthfull wave of that great griesy
  lake;
Soone shee that island far behind her lefte,
And now is come to that same place, where
  first she wefte.

XIX

By this time was the worthy Guyon brought
Unto the other side of that wide strond,
Where she was rowing, and for passage
  sought:
Him needed not long call; shee soone to
  hond
Her ferry brought, where him she byding
  fond
With his sad guide: him selfe she tooke
  a boord,
But the blacke palmer suffred still to stond,

Ne would for price or prayers once affoord,
To ferry that old man over the perlous
  foord.

XX

Guyon was loath to leave his guide behind,
Yet, being entred, might not backe retyre;
For the flitt barke, obaying to her mind,
Forth launched quickly, as she did desire,
Ne gave him leave to bid that aged sire
Adieu, but nimbly ran her wonted course
Through the dull billowes thicke as troubled
  mire,
Whom nether wind out of their seat could
  forse,
Nor timely tides did drive out of their
  sluggish sourse.

XXI

And by the way, as was her wonted guize,
Her mery fitt shee freshly gan to reare,
And did of joy and jollity devize,
Her selfe to cherish, and her guest to cheare.
The knight was courteous, and did not for-
  beare
Her honest merth and pleasaunce to partake;
But when he saw her toy, and gibe, and
  geare,
And passe the bonds of modest merimake,
Her dalliaunce he despisd, and follies did
  forsake.

XXII

Yet she still followed her former style,
And said, and did, all that mote him delight,
Till they arrived in that pleasaunt ile,
Where sleeping late she lefte her other
  knight.
But whenas Guyon of that land had sight,
He wist him selfe amisse, and angry said:
'Ah! dame, perdy ye have not doen me
  right,
Thus to mislead mee, whiles I you obaid:
Me litle needed from my right way to
  have straid.'

XXIII

'Faire sir,' quoth she, 'be not displeasd at
  all:
Who fares on sea may not commaund his
  way,
Ne wind and weather at his pleasure call:
The sea is wide, and easy for to stray;
The wind unstable, and doth never stay.
But here a while ye may in safety rest,

Till season serve new passage to assay:
Better safe port, then be in seas distrest.'
Therewith she laught, and did her earnest
  end in jest.

XXIV

But he, halfe discontent, mote nathelesse
Himselfe appease, and issewd forth on
  shore:
The joyes whereof, and happy fruitfulnesse,
Such as he saw, she gan him lay before,
And all, though pleasaunt, yet she made
  much more:
The fields did laugh, the flowres did freshly
  spring,
The trees did bud, and early blossomes bore,
And all the quire of birds did sweetly sing,
And told that gardins pleasures in their
  caroling.

XXV

And she, more sweete then any bird on
  bough,
Would oftentimes emongst them beare a
  part,
And strive to passe (as she could well
  enough)
Their native musicke by her skilful art:
So did she all, that might his constant
  hart
Withdraw from thought of warlike enter-
  prize,
And drowne in dissolute delights apart,
Where noise of armes, or vew of martiall
  guize,
Might not revive desire of knightly exercize.

XXVI

But he was wise, and wary of her will,
And ever held his hand upon his hart:
Yet would not seeme so rude, and thewed
  ill,
As to despise so curteous seeming part,
That gentle lady did to him impart:
But fairly tempring fond desire subdewd,
And ever her desired to depart.
She list not heare, but her disports pour-
  sewd,
And ever bad him stay, till time the tide
  renewd.

XXVII

And now by this, Cymochles howre was
  spent,
That he awoke out of his ydle dreme,

And shaking off his drowsy dreriment,
Gan him avize, howe ill did him beseme,
In slouthfull sleepe his molten hart to
  steme,
And quench the brond of his conceived
  yre.
Tho up he started, stird with shame ex-
  treme,
Ne staied for his damsell to inquire,
But marched to the strond, there passage
  to require.

XXVIII

And in the way he with Sir Guyon mett,
Accompanyde with Phædria the faire:
Eftsoones he gan to rage, and inly frett,
Crying: ' Let be that lady debonaire,
Thou recreaunt knight, and soone thy selfe
  prepaire
To batteile, if thou meane her love to
  gayn:
Loe ! loe already, how the fowles in aire
Doe flocke, awaiting shortly to obtayn
Thy carcas for their pray, the guerdon of
  thy payn.'

XXIX

And therewithall he fiersly at him flew,
And with importune outrage him assayld;
Who, soone prepard to field, his sword forth
  drew,
And him with equall valew countervayld:
Their mightie strokes their haberjeons dis-
  mayld,
And naked made each others manly spalles;
The mortall steele despiteously entayld
Deepe in their flesh, quite through the yron
  walles,
That a large purple stream adown their
  giambeux falles.

XXX

Cymocles, that had never mett before
So puissant foe, with envious despight
His prowd presumed force increased more,
Disdeigning to bee held so long in fight:
Sir Guyon, grudging not so much his
  might,
As those unknightly raylinges which he
  spoke,
With wrathfull fire his corage kindled
  bright,
Thereof devising shortly to be wroke,
And, doubling all his powres, redoubled
  every stroke.

XXXI

Both of them high attouce their hands en-
    haunst,
And both attonce their huge blowes down
    did sway:
Cymochles sword on Guyons shield yglaunst,
And thereof nigh one quarter sheard away;
But Guyons angry blade so fiers did play
On th' others helmett, which as Titan shone,
That quite it clove his plumed crest in tway,
And bared all his head unto the bone;
Wherewith astonisht, still he stood, as sence-
    lesse stone.

XXXII

Still as he stood, fayre Phædria, that be-
    held
That deadly daunger, soone atweene them
    ran;
And at their feet her selfe most humbly
    feld,
Crying with pitteous voyce, and count'nance
    wan,
' Ah, well away ! most noble lords, how can
Your cruell eyes endure so pitteous sight,
To shed your lives on ground ? Wo worth
    the man,
That first did teach the cursed steele to
    bight
In his owne flesh, and make way to the liv-
    ing spright !

XXXIII

' If ever love of lady did empierce
Your yron brestes, or pittie could find place,
Withhold your bloody handes from battaill
    fierce,
And sith for me ye fight, to me this grace
Both yield, to stay your deadly stryfe a
    space.'
They stayd a while; and forth she gan
    proceed:
' Most wretched woman, and of wicked race,
That am the authour of this hainous deed,
And cause of death betweene two doughtie
    knights do breed !

XXXIV

' But if for me ye fight, or me will serve,
Not this rude kynd of battaill, nor these
    armes
Are meet, the which doe men in bale to
    sterve,
And doolefull sorrow heape with deadly
    harmes:

Such cruell game my scarmoges disarmes:
Another warre, and other weapons, I
Doe love, where Love does give his sweet
    alarmes,
Without bloodshed, and where the enimy
Does yield unto his foe a pleasaunt victory.

XXXV

' Debatefull strife, and cruell enmity,
The famous name of knighthood fowly
    shend;
But lovely peace, and gentle amity,
And in amours the passing howres to spend,
The mightie martiall handes doe most
    commend;
Of love they ever greater glory bore,
Then of their armes: Mars is Cupidoes
    frend,
And is for Venus loves renowmed more,
Then all his wars and spoiles, the which he
    did of yore.'

XXXVI

Therewith she sweetly smyld. They
    though full bent
To prove extremities of bloody fight,
Yet at her speach their rages gan relent,
And calme the sea of their tempestuous
    spight:
Such powre have pleasing wordes; such is
    the might
Of courteous clemency in gentle hart.
Now after all was ceast, the Faery knight
Besought that damzell suffer him depart,
And yield him ready passage to that other
    part.

XXXVII

She no lesse glad, then he desirous, was
Of his departure thence; for of her joy
And vaine delight she saw he light did
    pas,
A foe of folly and immodest toy,
Still solemne sad, or still disdainfull coy,
Delighting all in armes and cruell warre,
That her sweet peace and pleasures did
    annoy,
Troubled with terrour and unquiet jarre,
That she well pleased was thence to amove
    him farre.

XXXVIII

Tho him she brought abord, and her swift
    bote
Forthwith directed to that further strand;

The which on the dull waves did lightly
    flote,
And soone arrived on the shallow sand,
Where gladsome Guyon salied forth to land,
And to that damsell thankes gave for re-
    ward.
Upon that shore he spyed Atin stand,
There by his maister left when late he far'd
In Phædrias flitt barck over that perlous
    shard.

XXXIX

Well could he him remember, sith of late
He with Pyrochles sharp debatement made:
Streight gan he him revyle, and bitter
    rate,
As shepheardes curre, that in darke even-
    inges shade
Hath tracted forth some salvage beastes
    trade:
'Vile miscreaunt!' said he, 'whether dost
    thou flye
The shame and death, which will thee soone
    invade?
What coward hand shall doe thee next to
    dye,
That art thus fowly fledd from famous
    enimy?'

XL

With that he stifly shooke his steelhead
    dart:
But sober Guyon hearing him so rayle,
Though somewhat moved in his mightie
    hart,
Yet with strong reason maistred passion
    fraile,
And passed fayrely forth. He, turning
    taile,
Backe to the strond retyrd, and there still
    stayd,
Awaiting passage, which him late did faile;
The whiles Cymochles with that wanton
    mayd
The hasty heat of his avowd revenge de-
    layd.

XLI

Whylest there the varlet stood, he saw
    from farre
An armed knight, that towardes him fast
    ran;
He ran on foot, as if in lucklesse warre
His forlorne steed from him the victour
    wan;

He seemed breathlesse, hartlesse, faint,
    and wan,
And all his armour sprinckled was with
    blood,
And soyld with durtie gore, that no man
    can
Discerne the hew thereof. He never stood,
But bent his hastie course towardes the ydle
    flood.

XLII

The varlett saw, when to the flood he came,
How without stop or stay he fiersly lept,
And deepe him selfe beducked in the same,
That in the lake his loftie crest was stept,
Ne of his safetie seemed care he kept,
But with his raging armes he rudely flasht
The waves about, and all his armour swept,
That all the blood and filth away was wasnt,
Yet still he bet the water, and the billowes
    dasht.

XLIII

Atin drew nigh, to weet what it mote
    bee;
For much he wondred at that uncouth
    sight:
Whom should he, but his own deare lord,
    there see,
His owne deare lord Pyrochles in sad
    plight,
Ready to drowne him selfe for fell de-
    spight.
'Harrow now out, and well away!' he
    cryde,
'What dismall day hath lent this cursed
    light,
To see my lord so deadly damnifyde?
Pyrochles, O Pyrochles, what is thee be-
    tyde?'

XLIV

'I burne, I burne, I burne!' then lowd he
    cryde,
'O how I burne with implacable fyre!
Yet nought can quench mine inly flaming
    syde,
Nor sea of licour cold, nor lake of myre,
Nothing but death can doe me to respyre.'
'Ah! be it,' said he, 'from Pyrochles farre,
After pursewing Death once to requyre,
Or think, that ought those puissant hands
    may marre:
Death is for wretches borne under unhappy
    starre.'

XLV

'Perdye, then is it fitt for me,' said he,
'That am, I weene, most wretched man
　alive,
Burning in flames, yet no flames can I see,
And dying dayly, dayly yet revive.
O Atin, helpe to me last death to give.'
The varlet at his plaint was grieved so
　sore,
That his deepe wounded hart in two did
　rive,
And his owne health remembring now no
　more,
Did follow that ensample which he blam'd
　afore.

XLVI

Into the lake he lept, his lord to ayd,
(So love the dread of daunger doth despise)
And of him catching hold, him strongly
　stayd
From drowning. But more happy he then
　wise,
Of that seas nature did him not avise.
The waves thereof so slow and sluggish
　were,
Engrost with mud, which did them fowle
　agrise,
That every weighty thing they did upbeare,
Ne ought mote ever sinck downe to the
　bottom there.

XLVII

Whiles thus they strugled in that ydle
　wave,
And strove in vaine, the one him selfe to
　drowne,
The other both from drowning for to save,
Lo! to that shore one in an auncient gowne,
Whose hoary locks great gravitie did
　crowne,
Holding in hand a goodly arming sword,
By fortune came, ledd with the troublous
　sowne:
Where drenched deepe he fownd in that
　dull ford
The carefull servaunt, stryving with his
　raging lord.

XLVIII

Him Atin spying, knew right well of yore,
And lowdly cald: 'Help, helpe! O Archi-
　mage,
To save my lord, in wretched plight for-
　lore;

Helpe with thy hand, or with thy counsell
　sage:
Weake handes, but counsell is most strong
　in age.'
Him when the old man saw, he woundred
　sore,
To see Pyrochles there so rudely rage:
Yet sithens helpe, he saw, he needed more
Then pitty, he in hast approched to the
　shore;

XLIX

And cald, 'Pyrochles! what is this I see?
What hellish fury hath at earst thee hent?
Furious ever I thee knew to bee,
Yet never in this straunge astonishment.'
'These flames, these flames,' he cryde, 'do
　me torment!'
'What flames,' quoth he, 'when I thee pre-
　sent see
In daunger rather to be drent then brent?'
'Harrow! the flames which me consume,'
　said hee,
'Ne can be quencht, within my secret
　bowelles bee.

L

'That cursed man, that cruel feend of hell,
Furor, oh! Furor hath me thus bedight:
His deadly woundes within my liver swell,
And his whott fyre burnes in mine entralles
　bright,
Kindled through his infernall brond of
　spight,
Sith late with him I batteill vaine would
　boste;
That now I weene Joves dreaded thunder
　light
Does scorch not halfe so sore, nor damned
　ghoste
In flaming Phlegeton does not so felly roste.'

LI

Which when as Archimago heard, his griefe
He knew right well, and him attonce dis-
　armd:
Then searcht his secret woundes, and made
　a priefe
Of every place, that was with bruzing
　harmd,
Or with the hidden fire too inly warmd.
Which doen, he balmes and herbes thereto
　applyde,
And evermore with mightie spels them
　charmd,

That in short space he has them qualifyde,
And him restor'd to helth, that would have
    algates dyde.

CANTO VII

Guyon findes Mamon in a delve,
    Sunning his threasure hore:
Is by him tempted, and led downe,
    To see his secrete store.

I

As pilot well expert in perilous wave,
That to a stedfast starre his course hath
    bent,
When foggy mistes or cloudy tempests have
The faithfull light of that faire lampe
    yblent,
And cover'd heaven with hideous dreriment,
Upon his card and compas firmes his eye,
The maysters of his long experiment,
And to them does the steddy helme apply,
Bidding his winged vessell fairely forward
    fly:

II

So Guyon, having lost his trustie guyde,
Late left beyond that Ydle Lake, proceedes
Yet on his way, of none accompanyde;
And evermore himselfe with comfort feedes
Of his owne vertues and praise-worthie
    deedes.
So long he yode, yet no adventure found,
Which Fame of her shrill trompet worthy
    reedes:
For still he traveild through wide wastfull
    ground,
That nought but desert wildernesse shewed
    all around.

III

At last he came unto a gloomy glade,
Cover'd with boughes and shrubs from
    heavens light,
Whereas he sitting found in secret shade
An uncouth, salvage, and uncivile wight,
Of griesly hew and fowle ill favour'd sight;
His face with smoke was tand, and eies were
    bleard,
His head and beard with sout were ill be-
    dight,
His cole-blacke hands did seeme to have
    ben seard
In smythes fire-spitting forge, and nayles
    like clawes appeard.

IV

His yron cote, all overgrowne with rust,
Was underneath enveloped with gold,
Whose glistring glosse, darkned with filthy
    dust,
Well yet appeared to have beene of old
A worke of rich entayle and curious mould,
Woven with antickes and wyld ymagery:
And in his lap a masse of coyne he told,
And turned upside downe, to feede his
    eye
And covetous desire with his huge threasury.

V

And round about him lay on every side
Great heapes of gold, that never could be
    spent:
Of which some were rude owre, not puri-
    fide
Of Mulcibers devouring element;
Some others were new driven, and distent
Into great ingowes, and to wedges square;
Some in round plates withouten moniment:
But most were stampt, and in their metal
    bare
The antique shapes of kings and kesars
    straung and rare.

VI

Soone as he Guyon saw, in great affright
And haste he rose, for to remove aside
Those pretious hils from straungers envious
    sight,
And downe them poured through an hole
    full wide
Into the hollow earth, them there to hide.
But Guyon, lightly to him leaping, stayd
His hand, that trembled as one terrifyde;
And though him selfe were at the sight dis-
    mayd,
Yet him perforce restraynd, and to him
    doubtfull sayd:

VII

'What art thou, man, (if man at all thou
    art)
That here in desert hast thine habitaunce,
And these rich heapes of welth doest hide
    apart
From the worldes eye, and from her right
    usaunce?'
Thereat, with staring eyes fixed askaunce,
In great disdaine, he answerd: 'Hardy
    Elfe,
That darest vew my direfull countenaunce,

I read thee rash and heedlesse of thy selfe,
To trouble my still seate, and heapes of
    pretious pelfe.

VIII

'God of the world and worldlings I me call,
Great Mammon, greatest god below the
    skye,
That of my plenty poure out unto all,
And unto none my graces do envye:
Riches, renowme, and principality,
Honour, estate, and all this worldes good,
For which men swinck and sweat inces-
    santly,
Fro me do flow into an ample flood,
And in the hollow earth have their eternall
    brood.

IX

'Wherefore, if me thou deigne to serve and
    sew,
At thy commaund, lo! all these mountaines
    bee;
Or if to thy great mind, or greedy vew,
All these may not suffise, there shall to
    thee
Ten times so much be nombred francke and
    free.'
'Mammon,' said he, 'thy godheads vaunt
    is vaine,
And idle offers of thy golden fee;
To them that covet such eye-glutting gaine
Proffer thy giftes, and fitter servaunts
    entertaine.

X

'Me ill besits, that in derdoing armes
And honours suit my vowed daies do spend,
Unto thy bounteous baytes and pleasing
    charmes,
With which weake men thou witchest, to
    attend:
Regard of worldly mucke doth fowly blend
And low abase the high heroicke spright,
That joyes for crownes and kingdomes to
    contend;
Faire shields, gay steedes, bright armes be
    my delight:
Those be the riches fit for an advent'rous
    knight.'

XI

'Vaine glorious Elfe,' saide he, 'doest not
    thou weet,
That money can thy wantes at will supply?

Sheilds, steeds, and armes, and all things
    for thee meet
It can purvay in twinckling of an eye;
And crownes and kingdomes to thee multi-
    ply.
Doe not I kings create, and throw the
    crowne
Sometimes to him that low in dust doth
    ly?
And him that raignd into his rowme thrust
    downe,
And whom I lust do heape with glory and
    renowne?'

XII

'All otherwise, saide he, 'I riches read,
And deeme them roote of all disquiet-
    nesse;
First got with guile, and then preserv'd
    with dread,
And after spent with pride and lavishnesse,
Leaving behind them griefe and heavinesse.
Infinite mischiefes of them doe arize,
Strife and debate, bloodshed and bitter-
    nesse,
Outrageous wrong and hellish covetize,
That noble heart, as great dishonour, doth
    despize.

XIII

'Ne thine be kingdomes, ne the scepters
    thine;
But realmes and rulers thou doest both con-
    found,
And loyall truth to treason doest incline:
Witnesse the guiltlesse blood pourd oft on
    ground,
The crowned often slaine, the slayer croun'd,
The sacred diademe in peeces rent,
And purple robe gored with many a wound;
Castles surprizd, great citties sackt and
    brent;
So mak'st thou kings, and gaynest wrong-
    full government.

XIV

'Long were to tell the troublous stormes,
    that tosse
The private state, and make the life un-
    sweet:
Who swelling sayles in Caspian sea doth
    crosse,
And in frayle wood on Adrian gulf doth
    fleet,
Doth not, I weene, so many evils meet.'

Then Mammon, wexing wroth, ' And why
    then,' sayd,
' Are mortall men so fond and undiscreet,
So evill thing to seeke unto their ayd,
And having not, complaine, and having it,
    upbrayd ? '

XV

' Indeede,' quoth he, ' through fowle intem-
    peraunce,
Frayle men are oft captiv'd to covetise:
But would they thinke, with how small
    allowaunce
Untroubled nature doth her selfe suffise,
Such superfluities they would despise,
Which with sad cares empeach our native
    joyes:
At the well head the purest streames arise:
But mucky filth his braunching armes an-
    noyes,
And with uncomely weedes the gentle wave
    accloyes.

XVI

' The antique world, in his first flowring
    youth,
Fownd no defect in his Creators grace,
But with glad thankes, and unreproved
    truth,
The guifts of soveraine bounty did embrace:
Like angels life was then mens happy cace:
But later ages pride, like corn-fed steed,
Abusd her plenty and fat swolne encreace
To all licentious lust, and gan exceed
The measure of her meane, and naturall
    first need.

XVII

' Then gan a cursed hand the quiet wombe
Of his great grandmother with steele to
    wound,
And the hid treasures in her sacred tombe
With sacriledge to dig. Therein he fownd
Fountaines of gold and silver to abownd,
Of which the matter of his huge desire
And pompous pride eftsoones he did com-
    pownd;
Then avarice gan through his veines inspire
His greedy flames, and kindled life-devour-
    ing fire.'

XVIII

' Sonne,' said he then, ' lett be thy bitter
    scorne,
And leave the rudenesse of that antique age

To them that liv'd therin in state forlorne.
Thou, that doest live in later times, must
    wage
Thy workes for wealth, and life for gold
    engage.
If then thee list my offred grace to use,
Take what thou please of all this surplus-
    age;
If thee list not, leave have thou to refuse:
But thing refused doe not afterward accuse.'

XIX

' Me list not,' said the Elfin knight, ' re-
    ceave
Thing offred, till I know it well be gott;
Ne wote I, but thou didst these goods
    bereave
From rightfull owner by unrighteous lott,
Or that blood guiltinesse or guile them
    blott.'
' Perdy,' quoth he, ' yet never eie did vew,
Ne tong did tell, ne hand these handled
    not;
But safe I have them kept in secret mew
From hevens sight, and powre of al which
    them poursew.'

XX

' What secret place,' quoth he, ' can safely
    hold
So huge a masse, and hide from heavens eie?
Or where hast thou thy wonne, that so
    much gold
Thou canst preserve from wrong and
    robbery ? '
' Come thou,' quoth he, ' and see.' So by
    and by,
Through that thick covert he him led,
    and fownd
A darkesome way, which no man could
    descry,
That deep descended through the hollow
    grownd,
And was with dread and horror compassed
    arownd.

XXI

At length they came into a larger space,
That stretcht it selfe into an ample playne,
Through which a beaten broad high way
    did trace,
That streight did lead to Plutoes griesly
    rayne:
By that wayes side there sate infernall
    Payne,

And fast beside him sat tumultuous Strife:
The one in hand an yron whip did strayne,
The other brandished a bloody knife,
And both did gnash their teeth, and both
    did threten life.

XXII

On thother side, in one consort, there sate
Cruell Revenge, and rancorous Despight,
Disloyall Treason, and hart-burning Hate;
But gnawing Gealosy, out of their sight
Sitting alone, his bitter lips did bight;
And trembling Feare still to and fro did fly,
And found no place, wher safe he shroud
    him might;
Lamenting Sorrow did in darknes lye;
And Shame his ugly face did hide from
    living eye.

XXIII

And over them sad Horror with grim hew
Did alwaies sore, beating his yron wings;
And after him owles and night-ravens flew,
The hatefull messengers of heavy things,
Of death and dolor telling sad tidings;
Whiles sad Celeno, sitting on a clifte,
A song of bale and bitter sorrow sings,
That hart of flint a sonder could have rifte:
Which having ended, after him she flyeth
    swifte.

XXIV

All these before the gates of Pluto lay;
By whom they passing, spake unto them
    nought.
But th' Elfin knight with wonder all the
    way
Did feed his eyes, and fild his inner thought.
At last him to a litle dore he brought,
That to the gate of hell, which gaped wide,
Was next adjoyning, ne them parted ought:
Betwixt them both was but a litle stride,
That did the house of Richesse from hell-
    mouth divide.

XXV

Before the dore sat selfe-consuming Care,
Day and night keeping wary watch and
    ward,
For feare least Force or Fraud should una-
    ware
Breake in, and spoile the treasure there in
    gard:
Ne would he suffer Sleepe once thether-
    ward

Approch, albe his drowsy den were next;
For next to Death is Sleepe to be compard:
Therefore his house is unto his annext;
Here Sleep, ther Richesse, and helgate them
    both betwext.

XXVI

So soone as Mammon there arrivd, the dore
To him did open and affoorded way;
Him followed eke Sir Guyon evermore,
Ne darkenesse him, ne daunger might dis-
    may.
Soone as he entred was, the dore streight
    way
Did shutt, and from behind it forth there
    lept
An ugly feend, more fowle then dismall day,
The which with monstrous stalke behind
    him stept,
And ever as he went, dew watch upon him
    kept.

XXVII

Well hoped hee, ere long that hardy guest,
If ever covetous hand, or lustfull eye,
Or lips he layd on thing that likte him best,
Or ever sleepe his eiestrings did untye,
Should be his pray. And therefore still on
    hye
He over him did hold his cruell clawes,
Threatning with greedy gripe to doe him
    dye,
And rend in peeces with his ravenous pawes,
If ever he transgrest the fatall Stygian
    lawes.

XXVIII

That houses forme within was rude and
    strong,
Lyke an huge cave, hewne out of rocky
    clifte,
From whose rough vaut the ragged breaches
    hong,
Embost with massy gold of glorious guifte,
And with rich metall loaded every rifte,
That heavy ruine they did seeme to threatt;
And over them Arachne high did lifte
Her cunning web, and spred her subtile nett,
Enwrapped in fowle smoke and clouds more
    black then jett.

XXIX

Both roofe, and floore, and walls were all
    of gold,
But overgrowne with dust and old decay,

And hid in darkenes, that none could be-
hold
The hew thereof: for vew of cherefull
day
Did never in that house it selfe display,
But a faint shadow of uncertein light;
Such as a lamp, whose life does fade away;
Or as the moone, cloathed with clowdy
night,
Does shew to him that walkes in feare and
sad affright.

XXX

In all that rowme was nothing to be seene,
But huge great yron chests and coffers
strong,
All bard with double bends, that none could
weene
Them to efforce by violence or wrong:
On every side they placed were along.
But all the grownd with sculs was scattered,
And dead mens bones, which round about
were flong;
Whose lives, it seemed, whilome there were
shed,
And their vile carcases now left unburied.

XXXI

They forward passe, ne Guyon yet spoke
word,
Till that they came unto an yron dore,
Which to them opened of his owne accord,
And shewd of richesse such exceeding store,
As eie of man did never see before,
Ne ever could within one place be fownd,
Though all the wealth, which is, or was of
yore,
Could gathered be through all the world
arownd,
And that above were added to that under
grownd.

XXXII

The charge thereof unto a covetous spright
Commaunded was, who thereby did attend,
And warily awaited day and night,
From other covetous feends it to defend,
Who it to rob and ransacke did intend.
Then Mammon, turning to that warriour,
said:
'Loe here the worldes blis! loe here the
end,
To which al men doe ayme, rich to be made!
Such grace now to be happy is before thee
laid.'

XXXIII

'Certes,' sayd he, 'I n'ill thine offred grace,
Ne to be made so happy doe intend:
Another blis before mine eyes I place,
Another happines, another end.
To them that list, these base regardes I
lend:
But I in armes, and in atchievements brave,
Do rather choose my flitting houres to
spend,
And to be lord of those that riches have,
Then them to have my selfe, and be their
servile sclave.'

XXXIV

Thereat the feend his gnashing teeth did
grate,
And griev'd, so long to lacke his greedie
pray;
For well he weened that so glorious bayte
Would tempt his guest to take thereof
assay:
Had he so doen, he had him snatcht away,
More light then culver in the faulcons fist.
Eternall God thee save from such decay!
But whenas Mammon saw his purpose mist,
Him to entrap unwares another way he
wist.

XXXV

Thence forward he him ledd, and shortly
brought
Unto another rowme, whose dore forthright
To him did open, as it had beene taught:
Therein an hundred raunges weren pight,
And hundred fournaces all burning bright:
By every fournace many feendes did byde,
Deformed creatures, horrible in sight;
And every feend his busie paines applyde,
To melt the golden metall, ready to be
tryde.

XXXVI

One with great bellowes gathered filling
ayre,
And with forst wind the fewell did inflame;
Another did the dying bronds repayre
With yron tongs, and sprinckled ofte the
same
With liquid waves, fiers Vulcans rage to
tame,
Who, maystring them, renewd his former
heat;
Some scumd the drosse, that from the met-
all came,

Some stird the molten owre with ladles great;
And every one did swincke, and every one
    did sweat.

XXXVII

But when an earthly wight they present saw,
Glistring in armes and battailous aray,
From their whot work they did themselves
    withdraw
To wonder at the sight: for, till that day,
They never creature saw, that cam that way.
Their staring eyes, sparckling with fervent
    fyre,
And ugly shapes did nigh the man dismay,
That, were it not for shame, he would re-
    tyre;
Till that him thus bespake their soveraine
    lord and syre:

XXXVIII

'Behold, thou Faeries sonne, with mortall
    eye,
That living eye before did never see:
The thing that thou didst crave so earnestly
To weet, whence all the wealth late shewd
    by mee
Proceeded, lo ! now is reveald to thee.
Here is the fountaine of the worldes good:
Now therefore, if thou wilt enriched bee,
Avise thee well, and chaunge thy wilfull
    mood;
Least thou perhaps hereafter wish, and be
    withstood.'

XXXIX

'Suffise it then, thou Money God,' quoth
    hee,
'That all thine ydle offers I refuse.
All that I need I have; what needeth mee
To covet more then I have cause to use ?
With such vaine shewes thy worldlinges
    vyle abuse:
But give me leave to follow mine emprise.'
Mammon was much displeasd, yet no'te he
    chuse
But beare the rigour of his bold mesprise,
And thence him forward ledd, him further
    to entise.

XL

He brought him through a darksom narrow
    strayt,
To a broad gate, all built of beaten gold:
The gate was open, but therein did wayt
A sturdie villein, stryding stiffe and bold,

As if that Highest God defy he would:
In his right hand an yron club he held,
But he himselfe was all of golden mould,
Yet had both life and sence, and well could
    weld
That cursed weapon, when his cruell foes
    he queld.

XLI

Disdayne he called was, and did disdayne
To be so cald, and who so did him call:
Sterne was his looke, and full of stomacke
    vayne,
His portaunce terrible, and stature tall,
Far passing th' hight of men terrestriall,
Like an huge gyant of the Titans race;
That made him scorne all creatures great
    and small,
And with his pride all others powre deface:
More fitt emongst black fiendes then men
    to have his place.

XLII

Soone as those glitterand armes he did
    espye,
That with their brightnesse made that dark-
    nes light,
His harmefull club he gan to hurtle hye,
And threaten batteill to the Faery knight;
Who likewise gan himselfe to batteill dight,
Till Mammon did his hasty hand withhold,
And counseld him abstaine from perilous
    fight:
For nothing might abash the villein bold,
Ne mortall steele emperce his miscreated
    mould.

XLIII

So having him with reason pacifyde,
And the fiers carle commaunding to for-
    beare,
He brought him in. The rowme was large
    and wyde,
As it some gyeld or solemne temple weare:
Many great golden pillours did upbeare
The massy roofe, and riches huge sustayne,
And every pillour decked was full deare
With crownes, and diademes, and titles
    vaine,
Which mortall princes wore, whiles they on
    earth did rayne.

XLIV

A route of people there assembled were,
Of every sort and nation under skye,

Which with great uprore preaced to draw
nere
To th' upper part, where was advaunced
hye
A stately siege of soveraine majestye;
And thereon satt a woman gorgeous gay,
And richly cladd in robes of royaltye,
That never earthly prince in such aray
His glory did enhaunce and pompous pryde
display.

XLV

Her face right wondrous faire did seeme to
bee,
That her broad beauties beam great bright-
nes threw
Through the dim shade, that all men might
it see:
Yet was not that same her owne native
hew,
But wrought by art and counterfetted shew,
Thereby more lovers unto her to call;
Nath'lesse most hevenly faire in deed and
vew
She by creation was, till she did fall;
Thenceforth she sought for helps to cloke
her crime withall.

XLVI

There as in glistring glory she did sitt,
She held a great gold chaine ylincked
well,
Whose upper end to highest heven was
knitt,
And lower part did reach to lowest hell;
And all that preace did rownd about her
swell,
To catchen hold of that long chaine, thereby
To climbe aloft, and others to excell:
That was Ambition, rash desire to sty,
And every linck thereof a step of dignity.

XLVII

Some thought to raise themselves to high
degree
By riches and unrighteous reward;
Some by close shouldring, some by flatteree;
Others through friendes, others for base
regard;
And all by wrong waies for themselves pre-
pard.
Those that were up themselves, kept
others low,
Those that were low themselves, held
others hard,

Ne suffred them to ryse or greater grow,
But every one did strive his fellow downe to
throw.

XLVIII

Which whenas Guyon saw, he gan inquire,
What meant that preace about that ladies
throne,
And what she was that did so high aspyre.
Him Mammon answered: 'That goodly one,
Whom all that folke with such contention
Doe flock about, my deare, my daughter is:
Honour and dignitie from her alone
Derived are, and all this worldes blis,
For which ye men doe strive: few gett, but
many mis.

XLIX

'And fayre Philotime she rightly hight,
The fairest wight that wonneth under skye,
But that this darksom neather world her
light
Doth dim with horror and deformity,
Worthie of heven and hye felicitie,
From whence the gods have her for envy
thrust:
But sith thou hast found favour in mine eye,
Thy spouse I will her make, if that thou
lust,
That she may thee advance for works and
merits just.'

L

'Gramercy, Mammon,' said the gentle
knight,
'For so great grace and offred high estate,
But I, that am fraile flesh and earthly wight,
Unworthy match for such immortall mate
My selfe well wote, and mine unequall fate:
And were I not, yet is my trouth yplight,
And love avowd to other lady late,
That to remove the same I have no might:
To chaunge love causelesse is reproch to
warlike knight.'

LI

Mammon emmoved was with inward wrath;
Yet, forcing it to fayne, him forth thence
ledd,
Through griesly shadowes by a beaten path,
Into a gardin goodly garnished
With hearbs and fruits, whose kinds mote
not be redd:
Not such as earth out of her fruitfull
woomb

Throwes forth to men, sweet and well
    savored,
But direfull deadly black, both leafe and
    bloom,
Fitt to adorne the dead and deck the drery
    toombe.

LII

There mournfull cypresse grew in greatest
    store,
And trees of bitter gall, and heben sad,
Dead sleeping poppy, and black helebore,
Cold coloquintida, and tetra mad,
Mortall samnitis, and cicuta bad,
With which th' unjust Atheniens made to dy
Wise Socrates, who thereof quaffing glad,
Pourd out his life and last philosophy
To the fayre Critias, his dearest belamy.

LIII

The Gardin of Proserpina this hight;
And in the midst thereof a silver seat,
With a thick arber goodly overdight,
In which she often usd from open heat
Her selfe to shroud, and pleasures to en-
    treat.
Next thereunto did grow a goodly tree,
With braunches broad dispredd and body
    great,
Clothed with leaves, that none the wood
    mote see,
And loaden all with fruit as thick as it
    might bee.

LIV

Their fruit were golden apples glistring
    bright,
That goodly was their glory to behold;
On earth like never grew, ne living wight
Like ever saw, but they from hence were
    sold;
For those, which Hercules with conquest
    bold
Got from great Atlas daughters, hence
    began,
And, planted there, did bring forth fruit of
    gold;
And those with which th' Eubœan young
    man wan
Swift Atalanta, when through craft he her
    out ran.

LV

Here also sprong that goodly golden fruit,
With which Acontius got his lover trew,

Whom he had long time sought with fruit-
    lesse suit:
Here eke that famous golden apple grew,
The which emongst the gods false Ate
    threw;
For which th' Idæan ladies disagreed,
Till partiall Paris dempt it Venus dew,
And had of her fayre Helen for his meed,
That many noble Greekes and Trojans
    made to bleed.

LVI

The warlike Elfe much wondred at this
    tree,
So fayre and great, that shadowed all the
    ground,
And his broad braunches, laden with rich
    fee,
Did stretch themselves without the utmost
    bound
Of this great gardin, compast with a mound:
Which over-hanging, they themselves did
    steepe
In a blacke flood, which flow'd about it
    round;
That is the river of Cocytus deepe,
In which full many soules do endlesse wayle
    and weepe.

LVII

Which to behold, he clomb up to the
    bancke,
And, looking downe, saw many damned
    wightes,
In those sad waves, which direfull deadly
    stancke,
Plonged continually of cruell sprightes,
That with their piteous cryes, and yelling
    shrightes,
They made the further shore resounden
    wide.
Emongst the rest of those same ruefull
    sightes,
One cursed creature he by chaunce espide,
That drenched lay full deepe, under the
    garden side.

LVIII

Deepe was he drenched to the upmost chin,
Yet gaped still, as coveting to drinke
Of the cold liquour which he waded in,
And stretching forth his hand, did often
    thinke
To reach the fruit which grew upon the
    bricke:

But both the fruit from hand, and flood
  from mouth,
Did fly abacke, and made him vainely
  swincke:
The whiles he sterv'd with hunger and
  with drouth,
He daily dyde, yet never throughly dyen
  couth.

LIX

The knight, him seeing labour so in vaine,
Askt who he was, and what he ment there-
  by:
Who, groning deepe, thus answerd him
  againe:
'Most cursed of all creatures under skye,
Lo ! Tantalus, I here tormented lye:
Of whom high Jove wont whylome feasted
  bee,
Lo ! here I now for want of food doe dye:
But if that thou be such as I thee see,
Of grace I pray thee, give to eat and drinke
  to mee.'

LX

'Nay, nay, thou greedy Tantalus,' quoth
  he,
' Abide the fortune of thy present fate,
And unto all that live in high degree
Ensample be of mind intemperate,
To teach them how to use their present
  state.'
Then gan the cursed wretch alowd to cry,
Accusing highest Jove and gods ingrate,
And eke blaspheming heaven bitterly,
As authour of unjustice, there to let him
  dye.

LXI

He lookt a litle further, and espyde
Another wretch, whose carcas deepe was
  drent
Within the river, which the same did hyde:
But both his handes, most filthy feculent,
Above the water were on high extent,
And faynd to wash themselves incessantly;
Yet nothing cleaner were for such intent,
But rather fowler seemed to the eye;
So lost his labour vaine and ydle industry.

LXII

The knight, him calling, asked who he was;
Who, lifting up his head, him answerd thus:
' I Pilate am, the falsest judge, alas !
And most unjust; that, by unrighteous

And wicked doome, to Jewes despiteous
Delivered up the Lord of Life to dye,
And did acquite a murdrer felonous:
The whiles my handes I washt in purity,
The whiles my soule was soyld with fowle
  iniquity.'

LXIII

Infinite moe, tormented in like paine,
He there beheld, too long here to be told:
Ne Mammon would there let him long re-
  mayne,
For terrour of the tortures manifold,
In which the damned soules he did behold,
But roughly him bespake: 'Thou fearefull
  foole,
Why takest not of that same fruite of gold,
Ne sittest downe on that same silver stoole,
To rest thy weary person in the shadow
  coole ? '

LXIV

All which he did, to do him deadly fall
In frayle intemperaunce through sinfull
  bayt;
To which if he inclyned had at all,
That dreadfull feend, which did behinde him
  wayt,
Would him have rent in thousand peeces
  strayt:
But he was wary wise in all his way,
And well perceived his deceiptfull sleight,
Ne suffred lust his safety to betray;
So goodly did beguile the guyler of his pray.

LXV

And now he has so long remained theare,
That vitall powres gan wexe both weake
  and wan,
For want of food and sleepe, which two up-
  beare,
Like mightie pillours, this frayle life of
  man,
That none without the same enduren can.
For now three dayes of men were full out-
  wrought,
Since he this hardy enterprize began:
Forthy great Mammon fayrely he besought,
Into the world to guyde him backe, as he
  him brought.

LXVI

The god, though loth, yet was constraynd
  t' obay,
For, lenger time then that, no living wight

Below the earth might suffred be to stay:
So backe againe him brought to living light.
But all so soone as his enfeebled spright
Gan sucke this vitall ayre into his brest,
As overcome with too exceeding might,
The life did flit away out of her nest,
And all his sences were with deadly fit opprest.

CANTO VIII

Sir Guyon, layd in swowne, is by
Acrates sonnes despoyld ;
Whom Arthure soone hath reskewed
And Paynim brethren foyld.

I

And is there care in heaven ? And is there
love
In heavenly spirits to these creatures bace,
That may compassion of their evilles move ?
There is: else much more wretched were
the cace
Of men then beasts. But O th' exceeding
grace
Of Highest God, that loves his creatures so,
And all his workes with mercy doth embrace,
That blessed angels he sends to and fro,
To serve to wicked man, to serve his wicked
foe !

II

How oft do they their silver bowers leave
To come to succour us, that succour want !
How oft do they with golden pineons cleave
The flitting skyes, like flying pursuivant,
Against fowle feendes to ayd us militant !
They for us fight, they watch and dewly
ward,
And their bright squadrons round about us
plant;
And all for love, and nothing for reward:
O why should hevenly God to men have
such regard ?

III

During the while that Guyon did abide
In Mamons house, the palmer, whom whyleare
That wanton mayd of passage had denide,
By further search had passage found elsewhere,
And, being on his way, approched neare
Where Guyon lay in traunce, when suddeinly

He heard a voyce, that called lowd and
cleare,
'Come hether ! come hether ! O come
hastily ! '
That all the fields resounded with the ruefull cry.

IV

The palmer lent his eare unto the noyce,
To weet who called so importunely:
Againe he heard a more efforced voyce,
That bad him come in haste. He by and
by
His feeble feet directed to the cry;
Which to that shady delve him brought at
last,
Where Mammon earst did sunne his threasury:
There the good Guyon he found slumbring
fast
In senceles dreame; which sight at first him
sore aghast.

V

Beside his head there satt a faire young
man,
Of wondrous beauty and of freshest yeares,
Whose tender bud to blossome new began,
And florish faire above his equall peares;
His snowy front, curled with golden heares,
Like Phoebus face adornd with sunny rayes,
Divinely shone, and two sharpe winged
sheares,
Decked with diverse plumes, like painted
jayes,
Were fixed at his backe, to cut his ayery
wayes.

VI

Like as Cupido on Idaean hill,
When having laid his cruell bow away,
And mortall arrowes, wherewith he doth
fill
The world with murdrous spoiles and bloody
pray,
With his faire mother he him dights to
play,
And with his goodly sisters, Graces three;
The goddesse, pleased with his wanton
play,
Suffers her selfe through sleepe beguild to
bee,
The whiles the other ladies mind theyr
mery glee.

VII

Whom when the palmer saw, abasht he was
Through fear and wonder, that he nought could say,
Till him the childe bespoke: 'Long lackt, alas!
Hath bene thy faithfull aide in hard assay,
Whiles deadly fitt thy pupill doth dismay.
Behold this heavy sight, thou reverend sire:
But dread of death and dolor doe away;
For life ere long shall to her home retire,
And he, that breathlesse seems, shal corage bold respire.

VIII

'The charge, which God doth unto me arrett,
Of his deare safety, I to thee commend;
Yet will I not forgoe, ne yet forgett,
The care thereof my selfe unto the end,
But evermore him succour, and defend
Against his foe and mine: watch thou, I pray;
For evill is at hand him to offend.'
So having said, eftsoones he gan display
His painted nimble wings, and vanisht quite away.

IX

The palmer seeing his lefte empty place,
And his slow eies beguiled of their sight,
Woxe sore affraid, and standing still a space,
Gaz'd after him, as fowle escapt by flight:
At last him turning to his charge behight,
With trembling hand his troubled pulse gan try,
Where finding life not yet dislodged quight,
He much rejoyst, and courd it tenderly,
As chicken newly hatcht, from dreaded destiny.

X

At last he spide where towards him did pace
Two Paynim knights, al armd as bright as skie,
And them beside an aged sire did trace,
And far before a light-foote page did flie,
That breathed strife and troublous enmitie.
Those were the two sonnes of Acrates old,
Who, meeting earst with Archimago slie,

Foreby that idle strond, of him were told,
That he which earst them combatted was Guyon bold.

XI

Which to avenge on him they dearly vowd,
Where ever that on ground they mote him find:
False Archimage provokte their corage prowd,
And stryful Atin in their stubborne mind
Coles of contention and whot vengeaunce tind.
Now bene they come whereas the Palmer sate,
Keeping that slombred corse to him assind:
Well knew they both his person, sith of late
With him in bloody armes they rashly did debate.

XII

Whom when Pyrochles saw, inflam'd with rage
That sire he fowl bespake: 'Thou dotard vile,
That with thy brutenesse shendst thy comely age,
Abandon soone, I read, the caytive spoile
Of that same outcast carcas, that ere while
Made it selfe famous through false trechery,
And crownd his coward crest with knightly stile:
Loe where he now inglorious doth lye,
To proove he lived il, that did thus fowly dye.'

XIII

To whom the palmer fearlesse answered:
'Certes, sir knight, ye bene too much to blame,
Thus for to blott the honor of the dead,
And with fowle cowardize his carcas shame,
Whose living handes immortalizd his name.
Vile is the vengeaunce on the ashes cold,
And envy base, to barke at sleeping fame:
Was never wight, to that treason of him told:
Your self his prowesse prov'd, and found him fiers and bold.'

XIV

Then sayd Cymochles: 'Palmer, thou doest dote,
Ne canst of prowesse ne of knighthood deeme,

Save as thou seest or hearst: but well I
  wote,
That of his puissaunce tryall made extreeme:
Yet gold al is not, that doth golden seeme,
Ne all good knights, that shake well speare
  and shield:
The worth of all men by their end esteeme,
And then dew praise or dew reproch them
  yield:
Bad therefore I him deeme that thus lies
  dead on field.'

XV

' Good or bad,' gan his brother fiers reply,
' What doe I recke, sith that he dide en-
  tire ?
Or what doth his bad death now satisfy
The greedy hunger of revenging yre,
Sith wrathfull hand wrought not her owne
  desire ?
Yet since no way is lefte to wreake my
  spight,
I will him reave of armes, the victors hire,
And of that shield, more worthy of good
  knight;
For why should a dead dog be deckt in
  armour bright ? '

XVI

' Fayr sir,' said then the palmer suppliaunt,
' For knighthoods love, doe not so fowle a
  deed,
Ne blame your honor with so shamefull
  vaunt
Of vile revenge. To spoile the dead of
  weed
Is sacrilege, and doth all sinnes exceed;
But leave these relicks of his living might
To decke his herce, and trap his tomb-blacke
  steed.'
' What herce or steed,' said he, ' should he
  have dight,
But be entombed in the raven or the
  kight ? '

XVII

With that, rude hand upon his shield he
  laid,
And th' other brother gan his helme unlace,
Both fiercely bent to have him disaraid;
Till that they spyde where towards them
  did pace

An armed knight, of bold and bounteous
  grace,
Whose squire bore after him an heben
  launce
And coverd shield. Well kend him so far
  space
Th' enchaunter by his armes and amenaunce,
When under him he saw his Lybian steed
  to praunce;

XVIII

And to those brethren sayd: ' Rise, rise
  bylive,
And unto batteil doe your selves addresse;
For yonder comes the prowest knight alive,
Prince Arthur, flowre of grace and nobil-
  esse,
That hath to Paynim knights wrought gret
  distresse,
And thousand Sar'zins fowly donne to
  dye.'
That word so deepe did in their harts im-
  presse,
That both eftsoones upstarted furiously,
And gan themselves prepare to batteill
  greedily.

XIX

But fiers Pyrochles, lacking his owne sword,
The want thereof now greatly gan to
  plaine,
And Archimage besought, him that afford,
Which he had brought for Braggadochio
  vaine.
' So would I,' said th' enchaunter, ' glad
  and faine
Beteeme to you this sword, you to defend,
Or ought that els your honor might main-
  taine,
But that this weapons powre I well have
  kend
To be contrary to the worke which ye in-
  tend.

XX

' For that same knights owne sword this is,
  of yore
Which Merlin made by his almightie art
For that his noursling, when he knighthood
  swore,
Therewith to doen his foes eternall smart.
The metall first he mixt with medæwart,
That no enchauntment from his dint might
  save;

Then it in flames of Aetna wrought apart,
And seven times dipped in the bitter wave
Of hellish Styx, which hidden vertue to it
    gave.

XXI

'The vertue is, that nether steele nor stone
The stroke thereof from entraunce may
    defend;
Ne ever may be used by his fone,
Ne forst his rightfull owner to offend;
Ne ever will it breake, ne ever bend:
Wherefore Morddure it rightfully is hight.
In vaine therefore, Pyrochles, should I lend
The same to thee, against his lord to fight,
For sure yt would deceive thy labor and
    thy might.'

XXII

'Foolish old man,' said then the Pagan
    wroth,
'That weenest words or charms may force
    withstond:
Soone shalt thou see, and then beleeve for
    troth,
That I can carve with this inchaunted brond
His lords owne flesh.'   Therewith out of
    his hond
That vertuous steele he rudely snatcht
    away,
And Guyons shield about his wrest he bond;
So ready dight, fierce battaile to assay,
And match his brother proud in battailous
    aray.

XXIII

By this, that straunger knight in presence
    came,
And goodly salued them; who nought
    againe
Him answered, as courtesie became,
But with sterne lookes, and stomachous
    disdaine,
Gave signes of grudge and discontentment
    vaine:
Then, turning to the palmer, he gan spy
Where at his feet, with sorrowfull demayne
And deadly hew, an armed corse did lye,
In whose dead face he redd great magna-
    nimity.

XXIV

Sayd he then to the palmer: 'Reverend syre,
What great misfortune hath betidd this
    knight?

Or did his life her fatall date expyre,
Or did he fall by treason, or by fight?
How ever, sure I rew his pitteous plight.'
'Not one, nor other,' sayd the palmer grave,
'Hath him befalne; but cloudes of deadly
    night
A while his heavy eylids cover'd have,
And all his sences drowned in deep sence-
    lesse wave.

XXV

'Which those his cruell foes, that stand
    hereby,
Making advauntage, to revenge their spight,
Would him disarme and treaten shame-
    fully;
Unworthie usage of redoubted knight.
But you, faire sir, whose honourable sight
Doth promise hope of helpe and timely
    grace,
Mote I beseech to succour his sad plight,
And by your powre protect his feeble cace.
First prayse of knighthood is, fowle outrage
    to deface.'

XXVI

'Palmer,' said he, 'no knight so rude, I
    weene,
As to doen outrage to a sleeping ghost:
Ne was there ever noble corage seene,
That in advauntage would his puissaunce
    bost:
Honour is least, where oddes appeareth
    most.
May bee, that better reason will aswage
The rash revengers heat.   Words well dis-
    post
Have secrete powre t' appease inflamed
    rage:
If not, leave unto me thy knights last pa-
    tronage.'

XXVII

Tho, turning to those brethren, thus be-
    spoke:
'Ye warlike payre, whose valorous great
    might,
It seemes, just wronges to vengeaunce doe
    provoke,
To wreake your wrath on this dead seeming
    knight,
Mote ought allay the storme of your de-
    spight,
And settle patience in so furious heat?
Not to debate the chalenge of your right,

But for this carkas pardon I entreat,
Whom fortune hath already laid in lowest
    seat.'

XXVIII

To whom Cymochles said: 'For what art
    thou,
That mak'st thy selfe his dayes-man, to
    prolong
The vengeaunce prest? Or who shall let
    me now,
On this vile body from to wreak my wrong,
And make his carkas as the outcast dong?
Why should not that dead carrion satis-
    fye
The guilt which, if he lived had thus long,
His life for dew revenge should deare
    abye?
The trespas still doth live, albee the person
    dye.'

XXIX

'Indeed,' then said the Prince, 'the evill
    donne
Dyes not, when breath the body first doth
    leave,
But from the grandsyre to the nephewes
    sonne,
And all his seede, the curse doth often
    cleave,
Till vengeaunce utterly the guilt bereave:
So streightly God doth judge. But gentle
    knight,
That doth against the dead his hand up-
    heave,
His honour staines with rancour and de-
    spight,
And great disparagment makes to his for-
    mer might.'

XXX

Pyrochles gan reply the second tyme,
And to him said: 'Now, felon, sure I read,
How that thou art partaker of his cryme:
Therefore by Termagaunt thou shalt be
    dead.'
With that, his hand, more sad then lomp of
    lead,
Uplifting high, he weened with Morddure,
His owne good sword Morddure, to cleave
    his head.
The faithfull steele such treason no'uld en-
    dure,
But swarving from the marke, his lordes
    life did assure.

XXXI

Yet was the force so furious and so fell,
That horse and man it made to reele
    asyde:
Nath'lesse the Prince would not forsake
    his sell,
For well of yore he learned had to ryde,
But full of anger fiersly to him cryde:
'False traitour miscreaunt! thou broken
    hast
The law of armes, to strike foe undefide.
But thou thy treasons fruit, I hope, shalt
    taste
Right sowre, and feele the law, the which
    thou hast defast.'

XXXII

With that, his balefull speare he fiercely
    bent
Against the Pagans brest, and therewith
    thought
His cursed life out of her lodg have rent:
But ere the point arrived where it ought,
That seven fold shield, which he from
    Guyon brought,
He cast between to ward the bitter stownd:
Through all those foldes the steelehead
    passage wrought,
And through his shoulder perst; wherwith
    to ground
He groveling fell, all gored in his gushing
    wound.

XXXIII

Which when his brother saw, fraught with
    great griefe
And wrath, he to him leaped furiously,
And fowly saide. 'By Mahoune, cursed
    thiefe,
That direfull stroke thou dearely shalt
    aby.'
Then, hurling up his harmefull blade on
    hy,
Smote him so hugely on his haughtie crest,
That from his saddle forced him to fly:
Els mote it needes downe to his manly
    brest
Have cleft his head in twaine, and life
    thence dispossest.

XXXIV

Now was the Prince in daungerous dis-
    tresse,
Wanting his sword, when he on foot should
    fight:

His single speare could doe him small re-
    dresse
Against two foes of so exceeding might,
The least of which was match for any
    knight.
And now the other, whom he earst did
    daunt,
Had reard him selfe againe to cruel fight,
Three times more furious and more puis-
    saunt,
Unmindfull of his wound, of his fate ignor-
    aunt.

XXXV

So both attonce him charge on either syde,
With hideous strokes and importable powre,
That forced him his ground to traverse
    wyde,
And wisely watch to ward that deadly
    stowre:
For in his shield, as thicke as stormie
    showre,
Their strokes did raine; yet did he never
    quaile,
Ne backward shrinke, but as a stedfast
    towre,
Whom foe with double battry doth assaile,
Them on her bulwarke beares, and bids
    them nought availe, —

XXXVI

So stoutly he withstood their strong assay;
Till that at last, when he advantage spyde,
His poynant speare he thrust with puissant
    sway
At proud Cymochles, whiles his shield was
    wyde,
That through his thigh the mortall steele
    did gryde:
He, swarving with the force, within his flesh
Did breake the launce, and let the head
    abyde:
Out of the wound the red blood flowed
    fresh,
That underneath his feet soone made a
    purple plesh.

XXXVII

Horribly then he gan to rage and rayle,
Cursing his gods, and him selfe damning
    deepe:
Als when his brother saw the red blood
    rayle
Adowne so fast, and all his armour steepe,
For very felnesse lowd he gan to weepe,

And said: 'Caytive, cursse on thy cruell hond,
That twise hath spedd ! yet shall it not thee
    keepe
From the third brunt of this my fatall
    brond:
Lo where the dreadfull Death behynd thy
    backe doth stond !'

XXXVIII

With that he strooke, and thother strooke
    withall,
That nothing seemd mote beare so mon-
    strous might:
The one upon his covered shield did fall,
And glauncing downe would not his owner
    byte:
But th' other did upon his troncheon smyte,
Which hewing quite a sunder, further way
It made, and on his hacqueton did lyte,
The which dividing with importune sway,
It seizd in his right side, and there the dint
    did stay.

XXXIX

Wyde was the wound, and a large luke-
    warme flood,
Red as the rose, thence gushed grievously,
That when the Paynym spyde the stream-
    ing blood,
Gave him great hart, and hope of victory.
On thother side, in huge perplexity
The Prince now stood, having his weapon
    broke;
Nought could he hurt, but still at warde
    did ly:
Yet with his troncheon he so rudely stroke
Cymochles twise, that twise him forst his
    foot revoke.

XL

Whom when the palmer saw in such dis-
    tresse,
Sir Guyons sword he lightly to him raught,
And said: 'Fayre sonne, great God thy
    right hand blesse,
To use that sword so well as he it ought.'
Glad was the knight, and with fresh courage
    fraught,
When as againe he armed felt his hond:
Then like a lyon, which hath long time
    saught
His robbed whelpes, and at the last them
    fond
Emongst the shepeheard swaynes, then
    wexeth wood and yond;

XLI

So fierce he laid about him, and dealt blowes
On either side, that neither mayie could
    hold,
Ne shield defend the thunder of his throwes:
Now to Pyrochles many strokes he told;
Eft to Cymochles twise so many fold:
Then backe againe turning his busie hond,
Them both atonce compeld with courage
    bold,
To yield wide way to his hart-thrilling
    brond;
And though they both stood stiffe, yet
    could not both withstond.

XLII

As salvage bull, whom two fierce mastives
    bayt,
When rancour doth with rage him once
    engore,
Forgets with wary warde them to awayt,
But with his dreadfull hornes them drives
    afore,
Or flings aloft, or treades downe in the
    flore,
Breathing out wrath, and bellowing dis-
    daine,
That all the forest quakes to heare him rore:
So rag'd Prince Arthur twixt his foemen
    twaine,
That neither could his mightie puissaunce
    sustaine.

XLIII

But ever at Pyrochles when he smitt,
Who Guyons shield cast ever him before,
Whereon the Faery Queenes pourtract was
    writt,
His hand relented, and the stroke forbore,
And his deare hart the picture gan adore;
Which oft the Paynim sav'd from deadly
    stowre.
But him henceforth the same can save no
    more;
For now arrived is his fatall howre,
That no'te avoyded be by earthly skill or
    powre.

XLIV

For when Cymochles saw the fowle re-
    proch,
Which them appeached, prickt with guiltie
    shame
And inward griefe, he fiercely gan approch,
Resolv'd to put away that loathly blame,

Or dye with honour and desert of fame;
And on the haubergh stroke the Prince so
    sore,
That quite disparted all the linked frame,
And pierced to the skin, but bit no more,
Yet made him twise to reele, that never
    moov'd afore.

XLV

Whereat renfierst with wrath and sharp
    regret,
He stroke so hugely with his borrowd blade,
That it empierst the Pagans burganet,
And cleaving the hard steele, did deepe in-
    vade
Into his head, and cruell passage made
Quite through his brayne. He, tombling
    downe on ground,
Breathd out his ghost, which, to th' infer-
    nall shade
Fast flying, there eternall torment found
For all the sinnes wherewith his lewd life
    did abound.

XLVI

Which when his german saw, the stony
    feare
Ran to his hart, and all his sence dismayd,
Ne thenceforth life ne corage did appeare;
But as a man, whom hellish feendes have
    frayd,
Long trembling still he stoode: at last thus
    sayd:
'Traytour, what hast thou doen? How
    ever may
Thy cursed hand so cruelly have swayd
Against that knight? Harrow and well
    away!
After so wicked deede why liv'st thou
    lenger day?'

XLVII

With that all desperate, as loathing light,
And with revenge desyring soone to dye,
Assembling all his force and utmost might,
With his owne swerd he fierce at him did
    flye,
And strooke, and foynd, and lasht out-
    rageously,
Withouten reason or regard. Well knew
The Prince, with pacience and sufferaunce
    sly
So hasty heat soone cooled to subdew:
Tho, when this breathlesse woxe, that bat-
    teil gan renew.

XLVIII

As when a windy tempest bloweth hye,
That nothing may withstand his stormy
    stowre,
The clowdes, as thinges affrayd, before him
    flye;
But all so soone as his outrageous powre
Is layd, they fiercely then begin to showre,
And, as in scorne of his spent stormy spight,
Now all attonce their malice forth do poure:
So did Prince Arthur beare himselfe in
    fight,
And suffred rash Pyrochles waste his ydle
    might.

XLIX

At last when as the Sarazin perceiv'd,
How that straunge sword refusd to serve
    his neede,
But, when he stroke most strong, the dint
    deceiv'd,
He flong it from him, and, devoyd of dreed,
Upon him lightly leaping without heed,
Twixt his two mighty armes engrasped fast,
Thinking to overthrowe and downe him tred:
But him in strength and skill the Prince
    surpast,
And through his nimble sleight did under
    him down cast.

L

Nought booted it the Paynim then to strive;
For as a bittur in the eagles clawe,
That may not hope by flight to scape alive,
Still waytes for death with dread and trem-
    bling aw,
So he, now subject to the victours law,
Did not once move, nor upward cast his eye,
For vile disdaine and rancour, which did
    gnaw
His hart in twaine with sad melancholy,
As one that loathed life, and yet despysd to
    dye.

LI

But full of princely bounty and great mind,
The conquerour nought cared him to slay,
But casting wronges and all revenge behind,
More glory thought to give life then decay,
And sayd: 'Paynim, this is thy dismall day;
Yet if thou wilt renounce thy miscreaunce,
And my trew liegeman yield thy selfe for ay,
Life will I graunt thee for thy valiaunce,
And all thy wronges will wipe out of my
    sovenaunce.'

LII

'Foole!' sayd the Pagan, 'I thy gift defye;
But use thy fortune, as it doth befall,
And say, that I not overcome doe dye,
But in despight of life for death doe call.'
Wroth was the Prince, and sory yet withall,
That he so wilfully refused grace;
Yet, sith his fate so cruelly did fall,
His shining helmet he gan soone unlace,
And left his headlesse body bleeding all the
    place.

LIII

By this, Sir Guyon from his traunce awakt,
Life having maystered her sencelesse foe;
And looking up, when as his shield he lakt,
And sword saw not, he wexed wondrous
    woe:
But when the palmer, whom he long ygoe
Had lost, he by him spyde, right glad he
    grew,
And saide: 'Deare sir, whom wandring to
    and fro
I long have lackt, I joy thy face to vew:
Firme is thy faith, whom daunger never
    fro me drew.

LIV

'But read, what wicked hand hath robbed
    mee
Of my good sword and shield?' The palmer,
    glad
With so fresh hew uprysing him to see,
Him answered: 'Fayre sonne, be no whit
    sad
For want of weapons; they shall soone be
    had.'
So gan he to discourse the whole debate,
Which that straunge knight for him sus-
    tained had,
And those two Sarazins confounded late,
Whose carcases on ground were horribly
    prostrate.

LV

Which when he heard, and saw the tokens
    trew,
His hart with great affection was embayd,
And to the Prince bowing with reverence
    dew,
As to the patrone of his life, thus sayd:
'My lord, my liege, by whose most gratious
    ayd
I live this day, and see my foes subdewd,
What may suffise to be for meede repayd

Of so great graces as ye have me shewd,
But to be ever bound — '

LVI

To whom the infant thus: 'Fayre sir,
  what need
Good turnes be counted, as a servile bond,
To bind their dooers to receive their meed ?
Are not all knightes by oath bound to
  withstond
Oppressours powre by armes and puissant
  hond ?
Suffise, that I have done my dew in place.'
So goodly purpose they together fond
Of kindnesse and of courteous aggrace;
The whiles false Archimage and Atin fled
  apace.

CANTO IX

The House of Temperance, in which
  Doth sober Alma dwell,
Besiegd of many foes, whom straunger
  knightes to flight compell.

I

OF all Gods workes, which doe this world
  adorne,
There is no one more faire and excellent,
Then is mans body both for powre and
  forme,
Whiles it is kept in sober government;
But none then it more fowle and indecent,
Distempred through misrule and passions
  bace:
It growes a monster, and incontinent
Doth loose his dignity and native grace.
Behold, who list, both one and other in this
  place.

II

After the Paynim brethren conquer'd were,
The Briton Prince recov'ring his stolne
  sword,
And Guyon his lost shield, they both yfere
Forth passed on their way in fayre accord,
Till him the Prince with gentle court did
  bord:
'Sir knight, mote I of you this court'sy
  read,
To weet why on your shield, so goodly
  scord,
Beare ye the picture of that ladies head ?
Full lively is the semblaunt, though the
  substance dead.'

III

'Fayre sir,' sayd he, 'if in that picture
  dead
Such life ye read, and vertue in vaine shew,
What mote ye weene, if the trew lively-
  head
Of that most glorious visage ye did vew ?
But yf the beauty of her mind ye knew,
That is, her bounty and imperiall powre,
Thousand times fairer then her mortal hew,
O how great wonder would your thoughts
  devoure,
And infinite desire into your spirite poure !

IV

'Shee is the mighty Queene of Faery,
Whose faire retraitt I in my shield doe
  beare;
Shee is the flowre of grace and chastity,
Throughout the world renowmed far and
  neare,
My liefe, my liege, my soveraine, my deare,
Whose glory shineth as the morning starre,
And with her light the earth enlumines
  cleare:
Far reach her mercies, and her praises
  farre,
As well in state of peace, as puissaunce in
  warre.'

V

'Thrise happy man,' said then the Briton
  knight,
'Whom gracious lott and thy great val-
  iaunce
Have made thee soldier of that princesse
  bright,
Which with her bounty and glad counten-
  aunce
Doth blesse her servaunts, and them high
  advaunce.
How may straunge knight hope ever to
  aspire,
By faithfull service and meete amenaunce.
Unto such blisse ? Sufficient were that hire
For losse of thousand lives, to die at her
  desire.'

VI

Said Guyon, 'Noble lord, what meed so
  great,
Or grace of earthly prince so soveraine,
But by your wondrous worth and warlike
  feat
Ye well may hope, and easely attaine ?

But were your will, her sold to entertaine,
And numbred be mongst Knights of May-
        denhed,
Great guerdon, well I wote, should you re-
        maine,
And in her favor high bee reckoned,
As Arthegall and Sophy now beene honored.'

VII

'Certes,' then said the Prince, 'I God avow,
That sith I armes and knighthood first did
        plight,
My whole desire hath beene, and yet is now,
To serve that Queene with al my powre and
        might.
Now hath the sunne with his lamp-burning
        light
Walkt round about the world, and I no
        lesse,
Sith of that goddesse I have sought the
        sight,
Yet no where can her find: such happinesse
Heven doth to me envy, and Fortune fa-
        vourlesse.'

VIII

'Fortune, the foe of famous chevisaunce,
Seldome,' said Guyon, 'yields to vertue aide,
But in her way throwes mischiefe and mis-
        chaunce,
Whereby her course is stopt and passage
        staid.
But you, faire sir, be not herewith dismaid,
But constant keepe the way in which ye
        stand;
Which were it not that I am els delaid
With hard adventure, which I have in hand,
I labour would to guide you through al Fary
        Land.'

IX

'Gramercy, sir,' said he; 'but mote I weete
What straunge adventure doe ye now pur-
        sew ?
Perhaps my succour or advizement meete
Mote stead you much your purpose to sub-
        dew.'
Then gan Sir Guyon all the story shew
Of false Acrasia, and her wicked wiles,
Which to avenge, the palmer him forth
        drew
From Faery court. So talked they, the
        whiles
They wasted had much way, and measurd
        many miles.

X

And now faire Phoebus gan decline in haste
His weary wagon to the westerne vale,
Whenas they spide a goodly castle, plaste
Foreby a river in a pleasaunt dale;
Which choosing for that evenings hospitale,
They thether marcht: but when they came
        in sight,
And from their sweaty coursers did avale,
They found the gates fast barred long ere
        night,
And every loup fast lockt, as fearing foes
        despight.

XI

Which when they saw, they weened fowle
        reproch
Was to them doen, their entraunce to for-
        stall,
Till that the squire gan nigher to approch,
And wind his horne under the castle wall,
That with the noise it shooke, as it would
        fall.
Eftsoones forth looked from the highest
        spire
The watch, and lowd unto the knights did
        call,
To weete what they so rudely did require:
Who gently answered, they entraunce did
        desire.

XII

'Fly, fly, good knights,' said he, 'fly fast
        away,
If that your lives ye love, as meete ye
        should;
Fly fast, and save your selves from neare
        decay;
Here may ye not have entraunce, though we
        would;
We would and would againe, if that we
        could;
But thousand enemies about us rave,
And with long siege us in this castle hould:
Seven yeares this wize they us besieged have,
And many good knights slaine, that have us
        sought to save.'

XIII

Thus as he spoke, loe ! with outragious cry
A thousand villeins rownd about them
        swarmd
Out of the rockes and caves adjoyning nye:
Vile caitive wretches, ragged, rude, de-
        formd,

All threatning death, all in straunge manner
    armd;
Some with unweldy clubs, some with long
    speares,
Some rusty knifes, some staves in fier
    warmd.
Sterne was their looke, like wild amazed
    steares,
Staring with hollow eies, and stiffe upstand-
    ing heares.

XIV

Fiersly at first those knights they did as-
    sayle,
And drove them to recoile: but, when
    againe
They gave fresh charge, their forces gan to
    fayle,
Unhable their encounter to sustaine;
For with such puissaunce and impetuous
    maine
Those champions broke on them, that forst
    them fly,
Like scattered sheepe, whenas the shepherds
    swaine
A lyon and a tigre doth espye,
With greedy pace forth rushing from the
    forest nye.

XV

A while they fled, but soone retournd
    againe
With greater fury then before was fownd;
And evermore their cruell capitaine
Sought with his raskall routs t' enclose
    them rownd,
And overronne to tread them to the grownd.
But soone the knights with their bright-
    burning blades
Broke their rude troupes, and orders did
    confownd,
Hewing and slashing at their idle shades;
For though they bodies seem, yet substaunce
    from them fades.

XVI

As when a swarme of gnats at eventide
Out of the fennes of Allan doe arise,
Their murmuring small trompetts sownden
    wide,
Whiles in the aire their clustring army
    flies,
That as a cloud doth seeme to dim the
    skies;
Ne man nor beast may rest, or take repast,

For their sharpe wounds and noyous in-
    juries,
Till the fierce northerne wind with blus-
    tring blast
Doth blow them quite away, and in the
    ocean cast.

XVII

Thus when they had that troublous rout
    disperst,
Unto the castle gate they come againe,
And entraunce crav'd, which was denied
    erst.
Now when report of that their perlous
    paine,
And combrous conflict which they did sus-
    taine,
Came to the ladies eare, which there did
    dwell,
Shee forth issewed with a goodly traine
Of squires and ladies equipaged well,
And entertained them right fairely, as befell.

XVIII

Alma she called was, a virgin bright,
That had not yet felt Cupides wanton rage;
Yet was shee wooed of many a gentle
    knight,
And many a lord of noble parentage,
That sought with her to lincke in marriage,
For shee was faire, as faire mote ever bee,
And in the flowre now of her freshest age;
Yet full of grace and goodly modestee,
That even heven rejoyced her sweete face
    to see.

XIX

In robe of lilly white she was arayd,
That from her shoulder to her heele downe
    raught;
The traine whereof loose far behind her
    strayd,
Braunched with gold and perle, most richly
    wrought,
And borne of two faire damsels, which were
    taught
That service well. Her yellow golden heare
Was trimly woven, and in tresses wrought,
Ne other tire she on her head did weare,
But crowned with a garland of sweete ro-
    siere.

XX

Goodly shee entertaind those noble knights,
And brought them up into her castle hall;

Where gentle court and gracious delight
Shee to them made, with mildnesse virgin-
all,
Shewing her selfe both wise and liberall.
There when they rested had a season dew,
They her besought, of favour speciall,
Of that faire castle to affoord them vew:
Shee graunted, and them leading forth, the
same did shew.

XXI

First she them led up to the castle wall,
That was so high as foe might not it clime,
And all so faire and fensible withall;
Not built of bricke, ne yet of stone and lime,
But of thing like to that Ægyptian slime,
Whereof King Nine whilome built Babell
towre:
But O great pitty that no lenger time
So goodly workemanship should not endure!
Soone it must turne to earth: no earthly
thing is sure.

XXII

The frame thereof seemd partly circulare,
And part triangulare: O worke divine!
Those two the first and last proportions are;
The one imperfect, mortall, fœminine,
Th' other immortall, perfect, masculine:
And twixt them both a quadrate was the
base,
Proportioned equally by seven and nine;
Nine was the circle sett in heavens place:
All which compacted made a goodly dia-
pase.

XXIII

Therein two gates were placed seemly well:
The one before, by which all in did pas,
Did th' other far in workmanship excell;
For not of wood, nor of enduring bras,
But of more worthy substance fram'd it
was:
Doubly disparted, it did locke and close,
That, when it locked, none might thorough
pas,
And when it opened, no man might it close;
Still open to their friendes, and closed to
their foes.

XXIV

Of hewen stone the porch was fayrely
wrought,
Stone more of valew, and more smooth
and fine,

Then jett or marble far from Ireland
brought;
Over the which was cast a wandring vine,
Enchaced with a wanton yvie twine.
And over it a fayre portcullis hong,
Which to the gate directly did incline,
With comely compasse and compacture
strong,
Nether unseemly short, nor yet exceeding
long.

XXV

Within the barbican a porter sate,
Day and night duely keeping watch and
ward;
Nor wight nor word mote passe out of the
gate,
But in good order, and with dew regard:
Utterers of secrets he from thence debard,
Bablers of folly, and blazers of cryme:
His larumbell might lowd and wyde be hard,
When cause requyrd, but never out of time;
Early and late it rong, at evening and at
prime.

XXVI

And rownd about the porch on every syde
Twise sixteene warders satt, all armed bright
In glistring steele, and strongly fortifyde:
Tall yeomen seemed they, and of great
might,
And were enraunged ready still for fight.
By them as Alma passed with her guestes,
They did obeysaunce, as beseemed right,
And then againe retourned to their restes:
The porter eke to her did lout with humble
gestes.

XXVII

Thence she them brought into a stately
hall,
Wherein were many tables fayre dispred,
And ready dight with drapets festivall,
Against the viaundes should be ministred.
At th' upper end there sate, yclad in red
Downe to the ground, a comely personage,
That in his hand a white rod menaged:
He steward was, hight Diet; rype of age,
And in demeanure sober, and in counsell
sage.

XXVIII

And through the hall there walked to and
fro
A jolly yeoman, marshall of the same,

Whose name was Appetite: he did bestow
Both guestes and meate, when ever in they
came,
And knew them how to order without
blame,
As him the steward badd. They both attone
Did dewty to their lady, as became;
Who, passing by, forth ledd her guestes
anone
Into the kitchin rowme, ne spard for nicenesse none.

XXIX

It was a vaut ybuilt for great dispence,
With many raunges reard along the wall,
And one great chimney, whose long tonnell
thence
The smoke forth threw: and in the midst
of all
There placed was a caudron wide and tall,
Upon a mightie fornace, burning whott,
More whott then Aetn', or flaming Mongi-
ball:
For day and night it brent, ne ceased not,
So long as any thing it in the caudron gott.

XXX

But to delay the heat, least by mischaunce
It might breake out, and set the whole on
fyre,
There added was by goodly ordinaunce
An huge great payre of bellowes, which did
styre
Continually, and cooling breath inspyre.
About the caudron many cookes accoyld,
With hookes and ladles, as need did re-
quyre:
The whyles the viaundes in the vessell
boyld,
They did about their businesse sweat, and
sorely toyld.

XXXI

The maister cooke was cald Concoction,
A carefull man, and full of comely guyse.
The kitchin clerke, that hight Digestion,
Did order all th' achates in seemely wise,
And set them forth, as well he could de-
vise.
The rest had severall offices assynd:
Some to remove the scum, as it did rise;
Others to beare the same away did mynd;
And others it to use according to his kynd.

XXXII

But all the liquour, which was fowle and
waste,
Not good nor serviceable elles for ought,
They in another great rownd vessell plaste,
Till by a conduit pipe it thence were
brought:
And all the rest, that noyous was and
nought,
By secret wayes, that none might it espy,
Was close convaid, and to the backgate
brought,
That cleped was Port Esquiline, whereby
It was avoided quite, and throwne out
privily.

XXXIII

Which goodly order and great workmans
skill
Whenas those knightes beheld, with rare
delight
And gazing wonder they their mindes did
fill;
For never had they seene so straunge a
sight.
Thence backe againe faire Alma led them
right,
And soone into a goodly parlour brought,
That was with royall arras richly dight,
In which was nothing pourtrahed nor
wrought,
Not wrought nor pourtrahed, but easie to
be thought.

XXXIV

And in the midst thereof upon the floure,
A lovely bevy of faire ladies sate,
Courted of many a jolly paramoure,
The which them did in modest wise amate,
And eachone sought his lady to aggrate:
And eke emongst them litle Cupid playd
His wanton sportes, being retourned late
From his fierce warres, and having from
him layd
His cruel bow, wherewith he thousands
hath dismayd.

XXXV

Diverse delights they fownd them selves to
please;
Some song in sweet consort, some laught for
joy,
Some plaid with strawes, some ydly satt at
ease;
But other some could not abide to toy,

All pleasaunce was to them griefe and
    annoy:
This fround, that faund, the third for
    shame did blush,
Another seemed envious, or coy,
Another in her teeth did gnaw a rush:
But at these straungers presence every one
    did hush.

XXXVI

Soone as the gracious Alma came in place,
They all attonce out of their seates arose,
And to her homage made, with humble
    grace:
Whom when the knights beheld, they gan
    dispose
Themselves to court, and each a damzell
    chose.
The Prince by chaunce did on a lady light,
That was right faire and fresh as morning
    rose,
But somwhat sad and solemne eke in sight,
As if some pensive thought constraind her
    gentle spright.

XXXVII

In a long purple pall, whose skirt with gold
Was fretted all about, she was arayd;
And in her hand a poplar braunch did hold:
To whom the Prince in courteous maner
    sayd:
'Gentle madame, why beene ye thus dis-
    mayd,
And your faire beautie doe with sadnes
    spill?
Lives any, that you hath thus ill apayd?
Or doen you love, or doen you lack your
    will?
What ever bee the cause, it sure beseemes
    you ill.'

XXXVIII

'Fayre sir,' said she, halfe in disdainefull
    wise,
'How is it, that this word in me ye blame,
And in your selfe doe not the same ad-
    vise?
Him ill beseemes, anothers fault to name,
That may unwares bee blotted with the
    same:
Pensive I yeeld I am, and sad in mind,
Through great desire of glory and of fame;
Ne ought I weene are ye therein behynd,
That have twelve monethes sought one, yet
    no where can her find.'

XXXIX

The Prince was inly moved at her speach,
Well weeting trew what she had rashly
    told,
Yet with faire semblaunt sought to hyde
    the breach,
Which chaunge of colour did perforce un-
    fold,
Now seeming flaming whott, now stony
    cold.
Tho, turning soft aside, he did inquyre
What wight she was, that poplar braunch
    did hold:
It answered was, her name was Prays-
    desire,
That by well doing sought to honour to
    aspyre.

XL

The whyles, the Faery knight did enter-
    tayne
Another damsell of that gentle crew,
That was right fayre, and modest of de-
    mayne,
But that too oft she chaung'd her native
    hew:
Straunge was her tyre, and all her garment
    blew,
Close rownd about her tuckt with many a
    plight:
Upon her fist the bird, which shonneth vew
And keepes in coverts close from living
    wight,
Did sitt, as yet ashamd, how rude Pan did
    her dight.

XLI

So long as Guyon with her commoned,
Unto the grownd she cast her modest eye,
And ever and anone with rosy red
The bashfull blood her snowy cheekes did
    dye,
That her became, as polisht yvory
Which cunning craftesman hand hath over-
    layd
With fayre vermilion or pure castory.
Great wonder had the knight, to see the
    mayd
So straungely passioned, and to her gently
    said:

XLII

'Fayre damzell, seemeth by your troubled
    cheare,
That either me too bold ye weene, this wise

You to molest, or other ill to feare
That in the secret of your hart close lyes,
From whence it doth, as cloud from sea,
    aryse.
If it be I, of pardon I you pray;
But if ought else that I mote not devyse,
I will, if please you it discure, assay
To ease you of that ill, so wisely as I may.'

XLIII

She answerd nought, but more abasht for
    shame,
Held downe her head, the whiles her lovely
    face
The flashing blood with blushing did inflame,
And the strong passion mard her modest
    grace,
That Guyon mervayld at her uncouth cace;
Till Alma him bespake: 'Why wonder yee,
Faire sir, at that which ye so much em-
    brace ?
She is the fountaine of your modestee;
You shamefast are, but Shamefastnes it
    selfe is shee.'

XLIV

Thereat the Elfe did blush in privitee,
And turnd his face away; but she the
    same
Dissembled faire, and faynd to oversee.
Thus they awhile with court and goodly game
Themselves did solace each one with his
    dame,
Till that great lady thence away them
    sought,
To vew her castles other wondrous frame.
Up to a stately turret she them brought,
Ascending by ten steps of alablaster
    wrought.

XLV

That turrets frame most admirable was,
Like highest heaven compassed around,
And lifted high above this earthly masse,
Which it survewd, as hils doen lower
    ground:
But not on ground mote like to this be
    found;
Not that, which antique Cadmus whylome
    built
In Thebes, which Alexander did confound;
Nor that proud towre of Troy, though
    richly guilt,
From which young Hectors blood by cruell
    Greekes was spilt.

XLVI

The roofe hereof was arched over head,
And deckt with flowers and herbars daint-
    ily:
Two goodly beacons, set in watches stead,
Therein gave light, and flamd continually;
For they of living fire most subtilly
Were made, and set in silver sockets bright,
Cover'd with lids deviz'd of substance sly,
That readily they shut and open might.
O who can tell the prayses of that makers
    might ?

XLVII

Ne can I tell, ne can I stay to tell
This parts great workemanship and won-
    drous powre,
That all this other worldes worke doth ex-
    cell,
And likest is unto that heavenly towre,
That God hath built for his owne blessed
    bowre.
Therein were divers rowmes, and divers
    stages,
But three the chiefest, and of greatest
    powre,
In which there dwelt three honorable sages,
The wisest men, I weene, that lived in
    their ages.

XLVIII

Not he, whom Greece, the nourse of all
    good arts,
By Phæbus doome, the wisest thought alive,
Might be compar'd to these by many parts:
Nor that sage Pylian syre, which did sur-
    vive
Three ages, such as mortall men contrive,
By whose advise old Priams cittie fell,
With these in praise of pollicies mote strive.
These three in these three rowmes did son-
    dry dwell,
And counselled faire Alma, how to governe
    well.

XLIX

The first of them could things to come fore-
    see;
The next could of thinges present best ad-
    vize;
The third things past could keepe in mem-
    oree:
So that no time nor reason could arize,
But that the same could one of these com-
    prize.

Forthy the first did in the forepart sit,
That nought mote hinder his quicke preju-
dize:
He had a sharpe foresight, and working wit,
That never idle was, ne once would rest a
whit.

L

His chamber was dispainted all with in
With sondry colours, in the which were writ
Infinite shapes of thinges dispersed thin;
Some such as in the world were never yit,
Ne can devized be of mortall wit;
Some daily seene, and knowen by their
names,
Such as in idle fantasies doe flit:
Infernall hags, centaurs, feendes, hippo-
dames,
Apes, lyons, aegles, owles, fooles, lovers,
children, dames.

LI

And all the chamber filled was with flyes,
Which buzzed all about, and made such
sound,
That they encombred all mens eares and
eyes,
Like many swarmes of bees assembled
round,
After their hives with honny do abound:
All those were idle thoughtes and fantasies,
Devices, dreames, opinions unsound,
Shewes, visions, sooth-sayes, and prophesies;
And all that fained is, as leasings, tales,
and lies.

LII

Emongst them all sate he which wonned
there,
That hight Phantastes by his nature trew,
A man of yeares yet fresh, as mote appere,
Of swarth complexion, and of crabbed hew,
That him full of melancholy did shew;
Bent hollow beetle browes, sharpe staring
eyes,
That mad or foolish seemd: one by his vew
Mote deeme him borne with ill-disposed
skyes,
When oblique Saturne sate in the house of
agonyes.

LIII

Whom Alma having shewed to her guestes,
Thence brought them to the second rowme,
whose wals

Were painted faire with memorable gestes
Of famous wisards, and with picturals
Of magistrates, of courts, of tribunals,
Of commen wealthes, of states, of pollicy,
Of lawes, of judgementes, and of decretals;
All artes, all science, all philosophy,
And all that in the world was ay thought
wittily.

LIV

Of those that rowme was full, and them
among
There sate a man of ripe and perfect age,
Who did them meditate all his life long,
That through continuall practise and usage,
He now was growne right wise and won-
drous sage.
Great plesure had those straunger knightes,
to see
His goodly reason and grave personage,
That his disciples both desyrd to bee;
But Alma thence them led to th' hindmost
rowme of three.

LV

That chamber seemed ruinous and old,
And therefore was removed far behind,
Yet were the wals, that did the same up-
hold,
Right firme and strong, though somwhat
they declind;
And therein sat an old old man, halfe blind,
And all decrepit in his feeble corse,
Yet lively vigour rested in his mind,
And recompenst him with a better scorse:
Weake body well is chang'd for minds re-
doubled forse.

LVI

This man of infinite remembraunce was,
And things foregone through many ages
held,
Which he recorded still, as they did pas,
Ne suffred them to perish through long eld,
As all things els, the which this world doth
weld,
But laid them up in his immortall scrine,
Where they for ever incorrupted dweld:
The warres he well remembred of King
Nine,
Of old Assaracus, and Inachus divine.

LVII

The yeares of Nestor nothing were to his,
Ne yet Mathusalem, though longest liv'd;

For he remembred both their infancis:
Ne wonder then, if that he were depriv'd
Of native strength now that he them sur-
    viv'd.
His chamber all was hangd about with
    rolls,
And old records from auncient times de-
    rivd,
Some made in books, some in long parch-
    ment scrolls,
That were all worm-eaten and full of canker
    holes.

LVIII

Amidst them all he in a chaire was sett,
Tossing and turning them withouten end;
But for he was unhable them to fett,
A litle boy did on him still attend,
To reach, when ever he for ought did send;
And oft when thinges were lost, or laid
    amis,
That boy them sought and unto him did
    lend:
Therefore he Anamnestes cleped is,
And that old man Eumnestes, by their pro-
    pertis.

LIX

The knightes, there entring, did him rever-
    ence dew,
And wondred at his endlesse exercise.
Then as they gan his library to vew,
And antique regesters for to avise,
There chaunced to the Princes hand to
    rize
An auncient booke, hight *Briton Moni-
    ments,*
That of this lands first conquest did devize,
And old division into regiments,
Till it reduced was to one mans governe-
    ments.

LX

Sir Guyon chaunst eke on another booke,
That hight *Antiquitee of Faery Lond:*
In which whenas he greedily did looke,
Th' ofspring of Elves and Faryes there he
    fond,
As it delivered was from hond to hond.
Whereat they, burning both with fervent
    fire
Their countreys auncestry to understond,
Crav'd leave of Alma and that aged sire,
To read those bookes; who gladly graunted
    their desire.

CANTO X

A chronicle of Briton kings,
    From Brute to Uthers rayne ;
And rolls of Elfin emperours,
    Till time of Gloriane.

I

WHO now shall give unto me words and
    sound,
Equall unto this haughty enterprise ?
Or who shall lend me wings, with which
    from ground
My lowly verse may loftily arise,
And lift it selfe unto the highest skyes ?
More ample spirit, then hetherto was wount,
Here needes me, whiles the famous aunces-
    tryes
Of my most dreaded Soveraigne I recount,
By which all earthly princes she doth far
    surmount.

II

Ne under sunne, that shines so wide and
    faire,
Whence all that lives does borrow life and
    light,
Lives ought that to her linage may com-
    paire,
Which, though from earth it be derived
    right,
Yet doth it selfe stretch forth to hevens
    hight,
And all the world with wonder overspred;
A labor huge, exceeding far my might:
How shall fraile pen, with feare disparaged,
Conceive such soveraine glory, and great
    bountyhed ?

III

Argument worthy of Mœonian quill,
Or rather worthy of great Phoebus rote,
Whereon the ruines of great Ossa hill,
And triumphes of Phlegræan Jove, he
    wrote,
That all the gods admird his lofty note.
But, if some relish of that hevenly lay
His learned daughters would to me report,
To decke my song withall, I would assay
Thy name, O soveraine Queene, to blazon
    far away.

IV

Thy name, O soveraine Queene, thy realme,
    and race,
From this renowmed Prince derived arre,

Who mightily upheld that royall mace,
Which now thou bear'st, to thee descended
    farre
From mighty kings and conquerours in
    warre,
Thy fathers and great grandfathers of old,
Whose noble deeds above the northern
    starre
Immortall Fame for ever hath enrold;
As in that old mans booke they were in
    order told.

V

The land, which warlike Britons now pos-
    sesse,
And therein have their mighty empire raysd,
In antique times was salvage wildernesse,
Unpeopled, unmannurd, unprovd, unpraysd;
Ne was it island then, ne was it paysd
Amid the ocean waves, ne was it sought
Of merchaunts farre, for profits therein
    praysd;
But was all desolate, and of some thought
By sea to have bene from the Celticke
    mayn-land brought.

VI

Ne did it then deserve a name to have,
Till that the venturous mariner that way,
Learning his ship from those white rocks
    to save,
Which all along the southerne sea-coast
    lay,
Threatning unheedy wrecke and rash de-
    cay,
For safeties sake that same his sea-marke
    made,
And namd it ALBION. But later day,
Finding in it fit ports for fishers trade,
Gan more the same frequent, and further
    to invade.

VII

But far in land a salvage nation dwelt
Of hideous giaunts, and halfe beastly men,
That never tasted grace, nor goodnes felt,
But like wild beastes lurking in loathsome
    den,
And flying fast as roebucke through the
    fen,
All naked without shame or care of cold,
By hunting and by spoiling liveden;
Of stature huge, and eke of corage bold,
That sonnes of men amazd their sternesse
    to behold.

VIII

But whence they sprong, or how they were
    begott,
Uneath is to assure; uneath to wene
That monstrous error, which doth some as-
    sott,
That Dioclesians fifty daughters shene
Into this land by chaunce have driven bene,
Where companing with feends and filthy
    sprights
Through vaine illusion of their lust unclene,
They brought forth geaunts, and such
    dreadfull wights
As far exceeded men in their immeasurd
    mights.

IX

They held this land, and with their filthi-
    nesse
Polluted this same gentle soyle long time:
That their owne mother loathd their
    beastlinesse,
And gan abhorre her broods unkindly crime,
All were they borne of her owne native
    slime:
Until that Brutus, anciently deriv'd
From roiall stocke of old Assaracs line,
Driven by fatall error, here arriv'd,
And them of their unjust possession de-
    priv'd.

X

But ere he had established his throne,
And spred his empire to the utmost shore,
He fought great batteils with his salvage
    fone;
In which he them defeated evermore,
And many giaunts left on groning flore,
That well can witnes yet unto this day
The westerne Hogh, besprincled with the
    gore
Of mighty Goëmot, whome in stout fray
Corineus conquered, and cruelly did slay.

XI

And eke that ample pitt, yet far renownd
For the large leape which Debon did com-
    pell
Coulin to make, being eight lugs of grownd,
Into the which retourning backe he fell:
But those three monstrous stones doe most
    excell
Which that huge sonne of hideous Albion,
Whose father Hercules in Fraunce did
    quell,

Great Godmer, threw, in fierce contention,
At bold Canutus; but of him was slaine
    anon.

XII

In meed of these great conquests by them
    gott,
Corineus had that province utmost west
To him assigned for his worthy lott,
Which of his name and memorable gest
He called Cornwaile, yet so called best:
And Debons shayre was that is Devonshyre:
But Canute had his portion from the rest,
The which he cald Canutium, for his hyre;
Now Cantium, which Kent we comenly in-
    quyre.

XIII

Thus Brute this realme unto his rule sub-
    dewd,
And raigned long in great felicity,
Lov'd of his freends, and of his foes es-
    chewd.
He left three sonnes, his famous progeny,
Borne of fayre Inogene of Italy;
Mongst whom he parted his imperiall state,
And Locrine left chiefe lord of Britany.
At last ripe age bad him surrender late
His life, and long good fortune, unto finall
    fate.

XIV

Locrine was left the soveraine lord of all;
But Albanact had all the northerne part,
Which of him selfe Albania he did call;
And Camber did possesse the westerne
    quart,
Which Severne now from Logris doth de-
    part:
And each his portion peaceably enjoyd,
Ne was there outward breach, nor grudge
    in hart,
That once their quiet government annoyd,
But each his paynes to others profit still
    employd.

XV

Untill a nation straung, with visage swart
And corage fierce, that all men did affray,
Which through the world then swarmd in
    every part,
And overflow'd all countries far away,
Like Noyes great flood, with their impor-
    tune sway,
This land invaded with like violence,

And did themselves through all the north
    display:
Untill that Locrine, for his realmes de-
    fence,
Did head against them make, and strong
    munificence.

XVI

He them encountred, a confused rout,
Foreby the river, that whylome was hight
The ancient Abus, where with courage stout
He them defeated in victorious fight,
And chaste so fiercely after fearefull flight,
That forst their chiefetain, for his safeties
    sake,
(Their chiefetain Humber named was aright,)
Unto the mighty streame him to betake,
Where he an end of batteill, and of life did
    make.

XVII

The king retourned proud of victory,
And insolent wox through unwonted ease,
That shortly he forgot the jeopardy,
Which in his land he lately did appease,
And fell to vaine voluptuous disease:
He lov'd faire Ladie Estrild, leudly lov'd,
Whose wanton pleasures him too much did
    please,
That quite his hart from Guendolene re-
    mov'd,
From Guendolene his wife, though alwaies
    faithful prov'd.

XVIII

The noble daughter of Corineus
Would not endure to bee so vile disdaind,
But, gathering force and corage valorous,
Encountred him in batteill well ordaind,
In which him vanquisht she to fly con-
    straind:
But she so fast pursewd, that him she
    tooke,
And threw in bands, where he till death
    remaind:
Als his faire leman, flying through a brooke,
She overhent, nought moved with her pite-
    ous looke.

XIX

But both her selfe, and eke her daughter
    deare,
Begotten by her kingly paramoure,
The faire Sabrina, almost dead with feare,
She there attached, far from all succoure;

The one she slew in that impatient stoure,
But the sad virgin, innocent of all,
Adowne the rolling river she did poure,
Which of her name now Severne men do
  call:
Such was the end that to disloyall love did
  fall.

XX

Then, for her sonne, which she to Locrin
  bore,
Madan, was young, unmeet the rule to
  sway,
In her owne hand the crowne she kept in
  store,
Till ryper yeares he raught, and stronger
  stay:
During which time her powre she did display
Through all this realme, the glory of her
  sex,
And first taught men a woman to obay:
But when her sonne to mans estate did
  wex,
She it surrendred, ne her selfe would lenger
  vex.

XXI

Tho Madan raignd, unworthie of his race:
For with all shame that sacred throne he
  fild:
Next Memprise, as unworthy of that place,
In which being consorted with Manild,
For thirst of single kingdom him he kild.
But Ebranck salved both their infamies
With noble deedes, and warreyd on Brun-
  child
In Henault, where yet of his victories
Brave moniments remaine, which yet that
  land envies.

XXII

An happy man in his first dayes he was,
And happy father of faire progeny:
For all so many weekes as the yeare has,
So many children he did multiply;
Of which were twentie sonnes, which did
  apply
Their mindes to prayse and chevalrous
  desyre:
Those germans did subdew all Germany,
Of whom it hight; but in the end their
  syre
With foule repulse from Fraunce was forced
  to retyre.

XXIII

Which blott his sonne succeeding in his seat,
The second Brute, the second both in name
And eke in semblaunce of his puissaunce
  great,
Right well recur'd, and did away that blame
With recompence of everlasting fame.
He with his victour sword first opened
The bowels of wide Fraunce, a forlorne
  dame,
And taught her first how to be conquered;
Since which, with sondrie spoiles she hath
  bene ransacked.

XXIV

Let Scaldis tell, and let tell Hania,
And let the marsh of Esthambruges tell,
What colour were their waters that same
  day,
And all the moore twixt Elversham and
  Dell,
With blood of Henalois, which therein fell.
How oft that day did sad Brunchildis see
The greene shield dyde in dolorous vermell!
That not *scuith guiridh* it mote seeme to bee,
But rather *y scuith gogh*, signe of sad
  crueltee.

XXV

His sonne, King Leill, by fathers labour
  long,
Enjoyd an heritage of lasting peace,
And built Cairleill, and built Cairleon strong.
Next Huddibras his realme did not en-
  crease,
But taught the land from wearie wars to
  cease.
Whose footsteps Bladud following, in artes
Exceld at Athens all the learned preace,
From whence he brought them to these
  salvage parts,
And with sweet science mollifide their
  stubborne harts.

XXVI

Ensample of his wondrous faculty,
Behold the boyling bathes at Cairbadon,
Which seeth with secret fire eternally,
And in their entrailles, full of quick
  brimston,
Nourish the flames which they are warmd
  upon,
That to their people wealth they forth do
  well,
And health to every forreyne nation:

Yet he at last, contending to excell
The reach of men, through flight into fond
    mischief fell.

XXVII

Next him King Leyr in happie peace long
    raynd,
But had no issue male him to succeed,
But three faire daughters, which were well
    uptraind
In all that seemed fitt for kingly seed:
Mongst whom his realme he equally decreed
To have divided. Tho, when feeble age
Nigh to his utmost date he saw proceed,
He cald his daughters, and with speeches
    sage
Inquyrd, which of them most did love her
    parentage.

XXVIII

The eldest Gonorill gan to protest,
That she much more then her owne life him
    lov'd;
And Regan greater love to him profest
Then all the world, when ever it were
    proov'd;
But Cordeill said she lov'd him as behoov'd:
Whose simple answere, wanting colours
    fayre
To paint it forth, him to displeasaunce
    moov'd,
That in his crown he counted her no hayre,
But twixt the other twain his kingdom whole
    did shayre.

XXIX

So wedded th' one to Maglan, king of
    Scottes,
And thother to the king of Cambria,
And twixt them shayrd his realme by equall
    lottes:
But without dowre the wise Cordelia
Was sent to Aggannip of Celtica.
Their aged syre, thus eased of his crowne,
A private life ledd in Albania,
With Gonorill, long had in great renowne,
That nought him griev'd to beene from rule
    deposed downe.

XXX

But true it is that, when the oyle is spent,
The light goes out, and weeke is throwne
    away;
So when he had resignd his regiment,
His daughter gan despise his drouping day,

And wearie wax of his continuall stay.
Tho to his daughter Regan he repayrd,
Who him at first well used every way;
But when of his departure she despayrd,
Her bountie she abated, and his cheare
    empayrd.

XXXI

The wretched man gan then avise to late,
That love is not, where most it is profest;
Too truely tryde in his extremest state.
At last, resolv'd likewise to prove the rest,
He to Cordelia him selfe addrest,
Who with entyre affection him receav'd,
As for her syre and king her seemed best;
And after all an army strong she leav'd,
To war on those which him had of his realme
    bereav'd.

XXXII

So to his crowne she him restord againe,
In which he dyde, made ripe for death by
    eld,
And after wild, it should to her remaine:
Who peaceably the same long time did weld,
And all mens harts in dew obedience held:
Till that her sisters children, woxen strong,
Through proud ambition against her rebeld,
And overcommen kept in prison long,
Till, weary of that wretched life, her selfe
    she hong.

XXXIII

Then gan the bloody brethren both to raine:
But fierce Cundah gan shortly to envy
His brother Morgan, prickt with proud
    disdaine,
To have a pere in part of soverainty;
And kindling coles of cruell enmity,
Raisd warre, and him in batteill overthrew:
Whence as he to those woody hilles did
    fly,
Which hight of him Glamorgan, there him
    slew:
Then did he raigne alone, when he none
    equall knew.

XXXIV

His sonne Rivall' his dead rowme did supply,
In whose sad time blood did from heaven
    rayne:
Next great Gurgustus, then faire Cæcily,
In constant peace their kingdomes did
    contayne:
After whom Lago and Kinmarke did rayne,

And Gorbogud, till far in yeares he grew:
Then his ambitious sonnes unto them
   twayne
Arraught the rule, and from their father
   drew:
Stout Ferrex and sterne Porrex him in prison
   threw.

XXXV

But O ! the greedy thirst of royall crowne,
That knowes no kinred, nor regardes no
   right,
Stird Porrex up to put his brother downe;
Who, unto him assembling forreigne might,
Made warre on him, and fell him selfe in
   fight:
Whose death t' avenge, his mother
   mercilesse,
Most mercilesse of women, Wyden hight,
Her other sonne fast sleeping did oppresse,
And with most cruell hand him murdred
   pittilesse.

XXXVI

Here ended Brutus sacred progeny,
Which had seven hundred yeares this scepter
   borne,
With high renowme and great felicity:
The noble braunch from th' antique stocke
   was torne
Through discord, and the roiall throne
   forlorne:
Thenceforth this realme was into factions
   rent,
Whilest each of Brutus boasted to be borne,
That in the end was left no moniment
Of Brutus, nor of Britons glorie auncient.

XXXVII

Then up arose a man of matchlesse might,
And wondrous wit to menage high affayres,
Who, stird with pitty of the stressed plight
Of this sad realme, cut into sondry shayres
By such as claymd themselves Brutes right-
   full hayres,
Gathered the princes of the people loose,
To taken counsell of their common cares;
Who, with his wisedom won, him streight
   did choose
Their king, and swore him fealty, to win or
   loose.

XXXVIII

Then made he head against his enimies,
And Ymner slew, of Logris miscreate;

Then Ruddoc and proud Stater, both allyes,
This of Albany newly nominate,
And that of Cambry king confirmed late,
He overthrew through his owne valiaunce;
Whose countries he redus'd to quiet state,
And shortly brought to civile governaunce,
Now one, which earst were many made
   through variaunce.

XXXIX

Then made he sacred lawes, which some
   men say
Were unto him reveald in vision,
By which he freed the traveilers high way,
The churches part, and ploughmans portion,
Restraining stealth and strong extortion;
The gratious Numa of Great Britany:
For, till his dayes, the chiefe dominion
By strength was wielded without pollicy;
Therefore he first wore crowne of gold for
   dignity.

XL

Donwallo dyde (for what may live for ay ?)
And left two sonnes, of pearelesse prowesse
   both,
That sacked Rome too dearely did assay,
The recompence of their perjured oth,
And ransackt Greece wel tryde, when they
   were wroth;
Besides subjected France and Germany,
Which yet their praises speake, all be they
   loth,
And inly tremble at the memory
Of Brennus and Belinus, kinges of Britany.

XLI

Next them did Gurgunt, great Belinus sonne,
In rule succeede, and eke in fathers praise:
He Easterland subdewd, and Denmarke
   wonne,
And of them both did foy and tribute raise,
The which was dew in his dead fathers daies:
He also gave to fugitives of Spayne,
Whom he at sea found wandring from their
   waies,
A seate in Ireland safely to remayne,
Which they should hold of him, as subject
   to Britayne.

XLII

After him raigned Guitheline his hayre,
The justest man and trewest in his daies,
Who had to wife Dame Mertia the fayre,
A woman worthy of immortall praise,

Which for this realme found many goodly
    layes,
And wholesome statutes to her husband
    brought:
Her many deemd to have beene of the
    Fayes,
As was Aegerie, that Numa tought:
Those yet of her be Mertian lawes both
    nam'd and thought.

XLIII

Her sonne Sisillus after her did rayne,
And then Kimarus, and then Danius;
Next whom Morindus did the crowne sus-
    tayne,
Who, had he not with wrath outrageous
And cruell rancour dim'd his valorous
And mightie deedes, should matched have
    the best:
As well in that same field victorious
Against the forreine Morands he exprest:
Yet lives his memorie, though carcas
    sleepe in rest.

XLIV

Five sonnes he left begotten of one wife,
All which successively by turnes did rayne;
First Gorboman, a man of vertuous life;
Next Archigald, who, for his proud dis-
    dayne,
Deposed was from princedome soverayne,
And pitteous Elidure put in his sted;
Who shortly it to him restord agayne,
Till by his death he it recovered;
But Peridure and Vigent him disthronized.

XLV

In wretched prison long he did remaine,
Till they outraigned had their utmost date,
And then therein reseized was againe,
And ruled long with honorable state,
Till he surrendred realme and life to fate.
Then all the sonnes of these five brethren
    raynd
By dew successe, and all their nephewes
    late;
Even thrise eleven descents the crowne re-
    taynd,
Till aged Hely by dew heritage it gaynd.

XLVI

He had two sonnes, whose eldest, called Lud,
Left of his life most famous memory,
And endlesse moniments of his great good:
The ruin'd wals he did reædifye

Of Troynovant, gainst force of enimy,
And built that gate which of his name is
    hight,
By which he lyes entombed solemnly.
He left two sonnes, too young to rule aright,
Androgeus and Tenantius, pictures of his
    might.

XLVII

Whilst they were young, Cassibalane their
    eme
Was by the people chosen in their sted,
Who on him tooke the roiall diademe,
And goodly well long time it governed;
Till the prowde Romanes him disquieted,
And warlike Cæsar, tempted with the name
Of this sweet island, never conquered,
And envying the Britons blazed fame,
(O hideous hunger of dominion!) hether
    came.

XLVIII

Yet twise they were repulsed backe againe,
And twise renforst backe to their ships to
    fly,
The whiles with blood they all the shore did
    staine,
And the gray ocean into purple dy:
Ne had they footing found at last perdie,
Had not Androgeus, false to native soyle,
And envious of uncles soveraintie,
Betrayd his countrey unto forreine spoyle:
Nought els but treason from the first this
    land did foyle.

XLIX

So by him Cæsar got the victory,
Through great bloodshed and many a sad
    assay,
In which himselfe was charged heavily
Of hardy Nennius, whom he yet did slay,
But lost his sword, yet to be seene this
    day.
Thenceforth this land was tributarie made
T' ambitious Rome, and did their rule obay,
Till Arthur all that reckoning defrayd;
Yet oft the Briton kings against them
    strongly swayd.

L

Next him Tenantius raignd; then Kimbe-
    line,
What time th' Eternall Lord in fleshly slime
Enwombed was, from wretched Adams line
To purge away the guilt of sinfull crime:

O joyous memorie of happy time,
That heavenly grace so plenteously displayd!
O too high ditty for my simple rime !
Soone after this the Romanes him warrayd,
For that their tribute he refusd to let be
payd.

LI

Good Claudius, that next was emperour,
An army brought, and with him batteile
fought,
In which the king was by a treachetour
Disguised slaine, ere any thereof thought:
Yet ceased not the bloody fight for ought;
For Arvirage his brothers place supplyde,
Both in his armes and crowne, and by that
draught
Did drive the Romanes to the weaker syde,
That they to peace agreed. So all was paci-
fyde.

LII

Was never king more highly magnifide,
Nor dredd of Romanes, then was Arvirage;
For which the emperour to him allide
His daughter Genuiss' in marriage:
Yet shortly he renounst the vassallage
Of Rome againe, who hether hastly sent
Vespasian, that with great spoile and rage
Forwasted all, till Genuissa gent
Persuaded him to ceasse, and her lord to
relent.

LIII

He dide; and him succeeded Marius,
Who joyd his dayes in great tranquillity:
Then Coyll, and after him good Lucius,
That first received Christianity,
The sacred pledge of Christes Evangely:
Yet true it is, that long before that day
Hither came Joseph of Arimathy,
Who brought with him the Holy Grayle,
(they say)
And preacht the truth; but since it greatly
did decay.

LIV

This good king shortly without issew dide,
Whereof great trouble in the kingdome
grew,
That did her selfe in sondry parts divide,
And with her powre her owne selfe over-
threw,
Whilest Romanes daily did the weake
subdew:

Which seeing stout Bunduca, up arose,
And taking armes, the Britons to her drew;
With whom she marched streight against
her foes,
And them unwares besides the Severne did
enclose.

LV

There she with them a cruell batteill tryde,
Not with so good successe as shee deserv'd,
By reason that the captaines on her syde,
Corrupted by Paulinus, from her swerv'd:
Yet such as were through former flight
preserv'd
Gathering againe, her host she did renew,
And with fresh corage on the victor serv'd:
But being all defeated, save a few,
Rather then fly, or be captiv'd, her selfe
she slew.

LVI

O famous moniment of womens prayse,
Matchable either to Semiramis,
Whom antique history so high doth rayse,
Or to Hypsiphil', or to Thomiris !
Her host two hundred thousand numbred
is;
Who, whiles good fortune favoured her
might,
Triumphed oft against her enemis;
And yet, though overcome in haplesse fight,
Shee triumphed on death, in enemies de-
spight.

LVII

Her reliques Fulgent having gathered,
Fought with Severus, and him overthrew;
Yet in the chace was slaine of them that fled:
So made them victors whome he did subdew.
Then gan Carausius tirannize anew,
And gainst the Romanes bent their proper
powre;
But him Allectus treacherously slew,
And tooke on him the robe of emperoure:
Nath'lesse the same enjoyed but short
happy howre.

LVIII

For Asclepiodate him overcame,
And left inglorious on the vanquisht playne,
Without or robe or rag to hide his shame.
Then afterwards he in his stead did raigne;
But shortly was by Coyll in batteill slaine:
Who after long debate, since Lucies tyme,
Was of the Britons first crownd soveraine.

Then gan this realme renew her passed
  prime:
He of his name Coylchester built of stone
  and lime.

LIX

Which when the Romanes heard, they
  hether sent
Constantius, a man of mickle might,
With whome King Coyll made an agree-
  ment,
And to him gave for wife his daughter
  bright,
Fayre Helena, the fairest living wight;
Who in all godly thewes, and goodly praise,
Did far excell, but was most famous hight
For skil in musicke of all in her daies,
Aswell in curious instruments as cunning
  laies.

LX

Of whom he did great Constantine begett,
Who afterward was emperour of Rome;
To which whiles absent he his mind did
  sett,
Octavius here lept into his roome,
And it usurped by unrighteous doome:
But he his title justifide by might,
Slaying Traherne, and having overcome
The Romane legion in dreadfull fight:
So settled he his kingdome, and confirmd
  his right.

LXI

But wanting yssew male, his daughter deare
He gave in wedlocke to Maximian,
And him with her made of his kingdome
  heyre,
Who soone by meanes thereof the empire
  wan,
Till murdred by the freends of Gratian.
Then gan the Hunnes and Picts invade
  this land,
During the raigne of Maximinian;
Who dying left none heire them to with-
  stand,
But that they overran all parts with easy
  hand.

LXII

The weary Britons, whose war-hable youth
Was by Maximian lately ledd away,
With wretched miseryes and woefull ruth
Were to those pagans made an open pray,
And daily spectacle of sad decay:

Whome Romane warres, which now fowr
  hundred yeares
And more had wasted, could no whit dismay;
Til by consent of Commons and of Peares,
They crownd the second Constantine with
  joyous teares.

LXIII

Who having oft in batteill vanquished
Those spoylefull Picts, and swarming East-
  erlings,
Long time in peace his realme established,
Yet oft annoyd with sondry bordragings
Of neighbour Scots, and forrein scatter-
  lings,
With which the world did in those dayes
  abound:
Which to outbarre, with painefull pyonings
From sea to sea he heapt a mighty mound,
Which from Alcluid to Panwelt did that
  border bownd.

LXIV

Three sonnes he dying left, all under age;
By meanes whereof, their uncle Vortigere
Usurpt the crowne during their pupillage;
Which th' infants tutors gathering to feare,
Them closely into Armorick did beare:
For dread of whom, and for those Picts an-
  noyes,
He sent to Germany, straunge aid to reare;
From whence eftsoones arrived here three
  hoyes
Of Saxons, whom he for his safety imployes.

LXV

Two brethren were their capitayns, which
  hight
Hengist and Horsus, well approv'd in warre,
And both of them men of renowmed might;
Who, making vantage of their civile jarre,
And of those forreyners which came from
  farre,
Grew great, and got large portions of land,
That in the realme ere long they stronger
  arre
Then they which sought at first their help-
  ing hand,
And Vortiger have forst the kingdome to
  aband.

LXVI

But by the helpe of Vortimere his sonne,
He is againe unto his rule restord;

And Hengist, seeming sad for that was
    donne,
Received is to grace and new accord,
Through his faire daughters face and flat-
    tring word.
Soone after which, three hundred lords he
    slew
Of British blood, all sitting at his bord;
Whose dolefull moniments who list to rew,
Th' eternall marks of treason may at Ston-
    heng vew.

LXVII

By this the sonnes of Constantine, which
    fled,
Ambrose and Uther, did ripe yeares at-
    tayne,
And here arriving, strongly challenged
The crowne, which Vortiger did long de-
    tayne;
Who, flying from his guilt, by them was
    slayne,
And Hengist eke soone brought to shame-
    full death.
Thenceforth Aurelius peaceably did rayne,
Till that through poyson stopped was his
    breath ;
So now entombed lies at Stoneheng by the
    heath.

LXVIII

After him Uther, which Pendragon hight,
Succeeding ——— There abruptly it did
    end,
Without full point, or other cesure right,
As if the rest some wicked hand did rend,
Or th' author selfe could not at least at-
    tend
To finish it: that so untimely breach
The Prince him selfe halfe seemed to of-
    fend;
Yet secret pleasure did offence empeach,
And wonder of antiquity long stopt his
    speach.

LXIX

At last, quite ravisht with delight, to heare
The royall ofspring of his native land,
Cryde out: 'Deare countrey ! O how dearely
    deare
Ought thy remembraunce and perpetual
    band
Be to thy foster childe, that from thy hand
Did commun breath and nouriture receave !
How brutish is it not to understand

How much to her we owe, that all us
    gave,
That gave unto us all, what ever good we
    have !'

LXX

But Guyon all this while his booke did read,
Ne yet has ended: for it was a great
And ample volume, that doth far excead
My leasure, so long leaves here to repeat:
It told, how first Prometheus did create
A man, of many parts from beasts deryv'd,
And then stole fire from heven, to animate
His worke, for which he was by Jove de-
    pryv'd
Of life him self, and hart-strings of an
    aegle ryv'd.

LXXI

That man so made he called Elfe, to weet
Quick, the first author of all Elfin kynd:
Who, wandring through the world with
    wearie feet,
Did in the gardins of Adonis fynd
A goodly creature, whom he deemd in
    mynd
To be no earthly wight, but either spright
Or angell, th' authour of all woman kynd;
Therefore a Fay he her according hight,
Of whom all Faryes spring, and fetch their
    lignage right.

LXXII

Of these a mighty people shortly grew,
And puissant kinges, which all the world
    warrayd,
And to them selves all nations did subdew.
The first and eldest, which that scepter
    swayd,
Was Elfin; him all India obayd,
And all that now America men call:
Next him was noble Elfinan, who laid
Cleopolis foundation first of all:
But Elfiline enclosd it with a golden wall.

LXXIII

His sonne was Elfinell, who overcame
The wicked Gobbelines in bloody field:
But Elfant was of most renowmed fame,
Who all of christall did Panthea build:
Then Elfar, who two brethren gyaunte;
    kild,
The one of which had two heades, th' othe
    three:
Then Elfinor, who was in magick skild;

He built by art upon the glassy see
A bridge of bras, whose sound hevens
thunder seem'd to bee.

LXXIV

He left three sonnes, the which in order
raynd,
And all their ofspring, in their dew de-
scents,
Even seven hundred princes, which main-
taynd
With mightie deedes their sondry govern-
ments;
That were too long their infinite contents
Here to record, ne much materiall;
Yet should they be most famous moni-
ments,
And brave ensample, both of martiall
And civil rule, to kinges and states imperiall.

LXXV

After all these Elficleos did rayne,
The wise Elficleos in great majestie,
Who mightily that scepter did sustayne,
And with rich spoyles and famous victorie
Did high advaunce the crowne of Faery:
He left two sonnes, of which faire Elferon,
The eldest brother, did untimely dy;
Whose emptie place the mightie Oberon
Doubly supplide, in spousall and dominion.

LXXVI

Great was his power and glorie over all
Which, him before, that sacred seate did
fill,
That yet remaines his wide memoriall:
He dying left the fairest Tanaquill,
Him to succeede therein, by his last will:
Fairer and nobler liveth none this howre,
Ne like in grace, ne like in learned skill;
Therefore they Glorian call that glorious
flowre:
Long mayst thou, Glorian, live, in glory and
great powre!

LXXVII

Beguyld thus with delight of novelties,
And naturall desire of countryes state,
So long they redd in those antiquities,
That how the time was fled they quite for-
gate;
Till gentle Alma, seeing it so late,
Perforce their studies broke, and them be-
sought
To thinke how supper did them long awaite:

So halfe unwilling from their bookes them
brought,
And fayrely feasted, as so noble knightes
she ought.

CANTO XI

The enimies of Temperaunce
Besiege her dwelling place:
Prince Arthure them repelles, and fowle
Maleger doth deface.

I

What warre so cruel, or what siege so
sore,
As that which strong affections doe apply
Against the forte of reason evermore,
To bring the sowle into captivity?
Their force is fiercer through infirmity
Of the fraile flesh, relenting to their rage,
And exercise most bitter tyranny
Upon the partes, brought into their bond-
age:
No wretchednesse is like to sinfull vellen-
age.

II

But in a body which doth freely yeeld
His partes to reasons rule obedient,
And letteth her, that ought, the scepter
weeld,
All happy peace and goodly government
Is setled there in sure establishment.
There Alma, like a virgin queene most
bright,
Doth florish in all beautie excellent,
And to her guestes doth bounteous banket
dight,
Attempred goodly well for health and for
delight.

III

Early, before the morne with cremosin ray
The windowes of bright heaven opened
had,
Through which into the world the dawning
day
Might looke, that maketh every creature
glad,
Uprose Sir Guyon, in bright armour clad,
And to his purposd journey him prepar'd:
With him the palmer eke in habit sad
Him selfe addrest to that adventure hard:
So to the rivers syde they both together
far'd.

IV

Where them awaited ready at the ford
The ferriman, as Alma had behight,
With his well rigged bote. They goe abord,
And he eftsoones gan launch his barke forth-
right.
Ere long they rowed were quite out of sight,
And fast the land behynd them fled away.
But let them pas, whiles winde and wether
right
Doe serve their turnes: here I a while must
stay,
To see a cruell fight doen by the Prince this
day.

V

For all so soone as Guyon thence was gon
Upon his voyage with his trustie guyde,
That wicked band of villeins fresh begon
That castle to assaile on every side,
And lay strong siege about it far and wyde.
So huge and infinite their numbers were,
That all the land they under them did hyde;
So fowle and ugly, that exceeding feare
Their visages imprest, when they approched
neare.

VI

Them in twelve troupes their captein did
dispart,
And round about in fittest steades did place,
Where each might best offend his proper
part,
And his contrary object most deface,
As every one seem'd meetest in that cace.
Seven of the same against the castle gate
In strong entrenchments he did closely
place,
Which with incessaunt force and endlesse
hate
They battred day and night, and entraunce
did awate.

VII

The other five, five sondry wayes he sett,
Against the five great bulwarkes of that
pyle,
And unto each a bulwarke did arrett,
T' assayle with open force or hidden guyle,
In hope thereof to win victorious spoile.
They all that charge did fervently apply
With greedie malice and importune toyle,
And planted there their huge artillery,
With which they dayly made most dread-
full battery.

VIII

The first troupe was a monstrous rablement
Of fowle misshapen wightes, of which some
were
Headed like owles, with beckes uncomely
bent,
Others like dogs, others like gryphons
dreare,
And some had wings, and some had clawes
to teare,
And every one of them had lynces eyes,
And every one did bow and arrowes beare;
All those were lawlesse lustes, corrupt
envyes,
And covetous aspects, all cruel enimyes.

IX

Those same against the bulwarke of the
Sight
Did lay strong siege and battailous assault,
Ne once did yield it respitt day nor night,
But soone as Titan gan his head exault,
And soone againe as he his light withhault,
Their wicked engins they against it bent:
That is, each thing by which the eyes may
fault:
But two, then all more huge and violent,
Beautie and money, they that bulwarke
sorely rent.

X

The second bulwarke was the Hearing
Sence,
Gainst which the second troupe dessignment
makes,
Deformed creatures, in straunge difference,
Some having heads like harts, some like to
snakes,
Some like wilde bores late rouzd out of the
brakes;
Slaunderous reproches, and fowle infamies,
Leasinges, backbytinges, and vaineglorious
crakes,
Bad counsels, prayses, and false flatteries;
All those against that fort did bend their
batteries.

XI

Likewise that same third fort, that is the
Smell,
Of that third troupe was cruelly assayd;
Whose hideous shapes were like to feendes
of hell,
Some like to houndes, some like to apes,
dismayd,

Some like to puttockes, all in plumes
arayd;
All shap't according their conditions:
For by those ugly formes weren pourtrayd
Foolish delights and fond abusions,
Which doe that sence besiege with light
illusions.

XII

And that fourth band, which cruell battry
bent
Against the fourth bulwarke, that is the
Taste,
Was, as the rest, a grysie rablement,
Some mouth'd like greedy oystriges, some
faste
Like loathly toades, some fashioned in the
waste
Like swine; for so deformd is luxury,
Surfeat, misdiet, and unthriftie waste,
Vaine feastes, and ydle superfluity:
All those this sences fort assayle incessantly.

XIII

But the fift troupe, most horrible of hew
And ferce of force, is dreadfull to report:
For some like snailes, some did like spyd-
ers shew,
And some like ugly urchins thick and short:
Cruelly they assayled that fift fort,
Armed with dartes of sensuall delight,
With stinges of carnall lust, and strong
effort
Of feeling pleasures, with which day and
night
Against that same fift bulwarke they con-
tinued fight.

XIV

Thus these twelve troupes with dreadfull
puissaunce
Against that castle restlesse siege did lay,
And evermore their hideous ordinaunce
Upon the bulwarkes cruelly did play,
That now it gan to threaten neare decay;
And evermore their wicked capitayn
Provoked them the breaches to assay,
Somtimes with threats, somtimes with hope
of gayn,
Which by the ransack of that peece they
should attayn.

XV

On th' other syde, th' assieged castles ward
Their stedfast stonds did mightily maintaine,

And many bold repulse and many hard
Atchievement wrought, with perill and with
payne,
That goodly frame from ruine to sustaine:
And those two brethren gyauntes did de-
fend
The walles so stoutly with their sturdie
mayne,
That never entraunce any durst pretend,
But they to direfull death their groning
ghosts did send.

XVI

The noble virgin, ladie of the place,
Was much dismayed with that dreadful
sight;
For never was she in so evill cace:
Till that the Prince, seeing her wofull plight,
Gan her recomfort from so sad affright,
Offring his service and his dearest life
For her defence, against that carle to fight,
Which was their chiefe and th' authour of
that strife:
She him remercied as the patrone of her
life.

XVII

Eftsoones himselfe in glitterand armes he
dight,
And his well proved weapons to him hent:
So taking courteous conge, he behight
Those gates to be unbar'd, and forth he went.
Fayre mote he thee, the prowest and most
gent
That ever brandished bright steele on hye:
Whom soone as that unruly rablement
With his gay squyre issewing did espye,
They reard a most outrageous dreadfull
yelling cry;

XVIII

And therewithall attonce at him let fly
Their fluttring arrowes, thicke as flakes of
snow,
And round about him flocke impetuously,
Like a great water flood, that, tombling low
From the high mountaines, threates to over-
flow
With suddein fury all the fertile playne,
And the sad husbandmans long hope doth
throw
A downe the streame, and all his vowes
make vayne,
Nor bounds nor banks his headlong ruine
may sustayne.

XIX

Upon his shield their heaped hayle he bore,
And with his sword disperst the raskall
flockes,
Which fled a sonder, and him fell before,
As withered leaves drop from their dryed
stockes,
When the wroth western wind does reave
their locks;
And under neath him his courageous steed,
The fierce Spumador, trode them downe like
docks;
The fierce Spumador borne of heavenly seed,
Such as Laomedon of Phæbus race did breed.

XX

Which suddeine horrour and confused cry
When as their capteine heard, in haste he
yode,
The cause to weet, and fault to remedy:
Upon a tygre swift and fierce he rode,
That as the winde ran underneath his lode,
Whiles his long legs nigh raught unto the
ground:
Full large he was of limbe, and shoulders
brode,
But of such subtile substance and unsound,
That like a ghost he seem'd, whose grave-
clothes were unbound.

XXI

And in his hand a bended bow was seene,
And many arrowes under his right side,
All deadly daungerous, all cruell keene,
Headed with flint, and fethers bloody dide,
Such as the Indians in their quivers hide:
Those could he well direct and streight as
line,
And bid them strike the marke which he
had eyde;
Ne was there salve, ne was there medicine,
That mote recure their wounds, so inly they
did tine.

XXII

As pale and wan as ashes was his looke,
His body leane and meagre as a rake,
And skin all withered like a dryed rooke,
Thereto as cold and drery as a snake,
That seemd to tremble evermore, and quake:
All in a canvas thin he was bedight,
And girded with a belt of twisted brake:
Upon his head he wore an helmet light,
Made of a dead mans skull, that seemd a
ghastly sight.

XXIII

Maleger was his name; and after him
There follow'd fast at hand two wicked
hags,
With hoary lockes all loose and visage grim;
Their feet unshod, their bodies wrapt in
rags,
And both as swift on foot as chased stags;
And yet the one her other legge had lame,
Which with a staffe, all full of litle snags,
She did support, and Impotence her name:
But th' other was Impatience, arm'd with
raging flame.

XXIV

Soone as the carle from far the Prince
espyde
Glistring in armes and warlike ornament,
His beast he felly prickt on either syde,
And his mischievous bow full readie bent,
With which at him a cruell shaft he sent:
But he was warie, and it warded well
Upon his shield, that it no further went,
But to the ground the idle quarrell fell:
Then he another and another did expell.

XXV

Which to prevent, the Prince his mortall
speare
Soone to him raught, and fierce at him did
ride,
To be avenged of that shot whyleare:
But he was not so hardy to abide
That bitter stownd, but turning quicke aside
His light-foot beast, fled fast away for feare:
Whom to poursue, the infant after hide,
So fast as his good courser could him beare;
But labour lost it was to weene approch
him neare.

XXVI

For as the winged wind his tigre fled,
That vew of eye could scarse him over-
take,
Ne scarse his feet on ground were seene to
tred:
Through hils and dales he speedy way did
make,
Ne hedge ne ditch his readie passage brake,
And in his flight the villein turn'd his face,
(As wonts the Tartar by the Caspian lake,
When as the Russian him in fight does
chace)
Unto his tygres taile, and shot at him
apace.

XXVII

Apace he shot, and yet he fled apace,
Still as the greedy knight nigh to him drew,
And oftentimes he would relent his pace,
That him his foe more fiercely should
    poursew:
Who when his uncouth manner he did vew,
He gan avize to follow him no more,
But keepe his standing, and his shaftes
    eschew,
Untill he quite had spent his perlous store,
And then assayle him fresh, ere he could
    shift for more.

XXVIII

But that lame hag, still as abroad he strew
His wicked arrowes, gathered them againe,
And to him brought, fresh batteill to re-
    new:
Which he espying, cast her to restraine
From yielding succour to that cursed swaine,
And her attaching, thought her hands to
    tye;
But soone as him dismounted on the plaine
That other hag did far away espye
Binding her sister, she to him ran hastily;

XXIX

And catching hold of him, as downe he lent,
Him backeward overthrew, and downe him
    stayd
With their rude handes and gryesly graple-
    ment,
Till that the villein, comming to their ayd,
Upon him fell, and lode upon him layd:
Full litle wanted, but he had him slaine,
And of the battell balefull end had made,
Had not his gentle squire beheld his paine,
And commen to his reskew, ere his bitter
    bane.

XXX

So greatest and most glorious thing on
    ground
May often need the helpe of weaker hand;
So feeble is mans state, and life unsound,
That in assuraunce it may never stand,
Till it dissolved be from earthly band.
Proofe be thou, Prince, the prowest man
    alyve,
And noblest borne of all in Britayne land;
Yet thee fierce Fortune did so nearely
    drive,
That had not Grace thee blest, thou should-
    est not survive.

XXXI

The squyre arriving, fiercely in his armes
Snatcht first the one, and then the other
    jade,
His chiefest letts and authors of his harmes,
And them perforce withheld with threatned
    blade,
Least that his lord they should behinde in-
    vade;
The whiles the Prince, prickt with reproch-
    ful shame,
As one awakte out of long slombring shade,
Revivyng thought of glory and of fame,
United all his powres to purge him selfe
    from blame.

XXXII

Like as a fire, the which in hollow cave
Hath long bene underkept and down sup-
    prest,
With murmurous disdayne doth inly rave,
And grudge, in so streight prison to be
    prest,
At last breakes forth with furious unrest,
And strives to mount unto his native seat;
All that did earst it hinder and molest,
Yt now devoures with flames and scorching
    heat,
And carries into smoake with rage and
    horror great.

XXXIII

So mightely the Briton Prince him rouzd
Out of his holde, and broke his caytive
    bands;
And as a beare, whom angry curres have
    touzd,
Having off-shakt them, and escapt their
    hands,
Becomes more fell, and all that him with-
    stands
Treads down and overthrowes. Now had
    the carle
Alighted from his tigre, and his hands
Discharged of his bow and deadly quar'le,
To seize upon his foe flatt lying on the
    marle.

XXXIV

Which now him turnd to disavantage deare,
For neither can he fly, nor other harme,
But trust unto his strength and manhood
    meare,
Sith now he is far from his monstrous
    swarme,

And of his weapons did him selfe disarme.
The knight, yet wrothfull for his late dis-
grace,
Fiercely advaunst his valorous right arme,
And him so sore smott with his yron mace,
That groveling to the ground he fell, and
fild his place.

XXXV

Wel weened hee that field was then his
owne,
And all his labor brought to happy end,
When suddein up the villeine overthrowne
Out of his swowne arose, fresh to contend,
And gan him selfe to second battaill bend,
As hurt he had not beene. Thereby there
lay
An huge great stone, which stood upon one
end,
And had not bene removed many a day;
Some land-marke seemd to bee, or signe of
sundry way.

XXXVI

The same he snatcht, and with exceeding
sway
Threw at his foe, who was right well aware
To shonne the engin of his meant decay;
It booted not to thinke that throw to
beare,
But grownd he gave, and lightly lept
areare:
Efte fierce retourning, as a faulcon fayre,
That once hath failed of her souse full
neare,
Remounts againe into the open ayre,
And unto better fortune doth her selfe pre-
payre.

XXXVII

So brave retourning, with his brandisht
blade,
He to the carle him selfe agayn addrest,
And strooke at him so sternely, that he
made
An open passage through his riven brest,
That halfe the steele behind his backe did
rest;
Which drawing backe, he looked ever more
When the hart blood should gush out of his
chest,
Or his dead corse should fall upon the
flore;
But his dead corse upon the flore fell nathe-
more.

XXXVIII

Ne drop of blood appeared shed to bee,
All were the wownd so wide and wonderous,
That through his carcas one might playnly
see.
Halfe in amaze with horror hideous,
And halfe in rage to be deluded thus,
Again through both the sides he strooke
him quight,
That made his spright to grone full piteous:
Yet nathemore forth fled his groning spright,
But freshly as at first, prepard himselfe to
fight.

XXXIX

Thereat he smitten was with great affright,
And trembling terror did his hart apall,
Ne wist he what to thinke of that same
sight,
Ne what to say, ne what to doe at all;
He doubted least it were some magicall
Illusion, that did beguile his sense,
Or wandring ghost, that wanted funerall,
Or aery spirite under false pretence,
Or hellish feend raysd up through divelish
science.

XL

His wonder far exceeded reasons reach,
That he began to doubt his dazeled sight,
And oft of error did him selfe appeach:
Flesh without blood, a person without
spright,
Wounds without hurt, a body without might,
That could doe harme, yet could not harmed
bee,
That could not die, yet seemd a mortall
wight,
That was most strong in most infirmitee;
Like did he never heare, like did he never
see.

XLI

A while he stood in this astonishment,
Yet would he not for all his great dismay
Give over to effect his first intent,
And th' utmost meanes of victory assay,
Or th' utmost yssew of his owne decay.
His owne good sword Mordure, that never
fayld
At need till now, he lightly threw away,
And his bright shield, that nought him
now avayld,
And with his naked hands him forcibly as-
sayld.

XLII

Twixt his two mighty armes him up he
    snatcht,
And crusht his carcas so against his brest,
That the disdainfull sowle he thence dis-
    patcht,
And th' ydle breath all utterly exprest:
Tho, when he felt him dead, adowne he
    kest
The lumpish corse unto the sencelesse
    grownd;
Adowne he kest it with so puissant wrest,
That backe againe it did alofte rebownd,
And gave against his mother Earth a grone-
    full sownd.

XLIII

As when Joves harnesse-bearing bird from
    hye
Stoupes at a flying heron with proud dis-
    dayne,
The stone-dead quarrey falls so forciblye,
That yt rebownds against the lowly playne,
A second fall redoubling backe agayne.
Then thought the Prince all peril sure was
    past,
And that he victor onely did remayne;
No sooner thought, then that the carle as
    fast
Gan heap huge strokes on him, as ere he
    down was cast.

XLIV

Nigh his wits end then woxe th' amazed
    knight,
And thought his labor lost and travell
    vayne,
Against this lifelesse shadow so to fight:
Yet life he saw, and felt his mighty mayne,
That, whiles he marveild still, did still him
    payne;
Forthy he gan some other wayes advize,
How to take life from that dead-living
    swayne,
Whom still he marked freshly to arize
From th' earth, and from her womb new
    spirits to reprize.

XLV

He then remembred well, that had bene
    sayd,
How th' Earth his mother was, and first
    him bore;
Shee eke, so often as his life decayd,
Did life with usury to him restore,

And reysd him up much stronger then be-
    fore,
So soone as he unto her wombe did fall;
Therefore to grownd he would him cast no
    more,
Ne him committ to grave terrestriall,
But beare him farre from hope of succour
    usuall.

XLVI

Tho up he caught him twixt his puissant
    hands,
And having scruzd out of his carrion corse
The lothfull life, now loosd from sinfull
    hands,
Upon his shoulders carried him perforse
Above three furlongs, taking his full course,
Untill he came unto a standing lake:
Him thereinto he threw without remorse,
Ne stird, till hope of life did him forsake:
So end of that carles dayes, and his owne
    paynes did make.

XLVII

Which when those wicked hags from far
    did spye,
Like two mad dogs they ran about the
    lands;
And th' one of them with dreadfull yelling
    crye,
Throwing away her broken chaines and
    bands,
And having quencht her burning fier brands,
Hedlong her selfe did cast into that lake;
But Impotence with her owne wilfull hands
One of Malegers cursed darts did take,
So ryv'd her trembling hart, and wicked
    end did make.

XLVIII

Thus now alone he conquerour remaines:
Tho, cumming to his squyre, that kept his
    steed,
Thought to have mounted, but his feeble
    vaines
Him faild thereto, and served not his need,
Through losse of blood, which from his
    wounds did bleed,
That he began to faint, and life decay:
But his good squyre, him helping up with
    speed,
With stedfast hand upon his horse did
    stay,
And led him to the castle by the beaten
    way.

XLIX

Where many groomes and squyres ready
　　were
To take him from his steed full tenderly,
And eke the fayrest Alma mett him there
With balme and wine and costly spicery,
To comfort him in his infirmity:
Eftesoones shee causd him up to be convayd,
And of his armes despoyled easily,
In sumptuous bed shee made him to be layd,
And al the while his wounds were dressing,
　　by him stayd.

CANTO XII

Guyon by palmers governaunce
Passing through perilles great,
Doth overthrow the Bowre of Blis,
And Acrasy defeat.

I

Now ginnes this goodly frame of Temper-
　　aunce
Fayrely to rise, and her adorned hed
To pricke of highest prayse forth to ad-
　　vaunce,
Formerly grounded and fast setteled
On firme foundation of true bountyhed:
And that brave knight, that for this vertue
　　fightes,
Now comes to point of that same perilous
　　sted,
Where Pleasure dwelles in sensuall de-
　　lights,
Mongst thousand dangers, and ten thousand
　　magick mights.

II

Two dayes now in that sea he sayled has,
Ne ever land beheld, ne living wight,
Ne ought save perill, still as he did pas:
Tho, when appeared the third morrow
　　bright,
Upon the waves to spred her trembling light,
An hideous roring far away they heard,
That all their sences filled with affright,
And streight they saw the raging surges
　　reard
Up to the skyes, that them of drowning
　　made affeard.

III

Said then the boteman, 'Palmer, stere
　　aright,
And keepe an even course; for yonder way

We needes must pas (God doe us well
　　acquight!)
That is the Gulfe of Greedinesse, they say,
That deepe engorgeth all this worldes pray;
Which having swallowd up excessively,
He soone in vomit up againe doth lay,
And belcheth forth his superfluity,
That all the seas for feare doe seeme away
　　to fly.

IV

'On thother syde an hideous rock is pight
Of mightie magnes stone, whose craggie
　　clift
Depending from on high, dreadfull to sight,
Over the waves his rugged armes doth lift,
And threatneth downe to throw his ragged
　　rift
On whoso cometh nigh; yet nigh it drawes
All passengers, that none from it can shift:
For whiles they fly that gulfes devouring
　　jawes,
They on this rock are rent, and sunck in
　　helples wawes.'

V

Forward they passe, and strongly he them
　　rowes,
Untill they nigh unto that gulfe arryve,
Where streame more violent and greedy
　　growes:
Then he with all his puisaunce doth stryve
To strike his oares, and mightily doth dryve
The hollow vessell through the threatfull
　　wave,
Which, gaping wide, to swallow them alyve
In th' huge abysse of his engulfing grave,
Doth rore at them in vaine, and with great
　　terrour rave.

VI

They, passing by, that grisely mouth did
　　see,
Sucking the seas into his entralles deepe,
That seemd more horrible then hell to bee,
Or that darke dreadfull hole of Tartare
　　steepe,
Through which the damned ghosts doen
　　often creep
Backe to the world, bad livers to torment:
But nought that falles into this direfull
　　deepe,
Ne that approcheth nigh the wyde descent,
May backe retourne, but is condemned to
　　be drent.

VII

On thother side they saw that perilous
    rocke,
Threatning it selfe on them to ruinate,
On whose sharp cliftes the ribs of vessels
    broke,
And shivered ships, which had beene
    wrecked late,
Yet stuck, with carcases exanimate
Of such, as having all their substance spent
In wanton joyes and lustes intemperate,
Did afterwardes make shipwrack violent,
Both of their life, and fame for ever fowly
    blent.

VIII

Forthy this hight the Rock of vile Reproch,
A daungerous and detestable place,
To which nor fish nor fowle did once ap-
    proch,
But yelling meawes, with seagulles hoars
    and bace,
And cormoyraunts, with birds of ravenous
    race,
Which still sat wayting on that wastfull
    clift
For spoile of wretches, whose unhappy cace,
After lost credit and consumed thrift,
At last them driven hath to this despaire-
    full drift.

IX

The palmer, seeing them in safetie past,
Thus saide: 'Behold th' ensamples in our
    sightes
Of lustfull luxurie and thriftlesse wast:
What now is left of miserable wightes,
Which spent their looser daies in leud de-
    lightes,
But shame and sad reproch, here to be
    red
By these rent reliques, speaking their ill
    plightes ?
Let all that live, hereby be counselled
To shunne Rock of Reproch, and it as death
    to dread.'

X

So forth they rowed, and that ferryman
With his stiffe oares did brush the sea so
    strong,
That the hoare waters from his frigot ran,
And the light bubles daunced all along,
Whiles the salt brine out of the billowes
    sprong.

At last far off they many islandes spy,
On every side floting the floodes emong:
Then said the knight: 'Lo ! I the land
    descry;
Therefore, old syre, thy course doe there-
    unto apply.'

XI

'That may not bee,' said then the ferry-
    man,
'Least wee unweeting hap to be fordonne:
For those same islands, seeming now and
    than,
Are not firme land, nor any certein wonne,
But stragling plots, which to and fro doe
    ronne
In the wide waters: therefore are they
    hight
The Wandring Islands. Therefore doe them
    shonne;
For they have ofte drawne many a wand-
    ring wight
Into most deadly daunger and distressed
    plight.

XII

'Yet well they seeme to him, that farre
    doth vew,
Both faire and fruitfull, and the grownd
    dispred
With grassy greene of delectable hew,
And the tall trees with leaves appareled,
Are deckt with blossoms dyde in white and
    red,
That mote the passengers thereto allure;
But whosoever once hath fastened
His foot thereon, may never it recure,
But wandreth ever more uncertein and un-
    sure.

XIII

'As th' isle of Delos whylome, men report,
Amid th' Aegæan sea long time did stray,
Ne made for shipping any certeine port,
Till that Latona traveiling that way,
Flying from Junoes wrath and hard assay,
Of her fayre twins was there delivered,
Which afterwards did rule the night and
    day;
Thenceforth it firmely was established,
And for Apolloes honor highly herried.'

XIV

They to him hearken, as beseemeth meete,
And passe on forward: so their way does ly,

That one of those same islands, which doe
    fleet
In the wide sea, they needes must passen
    by,
Which seemd so sweet and pleasaunt to the
    eye,
That it would tempt a man to touchen there:
Upon the banck they sitting did espy
A daintie damsell, dressing of her heare,
By whom a little skippet floting did appeare.

XV

She, them espying, loud to them can call,
Bidding them nigher draw unto the shore;
For she had cause to busie them withall;
And therewith lowdly laught: but nathe-
    more
Would they once turne, but kept on as afore:
Which when she saw, she left her lockes
    undight,
And running to her boat withouten ore,
From the departing land it launched light,
And after them did drive with all her power
    and might.

XVI

Whom overtaking, she in merry sort
Them gan to bord, and purpose diversly,
Now faining dalliaunce and wanton sport,
Now throwing forth lewd wordes immod-
    estly;
Till that the palmer gan full bitterly
Her to rebuke, for being loose and light:
Which not abiding, but more scornfully
Scoffing at him that did her justly wite,
She turnd her bote about, and from them
    rowed quite.

XVII

That was the wanton Phœdria, which late
Did ferry him over the Idle Lake:
Whom nought regarding, they kept on their
    gate,
And all her vaine allurements did forsake;
When them the wary boteman thus bespake:
' Here now behoveth us well to avyse,
And of our safety good heede to take;
For here before a perlous passage lyes,
Where many mermayds haunt, making false
    melodies.

XVIII

'But by the way there is a great quick-
    sand,
And a whirlepoole of hidden jeopardy:

Therefore, sir palmer, keepe an even hand;
For twixt them both the narrow way doth
    ly.'
Scarse had he saide, when hard at hand they
    spy
That quicksand nigh with water covered;
But by the checked wave they did descry
It plaine, and by the sea discoloured:
It called was the Quickesand of Unthrifty-
    hed.

XIX

They, passing by, a goodly ship did see,
Laden from far with precious merchandize,
And bravely furnished as ship might bee,
Which through great disaventure, or mes-
    prize,
Her selfe had ronne into that hazardize;
Whose mariners and merchants, with much
    toyle,
Labour'd in vaine to have recur'd their prize,
And the rich wares to save from pitteous
    spoyle;
But neither toyle nor traveill might her
    backe recoyle.

XX

On th' other side they see that perilous
    poole,
That called was the Whirlepoole of Decay,
In which full many had with haplesse doole
Beene suncke, of whom no memorie did
    stay:
Whose circled waters rapt with whirling
    sway,
Like to a restlesse wheele, still ronning
    round,
Did covet, as they passed by that way,
To draw their bote within the utmost bound
Of his wide labyrinth, and then to have
    them dround.

XXI

But th' heedfull boteman strongly fo. h did
    stretch
His brawnie armes, and all his bodie straine,
That th' utmost sandy breach they shortly
    fetch,
Whiles the dredd daunger does behind re-
    maine.
Suddeine they see from midst of all the
    maine
The surging waters like a mountaine rise,
And the great sea, puft up with proud dis-
    daine,

To swell above the measure of his guise,
As threatning to devoure all that his powre
   despise.

XXII

The waves come rolling, and the billowes
   rore
Outragiously, as they enraged were,
Or wrathfull Neptune did them drive be-
   fore
His whirling charet, for exceeding feare;
For not one puffe of winde there did ap-
   peare;
That all the three thereat woxe much
   afrayd,
Unweeting what such horrour straunge did
   reare.
Eftsoones they saw an hideous hoast arrayd
Of huge sea monsters, such as living sence
   dismayd.

XXIII

Most ugly shapes and horrible aspects,
Such as Dame Nature selfe mote feare to
   see,
Or shame that ever should so fowle defects
From her most cunning hand escaped bee;
All dreadfull pourtraicts of deformitee:
Spring-headed hydres, and sea-shouldring
   whales,
Great whirlpooles, which all fishes make to
   flee,
Bright scolopendraes, arm'd with silver
   scales,
Mighty monoceros with immeasured tayles,

XXIV

The dreadfull fish, that hath deserv'd the
   name
Of Death, and like him lookes in dreadfull
   hew,
The griesly wasserman, that makes his game
The flying ships with swiftnes to pursew,
The horrible sea-satyre, that doth shew
His fearefull face in time of greatest storme,
Huge ziffius, whom mariners eschew
No lesse then rockes, (as travellers in-
   forme,)
And greedy rosmarines with visages de-
   forme.

XXV

All these, and thousand thousands many
   more,
And more deformed monsters thousand fold,

With dreadfull noise and hollow rombling
   rore,
Came rushing, in the fomy waves enrold,
Which seem'd to fly for feare them to be-
   hold:
Ne wonder, if these did the knight appall;
For all, that here on earth we dreadfull
   hold,
Be but as bugs to fearen babes withall,
Compared to the creatures in the seas en-
   trall.

XXVI

' Feare nought,' then saide the palmer well
   aviz'd;
' For these same monsters are not these in
   deed,
But are into these fearefull shapes dis-
   guiz'd
By that same wicked witch, to worke us
   dreed,
And draw from on this journey to pro-
   ceed.'
Tho, lifting up his vertuous staffe on hye,
He smote the sea, which calmed was with
   speed,
And all that dreadfull armie fast gan flye
Into great Tethys bosome, where they
   hidden lye.

XXVII

Quit from that danger, forth their course
   they kept,
And as they went they heard a ruefull cry
Of one that wayld and pittifully wept,
That through the sea the resounding plaints
   did fly:
At last they in an island did espy
A seemely maiden, sitting by the shore,
That with great sorrow and sad agony
Seemed some great misfortune to deplore,
And lowd to them for succour called ever-
   more.

XXVIII

Which Guyon hearing, streight his palmer
   bad
To stere the bote towards that dolefull
   mayd,
That he might know and ease her sorrow
   sad:
Who, him avizing better, to him sayd:
' Faire sir, be not displeasd if disobayd:
For ill it were to hearken to her cry;
For she is inly nothing ill apayd,

But onely womanish fine forgery,
Your stubborne hart t' affect with fraile
infirmity.

XXIX

'To which when she your courage hath in-
clind
Through foolish pitty, then her guilefull
bayt
She will embosome deeper in your mind,
And for your ruine at the last awayt.'
The knight was ruled, and the boteman
strayt
Held on his course with stayed stedfast-
nesse,
Ne ever shroncke, ne ever sought to bayt
His tyred armes for toylesome wearinesse,
But with his oares did sweepe the watry
wildernesse.

XXX

And now they nigh approched to the sted,
Where as those mermayds dwelt: it was a
still
And calmy bay, on th' one side sheltered
With the brode shadow of an hoarie hill,
On th' other side an high rocke toured still,
That twixt them both a pleasaunt port they
made,
And did like an halfe theatre fulfill:
There those five sisters had continuall
trade,
And usd to bath themselves in that deceipt-
full shade.

XXXI

They were faire ladies, till they fondly
striv'd
With th' Heliconian maides for maystery;
Of whom they over-comen, were depriv'd
Of their proud beautie, and th' one moyity
Transformd to fish, for their bold surquedry;
But th' upper halfe their hew retayned still,
And their sweet skill in wonted melody;
Which ever after they abusd to ill,
T' allure weake traveillers, whom gotten
they did kill.

XXXII

So now to Guyon, as he passed by,
Their pleasaunt tunes they sweetly thus ap-
plyde:
'O thou fayre sonne of gentle Faery,
That art in mightie armes most magnifyde
Above all knights that ever batteill tryde,

O turne thy rudder hetherward a while:
Here may thy storme-bett vessell safely
ryde;
This is the port of rest from troublous toyle,
The worldes sweet in from paine and wea-
risome turmoyle.'

XXXIII

With that the rolling sea, resounding soft,
In his big base them fitly answered,
And on the rocke the waves breaking aloft,
A solemne meane unto them measured,
The whiles sweet Zephyrus lowd whisteled
His treble, a straunge kinde of harmony;
Which Guyons senses softly tickeled,
That he the boteman bad row easily,
And let him heare some part of their rare
melody.

XXXIV

But him the palmer from that vanity
With temperate advice discounselled,
That they it past, and shortly gan descry
The land, to which their course they leveled;
When suddeinly a grosse fog over spred
With his dull vapour all that desert has,
And heavens chearefull face enveloped,
That all things one, and one as nothing was,
And this great universe seemd one confused
mas.

XXXV

Thereat they greatly were dismayd, ne wist
How to direct theyr way in darkenes wide,
But feard to wander in that wastefull mist,
For tombling into mischiefe unespide:
Worse is the daunger hidden then describe.
Suddeinly an innumerable flight
Of harmefull fowles, about them fluttering,
cride,
And with their wicked wings them ofte did
smight,
And sore annoyed, groping in that griesly
night.

XXXVI

Even all the nation of unfortunate
And fatall birds about them flocked were,
Such as by nature men abhorre and hate;
The ill-faste owle, deaths dreadfull mes-
sengere,
The hoars night-raven, trump of dolefull
drere,
The lether-winged batt, dayes enimy,
The ruefull strich, still waiting on the bere,

The whistler shrill, that who so heares doth
    dy,
The hellish harpyes, prophets of sad destiny.

XXXVII

All those, and all that els does horror breed,
About them flew, and fild their sayles with
    feare:
Yet stayd they not, but forward did pro-
    ceed,
Whiles th' one did row, and th' other stifly
    steare;
Till that at last the weather gan to cleare,
And the faire land it selfe did playnly sheow.
Said then the palmer: 'Lo where does ap-
    peare
The sacred soile where all our perills grow;
Therfore, sir knight, your ready arms
    about you throw.'

XXXVIII

He hearkned, and his armes about him
    tooke,
The whiles the nimble bote so well her sped,
That with her crooked keele the land she
    strooke.
Then forth the noble Guyon sallied,
And his sage palmer, that him governed;
But th' other by his bote behind did stay.
They marched fayrly forth, of nought ydred,
Both firmely armd for every hard assay,
With constancy and care, gainst daunger
    and dismay.

XXXIX

Ere long they heard an hideous bellowing
Of many beasts, that roard outrageously,
As if that hungers poynt or Venus sting
Had them enraged with fell surquedry;
Yet nought they feard, but past on hardily,
Untill they came in vew of those wilde
    beasts:
Who all attonce, gaping full greedily,
And rearing fercely their upstarting crests,
Ran towards, to devoure those unexpected
    guests.

XL

But soone as they approcht with deadly
    threat,
The palmer over them his staffe upheld,
His mighty staffe, that could all charmes
    defeat:
Eftesoones their stubborne corages were
    queld,

And high advaunced crests downe meekely
    feld;
Instead of fraying, they them selves did
    feare,
And trembled, as them passing they be-
    held:
Such wondrous powre did in that staffe ap-
    peare,
All monsters to subdew to him that did it
    beare.

XLI

Of that same wood it fram'd was cunningly,
Of which Caduceus whilome was made,
Caduceus, the rod of Mercury,
With which he wonts the Stygian realmes
    invade,
Through ghastly horror and eternall shade;
Th' infernall feends with it he can asswage,
And Orcus tame, whome nothing can per-
    suade,
And rule the Furyes, when they most doe
    rage:
Such vertue in his staffe had eke this palmer
    sage.

XLII

Thence passing forth, they shortly doe ar-
    ryve
Whereas the Bowre of Blisse was situate;
A place pickt out by choyce of best alyve,
That Natures worke by art can imitate:
In which what ever in this worldly state
Is sweete, and pleasing unto living sense,
Or that may dayntest fantasy aggrate,
Was poured forth with plentifull dispence,
And made there to abound with lavish
    affluence.

XLIII

Goodly it was enclosed rownd about,
As well their entred guestes to keep within,
As those unruly beasts to hold without;
Yet was the fence thereof but weake and
    thin;
Nought feard theyr force, that fortilage to
    win,
But wisedomes powre, and temperaunces
    might,
By which the mightiest things efforced
    bin:
And eke the gate was wrought of sub-
    staunce light,
Rather for pleasure then for battery or
    fight.

XLIV

Yt framed was of precious yvory,
That seemd a worke of admirable witt;
And therein all the famous history
Of Jason and Medæa was ywritt;
Her mighty charmes, her furious loving fitt,
His goodly conquest of the golden fleece,
His falsed fayth, and love too lightly flitt,
The wondred Argo, which in venturous
   peece
First through the Euxine seas bore all the
   flowr of Greece.

XLV

Ye might have seene the frothy billowes
   fry
Under the ship, as thorough them she went,
That seemd the waves were into yvory,
Or yvory into the waves were sent;
And otherwhere the snowy substaunce
   sprent
With vermell, like the boyes blood therein
   shed,
A piteous spectacle did represent;
And otherwhiles with gold besprinkeled,
Yt seemd thenchaunted flame, which did
   Creusa wed.

XLVI

All this and more might in that goodly gate
Be red; that ever open stood to all
Which thether came: but in the porch there
   sate
A comely personage of stature tall,
And semblaunce pleasing, more then natur-
   all,
That traveilers to him seemd to entize;
His looser garment to the ground did fall,
And flew about his heeles in wanton wize,
Not fitt for speedy pace or manly exercize.

XLVII

They in that place him Genius did call:
Not that celestiall powre, to whom the care
Of life, and generation of all
That lives, perteines in charge particulare,
Who wondrous things concerning our wel-
   fare,
And straunge phantomes, doth lett us ofte
   forsee,
And ofte of secret ill bids us beware:
That is our selfe, whom though we doe
   not see,
Yet each doth in him selfe it well perceive
   to bee.

XLVIII

Therefore a god him sage antiquity
Did wisely make, and good Agdistes call:
But this same was to that quite contrary,
The foe of life, that good envyes to all,
That secretly doth us procure to fall,
Through guilefull semblants, which he
   makes us see.
He of this gardin had the governall,
And Pleasures porter was devizd to bee,
Holding a staffe in hand for more formali-
   tee.

XLIX

With diverse flowres he daintily was deckt,
And strowed rownd about, and by his side
A mighty mazer bowle of wine was sett,
As if it had to him bene sacrifide;
Wherewith all new-come guests he graty-
   fide:
So did he eke Sir Guyon passing by:
But he his ydle curtesie defide,
And overthrew his bowle disdainfully,
And broke his staffe, with which he charmed
   semblants sly.

L

Thus being entred, they behold arownd
A large and spacious plaine, on every
   side
Strowed with pleasauns, whose fayre grassy
   grownd
Mantled with greene, and goodly beautifide
With all the ornaments of Floraes pride,
Wherewith her mother Art, as halfe in
   scorne
Of niggard Nature, like a pompous bride
Did decke her, and too lavishly adorne,
When forth from virgin bowre she comes
   in th' early morne.

LI

Thereto the heavens always joviall,
Lookte on them lovely, still in stedfast
   state,
Ne suffred storme nor frost on them to
   fall,
Their tender buds or leaves to violate,
Nor scorching heat, nor cold intemperate,
T' afflict the creatures which therein did
   dwell,
But the milde ayre with season moderate
Gently attempred, and dispos'd so well,
That still it breathed forth sweet spirit and
   holesom smell.

LII

More sweet and holesome then the pleasaunt
    hill
Of Rhodope, on which the nimphe that bore
A gyaunt babe her selfe for griefe did kill;
Or the Thessalian Tempe, where of yore
Fayre Daphne Phœbus hart with love did
    gore;
Or Ida, where the gods lov'd to repayre,
When ever they their heavenly bowres for-
    lore;
Or sweet Parnasse, the haunt of Muses
    fayre;
Or Eden selfe, if ought with Eden mote
    compayre.

LIII

Much wondred Guyon at the fayre aspect
Of that sweet place, yet suffred no delight
To sincke into his sence, nor mind affect,
But passed forth, and lookt still forward
    right,
Brydling his will, and maystering his might:
Till that he came unto another gate,
No gate, but like one, being goodly dight
With bowes and braunches, which did broad
    dilate
Their clasping armes, in wanton wreathings
    intricate:

LIV

So fashioned a porch with rare device,
Archt over head with an embracing vine,
Whose bounches, hanging downe, seemd to
    entice
All passers by to taste their lushious wine,
And did them selves into their hands in-
    cline,
As freely offering to be gathered:
Some deepe empurpled as the hyacine,
Some as the rubine laughing sweetely red,
Some like faire emeraudes, not yet well
    ripened.

LV

And them amongst, some were of burnisht
    gold,
So made by art, to beautify the rest,
Which did themselves emongst the leaves
    enfold,
As lurking from the vew of covetous guest,
That the weake boughes, with so rich load
    opprest,
Did bow adowne, as overburdened.
Under that porch a comely dame did rest,

Clad in fayre weedes, but fowle disordered,
And garments loose, that seemd unmeet
    for womanhed.

LVI

In her left hand a cup of gold she held,
And with her right the riper fruit did reach,
Whose sappy liquor, that with fulnesse
    sweld,
Into her cup she scruzd, with daintie breach
Of her fine fingers, without fowle empeach,
That so faire winepresse made the wine
    more sweet:
Thereof she usd to give to drinke to each,
Whom passing by she happened to meet:
It was her guise, all straungers goodly so
    to greet.

LVII

So she to Guyon offred it to tast,
Who, taking it out of her tender hond,
The cup to ground did violently cast,
That all in peeces it was broken fond,
And with the liquor stained all the lond:
Whereat Excesse exceedingly was wroth,
Yet no'te the same amend, ne yet with-
    stond,
But suffered him to passe, all were she loth;
Who, nought regarding her displeasure, for-
    ward goth.

LVIII

There the most daintie paradise on ground
It selfe doth offer to his sober eye,
In which all pleasures plenteously abownd,
And none does others happinesse envye:
The painted flowres, the trees upshooting
    hye,
The dales for shade, the hilles for breath-
    ing space,
The trembling groves, the christall running
    by;
And that which all faire workes doth most
    aggrace,
The art, which all that wrought, appeared
    in no place.

LIX

One would have thought, (so cunningly the
    rude
And scorned partes were mingled with the
    fine,)
That Nature had for wantonesse ensude
Art, and that Art at Nature did repine;
So striving each th' other to undermine,

Each did the others worke more beautify;
So diff'ring both in willes agreed in fine:
So all agreed through sweete diversity,
This gardin to adorne with all variety.

LX

And in the midst of all a fountaine stood,
Of richest substance that on earth might
bee,
So pure and shiny that the silver flood
Through every channell running one might
see:
Most goodly it with curious ymageree
Was overwrought, and shapes of naked
boyes,
Of which some seemd with lively jollitee
To fly about playing their wanton toyes,
Whylest others did them selves embay in
liquid joyes.

LXI

And over all, of purest gold was spred
A trayle of yvie in his native hew:
For the rich metall was so coloured,
That wight, who did not well avis'd it vew,
Would surely deeme it to bee yvie trew:
Low his lascivious armes adown did creepe,
That themselves dipping in the silver dew,
Their fleecy flowres they tenderly did steepe,
Which drops of christall seemd for wantones
to weep.

LXII

Infinit streames continually did well
Out of this fountaine, sweet and faire to see,
The which into an ample laver fell,
And shortly grew to so great quantitie,
That like a litle lake it seemd to bee;
Whose depth exceeded not three cubits
hight,
That through the waves one might the
bottom see,
All pav'd beneath with jaspar shining bright,
That seemd the fountaine in that sea did
sayle upright.

LXIII

And all the margent round about was sett
With shady laurell trees, thence to defend
The sunny beames, which on the billowes
bett,
And those which therein bathed mote offend.
As Guyon hapned by the same to wend,
Two naked damzelles he therein espyde,
Which, therein bathing, seemed to contend

And wrestle wantonly, ne car'd to hyde
Their dainty partes from vew of any which
them eyd.

LXIV

Sometimes the one would lift the other
quight
Above the waters, and then downe againe
Her plong, as over maystered by might,
Where both awhile would covered remaine,
And each the other from to rise restraine;
The whiles their snowy limbes, as through
a vele,
So through the christall waves appeared
plaine:
Then suddeinly both would themselves un-
hele,
And th' amorous sweet spoiles to greedy
eyes revele.

LXV

As that faire starre, the messenger of
morne,
His deawy face out of the sea doth reare,
Or as the Cyprian goddesse, newly borne
Of th' oceans fruitfull froth, did first ap-
peare,
Such seemed they, and so their yellow heare
Christalline humor dropped downe apace.
Whom such when Guyon saw, he drew him
neare,
And somewhat gan relent his earnest pace;
His stubborne brest gan secret pleasaunce
to embrace.

LXVI

The wanton maidens, him espying, stood
Gazing a while at his unwonted guise;
Then th' one her selfe low ducked in the
flood,
Abasht that her a straunger did avise:
But thother rather higher did arise,
And her two lilly paps aloft displayd,
And all, that might his melting hart entyse
To her delights, she unto him bewrayd:
The rest, hidd underneath, him more de-
sirous made.

LXVII

With that the other likewise up arose,
And her faire lockes, which formerly were
bownd
Up in one knott, she low adowne did lose:
Which, flowing long and thick, her cloth'd
arownd,

And th' yvorie in golden mantle gownd:
So that faire spectacle from him was reft,
Yet that which reft it no lesse faire was
    fownd:
So hidd in lockes and waves from lookers
    theft,
Nought but her lovely face she for his look-
    ing left.

LXVIII

Withall she laughed, and she blusht with-
    all,
That blushing to her laughter gave more
    grace,
And laughter to her blushing, as did fall.
Now when they spyde the knight to slacke
    his pace,
Them to behold, and in his sparkling face
The secrete signes of kindled lust appeare,
Their wanton meriments they did encreace,
And to him beckned to approch more neare,
And shewd him many sights, that corage
    cold could reare.

LXIX

On which when gazing him the palmer saw,
He much rebukt those wandring eyes of
    his,
And, counseld well, him forward thence did
    draw.
Now are they come nigh to the Bowre of
    Blis,
Of her fond favorites so nam'd amis:
When thus the palmer: 'Now, sir, well
    avise;
For here the end of all our traveill is:
Here wonnes Acrasia, whom we must sur-
    prise,
Els she will slip away, and all our drift de-
    spise.'

LXX

Eftsoones they heard a most melodious
    sound,
Of all that mote delight a daintie eare,
Such as attonce might not on living ground,
Save in this paradise, be heard elswhere:
Right hard it was for wight which did it
    heare,
To read what manner musicke that mote
    bee:
For all that pleasing is to living eare
Was there consorted in one harmonee;
Birdes, voices, instruments, windes, waters,
    all agree.

LXXI

The joyous birdes, shrouded in chearefull
    shade,
Their notes unto the voice attempred sweet:
Th' angelicall soft trembling voyces made
To th' instruments divine respondence meet:
The silver sounding instruments did meet
With the base murmure of the waters fall·
The waters fall with difference discreet,
Now soft, now loud, unto the wind did call:
The gentle warbling wind low answered to
    all.

LXXII

There, whence that musick seemed heard
    to bee,
Was the faire witch, her selfe now solacing
With a new lover, whom, through sorceree
And witchcraft, she from farre did thether
    bring:
There she had him now laid a slombering,
In secret shade after long wanton joyes:
Whilst round about them pleasauntly did
    sing
Many faire ladies and lascivious boyes,
That ever mixt their song with light licen-
    tious toyes.

LXXIII

And all that while, right over him she
    hong,
With her false eyes fast fixed in his sight,
As seeking medicine whence she was stong,
Or greedily depasturing delight:
And oft inclining downe, with kisses light,
For feare of waking him, his lips bedewd,
And through his humid eyes did sucke his
    spright,
Quite molten into lust and pleasure lewd;
Wherewith she sighed soft, as if his case she
    rewd.

LXXIV

The whiles some one did chaunt this lovely
    lay: —
Ah ! see, who so fayre thing doest faine to
    see,
In springing flowre the image of thy day;
Ah ! see the virgin rose, how sweetly shee
Doth first peepe foorth with bashfull mo-
    destee,
That fairer seemes, the lesse ye see her
    may;
Lo ! see soone after, how more bold and
    free

Her bared bosome she doth broad dis-
    play;
Lo ! see soone after, how she fades and falls
    away.

LXXV

So passeth, in the passing of a day,
Of mortall life the leafe, the bud, the flowre,
Ne more doth florish after first decay,
That earst was sought to deck both bed
    and bowre
Of many a lady, and many a paramowre:
Gather therefore the rose, whilest yet is
    prime,
For soone comes age, that will her pride
    deflowre:
Gather the rose of love, whilest yet is time,
Whilest loving thou mayst loved be with
    equall crime.

LXXVI

He ceast, and then gan all the quire of
    birdes
Their diverse notes t' attune unto his lay,
As in approvaunce of his pleasing wordes.
The constant payre heard all that he did
    say,
Yet swarved not, but kept their forward
    way,
Through many covert groves and thickets
    close,
In which they creeping did at last display
That wanton lady, with her lover lose,
Whose sleepie head she in her lap did soft
    dispose.

LXXVII

Upon a bed of roses she was layd,
As faint through heat, or dight to pleasant
    sin,
And was arayd, or rather disarayd,
All in a vele of silke and silver thin,
That hid no whit her alablaster skin,
But rather shewd more white, if more
    might bee:
More subtile web Arachne cannot spin,
Nor the fine nets, which oft we woven
    see
Of scorched deaw, do not in th' ayre more
    lightly flee.

LXXVIII

Her snowy brest was bare to ready spoyle
Of hungry eies, which n'ote therewith be
    fild;
And yet through languour of her late sweet
    toyle,
Few drops, more cleare then nectar, forth
    distild,
That like pure orient perles adowne it
    trild;
And her faire eyes, sweet smyling in de-
    light,
Moystened their fierie beames, with which
    she thrild
Fraile harts, yet quenched not, like starry
    light,
Which, sparckling on the silent waves, does
    seeme more bright.

LXXIX

The young man, sleeping by her, seemd to
    be
Some goodly swayne of honorable place,
That certes it great pitty was to see
Him his nobility so fowle deface:
A sweet regard and amiable grace,
Mixed with manly sternesse, did appeare,
Yet sleeping, in his well proportiond face,
And on his tender lips the downy heare
Did now but freshly spring, and silken
    blossoms beare.

LXXX

His warlike armes, the ydle instruments
Of sleeping praise, were hong upon a tree,
And his brave shield, full of old moni-
    ments,
Was fowly ra'st, that none the signes might
    see;
Ne for them, ne for honour, cared hee,
Ne ought that did to his advauncement
    tend,
But in lewd loves, and wastfull luxuree,
His dayes, his goods, his bodie he did
    spend:
O horrible enchantment, that him so did
    blend !

LXXXI

The noble Elfe and carefull palmer drew
So nigh them, minding nought but lustfull
    game,
That suddein forth they on them rusht, and
    threw
A subtile net, which only for that same
The skilfull palmer formally did frame:
So held them under fast, the whiles the
    rest
Fled all away for feare of fowler shame.

The faire enchauntresse, so unwares op-
        prest,
Tryde all her arts and all her sleights,
        thence out to wrest.

LXXXII

And eke her lover strove : but all in
        vaine;
For that same net so cunningly was wound,
That neither guile nor force might it di-
        straine.
They tooke them both, and both them
        strongly bound
In captive bandes, which there they readie
        found:
But her in chaines of adamant he tyde;
For nothing else might keepe her safe and
        sound;
But Verdant (so he hight) he soone un-
        tyde,
And counsell sage in steed thereof to him
        applyde.

LXXXIII

But all those pleasaunt bowres and pallace
        brave
Guyon broke downe, with rigour pitti-
        lesse;
Ne ought their goodly workmanship might
        save
Them from the tempest of his wrathful-
        nesse,
But that their blisse he turn'd to baleful-
        nesse:
Their groves he feld, their gardins did de-
        face,
Their arbers spoyle, their cabinets sup-
        presse,
Their banket houses burne, their buildings
        race,
And, of the fayrest late, now made the
        fowlest place.

LXXXIV

Then led they her away, and eke that
        knight
They with them led, both sorrowfull and
        sad:
The way they came, the same retourn'd
        they right,
Till they arrived where they lately had
Charm'd those wild-beasts, that rag'd with
        furie mad:
Which, now awaking, fierce at them gan
        fly,

As in their mistresse reskew, whom they
        lad;
But them the palmer soone did pacify.
Then Guyon askt, what meant those beastes
        which there did ly.

LXXXV

Sayd he: 'These seeming beasts are men
        indeed,
Whom this enchauntresse hath transformed
        thus,
Whylome her lovers, which her lustes did
        feed,
Now turned into figures hideous,
According to their mindes like monstru-
        ous.'
'Sad end,' quoth he, 'of life intemperate,
And mournefull meed of joyes delicious !
But, palmer, if it mote thee so aggrate,
Let them returned be unto their former
        state.'

LXXXVI

Streight way he with his vertuous staffe
        them strooke,
And streight of beastes they comely men
        became;
Yet being men they did unmanly looke,
And stared ghastly, some for inward
        shame,
And some for wrath, to see their captive
        dame :
But one above the rest in speciall,
That had an hog beene late, hight Grylle by
        name,
Repyned greatly, and did him miscall,
That had from hoggish forme him brought
        to naturall.

LXXXVII

Saide Guyon: 'See the mind of beastly
        man,
That hath so soone forgot the excel-
        lence
Of his creation, when he life began,
That now he chooseth, with vile differ-
        ence,
To be a beast, and lacke intelligence.'
To whom the palmer thus: 'The donghill
        kinde
Delightes in filth and fowle incontinence:
Let Gryll be Gryll, and have his hoggish
        minde;
But let us hence depart, whilest wether
        serves and winde.'

THE THIRDE BOOKE
OF THE FAERIE QUEENE
CONTAYNING
THE LEGEND OF BRITOMARTIS
OR
OF CHASTITY

I

It falls me here to write of Chastity,
That fayrest vertue, far above the rest;
For which what needes me fetch from Faery
Forreine ensamples, it to have exprest?
Sith it is shrined in my Soveraines brest,
And formd so lively in each perfect part,
That to all ladies, which have it profest,
Neede but behold the pourtraict of her hart,
If pourtrayd it might bee by any living art.

II

But living art may not least part expresse,
Nor life-resembling pencill it can paynt,
All were it Zeuxis or Praxiteles:
His dædale hand would faile, and greatly
    faynt,
And her perfections with his error taynt:
Ne poets witt, that passeth painter farre
In picturing the parts of beauty daynt,
So hard a workemanship adventure darre,
For fear through want of words her excel-
    lence to marre.

III

How then shall I, apprentice of the skill
That whilome in divinest wits did rayne,
Presume so high to stretch mine humble
    quill?
Yet now my luckelesse lott doth me con-
    strayne
Hereto perforce. But, O dredd Soverayne,
Thus far forth pardon, sith that choicest
    witt
Cannot your glorious pourtraict figure
    playne,
That I in colour showes may shadow itt,
And antique praises unto present persons
    fitt.

IV

But if in living colours, and right hew,
Your selfe you covet to see pictured,
Who can it doe more lively, or more
    trew,

Then that sweete verse, with nectar sprinck-
    eled,
In which a gracious servaunt pictured
His Cynthia, his heavens fayrest light?
That with his melting sweetnes ravished,
And with the wonder of her beames bright,
My sences lulled are in slomber of delight.

V

But let that same delitious poet lend
A little leave unto a rusticke Muse
To sing his mistresse prayse, and let him
    mend,
If ought amis her liking may abuse:
Ne let his fayrest Cynthia refuse,
In mirrours more then one her selfe to
    see,
But either Gloriana let her chuse,
Or in Belphœbe fashioned to bee:
In th' one her rule, in th' other her rare
    chastitee.

CANTO I

Guyon encountreth Britomart:
Fayre Florimell is chaced:
Duessaes traines and Malecastaes
champions are defaced.

I

The famous Briton Prince and Faery
    knight,
After long wayes and perilous paines en-
    dur'd,
Having their weary limbes to perfect plight
Restord, and sory wounds right well recur'd,
Of the faire Alma greatly were procur'd
To make there lenger sojourne and abode;
But when thereto they might not be allur'd
From seeking praise and deeds of armes
    abrode,
They courteous conge tooke, and forth to-
    gether yode.

II

But the captiv'd Acrasia he sent,
Because of traveill long, a nigher way,
With a strong gard, all reskew to prevent,
And her to Faery court safe to convay,
That her for witnes of his hard assay
Unto his Faery Queene he might present:
But he him selfe betooke another way,
To make more triall of his hardiment,
And seeke adventures, as he with Prince
    Arthure went.

III

Long so they traveiled through wastefull
    wayes,
Where daungers dwelt, and perils most did
    wonne,
To hunt for glory and renowmed prayse:
Full many countreyes they did overronne,
From the uprising to the setting sunne,
And many hard adventures did atchieve;
Of all the which they honour ever wonne,
Seeking the weake oppressed to relieve,
And to recover right for such as wrong did
    grieve.

IV

At last, as through an open plaine they
    yode,
They spide a knight, that towards pricked
    fayre;
And him beside an aged squire there rode,
That seemd to couch under his shield three-
    square,
As if that age badd him that burden spare,
And yield it those that stouter could it
    wield:
He them espying, gan him selfe prepare,
And on his arme addresse his goodly shield,
That bore a lion passant in a golden field.

V

Which seeing good Sir Guyon, deare be-
    sought
The Prince, of grace, to let him ronne that
    turne.
He graunted: then the Faery quickly raught
His poynant speare, and sharply gan to
    spurne
His fomy steed, whose fiery feete did burne
The verdant gras, as he thereon did tread;
Ne did the other backe his foote returne,
But fiercely forward came withouten dread,
And bent his dreadful speare against the
    others head.

VI

They beene ymett, and both theyr points
    arriv'd;
But Guyon drove so furious and fell,
That seemd both shield and plate it would
    have riv'd:
Nathelesse it bore his foe not from his
    sell,
But made him stagger, as he were not
    well:
But Guyon selfe, ere well he was aware,

Nigh a speares length behind his crouper
    fell;
Yet in his fall so well him selfe he bare,
That mischievous mischaunce his life and
    limbs did spare.

VII

Great shame and sorrow of that fall he
    tooke;
For never yet, sith warlike armes he bore,
And shivering speare in bloody field first
    shooke,
He fownd him selfe dishonored so sore.
Ah! gentlest knight that ever armor bore,
Let not thee grieve dismounted to have
    beene,
And brought to grownd, that never wast
    before;
For not thy fault, but secret powre unseene:
That speare enchaunted was, which layd thee
    on the greene.

VIII

But weenedst thou what wight thee over-
    threw,
Much greater griefe and shamefuller re-
    grett
For thy hard fortune then thou wouldst
    renew,
That of a single damzell thou wert mett
On equall plaine, and there so hard be-
    sett:
Even the famous Britomart it was,
Whom straunge adventure did from Bri-
    tayne fett,
To seeke her lover, (love far sought, alas!)
Whose image shee had seene in Venus look-
    ing glas.

IX

Full of disdainefull wrath, he fierce up-
    rose,
For to revenge that fowle reprochefull
    shame,
And snatching his bright sword, began to
    close
With her on foot, and stoutly forward came;
Dye rather would he then endure that same.
Which when his palmer saw, he gan to
    feare
His toward perill and untoward blame,
Which by that new rencounter he should
    reare:
For death sate on the point of that en-
    chaunted speare.

X

And hasting towards him gan fayre per-
swade,
Not to provoke misfortune, nor to weene
His speares default to mend with cruell
blade:
For by his mightie science he had seene
The secrete vertue of that weapon keene,
That mortall puissaunce mote not with-
stond:
Nothing on earth mote alwaies happy beene.
Great hazard were it, and adventure fond,
To loose long gotten honour with one evill
hond.

XI

By such good meanes he him discounselled
From prosecuting his revenging rage;
And eke the Prince like treaty handeled,
His wrathfull will with reason to aswage,
And laid the blame, not to his carriage,
But to his starting steed, that swarv'd asyde,
And to the ill purveyaunce of his page,
That had his furnitures not firmely tyde:
So is his angry corage fayrly pacifyde.

XII

Thus reconcilement was betweene them
knitt,
Through goodly temperaunce and affection
chaste;
And either vowd with all their power and
witt,
To let not others honour be defaste
Of friend or foe, who ever it embaste,
Ne armes to beare against the others syde:
In which accord the Prince was also plaste,
And with that golden chaine of concord
tyde.
So goodly all agreed, they forth yfere did
ryde.

XIII

O goodly usage of those antique tymes,
In which the sword was servaunt unto right!
When not for malice and contentious
crymes,
But all for prayse, and proofe of manly
might,
The martiall brood accustomed to fight:
Then honour was the meed of victory,
And yet the vanquished had no despight:
Let later age that noble use envy,
Vyle rancor to avoid, and cruel sur-
quedry.

XIV

Long they thus traveiled in friendly wise,
Through countreyes waste and eke well
edifyde,
Seeking adventures hard, to exercise
Their puissaunce, whylome full dernly
tryde:
At length they came into a forest wyde,
Whose hideous horror and sad trembling
sownd
Full griesly seemd: therein they long did
ryde,
Yet tract of living creature none they
fownd,
Save beares, lyons, and buls, which romed
them arownd.

XV

All suddenly out of the thickest brush,
Upon a milkwhite palfrey all alone,
A goodly lady did foreby them rush,
Whose face did seeme as cleare as christall
stone,
And eke through feare as white as whales
bone:
Her garments all were wrought of beaten
gold,
And all her steed with tinsell trappings
shone,
Which fledd so fast that nothing mote him
hold,
And scarse them leasure gave, her passing
to behold.

XVI

Still as she fledd her eye she backward
threw,
As fearing evill that poursewd her fast;
And her faire yellow locks behind her flew,
Loosely disperst with puff of every blast:
All as a blazing starre doth farre outcast
His hearie beames, and flaming lockes di-
spredd,
At sight whereof the people stand aghast:
But the sage wisard telles, as he has redd,
That it importunes death and dolefull dre-
ryhedd.

XVII

So as they gazed after her a whyle,
Lo! where a griesly foster forth did rush,
Breathing out beastly lust her to defyle:
His tyreling jade he fiersly forth did push,
Through thicke and thin, both over banck
and bush,

In hope her to attaine by hooke or crooke,
That from his gory sydes the blood did
    gush:
Large were his limbes, and terrible his
    looke,
And in his clownish hand a sharp bore
    speare he shooke.

XVIII

Which outrage when those gentle knights
    did see,
Full of great envy and fell gealosy,
They stayd not to avise who first should
    bee,
But all spurd after fast as they mote fly,
To reskew her from shamefull villany.
The Prince and Guyon equally bylive
Her selfe pursewd, in hope to win thereby
Most goodly meede, the fairest dame alive:
But after the foule foster Timias did strive.

XIX

The whiles faire Britomart, whose constant
    mind
Would not so lightly follow beauties chace,
Ne reckt of ladies love, did stay behynd,
And them awayted there a certaine space,
To weet if they would turne backe to that
    place:
But when she saw them gone, she forward
    went,
As lay her journey, through that perlous
    pace,
With stedfast corage and stout hardiment;
Ne evil thing she feard, ne evill thing she
    ment.

XX

At last, as nigh out of the wood she came,
A stately castle far away she spyde,
To which her steps directly she did frame.
That castle was most goodly edifyde,
And plaste for pleasure nigh that forrest
    syde:
But faire before the gate a spatious playne,
Mantled with greene, it selfe did spredden
    wyde,
On which she saw six knights, that did
    darrayne
Fiers battaill against one, with cruel might
    and mayne.

XXI

Mainely they all attonce upon him laid,
And sore beset on every side arownd,

That nigh he breathlesse grew, yet nought
    dismaid,
Ne ever to them yielded foot of grownd,
All had he lost much blood through many
    a wownd,
But stoutly dealt his blowes, and every way,
To which he turned in his wrathfull stownd,
Made them recoile, and fly from dredd decay,
That none of all the six before him durst
    assay.

XXII

Like dastard curres, that, having at a bay
The salvage beast embost in wearie chace,
Dare not adventure on the stubborne pray,
Ne byte before, but rome from place to
    place,
To get a snatch, when turned is his face.
In such distresse and doubtfull jeopardy
When Britomart him saw, she ran apace
Unto his reskew, and with earnest cry
Badd those same sixe forbeare that single
    enimy.

XXIII

But to her cry they list not lenden eare,
Ne ought the more their mightie strokes
    surceasse,
But gathering him rownd about more neare,
Their direfull rancour rather did encrease;
Till that she, rushing through the thickest
    preasse,
Perforce disparted their compacted gyre,
And soone compeld to hearken unto peace:
Tho gan she myldly of them to inquyre
The cause of their dissention and outrageous
    yre.

XXIV

Whereto that single knight did answere
    frame:
' These six would me enforce by oddes of
    might,
To chaunge my liefe, and love another
    dame,
That death me liefer were then such de-
    spight,
So unto wrong to yield my wrested right:
For I love one, the truest one on grownd,
Ne list me chaunge; she th' Errant Dam-
    zell hight;
For whose deare sake full many a bitter
    stownd
I have endurd, and tasted many a bloody
    wownd.'

XXV

' Certes,' said she, ' then beene ye sixe to
    blame,
To weene your wrong by force to justify:
For knight to leave his lady were great
    shame,
That faithfull is, and better were to dy.
All losse is lesse, and lesse the infamy,
Then losse of love to him that loves but
    one:
Ne may love be compeld by maistery;
For soone as maistery comes, sweet Love
    anone
Taketh his nimble winges, and soone away
    is gone.'

XXVI

Then spake one of those six: ' There dwell-
    eth here,
Within this castle wall, a lady fayre,
Whose soveraine beautie hath no living
    pere;
Thereto so bounteous and so debonayre,
That never any mote with her compayre.
She hath ordaind this law, which we ap-
    prove,
That every knight, which doth this way re-
    payre,
In case he have no lady nor no love,
Shall doe unto her service, never to remove.

XXVII

' But if he have a lady or a love,
Then must he her forgoe with fowle de-
    fame,
Or els with us by dint of sword approve,
That she is fairer then our fairest dame;
As did this knight, before ye hether came.'
' Perdy,' said Britomart, ' the choise is hard:
But what reward had he that overcame ? '
' He should advaunced bee to high regard,'
Said they, ' and have our ladies love for his
    reward.

XXVIII

' Therefore aread, sir, if thou have a love.'
' Love have I sure,' quoth she, ' but lady
    none;
Yet will I not fro mine owne love remove,
Ne to your lady will I service done,
But wreake your wronges wrought to this
    knight alone,
And prove his cause.' With that, her mor-
    tall speare
She mightily aventred towards one,

And downe him smot ere well aware he
    weare;
Then to the next she rode, and downe the
    next did beare.

XXIX

Ne did she stay, till three on ground she
    layd,
That none of them himselfe could reare
    againe;
The fourth was by that other knight dis-
    mayd,
All were he wearie of his former paine,
That now there do but two of six re-
    maine;
Which two did yield before she did them
    smight.
' Ah ! ' sayd she then, ' now may ye all see
    plaine,
That truth is strong, and trew love most of
    might,
That for his trusty servaunts doth so
    strongly fight.'

XXX

' Too well we see,' saide they, ' and prove
    too well
Our faulty weakenes, and your matchlesse
    might:
Forthy, faire sir, yours be the damozell,
Which by her owne law to your lot doth
    light,
And we your liege men faith unto you
    plight.'
So underneath her feet their swords they
    mard,
And after, her besought, well as they
    might,
To enter in and reape the dew reward:
She graunted, and then in they all together
    far'd.

XXXI

Long were it to describe the goodly frame
And stately port of Castle Joyeous,
(For so that castle hight by commun name)
Where they were entertaynd with courteous
And comely glee of many gratious
Faire ladies, and of many a gentle knight,
Who through a chamber long and spa-
    cious,
Eftsoones them brought unto their ladies
    sight,
That of them cleeped was the Lady of De-
    light.

XXXII

But for to tell the sumptuous aray
Of that great chamber should be labour
    lost:
For living wit, I weene, cannot display
The roiall riches and exceeding cost
Of every pillour and of every post;
Which all of purest bullion framed were,
And with great perles and pretious stones
    embost,
That the bright glister of their beames
    cleare
Did sparckle forth great light, and glorious
    did appeare.

XXXIII

These stranger knights, through passing,
    forth were led
Into an inner rowme, whose royaltee
And rich purveyance might uneath be red;
Mote princes place beseeme so deckt to
    bee.
Which stately manner when as they did see,
The image of superfluous riotize,
Exceeding much the state of meane degree,
They greatly wondred whence so sump-
    teous guize
Might be maintaynd, and each gan diversely
    devize.

XXXIV

The wals were round about appareiled
With costly clothes of Arras and of Toure,
In which with cunning hand was pourtrahed
The love of Venus and her paramoure,
The fayre Adonis, turned to a flowre,
A worke of rare device and wondrous wit.
First did it shew the bitter balefull stowre,
Which her assayd with many a fervent
    fit,
When first her tender hart was with his
    beautie smit:

XXXV

Then with what sleights and sweet allure-
    ments she
Entyst the boy, as well that art she knew,
And wooed him her paramoure to bee;
Now making girlonds of each flowre that
    grew,
To crowne his golden lockes with honour
    dew;
Now leading him into a secret shade
From his beauperes, and from bright hea-
    vens vew,

Where him to sleepe she gently would per-
    swade,
Or bathe him in a fountaine by some covert
    glade.

XXXVI

And whilst he slept, she over him would
    spred
Her mantle, colour'd like the starry skyes,
And her soft arme lay underneath his hed,
And with ambrosiall kisses bathe his eyes;
And whilst he bath'd, with her two crafty
    spyes
She secretly would search each daintie lim,
And throw into the well sweet rosemaryes,
And fragrant violets, and paunces trim,
And ever with sweet nectar she did sprinkle
    him.

XXXVII

So did she steale his heedelesse hart away,
And joyd his love in secret unespyde.
But for she saw him bent to cruell play,
To hunt the salvage beast in forrest wyde,
Dreadfull of daunger, that mote him betyde,
She oft and oft adviz'd him to refraine
From chase of greater beastes, whose brut-
    ish pryde
Mote breede him scath unwares: but all in
    vaine;
For who can shun the chance that dest'ny
    doth ordaine ?

XXXVIII

Lo ! where beyond he lyeth languishing,
Deadly engored of a great wilde bore,
And by his side the goddesse groveling
Makes for him endlesse mone, and ever-
    more
With her soft garment wipes away the gore,
Which staynes his snowy skin with hatefull
    hew:
But when she saw no helpe might him
    restore,
Him to a dainty flowre she did transmew,
Which in that cloth was wrought, as if it
    lively grew.

XXXIX

So was that chamber clad in goodly wize:
And rownd about it many beds were dight,
As whylome was the antique worldes guize,
Some for untimely ease, some for delight,
As pleased them to use, that use it might:
And all was full of damzels and of squyres,

Daun, cing and reveling both day and night,
And swimming deepe in sensuall desyres;
And Cupid still emongest them kindled lust-
  full fyres.

XL

And all the while sweet musicke did divide
Her looser notes with Lydian harmony;
And all the while sweet birdes thereto
  applide
Their daintie layes and dulcet melody,
Ay caroling of love and jollity,
That wonder was to heare their trim con-
  sort.
Which when those knights beheld, with
  scornefull eye,
They sdeigned such lascivious disport,
And loath'd the loose demeanure of that
  wanton sort.

XLI

Thence they were brought to that great
  ladies vew,
Whom they found sitting on a sumptuous
  bed,
That glistred all with gold and glorious
  shew,
As the proud Persian queenes accustomed:
She seemd a woman of great bountihed
And of rare beautie, saving that askaunce
Her wanton eyes, ill signes of womanhed,
Did roll too lightly, and too often glaunce,
Without regard of grace or comely amen-
  aunce.

XLII

Long worke it were, and needlesse, to devize
Their goodly entertainement and great glee:
She caused them be led in courteous wize
Into a bowre, disarmed for to be,
And cheared well with wine and spiceree:
The Redcrosse Knight was soone disarmed
  there,
But the brave mayd would not disarmed
  bee,
But onely vented up her umbriere.
And so did let her goodly visage to appere.

XLIII

As when fayre Cynthia, in darkesome night,
Is in a noyous cloud enveloped,
Where she may finde the substance thin
  and light
Breakes forth her silver beames, and her
  bright hed

Discovers to the world discomfited;
Of the poore traveiler, that went astray,
With thousand blessings she is heried;
Such was the beautie and the shining ray,
With which fayre Britomart gave ligh
  unto the day.

XLIV

And eke those six, which lately with her
  fought,
Now were disarmd, and did them selves
  present
Unto her vew, and company unsought;
For they all seemed courteous and gent,
And all sixe brethren, borne of one pa-
  rent,
Which had them traynd in all civilitee,
And goodly taught to tilt and turnament;
Now were they liegmen to this ladie free,
And her knights service ought, to hold of
  her in fee.

XLV

The first of them by name Gardante hight,
A jolly person, and of comely vew;
The second was Parlante, a bold knight,
And next to him Jocante did ensew;
Basciante did him selfe most courteous
  shew;
But fierce Bacchante seemd too fell and
  keene;
And yett in armes Noctante greater grew:
All were faire knights, and goodly well be-
  seene,
But to faire Britomart they all but shad-
  owes beene.

XLVI

For shee was full of amiable grace,
And manly terror mixed therewithall,
That as the one stird up affections bace,
So th' other did mens rash desires apall,
And hold them backe, that would in error
  fall;
As hee that hath espide a vermeill rose,
To which sharpe thornes and breres the
  way forstall,
Dare not for dread his hardy hand ex-
  pose,
But wishing it far off, his ydle wish doth
  lose.

XLVII

Whom when the lady saw so faire a wight,
All ignorant of her contrary sex,

(For shee her weend a fresh and lusty
    knight)
Shee greatly gan enamoured to wex,
And with vaine thoughts her falsed fancy
    vex:
Her fickle hart conceived hasty fyre,
Like sparkes of fire which fall in sclender
    flex,
That shortly brent into extreme desyre,
And ransackt all her veines with passion
    entyre.

XLVIII

Eftsoones shee grew to great impatience,
And into termes of open outrage brust,
That plaine discovered her incontinence,
Ne reckt shee who her meaning did mis-
    trust;
For she was given all to fleshly lust,
And poured forth in sensuall delight,
That all regard of shame she had discust,
And meet respect of honor putt to flight:
So shamelesse beauty soone becomes a
    loathly sight.

XLIX

Faire ladies, that to love captived arre,
And chaste desires doe nourish in your
    mind,
Let not her fault your sweete affections
    marre,
Ne blott the bounty of all womankind,
'Mongst thousands good one wanton dame
    to find:
Emongst the roses grow some wicked
    weeds:
For this was not to love, but lust, inclind;
For love does alwaies bring forth boun-
    teous deeds,
And in each gentle hart desire of honor
    breeds.

L

Nought so of love this looser dame did
    skill,
But as a cole to kindle fleshly flame,
Giving the bridle to her wanton will,
And treading under foote her honest name:
Such love is hate, and such desire is shame.
Still did she rove at her with crafty glaunce
Of her false eies, that at her hart did
    ayme,
And told her meaning in her countenaunce;
But Britomart dissembled it with ignor-
    aunce.

LI

Supper was shortly dight, and downe they
    satt;
Where they were served with all sumptuous
    fare,
Whiles fruitfull Ceres and Lyæus fatt
Pour out their plenty, without spight or
    spare:
Nought wanted there that dainty was and
    rare;
And aye the cups their bancks did overflow,
And aye, betweene the cups, she did prepare
Way to her love, and secret darts did throw;
But Britomart would not such guilfull mes-
    sage know.

LII

So when they slaked had the fervent heat
Of appetite with meates of every sort,
The lady did faire Britomart entreat,
Her to disarme, and with delightfull sport
To loose her warlike limbs and strong
    effort:
But when shee mote not thereunto be wonne,
(For shee her sexe under that straunge pur-
    port
Did use to hide, and plaine apparaunce
    shonne,)
In playner wise to tell her grievaunce she
    begonne.

LIII

And all attonce discovered her desire
With sighes, and sobs, and plaints, and
    piteous griefe,
The outward sparkes of her inburning fire;
Which spent in vaine, at last she told her
    briefe,
That, but if she did lend her short reliefe,
And doe her comfort, she mote algates dye.
But the chaste damzell, that had never priefe
Of such malengine and fine forgerye,
Did easely beleeve her strong extremitye.

LIV

Full easy was for her to have beliefe,
Who by self-feeling of her feeble sexe,
And by long triall of the inward griefe,
Wherewith imperious love her hart did vexe,
Could judge what paines doe loving harts
    perplexe.
Who meanes no guile, be guiled soonest
    shall,
And to faire semblaunce doth light faith
    annexe:

The bird, that knowes not the false fowlers
    call,
Into his hidden nett full easely doth fall.

LV

Forthy she would not in discourteise wise
Scorne the faire offer of good will profest;
For great rebuke it is, love to despise,
Or rudely sdeigne a gentle harts request;
But with faire countenaunce, as beseemed
    best,
Her entertaynd; nath'lesse shee inly deemd
Her love too light, to wooe a wandring
    guest:
Which she misconstruing, thereby esteemd
That from like inward fire that outward
    smoke had steemd.

LVI

Therewith a while she her flit fancy fedd,
Till she mote winne fit time for her desire,
But yet her wound still inward freshly
    bledd,
And through her bones the false instilled fire
Did spred it selfe, and venime close inspire.
Tho were the tables taken all away,
And every knight, and every gentle squire
Gan choose his dame with *basciomani* gay,
With whom he ment to make his sport and
    courtly play.

LVII

Some fell to daunce, some fel to hazardry,
Some to make love, some to make mery-
    ment,
As diverse witts to diverse things apply;
And all the while faire Malecasta bent
Her crafty engins to her close intent.
By this th' eternall lampes, wherewith high
    Jove
Doth light the lower world, were halfe
    yspent,
And the moist daughters of huge Atlas
    strove
Into the ocean deepe to drive their weary
    drove.

LVIII

High time it seemed then for everie wight
Them to betake unto their kindly rest:
Eftesoones long waxen torches weren light,
Unto their bowres to guyden every guest:
Tho, when the Britonesse saw all the rest
Avoided quite, she gan her selfe despoile,
And safe committ to her soft fethered nest,

Wher through long watch, and late daies
    weary toile,
She soundly slept, and carefull thoughts did
    quite assoile.

LIX

Now whenas all the world in silence deepe
Yshrowded was, and every mortall wight
Was drowned in the depth of deadly sleepe,
Faire Malecasta, whose engrieved spright
Could find no rest in such perplexed plight,
Lightly arose out of her wearie bed,
And, under the blacke vele of guilty night,
Her with a scarlott mantle covered,
That was with gold and ermines faire en-
    veloped.

LX

Then panting softe, and trembling every
    joynt,
Her fearfull feete towards the bowre she
    mov'd,
Where she for secret purpose did appoynt
To lodge the warlike maide, unwisely loov'd;
And to her bed approching, first she proov'd
Whether she slept or wakte; with her softe
    hand
She softely felt if any member moov'd,
And lent her wary eare to understand
If any puffe of breath or signe of sence shee
    fond.

LXI

Which whenas none she fond, with easy
    shifte,
For feare least her unwares she should
    abrayd,
Th' embroderd quilt she lightly up did lifte,
And by her side her selfe she softly layd,
Of every finest fingers touch affrayd;
Ne any noise she made, ne word she spake,
But inly sigh'd. At last the royall mayd
Out of her quiet slomber did awake,
And chaungd her weary side, the better ease
    to take.

LXII

Where feeling one close couched by her
    side,
She lightly lept out of her filed bedd,
And to her weapon ran, in minde to gride
The loathed leachour. But the dame, halfe
    dedd
Through suddein feare and ghastly dreri-
    hedd,

Did shrieke alowd, that through the hous it
    rong,
And the whole family, therewith adredd,
Rashly out of their rouzed couches sprong,
And to the troubled chamber all in armes
    did throng.

LXIII

And those sixe knights, that ladies cham-
    pions,
And eke the Redcrosse Knight ran to the
    stownd,
Halfe armd and halfe unarmd, with them
    attons:
Where when confusedly they came, they
    fownd
Their lady lying on the sencelesse grownd;
On thother side, they saw the warlike
    mayd
Al in her snow-white smocke, with locks
    unbownd,
Threatning the point of her avenging blaed;
That with so troublous terror they were all
    dismayd.

LXIV

About their ladye first they flockt arownd;
Whom having laid in comfortable couch,
Shortly they reard out of her frosen
    swownd;
And afterwardes they gan with fowle re-
    proch
To stirre up strife, and troublous contecke
    broch:
But, by ensample of the last dayes losse,
None of them rashly durst to her approch,
Ne in so glorious spoile themselves embosse:
Her succourd eke the champion of the bloody
    crosse.

LXV

But one of those sixe knights, Gardante
    hight,
Drew out a deadly bow and arrow keene,
Which forth he sent with felonous despight,
And fell intent, against the virgin sheene:
The mortall steele stayd not till it was
    seene
To gore her side; yet was the wound not
    deepe,
But lightly rased her soft silken skin,
That drops of purple blood thereout did
    weepe,
Which did her lilly smock with staines of
    vermeil steep.

LXVI

Wherewith enrag'd, she fiercely at them
    flew,
And with her flaming sword about her layd,
That none of them foule mischiefe could
    eschew,
But with her dreadfull strokes were all dis-
    mayd:
Here, there, and every where about her
    swayd
Her wrathfull steele, that none mote it
    abyde;
And eke the Redcrosse Knight gave her good
    ayd,
Ay joyning foot to foot, and syde to syde,
That in short space their foes they have
    quite terrifyde.

LXVII

Tho whenas all were put to shamefull flight,
The noble Britomartis her arayd,
And her bright armes about her body dight:
For nothing would she lenger there be
    stayd,
Where so loose life, and so ungentle trade,
Was usd of knights and ladies seeming
    gent:
So, earely, ere the grosse earthes gryesy
    shade
Was all disperst out of the firmament,
They tooke their steeds, and forth upon
    their journey went.

CANTO II

The Redcrosse Knight to Britomart
    Describeth Artegall :
The wondrous myrrhour, by which she
    In love with him did fall.

I

HERE have I cause in men just blame to
    find,
That in their proper praise too partiall bee,
And not indifferent to woman kind,
To whom no share in armes and chevalree
They doe impart, ne maken memoree
Of their brave gestes and prowesse mar-
    tiall:
Scarse doe they spare to one, or two, or
    three,
Rowme in their writtes; yet the same writ-
    ing small
Does all their deedes deface, and dims their
    glories all.

II

But by record of antique times I finde,
That wemen wont in warres to beare most
sway,
And to all great exploites them selves in-
clind:
Of which they still the girlond bore away,
Till envious men, fearing their rules decay,
Gan coyne streight lawes to curb their lib-
erty:
Yet sith they warlike armes have laide
away,
They have exceld in artes and pollicy,
That now we foolish men that prayse gin
eke t' envy.

III

Of warlike puissaunce in ages spent,
Be thou, faire Britomart, whose prayse I
wryte;
But of all wisedom bee thou precedent,
O soveraine Queene, whose prayse I would
endyte,
Endite I would as dewtie doth excyte;
But ah! my rymes to rude and rugged arre,
When in so high an object they doe lyte,
And, striving fit to make, I feare doe
marre:
Thy selfe thy prayses tell, and make them
knowen farre.

IV

She, traveiling with Guyon, by the way
Of sondry thinges faire purpose gan to find,
T' abridg their journey long and lingring
day:
Mongst which it fell into that Fairies mind
To aske this Briton maid, what uncouth
wind
Brought her into those partes, and what
inquest
Made her dissemble her disguised kind:
Faire lady she him seemd, like lady drest,
But fairest knight alive, when armed was
her brest.

V

Thereat she sighing softly, had no powre
To speake a while, ne ready answere make,
But with hart-thrilling throbs and bitter
stowre,
As if she had a fever fitt, did quake,
And every daintie limbe with horrour
shake,
And ever and anone the rosy red

Flasht through her face, as it had beene a
flake
Of lightning through bright heven ful-
mined:
At last, the passion past, she thus him answered:

VI

' Faire sir, I let you weete, that from the
howre
I taken was from nourses tender pap,
I have beene trained up in warlike stowre,
To tossen speare and shield, and to affrap
The warlike ryder to his most mishap:
Sithence I loathed have my life to lead,
As ladies wont, in pleasures wanton lap,
To finger the fine needle and nyce thread;
Me lever were with point of foemans speare
be dead.

VII

' All my delight on deedes of armes is sett,
To hunt out perilles and adventures hard,
By sea, by land, where so they may be mett,
Onely for honour and for high regard,
Without respect of richesse or reward.
For such intent into these partes I came,
Withouten compasse or withouten card,
Far fro my native soyle, that is by name
The Greater Brytayne, here to seeke for
praise and fame.

VIII

' Fame blazed hath, that here in Faery Lond
Doe many famous knightes and ladies
wonne,
And many straunge adventures to bee fond,
Of which great worth and worship may be
wonne:
Which I to prove, this voyage have be-
gonne.
But mote I weet of you, right courteous
knight,
Tydings of one, that hath unto me donne
Late foule dishonour and reprochfull spight,
The which I seeke to wreake, and Arthegall
he hight.'

IX

The word gone out she backe againe would
call,
As her repenting so to have missayd,
But that he it uptaking ere the fall,
Her shortly answered: ' Faire martiall
mayd,

Certes ye misavised beene, t' upbrayd
A gentle knight with so unknightly blame:
For weet ye well, of all that ever playd
At tilt or tourney, or like warlike game,
The noble Arthegall hath ever borne the
    name.

X

'Forthy great wonder were it, if such
    shame
Should ever enter in his bounteous thought,
Or ever doe that mote deserven blame:
The noble corage never weeneth ought,
That may unworthy of it selfe be thought.
Therefore, faire damzell, be ye well aware,
Least that too farre ye have your sorrow
    sought:
You and your countrey both I wish welfare,
And honour both; for each of other worthy
    are.'

XI

The royall maid woxe inly wondrous glad,
To heare her love so highly magnifyde,
And joyd that ever she affixed had
Her hart on knight so goodly glorifyde,
How ever finely she it faind to hyde:
The loving mother, that nine monethes did
    beare,
In the deare closett of her painefull syde,
Her tender babe, it seeing safe appeare,
Doth not so much rejoyce as she rejoyced
    theare.

XII

But to occasion him to further talke,
To feed her humor with his pleasing style,
Her list in stryfull termes with him to
    balke,
And thus replyde: 'How ever, sir, ye fyle
Your courteous tongue, his prayses to com-
    pyle,
It ill beseemes a knight of gentle sort,
Such as ye have him boasted, to beguyle
A simple maide, and worke so hainous tort,
In shame of knighthood, as I largely can
    report.

XIII

'Let bee therefore my vengeaunce to dis-
    swade,
And read, where I that faytour false may
    find.'
'Ah! but if reason faire might you per-
    swade

To slake your wrath, and mollify your
    mind,'
Said he, 'perhaps ye should it better find:
For hardie thing it is, to weene by might
That man to hard conditions to bind,
Or ever hope to match in equall fight,
Whose prowesse paragone saw never living
    wight.

XIV

'Ne soothlich is it easie for to read
Where now on earth, or how, he may be
    fownd;
For he ne wonneth in one certeine stead,
But restlesse walketh all the world arownd,
Ay doing thinges that to his fame redownd,
Defending ladies cause and orphans right,
Where so he heares that any doth confownd
Them comfortlesse, through tyranny or
    might:
So is his soveraine honour raisde to hevens
    hight.'

XV

His feeling wordes her feeble sence much
    pleased,
And softly sunck into her molten hart:
Hart that is inly hurt is greatly eased
With hope of thing that may allegge his
    smart;
For pleasing wordes are like to magick
    art,
That doth the charmed snake in slomber
    lay:
Such secrete ease felt gentle Britomart,
Yet list the same efforce with faind gaine-
    say:
So dischord ofte in musick makes the
    sweeter lay:

XVI

And sayd: 'Sir knight, these ydle termes
    forbeare,
And sith it is uneath to finde his haunt,
Tell me some markes by which he may ap-
    peare,
If chaunce I him encounter paravaunt;
For perdy one shall other slay, or daunt:
What shape, what shield, what armes, what
    steed, what stedd,
And what so else his person most may
    vaunt,
All which the Redcrosse Knight to point
    aredd,
And him in everie part before her fashioned.

XVII

Yet him in everie part before she knew,
How ever list her now her knowledge
fayne,
Sith him whylome in Brytayne she did vew,
To her revealed in a mirrhour playne,
Whereof did grow her first engraffed payne,
Whose root and stalke so bitter yet did
taste,
That, but the fruit more sweetnes did con-
tayne,
Her wretched dayes in dolour she mote
waste,
And yield the pray of love to lothsome
death at last.

XVIII

By straunge occasion she did him behold,
And much more straungely gan to love his
sight,
As it in bookes hath written beene of old.
In Deheubarth, that now South-Wales is
hight,
What time King Ryence raign'd and dealed
right,
The great magitien Merlin had deviz'd,
By his deepe science and hell-dreaded
might,
A looking glasse, right wondrously aguiz'd,
Whose vertues through the wyde worlde
soone were solemniz'd.

XIX

It vertue had to shew in perfect sight
What ever thing was in the world contaynd,
Betwixt the lowest earth and hevens hight,
So that it to the looker appertaynd;
What ever foe had wrought, or frend had
faynd,
Therein discovered was, ne ought mote pas,
Ne ought in secret from the same remaynd;
Forthy it round and hollow shaped was,
Like to the world it selfe, and seemd a
world of glas.

XX

Who wonders not, that reades so wonderous worke?
But who does wonder, that has red the
towre,
Wherein th' Aegyptian Phao long did lurke
From all mens vew, that none might her
discoure,
Yet she might all men vew out of her
bowre?

Great Ptolomæe it for his lemans sake
Ybuilded all of glasse, by magicke powre,
And also it impregnable did make;
Yet when his love was false, he with a
peaze it brake.

XXI

Such was the glassy globe, that Merlin
made,
And gave unto King Ryence for his gard,
That never foes his kingdome might in-
vade,
But he it knew at home before he hard
Tydings thereof, and so them still debar'd.
It was a famous present for a prince,
And worthy worke of infinite reward,
That treasons could bewray, and foes con-
vince:
Happy this realme, had it remayned ever
since!

XXII

One day it fortuned fayre Britomart
Into her fathers closet to repayre;
For nothing he from her reserv'd apart,
Being his onely daughter and his hayre:
Where when she had espyde that mirrhour
fayre,
Her selfe awhile therein she vewd in vaine;
Tho her avizing of the vertues rare
Which thereof spoken were, she gan againe
Her to bethinke of that mote to her selfe
pertaine.

XXIII

But as it falleth, in the gentlest harts
Imperious Love hath highest set his throne,
And tyrannizeth in the bitter smarts
Of them that to him buxome are and prone:
So thought this mayd (as maydens use to
done)
Whom fortune for her husband would allot;
Not that she lusted after any one,
For she was pure from blame of sinfull blot,
Yet wist her life at last must lincke in that
same knot.

XXIV

Eftsoones there was presented to her eye
A comely knight, all arm'd in complete wize,
Through whose bright ventayle, lifted up
on hye,
His manly face, that did his foes agrize,
And frends to termes of gentle truce en-
tize,

Lookt foorth, as Phœbus face out of the east
Betwixt two shady mountaynes doth arize:
Portly his person was, and much increast
Through his heroicke grace and honorable
    gest.

XXV

His crest was covered with a couchant
    hownd,
And all his armour seemd of antique mould,
But wondrous massy and assured sownd,
And round about yfretted all with gold,
In which there written was, with cyphres
    old,
Achilles armes, which Arthegall did win.
And on his shield enveloped sevenfold
He bore a crowned litle ermilin,
That deckt the azure field with her fayre
    pouldred skin.

XXVI

The damzell well did vew his personage,
And liked well, ne further fastned not,
But went her way; ne her unguilty age
Did weene, unwares, that her unlucky lot
Lay hidden in the bottome of the pot:
Of hurt unwist most daunger doth redound:
But the false archer, which that arrow shot
So slyly that she did not feele the wound,
Did smyle full smoothly at her weetlesse
    wofull stound.

XXVII

Thenceforth the fether in her lofty crest,
Ruffed of love, gan lowly to availe,
And her prowd portaunce and her princely
    gest,
With which she earst tryumphed, now did
    quaile:
Sad, solemne, sowre, and full of fancies
    fraile
She woxe; yet wist she nether how, nor
    why;
She wist not, silly mayd, what she did aile,
Yet wist she was not well at ease perdy,
Yet thought it was not love, but some mel-
    ancholy.

XXVIII

So soone as Night had with her pallid hew
Defaste the beautie of the shyning skye,
And reft from men the worldes desired vew,
She with her nourse adowne to sleepe did
    lye;
But sleepe full far away from her did fly:

In stead thereof sad sighes and sorrowes
    deepe
Kept watch and ward about her warily,
That nought she did but wayle, and often
    steepe
Her dainty couch with teares, which closely
    she did weepe.

XXIX

And if that any drop of slombring rest
Did chaunce to still into her weary spright,
When feeble nature felt her selfe opprest,
Streight way with dreames, and with fantas-
    tick sight
Of dreadfull things, the same was put to
    flight,
That oft out of her bed she did astart,
As one with vew of ghastly feends affright:
Tho gan she to renew her former smart,
And thinke of that fayre visage, written in
    her hart.

XXX

One night, when she was tost with such un-
    rest,
Her aged nourse, whose name was Glauce
    hight,
Feeling her leape out of her loathed nest,
Betwixt her feeble armes her quickly keight
And downe againe in her warme bed her
    dight:
'Ah! my deare daughter, ah! my dearest
    dread,
What uncouth fit,' sayd she, 'what evill
    plight,
Hath thee opprest, and with sad dreary-
    head
Chaunged thy lively cheare, and living made
    thee dead?

XXXI

'For not of nought these suddein ghastly
    feares
All night afflict thy naturall repose;
And all the day, when as thine equall peares
Their fit disports with faire delight doe
    chose,
Thou in dull corners doest thy selfe inclose
Ne tastest princes pleasures, ne doest
    spred
Abroad thy fresh youths fayrest flowre, but
    lose
Both leafe and fruite, both too untimely
    shed,
As one in wilfull bale for ever buried.

XXXII

'The time that mortall men their weary
   cares
Do lay away, and all wilde beastes do rest,
And every river eke his course forbeares,
Then doth this wicked evill thee infest,
And rive with thousand throbs thy thrilled
   brest;
Like an huge Aetn' of deepe engulfed
   gryefe,
Sorrow is heaped in thy hollow chest,
Whence foorth it breakes in sighes and an-
   guish ryfe,
As smoke and sulphure mingled with con-
   fused stryfe.

XXXIII

'Ay me ! how much I feare least love it
   bee !
But if that love it be, as sure I read
By knowen signes and passions which I
   see,
Be it worthy of thy race and royall sead,
Then I avow by this most sacred head
Of my deare foster childe, to ease thy
   griefe,
And win thy will: therefore away doe
   dread;
For death nor daunger from thy dew re-
   liefe
Shall me debarre: tell me, therefore, my
   liefest liefe.'

XXXIV

So having sayd, her twixt her armes twaine
Shee streightly straynd, and colled tenderly,
And every trembling joynt and every vaine
Shee softly felt, and rubbed busily,
To doe the frosen cold away to fly;
And her faire deawy eies with kisses deare
Shee ofte did bathe, and ofte againe did
   dry;
And ever her importund, not to feare
To let the secret of her hart to her appeare.

XXXV

The damzell pauzd, and then thus fearfully:
'Ah ! nurse, what needeth thee to eke my
   paine ?
Is not enough that I alone doe dye,
But it must doubled bee with death of
   twaine ?
For nought for me but death there doth
   remaine.'

'O daughter deare,' said she, 'despeire no
   whit;
For never sore, but might a salve obtaine:
That blinded god, which hath ye blindly
   smit,
Another arrow hath your lovers hart to hit.'

XXXVI

'But mine is not,' quoth she, 'like other
   wownd;
For which no reason can finde remedy.'
'Was never such, but mote the like be
   fownd,'
Said she, 'and though no reason may apply
Salve to your sore, yet love can higher
   stye
Then reasons reach, and oft hath wonders
   donne.'
'But neither god of love nor god of skye
Can doe,' said she, 'that which cannot be
   donne.'
'Things ofte impossible,' quoth she, 'seeme
   ere begonne.'

XXXVII

'These idle wordes,' said she, ' doe nought
   aswage
My stubborne smart, but more annoiaunce
   breed:
For no no usuall fire, no usuall rage
Yt is, O nourse, which on my life doth feed,
And sucks the blood which from my hart
   doth bleed.
But since thy faithfull zele lets me not hyde
My crime, (if crime it be) I will it reed.
Nor prince, nor pere it is, whose love hath
   gryde
My feeble brest of late, and launched this
   wound wyde.

XXXVIII

'Nor man it is, nor other living wight;
For then some hope I might unto me draw;
But th' only shade and semblant of a knight,
Whose shape or person yet I never saw,
Hath me subjected to Loves cruell law:
The same one day, as me misfortune led,
I in my fathers wondrous mirrhour saw,
And, pleased with that seeming goodly-hed,
Unwares the hidden hooke with baite I swal-
   lowed.

XXXIX

'Sithens it hath infixed faster hold
Within my bleeding bowells, and so sore

Now ranckleth in this same fraile fleshly
  mould,
That all mine entrailes flow with poisnous
  gore,
And th' ulcer groweth daily more and more;
Ne can my ronning sore finde remedee,
Other then my hard fortune to deplore,
And languish as the leafe faln from the
  tree,
Till death make one end of my daies and
  miseree.'

XL

' Daughter,' said she, ' what need ye be dis-
  mayd,
Or why make ye such monster of your
  minde ?
Of much more uncouth thing I was affrayd;
Of filthy lust, contrary unto kinde:
But this affection nothing straunge I finde;
For who with reason can you aye reprove,
To love the semblaunt pleasing most your
  minde,
And yield your heart whence ye cannot re-
  move ?
No guilt in you, but in the tyranny of Love.

XLI

' Not so th' Arabian Myrrhe did sett her
  mynd,
Nor so did Biblis spend her pining hart,
But lov'd their native flesh against al kynd,
And to their purpose used wicked art:
Yet playd Pasiphaë a more monstrous part,
That lov'd a bul, and learnd a beast to
  bee:
Such shamefull lusts who loaths not, which
  depart
From course of nature and of modestee ?
Swete Love such lewdnes bands from his
  faire companee.

XLII

' But thine, my deare, (welfare thy heart,
  my deare)
Though straunge beginning had, yet fixed is
On one that worthy may perhaps appeare;
And certes seemes bestowed not amis:
Joy thereof have thou and eternall blis.'
With that upleaning on her elbow weake,
Her alablaster brest she soft did kis,
Which all that while shee felt to pant and
  quake,
As it an earth-quake were: at last she thus
  bespake:

XLIII

' Beldame, your words doe worke me litle
  ease;
For though my love be not so lewdly bent
As those ye blame, yet may it nought ap-
  pease
My raging smart, ne ought my flame relent,
But rather doth my helpelesse griefe aug-
  ment.
For they, how ever shamefull and unkinde,
Yet did possesse their horrible intent:
Short end of sorowes they therby did finde;
So was their fortune good, though wicked
  were their minde.

XLIV

' But wicked fortune mine, though minde be
  good,
Can have no end, nor hope of my desire,
But feed on shadowes, whiles I die for
  food,
And like a shadow wexe, whiles with entire
Affection I doe languish and expire.
I, fonder then Cephisus foolish chyld,
Who, having vewed in a fountaine shere
His face, was with the love thereof be-
  guyld;
I, fonder, love a shade, the body far exyld.'

XLV

' Nought like,' quoth shee, ' for that same
  wretched boy
Was of him selfe the ydle paramoure,
Both love and lover, without hope of
  joy;
For which he faded to a watry flowre.
But better fortune thine, and better howre,
Which lov'st the shadow of a warlike
  knight;
No shadow, but a body hath in powre:
That body, wheresoever that it light,
May learned be by cyphers, or by magicke
  might.

XLVI

' But if thou may with reason yet represse
The growing evill, ere it strength have
  gott,
And thee abandond wholy doe possesse,
Against it strongly strive, and yield thee
  nott,
Til thou in open fielde adowne be smott.
But if the passion mayster thy fraile might,
So that needs love or death must bee thy
  lott,

Then I avow to thee, by wrong or right
To compas thy desire, and find that loved
    knight.'

XLVII

Her chearefull words much cheard the
    feeble spright
Of the sicke virgin, that her downe she
    layd
In her warme bed to sleepe, if that she
    might;
And the old-woman carefully displayd
The clothes about her round with busy ayd,
So that at last a litle creeping sleepe
Surprisd her sence. Shee, therewith well
    apayd,
The dronken lamp down in the oyl did
    steepe,
And sett her by to watch, and sett her by
    to weepe.

XLVIII

Earely the morrow next, before that day
His joyous face did to the world revele,
They both uprose and tooke their ready way
Unto the church, their praiers to appele,
With great devotion, and with litle zele:
For the faire damzell from the holy herse
Her love-sicke hart to other thoughts did
    steale;
And that old dame said many an idle verse,
Out of her daughters hart fond fancies to
    reverse.

XLIX

Retourned home, the royall infant fell
Into her former fitt; forwhy no powre
Nor guidaunce of her selfe in her did dwell.
But th' aged nourse, her calling to her
    bowre,
Had gathered rew, and savine, and the
    flowre
Of camphora, and calamint, and dill,
All which she in a earthen pot did poure,
And to the brim with colt wood did it fill,
And many drops of milk and blood through
    it did spill.

L

Then, taking thrise three heares from of her
    head,
Them trebly breaded in a threefold lace,
And round about the pots mouth bound the
    thread,
And after having whispered a space

Certein sad words, with hollow voice and
    bace,
Shee to the virgin sayd, thrise sayd she itt:
'Come, daughter, come, come; spit upon my
    face,
Spitt thrise upon me, thrise upon me spitt;
Th' uneven nomber for this busines is most
    fitt.'

LI

That sayd, her rownd about she from her
    turnd,
She turned her contrary to the sunne,
Thrise she her turnd contrary, and returnd
All contrary, for she the right did shunne,
And ever what she did was streight un-
    donne.
So thought she to undoe her daughters love:
But love, that is in gentle brest begonne,
No ydle charmes so lightly may remove;
That well can witnesse, who by tryall it
    does prove.

LII

Ne ought it mote the noble mayd avayle,
Ne slake the fury of her cruell flame,
But that shee still did waste, and still did
    wayle,
That through long languour and hart-burn-
    ing brame
She shortly like a pyned ghost became,
Which long hath waited by the Stygian
    strond.
That when old Glauce saw, for feare least
    blame
Of her miscarriage should in her be fond,
She wist not how t' amend, nor how it to
    withstond.

CANTO III

Merlin bewrayes to Britomart
The state of Arthegall :
And shews the famous progeny,
Which from them springen shall.

I

Most sacred fyre, that burnest mightily
In living brests, ykindled first above,
Emongst th' eternall spheres and lamping
    sky,
And thence pourd into men, which men
    call Love;
Not that same which doth base affections
    move

In brutish mindes, and filthy lust inflame,
But that sweete fit that doth true beautie
    love,
And choseth Vertue for his dearest dame,
Whence spring all noble deedes and never
    dying fame:

II

Well did antiquity a god thee deeme,
That over mortall mindes hast so great
    might,
To order them as best to thee doth seeme,
And all their actions to direct aright:
The fatall purpose of divine foresight
Thou doest effect in destined descents,
Through deepe impression of thy secret
    might,
And stirredst up th' heroes high intents,
Which the late world admyres for wondrous
    moniments.

III

But thy dredd dartes in none doe triumph
    more,
Ne braver proofe, in any, of thy powre
Shew'dst thou, then in this royall maid of
    yore,
Making her seeke an unknowne paramoure,
From the worlds end, through many a bit-
    ter stowre:
From whose two loynes thou afterwardes
    did rayse
Most famous fruites of matrimoniall bowre,
Which through the earth have spredd their
    living prayse,
That Fame in tromp of gold eternally dis-
    playes.

IV

Begin then, O my dearest sacred dame,
Daughter of Phœbus and of Memorye,
That doest ennoble with immortall name
The warlike worthies, from antiquitye,
In thy great volume of eternitye:
Begin, O Clio, and recount from hence
My glorious Soveraines goodly auncestrye,
Till that by dew degrees and long protense,
Thou have it lastly brought unto her Ex-
    cellence.

V

Full many wayes within her troubled mind
Old Glauce cast, to cure this ladies griefe :
Full many waies she sought, but none could
    find,

Nor herbes, nor charmes, nor counsel, that
    is chiefe
And choisest med'cine for sick harts reliefe:
Forthy great care she tooke, and greater
    feare,
Least that it should her turne to fowle re-
    priefe
And sore reproch, when so her father deare
Should of his dearest daughters hard mis-
    fortune heare.

VI

At last she her avisde, that he which made
That mirrhour, wherein the sicke damosell
So straungely vewed her straunge lovers
    shade,
To weet, the learned Merlin, well could tell,
Under what coast of heaven the man did
    dwell,
And by what means his love might best be
    wrought:
For though beyond the Africk Ismael
Or th' Indian Peru he were, she thought
Him forth through infinite endevour to have
    sought.

VII

Forthwith them selves disguising both in
    straunge
And base atyre, that none might them be-
    wray,
To Maridunum, that is now by chaunge
Of name Cayr-Merdin cald, they tooke their
    way:
There the wise Merlin whylome wont (they
    say)
To make his wonne, low underneath the
    ground,
In a deepe delve, farre from the vew of
    day,
That of no living wight he mote be found,
When so he counseld with his sprights en-
    compast round.

VIII

And if thou ever happen that same way
To traveill, go to see that dreadfull place:
It is an hideous hollow cave (they say)
Under a rock, that lyes a litle space
From the swift Barry, tombling downe apace
Emongst the woody hilles of Dynevowre:
But dare thou not, I charge, in any cace,
To enter into that same balefull bowre,
For feare the cruell feendes should thee
    unwares devowre.

IX

But standing high aloft, low lay thine eare,
And there such ghastly noyse of yron
    chaines
And brasen caudrons thou shalt rombling
    heare,
Which thousand sprights with long enduring
    paines
Doe tosse, that it will stonn thy feeble
    braines;
And oftentimes great grones, and grievous
    stownds,
When too huge toile and labour them con-
    straines,
And oftentimes loud strokes, and ringing
    sowndes,
From under that deepe rock most horribly
    rebowndes.

X

The cause, some say, is this: A litle whyle
Before that Merlin dyde, he did intend
A brasen wall in compas to compyle
About Cairmardin, and did it commend
Unto these sprights, to bring to perfect end.
During which worke the Lady of the Lake,
Whom long he lov'd, for him in hast did
    send;
Who, thereby forst his workemen to for-
    sake,
Them bownd, till his retourne, their labour
    not to slake.

XI

In the meane time, through that false ladies
    traine,
He was surprisd, and buried under beare,
Ne ever to his worke returnd againe:
Nath'lesse those feends may not their work
    forbeare,
So greatly his commandement they feare,
But there doe toyle and traveile day and
    night,
Untill that brasen wall they up doe reare:
For Merlin had in magick more insight
Then ever him before or after living wight.

XII

For he by wordes could call out of the sky
Both sunne and moone, and make them
    him obay:
The land to sea, and sea to maineland dry,
And darksom night he eke could turne to
    day:
Huge hostes of men he could alone dismay,

And hostes of men of meanest thinges could
    frame,
When so him list his enimies to fray:
That to this day, for terror of his fame,
The feends do quake, when any him to
    them does name.

XIII

And sooth, men say that he was not the
    sonne
Of mortall syre or other living wight,
But wondrously begotten, and begonne
By false illusion of a guilefull spright,
On a faire lady nonne, that whilome hight
Matilda, daughter to Pubidius,
Who was the lord of Mathraval by right,
And coosen unto King Ambrosius:
Whence he indued was with skill so mer-
    veilous.

XIV

They, here ariving, staid a while without,
Ne durst adventure rashly in to wend,
But of their first intent gan make new dout,
For dread of daunger, which it might por-
    tend:
Untill the hardy mayd (with love to frend)
First entering, the dreadfull mage there
    fownd
Deepe busied bout worke of wondrous end,
And writing straunge characters in the
    grownd,
With which the stubborne feendes he to his
    service bownd.

XV

He nought was moved at their entraunce
    bold,
For of their comming well he wist afore;
Yet list them bid their businesse to un-
    fold,
As if ought in this world in secrete store
Were from him hidden, or unknowne of
    yore.
Then Glauce thus: ' Let not it thee offend,
That we thus rashly through thy darksom
    dore
Unwares have prest: for either fatall end,
Or other mightie cause, us two did hether
    send.'

XVI

He bad tell on; and then she thus began:
' Now have three moones with borrowd
    brothers light

Thrise shined faire, and thrise seemd dim
   and wan,
Sith a sore evill, which this virgin bright
Tormenteth, and doth plonge in dolefull
   plight,
First rooting tooke; but what thing it mote
   bee,
Or whence it sprong, I can not read aright;
But this I read, that, but if remedee
Thou her afford, full shortly I her dead
   shall see.'

XVII

Therewith th'enchaunter softly gan to smyle
At her smooth speeches, weeting inly well
That she to him dissembled womanish
   guyle,
And to her said: 'Beldame, by that ye tell,
More neede of leach-crafte hath your damo-
   zell,
Then of my skill: who helpe may have els-
   where,
In vaine seekes wonders out of magick
   spell.'
Th' old woman wox half blanck those
   wordes to heare;
And yet was loth to let her purpose plaine
   appeare;

XVIII

And to him said: 'Yf any leaches skill,
Or other learned meanes, could have redrest
This my deare daughters deepe engraffed
   ill,
Certes I should be loth thee to molest:
But this sad evill, which doth her infest,
Doth course of naturall cause farre exceed,
And housed is within her hollow brest,
That either seemes some cursed witches
   deed,
Or evill spright, that in her doth such tor-
   ment breed.'

XIX

The wisard could no lenger beare her bord,
But brusting forth in laughter, to her sayd:
'Glauce, what needes this colourable word,
To cloke the cause that hath it selfe be-
   wrayd?
Ne ye, fayre Britomartis, thus arayd,
More hidden are then sunne in cloudy vele;
Whom thy good fortune, having fate obayd,
Hath hether brought, for succour to appele:
The which the Powres to thee are pleased
   to revele.'

XX

The doubtfull mayd, seeing her selfe de-
   scryde,
Was all abasht, and her pure yvory
Into a cleare carnation suddeine dyde;
As fayre Aurora, rysing hastily,
Doth by her blushing tell that she did lye
All night in old Tithonus frosen bed,
Whereof she seemes ashamed inwardly.
But her olde nourse was nought dishartened,
But vauntage made of that which Merlin
   had ared;

XXI

And sayd: 'Sith then thou knowest all our
   griefe,
(For what doest not thou knowe?) of grace,
   I pray,
Pitty our playnt, and yield us meet reliefe.'
With that the prophet still awhile did stay,
And then his spirite thus gan foorth dis-
   play:
'Most noble virgin, that by fatall lore
Hast learn'd to love, let no whit thee dis-
   may
The hard beginne that meetes thee in the
   dorc,
And with sharpe fits thy tender hart op-
   presseth sore.

XXII

'For so must all things excellent begin,
And eke enrooted deepe must be that tree,
Whose big embodied braunches shall not
   lin,
Till they to hevens hight forth stretched bee.
For from thy wombe a famous progenee
Shall spring, out of the auncient Trojan
   blood,
Which shall revive the sleeping memoree
Of those same antique peres, the hevens
   brood,
Which Greeke and Asian rivers stayned with
   their blood.

XXIII

'Renowmed kings and sacred emperours,
Thy fruitfull ofspring, shall from thee de-
   scend;
Brave captaines and most mighty warriours,
That shall their conquests through all lands
   extend,
And their decayed kingdomes shall amend:
The feeble Britons, broken with long warre,
They shall upreare, and mightily defend

Against their forren foe, that commes from
    farre,
Till universall peace compound all civill
    jarre.

XXIV

'It was not, Britomart, thy wandring eye,
Glauncing unwares in charmed looking glas,
But the streight course of hevenly destiny,
Led with Eternall Providence, that has
Guyded thy glaunce, to bring His will to
    pas:
Ne is thy fate, ne is thy fortune ill,
To love the prowest knight that ever was:
Therefore submit thy wayes unto His will,
And doe, by all dew meanes, thy destiny
    fulfill.'

XXV

'But read,' saide Glauce, 'thou magitian,
What meanes shall she out seeke, or what
    waies take?
How shall she know, how shall she finde
    the man?
Or what needes her to toyle, sith Fates can
    make
Way for themselves, their purpose to per-
    take?'
Then Merlin thus: 'Indeede the Fates are
    firme,
And may not shrinck, though all the world
    do shake:
Yet ought mens good endevours them con-
    firme,
And guyde the heavenly causes to tneir con-
    stant terme.

XXVI

'The man, whom heavens have ordaynd to
    bee
The spouse of Britomart, is Arthegall:
He wonneth in the land of Fayeree,
Yet is no Fary borne, ne sib at all
To Elfes, but sprong of seed terrestriall,
And whylome by false Faries stolne away,
Whyles yet in infant cradle he did crall;
Ne other to himselfe is knowne this day,
But that he by an Elfe was gotten of a Fay.

XXVII

'But sooth he is the sonne of Gorlois,
And brother unto Cador, Cornish king,
And for his warlike feates renowmed is,
From where the day out of the sea doth
    spring

Untill the closure of the evening.
From thence him, firmely bound with faith-
    full band,
To this his native soyle thou backe shalt
    bring,
Strongly to ayde his countrey to withstand
The powre of forreine Paynims, which in-
    vade thy land.

XXVIII

'Great ayd thereto his mighty puissaunce
And dreaded name shall give in that sad
    day:
Where also proofe of thy prow valiaunce
Thou then shalt make, t' increase thy lovers
    pray.
Long time ye both in armes shall beare
    great sway,
Till thy wombes burden thee from them do
    call,
And his last fate him from thee take away,
Too rathe cut off by practise criminall
Of secrete foes, that him shall make in mis-
    chiefe fall.

XXIX

'With thee yet shall he leave, for memory
Of his late puissaunce, his ymage dead,
That living him in all activity
To thee shall represent. He from the head
Of his coosen Constantius, without dread,
Shall take the crowne, that was his fathers
    right,
And therewith crowne himselfe in th' others
    stead:
Then shall he issew forth with dreadfull
    might,
Against his Saxon foes in bloody field to
    fight.

XXX

'Like as a lyon, that in drowsie cave
Hath long time slept, himselfe so shall he
    shake,
And comming forth, shall spred his banner
    brave
Over the troubled South, that it shall make
The warlike Mertians for feare to quake:
Thrise shall he fight with them, and twise
    shall win,
But the third time shall fayre accordaunce
    make:
And if he then with victorie can lin,
He shall his dayes with peace bring to his
    earthly in.

XXXI

'His sonne, hight Vortipore, shall him suc-
ceede
In kingdome, but not in felicity;
Yet shall he long time warre with happy
speed,
And with great honour many batteills try:
But at the last to th' importunity
Of froward fortune shall be forst to yield.
But his sonne Malgo shall full mightily
Avenge his fathers losse, with speare and
shield,
And his proud foes discomfit in victorious
field.

XXXII

'Behold the man! and tell me, Britomart,
If ay more goodly creature thou didst see:
How like a gyaunt in each manly part
Beares he himselfe with portly majestee,
That one of th' old heroes seemes to bee!
He the six islands, comprovinciall
In auncient times unto Great Britainee,
Shall to the same reduce, and to him call
Their sondry kings to doe their homage
severall.

XXXIII

'All which his sonne Careticus awhile
Shall well defend, and Saxons powre sup-
presse,
Untill a straunger king, from unknowne
soyle
Arriving, him with multitude oppresse;
Great Gormond, having with huge mighti-
nesse
Ireland subdewd, and therein fixt his throne,
Like a swift otter, fell through empti-
nesse,
Shall overswim the sea with many one
Of his Norveyses, to assist the Britons fone.

XXXIV

'He in his furie all shall overronne,
And holy church with faithlesse handes de-
face,
That thy sad people, utterly fordonne,
Shall to the utmost mountaines fly apace:
Was never so great waste in any place,
Nor so fowle outrage doen by living men:
For all thy citties they shall sacke and race,
And the greene grasse that groweth they
shall bren,
That even the wilde beast shall dy in starved
den.

XXXV

'Whiles thus thy Britons doe in languour
pine,
Proud Etheldred shall from the North arise,
Serving th' ambitious will of Augustine,
And passing Dee with hardy enterprise,
Shall backe repulse the valiaunt Brockwell
twise,
And Bangor with massacred martyrs fill;
But the third time shall rew his foolhardise:
For Cadwan, pittying his peoples ill,
Shall stoutly him defeat, and thousand
Saxons kill.

XXXVI

'But after him, Cadwallin mightily
On his sonne Edwin all those wrongs shall
wreake;
Ne shall availe the wicked sorcery
Of false Pellite, his purposes to breake,
But him shall slay, and on a gallowes bleak
Shall give th' enchaunter his unhappy hire:
Then shall the Britons, late dismayd and
weake,
From their long vassallage gin to respire,
And on their Paynim foes avenge their
ranckled ire.

XXXVII

'Ne shall he yet his wrath so mitigate,
Till both the sonnes of Edwin he have
slayne,
Offricke and Osricke, twinnes unfortunate,
Both slaine in battaile upon Layburne
playne,
Together with the king of Louthiane,
Hight Adin, and the king of Orkeny,
Both joynt partakers of their fatall payne:
But Penda, fearefull of like desteny,
Shall yield him selfe his liegeman, and
sweare fealty.

XXXVIII

'Him shall he make his fatall instrument,
T' afflict the other Saxons unsubdewd;
He marching forth with fury insolent
Against the good King Oswald, who, in-
dewd
With heavenly powre, and by angels res-
kewd,
Al holding crosses in their hands on hye,
Shall him defeate withouten blood im-
brewd:
Of which that field for endlesse memory
Shall Hevenfield be cald to all posterity.

XXXIX

Whereat Cadwallin wroth, shall forth
    issew,
And an huge hoste into Northumber lead,
With which he godly Oswald shall subdew,
And crowne with martiredome his sacred
    head.
Whose brother Oswin, daunted with like
    dread,
With price of silver shall his kingdome buy,
And Penda, seeking him adowne to tread,
Shall tread adowne, and doe him fowly dye,
But shall with guifts his lord Cadwallin
    pacify.

XL

Then shall Cadwallin die, and then the
    raine
Of Britons eke with him attonce shall dye;
Ne shall the good Cadwallader, with paine
Or powre, be hable it to remedy,
When the full time, prefixt by destiny,
Shalbe expird of Britons regiment:
For Heven it selfe shall their successe envy,
And them with plagues and murrins
    pestilent
Consume, till all their warlike puissaunce
    be spent.

XLI

'Yet after all these sorrowes, and huge
    hills
Of dying people, during eight yeares space,
Cadwallader, not yielding to his ills,
From Armoricke, where long in wretched
    cace
He liv'd, retourning to his native place,
Shalbe by vision staide from his intent :
For th' Heavens have decreed to displace
The Britons for their sinnes dew punish-
    ment,
And to the Saxons over-give their govern-
    ment.

XLII

'Then woe, and woe, and everlasting woe,
Be to the Briton babe, that shalbe borne
To live in thraldome of his fathers foe !
Late king, now captive, late lord, now for-
    lorne,
The worlds reproch, the cruell victors
    scorne,
Banisht from princely bowre to wasteful
    wood !
O ! who shal helpe me to lament and mourne

The royall seed, the antique Trojan blood,
Whose empire lenger here then ever any
    stood ?'

XLIII

The damzell was full deepe empassioned,
Both for his griefe, and for her peoples sake,
Whose future woes so plaine he fashioned,
And sighing sore, at length him thus be-
    spake:
'Ah ! but will Hevens fury never slake,
Nor vengeaunce huge relent it selfe at last ?
Will not long misery late mercy make,
But shall their name for ever be defaste,
And quite from of the earth their memory
    be raste ?'

XLIV

'Nay, but the terme,' sayd he, 'is limited,
That in this thraldome Britons shall abide,
And the just revolution measured,
That they as straungers shalbe notifide:
For twise fowre hundreth yeares shalbe
    supplide,
Ere they to former rule restor'd shalbee,
And their importune fates all satisfide:
Yet during this their most obscuritee,
Their beames shall ofte breake forth, that
    men them faire may see.

XLV

'For Rhodoricke, whose surname shalbe
    Great,
Shall of him selfe a brave ensample shew,
That Saxon kings his frendship shall in-
    treat;
And Howell Dha shall goodly well indew
The salvage minds with skill of just and
    trew;
Then Griffyth Conan also shall up reare
His dreaded head, and the old sparkes re-
    new
Of native corage, that his foes shall feare
Least back againe the kingdom he from
    them should beare.

XLVI

'Ne shall the Saxons selves all peaceably
Enjoy the crowne, which they from Britons
    wonne
First ill, and after ruled wickedly:
For ere two hundred yeares be full out-
    ronne,
There shall a Raven, far from rising sunne,
With his wide wings upon them fiercely fly,

And bid his faithlesse chickens overonne
The fruitfull plaines, and with fell cruelty,
In their avenge, tread downe the victors
    surquedry.

XLVII

' Yet shall a third both these and thine sub-
    dew:
There shall a Lion from the sea-bord wood
Of Neustria come roring, with a crew
Of hungry whelpes, his battailous bold
    brood,
Whose clawes were newly dipt in cruddy
    blood,
That from the Daniske tyrants head shall
    rend
Th' usurped crowne, as if that he were
    wood,
And the spoile of the countrey conquered
Emongst his young ones shall divide with
    bountyhed.

XLVIII

' Tho, when the terme is full accomplishid,
There shall a sparke of fire, which hath
    long-while
Bene in his ashes raked up and hid,
Bee freshly kindled in the fruitfull ile
Of Mona, where it lurked in exile;
Which shall breake forth into bright burning
    flame,
And reach into the house that beares the
    stile
Of roiall majesty and soveraine name:
So shall the Briton blood their crowne
    agayn reclame.

XLIX

' Thenceforth eternall union shall be made
Betweene the nations different afore,
And sacred Peace shall lovingly persuade
The warlike minds to learne her goodly
    lore,
And civile armes to exercise no more:
Then shall a royall Virgin raine, which shall
Stretch her white rod over the Belgicke
    shore,
And the great Castle smite so sore with all,
That it shall make him shake, and shortly
    learne to fall.

L

' But yet the end is not.——' There Merlin
    stayd,
As overcomen of the spirites powre,

Or other ghastly spectacle dismayd,
That secretly he saw, yet note discoure:
Which suddein fitt and halfe extatick stoure
When the two fearefull wemen saw, they
    grew
Greatly confused in behaveoure:
At last the fury past, to former hew
Hee turnd againe, and chearfull looks as
    earst did shew.

LI

Then, when them selves they well in-
    structed had
Of all that needed them to be inquird,
They both, conceiving hope of comfort glad,
With lighter hearts unto their home re-
    tird;
Where they in secret counsell close con-
    spird,
How to effect so hard an enterprize,
And to possesse the purpose they desird:
Now this, now that twixt them they did
    devize,
And diverse plots did frame, to maske in
    strange disguise.

LII

At last the nourse in her foolhardy wit
Conceivd a bold devise, and thus bespake:
' Daughter, I deeme that counsel aye most
    fit,
That of the time doth dew advauntage
    take:
Ye see that good King Uther now doth
    make
Strong warre upon the Paynim brethren,
    hight
Octa and Oza, whome hee lately brake
Beside Cayr Verolame in victorious fight,
That now all Britany doth burne in armes
    bright.

LIII

' That therefore nought our passage may
    empeach,
Let us in feigned armes our selves disguize,
And our weake hands (whom need new
    strength shall teach)
The dreadfull speare and shield to exercize:
Ne certes, daughter, that same warlike
    wize,
I weene, would you misseeme; for ye beene
    tall
And large of limbe t' atchieve an hard em-
    prize,

Ne ought ye want, but skil, which practize
 small
Wil bring, and shortly make you a mayd
 martiall.

LIV

' And sooth, it ought your corage much in-
 flame,
To heare so often, in that royall hous,
From whence to none inferior ye came,
Bards tell of many wemen valorous,
Which have full many feats adventurous
Performd, in paragone of proudest men:
The bold Bunduca, whose victorious
Exployts made Rome to quake, stout
 Guendolen,
Renowmed Martia, and redoubted Emmi-
 len ;

LV

' And that which more then all the rest
 may sway,
Late dayes ensample, which these eyes be-
 held:
In the last field before Menevia,
Which Uther with tnose forrein pagans
 held,
I saw a Saxon virgin, the which feld
Great Ulfin thrise upon the bloody playne,
And had not Carados her hand withheld
From rash revenge, she had him surely
 slayne,
Yet Carados himselfe from her escapt with
 payne.'

LVI

' Ah ! read,' quoth Britomart, ' how is she
 hight ? '
' Fayre Angela,' quoth she, ' men do her call,
No whit lesse fayre then terrible in fight:
She hath the leading of a martiall
And mightie people, dreaded more then all
The other Saxons, which doe, for her sake
And love, themselves of her name Angles
 call.
Therefore, faire infant, her ensample make
Unto thy selfe, and equall corage to thee
 take.'

LVII

Her harty wordes so deepe into the mynd
Of the yong damzell sunke, that great desire
Of warlike armes in her forthwith they
 tynd,

And generous stout courage did inspyre,
That she resolv'd, unweeting to her syre,
Advent'rous knighthood on her selfe to
 don,
And counseld with her nourse, her maides
 attyre
To turne into a massy habergeon,
And bad her all things put in readinesse
 anon.

LVIII

Th' old woman nought that needed did
 omit;
But all thinges did conveniently purvay.
It fortuned (so time their turne did fitt)
A band of Britons, ryding on forray
Few dayes before, had gotten a great pray
Of Saxon goods, emongst the which was
 seene
A goodly armour, and full rich aray,
Which long'd to Angela, the Saxon queene,
All fretted round with gold, and goodly
 wel beseene.

LIX

The same, with all the other ornaments,
King Ryence caused to be hanged hy
In his chiefe church, for endlesse moni-
 ments
Of his successe and gladfull victory:
Of which her selfe avising readily,
In th' evening late old Glauce thether led
Faire Britomart, and that same armory
Downe taking, her therein appareled,
Well as she might, and with brave bauld-
 rick garnished.

LX

Beside those armes there stood a mightie
 speare,
Which Bladud made by magick art of yore,
And usd the same in batteill aye to beare:
Sith which it had beene here preserv'd in
 store,
For his great vertues proved long afore:
For never wight so fast in sell could sit,
But him perforce unto the ground it bore:
Both speare she tooke and shield, which
 hong by it:
Both speare and shield of great powre, for
 her purpose fit.

LXI

Thus when she had the virgin all arayd,
Another harnesse, which did hang thereby

About her selfe she dight, that the yong
          mayd
She might in equall armes accompany,
And as her squyre attend her carefully:
Tho to their ready steedes they clombe full
          light,
And through back waies, that none might
          them espy,
Covered with secret cloud of silent night,
Themselves they forth convaid, and passed
          forward right.

LXII

Ne rested they, till that to Faery Lond
They came, as Merlin them directed late:
Where meeting with this Redcrosse Knight,
          she fond
Of diverse thinges discourses to dilate,
But most of Arthegall and his estate.
At last their wayes so fell, that they mote
          part:
Then each to other well affectionate,
Frendship professed with unfained hart:
The Redcrosse Knight diverst, but forth
          rode Britomart.

CANTO IV

Bold Marinell of Britomart
Is throwne on the Rich Strond:
Faire Florimell of Arthure is
Long followed, but not fond.

I

WHERE is the antique glory now become,
That whylome wont in wemen to appeare ?
Where be the brave atchievements doen by
          some ?
Where be the batteilles, where the shield
          and speare,
And all the conquests which them high did
          reare,
That matter made for famous poets verse,
And boastfull men so oft abasht to heare ?
Beene they all dead, and laide in dolefull
          herse ?
Or doen they onely sleepe, and shall againe
          reverse ?

II

If they be dead, then woe is me therefore :
But if they sleepe, O let them soone awake !
For all too long I burne with envy sore,
To heare the warlike feates which Homere
          spake

Of bold Penthesilee, which made a lake
Of Greekish blood so ofte in Trojan plaine ;
But when I reade, how stout Debora strake
Proud Sisera, and how Camill' hath slaine
The huge Orsilochus, I swell with great
          disdaine.

III

Yet these, and all that els had puissaunce,
Cannot with noble Britomart compare,
Aswell for glorie of great valiaunce,
As for pure chastitie and vertue rare,
That all her goodly deedes do well declare.
Well worthie stock, from which the
          branches sprong
That in late yeares so faire a blossome bare
As thee, O Queene, the matter of my song,
Whose lignage from this lady I derive along.

IV

Who when, through speaches with the
          Redcrosse Knight,
She learned had th' estate of Arthegall,
And in each point her selfe informd aright,
A frendly league of love perpetuall
She with him bound, and congé tooke withall.
Then he forth on his journey did proceede,
To seeke adventures which mote him befall,
And win him worship through his warlike
          deed,
Which alwaies of his paines he made the
          chiefest meed.

V

But Britomart kept on her former course,
Ne ever dofte her armes, but all the way
Grew pensive through that amarous dis-
          course,
By which the Redcrosse Knight did earst
          display
Her lovers shape and chevalrous aray:
A thousand thoughts she fashiond in her
          mind,
And in her feigning fancie did pourtray
Him such as fittest she for love could find,
Wise, warlike, personable, courteous, and
          kind.

VI

With such selfe-pleasing thoughts her
          wound she fedd,
And thought so to beguile her grievous
          smart;
But so her smart was much more grievous
          bredd,

And the deepe wound more deep engord
    her hart,
That nought but death her dolour mote
    depart.
So forth she rode without repose or rest,
Searching all lands and each remotest part,
Following the guydaunce of her blinded
    guest,
Till that to the seacoast at length she her
    addrest.

VII

There she alighted from her light-foot
    beast,
And sitting downe upon the rocky shore,
Badd her old squyre unlace her lofty creast:
Tho, having vewd a while the surges hore,
That gainst the craggy clifts did loudly
    rore,
And in their raging surquedry disdaynd
That the fast earth affronted them so sore,
And their devouring covetize restraynd,
Thereat she sighed deepe, and after thus
    complaynd.

VIII

' Huge sea of sorrow and tempestuous griefe,
Wherein my feeble barke is tossed long,
Far from the hoped haven of reliefe,
Why doe thy cruel billowes beat so strong,
And thy moyst mountaynes each on others
    throng,
Threatning to swallow up my fearefull lyfe?
O! doe thy cruell wrath and spightfull
    wrong
At length allay, and stint thy stormy stryfe,
Which in these troubled bowels raignes
    and rageth ryfe.

IX

' For els my feeble vessell, crazd and crackt
Through thy strong buffets and outrageous
    blowes,
Cannot endure, but needes it must be wrackt
On the rough rocks, or on the sandy shal-
    lowes,
The whiles that Love it steres, and Fortune
    rowes:
Love, my lewd pilott, hath a restlesse minde,
And Fortune, boteswaine, no assuraunce
    knowes,
But saile withouten starres gainst tyde and
    winde:
How can they other doe, sith both are
    bold and blinde?

X

' Thou god of windes, that raignest in the
    seas,
That raignest also in the continent,
At last blow up some gentle gale of ease,
The which may bring my ship, ere it be rent,
Unto the gladsome port of her intent:
Then, when I shall my selfe in safety see,
A table, for eternall moniment
Of thy great grace, and my great jeopardee,
Great Neptune, I avow to hallow unto thee.'

XI

Then sighing softly sore, and inly deepe,
She shut up all her plaint in privy griefe;
For her great courage would not let her
    weepe;
Till that old Glauce gan with sharpe re-
    priefe
Her to restraine, and give her good reliefe,
Through hope of those which Merlin had
    her told
Should of her name and nation be chiefe,
And fetch their being from the sacred
    mould
Of her immortall womb, to be in heaven
    enrold.

XII

Thus as she her recomforted, she spyde
Where far away one, all in armour bright,
With hasty gallop towards her did ryde:
Her dolour soone she ceast, and on her
    dight
Her helmet, to her courser mounting light:
Her former sorrow into suddein wrath,
Both coosen passions of distroubled spright,
Converting, forth she beates the dusty path:
Love and despight attonce her courage kin-
    dled hath.

XIII

As when a foggy mist hath overcast
The face of heven, and the cleare ayre en-
    groste,
The world in darkenes dwels, till that at
    last
The watry southwinde, from the seabord
    coste
Upblowing, doth disperse the vapour lo'ste,
And poures it selfe forth in a stormy showre;
So the fayre Britomart, having disclo'ste
Her clowdy care into a wrathfull stowre,
The mist of griefe dissolv'd did into ven-
    geance powre.

XIV

Eftsoones her goodly shield addressing
    fayre,
That mortall speare she in her hand did
    take,
And unto battaill did her selfe prepayre.
The knight, approching, sternely her be-
    spake:
'Sir knight, that doest thy voyage rashly
    make
By this forbidden way in my despight,
Ne doest by others death ensample take,
I read thee soone retyre, whiles thou hast
    might,
Least afterwards it be too late to take thy
    flight.'

XV

Ythrild with deepe disdaine of his proud
    threat,
She shortly thus: 'Fly they, that need to fly;
Wordes fearen babes: I meane not thee
    entreat
To passe; but maugre thee will passe or
    dy:'
Ne lenger stayd for th' other to reply,
But with sharpe speare the rest made dearly
    knowne.
Strongly the straunge knight ran, and stur-
    dily
Strooke her full on the brest, that made
    her downe
Decline her head, and touch her crouper
    with her crown.

XVI

But she againe him in the shield did smite
With so fierce furie and great puissaunce,
That through his threesquare scuchin per-
    cing quite,
And through his mayled hauberque, by mis-
    chaunce
The wicked steele through his left side did
    glaunce:
Him so transfixed she before her bore
Beyond his croupe, the length of all her
    launce,
Till, sadly soucing on the sandy shore,
He tombled on an heape, and wallowd in
    his gore.

XVII

Like as the sacred oxe, that carelesse stands
With gilden hornes and flowry girlonds
    crownd,

Proud of his dying honor and deare bandes,
Whiles th' altars fume with frankincense
    arownd,
All suddeinly with mortall stroke astownd,
Doth groveling fall, and with his streaming
    gore
Distaines the pillours and the holy grownd,
And the faire flowres that decked him
    afore:
So fell proud Marinell upon the pretious
    shore.

XVIII

The martiall mayd stayd not him to la-
    ment,
But forward rode, and kept her ready
    way
Along the strond; which as she over-went,
She saw bestrowed all with rich aray
Of pearles and pretious stones of great as-
    say,
And all the gravell mixt with golden owre;
Whereat she wondred much, but would
    not stay
For gold, or perles, or pretious stones an
    howre,
But them despised all, for all was in her
    powre.

XIX

Whiles thus he lay in deadly stonishment,
Tydings hereof came to his mothers eare:
His mother was the blacke-browd Cymo-
    ent,
The daughter of great Nereus, which did
    beare
This warlike sonne unto an earthly peare,
The famous Dumarin; who on a day
Finding the nymph a sleepe in secret
    wheare,
As he by chaunce did wander that same
    way,
Was taken with her love, and by her closely
    lay.

XX

There he this knight of her begot, whom
    borne
She, of his father, Marinell did name,
And in a rocky cave, as wight forlorne,
Long time she fostred up, till he became
A mighty man at armes, and mickle fame
Did get through great adventures by him
    donne:
For never man he suffred by that same

Rich Strond to travell, whereas he did
wonne,
But that he must do battail with the sea-
nymphes sonne.

XXI

An hundred knights of honorable name
He had subdew'd, and them his vassals
made,
That through all Farie Lond his noble fame
Now blazed was, and feare did all invade,
That none durst passen through that peril-
ous glade.
And to advaunce his name and glory more,
Her sea-god syre she dearely did perswade,
T' endow her sonne with threasure and rich
store,
Bove all the sonnes that were of earthly
wombes ybore.

XXII

The god did graunt his daughters deare
demaund,
To doen his nephew in all riches flow:
Eftsoones his heaped waves he did com-
maund
Out of their hollow bosome forth to throw
All the huge threasure, which the sea below
Had in his greedy gulfe devoured deepe,
And him enriched through the overthrow
And wreckes of many wretches, which did
weepe
And often wayle their wealth, which he
from them did keepe.

XXIII

Shortly upon that shore there heaped was
Exceeding riches and all pretious things,
The spoyle of all the world, that it did pas
The wealth of th' East, and pompe of Per-
sian kings:
Gold, amber, yvorie, perles, owches, rings,
And all that els was pretious and deare,
The sea unto him voluntary brings,
That shortly he a great lord did appeare,
As was in all the lond of Faery, or else
wheare.

XXIV

Thereto he was a doughty dreaded knight,
Tryde often to the scath of many deare,
That none in equall armes him matchen
might:
The which his mother seeing, gan to feare
Least his too haughtie hardines might reare

Some hard mishap, in hazard of his life:
Forthy she oft him counseld to forbeare
The bloody batteill, and to stirre up strife,
But after all his warre to rest his wearie
knife.

XXV

And, for his more assuraunce, she inquir'd
One day of Proteus by his mighty spell
(For Proteus was with prophecy inspir'd)
Her deare sonnes destiny to her to tell,
And the sad end of her sweet Marinell.
Who, through foresight of his eternall skill,
Bad her from womankind to keepe him well:
For of a woman he should have much ill;
A virgin straunge and stout him should dis-
may or kill.

XXVI

Forthy she gave him warning every day,
The love of women not to entertaine;
A lesson too too hard for living clay,
From love in course of nature to refraine:
Yet he his mothers lore did well retaine,
And ever from fayre ladies love did fly;
Yet many ladies fayre did oft complaine,
That they for love of him would algates dy:
Dy who so list for him, he was loves enimy.

XXVII

But ah! who can deceive his destiny,
Or weene by warning to avoyd his fate?
That, when he sleepes in most security
And safest seemes, him soonest doth amate,
And findeth dew effect or soone or late.
So feeble is the powre of fleshly arme!
His mother bad him wemens love to hate,
For she of womans force did feare no harme;
So weening to have arm'd him, she did quite
disarme.

XXVIII

This was that woman, this that deadly
wownd,
That Proteus prophecide should him dismay,
The which his mother vainely did expownd,
To be hart-wownding love, which should
assay
To bring her sonne unto his last decay.
So ticle be the termes of mortall state
And full of subtile sophismes, which doe
play
With double sences, and with false debate,
T' approve the unknowen purpose of eter-
nall fate.

XXIX

Too trew the famous Marinell it fownd,
Who, through late triall, on that wealthy
strond
Inglorious now lies in sencelesse swownd,
Through heavy stroke of Britomartis hond.
Which when his mother deare did under-
stond,
And heavy tidings heard, whereas she playd
Amongst her watry sisters by a pond,
Gathering sweete daffadillyes, to have made
Gay girlonds, from the sun their forheads
fayr to shade,

XXX

Eftesoones both flowres and girlonds far
away
Shee flong, and her faire deawy locks yrent;
To sorrow huge she turnd her former play,
And gamesome merth to grievous dreri-
ment:
Shee threw her selfe downe on the contin-
ent,
Ne word did speake, but lay as in a swowne,
Whiles al her sisters did for her lament,
With yelling outcries, and with shrieking
sowne;
And every one did teare her girlond from
her crowne.

XXXI

Soone as shee up out of her deadly fitt
Arose, shee bad her charett to be brought,
And all her sisters, that with her did sitt,
Bad eke attonce their charetts to be sought:
Tho, full of bitter griefe and pensife
thought,
She to her wagon clombe; clombe all the
rest,
And forth together went, with sorow
fraught.
The waves, obedient to theyr beheast,
Them yielded ready passage, and their rage
surceast.

XXXII

Great Neptune stoode amazed at their
sight,
Whiles on his broad rownd backe they softly
slid,
And eke him selfe mournd at their mournfull plight,
Yet wist not what their wailing ment, yet
did,
For great compassion of their sorow, bid

His mighty waters to them buxome bee:
Eftesoones the roaring billowes still abid,
And all the griesly monsters of the see
Stood gaping at their gate, and wondred
them to see.

XXXIII

A teme of dolphins, raunged in aray,
Drew the smooth charett of sad Cymoent;
They were all taught by Triton to obay
To the long raynes at her commaunde-
ment:
As swifte as swallowes on the waves they
went,
That their brode flaggy finnes no fome did
reare,
Ne bubling rowndell they behinde them
sent;
The rest of other fishes drawen weare,
Which with their finny oars the swelling
sea did sheare.

XXXIV

Soone as they bene arriv'd upon the brim
Of the Rich Strond, their charets they
forlore,
And let their temed fishes softly swim
Along the margent of the fomy shore,
Least they their finnes should bruze, and
surbate sore
Their tender feete upon the stony grownd:
And comming to the place, where all in
gore
And cruddy blood enwallowed they fownd
The lucklesse Marinell, lying in deadly
swownd;

XXXV

His mother swowned thrise, and the third
time
Could scarce recovered bee out of her
paine;
Had she not beene devoide of mortall
slime,
Shee should not then have bene relyv'd
againe;
But soone as life recovered had the raine,
Shee made so piteous mone and deare wayment,
That the hard rocks could scarse from tears
refraine,
And all her sister nymphes with one consent
Supplide her sobbing breaches with sad
complement.

XXXVI

'Deare image of my selfe,' she sayd, 'that is,
The wretched sonne of wretched mother borne,
Is this thine high advauncement? O! is this
Th' immortall name, with which thee yet unborne
Thy gransire Nereus promist to adorne?
Now lyest thou of life and honor refte,
Now lyest thou a lumpe of earth forlorne,
Ne of thy late life memory is lefte,
Ne can thy irrevocable desteny bee wefte?

XXXVII

'Fond Proteus, father of false prophecis!
And they more fond, that credit to thee give!
Not this the worke of womans hand ywis,
That so deepe wound through these deare members drive.
I feared love: but they that love doe live,
But they that dye doe nether love nor hate.
Nath'lesse to thee thy folly I forgive,
And to my selfe and to accursed fate
The guilt I doe ascribe: deare wisedom bought too late.

XXXVIII

'O what availes it of immortall seed
To beene ybredd and never borne to dye?
Farre better I it deeme to die with speed,
Then waste in woe and waylfull miserye.
Who dyes the utmost dolor doth abye,
But who that lives is lefte to waile his losse:
So life is losse, and death felicity:
Sad life worse then glad death: and greater crosse
To see frends grave, then dead the grave self to engrosse.

XXXIX

'But if the heavens did his dayes envie,
And my short blis maligne, yet mote they well
Thus much afford me, ere that he did die,
That the dim eies of my deare Marinell
I mote have closed, and him bed farewell,
Sith other offices for mother meet
They would not graunt ——
Yett, maulgre them, farewell, my sweetest sweet!
Farewell, my sweetest sonne, sith we no more shall meet!'

XL

Thus when they all had sorowed their fill,
They softly gan to search his griesly wownd:
And that they might him handle more at will,
They him disarmd, and spredding on the grownd
Their watchet mantles frindgd with silver rownd,
They softly wipt away the gelly blood
From th' orifice; which having well upbownd,
They pourd in soveraine balme and nectar good,
Good both for erthly med'cine and for hevenly food.

XLI

Tho, when the lilly handed Liagore
(This Liagore whilome had learned skill
In leaches craft, by great Appolloes lore,
Sith her whilome upon high Pindus hill
He loved, and at last her wombe did fill
With hevenly seed, whereof wise Pæon sprong)
Did feele his pulse, shee knew there staied still
Some litle life his feeble sprites emong;
Which to his mother told, despeyre she from her flong.

XLII

Tho up him taking in their tender hands,
They easely unto her charett beare:
Her teme at her commaundement quiet stands,
Whiles they the corse into her wagon reare,
And strowe with flowres the lamentable beare:
Then all the rest into their coches clim,
And through the brackish waves their passage shear;
Upon great Neptunes necke they softly swim,
And to her watry chamber swiftly carry him.

XLIII

Deepe in the bottome of the sea, her bowre
Is built of hollow billowes heaped hye,
Like to thicke clouds that threat a stormy showre,
And vauted all within, like to the skye,

In which the gods doe dwell eternally:
There they him laide in easy couch well
    dight,
And sent in haste for Tryphon, to apply
Salves to his wounds, and medicines of
    might:
For Tryphon of sea gods the soveraine
    leach is hight.

XLIV

The whiles the nymphes sitt all about him
    rownd,
Lamenting his mishap and heavy plight;
And ofte his mother, vewing his wide
    wownd,
Cursed the hand that did so deadly smight
Her dearest sonne, her dearest harts de-
    light.
But none of all those curses overtooke
The warlike maide, th' ensample of that
    might;
But fairely well shee thryvd, and well did
    brooke
Her noble deeds, ne her right course for
    ought forsooke.

XLV

Yet did false Archimage her still pursew,
To bring to passe his mischievous intent,
Now that he had her singled from the crew
Of courteous knights, the Prince and Fary
    gent,
Whom late in chace of beauty excellent
Shee lefte, pursewing that same foster
    strong;
Of whose fowle outrage they impatient,
And full of firy zele, him followed long,
To reskew her from shame, and to revenge
    her wrong.

XLVI

Through thick and thin, through mountains
    and through playns,
Those two gret champions did attonce pur-
    sew
The fearefull damzell, with incessant payns:
Who from them fled, as light-foot hare from
    vew
Of hunter swifte and sent of howndes trew.
At last they came unto a double way,
Where, doubtfull which to take, her to res-
    kew,
Themselves they did dispart, each to assay
Whether more happy were to win so goodly
    pray.

XLVII

But Timias, the Princes gentle squyre,
That ladies love unto his lord forlent,
And with proud envy and indignant yre
After that wicked foster fiercely went.
So beene they three three sondry wayes
    ybent:
But fayrest fortune to the Prince befell;
Whose chaunce it was, that soone he did
    repent,
To take that way in which that damozell
Was fledd afore, affraid of him as feend
    of hell.

XLVIII

At last of her far of he gained vew:
Then gan he freshly pricke his fomy steed,
And ever as he nigher to her drew,
So evermore he did increase his speed,
And of each turning still kept wary heed:
Alowd to her he oftentimes did call,
To doe away vaine doubt and needlesse
    dreed:
Full myld to her he spake, and oft let
    fall
Many meeke wordes, to stay and comfort
    her withall.

XLIX

But nothing might relent her hasty flight;
So deepe the deadly feare of that foule
    swaine
Was earst impressed in her gentle spright:
Like as a fearefull dove, which through the
    raine
Of the wide ayre her way does cut amaine,
Having farre off espyde a tassell gent,
Which after her his nimble winges doth
    straine,
Doubleth her hast for feare to bee for-
    hent,
And with her pineons cleaves the liquid
    firmament.

L

With no lesse hast, and eke with no lesse
    dreed,
That fearefull ladie fledd from him that
    ment
To her no evill thought nor evill deed;
Yet former feare of being fowly shent
Carried her forward with her first intent:
And though, oft looking backward, well
    she vewde
Her selfe freed from that foster insolent,

And that it was a knight which now her
sewde,
Yet she no lesse the knight feard then that
villein rude.

LI

His uncouth shield and straunge armes her
dismayd,
Whose like in Faery Lond were seldom
seene,
That fast she from him fledd, no lesse afrayd
Then of wilde beastes if she had chased
beene:
Yet he her followd still with corage keene,
So long that now the golden Hesperus
Was mounted high in top of heaven sheene,
And warnd his other brethren joyeous
To light their blessed lamps in Joves eter-
nall hous.

I I I

All suddeinly dim wox the dampish ayre,
And griesly shadowes covered heaven bright,
That now with thousand starres was decked
fayre;
Which when the Prince beheld, a lothfull
sight,
And that perforce, for want of lenger light,
He mote surceasse his suit, and lose the
hope
Of his long labour, he gan fowly wyte
His wicked fortune, that had turnd aslope,
And cursed Night, that reft from him so
goodly scope.

LIII

Tho, when her wayes he could no more de-
scry,
But to and fro at disaventure strayd,
Like as a ship, whose lodestar suddeinly
Covered with cloudes her pilott hath dis-
mayd,
His wearisome pursuit perforce he stayd,
And from his loftie steed dismounting low,
Did let him forage. Downe himselfe he
layd
Upon the grassy ground, to sleepe a throw;
The cold earth was his couch, the hard
steele his pillow.

LIV

But gentle Sleepe envyde him any rest;
In stead thereof sad sorow and disdaine
Of his hard hap did vexe his noble brest,
And thousand fancies bett his ydle brayne

With their light wings, the sights of sem-
blants vaine;
Oft did he wish that lady faire mote bee
His Faery Queene, for whom he did com-
plaine;
Or that his Faery Queene were such as
shee;
And ever hasty Night he blamed bitterlie.

LV

'Night, thou foule mother of annoyaunce
sad,
Sister of heavie Death, and nourse of Woe,
Which wast begot in heaven, but for thy
bad
And brutish shape thrust downe to hell be-
low,
Where by the grim floud of Cocytus slow
Thy dwelling is, in Herebus black hous,
(Black Herebus, thy husband, is the foe
Of all the gods) where thou ungratious
Halfe of thy dayes doest lead in horrour
hideous:

LVI

'What had th' Eternall Maker need of thee,
The world in his continuall course to keepe,
That doest all thinges deface, ne lettest see
The beautie of his worke? Indeed, in
sleepe
The slouthfull body that doth love to steep
His lustlesse limbes, and drowne his baser
mind,
Doth praise thee oft, and oft from Stygian
deepe
Calles thee, his goddesse in his errour blind,
And great Dame Natures handmaide chear-
ing every kind.

LVII

'But well I wote, that to an heavy hart
Thou art the roote and nourse of bitter
cares,
Breeder of new, renewer of old smarts:
In stead of rest thou lendest rayling teares,
In stead of sleepe thou sendest troublous
feares
And dreadfull visions, in the which alive
The dreary image of sad death appeares:
So from the wearie spirit thou doest drive
Desired rest, and men of happinesse deprive.

LVIII

'Under thy mantle black there hidden lye
Light-shonning thefte, and traiterous intent,

Abhorred bloodshed, and vile felony,
Shamefull deceipt, and daunger imminent,
Fowle horror, and eke hellish dreriment:
All these, I wote, in thy protection bee,
And light doe shonne, for feare of being
    shent:
For light ylike is loth'd of them and thee,
And all that lewdnesse love doe hate the
    light to see.

LIX

' For Day discovers all dishonest wayes,
And sheweth each thing as it is in deed:
The prayses of High God he faire dis-
    playes,
And His large bountie rightly doth areed.
Dayes dearest children be the blessed seed
Which Darknesse shall subdue and heaven
    win:
Truth is his daughter; he her first did
    breed,
Most sacred virgin, without spot of sinne.
Our life is day, but death with darknesse
    doth begin.

LX

' O when will Day then turne to me againe,
And bring with him his long expected light ?
O Titan, hast to reare thy joyous waine:
Speed thee to spred abroad thy beames
    bright,
And chace away this too long lingring
    Night;
Chace her away, from whence she came, to
    hell:
She, she it is, that hath me done despight:
There let her with the damned spirits dwell,
And yield her rowme to Day, that can it
    governe well.'

LXI

Thus did the Prince that wearie night out-
    weare
In restlesse anguish and unquiet paine;
And earely, ere the Morrow did upreare
His deawy head out of the ocean maine,
He up arose, as halfe in great disdaine,
And clombe unto his steed. So forth he
    went,
With heavy looke and lumpish pace, that
    plaine
In him bewraid great grudge and mal-
    talent:
His steed eke seemd t' apply his steps to
    his intent.

CANTO V

Prince Arthur heares of Florimell:
    Three fosters Timias wound ;
Belphebe findes him almost dead,
    And reareth out of sownd.

I

WONDER it is to see in diverse mindes
How diversly Love doth his pageaunts play,
And shewes his powre in variable kindes:
The baser wit, whose ydle thoughts alway
Are wont to cleave unto the lowly clay,
It stirreth up to sensuall desire,
And in lewd slouth to wast his carelesse
    day:
But in brave sprite it kindles goodly fire,
That to all high desert and honour doth
    aspire.

II

Ne suffereth it uncomely idlenesse
In his free thought to build her sluggish
    nest;
Ne suffereth it thought of ungentlenesse
Ever to creepe into his noble brest;
But to the highest and the worthiest
Lifteth it up, that els would lowly fall:
It lettes not fall, it lettes it not to rest:
It lettes not scarse this Prince to breath at
    all,
But to his first poursuit him forward still
    doth call.

III

Who long time wandred through the forest
    wyde,
To finde some issue thence, till that at last
He met a dwarfe, that seemed terrifyde
With some late perill, which he hardly past,
Or other accident which him aghast;
Of whom he asked, whence he lately came,
And whether now he traveiled so fast:
For sore he swat, and ronning through that
    same
Thicke forest, was bescracht, and both his
    feet nigh lame.

IV

Panting for breath, and almost out of hart,
The dwarfe him answerd: 'Sir, ill mote I
    stay
To tell the same. I lately did depart
From Faery court, where I have many a
    day
Served a gentle lady of great sway

And high accompt through out all Elfin
    Land,
Who lately left the same, and tooke this
    way:
Her now I seeke, and if ye understand
Which way she fared hath, good sir, tell
    out of hand.'

V

' What mister wight,' saide he, ' and how
    arayd ? '
' Royally clad,' quoth he, ' in cloth of gold,
As meetest may beseeme a noble mayd;
Her faire lockes in rich circlet be enrold,
A fayrer wight did never sunne behold;
And on a palfrey rydes more white then
    snow,
Yet she her selfe is whiter manifold:
The surest signe, whereby ye may her
    know,
Is, that she is the fairest wight alive, I trow.'

VI

' Now certes, swaine,' saide he, ' such one,
    I weene,
Fast flying through this forest from her fo,
A foule ill favoured foster, I have seene;
Her selfe, well as I might, I reskewd tho,
But could not stay, so fast she did foregoe,
Carried away with wings of speedy feare.'
' Ah, dearest God ! ' quoth he, ' that is great
    woe,
And wondrous ruth to all that shall it
    heare.
But can ye read, sir, how I may her finde,
    or where ? '

VII

' Perdy, me lever were to weeten that,'
Saide he, ' then ransome of the richest
    knight,
Or all the good that ever yet I gat:
But froward Fortune, and too forward
    Night,
Such happinesse did, maulgre, to me spight,
And fro me reft both life and light attone.
But, dwarfe, aread what is that lady bright,
That through this forrest wandreth thus
    alone;
For of her errour straunge I have great
    ruth and mone.'

VIII

' That ladie is,' quoth he, ' where so she bee,
The bountiest virgin and most debonaire

That ever living eye, I weene, did see;
Lives none this day that may with her com-
    pare
In stedfast chastitie and vertue rare,
The goodly ornaments of beautie bright;
And is ycleped Florimell the Fayre,
Faire Florimell, belov'd of many a knight,
Yet she loves none but one, that Marinell is
    hight.

IX

' A sea-nymphes sonne, that Marinell is
    hight,
Of my deare dame is loved dearely well;
In other none, but him, she sets delight,
All her delight is set on Marinell;
But he sets nought at all by Florimell:
For ladies love his mother long ygoe
Did him, they say, forwarne through sacred
    spell.
But fame now flies, that of a forreine foe
He is yslaine, which is the ground of all
    our woe.

X

' Five daies there be since he (they say)
    was slaine,
And fowre, since Florimell the court for-
    went,
And vowed never to returne againe,
Till him alive or dead she did invent.
Therefore, faire sir, for love of knighthood
    gent
And honour of trew ladies, if ye may
By your good counsell, or bold hardi-
    ment,
Or succour her, or me direct the way,
Do one or other good, I you most humbly
    pray.

XI

' So may ye gaine to you full great re-
    nowme
Of all good ladies through the world so
    wide,
And haply in her hart finde highest rowme,
Of whom ye seeke to be most magnifide:
At least eternall meede shall you abide.'
To whom the Prince: ' Dwarfe, comfort to
    thee take:
For till thou tidings learne, what her be-
    tide,
I here avow thee never to forsake.
Ill weares he armes, that nill them use for
    ladies sake.'

XII

So with the dwarfe he backe retourn'd
 againe,
To seeke his lady, where he mote her
 finde;
But by the way he greatly gan complaine
The want of his good squire, late left be-
 hinde,
For whom he wondrous pensive grew in
 minde,
For doubt of daunger, which mote him be-
 tide;
For him he loved above all mankinde,
Having him trew and faithfull ever tride,
And bold, as ever squyre that waited by
 knights side.

XIII

Who all this while full hardly was assayd
Of deadly daunger, which to him betidd;
For whiles his lord pursewd that noble
 mayd,
After that foster fowle he fiercely ridd,
To bene avenged of the shame he did
To that faire damzell. Him he chaced
 long
Through the thicke woods, wherein he would
 have hid
His shamefull head from his avengement
 strong,
And oft him threatned death for his outra-
 geous wrong.

XIV

Nathlesse the villein sped himselfe so well,
Whether through swiftnesse of his speedie
 beast,
Or knowledge of those woods, where he did
 dwell,
That shortly he from daunger was releast,
And out of sight escaped at the least;
Yet not escaped from the dew reward
Of his bad deedes, which daily he increast,
Ne ceased not, till him oppressed hard
The heavie plague that for such leachours
 is prepard.

XV

For soone as he was vanisht out of sight,
His coward courage gan emboldned bee,
And cast t' avenge him of that fowle de-
 spight,
Which he had borne of his bold enimee.
Tho to his brethren came; for they were
 three

Ungratious children of one gracelesse syre;
And unto them complayned how that he
Had used beene of that foolehardie squyre:
So them with bitter words he stird to
 bloodie yre.

XVI

Forthwith themselves with their sad instru-
 ments
Of spoyle and murder they gan arme by-
 live,
And with him foorth into the forrest went,
To wreake the wrath, which he did earst
 revive
In their sterne brests, on him which late
 did drive
Their brother to reproch and shamefull
 flight:
For they had vow'd, that never he alive
Out of that forest should escape their
 might;
Vile rancour their rude harts had fild with
 such despight.

XVII

Within that wood there was a covert glade,
Foreby a narrow foord, to them well knowne,
Through which it was uneath for wight to
 wade,
And now by fortune it was overflowne:
By that same way they knew that squyre
 unknowne
Mote algates passe; forthy themselves they
 set
There in await, with thicke woods over
 growne,
And all the while their malice they did
 whet
With cruell threats, his passage through
 the ford to let.

XVIII

It fortuned, as they devized had,
The gentle squyre came ryding that same
 way,
Unweeting of their wile and treason bad,
And through the ford to passen did as-
 say;
But that fierce foster, which late fled away,
Stoutly foorth stepping on the further
 shore,
Him boldly bad his passage there to stay,
Till he had made amends, and full restore
For all the damage which he had him doen
 afore.

XIX

With that, at him a quiv'ring dart he threw,
With so fell force and villeinous despite,
That through his haberjeon the forkehead
    flew,
And through the linked mayles empierced
    quite,
But had no powre in his soft flesh to bite:
That stroke the hardy squire did sore dis-
    please,
But more that him he could not come to
    smite;
For by no meanes the high banke he could
    sease,
But labour'd long in that deepe ford with
    vaine disease.

XX

And still the foster with his long bore-
    speare
Him kept from landing at his wished will.
Anone one sent out of the thicket neare
A cruell shaft, headed with deadly ill,
And fethered with an unlucky quill:
The wicked steele stayd not, till it did light
In his left thigh, and deepely did it thrill:
Exceeding griefe that wound in him em-
    pight,
But more that with his foes he could not
    come to fight.

XXI

At last, through wrath and vengeaunce
    making way,
He on the bancke arryvd with mickle payne,
Where the third brother him did sore as-
    say,
And drove at him with all his might and
    mayne
A forest bill, which both his hands did
    strayne;
But warily he did avoide the blow,
And with his speare requited him agayne,
That both his sides were thrilled with the
    throw,
And a large streame of blood out of the
    wound did flow.

XXII

He, tombling downe, with gnashing teeth
    did bite
The bitter earth, and bad to lett him in
Into the balefull house of endlesse night,
Where wicked ghosts doe waile their for-
    mer sin.

Tho gan the battaile freshly to begin;
For nathemore for that spectacle bad
Did th' other two their cruell vengeaunce
    blin,
But both attonce on both sides him bestad,
And load upon him layd, his life for to
    have had.

XXIII

Tho when that villayn he aviz'd, which late
Affrighted had the fairest Florimell,
Full of fiers fury and indignant hate,
To him he turned, and with rigor fell
Smote him so rudely on the pannikell,
That to the chin he clefte his head in
    twaine:
Downe on the ground his carkas groveling
    fell;
His sinfull sowle, with desperate disdaine,
Out of her fleshly ferme fled to the place
    of paine.

XXIV

That seeing now the only last of three,
Who with that wicked shafte him wounded
    had,
Trembling with horror, as that did foresee
The fearefull end of his avengement sad,
Through which he follow should his breth-
    ren bad,
His bootelesse bow in feeble hand upcaught,
And therewith shott an arrow at the lad;
Which, fayntly fluttring, scarce his helmet
    raught,
And glauncing fel to ground, but him an-
    noyed naught.

XXV

With that he would have fled into the wood;
But Timias him lightly overhent,
Right as he entring was into the flood,
And strooke at him with force so violent,
That headlesse him into the foord he sent;
The carcas with the streame was carried
    downe,
But th' head fell backeward on the contin-
    ent.
So mischief fel upon the meaners crowne;
They three be dead with shame, the squire
    lives with renowne.

XXVI

He lives, but takes small joy of his re-
    nowne;
For of that cruell wound he bled so sore,

That from his steed he fell in deadly
　　swowne;
Yet still the blood forth gusht in so great
　　store,
That he lay wallowd all in his owne gore.
Now God thee keepe, thou gentlest squire
　　alive,
Els shall thy loving lord thee see no more,
But both of comfort him thou shalt de-
　　prive,
And eke thy selfe of honor, which thou
　　didst atchive.

XXVII

Providence hevenly passeth living thought,
And doth for wretched mens reliefe make
　　way;
For loe ! great grace or fortune thether
　　brought
Comfort to him that comfortlesse now
　　lay.
In those same woods, ye well remember
　　may
How that a noble hunteresse did wonne,
Shee that base Braggadochio did affray,
And made him fast out of the forest ronne;
Belphœbe was her name, as faire as Phœ-
　　bus sunne.

XXVIII

She on a day, as shee pursewd the chace
Of some wilde beast, which with her arrowes
　　keene
She wounded had, the same along did
　　trace
By tract of blood, which she had freshly
　　seene
To have besprinckled all the grassy greene;
By the great persue, which she there per-
　　ceav'd,
Well hoped shee the beast engor'd had
　　beene,
And made more haste, the life to have be-
　　reav'd:
But ah ! her expectation greatly was de-
　　ceav'd.

XXIX

Shortly she came whereas that woefull
　　squire,
With blood deformed, lay in deadly
　　swownd:
In whose faire eyes, like lamps of quenched
　　fire,
The christall humor stood congealed rownd;

His locks, like faded leaves fallen to
　　grownd,
Knotted with blood in bounches rudely ran;
And his sweete lips, on which before that
　　stownd
The bud of youth to blossome faire began,
Spoild of their rosy red, were woxen pale
　　and wan.

XXX

Saw never living eie more heavy sight,
That could have made a rocke of stone to
　　rew,
Or rive in twaine: which when that lady
　　bright,
Besides all hope, with melting eies did
　　vew,
All suddeinly abasht shee chaunged hew,
And with sterne horror backward gan to
　　start:
But when shee better him beheld, shee grew
Full of soft passion and unwonted smart:
The point of pitty perced through her ten-
　　der hart.

XXXI

Meekely shee bowed downe, to weete if
　　life
Yett in his frosen members did remaine;
And feeling by his pulses beating rife
That the weake sowle her seat did yett re-
　　taine,
She cast to comfort him with busy paine:
His double folded necke she reard upright,
And rubd his temples and each trembling
　　vaine;
His mayled haberjeon she did undight,
And from his head his heavy burganet did
　　light.

XXXII

Into the woods thenceforth in haste shee
　　went,
To seeke for hearbes that mote him rem-
　　edy;
For shee of herbes had great intendiment,
Taught of the nymphe, which from her in-
　　fancy
Her nourced had in trew nobility:
There, whether yt divine tobacco were,
Or panachæa, or polygony,
Shee fownd, and brought it to her patient
　　deare,
Who al this while lay bleding out his hart-
　　blood neare.

XXXIII

The soveraine weede betwixt two marbles
plaine
Shee pownded small, and did in peeces
bruze,
And then atweene her lilly handes twaine
Into his wound the juice thereof did scruze,
And round about, as she could well it uze,
The flesh therewith shee suppled and did
steepe,
T' abate all spasme and soke the swelling
bruze,
And after having searcht the intuse deepe,
She with her scarf did bind the wound from
cold to keepe.

XXXIV

By this he had sweet life recur'd agayne,
And, groning inly deepe, at last his eies,
His watry eies, drizling like deawy rayne,
He up gan lifte toward the azure skies,
From whence descend all hopelesse reme-
dies :
Therewith he sigh'd, and turning him aside,
The goodly maide ful of divinities
And gifts of heavenly grace he by him spide,
Her bow and gilden quiver lying him be-
side.

XXXV

'Mercy! deare Lord,' said he, 'what grace
is this,
That thou hast shewed to me, sinfull wight,
To send thine angell from her bowre of
blis,
To comfort me in my distressed plight ?
Angell, or goddesse doe I call thee right ?
What service may I doe unto thee meete,
That hast from darkenes me returnd to
light,
And with thy hevenly salves and med'cines
sweete
Hast drest my sinfull wounds ? I kisse thy
blessed feete.

XXXVI

Thereat she blushing said: 'Ah ! gentle
squire,
Nor goddesse I, nor angell, but the mayd
And daughter of a woody nymphe, desire
No service but thy safety and ayd;
Which if thou gaine, I shalbe well apayd.
Wee mortall wights, whose lives and for-
tunes bee
To commun accidents stil open layd,

Are bownd with commun bond of fraïltee,
To succor wretched wights, whom we captived see.'

XXXVII

By this her damzells, which the former
chace
Had undertaken after her, arryv'd,
As did Belphœbe, in the bloody place,
And thereby deemd the beast had bene de-
priv'd
Of life, whom late their ladies arrow ryv'd:
Forthy the bloody tract they followd fast,
And every one to ronne the swiftest stryv'd;
But two of them the rest far overpast,
And where their lady was arrived at the
last.

XXXVIII

Where when they saw that goodly boy, with
blood
Defowled, and their lady dresse his wownd,
They wondred much, and shortly under-
stood
How him in deadly case theyr lady fownd,
And reskewed out of the heavy stownd.
Eftsoones his warlike courser, which was
strayd
Farre in the woodes, whiles that he lay in
swownd,
She made those damzels search, which be-
ing stayd,
They did him set theron, and forth with
them convayd.

XXXIX

Into that forest farre they thence him
led,
Where was their dwelling, in a pleasant
glade
With mountaines rownd about environed,
And mightie woodes, which did the valley
shade,
And like a stately theatre it made,
Spreading it selfe into a spatious plaine;
And in the midst a little river plaide
Emongst the pumy stones, which seemd to
plaine
With gentle murmure that his cours they
did restraine.

XL

Beside the same a dainty place there lay,
Planted with mirtle trees and laurells
greene,

In which the birds song many a lovely lay
Of Gods high praise, and of their loves
    sweet teene,
As it an earthly paradize had beene:
In whose enclosed shadow there was pight
A faire pavilion, scarcely to be seene,
The which was al within most richly dight,
That greatest princes living it mote well
    delight.

XLI

Thether they brought that wounded squyre,
    and layd
In easie couch his feeble limbes to rest.
He rested him a while, and then the mayd
His readie wound with better salves new
    drest:
Daily she dressed him, and did the best,
His grievous hurt to guarish, that she might,
That shortly she his dolour hath redrest,
And his foule sore reduced to faire plight:
It she reduced, but himselfe destroyed
    quight.

XLII

O foolish physick, and unfruitfull paine,
That heales up one and makes another
    wound !
She his hurt thigh to him recurd againe
But hurt his hart, the which before was
    sound,
Through an unwary dart, which did rebownd
From her faire eyes and gratious counten-
    aunce.
What bootes it him from death to be un-
    bownd,
To be captived in endlesse duraunce
Of sorrow and despeyre without alegge-
    aunce ?

XLIII

Still as his wound did gather, and grow
    hole,
So still his hart woxe sore, and health de-
    cayd:
Madnesse to save a part, and lose the whole !
Still whenas he beheld the heavenly mayd,
Whiles dayly playsters to his wownd she
    layd,
So still his malady the more increast,
The whiles her matchlesse beautie him dis-
    mayd.
Ah God ! what other could he doe at least,
But love so fayre a lady, that his life re-
    least ?

XLIV

Long while he strove in his corageous brest,
With reason dew the passion to subdew,
And love for to dislodge out of his nest:
Still when her excellencies he did vew,
Her soveraine bountie and celestiall hew,
The same to love he strongly was con-
    straynd:
But when his meane estate he did revew,
He from such hardy boldnesse was re-
    straynd,
And of his lucklesse lott and cruell love
    thus playnd.

XLV

'Unthankfull wretch,' said he, ' is this the
    meed,
With which her soverain mercy thou doest
    quight?
Thy life she saved by her gratious deed,
But thou doest weene with villeinous de-
    spight
To blott her honour and her heavenly light.
Dye rather, dye, then so disloyally
Deeme of her high desert, or seeme so
    light:
Fayre death it is, to shonne more shame,
    to dy:
Dye rather, dy, then ever love disloyally.

XLVI

' But if to love disloyalty it bee,
Shall I then hate her, that from deathes
    dore
Me brought? ah! farre be such reproch fro
    mee!
What can I lesse doe, then her love there-
    fore,
Sith I her dew reward cannot restore?
Dye rather, dye, and dying doe her serve,
Dying her serve, and living her adore;
Thy life she gave, thy life she doth de-
    serve:
Dye rather, dye, then ever from her service
    swerve.

XLVII

' But, foolish boy, what bootes thy service
    bace
To her, to whom the hevens doe serve and
    sew ?
Thou a meane squyre, of meeke and lowly
    place,
She hevenly borne, and of celestiall hew.
How then ? of all Love taketh equall vew:

And doth not Highest God vouchsafe to
take
The love and service of the basest crew?
If she will not, dye meekly for her sake:
Dye rather, dye, then ever so faire love
forsake.'

XLVIII

Thus warreid he long time against his will,
Till that through weaknesse he was forst
at last
To yield himselfe unto the mightie ill:
Which, as a victour proud, gan ransack fast
His inward partes, and all his entrayles
wast,
That neither blood in face nor life in hart
It left, but both did quite drye up and
blast;
As percing levin, which the inner part
Of every thing consumes and calcineth by
art.

XLIX

Which seeing fayre Belphoebe, gan to feare
Least that his wound were inly well not
heald,
Or that the wicked steele empoysned were:
Litle shee weend that love he close con-
ceald:
Yet still he wasted, as the snow congeald,
When the bright sunne his beames theron
doth beat;
Yet never he his hart to her reveald,
But rather chose to dye for sorow great,
Then with dishonorable termes her to en-
treat.

L

She, gracious lady, yet no paines did spare,
To doe him ease, or doe him remedy:
Many restoratives of vertues rare
And costly cordialles she did apply,
To mitigate his stubborne malady:
But that sweet cordiall, which can restore
A love-sick hart, she did to him envy;
To him, and to all th' unworthy world for-
lore,
She did envy that soveraine salve, in secret
store.

LI

That daintie rose, the daughter of her
morne,
More deare then life she tendered, whose
flowre

The girlond of her honour did adorne:
Ne suffred she the middayes scorching
powre,
Ne the sharp northerne wind thereon to
showre,
But lapped up her silken leaves most chayre,
When so the froward skye began to lowre:
But soone as calmed was the christall ayre,
She did it fayre dispred, and let to florish
fayre.

LII

Eternall God, in his almightie powre,
To make ensample of his heavenly grace,
In paradize whylome did plant this flowre;
Whence he it fetcht out of her native place,
And did in stocke of earthly flesh enrace,
That mortall men her glory should admyre.
In gentle ladies breste and bounteous race
Of woman kind it fayrest flowre doth spyre,
And beareth fruit of honour and all chast
desyre.

LIII

Fayre ympes of beautie, whose bright
shining beames
Adorne the world with like to heavenly
light,
And to your willes both royalties and
reames
Subdew, through conquest of your wondrous might,
With this fayre flowre your goodly girlonds
dight
Of chastity and vertue virginall,
That shall embellish more your beautie
bright,
And crowne your heades with heavenly
coronall,
Such as the angels weare before Gods tri-
bunall.

LIV

To youre faire selves a faire ensample
frame
Of this faire virgin, this Belphebe fayre,
To whom, in perfect love and spotlesse fame
Of chastitie, none living may compayre:
Ne poysnous envy justly can empayre
The prayse of her fresh flowring mayden-
head;
Forthy she standeth on the highest stayre
Of th' honorable stage of womanhead,
That ladies all may follow her ensample
dead.

LV

In so great prayse of stedfast chastity
Nathlesse she was so courteous and kynde,
Tempred with grace and goodly modesty,
That seemed those two vertues strove to
    fynd
The higher place in her heroick mynd:
So striving each did other more augment,
And both encreast the prayse of woman
    kynde,
And both encreast her beautie excellent;
So all did make in her a perfect comple-
    ment.

CANTO VI

The birth of fayre Belphoebe and
Of Amorett is told :
The Gardins of Adonis fraught
With pleasures manifold.

I

WELL may I weene, faire ladies, all this
    while
Ye wonder how this noble damozell
So great perfections did in her compile,
Sith that in salvage forests she did dwell,
So farre from court and royall citadell,
The great schoolmaistresse of all courtesy:
Seemeth that such wilde woodes should far
    expell
All civile usage and gentility,
And gentle sprite deforme with rude rus-
    ticity.

II

But to this faire Belphœbe in her berth
The hevens so favorable were and free,
Looking with myld aspect upon the earth
In th' horoscope of her nativitee,
That all the gifts of grace and chastitee
On her they poured forth of plenteous horne;
Jove laught on Venus from his soverayne
    see,
And Phœbus with faire beames did her
    adorne,
And all the Graces rockt her cradle being
    borne.

III

Her berth was of the wombe of morning
    dew,
And her conception of the joyous prime,
And all her whole creation did her shew
Pure and unspotted from all loathly crime,
That is ingenerate in fleshly slime.
So was this virgin borne, so was she bred,
So was she trayned up from time to time
In all chaste vertue and true bounti-hed,
Till to her dew perfection she was ripened

IV

Her mother was the faire Chrysogonee,
The daughter of Amphisa, who by race
A Faerie was, yborne of high degree:
She bore Belphæbe, she bore in like cace
Fayre Amoretta in the second place:
These two were twinnes, and twixt them
    two did share
The heritage of all celestiall grace;
That all the rest it seemd they robbed bare
Of bounty, and of beautie, and all vertues
    rare.

V

It were a goodly storie to declare
By what straunge accident faire Chrysogone
Conceiv'd these infants, and how them she
    bare,
In this wilde forrest wandring all alone,
After she had nine moneths fulfild and
    gone:
For not as other wemens commune brood
They were enwombed in the sacred throne
Of her chaste bodie, nor with commune
    food,
As other wemens babes, they sucked vitall
    blood.

VI

But wondrously they were begot and bred,
Through influence of th' hevens fruitfull
    ray,
As it in antique bookes is mentioned.
It was upon a sommers shinie day,
When Titan faire his beames did display,
In a fresh fountaine, far from all mens vew,
She bath'd her brest, the boyling heat t'
    allay;
She bath'd with roses red and violets blew,
And all the sweetest flowres that in the
    forrest grew:

VII

Till, faint through yrkesome wearines,
    adowne
Upon the grassy ground her selfe she layd
To sleepe, the whiles a gentle slombring
    swowne
Upon her fell all naked bare displayd:

The sunbeames bright upon her body
    playd,
Being through former bathing mollifide,
And pierst into her wombe, where they
    embayd
With so sweet sence and secret power un-
    spide,
That in her pregnant flesh they shortly
    fructifide.

VIII

Miraculous may seeme to him that reades
So straunge ensample of conception;
But reason teacheth that the fruitfull
    seades
Of all things living, through impression
Of the sunbeames in moyst complexion,
Doe life conceive and quickned are by
    kynd:
So, after Nilus inundation,
Infinite shapes of creatures men doe fynd,
Informed in the mud, on which the sunne
    hath shynd.

IX

Great father he of generation
Is rightly cald, th' authour of life and
    light;
And his faire sister for creation
Ministreth matter fit, which, tempred right
With heate and humour, breedes the living
    wight.
So sprong these twinnes in womb of Chryso-
    gone;
Yet wist she nought thereof, but, sore af-
    fright,
Wondred to see her belly so upblone,
Which still increast, till she her terme had
    full outgone.

X

Whereof conceiving shame and foule dis-
    grace,
Albe her guiltlesse conscience her cleard,
She fled into the wildernesse a space,
Till that unweeldy burden she had reard,
And shund dishonor, which as death she
    feard:
Where, wearie of long traveill, downe to
    rest
Her selfe she set, and comfortably cheard;
There a sad cloud of sleepe her over-
    kest,
And seized every sence with sorrow sore
    opprest.

XI

It fortuned, faire Venus having lost
Her little sonne, the winged God of Love,
Who for some light displeasure, which him
    crost,
Was from her fled, as flit as ayery dove,
And left her blisfull bowre of joy above;
(So from her often he had fled away,
When she for ought him sharpely did re-
    prove,
And wandred in the world in straunge aray,
Disguiz'd in thousand shapes, that none
    might him bewray;)

XII

Him for to seeke, she left her heavenly
    hous,
The house of goodly formes and faire
    aspects,
Whence all the world derives the glorious
Features of beautie, and all shapes select,
With which High God his workmanship
    hath deckt;
And searched everie way through which his
    wings
Had borne him, or his tract she mote de-
    tect:
She promist kisses sweet, and sweeter
    things,
Unto the man that of him tydings to her
    brings.

XIII

First she him sought in court, where most
    he us'd
Whylome to haunt, but there she found him
    not;
But many there she found, which sore ac-
    cus'd
His falshood, and with fowle infamous blot
His cruell deedes and wicked wyles did
    spot:
Ladies and lordes she every where mote
    heare
Complayning, how with his empoysned
    shot
Their wofull harts he wounded had whyl-
    eare,
And so had left them languishing twixt
    hope and feare.

XIV

She then the cities sought from gate to
    gate,
And everie one did aske, did he him see?

And everie one her answerd, that too late
He had him seene, and felt the crueltee
Of his sharpe dartes and whot artilleree;
And every one threw forth reproches rife
Of his mischievous deedes, and sayd that
hee
Was the disturber of all civill life,
The enimy of peace, and authour of all
strife.

XV

Then in the countrey she abroad him
sought,
And in the rurall cottages inquir'd,
Where also many plaintes to her were
brought,
How he their heedelesse harts with love
had fir'd,
And his false venim through their veines
inspir'd;
And eke the gentle shepheard swaynes,
which sat
Keeping their fleecy flockes, as they were
hyr'd,
She sweetly heard complaine both how and
what
Her sonne had to them doen; yet she did
smile thereat.

XVI

But when in none of all these she him got,
She gan avize where els he mote him hyde:
At last she her bethought, that she had
not
Yet sought the salvage woods and forests
wyde,
In which full many lovely nymphes abyde,
Mongst whom might be that he did closely
lye,
Or that the love of some of them him
tyde:
Forthy she thether cast her course t' apply,
To search the secret haunts of Dianes com-
pany.

XVII

Shortly unto the wastefull woods she came,
Whereas she found the goddesse with her
crew,
After late chace of their embrewed game,
Sitting beside a fountaine in a rew;
Some of them washing with the liquid dew
From of their dainty limbs the dusty sweat
And soyle, which did deforme their lively
hew;

Others lay shaded from the scorching heat;
The rest upon her person gave attendance
great.

XVIII

She, having hong upon a bough on high
Her bow and painted quiver, had unlaste
Her silver buskins from her nimble thigh,
And her lanck loynes ungirt, and brests un-
braste,
After her heat the breathing cold to taste;
Her golden lockes, that late in tresses
bright
Embreaded were for hindring of her haste,
Now loose about her shoulders hong un-
dight,
And were with sweet ambrosia all be-
sprinckled light.

XIX

Soone as she Venus saw behinde her backe,
She was asham'd to be so loose surpriz'd,
And woxe halfe wroth against her damzels
slacke,
That had not her thereof before aviz'd,
But suffred her so carelesly disguiz'd
Be overtaken.   Soone her garments loose
Upgath'ring, in her bosome she compriz'd,
Well as she might, and to the goddesse
rose,
Whiles all her nymphes did like a girlond
her enclose.

XX

Goodly she gan faire Cytherea greet,
And shortly asked her, what cause her
brought
Into that wildernesse for her unmeet,
From her sweete bowres, and beds with
pleasures fraught:
That suddein chaung she straung adven-
ture thought.
To whom halfe weeping she thus answered:
That she her dearest sonne Cupido sought,
Who in his frowardnes from her was fled;
That she repented sore to have him angered.

XXI

Thereat Diana gan to smile, in scorne
Of her vaine playnt, and to her scoffing
sayd:
'Great pitty sure that ye be so forlorne
Of your gay sonne, that gives ye so good
ayd
To your disports: ill mote ye bene apayd!'

But she was more engrieved, and replide:
' Faire sister, ill beseemes it to upbrayd
A dolefull heart with so disdainfull pride;
The like that mine, may be your paine an-
    other tide.

XXII

' As you in woods and wanton wildernesse
Your glory sett, to chace the salvage beasts,
So my delight is all in joyfulnesse,
In beds, in bowres, in banckets, and in
    feasts:
And ill becomes you, with your lofty creasts,
To scorne the joy that Jove is glad to seeke;
We both are bownd to follow heavens be-
    heasts,
And tend our charges with obeisaunce
    meeke:
Spare, gentle sister, with reproch my paine
    to eeke.

XXIII

' And tell me if that ye my sonne have heard
To lurke emongst your nimphes in secret
    wize,
Or keepe their cabins: much I am affeard,
Least he like one of them him selfe disguize,
And turne his arrowes to their exercize:
So may he long him selfe full easie hide:
For he is faire, and fresh in face and guize,
As any nimphe (let not it be envide.) '
So saying, every nimph full narrowly shee
    eide.

XXIV

But Phœbe therewith sore was angered,
And sharply saide: ' Goe, dame; goe, seeke
    your boy,
Where you him lately lefte, in Mars his bed:
He comes not here; we scorne his foolish
    joy,
Ne lend we leisure to his idle toy:
But if I catch him in this company,
By Stygian lake I vow, whose sad annoy
The gods doe dread, he dearly shall abye:
Ile clip his wanton wings, that he no more
    shall flye.'

XXV

Whom whenas Venus saw so sore displeasd,
Shee inly sory was, and gan relent
What shee had said: so her she soone ap-
    peasd
With sugred words and gentle blandish-
    ment,

Which as a fountaine from her sweete lips
    went,
And welled goodly forth, that in short space
She was well pleasd, and forth her damzells
    sent
Through all the woods, to search from place
    to place,
If any tract of him or tidings they mote
    trace.

XXVI

To search the God of Love her nimphes she
    sent,
Throughout the wandring forest every
    where:
And after them her selfe eke with her went
To seeke the fugitive both farre and nere.
So long they sought, till they arrived were
In that same shady covert whereas lay
Faire Crysogone in slombry traunce whilere:
Who in her sleepe (a wondrous thing to
    say)
Unwares had borne two babes, as faire as
    springing day.

XXVII

Unwares she them conceivd, unwares she
    bore:
She bore withouten paine that she conceiv'd
Withouten pleasure: ne her need implore
Lucinaes aide: which when they both per-
    ceiv'd,
They were through wonder nigh of sence
    berev'd,
And gazing each on other, nought bespake:
At last they both agreed, her seeming griev'd
Out of her heavie swowne not to awake,
But from her loving side the tender babes
    to take.

XXVIII

Up they them tooke, eachone a babe up-
    tooke,
And with them carried, to be fostered:
Dame Phæbe to a nymphe her babe be-
    tooke,
To be upbrought in perfect maydenhed,
And, of her selfe, her name Belphœbe
    red:
But Venus hers thence far away convayd,
To be upbrought in goodly womanhed,
And in her little Loves stead, which was
    strayd,
Her Amoretta cald, to comfort her dis-
    mayd.

XXIX

Shee brought her to her joyous paradize,
Wher most she wonnes, when she on earth
    does dwell:
So faire a place as Nature can devize:
Whether in Paphos, or Cytheron hill,
Or it in Gnidus bee, I wote not well;
But well I wote by triall, that this same
All other pleasaunt places doth excell,
And called is by her lost lovers name,
The Gardin of Adonis, far renowmd by
    fame.

XXX

.n that same gardin all the goodly flowres,
Wherewith Dame Nature doth her beautify,
And decks the girlonds of her paramoures,
Are fetcht: there is the first seminary
Of all things that are borne to live and
    dye,
According to their kynds. Long worke it
    were,
Here to account the endlesse progeny
Of all the weeds that bud and blossome
    there;
But so much as doth need must needs be
    counted here.

XXXI

It sited was in fruitfull soyle of old,
And girt in with two walls on either side,
The one of yron, the other of bright gold,
That none might thorough breake, nor over-
    stride:
And double gates it had, which opened
    wide,
By which both in and out men moten pas;
Th' one faire and fresh, the other old and
    dride:
Old Genius the porter of them was,
Old Genius, the which a double nature has.

XXXII

He letteth in, he letteth out to wend,
All that to come into the world desire:
A thousand thousand naked babes attend
About him day and night, which doe re-
    quire
That he with fleshly weeds would them
    attire:
Such as him list, such as eternall Fate
Ordained hath, he clothes with sinfull mire,
And sendeth forth to live in mortall state,
Till they agayn returne backe by the hinder
    gate.

XXXIII

After that they againe retourned beene,
They in that gardin planted bee agayne,
And grow afresh, as they had never seene
Fleshly corruption nor mortall payne.
Some thousand yeares so doen they there
    remayne,
And then of him are clad with other hew,
Or sent into the chaungefull world agayne,
Till thether they retourne, where first they
    grew:
So like a wheele arownd they ronne from
    old to new.

XXXIV

Ne needs there gardiner to sett or sow,
To plant or prune: for of their owne ac-
    cord
All things, as they created were, doe grow,
And yet remember well the mighty word,
Which first was spoken by th' Almighty
    Lord,
That bad them to increase and multiply:
Ne doe they need with water of the ford
Or of the clouds to moysten their roots
    dry;
For in themselves eternall moisture they
    imply.

XXXV

Infinite shapes of creatures there are bred,
And uncouth formes, which none yet ever
    knew;
And every sort is in a sondry bed
Sett by it selfe, and ranckt in comely rew:
Some fitt for reasonable sowles t' indew,
Some made for beasts, some made for birds
    to weare,
And all the fruitfull spawne of fishes hew
In endlesse rancks along enraunged were,
That seemd the ocean could not containe
    them there.

XXXVI

Daily they grow, and daily forth are sent
Into the world, it to replenish more;
Yet is the stocke not lessened nor spent,
But still remaines in everlasting store,
As it at first created was of yore:
For in the wide wombe of the world there
    lyes,
In hatefull darknes and in deepe horrore,
An huge eternal chaos, which supplyes
The substaunces of Natures fruitfull pro-
    genyes.

XXXVII

All things from thence doe their first being
    fetch,
And borrow matter whereof they are made,
Which, whenas forme and feature it does
    ketch,
Becomes a body, and doth then invade
The state of life out of the griesly shade.
That substaunce is eterne, and bideth so,
Ne when the life decayes, and forme does
    fade,
Doth it consume and into nothing goe,
But chaunged is, and often altred to and
    froe.

XXXVIII

The substaunce is not chaungd nor altered,
But th' only forme and outward fashion;
For every substaunce is conditioned
To chaunge her hew, and sondry formes to
    don,
Meet for her temper and complexion:
For formes are variable, and decay
By course of kinde and by occasion;
And that faire flowre of beautie fades
    away,
As doth the lilly fresh before the sunny
    ray.

XXXIX

Great enimy to it, and to all the rest,
That in the Gardin of Adonis springs,
Is wicked Tyme, who, with his scyth ad-
    drest,
Does mow the flowring herbes and goodly
    things,
And all their glory to the ground downe
    flings,
Where they do wither and are fowly mard:
He flyes about, and with his flaggy winges
Beates downe both leaves and buds without
    regard,
Ne ever pitty may relent his malice hard.

XL

Yet pitty often did the gods relent,
To see so faire thinges mard and spoiled
    quight:
And their great mother Venus did lament
The losse of her deare brood, her deare de-
    light:
Her hart was pierst with pitty at the sight,
When walking through the gardin them she
    saw,
Yet no'te she find redresse for such despight:

For all that lives is subject to that law:
All things decay in time, and to their end
    doe draw.

XLI

But were it not, that Time their troubler is,
All that in this delightfull gardin growes
Should happy bee, and have immortall blis:
For here all plenty and all pleasure flowes,
And sweete Love gentle fitts emongst them
    throwes,
Without fell rancor or fond gealosy:
Franckly each paramor his leman knowes,
Each bird his mate, ne any does envy
Their goodly meriment and gay felicity.

XLII

There is continuall spring, and harvest
    there
Continuall, both meeting at one tyme:
For both the boughes doe laughing blossoms
    beare,
And with fresh colours decke the wanton
    pryme,
And eke attonce the heavy trees they
    clyme,
Which seeme to labour under their fruites
    lode:
The whiles the joyous birdes make their
    pastyme
Emongst the shady leaves, their sweet
    abode,
And their trew loves without suspition tell
    abrode.

XLIII

Right in the middest of that paradise
There stood a stately mount, on whose
    round top
A gloomy grove of mirtle trees did rise,
Whose shady boughes sharp steele did
    never lop,
Nor wicked beastes their tender buds did
    crop,
But like a girlond compassed the hight,
And from their fruitfull sydes sweet gum
    did drop,
That all the ground, with pretious deaw
    bedight,
Threw forth most dainty odours, and most
    sweet delight.

XLIV

And in the thickest covert of that shade
There was a pleasaunt arber, not by art,

But of the trees owne inclination made,
Which knitting their rancke braunches part
 to part,
With wanton yvie twyne entrayld athwart,
And eglantine and caprifole emong,
Fashiond above within their inmost part,
That nether Phoebus beams could through
 them throng,
Nor Aeolus sharp blast could worke them
 any wrong.

XLV

And all about grew every sort of flowre,
To which sad lovers were transformde of
 yore;
Fresh Hyacinthus, Phœbus paramoure
And dearest love,
Foolish Narcisse, that likes the watry shore,
Sad Amaranthus, made a flowre but late,
Sad Amaranthus, in whose purple gore
Me seemes I see Amintas wretched fate,
To whom sweet poets verse hath given end-
 lesse date.

XLVI

There wont fayre Venus often to enjoy
Her deare Adonis joyous company,
And reape sweet pleasure of the wanton
 boy:
There yet, some say, in secret he does ly,
Lapped in flowres and pretious spycery,
By her hid from the world, and from the
 skill
Of Stygian gods, which doe her love envy;
But she her selfe, when ever that she will,
Possesseth him, and of his sweetnesse takes
 her fill.

XLVII

And sooth, it seemes, they say: for he may
 not
For ever dye, and ever buried bee
In balefull night, where all thinges are for-
 got;
All be he subject to mortalitie,
Yet is eterne in mutabilitie,
And by succession made perpetuall,
Transformed oft, and chaunged diverslie:
For him the father of all formes they call;
Therfore needs mote he live, that living
 gives to all.

XLVIII

There now he liveth in eternall blis,
Joying his goddesse, and of her enjoyd:

Ne feareth he henceforth that foe of his,
Which with his cruell tuske him deadly
 cloyd:
For that wilde bore, the which him once
 annoyd,
She firmely hath emprisoned for ay,
That her sweet love his malice mote avoyd,
In a strong rocky cave, which is, they
 say,
Hewen underneath that mount, that none
 him losen may.

XLIX

There now he lives in everlasting joy,
With many of the gods in company,
Which thether haunt, and with the winged
 boy
Sporting him selfe in safe felicity:
Who, when he hath with spoiles and cru-
 elty
Ransackt the world, and in the wofull
 harts
Of many wretches set his triumphes hye,
Thether resortes, and laying his sad dartes
Asyde, with faire Adonis playes his wanton
 partes.

L

And his trew love, faire Psyche, with him
 playes,
Fayre Psyche to him lately reconcyld,
After long troubles and unmeet upbrayes,
With which his mother Venus her revyld,
And eke himselfe her cruelly exyld:
But now in stedfast love and happy state
She with him lives, and hath him borne a
 chyld,
Pleasure, that doth both gods and men
 aggrate,
Pleasure, the daughter of Cupid and Psyche
 late.

LI

Hether great Venus brought this infant
 fayre,
The yonger daughter of Chrysogonee,
And unto Psyche with great trust and care
Committed her, yfostered to bee,
And trained up in trew feminitee:
Who no lesse carefully her tendered
Then her owne daughter Pleasure, to whom
 shee
Made her companion, and her lessoned
In all the lore of love and goodly woman-
 head.

LII

In which when she to perfect ripenes grew,
Of grace and beautie noble paragone,
She brought her forth into the worldes vew,
To be th' ensample of true love alone,
And lodestarre of all chaste affection
To all fayre ladies, that doe live on grownd.
To Faery court she came, where many one
Admyrd her goodly haveour, and fownd
His feeble hart wide launched with loves cruel wownd.

LIII

But she to none of them her love did cast,
Save to the noble knight, Sir Scudamore,
To whom her loving hart she linked fast
In faithfull love, t' abide for evermore,
And for his dearest sake endured sore,
Sore trouble of an hainous enimy,
Who her would forced have to have forlore
Her former love and stedfast loialty,
As ye may elswhere reade that ruefull history.

LIV

But well I weene ye first desire to learne
What end unto that fearefull damozell,
Which fledd so fast from that same foster stearne,
Whom with his brethren Timias slew, befell:
That was, to weet, the goodly Florimell,
Who, wandring for to seeke her lover deare,
Her lover deare, her dearest Marinell,
Into misfortune fell, as ye did heare,
And from Prince Arthure fled with wings of idle feare.

CANTO VII

The witches sonne loves Florimell:
She flyes, he faines to dy.
Satyrane saves the Squyre of Dames
From gyaunts tyranny.

I

Like as an hynd forth singled from the heard,
That hath escaped from a ravenous beast,
Yet flyes away of her owne feete afeard,
And every leafe, that shaketh with the least
Murmure of winde, her terror hath encreast;
So fledd fayre Florimell from her vaine feare,
Long after she from perill was releast:
Each shade she saw, and each noyse she did heare,
Did seeme to be the same which she escapt whileare.

II

All that same evening she in flying spent,
And all that night her course continewed:
Ne did she let dull sleepe once to relent,
Nor wearinesse to slack her hast, but fled
Ever alike, as if her former dred
Were hard behind, her ready to arrest:
And her white palfrey, having conquered
The maistring raines out of her weary wrest,
Perforce her carried where ever he thought best.

III

So long as breath and hable puissaunce
Did native corage unto him supply,
His pace he freshly forward did advaunce,
And carried her beyond all jeopardy;
But nought that wanteth rest can long aby:
He, having through incessant traveill spent
His force, at last perforce adowne did ly,
Ne foot could further move. The lady gent
Thereat was suddein strook with great astonishment;

IV

And forst t' alight, on foot mote algates fare,
A traveiler unwonted to such way:
Need teacheth her this lesson hard and rare,
That Fortune all in equall launce doth sway,
And mortall miseries doth make her play.
So long she traveild, till at length she came
To an hilles side, which did to her bewray
A litle valley, subject to the same,
All coverd with thick woodes, that quite it overcame.

V

Through the tops of the high trees she did descry
A litle smoke, whose vapour thin and light,
Reeking aloft, uprolled to the sky:
Which chearefull signe did send unto her sight

That in the same did wonne some living
    wight.
Eftsoones her steps she thereunto applyd,
And came at last, in weary wretched plight,
Unto the place, to which her hope did
    guyde,
To finde some refuge there, and rest her
    wearie syde.

VI

There in a gloomy hollow glen she found
A little cottage, built of stickes and reedes
In homely wize, and wald with sods around,
In which a witch did dwell, in loathly
    weedes,
And wilfull want, all carelesse of her
    needes;
So choosing solitarie to abide,
Far from all neighbours, that her divelish
    deedes
And hellish arts from people she might
    hide,
And hurt far off unknowne whom ever she
    envide.

VII

The damzell there arriving entred in;
Where sitting on the flore the hag she
    found,
Busie (as seem'd) about some wicked gin:
Who, soone as she beheld that suddein
    stound,
Lightly upstarted from the dustie ground,
And with fell looke and hollow deadly
    gaze
Stared on her awhile, as one astound,
Ne had one word to speake, for great
    amaze,
But shewd by outward signes that dread
    her sence did daze.

VIII

At last, turning her feare to foolish wrath,
She askt, what devill had her thether
    brought,
And who she was, and what unwonted path
Had guided her, unwelcomed, unsought.
To which the damzell, full of doubtfull
    thought,
Her mildly answer'd : 'Beldame, be not
    wroth
With silly virgin, by adventure brought
Unto your dwelling, ignorant and loth,
That crave but rowme to rest, while tem-
    pest overblo'th.'

IX

With that, adowne out of her christall
    eyne
Few trickling teares she softly forth let
    fall,
That like to orient perles did purely shyne
Upon her snowy cheeke; and therewithall
She sighed soft, that none so bestiall
Nor salvage hart, but ruth of her sad
    plight
Would make to melt, or pitteously appall;
And that vile hag, all were her whole de-
    light
In mischiefe, was much moved at so pit-
    teous sight;

X

And gan recomfort her in her rude wyse,
With womanish compassion of her plaint,
Wiping the teares from her suffused eyes,
And bidding her sit downe, to rest her
    faint
And wearie limbs awhile. She nothing
    quaint
Nor s'deignfull of so homely fashion,
Sith brought she was now to so hard con-
    straint,
Sate downe upon the dusty ground anon,
As glad of that small rest, as bird of tem-
    pest gon.

XI

Tho gan she gather up her garments rent,
And her loose lockes to dight in order dew,
With golden wreath and gorgeous orna-
    ment;
Whom such whenas the wicked hag did
    vew,
She was astonisht at her heavenly hew,
And doubted her to deeme an earthly
    wight,
But or some goddesse, or of Dianes crew,
And thought her to adore with humble
    spright:
T' adore thing so divine as beauty were but
    right.

XII

This wicked woman had a wicked sonne,
The comfort of her age and weary dayes,
A laesy loord, for nothing good to donne,
But stretched forth in ydlenesse alwayes,
Ne ever cast his mind to covet prayse,
Or ply him selfe to any honest trade,
But all the day before the sunny rayes

He us'd to slug, or sleepe in slothfull shade:
Such laesinesse both lewd and poore attonce him made.

XIII

He, comming home at undertime, there
found
The fayrest creature that he ever saw
Sitting beside his mother on the ground;
The sight whereof did greatly him adaw,
And his base thought with terrour and with
aw
So inly smot, that, as one which hath gaz'd
On the bright sunne unwares, doth soone
withdraw
His feeble eyne, with too much brightnes
daz'd,
So stared he on her, and stood long while
amaz'd.

XIV

Softly at last he gan his mother aske,
What mister wight that was, and whence
deriv'd,
That in so straunge disguizement there did
maske,
And by what accident she there arriv'd:
But she, as one nigh of her wits depriv'd,
With nought but ghastly lookes him an-
swered,
Like to a ghost, that lately is reviv'd
From Stygian shores, where late it wan-
dered;
So both at her, and each at other wondered.

XV

But the fayre virgin was so meeke and
myld,
That she to them vouchsafed to embace
Her goodly port, and to their senses vyld
Her gentle speach applyde, that in short
space
She grew familiare in that desert place.
During which time the chorle, through her
so kind
And courteise use, conceiv'd affection bace,
And cast to love her in his brutish mind;
No love, but brutish lust, that was so beastly
tind.

XVI

Closely the wicked flame his bowels brent,
And shortly grew into outrageous fire;
Yet had he not the hart, nor hardiment,
As unto her to utter his desire;

His caytive thought durst not so high
aspire:
But with soft sighes and lovely semblaunces
He ween'd that his affection entire
She should aread; many resemblaunces
To her he made, and many kinde remem-
braunces.

XVII

Oft from the forrest wildings he did bring,
Whose sides empurpled were with smyling
red,
And oft young birds, which he had taught
to sing
His maistresse praises sweetly caroled;
Girlonds of flowres sometimes for her faire
hed
He fine would dight; sometimes the squirrell
wild
He brought to her in bands, as conquered
To be her thrall, his fellow servant vild;
All which she of him tooke with counten-
ance meeke and mild.

XVIII

But, past awhile, when she fit season saw
To leave that desert mansion, she cast
In secret wize her selfe thence to withdraw,
For feare of mischiefe, which she did fore-
cast
Might be by the witch or that her sonne
compast:
Her wearie palfrey closely, as she might,
Now well recovered after long repast,
In his proud furnitures she freshly dight,
His late miswandred wayes now to remea-
sure right.

XIX

And earely, ere the dawning day appeard,
She forth issewed, and on her journey went;
She went in perill, of each noyse affeard,
And of each shade that did it selfe present;
For still she feared to be overhent
Of that vile hag, or her uncivile sonne:
Who when, too late awaking, well they
kent
That their fayre guest was gone, they both
begonne
To make exceeding mone, as they had
beene undonne.

XX

But that lewd lover did the most lament
For her depart, that ever man did heare;

He knockt his brest with desperate intent,
And scratcht his face, and with his teeth
    did teare
His rugged flesh, and rent his ragged heare:
That his sad mother, seeing his sore plight,
Was greatly woe begon, and gan to feare
Least his fraile senses were emperisht
    quight,
And love to frenzy turnd, sith love is fran-
    ticke hight.

XXI

All wayes shee sought, him to restore to
    plight,
With herbs, with charms, with counsel, and
    with teares,
But tears, nor charms, nor herbs, nor coun-
    sell might
Asswage the fury which his entrails teares:
So strong is passion that no reason heares.
Tho, when all other helpes she saw to faile,
She turnd her selfe backe to her wicked
    leares,
And by her divelish arts thought to pre-
    vaile,
To bring her backe againe, or worke her finall
    bale.

XXII

Eftesoones out of her hidden cave she cald
An hideous beast, of horrible aspect,
That could the stoutest corage have appald;
Monstrous, mishapt, and all his backe was
    spect
With thousand spots of colours queint elect;
Thereto so swifte that it all beasts did pas:
Like never yet did living eie detect;
But likest it to an hyena was,
That feeds on wemens flesh, as others feede
    on gras.

XXIII

It forth she cald, and gave it streight in
    charge,
Through thicke and thin her to poursew
    apace,
Ne once to stay to rest, or breath at large,
Till her he had attaind, and brought in
    place,
Or quite devourd her beauties scornefull
    grace.
The monster, swifte as word that from her
    went,
Went forth in haste, and did her footing
    trace

So sure and swiftly, through his perfeet
    sent
And passing speede, that shortly he her
    overhent.

XXIV

Whom when the fearefull damzell nigh
    espide,
No need to bid her fast away to flie;
That ugly shape so sore her terrifide,
That it she shund no lesse then dread to
    die;
And her flitt palfrey did so well apply
His nimble feet to her conceived feare,
That whilest his breath did strength to him
    supply,
From perill free he her away did beare:
But when his force gan faile, his pace gan
    wex areare.

XXV

Which whenas she perceiv'd, she was dis-
    mayd
At that same last extremity ful sore,
And of her safety greatly grew afrayd:
And now she gan approch to the sea shore,
As it befell, that she could flie no more,
But yield her selfe to spoile of greedi-
    nesse:
Lightly she leaped, as a wight forlore,
From her dull horse, in desperate distresse,
And to her feet betooke her doubtfull sick-
    ernesse.

XXVI

Not halfe so fast the wicked Myrrha fled
From dread of her revenging fathers hond,
Nor halfe so fast, to save her maydenhed,
Fled fearfull Daphne on th' Ægæan strond,
As Florimell fled from that monster yond,
To reach the sea ere she of him were
    raught:
For in the sea to drowne her selfe she fond,
Rather then of the tyrant to be caught:
Thereto fear gave her wings, and need her
    corage taught.

XXVII

It fortuned (High God did so ordaine)
As shee arrived on the roring shore,
In minde to leape into the mighty maine,
A little bote hoving her before,
In which there slept a fisher old and pore,
The whiles his nets were drying on the sand:
Into the same shee lept, and with the ore

Did thrust the shallop from the floting
    strand:
So safety fownd at sea, which she fownd
    not at land.

XXVIII

The monster, ready on the pray to sease,
Was of his forward hope deceived quight,
Ne durst assay to wade the perlous seas,
But, greedily long gaping at the sight,
At last in vaine was forst to turne his flight,
And tell the idle tidings to his dame:
Yet, to avenge his divelishe despight,
He sett upon her palfrey tired lame,
And slew him cruelly, ere any reskew came.

XXIX

And after having him embowelled,
To fill his hellish gorge, it chaunst a knight
To passe that way, as forth he traveiled:
Yt was a goodly swaine, and of great might,
As ever man that bloody field did fight;
But in vain sheows, that wont yong knights
    bewitch,
And courtly services tooke no delight,
But rather joyd to bee then seemen sich:
For both to be and seeme to him was labor
    lich.

XXX

It was to weete the good Sir Satyrane,
That raungd abrode to seeke adventures
    wilde,
As was his wont, in forest and in plaine:
He was all armd in rugged steele unfilde,
As in the smoky forge it was compilde,
And in his scutchin bore a satyres hedd:
He comming present, where the monster
    vilde
Upon that milke-white palfreyes carcas
    fedd,
Unto his reskew ran, and greedily him
    spedd.

XXXI

There well perceivd he, that it was the
    horse
Whereon faire Florimell was wont to ride,
That of that feend was rent without re-
    morse:
Much feared he, least ought did ill betide
To that faire maide, the flowre of wemens
    pride;
For her he dearely loved, and in all
His famous conquests highly magnifide:

Besides, her golden girdle, which did fall
From her in flight, he fownd, that did him
    sore apall.

XXXII

Full of sad feare and doubtfull agony,
Fiercely he flew upon that wicked feend;
And with huge strokes and cruell battery
Him forst to leave his pray, for to attend
Him selfe from deadly daunger to defend:
Full many wounds in his corrupted flesh
He did engrave, and muchell blood did spend,
Yet might not doe him die, but aie more fresh
And fierce he still appeard, the more he did
    him thresh.

XXXIII

He wist not how him to despoile of life,
Ne how to win the wished victory,
Sith him he saw still stronger grow through
    strife.
And him selfe weaker through infirmity:
Greatly he grew enrag'd, and furiously
Hurling his sword away, he lightly lept
Upon the beast, that with great cruelty
Rored and raged to be underkept;
Yet he perforce him held, and strokes upon
    him hept.

XXXIV

As he that strives to stop a suddein flood,
And in strong bancks his violence containe,
Forceth it swell above his wonted mood,
And largely overflow the fruitfull plaine,
That all the countrey seemes to be a maine,
And the rich furrowes flote, all quite for-
    donne:
The wofull husbandman doth lowd com-
    plaine,
To see his whole yeares labor lost so soone,
For which to God he made so many an idle
    boone:

XXXV

So him he held, and did through might
    amate:
So long he held him, and him bett so long,
That at the last his fiercenes gan abate,
And meekely stoup unto the victor strong:
Who, to avenge the implacable wrong,
Which he supposed donne to Florimell,
Sought by all meanes his dolor to prolong,
Sith dint of steele his carcas could not quell,
His maker with her charmes had framed him
    so well.

XXXVI

The golden ribband, which that virgin wore
About her sclender waste, he tooke in hand,
And with it bownd the beast, that lowd did
　　rore
For great despight of that unwonted band,
Yet dared not his victor to withstand,
But trembled like a lambe fled from the
　　pray,
And all the way him followd on the strand,
As he had long bene learned to obay;
Yet never learned he such service till that
　　day.

XXXVII

Thus as he led the beast along the way,
He spide far of a mighty giauntesse,
Fast flying on a courser dapled gray
From a bold knight, that with great hardi-
　　nesse
Her hard pursewd, and sought for to sup-
　　presse:
She bore before her lap a dolefull squire,
Lying athwart her horse in great distresse,
Fast bounden hand and foote with cords of
　　wire,
Whom she did meane to make the thrall of
　　her desire.

XXXVIII

Which whenas Satyrane beheld, in haste
He lefte his captive beast at liberty,
And crost the nearest way, by which he
　　cast
Her to encounter ere she passed by:
But she the way shund nathemore forthy,
But forward gallopt fast; which when he
　　spyde,
His mighty speare he couched warily,
And at her ran: she having him descryde,
Her selfe to fight addrest, and threw her
　　lode aside.

XXXIX

Like as a goshauke, that in foote doth
　　beare
A trembling culver, having spide on hight
An eagle, that with plumy wings doth
　　sheare
The subtile ayre, stouping with all his
　　might,
The quarrey throwes to ground with fell
　　despight,
And to the batteill doth her selfe prepare:
So ran the geauntesse unto the fight;

(continued)

Her fyrie eyes with furious sparkes did
　　stare,
And with blasphemous bannes High God in
　　peeces tare.

XL

She caught in hand an huge great yron
　　mace,
Wherewith she many had of life depriv'd;
But ere the stroke could seize his aymed
　　place,
His speare amids her sun-brode shield ar-
　　riv'd;
Yet nathemore the steele a sonder riv'd,
All were the beame in bignes like a mast,
Ne her out of the stedfast sadle driv'd,
But glauncing on the tempred metall, brast
In thousand shivers, and so forth beside her
　　past.

XLI

Her steed did stagger with that puissaunt
　　strooke,
But she no more was moved with that
　　might,
Then it had lighted on an aged oke;
Or on the marble pillour, that is pight
Upon the top of Mount Olympus hight,
For the brave youthly champions to assay,
With burning charet wheeles it nigh to
　　smite:
But who that smites it mars his joyous
　　play,
And is the spectacle of ruinous decay.

XLII

Yet therewith sore enrag'd, with sterne re-
　　gard
Her dreadfull weapon she to him addrest,
Which on his helmet martelled so hard,
That made him low incline his lofty crest,
And bowd his battred visour to his brest:
Wherewith he was so stund that he n'ote
　　ryde,
But reeled to and fro from east to west:
Which when his cruell enimy espyde,
She lightly unto him adjoyned syde to syde;

XLIII

And on his collar laying puissant hand,
Out of his wavering seat him pluckt per-
　　forse,
Perforse him pluckt, unable to withstand,
Or helpe himselfe, and laying thwart her
　　horse,

In loathly wise like to a carrion corse,
She bore him fast away. Which when the
knight
That her pursewed saw, with great remorse
He nere was touched in his noble spright,
And gan encrease his speed, as she encreast
her flight.

XLIV

Whom when as nigh approching she espyde,
She threw away her burden angrily;
For she list not the batteill to abide,
But made her selfe more light, away to
fly:
Yet her the hardy knight pursewd so nye
That almost in the backe he oft her strake:
But still, when him at hand she did espy,
She turnd, and semblaunce of faire fight
did make;
But when he stayd, to flight againe she did
her take.

XLV

By this the good Sir Satyrane gan wake
Out of his dreame, that did him long en-
traunce,
And seeing none in place, he gan to make
Exceeding mone, and curst that cruell
chaunce,
Which reft from him so faire a chevisaunce:
At length he spyde whereas that wofull
squyre,
Whom he had reskewed from captivaunce
Of his strong foe, lay tombled in the myre,
Unable to arise, or foot or hand to styre.

XLVI

To whom approching, well he mote per-
ceive
In that fowle plight a comely personage,
And lovely face, made fit for to deceive
Fraile ladies hart with loves consuming
rage,
Now in the blossome of his freshest age:
He reard him up, and loosd his yron bands,
And after gan inquire his parentage,
And how he fell into that gyaunts hands,
And who that was, which chaced her along
the lands.

XLVII

Then trembling yet through feare, the
squire bespake:
'That geauntesse Argante is behight,
A daughter of the Titans which did make

Warre against heven, and heaped hils on
hight,
To scale the skyes, and put Jove from his
right:
Her syre Typhoeus was, who, mad through
merth,
And dronke with blood of men, slaine by his
might,
Through incest her of his owne mother
Earth
Whylome begot, being but halfe twin of
that berth.

XLVIII

'For at that berth another babe she bore,
To weet, the mightie Ollyphant, that
wrought
Great wreake to many errant knights of
yore,
And many hath to foule confusion brought.
These twinnes, men say, (a thing far pass-
ing thought)
Whiles in their mothers wombe enclosd
they were,
Ere they into the lightsom world were
brought,
In fleshly lust were mingled both yfere,
And in that monstrous wise did to the
world appere.

XLIX

'So liv'd they ever after in like sin,
Gainst natures law and good behaveoure:
But greatest shame was to that maiden
twin,
Who, not content so fowly to devoure
Her native flesh, and staine her brothers
bowre,
Did wallow in all other fleshly myre,
And suffred beastes her body to deflowre,
So whot she burned in that lustfull fyre:
Yet all that might not slake her sensuall
desyre.

L

'But over all the countrie she did raunge,
To seeke young men, to quench her flaming
thrust,
And feed her fancy with delightfull
chaunge:
Whom so she fittest findes to serve her lust,
Through her maine strength, in which she
most doth trust,
She with her bringes into a secret ile,
Where in eternall bondage dye he must,

Or be the vassall of her pleasures vile,
And in all shamefull sort him selfe with
   her defile.

LI

'Me, seely wretch, she so at vauntage
   caught,
After she long in waite for me did lye,
And meant unto her prison to have brought,
Her lothsom pleasure there to satisfye;
That thousand deathes me lever were to
   dye,
Then breake the vow, that to faire Colum-
   bell
I plighted have, and yet keepe stedfastly.
As for my name, it mistreth not to tell;
Call me the Squyre of Dames; that me
   beseemeth well.

LII

'But that bold knight, whom ye pursuing
   saw
That geauntesse, is not such as she seemd,
But a faire virgin, that in martiall law
And deedes of armes above all dames is
   deemd,
And above many knightes is eke esteemd,
For her great worth; she Palladine is hight:
She you from death, you me from dread,
   redeemd.
Ne any may that monster match in fight,
But she, or such as she, that is so chaste a
   wight.'

LIII

'Her well beseemes that quest,' quoth Sa-
   tyrane:
'But read, thou Squyre of Dames, what
   vow is this,
Which thou upon thy selfe hast lately ta'ne?'
'That shall I you recount,' quoth he, 'ywis,
So be ye pleasd to pardon all amis.
That gentle lady whom I love and serve,
After long suit and wearie servicis,
Did aske me how I could her love deserve,
And how she might be sure that I would
   never swerve.

LIV

'I, glad by any meanes her grace to gaine,
Badd her commaund my life to save or spill.
Eftsoones she badd me, with incessaunt
   paine
To wander through the world abroad at
   will,

And every where, where with my power or
   skill
I might doe service unto gentle dames,
That I the same should faithfully fulfill,
And at the twelve monethes end should
   bring their names
And pledges, as the spoiles of my victorious
   games.

LV

'So well I to faire ladies service did,
And found such favour in their loving
   hartes,
That, ere the yeare his course had com-
   passid,
Thre hundred pledges for my good desartes,
And thrise three hundred thanks for my
   good partes,
I with me brought, and did to her present:
Which when she saw, more bent to eke my
   smartes
Then to reward my trusty true intent,
She gan for me devise a grievous punish-
   ment:

LVI

'To weet, that I my traveill should resume,
And with like labour walke the world
   arownd,
Ne ever to her presence should presume,
Till I so many other dames had fownd,
The which, for all the suit I could pro-
   pownd,
Would me refuse their pledges to afford,
But did abide for ever chaste and sownd.'
'Ah! gentle squyre,' quoth he, 'tell at one
   word,
How many fowndst thou such to put in thy
   record?'

LVII

'In deed, sir knight,' said he, 'one word
   may tell
All that I ever fownd so wisely stayd;
For onely three they were disposd so well,
And yet three yeares I now abrode have
   strayd,
To fynd them out.' 'Mote I,' then laughing
   sayd
The knight, 'inquire of thee, what were
   those three,
The which thy proffred curtesie denayd?
Or ill they seemed sure avizd to bee,
Or brutishly brought up, that nev'r did
   fashions see.'

LVIII

'The first which then refused me,' said hee,
'Certes was but a common courtisane,
Yet flat refusd to have adoe with mee,
Because I could not give her many a jane.'
(Thereat full hartely laughed Satyrane.)
'The second was an holy nunne to chose,
Which would not let me be her chappel-
lane,
Because she knew, she sayd, I would dis-
close
Her counsell, if she should her trust in me
repose.

LIX

'The third a damzell was of low degree,
Whom I in countrey cottage fownd by
chaunce:
Full litle weened I, that chastitee
Had lodging in so meane a maintenaunce;
Yet was she fayre, and in her countenaunce
Dwelt simple truth in seemely fashion.
Long thus I woo'd her with dew observ-
aunce,
In hope unto my pleasure to have won,
But was as far at last, as when I first begon.

LX

'Safe her, I never any woman found,
That chastity did for it selfe embrace,
But were for other causes firme and sound,
Either for want of handsome time and
place,
Or else for feare of shame and fowle dis-
grace.
Thus am I hopelesse ever to attaine
My ladies love, in such a desperate case,
But all my dayes am like to waste in vaine,
Seeking to match the chaste with th' un-
chaste ladies traine.'

LXI

'Perdy,' sayd Satyrane, 'thou Squyre of
Dames,
Great labour fondly hast thou hent in hand,
To get small thankes, and therewith many
blames,
That may emongst Alcides labours stand.'
Thence backe returning to the former land,
Where late he left the beast he overcame,
He found him not; for he had broke his
band,
And was returnd againe unto his dame,
To tell what tydings of fayre Florimell be-
came.

CANTO VIII

The witch creates a snowy lady,
 like to Florimell:
Who, wronged by carle, by Proteus sav'd,
 Is sought by Paridell.

I

So oft as I this history record,
My hart doth melt with meere compassion,
To thinke how causelesse of her owne accord
This gentle damzell, whom I write upon,
Should plonged be in such affliction,
Without all hope of comfort or reliefe,
That sure I weene, the hardest hart of stone
Would hardly finde to aggravate her griefe;
For misery craves rather mercy then re-
priefe.

II

But that accursed hag, her hostesse late,
Had so enranckled her malitious hart,
That she desyrd th' abridgement of her fate,
Or long enlargement of her painefull smart.
Now when the beast, which by her wicked
art
Late foorth she sent, she backe retourning
spyde,
Tyde with her broken girdle, it a part
Of her rich spoyles, whom he had earst de-
stroyd,
She weend, and wondrous gladnes to her
hart applyde.

III

And with it ronning hast'ly to her sonne,
Thought with that sight him much to have
reliv'd;
Who thereby deeming sure the thing as
donne,
His former griefe with furie fresh reviv'd,
Much more then earst, and would have al-
gates riv'd
The hart out of his brest: for sith her dedd
He surely dempt, himselfe he thought de-
priv'd
Quite of all hope, wherewith he long had
fedd
His foolish malady, and long time had mis-
ledd.

IV

With thought whereof, exceeding mad he
grew,
And in his rage his mother would have
slaine,

Had she not fled into a secret mew,
Where she was wont her sprightes to enter-
        taine,
The maisters of her art: there was she faine
To call them all in order to her ayde,
And them conjure, upon eternall paine,
To counsell her so carefully dismayd,
How she might heale her sonne, whose
        senses were decayd.

V

By their advise, and her owne wicked wit,
She there deviz'd a wondrous worke to
        frame,
Whose like on earth was never framed
        yit,
That even Nature selfe envide the same,
And grudg'd to see the counterfet should
        shame
The thing it selfe. In hand she boldly
        tooke
To make another like the former dame,
Another Florimell, in shape and looke
So lively and so like that many it mistooke.

VI

The substance, whereof she the body made,
Was purest snow in massy mould congeald,
Which she had gathered in a shady glade
Of the Riphœan hils, to her reveald
By errant sprights, but from all men con-
        ceald:
The same she tempred with fine mercury,
And virgin wex, that never yet was seald,
And mingled them with perfect vermily,
That like a lively sanguine it seemd to the
        eye.

VII

In stead of eyes, two burning lampes she
        set
In silver sockets, shyning like the skyes,
And a quicke moving spirit did arret
To stirre and roll them, like a womans eyes:
In stead of yellow lockes, she did devyse,
With golden wyre to weave her curled head;
Yet golden wyre was not so yellow thryse
As Florimells fayre heare: and in the stead
Of life, she put a spright to rule the carcas
        dead:

VIII

A wicked spright, yfraught with **fawning**
        guyle
And fayre resemblance. above all the rest

Which with the Prince of Darkenes fell
        somewhyle
From heavens blis and everlasting rest:
Him needed not instruct, which way were
        best
Him selfe to fashion likest Florimell,
Ne how to speake, ne how to use his gest;
For he in counterfesaunce did excell,
And all the wyles of wemens wits knew
        passing well.

IX

Him shaped thus she deckt in garments
        gay,
Which Florimell had left behind her late,
That who so then her saw would surely say,
It was her selfe whom it did imitate,
Or fayrer then her selfe, if ought algate
Might fayrer be. And then she forth her
        brought
Unto her sonne, that lay in feeble state;
Who seeing her gan streight upstart, and
        thought
She was the lady selfe, whom he so long had
        sought.

X

Tho, fast her clipping twixt his armes
        twayne,
Extremely joyed in so happy sight,
And soone forgot his former sickely payne;
But she, the more to seeme such as she
        hight,
Coyly rebutted his embracement light;
Yet still with gentle countenaunce retain'd
Enough to hold a foole in vaine delight:
Him long she so with shadowes entertain'd,
As her creatresse had in charge to her or-
        dain'd.

XI

Till on a day, as he disposed was
To walke the woodes with that his idole
        faire,
Her to disport, and idle time to pas
In th' open freshnes of the gentle aire,
A knight that way there chaunced to re-
        paire;
Yet knight he was not, but a boastfull
        swaine,
That deedes of armes had ever in despaire,
Proud Braggadocchio, that in vaunting
        vaine
His glory did repose, and credit did main-
        taine.

XII

He, seeing with that chorle so faire a wight,
Decked with many a costly ornament,
Much merveiled thereat, as well he might,
And thought that match a fowle disparagement:
His bloody speare eftesoones he boldly bent
Against the silly clowne, who, dead through feare,
Fell streight to ground in great astonishment:
'Villein,' sayd he, 'this lady is my deare;
Dy, if thou it gainesay: I will away her beare.'

XIII

The fearefull chorle durst not gainesay, nor dooe,
But trembling stood, and yielded him the pray;
Who, finding litle leasure her to wooe,
On Tromparts steed her mounted without stay,
And without reskew led her quite away.
Proud man himselfe then Braggadochio deem'd,
And next to none, after that happy day,
Being possessed of that spoyle, which seem'd
The fairest wight on ground, and most of men esteem'd.

XIV

But when hee saw him selfe free from poursute,
He gan make gentle purpose to his dame,
With termes of love and lewdnesse dissolute;
For he could well his glozing speaches frame
To such vaine uses, that him best became:
But she thereto would lend but light regard,
As seeming sory that she ever came
Into his powre, that used her so hard,
To reave her honor, which she more then life prefard.

XV

Thus as they two of kindnes treated long,
There them by chaunce encountred on the way
An armed knight, upon a courser strong,
Whose trampling feete upon the hollow lay
Seemed to thunder, and did nigh affray
That capons corage: yet he looked grim,
And faynd to cheare his lady in dismay,
Who seemd for feare to quake in every lim,
And her to save from outrage meekely prayed him.

XVI

Fiercely that straunger forward came, and nigh
Approching, with bold words and bitter threat,
Bad that same boaster, as he mote on high,
To leave to him that lady for excheat,
Or bide him batteill without further treat.
That challenge did too peremptory seeme,
And fild his senses with abashment great;
Yet, seeing nigh him jeopardy extreme,
He it dissembled well, and light seemd to esteeme;

XVII

Saying, 'Thou foolish knight! that weenst with words
To steale away that I with blowes have wonne,
And broght throgh points of many perilous swords:
But if thee list to see thy courser ronne,
Or prove thy selfe, this sad encounter shonne,
And seeke els without hazard of thy hedd.'
At those prowd words that other knight begonne
To wex exceeding wroth, and him aredd
To turne his steede about, or sure he should be dedd.

XVIII

'Sith then,' said Braggadochio, 'needes thou wilt
Thy daies abridge, through proofe of puissaunce,
Turne we our steeds, that both in equall tilt
May meete againe, and each take happy chaunce.'
This said, they both a furlongs mountenaunce
Retird their steeds, to ronne in even race:
But Braggadochio with his bloody launce
Once having turnd, no more returnd his face,
But lefte his love to losse, and fled him selfe apace.

XIX

The knight, him seeing flie, had no regard
Him to poursew, but to the lady rode,

And having her from Trompart lightly reard,
Upon his courser sett the lovely lode,
And with her fled away without abode.
Well weened he, that fairest Florimell
It was, with whom in company he yode,
And so her selfe did alwaies to him tell;
So made him thinke him selfe in heven, that
    was in hell.

XX

But Florimell her selfe was far away,
Driven to great distresse by fortune
    straunge,
And taught the carefull mariner to play,
Sith late mischaunce had her compeld to
    chaunge
The land for sea, at randon there to raunge:
Yett there that cruell queene avengeresse,
Not satisfyde so far her to estraunge
From courtly blis and wonted happinesse,
Did heape on her new waves of weary
    wretchednesse.

XXI

For being fled into the fishers bote,
For refuge from the monsters cruelty,
Long so she on the mighty maine did flote,
And with the tide drove forward carelesly;
For th' ayre was milde, and cleared was
    the skie,
And all his windes Dan Aeolus did keepe
From stirring up their stormy enmity,
As pittying to see her waile and weepe;
But all the while the fisher did securely
    sleepe.

XXII

At last when droncke with drowsinesse he
    woke,
And saw his drover drive along the streame,
He was dismayd, and thrise his brest he
    stroke,
For marveill of that accident extreame;
But when he saw that blazing beauties
    beame,
Which with rare light his bote did beauti-
    fye,
He marveild more, and thought he yet did
    dreame
Not well awakte, or that some extasye
Assotted had his sence, or dazed was his eye.

XXIII

But when her well avizing, hee perceiv'd
To be no vision nor fantasticke sight,

Great comfort of her presence he conceiv'd,
And felt in his old corage new delight
To gin awake, and stir his frosen spright:
Tho rudely askte her, how she thether came.
'Ah!' sayd she, 'father, I note read aright
What hard misfortune brought me to this
    same;
Yet am I glad that here I now in safety
    ame.

XXIV

'But thou good man, sith far in sea we bee,
And the great waters gin apace to swell,
That now no more we can the mayn-land
    see,
Have care, I pray, to guide the cock-bote
    well,
Least worse on sea then us on land befell.'
Thereat th' old man did nought but fondly
    grin,
And saide, his boat the way could wisely
    tell:
But his deceiptfull eyes did never lin
To looke on her faire face, and marke her
    snowy skin.

XXV

The sight whereof in his congealed flesh
Infixt such secrete sting of greedy lust,
That the drie withered stocke it gan refresh,
And kindled heat, that soone in flame forth
    brust:
The driest wood is soonest burnt to dust.
Rudely to her he lept, and his rough hand,
Where ill became him, rashly would have
    thrust;
But she with angry scorne him did with-
    stond,
And shamefully reproved for his rudenes
    fond.

XXVI

But he, that never good nor maners knew,
Her sharpe rebuke full litle did esteeme;
Hard is to teach an old horse amble trew.
The inward smoke, that did before but
    steeme,
Broke into open fire and rage extreme;
And now he strength gan adde unto his will,
Forcyng to doe that did him fowle mis-
    seeme:
Beastly he threwe her downe, ne car'd to
    spill
Her garments gay with scales of fish, that
    all did fill.

XXVII

The silly virgin strove him to withstand,
All that she might, and him in vaine revild:
Shee strugled strongly both with foote and
    hand,
To save her honor from that villaine vilde,
And cride to heven, from humane helpe
    exild.
O ye brave knights, that boast this ladies
    love,
Where be ye now, when she is nigh defild
Of filthy wretch? Well may she you re-
    prove
Of falsehood or of slouth, when most it may
    behove.

XXVIII

But if that thou, Sir Satyran, didst weete,
Or thou, Sir Peridure, her sory state,
How soone would yee assemble many a
    fleete,
To fetch from sea that ye at land lost late!
Towres, citties, kingdomes ye would ruin-
    ate,
In your avengement and dispiteous rage,
Ne ought your burning fury mote abate;
But if Sir Calidore could it presage,
No living creature could his cruelty as-
    swage.

XXIX

But sith that none of all her knights is nye,
See how the heavens, of voluntary grace
And soveraine favor towards chastity,
Doe succor send to her distressed cace:
So much High God doth innocence embrace.
It fortuned, whilest thus she stifly strove,
And the wide sea importuned long space
With shrilling shriekes, Proteus abrode did
    rove,
Along the fomy waves driving his finny
    drove.

XXX

Proteus is shepheard of the seas of yore,
And hath the charge of Neptunes mighty
    heard,
An aged sire with head all frowy hore,
And sprinckled frost upon his deawy beard:
Who when those pittifull outcries he heard
Through all the seas so ruefully resownd,
His charett swifte in hast he thether steard,
Which, with a teeme of scaly phocas bownd,
Was drawne upon the waves, that fomed
    him arownd.

XXXI

And comming to that fishers wandring bote,
That went at will, withouten card or sayle,
He therein saw that yrkesome sight, which
    smote
Deepe indignation and compassion frayle
Into his hart attonce: streight did he hayle
The greedy villein from his hoped pray,
Of which he now did very litle fayle,
And with his staffe, that drives his heard
    astray,
Him bett so sore, that life and sence did
    much dismay.

XXXII

The whiles the pitteous lady up did ryse,
Ruffled and fowly raid with filthy soyle,
And blubbred face with teares of her faire
    eyes:
Her heart nigh broken was with weary
    toyle,
To save her selfe from that outrageous
    spoyle:
But when she looked up, to weet what
    wight
Had her from so infamous fact assoyld,
For shame, but more for feare of his grim
    sight,
Downe in her lap she hid her face, and
    lowdly shright.

XXXIII

Her selfe not saved yet from daunger
    dredd
She thought, but chaung'd from one to
    other feare:
Like as a fearefull partridge, that is fledd
From the sharpe hauke, which her attached
    neare,
And fals to ground, to seeke for succor
    theare,
Whereas the hungry spaniells she does
    spye,
With greedy jawes her ready for to teare;
In such distresse and sad perplexity
Was Florimell, when Proteus she did see
    thereby.

XXXIV

But he endevored with speaches milde
Her to recomfort, and accourage bold,
Bidding her feare no more her foeman
    vilde,
Nor doubt himselfe; and who he was her
    told.

Yet all that could not from affright her hold,
Ne to recomfort her at all prevayld;
For her faint hart was with the frosen cold
Benumbd so inly, that her wits nigh fayld,
And all her sences with abashment quite
    were quayld.

XXXV

Her up betwixt his rugged hands he reard,
And with his frory lips full softly kist,
Whiles the cold ysickles from his rough
    beard
Dropped adowne upon her yvory brest:
Yet he him selfe so busily addrest,
That her out of astonishment he wrought,
And out of that same fishers filthy nest
Removing her, into his charet brought,
And there with many gentle termes her
    faire besought.

XXXVI

But that old leachour, which with bold as-
    sault
That beautie durst presume to violate,
He cast to punish for his hainous fault:
Then tooke he him, yet trembling sith of
    late,
And tyde behind his charet, to aggrate
The virgin, whom he had abusde so sore:
So drag'd him through the waves in scorn-
    full state,
And after cast him up upon the shore;
But Florimell with him unto his bowre he
    bore.

XXXVII

His bowre is in the bottom of the maine,
Under a mightie rocke, gainst which doe
    rave
The roring billowes in their proud disdaine,
That with the angry working of the wave
Therein is eaten out an hollow cave,
That seemes rough masons hand with en-
    gines keene
Had long while laboured it to engrave:
There was his wonne, ne living wight was
    seene,
Save one old nymph, hight Panope, to
    keepe it cleane.

XXXVIII

Thether he brought the sory Florimell,
And entertained her the best he might,
And Panope her entertaind eke well,
As an immortall mote a mortall wight,

To winne her liking unto his delight:
With flattering wordes he sweetly wooed
    her,
And offered faire guiftes, t' allure her sight;
But she both offers and the offerer
Despysde, and all the fawning of the flat-
    terer.

XXXIX

Dayly he tempted her with this or that,
And never suffred her to be at rest:
But evermore she him refused flat,
And all his fained kindnes did detest;
So firmely she had sealed up her brest.
Sometimes he boasted that a god he hight;
But she a mortall creature loved best:
Then he would make him selfe a mortall
    wight;
But then she said she lov'd none but a
    Faery knight.

XL

Then like a Faerie knight him selfe he
    drest;
For every shape on him he could endew:
Then like a king he was to her exprest,
And offred kingdoms unto her in vew,
To be his leman and his lady trew:
But when all this he nothing saw prevaile,
With harder meanes he cast her to subdew,
And with sharpe threates her often did as-
    sayle,
So thinking for to make her stubborne
    corage quayle.

XLI

To dreadfull shapes he did him selfe trans-
    forme,
Now like a gyaunt, now like to a feend,
Then like a centaure, then like to a storme,
Raging within the waves: thereby he weend
Her will to win unto his wished eend
But when with feare, nor favour, nor with
    all
He els could doe, he saw him selfe es-
    teemd,
Downe in a dongeon deepe he let her fall,
And threatned there to make her his eter-
    nall thrall.

XLII

Eternall thraldome was to her more liefe,
Then losse of chastitie, or chaunge of love:
Dye had she rather in tormenting griefe,
Then any should of falsenesse her reprove,

Or loosenes, that she lightly did remove.
Most vertuous virgin! glory be thy meed,
And crowne of heavenly prayse with saintes
    above,
Where most sweet hymmes of this thy fa-
    mous deed
Are still emongst them song, that far my
    rymes exceed.

XLIII

Fit song of angels caroled to bee!
But yet what so my feeble Muse can frame,
Shalbe t' advance thy goodly chastitee,
And to enroll thy memorable name
In th' heart of every honourable dame,
That they thy vertuous deedes may imitate,
And be partakers of thy endlesse fame.
Yt yrkes me leave thee in this wofull state,
To tell of Satyrane, where I him left of
    late.

XLIV

Who having ended with that Squyre of
    Dames
A long discourse of his adventures vayne,
The which himselfe, then ladies, more de-
    fames,
And finding not th' hyena to be slayne,
With that same squyre retourned back
    agayne
To his first way. And as they forward went,
They spyde a knight fayre pricking on the
    playne,
As if he were on some adventure bent,
And in his port appeared manly hardiment.

XLV

Sir Satyrane him towardes did addresse,
To weet what wight he was, and what his
    quest:
And comming nigh, eftsoones he gan to
    gesse
Both by the burning hart which on his
    brest
He bare, and by the colours in his crest,
That Paridell it was: tho to him yode,
And him saluting as beseemed best,
Gan first inquire of tydinges farre abrode;
And afterwardes, on what adventure now
    he rode.

XLVI

Who thereto answering said: 'The tyd-
    inges bad,
Which now in Faery court all men doe tell,
Which turned hath great mirth to mourning
    sad,
Is the late ruine of proud Marinell,
And suddein parture of faire Florimell,
To find him forth: and after her are gone
All the brave knightes, that doen in armes
    excell,
To savegard her, ywandred all alone;
Emongst the rest my lott (unworthy') is to
    be one.'

XLVII

' Ah! gentle knight,' said then Sir Satyrane,
' Thy labour all is lost, I greatly dread,
That hast a thanklesse service on thee
    ta'ne,
And offrest sacrifice unto the dead.
For dead, I surely doubt, thou maist aread
Henceforth for ever Florimell to bee,
That all the noble knights of Mayden-
    head,
Which her ador'd, may sore repent with
    mee,
And all faire ladies may for ever sory
    bee.'

XLVIII

Which wordes when Paridell had heard, his
    hew
Gan greatly chaung, and seemd dismaid to
    bee;
Then said: ' Fayre sir, how may I weene it
    trew,
That ye doe tell in such uncerteintee?
Or speake ye of report, or did ye see
Just cause of dread, that makes ye doubt
    so sore?
For, perdie, elles how mote it ever bee,
That ever hand should dare for to engore
Her noble blood? The hevens such cruel-
    tie abhore.'

XLIX

' These eyes did see, that they will ever
    rew
To have seene,' quoth he, ' when as a mon-
    strous beast
The palfrey whereon she did travell slew,
And of his bowels made his bloody feast:
Which speaking token sheweth at the least
Her certeine losse, if not her sure decay:
Besides, that more suspicion encreast,
I found her golden girdle cast astray,
Distaynd with durt and blood, as relique of
    the pray.'

L

' Ay me ! ' said Paridell, ' the signes be sadd,
And but God turne the same to good sooth
    say,
That ladies safetie is sore to be dradd:
Yet will I not forsake my forward way,
Till triall doe more certeine truth bewray.'
' Faire sir,' quoth he, ' well may it you suc-
    ceed:
Ne long shall Satyrane behind you stay,
But to the rest, which in this quest proceed,
My labour adde, and be partaker of their
    speed.'

LI

' Ye noble knights,' said then the Squyre of
    Dames,
' Well may yee speede in so praiseworthy
    payne:
But sith the sunne now ginnes to slake his
    beames
In deawy vapours of the westerne mayne,
And lose the teme out of his weary wayne,
Mote not mislike you also to abate
Your zealous hast, till morrow next againe
Both light of heven and strength of men
    relate:
Which if ye please, to yonder castle turne
    your gate.'

LII

That counsell pleased well; so all yfere
Forth marched to a castle them before;
Where soone arryving, they restrained were
Of ready entraunce, which ought evermore
To errant knights be commune: wondrous
    sore
Thereat displeasd they were, till that young
    squyre
Gan them informe the cause why that same
    dore
Was shut to all which lodging did desyre:
The which to let you weet will further time
    requyre.

CANTO IX

Malbecco will no straunge knights host,
    For peevish gealosy:
Paridell giusts with Britomart:
    Both shew their auncestry.

I

REDOUBTED knights, and honorable dames,
To whom I levell all my labours end,

Right sore I feare, least with unworthie
    blames
This odious argument my rymes should
    shend,
Or ought your goodly patience offend,
Whiles of a wanton lady I doe write,
Which with her loose incontinence doth
    blend
The shyning glory of your soveraine light;
And knighthood fowle defaced by a faith-
    lesse knight.

II

But never let th' ensample of the bad
Offend the good: for good, by paragone
Of evill, may more notably be rad,
As white seemes fayrer, macht with blacke
    attone;
Ne all are shamed by the fault of one:
For lo ! in heven, whereas all goodnes is,
Emongst the angels, a whole legione
Of wicked sprightes did fall from happy
    blis;
What wonder then, if one of women all did
    mis ?

III

Then listen, lordings, if ye list to weet
The cause why Satyrane and Paridell
Mote not be entertaynd, as seemed meet,
Into that castle (as that squyre does tell.)
' Therein a cancred crabbed carle does
    dwell,
That has no skill of court nor courtesie,
Ne cares what men say of him ill or well;
For all his dayes he drownes in privitie,
Yet has full large to live, and spend at
    libertie.

IV

' But all his mind is set on mucky pelfe,
To hoord up heapes of evill gotten masse,
For which he others wrongs and wreckes
    himselfe;
Yet is he lincked to a lovely lasse,
Whose beauty doth her bounty far surpasse,
The which to him both far unequall yeares
And also far unlike conditions has;
For she does joy to play emongst her peares,
And to be free from hard restraynt and
    gealous feares.

V

' But he is old, and withered like hay,
Unfit faire ladies service to supply,

The privie guilt whereof makes him alway
Suspect her truth, and keepe continuall spy
Upon her with his other blincked eye;
Ne suffreth he resort of living wight
Approch to her, ne keepe her company,
But in close bowre her mewes from all mens
    sight,
Depriv'd of kindly joy and naturall delight.

VI

' Malbecco he, and Hellenore she hight,
Unfitly yokt together in one teeme:
That is the cause why never any knight
Is suffred here to enter, but he seeme
Such as no doubt of him he neede mis-
    deeme.'
Thereat Sir Satyrane gan smyle, and say:
' Extremely mad the man I surely deeme,
That weenes with watch and hard restraynt
    to stay
A womans will, which is disposd to go astray.

VII

' In vaine he feares that which he cannot
    shonne:
For who wotes not, that womans subtiltyes
Can guylen Argus, when she list misdonne ?
It is not yron bandes, nor hundred eyes,
Nor brasen walls, nor many wakefull spyes,
That can withhold her wilfull wandring
    feet;
But fast goodwill with gentle courtesyes,
And timely service to her pleasures meet,
May her perhaps containe, that else would
    algates fleet.'

VIII

' Then is he not more mad,' sayd Paridell,
' That hath himselfe unto such service sold,
In dolefull thraldome all his dayes to
    dwell ?
For sure a foole I doe him firmely hold,
That loves his fetters, though they were of
    gold.
But why doe wee devise of others ill,
Whyles thus we suffer this same dotard old
To keepe us out, in scorne, of his owne will,
And rather do not ransack all, and him selfe
    kill ? '

IX

' Nay, let us first,' sayd Satyrane, ' entreat
The man by gentle meanes, to let us in;
And afterwardes affray with cruell threat,
Ere that we to efforce it doe begin:

Then if all fayle, we will by force it win,
And eke reward the wretch for his mes-
    prise,
As may be worthy of his haynous sin.'
That counsell pleasd: then Paridell did rise,
And to the castle gate approcht in quiet
    wise.

X

Whereat soft knocking, entrance he de-
    syrd.
The good man selfe, which then the porter
    playd,
Him answered, that all were now retyrd
Unto their rest, and all the keyes convayd
Unto their maister, who in bed was layd,
That none him durst awake out of his
    dreme;
And therefore them of patience gently
    prayd.
Then Paridell began to chaunge his theme,
And threatned him with force and punish-
    ment extreme.

XI

But all in vaine; for nought mote him re-
    lent:
And now so long before the wicket fast
They wayted, that the night was forward
    spent,
And the faire welkin, fowly overcast,
Gan blowen up a bitter stormy blast,
With showre and hayle so horrible and
    dred,
That this faire many were compeld at last
To fly for succour to a little shed,
The which beside the gate for swyne was
    ordered.

XII

It fortuned, soone after they were gone,
Another knight, whom tempest thether
    brought,
Came to that castle, and with earnest
    mone,
Like as the rest, late entrance deare be-
    sought;
But like so as the rest, he prayd for
    nought,
For flatly he of entrance was refusd.
Sorely thereat he was displeasd, and
    thought
How to avenge himselfe so sore abusd,
And evermore the carle of courtesie ac-
    cusd.

XIII

But to avoyde th' intollerable stowre,
He was compeld to seeke some refuge
    neare,
And to that shed, to shrowd him from the
    showre,
He came, which full of guests he found
    whyleare,
So as he was not let to enter there:
Whereat he gan to wex exceeding wroth,
And swore that he would lodge with them
    yfere,
Or them dislodg, all were they liefe or
    loth;
And so defyde them each, and so defyde
    them both.

XIV

Both were full loth to leave that needfull
    tent,
And both full loth in darkenesse to debate;
Yet both full liefe him lodging to have lent,
And both full liefe his boasting to abate;
But chiefely Paridell his hart did grate,
To heare him threaten so despightfully,
As if he did a dogge in kenell rate,
That durst not barke; and rather had he dy
Then, when he was defyde, in coward cor-
    ner ly.

XV

Tho, hastily remounting to his steed,
He forth issew'd; like as a boystrous winde,
Which in th' earthes hollow caves hath long
    ben hid,
And shut up fast within her prisons blind,
Makes the huge element, against her kinde,
To move and tremble as it were aghast,
Untill that it an issew forth may finde;
Then forth it breakes, and with his furious
    blast
Confounds both land and seas, and skyes
    doth overcast.

XVI

Their steel-hed speares they strongly coucht,
    and met
Together with impetuous rage and forse,
That with the terrour of their fierce affret,
They rudely drove to ground both man and
    horse,
That each awhile lay like a sencelesse corse.
But Paridell, sore brused with the blow,
Could not arise, the counterchaunge to
    scorse,

Till that young squyre him reared from
    below;
Then drew he his bright sword, and gan
    about him throw.

XVII

But Satyrane, forth stepping, did them
    stay,
And with faire treaty pacifide their yre:
Then, when they were accorded from the
    fray,
Against that castles lord they gan conspire,
To heape on him dew vengeaunce for his
    hire.
They beene agreed, and to the gates they
    goe,
To burne the same with unquenchable
    fire,
And that uncurteous carle, their commune
    foe,
To doe fowle death to die, or wrap in
    grievous woe.

XVIII

Malbecco seeing them resolvd in deed
To flame the gates, and hearing them to
    call
For fire in earnest, ran with fearfull speed,
And to them calling from the castle wall,
Besought them humbly him to beare with
    all,
As ignorant of servants bad abuse,
And slacke attendaunce unto straungers
    call.
The knights were willing all things to ex-
    cuse,
Though nought belev'd, and entraunce late
    did not refuse.

XIX

They beene ybrought into a comely bowre,
And servd of all things that mote needfull
    bee;
Yet secretly their hoste did on them lowre,
And welcomde more for feare then chari-
    tee;
But they dissembled what they did not see,
And welcomed themselves. Each gan un-
    dight
Their garments wett, and weary armour
    free,
To dry them selves by Vulcanes flaming
    light,
And eke their lately bruzed parts to bring
    in plight.

XX

And eke tha t straunger knight emongst
the re·t
Was for like need enforst to disaray:
Tho, whenas vailed was her lofty crest,
Her golden locks, that were in tramells
gay
Upbounden, did them selves adowne dis-
play,
And raught unto her heeles; like sunny
beames,
That in a cloud their light did long time
stay,
Their vapour vaded, shewe their golden
gleames,
And through the persant aire shoote forth
their azure streames.

XXI

Shee also dofte her heavy haberjeon,
Which the faire feature of her limbs did
hyde,
And her well plighted frock, which she did
won
To tucke about her short, when she did
ryde,
Shee low let fall, that flowd from her
lanck syde
Downe to her foot with carelesse modes-
tee.
Then of them all she plainly was espyde
To be a woman wight, unwist to bee,
The fairest woman wight that ever eie did
see.

XXII

Like as Minerva, being late returnd
From slaughter of the giaunts conquered;
Where proud Encelade, whose wide nose-
thrils burnd
With breathed flames, like to a furnace
redd,
Transfixed with her speare, downe tombled
dedd
From top of Hemus, by him heaped hye;
Hath loosd her helmet from her lofty hedd,
And her Gorgonian shield gins to untye
From her lefte arme, to rest in glorious
victorye.

XXIII

Which whenas they beheld, they smitten
were
With great amazement of so wondrous
sight,

And each on other, and they all on her,
Stood gazing, as if suddein great affright
Had them surprizd. At last avizing right
Her goodly personage and glorious hew,
Which they so much mistooke, they tooke
delight
In their first error, and yett still anew
With wonder of her beauty fed their hongry
vew.

XXIV

Yet note their hongry vew be satisfide,
But seeing, still the more desir'd to see,
And ever firmely fixed did abide
In contemplation of divinitee:
But most they mervaild at her chevalree
And noble prowesse, which they had ap-
prov'd,
That much they faynd to know who she
mote bee;
Yet none of all them her thereof amov'd,
Yet every one her likte, and every one her
lov'd.

XXV

And Paridell, though partly discontent
With his late fall and fowle indignity,
Yet was soone wonne his malice to relent,
Through gratious regard of her faire eye,
And knightly worth, which he too late did
try,
Yet tried did adore. Supper was dight;
Then they Malbecco prayd of courtesy,
That of his lady they might have the sight,
And company at meat, to doe them more
delight.

XXVI

But he, to shifte their curious request,
Gan causen why she could not come in
place;
Her crased helth, her late recourse to rest,
And humid evening, ill for sicke folkes cace;
But none of those excuses could take place,
Ne would they eate, till she in presence
came.
Shee came in presence with right comely
grace,
And fairely them saluted, as became,
And shewd her selfe in all a gentle cour-
teous dame.

XXVII

They sate to meat, and Satyrane his chaunce
Was her before, and Paridell beside;

But he him selfe sate looking still askaunce
Gainst Britomart, and ever closely eide
Sir Satyrane, that glaunces might not glide:
But his blinde eie, that sided Paridell,
All his demeasnure from his sight did hide:
On her faire face so did he feede his fill,
And sent close messages of love to her at
will.

XXVIII

And ever and anone, when none was ware,
With speaking lookes, that close embassage
bore,
He rov'd at her, and told his secret care:
For all that art he learned had of yore.
Ne was she ignoraunt of that leud lore,
But in his eye his meaning wisely redd,
And with the like him aunswerd evermore:
Shee sent at him one fyrie dart, whose hedd
Empoisned was with privy lust and gealous
dredd.

XXIX

He from that deadly throw made no de-
fence,
But to the wound his weake heart opened
wyde:
The wicked engine through false influence
Past through his eies, and secretly did
glyde
Into his heart, which it did sorely gryde.
But nothing new to him was that same
paine,
Ne paine at all; for he so ofte had tryde
The powre thereof, and lov'd so oft in
vaine,
That thing of course he counted, love to en-
tertaine.

XXX

Thenceforth to her he sought to intimate
His inward griefe, by meanes to him well
knowne:
Now Bacchus fruit out of the silver plate
He on the table dasht, as overthrowne,
Or of the fruitfull liquor overflowne,
And by the dauncing bubbles did divine,
Or therein write to lett his love be showne;
Which well she redd out of the learned line:
A sacrament prophane in mistery of wine.

XXXI

And when so of his hand the pledge she
raught,
The guilty cup she fained to mistake,

And in her lap did shed her idle draught,
Shewing desire her inward flame to slake.
By such close signes they secret way did
make
Unto their wils, and one eies watch escape:
Two eies him needeth, for to watch and
wake,
Who lovers will deceive. Thus was the ape,
By their faire handling, put into Malbeccoes
cape.

XXXII

Now when of meats and drinks they had
their fill,
Purpose was moved by that gentle dame
Unto those knights adventurous, to tell
Of deeds of armes which unto them be-
came,
And every one his kindred and his name.
Then Paridell, in whom a kindly pride
Of gratious speach and skill his words to
frame
Abounded, being glad of so fitte tide
Him to commend to her, thus spake, of al
well eide:

XXXIII

'Troy, that art now nought but an idle
name,
And in thine ashes buried low dost lie,
Though whilome far much greater then
thy fame,
Before that angry gods and cruell skie
Upon thee heapt a direfull destinie,
What boots it boast thy glorious descent,
And fetch from heven thy great genealogie
Sith all thy worthie prayses being blent,
Their ofspring hath embaste, and later glory
shent?

XXXIV

'Most famous worthy of the world, by
whome
That warre was kindled which did Troy in
flame,
And stately towres of Ilion whilome
Brought unto balefull ruine, was by name
Sir Paris, far renowmd through noble fame
Who, through great prowesse and bold
hardinesse,
From Lacedæmon fetcht the fayrest dame
That ever Greece did boast, or knight pos-
sesse,
Whom Venus to him gave for meed of wor-
thinesse:

XXXV

Fayre Helene, flowre of beautie excellent,
And girlond of the mighty conquerours,
That madest many ladies deare lament
The heavie losse of their brave paramours,
Which they far off beheld from Trojan
    toures,
And saw the fieldes of faire Scamander
    strowne
With carcases of noble warrioures,
Whose fruitlesse lives were under furrow
    sowne,
And Xanthus sandy bankes with blood all
    overflowne.

XXXVI

From him my linage I derive aright,
Who long before the ten yeares siege of
    Troy,
Whiles yet on Ida he a shepeheard hight,
On faire Oenone got a lovely boy,
Whom, for remembrance of her passed joy,
She of his father Parius did name;
Who, after Greekes did Priams realme de-
    stroy,
Gathred the Trojan reliques sav'd from
    flame,
And with them sayling thence, to th' isle of
    Paros came.

XXXVII

That was by him cald Paros, which before
Hight Nausa; there he many yeares did
    raine,
And built Nausicle by the Pontick shore,
The which he dying lefte next in remaine
To Paridas his sonne,
From whom I, Paridell, by kin descend;
But, for faire ladies love and glories gaine,
My native soile have lefte, my dayes to
    spend
In seewing deeds of armes, my lives and
    labors end.'

XXXVIII

Whenas the noble Britomart heard tell
Of Trojan warres and Priams citie sackt,
The ruefull story of Sir Paridell,
She was empassiond at that piteous act,
With zelous envy of Greekes cruell fact
Against that nation, from whose race of old
She heard that she was lineally extract:
For noble Britons sprong from Trojans bold,
And Troynovant was built of old Troyes
    ashes cold.

XXXIX

Then sighing soft awhile, at last she thus:
'O lamentable fall of famous towne,
Which raignd so many yeares victorious,
And of all Asie bore the soveraine crowne,
In one sad night consumd and throwen
    downe !
What stony hart, that heares thy haplesse
    fate,
Is not empierst with deepe compassiowne,
And makes ensample of mans wretched
    state,
That floures so fresh at morne, and fades
    at evening late ?

XL

' Behold, sir, how your pitifull complaint
Hath fownd another partner of your payne:
For nothing may impresse so deare con-
    straint,
As countries cause and commune foes dis-
    dayne.
But if it should not grieve you, backe
    agayne
To turne your course, I would to heare de-
    syre
What to Aeneas fell; sith that men sayne
He was not in the cities wofull fyre
Consum'd, but did him selfe to safety re-
    tyre.'

XLI

' Anchyses sonne, begott of Venus fayre,'
Said he, ' out of the flames for safegard fled,
And with a remnant did to sea repayre,
Where he through fatall errour long was
    led
Full many yeares, and weetlesse wandered
From shore to shore, emongst the Lybick
    sandes,
Ere rest he fownd. Much there he suf-
    fered,
And many perilles past in forreine landes,
To save his people sad from victours venge-
    full handes.

XLII

' At last in Latium he did arryve,
Where he with cruell warre was entertaind
Of th' inland folke, which sought him backe
    to drive,
Till he with old Latinus was constraind
To contract wedlock; (so the Fates ordaind;)
Wedlocke contract in blood, and eke in
    blood

Accomplished, that many deare complaind:
The rivall slaine, the victour, through the
    flood
Escaped hardly, hardly praisd his wedlock
    good.

XLIII

' Yet after all, he victour did survive,
And with Latinus did the kingdom part.
But after, when both nations gan to strive,
Into their names the title to convart,
His sonne Iülus did from thence depart
With all the warlike youth of Trojans
    bloud,
And in Long Alba plast his throne apart,
Where faire it florished, and long time
    stoud,
Till Romulus, renewing it, to Rome re-
    moud.'

XLIV

' There, there,' said Britomart, 'a fresh ap-
    peard
The glory of the later world to spring,
And Troy againe out of her dust was reard,
To sitt in second seat of soveraine king
Of all the world under her governing.
But a third kingdom yet is to arise
Out of the Trojans scattered ofspring,
That, in all glory and great enterprise,
Both first and second Troy shall dare to
    equalise.

XLV

' It Troynovant is hight, that with the
    waves
Of wealthy Thamis washed is along,
Upon whose stubborne neck, whereat he
    raves
With roring rage, and sore him selfe does
    throng,
That all men feare to tempt his billowes
    strong,
She fastned hath her foot, which standes so
    hy,
That it a wonder of the world is song
In forreine landes, and all which passen by,
Beholding it from farre, doe thinke it
    threates the skye.

XLVI

' The Trojan Brute did first that citie
    fownd,
And Hygate made the meare thereof by
    west,

And Overt gate by north: that is the
    bownd
Toward the land; two rivers bownd the
    rest.
So huge a scope at first him seemed best,
To be the compasse of his kingdomes seat:
So huge a mind could not in lesser rest,
Ne in small meares containe his glory great,
That Albion had conquered first by warlike
    feat.'

XLVII

' Ah ! fairest lady knight,' said Paridell,
' Pardon, I pray, my heedlesse oversight,
Who had forgot that whylome I hard tell
From aged Mnemon; for my wits beene
    light.
Indeed he said (if I remember right)
That of the antique Trojan stocke there
    grew
Another plant, that raught to wondrous
    hight,
And far abroad his mightie braunches threw
Into the utmost angle of the world he
    knew.

XLVIII

' For that same Brute, whom much he did
    advaunce
In all his speach, was Sylvius his sonne,
Whom having slain through luckles ar-
    rowes glaunce,
He fled for feare of that he had misdonne,
Or els for shame, so fowle reproch to
    shonne,
And with him ledd to sea an youthly trayne,
Where wearie wandring they long time did
    wonne,
And many fortunes prov'd in th' ocean
    mayne,
And great adventures found, that now were
    long to sayne.

XLIX

' At last by fatall course they driven were
Into an island spatious and brode,
The furthest north that did to them ap-
    peare:
Which, after rest, they seeking farre abrode,
Found it the fittest soyle for their abode,
Fruitfull of all thinges fitt for living foode,
But wholy waste and void of peoples trode,
Save an huge nation of the geaunts broode,
That fed on living flesh, and dronck mens
    vitall blood.

L

'Whom he, through wearie wars and la-
bours long,
Subdewd with losse of many Britons bold:
In which the great Goemagot of strong
Corineus, and Coulin of Debon old,
Were overthrowne and laide on th' earth
full cold,
Which quaked under their so hideous masse:
A famous history to bee enrold
In everlasting moniments of brasse,
That all the antique worthies merits far did
passe.

LI

'His worke great Troynovant, his worke is
eke
Faire Lincolne, both renowmed far away,
That who from east to west will endlong
seeke,
Cannot two fairer cities find this day,
Except Cleopolis: so heard I say
Old Mnemon. Therefore, sir, I greet you
well,
Your countrey kin, and you entyrely pray
Of pardon for the strife which late befell
Betwixt us both unknowne.' So ended
Paridell.

LII

But all the while that he these speeches
spent,
Upon his lips hong faire Dame Hellenore,
With vigilant regard and dew attent,
Fashioning worldes of fancies evermore
In her fraile witt, that now her quite for-
lore:
The whiles unwares away her wondring eye
And greedy eares her weake hart from her
bore:
Which he perceiving, ever privily,
In speaking, many false belgardes at her
let fly.

LIII

So long these knightes discoursed diversly
Of straunge affaires, and noble hardiment,
Which they had past with mickle jeopardy,
That now the humid night was farforth
spent,
And hevenly lampes were halfendeale
ybrent:
Which th' old man seeing wel, who too long
thought
Every discourse and every argument,

Which by the houres he measured, besought
Them go to rest. So all unto their bowres
were brought.

CANTO X

Paridell rapeth Hellenore:
Malbecco her poursewes:
Fynds emongst Satyres, whence with him
To turne she doth refuse.

I

THE morow next, so soone as Phœbus lamp
Bewrayed had the world with early light,
And fresh Aurora had the shady damp
Out of the goodly heven amoved quight,
Faire Britomart and that same Faery
knight
Uprose, forth on their journey for to wend:
But Paridell complaynd, that his late fight
With Britomart so sore did him offend,
That ryde he could not, till his hurts he did
amend.

II

So foorth they far'd, but he behind them
stayd,
Maulgre his host, who grudged grivously
To house a guest that would be needes
obayd,
And of his owne him left not liberty:
Might wanting measure moveth surquedry.
Two things he feared, but the third was
death:
That fiers youngmans unruly maystery;
His money, which he lov'd as living breath;
And his faire wife, whom honest long he
kept uneath.

III

But patience perforce, he must abie
What fortune and his fate on him will lay;
Fond is the feare that findes no remedie;
Yet warily he watcheth every way,
By which he feareth evill happen may:
So th' evill thinkes by watching to prevent;
Ne doth he suffer her, nor night nor day,
Out of his sight her selfe once to absent.
So doth he punish her and eke himselfe
torment.

IV

But Paridell kept better watch then hee,
A fit occasion for his turne to finde.

False Love, why do men say thou canst not
    see,
And in their foolish fancy feigne thee blinde,
That with thy charmes the sharpest sight
    doest binde,
And to thy will abuse ? Thou walkest free,
And seest every secret of the minde;
Thou seest all, yet none at all sees thee;
All that is by the working of thy deitee.

V

So perfect in that art was Paridell,
That he Malbeccoes halfen eye did wyle;
His halfen eye he wiled wondrous well,
And Hellenors both eyes did eke beguyle,
Both eyes and hart attonce, during the
    whyle
That he there sojourned his woundes to
    heale;
That Cupid selfe, it seeing, close did smyle,
To weet how he her love away did steale,
And bad that none their joyous treason
    should reveale.

VI

The learned lover lost no time nor tyde,
That least avantage mote to him afford,
Yet bore so faire a sayle, that none espyde
His secret drift, till he her layd abord.
When so in open place and commune bord
He fortun'd her to meet, with commune
    speach
He courted her, yet bayted every word,
That his ungentle hoste n'ote him appeach
Of vile ungentlenesse, or hospitages breach.

VII

But when apart (if ever her apart)
He found, then his false engins fast he
    plyde,
And all the sleights unbosomd in his hart;
He sigh'd, he sobd, he swownd, he perdy
    dyde,
And cast himselfe on ground her fast be-
    syde:
Tho, when againe he him bethought to live,
He wept, and wayld, and false laments be-
    lyde,
Saying, but if she mercie would him give,
That he mote algates dye, yet did his death
    forgive.

VIII

And otherwhyles with amorous delights
And pleasing toyes he would her entertaine,

Now singing sweetly, to surprize her
    sprights,
Now making layes of love and lovers paine,
Bransles, ballads, virelayes, and verses
    vaine;
Oft purposes, oft riddles he devysd,
And thousands like, which flowed in his
    braine,
With which he fed her fancy, and entysd
To take to his new love, and leave her old
    despysd.

IX

And every where he might, and everie
    while,
He did her service dewtifull, and sewd
At hand with humble pride and pleasing
    guile,
So closely yet, that none but she it vewd,
Who well perceived all, and all indewd.
Thus finely did he his false nets dispred,
With which he many weake harts had sub-
    dewd
Of yore, and many had ylike misled:
What wonder then, if she were likewise
    carried ?

X

No fort so fensible, no wals so strong,
But that continuall battery will rive,
Or daily siege, through dispurvayaunce
    long
And lacke of reskewes, will to parley drive;
And peece, that unto parley eare will give,
Will shortly yield it selfe, and will be made
The vassall of the victors will bylive:
That stratageme had oftentimes assayd
This crafty paramoure, and now it plaine
    displayd.

XI

For through his traines he her intrapped
    hath,
That she her love and hart hath wholy
    sold
To him, without regard of gaine or scath,
Or care of credite, or of husband old,
Whom she hath vow'd to dub a fayre cuc-
    quold.
Nought wants but time and place, which
    shortly shee
Devized hath, and to her lover told.
It pleased well: so well they both agree;
So readie rype to ill, ill wemens counsels
    bee.

XII

Darke was the evening, fit for lovers stealth,
When chaunst Malbecco busie be elsewhere,
She to his closet went, where all his wealth
Lay hid: thereof she countlesse summes did
    reare,
The which she meant away with her to
    beare;
The rest she fyr'd for sport, or for despight;
As Hellene, when she saw aloft appeare
The Trojane flames, and reach to hevens
    hight,
Did clap her hands, and joyed at that dole-
    full sight.

XIII

This second Helene, fayre Dame Hellenore,
The whiles her husband ran with sory haste,
To quench the flames which she had tyn'd
    before,
Laught at his foolish labour spent in waste,
And ran into her lovers armes right fast;
Where streight embraced, she to him did cry
And call alowd for helpe, ere helpe were
    past,
For lo! that guest did beare her forcibly,
And meant to ravish her, that rather had to
    dy.

XIV

The wretched man, hearing her call for ayd,
And ready seeing him with her to fly,
In his disquiet mind was much dismayd:
But when againe he backeward cast his eye,
And saw the wicked fire so furiously
Consume his hart, and scorch his idoles
    face,
He was therewith distressed diversely,
Ne wist he how to turne, nor to what place:
Was never wretched man in such a wofull
    cace.

XV

Ay when to him she cryde, to her he turnd,
And left the fire; love money overcame:
But when he marked how his money burnd,
He left his wife; money did love disclame:
Both was he loth to loose his loved dame,
And loth to leave his liefest pelfe behinde,
Yet sith he n'ote save both, he sav'd that
    same
Which was the dearest to his dounghill
    minde,
The god of his desire, the joy of misers
    blinde.

XVI

Thus whilest all things in troublous uprore
    were,
And all men busie to suppresse the flame,
The loving couple neede no reskew feare,
But leasure had and liberty to frame
Their purpost flight, free from all mens re-
    clame;
And Night, the patronesse of love-stealth
    fayre,
Gave them safeconduct, till to end they
    came:
So beene they gone yfere, a wanton payre
Of lovers loosely knit, where list them to
    repayre.

XVII

Soone as the cruell flames yslaked were,
Malbecco, seeing how his losse did lye,
Out of the flames, which he had quencht
    whylere,
Into huge waves of griefe and gealosye
Full deepe emplonged was, and drowned
    nye
Twixt inward doole and felonous despight:
He rav'd, he wept, he stampt, he lowd did
    cry,
And all the passions that in man may light
Did him attonce oppresse, and vex his cay-
    tive spright.

XVIII

Long thus he chawd the cud of inward
    griefe,
And did consume his gall with anguish sore:
Still when he mused on his late mischiefe,
Then still the smart thereof increased more,
And seemd more grievous then it was be-
    fore:
At last, when sorrow he saw booted nought,
Ne griefe might not his love to him re-
    store,
He gan devise how her he reskew mought;
Ten thousand wayes he cast in his confused
    thought.

XIX

At last resolving, like a pilgrim pore,
To search her forth, where so she might be
    fond,
And bearing with him treasure in close
    store,
The rest he leaves in ground: so takes in
    hond
To seeke her endlong both by sea and lond.

Long he her sought, he sought her far and
nere,
And every where that he mote understand
Of knights and ladies any meetings were,
And of eachone he mett he tidings did in-
quere.

XX

But all in vaine; his woman was too wise,
Ever to come into his clouch againe,
And hee too simple ever to surprise
The jolly Paridell, for all his paine.
One day, as hee forpassed by the plaine
With weary pace, he far away espide
A couple, seeming well to be his twaine,
Which hoved close under a forest side,
As if they lay in wait, or els them selves
did hide.

XXI

Well weened hee that those the same mote
bee,
And as he better did their shape avize,
Him seemed more their maner did agree;
For th' one was armed all in warlike wize,
Whom to be Paridell he did devize;
And th' other, al yclad in garments light,
Discolourd like to womanish disguise,
He did resemble to his lady bright,
And ever his faint hart much earned at the
sight.

XXII

And ever faine he towards them would goe,
But yet durst not for dread approchen nie,
But stood aloofe, unweeting what to doe,
Till that prickt forth with loves extremity,
That is the father of fowle gealosy,
He closely nearer crept, the truth to weet:
But, as he nigher drew, he easily
Might scerne that it was not his sweetest
sweet,
Ne yet her belamour, the partner of his
sheet.

XXIII

But it was scornefull Braggadochio,
That with his servant Trompart hoverd
there,
Sith late he fled from his too earnest foe:
Whom such whenas Malbecco spyed clere,
He turned backe, and would have fled
arere;
Till Trompart ronning hastely. him did stay,
And bad before his soveraine lord appere:

That was him loth, yet durst he not gainesay,
And comming him before, low louted on
the lay.

XXIV

The boaster at him sternely bent his browe,
As if he could have kild him with his looke,
That to the ground him meekely made to
bowe,
And awfull terror deepe into him strooke,
That every member of his body quooke.
Said he, 'Thou man of nought, what doest
thou here,
Unfitly furnisht with thy bag and booke,
Where I expected one with shield and
spere,
To prove some deeds of armes upon an
equall pere?'

XXV

The wretched man at his imperious speach
Was all abasht, and low prostrating, said:
'Good sir, let not my rudenes be no breach
Unto your patience, ne be ill ypaid;
For I unwares this way by fortune straid,
A silly pilgrim driven to distresse,
That seeke a lady—' There he suddein
staid,
And did the rest with grievous sighes sup-
presse,
While teares stood in his eies, few drops of
bitternesse.

XXVI

'What lady, man?' said Trompart. 'Take
good hart,
And tell thy griefe, if any hidden lye:
Was never better time to shew thy smart
Then now that noble succor is thee by,
That is the whole worlds commune remedy.
That chearfull word his weak heart much
did cheare,
And with vaine hope his spirits faint sup-
ply,
That bold he sayd: 'O most redoubted pere
Vouchsafe with mild regard a wretches cace
to heare.'

XXVII

Then sighing sore, 'It is not long,' said
hee,
'Sith I enjoyd the gentlest dame alive;
Of whom a knight, no knight at all perdee
But shame of all that doe for honor strive

By treacherous deceipt did me deprive;
Through open outrage he her bore away,
And with fowle force unto his will did
    drive,
Which al good knights, that armes do bear
    this day,
Are bownd for to revenge and punish if
    they may.

XXVIII

'And you, most noble lord, that can and
    dare
Redresse the wrong of miserable wight,
Cannot employ your most victorious speare
In better quarell then defence of right,
And for a lady gainst a faithlesse knight:
So shall your glory bee advaunced much,
And all faire ladies magnify your might,
And eke my selfe, albee I simple such,
Your worthy paine shall wel reward with
    guerdon rich.'

XXIX

With that out of his bouget forth he drew
Great store of treasure, therewith him to
    tempt;
But he on it lookt scornefully askew,
As much disdeigning to be so misdempt,
Or a war-monger to be basely nempt;
And sayd: 'Thy offers base I greatly loth,
And eke thy words uncourteous and un-
    kempt:
I tread in dust thee and thy money both,
That, were it not for shame —' So turned
    from him wroth.

XXX

But Trompart, that his maistres humor
    knew,
In lofty looks to hide an humble minde,
Was inly tickled with that golden vew,
And in his eare him rownded close be-
    hinde:
Yet stoupt he not, but lay still in the
    winde,
Waiting advauntage on the pray to sease;
Till Trompart, lowly to the grownd in-
    clinde,
Besought him his great corage to appease,
And pardon simple man, that rash did him
    displease.

XXXI

Big looking like a doughty doucepere,
At last he thus: 'Thou clod of vilest clay,

I pardon yield, and with thy rudenes beare;
But weete henceforth, that all that golden
    pray,
And all that els the vaine world vaunten
    may,
I loath as doung, ne deeme my dew re-
    ward:
Fame is my meed, and glory vertues pay:
But minds of mortal men are muchell mard
And mov'd amisse with massy mucks un-
    meet regard.

XXXII

'And more, I graunt to thy great misery
Gratious respect; thy wife shall backe be
    sent,
And that vile knight, who ever that he bee,
Which hath thy lady reft, and knighthood
    shent,
By Sanglamort my sword, whose deadly
    dent
The blood hath of so many thousands shedd,
I sweare, ere long shall dearly it repent;
Ne he twixt heven and earth shall hide his
    hedd,
But soone he shalbe fownd, and shortly
    doen be dedd.'

XXXIII

The foolish man thereat woxe wondrous
    blith,
As if the word so spoken were halfe donne,
And humbly thanked him a thousand sith,
That had from death to life him newly
    wonne.
Tho forth the boaster marching, brave be-
    gonne
His stolen steed to thunder furiously,
As if he heaven and hell would overonne,
And all the world confound with cruelty,
That much Malbecco joyed in his jollity.

XXXIV

Thus long they three together traveiled,
Through many a wood and many an un-
    couth way,
To seeke his wife, that was far wandered:
But those two sought nought but the pre-
    sent pray,
To weete, the treasure which he did be-
    wray,
On which their eies and harts were wholly
    sett,
With purpose how they might it best be-
    tray;

For sith the howre that first he did them
    lett
The same behold, therwith their keene de-
    sires were whett.

XXXV

It fortuned, as they together far'd,
They spide, where Paridell came pricking
    fast
Upon the plaine, the which him selfe pre-
    par'd
To giust with that brave straunger knight
    a cast,
As on adventure by the way he past:
Alone he rode without his paragone;
For having filcht her bells, her up he cast
To the wide world, and let her fly alone;
He nould be clogd. So had he served many
    one.

XXXVI

The gentle lady, loose at randon lefte,
The greene-wood long did walke, and wan-
    der wide
At wilde adventure, like a forlorne wefte,
Till on a day the Satyres her espide
Straying alone withouten groome or guide:
Her up they tooke, and with them home her
    ledd,
With them as housewife ever to abide,
To milk their gotes, and make them cheese
    and bredd,
And every one as commune good her hand-
    eled:

XXXVII

That shortly she Malbecco has forgott,
And eke Sir Paridell, all were he deare;
Who from her went to seeke another lott,
And now by fortune was arrived here,
Where those two guilers with Malbecco
    were.
Soone as the oldman saw Sir Paridell,
He fainted, and was almost dead with
    feare,
Ne word he had to speake, his griefe to
    tell,
But to him louted low, and greeted goodly
    well;

XXXVIII

And after asked him for Hellenore.
'I take no keepe of her,' sayd Paridell,
'She wonneth in the forrest there before.'
So forth he rode, as his adventure fell;

The whiles the boaster from his loftie sell
Faynd to alight, something amisse to mend;
But the fresh swayne would not his leasure
    dwell,
But went his way; whom when he passed
    kend,
He up remounted light, and after faind to
    wend.

XXXIX

'Perdy nay,' said Malbecco, 'shall ye not:
But let him passe as lightly as he came:
For litle good of him is to be got,
And mickle perill to bee put to shame.
But let us goe to seeke my dearest dame,
Whom he hath left in yonder forest wyld:
For of her safety in great doubt I ame,
Least salvage beastes her person have de-
    spoyld:
Then all the world is lost, and we in vaine
    have toyld.'

XL

They all agree, and forward them addrest:
'Ah! but,' said crafty Trompart, 'weete ye
    well,
That yonder in that wastefull wildernesse
Huge monsters haunt, and many dangers
    dwell;
Dragons, and minotaures, and feendes of
    hell,
And many wilde woodmen, which robbe and
    rend
All travellers; therefore advise ye well,
Before ye enterprise that way to wend:
One may his journey bring too soone to
    evill end.'

XLI

Malbecco stopt in great astonishment,
And with pale eyes fast fixed on the rest,
Their counsell crav'd, in daunger imminent.
Said Trompart: 'You, that are the most
    opprest
With burdein of great treasure, I thinke
    best
Here for to stay in safetie behynd;
My lord and I will search the wide forest.'
That counsell pleased not Malbeccoes mynd:
For he was much afraid, him selfe alone to
    fynd.

XLII

'Then is it best,' said he, 'that ye doe leave
Your treasure here in some security,

Either fast closed in some hollow greave,
Or buried in the ground from jeopardy,
Till we returne againe in safety:
As for us two, least doubt of us ye have,
Hence farre away we will blyndfolded ly,
Ne privy bee unto your treasures grave.'
It pleased: so he did. Then they march
    forward brave.

XLIII

Now when amid the thickest woodes they
    were,
They heard a noyse of many bagpipes
    shrill,
And shrieking hububs them approching
    nere,
Which all the forest did with horrour fill:
That dreadfull sound the bosters hart did
    thrill
With such amazment, that in hast he fledd,
Ne ever looked back for good or ill,
And after him eke fearefull Trompart
    spedd;
The old man could not fly, but fell to
    ground half dedd.

XLIV

Yet afterwardes close creeping as he might,
He in a bush did hyde his fearefull hedd.
The jolly Satyres, full of fresh delight,
Came dauncing forth, and with them nim-
    bly ledd
Faire Helenore, with girlonds all bespredd,
Whom their May-lady they had newly
    made:
She, proude of that new honour which they
    redd,
And of their lovely fellowship full glade,
Daunst lively, and her face did with a law-
    rell shade.

XLV

The silly man that in the thickett lay
Saw all this goodly sport, and grieved sore,
Yet durst he not against it doe or say,
But did his hart with bitter thoughts en-
    gore,
To see th' unkindnes of his Hellenore.
All day they daunced with great lustyhedd,
And with their horned feet the greene gras
    wore,
The whiles their gotes upon the brouzes
    fedd,
Till drouping Phœbus gan to hyde his
    golden hedd.

XLVI

Tho up they gan their mery pypes to trusse,
And all their goodly heardes did gather
    rownd,
But every Satyre first did give a busse
To Hellenore: so busses did abound.
Now gan the humid vapour shed the grownd
With perly deaw, and th' earthes gloomy
    shade
Did dim the brightnesse of the welkin
    rownd,
That every bird and beast awarned made
To shrowd themselves, whiles sleepe their
    sences did invade.

XLVII

Which when Malbecco saw, out of his bush
Upon his hands and feete he crept full
    light,
And like a gote emongst the gotes did rush,
That through the helpe of his faire hornes
    on hight,
And misty dampe of misconceyving night,
And eke through likenesse of his gotish
    beard,
He did the better counterfeite aright:
So home he marcht emongst the horned
    heard,
That none of all the Satyres him espyde or
    heard.

XLVIII

At night, when all they went to sleepe, he
    vewd
Whereas his lovely wife emongst them lay,
Embraced of a Satyre rough and rude,
Who all the night did minde his joyous
    play:
Nine times he heard him come aloft ere
    day,
That all his hart with gealosy did swell;
But yet that nights ensample did bewray,
That not for nought his wife them loved so
    well,
When one so oft a night did ring his matins
    bell.

XLIX

So closely as he could, he to them crept,
When wearie of their sport to sleepe they
    fell,
And to his wife, that now full soundly slept,
He whispered in her eare, and did her tell,
That it was he, which by her side did
    dwell,

And therefore prayd her wake, to heare
    him plaine.
As one out of a dreame not waked well,
She turnd her, and returned backe againe:
Yet her for to awake he did the more con-
    straine.

L

At last with irkesom trouble she abrayd;
And then perceiving, that it was indeed
Her old Malbecco, which did her upbrayd
With loosenesse of her love and loathly
    deed,
She was astonisht with exceeding dreed,
And would have wakt the Satyre by her
    syde;
But he her prayd, for mercy or for meed,
To save his life, ne let him be descryde,
But hearken to his lore, and all his counsell
    hyde.

LI

Tho gan he her perswade to leave that lewd
And loathsom life, of God and man ab-
    hord,
And home returne, where all should be re-
    newd
With perfect peace and bandes of fresh ac-
    cord,
And she receivd againe to bed and bord,
As if no trespas ever had beene donne:
But she it all refused at one word,
And by no meanes would to his will be
    wonne,
But chose emongst the jolly Satyres still to
    wonne.

LII

He wooed her till day spring he espyde;
But all in vaine: and then turnd to the
    heard,
Who butted him with hornes on every syde,
And trode downe in the durt, where his
    hore beard
Was fowly dight, and he of death afeard.
Early, before the heavens fairest light
Out of the ruddy east was fully reard,
The heardes out of their foldes were loosed
    quight,
And he emongst the rest crept forth in sory
    plight.

LIII

So soone as he the prison dore did pas,
He ran as fast as both his feet could beare,
And never looked who behind him was,
Ne scarsely who before: like as a beare,
That creeping close, amongst the hives to
    reare
An hony combe, the wakefull dogs espy,
And him assayling, sore his carkas teare,
That hardly he with life away does fly,
Ne stayes, till safe him selfe he see from
    jeopardy.

LIV

Ne stayd he, till he came unto the place,
Where late his treasure he entombed
    had;
Where when he found it not (for Trom-
    part bace
Had it purloyned for his maister bad)
With extreme fury he became quite mad,
And ran away, ran with him selfe away:
That who so straungely had him seene be-
    stadd,
With upstart haire and staring eyes dis-
    may,
From Limbo lake him late escaped sure
    would say.

LV

High over hilles and over dales he fledd,
As if the wind him on his winges had
    borne,
Ne banck nor bush could stay him, when he
    spedd
His nimble feet, as treading still on thorne:
Griefe, and despight, and gealosy, and
    scorne
Did all the way him follow hard behynd,
And he himselfe himselfe loath'd so for-
    lorne,
So shamefully forlorne of womankynd;
That, as a snake, still lurked in his wounded
    mynd.

LVI

Still fled he forward, looking backward
    still,
Ne stayd his flight, nor fearefull agony,
Till that he came unto a rocky hill,
Over the sea suspended dreadfully,
That living creature it would terrify
To looke adowne, or upward to the hight:
From thence he threw him selfe dispite-
    ously,
All desperate of his fore-damned spright,
That seemd no help for him was left in liv-
    ing sight.

LVII

But through long anguish and selfe-murd-
    ring thought,
He was so wasted and forpined quight,
That all his substance was consum'd to
    nought,
And nothing left, but like an aery spright,
That on the rockes he fell so flit and light,
That he thereby receiv'd no hurt at all;
But chaunced on a craggy cliff to light;
Whence he with crooked clawes so long did
    crall,
That at the last he found a cave with en-
    trance small.

LVIII

Into the same he creepes, and thenceforth
    there
Resolv'd to build his balefull mansion,
In drery darkenes, and continuall feare
Of that rocks fall, which ever and anon
Threates with huge ruine him to fall upon,
That he dare never sleepe, but that one eye
Still ope he keepes for that occasion;
Ne ever rests he in tranquillity,
The roring billowes beat his bowre so boyst-
    rously.

LIX

Ne ever is he wont on ought to feed
But todes and frogs, his pasture poyson-
    ous,
Which in his cold complexion doe breed
A filthy blood, or humour rancorous,
Matter of doubt and dread suspitious,
That doth with curelesse care consume the
    hart,
Corrupts the stomacke with gall vitious,
Croscuts the liver with internall smart,
And doth transfixe the soule with deathes
    eternall dart.

LX

Yet can he never dye, but dying lives,
And doth himselfe with sorrow new sus-
    taine,
That death and life attonce unto him gives,
And painefull pleasure turnes to pleasing
    paine.
There dwels he ever, miserable swaine,
Hatefull both to him selfe and every wight;
Where he, through privy griefe and hor-
    rour vaine,
Is woxen so deform'd, that he has quight
Forgot he was a man, and Gelosy is hight.

CANTO XI

Britomart chaceth Ollyphant;
Findes Scudamour distrest :
Assayes the house of Busyrane,
Where Loves spoyles are exprest.

I

O HATEFULL hellish snake! what Furie
    furst
Brought thee from balefull house of Pro-
    serpine,
Where in her bosome she thee long had
    nurst,
And fostred up with bitter milke of tine,
Fowle Gealosy! that turnest love divine
To joylesse dread, and mak'st the loving
    hart
With hatefull thoughts to languish and to
    pine,
And feed it selfe with selfe-consuming
    smart?
Of all the passions in the mind thou vilest
    art.

II

O let him far be banished away,
And in his stead let Love for ever dwell,
Sweete Love, that doth his golden wings
    embay
In blessed nectar, and pure pleasures
    well,
Untroubled of vile feare or bitter fell.
And ye, faire ladies, that your kingdomes
    make
In th' harts of men, them governe wisely
    well,
And of faire Britomart ensample take,
That was as trew in love as turtle to her
    make.

III

Who with Sir Satyrane, as earst ye red,
Forth ryding from Malbeccoes hostlesse
    hous,
Far off aspyde a young man, the which
    fled
From an huge geaunt, that with hideous
And hatefull outrage long him chaced
    thus;
It was that Ollyphant, the brother deare
Of that Argante vile and vitious,
From whom the Squyre of Dames was reft
    whylere;
This all as bad as she, and worse, if worse
    ought were.

IV

For as the sister did in feminine
And filthy lust exceede all woman kinde,
So he surpassed his sex masculine,
In beastly use, all that I ever finde:
Whom when as Britomart beheld behinde
The fearefull boy so greedily poursew,
She was emmoved in her noble minde
T' employ her puissaunce to his reskew,
And pricked fiercely forward, where she
did him vew.

V

Ne was Sir Satyrane her far behinde,
But with like fiercenesse did ensew the
chace:
Whom when the gyaunt saw, he soone re-
sinde
His former suit, and from them fled apace:
They after both, and boldly bad him bace,
And each did strive the other to outgoe;
But he them both outran a wondrous space,
For he was long, and swift as any roe,
And now made better speed, t' escape his
feared foe.

VI

It was not Satyrane, whom he did feare,
But Britomart the flowre of chastity;
For he the powre of chaste hands might not
beare,
But alwayes did their dread encounter fly:
And now so fast his feet he did apply,
That he has gotten to a forrest neare,
Where he is shrowded in security.
The wood they enter, and search everie
where;
They searched diversely, so both divided
were.

VII

Fayre Britomart so long him followed,
That she at last came to a fountaine sheare,
By which there lay a knight all wallowed
Upon the grassy ground, and by him neare
His haberjeon, his helmet, and his speare:
A little of, his shield was rudely throwne,
On which the Winged Boy in colours cleare
Depeincted was, full easie to be knowne,
And he thereby, where ever it in field was
showne.

VIII

His face upon the grownd did groveling ly,
As if he had beene slombring in the shade,
That the brave mayd would not for courtesy
Out of his quiet slomber him abrade,
Nor seeme too suddeinly him to invade:
Still as she stood, she heard with grievous
throb
Him grone, as if his hart were peeces made,
And with most painefull pangs to sigh and
sob,
That pitty did the virgins hart of patience
rob.

IX

At last forth breaking into bitter plaintes
He sayd: 'O soverayne Lord, that sit'st on
hye,
And raignst in blis emongst thy blessed
saintes,
How suffrest thou such shamefull cruelty,
So long unwreaked of thine enimy ?
Or hast thou, Lord, of good mens cause no
heed ?
Or doth thy justice sleepe, and silently ?
What booteth then the good and righteous
deed,
If goodnesse find no grace, nor righteousnes
no meed ?

X

'If good find grace, and righteousnes re-
ward,
Why then is Amoret in caytive band,
Sith that more bounteous creature never
far'd
On foot upon the face of living land ?
Or if that hevenly justice may withstand
The wrongfull outrage of unrighteous men,
Why then is Busirane with wicked hand
Suffred, these seven monethes day in secret
den
My lady and my love so cruelly to pen ?

XI

'My lady and my love is cruelly pend
In dolefull darkenes from the vew of day,
Whilest deadly torments doe her chast
brest rend,
And the sharpe steele doth rive her hart in
tway,
All for she Scudamore will not denay.
Yet thou, vile man, vile Scudamore, art
sound,
Ne canst her ayde, ne canst her foe dismay;
Unworthy wretch to tread upon the ground,
For whom so faire a lady feeles so sore a
wound.'

XII

There an huge heape of singulfes did op-
    presse
His strugling soule, and swelling throbs
    empeach
His foltring toung with pangs of drerinesse,
Choking the remnant of his plaintife speach,
As if his dayes were come to their last
    reach.
Which when she heard, and saw the ghastly
    fit,
Threatning into his life to make a breach,
Both with great ruth and terrour she was
    smit,
Fearing least from her cage the wearie
    soule would flit.

XIII

Tho stouping downe, she him amoved light;
Who, therewith somewhat starting, up gan
    looke,
And seeing him behind a stranger knight,
Whereas no living creature he mistooke,
With great indignaunce he that sight for-
    sooke,
And downe againe himselfe disdainefully
Abjecting, th' earth with his faire forhead
    strooke:
Which the bold virgin seeing, gan apply
Fit medcine to his griefe, and spake thus
    courtesly:

XIV

'Ah! gentle knight, whose deepe con-
    ceived griefe
Well seemes t' exceede the powre of pa-
    tience,
Yet if that hevenly grace some good re-
    liefe
You send, submit you to High Providence,
And ever in your noble hart prepense,
That all the sorrow in the world is lesse
Then vertues might and values confidence.
For who nill bide the burden of distresse
Must not here thinke to live: for life is
    wretchednesse.

XV

'Therefore, faire sir, doe comfort to you
    take,
And freely read what wicked felon so
Hath outrag'd you, and thrald your gentle
    make.
Perhaps this hand may helpe to ease your
    woe,

And wreake your sorrow on your cruell
    foe;
At least it faire endevour will apply.'
Those feeling words so neare the quicke
    did goe,
That up his head he reared easily,
And leaning on his elbowe, these few words
    lett fly:

XVI

'What boots it plaine that cannot be re-
    drest,
And sow vaine sorrow in a fruitlesse eare,
Sith powre of hand, nor skill of learned
    brest,
Ne worldly price cannot redeeme my deare
Out of her thraldome and continuall feare?
For he, the tyrant, which her hath in ward
By strong enchauntments and blacke mag-
    icke leare,
Hath in a dungeon deepe her close embard,
And many dreadfull feends hath pointed to
    her gard.

XVII

'There he tormenteth her most terribly,
And day and night afflicts with mortall
    paine,
Because to yield him love she doth deny,
Once to me yold, not to be yolde againe:
But yet by torture he would her con-
    straine
Love to conceive in her disdainfull brest;
Till so she doe, she must in doole remaine,
Ne may by living meanes be thence relest:
What boots it then to plaine that cannot be
    redrest?'

XVIII

With this sad hersall of his heavy stresse
The warlike damzell was empassiond sore,
And sayd: 'Sir knight, your cause is no-
    thing lesse
Then is your sorrow, certes, if not more;
For nothing so much pitty doth implore,
As gentle ladyes helplesse misery.
But yet, if please ye listen to my lore,
I will, with proofe of last extremity,
Deliver her fro thence, or with her for you
    dy.'

XIX

'Ah! gentlest knight alive,' sayd Scuda-
    more,
'What huge heroicke magnanimity

Dwells in thy bounteous brest? what
    couldst thou more,
If shee were thine, and thou as now am I?
O spare thy happy daies, and them apply
To better boot, but let me die, that ought;
More is more losse: one is enough to dy.'
'Life is not lost,' said she, 'for which is
    bought
Endlesse renowm, that more then death is
    to be sought.'

XX

Thus shee at length persuaded him to rise,
And with her wend, to see what new suc-
    cesse
Mote him befall upon new enterprise:
His armes, which he had vowed to dispro-
    fesse,
She gathered up and did about him dresse,
And his forwandred steed unto him gott:
So forth they both yfere make their pro-
    gresse,
And march not past the mounteaunce of a
    shott,
Till they arriv'd whereas their purpose they
    did plott.

XXI

There they dismounting, drew their weap-
    ons bold,
And stoutly came unto the castle gate,
Whereas no gate they found, them to with-
    hold,
Nor ward to wait at morne and evening
    late;
But in the porch, that did them sore amate,
A flaming fire, ymixt with smouldry smoke
And stinking sulphure, that with griesly
    hate
And dreadfull horror did all entraunce
    choke,
Enforced them their forward footing to
    revoke.

XXII

Greatly thereat was Britomart dismayd,
Ne in that stownd wist how her selfe to
    beare;
For daunger vaine it were to have assayd
That cruell element, which all things feare,
Ne none can suffer to approchen neare:
And turning backe to Scudamour, thus
    sayd:
'What monstrous enmity provoke we
    heare,

Foolhardy as th' Earthes children, the which
    made
Batteill against the gods? so we a god in-
    vade.

XXIII

'Daunger without discretion to attempt
Inglorious and beastlike is: therefore, sir
    knight,
Aread what course of you is safest dempt,
And how we with our foe may come to
    fight.'
'This is,' quoth he, 'the dolorous despight,
Which earst to you I playnd: for neither
    may
This fire be quencht by any witt or might,
Ne yet by any meanes remov'd away;
So mighty be th' enchauntments which the
    same do stay.

XXIV

'What is there ells, but cease these fruit-
    lesse paines,
And leave me to my former languishing?
Faire Amorett must dwell in wicked chaines,
And Scudamore here die with sorrowing.'
'Perdy, not so,' saide shee; 'for shameful
    thing
Yt were t' abandon noble chevisaunce,
For shewe of perill, without venturing:
Rather let try extremities of chaunce,
Then enterprised praise for dread to dis-
    avaunce.'

XXV

Therewith, resolv'd to prove her utmost
    might,
Her ample shield she threw before her
    face,
And her swords point directing forward
    right,
Assayld the flame, the which eftesoones
    gave place,
And did it selfe divide with equall space,
That through she passed, as a thonder bolt
Perceth the yielding ayre, and doth dis-
    place
The soring clouds into sad showres ymolt;
So to her yold the flames, and did their
    force revolt.

XXVI

Whome whenas Scudamour saw past the
    fire,
Safe and untoucht, he likewise gan assay,

With greedy will and envious desire,
And bad the stubborne flames to yield him
way:
But cruell Mulciber would not obay
His threatfull pride, but did the more aug-
ment
His mighty rage, and with imperious sway
Him forst (maulgre) his fercenes to relent,
And backe retire, all scorcht and pitifully
brent.

XXVII

With huge impatience he inly swelt,
More for great sorrow that he could not pas
Then for the burning torment which he felt;
That with fell woodnes he effierced was,
And wilfully him throwing on the gras,
Did beat and bounse his head and brest ful
sore;
The whiles the championesse now entred
has
The utmost rowme, and past the formost
dore,
The utmost rowme, abounding with all pre-
cious store.

XXVIII

For round about, the walls yclothed were
With goodly arras of great majesty,
Woven with gold and silke so close and
nere,
That the rich metall lurked privily,
As faining to be hidd from envious eye;
Yet here, and there, and every where un-
wares
It shewd it selfe, and shone unwillingly;
Like a discolourd snake, whose hidden snares
Through the greene gras his long bright
burnisht back declares.

XXIX

And in those tapets weren fashioned
Many faire pourtraicts, and many a faire
feate;
And all of love, and al of lusty-hed,
As seemed by their semblaunt, did entreat;
And eke all Cupids warres they did repeate,
And cruell battailes, which he whilome
fought
Gainst all the gods, to make his empire
great;
Besides the huge massacres, which he
wrought
On mighty kings and kesars, into thraldome
brought.

XXX

Therein was writt, how often thondring
Jove
Had felt the point of his hart percing dart,
And leaving heavens kingdome, here did
rove
In straunge disguize, to slake his scalding
smart;
Now like a ram, faire Helle to pervart,
Now like a bull, Europa to withdraw:
Ah! how the fearefull ladies tender hart
Did lively seeme to tremble, when she saw
The huge seas under her t' obay her ser-
vaunts law!

XXXI

Soone after that, into a golden showre
Him selfe he chaung'd, faire Danaë to vew,
And through the roofe of her strong brasen
towre
Did raine into her lap an hony dew,
The whiles her foolish garde, that litle knew
Of such deceipt, kept th' yron dore fast
bard,
And watcht, that none should enter nor is-
sew;
Vaine was the watch, and bootlesse all the
ward,
Whenas the god to golden hew him selfe
transfard.

XXXII

Then was he turnd into a snowy swan,
To win faire Leda to his lovely trade:
O wondrous skill and sweet wit of the man,
That her in daffadillies sleeping made,
From scorching heat her daintie limbes to
shade:
Whiles the proud bird, ruffing his fethers
wyde
And brushing his faire brest, did her in-
vade!
Shee slept, yet twixt her eielids closely
spyde
How towards her he rusht, and smiled at
his pryde.

XXXIII

Then shewd it how the Thebane Semelee,
Deceivd of gealous Juno, did require
To see him in his soverayne majestee,
Armd with his thunderbolts and lightning
fire,
Whens dearely she with death bought her
desire.

But faire Alcmena better match did make,
Joying his love in likenes more entire:
Three nights in one they say that for her
    sake
He then did put, her pleasures lenger to
    partake.

XXXIV

Twise was he seene in soaring eagles shape,
And with wide winges to beat the buxome
    ayre:
Once, when he with Asterie did scape,
Againe, when as the Trojane boy so fayre
He snatcht from Ida hill, and with him bare:
Wondrous delight it was, there to behould
How the rude shepheards after him did stare,
Trembling through feare least down he
    fallen should,
And often to him calling to take surer
    hould.

XXXV

In Satyres shape Antiopa he snatcht:
And like a fire, when he Aegin' assayd:
A shepeheard, when Mnemosyne he catcht:
And like a serpent to the Thracian mayd.
Whyles thus on earth great Jove these pa-
    geaunts playd,
The Winged Boy did thrust into his throne,
And scoffing, thus unto his mother sayd:
'Lo! now the hevens obey to me alone,
And take me for their Jove, whiles Jove to
    earth is gone.'

XXXVI

And thou, faire Phœbus, in thy colours
    bright
Wast there enwoven, and the sad distresse
In which that boy thee plonged, for de-
    spight
That thou bewray'dst his mothers wanton-
    nesse,
When she with Mars was meynt in joyful-
    nesse:
Forthy he thrild thee with a leaden dart,
To love faire Daphne, which thee loved
    lesse:
Lesse she thee lov'd then was thy just de-
    sart,
Yet was thy love her death, and her death
    was thy smart.

XXXVII

So lovedst thou the lusty Hyacinct,
So lovedst thou the faire Coronis deare:

Yet both are of thy haplesse hand ex-
    tinct,
Yet both in flowres doe live, and love thee
    beare,
The one a paunce, the other a sweet breare:
For griefe whereof, ye mote have lively
    seene
The god himselfe rending his golden heare,
And breaking quite his garlond ever greene,
With other signes of sorrow and impatient
    teene.

XXXVIII

Both for those two, and for his owne deare
    sonne,
The sonne of Climene, he did repent,
Who, bold to guide the charet of the
    sunne,
Himselfe in thousand peeces fondly rent,
And all the world with flashing fire brent:
So like, that all the walles did seeme to
    flame.
Yet cruell Cupid, not herewith content,
Forst him eftsoones to follow other game,
And love a shephards daughter for his
    dearest dame.

XXXIX

He loved Isse for his dearest dame,
And for her sake her cattell fedd a while,
And for her sake a cowheard vile became,
The servant of Admetus, cowheard vile,
Whiles that from heaven he suffered ex-
    ile.
Long were to tell each other lovely fitt,
Now like a lyon, hunting after spoile,
Now like a stag, now like a faulcon flit:
All which in that faire arras was most lively
    writ.

XL

Next unto him was Neptune pictured,
In his divine resemblance wondrous lyke:
His face was rugged, and his hoarie hed
Dropped with brackish deaw; his threeforkt
    pyke
He stearnly shooke, and therewith fierce
    did stryke
The raging billowes, that on every syde
They trembling stood, and made a long
    broad dyke,
That his swift charet might have passage
    wyde,
Which foure great hippodames did draw in
    temewise tyde.

XLI

His seahorses did seeme to snort amayne,
And from their nosethrilles blow the brynie
    streame,
That made the sparckling waves to smoke
    agayne,
And flame with gold, but the white fomy
    creame
Did shine with silver, and shoot forth his
    beame.
The god himselfe did pensive seeme and
    sad,
And hong adowne his head, as he did
    dreame:
For privy love his brest empierced had,
Ne ought but deare Bisaltis ay could make
    him glad.

XLII

He loved eke Iphimedia deare,
And Aeolus faire daughter, Arne hight,
For whom he turnd him selfe into a steare,
And fedd on fodder, to beguile her sight.
Also to win Deucalions daughter bright,
He turnd him selfe into a dolphin fayre;
And like a winged horse he tooke his flight,
To snaky-locke Medusa to repayre,
On whom he got faire Pegasus, that flitteth
    in the ayre.

XLIII

Next Saturne was, (but who would ever
    weene
That sullein Saturne ever weend to love?
Yet love is sullein, and Saturnlike seene,
As he did for Erigone it prove,)
That to a centaure did him selfe transmove.
So proov'd it eke that gratious god of wine,
When, for to compasse Philliras hard love,
He turnd himself into a fruitfull vine,
And into her faire bosome made his grapes
    decline.

XLIV

Long were to tell the amorous assayes,
And gentle pangues, with which he maked
    meeke
The mightie Mars, to learne his wanton
    playes:
How oft for Venus, and how often eek
For many other nymphes he sore did
    shreek,
With womanish teares, and with unwarlike
    smarts,
Privily moystening his horrid cheeke.

There was he painted full of burning
    dartes,
And many wide woundes launched through
    his inner partes.

XLV

Ne did he spare (so cruell was the elfe)
His owne deare mother, (ah! why should
    he so?)
Ne did he spare sometime to pricke him-
    selfe,
That he might taste the sweet consuming
    woe,
Which he had wrought to many others moe.
But to declare the mournfull tragedyes,
And spoiles, wherewith he all the ground
    did strow,
More eath to number with how many eyes
High heven beholdes sad lovers nightly
    theeveryes.

XLVI

Kings, queenes, lords, ladies, knights, and
    damsels gent
Were heap'd together with the vulgar sort,
And mingled with the raskall rablement,
Without respect of person or of port,
To shew Dan Cupids powre and great
    effort:
And round about, a border was entrayld
Of broken bowes and arrowes shivered
    short,
And a long bloody river through them rayld,
So lively and so like that living sence it
    fayld.

XLVII

And at the upper end of that faire rowme,
There was an altar built of pretious stone,
Of passing valew and of great renowme,
On which there stood an image all alone
Of massy gold, which with his owne light
    shone;
And winges it had with sondry colours
    dight,
More sondry colours then the proud pavone
Beares in his boasted fan, or Iris bright,
When her discolourd bow she spreds
    through hevens hight.

XLVIII

Blyndfold he was, and in his cruell fist
A mortall bow and arrowes keene did hold,
With which he shot at randon, when him
    list,

Some headed with sad lead, some with pure
    gold;
(Ah! man, beware how thou those dartes
    behold.)
A wounded dragon under him did ly,
Whose hideous tayle his lefte foot did en-
    fold,
And with a shaft was shot through either
    eye,
That no man forth might draw, ne no man
    remedye.

XLIX

And underneath his feet was written thus,
Unto the victor of the gods this bee:
And all the people in that ample hous
Did to that image bowe their humble
    knee,
And oft committed fowle idolatree.
That wondrous sight faire Britomart
    amazd,
Ne seeing could her wonder satisfie,
But ever more and more upon it gazd,
The whiles the passing brightnes her fraile
    sences dazd.

L

Tho as she backward cast her busie eye,
To search each secrete of that goodly
    sted,
Over the dore thus written she did spye,
Bee bold: she oft and oft it over-red,
Yet could not find what sence it figured:
But what so were therein or writ or
    ment,
She was no whit thereby discouraged
From prosecuting of her first intent,
But forward with bold steps into the next
    roome went.

LI

Much fayrer then the former was that
    roome,
And richlier by many partes arayd;
For not with arras made in painefull loome,
But with pure gold, it all was overlayd,
Wrought with wilde antickes, which their
    follies playd
In the rich metall, as they living were:
A thousand monstrous formes therein were
    made,
Such as false Love doth oft upon him
    weare,
For Love in thousand monstrous formes
    doth oft appeare.

LII

And all about, the glistring walles were
    hong
With warlike spoiles and with victorious
    prayes
Of mightie conquerours and captaines
    strong,
Which were whilome captived in their
    dayes
To cruell Love, and wrought their owne
    decayes:
Their swerds and speres were broke, and
    hauberques rent,
And their proud girlonds of tryumphant
    bayes
Troden in dust with fury insolent,
To shew the victors might and mercilesse
    intent.

LIII

The warlike mayd, beholding earnestly
The goodly ordinaunce of this rich place,
Did greatly wonder, ne could satisfy
Her greedy eyes with gazing a long space;
But more she mervaild that no footings
    trace
Nor wight appear'd, but wastefull empti-
    nesse
And solemne silence over all that place:
Straunge thing it seem'd, that none was to
    possesse
So rich purveyaunce, ne them keepe with
    carefulnesse.

LIV

And as she lookt about, she did behold
How over that same dore was likewise
    writ,
Be bolde, be bolde, and every where *Be bold,*
That much she muz'd, yet could not con
    strue it
By any ridling skill or commune wit.
At last she spyde at that rowmes upper end
Another yron dore, on which was writ,
Be not too bold; whereto though she did bend
Her earnest minde, yet wist not what it
    might intend.

LV

Thus she there wayted untill eventyde,
Yet living creature none she saw appeare:
And now sad shadowes gan the world to
    hyde
From mortall vew, and wrap in darkenes
    dreare:

Yet nould she d'off her weary armes, for
    feare
Of secret daunger, ne let sleepe oppresse
Her heavy eyes with natures burdein deare,
But drew her selfe aside in sickernesse,
And her welpointed wepons did about her
    dresse.

CANTO XII

The maske of Cupid, and th' enchanted
    chamber are displayd,
Whence Britomart redeemes faire
    Amoret through charmes decayd.

I

Tho, when as chearelesse night ycovered
    had
Fayre heaven with an universall clowd,
That every wight, dismayd with darkenes
    sad,
In silence and in sleepe themselves did
    shrowd,
She heard a shrilling trompet sound alowd,
Signe of nigh battaill, or got victory:
Nought therewith daunted was her courage
    prowd,
But rather stird to cruell enmity,
Expecting ever when some foe she might
    descry.

II

With that, an hideous storme of winde
    arose,
With dreadfull thunder and lightning
    atwixt,
And an earthquake, as if it streight would
    lose
The worlds foundations from his centre fixt:
A direfull stench of smoke and sulphure
    mixt
Ensewd, whose noyaunce fild the fearefull
    sted,
From the fourth howre of night untill the
    sixt;
Yet the bold Britonesse was nought ydred,
Though much emmov'd, but stedfast still
    persevered.

III

All suddeinly a stormy whirlwind blew
Throughout the house, that clapped every
    dore,
With which that yron wicket open flew,
As it with mighty levers had bene tore;

And forth yssewd, as on the readie flore
Of some theatre, a grave personage,
That in his hand a braunch of laurell bore,
With comely haveour and count'nance sage,
Yclad in costly garments, fit for tragicke
    stage.

IV

Proceeding to the midst, he stil did stand,
As if in minde he somewhat had to say,
And to the vulgare beckning with his hand,
In signe of silence, as to heare a play,
By lively actions he gan bewray
Some argument of matter passioned;
Which doen, he backe retyred soft away,
And passing by, his name discovered,
Ease, on his robe in golden letters cyphered.

V

The noble mayd, still standing, all this
    vewd,
And merveild at his straunge intendiment:
With that a joyous fellowship issewd
Of minstrales, making goodly meriment,
With wanton bardes, and rymers impu-
    dent,
All which together song full chearefully
A lay of loves delight, with sweet concent:
After whom marcht a jolly company,
In manner of a maske, enranged orderly.

VI

The whiles a most delitious harmony
In full straunge notes was sweetly heard to
    sound,
That the rare sweetnesse of the melody
The feeble sences wholy did confound,
And the frayle soule in deepe delight nigh
    drownd:
And when it ceast, shrill trompets lowd did
    bray,
That their report did far away rebound,
And when they ceast, it gan againe to play,
The whiles the maskers marched forth in
    trim aray.

VII

The first was Fansy, like a lovely boy,
Of rare aspect and beautie without peare,
Matchable ether to that ympe of Troy,
Whom Jove did love and chose his cup to
    beare,
Or that same daintie lad, which was so
    deare
To great Alcides, that, when as he dyde,

He wailed womanlike with many a teare,
And every wood and every valley wyde
He fild with Hylas name; the nymphes eke
    Hylas cryde.

VIII

His garment nether was of silke nor say,
But paynted plumes, in goodly order dight,
Like as the sunburnt Indians do aray
Their tawney bodies, in their proudest
    plight:
As those same plumes, so seemd he vaine
    and light,
That by his gate might easily appeare;
For still he far'd as dauncing in delight,
And in his hand a windy fan did beare,
That in the ydle ayre he mov'd still here
    and theare.

IX

And him beside marcht amorous Desyre,
Who seemd of ryper yeares then th' other
    swayne,
Yet was that other swayne this elders syre,
And gave him being, commune to them
    twayne:
His garment was disguysed very vayne,
And his embrodered bonet sat awry;
Twixt both his hands few sparks he close
    did strayne,
Which still he blew, and kindled busily,
That soone they life conceiv'd, and forth in
    flames did fly.

X

Next after him went Doubt, who was yclad
In a discolour'd cote of straunge disguyse,
That at his backe a brode capuccio had,
And sleeves dependaunt Albanese-wyse:
He lookt askew with his mistrustfull eyes,
And nycely trode, as thornes lay in his way,
Or that the flore to shrinke he did avyse,
And on a broken reed he still did stay
His feeble steps, which shrunck when hard
    thereon he lay.

XI

With him went Daunger, cloth'd in ragged
    weed,
Made of beares skin, that him more dread-
    full made,
Yet his owne face was dreadfull, ne did
    need
Straunge horrour to deforme his griesly
    shade:

A net in th' one hand, and a rusty blade
In th' other was, this Mischiefe, that Mis-
    hap;
With th' one his foes he threatned to in-
    vade,
With th' other he his friends ment to en-
    wrap:
For whom he could not kill he practizd to
    entrap.

XII

Next him was Feare, all arm'd from top to
    toe,
Yet thought himselfe not safe enough
    thereby,
But feard each shadow moving too or
    froe,
And his owne armes when glittering he did
    spy,
Or clashing heard, he fast away did fly,
As ashes pale of hew, and wingyheeld;
And evermore on Daunger fixt his eye,
Gainst whom he alwayes bent a brasen
    shield,
Which his right hand unarmed fearefully
    did wield.

XIII

With him went Hope in rancke, a hand-
    some mayd,
Of chearefull looke and lovely to behold;
In silken samite she was light arayd,
And her fayre lockes were woven up in
    gold;
She alway smyld, and in her hand did hold
An holy water sprinckle, dipt in deowe,
With which she sprinckled favours mani-
    fold
On whom she list, and did great liking
    sheowe,
Great liking unto many, but true love to
    feowe.

XIV

And after them Dissemblaunce and Sus-
    pect
Marcht in one rancke, yet an unequall
    paire:
For she was gentle and of milde aspect,
Courteous to all and seeming debonaire,
Goodly adorned and exceeding faire:
Yet was that all but paynted and pour-
    loynd,
And her bright browes were deckt with
    borrowed haire:

Her deeds were forged, and her words false
    coynd,
And alwaies in her hand two clewes of
    silke she twynd.

XV

But he was fowle, ill favoured, and grim,
Under his eiebrowes looking still askaunce;
And ever as Dissemblaunce laught on him,
He lowrd on her with daungerous eye-
    glaunce,
Shewing his nature in his countenaunce;
His rolling eies did never rest in place,
But walkte each where, for feare of hid
    mischaunce;
Holding a lattis still before his face,
Through which he stil did peep, as forward
    he did pace.

XVI

Next him went Griefe and Fury matcht
    yfere;
Griefe all in sable sorrowfully clad,
Downe hanging his dull head, with heavy
    chere,
Yet inly being more then seeming sad:
A paire of pincers in his hand he had,
With which he pinched people to the hart,
That from thenceforth a wretched life they
    ladd,
In wilfull languor and consuming smart,
Dying each day with inward wounds of
    dolours dart.

XVII

But Fury was full ill appareiled
In rags, that naked nigh she did appeare,
With ghastly looks and dreadfull drerihed;
For from her backe her garments she did
    teare,
And from her head ofte rent her snarled
    heare:
In her right hand a firebrand shee did tosse
About her head, still roming here and there;
As a dismayed deare in chace embost,
Forgetfull of his safety, hath his right
    way lost.

XVIII

After them went Displeasure and Pleas-
    aunce,
He looking lompish and full sullein sad,
And hanging downe his heavy countenaunce;
She chearfull fresh and full of joyaunce
    glad,

As if no sorrow she ne felt ne drad;
That evill matched paire they seemd to
    bee:
An angry waspe th' one in a viall had,
Th' other in hers an hony-laden bee.
Thus marched these six couples forth in
    faire degree.

XIX

After all these there marcht a most faire
    dame,
Led of two grysie villeins, th' one De-
    spight,
The other cleped Cruelty by name:
She, dolefull lady, like a dreary spright
Cald by strong charmes out of eternall
    night,
Had deathes owne ymage figurd in her face,
Full of sad signes, fearfull to living sight,
Yet in that horror shewd a seemely grace,
And with her feeble feete did move a
    comely pace.

XX

Her brest all naked, as nett yvory,
Without adorne of gold or silver bright,
Wherewith the craftesman wonts it beaut-
    ify,
Of her dew honour was despoyled quight,
And a wide wound therein (O ruefull
    sight!)
Entrenched deep with knyfe accursed
    keene,
Yet freshly bleeding forth her fainting
    spright,
(The worke of cruell hand) was to be
    seene,
That dyde in sanguine red her skin all
    snowy cleene.

XXI

At that wide orifice her trembling hart
Was drawne forth, and in silver basin layd,
Quite through transfixed with a deadly dart,
And in her blood yet steeming fresh em-
    bayd:
And those two villeins, which her steps up-
    stayd,
When her weake feete could scarcely her
    sustaine,
And fading vitall powers gan to fade,
Her forward still with torture did con-
    straine,
And evermore encreased her consuming
    paine.

XXII

Next after her, the Winged God him selfe
Came riding on a lion ravenous,
Taught to obay the menage of that elfe,
That man and beast with powre imperious
Subdeweth to his kingdome tyrannous:
His blindfold eies he had a while unbinde,
That his proud spoile of that same dolorous
Faire dame he might behold in perfect
    kinde,
Which seene, he much rejoyced in his
    cruell minde.

XXIII

Of which ful prowd, him selfe up rearing
    hye,
He looked round about with sterne dis-
    dayne,
And did survay his goodly company:
And marshalling the evill ordered trayne,
With that the darts which his right hand
    did straine
Full dreadfully he shooke, that all did
    quake,
And clapt on hye his coulourd winges
    twaine,
That all his many it affraide did make:
Tho, blinding him againe, his way he forth
    did take.

XXIV

Behinde him was Reproch, Repentaunce,
    Shame;
Reproch the first, Shame next, Repent be-
    hinde:
Repentaunce feeble, sorowfull, and lame;
Reproch despightfull, carelesse, and un-
    kinde;
Shame most ill favourd, bestiall, and blinde:
Shame lowrd, Repentaunce sigh'd, Reproch
    did scould;
Reproch sharpe stings, Repentaunce whips
    entwinde,
Shame burning brond-yrons in her hand did
    hold:
All three to each unlike, yet all made in
    one mould.

XXV

And after them a rude confused rout
Of persons flockt, whose names is hard to
    read:
Emongst them was sterne Strife, and An-
    ger stout,
Unquiet Care, and fond Unthriftyhead,

Lewd Losse of Time, and Sorrow seeming
    dead,
Inconstant Chaunge, and false Disloyalty,
Consuming Riotise, and guilty Dread
Of Heavenly Vengeaunce, faint Infirmity,
Vile Poverty, and lastly Death with Infamy.

XXVI

There were full many moe like maladies,
Whose names and natures I note readen
    well;
So many moe, as there be phantasies
In wavering wemens witt, that none can
    tell,
Or paines in love, or punishments in hell;
All which disguized marcht in masking
    wise
About the chamber with that damozell,
And then returned, having marched thrise,
Into the inner rowme, from whence they
    first did rise.

XXVII

So soone as they were in, the dore streight
    way
Fast locked, driven with that stormy blast
Which first it opened; and bore all away.
Then the brave maid, which al this while
    was plast
In secret shade, and saw both first and last,
Issewed forth, and went unto the dore,
To enter in, but fownd it locked fast:
It vaine she thought with rigorous uprore
For to efforce, when charmes had closed it
    afore.

XXVIII

Where force might not availe, there sleights
    and art
She cast to use, both fitt for hard emprize:
Forthy from that same rowme not to depart
Till morrow next shee did her selfe avize,
When that same maske againe should forth
    arize.
The morrowe next appeard with joyous
    cheare,
Calling men to their daily exercize:
Then she, as morrow fresh, her selfe did
    reare
Out of her secret stand, that day for to out-
    weare.

XXIX

All that day she outwore in wandering,
And gazing on that chambers ornament,

Till that againe the second evening
Her covered with her sable vestiment,
Wherewith the worlds faire beautie she hath
    blent:
Then, when the second watch was almost
    past,
That brasen dore flew open, and in went
Bold Britomart, as she had late forecast,
Nether of ydle showes nor of false charmes
    aghast.

XXX

So soone as she was entred, rownd about
Shee cast her eies, to see what was be-
    come
Of all those persons which she saw without:
But lo! they streight were vanisht all and
    some,
Ne living wight she saw in all that roome,
Save that same woefull lady, both whose
    hands
Were bounden fast, that did her ill become,
And her small waste girt rownd with yron
    bands,
Unto a brasen pillour, by the which she
    stands.

XXXI

And her before, the vile enchaunter sate,
Figuring straunge characters of his art:
With living blood he those characters wrate,
Dreadfully dropping from her dying hart,
Seeming transfixed with a cruell dart;
And all perforce to make her him to love.
Ah! who can love the worker of her smart?
A thousand charmes he formerly did prove;
Yet thousand charmes could not her stedfast
    hart remove.

XXXII

Soone as that virgin knight he saw in place,
His wicked bookes in hast he overthrew,
Not caring his long labours to deface;
And fiercely running to that lady trew,
A murdrous knife out of his pocket drew,
The which he thought, for villeinous de-
    spight,
In her tormented bodie to embrew:
But the stout damzell to him leaping light,
His cursed hand withheld, and maistered his
    might.

XXXIII

From her, to whom his fury first he ment,
The wicked weapon rashly he did wrest,
And turning to herselfe his fell intent,
Unwares it strooke into her snowie chest,
That litle drops empurpled her faire brest.
Exceeding wroth therewith the virgin grew,
Albe the wound were nothing deepe im-
    prest,
And fiercely forth her mortall blade she
    drew,
To give him the reward for such vile outrage
    dew.

XXXIV

So mightily she smote him, that to ground
He fell halfe dead; next stroke him should
    have slaine,
Had not the lady, which by him stood bound,
Dernly unto her called to abstaine
From doing him to dy; for else her paine
Should be remedilesse, sith none but hee,
Which wrought it, could the same recure
    againe.
Therewith she stayd her hand, loth stayd to
    bee;
For life she him envyde, and long'd revenge
    to see:

XXXV

And to him said: 'Thou wicked man! whose
    meed
For so huge mischiefe and vile villany
Is death, or if that ought doe death exceed,
Be sure that nought may save thee from to
    dy,
But if that thou this dame doe presently
Restore unto her health and former state;
This doe and live, els dye undoubtedly.'
He, glad of life, that lookt for death but
    late,
Did yield him selfe right willing to prolong
    his date:

XXXVI

And rising up, gan streight to overlooke
Those cursed leaves, his charmes back to
    reverse;
Full dreadfull thinges out of that balefull
    booke
He red, and measur'd many a sad verse,
That horrour gan the virgins hart to perse,
And her faire locks up stared stiffe on end,
Hearing him those same bloody lynes re-
    herse;
And all the while he red, she did extend
Her sword high over him, if ought he did
    offend.

XXXVII

Anon she gan perceive the house to quake,
And all the dores to rattle round about;
Yet all that did not her dismaied make,
Nor slack her threatfull hand for daungers
    dout,
But still with stedfast eye and courage stout
Abode, to weet what end would come of all.
At last that mightie chaine, which round
    about
Her tender waste was wound, adowne gan
    fall,
And that great brasen pillour broke in
    peeces small.

XXXVIII

The cruell steele, which thrild her dying
    hart,
Fell softly forth, as of his owne accord,
And the wyde wound, which lately did dis-
    part
Her bleeding brest, and riven bowels gor'd,
Was closed up, as it had not beene bor'd,
And every part to safety full sownd,
As she were never hurt, was soone restor'd:
Tho, when she felt her selfe to be unbownd,
And perfect hole, prostrate she fell unto
    the grownd.

XXXIX

Before faire Britomart she fell prostrate,
Saying: 'Ah, noble knight! what worthy
    meede
Can wretched lady, quitt from wofull state,
Yield you in lieu of this your gracious
    deed?
Your vertue selfe her owne reward shall
    breed,
Even immortall prayse and glory wyde,
Which I, your vassall, by your prowesse
    freed,
Shall through the world make to be noti-
    fyde,
And goodly well advaunce, that goodly well
    was tryde.'

XL

But Britomart, uprearing her from grownd,
Said: 'Gentle dame, reward enough I
    weene,
For many labours more then I have found,
This, that in safetie now I have you seene,
And meane of your deliverance have beene:
Henceforth, faire lady, comfort to you
    take,

And put away remembraunce of late teene;
In sted thereof, know that your loving
    make
Hath no lesse griefe endured for your gen-
    tle sake.'

XLI

She much was cheard to heare him men-
    tiond,
Whom of all living wightes she loved best.
Then laid the noble championesse strong
    hond
Upon th' enchaunter, which had her dis-
    trest
So sore, and with foule outrages opprest:
With that great chaine, wherewith not long
    ygoe
He bound that pitteous lady prisoner, now
    ...iest,
Himselfe she bound, more worthy to be so,
And captive with her led to wretchednesse
    and wo.

XLII

Returning back, those goodly rowmes,
    which erst
She saw so rich and royally arayd,
Now vanisht utterly and cleane subverst
She found, and all their glory quite de-
    cayd,
That sight of such a chaunge her much
    dismayd.
Thence forth descending to that perlous
    porch,
Those dreadfull flames she also found de-
    layd,
And quenched quite, like a consumed torch,
That erst all entrers wont so cruelly to
    scorch.

XLIII

More easie issew now then entrance late
She found: for now that fained dreadfull
    flame,
Which chokt the porch of that enchaunted
    gate,
And passage bard to all that thither came,
Was vanisht quite, as it were not the same,
And gave her leave at pleasure forth to
    passe.
Th' enchaunter selfe, which all that fraud
    did frame,
To have efforst the love of that faire lasse,
Seeing his worke now wasted, deepe en-
    grieved was.

XLIV

But when the victoresse arrived there
Where late she left the pensife Scuda-
more
With her own trusty squire, both full of
feare,
Neither of them she found where she them
lore:
Thereat her noble hart was stonisht sore;
But most faire Amoret, whose gentle spright
Now gan to feede on hope, which she be-
fore
Conceived had, to see her own deare knight,
Being thereof beguyld, was fild with new
affright.

XLV

But he, sad man, when he had long in drede
Awayted there for Britomarts returne,
Yet saw her not, nor signe of her good speed,
His expectation to despaire did turne,
Misdeeming sure that her those flames did
burne;
And therefore gan advize with her old
squire,
Who her deare nourslings losse no lesse did
mourne,
Thence to depart for further aide t' en-
quire:
Where let them wend at will, whilest here
I doe respire.

THE SECOND PART OF THE
FAERIE QUEENE

CONTAINING

THE FOURTH, FIFTH, AND SIXTH BOOKES

BY ED. SPENSER

IMPRINTED AT LONDON FOR WILLIAM
PONSONBY. 1596

THE FOURTH BOOKE
OF THE FAERIE QUEENE

CONTAINING

THE LEGEND OF CAMBEL AND
TRIAMOND

OR

OF FRIENDSHIP

I

THE rugged forhead that with grave fore-
sight
Welds kingdomes causes and affaires of state,
My looser rimes (I wote) doth sharply wite,
For praising love, as I have done of late,
And magnifying lovers deare debate;
By which fraile youth is oft to follie led,
Through false allurement of that pleasing
baite,
That better were in vertues discipled,
Then with vaine poemes weeds to have
their fancies fed.

II

Such ones ill judge of love, that cannot
love,
Ne in their frosen hearts feele kindly
flame:
Forthy they ought not thing unknowne re-
prove,
Ne naturall affection faultlesse blame,
For fault of few that have abusd the
same.
For it of honor and all vertue is
The roote, and brings forth glorious flowres
of fame,
That crowne true lovers with immortall
blis,
The meed of them that love, and do not
live amisse.

III

Which who so list looke backe to former
ages,
And call to count the things that then were
donne,

Shall find, that all the workes of those wise
sages,
And brave exploits which great heroes
wonne,
In love were either ended or begunne:
Witnesse the father of philosophie,
Which to his Critias, shaded oft from sunne,
Of love full manie lessons did apply,
The which these Stoicke censours cannot
well deny.

IV

To such therefore I do not sing at all,
But to that sacred saint my soveraigne
Queene,
In whose chast breast all bountie naturall
And treasures of true love enlocked beene,
Bove all her sexe that ever yet was seene:
To her I sing of love, that loveth best
And best is lov'd of all alive, I weene;
To her this song most fitly is addrest,
The queene of love, and prince of peace
from heaven blest.

V

Which that she may the better deigne to
heare,
Do thou, dred infant, Venus dearling
dove,
From her high spirit chase imperious feare,
And use of awfull majestie remove:
In sted thereof with drops of melting love,
Deawd with ambrosiall kisses, by thee
gotten
From thy sweete smyling mother from
above,
Sprinckle her heart, and haughtie courage
soften,
That she may hearke to love, and reade
this lesson often.

CANTO I

Fayre Britomart saves Amoret:
Duessa discord breedes
Twixt Scudamour and Blandamour:
Their fight and warlike deedes.

I

OF lovers sad calamities of old
Full many piteous stories doe remaine,
But none more piteous ever was ytold,
Then that of Amorets hart-binding chaine,
And this of Florimels unworthie paine:
The deare compassion of whose bitter fit

My softened heart so sorely doth constraine,
That I with teares full oft doe pittie it,
And oftentimes doe wish it never had bene
writ.

II

For from the time that Scudamour her
bought
In perilous fight, she never joyed day;
A perilous fight when he with force her
brought
From twentie knights, that did him all as-
say:
Yet fairely well he did them all dismay,
And with great glorie both the Shield of
Love
And eke the ladie selfe he brought away;
Whom having wedded, as did him behove,
A new unknowen mischiefe did from him
remove.

III

For that same vile enchauntour Busyran,
The very selfe same day that she was
wedded,
Amidst the bridale feast, whilest every
man,
Surcharg'd with wine, were heedlesse and
ill hedded,
All bent to mirth before the bride was
bedded,
Brought in that Mask of Love which late
was showen:
And there the ladie ill of friends bestedded,
By way of sport, as oft in maskes is knowen,
Conveyed quite away to living wight un-
knowen.

IV

Seven moneths he so her kept in bitter
smart,
Because his sinful lust she would not serve,
Untill such time as noble Britomart
Released her, that else was like to sterve,
Through cruell knife that her deare heart
did kerve.
And now she is with her upon the way,
Marching in lovely wise, that could deserve
No spot of blame, though spite did oft as-
say
To blot her with dishonor of so faire a pray.

V

Yet should it be a pleasant tale, to tell
The diverse usage, and demeanure daint,

That each to other made, as oft befell.
For Amoret right fearefull was and faint,
Lest she with blame her honor should at-
　taint,
That everie word did tremble as she
　spake,
And everie looke was coy and wondrous
　quaint,
And everie limbe that touched her did
　quake:
Yet could she not but curteous countenance
　to her make.

VI

For well she wist, as true it was indeed,
That her lives lord and patrone of her
　health
Right well deserved, as his duefull meed,
Her love, her service, and her utmost
　wealth:
All is his justly, that all freely dealth.
Nathlesse her honor, dearer then her life,
She sought to save, as thing reserv'd from
　stealth;
Die had she lever with enchanters knife,
Then to be false in love, profest a virgine
　wife.

VII

Thereto her feare was made so much the
　greater
Through fine abusion of that Briton mayd:
Who, for to hide her fained sex the better
And maske her wounded mind, both did
　and sayd
Full many things so doubtfull to be wayd,
That well she wist not what by them to
　gesse;
For other whiles to her she purpos made
Of love, and otherwhiles of lustfulnesse,
That much she feard his mind would grow
　to some excesse.

VIII

His will she feard; for him she surely
　thought
To be a man, such as indeed he seemed,
And much the more, by that he lately
　wrought,
When her from deadly thraldome he re-
　deemed,
For which no service she too much es-
　teemed:
Yet dread of shame and doubt of fowle
　dishonor

Made her not yeeld so much as due she
　deemed.
Yet Britomart attended duly on her,
As well became a knight, and did to her all
　honor.

IX

It so befell one evening, that they came
Unto a castell, lodged there to bee,
Where many a knight, and many a lovely
　dame,
Was then assembled, deeds of armes to see:
Amongst all which was none more faire
　then shee,
That many of them mov'd to eye her sore.
The custome of that place was such, that hee
Which had no love nor lemman there in
　store
Should either winne him one, or lye with-
　out the dore.

X

Amongst the rest there was a jolly knight,
Who, being asked for his love, avow'd
That fairest Amoret was his by right,
And offred that to justifie alowd.
The warlike virgine, seeing his so prowd
And boastfull chalenge, wexed inlie wroth,
But for the present did her anger shrowd;
And sayd, her love to lose she was full loth,
But either he should neither of them have,
　or both.

XI

So foorth they went, and both together
　giusted;
But that same younker soone was over
　throwne,
And made repent that he had rashly lusted
For thing unlawfull, that was not his owne:
Yet since he seemed valiant, though un-
　knowne,
She, that no lesse was courteous then stout,
Cast how to salve, that both the custome
　showne
Were kept, and yet that knight not locked
　out;
That seem'd full hard t' accord two things
　so far in dout.

XII

The seneschall was cal'd to deeme the
　right:
Whom she requir'd, that first fayre Amoret
Might be to her allow'd, as to a knight

That did her win and free from chalenge
　　set:
Which straight to her was yeelded without
　　let.
Then, since that strange knights love from
　　him was quitted,
She claim'd that to her selfe, as ladies
　　det,
He as a knight might justly be admitted;
So none should be out shut, sith all of loves
　　were fitted.

XIII

With that, her glistring helmet she un-
　　laced;
Which doft, her golden lockes, that were
　　up bound
Still in a knot, unto her heeles downe
　　traced,
And like a silken veile in compasse round
About her backe and all her bodie wound:
Like as the shining skie in summers night,
What time the dayes with scorching heat
　　abound,
Is creasted all with lines of firie light,
That it prodigious seemes in common peo-
　　ples sight.

XIV

Such when those knights and ladies all
　　about
Beheld her, all were with amazement smit,
And every one gan grow in secret dout
Of this and that, according to each wit:
Some thought that some enchantment
　　faygned it;
Some, that Bellona in that warlike wise
To them appear'd, with shield and armour
　　fit;
Some, that it was a maske of strange dis-
　　guise:
So diversely each one did sundrie doubts
　　devise.

XV

But that young knight, which through her
　　gentle deed
Was to that goodly fellowship restor'd,
Ten thousand thankes did yeeld her for her
　　meed,
And, doubly overcommen, her ador'd:
So did they all their former strife accord;
And eke fayre Amoret, now freed from
　　feare,
More franke affection did to her afford,

And to her bed, which she was wont for-
　　beare,
Now freely drew, and found right safe
　　assurance theare.

XVI

Where all that night they of their loves did
　　treat,
And hard adventures, twixt themselves
　　alone,
That each the other gan with passion great
And griefull pittie privately bemone.
The morow next, so soone as Titan shone,
They both uprose, and to their waies them
　　dight:
Long wandred they, yet never met with
　　none
That to their willes could them direct
　　aright,
Or to them tydings tell that mote their
　　harts delight.

XVII

Lo ! thus they rode, till at the last they
　　spide
Two armed knights, that toward them did
　　pace,
And ech of them had ryding by his side
A ladie, seeming in so farre a space;
But ladies none they were, albee in face
And outward shew faire semblance they did
　　beare;
For under maske of beautie and good
　　grace
Vile treason and fowle falshood hidden
　　were,
That mote to none but to the warie wise
　　appeare.

XVIII

The one of them the false Duessa hight,
That now had chang'd her former wonted
　　hew:
For she could d'on so manie shapes in
　　sight,
As ever could cameleon colours new;
So could she forge all colours, save the
　　trew.
The other no whit better was then shee,
But that, such as she was, she plaine did
　　shew;
Yet otherwise much worse, if worse might
　　bee,
And dayly more offensive unto each de-
　　gree.

XIX

Her name was Ate, mother of debate
And all dissention, which doth dayly grow
Amongst fraile men, that many a publike
    state
And many a private oft doth overthrow.
Her false Duessa, who full well did know
To be most fit to trouble noble knights,
Which hunt for honor, raised from below
Out of the dwellings of the damned sprights,
Where she in darknes wastes her cursed
    daies and nights.

XX

Hard by the gates of hell her dwelling is,
There whereas all the plagues and harmes
    abound,
Which punish wicked men, that walke
    amisse.
It is a darksome delve farre under ground,
With thornes and barren brakes environd
    round,
That none the same may easily out win;
Yet many waies to enter may be found,
But none to issue forth when one is in:
For discord harder is to end then to begin.

XXI

And all within, the riven walls were hung
With ragged monuments of times forepast,
All which the sad effects of discord sung:
There were rent robes and broken scepters
    plast,
Altars defyl'd, and holy things defast,
Disshivered speares, and shields ytorne in
    twaine,
Great cities ransackt, and strong castles
    rast,
Nations captived, and huge armies slaine:
Of all which ruines there some relicks did
    remaine.

XXII

There was the signe of antique Babylon,
Of fatall Thebes, of Rome that raigned
    long,
Of sacred Salem, and sad Ilion,
For memorie of which on high there hong
The golden apple, cause of all their wrong,
For which the three faire goddesses did
    strive:
There also was the name of Nimrod strong,
Of Alexander, and his princes five,
Which shar'd to them the spoiles that he
    had got alive:

XXIII

And there the relicks of the drunken fray,
The which amongst the Lapithees befell:
And of the bloodie feast, which sent away
So many Centaures drunken soules to hell,
That under great Alcides furie fell:
And of the dreadfull discord, which did
    drive
The noble Argonauts to outrage fell,
That each of life sought others to deprive,
All mindlesse of the Golden Fleece, which
    made them strive.

XXIV

And eke of private persons many moe,
That were too long a worke to count them
    all;
Some of sworne friends, that did their
    faith forgoe;
Some of borne brethren, prov'd unnaturall;
Some of deare lovers, foes perpetuall:
Witnesse their broken bandes there to be
    seene,
Their girlonds rent, their bowres despoyled
    all;
The moniments whereof there byding
    beene,
As plaine as at the first, when they were
    fresh and greene.

XXV

Such was her house within; but all without,
The barren ground was full of wicked
    weedes,
Which she her selfe had sowen all about,
Now growen great, at first of little seedes,
The seedes of evill wordes and factious
    deedes;
Which, when to ripenesse due they growen
    arre,
Bring foorth an infinite increase, that
    breedes
Tumultuous trouble and contentious jarre,
The which most often end in bloudshed
    and in warre.

XXVI

And those same cursed seedes doe also
    serve
To her for bread, and yeeld her living food:
For life it is to her, when others sterve
Through mischievous debate and deadly
    feood,
That she may sucke their life and drinke
    their blood,

With which she from her childhood had
  bene fed:
For she at first was borne of hellish brood,
And by infernall furies nourished,
That by her monstrous shape might easily
  be red.

XXVII

Her face most fowle and filthy was to see,
With squinted eyes contrarie wayes in-
  tended,
And loathly mouth, unmeete a mouth to
  bee,
That nought but gall and venim compre-
  hended,
And wicked wordes that God and man
  offended:
Her lying tongue was in two parts divided,
And both the parts did speake, and both
  contended;
And as her tongue, so was her hart dis-
  cided,
That never thoght one thing, but doubly stil
  was guided.

XXVIII

Als as she double spake, so heard she
  double,
With matchlesse eares deformed and dis-
  tort,
Fild with false rumors and seditious trou-
  ble,
Bred in assemblies of the vulgar sort,
That still are led with every light report.
And as her eares, so eke her feet were odde,
And much unlike, th' one long, the other
  short,
And both misplast; that, when th' one for-
  ward yode,
The other backe retired, and contrarie
  trode.

XXIX

Likewise unequall were her handes twaine:
That one did reach, the other pusht away;
That one did make, the other mard againe,
And sought to bring all things unto decay;
Whereby great riches, gathered manie a
  day,
She in short space did often bring to
  nought,
And their possessours often did dismay:
For all her studie was and all her thought,
How she might overthrow the things that
  Concord wrought.

XXX

So much her malice did her might surpas,
That even th' Almightie selfe she did
  maligne,
Because to man so mercifull he was,
And unto all his creatures so benigne,
Sith she her selfe was of his grace indigne:
For all this worlds faire workmanship she
  tride
Unto his last confusion to bring,
And that great golden chaine quite to
  divide,
With which it blessed Concord hath to-
  gether tide.

XXXI

Such was that hag which with Duessa
  roade,
And serving her in her malitious use,
To hurt good knights, was as it were her
  baude,
To sell her borrowed beautie to abuse.
For though, like withered tree that wanteth
  juyce,
She old and crooked were, yet now of late
As fresh and fragrant as the floure deluce
She was become, by chaunge of her estate,
And made full goodly joyance to her new
  found mate.

XXXII

Her mate, he was a jollie youthfull knight,
That bore great sway in armes and chiv-
  alrie,
And was indeed a man of mickle might:
His name was Blandamour, that did descrie
His fickle mind full of inconstancie.
And now himselfe he fitted had right well
With two companions of like qualitie,
Faithlesse Duessa, and false Paridell,
That whether were more false, full hard it
  is to tell.

XXXIII

Now when this gallant with his goodly crew
From farre espide the famous Britomart,
Like knight adventurous in outward vew,
With his faire paragon, his conquests part,
Approching nigh, eftsoones his wanton hart
Was tickled with delight, and jesting sayd:
' Lo ! there, Sir Paridel, for your desart,
Good lucke presents you with yond lovely
  mayd,
For pitie that ye want a fellow for your
  ayd.'

XXXIV

By that the lovely paire drew nigh to hond:
Whom when as Paridel more plaine be-
    held,
Albee in heart he like affection fond,
Yet mindfull how he late by one was feld,
That did those armes and that same scutch-
    ion weld,
He had small lust to buy his love so deare,
But answerd: 'Sir, him wise I never held,
That, having once escaped perill neare,
Would afterwards afresh the sleeping evill
    reare.

XXXV

'This knight too late his manhood and his
    might
I did assay, that me right dearely cost,
Ne list I for revenge provoke new fight,
Ne for light ladies love, that soone is lost.'
The hot-spurre youth so scorning to be crost,
'Take then to you this dame of mine,' quoth
    hee,
'And I, without your perill or your cost,
Will chalenge yond same other for my
    fee.'
So forth he fiercely prickt, that one him
    scarce could see.

XXXVI

The warlike Britonesse her soone addrest,
And with such uncouth welcome did re-
    ceave
Her fayned paramour, her forced guest,
That, being forst his saddle soone to leave,
Him selfe he did of his new love deceave,
And made him selfe thensample of his follie.
Which done, she passed forth, not taking
    leave,
And left him now as sad as whilome jollie,
Well warned to beware with whom he dar'd
    to dallie.

XXXVII

Which when his other companie beheld,
They to his succour ran with readie ayd:
And finding him unable once to weld,
They reared him on horsebacke, and up-
    stayd,
Till on his way they had him forth con-
    vayd:
And all the way, with wondrous griefe of
    mynd
And shame, he shewd him selfe to be dis-
    mayd,

More for the love which he had left be-
    hynd,
Then that which he had to Sir Paridel re-
    synd.

XXXVIII

Nathlesse he forth did march well as he
    might,
And made good semblance to his companie,
Dissembling his disease and evill plight;
Till that ere long they chaunced to espie
Two other knights, that towards them did
    ply
With speedie course, as bent to charge
    them new.
Whom when as Blandamour approching nie
Perceiv'd to be such as they seemd in vew,
He was full wo, and gan his former griefe
    renew.

XXXIX

For th' one of them he perfectly describe
To be Sir Scudamour, by that he bore
The God of Love with wings displayed wide,
Whom mortally he hated evermore,
Both for his worth, that all men did adore,
And eke because his love he wonne by
    right:
Which when he thought, it grieved him
    full sore,
That, through the bruses of his former
    fight,
He now unable was to wreake his old de-
    spight.

XL

Forthy he thus to Paridel bespake:
'Faire sir, of friendship let me now you
    pray,
That as I late adventured for your sake,
The hurts whereof me now from battell stay,
Ye will me now with like good turne repay,
And justifie my cause on yonder knight.'
'Ah! sir,' said Paridel, 'do not dismay
Your selfe for this; my selfe will for you
    fight,
As ye have done for me: the left hand rubs
    the right.'

XLI

With that he put his spurres unto his steed,
With speare in rest, and toward him did
    fare,
Like shaft out of a bow preventing speed.
But Scudamour was shortly well aware

Of his approch, and gan him selfe prepare
Him to receive with entertainment meete.
So furiously they met, that either bare
The other downe under their horses feete,
That what of them became themselves did
    scarsly weete.

XLII

As when two billowes in the Irish sowndes,
Forcibly driven with contrarie tydes,
Do meete together, each abacke rebowndes
With roaring rage; and dashing on all sides,
That filleth all the sea with fome, divydes
The doubtfull current into divers wayes:
So fell those two in spight of both their
    prydes;
But Scudamour himselfe did soone uprayse,
And mounting light, his foe for lying long
    upbrayes.

XLIII

Who, rolled on an heape, lay still in
    swound,
All carelesse of his taunt and bitter rayle;
Till that the rest, him seeing lie on ground,
Ran hastily, to weete what did him ayle:
Where finding that the breath gan him to
    fayle,
With busie care they strove him to awake,
And doft his helmet, and undid his mayle:
So much they did, that at the last they
    brake
His slomber, yet so mazed that he nothing
    spake.

XLIV

Which when as Blandamour beheld, he
    sayd:
'False faitour Scudamour, that hast by
    slight
And foule advantage this good knight dis-
    mayd,
A knight much better then thy selfe be-
    hight,
Well falles it thee that I am not in plight,
This day, to wreake the dammage by thee
    donne:
Such is thy wont, that still when any knight
Is weakned, then thou doest him overronne:
So hast thou to thy selfe false honour often
    wonne.'

XLV

He little answer'd, but in manly heart
His mightie indignation did forbeare,
Which was not yet so secret, but some part
Thereof did in his frouning face appeare:
Like as a gloomie cloud, the which doth
    beare
An hideous storme, is by the northerne
    blast
Quite overblowne, yet doth not passe so
    cleare,
But that it all the skie doth overcast
With darknes dred, and threatens all the
    world to wast.

XLVI

'Ah! gentle knight,' then false Duessa
    sayd,
'Why do ye strive for ladies love so sore,
Whose chiefe desire is love and friendly
    aid
Mongst gentle knights to nourish ever-
    more?
Ne be ye wroth, Sir Scudamour, therefore,
That ye your love list love another knight,
Ne do your selfe dislike a whit the more;
For love is free, and led with selfe de-
    light,
Ne will enforced be with maisterdome or
    might.'

XLVII

So false Duessa, but vile Ate thus:
'Both foolish knights, I can but laugh at
    both,
That strive and storme, with stirre outra-
    geous,
For her that each of you alike doth loth,
And loves another, with whom now she goth
In lovely wise, and sleepes, and sports, and
    playes;
Whilest both you here with many a cursed
    oth
Sweare she is yours, and stirre up bloudie
    frayes,
To win a willow bough, whilest other
    weares the bayes.'

XLVIII

'Vile hag,' sayd Scudamour, 'why dost
    thou lye?
And falsly seekst a vertuous wight to
    shame?'
'Fond knight,' sayd she, 'the thing that
    with this eye
I saw, why should I doubt to tell the same?'
'Then tell,' quoth Blandamour, 'and feare
    no blame,

Tell what thou saw'st, maulgre who so it
    heares.'
' I saw,' quoth she, ' a stranger knight,
    whose name
I wote not well, but in his shield he beares
(That well I wote) the heads of many
    broken speares.

XLIX

' I saw him have your Amoret at will,
I saw him kisse, I saw him her embrace,
I saw him sleepe with her all night his fill,
All manie nights, and manie by in place,
That present were to testifie the case.'
Which when as Scudamour did heare, his
    heart
Was thrild with inward griefe, as when in
    chace
The Parthian strikes a stag with shivering
    dart,
The beast astonisht stands in middest of his
    smart.

L

So stood Sir Scudamour, when this he
    heard,
Ne word he had to speake for great dis-
    may,
But lookt on Glauce grim, who woxe
    afeard
Of outrage for the words which she heard say,
Albee untrue she wist them by assay.
But Blandamour, whenas he did espie
His chaunge of cheere, that anguish did be-
    wray,
He woxe full blithe, as he had got thereby,
And gan thereat to triumph without vic-
    torie.

LI

' Lo! recreant,' sayd he, ' the fruitlesse end
Of thy vaine boast, and spoile of love mis-
    gotten,
Whereby the name of knight-hood thou
    dost shend,
And all true lovers with dishonor blotten:
All things not rooted well will soone be
    rotten.'
' Fy, fy! false knight,' then false Duessa
    cryde,
' Unworthy life, that love with guile hast
    gotten;
Be thou, where ever thou do go or ryde,
Loathed of ladies all, and of all knights
    defyde.'

LII

But Scudamour, for passing great despight,
Staid not to answer, scarcely did refraine,
But that in all those knights and ladies sight
He for revenge had guiltlesse Glauce
    slaine:
But being past, he thus began amaine:
' False traitour squire, false squire of fals-
    est knight,
Why doth mine hand from thine avenge
    abstaine,
Whose lord hath done my love this foule
    despight?
Why do I not it wreake on thee now in my
    might?

LIII

' Discourteous, disloyall Britomart,
Untrue to God, and unto man unjust,
What vengeance due can equall thy desart,
That hast with shamefull spot of sinfull
    lust
Defil'd the pledge committed to thy trust?
Let ugly shame and endlesse infamy
Colour thy name with foule reproaches rust.
Yet thou, false squire, his fault shalt deare
    aby,
And with thy punishment his penance shalt
    supply.'

LIV

The aged dame, him seeing so enraged,
Was dead with feare; nathlesse, as neede
    required,
His flaming furie sought to have assuaged
With sober words, that sufferance desired
Till time the tryall of her truth expyred:
And evermore sought Britomart to cleare.
But he the more with furious rage was
    fyred,
And thrise his hand to kill her did upreare,
And thrise he drew it backe: so did at last
    forbeare.

CANTO II

Blandamour winnes false Florimell;
    Paridell for her strives;
They are accorded: Agape
    Doth lengthen her sonnes lives.

I

FIREBRAND of hell, first tynd in Phlegeton
By thousand furies, and from thence out
    throwen

Into this world, to worke confusion
And set it all on fire by force unknowen,
Is wicked discord, whose small sparkes
    once blowen
None but a god or godlike man can slake;
Such as was Orpheus, that when strife was
    growen
Amongst those famous ympes of Greece,
    did take
His silver harpe in hand, and shortly friends
    them make;

II

Or such as that celestiall Psalmist was,
That when the wicked feend his lord tor-
    mented,
With heavenly notes, that did all other pas,
The outrage of his furious fit relented.
Such musicke is wise words with time con-
    cented,
To moderate stiffe mindes, disposd to
    strive:
Such as that prudent Romane well in-
    vented,
What time his people into partes did rive,
Them reconcyld againe, and to their homes
    did drive.

III

Such us'd wise Glauce to that wrathfull
    knight,
To calme the tempest of his troubled
    thought:
Yet Blandamour, with termes of foule
    despight,
And Paridell her scornd, and set at nought,
As old and crooked and not good for ought.
Both they unwise, and warelesse of the
    evill
That by themselves unto themselves is
    wrought,
Through that false witch, and that foule
    aged drevill,
The one a feend, the other an incarnate
    devill.

IV

With whom as they thus rode accompanide,
They were encountred of a lustie knight,
That had a goodly ladie by his side,
To whom he made great dalliance and
    delight.
It was to weete the bold Sir Ferraugh
    hight,
He that from Braggadocchio whilome reft

The snowy Florimell, whose beautie bright
Made him seeme happie for so glorious
    theft;
Yet was it in due triall but a wandring weft.

V

Which when as Blandamour, whose fancie
    light
Was alwaies flitting, as the wavering wind,
After each beautie that appeard in sight,
Beheld, eftsoones it prickt his wanton mind
With sting of lust, that reasons eye did
    blind,
That to Sir Paridell these words he sent:
'Sir knight, why ride ye dumpish thus
    behind,
Since so good fortune doth to you present
So fayre a spoyle, to make you joyous
    meriment?'

VI

But Paridell, that had too late a tryall
Of the bad issue of his counsell vaine,
List not to hearke, but made this faire
    denyall:
'Last turne was mine, well proved to my
    paine;
This now be yours; God send you better
    gaine.'
Whose scoffed words he taking halfe in
    scorne,
Fiercely forth prickt his steed, as in
    disdaine,
Against that knight, ere he him well could
    torne;
By meanes whereof he hath him lightly
    overborne.

VII

Who, with the sudden stroke astonisht sore
Upon the ground a while in slomber lay;
The whiles his love away the other bore,
And shewing her, did Paridell upbray:
'Lo! sluggish knight, the victors happie
    pray!
So Fortune friends the bold·' whom Paridell
Seeing so faire indeede, as he did say,
His hart with secret envie gan to swell,
And inly grudge at him, that he had sped so
    well.

VIII

Nathlesse proud man himselfe the other
    deemed,
Having so peerelesse paragon ygot:

For sure the fayrest Florimell him seemed
To him was fallen for his happie lot,
Whose like alive on earth he weened
  not:
Therefore he her did court, did serve, did
  wooe,
With humblest suit that he imagine mot,
And all things did devise, and all things
  dooe,
That might her love prepare, and liking win
  theretoo.

IX

She, in regard thereof, him recompenst
With golden words and goodly counten-
  ance,
And such fond favours sparingly dis-
  penst:
Sometimes him blessing with a light eye-
  glance,
And coy lookes tempring with loose dalli-
  ance;
Sometimes estranging him in sterner wise;
That, having cast him in a foolish trance,
He seemed brought to bed in Paradise,
And prov'd himselfe most foole in what he
  seem'd most wise.

X

So great a mistresse of her art she was,
And perfectly practiz'd in womans craft,
That though therein himselfe he thought to
  pas,
And by his false allurements wylie draft
Had thousand women of their love be-
  raft,
Yet now he was surpriz'd: for that false
  spright,
Which that same witch had in this forme
  engraft,
Was so expert in every subtile slight,
That it could overreach the wisest earthly
  wight.

XI

Yet he to her did dayly service more,
And dayly more deceived was thereby;
Yet Paridell him envied therefore,
As seeming plast in sole felicity:
So blind is lust, false colours to descry.
But Ate soone discovering his desire,
And finding now fit opportunity
To stirre up strife twixt love and spight and
  ire,
Did privily put coles unto his secret fire.

XII

By sundry meanes thereto she prickt him
  forth,
Now with remembrance of those spightfull
  speaches,
Now with opinion of his owne more worth,
Now with recounting of like former
  breaches
Made in their friendship, as that hag him
  teaches:
And ever when his passion is allayd,
She it revives and new occasion reaches:
That, on a time, as they together way'd,
He made him open chalenge, and thus
  boldly sayd:

XIII

'Too boastfull Blandamour, too long I
  beare
The open wrongs thou doest me day by
  day:
Well know'st thou, when we friendship first
  did sweare,
The covenant was, that every spoyle or
  pray
Should equally be shard betwixt us tway:
Where is my part, then, of this ladie bright,
Whom to thy selfe thou takest quite away?
Render therefore therein to me my right,
Or answere for thy wrong, as shall fall out
  in fight.'

XIV

Exceeding wroth thereat was Blandamour,
And gan this bitter answere to him make:
'Too foolish Paridell, that fayrest floure
Wouldst gather faine, and yet no paines
  wouldst take!
But not so easie will I her forsake;
This hand her wonne, this hand shall her
  defend.'
With that they gan their shivering speares
  to shake,
And deadly points at eithers breast to bend,
Forgetfull each to have bene ever others
  frend.

XV

Their firie steedes with so untamed forse
Did beare them both to fell avenges end,
That both their speares, with pitilesse re-
  morse,
Through shield and mayle and haberjeon
  did wend,
And in their flesh a griesly passage rend,

That with the furie of their owne affret
Each other, horse and man, to ground did
send;
Where lying still awhile, both did forget
The perilous present stownd in which their
lives were set.

XVI

As when two warlike brigandines at sea,
With murdrous weapons arm'd to cruell
fight,
Doe meete together on the watry lea,
They stemme ech other with so fell de-
spight,
That with the shocke of their owne heed-
lesse might,
Their wooden ribs are shaken nigh a son-
der;
They which from shore behold the dread-
full sight
Of flashing fire, and heare the ordenance
thonder,
Do greatly stand amaz'd at such unwonted
wonder.

XVII

At length they both upstarted in amaze,
As men awaked rashly out of dreme,
And round about themselves a while did
gaze;
Till, seeing her that Florimell did seme,
In doubt to whom she victorie should
deeme,
Therewith their dulled sprights they edgd
anew,
And drawing both their swords with rage
extreme,
Like two mad mastiffes each on other flew,
And shields did share, and mailes did rash,
and helmes did hew.

XVIII

So furiously each other did assayle,
As if their soules they would attonce have
rent
Out of their brests, that streames of bloud
did rayle
Adowne, as if their springs of life were
spent;
That all the ground with purple bloud was
sprent,
And all their armours staynd with bloudie
gore;
Yet scarcely once to breath would they relent,

So mortall was their malice and so sore
Become of fayned friendship which they
vow'd afore.

XIX

And that which is for ladies most besit-
ting,
To stint all strife, and foster friendly
peace,
Was from those dames so farre and so un-
fitting,
As that, in stead of praying them surcease,
They did much more their cruelty en-
crease;
Bidding them fight for honour of their
love,
And rather die then ladies cause release.
With which vaine termes so much they did
them move,
That both resolv'd the last extremities to
prove.

XX

There they, I weene, would fight untill this
day,
Had not a squire, even he the Squire of
Dames,
By great adventure travelled that way;
Who seeing both bent to so bloudy games,
And both of old well knowing by their
names,
Drew nigh, to weete the cause of their de-
bate:
And first laide on those ladies thousand
blames,
That did not seeke t' appease their deadly
hate,
But gazed on their harmes, not pitting
their estate.

XXI

And then those knights he humbly did be-
seech
To stay their hands, till he a while had
spoken:
Who lookt a little up at that his speech,
Yet would not let their battell so be broken,
Both greedie fiers on other to be wroken.
Yet he to them so earnestly did call,
And them conjur'd by some well knowen
token,
That they at last their wrothfull hands let
fall,
Content to heare him speake, and glad to
rest withall.

XXII

First he desir'd their cause of strife to see:
They said, it was for love of Florimell.
'Ah! gentle knights,' quoth he, 'how may
    that bee,
And she so farre astray, as none can tell?'
'Fond squire,' full angry then sayd Pari-
    dell,
'Seest not the ladie there before thy face?'
He looked backe, and her advizing well,
Weend, as he said, by that her outward
    grace,
That fayrest Florimell was present there in
    place.

XXIII

Glad man was he to see that joyous sight,
For none alive but joy'd in Florimell,
And lowly to her lowting, thus behight:
'Fayrest of faire, that fairenesse doest ex-
    cell,
This happie day I have to greete you well,
In which you safe I see, whom thousand late
Misdoubted lost through mischiefe that be-
    fell;
Long may you live in health and happie
    state.'
She litle answer'd him, but lightly did
    aggrate.

XXIV

Then turning to those knights, he gan
    a new:
'And you, Sir Blandamour and Paridell,
That for this ladie present in your vew
Have rays'd this cruell warre and outrage
    fell,
Certes, me seemes, bene not advised well,
But rather ought in friendship for her sake
To joyne your force, their forces to repell
That seeke perforce her from you both to
    take,
And of your gotten spoyle their owne tri-
    umph to make.'

XXV

Thereat Sir Blandamour, with countenance
    sterne,
All full of wrath, thus fiercely him be-
    spake:
'A read, thou squire, that I the man may
    learne,
That dare fro me thinke Florimell to take.'
'Not one,' quoth he, 'but many doe par-
    take

Herein, as thus: It lately so befell,
That Satyran a girdle did uptake
Well knowne to appertaine to Florimell,
Which for her sake he wore, as him be-
    seemed well.

XXVI

'But when as she her selfe was lost and
    gone,
Full many knights, that loved her like
    deare,
Thereat did greatly grudge, that he alone
That lost faire ladies ornament should
    weare,
And gan therefore close spight to him to
    beare:
Which he to shun, and stop vile envies
    sting,
Hath lately caus'd to be proclaim'd each
    where
A solemne feast, with publike turneying,
To which all knights with them their ladies
    are to bring.

XXVII

'And of them all she that is fayrest found
Shall have that golden girdle for reward,
And of those knights who is most stout on
    ground
Shall to that fairest ladie be prefard.
Since therefore she her selfe is now your
    ward,
To you that ornament of hers pertaines
Against all those that chalenge it to gard,
And save her honour with your ventrous
    paines;
That shall you win more glory then ye here
    find gaines.'

XXVIII

When they the reason of his words had
    hard,
They gan abate the rancour of their rage,
And with their honours and their loves re-
    gard
The furious flames of malice to asswage.
Tho each to other did his faith engage,
Like faithfull friends thenceforth to joyne
    in one
With all their force, and battell strong to
    wage
Gainst all those knights, as their professed
    fone,
That chaleng'd ought in Florimell, save
    they alone.

XXIX

So well accorded forth they rode together
In friendly sort, that lasted but a while,
And of all old dislikes they made faire
　　weather;
Yet all was forg'd and spred with golden
　　foyle,
That under it hidde hate and hollow guyle.
Ne certes can that friendship long endure,
How ever gay and goodly be the style,
That doth ill cause or evill end enure:
For vertue is the band that bindeth harts
　　most sure.

XXX

Thus as they marched all in close disguise
Of fayned love, they chaunst to overtake
Two knights, that lincked rode in lovely
　　wise,
As if they secret counsels did partake;
And each not farre behinde him had his
　　make,
To weete, two ladies of most goodly hew,
That twixt themselves did gentle purpose
　　make,
Unmindfull both of that discordfull crew,
The which with speedie pace did after them
　　pursew.

XXXI

Who, as they now approched nigh at hand,
Deeming them doughtie as they did ap-
　　peare,
They sent that squire afore, to understand
What mote they be: who, viewing them
　　more neare,
Returned readie newes, that those same
　　weare
Two of the prowest knights in Faery Lond,
And those two ladies their two lovers
　　deare;
Couragious Cambell, and stout Triamond,
With Canacee and Cambine linckt in lovely
　　bond.

XXXII

Whylome, as antique stories tellen us,
Those two were foes the fellonest on
　　ground,
And battell made the dreddest daungerous
That ever shrilling trumpet did resound;
Though now their acts be no where to be
　　found,
As that renowmed poet them compyled
With warlike numbers and heroicke sound,

Dan Chaucer, well of English undefyled,
On Fames eternall beadroll worthie to be
　　fyled.

XXXIII

But wicked Time, that all good thoughts
　　doth waste,
And workes of noblest wits to nought out
　　weare,
That famous moniment hath quite defaste,
And robd the world of threasure endlesse
　　deare,
The which mote have enriched all us heare.
O cursed Eld, the cankerworme of writs!
How may these rimes, so rude as doth ap-
　　peare,
Hope to endure, sith workes of heavenly wits
Are quite devourd, and brought to nought
　　by little bits?

XXXIV

Then pardon, O most sacred happie spirit,
That I thy labours lost may thus revive,
And steale from thee the meede of thy due
　　merit,
That none durst ever whilest thou wast
　　alive,
And, being dead, in vaine yet many strive:
Ne dare I like, but through infusion sweete
Of thine owne spirit, which doth in me sur-
　　vive,
I follow here the footing of thy feete,
That with thy meaning so I may the rather
　　meete.

XXXV

Cambelloes sister was fayre Canacee,
That was the learnedst ladie in her dayes,
Well seene in everie science that mote bee,
And every secret worke of Natures wayes,
In wittie riddles, and in wise soothsayes,
In power of herbes, and tunes of beasts and
　　burds;
And, that augmented all her other prayse,
She modest was in all her deedes and words,
And wondrous chast of life, yet lov'd of
　　knights and lords.

XXXVI

Full many lords and many knights her
　　loved,
Yet she to none of them her liking lent,
Ne ever was with fond affection moved,
But rul'd her thoughts with goodly gov-
　　ernement.

For dread of blame and honours blemish-
     ment;
And eke unto her lookes a law she made,
That none of them once out of order went,
But, like to warie centonels well stayd,
Still watcht on every side, of secret foes
     affrayd.

XXXVII

So much the more as she refusd to love,
So much the more she loved was and
     sought,
That oftentimes unquiet strife did move
Amongst her lovers, and great quarrels
     wrought,
That oft for her in bloudie armes they
     fought.
Which whenas Cambell, that was stout and
     wise,
Perceiv'd would breede great mischiefe, he
     bethought
How to prevent the perill that mote rise,
And turne both him and her to honour in
     this wise.

XXXVIII

One day, when all that troupe of warlike
     wooers
Assembled were, to weet whose she should
     bee,
All mightie men and dreadfull derring
     dooers,
(The harder it to make them well agree)
Amongst them all this end he did decree;
That of them all, which love to her did make,
They by consent should chose the stoutest
     three,
That with himselfe should combat for her
     sake,
And of them all the victour should his sis-
     ter take.

XXXIX

Bold was the chalenge, as himselfe was
     bold,
And courage full of haughtie hardiment,
Approved oft in perils manifold,
Which he atchiev'd to his great ornament:
But yet his sisters skill unto him lent
Most confidence and hope of happie speed,
Conceived by a ring which she him sent,
That, mongst the manie vertues which we
     reed,
Had power to staunch al wounds that mor-
     tally did bleed.

XL

Well was that rings great vertue knowen
     to all,
That dread thereof, and his redoubted
     might,
Did all that youthly rout so much appall,
That none of them durst undertake the
     fight;
More wise they weend to make of love de-
     light,
Then life to hazard for faire ladies looke,
And yet uncertaine by such outward sight,
Though for her sake they all that perill
     tooke,
Whether she would them love, or in her
     liking brooke.

XLI

Amongst those knights there were three
     brethren bold,
Three bolder brethren never were yborne,
Borne of one mother in one happie mold,
Borne at one burden in one happie morne;
Thrise happie mother, and thrise happie
     morne,
That bore three such, three such not to be
     fond !
Her name was Agape, whose children
     werne
All three as one; the first hight Priamond,
The second Dyamond, the youngest Tria-
     mond.

XLII

Stout Priamond, but not so strong to strike,
Strong Diamond, but not so stout a knight,
But Triamond was stout and strong alike:
On horsebacke used Triamond to fight,
And Priamond on foote had more delight,
But horse and foote knew Diamond to
     wield:
With curtaxe used Diamond to smite,
And Triamond to handle speare and shield,
But speare and curtaxe both usd Priamond
     in field.

XLIII

These three did love each other dearely
     well,
And with so firme affection were allyde,
As if but one soule in them all did dwell,
Which did her powre into three parts di-
     vyde;
Like three faire branches budding farre
     and wide.

That from one roote deriv'd their vitall sap:
And like that roote that doth her life divide
    Their mother was, and had full blessed hap,
These three so noble babes to bring forth at one clap.

XLIV

Their mother was a Fay, and had the skill
Of secret things, and all the powres of nature,
Which she by art could use unto her will,
And to her service bind each living creature,
Through secret understanding of their feature.
    Thereto she was right faire, when so her face
She list discover, and of goodly stature;
But she, as Fayes are wont, in privie place
Did spend her dayes, and lov'd in forests wyld to space.

XLV

There on a day a noble youthly knight,
Seeking adventures in the salvage wood,
Did by great fortune get of her the sight,
As she sate carelesse by a cristall flood,
Combing her golden lockes, as seemd her good;
    And unawares upon her laying hold,
That strove in vaine him long to have withstood,
Oppressed her, and there (as it is told)
Got these three lovely babes, that prov'd three champions bold.

XLVI

Which she with her long fostred in that wood,
Till that to ripenesse of mans state they grew:
Then, shewing forth signes of their fathers blood,
They loved armes, and knighthood did ensew,
Seeking adventures, where they anie knew.
    Which when their mother saw, she gan to dout
Their safetie, least by searching daungers new,
And rash provoking perils all about,
Their days mote be abridged through their corage stout.

XLVII

Therefore desirous th' end of all their dayes
To know, and them t' enlarge with long extent,
By wondrous skill and many hidden wayes
To the three Fatall Sisters house she went.
Farre under ground from tract of living went,
    Downe in the bottome of the deepe Abysse,
Where Demogorgon, in dull darknesse pent,
Farre from the view of gods and heavens blis,
The hideous Chaos keepes, their dreadfull dwelling is.

XLVIII

There she them found, all sitting round about
The direfull distaffe standing in the mid,
And with unwearied fingers drawing out
The lines of life, from living knowledge hid.
Sad Clotho held the rocke, the whiles the thrid
    By griesly Lachesis was spun with paine,
That cruell Atropos eftsoones undid,
With cursed knife cutting the twist in twaine:
Most wretched men, whose dayes depend on thrids so vaine!

XLIX

She them saluting, there by them sate still,
Beholding how the thrids of life they span:
And when at last she had beheld her fill,
Trembling in heart, and looking pale and wan,
Her cause of comming she to tell began.
    To whom fierce Atropos: 'Bold Fay, that durst
Come see the secret of the life of man,
Well worthie thou to be of Jove accurst,
And eke thy childrens thrids to be a sunder burst.'

L

Whereat she sore affrayd, yet her besought
To graunt her boone, and rigour to abate,
That she might see her childrens thrids forth brought,
And know the measure of their utmost date,
To them ordained by eternall Fate:

Which Clotho graunting, shewed her the
    same:
That when she saw, it did her much amate
To see their thrids so thin as spiders frame,
And eke so short, that seemd their ends out
    shortly came.

LI

She then began them humbly to intreate
To draw them longer out, and better twine,
That so their lives might be prolonged late.
But Lachesis thereat gan to repine,
And sayd: 'Fond dame! that deem'st of
    things divine
As of humane, that they may altred bee,
And chaung'd at pleasure for those impes of
    thine:
Not so; for what the Fates do once decree,
Not all the gods can chaunge, nor Jove him
    self can free.'

LII

'Then since,' quoth she, 'the terme of each
    mans life
For nought may lessened nor enlarged bee,
Graunt this, that when ye shred with fatall
    knife
His line which is the eldest of the three,
Which is of them the shortest, as I see,
Eftsoones his life may passe into the next;
And when the next shall likewise ended
    bee,
That both their lives may likewise be
    annext
Unto the third, that his may so be trebly
    wext.'

LIII

They graunted it; and then that carefull
    Fay
Departed thence with full contented mynd;
And comming home, in warlike fresh aray
Them found all three, according to their
    kynd:
But unto them what destinie was assynd,
Or how their lives were eekt, she did not
    tell;
But evermore, when she fit time could fynd,
She warned them to tend their safeties well,
And love each other deare, what ever them
    befell.

LIV

So did they surely during all their dayes,
And never discord did amongst them fall;

Which much augmented all their other
    praise.
And now, t' increase affection naturall,
In love of Canacee they joyned all:
Upon which ground this same great battell
    grew,
Great matter growing of beginning small;
The which, for length, I will not here
    pursew,
But rather will reserve it for a canto new.

CANTO III

The battell twixt three brethren with
    Cambell for Canacee:
Cambina with true friendships bond
Doth their long strife agree.

I

O why doe wretched men so much desire
To draw their dayes unto the utmost date,
And doe not rather wish them soone expire,
Knowing the miserie of their estate,
And thousand perills which them still awate,
Tossing them like a boate amid the mayne,
That every houre they knocke at Deathes
    gate?
And he that happie seemes and least in
    payne,
Yet is as nigh his end as he that most doth
    playne.

II

Therefore this Fay I hold but fond and
    vaine,
The which, in seeking for her children three
Long life, thereby did more prolong their
    paine.
Yet whilest they lived none did ever see
More happie creatures then they seem'd to
    bee,
Nor more ennobled for their courtesie,
That made them dearely lov'd of each
    degree,
Ne more renowmed for their chevalrie,
That made them dreaded much of all men
    farre and nie.

III

These three that hardie chalenge tooke in
    hand,
For Canacee with Cambell for to fight:
The day was set, that all might understand,
And pledges pawnd the same to keepe
    a right:

That day, the dreddest day that living
    wight
Did ever see upon this world to shine,
So soone as heavens window shewed light,
These warlike champions, all in armour shine,
Assembled were in field, the chalenge to
    define.

IV

The field with listes was all about enclos'd,
To barre the prease of people farre away;
And at th' one side sixe judges were dis-
    pos'd,
To view and deeme the deedes of armes
    that day;
And on the other side, in fresh aray,
Fayre Canacee upon a stately stage
Was set, to see the fortune of that fray,
And to be seene, as his most worthie wage
That could her purchase with his lives ad-
    ventur'd gage.

V

Then entred Cambell first into the list,
With stately steps and fearelesse counten-
    ance,
As if the conquest his he surely wist.
Soone after did the brethren three advance,
In brave aray and goodly amenance,
With scutchins gilt and banners broad dis-
    playd;
And marching thrise in warlike ordinance,
Thrise lowted lowly to the noble mayd,
The whiles shril trompets and loud clarions
    sweetly playd.

VI

Which doen, the doughty chalenger came
    forth,
All arm'd to point, his chalenge to abet:
Gainst whom Sir Priamond, with equall
    worth
And equall armes, himselfe did forward
    set.
A trompet blew; they both together met
With dreadfull force and furious intent,
Carelesse of perill in their fiers affret,
As if that life to losse they had forelent,
And cared not to spare that should be
    shortly spent.

VII

Right practicke was Sir Priamond in fight,
And throughly skild in use of shield and
    speare·

Ne lesse approved was Cambelloes might,
Ne lesse his skill in weapons did appeare,
That hard it was to weene which harder
    were.
Full many mightie strokes on either side
Were sent, that seemed death in them to
    beare,
But they were both so watchfull and well
    eyde,
That they avoyded were, and vainely by
    did slyde.

VIII

Yet one of many was so strongly bent
By Priamond, that with unluckie glaunce
Through Cambels shoulder it unwarely
    went,
That forced him his shield to disadvaunce:
Much was he grieved with that gracelesse
    chaunce,
Yet from the wound no drop of bloud there
    fell,
But wondrous paine, that did the more en-
    haunce
His haughtie courage to advengement fell:
Smart daunts not mighty harts, but makes
    them more to swell.

IX

With that, his poynant speare he fierce
    aventred,
With doubled force, close underneath his
    shield,
That through the mayles into his thigh it
    entred,
And there arresting, readie way did yield
For bloud to gush forth on the grassie
    field;
That he for paine himselfe not right up-
    reare,
But too and fro in great amazement reel'd,
Like an old oke, whose pith and sap is
    seare,
At puffe of every storme doth stagger here
    and theare.

X

Whom so dismayd when Cambell had
    espide,
Againe he drove at him with double might,
That nought mote stay the steele, till in his
    side
The mortall point most cruelly empight:
Where fast infixed, whilest he sought by
    slight

It forth to wrest, the staffe a sunder brake,
And left the head behind: with which despight
He all enrag'd, his shivering speare did
shake,
And charging him a fresh, thus felly him
bespake:

XI

'Lo ! faitour, there thy meede unto thee
take,
The meede of thy mischalenge and abet:
Not for thine owne, but for thy sisters
sake,
Have I thus long thy life unto thee let:
But to forbeare doth not forgive the det.'
The wicked weapon heard his wrathfull
vow,
And passing forth with furious affret,
Pierst through his bever quite into his brow,
That with the force it backward forced him
to bow.

XII

Therewith a sunder in the midst it brast,
And in his hand nought but the troncheon
left;
The other halfe behind yet sticking fast
Out of his headpeece Cambell fiercely reft,
And with such furie backe at him it heft,
That, making way unto his dearest life,
His weasand pipe it through his gorget
cleft:
Thence streames of purple bloud issuing
rife
Let forth his wearie ghost, and made an
end of strife.

XIII

His wearie ghost, assoyld from fleshly band,
Did not, as others wont, directly fly
Unto her rest in Plutoes griesly land,
Ne into ayre did vanish presently,
Ne chaunged was into a starre in sky:
But through traduction was eftsoones de-
rived,
Like as his mother prayd the Destinie,
Into his other brethren that survived,
In whom he liv'd a new, of former life de-
prived.

XIV

Whom when on ground his brother next
beheld,
Though sad and sorie for so heavy sight,
Yet leave unto his sorrow did not yeeld;
But rather stird to vengeance and despight,
Through secret feeling of his generous
spright,
Rusht fiercely forth, the battell to renew,
As in reversion of his brothers right;
And chalenging the virgin as his dew.
His foe was soone addrest: the trompets
freshly blew.

XV

With that they both together fiercely met,
As if that each ment other to devoure;
And with their axes both so sorely bet,
That neither plate nor mayle, whereas their
powre
They felt, could once sustaine the hideous
stowre,
But rived were like rotten wood a sunder,
Whilest through their rifts the ruddie
bloud did showre,
And fire did flash, like lightning after
thunder,
That fild the lookers on attonce with ruth
and wonder.

XVI

As when two tygers, prickt with hungers
rage,
Have by good fortune found some beasts
fresh spoyle,
On which they weene their famine to as-
swage,
And gaine a feastfull guerdon of their toyle;
Both falling out doe stirre up strifefull
broyle,
And cruell battell twixt themselves doe
make,
Whiles neither lets the other touch the
soyle,
But either sdeignes with other to partake:
So cruelly these knights strove for that
ladies sake.

XVII

Full many strokes, that mortally were
ment,
The whiles were enterchaunged twixt them
two;
Yet they were all with so good wariment
Or warded, or avoyded and let goe,
That still the life stood fearelesse of her
foe:
Till Diamond, disdeigning long delay
Of doubtfull fortune wavering to and fro,

Resolv'd to end it one or other way;
And heav'd his murdrous axe at him with
  mighty sway.

XVIII

The dreadfull stroke, in case it had arrived
Where it was ment, (so deadly it was ment)
The soule had sure out of his bodie rived,
And stinted all the strife incontinent.
But Cambels fate that fortune did prevent:
For seeing it at hand, he swarv'd asyde,
And so gave way unto his fell intent:
Who, missing of the marke which he had
  eyde,
Was with the force nigh feld whilst his
  right foot did slyde.

XIX

As when a vulture greedie of his pray,
Through hunger long, that hart to him doth
  lend,
Strikes at an heron with all his bodies
  sway,
That from his force seemes nought may it
  defend;
The warie fowle, that spies him toward
  bend
His dreadfull souse, avoydes it, shunning
  light,
And maketh him his wing in vaine to spend;
That with the weight of his owne weeld-
  lesse might,
He falleth nigh to ground, and scarse re-
  covereth flight.

XX

Which faire adventure when Cambello
  spide,
Full lightly, ere himselfe he could recover,
From daungers dread to ward his naked
  side,
He can let drive at him with all his power,
And with his axe him smote in evill hower,
That from his shoulders quite his head he
  reft:
The headlesse tronke, as heedlesse of that
  stower,
Stood still a while, and his fast footing kept,
Till, feeling life to fayle, it fell, and deadly
  slept.

XXI

They which that piteous spectacle beheld
Were much amaz'd the headlesse tronke to
  see

Stand up so long, and weapon vaine to weld,
Unweeting of the Fates divine decree
For lifes succession in those brethren three.
For notwithstanding that one soule was
  reft,
Yet, had the bodie not dismembred bee,
It would have lived, and revived eft;
But finding no fit seat, the lifelesse corse it
  left.

XXII

It left; but that same soule which therein
  dwelt,
Streight entring into Triamond, him fild
With double life and griefe; which when
  he felt,
As one whose inner parts had bene ythrild
With point of steele, that close his hartbloud
  spild,
He lightly lept out of his place of rest,
And rushing forth into the emptie field,
Against Cambello fiercely him addrest;
Who him affronting soone to fight was
  readie prest.

XXIII

Well mote ye wonder how that noble knight,
After he had so often wounded beene,
Could stand on foot now to renew the fight.
But had ye then him forth advauncing
  seene,
Some newborne wight ye would him surely
  weene,
So fresh he seemed and so fierce in sight;
Like as a snake, whom wearie winters
  teene
Hath worne to nought, now feeling som-
  mers might,
Casts off his ragged skin and freshly doth
  him dight.

XXIV

All was through vertue of the ring he wore,
The which not onely did not from him let
One drop of bloud to fall, but did restore
His weakned powers, and dulled spirits
  whet,
Through working of the stone therein yset,
Else how could one of equall might with
  most,
Against so many no lesse mightie met,
Once thinke to match three such on equall
  cost,
Three such as able were to match a puissant
  host?

XXV

Yet nought thereof was Triamond adredde,
Ne desperate of glorious victorie,
But sharpely him assayld, and sore be-
    stedde,
With heapes of strokes, which he at him let
    flie
As thicke as hayle forth poured from the
    skie:
He stroke, he soust, he foynd, he hewd, he
    lasht,
And did his yron brond so fast applie,
That from the same the fierie sparkles
    flasht,
As fast as water-sprinkles gainst a rocke
    are dasht.

XXVI

Much was Cambello daunted with his
    blowes,
So thicke they fell, and forcibly were sent,
That he was forst from daunger of the
    throwes
Backe to retire, and somewhat to relent,
Till th' heat of his fierce furie he had spent:
Which when for want of breath gan to
    abate,
He then afresh with new encouragement
Did him assayle, and mightily amate,
As fast as forward erst, now backward to
    retrate.

XXVII

Like as the tide, that comes fro th' ocean
    mayne,
Flowes up the Shenan with contrarie forse,
And overruling him in his owne rayne,
Drives backe the current of his kindly
    course,
And makes it seeme to have some other
    sourse:
But when the floud is spent, then backe
    againe,
His borrowed waters forst to redisbourse,
He sends the sea his owne with double
    gaine,
And tribute eke withall, as to his soveraine.

XXVIII

Thus did the battell varie to and fro,
With diverse fortune doubtfull to be
    deemed:
Now this the better had, now had his fo;
Then he halfe vanquisht, then the other
    seemed;

Yet victors both them selves alwayes
    esteemed.
And all the while the disentrayled blood
Adowne their sides like litle rivers stremed,
That with the wasting of his vitall flood
Sir Triamond at last full faint and feeble
    stood.

XXIX

But Cambell still more strong and greater
    grew,
Ne felt his blood to wast, ne powres em-
    perisht,
Through that rings vertue, that with vigour
    new,
Still when as he enfeebled was, him
    cherisht,
And all his wounds and all his bruses
    guarisht:
Like as a withered tree, through husbands
    toyle,
Is often seene full freshly to have florisht,
And fruitfull apples to have borne awhile,
As fresh as when it first was planted in the
    soyle.

XXX

Through which advantage, in his strength
    he rose,
And smote the other with so wondrous
    might,
That through the seame which did his
    hauberk close
Into his throate and life it pierced quight,
That downe he fell as dead in all mens
    sight:
Yet dead he was not, yet he sure did die,
As all men do that lose the living spright:
So did one soule out of his bodie flie
Unto her native home from mortall miserie.

XXXI

But nathelesse whilst all the lookers on
Him dead behight, as he to all appeard,
All unawares he started up anon,
As one that had out of a dreame bene
    reard,
And fresh assayld his foe; who halfe af-
    feard
Of th' uncouth sight, as he some ghost had
    seene,
Stood still amaz'd, holding his idle sweard;
Till, having often by him stricken beene,
He forced was to strike, and save him selfe
    from teene.

XXXII

Yet from thenceforth more warily he
   fought,
As one in feare the Stygian gods t' offend,
Ne followd on so fast, but rather sought
Him selfe to save, and daunger to defend,
Then life and labour both in vaine to spend.
Which Triamond perceiving, weened sure
He gan to faint toward the battels end,
And that he should not long on foote en-
   dure,
A signe which did to him the victorie as-
   sure.

XXXIII

Whereof full blith, eftsoones his mightie
   hand
He heav'd on high, in mind with that same
   blow
To make an end of all that did withstand:
Which Cambell seeing come, was nothing
   slow
Him selfe to save from that so deadly
   throw;
And at that instant reaching forth his
   sweard,
Close underneath his shield, that scarce did
   show,
Stroke him, as he his hand to strike upreard,
In th' arm-pit full, that through both sides
   the wound appeard.

XXXIV

Yet still that direfull stroke kept on his
   way,
And falling heavie on Cambelloes crest,
Strooke him so hugely that in swowne he
   lay,
And in his head an hideous wound imprest:
And sure, had it not happily found rest
Upon the brim of his brode plated shield,
It would have cleft his braine downe to his
   brest.
So both at once fell dead upon the field,
And each to other seemd the victorie to
   yield.

XXXV

Which when as all the lookers on beheld,
They weened sure the warre was at an end,
And judges rose, and marshals of the field
Broke up the listes, their armes away to
   rend;
And Canacee gan wayle her dearest frend.

All suddenly they both upstarted light,
The one out of the swownd which him did
   blend,
The other breathing now another spright,
And fiercely each assayling, gan afresh to
   fight.

XXXVI

Long while they then continued in that wize,
As if but then the battell had begonne:
Strokes, wounds, wards, weapons, all they
   did despise,
Ne either car'd to ward, or perill shonne,
Desirous both to have the battell donne;
Ne either cared life to save or spill,
Ne which of them did winne, ne which were
   wonne.
So wearie both of fighting had their fill,
That life it selfe seemd loathsome, and
   long safetie ill.

XXXVII

Whilst thus the case in doubtfull ballance
   hong,
Unsure to whether side it would incline,
And all mens eyes and hearts, which there
   among
Stood gazing, filled were with rufull tine,
And secret feare to see their fatall fine,
All suddenly they heard a troublous noyes,
That seemd some perilous tumult to de-
   sine,
Confusd with womens cries and shouts of
   boyes,
Such as the troubled theaters oftimes an-
   noyes.

XXXVIII

Thereat the champions both stood still a
   space,
To weeten what that sudden clamour ment;
Lo ! where they spyde with speedie whirl-
   ing pace
One in a charet of straunge furniment
Towards them driving like a storme out
   sent.
The charet decked was in wondrous wize
With gold and many a gorgeous ornament,
After the Persian Monarks antique guize,
Such as the maker selfe could best by art
   devize.

XXXIX

And drawne it was (that wonder is to tell)
Of two grim lyons, taken from the wood

In which their powre all others did excell;
Now made forget their former cruell mood,
T' obey their riders hest, as seemed good.
And therein sate a ladie passing faire
And bright, that seemed borne of angels
    brood,
And with her beautie bountie did compare,
Whether of them in her should have the
    greater share.

XL

Thereto she learned was in magicke leare,
And all the artes that subtill wits discover,
Having therein bene trained many a yeare,
And well instructed by the Fay her mother,
That in the same she farre exceld all other.
Who, understanding by her mightie art
Of th' evill plight in which her dearest
    brother
Now stood, came forth in hast to take his
    part,
And pacifie the strife which causd so deadly
    smart.

XLI

And as she passed through th' unruly preace
Of people thronging thicke her to behold,
Her angrie teame, breaking their bonds of
    peace,
Great heapes of them, like sheepe in nar-
    row fold,
For hast did over-runne, in dust enrould;
That, thorough rude confusion of the rout,
Some fearing shriekt, some being harmed
    hould,
Some laught for sport, some did for wonder
    shout,
And some, that would seeme wise, their
    wonder turnd to dout.

XLII

In her right hand a rod of peace shee
    bore,
About the which two serpents weren wound,
Entrayled mutually in lovely lore,
And by the tailes together firmely bound,
And both were with one olive garland
    crownd,
Like to the rod which Maias sonne doth
    wield,
Wherewith the hellish fiends he doth con-
    found.
And in her other hand a cup she hild,
The which was with Nepenthe to the brim
    upfild.

XLIII

Nepenthe is a drinck of soverayne grace,
Devized by the gods, for to asswage
Harts grief, and bitter gall away to chace,
Which stirs up anguish and contentious
    rage:
In stead thereof sweet peace and quietage
It doth establish in the troubled mynd.
Few men, but such as sober are and sage,
Are by the gods to drinck thereof assynd;
But such as drinck, eternall happinesse do
    fynd.

XLIV

Such famous men, such worthies of the
    earth,
As Jove will have advaunced to the skie,
And there made gods, though borne of mor-
    tall berth,
For their high merits and great dignitie,
Are wont, before they may to heaven flie,
To drincke hereof, whereby all cares fore-
    past
Are washt away quite from their memorie.
So did those olde heroes hereof taste,
Before that they in blisse amongst the gods
    were plaste.

XLV

Much more of price and of more gratious
    powre
Is this, then that same water of Ardenne,
The which Rinaldo drunck in happie howre,
Described by that famous Tuscane penne:
For that had might to change the hearts of
    men
Fro love to hate, a change of evill choise:
But this doth hatred make in love to brenne,
And heavy heart with comfort doth rejoyce.
Who would not to this vertue rather yeeld
    his voice?

XLVI

At last arriving by the listes side,
Shee with her rod did softly smite the raile,
Which straight flew ope, and gave her way
    to ride.
Eftsoones out of her coch she gan availe,
And pacing fairely forth, did bid all haile,
First to her brother, whom she loved deare,
That so to see him made her heart to quaile:
And next to Cambell, whose sad ruefull
    cheare
Made her to change her hew, and hidden
    love t' appeare.

XLVII

They lightly her requit (for small delight
They had as then her long to entertaine,)
And eft them turned both againe to fight:
Which when she saw, downe on the bloudy
    plaine
Her selfe she threw, and teares gan shed
    amaine;
Amongst her teares immixing prayers
    meeke,
And with her prayers reasons, to restraine
From blouddy strife; and blessed peace to
    seeke,
By all that unto them was deare, did them
    beseeke.

XLVIII

But when as all might nought with them
    prevaile,
Shee smote them lightly with her powre-
    full wand.
Then suddenly as if their hearts did faile,
Their wrathfull blades downe fell out of
    their hand,
And they like men astonisht still did stand.
Thus whilest their minds were doubtfully
    distraught,
And mighty spirites bound with mightier
    band,
Her golden cup to them for drinke she
    raught,
Whereof, full glad for thirst, ech drunk an
    harty draught.

XLIX

Of which so soone as they once tasted had,
Wonder it is that sudden change to see:
Instead of strokes, each other kissed glad,
And lovely haulst, from feare of treason
    free,
And plighted hands for ever friends to be.
When all men saw this sudden change of
    things,
So mortall foes so friendly to agree,
For passing joy, which so great marvaile
    brings,
They all gan shout aloud, that all the
    heaven rings.

L

All which when gentle Canacee beheld,
In hast she from her lofty chaire descended,
Too weet what sudden tidings was befeld:
Where when she saw that cruell war so
    ended,

And deadly foes so faithfully affrended,
In lovely wise she gan that lady greet,
Which had so great dismay so well
    amended,
And entertaining her with curt'sies meet,
Profest to her true friendship and affection
    sweet.

LI

Thus when they all accorded goodly were,
The trumpets sounded, and they all arose,
Thence to depart with glee and gladsome
    chere.
Those warlike champions both together
    chose
Homeward to march, themselves there to
    repose,
And wise Cambina, taking by her side
Faire Canacee, as fresh as morning rose,
Unto her coch remounting, home did ride,
Admir'd of all the people and much glori-
    fide.

LII

Where making joyous feast theire daies
    they spent
In perfect love, devoide of hatefull strife,
Allide with bands of mutuall couplement;
For Triamond had Canacee to wife,
With whom he ledd a long and happie life;
And Cambel tooke Cambina to his fere,
The which as life were each to other liefe.
So all alike did love, and loved were,
That since their days such lovers were not
    found elswhere.

CANTO IV

Satyrane makes a turneyment
    For love of Florimell :
Britomart winnes the prize from all,
    And Artegall doth quell.

I

IT often fals, (as here it earst befell)
That mortall foes doe turne to faithfull
    frends,
And friends profest are chaungd to foemen
    fell:
The cause of both, of both their minds de-
    pends,
And th' end of both, likewise of both their
    ends:
For enmitie, that of no ill proceeds,
But of occasion, with th' occasion ends:

And friendship, which a faint affection
    breeds
Without regard of good, dyes like ill
    grounded seeds.

II

That well (me seemes) appeares by that of
    late
Twixt Cambell and Sir Triamond befell,
As els by this, that now a new debate
Stird up twixt Blandamour and Paridell,
The which by course befals me here to
    tell:
Who having those two other knights espide,
Marching afore, as ye remember well,
Sent forth their squire to have them both
    descride,
And eke those masked ladies riding them
    beside.

III

Who backe returning, told as he had seene,
That they were doughtie knights of
    dreaded name,
And those two ladies their two loves un-
    seene;
And therefore wisht them without blot or
    blame
To let them passe at will, for dread of
    shame.
But Blandamour, full of vainglorious
    spright,
And rather stird by his discordfull dame,
Upon them gladly would have prov'd his
    might,
But that he yet was sore of his late luck-
    lesse fight.

IV

Yet, nigh approching, he them fowle be-
    spake,
Disgracing them, him selfe thereby to
    grace,
As was his wont, so weening way to make
To ladies love, where so he came in place,
And with lewd termes their lovers to de-
    face.
Whose sharpe provokement them incenst
    so sore,
That both were bent t' avenge his usage
    base,
And gan their shields addresse them selves
    afore:
For evill deedes may better then bad words
    be bore.

V

But faire Cambina with perswasions myld
Did mitigate the fiercenesse of their mode,
That for the present they were reconcyld,
And gan to treate of deeds of armes abrode,
And strange adventures, all the way they
    rode:
Amongst the which they told, as then be-
    fell,
Of that great turney which was blazed
    brode,
For that rich girdle of faire Florimell,
The prize of her which did in beautie most
    excell.

VI

To which folke-mote they all with one con-
    sent,
Sith each of them his ladie had him by,
Whose beautie each of them thought ex-
    cellent,
Agreed to travell, and their fortunes try.
So as they passed forth, they did espy
One in bright armes, with ready speare in
    rest,
That toward them his course seem'd to ap-
    ply;
Gainst whom Sir Paridell himselfe ad-
    drest,
Him weening, ere he nigh approcht, to have
    represt.

VII

Which th' other seeing, gan his course re-
    lent,
And vaunted speare eftsoones to disad-
    vaunce,
As if he naught but peace and pleasure
    ment,
Now falne into their fellowship by chance,
Whereat they shewed curteous counten-
    aunce.
So as he rode with them accompanide,
His roving eie did on the lady glaunce
Which Blandamour had riding by his side:
Whom sure he weend that he some wher
    tofore had eide.

VIII

It was to weete that snowy Florimell,
Which Ferrau late from Braggadochio
    wonne;
Whom he now seeing, her remembred well,
How, having reft her from the witches
    sonne,

He soone her lost: wherefore he now be-
     gunne
To challenge her anew, as his owne prize,
Whom formerly he had in battell wonne,
And proffer made by force her to reprize:
Which scornefull offer Blandamour gan
     soone despize;

IX

And said: 'Sir knight, sith ye this lady
     clame,
Whom he that hath were loth to lose so
     light,
(For so to lose a lady were great shame,)
Yee shall her winne, as I have done, in fight:
And lo! shee shall be placed here in sight,
Together with this hag beside her set,
That who so winnes her may her have by
     right:
But he shall have the hag that is ybet,
And with her alwaies ride, till he another
     get.'

X

That offer pleased all the company,
So Florimell with Ate forth was brought,
At which they all gan laugh full merrily:
But Braggadochio said, he never thought
For such an hag, that seemed worse then
     nought,
His person to emperill so in fight:
But if to match that lady they had sought
Another like, that were like faire and
     bright,
His life he then would spend to justifie his
     right.

XI

At which his vaine excuse they all gan
     smile,
As scorning his unmanly cowardize:
And Florimell him fowly gan revile,
That for her sake refus'd to enterprize
The battell, offred in so knightly wize:
And Ate eke provokt him privily
With love of her, and shame of such mes-
     prize.
But naught he car'd for friend or enemy,
For in base mind nor friendship dwels nor
     enmity.

XII

But Cambell thus did shut up all in jest:
'Brave knights and ladies, certes ye doe
     wrong

To stirre up strife, when most us needeth
     rest,
That we may us reserve both fresh and
     strong
Against the turneiment, which is not long,
When who so list to fight may fight his fill.
Till then your challenges ye may prolong;
And then it shall be tried, if ye will,
Whether shall have the hag, or hold the
     lady still.'

XIII

They all agreed; so, turning all to game
And pleasaunt bord, they past forth on
     their way,
And all that while, where so they rode or
     came,
That masked mock-knight was their sport
     and play.
Till that at length, upon th' appointed day,
Unto the place of turneyment they came;
Where they before them found in fresh
     aray
Manie a brave knight and manie a daintie
     dame
Assembled, for to get the honour of that
     game.

XIV

There this faire crewe arriving did divide
Them selves asunder: Blandamour with
     those
Of his on th' one; the rest on th' other
     side.
But boastfull Braggadocchio rather chose,
For glorie vaine, their fellowship to lose,
That men on him the more might gaze
     alone.
The rest them selves in troupes did else
     dispose,
Like as it seemed best to every one;
The knights in couples marcht, with ladies
     linckt attone.

XV

Then first of all forth came Sir Satyrane,
Bearing that precious relicke in an arke
Of gold, that bad eyes might it not pro-
     phane:
Which drawing softly forth out of the
     darke,
He open shewd, that all men it mote marke:
A gorgeous girdle, curiously embost
With pearle and precious stone, worth
     many a marke;

Yet did the workmanship farre passe the
    cost:
It was the same which lately Florimel had
    lost.

XVI

That same aloft he hong in open vew,
To be the prize of beautie and of might;
The which eftsoones discovered, to it drew
The eyes of all, allur'd with close delight,
And hearts quite robbed with so glorious
    sight,
That all men threw out vowes and wishes
    vaine.
Thrise happie ladie, and thrise happie
    knight,
Them seemd, that could so goodly riches
    gaine,
So worthie of the perill, worthy of the
    paine.

XVII

Then tooke the bold Sir Satyrane in hand
An huge great speare, such as he wont to
    wield,
And vauncing forth from all the other
    band
Of knights, addrest his maiden-headed
    shield,
Shewing him selfe all ready for the field.
Gainst whom there singled from the other
    side
A Painim knight, that well in armes was
    skild,
And had in many a battell oft bene tride,
Hight Bruncheval the bold, who fiersly
    forth did ride.

XVIII

So furiously they both together met,
That neither could the others force sus-
    taine:
As two fierce buls, that strive the rule to
    get
Of all the heard, meete with so hideous
    maine,
That both, rebutted, tumble on the plaine;
So these two champions to the ground were
    feld,
Where in a maze they both did long
    remaine,
And in their hands their idle troncheons
    held,
Which neither able were to wag, or once to
    weld.

XIX

Which when the noble Ferramont espide,
He pricked forth in ayd of Satyran;
And him against Sir Blandamour did ride
With all the strength and stifnesse that he
    can.
But the more strong and stiffely that he
    ran,
So much more sorely to the ground he fell,
That on an heape were tumbled horse and
    man.
Unto whose rescue forth rode Paridell;
But him likewise with that same speare he
    eke did quell.

XX

Which Braggadocchio seeing, had no will
To hasten greatly to his parties ayd,
Albee his turne were next; but stood there
    still,
As one that seemed doubtfull or dismayd.
But Triamond, halfe wroth to see him staid,
Sternly stept forth, and raught away his
    speare,
With which so sore he Ferramont assaid,
That horse and man to ground he quite did
    beare,
That neither could in hast themselves
    againe upreare.

XXI

Which to avenge, Sir Devon him did dight,
But with no better fortune then the rest,
For him likewise he quickly downe did
    smight;
And after him Sir Douglas him addrest,
And after him Sir Paliumord forth prest,
But none of them against his strokes could
    stand;
But all the more, the more his praise in-
    crest:
For either they were left uppon the land,
Or went away sore wounded of his haplesse
    hand.

XXII

And now by this, Sir Satyrane abraid
Out of the swowne, in which too long he
    lay;
And looking round about, like one dismaid,
When as he saw the mercilesse affray
Which doughty Triamond had wrought
    that day
Unto the noble Knights of Maidenhead,
His mighty heart did almost rend in tway

For very gall, that rather wholly dead
Himselfe he wisht have beene, then in so
    bad a stead.

XXIII

Eftsoones he gan to gather up around
His weapons, which lay scattered all
    abrode,
And as it fell, his steed he ready found.
On whom remounting, fiercely forth he
    rode,
Like sparke of fire that from the andvile
    glode,
There where he saw the valiant Triamond
Chasing, and laying on them heavy lode,
That none his force were able to with-
    stond,
So dreadfull were his strokes, so deadly was
    his hond.

XXIV

With that, at him his beamlike speare he
    aimed,
And thereto all his power and might
    applide:
The wicked steele for mischiefe first or-
    dained,
And having now misfortune got for guide,
Staid not till it arrived in his side,
And therein made a very griesly wound,
That streames of bloud his armour all
    bedide.
Much was he daunted with that direfull
    stound,
That scarse he him upheld from falling in a
    sound.

XXV

Yet as he might, himselfe he soft withdrew
Out of the field, that none perceiv'd it
    plaine.
Then gan the part of chalengers anew
To range the field, and victorlike to raine,
That none against them battell durst main-
    taine.
By that the gloomy evening on them fell,
That forced them from fighting to refraine,
And trumpets sound to cease did them com-
    pell.
So Satyrane that day was judg'd to beare
    the bell.

XXVI

The morrow next the turney gan anew,
And with the first the hardy Satyrane

Appear'd in place, with all his noble crew:
On th' other side full many a warlike
    swaine
Assembled were, that glorious prize to
    gaine.
But mongst them all was not Sir Triamond;
Unable he new battell to darraine,
Through grievaunce of his late received
    wound,
That doubly did him grieve, when so him-
    selfe he found.

XXVII

Which Cambell seeing, though he could not
    salve,
Ne done undoe, yet for to salve his name,
And purchase honour in his friends behalve,
This goodly counterfesaunce he did frame:
The shield and armes, well knowne to be
    the same
Which Triamond had worne, unwares to
    wight,
And to his friend unwist, for doubt of
    blame,
If he misdid, he on himselfe did dight,
That none could him discerne, and so went
    forth to fight.

XXVIII

There Satyrane lord of the field he found,
Triumphing in great joy and jolity;
Gainst whom none able was to stand on
    ground;
That much he gan his glorie to envy,
And cast t' avenge his friends indignity.
A mightie speare eftsoones at him he bent;
Who, seeing him come on so furiously,
Met him mid-way with equall hardiment,
That forcibly to ground they both together
    went.

XXIX

They up againe them selves can lightly
    reare,
And to their tryed swords them selves be-
    take;
With which they wrought such wondrous
    marvels there,
That all the rest it did amazed make,
Ne any dar'd their perill to partake;
Now cuffing close, now chacing to and fro,
Now hurtling round advantage for to take:
As two wild boares together grapling go,
Chaufing and foming choler each against
    his fo.

XXX

So as they courst, and turneyd here and
theare,
It chaunst Sir Satyrane his steed at last,
Whether through foundring, or through
sodein feare,
To stumble, that his rider nigh he cast;
Which vauntage Cambell did pursue so
fast,
That ere him selfe he had recovered well,
So sore he sowst him on the compast creast,
That forced him to leave his loftie sell,
And rudely tumbling downe under his
horse feete fell.

XXXI

Lightly Cambello leapt downe from his
steed,
For to have rent his shield and armes away,
That whylome wont to be the victors
meed;
When all unwares he felt an hideous sway
Of many swords, that lode on him did lay.
An hundred knights had him enclosed
round,
To rescue Satyrane out of his pray;
All which at once huge strokes on him did
pound,
In hope to take him prisoner, where he
stood on ground.

XXXII

He with their multitude was nought dis-
mayd,
But with stout courage turnd upon them
all,
And with his brondiron round about him
layd;
Of which he dealt large almes, as did befall:
Like as a lion, that by chaunce doth fall
Into the hunters toile, doth rage and rore,
In royall heart disdaining to be thrall.
But all in vaine: for what might one do
more ?
They have him taken captive, though it
grieve him sore.

XXXIII

Whereof when newes to Triamond was
brought,
There as he lay, his wound he soone forgot,
And starting up, streight for his armour
sought:
In vaine he sought; for there he found it
not;

Cambello it away before had got:
Cambelloes armes therefore he on him
threw,
And lightly issewd forth to take his lot.
There he in troupe found all that warlike
crew,
Leading his friend away, full sorie to his
vew.

XXXIV

Into the thickest of that knightly preasse
He thrust, and smote downe all that was
betweene,
Caried with fervent zeale, ne did he ceasse,
Till that he came where he had Cambell
seene,
Like captive thral two other knights
atweene:
There he amongst them cruell havocke
makes,
That they which lead him soone enforced
beene
To let him loose, to save their proper
stakes;
Who being freed, from one a weapon
fiercely takes.

XXXV

With that he drives at them with dreadfull
might,
Both in remembrance of his friends late
harme,
And in revengement of his owne despight;
So both together give a new allarme,
As if but now the battell wexed warme.
As when two greedy wolves doe breake by
force
Into an heard, farre from the husband
farme,
They spoile and ravine without all re-
morse;
So did these two through all the field their
foes enforce.

XXXVI

Fiercely they followd on their bolde em-
prize,
Till trumpets sound did warne them all to
rest;
Then all with one consent did yeeld the
prize
To Triamond and Cambell as the best.
But Triamond to Cambell it relest,
And Cambell it to Triamond transferd;
Each labouring t' advance the others gest,

And make his praise before his owne pre-
    ferd:
So that the doome was to another day dif-
    ferd.

XXXVII

The last day came, when all those knightes
    againe
Assembled were their deedes of armes to
    shew.
Full many deedes that day were shewed
    plaine:
But Satyrane, bove all the other crew,
His wondrous worth declared in all mens
    view;
For from the first he to the last endured,
And though some while Fortune from him
    withdrew,
Yet evermore his honour he recured,
And with unwearied powre his party still
    assured.

XXXVIII

Ne was there knight that ever thought of
    armes,
But that his utmost prowesse there made
    knowen;
That by their many wounds, and carelesse
    harmes,
By shivered speares, and swords all under
    strowen,
By scattered shields was easie to be showen.
There might ye see loose steeds at randon
    ronne,
Whose luckelesse riders late were over-
    throwen,
And squiers make hast to helpe their lords
    fordonne:
But still the Knights of Maidenhead the
    better wonne.

XXXIX

Till that there entred on the other side
A straunger knight, from whence no man
    could reed,
In queynt disguise, full hard to be describe.
For all his armour was like salvage weed,
With woody mosse bedight, and all his
    steed
With oaken leaves attrapt, that seemed
    fit
For salvage wight, and thereto well agreed
His word, which on his ragged shield was
    writ,
Salvagesse sans finesse, shewing secret wit.

XL

He, at his first incomming, charg'd his spere
At him that first appeared in his sight:
That was to weet the stout Sir Sangliere,
Who well was knowen to be a valiant
    knight,
Approved oft in many a perlous fight.
Him at the first encounter downe he smote,
And overbore beyond his crouper quight,
And after him another knight, that hote
Sir Brianor, so sore, that none him life be-
    hote.

XLI

Then, ere his hand he reard, he overthrew
Seven knights, one after other, as they
    came:
And when his speare was brust, his sword
    he drew,
The instrument of wrath, and with the
    same
Far'd like a lyon in his bloodie game,
Hewing and slashing shields and helmets
    bright,
And beating downe what ever nigh him
    came,
That every one gan shun his dreadfull sight,
No lesse then death it selfe, in daungerous
    affright.

XLII

Much wondred all men, what, or whence he
    came,
That did amongst the troupes so tyrannize;
And each of other gan inquire his name.
But when they could not learne it by no
    wize,
Most answerable to his wyld disguize
It seemed, him to terme the Salvage Knight.
But certes his right name was otherwize,
Though knowne to few that Arthegall he
    hight,
The doughtiest knight that liv'd that day,
    and most of might.

XLIII

Thus was Sir Satyrane with all his band
By his sole manhood and atchievement
    stout
Dismayd, that none of them in field durst
    stand,
But beaten were, and chased all about,
So he continued all that day throughout,
Till evening, that the sunne gan downward
    bend.

Then rushed forth out of the thickest rout
A stranger knight, that did his glorie shend:
So nought may be esteemed happie till the
    end.

XLIV

He at his entrance charg'd his powrefull
    speare
At Artegall, in middest of his pryde,
And therewith smote him on his umbriere
So sore, that, tombling backe, he downe did
    slyde
Over his horses taile above a stryde:
Whence litle lust he had to rise againe.
Which Cambell seeing, much the same en-
    vyde,
And ran at him with all his might and
    maine;
But shortly was likewise seene lying on
    the plaine.

XLV

Whereat full inly wroth was Triamond,
And cast t' avenge the shame doen to his
    freend:
But by his friend himselfe eke soone he
    fond,
In no lesse neede of helpe then him he
    weend.
All which when Blandamour from end to
    end
Beheld, he woxe therewith displeased sore,
And thought in mind it shortly to amend:
His speare he feutred, and at him it bore;
But with no better fortune then the rest
    afore.

XLVI

Full many others at him likewise ran:
But all of them likewise dismounted were.
Ne certes wonder; for no powre of man
Could bide the force of that enchaunted
    speare,
The which this famous Britomart did beare;
With which she wondrous deeds of arms
    atchieved,
And overthrew what ever came her neare,
That all those stranger knights full sore
    agrieved,
And that late weaker band of chalengers
    relieved.

XLVII

Like as in sommers day, when raging heat
Doth burne the earth, and boyled rivers drie,

That all brute beasts, forst to refraine fro
    meat,
Doe hunt for shade, where shrowded they
    may lie,
And missing it, faine from themselves to
    flie;
All travellers tormented are with paine:
A watry cloud doth overcast the skie,
And poureth forth a sudden shoure of raine,
That all the wretched world recomforteth
    againe.

XLVIII

So did the warlike Britomart restore
The prize to Knights of Maydenhead that
    day,
Which else was like to have bene lost, and
    bore
The prayse of prowesse from them all
    away.
Then shrilling trompets loudly gan to bray,
And bad them leave their labours and long
    toyle
To joyous feast and other gentle play,
Where beauties prize shold win that pre-
    tious spoyle:
Where I with sound of trompe will also rest
    a whyle.

CANTO V

The ladies for the girdle strive
Of famous Florimell:
Scudamour, comming to Cares house,
Doth sleepe from him expell.

I

It hath bene through all ages ever seene,
That with the praise of armes and chevalrie
The prize of beautie still hath joyned beene;
And that for reasons speciall privitie:
For either doth on other much relie.
For he me seemes most fit the faire to
    serve,
That can her best defend from villenie;
And she most fit his service doth deserve,
That fairest is and from her faith will
    never swerve.

II

So fitly now here commeth next in place,
After the proofe of prowesse ended well,
The controverse of beauties soveraine
    grace;
In which, to her that doth the most excell

Shall fall the girdle of faire Florimell:
That many wish to win for glorie vaine,
And not for vertuous use, which some doe
    tell
That glorious belt did in it selfe containe,
Which ladies ought to love, and seeke for
    to obtaine.

III

That girdle gave the vertue of chast love
And wivehood true to all that did it beare;
But whosoever contrarie doth prove
Might not the same about her middle
    weare:
But it would loose, or else a sunder teare.
Whilome it was (as Faeries wont report)
Dame Venus girdle, by her steemed deare,
What time she usd to live in wively sort;
But layd aside, when so she usd her looser
    sport.

IV

Her husband Vulcan whylome for her
    sake,
When first he loved her with heart entire,
This pretious ornament, they say, did make,
And wrought in Lemno with unquenched
    fire:
And afterwards did for her loves first hire
Give it to her, for ever to remaine,
Therewith to bind lascivious desire,
And loose affections streightly to restraine;
Which vertue it for ever after did retaine.

V

The same one day, when she her selfe dis-
    posd
To visite her beloved paramoure,
The God of Warre, she from her middle
    loosd,
And left behind her in her secret bowre,
On Acidalian mount, where many an howre
She with the pleasant Graces wont to play.
There Florimell in her first ages flowre
Was fostered by those Graces, (as they say)
And brought with her from thence that
    goodly belt away.

VI

That goodly belt was Cestus hight by name,
And as her life by her esteemed deare.
No wonder then, if that to winne the same
So many ladies sought, as shall appeare;
For pearelesse she was thought, that did it
    beare.

And now by this their feast all being ended,
The judges which thereto selected were
Into the Martian field adowne descended,
To deeme this doutfull case, for which
    they all contended.

VII

But first was question made, which of those
    knights
That lately turneyd had the wager wonne:
There was it judged by those worthie
    wights,
That Satyrane the first day best had donne:
For he last ended, having first begonne.
The second was to Triamond behight,
For that he sav'd the victour from for-
    donne:
For Cambell victour was in all mens sight,
Till by mishap he in his foemens hand did
    light.

VIII

The third dayes prize unto that straunger
    knight,
Whom all men term'd Knight of the
    Hebene Speare,
To Britomart, was given by good right;
For that with puissant stroke she downe
    did beare
The Salvage Knight, that victour was
    whileare,
And all the rest which had the best afore,
And to the last unconquer'd did appeare;
For last is deemed best. To her therefore
The fayrest ladie was adjudgd for para-
    more.

IX

But thereat greatly grudged Arthegall,
And much repynd, that both of victors
    meede
And eke of honour she did him forestall.
Yet mote he not withstand what was de-
    creede;
But inly thought of that despightfull deede
Fit time t' awaite avenged for to bee.
This being ended thus, and all agreed,
Then next ensew'd the paragon to see
Of beauties praise, and yeeld the fayrest
    her due fee.

X

Then first Cambello brought unto their
    view
His faire Cambina, covered with a veale;

Which being once withdrawne, most per-
    fect hew
And passing beautie did eftsoones reveale,
That able was weake harts away to steale.
Next did Sir Triamond unto their sight
The face of his deare Canacee unheale;
Whose beauties beame eftsoones did shine
    so bright,
That daz'd the eyes of all, as with exceed-
    ing light.

XI

And after her did Paridell produce
His false Duessa, that she might be seene,
Who with her forged beautie did seduce
The hearts of some, that fairest her did
    weene;
As diverse wits affected divers beene.
Then did Sir Ferramont unto them shew
His Lucida, that was full faire and sheene:
And after these an hundred ladies moe
Appear'd in place, the which each other did
    outgoe.

XII

All which who so dare thinke for to enchace,
Him needeth sure a golden pen, I weene,
To tell the feature of each goodly face.
For since the day that they created beene,
So many heavenly faces were not seene
Assembled in one place: ne he that thought
For Chian folke to pourtraict beauties queene,
By view of all the fairest to him brought,
So many faire did see, as here he might
    have sought.

XIII

At last, the most redoubted Britonesse
Her lovely Amoret did open shew;
Whose face discovered, plainely did ex-
    presse
The heavenly pourtraict of bright angels
    hew.
Well weened all, which her that time did
    vew,
That she should surely beare the bell away,
Till Blandamour, who thought he had the
    trew
And very Florimell, did her display:
The sight of whom once seene did all the
    rest dismay.

XIV

For all afore that seemed fayre and bright,
Now base and contemptible did appeare,

Compar'd to her, that shone as Phebes light
Amongst the lesser starres in evening
    cleare.
All that her saw with wonder ravisht weare,
And weend no mortall creature she should
    bee,
But some celestiall shape, that flesh did
    beare:
Yet all were glad there Florimell to see;
Yet thought that Florimell was not so
    faire as shee.

XV

As guilefull goldsmith that, by secret skill,
With golden foyle doth finely over spred
Some baser metall, which commend he will
Unto the vulgar for good gold insted,
He much more goodly glosse thereon doth
    shed,
To hide his falshood, then if it were trew:
So hard this idole was to be ared,
That Florimell her selfe in all mens vew
She seem'd to passe: so forged things do
    fairest shew.

XVI

Then was that golden belt by doome of
    all
Graunted to her, as to the fayrest dame.
Which being brought, about her middle
    small
They thought to gird, as best it her be-
    came;
But by no meanes they could it thereto
    frame.
For, ever as they fastned it, it loos'd
And fell away, as feeling secret blame.
Full oft about her wast she it enclos'd;
And it as oft was from about her wast dis-
    clos'd.

XVII

That all men wondred at the uncouth sight,
And each one thought as to their fancies
    came.
But she her selfe did thinke it doen for
    spight,
And touched was with secret wrath and
    shame
Therewith, as thing deviz'd her to defame.
Then many other ladies likewise tride
About their tender loynes to knit the same;
But it would not on none of them abide,
But when they thought it fast, eftsoones it
    was untide.

XVIII

Which when that scornefull Squire of
    Dames did vew,
He lowdly gan to laugh, and thus to jest:
' Alas for pittie, that so faire a crew,
As like can not be seene from east to west,
Cannot find one this girdle to invest !
Fie on the man that did it first invent,
To shame us all with this, *Ungirt unblest !*
Let never ladie to his love assent,
That hath this day so many so unmanly
    shent.'

XIX

Thereat all knights gan laugh, and ladies
    lowre:
Till that at last the gentle Amoret
Likewise assayd, to prove that girdles
    powre;
And having it about her middle set,
Did find it fit withouten breach or let.
Whereat the rest gan greatly to envie:
But Florimell exceedingly did fret,
And snatching from her hand halfe angrily
The belt againe, about her bodie gan it tie.

XX

Yet nathemore would it her bodie fit;
Yet nathelesse to her, as her dew right,
It yeelded was by them that judged it:
And she her selfe adjudged to the knight
That bore the hebene speare, as wonne in
    fight.
But Britomart would not thereto assent,
Ne her owne Amoret forgoe so light
For that strange dame, whose beauties
    wonderment
She lesse esteem'd then th' others vertuous
    government.

XXI

Whom when the rest did see her to re-
    fuse,
They were full glad, in hope themselves to
    get her:
Yet at her choice they all did greatly muse.
But after that, the judges did arret her
Unto the second best, that lov'd her better;
That was the Salvage Knight: but he was
    gone
In great displeasure, that he could not get
    her.
Then was she judged Triamond his one;
But Triamond lov'd Canacee, and other
    none.

XXII

Tho unto Satyran she was adjudged,
Who was right glad to gaine so goodly
    meed :
But Blandamour thereat full greatly
    grudged,
And litle prays'd his labours evill speed,
That, for to winne the saddle, lost the steed.
Ne lesse thereat did Paridell complaine,
And thought t' appeale from that which
    was decreed
To single combat with Sir Satyrane.
Thereto him Ate stird, new discord to
    maintaine.

XXIII

And eke with these, full many other knights
She through her wicked working did in-
    cense,
Her to demaund, and chalenge as their
    rights,
Deserved for their perils recompense.
Amongst the rest, with boastfull vaine
    pretense
Stept Braggadochio forth, and as his thrall
Her claym'd, by him in battell wonne long
    sens:
Whereto her selfe he did to witnesse call;
Who being askt, accordingly confessed all.

XXIV

Thereat exceeding wroth was Satyran;
And wroth with Satyran was Blandamour;
And wroth with Blandamour was Erivan;
And at them both Sir Paridell did loure.
So all together stird up strifull stoure,
And readie were new battell to darraine.
Each one profest to be her paramoure,
And vow'd with speare and shield it to
    maintaine;
Ne judges powre, ne reasons rule, mote
    them restraine.

XXV

Which troublous stirre when Satyrane
    aviz'd,
He gan to cast how to appease the same,
And, to accord them all, this meanes
    deviz'd:
First in the midst to set that fayrest dame,
To whom each one his chalenge should
    disclame,
And he himselfe his right would eke
    releasse:
Then looke, to whom she voluntarie came,

He should without disturbance her possesse:
Sweete is the love that comes alone with
   willingnesse.

XXVI

They all agreed, and then that snowy mayd
Was in the middest plast among them all:
All on her gazing wisht, and vowd, and prayd,
And to the Queene of Beautie close did call,
That she unto their portion might befall.
Then when she long had lookt upon each
   one,
As though she wished to have pleasd them
   all,
At last to Braggadochio selfe alone
She came of her accord, in spight of all his
   fone.

XXVII

Which when they all beheld, they chaft, and
   rag'd,
And woxe nigh mad for very harts despight,
That from revenge their willes they scarse
   asswag'd:
Some thought from him her to have reft by
   might;
Some proffer made with him for her to
   fight.
But he nought car'd for all that they could
   say:
For he their words as wind esteemed light.
Yet not fit place he thought it there to stay,
But secretly from thence that night her
   bore away.

XXVIII

They which remaynd, so soone as they
   perceiv'd
That she was gone, departed thence with
   speed,
And follow'd them, in mind her to have
   reav'd
From wight unworthie of so noble meed.
In which poursuit how each one did suc-
   ceede,
Shall else be told in order, as it fell.
But now of Britomart it here doth neede,
The hard adventures and strange haps to
   tell;
Since with the rest she went not after
   Florimell.

XXIX

For soone as she them saw to discord set,
Her list no longer in that place abide;

But taking with her lovely Amoret,
Upon her first adventure forth did ride,
To seeke her lov'd, making blind Love her
   guide.
Unluckie mayd, to seeke her enemie !
Unluckie mayd, to seeke him farre and
   wide,
Whom, when he was unto her selfe most
   nie,
She through his late disguizement could
   him not descrie !

XXX

So much the more her griefe, the more her
   toyle:
Yet neither toyle nor griefe she once did
   spare,
In seeking him that should her paine
   assoyle;
Whereto great comfort in her sad misfare
Was Amoret, companion of her care:
Who likewise sought her lover long mis-
   went,
The gentle Scudamour, whose hart whil-
   eare
That stryfull hag with gealous discontent
Had fild, that he to fell reveng was fully
   bent.

XXXI

Bent to revenge on blamelesse Britomart
The crime which cursed Ate kindled earst,
The which like thornes did pricke his geal-
   ous hart,
And through his soule like poysned arrow
   perst,
That by no reason it might be reverst,
For ought that Glauce could or doe or
   say.
For aye the more that she the same re-
   herst,
The more it gauld and griev'd him night
   and day,
That nought but dire revenge his anger
   mote defray.

XXXII

So as they travelled, the drouping night,
Covered with cloudie storme and bitter
   showre,
That dreadfull seem'd to every living wight,
Upon them fell, before her timely howre;
That forced them to seeke some covert
   bowre,

Where they might hide their heads in quiet
  rest,
And shrowd their persons from that stormie
  stowre.
Not farre away, not meete for any guest,
They spide a little cottage, like some
  poore mans nest.

XXXIII

Under a steepe hilles side it placed was,
There where the mouldred earth had cav'd
  the banke;
And fast beside a little brooke did pas
Of muddie water, that like puddle stanke,
By which few crooked sallowes grew in
  ranke:
Wherto approaching nigh, they heard the
  sound
Of many yron hammers beating ranke,
And answering their wearie turnes around,
That seemed some blacksmith dwelt in that
  desert ground.

XXXIV

There entring in, they found the goodman
  selfe
Full busily unto his worke ybent;
Who was to weet a wretched wearish elfe,
With hollow eyes and rawbone cheekes for-
  spent,
As if he had in prison long bene pent:
Full blacke and griesly did his face ap-
  peare,
Besmeard with smoke that nigh his eye-
  sight blent;
With rugged beard, and hoarie shagged
  heare,
The which he never wont to combe, or
  comely sheare.

XXXV

Rude was his garment, and to rags all rent,
Ne better had he, ne for better cared:
With blistred hands emongst the cinders
  brent,
And fingers filthie, with long nayles un-
  pared,
Right fit to rend the food on which he fared.
His name was Care; a blacksmith by his
  trade,
That neither day nor night from working
  spared,
But to small purpose yron wedges made;
Those be unquiet thoughts, that carefull
  minds invade.

XXXVI

In which his worke he had sixe servants
  prest,
About the andvile standing evermore,
With huge great hammers, that did never
  rest
From heaping stroakes, which thereon
  soused sore:
All sixe strong groomes, but one then other
  more:
For by degrees they all were disagreed;
So likewise did the hammers which they
  bore
Like belles in greatnesse orderly succeed,
That he which was the last the first did
  farre exceede.

XXXVII

He like a monstrous gyant seem'd in sight,
Farre passing Bronteus or Pyracmon great,
The which in Lipari doe day and night
Frame thunderbolts for Joves avengefull
  threate.
So dreadfully he did the andvile beat,
That seem'd to dust he shortly would it
  drive:
So huge his hammer and so fierce his
  heat,
That seem'd a rocke of diamond it could
  rive,
And rend a sunder quite, if he thereto list
  strive.

XXXVIII

Sir Scudamour, there entring, much ad-
  mired
The manner of their worke and wearie
  paine;
And having long beheld, at last enquired
The cause and end thereof: but all in
  vaine;
For they for nought would from their
  worke refraine,
Ne let his speeches come unto their eare;
And eke the breathfull bellowes blew
  amaine,
Like to the northren winde, that none could
  heare:
Those Pensifenesse did move; and Sighes
  the bellows weare.

XXXIX

Which when that warriour saw, he said no
  more,
But in his armour layd him downe to rest:

To rest he layd him downe upon the flore,
(Whylome for ventrous knights the bedding best,)
And thought his wearie limbs to have redrest.
And that old aged dame, his faithfull squire,
Her feeble joynts layd eke a downe to rest;
That needed much her weake age to desire,
After so long a travell, which them both did tire.

XL

There lay Sir Scudamour long while expecting
When gentle sleepe his heavie eyes would close;
Oft chaunging sides, and oft new place electing,
Where better seem'd he mote himselfe repose;
And oft in wrath he thence againe uprose;
And oft in wrath he layd him downe againe.
But wheresoever he did himselfe dispose,
He by no meanes could wished ease obtaine:
So every place seem'd painefull, and ech changing vaine.

XLI

And evermore, when he to sleepe did thinke,
The hammers sound his senses did molest;
And evermore, when he began to winke,
The bellowes noyse disturb'd his quiet rest,
Ne suffred sleepe to settle in his brest.
And all the night the dogs did barke and howle
About the house, at sent of stranger guest:
And now the crowing cocke, and now the owle
Lowde shriking, him afflicted to the very sowle.

XLII

And if by fortune any litle nap
Upon his heavie eye-lids chaunst to fall,
Eftsoones one of those villeins him did rap
Upon his headpeece with his yron mall,
That he was soone awaked therewithall,
And lightly started up as one affrayd,
Or as if one him suddenly did call:
So oftentimes he out of sleepe abrayd,
And then lay musing long on that him ill apayd.

XLIII

So long he muzed, and so long he lay,
That at the last his wearie sprite opprest
With fleshly weaknesse, which no creature may
Long time resist, gave place to kindly rest,
That all his senses did full soone arrest:
Yet, in his soundest sleepe, his dayly feare
His ydle braine gan busily molest,
And made him dreame those two disloyall were:
The things that day most minds, at night doe most appeare.

XLIV

With that, the wicked carle, the maister smith,
A paire of redwhot yron tongs did take
Out of the burning cinders, and therewith
Under his side him nipt, that, forst to wake,
He felt his hart for very paine to quake,
And started up avenged for to be
On him the which his quiet slomber brake:
Yet, looking round about him, none could see;
Yet did the smart remaine, though he himselfe did flee.

XLV

In such disquiet and hartfretting payne
He all that night, that too long night, did passe.
And now the day out of the ocean mayne
Began to peepe above this earthly masse,
With pearly dew sprinkling the morning grasse:
Then up he rose like heavie lumpe of lead,
That in his face, as in a looking glasse,
The signes of anguish one mote plainely read,
And ghesse the man to be dismayd with gealous dread.

XLVI

Unto his lofty steede he clombe anone,
And forth upon his former voiage fared,
And with him eke that aged squire attone;
Who, whatsoever perill was prepared,
Both equall paines and equall perill shared:
The end whereof and daungerous event
Shall for another canticle be spared:
But here my wearie teeme, nigh over spent,
Shall breath it selfe awhile, after so long a went.

CANTO VI

Both Scudamour and Arthegall
Doe fight with Britomart :
He sees her face ; doth fall in love,
And soone from her depart.

I

WHAT equall torment to the griefe of mind,
And pyning anguish hid in gentle hart,
That inly feeds it selfe with thoughts un-
　　kind,
And nourisheth her owne consuming
　　smart ?
What medicine can any leaches art
Yeeld such a sore, that doth her grievance
　　hide,
And will to none her maladie impart ?
Such was the wound that Scudamour did
　　gride ;
For which Dan Phebus selfe cannot a salve
　　provide.

II

Who having left that restlesse House of Care,
The next day, as he on his way did ride,
Full of melancholie and sad misfare,
Through misconceipt, all unawares espide
An armed knight under a forrest side,
Sitting in shade beside his grazing steede ;
Who, soone as them approaching he de-
　　scride,
Gan towards them to pricke with eger
　　speede,
That seem'd he was full bent to some mis-
　　chievous deede.

III

Which Scudamour perceiving, forth issewed
To have rencountred him in equall race ;
But soone as th' other, nigh approaching,
　　vewed
The armes he bore, his speare he gan abase,
And voide his course : at which so suddain
　　case
He wondred much. But th' other thus can
　　say :
' Ah ! gentle Scudamour, unto your grace
I me submit, and you of pardon pray,
That almost had against you trespassed this
　　day.'

IV

Whereto thus Scudamour : ' Small harme it
　　were
For any knight upon a ventrous knight
Without displeasance for to prove his
　　spere.
But reade you, sir, sith ye my name have
　　hight,
What is your owne, that I mote you re-
　　quite ? '
' Certes,' sayd he, ' ye mote as now excuse
Me from discovering you my name aright :
For time yet serves that I the same re-
　　fuse ;
But call ye me the Salvage Knight, as
　　others use.'

V

' Then this, Sir Salvage Knight,' quoth he,
　　' areede ;
Or doe you here within this forrest wonne,
That seemeth well to answere to your
　　weede ?
Or have ye it for some occasion donne ?
That rather seemes, sith knowen armes ye
　　shonne.'
' This other day,' sayd he, ' a stranger
　　knight
Shame and dishonour hath unto me donne ;
On whom I waite to wreake that foule de-
　　spight,
When ever he this way shall passe by day
　　or night.'

VI

' Shame be his meede,' quoth he, ' that
　　meaneth shame.
But what is he by whom ye shamed were ? '
' A stranger knight,' sayd he, ' unknowne
　　by name,
But knowne by fame, and by an hebene
　　speare,
With which he all that met him downe did
　　beare.
He in an open turney, lately held,
Fro me the honour of that game did
　　reare ;
And having me, all wearie earst, downe
　　feld,
The fayrest ladie reft, and ever since with-
　　held.'

VII

When Scudamour heard mention of that
　　speare,
He wist right well that it was Britomart,
The which from him his fairest love did
　　beare.
Tho gan he swell in every inner part,

For fell despight, and gnaw his gealous
    hart,
That thus he sharply sayd: 'Now by my
    head,
Yet is not this the first unknightly part,
Which that same knight, whom by his
    launce I read,
Hath doen to noble knights, that many
    makes him dread.

VIII

' For lately he my love hath fro me reft,
And eke defiled with foule villanie
The sacred pledge which in his faith was
    left,
In shame of knighthood and fidelitie;
The which ere long full deare he shall abie.
And if to that avenge by you decreed
This hand may helpe, or succour aught sup-
    plie,
It shall not fayle, when so ye shall it need.'
So both to wreake their wrathes on Brito-
    mart agreed.

IX

Whiles thus they communed, lo! farre
    away
A knight soft ryding towards them they
    spyde,
Attyr'd in forraine armes and straunge
    aray:
Whom when they nigh approcht, they
    plaine descryde
To be the same for whom they did abyde.
Sayd then Sir Scudamour, ' Sir Salvage
    Knight,
Let me this crave, sith first I was defyde,
That first I may that wrong to him requite:
And, if I hap to fayle, you shall recure my
    right.'

X

Which being yeelded, he his threatfull
    speare
Gan fewter, and against her fiercely ran.
Who soone as she him saw approaching
    neare
With so fell rage, her selfe she lightly gan
To dight, to welcome him well as she can:
But entertaind him in so rude a wise,
That to the ground she smote both horse
    and man;
Whence neither greatly hasted to arise,
But on their common harmes together did
    devise.

XI

But Artegall, beholding his mischaunce,
New matter added to his former fire;
And eft aventring his steeleheaded launce,
Against her rode, full of despiteous ire,
That nought but spoyle and vengeance did
    require.
But to himselfe his felonous intent
Returning, disappointed his desire,
Whiles unawares his saddle he forwent,
And found himselfe on ground in great
    amazement.

XII

Lightly he started up out of that stound,
And snatching forth his direfull deadly
    blade,
Did leape to her, as doth an eger hound
Thrust to an hynd within some covert glade,
Whom without perill he cannot invade.
With such fell greedines he her assayled,
That though she mounted were, yet he her
    made
To give him ground, (so much his force
    prevayled)
And shun his mightie strokes, gainst which
    no armes avayled.

XIII

So as they coursed here and there, it
    chaunst
That, in her wheeling round, behind her
    crest
So sorely he her strooke, that thence it
    glaunst
Adowne her backe, the which it fairely
    blest
From foule mischance; ne did it ever rest,
Till on her horses hinder parts it fell;
Where byting deepe, so deadly it imprest,
That quite it chynd his backe behind the
    sell,
And to alight on foote her algates did com-
    pell.

XIV

Like as the lightning brond from riven
    skie,
Throwne out by angry Jove in his ven-
    geance,
With dreadfull force falles on some steeple
    hie;
Which battring, downe it on the church
    doth glance,
And teares it all with terrible mischance.

Yet she no whit dismayd, her steed forsooke,
And casting from her that enchaunted
 lance,
Unto her sword and shield her soone betooke;
And therewithall at him right furiously she
 strooke.

XV

So furiously she strooke in her first heat,
Whiles with long fight on foot he breath-
 lesse was,
That she him forced backward to retreat,
And yeeld unto her weapon way to pas:
Whose raging rigour neither steele nor
 bras
Could stay, but to the tender flesh it went,
And pour'd the purple bloud forth on the
 gras;
That all his mayle yriv'd, and plates yrent,
Shew'd all his bodie bare unto the cruell
 dent.

XVI

At length, when as he saw her hastie heat
Abate, and panting breath begin to fayle,
He, through long sufferance growing now
 more great,
Rose in his strength, and gan her fresh as-
 sayle,
Heaping huge strokes, as thicke as showre
 of hayle,
And lashing dreadfully at every part,
As if he thought her soule to disentrayle.
Ah! cruell hand, and thrise more cruell
 hart,
That workst such wrecke on her to whom
 thou dearest art!

XVII

What yron courage ever could endure,
To worke such outrage on so faire a
 creature?
And in his madnesse thinke with hands
 impure
To spoyle so goodly workmanship of nature,
The Maker selfe resembling in her feature?
Certes some hellish furie, or some feend,
This mischiefe framd, for their first loves
 defeature,
To bath their hands in bloud of dearest
 freend,
Thereby to make their loves beginning their
 lives end.

XVIII

Thus long they trac'd and traverst to and
 fro,
Sometimes pursewing, and sometimes pur-
 sewed,
Still as advantage they espyde thereto:
But toward th' end Sir Arthegall renewed
His strength still more, but she still more
 decrewed.
At last his lucklesse hand he heav'd on
 hie,
Having his forces all in one accrewed,
And therewith stroke at her so hideouslie,
That seemed nought but death mote be her
 destinie.

XIX

The wicked stroke upon her helmet
 chaunst,
And with the force which in it selfe it bore
Her ventayle shard away, and thence forth
 glaunst
Adowne in vaine, ne harm'd her any more.
With that, her angels face, unseene afore,
Like to the ruddie morne appeard in sight,
Deawed with silver drops, through sweat-
 ing sore,
But somewhat redder then beseem'd aright,
Through toylesome heate and labour of her
 weary fight.

XX

And round about the same, her yellow
 heare,
Having through stirring loosd their wonted
 band,
Like to a golden border did appeare,
Framed in goldsmithes forge with cunning
 hand:
Yet goldsmithes cunning could not under-
 stand
To frame such subtile wire, so shinie cleare.
For it did glister like the golden sand,
The which Pactolus, with his waters shere,
Throwes forth upon the rivage round about
 him nere.

XXI

And as his hand he up againe did reare,
Thinking to worke on her his utmost
 wracke,
His powrelesse arme, benumbd with secret
 feare,
From his revengefull purpose shronke
 abacke,

And cruell sword out of his fingers slacke
Fell downe to ground, as if the steele had
    sence,
And felt some ruth, or sence his hand did
    lacke,
Or both of them did thinke, obedience
To doe to so divine a beauties excellence.

XXII

And he himselfe long gazing thereupon,
At last fell humbly downe upon his knee,
And of his wonder made religion,
Weening some heavenly goddesse he did
    see,
Or else unweeting what it else might bee;
And pardon her besought his errour frayle,
That had done outrage in so high degree:
Whilest trembling horrour did his sense
    assayle,
And made ech member quake, and manly
    hart to quayle.

XXIII

Nathelesse she, full of wrath for that late
    stroke,
All that long while upheld her wrathfull
    hand,
With fell intent on him to bene ywroke:
And looking sterne, still over him did stand,
Threatning to strike, unlesse he would
    withstand:
And bad him rise, or surely he should die.
But, die or live, for nought he would
    upstand,
But her of pardon prayd more earnestlie,
Or wreake on him her will for so great
    injurie.

XXIV

Which when as Scudamour, who now
    abrayd,
Beheld, where as he stood not farre aside,
He was therewith right wondrously dismayd,
And drawing nigh, when as he plaine
    descride
That peerelesse paterne of Dame Natures
    pride,
And heavenly image of perfection,
He blest himselfe, as one sore terrifide,
And turning feare to faint devotion,
Did worship her as some celestiall vision.

XXV

But Glauce, seeing all that chaunced there,
Well weeting how their errour to assoyle,

Full glad of so good end, to them drew
    nere,
And her salewd with seemly belaccoyle,
Joyous to see her safe after long toyle:
Then her besought, as she to her was deare,
To graunt unto those warriours truce a
    whyle;
Which yeelded, they their bevers up did
    reare,
And shew'd themselves to her, such as
    indeed they were.

XXVI

When Britomart with sharpe avizefull eye
Beheld the lovely face of Artegall,
Tempred with sternesse and stout majestie,
She gan eftsoones it to her mind to call,
To be the same which in her fathers hall
Long since in that enchaunted glasse she
    saw.
Therewith her wrathfull courage gan
    appall,
And haughtie spirits meekely to adaw,
That her enhaunced hand she downe can
    soft withdraw.

XXVII

Yet she it forst to have againe upheld,
As fayning choler, which was turn'd to
    cold:
But ever when his visage she beheld,
Her hand fell downe, and would no longer
    hold
The wrathfull weapon gainst his count-
    nance bold:
But when in vaine to fight she oft assayd,
She arm'd her tongue, and thought at him
    to scold;
Nathelesse her tongue not to her will obayd,
But brought forth speeches myld, when she
    would have missayd.

XXVIII

But Scudamour now woxen inly glad,
That all his gealous feare he false had
    found,
And how that hag his love abused had
With breach of faith and loyaltie unsound,
The which long time his grieved hart did
    wound,
Him thus bespake: 'Certes, Sir Artegall,
I joy to see you lout so low on ground,
And now become to live a ladies thrall,
That whylome in your minde wont to de-
    spise them all.'

XXIX

Soone as she heard the name of Artegall,
Her hart did leape, and all her hart-strings
    tremble,
For sudden joy, and secret feare withall,
And all her vitall powres, with motion
    nimble,
To succour it, themselves gan there assem-
    ble,
That by the swift recourse of flushing
    blood
Right plaine appeard, though she it would
    dissemble,
And fayned still her former angry mood,
Thinking to hide the depth by troubling of
    the flood.

XXX

When Glauce thus gan wisely all upknit:
'Ye gentle knights, whom fortune here
    hath brought,
To be spectators of this uncouth fit,
Which secret fate hath in this ladie
    wrought,
Against the course of kind, ne mervaile
    nought,
Ne thenceforth feare the thing that hether-
    too
Hath troubled both your mindes with idle
    thought,
Fearing least she your loves away should
    woo,
Feared in vaine, sith meanes ye see there
    wants theretoo.

XXXI

'And you, Sir Artegall, the Salvage Knight,
Henceforth may not disdaine that womans
    hand
Hath conquered you anew in second fight:
For whylome they have conquerd sea and
    land,
And heaven it selfe, that nought may them
    withstand:
Ne henceforth be rebellious unto love,
That is the crowne of knighthood, and the
    band
Of noble minds derived from above,
Which being knit with vertue, never will
    remove.

XXXII

'And you, faire ladie knight, my dearest
    dame,
Relent the rigour of your wrathfull will,
Whose fire were better turn'd to other
    flame;
And wiping out remembrance of all ill,
Graunt him your grace, but so that he ful-
    fill
The penance which ye shall to him em-
    part:
For lovers heaven must passe by sorrowes
    hell.'
Thereat full inly blushed Britomart;
But Artegall, close smyling, joy'd in secret
    hart.

XXXIII

Yet durst he not make love so suddenly,
Ne thinke th' affection of her hart to
    draw
From one to other so quite contrary:
Besides her modest countenance he saw
So goodly grave, and full of princely aw,
That it his ranging fancie did refraine,
And looser thoughts to lawfull bounds with
    draw,
Whereby the passion grew more fierce and
    faine,
Like to a stubborne steede whom strong
    hand would restraine.

XXXIV

But Scudamour, whose hart twixt doubtfull
    feare
And feeble hope hung all this while sus-
    pence,
Desiring of his Amoret to heare
Some gladfull newes and sure intelligence,
Her thus bespake: 'But, sir, without
    offence
Mote I request you tydings of my love,
My Amoret, sith you her freed fro thence,
Where she, captived long, great woes did
    prove;
That where ye left, I may her seeke, as
    doth behove.'

XXXV

To whom thus Britomart: 'Certes, sir
    knight,
What is of her become, or whether reft,
I can not unto you aread a right.
For from that time I from enchaunters
    theft
Her freed, in which ye her all hopelesse
    left,
I her preserv'd from perill and from feare,
And evermore from villenie her kept:

Ne ever was there wight to me more deare
Then she, ne unto whom I more true love
  did beare.

XXXVI

'Till on a day, as through a desert wyld
We travelled, both wearie of the way,
We did alight, and sate in shadow myld;
Where fearelesse I to sleepe me downe did
  lay.
But when as I did out of sleepe abray,
I found her not where I her left whyleare,
But thought she wandred was, or gone
  astray.
I cal'd her loud, I sought her farre and
  neare;
But no where could her find, nor tydings of
  her heare.'

XXXVII

When Scudamour those heavie tydings
  heard,
His hart was thrild with point of deadly
  feare;
Ne in his face or bloud or life appeard,
But senselesse stood, like to a mazed steare
That yet of mortall stroke the stound doth
  beare:
Till Glauce thus: 'Faire sir, be nought dis-
  mayd
With needelesse dread, till certaintie ye
  heare:
For yet she may be safe though somewhat
  strayd;
Its best to hope the best, though of the
  worst affrayd.'

XXXVIII

Nathlesse he hardly of her chearefull
  speech
Did comfort take, or in his troubled sight
Shew'd change of better cheare, so sore a
  breach
That sudden newes had made into his
  spright;
Till Britomart him fairely thus behight:
'Great cause of sorrow certes, sir, ye have:
But comfort take: for by this heavens light
I vow, you dead or living not to leave,
Till I her find, and wreake on him that did
  her reave.'

XXXIX

Therewith he rested, and well pleased was.
So peace being confirm'd amongst them all,

They tooke their steeds, and forward thence
  did pas
Unto some resting place, which mote be-
  fall,
All being guided by Sir Artegall:
Where goodly solace was unto them made,
And dayly feasting both in bowre and hall,
Untill that they their wounds well healed
  had,
And wearie limmes recur'd after late usage
  bad.

XL

In all which time, Sir Artegall made way
Unto the love of noble Britomart,
And with meeke service and much suit did
  lay
Continuall siege unto her gentle hart:
Which being whylome launcht with lovely
  dart,
More eath was new impression to receive,
How ever she her paynd with womanish art
To hide her wound, that none might it per-
  ceive:
Vaine is the art that seekes it selfe for to
  deceive.

XLI

So well he woo'd her, and so well he
  wrought her,
With faire entreatie and sweet blandish-
  ment,
That at the length unto a bay he brought her,
So as she to his speeches was content
To lend an eare, and softly to relent.
At last, through many vowes which forth he
  pour'd,
And many othes, she yeelded her consent
To be his love, and take him for her lord,
Till they with mariage meet might finish
  that accord.

XLII

Tho, when they had long time there taken
  rest,
Sir Artegall, who all this while was bound
Upon an hard adventure yet in quest,
Fit time for him thence to depart it found,
To follow that which he did long propound;
And unto her his congee came to take.
But her therewith full sore displeasd he
  found,
And loth to leave her late betrothed make,
Her dearest love full loth so shortly to for-
  sake

XLIII

Yet he with strong perswasions her as-
      swaged,
And wonne her will to suffer him depart;
For which his faith with her he fast
      engaged,
And thousand vowes from bottome of his
      hart,
That all so soone as he by wit or art
Could that atchieve, whereto he did aspire,
He unto her would speedily revert:
No longer space thereto he did desire,
But till the horned moone three courses
      did expire.

XLIV

With which she for the present was ap-
      peased,
And yeelded leave, how ever malcontent
She inly were, and in her mind displeased.
So, early in the morrow next, he went
Forth on his way, to which he was ybent;
Ne wight him to attend, or way to guide,
As whylome was the custome ancient
Mongst knights, when on adventures they
      did ride,
Save that she algates him a while accom-
      panide.

XLV

And by the way she sundry purpose found
Of this or that, the time for to delay,
And of the perils whereto he was bound,
The feare whereof seem'd much her to
      affray:
But all she did was but to weare out day.
Full oftentimes she leave of him did take;
And eft againe deviz'd some what to say,
Which she forgot, whereby excuse to make:
So loth she was his companie for to for-
      sake.

XLVI

At last, when all her speeches she had
      spent,
And new occasion fayld her more to find,
She left him to his fortunes government,
And backe returned with right heavie mind
To Scudamour, who she had left behind:
With whom she went to seeke faire Amo-
      ret,
Her second care, though in another kind:
For vertues onely sake, which doth beget
True love and faithfull friendship, she by
      her did set.

XLVII

Backe to that desert forrest they retyred,
Where sorie Britomart had lost her late;
There they her sought, and every where in-
      quired,
Where they might tydings get of her estate:
Yet found they none. But by what hap-
      lesse fate
Or hard misfortune she was thence convayd,
And stolne away from her beloved mate,
Were long to tell; therefore I here will
      stay
Untill another tyde, that I it finish may.

CANTO VII

Amoret rapt by greedie Lust
  Belphebe saves from dread :
The squire her loves, and being blam'd,
  His dayes in dole doth lead.

I

GREAT God of Love, that with thy cruell
      darts
Doest conquer greatest conquerors on
      ground,
And setst thy kingdome in the captive harts
Of kings and keasars, to thy service bound,
What glorie or what guerdon hast thou
      found
In feeble ladies tyranning so sore,
And adding anguish to the bitter wound,
With which their lives thou lanchedst long
      afore,
By heaping stormes of trouble on them
      daily more ?

II

So whylome didst thou to faire Florimell;
And so and so to noble Britomart:
So doest thou now to her of whom I tell,
The lovely Amoret, whose gentle hart
Thou martyrest with sorow and with smart
In salvage forrests and in deserts wide,
With beares and tygers taking heavie part,
Withouten comfort, and withouten guide,
That pittie is to heare the perils which she
      tride.

III

So soone as she with that brave Britonesse
Had left that turneyment for beauties prise
They travel'd long; that now for weari-
      nesse,
Both of the way and warlike exercise,

Both through a forest ryding did devise
T' alight, and rest their wearie limbs
awhile.
There heavie sleepe the eye-lids did sur-
prise
Of Britomart, after long tedious toyle,
That did her passed paines in quiet rest
assoyle.

IV

The whiles faire Amoret, of nought affeard,
Walkt through the wood, for pleasure or
for need;
When suddenly behind her backe she heard
One rushing forth out of the thickest weed,
That ere she backe could turne to taken
heed,
Had unawares her snatched up from
ground.
Feebly she shriekt, but so feebly indeed,
That Britomart heard not the shrilling
sound,
There where through weary travel she lay
sleeping sound.

V

It was to weet a wilde and salvage man,
Yet was no man, but onely like in shape,
And eke in stature higher by a span,
All overgrowne with haire, that could
awhape
An hardy hart, and his wide mouth did
gape
With huge great teeth, like to a tusked
bore:
For he liv'd all on ravin and on rape
Of men and beasts; and fed on fleshly gore,
The signe whereof yet stain'd his bloudy
lips afore.

VI

His neather lip was not like man nor beast,
But like a wide deepe poke, downe hanging
low,
In which he wont the relickes of his feast
And cruell spoyle, which he had spard, to
stow:
And over it his huge great nose did grow,
Full dreadfully empurpled all with bloud;
And downe both sides two wide long eares
did glow,
And raught downe to his waste, when up he
stood,
More great then th' eares of elephants by
Indus flood.

VII

His wast was with a wreath of yvie greene
Engirt about, ne other garment wore:
For all his haire was like a garment seene;
And in his hand a tall young oake he bore,
Whose knottie snags were sharpned all
afore,
And beath'd in fire for steele to be in sted.
But whence he was, or of what wombe
ybore,
Of beasts, or of the earth, I have not red:
But certes was with milke of wolves and
tygres fed.

VIII

This ugly creature in his armes her snatcht,
And through the forrest bore her quite
away,
With briers and bushes all to-rent and
scratcht;
Ne care he had, ne pittie of the pray,
Which many a knight had sought so many a
day.
He stayed not, but in his armes her bear-
ing
Ran, till he came to th' end of all his
way,
Unto his cave, farre from all peoples
hearing,
And there he threw her in, nought feeling,
ne nought fearing.

IX

For she, deare ladie, all the way was dead,
Whilest he in armes her bore; but when she
felt
Her selfe downe soust, she waked out of
dread
Streight into griefe, that her deare hart
nigh swelt,
And eft gan into tender teares to melt.
Then when she lookt about, and nothing
found
But darknesse and dread horrour, where
she dwelt,
She almost fell againe into a swound,
Ne wist whether above she were, or under
ground.

X

With that she heard some one close by her
side
Sighing and sobbing sore, as if the paine
Her tender hart in peeces would divide:
Which she long listning, softly askt againe

What mister wight it was that so did
      plaine ?
To whom thus aunswer'd was : 'Ah,
      wretched wight !
That seekes to know anothers griefe in
      vaine,
Unweeting of thine owne like haplesse
      plight:
Selfe to forget to mind another, is
      oversight.'

XI

'Aye me !' said she, 'where am I, or with
      whom ?
Emong the living, or emong the dead ?
What shall of me, unhappy maid, become ?
Shall death be th' end, or ought else worse,
      aread.'
'Unhappy mayd,' then answer'd she, 'whose
      dread
Untride is lesse then when thou shalt it try:
Death is to him that wretched life doth
      lead,
Both grace and gaine; but he in hell doth
      lie,
That lives a loathed life, and wishing can-
      not die.

XII

'This dismall day hath thee a caytive
      made,
And vassall to the vilest wretch alive,
Whose cursed usage and ungodly trade
The heavens abhorre, and into darkenesse
      drive.
For on the spoile of women he doth live,
Whose bodies chast, when ever in his
      powre
He may them catch, unable to gainestrive,
He with his shamefull lust doth first de-
      flowre,
And afterwards themselves doth cruelly
      devoure.

XIII

'Now twenty daies, by which the sonnes of
      men
Divide their works, have past through
      heven sheene,
Since I was brought into this dolefull den;
During which space these sory eies have
      seen
Seaven women by him slaine, and eaten
      clene.
And now no more for him but I alone,

And this old woman, here remaining beene;
Till thou cam'st hither to augment our
      mone;
And of us three to morrow he will sure
      eate one.'

XIV

'Ah ! dreadfull tidings which thou doest
      declare,'
Quoth she, 'of all that ever hath bene
      knowen !
Full many great calamities and rare
This feeble brest endured hath, but none
Equall to this, where ever I have gone.
But what are you, whom like unlucky lot
Hath linckt with me in the same chaine at-
      tone ?'
'To tell,' quoth she, 'that which ye see,
      needs not;
A wofull wretched maid, of God and man
      forgot.

XV

'But what I was it irkes me to reherse;
Daughter unto a lord of high degree,
That joyd in happy peace, till Fates per-
      verse
With guilefull Love did secretly agree,
To overthrow my state and dignitie.
It was my lot to love a gentle swaine,
Yet was he but a squire of low degree;
Yet was he meet, unlesse mine eye did
      faine,
By any ladies side for leman to have laine

XVI

'But, for his meannesse and disparagement
My sire, who me too dearely well did love
Unto my choise by no meanes would assent
But often did my folly fowle reprove,
Yet nothing could my fixed mind remove,
But whether willed or nilled friend or foe,
I me resolv'd the utmost end to prove,
And rather then my love abandon so,
Both sire, and friends, and all for ever to
      forgo.

XVII

'Thenceforth I sought by secret meanes to
      worke
Time to my will, and from his wrathful
      sight
To hide th' intent which in my heart did
      lurke,
Till I thereto had all things ready dight.

So on a day, unweeting unto wight,
I with that squire agreede away to flit,
And in a privy place, betwixt us hight,
Within a grove appointed him to meete;
To which I boldly came upon my feeble
  feete.

XVIII

'But ah! unhappy houre me thither
  brought:
For in that place where I him thought to
  find,
There was I found, contrary to my thought,
Of this accursed carle of hellish kind,
The shame of men, and plague of woman-
  kind;
Who trussing me, as eagle doth his pray,
Me hether brought with him, as swift as
  wind,
Where yet untouched till this present day,
I rest his wretched thrall, the sad Æmylia.'

XIX

'Ah! sad Æmylia,' then sayd Amoret,
'Thy ruefull plight I pitty as mine owne.
But read to me, by what devise or wit
Hast thou, in all this time, from him un-
  knowne
Thine honor sav'd, though into thraldome
  throwne?'
'Through helpe,' quoth she, 'of this old
  woman here
I have so done, as she to me hath showne:
For ever, when he burnt in lustfull fire,
She in my stead supplide his bestiall desire.'

XX

Thus of their evils as they did discourse,
And each did other much bewaile and mone,
Loe! where the villaine selfe, their sor-
  rowes sourse,
Came to the cave, and rolling thence the
  stone,
Which wont to stop the mouth thereof,
  that none
Might issue forth, came rudely rushing in,
And spredding over all the flore alone,
Gan dight him selfe unto his wonted sinne;
Which ended, then his bloudy banket should
  beginne.

XXI

Which when as fearefull Amoret perceived,
She staid not the utmost end thereof to try,

But like a ghastly gelt, whose wits are
  reaved,
Ran forth in hast with hideous outcry,
For horrour of his shamefull villany.
But after her full lightly he uprose,
And her pursu'd as fast as she did flie:
Full fast she flies, and farre afore him goes,
Ne feeles the thorns and thickets pricke her
  tender toes.

XXII

Nor hedge, nor ditch, nor hill, nor dale she
  staies,
But overleapes them all, like robucke light,
And through the thickest makes her nigh-
  est waies;
And evermore when with regardfull sight
She, looking backe, espies that griesly wight
Approching nigh, she gins to mend her pace,
And makes her feare a spur to hast her
  flight:
More swift then Myrrh' or Daphne in her
  race,
Or any of the Thracian Nimphes in sal-
  vage chase.

XXIII

Long so she fled, and so he follow'd long;
Ne living aide for her on earth appeares,
But if the heavens helpe to redresse her
  wrong,
Moved with pity of her plenteous teares.
It fortuned, Belphebe with her peares,
The woody nimphs, and with that lovely
  boy,
Was hunting then the libbards and the
  beares,
In these wild woods, as was her wonted joy,
To banish sloth, that oft doth noble mindes
  annoy.

XXIV

It so befell, as oft it fals in chace,
That each of them from other sundred
  were,
And that same gentle squire arriv'd in
  place
Where this same cursed caytive did ap-
  peare,
Pursuing that faire lady full of feare;
And now he her quite overtaken had;
And now he her away with him did beare
Under his arme, as seeming wondrous glad,
That by his grenning laughter mote farre
  off be rad.

XXV

Which drery sight the gentle squire espy-
        ing,
Doth hast to crosse him by the nearest way,
Led with that wofull ladies piteous crying,
And him assailes with all the might he
        may:
Yet will not he the lovely spoile downe lay,
But with his craggy club in his right hand
Defends him selfe, and saves his gotten
        pray.
Yet had it bene right hard him to with-
        stand,
But that he was full light and nimble on
        the land.

XXVI

Thereto the villaine used craft in fight;
For ever when the squire his javelin
        shooke,
He held the lady forth before him right,
And with her body, as a buckler, broke
The puissance of his intended stroke.
And if it chaunst, (as needs it must in
        fight)
Whilest he on him was greedy to be wroke,
That any little blow on her did light,
Then would he laugh aloud, and gather
        great delight.

XXVII

Which subtill sleight did him encumber
        much,
And made him oft, when he would strike,
        forbeare;
For hardly could he come the carle to
        touch,
But that he her must hurt, or hazard neare:
Yet he his hand so carefully did beare,
That at the last he did himselfe attaine,
And therein left the pike head of his speare
A streame of coleblacke bloud thence gusht
        amaine,
That all her silken garments did with bloud
        bestaine.

XXVIII

With that he threw her rudely on the flore,
And laying both his hands upon his glave,
With dreadfull strokes let drive at him so
        sore,
That forst him flie abacke, himselfe to save:
Yet he therewith so felly still did rave,
That scarse the squire his hand could once
        upreare,

But, for advantage, ground unto him gave;
Tracing and traversing, now here, now there;
For bootlesse thing it was to think such
        blowes to beare.

XXIX

Whilest thus in battell they embusied were,
Belphebe, raunging in that forrest wide,
The hideous noise of their huge strokes did
        heare,
And drew thereto, making her eare her
        guide.
Whom when that theefe approching nigh
        espide,
With bow in hand, and arrowes ready bent,
He by his former combate would not bide,
But fled away with ghastly dreriment,
Well knowing her to be his deaths sole in-
        strument.

XXX

Whom seeing flie, she speedily poursewed
With winged feete, as nimble as the winde,
And ever in her bow she ready shewed
The arrow to his deadly marke desynde:
As when Latonaes daughter, cruell kynde,
In vengement of her mothers great dis-
        grace,
With fell despight her cruell arrowes tynde
Gainst wofull Niobes unhappy race,
That all the gods did mone her miserable
        case.

XXXI

So well she sped her and so far she ventred,
That ere unto his hellish den he raught,
Even as he ready was there to have entred,
She sent an arrow forth with mighty
        draught,
That in the very dore him overcaught,
And in his nape arriving, through it thrild
His greedy throte, therewith in two dis-
        traught,
That all his vitall spirites thereby spild,
And all his hairy brest with gory bloud
        was fild.

XXXII

Whom when on ground she groveling saw
        to rowle,
She ran in hast his life to have bereft:
But ere she could him reach, the sinfull
        sowle,
Having his carrion corse quite sencelesse
        left,

Was fled to hell, surcharg'd with spoile and
  theft.
Yet over him she there long gazing stood,
And oft admir'd his monstrous shape, and
  oft
His mighty limbs, whilest all with filthy
  bloud
The place there overflowne seemd like a
  sodaine flood.

XXXIII

Thenceforth she past into his dreadfull den,
Where nought but darkesome drerinesse
  she found,
Ne creature saw, but hearkned now and
  then
Some litle whispering, and soft groning
  sound.
With that she askt, what ghosts there
  under ground
Lay hid in horrour of eternall night;
And bad them, if so be they were not
  bound,
To come and shew themselves before the
. light,
Now freed from feare and danger of that
  dismall wight.

XXXIV

Then forth the sad Æmylia issewed,
Yet trembling every joynt through former
  feare;
And after her the hag, there with her
  mewed,
A foule and lothsome creature, did ap-
  peare;
A leman fit for such a lover deare:
That mov'd Belphebe her no lesse to hate,
Then for to rue the others heavy cheare;
Of whom she gan enquire of her estate:
Who all to her at large, as hapned, did re-
  late.

XXXV

Thence she them brought toward the place
  where late
She left the gentle squire with Amoret:
There she him found by that new lovely
  mate,
Who lay the whiles in swoune, full sadly
  set,
From her faire eyes wiping the deawy
  wet,
Which softly stild, and kissing them
  atweene,

And handling soft the hurts which she did
  get:
For of that carle she sorely bruz'd had
  beene,
Als of his owne rash hand one wound was
  to be seene.

XXXVI

Which when she saw, with sodaine glaunc-
  ing eye,
Her noble heart with sight thereof was fild
With deepe disdaine, and great indignity,
That in her wrath she thought them both
  have thrild
With that selfe arrow which the carle had
  kild:
Yet held her wrathfull hand from ven-
  geance sore,
But drawing nigh, ere he her well beheld,
' Is this the faith? ' she said, — and said no
  more,
But turnd her face, and fled away for ever-
  more.

XXXVII

He, seeing her depart, arose up light,
Right sore agrieved at her sharpe reproofe,
And follow'd fast: but when he came in
  sight,
He durst not nigh approch, but kept aloofe,
For dread of her displeasures utmost proofe.
And evermore, when he did grace entreat,
And framed speaches fit for his behoofe,
Her mortall arrowes she at him did threat,
And forst him backe with fowle dishonor
  to retreat.

XXXVIII

At last, when long he follow'd had in vaine,
Yet found no ease of griefe, nor hope of
  grace,
Unto those woods he turned backe againe,
Full of sad anguish and in heavy case:
And finding there fit solitary place
For wofull wight, chose out a gloomy glade,
Where hardly eye mote see bright heavens
  face,
For mossy trees, which covered all with
  shade
And sad melancholy: there he his cabin
  made.

XXXIX

His wonted warlike weapons all he broke,
And threw away, with vow to use no more,

Ne thenceforth ever strike in battell stroke,
Ne ever word to speake to woman more;
But in that wildernesse, of men forlore,
And of the wicked world forgotten quight,
His hard mishap in dolor to deplore,
And wast his wretched daies in wofull
plight;
So on him selfe to wreake his follies owne
despight.

XL

And eke his garment, to be thereto meet,
He wilfully did cut and shape anew;
And his faire lockes, that wont with oint-
ment sweet
To be embaulm'd, and sweat out dainty dew,
He let to grow and griesly to concrew,
Uncomb'd, uncurl'd, and carelesly unshed;
That in short time his face they overgrew,
And over all his shoulders did dispred,
That who he whilome was, uneath was to
be red.

XLI

There he continued in this carefull plight,
Wretchedly wearing out his youthly yeares,
Through wilfull penury consumed quight,
That like a pined ghost he soone appeares.
For other food then that wilde forrest
beares,
Ne other drinke there did he ever tast,
Then running water, tempred with his
teares,
The more his weakened body so to wast:
That out of all mens knowledge he was
worne at last.

XLII

For on a day, by fortune as it fell,
His owne deare lord, Prince Arthure, came
that way,
Seeking adventures, where he mote heare
tell;
And as he through the wandring wood did
stray,
Having espide this cabin far away,
He to it drew, to weet who there did wonne;
Weening therein some holy hermit lay,
That did resort of sinfull people shonne;
Or else some woodman shrowded there
from scorching sunne.

XLIII

Arriving there, he found this wretched man,
Spending his daies in dolour and despaire,

And through long fasting woxen pale and
wan,
All overgrowen with rude and rugged haire;
That albeit his owne deare squire he were,
Yet he him knew not, ne aviz'd at all,
But like strange wight, whom he had
seene no where,
Saluting him, gan into speach to fall,
And pitty much his plight, that liv'd like
outcast thrall.

XLIV

But to his speach he aunswered no whit,
But stood still mute, as if he had beene
dum,
Ne signe of sence did shew, ne common
wit,
As one with griefe and anguishe overcum,
And unto every thing did aunswere mum:
And ever when the Prince unto him spake,
He louted lowly, as did him becum,
And humble homage did unto him make,
Midst sorrow shewing joyous semblance
for his sake.

XLV

At which his uncouth guise and usage
quaint
The Prince did wonder much, yet could
not ghesse
The cause of that his sorrowfull constraint;
Yet weend by secret signes of manlinesse,
Which close appeard in that rude brutish-
nesse,
That he whilome some gentle swaine had
beene,
Traind up in feats of armes and knightli-
nesse;
Which he observ'd, by that he him had
seene
To weld his naked sword, and try the
edges keene;

XLVI

And eke by that he saw on every tree
How he the name of one engraven had,
Which likly was his liefest love to be,
For whom he now so sorely was bestad;
Which was by him BELPHEBE rightly rad.
Yet who was that Belphebe he ne wist;
Yet saw he often how he wexed glad,
When he it heard, and how the ground he
kist,
Wherein it written was, and how himselfe
he blist.

XLVII

Tho, when he long had marked his de-
    meanor,
And saw that all he said and did was vaine,
Ne ought mote make him change his
    wonted tenor,
Ne ought mote ease or mitigate his paine,
He left him there in languor to remaine,
Till time for him should remedy provide,
And him restore to former grace againe.
Which for it is too long here to abide,
I will deferre the end untill another tide.

CANTO VIII

The gentle squire recovers grace :
  Sclaunder her guests doth staine :
Corflambo chaseth Placidas,
  And is by Arthure slaine.

I

WELL said the wiseman, now prov'd true
    by this,
Which to this gentle squire did happen late,
That the displeasure of the mighty is
Then death it selfe more dread and de-
    sperate.
For naught the same may calme ne miti-
    gate,
Till time the tempest doe thereof delay
With sufferaunce soft, which rigour can
    abate,
And have the sterne remembrance wypt
    away
Of bitter thoughts, which deepe therein in-
    fixed lay.

II

Like as it fell to this unhappy boy,
Whose tender heart the faire Belphebe had
With one sterne looke so daunted, that no
    joy
In all his life, which afterwards he lad,
He ever tasted; but with penaunce sad
And pensive sorrow pind and wore away,
Ne ever laught, ne once shew'd counten-
    ance glad;
But alwaies wept and wailed night and day,
As blasted bloosme through heat doth
    languish and decay.

III

Till on a day, as in his wonted wise
His doole he made, there chaunst a turtle
    dove
To come where he his dolors did devise,
That likewise late had lost her dearest love,
Which losse her made like passion also
    prove.
Who seeing his sad plight, her tender heart
With deare compassion deeply did emmove,
That she gan mone his undeserved smart,
And with her dolefull accent beare with
    him a part.

IV

Shee sitting by him, as on ground he lay,
Her mournefull notes full piteously did
    frame,
And thereof made a lamentable lay,
So sensibly compyld, that in the same
Him seemed oft he heard his owne right
    name.
With that he forth would poure so plente-
    ous teares,
And beat his breast unworthy of such blame,
And knocke his head, and rend his rugged
    heares,
That could have perst the hearts of tigres
    and of beares.

V

Thus, long this gentle bird to him did use
Withouten dread of perill to repaire
Unto his wonne, and with her mournefull
    muse
Him to recomfort in his greatest care,
That much did ease his mourning and mis-
    fare:
And every day, for guerdon of her song,
He part of his small feast to her would
    share;
That, at the last, of all his woe and wrong
Companion she became, and so continued
    long.

VI

Upon a day, as she him sate beside,
By chance he certaine miniments forth
    drew,
Which yet with him as relickes did abide
Of all the bounty which Belphebe threw
On him, whilst goodly grace she did him
    shew:
Amongst the rest a jewell rich he found,
That was a ruby of right perfect hew,
Shap'd like a heart yet bleeding of the
    wound,
And with a litle golden chaine about it
    bound.

VII

The same he tooke, and with a riband new,
In which his ladies colours were, did bind
About the turtles necke, that with the vew
Did greatly solace his engrieved mind.
All unawares the bird, when she did find
Her selfe so deckt, her nimble wings dis-
    plaid,
And flew away, as lightly as the wind:
Which sodaine accident him much dismaid,
And looking after long, did marke which
    way she straid.

VIII

But when as long he looked had in vaine,
Yet saw her forward still to make her flight,
His weary eie returnd to him againe,
Full of discomfort and disquiet plight,
That both his juell he had lost so light,
And eke his deare companion of his care.
But that sweet bird departing flew forth
    right
Through the wide region of the wastfull
    aire,
Untill she came where wonned his Belphebe
    faire.

IX

There found she her (as then it did betide)
Sitting in covert shade of arbors sweet,
After late weary toile, which she had tride
In salvage chase, to rest as seem'd her
    meet.
There she alighting, fell before her feet,
And gan to her her mournfull plaint to
    make,
As was her wont, thinking to let her weet
The great tormenting griefe that for her
    sake
Her gentle squire through her displeasure
    did pertake.

X

She her beholding with attentive eye,
At length did marke about her purple brest
That precious juell, which she formerly
Had knowne right well, with colourd rib-
    bands drest:
Therewith she rose in hast, and her addrest
With ready hand it to have reft away:
But the swift bird obayd not her behest,
But swarv'd aside, and there againe did
    stay;
She follow'd her, and thought againe it to
    assay.

XI

And ever when she nigh approcht, the dove
Would flit a litle forward, and then stay,
Till she drew neare, and then againe re-
    move;
So tempting her still to pursue the pray,
And still from her escaping soft away:
Till that at length into that forrest wide
She drew her far, and led with slow delay.
In th' end she her unto that place did guide,
Whereas that wofull man in languor did
    abide.

XII

Eftsoones she flew unto his fearelesse hand,
And there a piteous ditty new deviz'd,
As if she would have made her understand
His sorrowes cause, to be of her despis'd.
Whom when she saw in wretched weedes
    disguiz'd,
With heary glib deform'd, and meiger face,
Like ghost late risen from his grave
    agryz'd,
She knew him not, but pittied much his
    case,
And wisht it were in her to doe him any
    grace.

XIII

He her beholding, at her feet downe fell,
And kist the ground on which her sole did
    tread,
And washt the same with water, which did
    well
From his moist eies, and like two streames
    procead;
Yet spake no word whereby she might
    aread
What mister wight he was, or what he
    ment;
But as one daunted with her presence
    dread,
Onely few ruefull lookes unto her sent,
As messengers of his true meaning and in-
    tent.

XIV

Yet nathemore his meaning she ared,
But wondred much at his so selcouth case,
And by his persons secret seemlyhed
Well weend that he had beene some man
    of place,
Before misfortune did his hew deface:
That, being mov'd with ruth, she thus be-
    spake:

'Ah, wofull man! what Heavens hard disgrace,
Or wrath of cruell wight on thee ywrake,
Or selfe disliked life, doth thee thus
wretched make?

XV

'If Heaven, then none may it redresse or
blame,
Sith to his powre we all are subject borne;
If wrathfull wight, then fowle rebuke and
shame
Be theirs, that have so cruell thee forlorne;
But if through inward griefe or wilfull
scorne
Of life it be, then better doe advise;
For he whose daies in wilfull woe are
worne,
The grace of his Creator doth despise,
That will not use his gifts for thanklesse
nigardise.'

XVI

When so he heard her say, eftsoones he
brake
His sodaine silence, which he long had pent,
And sighing inly deepe, her thus bespake:
'Then have they all themselves against me
bent:
For Heaven, first author of my languish-
ment,
Envying my too great felicity,
Did closely with a cruell one consent
To cloud my daies in dolefull misery,
And make me loath this life, still longing
for to die.

XVII

'Ne any but your selfe, O dearest dred,
Hath done this wrong, to wreake on
worthlesse wight
Your high displesure, through misdeeming
bred:
That, when your pleasure is to deeme aright,
Ye may redresse, and me restore to light.'
Which sory words her mightie hart did
mate
With mild regard, to see his ruefull plight,
That her inburning wrath she gan abate,
And him receiv'd againe to former favours
state.

XVIII

In which he long time afterwards did lead
An happie life with grace and good accord,

Fearlesse of fortunes chaunge or envies
dread,
And eke all mindlesse of his owne deare
lord,
The noble Prince, who never heard one
word
Of tydings, what did unto him betide,
Or what good fortune did to him afford,
But through the endlesse world did wander
wide,
Him seeking evermore, yet no where him
describe.

XIX

Till on a day, as through that wood he
rode,
He chaunst to come where those two ladies
late,
Æmylia and Amoret, abode,
Both in full sad and sorrowfull estate;
The one right feeble through the evill rate
Of food, which in her duresse she had
found:
The other almost dead and desperate
Through her late hurts, and through that
haplesse wound
With which the squire in her defence her
sore astound.

XX

Whom when the Prince beheld, he gan to
rew
The evill case in which those ladies lay;
But most was moved at the piteous vew,
Of Amoret, so neare unto decay,
That her great daunger did him much
dismay.
Eftsoones that pretious liquour forth he
drew,
Which he in store about him kept alway,
And with few drops thereof did softly dew
Her wounds, that unto strength restor'd her
soone anew.

XXI

Tho, when they both recovered were right
well,
He gan of them inquire, what evill guide
Them thether brought, and how their
harmes befell.
To whom they told all that did them be-
tide,
And how from thraldome vile they were
untide
Of that same wicked carle, by virgins hond;

Whose bloudie corse they shew'd him there
    beside,
And eke his cave, in which they both were
    bond:
At which he wondred much, when all those
    signes he fond.

XXII

And evermore he greatly did desire
To know, what virgin did them thence
    unbind;
And oft of them did earnestly inquire,
Where was her won, and how he mote her
    find.
But when as nought according to his mind
He could outlearne, he them from ground
    did reare,
(No service lothsome to a gentle kind)
And on his warlike beast them both did beare,
Himselfe by them on foot, to succour them
    from feare.

XXIII

So when that forrest they had passed well,
A litle cotage farre away they spide,
To which they drew, ere night upon them
    fell;
And entring in, found none therein abide,
But one old woman sitting there beside,
Upon the ground, in ragged rude attyre,
With filthy lockes about her scattered wide,
Gnawing her nayles for felnesse and for yre,
And there out sucking venime to her parts
    entyre.

XXIV

A foule and loathly creature sure in sight,
And in conditions to be loath'd no lesse:
For she was stuft with rancour and despight
Up to the throat; that oft with bitternesse
It forth would breake, and gush in great
    excesse,
Pouring out streames of poyson and of gall
Gainst all that truth or vertue doe professe;
Whom she with leasings lewdly did miscall,
And wickedly backbite: her name men
    Sclaunder call.

XXV

Her nature is, all goodnesse to abuse,
And causelesse crimes continually to frame,
With which she guiltlesse persons may ac-
    cuse,
And steale away the crowne of their good
    name;

Ne ever knight so bold, ne ever dame
So chast and loyall liv'd, but she would
    strive
With forged cause them falsely to defame;
Ne ever thing so well was doen alive,
But she with blame would blot, and of due
    praise deprive.

XXVI

Her words were not, as common words are
    ment,
T' expresse the meaning of the inward
    mind,
But noysome breath, and poysnous spirit
    sent
From inward parts, with cancred malice
    lind,
And breathed forth with blast of bitter
    wind;
Which passing through the eares would
    pierce the hart,
And wound the soule it selfe with griefe
    unkind:
For like the stings of aspes, that kill with
    smart,
Her spightfull words did pricke and wound
    the inner part.

XXVII

Such was that hag, unmeet to host such
    guests,
Whom greatest princes court would wel-
    come fayne;
But neede, that answers not to all requests,
Bad them not looke for better entertayne;
And eke that age despysed nicenesse vaine,
Enur'd to hardnesse and to homely fare,
Which them to warlike discipline did
    trayne,
And manly limbs endur'd with litle care
Against all hard mishaps and fortunelesse
    misfare.

XXVIII

Then all that evening, welcommed with
    cold
And chearelesse hunger, they together
    spent;
Yet found no fault, but that the hag did
    scold
And rayle at them with grudgefull discon-
    tent,
For lodging there without her owne con-
    sent:
Yet they endured all with patience milde,

And unto rest themselves all onely lent;
Regardlesse, of that queane so base and
   vilde
To be unjustly blamd, and bitterly revilde.

XXIX

Here well I weene, when as these rimes be
   red
With misregard, that some rash witted
   wight,
Whose looser thought will lightly be mis-
   led,
These gentle ladies will misdeeme too light,
For thus conversing with this noble knight;
Sith now of dayes such temperance is rare
And hard to finde, that heat of youthfull
   spright
For ought will from his greedie pleasure
   spare:
More hard for hungry steed t' abstaine
   from pleasant lare.

XXX

But antique age, yet in the infancie
Of time, did live then like an innocent,
In simple truth and blamelesse chastitie,
Ne then of guile had made experiment,
But voide of vile and treacherous intent,
Held vertue for it selfe in soveraine awe:
Then loyall love had royall regiment,
And each unto his lust did make a lawe,
From all forbidden things his liking to with-
   draw.

XXXI

The lyon there did with the lambe consort,
And eke the dove sate by the faulcons side,
Ne each of other feared fraud or tort,
But did in safe securitie abide,
Withouten perill of the stronger pride:
But when the world woxe old, it woxe
   warre old
(Whereof it hight) and having shortly tride
The traines of wit, in wickednesse woxe
   bold,
And dared of all sinnes the secrets to un-
   fold.

XXXII

Then beautie, which was made to repre-
   sent
The great Creatours owne resemblance
   bright,
Unto abuse of lawlesse lust was lent,
And made the baite of bestiall delight:

Then faire grew foule, and foule grew faire
   in sight,
And that which wont to vanquish God and
   man
Was made the vassall of the victors might;
Then did her glorious flowre wex dead and
   wan,
Despisd and troden downe of all that overran.

XXXIII

And now it is so utterly decayd,
That any bud thereof doth scarse remaine,
But if few plants, preserv'd through heav-
   enly ayd,
In princes court doe hap to sprout againe,
Dew'd with her drops of bountie soveraine,
Which from that goodly glorious flowre
   proceed,
Sprung of the auncient stocke of princes
   straine,
Now th' onely remnant of that royall breed,
Whose noble kind at first was sure of heav-
   enly seed.

XXXIV

Tho, soone as day discovered heavens face
To sinfull men with darknes overdight,
This gentle crew gan from their eye-lids
   chace
The drowzie humour of the dampish night,
And did themselves unto their journey dight.
So forth they yode, and forward softly
   paced,
That them to view had bene an uncouth
   sight,
How all the way the Prince on footpace
   traced,
The ladies both on horse, together fast em-
   braced.

XXXV

Soone as they thence departed were afore,
That shamefull hag, the slaunder of her sexe,
Them follow'd fast, and them reviled sore,
Him calling theefe, them whores; that much
   did vexe
His noble hart: thereto she did annexe
False crimes and facts, such as they never
   ment,
That those two ladies much asham'd did
   wexe:
The more did she pursue her lewd intent,
And rayl'd and rag'd, till she had all her
   poyson spent.

XXXVI

At last, when they were passed out of sight,
Yet she did not her spightfull speach for-
  beare,
But after them did barke, and still back-
  bite,
Though there were none her hatefull words
  to heare:
Like as a curre doth felly bite and teare
The stone which passed straunger at him
  threw;
So she them seeing past the reach of eare,
Against the stones and trees did rayle
  anew,
Till she had duld the sting which in her
  tongs end grew.

XXXVII

They, passing forth, kept on their readie
  way,
With easie steps so soft as foot could stryde,
Both for great feeblesse, which did oft as-
  say
Faire Amoret, that scarcely she could ryde,
And eke through heavie armes, which sore
  annoyd
The Prince on foot, not wonted so to fare;
Whose steadie hand was faine his steede to
  guyde,
And all the way from trotting hard to
  spare;
So was his toyle the more, the more that
  was his care.

XXXVIII

At length they spide where towards them
  with speed
A squire came gallopping, as he would flie,
Bearing a litle dwarfe before his steed,
That all the way full loud for aide did crie,
That seem'd his shrikes would rend the
  brasen skie:
Whom after did a mightie man pursew,
Ryding upon a dromedare on hie,
Of stature huge, and horrible of hew,
That would have maz'd a man his dreadfull
  face to vew.

XXXIX

For from his fearefull eyes two fierie
  beames,
More sharpe then points of needles, did
  proceede,
Shooting forth farre away two flaming
  streames,

Full of sad powre, that poysonous bale did
  breede
To all that on him lookt without good
  heed,
And secretly his enemies did slay:
Like as the basiliske, of serpents seede,
From powrefull eyes close venim doth con-
  vay
Into the lookers hart, and killeth farre away.

XL

He all the way did rage at that same squire,
And after him full many threatnings threw,
With curses vaine in his avengefull ire:
But none of them (so fast away he flew)
Him overtooke before he came in vew.
Where when he saw the Prince in armour
  bright,
He cald to him aloud, his case to rew,
And rescue him through succour of his
  might,
From that his cruell foe, that him pursewd
  in sight.

XLI

Eftsoones the Prince tooke downe those
  ladies twaine
From loftie steede, and mounting in their
  stead,
Came to that squire, yet trembling every
  vaine:
Of whom he gan enquire his cause of dread:
Who as he gan the same to him aread,
Loe! hard behind his backe his foe was
  prest,
With dreadfull weapon aymed at his head,
That unto death had doen him unredrest,
Had not the noble Prince his readie stroke
  represt.

XLII

Who, thrusting boldly twixt him and the
  blow,
The burden of the deadly brunt did beare
Upon his shield, which lightly he did throw
Over his head, before the harme came
  neare.
Nathlesse it fell with so despiteous dreare
And heavie sway, that hard unto his crowne
The shield it drove, and did the covering
  reare:
Therewith both squire and dwarfe did
  tomble downe
Unto the earth, and lay long while in
  senselesse swowne.

XLIII

Whereat the Prince full wrath, his strong
        right hand
In full avengement heaved up on hie,
And stroke the Pagan with his steely brand
So sore, that to his saddle bow thereby
He bowed low, and so a while did lie:
And sure, had not his massie yron mace
Betwixt him and his hurt bene happily,
It would have cleft him to the girding place;
Yet, as it was, it did astonish him long
        space.

XLIV

But when he to himselfe returnd againe,
All full of rage he gan to curse and sweare,
And vow by Mahoune that he should be
        slaine.
With that his murdrous mace he up did
        reare,
That seemed nought the souse thereof
        could beare,
And therewith smote at him with all his
        might.
But ere that it to him approched neare,
The royall child, with readie quicke fore-
        sight,
Did shun the proofe thereof and it avoyded
        light.

XLV

But ere his hand he could recure againe,
To ward his bodie from the balefull stound,
He smote at him with all his might and
        maine,
So furiously, that, ere he wist, he found
His head before him tombling on the
        ground.
The whiles his babling tongue did yet blas-
        pheme
And curse his god, that did him so con-
        found;
The whiles his life ran foorth in bloudie
        streame,
His soule descended downe into the Stygian
        reame.

XLVI

Which when that squire beheld, he woxe
        full glad
To see his foe breath out his spright in
        vaine:
But that same dwarfe right sorie seem'd
        and sad,
And howld aloud to see his lord there slaine,

And rent his haire and scratcht his face
        for paine.
Then gan the Prince at leasure to inquire
Of all the accident, there hapned plaine,
And what he was, whose eyes did flame with
        fire;
All which was, thus to him declared by that
        squire.

XLVII

' This mightie man,' quoth he, ' whom you
        have slaine,
Of an huge geauntesse whylome was bred;
And by his strength rule to himselfe did
        gaine
Of many nations into thraldome led,
And mightie kingdomes of his force adred;
Whom yet he conquer'd not by bloudie
        fight,
Ne hostes of men with banners brode di-
        spred,
But by the powre of his infectious sight,
With which he killed all that came within
        his might.

XLVIII

' Ne was he ever vanquished afore,
But ever vanquisht all with whom he
        fought;
Ne was there man so strong, but he downe
        bore,
Ne woman yet so faire, but he her brought
Unto his bay, and captived her thought.
For most of strength and beautie his de-
        sire
Was spoyle to make, and wast them unto
        nought,
By casting secret flakes of lustfull fire
From his false eyes, into their harts and
        parts entire.

XLIX

' Therefore Corflambo was he cald aright,
Though namelesse there his bodie now doth
        lie;
Yet hath he left one daughter that is
        hight
The faire Pœana; who seemes outwardly
So faire as ever yet saw living eie:
And were her vertue like her beautie
        bright,
She were as faire as any under skie.
But ah ! she given is to vaine delight,
And eke too loose of life, and eke of love
        too light.

L

'So as it fell, there was a gentle squire,
That lov'd a ladie of high parentage;
But for his meane degree might not aspire
To match so high, her friends with counsell
    sage
Dissuaded her from such a disparage.
But she, whose hart to love was wholly
    lent,
Out of his hands could not redeeme her
    gage,
But firmely following her first intent,
Resolv'd with him to wend, gainst all her
    friends consent.

LI

'So twixt themselves they pointed time and
    place,
To which when he according did repaire,
An hard mishap and disaventrous case
Him chaunst; in stead of his Æmylia faire,
This gyants sonne, that lies there on the
    laire
An headlesse heape, him unawares there
    caught,
And, all dismayd through mercilesse de-
    spaire,
Him wretched thrall unto his dongeon
    brought,
Where he remaines, of all unsuccour'd and
    unsought.

LII

'This gyants daughter came upon a day
Unto the prison in her joyous glee,
To view the thrals which there in bondage
    lay:
Amongst the rest she chaunced there to see
This lovely swaine, the squire of low de-
    gree;
To whom she did her liking lightly cast,
And wooed him her paramour to bee:
From day to day she woo'd and prayd him
    fast,
And for his love him promist libertie at last.

LIII

'He, though affide unto a former love,
To whom his faith he firmely ment to hold,
Yet seeing not how thence he mote remove,
But by that meanes which fortune did un-
    fold,
Her graunted love, but with affection cold,
To win her grace his libertie to get.
Yet she him still detaines in captive hold,

Fearing least, if she should him freely set,
He would her shortly leave, and former
    love forget.

LIV

'Yet so much favour she to him hath hight
Above the rest, that he sometimes may
    space
And walke about her gardens of delight,
Having a keeper still with him in place;
Which keeper is this dwarfe, her dearling
    base,
To whom the keyes of every prison dore
By her committed be, of speciall grace,
And at his will may whom he list restore,
And whom he list reserve, to be afflicted
    more.

LV

'Whereof when tydings came unto mine
    eare,
Full inly sorie, for the fervent zeale
Which I to him as to my soule did beare,
I thether went; where I did long conceale
My selfe, till that the dwarfe did me re-
    veale,
And told his dame her squire of low de-
    gree
Did secretly out of her prison steale;
For me he did mistake that squire to bee;
For never two so like did living creature
    see.

LVI

'Then was I taken and before her brought:
Who, through the likenesse of my outward
    hew,
Being likewise beguiled in her thought,
Gan blame me much for being so untrew,
To seeke by flight her fellowship t' eschew,
That lov'd me deare, as dearest thing alive.
Thence she commaunded me to prison new;
Whereof I glad did not gainesay nor strive,
But suffred that same dwarfe me to her
    dongeon drive.

LVII

'There did I finde mine onely faithfull
    frend
In heavy plight and sad perplexitie;
Whereof I sorie, yet my selfe did bend
Him to recomfort with my companie.
But him the more agreev'd I found thereby.
For all his joy, he said, in that distresse,
Was mine and his Æmylias libertie.

Æmylia well he lov'd, as I mote ghesse;
Yet greater love to me then her he did
professe.

LVIII

'But I with better reason him aviz'd,
And shew'd him how, through error and
mis-thought
Of our like persons, eath to be disguiz'd,
Or his exchange or freedome might be
wrought.
Whereto full loth was he, ne would for
ought
Consent that I, who stood all fearelesse
free,
Should wilfully be into thraldome brought,
Till Fortune did perforce it so decree.
Yet, overrul'd at last, he did to me agree.

LIX

'The morrow next, about the wonted
howre,
The dwarfe cald at the doore of Amyas,
To come forthwith unto his ladies bowre.
In steed of whom forth came I, Placidas,
And undiscerned forth with him did pas.
There with great joyance and with glad-
some glee
Of faire Pœana I received was,
And oft imbrast, as if that I were hee,
And with kind words accoyd, vowing great
love to mee.

LX

'Which I, that was not bent to former love,
As was my friend, that had her long refusd,
Did well accept, as well it did behove,
And to the present neede it wisely usd.
My former hardnesse first I faire excusd;
And after promist large amends to make.
With such smooth termes her error I
abusd,
To my friends good more then for mine
owne sake,
For whose sole libertie I love and life did
stake.

LXI

'Thenceforth I found more favour at her
hand,
That to her dwarfe, which had me in his
charge,
She bad to lighten my too heavie band,
And graunt more scope to me to walke at
large.

So on a day, as by the flowrie marge
Of a fresh streame I with that elfe did
play,
Finding no meanes how I might us enlarge,
But if that dwarfe I could with me con-
vay,
I lightly snatcht him up, and with me bore
away.

LXII

'Thereat he shriekt aloud, that with his
cry
The tyrant selfe came forth with yelling
bray,
And me pursew'd; but nathemore would I
Forgoe the purchase of my gotten pray,
But have perforce him hether brought
away.'
Thus as they talked, loe ! where nigh at
hand
Those ladies two, yet doubtfull through dis-
may,
In presence came, desirous t' understand
Tydings of all which there had hapned on
the land.

LXIII

Where soone as sad Æmylia did espie
Her captive lovers friend, young Placidas,
All mindlesse of her wonted modestie,
She to him ran, and him with streight em-
bras
Enfolding said: 'And lives yet Amyas ?'
'He lives,' quoth he, 'and his Æmylia
loves.'
'Then lesse,' said she, 'by all the woe I
pas,
With which my weaker patience Fortune
proves.
But what mishap thus long him fro my
selfe removes ?'

LXIV

Then gan he all this storie to renew,
And tell the course of his captivitie;
That her deare hart full deeply made to
rew,
And sigh full sore, to heare the miserie,
In which so long he mercilesse did lie.
Then, after many teares and sorrowes
spent,
She deare besought the Prince of remedie:
Who thereto did with readie will consent,
And well perform'd, as shall appeare by
his event.

CANTO IX

The squire of low degree, releast,
Pœana takes to wife:
Britomart fightes with many knights;
Prince Arthur stints their strife.

I

HARD is the doubt, and difficult to deeme,
When all three kinds of love together meet,
And doe dispart the hart with powre extreme,
Whether shall weigh the balance downe;
to weet,
The deare affection unto kindred sweet,
Or raging fire of love to woman kind,
Or zeale of friends combynd with vertues
meet.
But of them all, the band of vertuous mind,
Me seemes, the gentle hart should most
assured bind.

II

For naturall affection soone doth cesse,
And quenched is with Cupids greater flame:
But faithfull friendship doth them both
suppresse,
And them with maystring discipline doth
tame,
Through thoughts aspyring to eternall fame.
For as the soule doth rule the earthly masse,
And all the service of the bodie frame,
So love of soule doth love of bodie passe,
No lesse then perfect gold surmounts the
meanest brasse.

III

All which who list by tryall to assay,
Shall in this storie find approved plaine;
In which these squires true friendship more
did sway,
Then either care of parents could refraine,
Or love of fairest ladie could constraine.
For though Pœana were as faire as morne,
Yet did this trustie squire with proud disdaine
For his friends sake her offred favours
scorne,
And she her selfe her syre, of whom she
was yborne.

IV

Now after that Prince Arthur graunted
had
To yeeld strong succour to that gentle
swayne,

Who now long time had lyen in prison
sad,
He gan advise how best he mote darrayne
That enterprize, for greatest glories gayne.
That headlesse tyrants tronke he reard
from ground,
And having ympt the head to it agayne,
Upon his usuall beast it firmely bound,
And made it so to ride as it alive was found.

V

Then did he take that chaced squire, and
layd
Before the ryder, as he captive were,
And made his dwarfe, though with unwilling ayd,
To guide the beast that did his maister
beare,
Till to his castle they approched neare.
Whom when the watch, that kept continuall
ward,
Saw comming home, all voide of doubtfull
feare,
He, running downe, the gate to him unbard;
Whom straight the Prince ensuing, in together far'd.

VI

There he did find in her delitious boure
The faire Pœana playing on a rote,
Complayning of her cruell paramoure,
And singing all her sorrow to the note,
As she had learned readily by rote:
That with the sweetnesse of her rare delight
The Prince halfe rapt, began on her to dote:
Till, better him bethinking of the right,
He her unwares attacht, and captive held
by might.

VII

Whence being forth produc'd, when she
perceived
Her owne deare sire, she cald to him for
aide.
But when of him no aunswere she received,
But saw him sencelesse by the squire upstaide,
She weened well that then she was betraide:
Then gan she loudly cry, and weepe, and
waile,
And that same squire of treason to upbraide:

But all in vaine; her plaints might not prevaile;
Ne none there was to reskue her, ne none
to baile.

VIII

Then tooke he that same dwarfe, and him
compeld
To open unto him the prison dore,
And forth to bring those thrals which there
he held.
Thence forth were brought to him above a
score
Of knights and squires to him unknowne
afore:
All which he did from bitter bondage free,
And unto former liberty restore.
Amongst the rest, that squire of low degree
Came forth full weake and wan, not like
him selfe to bee.

IX

Whom soone as faire Æmylia beheld,
And Placidas, they both unto him ran,
And him embracing fast betwixt them
held,
Striving to comfort him all that they can,
And kissing oft his visage pale and wan;
That faire Pæana, them beholding both,
Gan both envy, and bitterly to ban;
Through jealous passion weeping inly wroth,
To see the sight perforce, that both her
eyes were loth.

X

But when a while they had together beene,
And diversly conferred of their case,
She, though full oft she both of them had
seene
A sunder, yet not ever in one place,
Began to doubt, when she them saw em-
brace,
Which was the captive squire she lov'd so
deare,
Deceived through great likenesse of their
face,
For they so like in person did appeare,
That she uneath discerned, whether whether
weare.

XI

And eke the Prince, when as he them
avized,
Their like resemblaunce much admired
there,

And mazd how Nature had so well dis-
guized
Her worke, and counterfet her selfe so
nere,
As if that by one patterne seene somewhere
She had them made a paragone to be,
Or whether it through skill or errour were.
Thus gazing long, at them much wondred
he;
So did the other knights and squires, which
them did see.

XII

Then gan they ransacke that same castle
strong,
In which he found great store of hoorded
threasure,
The which that tyrant gathered had by
wrong
And tortious powre, without respect or
measure,
Upon all which the Briton Prince made
seasure,
And afterwards continu'd there a while,
To rest him selfe, and solace in soft pleas-
ure
Those weaker ladies after weary toile;
To whom he did divide part of his pur-
chast spoile.

XIII

And for more joy, that captive lady faire,
The faire Pæana, he enlarged free,
And by the rest did set in sumptuous chaire,
To feast and frollicke; nathemore would
she
Shew gladsome countenaunce nor pleasaunt
glee,
But grieved was for losse both of her sire,
And eke of lordship, with both land and
fee:
But most she touched was with griefe en-
tire
For losse of her new love, the hope of her
desire.

XIV

But her the Prince, through his well wonted
grace,
To better termes of myldnesse did entreat
From that fowle rudenesse which did her
deface;
And that same bitter corsive, which did eat
Her tender heart, and made refraine from
meat,

He with good thewes and speaches well applyde
Did mollifie, and calme her raging heat.
For though she were most faire, and goodly
dyde,
Yet she it all did mar with cruelty and
pride.

XV

And for to shut up all in friendly love,
Sith love was first the ground of all her
griefe,
That trusty squire he wisely well did move
Not to despise that dame, which lov'd him
liefe,
Till he had made of her some better priefe,
But to accept her to his wedded wife.
Thereto he offred for to make him chiefe
Of all her land and lordship during life:
He yeelded, and her tooke; so stinted all
their strife.

XVI

From that day forth in peace and joyous
blis
They liv'd together long without debate,
Ne private jarre, ne spite of enemis
Could shake the safe assuraunce of their
state.
And she, whom Nature did so faire create
That she mote match the fairest of her
daies,
Yet with lewd loves and lust intemperate
Had it defaste, thenceforth reformd her
waies,
That all men much admyrde her change,
and spake her praise.

XVII

Thus when the Prince had perfectly com-
pylde
These paires of friends in peace and setled
rest,
Him selfe, whose minde did travell as with
chylde
Of his old love, conceav'd in secret brest,
Resolved to pursue his former quest;
And taking leave of all, with him did beare
Faire Amoret, whom Fortune by bequest
Had left in his protection whileare,
Exchanged out of one into an other feare.

XVIII

Feare of her safety did her not constraine,
For well she wist now in a mighty hond

Her person, late in perill, did remaine,
Who able was all daungers to withstond:
But now in feare of shame she more did
stond,
Seeing her selfe all soly succourlesse,
Left in the victors powre, like vassall bond;
Whose will her weakenesse could no way
represse,
In case his burning lust should breake into
excesse.

XIX

But cause of feare sure had she none at
all
Of him, who goodly learned had of yore
The course of loose affection to forstall,
And lawlesse lust to rule with reasons lore;
That all the while he by his side her bore,
She was as safe as in a sanctuary.
Thus many miles they two together wore,
To seeke their loves dispersed diversly,
Yet neither shewed to other their hearts
privity.

XX

At length they came, whereas a troupe of
knights
They saw together skirmishing, as seemed:
Sixe they were all, all full of fell despight,
But foure of them the battell best be-
seemed,
That which of them was best mote not be
deemed.
Those foure were they from whom false
Florimell
By Braggadochio lately was redeemed;
To weet, sterne Druon, and lewd Clari-
bell,
Love-lavish Blandamour, and lustfull Pari-
dell.

XXI

Druons delight was all in single life,
And unto ladies love would lend no leasure:
The more was Claribell enraged rife
With fervent flames, and loved out of
measure:
So eke lov'd Blandamour, but yet at
pleasure
Would change his liking, and new lemans
prove:
But Paridell of love did make no threasure,
But lusted after all that him did move.
So diversly these foure disposed were to
love.

XXII

But those two other, which beside them
    stoode,
Were Britomart and gentle Scudamour;
Who all the while beheld their wrathfull
    moode,
And wondred at their impacable stoure,
Whose like they never saw till that same
    houre:
So dreadfull strokes each did at other drive,
And laid on load with all their might and
    powre,
As if that every dint the ghost would rive
Out of their wretched corses, and their
    lives deprive.

XXIII

As when Dan Æolus, in great displeasure,
For losse of his deare love by Neptune
    hent,
Sends forth the winds out of his hidden
    threasure,
Upon the sea to wreake his fell intent;
They, breaking forth with rude unruliment
From all foure parts of heaven, doe rage
    full sore,
And tosse the deepes, and teare the firma-
    ment,
And all the world confound with wide up-
    rore,
As if in stead thereof they Chaos would re-
    store.

XXIV

Cause of their discord and so fell debate
Was for the love of that same snowy
    maid,
Whome they had lost in turneyment of
    late,
And seeking long, to weet which way she
    straid,
Met here together, where, through lewd
    upbraide
Of Ate and Duessa, they fell out,
And each one taking part in others aide,
This cruell conflict raised thereabout,
Whose dangerous successe depended yet in
    dout.

XXV

For sometimes Paridell and Blandamour
The better had, and bet the others backe;
Eftsoones the others did the field recoure,
And on their foes did worke full cruell
    wracke:

Yet neither would their fiendlike fury
    slacke,
But evermore their malice did augment;
Till that uneath they forced were, for lacke
Of breath, their raging rigour to relent,
And rest themselves for to recover spirits
    spent.

XXVI

Then gan they change their sides, and new
    parts take;
For Paridell did take to Druons side,
For old despight, which now forth newly
    brake
Gainst Blandamour, whom alwaies he en-
    vide;
And Blandamour to Claribell relide:
So all afresh gan former fight renew.
As when two barkes, this caried with the
    tide,
That with the wind, contrary courses sew,
If wind and tide doe change, their courses
    change anew.

XXVII

Thenceforth they much more furiously gan
    fare,
As if but then the battell had begonne,
Ne helmets bright ne hawberks strong did
    spare,
That through the clifts the vermeil bloud
    out sponne,
And all adowne their riven sides did ronne.
Such mortall malice wonder was to see
In friends profest, and so great outrage
    donne:
But sooth is said, and tride in each degree,
Faint friends when they fall out most cruell
    fomen bee.

XXVIII

Thus they long while continued in fight,
Till Scudamour and that same Briton maide
By fortune in that place did chance to
    light:
Whom soone as they with wrathfull eie
    bewraide,
They gan remember of the fowle upbraide,
The which that Britonesse had to them
    donne,
In that late turney for the snowy maide;
Where she had them both shamefully for-
    donne,
And eke the famous prize of beauty from
    them wonne.

XXIX

Eftsoones all burning with a fresh desire
Of fell revenge, in their malicious mood
They from them selves gan turne their furious ire,
And cruell blades, yet steeming with whot bloud,
Against those two let drive, as they were wood:
Who wondring much at that so sodaine fit,
Yet nought dismayd, them stoutly well withstood;
Ne yeelded foote, ne once abacke did flit,
But being doubly smitten, likewise doubly smit.

XXX

The warlike dame was on her part assaid
Of Claribell and Blandamour attone;
And Paridell and Druon fiercely laid
At Scudamour, both his professed fone.
Foure charged two, and two surcharged one;
Yet did those two them selves so bravely beare,
That the other litle gained by the lone,
But with their owne repayed duely weare,
And usury withall: such gaine was gotten deare.

XXXI

Full oftentimes did Britomart assay
To speake to them, and some emparlance move;
But they for nought their cruell hands would stay,
Ne lend an eare to ought that might behove:
As when an eager mastiffe once doth prove
The tast of bloud of some engored beast,
No words may rate, nor rigour him remove
From greedy hold of that his blouddy feast:
So litle did they hearken to her sweet beheast.

XXXII

Whom when the Briton Prince a farre beheld
With ods of so unequall match opprest,
His mighty heart with indignation sweld,
And inward grudge fild his heroicke brest:
Eftsoones him selfe he to their aide addrest,
And thrusting fierce into the thickest preace,
Divided them, how ever loth to rest,
And would them faine from battell to surceasse,
With gentle words perswading them to friendly peace.

XXXIII

But they so farre from peace or patience were,
That all at once at him gan fiercely flie,
And lay on load, as they him downe would beare:
Like to a storme, which hovers under skie,
Long here and there and round about doth stie,
At length breakes downe in raine, and haile, and sleet,
First from one coast, till nought thereof be drie;
And then another, till that likewise fleet;
And so from side to side till all the world it weet.

XXXIV

But now their forces greatly were decayd,
The Prince yet being fresh untoucht afore;
Who them with speaches milde gan first disswade
From such foule outrage, and them long forbore:
Till, seeing them through suffrance hartned more,
Him selfe he bent their furies to abate,
And layd at them so sharpely and so sore,
That shortly them compelled to retrate,
And being brought in daunger, to relent too late

XXXV

But now his courage being throughly fired,
He ment to make them know their follies prise,
Had not those two him instantly desired
T' asswage his wrath, and pardon their mesprise.
At whose request he gan him selfe advise
To stay his hand, and of a truce to treat
In milder tearmes, as list them to devise:
Mongst which, the cause of their so cruell heat
He did them aske: who all that passed gan repeat;

XXXVI

And told at large how that same errant
    knight,
To weet, faire Britomart, them late had
    foyled
In open turney, and by wrongfull fight
Both of their publicke praise had them de-
    spoyled,
And also of their private loves beguyled;
Of two full hard to read the harder theft.
But she that wrongfull challenge soone as-
    soyled,
And shew'd that she had not that lady reft,
(As they supposd) but her had to her lik-
    ing left.

XXXVII

To whom the Prince thus goodly well re-
    plied:
'Certes, sir knights, ye seemen much to
    blame,
To rip up wrong that battell once hath
    tried;
Wherein the honor both of armes ye shame,
And eke the love of ladies foule defame;
To whom the world this franchise ever
    yeelded,
That of their loves choise they might free-
    dom clame,
And in that right should by all knights be
    shielded:
Gainst which, me seemes, this war ye
    wrongfully have wielded.'

XXXVIII

'And yet,' quoth she, 'a greater wrong re-
    maines:
For I thereby my former love have lost,
Whom seeking ever since, with endlesse
    paines,
Hath me much sorrow and much travell
    cost:
Aye me, to see that gentle maide so tost!'
But Scudamour, then sighing deepe, thus
    saide:
'Certes her losse ought me to sorrow most,
Whose right she is, where ever she be
    straide,
Through many perils wonne, and many for-
    tunes waide.

XXXIX

'For from the first that I her love profest,
Unto this houre, this present lucklesse
    howre,

I never joyed happinesse nor rest,
But thus turmoild from one to other
    stowre,
I wast my life, and doe my daies devowre
In wretched anguishe and incessant woe,
Passing the measure of my feeble powre,
That, living thus a wretch and loving so,
I neither can my love, ne yet my life forgo.'

XL

Then good Sir Claribell him thus bespake:
'Now were it not, Sir Scudamour, to you
Dislikefull paine, so sad a taske to take,
Mote we entreat you, sith this gentle crew
Is now so well accorded all anew,
That, as we ride together on our way,
Ye will recount to us in order dew
All that adventure, which ye did assay
For that faire ladies love: past perils well
    apay.'

XLI

So gan the rest him likewise to require,
But Britomart did him importune hard
To take on him that paine: whose great
    desire
He glad to satisfie, him selfe prepar'd
To tell through what misfortune he had
    far'd
In that atchievement, as to him befell;
And all those daungers unto them de-
    clar'd,
Which sith they cannot in this canto well
Comprised be, I will them in another tell.

CANTO X

Scudamour doth his conquest tell
    Of vertuous Amoret:
Great Venus temple is describ'd,
    And lovers life forth set.

I

'True he it said, what ever man it sayd,
That love with gall and hony doth abound,
But if the one be with the other wayd,
For every dram of hony therein found,
A pound of gall doth over it redound.
That I too true by triall have approved:
For since the day that first with deadly
    wound
My heart was launcht, and learned to have
    loved,
I never joyed howre, but still with care
    was moved.

II

'And yet such grace is given them from
  above,
That all the cares and evill which they
  meet
May nought at all their setled mindes re-
  move,
But seeme, gainst common sence, to them
  most sweet;
As bosting in their martyrdome unmeet.
So all that ever yet I have endured
I count as naught, and tread downe under
  feet,
Since of my love at length I rest assured,
That to disloyalty she will not be allured.

III

'Long were to tell the travell and long
  toile,
Through which this Shield of Love I late
  have wonne,
And purchased this peerelesse beauties
  spoile,
That harder may be ended, then begonne:
But since ye so desire, your will be donne.
Then hearke, ye gentle knights and ladies
  free,
My hard mishaps, that ye may learne to
  shonne;
For though sweet love to conquer glorious
  bee,
Yet is the paine thereof much greater then
  the fee.

IV

'What time the fame of this renowmed
  prise
Flew first abroad, and all mens eares pos-
  sest,
I, having armes then taken, gan avise
To winne me honour by some noble gest,
And purchase me some place amongst the
  best.
I boldly thought (so young mens thoughts
  are bold)
That this same brave emprize for me did
  rest,
And that both shield and she whom I be-
  hold
Might be my lucky lot; sith all by lot we
  hold.

V

'So on that hard adventure forth I went,
And to the place of perill shortly came.

That was a temple faire and auncient,
Which of great mother Venus bare the
  name,
And farre renowmed through exceeding
  fame;
Much more then that which was in Paphos
  built,
Or that in Cyprus, both long since this
  same,
Though all the pillours of the one were
  guilt,
And all the others pavement were with
  yvory spilt.

VI

'And it was seated in an island strong,
Abounding all with delices most rare,
And wall'd by nature gainst invaders
  wrong,
That none mote have accesse, nor inward
  fare,
But by one way, that passage did prepare.
It was a bridge ybuilt in goodly wize,
With curious corbes and pendants graven
  faire,
And, arched all with porches, did arize
On stately pillours, fram'd after the
  Doricke guize.

VII

'And for defence thereof, on th' other end
There reared was a castle faire and strong,
That warded all which in or out did wend,
And flancked both the bridges sides along,
Gainst all that would it faine to force or
  wrong.
And therein wonned twenty valiant
  knights;
All twenty tride in warres experience long;
Whose office was, against all manner
  wights
By all meanes to maintaine that castels
  ancient rights.

VIII

'Before that castle was an open plaine,
And in the midst thereof a piller placed;
On which this shield, of many sought in
  vaine,
The Shield of Love, whose guerdon me hath
  graced,
Was hangd on high with golden ribbands
  laced;
And in the marble stone was written this,
With golden letters goodly well enchaced:

Blessed the man that well can use his blis:
Whose ever be the shield, faire Amoret be his.

IX

'Which when I red, my heart did inly
    earne,
And pant with hope of that adventures hap:
Ne stayed further newes thereof to learne,
But with my speare upon the shield did rap,
That all the castle ringed with the clap.
Streight forth issewd a knight all arm'd to
    proofe,
And bravely mounted to his most mishap:
Who, staying nought to question from
    aloofe,
Ran fierce at me, that fire glaunst from his
    horses hoofe.

X

'Whom boldly I encountred as I could,
And by good fortune shortly him unseated.
Eftsoones out sprung two more of equall
    mould;
But I them both with equall hap defeated:
So all the twenty I likewise entreated,
And left them groning there upon the
    plaine.
Then, preacing to the pillour, I repeated
The read thereof for guerdon of my paine,
And taking downe the shield, with me did it
    retaine.

XI

'So forth without impediment I past,
Till to the bridges utter gate I came:
The which I found sure lockt and chained
    fast.
I knockt, but no man aunswred me by
    name;
I cald, but no man answerd to my clame.
Yet I persever'd still to knocke and call,
Till at the last I spide within the same
Where one stood peeping through a crevis
    small,
To whom I cald aloud, halfe angry
    therewithall.

XII

'That was to weet the porter of the place,
Unto whose trust the charge thereof was
    lent:
His name was Doubt, that had a double
    face,
Th' one forward looking, th' other backe-
    ward bent,

Therein resembling Janus auncient,
Which hath in charge the ingate of the
    yeare:
And evermore his eyes about him went,
As if some proved perill he did feare,
Or did misdoubt some ill, whose cause did
    not appeare.

XIII

'On th' one side he, on th' other sate Delay,
Behinde the gate, that none her might
    espy;
Whose manner was, all passengers to stay
And entertaine with her occasions sly;
Through which some lost great hope un-
    heedily,
Which never they recover might againe;
And others, quite excluded forth, did ly
Long languishing there in unpittied paine,
And seeking often entraunce afterwards in
    vaine.

XIV

'Me when as he had privily espide
Bearing the shield which I had conquerd
    late,
He kend it streight, and to me opened wide.
So in I past, and streight he closd the gate.
But being in, Delay in close awaite
Caught hold on me, and thought my steps
    to stay,
Feigning full many a fond excuse to prate,
And time to steale, the threasure of mans
    day,
Whose smallest minute lost no riches
    render may.

XV

'But by no meanes my way I would
    forslow,
For ought that ever she could doe or say,
But from my lofty steede dismounting low,
Past forth on foote, beholding all the way
The goodly workes, and stones of rich
    assay,
Cast into sundry shapes by wondrous skill,
That like on earth no where I recken may:
And underneath, the river rolling still
With murmure soft, that seem'd to serve
    the workmans will.

XVI

'Thence forth I passed to the second gate,
The Gate of Good Desert, whose goodly
    pride

And costly frame were long here to relate.
The same to all stoode alwaies open wide:
But in the porch did evermore abide
An hideous giant, dreadfull to behold,
That stopt the entraunce with his spacious
stride,
And with the terrour of his countenance
bold
Full many did affray, that else faine enter
would.

XVII

' His name was Daunger, dreaded over all,
Who day and night did watch and duely
ward,
From fearefull cowards entrance to for-
stall,
And faint-heart-fooles, whom shew of perill
hard
Could terrifie from Fortunes faire adward:
For oftentimes faint hearts, at first espiall
Of his grim face, were from approaching
scard:
Unworthy they of grace, whom one deniall
Excludes from fairest hope, withouten fur-
ther triall.

XVIII

' Yet many doughty warriours, often tride
In greater perils to be stout and bold,
Durst not the sternnesse of his looke abide,
But soone as they his countenance did be-
hold,
Began to faint, and feele their corage cold.
Againe, some other, that in hard assaies
Were cowards knowne, and litle count did
hold,
Either through gifts, or guile, or such like
waies,
Crept in by stouping low, or stealing of the
kaies.

XIX

' But I, though meanest man of many moe,
Yet much disdaining unto him to lout,
Or creepe betweene his legs, so in to goe,
Resolv'd him to assault with manhood stout,
And either beat him in or drive him out.
Eftsoones, advauncing that enchaunted
shield,
With all my might I gan to lay about:
Which when he saw, the glaive which he
did wield
He gan forthwith t' avale, and way unto
me yield.

XX

' So as I entred, I did backeward looke,
For feare of harme, that might lie hidden
there;
And loe! his hindparts, whereof heed I
tooke,
Much more deformed fearefull ugly were,
Then all his former parts did earst appere:
For Hatred, Murther, Treason, and De-
spight,
With many moe, lay in ambushment there,
Awayting to entrap the warelesse wight,
Which did not them prevent with vigilant
foresight.

XXI

' Thus having past all perill, I was come
Within the compasse of that islands space;
The which did seeme, unto my simple
doome,
The onely pleasant and delightfull place
That ever troden was of footings trace.
For all that Nature by her mother wit
Could frame in earth, and forme of sub-
stance base,
Was there, and all that Nature did omit,
Art, playing second Natures part, supplyed
it.

XXII

' No tree, that is of count, in greenewood
growes,
From lowest juniper to ceder tall,
No flowre in field, that daintie odour
throwes,
And deckes his branch with blossomes over
all,
But there was planted, or grew naturall:
Nor sense of man so coy and curious nice,
But there mote find to please it selfe with-
all;
Nor hart could wish for any queint device,
But there it present was, and did fraile
sense entice.

XXIII

' In such luxurious plentie of all pleasure,
It seem'd a second paradise to ghesse,
So lavishly enricht with Natures threasure,
That if the happie soules, which doe pos-
sesse
Th' Elysian fields and live in lasting blesse,
Should happen this with living eye to see,
They soone would loath their lesser happi-
nesse,

And wish to life return'd againe to bee,
That in this joyous place they mote have
      joyance free.

XXIV

' Fresh shadowes, fit to shroud from sunny
      ray;
Faire lawnds, to take the sunne in season
      dew;
Sweet springs, in which a thousand nymphs
      did play;
Soft rombling brookes, that gentle slomber
      drew;
High reared mounts, the lands about to
      vew;
Low looking dales, disloignd from common
      gaze;
Delightfull bowres, to solace lovers trew;
False labyrinthes, fond runners eyes to daze;
All which by Nature made did Nature selfe
      amaze.

XXV

' And all without were walkes and alleyes
      dight
With divers trees, enrang'd in even rankes;
And here and there were pleasant arbors
      pight,
And shadie seates, and sundry flowring
      bankes,
To sit and rest the walkers wearie shankes;
And therein thousand payres of lovers walkt,
Praysing their god, and yeelding him great
      thankes,
Ne ever ought but of their true loves talkt,
Ne ever for rebuke or blame of any balkt.

XXVI

' All these together by themselves did sport
Their spotlesse pleasures, and sweet loves
      content.
But farre away from these, another sort
Of lovers lincked in true harts consent;
Which loved not as these, for like intent,
But on chast vertue grounded their desire,
Farre from all fraud, or fayned blandish-
      ment;
Which, in their spirits kindling zealous fire,
Brave thoughts and noble deedes did ever-
      more aspire.

XXVII

' Such were great Hercules, and Hyllus
      deare;
Trew Jonathan, and David trustie tryde;

Stout Theseus, and Pirithous his feare;
Pylades, and Orestes by his syde;
Myld Titus and Gesippus without pryde;
Damon and Pythias, whom death could not
      sever:
All these, and all that ever had bene tyde
In bands of friendship, there did live for
      ever;
Whose lives although decay'd, yet loves
      decayed never.

XXVIII

' Which when as I, that never tasted blis
Nor happie howre, beheld with gazefull
      eye,
I thought there was none other heaven then
      this;
And gan their endlesse happinesse envye,
That, being free from feare and gealosye,
Might frankely there their loves desire
      possesse;
Whilest I through paines and perlous
      jeopardie
Was forst to seeke my lifes deare patron-
      esse:
Much dearer be the things which come
      through hard distresse.

XXIX

' Yet all those sights, and all that else I
      saw,
Might not my steps withhold, but that
      forthright
Unto that purposd place I did me draw,
Where as my love was lodged day and
      night:
The temple of great Venus, that is hight
The Queene of Beautie, and of Love the
      mother,
There worshipped of every living wight;
Whose goodly workmanship farre past all
      other
That ever were on earth, all were they set
      together.

XXX

' Not that same famous temple of Diane,
Whose hight all Ephesus did oversee,
And which all Asia sought with vowes pro-
      phane,
One of the worlds seven wonders sayd to
      bee,
Might match with this by many a degree:
Nor that which that wise king of Jurie
      framed,

With endlesse cost, to be th' Almighties
　　see;
Nor all that else through all the world is
　　named
To all the heathen gods, might like to this
　　be clamed.

XXXI

' I, much admyring that so goodly frame,
Unto the porch approcht, which open
　　stood;
But therein sate an amiable dame,
That seem'd to be of very sober mood,
And in her semblant shewed great woman-
　　hood:
Strange was her tyre; for on her head a
　　crowne
She wore, much like unto a Danisk hood,
Poudred with pearle and stone, and all her
　　gowne
Enwoven was with gold, that raught full
　　low a downe.

XXXII

' On either side of her two young men
　　stood,
Both strongly arm'd, as fearing one an-
　　other;
Yet were they brethren both of halfe the
　　blood,
Begotten by two fathers of one mother,
Though of contrarie natures each to other:
The one of them hight Love, the other
　　Hate;
Hate was the elder, Love the younger
　　brother;
Yet was the younger stronger in his state
Then th' elder, and him maystred still in
　　all debate.

XXXIII

' Nathlesse that dame so well them tem-
　　pred both,
That she them forced hand to joyne in
　　hand,
Albe that Hatred was thereto full loth,
And turn'd his face away, as he did stand,
Unwilling to behold that lovely band.
Yet she was of such grace and vertuous
　　might,
That her commaundment he could not
　　withstand,
But bit his lip for felonous despight,
And gnasht his yron tuskes at that dis-
　　pleasing sight.

XXXIV

' Concord she cleeped was in common reed,
Mother of blessed Peace and Friendship
　　trew;
They both her twins, both borne of heav-
　　enly seed,
And she her selfe likewise divinely grew;
The which right well her workes divine
　　did shew:
For strength and wealth and happinesse
　　she lends,
And strife and warre and anger does sub-
　　dew;
Of litle much, of foes she maketh frends,
And to afflicted minds sweet rest and quiet
　　sends.

XXXV

' By her the heaven is in his course con-
　　tained,
And all the world in state unmoved stands,
As their Almightie Maker first ordained,
And bound them with inviolable bands;
Else would the waters overflow the lands,
And fire devoure the ayre, and hell them
　　quight,
But that she holds them with her blessed
　　hands.
She is the nourse of pleasure and delight,
And unto Venus grace the gate doth open
　　right.

XXXVI

' By her I entring halfe dismayed was,
But she in gentle wise me entertayned,
And twixt her selfe and Love did let me
　　pas;
But Hatred would my entrance have re-
　　strayned,
And with his club me threatned to have
　　brayned,
Had not the ladie with her powrefull
　　speach
Him from his wicked will uneath re-
　　frayned;
And th' other eke his malice did empeach,
Till I was throughly past the perill of his
　　reach.

XXXVII

' Into the inmost temple thus I came,
Which fuming all with frankensence I
　　found,
And odours rising from the altars flame.
Upon an hundred marble pillors round

The roofe up high was reared from the
   ground,
All deckt with crownes, and chaynes, and
   girlands gay,
And thousand pretious gifts worth many a
   pound,
The which sad lovers for their vowes did
   pay;
And all the ground was strow'd with flowres, as fresh as May.

XXXVIII

' An hundred altars round about were set,
All flaming with their sacrifices fire,
That with the steme thereof the temple
   swet,
Which rould in clouds to heaven did aspire,
And in them bore true lovers vowes en-
   tire:
And eke an hundred brasen caudrons
   bright,
To bath in joy and amorous desire,
Every of which was to a damzell hight;
For all the priests were damzels, in soft
   linnen dight.

XXXIX

' Right in the midst the goddesse selfe did
   stand
Upon an altar of some costly masse,
Whose substance was uneath to understand:
For neither pretious stone, nor durefull
   brasse,
Nor shining gold, nor mouldring clay it was;
But much more rare and pretious to es-
   teeme,
Pure in aspect, and like to christall glasse,
Yet glasse was not, if one did rightly
   deeme,
But being faire and brickle, likest glasse
   did seeme.

XL

' But it in shape and beautie did excell
All other idoles which the heathen adore,
Farre passing that which by surpassing skill
Phidias did make in Paphos isle of yore,
With which that wretched Greeke, that life
   forlore,
Did fall in love: yet this much fairer shined,
But covered with a slender veile afore;
And both her feete and legs together
   twyned
Were with a snake, whose head and tail
   were fast combyned.

XLI

' The cause why she was covered with a
   vele
Was hard to know, for that her priests the
   same
From peoples knowledge labour'd to con-
   cele.
But sooth it was not sure for womanish
   shame,
Nor any blemish, which the worke mote
   blame;
But for, they say, she hath both kinds in
   one,
Both male and female, both under one
   name:
She syre and mother is her selfe alone,
Begets and eke conceives, ne needeth other
   none.

XLII

' And all about her necke and shoulders flew
A flocke of litle loves, and sports, and
   joyes,
With nimble wings of gold and purple hew,
Whose shapes seem'd not like to terrestriall
   boyes,
But like to angels playing heavenly toyes;
The whilest their eldest brother was away,
Cupid, their eldest brother: he enjoyes
The wide kingdome of Love with lordly
   sway,
And to his law compels all creatures to
   obay.

XLIII

' And all about her altar, scattered lay
Great sorts of lovers piteously complayn-
   ing,
Some of their losse, some of their loves de-
   lay,
Some of their pride, some paragons dis-
   dayning,
Some fearing fraud, some fraudulently
   fayning,
As every one had cause of good or ill.
Amongst the rest some one, through loves
   constrayning,
Tormented sore, could not containe it still,
But thus brake forth, that all the temple it
   did fill:

XLIV

' " Great Venus, queene of beautie and of
   grace,
The joy of gods and men, that under skie

Doest fayrest shine, and most adorne thy
    place,
That with thy smyling looke doest pacifie
The raging seas, and makst the stormes to
    flie;
Thee, goddesse, thee the winds, the clouds
    doe feare,
And when thou spredst thy mantle forth
    on hie,
The waters play, and pleasant lands ap-
    peare,
And heavens laugh, and al the world shews
    joyous cheare.

XLV

' " Then doth the dædale earth throw forth
    to thee
Out of her fruitfull lap aboundant flowres;
And then all living wights, soone as they
    see
The Spring breake forth out of his lusty
    bowres,
They all doe learne to play the para-
    mours:
First doe the merry birds, thy prety pages,
Privily pricked with thy lustfull powres,
Chirpe loud to thee out of their leavy
    cages,
And thee their mother call to coole their
    kindly rages.

XLVI

'" Then doe the salvage beasts begin to
    play
Their pleasant friskes, and loath their
    wonted food;
The lyons rore, the tygres loudly bray,
The raging buls rebellow through the
    wood,
And breaking forth, dare tempt the deep-
    est flood,
To come where thou doest draw them with
    desire:
So all things else, that nourish vitall blood,
Soone as with fury thou doest them in-
    spire,
In generation seeke to quench their inward
    fire.

XLVII

" So all the world by thee at first was
    made,
And dayly yet thou doest the same repayre:
Ne ought on earth that merry is and glad,
Ne ought on earth that lovely is and fayre,

But thou the same for pleasure didst pre-
    payre.
Thou art the root of all that joyous is,
Great god of men and women, queene of
    th' ayre,
Mother of laughter, and welspring of blisse,
O graunt that of my love at last I may not
    misse."

XLVIII

' So did he say: but I with murmure soft,
That none might heare the sorrow of my
    hart,
Yet inly groning deepe and sighing oft,
Besought her to graunt ease unto my
    smart,
And to my wound her gratious help impart.
Whilest thus I spake, behold ! with happy
    eye
I spyde where at the idoles feet apart
A bevie of fayre damzels close did lye,
Wayting when as the antheme should be
    sung on hye.

XLIX

' The first of them did seeme of ryper
    yeares
And graver countenance then all the rest;
Yet all the rest were eke her equall peares,
Yet unto her obayed all the best.
Her name was Womanhood, that she ex-
    prest
By her sad semblant and demeanure wyse.
For stedfast still her eyes did fixed rest,
Ne rov'd at randon, after gazers guyse,
Whose luring baytes oftimes doe heedlesse
    harts entyse.

L

' And next to her sate goodly Shamefast-
    nesse,
Ne ever durst her eyes from ground up-
    reare,
Ne ever once did looke up from her desse,
As if some blame of evill she did feare,
That in her cheekes made roses oft ap-
    peare:
And her against sweet Cherefulnesse was
    placed,
Whose eyes, like twinkling stars in evening
    cleare,
Were deckt with smyles, that all sad hu-
    mors chaced,
And darted forth delights, the which her
    goodly graced.

LI

' And next to her sate sober Modestie,
Holding her hand upon her gentle hart;
And her against sate comely Curtesie,
That unto every person knew her part;
And her before was seated overthwart
Soft Silence, and submisse Obedience,
Both linckt together never to dispart,
Both gifts of God not gotten but from
     thence,
Both girlonds of his saints against their
     foes offence.

LII

' Thus sate they all a round in seemely rate.
And in the midst of them a goodly mayd,
Even in the lap of Womanhood, there
     sate,
The which was all in lilly white arayd,
With silver streames amongst the linnen
     stray'd;
Like to the Morne, when first her shyning
     face
Hath to the gloomy world it selfe be-
     wray'd :
That same was fayrest Amoret in place,
Shyning with beauties light and heavenly
     vertues grace.

LIII

' Whom soone as I beheld, my hart gan
     throb,
And wade in doubt, what best were to be
     donne:
For sacrilege me seem'd the church to rob,
And folly seem'd to leave the thing un-
     donne,
Which with so strong attempt I had be-
     gonne.
Tho, shaking off all doubt and shamefast
     feare,
Which ladies love I heard had never wonne
Mongst men of worth, I to her stepped
     neare,
And by the lilly hand her labour'd up to
     reare.

LIV

' Thereat that formost matrone me did
     blame,
And sharpe rebuke, for being over bold;
Saying it was to knight unseemely shame,
Upon a recluse virgin to lay hold,
That unto Venus services was sold.
To whom I thus : " Nay, but it fitteth best

For Cupids man with Venus mayd to hold;
For ill your goddesse services are drest
By virgins, and her sacrifices let to rest."

LV

' With that my shield I forth to her did
     show,
Which all that while I closely had conceld;
On which when Cupid with his killing bow
And cruell shafts emblazond she beheld,
At sight thereof she was with terror queld,
And said no more : but I, which all that
     while
The pledge of faith, her hand, engaged held,
Like warie hynd within the weedie soyle,
For no intreatie would forgoe so glorious
     spoyle.

LVI

' And evermore upon the goddesse face
Mine eye was fixt, for feare of her offence:
Whom when I saw with amiable grace
To laugh at me, and favour my pretence,
I was emboldned with more confidence,
And nought for nicenesse nor for envy
     sparing,
In presence of them all forth led her
     thence,
All looking on, and like astonisht staring,
Yet to lay hand on her not one of all them
     daring.

LVII

' She often prayd, and often me besought,
Sometime with tender teares to let her goe,
Sometime with witching smyles: but yet,
     for nought
That ever she to me could say or doe,
Could she her wished freedome fro me
     wooe;
But forth I led her through the temple
     gate,
By which I hardly past with much adoe:
But that same ladie, which me friended
     late
In entrance, did me also friend in my re-
     trate.

LVIII

' No lesse did Daunger threaten me with
     dread,
When as he saw me, maugre all his powre,
That glorious spoyle of beautie with me
     lead,
Then Cerberus, when Orpheus did recoure

His leman from the Stygian princes boure.
But evermore my shield did me defend
Against the storme of every dreadfull
    stoure:
Thus safely with my love I thence did
    wend.'
So ended he his tale, where I this canto
    end.

CANTO XI

Marinells former wound is heald;
He comes to Proteus hall,
Where Thames doth the Medway wedd,
And feasts the sea-gods all.

I

But ah for pittie that I have thus long
Left a fayre ladie languishing in payne!
Now well away! that I have doen such
    wrong,
To let faire Florimell in bands remayne,
In bands of love, and in sad thraldomes
    chayne!
From which unlesse some heavenly powre
    her free
By miracle, not yet appearing playne,
She lenger yet is like captiv'd to bee:
That even to thinke thereof it inly pitties
    mee.

II

Here neede you to remember, how erewhile
Unlovely Proteus, missing to his mind
That virgins love to win by wit or wile,
Her threw into a dongeon deepe and blind,
And there in chaynes her cruelly did bind,
In hope thereby her to his bent to draw:
For when as neither gifts nor graces kind
Her constant mind could move at all, he
    saw,
He thought her to compell by crueltie and
    awe.

III

Deepe in the bottome of an huge great
    rocke
The dongeon was, in which her bound he
    left,
That neither yron barres, nor brasen locke,
Did neede to gard from force or secret theft
Of all her lovers, which would her have
    reft.
For wall'd it was with waves, which rag'd
    and ror'd

As they the cliffe in peeces would have
    cleft;
Besides, ten thousand monsters foule ab-
    hor'd
Did waite about it, gaping griesly, all be-
    gor'd.

IV

And in the midst thereof did horror dwell,
And darkenesse dredd, that never viewed
    day,
Like to the balefull house of lowest hell,
In which old Styx her aged bones alway,
Old Styx the grandame of the gods, doth
    lay.
There did this lucklesse mayd seven months
    abide,
Ne ever evening saw, ne mornings ray,
Ne ever from the day the night descride,
But thought it all one night, that did no
    houres divide.

V

And all this was for love of Marinell,
Who her despysd (ah! who would her de-
    spyse?)
And wemens love did from his hart expell,
And all those joyes that weake mankind
    entyse.
Nathlesse his pride full dearely he did
    pryse;
For of a womans hand it was ywroke,
That of the wound he yet in languor lyes,
Ne can be cured of that cruell stroke
Which Britomart him gave, when he did
    her provoke.

VI

Yet farre and neare the nymph, his mother,
    sought,
And many salves did to his sore applie,
And many herbes did use. But when as
    nought
She saw could ease his rankling maladie,
At last to Tryphon she for helpe did hie,
(This Tryphon is the seagods surgeon hight)
Whom she besought to find some remedie:
And for his paines a whistle him behight,
That of a fishes shell was wrought with rare
    delight.

VII

So well that leach did hearke to her re-
    quest,
And did so well employ his carefull paine,

That in short space his hurts he had redrest,
And him restor'd to healthfull state againe:
In which he long time after did remaine
There with the nymph his mother, like her
thrall;
Who sore against his will did him retaine,
For feare of perill, which to him mote fall,
Through his too ventrous prowesse proved
over all.

VIII

It fortun'd then, a solemne feast was there
To all the sea-gods and their fruitfull seede,
In honour of the spousalls which then were
Betwixt the Medway and the Thames
agreed.
Long had the Thames (as we in records
reed)
Before that day her wooed to his bed;
But the proud nymph would for no worldly
meed,
Nor no entreatie to his love be led;
Till now at last relenting, she to him was
wed.

IX

So both agreed that this their bridale feast
Should for the gods in Proteus house be
made;
To which they all repayr'd, both most and
least,
Aswell which in the mightie ocean trade,
As that in rivers swim, or brookes doe wade.
All which not if an hundred tongues to tell,
And hundred mouthes, and voice of brasse I
had,
And endlesse memorie, that mote excell,
In order as they came, could I recount them
well.

X

Helpe therefore, O thou sacred imp of
Jove,
The noursling of Dame Memorie his deare,
To whom those rolles, layd up in heaven
above,
And records of antiquitie appeare,
To which no wit of man may comen neare;
Helpe me to tell the names of all those
floods,
And all those nymphes, which then assem-
bled were
To that great banquet of the watry gods,
And all their sundry kinds, and all their hid
abodes.

XI

First came great Neptune with his three-
forkt mace,
That rules the seas, and makes them rise
or fall;
His dewy lockes did drop with brine apace
Under his diademe imperiall:
And by his side his queene with coronall,
Faire Amphitrite, most divinely faire,
Whose yvorie shoulders weren covered all,
As with a robe, with her owne silver haire,
And deckt with pearles, which th' Indian
seas for her prepaire.

XII

These marched farre afore the other crew;
And all the way before them as they went,
Triton his trompet shrill before them blew,
For goodly triumph and great jollyment,
That made the rockes to roare, as they
were rent.
And after them the royall issue came,
Which of them sprung by lineall descent:
First the sea-gods, which to themselves doe
clame
The powre to rule the billowes, and the
waves to tame:

XIII

Phorcys, the father of that fatall brood,
By whom those old heroes wonne such
fame;
And Glaucus, that wise southsayes under-
stood;
And tragicke Inoes sonne, the which be-
came
A god of seas through his mad mothers
blame,
Now hight Palemon, and is saylers frend;
Great Brontes, and Astræus, that did shame
Himselfe with incest of his kin unkend;
And huge Orion, that doth tempests still
portend;

XIV

The rich Cteatus, and Eurytus long;
Neleus and Pelias, lovely brethren both;
Mightie Chrysaor, and Caïcus strong;
Eurypulus, that calmes the waters wroth;
And faire Euphœmus, that upon them goth
As on the ground, without dismay or dread;
Fierce Eryx, and Alebius that know'th
The waters depth, and doth their bottome
tread;
And sad Asopus, comely with his hoarie head.

XV

There also some most famous founders
    were
Of puissant nations, which the world pos-
    sest;
Yet sonnes of Neptune, now assembled
    here:
Ancient Ogyges, even th' auncientest,
And Inachus renowmd above the rest;
Phœnix, and Aon, and Pelasgus old,
Great Belus, Phœax, and Agenor best;
And mightie Albion, father of the bold
And warlike people which the Britaine
    Islands hold.

XVI

For Albion the sonne of Neptune was,
Who, for the proofe of his great puissance,
Out of his Albion did on dry-foot pas
Into old Gall, that now is cleeped France,
To fight with Hercules, that did advance
To vanquish all the world with matchlesse
    might,
And there his mortall part by great mis-
    chance
Was slaine: but that which is th' immortall
    spright
Lives still, and to this feast with Neptunes
    seed was dight.

XVII

But what doe I their names seeke to re-
    herse,
Which all the world have with their issue
    fild?
How can they all in this so narrow verse
Contayned be, and in small compasse hild?
Let them record them, that are better skild,
And know the moniments of passed age:
Onely what needeth shall be here fulfild,
T' expresse some part of that great equip-
    age,
Which from great Neptune do derive their
    parentage.

XVIII

Next came the aged Ocean, and his dame,
Old Tethys, th' oldest two of all the rest,
For all the rest of those two parents came,
Which afterward both sea and land pos-
    sest:
Of all which Nereus, th' eldest and the best,
Did first proceed, then which none more
    upright,
Ne more sincere in word and deed profest;

Most voide of guile, most free from fowle
    despight,
Doing him selfe, and teaching others to doe
    right.

XIX

Thereto he was expert in prophecies,
And could the ledden of the gods unfold,
Through which, when Paris brought his
    famous prise,
The faire Tindarid lasse, he him fortold,
That her all Greece with many a champion
    bold
Should fetch againe, and finally destroy
Proud Priams towne. So wise is Nereus
    old,
And so well skild; nathlesse he takes great
    joy
Oft-times amongst the wanton nymphs to
    sport and toy.

XX

And after him the famous rivers came,
Which doe the earth enrich and beauti-
    fie:
The fertile Nile, which creatures new doth
    frame;
Long Rhodanus, whose sourse springs from
    the skie;
Faire Ister, flowing from the mountaines
    hie;
Divine Scamander, purpled yet with blood
Of Greekes and Trojans, which therein did
    die;
Pactolus glistring with his golden flood,
And Tygris fierce, whose streames of none
    may be withstood;

XXI

Great Ganges, and immortall Euphrates,
Deepe Indus, and Mæander intricate,
Slow Peneus, and tempestuous Phasides,
Swift Rhene, and Alpheus still immacu-
    late;
Ooraxes, feared for great Cyrus fate;
Tybris, renowmed for the Romaines fame;
Rich Oranochy, though but knowen late;
And that huge river, which doth beare his
    name
Of warlike Amazons, which doe possesse
    the same.

XXII

Joy on those warlike women, which so long
Can from all men so rich a kingdome hold!

And shame on you, O men, which boast
  your strong
And valiant hearts, in thoughts lesse hard
  and bold,
Yet quaile in conquest of that land of gold !
But this to you, O Britons, most pertaines,
To whom the right hereof it selfe hath
  sold;
The which, for sparing litle cost or paines,
Loose so immortall glory, and so endlesse
  gaines.

XXIII

Then was there heard a most celestiall
  sound
Of dainty musicke, which did next ensew
Before the spouse: that was Arion crownd;
Who, playing on his harpe, unto him drew
The eares and hearts of all that goodly
  crew,
That even yet the dolphin, which him bore
Through the Agæan seas from pirates vew,
Stood still by him astonisht at his lore,
And all the raging seas for joy forgot to
  rore.

XXIV

So went he playing on the watery plaine.
Soone after whom the lovely bridegroome
  came,
The noble Thamis, with all his goodly
  traine;
But him before there went, as best became,
His auncient parents, namely th' auncient
  Thame:
But much more aged was his wife then he,
The Ouze, whom men doe Isis rightly
  name;
Full weake and crooked creature seemed
  shee,
And almost blind through eld, that scarce
  her way could see.

XXV

Therefore on either side she was sustained
Of two smal grooms, which by their names
  were hight
The Churne and Charwell, two small
  streames, which pained
Them selves her footing to direct aright,
Which fayled oft through faint and feeble
  plight:
But Thame was stronger, and of better
  stay;
Yet seem'd full aged by his outward sight,
With head all hoary, and his beard all gray,
Deawed with silver drops, that trickled
  downe alway.

XXVI

And eke he somewhat seem'd to stoupe
  afore
With bowed backe, by reason of the lode
And auncient heavy burden which he bore
Of that faire city, wherein make abode
So many learned impes, that shoote abrode,
And with their braunches spred all Britany,
No lesse then do her elder sisters broode.
Joy to you both, ye double noursery
Of arts ! but, Oxford, thine doth Thame
  most glorify.

XXVII

But he their sonne full fresh and jolly was,
All decked in a robe of watchet hew,
On which the waves, glittering like christall
  glas,
So cunningly enwoven were, that few
Could weenen whether they were false or
  trew.
And on his head like to a coronet
He wore, that seemed strange to common
  vew,
In which were many towres and castels set,
That it encompast round as with a golden
  fret.

XXVIII

Like as the mother of the gods, they say,
In her great iron charet wonts to ride,
When to Joves pallace she doth take her
  way,
Old Cybele, arayd with pompous pride,
Wearing a diademe embattild wide
With hundred turrets, like a turribant.
With such an one was Thamis beautifide;
That was to weet the famous Troynovant,
In which her kingdomes throne is chiefly
  resiant.

XXIX

And round about him many a pretty page
Attended duely, ready to obay;
All little rivers, which owe vassallage
To him, as to their lord, and tribute pay:
The chaulky Kenet, and the Thetis gray,
The morish Cole, and the soft sliding
  Breane,
The wanton Lee, that oft doth loose his
  way.

And the still Darent, in whose waters
    cleane
Ten thousand fishes play, and decke his
    pleasant streame.

XXX

Then came his neighbour flouds, which
    nigh him dwell,
And water all the English soile through-
    out;
They all on him this day attended well,
And with meet service waited him about;
Ne none disdained low to him to lout:
No, not the stately Severne grudg'd at
    all,
Ne storming Humber, though he looked
    stout;
But both him honor'd as their principall,
And let their swelling waters low before
    him fall.

XXXI

There was the speedy Tamar, which de-
    vides
The Cornish and the Devonish confines;
Through both whose borders swiftly downe
    it glides,
And meeting Plim, to Plimmouth thence
    declines:
And Dart, nigh chockt with sands of tinny
    mines.
But Avon marched in more stately path,
Proud of his adamants, with which he
    shines
And glisters wide, as als' of wondrous
    Bath,
And Bristow faire, which on his waves he
    builded hath.

XXXII

And there came Stoure with terrible aspect,
Bearing his sixe deformed heads on hye,
That doth his course through Blandford
    plains direct,
And washeth Winborne meades in season
    drye.
Next him went Wylibourne with passage
    slye,
That of his wylinesse his name doth take,
And of him selfe doth name the shire
    thereby:
And Mole, that like a nousling mole doth
    make
His way still under ground, till Thamis he
    overtake.

XXXIII

Then came the Rother, decked all with
    woods
Like a wood god, and flowing fast to Rhy:
And Sture, that parteth with his pleasant
    floods
The easterne Saxons from the southerne ny,
And Clare and Harwitch both doth beau-
    tify:
Him follow'd Yar, soft washing Norwitch
    wall,
And with him brought a present joyfully
Of his owne fish unto their festivall,
Whose like none else could shew, the which
    they ruffins call.

XXXIV

Next these the plenteous Ouse came far
    from land,
By many a city, and by many a towne,
And many rivers taking under hand
Into his waters, as he passeth downe,
The Cle, the Were, the Grant, the Sture,
    the Rowne,
Thence doth by Huntingdon and Cambridge
    flit,
My mother Cambridge, whom as with a
    crowne
He doth adorne, and is adorn'd of it
With many a gentle muse, and many a
    learned wit.

XXXV

And after him the fatall Welland went,
That if old sawes prove true (which God
    forbid)
Shall drowne all Holland with his excre-
    ment,
And shall see Stamford, though now
    homely hid,
Then shine in learning, more then ever
    did
Cambridge or Oxford, Englands goodly
    beames.
And next to him the Nene downe softly
    slid;
And bounteous Trent, that in him selfe en-
    seames
Both thirty sorts of fish and thirty sundry
    streames.

XXXVI

Next these came Tyne, along whose stony
    bancke
Tha' Romaine monarch built a brasen wall,

Which mote the feebled Britons strongly
flancke
Against the Picts, that swarmed over all,
Which yet thereof Gualsever they doe call:
And Twede, the limit betwixt Logris land
And Albany: and Eden, though but small,
Yet often stainde with bloud of many a band
Of Scots and English both, that tyned on
his strand.

XXXVII

Then came those sixe sad brethren, like
forlorne,
That whilome were (as antique fathers tell)
Sixe valiant knights, of one faire nymphe
yborne,
Which did in noble deedes of armes excell,
And wonned there where now Yorke people
dwell:
Still Ure, swift Werfe, and Oze the most
of might,
High Swale, unquiet Nide, and troublous
Skell;
All whom a Scythian king, that Humber
hight,
Slew cruelly, and in the river drowned
quight.

XXXVIII

But past not long, ere Brutus warlicke
sonne,
Locrinus, them aveng'd, and the same date,
Which the proud Humber unto them had
donne,
By equall dome repayd on his owne pate:
For in the selfe same river, where he late
Had drenched them, he drowned him
againe;
And nam'd the river of his wretched fate;
Whose bad condition yet it doth retaine,
Oft tossed with his stormes, which therein
still remaine.

XXXIX

These after, came the stony shallow Lone,
That to old Loncaster his name doth lend;
And following Dee, which Britons long
ygone
Did call divine, that doth by Chester tend;
And Conway, which out of his streame doth
send
Plenty of pearles to decke his dames with-
all;
And Lindus, that his pikes doth most com-
mend,

Of which the auncient Lincolne men doe
call:
All these together marched toward Proteus hall.

XL

Ne thence the Irishe rivers absent were:
Sith no lesse famous then the rest they bee,
And joyne in neighbourhood of kingdome
nere,
Why should they not likewise in love agree,
And joy likewise this solemne day to see?
They saw it all, and present were in place;
Though I them all, according their degree,
Cannot recount, nor tell their hidden race,
Nor read the salvage cuntreis thorough
which they pace.

XLI

There was the Liffy rolling downe the lea,
The sandy Slane, the stony Aubrian,
The spacious Shenan spreading like a sea,
The pleasant Boyne, the fishy fruitfull Ban,
Swift Awniduff, which of the English man
Is cal'de Blackewater, and the Liffar deep,
Sad Trowis, that once his people overran,
Strong Allo tombling from Slewlogher
steep,
And Mulla mine, whose waves I whilom
taught to weep.

XLII

And there the three renowmed brethren
were,
Which that great gyant Blomius begot
Of the faire nimph Rheusa wandring there.
One day, as she to shunne the season whot,
Under Slewbloome in shady grove was got,
This gyant found her, and by force de-
flowr'd;
Whereof conceiving, she in time forth
brought
These three faire sons, which, being thence
forth powrd,
In three great rivers ran, and many
countreis scowrd.

XLIII

The first, the gentle Shure, that, making
way
By sweet Clonmell, adornes rich Waterford;
The next, the stubborne Newre, whose
waters gray
By faire Kilkenny and Rosseponte boord;

The third, the goodly Barow, which doth
　　hoord
Great heapes of salmons in his deepe
　　bosome:
All which long sundred, doe at last accord
To joyne in one, ere to the sea they come,
So, flowing all from one, all one at last
　　become.

XLIV

There also was the wide embayed Mayre,
The pleasaunt Bandon, crownd with many a
　　wood,
The spreading Lee, that like an island
　　fayre
Encloseth Corke with his devided flood;
And balefull Oure, late staind with English
　　blood:
With many more, whose names no tongue
　　can tell.
All which that day in order seemly good
Did on the Thamis attend, and waited
　　well
To doe their duefull service, as to them
　　befell.

XLV

Then came the bride, the lovely Medua
　　came,
Clad in a vesture of unknowen geare,
And uncouth fashion, yet her well became;
That seem'd like silver, sprinckled here and
　　theare
With glittering spangs, that did like starres
　　appeare,
And wav'd upon, like water chamelot,
To hide the metall, which yet every where
Bewrayd it selfe, to let men plainely wot,
It was no mortall worke, that seem'd and
　　yet was not.

XLVI

Her goodly lockes adowne her backe did
　　flow
Unto her waste, with flowres bescattered,
The which ambrosiall odours forth did
　　throw
To all about, and all her shoulders spred
As a new spring; and likewise on her hed
A chapelet of sundry flowers she wore,
From under which the deawy humour shed
Did tricle downe her haire, like to the
　　hore
Congealed litle drops, which doe the morne
　　adore

XLVII

On her two pretty handmaides did attend,
One cald the Theise, the other cald the
　　Crane;
Which on her waited, things amisse to
　　mend,
And both behind upheld her spredding
　　traine;
Under the which her feet appeared plaine,
Her silver feet, faire washt against this
　　day:
And her before there paced pages twaine,
Both clad in colours like, and like array,
The Doune and eke the Frith, both which
　　prepard her way.

XLVIII

And after these the sea nymphs marched
　　all,
All goodly damzels, deckt with long greene
　　haire,
Whom of their sire Nereides men call,
All which the Oceans daughter to him
　　bare,
The gray eyde Doris: all which fifty are;
All which she there on her attending had:
Swift Proto, milde Eucrate, Thetis faire,
Soft Spio, sweete Eudore, Sao sad,
Light Doto, wanton Glauce, and Galene
　　glad,

XLIX

White hand Eunica, proud Dynamene,
Joyous Thalia, goodly Amphitrite,
Lovely Pasithee, kinde Eulimene,
Light foote Cymothoe, and sweete Melite,
Fairest Pherusa, Phao lilly white,
Wondred Agave, Poris, and Nesæa,
With Erato, that doth in love delite,
And Panopæ, and wise Protomedæa,
And snowy neckd Doris, and milkewhite
　　Galathæa,

L

Speedy Hippothoe, and chaste Actea,
Large Lisianassa, and Pronæa sage,
Evagore, and light Pontoporea,
And she that with her least word can
　　asswage
The surging seas, when they do sorest rage,
Cymodoce, and stout Autonoe,
And Neso, and Eione well in age,
And seeming still to smile, Glauconome,
And she that hight of many heastes
　　Polynome,

LI

Fresh Alimeda, deckt with girlond greene,
Hyponeo, with salt bedewed wrests,
Laomedia, like the christall sheene,
Liagore, much praisd for wise behests,
And Psamathe, for her brode snowy brests,
Cymo, Eupompe, and Themiste just,
And she that vertue loves and vice detests,
Evarna, and Menippe true in trust,
And Nemertea, learned well to rule her lust.

LII

All these the daughters of old Nereus were,
Which have the sea in charge to them as-
    sinde,
To rule his tides, and surges to uprere,
To bring forth stormes, or fast them to up-
    binde,
And sailers save from wreckes of wrath-
    full winde.
And yet besides, three thousand more there
    were
Of th' Oceans seede, but Joves and Phœbus
    kinde;
The which in floods and fountaines doe ap-
    pere,
And all mankinde do nourish with their
    waters clere.

LIII

The which, more eath it were for mortall
    wight
To tell the sands, or count the starres on
    hye,
Or ought more hard, then thinke to reckon
    right.
But well I wote that these which I descry
Were present at this great solemnity:
And there, amongst the rest, the mother was
Of luckelesse Marinell, Cymodoce;
Which, for my Muse her selfe now tyred
    has,
Unto an other canto I will overpas.

CANTO XII

Marin, for love of Florimell,
    In languor wastes his life:
The nymph his mother getteth her,
    And gives to him for wife.

I

O WHAT an endlesse worke have I in
    hand,
To count the seas abundant progeny,
Whose fruitfull seede farre passeth those
    in land,
And also those which wonne in th' azure
    sky !
For much more eath to tell the starres on
    hy,
Albe they endlesse seeme in estimation,
Then to recount the seas posterity:
So fertile be the flouds in generation,
So huge their numbers, and so numberlesse
    their nation.

II

Therefore the antique wisards well in-
    vented,
That Venus of the fomy sea was bred;
For that the seas by her are most aug-
    mented.
Witnesse th' exceeding fry which there are
    fed,
And wondrous sholes, which may of none
    be red.
Then blame me not, if I have err'd in
    count
Of gods, of nymphs, of rivers yet unred:
For though their numbers do much more
    surmount,
Yet all those same were there, which erst I
    did recount.

III

All those were there, and many other more,
Whose names and nations were too long to
    tell,
That Proteus house they fild even to the
    dore;
Yet were they all in order, as befell,
According their degrees disposed well.
Amongst the rest was faire Cymodoce,
The mother of unlucky Marinell,
Who thither with her came, to learne and
    see
The manner of the gods when they at ban-
    quet be.

IV

But for he was halfe mortall, being bred
Of mortall sire, though of immortall
    wombe,
He might not with immortall food be fed,
Ne with th' eternall gods to bancket come;
But walkt abrode, and round about did
    rome,
To view the building of that uncouth place,
That seem'd unlike unto his earthly home:

Where, as he to and fro by chaunce did
    trace,
There unto him betid a disaventrous case.

V

Under the hanging of an hideous clieffe
He heard the lamentable voice of one
That piteously complaind her carefull
    grieffe,
Which never she before disclosd to none,
But to her selfe her sorrow did bemone.
So feelingly her case she did complaine,
That ruth it moved in the rocky stone,
And made it seeme to feele her grievous
    paine,
And oft to grone with billowes beating from
    the maine.

VI

'Though vaine I see my sorrowes to unfold,
And count my cares, when none is nigh to
    heare,
Yet, hoping griefe may lessen being told,
I will them tell though unto no man neare:
For Heaven, that unto all lends equall eare,
Is farre from hearing of my heavy plight;
And lowest Hell, to which I lie most neare,
Cares not what evils hap to wretched wight;
And greedy seas doe in the spoile of life
    delight.

VII

'Yet loe! the seas I see by often beating
Doe pearce the rockes, and hardest mar-
    ble weares;
But his hard rocky hart for no entreating
Will yeeld, but when my piteous plaints he
    heares,
Is hardned more with my aboundant teares.
Yet though he never list to me relent,
But let me waste in woe my wretched
    yeares,
Yet will I never of my love repent,
But joy that for his sake I suffer prisonment.

VIII

'And when my weary ghost, with griefe
    outworne,
By timely death shall winne her wished
    rest,
Let then this plaint unto his eares be borne,
That blame it is to him, that armes pro-
    fest,
To let her die, whom he might have re-
    drest.'

There did she pause, inforced to give place
Unto the passion that her heart opprest;
And after she had wept and wail'd a space,
She gan afresh thus to renew her wretched
    case:

IX

'Ye gods of seas, if any gods at all
Have care of right, or ruth of wretches
    wrong,
By one or other way me, woefull thrall,
Deliver hence out of this dungeon strong,
In which I daily dying am too long.
And if ye deeme me death for loving one
That loves not me, then doe it not prolong,
But let me die and end my daies attone,
And let him live unlov'd, or love him selfe
    alone.

X

'But if that life ye unto me decree,
Then let mee live as lovers ought to do,
And of my lifes deare love beloved be:
And if he shall through pride your doome
    undo,
Do you by duresse him compell thereto,
And in this prison put him here with me:
One prison fittest is to hold us two:
So had I rather to be thrall then free;
Such thraldome or such freedome let it
    surely be.

XI

'But O vaine judgement, and conditions
    vaine,
The which the prisoner points unto the free!
The whiles I him condemne, and deeme his
    paine,
He where he list goes loose, and laughes at
    me.
So ever loose, so ever happy be.
But where so loose or happy that thou art,
Know, Marinell, that all this is for thee.'
With that she wept and wail'd, as if her
    hart
Would quite have burst through great
    abundance of her smart.

XII

All which complaint when Marinell had
    heard,
And understood the cause of all her care
To come of him, for using her so hard,
His stubborne heart, that never felt mis-
    fare,

Was toucht with soft remorse and pitty rare;
That even for griefe of minde he oft did
    grone,
And inly wish that in his powre it weare
Her to redresse: but since he meanes found
    none,
He could no more but her great misery be-
    mone.

XIII

Thus whilst his stony heart with tender
    ruth
Was toucht, and mighty courage mollifide,
Dame Venus sonne, that tameth stubborne
    youth
With iron bit, and maketh him abide,
Till like a victor on his backe he ride,
Into his mouth his maystring bridle threw,
That made him stoupe, till he did him be-
    stride:
Then gan he make him tread his steps
    anew,
And learne to love, by learning lovers
    paines to rew.

XIV

Now gan he in his grieved minde devise,
How from that dungeon he might her en-
    large:
Some while he thought, by faire and hum-
    ble wise
To Proteus selfe to sue for her discharge;
But then he fear'd his mothers former
    charge
Gainst womens love, long given him in
    vaine:
Then gan he thinke, perforce with sword
    and targe
Her forth to fetch, and Proteus to con-
    straine;
But soone he gan such folly to forthinke
    againe.

XV

Then did he cast to steale her thence away,
And with him beare, where none of her
    might know.
But all in vaine: forwhy he found no way
To enter in, or issue forth below:
For all about that rocke the sea did flow.
And though unto his will she given were,
Yet without ship or bote her thence to row,
He wist not how her thence away to bere;
And daunger well he wist long to continue
    there.

XVI

At last when as no meanes he could in-
    vent,
Backe to him selfe he gan returne the
    blame,
That was the author of her punishment;
And with vile curses and reprochfull shame
To damne him selfe by every evill name;
And deeme unworthy or of love or life,
That had despisde so chast and faire a
    dame,
Which him had sought through trouble and
    long strife,
Yet had refusde a god that her had sought
    to wife.

XVII

In this sad plight he walked here and there,
And romed round about the rocke in vaine,
As he had lost him selfe, he wist not where;
Oft listening if he mote her heare againe,
And still bemoning her unworthy paine:
Like as an hynde whose calfe is falne un-
    wares
Into some pit, where she him heares com-
    plaine,
An hundred times about the pit side fares,
Right sorrowfully mourning her bereaved
    cares.

XVIII

And now by this the feast was throughly
    ended,
And every one gan homeward to resort.
Which seeing, Marinell was sore offended,
That his departure thence should be so
    short,
And leave his love in that sea-walled fort.
Yet durst he not his mother disobay;
But her attending in full seemly sort,
Did march amongst the many all the way:
And all the way did inly mourne, like one
    astray.

XIX

Being returned to his mothers bowre,
In solitary silence far from wight,
He gan record the lamentable stowre
In which his wretched love lay day and
    night,
For his deare sake, that ill deserv'd that
    plight:
The thought whereof empierst his hart so
    deepe,
That of no worldly thing he tooke delight;

Ne dayly food did take, ne nightly sleepe,
But pyn'd, and mourn'd, and languisht, and
    alone did weepe;

XX

That in short space his wonted chearefull
    hew
Gan fade, and lively spirits deaded quight:
His cheeke bones raw, and eie-pits hollow
    grew,
And brawney armes had lost their knowen
    might,
That nothing like himselfe he seem'd in
    sight.
Ere long so weake of limbe, and sicke of
    love
He woxe, that lenger he note stand up-
    right,
But to his bed was brought, and layd above,
Like ruefull ghost, unable once to stirre or
    move.

XXI

Which when his mother saw, she in her
    mind
Was troubled sore, ne wist well what to
    weene,
Ne could by search nor any meanes out
    find
The secret cause and nature of his teene,
Whereby she might apply some medicine;
But weeping day and night, did him attend,
And mourn'd to see her losse before her
    eyne,
Which griev'd her more that she it could
    not mend:
To see an helpelesse evill double griefe
    doth lend.

XXII

Nought could she read the roote of his
    disease,
Ne weene what mister maladie it is,
Whereby to seeke some meanes it to ap-
    pease.
Most did she thinke, but most she thought
    amis,
That that same former fatall wound of his
Whyleare by Tryphon was not throughly
    healed,
But closely rankled under th' orifis:
Least did she thinke, that which he most
    concealed,
That love it was, which in his hart lay
    unrevealed.

XXIII

Therefore to Tryphon she againe doth hast,
And him doth chyde as false and fraudu-
    lent,
That fayld the trust which she in him had
    plast,
To cure her sonne, as he his faith had lent:
Who now was falne into new languishment
Of his old hurt, which was not throughly
    cured.
So backe he came unto her patient:
Where searching every part, her well as-
    sured,
That it was no old sore which his new paine
    procured;

XXIV

But that it was some other maladie,
Or griefe unknowne, which he could not
    discerne:
So left he her withouten remedie.
Then gan her heart to faint, and quake, and
    earne,
And inly troubled was, the truth to learne.
Unto himselfe she came, and him besought,
Now with faire speches, now with threat-
    nings sterne,
If ought lay hidden in his grieved thought,
It to reveale: who still her answered, there
    was nought.

XXV

Nathlesse she rested not so satisfide,
But leaving watry gods, as booting nought,
Unto the shinie heaven in haste she hide,
And thence Apollo, king of leaches,
    brought.
Apollo came; who, soone as he had sought
Through his disease, did by and by out
    find
That he did languish of some inward
    thought,
The which afflicted his engrieved mind;
Which love he red to be, that leads each
    living kind.

XXVI

Which when he had unto his mother told,
She gan thereat to fret and greatly grieve;
And comming to her sonne, gan first to
    scold
And chyde at him, that made her misbe-
    lieve:
But afterwards she gan him soft to shrieve,
And wooe with faire intreatie, to disclose

Which of the nymphes his heart so sore did
    mieve;
For sure she weend it was some one of
    those
Which he had lately seene, that for his love
    he chose.

XXVII

Now lesse she feared that same fatall read,
That warned him of womens love beware:
Which being ment of mortall creatures
    sead,
For love of nymphes she thought she need
    not care,
But promist him, what ever wight she
    weare,
That she her love to him would shortly
    gaine:
So he her told: but soone as she did heare
That Florimell it was, which wrought his
    paine,
She gan a fresh to chafe, and grieve in every
    vaine.

XXVIII

Yet since she saw the streight extremitie,
In which his life unluckily was layd,
It was no time to scan the prophecie,
Whether old Proteus true or false had sayd,
That his decay should happen by a mayd:
It's late, in death, of daunger to advize,
Or love forbid him that is life denayd:
But rather gan in troubled mind devize
How she that ladies libertie might enter-
    prize.

XXIX

To Proteus selfe to sew she thought it
    vaine,
Who was the root and worker of her woe,
Nor unto any meaner to complaine;
But unto great King Neptune selfe did goe,
And on her knee before him falling lowe,
Made humble suit unto his Majestie,
To graunt to her her sonnes life, which his
    foe,
A cruell tyrant, had presumpteouslie
By wicked doome condemn'd a wretched
    death to die.

XXX

To whom God Neptune, softly smyling,
    thus:
'Daughter, me seemes of double wrong ye
    plaine,

Gainst one that hath both wronged you and
    us:
For death t' adward I ween'd did apper-
    taine
To none but to the seas sole soveraine.
Read therefore who it is, which this hath
    wrought,
And for what cause; the truth discover
    plaine.
For never wight so evill did or thought,
But would some rightfull cause pretend,
    though rightly nought.'

XXXI

To whom she answerd: 'Then it is by name
Proteus, that hath ordayn'd my sonne to
    die;
For that a waift, the which by fortune
    came
Upon your seas, he claym'd as propertie:
And yet nor his, nor his in equitie,
But yours the waift by high prerogative.
Therefore I humbly crave your Majestie,
It to replevie, and my sonne reprive:
So shall you by one gift save all us three
    alive.'

XXXII

He graunted it: and streight his warrant
    made,
Under the sea-gods seale autenticall,
Commaunding Proteus straight t' enlarge
    the mayd
Which, wandring on his seas imperiall,
He lately tooke, and sithence kept as thrall.
Which she receiving with meete thankeful-
    nesse,
Departed straight to Proteus therewithall:
Who, reading it with inward loathfulnesse,
Was grieved to restore the pledge he did
    possesse.

XXXIII

Yet durst he not the warrant to withstand,
But unto her delivered Florimell.
Whom she receiving by the lilly hand,
Admyr'd her beautie much, as she mote
    well;
For she all living creatures did excell;
And was right joyous, that she gotten had
So faire a wife for her sonne Marinell.
So home with her she streight the virgin
    lad,
And shewed her to him, then being sore
    bestad.

XXXIV

Who soone as he beheld that angels face,
Adorn'd with all divine perfection,
His cheared heart eftsoones away gan chace
Sad death, revived with her sweet inspection,
And feeble spirit inly felt refection;
As withered weed through cruell winters tine,
That feeles the warmth of sunny beames reflection,
Liftes up his head, that did before decline,
And gins to spread his leafe before the faire sunshine.

XXXV

Right so himselfe did Marinell upreare,
When he in place his dearest love did spy;
And though his limbs could not his bodie beare,
Ne former strength returne so suddenly,
Yet chearefull signes he shewed outwardly.
Ne lesse was she in secret hart affected,
But that she masked it with modestie,
For feare she should of lightnesse be detected:
Which to another place I leave to be perfected.

THE FIFTH BOOKE
OF THE FAERIE QUEENE
CONTAYNING
THE LEGEND OF ARTEGALL
OR
OF JUSTICE

I

So oft as I with state of present time
The image of the antique world compare,
When as mans age was in his freshest prime,
And the first blossome of faire vertue bare,
Such oddes I finde twixt those, and these which are,
As that, through long continuance of his course,
Me seemes the world is runne quite out of square
From the first point of his appointed sourse,
And being once amisse, growes daily wourse and wourse.

II

For from the golden age, that first was named,
It 's now at earst become a stonie one;
And men themselves, the which at first were framed
Of earthly mould, and form'd of flesh and bone,
Are now transformed into hardest stone:
Such as behind their backs (so backward bred)
Were throwne by Pyrrha and Deucalione:
And if then those may any worse be red,
They into that ere long will be degendered.

III

Let none then blame me, if in discipline
Of vertue and of civill uses lore,
I doe not forme them to the common line
Of present dayes, which are corrupted sore,
But to the antique use which was of yore,
When good was onely for it selfe desyred,
And all men sought their owne, and none no more;
When Justice was not for most meed outhyred,
But simple Truth did rayne, and was of all admyred.

IV

For that which all men then did vertue call
Is now cald vice; and that which vice was hight,
Is now hight vertue, and so us'd of all:
Right now is wrong, and wrong that was is right,
As all things else in time are chaunged quight.
Ne wonder; for the heavens revolution
Is wandred farre from where it first was pight,
And so doe make contrarie constitution
Of all this lower world, toward his dissolution.

V

For who so list into the heavens looke,
And search the courses of the rowling spheares,
Shall find that from the point where they first tooke
Their setting forth, in these few thousand yeares

They all are wandred much; that plaine
appeares.
For that same golden fleecy Ram, which
bore
Phrixus and Helle from their stepdames
feares,
Hath now forgot where he was plast of
yore,
And shouldred hath the Bull, which fayre
Europa bore.

VI

And eke the Bull hath with his bow-bent
horne
So hardly butted those two Twinnes of
Jove,
That they have crusht the Crab, and quite
him borne
Into the great Nemœan Lions grove.
So now all range, and doe at randon rove
Out of their proper places farre away,
And all this world with them amisse doe
move,
And all his creatures from their course
astray,
Till they arrive at their last ruinous de-
cay.

VII

Ne is that same great glorious lampe of
light,
That doth enlumine all these lesser fyres,
In better case, ne keepes his course more
right,
But is miscaried with the other spheres.
For since the terme of fourteene hundred
yeres,
That learned Ptolomæe his hight did
take,
He is declyned from that marke of theirs
Nigh thirtie minutes to the southerne lake;
That makes me feare in time he will us quite
forsake.

VIII

And if to those Ægyptian wisards old,
Which in star-read were wont have best in-
sight,
Faith may be given, it is by them told,
That since the time they first tooke the
sunnes hight,
Foure times his place he shifted hath in
sight,
And twice hath risen where he now doth
west.

And wested twice where he ought rise
aright.
But most is Mars amisse of all the rest,
And next to him old Saturne, that was wont
be best.

IX

For during Saturnes ancient raigne it's
sayd
That all the world with goodnesse did
abound:
All loved vertue, no man was affrayd
Of force, ne fraud in wight was to be found:
No warre was knowne, no dreadfull trom-
pets sound,
Peace universall rayn'd mongst men and
beasts,
And all things freely grew out of the
ground:
Justice sate high ador'd with solemne
feasts,
And to all people did divide her dred be-
heasts.

X

Most sacred vertue she of all the rest,
Resembling God in his imperiall might;
Whose soveraine powre is herein most
exprest,
That both to good and bad he dealeth
right,
And all his workes with justice hath be-
dight.
That powre he also doth to princes lend,
And makes them like himselfe in glorious
sight,
To sit in his owne seate, his cause to end,
And rule his people right, as he doth re-
commend.

XI

Dread soverayne goddesse, that doest high-
est sit
In seate of judgement, in th' Almighties
stead,
And with magnificke might and wondrous
wit
Doest to thy people righteous doome aread,
That furthest nations filles with awfull
dread,
Pardon the boldnesse of thy basest thrall,
That dare discourse of so divine a read,
As thy great justice praysed over all:
The instrument whereof, loe! here thy
Artegall.

CANTO I

Artegall trayn'd in Justice lore
Irenaes quest pursewed;
He doeth avenge on Sanglier
His ladies bloud embrewed.

I

THOUGH vertue then were held in highest
        price,
In those old times of which I doe intreat,
Yet then likewise the wicked seede of
        vice
Began to spring; which shortly grew full
        great,
And with their boughes the gentle plants
        did beat.
But evermore some of the vertuous race
Rose up, inspired with heroicke heat,
That cropt the branches of the sient base,
And with strong hand their fruitfull ranck-
        nes did deface.

II

Such first was Bacchus, that with furious
        might
All th' East, before untam'd, did overronne,
And wrong repressed, and establisht right,
Which lawlesse men had formerly fordonne:
There Justice first her princely rule be-
        gonne.
Next Hercules his like ensample shewed,
Who all the West with equall conquest
        wonne,
And monstrous tyrants with his club sub-
        dewed;
The club of Justice dread, with kingly
        powre endewed.

III

And such was he of whom I have to tell,
The champion of true Justice, Artegall:
Whom (as ye lately mote remember well)
An hard adventure, which did then befall,
Into redoubted perill forth did call;
That was to succour a distressed dame,
Whom a strong tyrant did unjustly thrall,
And from the heritage which she did clame
Did with strong hand withhold: Grantorto
        was his name.

IV

Wherefore the lady, which Eirena hight,
Did to the Faery Queene her way addresse,
To whom complayning her afflicted plight,
She her besought of gratious redresse.
That soveraine queene, that mightie em-
        peresse,
Whose glorie is to aide all suppliants
        pore,
And of weake princes to be patronesse,
Chose Artegall to right her to restore;
For that to her he seem'd best skild in
        righteous lore.

V

For Artegall in justice was upbrought
Even from the cradle of his infancie,
And all the depth of rightfull doome was
        taught
By faire Astræa, with great industrie,
Whilest here on earth she lived mortallie.
For till the world from his perfection fell
Into all filth and foule iniquitie,
Astræa here mongst earthly men did dwell,
And in the rules of justice them instructed
        well.

VI

Whiles through the world she walked in
        this sort,
Upon a day she found this gentle childe,
Amongst his peres playing his childish
        sport:
Whom seeing fit, and with no crime de-
        filde,
She did allure with gifts and speaches
        milde
To wend with her. So thence him farre
        she brought
Into a cave from companie exilde,
In which she noursled him, till yeares he
        raught,
And all the discipline of justice there him
        taught.

VII

There she him taught to weigh both right
        and wrong
In equall ballance with due recompence,
And equitie to measure out along,
According to the line of conscience,
When so it needs with rigour to dis-
        pence.
Of all the which, for want there of man-
        kind,
She caused him to make experience
Upon wyld beasts, which she in woods
        did find,
With wrongfull powre oppressing others of
        their kind.

VIII

Thus she him trayned, and thus she him
taught,
In all the skill of deeming wrong and
right,
Untill the ripenesse of mans yeares he
raught;
That even wilde beasts did feare his awfull
sight,
And men admyr'd his overruling might;
Ne any liv'd on ground, that durst with-
stand
His dreadfull heast, much lesse him match
in fight,
Or bide the horror of his wreakfull hand,
When so he list in wrath lift up his steely
brand.

IX

Which steely brand, to make him dreaded
more,
She gave unto him, gotten by her slight
And earnest search, where it was kept in
store
In Joves eternall house, unwist of wight,
Since he himselfe it us'd in that great fight
Against the Titans, that whylome rebelled
Gainst highest heaven; Chrysaor it was
hight;
Chrysaor that all other swords excelled,
Well prov'd in that same day, when Jove
those gyants quelled.

X

For of most perfect metall it was made,
Tempred with adamant amongst the same,
And garnisht all with gold upon the blade
In goodly wise, whereof it tooke his name,
And was of no lesse vertue then of fame:
For there no substance was so firme and
hard,
But it would pierce or cleave, where so it
came;
Ne any armour could his dint out ward;
But wheresoever it did light, it throughly
shard.

XI

Now when the world with sinne gan to
abound,
Astræa loathing lenger here to space
Mongst wicked men, in whom no truth she
found,
Return'd to heaven, whence she deriv'd her
race;

Where she hath now an everlasting place,
Mongst those twelve signes which nightly
we doe see
The heavens bright-shining baudricke to en-
chace;
And is the Virgin, sixt in her degree,
And next her selfe her righteous ballance
hanging bee.

XII

But when she parted hence, she left her
groome,
An yron man, which did on her attend
Alwayes, to execute her stedfast doome,
And willed him with Artegall to wend,
And doe what ever thing he did intend.
His name was Talus, made of yron mould,
Immoveable, resistlesse, without end;
Who in his hand an yron flaile did hould,
With which he thresht out falshood, and
did truth unfould.

XIII

He now went with him in this new inquest,
Him for to aide, if aide he chaunst to neede,
Against that cruell tyrant, which opprest
The faire Irena with his foule misdeede,
And kept the crowne in which she should
succeed.
And now together on their way they bin,
When as they saw a squire in squallid weed,
Lamenting sore his sorowfull sad tyne,
With many bitter teares shed from his
blubbred eyne.

XIV

To whom as they approched, they espide
A sorie sight, as ever seene with eye;
An headlesse ladie lying him beside,
In her owne blood all wallow'd wofully,
That her gay clothes did in discolour die.
Much was he moved at that ruefull sight;
And flam'd with zeale of vengeance in-
wardly,
He askt who had that dame so fouly dight;
Or whether his owne hand, or whether
other wight?

XV

' Ah, woe is me, and well away !' quoth hee,
Bursting forth teares, like springs out of a
banke,
' That ever I this dismall day did see !
Full farre was I from thinking such a
pranke;

Yet litle losse it were, and mickle thanke,
If I should graunt that I have doen the
same,
That I mote drinke the cup whereof she
dranke:
But that I should die guiltie of the blame,
The which another did, who now is fled
with shame.'

XVI

'Who was it then,' sayd Artegall, ' that
wrought ?
And why ? doe it declare unto me trew.'
' A knight,' said he, ' if knight he may be
thought,
That did his hand in ladies bloud embrew,
And for no cause, but as I shall you shew.
This day as I in solace sate hereby
With a fayre love, whose losse I now do
rew,
There came this knight, having in com-
panie
This lucklesse ladie, which now here doth
headlesse lie.

XVII

' He, whether mine seem'd fayrer in his
eye,
Or that he wexed weary of his owne,
Would change with me; but I did it denye;
So did the ladies both, as may be knowne:
But he, whose spirit was with pride up-
blowne,
Would not so rest contented with his right,
But having from his courser her downe
throwne,
Fro me reft mine away by lawlesse might,
And on his steed her set, to beare her out
of sight.

XVIII

' Which when his ladie saw, she follow'd
fast,
And on him catching hold, gan loud to crie
Not so to leave her, nor away to cast,
But rather of his hand besought to die.
With that his sword he drew all wrath-
fully,
And at one stroke cropt off her head with
scorne,
In that same place whereas it now doth
lie.
So he my love away with him hath borne,
And left me here, both his and mine owne
love to morne.'

XIX

' Aread,' sayd he, ' which way then did he
make ?
And by what markes may he be knowne
againe ? '
' To hope,' quoth he, ' him soone to over-
take,
That hence so long departed, is but vaine:
But yet he pricked over yonder plaine,
And as I marked, bore upon his shield,
By which it's easie him to know againe,
A broken sword within a bloodie field;
Expressing well his nature, which the same
did wield.'

XX

No sooner sayd, but streight he after sent
His yron page, who him pursew'd so light,
As that it seem'd above the ground he went:
For he was swift as swallow in her flight,
And strong as lyon in his lordly might.
It was not long before he overtooke
Sir Sanglier (so cleeped was that knight);
Whom at the first he ghessed by his looke,
And by the other markes which of his shield
he tooke.

XXI

He bad him stay, and backe with him re-
tire;
Who, full of scorne to be commaunded so,
The lady to alight did eft require,
Whilest he reformed that uncivill fo:
And streight at him with all his force did
go.
Who mov'd no more therewith, then when
a rocke
Is lightly stricken with some stones throw;
But to him leaping, lent him such a knocke,
That on the ground he layd him like a
sencelesse blocke.

XXII

But ere he could him selfe recure againe,
Him in his iron paw he seized had;
That when he wak't out of his warelesse
paine,
He found him selfe, unwist, so ill bestad,
That lim he could not wag. Thence he
him lad,
Bound like a beast appointed to the stall:
The sight whereof the lady sore adrad,
And fain'd to fly for feare of being thrall;
But he her quickly stayd, and forst to wend
withall.

XXIII

When to the place they came, where
    Artegall
By that same carefull squire did then abide,
He gently gan him to demaund of all,
That did betwixt him and that squire betide.
Who with sterne countenance and indignant
    pride
Did aunswere, that of all he guiltlesse
    stood,
And his accuser thereupon defide:
For neither he did shed that ladies bloud,
Nor tooke away his love, but his owne
    proper good.

XXIV

Well did the squire perceive him selfe too
    weake,
To aunswere his defiaunce in the field,
And rather chose his challenge off to
    breake,
Then to approve his right with speare and
    shield,
And rather guilty chose him selfe to yield.
But Artegall by signes perceiving plaine
That he it was not which that lady kild,
But that strange knight, the fairer love to
    gaine,
Did cast about by sleight the truth there-
    out to straine;

XXV

And sayd: 'Now sure this doubtfull causes
    right
Can hardly but by sacrament be tride,
Or else by ordele, or by blooddy fight;
That ill perhaps mote fall to either side.
But if ye please that I your cause decide,
Perhaps I may all further quarrell end,
So ye will sweare my judgement to abide.'
Thereto they both did franckly condiscend,
And to his doome with listfull eares did
    both attend.

XXVI

'Sith then,' sayd he, 'ye both the dead
    deny,
And both the living lady claime your right,
Let both the dead and living equally
Devided be betwixt you here in sight,
And each of either take his share aright.
But looke, who does dissent from this my
    read,
He for a twelve moneths day shall in de-
    spight

Beare for his penaunce that same ladies
    head;
To witnesse to the world that she by him is
    dead.'

XXVII

Well pleased with that doome was San-
    gliere,
And offred streight the lady to be slaine.
But that same squire, to whom she was
    more dere,
When as he saw she should be cut in twaine,
Did yield, she rather should with him re-
    maine
Alive, then to him selfe be shared dead;
And rather then his love should suffer
    paine,
He chose with shame to beare that ladies
    head.
True love despiseth shame, when life is
    cald in dread.

XXVIII

Whom when so willing Artegall perceaved,
'Not so, thou squire,' he sayd, 'but thine
    I deeme
The living lady, which from thee he
    reaved:
For worthy thou of her doest rightly seeme.
And you, sir knight, that love so light es-
    teeme,
As that ye would for little leave the same,
Take here your owne, that doth you best
    beseeme,
And with it beare the burden of defame;
Your owne dead ladies head, to tell abrode
    your shame.'

XXIX

But Sangliere disdained much his doome,
And sternly gan repine at his beheast;
Ne would for ought obay, as did become,
To beare that ladies head before his
    breast:
Untill that Talus had his pride represt,
And forced him, maulgre, it up to reare.
Who when he saw it bootelesse to resist,
He tooke it up, and thence with him did
    beare,
As rated spaniell takes his burden up for
    feare.

XXX

Much did that squire Sir Artegall adore,
For his great justice, held in high regard;

And as his squire him offred evermore
To serve, for want of other meete reward,
And wend with him on his adventure hard.
But he thereto would by no meanes con-
　　sent;
But leaving him, forth on his journey far'd:
Ne wight with him but onely Talus went;
They two enough t'encounter an whole
　　regiment.

CANTO II

Artegall heares of Florimell ;
　Does with the Pagan fight :
Him slaies, drownes Lady Munera,
　Does race her castle quight

I

NOUGHT is more honorable to a knight,
Ne better doth beseeme brave chevalry,
Then to defend the feeble in their right,
And wrong redresse in such as wend awry.
Whilome those great heroes got thereby
Their greatest glory, for their rightfull
　　deedes,
And place deserved with the gods on hy.
Herein the noblesse of this knight exceedes,
Who now to perils great for justice sake
　　proceedes.

II

To which as he now was uppon the way,
He chaunst to meet a dwarfe in hasty
　　course;
Whom he requir'd his forward hast to
　　stay,
Till he of tidings mote with him discourse.
Loth was the dwarfe, yet did he stay per-
　　forse,
And gan of sundry newes his store to tell,
As to his memory they had recourse:
But chiefely of the fairest Florimell,
How she was found againe, and spousde to
　　Marinell.

III

For this was Dony, Florimels owne dwarfe,
Whom having lost (as ye have heard
　　whyleare)
And finding in the way the scattred scarfe,
The fortune of her life long time did feare.
But of her health when Artegall did heare,
And safe returne, he was full inly glad,
And askt him where and when her bridale
　　cheare

Should be solemniz'd: for if time he had,
He would be there, and honor to her
　　spousall ad.

IV

'Within three daies,' quoth he, 'as I do here,
It will be at the Castle of the Strond;
What time, if naught me let, I will be there
To doe her service, so as I am bond.
But in my way a little here beyond
A cursed cruell Sarazin doth wonne,
That keepes a bridges passage by strong
　　hond,
And many errant knights hath there for-
　　donne;
That makes all men for feare that passage
　　for to shonne.'

V

'What mister wight,' quoth he, 'and how
　　far hence
Is he, that doth to travellers such harmes?'
'He is,' said he, 'a man of great defence;
Expert in battell and in deedes of armes;
And more emboldned by the wicked
　　charmes,
With which his daughter doth him still
　　support;
Having great lordships got and goodly
　　farmes,
Through strong oppression of his powre
　　extort;
By which he stil them holds, and keepes
　　with strong effort.

VI

'And dayly he his wrongs encreaseth more;
For never wight he lets to passe that way,
Over his bridge, albee he rich or poore,
But he him makes his passage-penny pay:
Else he doth hold him backe or beat away.
Thereto he hath a groome of evill guize,
Whose scalp is bare, that bondage doth be-
　　wray,
Which pols and pils the poore in piteous
　　wize,
But he him selfe uppon the rich doth
　　tyrannize.

VII

'His name is hight Pollente, rightly so,
For that he is so puissant and strong,
That with his powre he all doth overgo,
And makes them subject to his mighty
　　wrong;

And some by sleight he eke doth under-
fong:
For on a bridge he custometh to fight,
Which is but narrow, but exceeding lcng;
And in the same are many trap fals pight,
Through which the rider downe doth fall
through oversight.

VIII

' And underneath the same a river flowes,
That is both swift and dangerous deepe
withall;
Into the which whom so he overthrowes,
All destitute of helpe doth headlong fall;
But he him selfe, through practise usuall,
Leapes forth into the floud, and there as-
saies
His foe confused through his sodaine fall,
That horse and man he equally dismaies,
And either both them drownes, or trayter-
ously slaies.

IX

' Then doth he take the spoile of them at
will,
And to his daughter brings, that dwels
thereby:
Who all that comes doth take, and there-
with fill
The coffers of her wicked threasury;
Which she with wrongs hath heaped up so
hy,
That many princes she in wealth exceedes,
And purchast all the countrey lying ny
With the revenue of her plenteous meedes:
Her name is Munera, agreeing with her
deedes.

X

' Thereto she is full faire, and rich attired,
With golden hands and silver feete beside,
That many lords have her to wife desired:
But she them all despiseth for great pride.'
' Now by my life,' sayd he, ' and God to
guide,
None other way will I this day betake,
But by that bridge, whereas he doth abide:
Therefore me thither lead.' No more he
spake,
But thitherward forthright his ready way
did make.

XI

Unto the place he came within a while,
Where on the bridge he ready armed saw

The Sarazin, awayting for some spoile.
Who as they to the passage gan to draw,
A villaine to them came with scull all raw,
That passage money did of them require,
According to the custome of their law.
To whom he aunswerd wroth, ' Loe ! there
thy hire;'
And with that word him strooke, that
streight he did expire.

XII

Which when the Pagan saw, he wexed
wroth,
And streight him selfe unto the fight ad-
drest,
Ne was Sir Artegall behinde: so both
Together ran with ready speares in rest.
Right in the midst, whereas they brest to
brest
Should meete, a trap was letten downe to
fall
Into the floud: streight leapt the carle un-
blest,
Well weening that his foe was falne withall:
But he was well aware, and leapt before
his fall.

XIII

There being both together in the floud,
They each at other tyrannously flew;
Ne ought the water cooled their whot
bloud,
But rather in them kindled choler new.
But there the Paynim, who that use well
knew
To fight in water, great advantage had,
That oftentimes him nigh he overthrew:
And eke the courser whereuppon he rad
Could swim like to a fish, whiles he his
backe bestrad.

XIV

Which oddes when as Sir Artegall espide,
He saw no way but close with him in hast;
And to him driving strongly downe the
tide,
Upon his iron coller griped fast,
That with the straint his wesand nigh he
brast.
There they together strove and struggled
long,
Either the other from his steede to cast;
Ne ever Artegall his griple strong
For any thing wold slacke, but still uppon
him hong.

XV

As when a dolphin and a sele are met
In the wide champian of the ocean plaine:
With cruell chaufe their courages they whet,
The maysterdome of each by force to
    gaine,
And dreadfull battaile twixt them do dar-
    raine:
They snuf, they snort, they bounce, they
    rage, they rore,
That all the sea, disturbed with their traine,
Doth frie with fome above the surges hore:
Such was betwixt these two the trouble-
    some uprore.

XVI

So Artegall at length him forst forsake
His horses backe, for dread of being
    drownd,
And to his handy swimming him betake.
Eftsoones him selfe he from his hold un-
    bownd,
And then no ods at all in him he fownd:
For Artegall in swimming skilfull was,
And durst the depth of any water sownd.
So ought each knight, that use of perill has,
In swimming be expert, through waters
    force to pas.

XVII

Then very doubtfull was the warres event,
Uncertaine whether had the better side:
For both were skild in that experiment,
And both in armes well traind and throughly
    tride.
But Artegall was better breath'd beside,
And towards th' end grew greater in his
    might,
That his faint foe no longer could abide
His puissance, ne beare him selfe upright,
But from the water to the land betooke his
    flight.

XVIII

But Artegall pursewd him still so neare,
With bright Chrysaor in his cruell hand,
That, as his head he gan a litle reare
Above the brincke, to tread upon the land,
He smote it off, that tumbling on the strand
It bit the earth for very fell despight,
And gnashed with his teeth, as if he band
High God, whose goodnesse he despaired
    quight,
Or curst the hand which did that vengeance
    on him dight.

XIX

His corps was carried downe along the lee,
Whose waters with his filthy bloud it
    stayned:
But his blasphemous head, that all might
    see,
He pitcht upon a pole on high ordayned;
Where many years it afterwards remayned,
To be a mirrour to all mighty men,
In whose right hands great power is con-
    tayned,
That none of them the feeble overren,
But alwaies doe their powre within just
    compasse pen.

XX

That done, unto the castle he did wend,
In which the Paynims daughter did abide,
Guarded of many which did her defend:
Of whom he entrance sought, but was de-
    nide,
And with reprochfull blasphemy defide,
Beaten with stones downe from the battil-
    ment,
That he was forced to withdraw aside;
And bad his servant Talus to invent
Which way he enter might without endan-
    germent.

XXI

Eftsoones his page drew to the castle gate,
And with his iron flaile at it let flie,
That all the warders it did sore amate,
The which erewhile spake so reprochfully,
And made them stoupe, that looked earst
    so hie.
Yet still he bet and bounst upon the dore,
And thundred strokes thereon so hideous-
    lie,
That all the peece he shaked from the
    flore,
And filled all the house with feare and
    great uprore.

XXII

With noise whereof the lady forth appeared
Upon the castle wall; and when she saw
The daungerous state in which she stood,
    she feared
The sad effect of her neare overthrow;
And gan entreat that iron man below
To cease his outrage, and him faire be-
    sought,
Sith neither force of stones which they did
    throw,

Nor powr of charms, which she against him
wrought,
Might otherwise prevaile, or make him
cease for ought.

XXIII

But when as yet she saw him to proceede,
Unmov'd with praiers or with piteous
thought,
She ment him to corrupt with goodly
meede;
And causde great sackes with endlesse
riches fraught,
Unto the battilment to be upbrought,
And powred forth over the castle wall,
That she might win some time, though
dearly bought,
Whilest he to gathering of the gold did
fall.
But he was nothing mov'd nor tempted
therewithall;

XXIV

But still continu'd his assault the more,
And layd on load with his huge yron
flaile,
That at the length he has yrent the dore,
And made way for his maister to assaile.
Who being entred, nought did then availe
For wight, against his powre them selves to
reare:
Each one did flie; their hearts began to
faile;
And hid them selves in corners here and
there;
And eke their dame halfe dead did hide
her self for feare.

XXV

Long they her sought, yet no where could
they finde her,
That sure they ween'd she was escapt
away:
But Talus, that could like a limehound
winde her,
And all things secrete wisely could be-
wray,
At length found out whereas she hidden
lay
Under an heape of gold. Thence he her
drew
By the faire lockes, and fowly did array,
Withouten pitty of her goodly hew,
That Artegall him selfe her seemelesse
plight did rew.

XXVI

Yet for no pitty would he change the cours
Of justice, which in Talus hand did lye;
Who rudely hayld her forth without re
morse,
Still holding up her suppliant hands o
hye,
And kneeling at his feete submissively.
But he her suppliant hands, those hands o
gold,
And eke her feete, those feete of silver
trye,
Which sought unrighteousnesse, and just
ice sold,
Chopt off, and nayld on high, that all
might them behold.

XXVII

Her selfe then tooke he by the sclender
wast,
In vaine loud crying, and into the flood
Over the castle wall adowne her cast,
And there her drowned in the durty mud:
But the streame washt away her guilty
blood.
Thereafter all that mucky pelfe he tooke,
The spoile of peoples evill gotten good,
The which her sire had scrap't by hooke
and crooke,
And burning all to ashes, powr'd it downe
the brooke.

XXVIII

And lastly all that castle quite he raced,
Even from the sole of his foundation,
And all the hewen stones thereof defaced,
That there mote be no hope of reparation,
Nor memory thereof to any nation.
All which when Talus throughly had per-
fourmed,
Sir Artegall undid the evill fashion,
And wicked customes of that bridge re-
fourmed:
Which done, unto his former journey he
retourned.

XXIX

In which they measur'd mickle weary
way,
Till that at length nigh to the sea they
drew;
By which as they did travell on a day,
They saw before them, far as they could
vew,
Full many people gathered in a crew;

Whose great assembly they did much ad-
　　mire;
For never there the like resort they knew.
So towardes them they coasted, to enquire
What thing so many nations met did there
　　desire.

XXX

There they beheld a mighty gyant stand
Upon a rocke, and holding forth on hie
An huge great paire of ballance in his
　　hand,
With which he boasted in his surquedrie,
That all the world he would weigh equallie,
If ought he had the same to counterpoys.
For want whereof he weighed vanity,
And fild his ballaunce full of idle toys:
Yet was admired much of fooles, women,
　　and boys.

XXXI

He sayd that he would all the earth up-
　　take,
And all the sea, devided each from either:
So would he of the fire one ballaunce make,
And one of th' ayre, without or wind or
　　wether:
Then would he ballaunce heaven and hell
　　together,
And all that did within them all containe;
Of all whose weight he would not misse a
　　fether:
And looke what surplus did of each re-
　　maine,
He would to his owne part restore the same
　　againe.

XXXII

Forwhy, he sayd, they all unequall were,
And had encroched uppon others share,
Like as the sea (which plaine he shewed
　　there)
Had worne the earth, so did the fire the
　　aire,
So all the rest did others parts empaire,
And so were realmes and nations run awry.
All which he undertooke for to repaire,
In sort as they were formed aunciently;
And all things would reduce unto equality.

XXXIII

Therefore the vulgar did about him flocke,
And cluster thicke unto his leasings vaine,
Like foolish flies about an hony crocke,
In hope by him great benefite to gaine,

And uncontrolled freedome to obtaine.
All which when Artegall did see and heare,
How he mis-led the simple peoples traine,
In sdeignfull wize he drew unto him neare,
And thus unto him spake, without regard
　　or feare:

XXXIV

'Thou that presum'st to weigh the world
　　anew,
And all things to an equall to restore,
In stead of right me seemes great wrong
　　dost shew,
And far above thy forces pitch to sore.
For ere thou limit what is lesse or more
In every thing, thou oughtest first to know,
What was the poyse of every part of yore:
And looke then, how much it doth over-
　　flow,
Or faile thereof, so much is more then just
　　to trow.

XXXV

'For at the first they all created were
In goodly measure by their Makers might,
And weighed out in ballaunces so nere,
That not a dram was missing of their
　　right:
The earth was in the middle centre pight,
In which it doth immoveable abide,
Hemd in with waters like a wall in sight;
And they with aire, that not a drop can
　　slide:
Al which the heavens containe, and in their
　　courses guide.

XXXVI

'Such heavenly justice doth among them
　　raine,
That every one doe know their certaine
　　bound,
In which they doe these many yeares re-
　　maine,
And mongst them al no change hath yet
　　beene found.
But if thou now shouldst weigh them new
　　in pound,
We are not sure they would so long re-
　　maine:
All change is perillous, and all chaunce un-
　　sound.
Therefore leave off to weigh them all
　　againe,
Till we may be assur'd they shall their
　　course retaine.'

XXXVII

'Thou foolishe Elfe,' said then the gyant
    wroth,
'Seest not, how badly all things present
    bee,
And each estate quite out of order goth?
The sea it selfe doest thou not plainely see
Encroch uppon the land there under thee;
And th' earth it selfe how daily its increast
By all that dying to it turned be?
Were it not good that wrong were then
    surceast,
And from the most, that some were given
    to the least?

XXXVIII

'Therefore I will throw downe these moun-
    taines hie,
And make them levell with the lowly
    plaine:
These towring rocks, which reach unto the
    skie,
I will thrust downe into the deepest maine,
And as they were, them equalize againe.
Tyrants, that make men subject to their
    law,
I will suppresse, that they no more may
    raine;
And lordings curbe, that commons over-aw;
And all the wealth of rich men to the poore
    will draw.'

XXXIX

'Of things unseene how canst thou deeme
    aright,'
Then answered the righteous Artegall,
'Sith thou misdeem'st so much of things in
    sight?
What though the sea with waves continuall
Doe eate the earth? it is no more at all,
Ne is the earth the lesse, or loseth ought:
For whatsoever from one place doth fall
Is with the tide unto an other brought:
For there is nothing lost, that may be
    found, if sought.

XL

'Likewise the earth is not augmented more
By all that dying into it doe fade:
For of the earth they formed were of yore;
How ever gay their blossome or their blade
Doe flourish now, they into dust shall vade.
What wrong then is it, if that when they die,
They turne to that whereof they first were
    made?

All in the powre of their great Maker lie:
All creatures must obey the voice of the
    Most Hie.

XLI

'They live, they die, like as He doth ordaine,
Ne ever any asketh reason why.
The hils doe not the lowly dales disdaine;
The dales doe not the lofty hils envy.
He maketh kings to sit in soveraity;
He maketh subjects to their powre obay;
He pulleth downe, He setteth up on hy;
He gives to this, from that He takes away:
For all we have is His: what He list doe,
    He may.

XLII

'What ever thing is done, by Him is donne,
Ne any may His mighty will withstand;
Ne any may His soveraine power shonne,
Ne loose that He hath bound with stedfast
    band.
In vaine therefore doest thou now take in
    hand,
To call to count, or weigh His workes anew,
Whose counsels depth thou canst not under-
    stand;
Sith of things subject to thy daily vew
Thou doest not know the causes, nor their
    courses dew.

XLIII

'For take thy ballaunce, if thou be so wise,
And weigh the winde that under heaven
    doth blow;
Or weigh the light that in the East doth rise;
Or weigh the thought that from mans mind
    doth flow.
But if the weight of these thou canst not
    show,
Weigh but one word which from thy lips
    doth fall:
For how canst thou those greater secrets
    know,
That doest not know the least thing of
    them all?
Ill can he rule the great, that cannot reach
    the small.'

XLIV

Therewith the gyant much abashed sayd,
That he of little things made reckoning
    light,
Yet the least word that ever could be layd
Within his ballaunce he could way aright.

'Which is,' sayd he, 'more heavy then in
weight,
The right or wrong, the false or else the
trew?'
He answered that he would try it streight:
So he the words into his ballaunce threw;
But streight the winged words out of his
ballaunce flew.

XLV

Wroth wext he then, and sayd that words
were light,
Ne would within his ballaunce well abide:
But he could justly weigh the wrong or
right.
'Well then,' sayd Artegall, 'let it be tride.
First in one ballance set the true aside.'
He did so first; and then the false he
layd
In th' other scale; but still it downe did
slide,
And by no meane could in the weight be
stayd:
For by no meanes the false will with the
truth be wayd.

XLVI

'Now take the right likewise,' sayd Arte-
gale,
'And counterpeise the same with so much
wrong.'
So first the right he put into one scale;
And then the gyant strove with puissance
strong
To fill the other scale with so much wrong.
But all the wrongs that he therein could
lay
Might not it peise; yet did he labour long,
And swat, and chauf'd, and proved every
way:
Yet all the wrongs could not a litle right
downe way.

XLVII

Which when he saw, he greatly grew in
rage,
And almost would his balances have broken:
But Artegall him fairely gan asswage,
And said: 'Be not upon thy balance wroken;
For they doe nought but right or wrong be-
token;
But in the mind the doome of right must
bee:

And so likewise of words, the which be
spoken,
The eare must be the ballance, to decree
And judge, whether with truth or falshood
they agree.

XLVIII

'But set the truth and set the right aside,
For they with wrong or falshood will not
fare;
And put two wrongs together to be tride,
Or else two falses, of each equall share,
And then together doe them both compare:
For truth is one, and right is ever one.'
So did he, and then plaine it did appeare,
Whether of them the greater were attone.
But right sate in the middest of the beame
alone.

XLIX

But he the right from thence did thrust
away,
For it was not the right which he did seeke;
But rather strove extremities to way,
Th' one to diminish, th' other for to eeke:
For of the meane he greatly did misleeke.
Whom when so lewdly minded Talus found,
Approching nigh unto him, cheeke by
cheeke,
He shouldered him from off the higher
ground,
And down the rock him throwing, in the
sea him dround.

L

Like as a ship, whom cruell tempest drives
Upon a rocke with horrible dismay,
Her shattered ribs in thousand peeces rives,
And spoyling all her geares and goodly ray,
Does make her selfe misfortunes piteous
pray:
So downe the cliffe the wretched gyant
tumbled;
His battred ballances in peeces lay,
His timbered bones all broken rudely rum-
bled:
So was the high aspyring with huge ruine
humbled.

LI

That when the people, which had there
about
Long wayted, saw his sudden desolation,
They gan to gather in tumultuous rout,
And mutining, to stirre up civill faction,

For certaine losse of so great expectation.
For well they hoped to have got great
    good,
And wondrous riches by his innovation.
Therefore resolving to revenge his blood,
They rose in armes, and all in battell order
    stood.

LII

Which lawlesse multitude him comming
    too,
In warlike wise, when Artegall did vew,
He much was troubled, ne wist what to
    doo.
For loth he was his noble hands t' embrew
In the base blood of such a rascall crew;
And otherwise, if that he should retire,
He fear'd least they with shame would him
    pursew.
Therefore he Talus to them sent, t' inquire
The cause of their array, and truce for to
    desire.

LIII

But soone as they him nigh approching
    spide,
They gan with all their weapons him as-
    say,
And rudely stroke at him on every side:
Yet nought they could him hurt, ne ought
    dismay.
But when at them he with his flaile gan
    lay,
He like a swarme of flyes them overthrew;
Ne any of them durst come in his way,
But here and there before his presence
    flew,
And hid themselves in holes and bushes
    from his vew.

LIV

As when a faulcon hath with nimble flight
Flowne at a flush of ducks, foreby the
    brooke,
The trembling foule, dismayd with dread-
    full sight
Of death, the which them almost overtooke,
Doe hide themselves from her astonying
    looke
Amongst the flags and covert round about.
When Talus saw they all the field for-
    sooke,
And none appear'd of all that raskall rout,
To Artegall he turn'd, and went with him
    throughout.

CANTO III

The spousals of faire Florimell,
    Where turney many knights :
There Braggadochio is uncas'd
    In all the ladies sights.

I

After long stormes and tempests over-
    blowne,
The sunne at length his joyous face doth
    cleare:
So when as Fortune all her spight hath
    showne,
Some blisfull houres at last must needes
    appeare;
Else should afflicted wights oftimes de-
    speire.
So comes it now to Florimell by tourne,
After long sorrowes suffered whyleare,
In which captiv'd she many moneths did
    mourne,
To tast of joy, and to wont pleasures to re-
    tourne.

II

Who being freed from Proteus cruell band
By Marinell, was unto him affide,
And by him brought againe to Faerie Land;
Where he her spous'd, and made his joyous
    bride.
The time and place was blazed farre and
    wide,
And solemne feasts and giusts ordain'd
    therefore.
To which there did resort from every
    side
Of lords and ladies infinite great store;
Ne any knight was absent, that brave cour-
    age bore.

III

To tell the glorie of the feast that day,
The goodly service, the devicefull sights,
The bridegromes state, the brides most
    rich aray,
The pride of ladies, and the worth of
    knights,
The royall banquets, and the rare de-
    lights
Were worke fit for an herauld, not for
    me:
But for so much as to my lot here lights,
That with this present treatise doth agree,
True vertue to advance, shall here re-
    counted bee.

IV

When all men had with full satietie
Of meates and drinkes their appetites suf-
    fiz'd,
To deedes of armes and proofe of chevalrie
They gan themselves addresse, full rich
    aguiz'd,
As each one had his furnitures deviz'd.
And first of all issu'd Sir Marinell,
And with him sixe knights more, which en-
    terpriz'd
To chalenge all in right of Florimell,
And to maintaine that she all others did
    excell.

V

The first of them was hight Sir Orimont,
A noble knight, and tride in hard assayes;
The second had to name Sir Bellisont,
But second unto none in prowesse prayse;
The third was Brunell, famous in his dayes;
The fourth Ecastor, of exceeding might;
The fift Armeddan, skild in lovely layes;
The sixt was Lansack, a redoubted knight:
All sixe well seene in armes, and prov'd in
    many a fight.

VI

And them against came all that list to
    giust,
From every coast and countrie under sunne:
None was debard, but all had leave that
    lust.
The trompets sound; then all together
    ronne.
Full many deedes of armes that day were
    donne,
And many knights unhorst, and many
    wounded,
As fortune fell; yet litle lost or wonne:
But all that day the greatest prayse re-
    dounded
To Marinell, whose name the heralds loud
    resounded.

VII

The second day, so soone as morrow light
Appear'd in heaven, into the field they
    came,
And there all day continew'd cruell fight,
With divers fortune fit for such a game,
In which all strove with perill to winne
    fame.
Yet whether side was victor note be ghest:
But at the last the trompets did proclame

That Marinell that day deserved best.
So they disparted were, and all men went
    to rest.

VIII

The third day came, that should due tryall
    lend
Of all the rest, and then this warlike crew
Together met, of all to make an end.
There Marinell great deeds of armes did
    shew;
And through the thickest like a lyon flew,
Rashing off helmes, and ryving plates a
    sonder,
That every one his daunger did eschew.
So terribly his dreadfull strokes did thonder,
That all men stood amaz'd, and at his
    might did wonder.

IX

But what on earth can alwayes happie
    stand?
The greater prowesse greater perils find.
So farre he past amongst his enemies band,
That they have him enclosed so behind,
As by no meanes he can himselfe outwind.
And now perforce they have him prisoner
    taken;
And now they doe with captive bands him
    bind;
And now they lead him thence, of all for-
    saken,
Unlesse some succour had in time him over-
    taken.

X

It fortun'd whylest they were thus ill beset,
Sir Artegall into the tilt-yard came,
With Braggadochio, whom he lately met
Upon the way, with that his snowy dame.
Where when he understood by common
    fame
What evill hap to Marinell betid,
He much was mov'd at so unworthie shame,
And streight that boaster prayd, with whom
    he rid,
To change his shield with him, to be the
    better hid.

XI

So forth he went, and soone them over hent,
Where they were leading Marinell away;
Whom he assayld with dreadlesse hardiment,
And forst the burden of their prize to stay.
They were an hundred knights of that array;

Of which th' one halfe upon himselfe did set,
The other stayd behind to gard the pray.
But he ere long the former fiftie bet;
And from the other fiftie soone the prisoner
    fet.

XII

So backe he brought Sir Marinell againe;
Whom having quickly arm'd againe anew,
They both together joyned might and
    maine,
To set afresh on all the other crew.
Whom with sore havocke soone they over-
    threw,
And chaced quite out of the field, that none
Against them durst his head to perill shew.
So were they left lords of the field alone:
So Marinell by him was rescu'd from his
    fone.

XIII

Which when he had perform'd, then backe
    againe
To Braggadochio did his shield restore:
Who all this while behind him did remaine,
Keeping there close with him in pretious
    store
That his false ladie, as ye heard afore.
Then did the trompets sound, and judges
    rose,
And all these knights, which that day ar-
    mour bore,
Came to the open hall, to listen whose
The honour of the prize should be adjudg'd
    by those.

XIV

And thether also came in open sight
Fayre Florimell, into the common hall,
To greet his guerdon unto every knight,
And best to him to whom the best should
    fall.
Then for that stranger knight they loud
    did call,
To whom that day they should the girlond
    yield:
Who came not forth: but for Sir Artegall
Came Braggadochio, and did shew his shield,
Which bore the sunne brode blazed in a
    golden field.

XV

The sight whereof did all with gladnesse
    fill:
So unto him they did addeeme the prise

Of all that tryumph. Then the trompets
    shrill
Don Braggadochios name resounded thrise:
So courage lent a cloke to cowardise.
And then to him came fayrest Florimell,
And goodly gan to greet his brave em-
    prise,
And thousand thankes him yeeld, that had
    so well
Approv'd that day that she all others did
    excell.

XVI

To whom the boaster, that all knights did
    blot,
With proud disdaine did scornefull answere
    make,
That what he did that day, he did it not
For her, but for his owne deare ladies
    sake,
Whom on his perill he did undertake,
Both her and eke all others to excell:
And further did uncomely speaches crake.
Much did his words the gentle ladie quell,
And turn'd aside for shame to heare what
    he did tell.

XVII

Then forth he brought his snowy Florimele,
Whom Trompart had in keeping there be-
    side,
Covered from peoples gazement with a
    vele.
Whom when discovered they had throughly
    eide,
With great amazement they were stupe-
    fide;
And said, that surely Florimell it was,
Or if it were not Florimell so tride,
That Florimell her selfe she then did pas.
So feeble skill of perfect things the vulgar
    has.

XVIII

Which when as Marinell beheld likewise,
He was therewith exceedingly dismayd;
Ne wist he what to thinke, or to devise,
But, like as one whom feends had made
    affrayd,
He long astonisht stood, ne ought he sayd,
Ne ought he did, but with fast fixed eies
He gazed still upon that snowy mayd;
Whom ever as he did the more avize,
The more to be true Florimell he did sur-
    mize.

XIX

As when two sunnes appeare in the azure
  skye,
Mounted in Phœbus charet fierie bright,
Both darting forth faire beames to each
  mans eye,
And both adorn'd with lampes of flaming
  light,
All that behold so strange prodigious
  sight,
Not knowing Natures worke, nor what to
  weene,
Are rapt with wonder and with rare af-
  fright:
So stood Sir Marinell, when he had seene
The semblant of this false by his faire
  beauties queene.

XX

All which when Artegall, who all this
  while
Stood in the preasse close covered, well
  advewed,
And saw that boasters pride and gracelesse
  guile,
He could no longer beare, but forth issewed,
And unto all himselfe there open shewed,
And to the boaster said: 'Thou losell
  base,
That hast with borrowed plumes thy selfe
  endewed,
And others worth with leasings doest deface,
When they are all restor'd, thou shalt rest
  in disgrace.

XXI

'That shield, which thou doest beare, was
  it indeed,
Which this dayes honour sav'd to Marinell;
But not that arme, nor thou the man, I
  reed,
Which didst that service unto Florimell.
For proofe shew forth thy sword, and let
  it tell
What strokes, what dreadfull stoure it
  stird this day:
Or shew the wounds which unto thee befell;
Or shew the sweat with which thou diddest
  sway
So sharpe a battell, that so many did dismay.

XXII

'But this the sword which wrought those
  cruell stounds,
And this the arme the which that shield
  did beare,
And these the signes,' (so shewed forth his
  wounds)
'By which that glorie gotten doth appeare.
As for this ladie, which he sheweth here,
Is not (I wager) Florimell at all;
But some fayre franion, fit for such a fere,
That by misfortune in his hand did fall.'
For proofe whereof, he bad them Florimell
  forth call.

XXIII

So forth the noble ladie was ybrought,
Adorn'd with honor and all comely grace:
Whereto her bashfull shamefastnesse
  ywrought
A great increase in her faire blushing face;
As roses did with lillies interlace.
For of those words, the which that boaster
  threw,
She inly yet conceived great disgrace.
Whom when as all the people such did
  vew,
They shouted loud, and signes of gladnesse
  all did shew.

XXIV

Then did he set her by that snowy one,
Like the true saint beside the image set,
Of both their beauties to make paragone,
And triall, whether should the honor get.
Streight way so soone as both together met,
Th' enchaunted damzell vanisht into
  nought:
Her snowy substance melted as with heat,
Ne of that goodly hew remayned ought,
But th' emptie girdle, which about her
  wast was wrought.

XXV

As when the daughter of Thaumantes faire
Hath in a watry cloud displayed wide
Her goodly bow, which paints the liquid
  ayre;
That all men wonder at her colours pride;
All suddenly, ere one can looke aside,
The glorious picture vanisheth away,
Ne any token doth thereof abide:
So did this ladies goodly forme decay,
And into nothing goe, ere one could it be-
  wray.

XXVI

Which when as all that present were be-
  held,
They stricken were with great astonishment,
And their faint harts with senselesse hor-
  rour queld,
To see the thing, that seem'd so excellent,
So stolen from their fancies wonderment;
That what of it became none understood.
And Braggadochio selfe with dreriment
So daunted was, in his despeyring mood,
That like a lifelesse corse immoveable he
  stood.

XXVII

But Artegall that golden belt uptooke,
The which of all her spoyle was onely left;
Which was not hers, as many it mistooke,
But Florimells owne girdle, from her reft,
While she was flying, like a weary weft,
From that foule monster which did her
  compell
To perils great; which he unbuckling eft,
Presented to the fayrest Florimell;
Who round about her tender wast it fitted
  well.

XXVIII

Full many ladies often had assayd
About their middles that faire belt to knit;
And many a one suppos'd to be a mayd:
Yet it to none of all their loynes would fit,
Till Florimell about her fastned it.
Such power it had, that to no womans wast
By any skill or labour it would sit,
Unlesse that she were continent and chast,
But it would lose or breake, that many had
  disgrast.

XXIX

Whilest thus they busied were bout Flori-
  mell,
And boastfull Braggadochio to defame,
Sir Guyon, as by fortune then befell,
Forth from the thickest preasse of people
  came,
His owne good steed, which he had stolne,
  to clame;
And th' one hand seizing on his golden bit,
With th' other drew his sword: for with
  the same
He ment the thiefe there deadly to have
  smit:
And had he not bene held, he nought had
  fayld of it.

XXX

Thereof great hurly burly moved was
Throughout the hall, for that same war-
  like horse:
For Braggadochio would not let him pas;
And Guyon would him algates have per-
  forse,
Or it approve upon his carrion corse.
Which troublous stirre when Artegall per-
  ceived,
He nigh them drew to stay th' avengers
  forse,
And gan inquire how was that steed be-
  reaved,
Whether by might extort, or else by slight
  deceaved.

XXXI

Who all that piteous storie, which befell
About that wofull couple which were slaine,
And their young bloodie babe, to him gan
  tell;
With whom whiles he did in the wood re-
  maine,
His horse purloyned was by subtill traine:
For which he chalenged the thiefe to fight.
But he for nought could him thereto con-
  straine;
For as the death he hated such despight,
And rather had to lose, then trie in armes
  his right.

XXXII

Which Artegall well hearing, though no
  more
By law of armes there neede ones right to
  trie,
As was the wont of warlike knights of
  yore,
Then that his foe should him the field de-
  nie,
Yet further right by tokens to descrie,
He askt what privie tokens he did beare.
' If that,' said Guyon, ' may you satisfie,
Within his mouth a blacke spot doth ap-
  peare,
Shapt like a horses shoe, who list to seeke
  it there.'

XXXIII

Whereof to make due tryall, one did take
The horse in hand, within his mouth to
  looke:
But with his heeles so sorely he him strake,
That all his ribs he quite in peeces broke,

That never word from that day forth he
　　spoke.
Another, that would seeme to have more
　　wit,
Him by the bright embrodered hedstall
　　tooke:
But by the shoulder him so sore he bit,
That he him maymed quite, and all his
　　shoulder split.

XXXIV

Ne he his mouth would open unto wight,
Untill that Guyon selfe unto him spake,
And called Brigadore (so was he hight);
Whose voice so soone as he did under-
　　take,
Eftsoones he stood as still as any stake,
And suffred all his secret marke to see:
And when as he him nam'd, for joy he
　　brake
His bands, and follow'd him with gladfull
　　glee,
And friskt, and flong aloft, and louted low
　　on knee.

XXXV

Thereby Sir Artegall did plaine areed,
That unto him the horse belong'd, and
　　sayd:
'Lo there, Sir Guyon, take to you the
　　steed,
As he with golden saddle is arayd;
And let that losell, plainely now displayd,
Hence fare on foot, till he an horse have
　　gayned.'
But the proud boaster gan his doome up-
　　brayd,
And him revil'd, and rated, and disdayned,
That judgement so unjust against him had
　　ordayned.

XXXVI

Much was the knight incenst with his lewd
　　word,
To have revenged that his villeny;
And thrise did lay his hand upon his sword,
To have him slaine, or dearely doen aby.
But Guyon did his choler pacify,
Saying, 'Sir knight, it would dishonour
　　bee
To you, that are our judge of equity,
To wreake your wrath on such a carle as
　　hee:
It's punishment enough, that all his shame
　　doe see.'

XXXVII

So did he mitigate Sir Artegall;
But Talus by the backe the boaster hent,
And drawing him out of the open hall,
Upon him did inflict this punishment:
First he his beard did shave, and fowly
　　shent;
Then from him reft his shield, and it ren-
　　verst,
And blotted out his armes with falshood
　　blent,
And himselfe baffuld, and his armes un-
　　herst,
And broke his sword in twaine, and all his
　　armour sperst.

XXXVIII

The whiles his guilefull groome was fled
　　away:
But vaine it was to thinke from him to
　　flie.
Who overtaking him did disaray,
And all his face deform'd with infamie,
And out of court him scourged openly.
So ought all faytours, that true knighthood
　　shame,
And armes dishonour with base villanie,
From all brave knights be banisht with
　　defame:
For oft their lewdnes blotteth good deserts
　　with blame.

XXXIX

Now when these counterfeits were thus
　　uncased
Out of the foreside of their forgerie,
And in the sight of all men cleane dis-
　　graced,
All gan to jest and gibe full merilie
At the remembrance of their knaverie.
Ladies can laugh at ladies, knights at
　　knights,
To thinke with how great vaunt of braverie
He them abused, through his subtill slights,
And what a glorious shew he made in all
　　their sights.

XL

There leave we them in pleasure and re-
　　past
Spending their joyous dayes and gladfull
　　nights,
And taking usurie of time forepast,
With all deare delices and rare delights,
Fit for such ladies and such lovely knights:

And turne we here to this faire furrowes
 end
Our wearie yokes, to gather fresher sprights,
That, when as time to Artegall shall tend,
We on his first adventure may him forward
 send.

CANTO IV

Artegall dealeth right betwixt
Two brethren that doe strive :
Saves Terpine from the gallow tree,
And doth from death reprive.

I

WHO so upon him selfe will take the skill
True justice unto people to divide,
Had neede have mightie hands, for to fulfill
That which he doth with righteous doome
 decide,
And for to maister wrong and puissant
 pride.
For vaine it is to deeme of things aright,
And makes wrong doers justice to deride,
Unlesse it be perform'd with dreadlesse
 might :
For powre is the right hand of Justice
 truely hight.

II

Therefore whylome to knights of great
 emprise
The charge of Justice given was in trust,
That they might execute her judgements
 wise,
And with their might beat downe licentious
 lust,
Which proudly did impugne her sentence
 just.
Whereof no braver president this day
Remaines on earth, preserv'd from yron
 rust
Of rude oblivion, and long times decay,
Then this of Artegall, which here we have
 to say.

III

Who, having lately left that lovely payre,
Enlincked fast in wedlockes loyall bond,
Bold Marinell with Florimell the fayre,
With whom great feast and goodly glee he
 fond,
Departed from the Castle of the Strond,
To follow his adventures first intent,
Which long agoe he taken had in hond :

Ne wight with him for his assistance went,
But that great yron groome, his gard and
 government.

IV

With whom as he did passe by the sea
 shore,
He chaunst to come whereas two comely
 squires,
Both brethren, whom one wombe together
 bore,
But stirred up with different desires,
Together strove, and kindled wrathfull
 fires :
And them beside two seemely damzels
 stood,
By all meanes seeking to asswage their ires,
Now with faire words ; but words did little
 good,
Now with sharpe threats ; but threats the
 more increast their mood.

V

And there before them stood a coffer
 strong,
Fast bound on every side with iron bands,
But seeming to have suffred mickle wrong,
Either by being wreckt uppon the sands,
Or being carried farre from forraine lands.
Seem'd that for it these squires at ods did
 fall,
And bent against them selves their cruell
 hands.
But evermore, those damzels did forestall
Their furious encounter, and their fierce-
 nesse pall.

VI

But firmely fixt they were, with dint of
 sword
And battailes doubtfull proofe their rights
 to try,
Ne other end their fury would afford,
But what to them fortune would justify.
So stood they both in readinesse, thereby
To joyne the combate with cruell intent ;
When Artegall arriving happily,
Did stay a while their greedy bickerment,
Till he had questioned the cause of their
 dissent.

VII

To whom the elder did this aunswere
 frame :
' Then weete ye, sir, that we two brethren be,

To whom our sire, Milesio by name,
Did equally bequeath his lands in fee,
Two ilands, which ye there before you see
Not farre in sea; of which the one appeares
But like a little mount of small degree;
Yet was as great and wide ere many yeares,
As that same other isle, that greater bredth
        now beares.

VIII

' But tract of time, that all things doth de-
        cay,
And this devouring sea, that naught doth
        spare,
The most part of my land hath washt
        away,
And throwne it up unto my brothers share:
So his encreased, but mine did empaire.
Before which time I lov'd, as was my lot,
That further mayd, hight Philtera the faire,
With whom a goodly dowre I should have
        got,
And should have joyned bene to her in
        wedlocks knot.

IX

' Then did my younger brother Amidas
Love that same other damzell, Lucy bright,
To whom but little dowre allotted was;
Her vertue was the dowre that did delight.
What better dowre can to a dame be hight?
But now when Philtra saw my lands decay,
And former livelod fayle, she left me
        quight,
And to my brother did ellope streight way:
Who, taking her from me, his owne love
        left astray.

X

' She seeing then her selfe forsaken so,
Through dolorous despaire, which she con-
        ceyved,
Into the sea her selfe did headlong throw,
Thinking to have her griefe by death be-
        reaved.
But see how much her purpose was de-
        ceaved.
Whilest thus amidst the billowes beating
        of her
Twixt life and death, long to and fro she
        weaved,
She chaunst unwares to light uppon this
        coffer,
Which to her in that daunger hope of life
        did offer.

XI

' The wretched mayd, that earst desir'd to
        die,
When as the paine of death she tasted had,
And but halfe seene his ugly visnomie,
Gan to repent that she had beene so mad,
For any death to chaunge life, though most
        bad:
And catching hold of this sea-beaten chest,
The lucky pylot of her passage sad,
After long tossing in the seas distrest,
Her weary barke at last uppon mine isle
        did rest.

XII

' Where I, by chaunce then wandring on the
        shore,
Did her espy, and through my good endev-
        our
From dreadfull mouth of death, which
        threatned sore
Her to have swallow'd up, did helpe to
        save her.
She then, in recompence of that great fa-
        vour
Which I on her bestowed, bestowed on
        me
The portion of that good which fortune
        gave her,
Together with her selfe in dowry free;
Both goodly portions, but of both the bet-
        ter she.

XIII

' Yet in this coffer, which she with her
        brought,
Great threasure sithence we did finde con-
        tained;
Which as our owne we tooke, and so it
        thought.
But this same other damzell since hath
        fained,
That to her selfe that threasure apper-
        tained;
And that she did transport the same by
        sea,
To bring it to her husband new ordained,
But suffred cruell shipwracke by the way.
But whether it be so or no, I can not say.

XIV

' But whether it indeede be so or no,
This doe I say, that what so good or ill
Or God or Fortune unto me did throw,
Not wronging any other by my will,

I hold mine owne, and so will hold it still.
And though my land he first did winne
    away,
And then my love (though now it little
    skill)
Yet my good lucke he shall not likewise
    pray;
But I will it defend, whilst ever that I
    may.'

XV

So having sayd, the younger did ensew:
' Full true it is, what so about our land
My brother here declared hath to you:
But not for it this ods twixt us doth stand,
But for this threasure throwne uppon his
    strand;
Which well I prove, as shall appeare by
    triall,
To be this maides with whom I fastned
    hand,
Known by good markes and perfect good
    espiall,
Therefore it ought be rendred her without
    deniall.'

XVI

When they thus ended had, the knight be-
    gan:
Certes your strife were easie to accord,
Would ye remit it to some righteous man.'
Unto your selfe,' said they, ' we give our
    word,
To bide what judgement ye shall us af-
    ford.'
Then for assuraunce to my doome to
    stand,
Under my foote let each lay downe his
    sword,
And then you shall my sentence under-
    stand.'
So each of them layd downe his sword out
    of his hand.

XVII

Then Artegall thus to the younger sayd:
Now tell me, Amidas, if that ye may,
Your brothers land, the which the sea hath
    layd
Unto your part, and pluckt from his away,
By what good right doe you withhold this
    day ?'
What other right,' quoth he, ' should you
    esteeme,
But that the sea it to my share did lay ?'

' Your right is good,' sayd he, ' and so I
    deeme,
That what the sea unto you sent your own
    should seeme.'

XVIII

Then turning to the elder thus he sayd:
' Now, Bracidas, let this likewise be showne:
Your brothers threasure, which from him is
    strayd,
Being the dowry of his wife well knowne,
By what right doe you claime to be your
    owne ? '
' What other right,' quoth he, ' should you
    esteeme,
But that the sea hath it unto me throwne ? '
' Your right is good,' sayd he, ' and so I
    deeme,
That what the sea unto you sent your own
    should seeme.

XIX

' For equall right in equall things doth
    stand;
For what the mighty sea hath once possest,
And plucked quite from all possessors hand,
Whether by rage of waves, that never
    rest,
Or else by wracke, that wretches hath dis-
    trest,
He may dispose by his imperiall might,
As thing at randon left, to whom he list.
So, Amidas, the land was yours first hight,
And so the threasure yours is, Bracidas, by
    right.'

XX

When he his sentence thus pronounced had,
Both Amidas and Philtra were displeased:
But Bracidas and Lucy were right glad,
And on the threasure by that judgement
    seased.
So was their discord by this doome ap-
    peased,
And each one had his right. Then Arte-
    gall,
When as their sharpe contention he had
    ceased,
Departed on his way, as did befall,
To follow his old quest, the which him
    forth did call.

XXI

So as he travelled upon the way,
He chaunst to come, where happily he spide

A rout of many people farre away;
To whom his course he hastily applide,
To weete the cause of their assemblaunce
    wide.
To whom when he approched neare in sight,
(An uncouth sight) he plainely then de-
    scride
To be a troupe of women warlike dight,
With weapons in their hands, as ready for
    to fight.

XXII

And in the midst of them he saw a knight,
With both his hands behinde him pinnoed
    hard,
And round about his necke an halter tight,
As ready for the gallow tree prepard:
His face was covered, and his head was
    bar'd,
That who he was uneath was to descry;
And with full heavy heart with them he
    far'd,
Griev'd to the soule, and groning in-
    wardly,
That he of womens hands so base a death
    should dy.

XXIII

But they like tyrants, mercilesse the more,
Rejoyced at his miserable case,
And him reviled, and reproched sore
With bitter taunts, and termes of vile dis-
    grace.
Now when as Artegall, arriv'd in place,
Did aske what cause brought that man to
    decay,
They round about him gan to swarme
    apace,
Meaning on him their cruell hands to lay,
And to have wrought unwares some vil-
    lanous assay.

XXIV

But he was soone aware of their ill minde,
And drawing backe deceived their intent;
Yet though him selfe did shame on woman-
    kinde
His mighty hand to shend, he Talus sent
To wrecke on them their follies hardy-
    ment:
Who with few sowces of his yron flaile
Dispersed all their troupe incontinent,
And sent them home to tell a piteous tale
Of their vaine prowesse turned to their pro-
    per bale.

XXV

But that same wretched man, ordaynd to
    die,
They left behind them, glad to be so quit:
Him Talus tooke out of perplexitie,
And horrour of fowle death for knight unfit,
Who more then losse of life ydreaded it;
And him restoring unto living light,
So brought unto his lord, where he did sit,
Beholding all that womanish weake fight;
Whom soone as he beheld, he knew, and
    thus behight:

XXVI

' Sir Turpine, haplesse man, what make
    you here ?
Or have you lost your selfe and your dis-
    cretion,
That ever in this wretched case ye were ?
Or have ye yeelded you to proude oppres-
    sion
Of womens powre, that boast of mens sub-
    jection ?
Or else what other deadly dismall day
Is falne on you, by heavens hard direction,
That ye were runne so fondly far astray,
As for to lead your selfe unto your owne
    decay ?'

XXVII

Much was the man confounded in his mind,
Partly with shame, and partly with dismay,
That all astonisht he him selfe did find,
And little had for his excuse to say,
But onely thus: ' Most haplesse well ye
    may
Me justly terme, that to this shame am
    brought,
And made the scorne of knighthod this
    same day.
But who can scape what his owne fate hath
    wrought ?
The worke of heavens will surpasseth hu-
    maine thought.'

XXVIII

' Right true: but faulty men use oftentimes
To attribute their folly unto fate,
And lay on heaven the guilt of their owne
    crimes.
But tell, Sir Terpin, ne let you amate
Your misery, how fell ye in this state ?'
' Then sith ye needs,' quoth he, ' will know
    my shame,
And all the ill which chaunst to me of late

I shortly will to you rehearse the same,
In hope ye will not turne misfortune to my
   blame.

XXIX

'Being desirous (as all knights are woont)
Through hard adventures deedes of armes
   to try,
And after fame and honour for to hunt,
I heard report that farre abrode did fly,
That a proud Amazon did late defy
All the brave knights that hold of Maiden-
   head,
And unto them wrought all the villany
That she could forge in her malicious head,
Which some hath put to shame, and many
   done be dead.

XXX

'The cause, they say, of this her cruell
   hate,
Is for the sake of Bellodant the bold,
To whom she bore most fervent love of
   late,
And wooed him by all the waies she could:
But when she saw at last, that he ne would
For ought or nought be wonne unto her
   will,
She turn'd her love to hatred manifold,
And for his sake vow'd to doe all the ill
Which she could doe to knights; which
   now she doth fulfill.

XXXI

'For all those knights, the which by force
   or guile
She doth subdue, she fowly doth entreate.
First she doth them of warlike armes de-
   spoile,
And cloth in womens weedes: and then
   with threat
Doth them compell to worke, to earne their
   meat,
To spin, to card, to sew, to wash, to wring;
Ne doth she give them other thing to
   eat,
But bread and water, or like feeble thing,
Them to disable from revenge adventuring.

XXXII

'But if through stout disdaine of manly
   mind,
Any her proud observaunce will withstand,
Uppon that gibbet, which is there behind,
She causeth them be hang'd up out of hand;

In which condition I right now did stand.
For being overcome by her in fight,
And put to that base service of her band,
I rather chose to die in lives despight,
Then lead that shamefull life, unworthy of
   a knight.'

XXXIII

'How hight that Amazon,' sayd Artegall,
'And where and how far hence does she
   abide?'
'Her name,' quoth he, 'they Radigund doe
   call,
A princesse of great powre and greater
   pride,
And queene of Amazons, in armes well
   tride
And sundry battels, which she hath at-
   chieved
With great successe, that her hath glorifide,
And made her famous, more then is be-
   lieved;
Ne would I it have ween'd, had I not late
   it prieved.'

XXXIV

'Now sure,' said he, 'and by the faith that I
To Maydenhead and noble knighthood owe,
I will not rest, till I her might doe trie,
And venge the shame that she to knights
   doth show.
Therefore, Sir Terpin, from you lightly
   throw
This squalid weede, the patterne of di-
   spaire,
And wend with me, that ye may see and
   know,
How fortune will your ruin'd name repaire,
And knights of Maidenhead, whose praise
   she would empaire.'

XXXV

With that, like one that hopelesse was re-
   pryv'd
From deathes dore, at which he lately lay,
Those yron fetters wherewith he was gyv'd,
The badges of reproch, he threw away,
And nimbly did him dight to guide the
   way
Unto the dwelling of that Amazone,
Which was from thence not past a mile or
   tway:
A goodly citty and a mighty one,
The which of her owne name she called
   Radegone.

XXXVI

Where they arriving, by the watchman were
Descried streight, who all the citty warned,
How that three warlike persons did appeare,
Of which the one him seem'd a knight all armed,
And th' other two well likely to have harmed.
Eftsoones the people all to harnesse ran,
And like a sort of bees in clusters swarmed:
Ere long their queene her selfe, halfe like a man,
Came forth into the rout, and them t' array began.

XXXVII

And now the knights, being arrived neare,
Did beat upon the gates to enter in,
And at the porter, skorning them so few,
Threw many threats, if they the towne did win,
To teare his flesh in peeces for his sin.
Which when as Radigund there comming heard,
Her heart for rage did grate, and teeth did grin:
She bad that streight the gates should be unbard,
And to them way to make, with weapons well prepard.

XXXVIII

Soone as the gates were open to them set,
They pressed forward, entraunce to have made.
But in the middle way they were ymet
With a sharpe showre of arrowes, which them staid,
And better bad advise, ere they assaid
Unknowen perill of bold womens pride.
Then all that rout uppon them rudely laid,
And heaped strokes so fast on every side,
And arrowes haild so thicke, that they could not abide.

XXXIX

But Radigund her selfe, when she espide
Sir Terpin, from her direfull doome acquit,
So cruell doale amongst her maides divide,
T' avenge that shame they did on him commit,
All sodainely enflam'd with furious fit,
Like a fell lionesse at him she flew,
And on his head-peece him so fiercely smit
That to the ground him quite she overthrew,
Dismayd so with the stroke that he n
colours knew.

XL

Soone as she saw him on the ground t
grovell,
She lightly to him leapt, and in his necke
Her proud foote setting, at his head di
levell,
Weening at once her wrath on him t
wreake,
And his contempt, that did her judg'men
breake.
As when a beare hath seiz'd her cruel
clawes
Upon the carkasse of some beast to
weake,
Proudly stands over, and a while dot
pause,
To heare the piteous beast pleading he
plaintiffe cause.

XLI

Whom when as Artegall in that distresse
By chaunce beheld, he left the bloud
slaughter
In which he swam, and ranne to his r
dresse.
There her assayling fiercely fresh, h
raught her
Such an huge stroke, that it of sence di
traught her:
And had she not it warded warily,
It had depriv'd her mother of a daughter.
Nathlesse for all the powre she did apply
It made her stagger oft, and stare wit
ghastly eye.

XLII

Like to an eagle in his kingly pride,
Soring through his wide empire of the air
To weather his brode sailes, by chaunc
hath spide
A goshauke, which hath seized for he
share
Uppon some fowle, that should her fea
prepare;
With dreadfull force he flies at her byliv
That with his souce, which none endure
dare,
Her from the quarrey he away doth driv
And from her griping pounce the gree
prey doth rive.

XLIII

But soone as she her sence recover'd had,
She fiercely towards him her selfe gan dight,
Through vengeful wrath and sdeignfull
    pride half mad:
For never had she suffred such despight.
But ere she could joyne hand with him to
    fight,
Her warlike maides about her flockt so
    fast,
That they disparted them, maugre their
    might,
And with their troupes did far a sunder
    cast:
But mongst the rest the fight did untill
    evening last.

XLIV

And every while that mighty yron man,
With his strange weapon, never wont in
    warre,
Them sorely vext, and courst, and overran,
And broke their bowes, and did their shoot-
    ing marre,
That none of all the many once did darre
Him to assault, nor once approach him nie,
But like a sort of sheepe dispersed farre
For dread of their devouring enemie,
Through all the fields and vallies did be-
    fore him flie.

XLV

But when as daies faire shinie-beame,
    yclowded
With fearefull shadowes of deformed night,
Warn'd man and beast in quiet rest be
    shrowded,
Bold Radigund, with sound of trumpe on
    hight,
Causd all her people to surcease from
    fight,
And gathering them unto her citties gate,
Made them all enter in before her sight,
And all the wounded, and the weake in
    state,
To be convayed in, ere she would once
    retrate.

XLVI

When thus the field was voided all away,
And all things quieted, the Elfin knight,
Weary of toile and travell of that day,
Causd his pavilion to be richly pight
Before the city gate, in open sight;
Where he him selfe did rest in safety,

Together with Sir Terpin, all that night:
But Talus usde in times of jeopardy
To keepe a nightly watch, for dread of
    treachery.

XLVII

But Radigund full of heart-gnawing griefe,
For the rebuke which she sustain'd that
    day,
Could take no rest, ne would receive re-
    liefe,
But tossed in her troublous minde, what
    way
She mote revenge that blot which on her
    lay.
There she resolv'd her selfe in single fight
To try her fortune, and his force assay,
Rather then see her people spoiled quight,
As she had seene that day, a disaventerous
    sight.

XLVIII

She called forth to her a trusty mayd,
Whom she thought fittest for that busi-
    nesse,
(Her name was Clarin,) and thus to her
    sayd:
'Goe, damzell, quickly, doe thy selfe ad-
    dresse,
To doe the message which I shall expresse.
Goe thou unto that stranger Faery knight,
Who yeester day drove us to such di-
    stresse;
Tell, that to morrow I with him wil fight,
And try in equall field, whether hath
    greater might.

XLIX

'But these conditions doe to him propound
That if I vanquishe him, he shall obay
My law, and ever to my lore be bound;
And so will I, if me he vanquish may,
What ever he shall like to doe or say.
Goe streight, and take with thee, to wit-
    nesse it,
Sixe of thy fellowes of the best array,
And beare with you both wine and jun-
    cates fit,
And bid him eate; henceforth he oft shall
    hungry sit.'

L

The damzell streight obayd, and putting all
In readinesse, forth to the towne-gate
    went,

Where sounding loud a trumpet from the
　　wall,
Unto those warlike knights she warning
　　sent.
Then Talus, forth issuing from the tent,
Unto the wall his way did fearelesse take,
To weeten what that trumpets sounding
　　ment:
Where that same damzell lowdly him be-
　　spake,
And shew'd that with his lord she would
　　emparlaunce make.

LI

So he them streight conducted to his lord,
Who, as he could, them goodly well did
　　greete,
Till they had told their message word by
　　word:
Which he accepting well, as he could weete,
Them fairely entertaynd with curt'sies
　　meete,
And gave them gifts and things of deare
　　delight.
So backe againe they homeward turnd
　　their feete.
But Artegall him selfe to rest did dight,
That he mote fresher be against the next
　　daies fight.

CANTO V

Artegall fights with Radigund,
　　And is subdewd by guile:
He is by her emprisoned,
　　But wrought by Clarins wile.

I

So soone as day forth dawning from the
　　East,
Nights humid curtaine from the heavens
　　withdrew,
And earely calling forth both man and
　　beast,
Comaunded them their daily workes re-
　　new,
These noble warriors, mindefull to pursew
The last daies purpose of their vowed
　　fight,
Them selves thereto preparde in order
　　dew;
The knight, as best was seeming for a
　　knight,
And th' Amazon, as best it likt her selfe to
　　dight:

II

All in a camis light of purple silke
Woven uppon with silver, subtly wrought,
And quilted uppon sattin white as milke,
Trayled with ribbands diversly distraught,
Like as the workeman had their courses
　　taught;
Which was short tucked for light motion
Up to her ham, but, when she list, it raught
Downe to her lowest heele, and thereuppon
She wore for her defence a mayled haber-
　　geon.

III

And on her legs she painted buskins wore,
Basted with bends of gold on every side,
And mailes betweene, and laced close afore:
Uppon her thigh her cemitare was tide,
With an embrodered belt of mickell pride;
And on her shoulder hung her shield, be-
　　deckt
Uppon the bosse with stones, that shined
　　wide
As the faire moone in her most full aspect,
That to the moone it mote be like in each
　　respect.

IV

So forth she came out of the citty gate,
With stately port and proud magnificence,
Guarded with many damzels, that did waite
Uppon her person for her sure defence,
Playing on shaumes and trumpets, that
　　from hence
Their sound did reach unto the heavens
　　hight.
So forth into the field she marched thence,
Where was a rich pavilion ready pight,
Her to receive, till time they should begin
　　the fight.

V

Then forth came Artegall out of his tent,
All arm'd to point, and first the lists did
　　enter:
Soone after eke came she, with fell intent
And countenaunce fierce, as having fully
　　bent her,
That battels utmost triall to adventer.
The lists were closed fast, to barre the rout
From rudely pressing to the middle center
Which in great heapes them circled all
　　about,
Wayting how fortune would resolve that
　　daungerous dout.

VI

The trumpets sounded, and the field began;
With bitter strokes it both began and
ended.
She at the first encounter on him ran
With furious rage, as if she had intended
Out of his breast the very heart have
rended:
But he, that had like tempests often tride,
From that first flaw him selfe right well
defended.
The more she rag'd, the more he did abide;
She hewd, she foynd, she lasht, she laid on
every side.

VII

Yet still her blowes he bore, and her for-
bore,
Weening at last to win advantage new;
Yet still her crueltie increased more,
And though powre faild, her courage did
accrew;
Which fayling, he gan fiercely her pursew.
Like as a smith that to his cunning feat
The stubborne mettall seeketh to subdew,
Soone as he feeles it mollifide with heat,
With his great yron sledge doth strongly
on it beat.

VIII

So did Sir Artegall upon her lay,
As if she had an yron andvile beene,
That flakes of fire, bright as the sunny
ray,
Out of her steely armes were flashing seene,
That all on fire ye would her surely weene.
But with her shield so well her selfe she
warded
From the dread daunger of his weapon
keene,
That all that while her life she safely
garded:
But he that helpe from her against her will
discarded.

IX

For with his trenchant blade at the next
blow
Halfe of her shield he shared quite away,
That halfe her side it selfe did naked show,
And thenceforth unto daunger opened way.
Much was she moved with the mightie
sway
Of that sad stroke, that halfe enrag'd she
grew,

And like a greedie beare unto her pray,
With her sharpe cemitare at him she flew,
That glauncing downe his thigh, the purple
bloud forth drew.

X

Thereat she gan to triumph with great
boast,
And to upbrayd that chaunce which him
misfell,
As if the prize she gotten had almost,
With spightfull speaches, fitting with her
well;
That his great hart gan inwardly to swell
With indignation at her vaunting vaine,
And at her strooke with puissance feareful)
fell;
Yet with her shield she warded it againe,
That shattered all to peeces round aboat
the plaine.

XI

Having her thus disarmed of her shield,
Upon her helmet he againe her strooke,
That downe she fell upon the grassie field,
In sencelesse swoune, as if her life for-
sooke,
And pangs of death her spirit overtooke.
Whom when he saw before his foote pro-
strated,
He to her lept with deadly dreadfull looke,
And her sunshynie helmet soone unlaced,
Thinking at once both head and helmet to
have raced.

XII

But when as he discovered had her face,
He saw, his senses straunge astonishment,
A miracle of Natures goodly grace
In her faire visage voide of ornament,
But bath'd in bloud and sweat together
ment;
Which, in the rudenesse of that evill plight,
Bewrayd the signes of feature excellent:
Like as the moone, in foggie winters night,
Doth seeme to be her selfe, though dark-
ned be her light.

XIII

At sight thereof his cruell minded hart
Empierced was with pittifull regard,
That his sharpe sword he threw from him
apart,
Cursing his hand that had that visage mard:
No hand so cruell, nor no hart so hard,

But ruth of beautie will it mollifie.
By this upstarting from her swoune, she
    star'd
A while about her with confused eye;
Like one that from his dreame is waked
    suddenlye.

XIV

Soone as the knight she there by her did
    spy,
Standing with emptie hands all weapon-
    lesse,
With fresh assault upon him she did fly,
And gan renew her former cruelnesse:
And though he still retyr'd, yet nathelesse
With huge redoubled strokes she on him
    layd;
And more increast her outrage mercilesse,
The more that he with meeke intreatie
    prayd,
Her wrathful hand from greedy vengeance
    to have stayd.

XV

Like as a puttocke having spyde in sight
A gentle faulcon sitting on an hill,
Whose other wing, now made unmeete for
    flight,
Was lately broken by some fortune ill;
The foolish kyte, led with licentious will,
Doth beat upon the gentle bird in vaine,
With many idle stoups her troubling still:
Even so did Radigund with bootlesse paine
Annoy this noble knight, and sorely him
    constraine.

XVI

Nought could he do, but shun the dred
    despight
Of her fierce wrath, and backward still
    retyre,
And with his single shield, well as he might,
Beare off the burden of her raging yre;
And evermore he gently did desyre
To stay her stroks, and he himselfe would
    yield:
Yet nould she hearke, ne let him once
    respyre,
Till he to her delivered had his shield,
And to her mercie him submitted in plaine
    field.

XVII

So was he overcome, not overcome,
But to her yeelded of his owne accord;

Yet was he justly damned by the doome
Of his owne mouth, that spake so warelesse
    word,
To be her thrall, and service her afford.
For though that he first victorie obtayned,
Yet after, by abandoning his sword,
He wilfull lost that he before attayned.
No fayrer conquest then that with goodwill
    is gayned.

XVIII

Tho with her sword on him she flatling
    strooke,
In signe of true subjection to her powre,
And as her vassall him to thraldome tooke.
But Terpine, borne to' a more unhappy
    howre,
As he on whom the lucklesse starres did
    lowre,
She causd to be attacht, and forthwith led
Unto the crooke, t' abide the balefull stowre
From which he lately had through reskew
    fled:
Where he full shamefully was hanged by
    the hed.

XIX

But when they thought on Talus hands to
    lay,
He with his yron flaile amongst them
    thondred,
That they were fayne to let him scape away
Glad from his companie to be so sondred;
Whose presence all their troups so much
    encombred,
That th' heapes of those which he did wound
    and slay,
Besides the rest dismayd, might not be
    nombred:
Yet all that while he would not once assay
To reskew his owne lord, but thought it
    just t' obay.

XX

Then tooke the Amazon this noble knight,
Left to her will by his owne wilfull blame,
And caused him to be disarmed quight
Of all the ornaments of knightly name,
With which whylome he gotten had great
    fame:
In stead whereof she made him to be dight
In womans weedes, that is to manhood
    shame,
And put before his lap a napron white,
In stead of curiets and bases fit for fight.

XXI

So being clad, she brought him from the
     field,
In which he had bene trayned many a day,
Into a long large chamber, which was sield
With moniments of many knights decay,
By her subdewed in victorious fray:
Amongst the which she causd his warlike
     armes
Be hang'd on high, that mote his shame
     bewray;
And broke his sword, for feare of further
     harmes,
With which he wont to stirre up battailous
     alarmes.

XXII

There entred in, he round about him saw
Many brave knights, whose names right
     well he knew,
There bound t' obay that Amazons proud
     law,
Spinning and carding all in comely rew,
That his bigge hart loth'd so uncomely vew.
But they were forst, through penurie and
     pyne,
To doe those workes to them appointed
     dew:
For nought was given them to sup or dyne,
But what their hands could earne by twist-
     ing linnen twyne.

XXIII

Amongst them all she placed him most
     low,
And in his hand a distaffe to him gave,
That he thereon should spin both flax and
     tow;
A sordid office for a mind so brave:
So hard it is to be a womans slave.
Yet he it tooke in his owne selfes despight,
And thereto did himselfe right well behave,
Her to obay, sith he his faith had plight,
Her vassall to become, if she him wonne in
     fight.

XXIV

Who had him seene, imagine mote thereby
That whylome hath of Hercules bene told,
How for Iolas sake he did apply
His mightie hands the distaffe vile to hold,
For his huge club, which had subdew'd of
     old
So many monsters which the world annoyed;
His lyons skin chaungd to a pall of gold,

In which, forgetting warres, he onely joyed
In combats of sweet love, and with his mis-
     tresse toyed.

XXV

Such is the crueltie of women kynd,
When they have shaken off the shamefast
     band,
With which wise Nature did them strongly
     bynd,
T' obay the heasts of mans well ruling
     hand,
That then all rule and reason they with-
     stand,
To purchase a licentious libertie.
But vertuous women wisely understand,
That they were borne to base humilitie,
Unlesse the heavens them lift to lawfull
     soveraintie.

XXVI

Thus there long while continu'd Artegall,
Serving proud Radigund with true subjec-
     tion;
How ever it his noble heart did gall
T' obay a womans tyrannous direction,
That might have had of life or death
     election:
But having chosen, now he might not
     chaunge.
During which time, the warlike Amazon,
Whose wandring fancie after lust did
     raunge,
Gan cast a secret liking to this captive
     straunge.

XXVII

Which long concealing in her covert brest,
She chaw'd the cud of lovers carefull plight;
Yet could it not so thoroughly digest,
Being fast fixed in her wounded spright,
But it tormented her both day and night:
Yet would she not thereto yeeld free ac-
     cord,
To serve the lowly vassall of her might,
And of her servant make her soverayne
     lord:
So great her pride, that she such basenesse
     much abhord.

XXVIII

So much the greater still her anguish grew,
Through stubborne handling of her love-
     sicke hart;
And still the more she strove it to subdew,

The more she still augmented her owne
   smart,
And wyder made the wound of th' hidden
   dart.
At last, when long she struggled had in
   vaine,
She gan to stoupe, and her proud mind
   convert
To meeke obeysance of Loves mightie raine,
And him entreat for grace, that had procur'd her paine.

XXIX

Unto her selfe in secret she did call
Her nearest handmayd, whom she most did
   trust,
And to her said: 'Clarinda, whom of all
I trust a live, sith I thee fostred first;
Now is the time that I untimely must
Thereof make tryall, in my greatest need:
It is so hapned that the heavens unjust,
Spighting my happie freedome, have agreed
To thrall my looser life, or my last bale
   to breed.'

XXX

With that she turn'd her head, as halfe
   abashed,
To hide the blush which in her visage
   rose,
And through her eyes like sudden light-
   ning flashed,
Decking her cheeke with a vermilion rose:
But soone she did her countenance com-
   pose,
And to her turning, thus began againe:
' This griefes deepe wound I would to thee
   disclose,
Thereto compelled through hart-murdring
   paine,
But dread of shame my doubtfull lips doth
   still restraine.'

XXXI

' Ah ! my deare dread,' said then the faithfull mayd,
' Can dread of ought your dreadlesse hart
   withhold,
That many hath with dread of death dismayd,
And dare even deathes most dreadfull face
   behold ?
Say on, my soverayne ladie, and be bold:
Doth not your handmayds life at your foot
   lie ? '

Therewith much comforted, she gan unfold
The cause of her conceived maladie,
As one that would confesse, yet faine would
   it denie.

XXXII

' Clarin,' sayd she, ' thou seest yond Fayry
   knight,
Whom not my valour, but his owne brave
   mind
Subjected hath to my unequall might:
What right is it, that he should thraldome
   find,
For lending life to me, a wretch unkind,
That for such good him recompence with ill?
Therefore I cast how I may him unbind,
And by his freedome get his free goodwill;
Yet so, as bound to me he may continue still:

XXXIII

' Bound unto me, but not with such hard
   bands
Of strong compulsion and streight violence,
As now in miserable state he stands;
But with sweet love and sure benevolence,
Voide of malitious mind or foule offence.
To which if thou canst win him any way,
Without discoverie of my thoughts pretence,
Both goodly meede of him it purchase may,
And eke with gratefull service me right
   well apay.

XXXIV

' Which that thou mayst the better bring to
   pas,
Loe here this ring, which shall thy warrant
   bee,
And token true to old Eumenias,
From time to time, when thou it best shalt
   see,
That in and out thou mayst have passage
   free.
Goe now, Clarinda; well thy wits advise,
And all thy forces gather unto thee,
Armies of lovely lookes, and speeches wise,
With which thou canst even Jove himselfe
   to love entise.'

XXXV

The trustie mayd, conceiving her intent,
Did with sure promise of her good indevour
Give her great comfort and some harts con-
   tent.
So from her parting, she thenceforth did
   labour

By all the meanes she might, to curry
    favour
With th' Elfin knight, her ladies best be-
    loved:
With daily shew of courteous kind behav-
    iour,
Even at the markewhite of his hart she
    roved,
And with wide glauncing words, one day
    she thus him proved:

XXXVI

'Unhappie knight, upon whose hopelesse
    state
Fortune, envying good, hath felly frowned,
And cruell heavens have heapt an heavy
    fate;
I rew that thus thy better dayes are
    drowned
In sad despaire, and all thy senses swowned
In stupid sorow, sith thy juster merit
Might else have with felicitie bene crowned:
Looke up at last, and wake thy dulled spirit,
To thinke how this long death thou mightest
    disinherit.'

XXXVII

Much did he marvell at her uncouth speach,
Whose hidden drift he could not well
    perceive;
And gan to doubt, least she him sought t'
    appeach
Of treason, or some guilefull traine did
    weave,
Through which she might his wretched
    life bereave.
Both which to barre, he with this answere
    met her:
'Faire damzell, that with ruth (as I per-
    ceave)
Of my mishaps, art mov'd to wish me
    better,
For such your kind regard I can but rest
    your detter.

XXXVIII

'Yet weet ye well, that to a courage great
It is no lesse beseeming well, to beare
The storme of Fortunes frowne, or Heavens
    threat,
Then in the sunshine of her countenance
    cleare
Timely to joy and carrie comely cheare.
For though this cloud have now me over-
    cast,

Yet doe I not of better times despeyre;
And, though unlike, they should for ever
    last,
Yet in my truthes assurance I rest fixed
    fast.'

XXXIX

'But what so stonie mind,' she then replyde,
'But, if in his owne powre occasion lay,
Would to his hope a windowe open wyde,
And to his fortunes helpe make readie
    way?'
'Unworthy sure,' quoth he, 'of better day,
That will not take the offer of good hope,
And eke pursew, if he attaine it may.'
Which speaches she applying to the scope
Of her intent, this further purpose to him
    shope:

XL

'Then why doest not, thou ill advized man,
Make meanes to win thy libertie forlorne,
And try if thou by faire entreatie can
Move Radigund? who, though she still have
    worne
Her dayes in warre, yet (weet thou) was
    not borne
Of beares and tygres, nor so salvage
    mynded,
As that, albe all love of men she scorne,
She yet forgets that she of men was
    kynded:
And sooth oft seene, that proudest harts
    base love hath blynded.'

XLI

'Certes, Clarinda, not of cancred will,'
Sayd he, 'nor obstinate disdainefull mind,
I have forbore this duetie to fulfill:
For well I may this weene, by that I fynd,
That she, a queene, and come of princely
    kynd,
Both worthie is for to be sewd unto,
Chiefely by him whose life her law doth
    bynd,
And eke of powre her owne doome to undo,
And als' of princely grace to be inclyn'd
    thereto.

XLII

'But want of meanes hath bene mine onely
    let
From seeking favour, where it doth abound;
Which if I might by your good office get,
I to your selfe should rest for ever bound,

And readie to deserve what grace I found.'
She feeling him thus bite upon the bayt,
Yet doubting least his hold was but un-
　　sound,
And not well fastened, would not strike
　　him strayt,
But drew him on with hope, fit leasure to
　　awayt.

XLIII

But foolish mayd! whyles, heedlesse of the
　　hooke,
She thus oft times was beating off and
　　on,
Through slipperie footing fell into the
　　brooke,
And there was caught to her confusion.
For seeking thus to salve the Amazon,
She wounded was with her deceipts owne
　　dart,
And gan thenceforth to cast affection,
Conceived close in her beguiled hart,
To Artegall, through pittie of his causelesse
　　smart.

XLIV

Yet durst she not disclose her fancies
　　wound,
Ne to himselfe, for doubt of being sdayned,
Ne yet to any other wight on ground,
For feare her mistresse shold have know-
　　ledge gayned,
But to her selfe it secretly retayned,
Within the closet of her covert brest:
The more thereby her tender hart was
　　payned.
Yet to awayt fit time she weened best,
And fairely did dissemble her sad thoughts
　　unrest.

XLV

One day her ladie, calling her apart,
Gan to demaund of her some tydings good,
Touching her loves successe, her lingring
　　smart.
Therewith she gan at first to change her
　　mood,
As one adaw'd, and halfe confused stood;
But quickly she it overpast, so soone
As she her face had wypt, to fresh her
　　blood:
Tho gan she tell her all that she had
　　donne,
And all the wayes she sought, his love for
　　to have wonne:

XLVI

But sayd, that he was obstinate and sterne,
Scorning her offers and conditions vaine;
Ne would be taught with any termes to lerne
So fond a lesson as to love againe.
Die rather would he in penurious paine,
And his abridged dayes in dolour wast,
Then his foes love or liking entertaine:
His resolution was, both first and last,
His bodie was her thrall, his hart was
　　freely plast.

XLVII

Which when the cruell Amazon perceived,
She gan to storme, and rage, and rend her
　　gall,
For very fell despight, which she conceived,
To be so scorned of a base borne thrall,
Whose life did lie in her least eye-lids fall;
Of which she vow'd with many a cursed
　　threat,
That she therefore would him ere long for-
　　stall.
Nathlesse, when calmed was her furious
　　heat,
She chang'd that threatfull mood, and
　　mildly gan entreat:

XLVIII

'What now is left, Clarinda? what re-
　　maines,
That we may compasse this our enterprize?
Great shame to lose so long employed
　　paines,
And greater shame t' abide so great mis
　　prize,
With which he dares our offers thus de-
　　spize.
Yet that his guilt the greater may appeare,
And more my gratious mercie by this wize
I will a while with his first folly beare,
Till thou have tride againe, and tempted
　　him more neare.

XLIX

'Say and do all that may thereto prevaile;
Leave nought unpromist that may him per-
　　swade,
Life, freedome, grace, and gifts of great
　　availe,
With which the gods themselves are
　　mylder made:
Thereto adde art, even womens witty trade
The art of mightie words, that men ca
　　charme;

With which in case thou canst him not invade,
Let him feele hardnesse of thy heavie
  arme:
Who will not stoupe with good shall be
  made stoupe with harme.

L

'Some of his diet doe from him with-
  draw;
For I him find to be too proudly fed:
Give him more labour, and with streighter
  law,
That he with worke may be forwearied:
Let him lodge hard, and lie in strawen bed,
That may pull downe the courage of his
  pride;
And lay upon him, for his greater dread,
Cold yron chaines, with which let him be
  tide;
And let what ever he desires be him de-
  nide.

LI

'When thou hast all this doen, then bring
  me newes
Of his demeane: thenceforth not like a
  lover,
But like a rebell stout I will him use.
For I resolve this siege not to give over,
Till I the conquest of my will recover.'
So she departed, full of griefe and sdaine,
Which inly did to great impatience move
  her.
But the false mayden shortly turn'd againe
Unto the prison, where her hart did thrall
  remaine.

LII

There all her subtill nets she did unfold,
And all the engins of her wit display;
In which she meant him warelesse to en-
  fold,
And of his innocence to make her pray.
So cunningly she wrought her crafts assay,
That both her ladie, and her selfe withall,
And eke the knight attonce she did betray:
But most the knight, whom she with guile-
  full call
Did cast for to allure, into her trap to fall.

LIII

As a bad nurse, which, fayning to receive
In her owne mouth the food ment for her
  chyld,

Withholdes it to her selfe, and doeth de-
  ceive
The infant, so for want of nourture spoyld:
Even so Clarinda her owne dame beguyld,
And turn'd the trust which was in her
  affyde
To feeding of her private fire, which boyld
Her inward brest, and in her entrayles
  fryde,
The more that she it sought to cover and
  to hyde.

LIV

For comming to this knight, she purpose
  fayned,
How earnest suit she earst for him had made
Unto her queene, his freedome to have
  gayned;
But by no meanes could her thereto per-
  swade:
But that, in stead thereof, she sternely bade
His miserie to be augmented more,
And many yron bands on him to lade;
All which nathlesse she for his love for-
  bore:
So praying him t' accept her service ever-
  more.

LV

And more then that, she promist that she
  would,
In case she might finde favour in his eye,
Devize how to enlarge him out of hould.
The Fayrie, glad to gaine his libertie,
Can yeeld great thankes for such her curte-
  sie;
And with faire words, fit for the time and
  place,
To feede the humour of her maladie,
Promist, if she would free him from that
  case,
He wold, by all good means he might, de-
  serve such grace.

LVI

So daily he faire semblant did her shew,
Yet never meant he in his noble mind,
To his owne absent love to be untrew:
Ne ever did deceiptfull Clarin find
In her false hart, his bondage to unbind;
But rather how she mote him faster tye,
Therefore unto her mistresse most unkind
She daily told, her love he did defye,
And him she told, her dame his freedome
  did denye.

LVII

Yet thus much friendship she to him did
show,
That his scarse diet somewhat was amended,
And his worke lessened, that his love mote
grow:
Yet to her dame him still she discom-
mended,
That she with him mote be the more
offended.
Thus he long while in thraldome there
remayned,
Of both beloved well, but litle frended;
Untill his owne true love his freedome
gayned,
Which in an other canto will be best con-
tayned.

CANTO VI

Talus brings newes to Britomart
Of Artegals mishap:
She goes to seeke him, Dolon meetes,
Who seekes her to entrap.

I

SOME men, I wote, will deeme in Artegall
Great weaknesse, and report of him much
ill,
For yeelding so himselfe a wretched thrall
To th' insolent commaund of womens will;
That all his former praise doth fowly spill.
But he the man, that say or doe so dare,
Be well adviz'd that he stand stedfast still:
For never yet was wight so well aware,
But he at first or last was trapt in womens
snare.

II

Yet in the streightnesse of that captive
state,
This gentle knight himselfe so well behaved,
That notwithstanding all the subtill bait,
With which those Amazons his love still
craved,
To his owne love his loialtie he saved:
Whose character in th' adamantine mould
Of his true hart so firmely was engraved,
That no new loves impression ever could
Bereave it thence: such blot his honour
blemish should.

III

Yet his owne love, the noble Britomart,
Scarse so conceived in her jealous thought,
What time sad tydings of his balefull smart
In womans bondage Talus to her brought
Brought in untimely houre, ere it was
sought.
For after that the utmost date, assynde
For his returne, she waited had for nought,
She gan to cast in her misdoubtfull mynde
A thousand feares, that love-sicke fancies
faine to fynde.

IV

Sometime she feared, least some hard mis-
hap
Had him misfalne in his adventurous quest;
Sometime least his false foe did him entrap
In traytrous traine, or had unwares opprest:
But most she did her troubled mynd molest,
And secretly afflict with jealous feare,
Least some new love had him from her
possest;
Yet loth she was, since she no ill did heare,
To thinke of him so ill: yet could she not
forbeare.

V

One while she blam'd her selfe; another
whyle
She him condemn'd, as trustlesse and un-
trew:
And then, her griefe with errour to beguyle,
She fayn'd to count the time againe anew,
As if before she had not counted trew.
For houres but dayes; for weekes, that
passed were,
She told but moneths, to make them seeme
more few:
Yet when she reckned them, still drawing
neare,
Each hour did seeme a moneth, and every
moneth a yeare.

VI

But when as yet she saw him not returne,
She thought to send some one to seeke him
out;
But none she found so fit to serve that
turne,
As her owne selfe, to ease her selfe of dout.
Now she deviz'd, amongst the warlike rout
Of errant knights, to seeke her errant
knight;
And then againe resolv'd to hunt him out
Amongst loose ladies, lapped in delight:
And then both knights envide, and ladies
eke did spight.

VII

One day, when as she long had sought for ease
In every place, and every place thought best,
Yet found no place that could her liking please,
She to a window came, that opened west,
Towards which coast her love his way adrest.
There looking forth, shee in her heart did find
Many vaine fancies, working her unrest;
And sent her winged thoughts, more swift then wind,
To beare unto her love the message of her mind.

VIII

There as she looked long, at last she spide
One comming towards her with hasty speede:
Well weend she then, ere him she plaine describe,
That it was one sent from her love indeede.
Who when he nigh approcht, shee mote arede
That it was Talus, Artegall his groome;
Whereat her heart was fild with hope and drede;
Ne would she stay till he in place could come,
But ran to meete him forth, to know his tidings somme.

IX

Even in the dore him meeting, she begun:
' And where is he thy lord, and how far hence ?
Declare at once; and hath he lost or wun ? '
The yron man, albe he wanted sence
And sorrowes feeling, yet with conscience
Of his ill newes, did inly chill and quake,
And stood still mute, as one in great suspence,
As if that by his silence he would make
Her rather reade his meaning, then him selfe it spake.

X

Till she againe thus sayd: ' Talus, be bold,
And tell what ever it be, good or bad,
That from thy tongue thy hearts intent doth hold.'
To whom he thus at length: ' The tidings sad,
That I would hide, will needs, I see, be rad.
My lord, your love, by hard mishap doth lie
In wretched bondage, wofully bestad.'
' Ay me,' quoth she, ' what wicked destinie !
And is he vanquisht by his tyrant enemy ? '

XI

' Not by that tyrant, his intended foe;
But by a tyrannesse,' he then replide,
' That him captived hath in haplesse woe.'
' Cease, thou bad newes-man; badly doest thou hide
Thy maisters shame, in harlots bondage tide.
The rest my selfe too readily can spell.'
With that in rage she turn'd from him aside,
Forcing in vaine the rest to her to tell,
And to her chamber went like solitary cell.

XII

There she began to make her monefull plaint
Against her knight, for being so untrew;
And him to touch with falshoods fowle attaint,
That all his other honour overthrew.
Oft did she blame her selfe, and often rew,
For yeelding to a straungers love so light,
Whose life and manners straunge she never knew;
And evermore she did him sharpely twight
For breach of faith to her, which he had firmely plight.

XIII

And then she in her wrathfull will did cast,
How to revenge that blot of honour blent;
To fight with him, and goodly die her last:
And then againe she did her selfe torment,
Inflicting on her selfe his punishment.
A while she walkt, and chauft; a while she threw
Her selfe uppon her bed, and did lament:
Yet did she not lament with loude alew,
As women wont, but with deepe sighes, and singulfs few.

XIV

Like as a wayward childe, whose sounder sleepe
Is broken with some fearefull dreames affright,
With froward will doth set him selfe to weepe;
Ne can be stild for all his nurses might,

But kicks, and squals, and shriekes for fell
  despight;
Now scratching her, and her loose locks
  misusing;
Now seeking darkenesse, and now seeking
  light;
Then craving sucke, and then the sucke refusing:
Such was this ladies fit, in her loves fond
  accusing.

XV

But when she had with such unquiet fits
Her selfe there close afflicted long in vaine,
Yet found no easement in her troubled wits,
She unto Talus forth return'd againe,
By change of place seeking to ease her
  paine;
And gan enquire of him, with mylder mood,
The certaine cause of Artegals detaine ;
And what he did, and in what state he
  stood,
And whether he did woo, or whether he
  were woo'd.

XVI

' Ah wellaway ! ' sayd then the yron man,
' That he is not the while in state to woo;
But lies in wretched thraldome, weake and
  wan,
Not by strong hand compelled thereunto,
But his owne doome, that none can now
  undoo.'
' Sayd I not then,' quoth shee, ' erwhile
  aright,
That this is thinge compacte betwixt you
  two,
Me to deceive of faith unto me plight,
Since that he was not forst, nor overcome
  in fight ? '

XVII

With that he gan at large to her dilate
The whole discourse of his captivance sad,
In sort as ye have heard the same of late.
All which when she with hard enduraunce
  had
Heard to the end, she was right sore bestad,
With sodaine stounds of wrath and griefe
  attone:
Ne would abide, till she had aunswere made,
But streight her selfe did dight, and armor
  don;
And mounting to her steede, bad Talus
  guide her on.

XVIII

So forth she rode uppon her ready way,
To seeke her knight, as Talus her did
  guide:
Sadly she rode, and never word did say,
Nor good nor bad, ne ever lookt aside,
But still right downe, and in her thought did
  hide
The felnesse of her heart, right fully bent
To fierce avengement of that womans pride,
Which had her lord in her base prison
  pent,
And so great honour with so fowle reproch
  had blent.

XIX

So as she thus melancholicke did ride,
Chawing the cud of griefe and inward paine,
She chaunst to meete toward the even-tide
A knight, that softly paced on the plaine,
As if him selfe to solace he were faine.
Well shot in yeares he seem'd, and rather
  bent
To peace, then needlesse trouble to con-
  straine;
As well by view of that his vestiment,
As by his modest semblant, that no evill
  ment.

XX

He, comming neare, gan gently her salute
With curteous words, in the most comely
  wize;
Who though desirous rather to rest mute,
Then termes to entertaine of common guize,
Yet rather then she kindnesse would de-
  spize,
She would her selfe displease, so him re-
  quite.
Then gan the other further to devize
Of things abrode, as next to hand did light,
And many things demaund, to which she
  answer'd light.

XXI

For little lust had she to talke of ought,
Or ought to heare, that mote delightfull
  bee;
Her minde was whole possessed of one
  thought,
That gave none other place.   Which when
  as hee
By outward signes (as well he might) did
  see,
He list no lenger to use lothfull speach,

But her besought to take it well in gree,
Sith shady dampe had dimd the heavens
    reach,
To lodge with him that night, unles good
    cause empeach.

XXII

The championesse, now seeing night at
    dore,
Was glad to yeeld unto his good request:
And with him went without gaine-saying
    more.
Not farre away, but little wide by west,
His dwelling was, to which he him addrest;
Where soone arriving, they received were
In seemely wise, as them beseemed best:
For he their host them goodly well did
    cheare,
And talk't of pleasant things, the night
    away to weare.

XXIII

Thus passing th' evening well, till time of
    rest,
Then Britomart unto a bowre was brought;
Where groomes awayted her to have un-
    drest.
But she ne would undressed be for ought,
Ne doffe her armes, though he her much
    besought.
For she had vow'd, she sayd, not to for-
    go
Those warlike weedes, till she revenge had
    wrought
Of a late wrong uppon a mortall foe;
Which she would sure performe, betide her
    wele or wo.

XXIV

Which when their host perceiv'd, right dis-
    content
In minde he grew, for feare least by that
    art
He should his purpose misse, which close
    he ment:
Yet taking leave of her, he did depart.
There all that night remained Britomart,
Restlesse, recomfortlesse, with heart deepe
    grieved,
Not suffering the least twinckling sleepe
    to start
Into her eye, which th' heart mote have
    relieved,
But if the least appear'd, her eyes she
    streight reprieved.

XXV

' Ye guilty eyes,' sayd she, ' the which with
    guyle
My heart at first betrayd, will ye betray
My life now to, for which a little whyle
Ye will not watch ? False watches, well-
    away !
I wote when ye did watch both night and
    day
Unto your losse: and now needes will ye
    sleepe ?
Now ye have made my heart to wake al-
    way,
Now will ye sleepe ? ah ! wake, and rather
    weepe,
To thinke of your nights want, that should
    yee waking keepe.'

XXVI

Thus did she watch, and weare the weary
    night
In waylfull plaints, that none was to ap-
    pease;
Now walking soft, now sitting still upright,
As sundry chaunge her seemed best to ease.
Ne lesse did Talus suffer sleepe to seaze
His eye-lids sad, but watcht continually,
Lying without her dore in great disease;
Like to a spaniell wayting carefully,
Least any should betray his lady treacher-
    ously.

XXVII

What time the native belman of the night,
The bird that warned Peter of his fall,
First rings his silver bell t' each sleepy
    wight,
That should their mindes up to devotion
    call,
She heard a wondrous noise below the hall.
All sodainely the bed, where she should lie,
By a false trap was let adowne to fall
Into a lower roome, and by and by
The loft was raysd againe, that no man
    could it spie.

XXVIII

With sight whereof she was dismayd right
    sore,
Perceiving well the treason which was
    ment:
Yet stirred not at all for doubt of more,
But kept her place with courage confident,
Wayting what would ensue of that event.
It was not long before she heard the sound

Of armed men, comming with close intent
Towards her chamber; at which dreadfull
    stound
She quickly caught her sword, and shield
    about her bound.

XXIX

With that there came unto her chamber
    dore
Two knights, all armed ready for to fight,
And after them full many other more,
A raskall rout, with weapons rudely dight.
Whom soone as Talus spide by glims of
    night,
He started up, there where on ground he
    lay,
And in his hand his thresher ready keight.
They seeing that, let drive at him streight
    way,
And round about him preace in riotous
    aray.

XXX

But soone as he began to lay about
With his rude yron flaile, they gan to flie,
Both armed knights and eke unarmed rout:
Yet Talus after them apace did plie,
Where ever in the darke he could them
    spie;
That here and there like scattred sheepe
    they lay.
Then backe returning, where his dame did
    lie,
He to her told the story of that fray,
And all that treason there intended did
    bewray.

XXXI

Wherewith though wondrous wroth, and
    inly burning
To be avenged for so fowle a deede,
Yet being forst to abide the daies return-
    ing,
She there remain'd, but with right wary
    heede,
Least any more such practise should pro-
    ceede.
Now mote ye know (that which to Brito-
    mart
Unknowen was) whence all this did pro-
    ceede,
And for what cause so great mischievous
    smart
Was ment to her, that never evill ment in
    hart.

XXXII

The goodman of this house was Dolon
    hight,
A man of subtill wit and wicked minde,
That whilome in his youth had bene a knight,
And armes had borne, but little good
    could finde,
And much lesse honour by that warlike
    kinde
Of life: for he was nothing valorous,
But with slie shiftes and wiles did under-
    minde
All noble knights which were adventurous,
And many brought to shame by treason
    treacherous.

XXXIII

He had three sonnes, all three like fathers
    sonnes,
Like treacherous, like full of fraud and
    guile,
Of all that on this earthly compasse wonnes:
The eldest of the which was slaine erewhile
By Artegall, through his owne guilty wile;
His name was Guizor; whose untimely fate
For to avenge, full many treasons vile
His father Dolon had deviz'd of late
With these his wicked sons, and shewd his
    cankred hate.

XXXIV

For sure he weend that this his present
    guest
Was Artegall, by many tokens plaine;
But chiefly by that yron page he ghest,
Which still was wont with Artegall re-
    maine;
And therefore ment him surely to have
    slaine.
But by Gods grace, and her good heedinesse,
She was preserved from their traytrous
    traine.
Thus she all night wore out in watchfulnesse,
Ne suffred slothfull sleepe her eyelids to
    oppresse.

XXXV

The morrow next, so soone as dawning
    houre
Discovered had the light to living eye,
She forth yssew'd out of her loathed bowre,
With full intent t' avenge that villany
On that vilde man and all his family:
And comming down to seeke them where
    they wond,

Nor sire, nor sonnes, nor any could she spie:
Each rowme she sought, but them all
      empty fond:
They all were fled for feare, but whether,
      nether kond.

XXXVI

She saw it vaine to make there lenger stay,
But tooke her steede, and thereon mount-
      ing light,
Gan her addresse unto her former way.
She had not rid the mountenance of a flight,
But that she saw there present in her sight
Those two false brethren, on that perillous
      bridge
On which Pollente with Artegall did fight.
Streight was the passage like a ploughed
      ridge,
That, if two met, the one mote needes fall
      over the lidge.

XXXVII

There they did thinke them selves on her
      to wreake:
Who as she nigh unto them drew, the one
These vile reproches gan unto her speake:
' Thou recreant false traytor, that with lone
Of armes hast knighthood stolne, yet knight
      art none,
No more shall now the darkenesse of the
      night
Defend thee from the vengeance of thy fone,
But with thy bloud thou shalt appease the
      spright
Of Guizor, by thee slaine, and murdred by
      thy slight.'

XXXVIII

Strange were the words in Britomartis eare;
Yet stayd she not for them, but forward
      fared,
Till to the perillous bridge she came, and
      there
Talus desir'd that he might have prepared
The way to her, and those two losels scared.
But she thereat was wroth, that for despight
The glauncing sparkles through her bever
      glared,
And from her eies did flash out fiery light,
Like coles that through a silver censer
      sparkle bright.

XXXIX

She stayd not to advise which way to take;
But putting spurres unto her fiery beast,

Thorough the midst of them she way did
      make.
The one of them, which most her wrath
      increast,
Uppon her speare she bore before her breast,
Till to the bridges further end she past,
Where falling downe, his challenge he re-
      least:
The other over side the bridge she cast
Into the river, where he drunke his deadly
      last.

XL

As when the flashing levin haps to light
Uppon two stubborne oakes, which stand so
      neare
That way betwixt them none appeares in
      sight;
The engin fiercely flying forth, doth teare
Th' one from the earth, and through the
      aire doth beare;
The other it with force doth overthrow
Uppon one side, and from his rootes doth
      reare:
So did the Championesse those two there
      strow,
And to their sire their carcasses left to be-
      stow.

CANTO VII

Britomart comes to Isis Church,
   Where shee strange visions sees:
She fights with Radigund, her slaies,
   And Artegall thence frees.

I

NOUGHT is on earth more sacred or divine,
That gods and men doe equally adore,
Then this same vertue that doth right de-
      fine:
For th' hevens themselves, whence mortal
      men implore
Right in their wrongs, are rul'd by right-
      eous lore
Of highest Jove, who doth true justice
      deale
To his inferiour gods, and evermore
Therewith containes his heavenly common-
      weale:
The skill whereof to princes hearts he doth
      reveale.

II

Well therefore did the antique world invent,
That Justice was a god of soveraine grace,

And altars unto him, and temples lent,
And heavenly honours in the highest place;
Calling him great Osyris, of the race
Of th' old Ægyptian kings, that whylome
    were;
With fayned colours shading a true case:
For that Osyris, whilest he lived here,
The justest man alive and truest did ap-
    peare.

III

His wife was Isis, whom they likewise made
A goddesse of great powre and soveraynty,
And in her person cunningly did shade
That part of justice which is equity,
Whereof I have to treat here presently.
Unto whose temple when as Britomart
Arrived, shee with great humility
Did enter in, ne would that night depart;
But Talus mote not be admitted to her part.

IV

There she received was in goodly wize
Of many priests, which duely did attend
Uppon the rites and daily sacrifize,
All clad in linnen robes with silver hemd;
And on their heads, with long locks comely
    kemd,
They wore rich mitres shaped like the
    moone,
To shew that Isis doth the moone portend;
Like as Osyris signifies the sunne:
For that they both like race in equall just-
    ice runne.

V

The championesse them greeting, as she
    could,
Was thence by them into the temple led;
Whose goodly building when she did be-
    hould,
Borne uppon stately pillours, all dispred
With shining gold, and arched over hed,
She wondred at the workemans passing
    skill,
Whose like before she never saw nor red;
And thereuppon long while stood gazing
    still,
But thought that she thereon could never
    gaze her fill.

VI

Thence forth unto the idoll they her
    brought,
The which was framed all of silver fine,

So well as could with cunning hand be
    wrought,
And clothed all in garments made of line,
Hemd all about with fringe of silver twine.
Uppon her head she wore a crowne of gold,
To shew that she had powre in things di-
    vine;
And at her feete a crocodile was rold,
That with his wreathed taile her middle did
    enfold.

VII

One foote was set uppon the crocodile,
And on the ground the other fast did stand,
So meaning to suppresse both forged guile
And open force: and in her other hand
She stretched forth a long white sclender
    wand.
Such was the goddesse; whom when Brito-
    mart
Had long beheld, her selfe uppon the land
She did prostrate, and with right humble
    hart,
Unto her selfe her silent prayers did im-
    part.

VIII

To which the idoll as it were inclining,
Her wand did move with amiable looke,
By outward shew her inward sence desin-
    ing.
Who well perceiving how her wand she
    shooke,
It as a token of good fortune tooke.
By this the day with dampe was overcast,
And joyous light the house of Jove for-
    sooke:
Which when she saw, her helmet she un-
    laste,
And by the altars side her selfe to slumber
    plaste.

IX

For other beds the priests there used none,
But on their mother Earths deare lap did
    lie,
And bake their sides uppon the cold hard
    stone,
T' enure them selves to sufferaunce thereby
And proud rebellious flesh to mortify.
For, by the vow of their religion,
They tied were to stedfast chastity,
And continence of life, that, all forgon,
They mote the better tend to their devo-
    tion.

X

Therefore they mote not taste of fleshly
food,
Ne feed on ought the which doth bloud
containe,
Ne drinke of wine, for wine they say is
blood,
Even the bloud of gyants, which were
slaine
By thundring Jove in the Phlegrean plaine:
For which the Earth (as they the story
tell)
Wroth with the gods, which to perpetuall
paine
Had damn'd her sonnes, which gainst them
did rebell,
With inward griefe and malice did against
them swell.

XI

And of their vitall bloud, the which was
shed
Into her pregnant bosome, forth she brought
The fruitfull vine, whose liquor blouddy
red,
Having the mindes of men with fury fraught,
Mote in them stirre up old rebellious
thought,
To make new warre against the gods againe:
Such is the powre of that same fruit, that
nought
The fell contagion may thereof restraine,
Ne within reasons rule her madding mood
containe.

XII

There did the warlike maide her selfe re-
pose,
Under the wings of Isis all that night,
And with sweete rest her heavy eyes did
close,
After that long daies toile and weary plight.
Where whilest her earthly parts with soft
delight
Of sencelesse sleepe did deeply drowned lie,
There did appeare unto her heavenly spright
A wondrous vision, which did close implie
The course of all her fortune and posteritie.

XIII

Her seem'd, as she was doing sacrifize
To Isis, deckt with mitre on her hed
And linnen stole, after those priestes guize,
All sodainely she saw transfigured
Her linnen stole to robe of scarlet red,

And moone-like mitre to a crowne of gold,
That even she her selfe much wondered
At such a chaunge, and joyed to behold
Her selfe adorn'd with gems and jewels
manifold.

XIV

And in the midst of her felicity,
An hideous tempest seemed from below
To rise through all the temple sodainely,
That from the altar all about did blow
The holy fire, and all the embers strow
Uppon the ground, which, kindled privily,
Into outragious flames unwares did grow,
That all the temple put in jeopardy
Of flaming, and her selfe in great per-
plexity.

XV

With that the crocodile, which sleeping lay
Under the idols feete in fearelesse bowre,
Seem'd to awake in horrible dismay,
As being troubled with that stormy stowre;
And gaping greedy wide, did streight de-
voure
Both flames and tempest: with which
growen great,
And swolne with pride of his owne peere-
lesse powre,
He gan to threaten her likewise to eat;
But that the goddesse with her rod him
backe did beat.

XVI

Tho turning all his pride to humblesse
meeke,
Him selfe before her feete he lowly threw,
And gan for grace and love of her to seeke:
Which she accepting, he so neare her drew,
That of his game she soone enwombed
grew,
And forth did bring a lion of great might;
That shortly did all other beasts subdew.
With that she waked, full of fearefull
fright,
And doubtfully dismayd through that so
uncouth sight.

XVII

So thereuppon long while she musing lay,
With thousand thoughts feeding her fan-
tasie,
Untill she spide the lampe of lightsome
day,
Up-lifted in the porch of heaven hie.

Then up she rose fraught with melancholy,
And forth into the lower parts did pas;
Whereas the priestes she found full busily
About their holy things for morrow mas:
Whom she saluting faire, faire resaluted
  was.

XVIII

But, by the change of her unchearefull
  looke,
They might perceive she was not well in
  plight;
Or that some pensivenesse to heart she
  tooke.
Therefore thus one of them, who seem'd in
  sight
To be the greatest and the gravest wight,
To her bespake: 'Sir knight, it seemes to
  me,
That, thorough evill rest of this last night,
Or ill apayd or much dismayd ye be,
That by your change of cheare is easie for
  to see.'

XIX

'Certes,' sayd she, 'sith ye so well have
  spide
The troublous passion of my pensive mind,
I will not seeke the same from you to hide,
But will my cares unfolde, in hope to find
Your aide, to guide me out of errour blind.'
'Say on,' quoth he, 'the secret of your hart:
For by the holy vow which me doth bind
I am adjur'd, best counsell to impart
To all that shall require my comfort in their
  smart.'

XX

Then gan she to declare the whole discourse
Of all that vision which to her appeard,
As well as to her minde it had recourse.
All which when he unto the end had heard,
Like to a weake faint-hearted man he fared,
Through great astonishment of that strange
  sight;
And with long locks up-standing, stifly stared
Like one adawed with some dreadfull
  spright.
So fild with heavenly fury, thus he her be-
  hight:

XXI

'Magnificke virgin, that in queint disguise
Of British armes doest maske thy royall
  blood,

So to pursue a perillous emprize,
How couldst thou weene, through that dis-
  guized hood,
To hide thy state from being understood?
Can from th' immortall gods ought hidden
  bee?
They doe thy linage, and thy lordly brood,
They doe thy sire, lamenting sore for thee,
They doe thy love, forlorne in womens
  thraldome, see.

XXII

'The end whereof, and all the long event,
They doe to thee in this same dreame dis-
  cover.
For that same crocodile doth represent
The righteous knight that is thy faithfull
  lover,
Like to Osyris in all just endever.
For that same crocodile Osyris is,
That under Isis feete doth sleepe for ever:
To shew that clemence oft, in things amis,
Restraines those sterne behests and cruell
  doomes of his.

XXIII

'That knight shall all the troublous stormes
  asswage,
And raging flames, that many foes shall
  reare,
To hinder thee from the just heritage
Of thy sires crowne, and from thy countrey
  deare.
Then shalt thou take him to thy loved fere,
And joyne in equall portion of thy realme:
And afterwards a sonne to him shalt beare,
That lion-like shall shew his powre ex-
  treame.
So blesse thee God, and give thee joyance
  of thy dreame.'

XXIV

All which when she unto the end had
  heard,
She much was eased in her troublous
  thought,
And on those priests bestowed rich reward:
And royall gifts of gold and silver wrought
She for a present to their goddesse brought.
Then taking leave of them, she forward
  went,
To seeke her love, where he was to be
  sought;
Ne rested till she came without relent
Unto the land of Amazons, as she was bent.

XXV

Whereof when newes to Radigund was
brought,
Not with amaze, as women wonted bee,
She was confused in her troublous thought,
But fild with courage and with joyous glee,
As glad to heare of armes, the which now
she
Had long surceast, she bad to open bold,
That she the face of her new foe might see.
But when they of that yron man had told,
Which late her folke had slaine, she bad
them forth to hold.

XXVI

So there without the gate (as seemed best)
She caused her pavilion be pight;
In which stout Britomart her selfe did rest,
Whiles Talus watched at the dore all night.
All night likewise, they of the towne in
fright
Uppon their wall good watch and ward did
keepe.
The morrow next, so soone as dawning light
Bad doe away the dampe of drouzie sleepe,
The warlike Amazon out of her bowre did
peepe;

XXVII

And caused streight a trumpet loud to
shrill,
To warne her foe to battell soone be prest:
Who, long before awoke, (for she ful ill
Could sleepe all night, that in unquiet brest
Did closely harbour such a jealous guest)
Was to the battell whilome ready dight.
Eftsoones that warriouresse with haughty
crest
Did forth issue, all ready for the fight:
On th' other side her foe appeared soone in
sight.

XXVIII

But ere they reared hand, the Amazone
Began the streight conditions to propound,
With which she used still to tye her fone:
To serve her so, as she the rest had bound.
Which when the other heard, she sternly
frownd
For high disdaine of such indignity,
And would no lenger treat, but bad them
sound.
For her no other termes should ever tie,
Then what prescribed were by lawes of
chevalrie.

XXIX

The trumpets sound, and they together run
With greedy rage, and with their faulchins
smot;
Ne either sought the others strokes to shun,
But through great fury both their skill
forgot,
And practicke use in armes: ne spared not
Their dainty parts, which Nature had created
So faire and tender, without staine or spot,
For other uses then they them translated;
Which they now hackt and hewd, as if such
use they hated.

XXX

As when a tygre and a lionesse
Are met at spoyling of some hungry pray,
Both challenge it with equall greedinesse:
But first the tygre clawes thereon did lay;
And therefore loth to loose her right away,
Doth in defence thereof full stoutly stond:
To which the lion strongly doth gainesay,
That she to hunt the beast first tooke in
hond;
And therefore ought it have, where ever
she it fond.

XXXI

Full fiercely layde the Amazon about,
And dealt her blowes unmercifully sore:
Which Britomart withstood with courage
stout,
And them repaide againe with double more.
So long they fought, that all the grassie
flore
Was fild with bloud, which from their sides
did flow,
And gushed through their armes, that all
in gore
They trode, and on the ground their lives
did strow,
Like fruitles seede, of which untimely
death should grow.

XXXII

At last proud Radigund with fell despight,
Having by chaunce espide advantage neare,
Let drive at her with all her dreadfull
might,
And thus upbrayding said: ' This token
beare
Unto the man whom thou doest love so
deare;
And tell him for his sake thy life thou
gavest.'

Which spitefull words she sore engriev'd to
    heare,
Thus answer'd: 'Lewdly thou my love de-
    pravest,
Who shortly must repent that now so
    vainely bravest.'

XXXIII

Nath'lesse that stroke so cruell passage
    found,
That, glauncing on her shoulder plate, it bit
Unto the bone, and made a griesly wound,
That she her shield through raging smart
    of it
Could scarse uphold; yet soone she it re-
    quit:
For having force increast through furious
    paine,
She her so rudely on the helmet smit,
That it empierced to the very braine,
And her proud person low prostrated on
    the plaine.

XXXIV

Where being layd, the wrothfull Britonesse
Stayd not till she came to her selfe againe,
But in revenge both of her loves distresse,
And her late vile reproch, though vaunted
    vaine,
And also of her wound, which sore did
    paine,
She with one stroke both head and helmet
    cleft.
Which dreadfull sight when all her warlike
    traine
There present saw, each one, of sence bereft,
Fled fast into the towne, and her sole vic-
    tor left.

XXXV

But yet so fast they could not home retrate,
But that swift Talus did the formost win;
And pressing through the preace unto the
    gate,
Pelmell with them attonce did enter in.
There then a piteous slaughter did begin:
For all that ever came within his reach
He with his yron flaile did thresh so thin,
That he no worke at all left for the leach:
Like to an hideous storme, which nothing
    may empeach.

XXXVI

And now by this the noble conqueresse
Her selfe came in, her glory to partake;

Where, though revengefull vow she did
    professe,
Yet when she saw the heapes which he did
    make
Of slaughtred carkasses, her heart did
    quake
For very ruth, which did it almost rive,
That she his fury willed him to slake:
For else he sure had left not one alive,
But all, in his revenge, of spirite would
    deprive.

XXXVII

Tho, when she had his execution stayd,
She for that yron prison did enquire,
In which her wretched love was captive layd:
Which breaking open with indignant ire,
She entred into all the partes entire:
Where when she saw that lothly uncouth
    sight,
Of men disguiz'd in womanishe attire,
Her heart gan grudge, for very deepe
    despight
Of so unmanly maske, in misery misdight.

XXXVIII

At last when as to her owne love she came,
Whom like disguize no lesse deformed had,
At sight thereof abasht with secrete shame,
She turnd her head aside, as nothing glad
To have beheld a spectacle so bad.
And then too well beleev'd that which tofore
Jealous suspect as true untruely drad:
Which vaine conceipt now nourishing no
    more,
She sought with ruth to salve his sad mis-
    fortunes sore.

XXXIX

Not so great wonder and astonishment
Did the most chast Penelope possesse,
To see her lord, that was reported drent,
And dead long since in dolorous distresse,
Come home to her in piteous wretchednesse,
After long travell of full twenty yeares,
That she knew not his favours likelynesse,
For many scarres and many hoary heares,
But stood long staring on him, mongst un-
    certaine feares.

XL

'Ah! my deare lord, what sight is this?'
    quoth she;
'What May-game hath misfortune made of
    you?

Where is that dreadfull manly looke ?
  where be
Those mighty palmes, the which ye wont
  t' embrew
In bloud of kings, and great hoastes to
  subdew ?
Could ought on earth so wondrous change
  have wrought,
As to have robde you of that manly hew ?
Could so great courage stouped have to
  ought ?
Then farewell, fleshly force; I see thy pride
  is nought.'

XLI

Thenceforth she streight into a bowre him
  brought,
And causd him those uncomely weedes un-
  dight,
And in their steede for other rayment
  sought,
Whereof there was great store, and ar-
  mors bright,
Which had bene reft from many a noble
  knight;
Whom that proud Amazon subdewed had,
Whilest fortune favourd her successe in
  fight:
In which when as she him anew had clad,
She was reviv'd, and joyd much in his
  semblance glad.

XLII

So there a while they afterwards remained,
Him to refresh, and her late wounds to
  heale:
During which space she there as princes
  rained,
And changing all that forme of common
  weale,
The liberty of women did repeale,
Which they had long usurpt; and them re-
  storing
To mens subjection, did true justice deale:
That all they, as a goddesse her adoring,
Her wisedome did admire, and hearkned to
  her loring.

XLIII

For all those knights, which long in captive
  shade
Had shrowded bene, she did from thraldome
  free,
And magistrates of all that city made,
And gave to them great living and large fee:

And that they should for ever faithfull bee,
Made them sweare fealty to Artegall:
Who when him selfe now well recur'd did
  see,
He purposd to proceed, what so be fall,
Uppon his first adventure, which him forth
  did call.

XLIV

Full sad and sorrowfull was Britomart
For his departure, her new cause of griefe;
Yet wisely moderated her owne smart,
Seeing his honor, which she tendred chiefe,
Consisted much in that adventures priefe.
The care whereof, and hope of his successe,
Gave unto her great comfort and reliefe,
That womanish complaints she did represse,
And tempred for the time her present
  heavinesse.

XLV

There she continu'd for a certaine space,
Till through his want her woe did more in-
  crease:
Then, hoping that the change of aire and
  place
Would change her paine, and sorrow some-
  what ease,
She parted thence, her anguish to appease.
Meane while her noble lord, Sir Artegall,
Went on his way, ne ever howre did cease,
Till he redeemed had that lady thrall:
That for another canto will more fitly fall.

CANTO VIII

Prince Arthure and Sir Artegall
   Free Samient from feare :
They slay the Soudan, drive his wife
   Adicia to despaire.

I

NOUGHT under heaven so strongly doth
  allure
The sence of man, and all his minde pos-
  sesse,
As beauties lovely baite, that doth procure
Great warriours oft their rigour to represse,
And mighty hands forget their manlinesse;
Drawne with the powre of an heart-robbing
  eye,
And wrapt in fetters of a golden tresse,
That can with melting pleasaunce mollifye
Their hardned hearts, enur'd to bloud and
  cruelty.

II

So whylome learnd that mighty Jewish
        swaine,
Each of whose lockes did match a man in
        might,
To lay his spoiles before his lemans traine:
So also did that great Oetean knight
For his loves sake his lions skin undight:
And so did warlike Antony neglect
The worlds whole rule for Cleopatras sight.
Such wondrous powre hath wemens faire
        aspect,
To captive men, and make them all the
        world reject.

III

Yet could it not sterne Artegall retaine,
Nor hold from suite of his avowed quest,
Which he had undertane to Gloriane;
But left his love, albe her strong request,
Faire Britomart, in languor and unrest,
And rode him selfe uppon his first in-
        tent:
Ne day nor night did ever idly rest;
Ne wight but onely Talus with him went,
The true guide of his way and vertuous
        government.

IV

So travelling, he chaunst far off to heed
A damzell, flying on a palfrey fast
Before two knights, that after her did
        speed
With all their powre, and her full fiercely
        chast
In hope to have her overhent at last:
Yet fled she fast, and both them farre out-
        went,
Carried with wings of feare, like fowle
        aghast,
With locks all loose, and rayment all to-
        rent;
And ever as she rode, her eye was backe-
        ward bent.

V

Soone after these he saw another knight,
That after those two former rode apace,
With speare in rest, and prickt with all his
        might:
So ran they all, as they had bene at bace,
They being chased, that did others chase.
At length he saw the hindmost overtake
One of those two, and force him turne his
        face;

How ever loth he were his way to slake,
Yet mote he algates now abide, and an-
        swere make.

VI

But th' other still pursu'd the fearefull
        mayd;
Who still from him as fast away did flie,
Ne once for ought her speedy passage
        stayd,
Till that at length she did before her spie
Sir Artegall, to whom she streight did hie
With gladfull hast, in hope of him to get
Succour against her greedy enimy:
Who, seeing her approch, gan forward set,
To save her from her feare, and him from
        force to let.

VII

But he like hound full greedy of his pray,
Being impatient of impediment,
Continu'd still his course, and by the way
Thought with his speare him quight have
        overwent.
So both together, ylike felly bent,
Like fiercely met. But Artegall was
        stronger,
And better skild in tilt and turnament,
And bore him quite out of his saddle,
        longer
Then two speares length: so mischiefe
        overmatcht the wronger.

VIII

And in his fall misfortune him mistooke;
For on his head unhappily he pight,
That his owne waight his necke asunder
        broke,
And left there dead. Meane while the
        other knight
Defeated had the other faytour quight,
And all his bowels in his body brast:
Whom leaving there in that dispiteous
        plight,
He ran still on, thinking to follow fast
His other fellow Pagan, which before him
        past.

IX

In stead of whom finding there ready prest
Sir Artegall, without discretion
He at him ran, with ready speare in rest:
Who, seeing him come still so fiercely on,
Against him made againe. So both anon
Together met, and strongly either strooke

And broke their speares; yet neither has forgon
His horses backe, yet to and fro long shooke,
And tottred like two towres, which through
a tempest quooke.

X

But when againe they had recovered sence,
They drew their swords, in mind to make amends
For what their speares had fayld of their pretence.
Which when the damzell, who those deadly ends
Of both her foes had seene, and now her frends
For her beginning a more fearefull fray,
She to them runnes in hast, and her haire rends,
Crying to them their cruell hands to stay,
Untill they both doe heare what she to them will say.

XI

They stayd their hands, when she thus gan to speake:
'Ah! gentle knights, what meane ye thus unwise
Upon your selves anothers wrong to wreake?
I am the wrong'd, whom ye did enterprise
Both to redresse, and both redrest likewise:
Witnesse the Paynims both, whom ye may see
There dead on ground. What doe ye then devise
Of more revenge? if more, then I am shee
Which was the roote of all; end your revenge on mee.'

XII

Whom when they heard so say, they lookt about,
To weete if it were true, as she had told;
Where when they saw their foes dead out of doubt,
Eftsoones they gan their wrothfull hands to hold,
And ventailes reare, each other to behold.
Tho, when as Artegall did Arthure vew,
So faire a creature, and so wondrous bold,
He much admired both his heart and hew,
And touched with intire affection, nigh him drew,

XIII

Saying: 'Sir knight, of pardon I you pray,
That all unweeting have you wrong'd thus sore,
Suffring my hand against my heart to stray:
Which if ye please forgive, I will therefore
Yeeld for amends my selfe yours evermore,
Or what so penaunce shall by you be red.'
To whom the Prince: 'Certes, me needeth more
To crave the same, whom errour so misled,
As that I did mistake the living for the ded.

XIV

'But sith ye please that both our blames shall die,
Amends may for the trespasse soone be made,
Since neither is endamadg'd much thereby.'
So can they both them selves full eath perswade
To faire accordaunce, and both faults to shade,
Either embracing other lovingly,
And swearing faith to either on his blade,
Never thenceforth to nourish enmity,
But either others cause to maintaine mutually.

XV

Then Artegall gan of the Prince enquire,
What were those knights, which there on ground were layd,
And had receiv'd their follies worthy hire,
And for what cause they chased so that mayd.
'Certes, I wote not well,' the Prince then sayd,
'But by adventure found them faring so,
As by the way unweetingly I strayd,
And lo the damzell selfe, whence all did grow,
Of whom we may at will the whole occasion know.'

XVI

Then they that damzell called to them nie,
And asked her, what were those two her fone,
From whom she earst so fast away did flie;
And what was she her selfe so woe begone,
And for what cause pursu'd of them attone.
To whom she thus: 'Then wote ye well, that I
Doe serve a queene, that not far hence doth wone,

A princesse of great powre and majestie,
Famous through all the world, and honor'd
    far and nie.

XVII

' Her name Mercilla most men use to call;
That is a mayden queene of high renowne,
For her great bounty knowen over all,
And soveraine grace, with which her royall
    crowne
She doth support, and strongly beateth
    downe
The malice of her foes, which her envy,
And at her happinesse do fret and frowne:
Yet she her selfe the more doth magnify,
And even to her foes her mercies multiply.

XVIII

' Mongst many which maligne her happy
    state,
There is a mighty man, which wonnes here
    by,
That with most fell despight and deadly
    hate
Seekes to subvert her crowne and dignity,
And all his powre doth thereunto apply:
And her good knights, of which so brave a
    band
Serves her as any princesse under sky,
He either spoiles, if they against him stand,
Or to his part allures, and bribeth under
    hand.

XIX

' Ne him sufficeth all the wrong and ill,
Which he unto her people does each day,
But that he seekes by traytrous traines to
    spill
Her person, and her sacred selfe to slay:
That, O ye heavens, defend, and turne away
From her unto the miscreant him selfe,
That neither hath religion nor fay,
But makes his god of his ungodly pelfe,
And idols serves; so let his idols serve the
    elfe.

XX

' To all which cruell tyranny, they say,
He is provokt, and stird up day and night
By his bad wife, that hight Adicia,
Who counsels him, through confidence of
    might,
To breake all bonds of law and rules of
    right.
For she her selfe professeth mortall foe

To Justice, and against her still doth fight,
Working to all that love her deadly woe,
And making all her knights and people to
    doe so.

XXI

' Which my liege lady seeing, thought it
    best,
With that his wife in friendly wise to deale,
For stint of strife and stablishment of rest
Both to her selfe and to her common weale,
And all forepast displeasures to repeale.
So me in message unto her she sent,
To treat with her, by way of enterdeale,
Of finall peace and faire attonement,
Which might concluded be by mutuall con-
    sent.

XXII

' All times have wont safe passage to afford
To messengers that come for causes just:
But this proude dame, disdayning all accord,
Not onely into bitter termes forth brust,
Reviling me, and rayling as she lust,
But lastly, to make proofe of utmost
    shame,
Me like a dog she out of dores did thrust,
Miscalling me by many a bitter name,
That never did her ill, ne once deserved
    blame.

XXIII

' And lastly, that no shame might wanting
    be,
When I was gone, soone after me she sent
These two false knights, whom there ye ly-
    ing see,
To be by them dishonoured and shent:
But thankt be God, and your good hardi-
    ment,
They have the price of their owne folly
    payd.'
So said this damzell, that hight Samient,
And to those knights, for their so noble ayd,
Her selfe most gratefull shew'd, and heap-
    ed thanks repayd.

XXIV

But they now having throughly heard, and
    seene
Al those great wrongs, the which that
    mayd complained
To have bene done against her lady queene
By that proud dame, which her so much
    disdained,

Were moved much thereat, and twixt them
    fained
With all their force to worke avengement
    strong
Uppon the Souldan selfe, which it mayn-
    tained,
And on his lady, th' author of that wrong,
And uppon all those knights that did to her
    belong.

XXV

But thinking best by counterfet disguise
To their deseigne to make the easier way,
They did this complot twixt them selves de-
    vise:
First, that Sir Artegall should him array
Like one of those two knights which dead
    there lay;
And then that damzell, the sad Samient,
Should as his purchast prize with him
    convay
Unto the Souldans court, her to present
Unto his scornefull lady, that for her had
    sent.

XXVI

So as they had deviz'd, Sir Artegall
Him clad in th' armour of a Pagan
    knight,
And taking with him, as his vanquisht
    thrall,
That damzell, led her to the Souldans
    right.
Where soone as his proud wife of her had
    sight,
Forth of her window as she looking lay,
She weened streight it was her Paynim
    knight,
Which brought that damzell as his purchast
    pray;
And sent to him a page, that mote direct
    his way.

XXVII

Who bringing them to their appointed place,
Offred his service to disarme the knight;
But he refusing him to let unlace,
For doubt to be discovered by his sight,
Kept himselfe still in his straunge armour
    dight.
Soone after whom the Prince arrived there,
And sending to the Souldan in despight
A bold defyance, did of him requere
That damzell, whom he held as wrongfull
    prisonere.

XXVIII

Wherewith the Souldan all with furie
    fraught,
Swearing and banning most blasphemously,
Commaunded straight his armour to be
    brought,
And mounting straight upon a charret hye,
(With yron wheeles and hookes arm'd
    dreadfully,
And drawne of cruell steedes, which he
    had fed
With flesh of men, whom through fell
    tyranny
He slaughtred had, and ere they were halfe
    ded,
Their bodies to his beasts for provender did
    spred,)

XXIX

So forth he came, all in a cote of plate,
Burnisht with bloudie rust; whiles on the
    greene
The Briton Prince him readie did awayte,
In glistering armes right goodly well be-
    seene,
That shone as bright as doth the heaven
    sheene;
And by his stirrup Talus did attend,
Playing his pages part, as he had beene
Before directed by his lord; to th' end
He should his flaile to finall execution bend.

XXX

Thus goe they both together to their geare,
With like fierce minds, but meanings dif-
    ferent:
For the proud Souldan, with presumpteous
    cheare,
And countenance sublime and insolent,
Sought onely slaughter and avengement:
But the brave Prince for honour and for
    right,
Gainst tortious powre and lawlesse regi-
    ment,
In the behalfe of wronged weake did fight:
More in his causes truth he trusted then in
    might.

XXXI

Like to the Thracian tyrant, who, they
    say,
Unto his horses gave his guests for meat,
Till he himselfe was made their greedie
    pray,
And torne in peeces by Alcides great:

So thought the Souldan in his follies threat,
Either the Prince in peeces to have torne
With his sharpe wheeles, in his first rages
    heat,
Or under his fierce horses feet have borne,
And trampled downe in dust his thoughts
    disdained scorne.

XXXII

But the bold child that perill well espying,
If he too rashly to his charet drew,
Gave way unto his horses speedie flying,
And their resistlesse rigour did eschew.
Yet, as he passed by, the Pagan threw
A shivering dart with so impetuous force,
That, had he not it shun'd with heedfull
    vew,
It had himselfe transfixed, or his horse,
Or made them both one masse withouten
    more remorse.

XXXIII

Oft drew the Prince unto his charret nigh,
In hope some stroke to fasten on him
    neare;
But he was mounted in his seat so high,
And his wingfooted coursers him did beare
So fast away, that ere his readie speare
He could advance, he farre was gone and
    past.
Yet still he him did follow every where,
And followed was of him likewise full
    fast,
So long as in his steedes the flaming breath
    did last.

XXXIV

Againe the Pagan threw another dart,
Of which he had with him abundant store,
On every side of his embatteld cart,
And of all other weapons lesse or more,
Which warlike uses had deviz'd of yore.
The wicked shaft, guyded through th' ayrie
    wyde
By some bad spirit, that it to mischiefe
    bore,
Stayd not, till through his curat it did
    glyde,
And made a griesly wound in his enriven
    side.

XXXV

Much was he grieved with that haplesse
    throe,
That opened had the welspring of his blood;

But much the more that to his hatefull foe
He mote not come, to wreake his wrathfull
    mood.
That made him rave, like to a lyon wood,
Which, being wounded of the huntsmans
    hand,
Can not come neare him in the covert
    wood,
Where he with boughes hath built his
    shady stand,
And fenst himselfe about with many a
    flaming brand.

XXXVI

Still when he sought t' approch unto him
    ny,
His charret wheeles about him whirled
    round,
And made him backe againe as fast to fly;
And eke his steedes, like to an hungry
    hound,
That hunting after game hath carrion
    found,
So cruelly did him persew and chace,
That his good steed, all were he much re-
    nound
For noble courage and for hardie race,
Durst not endure their sight, but fled from
    place to place.

XXXVII

Thus long they trast and traverst to and
    fro,
Seeking by every way to make some
    breach,
Yet could the Prince not nigh unto him goe,
That one sure stroke he might unto him
    reach.
Whereby his strengthes assay he might
    him teach.
At last from his victorious shield he drew
The vaile which did his powrefull light em-
    peach;
And comming full before his horses vew,
As they upon him prest, it plaine to them
    did shew.

XXXVIII

Like lightening flash, that hath the gazer
    burned,
So did the sight thereof their sense dismay,
That backe againe upon themselves they
    turned,
And with their ryder ranne perforce away:
Ne could the Souldan them from flying stay

With raynes, or wonted rule, as well he
    knew.
Nought feared they what he could do or
    say,
But th' onely feare that was before their
    vew;
From which, like mazed deare, dismayfully
    they flew.

XXXIX

Fast did they fly as them their feete could
    beare,
High over hilles, and lowly over dales,
As they were follow'd of their former
    feare.
In vaine the Pagan bannes, and sweares,
    and rayles,
And backe with both his hands unto him
    hayles
The resty raynes, regarded now no more:
He to them calles and speakes, yet nought
    avayles;
They heare him not, they have forgot his
    lore,
But go which way they list; their guide
    they have forlore.

XL

As when the firie-mouthed steeds, which
    drew
The sunnes bright wayne to Phaetons de-
    cay,
Soone as they did the monstrous Scorpion
    vew,
With ugly craples crawling in their way,
The dreadfull sight did them so sore affray,
That their well knowen courses they for-
    went,
And leading th' ever-burning lampe astray,
This lower world nigh all to ashes brent,
And left their scorched path yet in the
    firmament.

XLI

Such was the furie of these head-strong
    steeds,
Soone as the infants sunlike shield they
    saw,
That all obedience both to words and deeds
They quite forgot, and scornd all former
    law:
Through woods, and rocks, and mountaines
    they did draw
The yron charet, and the wheeles did teare,
And tost the Paynim, without feare or awe;

From side to side they tost him here and
    there,
Crying to them in vaine, that nould his cry-
    ing heare.

XLII

Yet still the Prince pursew'd him close be-
    hind,
Oft making offer him to smite, but found
No easie meanes according to his mind.
At last they have all overthrowne to
    ground,
Quite topside turvey, and the Pagan hound
Amongst the yron hookes and graples keene
Torne all to rags, and rent with many a
    wound,
That no whole peece of him was to be
    seene,
But scattred all about, and strow'd upon
    the greene.

XLIII

Like as the cursed sonne of Theseus,
That, following his chace in dewy morne,
To fly his stepdames loves outrageous,
Of his owne steedes was all to peeces torne,
And his faire limbs left in the woods for-
    lorne;
That for his sake Diana did lament,
And all the wooddy nymphes did wayle and
    mourne:
So was this Souldan rapt and all to-rent,
That of his shape appear'd no litle moni-
    ment.

XLIV

Onely his shield and armour, which there
    lay,
Though nothing whole, but all to-brusd and
    broken,
He up did take, and with him brought away,
That mote remaine for an eternall token
To all mongst whom this storie should be
    spoken,
How worthily, by Heavens high decree,
Justice that day of wrong her selfe had
    wroken,
That all men which that spectacle did see,
By like ensample mote for ever warned bee.

XLV

So on a tree, before the tyrants dore,
He caused them be hung in all mens sight,
To be a moniment for evermore.
Which when his ladie from the castles hight

Beheld, it much appald her troubled spright:
Yet not, as women wont, in dolefull fit
She was dismayd, or faynted through
    affright,
But gathered unto her her troubled wit,
And gan eftsoones devize to be aveng'd for
    it.

XLVI

Streight downe she ranne, like an enraged
    cow,
That is berobbed of her youngling dere,
With knife in hand, and fatally did vow
To wreake her on that mayden messengere,
Whom she had causd be kept as prisonere
By Artegall, misween'd for her owne knight,
That brought her backe. And comming
    present there,
She at her ran with all her force and might,
All flaming with revenge and furious de-
    spight.

XLVII

Like raging Ino, when with knife in hand
She threw her husbands murdred infant
    out;
Or fell Medea, when on Colchicke strand
Her brothers bones she scattered all about;
Or as that madding mother, mongst the
    rout
Of Bacchus priests, her owne deare flesh
    did teare.
Yet neither Ino, nor Medea stout,
Nor all the Mœnades so furious were,
As this bold woman, when she saw that
    damzell there.

XLVIII

But Artegall, being thereof aware,
Did stay her cruell hand, ere she her
    raught,
And as she did her selfe to strike prepare,
Out of her fist the wicked weapon caught:
With that, like one enfelon'd or distraught,
She forth did rome, whether her rage her
    bore,
With franticke passion and with furie
    fraught;
And breaking forth out at a posterne dore,
Unto the wyld wood ranne, her dolours to
    deplore.

XLIX

As a mad bytch, when as the franticke fit
Her burning tongue with rage inflamed hath,

Doth runne at randon, and with furious
    bit
Snatching at every thing, doth wreake her
    wrath
On man and beast that commeth in her
    path.
There they doe say that she transformed
    was
Into a tygre, and that tygres scath
In crueltie and outrage she did pas,
To prove her surname true, that she im-
    posed has.

L

Then Artegall himselfe discovering plaine,
Did issue forth gainst all that warlike rout
Of knights and armed men, which did
    maintaine
That ladies part, and to the Souldan lout:
All which he did assault with courage stout,
All were they nigh an hundred knights of
    name,
And like wyld goates them chaced all about,
Flying from place to place with cowheard
    shame,
So that with finall force them all he over-
    came.

LI

Then caused he the gates be opened wyde,
And there the Prince, as victour of that
    day,
With tryumph entertayn'd and glorifyde,
Presenting him with all the rich array
And roiall pompe, which there long hidden
    lay,
Purchast through lawlesse powre and tor-
    tious wrong
Of that proud Souldan, whom he earst did
    slay.
So both, for rest there having stayd not
    long,
Marcht with that mayd, fit matter for an-
    other song.

CANTO IX

Arthur and Artegall catch Guyle,
    Whom Talus doth dismay:
They to Mercillaes pallace come,
    And see her rich array.

I

WHAT tygre, or what other salvage wight,
Is so exceeding furious and fell

As Wrong, when it hath arm'd it selfe with
  might ?
Not fit mongst men, that doe with reason
  mell,
But mongst wyld beasts and salvage woods
  to dwell;
Where still the stronger doth the weake devoure,
And they that most in boldnesse doe excell
Are dreadded most, and feared for their
  powre:
Fit for Adicia, there to build her wicked
  bowre.

II

There let her wonne farre from resort of
  men,
Where righteous Artegall her late exyled;
There let her ever keepe her damned den,
Where none may be with her lewd parts
  defyled,
Nor none but beasts may be of her de-
  spoyled:
And turne we to the noble Prince, where
  late
We did him leave, after that he had foyled
The cruell Souldan, and with dreadfull
  fate
Had utterly subverted his unrighteous
  state.

III

Where having with Sir Artegall a space
Well solast in that Souldans late delight,
They both resolving now to leave the place,
Both it and all the wealth therein behight
Unto that damzell in her ladies right,
And so would have departed on their way.
But she them woo'd by all the meanes she
  might,
And earnestly besought, to wend that day
With her, to see her ladie thence not farre
  away.

IV

By whose entreatie both they overcommen,
Agree to goe with her, and by the way,
(As often falles) of sundry things did com-
  men.
Mongst which that damzell did to them
  bewray
A straunge adventure, which not farre
  thence lay;
To weet, a wicked villaine, bold and stout,
Which wonned in a rocke not farre away,

That robbed all the countrie there about,
And brought the pillage home, whence
  none could get it out.

V

Thereto both his owne wylie wit (she sayd)
And eke the fastnesse of his dwelling place,
Both unassaylable, gave him great ayde:
For he so crafty was to forge and face,
So light of hand, and nymble of his pace,
So smooth of tongue, and subtile in his tale,
That could deceive one looking in his face;
Therefore by name Malengin they him call,
Well knowen by his feates, and famous
  over all.

VI

Through these his slights he many doth
  confound,
And eke the rocke, in which he wonts to
  dwell,
Is wondrous strong, and hewen farre under
  ground
A dreadfull depth, how deepe no man can
  tell;
But some doe say, it goeth downe to hell.
And all within, it full of wyndings is,
And hidden wayes, that scarse an hound
  by smell
Can follow out those false footsteps of his,
Ne none can backe returne that once are
  gone amis.

VII

Which when those knights had heard, their
  harts gan earne
To understand that villeins dwelling place,
And greatly it desir'd of her to learne,
And by which way they towards it should
  trace.
'Were not,' sayd she, 'that it should let
  your pace
Towards my ladies presence by you ment,
I would you guyde directly to the place.'
'Then let not that,' said they, 'stay your
  intent;
For neither will one foot, till we that carle
  have hent.'

VIII

So forth they past, till they approched ny
Unto the rocke where was the villains
  won:
Which when the damzell neare at hand did
  spy,

She warn'd the knights thereof: who there-
　　upon
Gan to advize what best were to be done.
So both agreed to send that mayd afore,
Where she might sit nigh to the den alone,
Wayling, and raysing pittifull uprore,
As if she did some great calamitie de-
　　plore.

IX

With noyse whereof when as the caytive
　　carle
Should issue forth, in hope to find some
　　spoyle,
They in awayt would closely him ensnarle,
Ere to his den he backward could recoyle,
And so would hope him easily to foyle.
The damzell straight went, as she was di-
　　rected,
Unto the rocke, and there upon the soyle
Having her selfe in wretched wize ab-
　　jected,
Gan weepe and wayle, as if great griefe
　　had her affected.

X

The cry whereof entring the hollow cave,
Eftsoones brought forth the villaine, as
　　they ment,
With hope of her some wishfull boot to
　　have.
Full dreadfull wight he was, as ever went
Upon the earth, with hollow eyes deepe
　　pent,
And long curld locks, that downe his
　　shoulders shagged,
And on his backe an uncouth vestiment
Made of straunge stuffe, but all to-worne
　　and ragged,
And underneath his breech was all to-torne
　　and jagged.

XI

And in his hand an huge long staffe he
　　held,
Whose top was arm'd with many an yron
　　hooke,
Fit to catch hold of all that he could weld,
Or in the compasse of his clouches tooke;
And ever round about he cast his looke.
Als at his backe a great wyde net he bore,
With which he seldome fished at the brooke,
But usd to fish for fooles on the dry shore,
Of which he in faire weather wont to take
　　great store.

XII

Him when the damzell saw fast by her side,
So ugly creature, she was nigh dismayd,
And now for helpe aloud in earnest cride.
But when the villaine saw her so affrayd,
He gan with guilefull words her to per-
　　swade
To banish feare, and with Sardonian smyle
Laughing on her, his false intent to shade,
Gan forth to lay his bayte her to beguyle,
That from her self unwares he might her
　　steale the whyle.

XIII

Like as the fouler on his guilefull pype
Charmes to the birds full many a pleasant
　　lay,
That they the whiles may take lesse heedie
　　keepe,
How he his nets doth for their ruine lay:
So did the villaine to her prate and play,
And many pleasant trickes before her show,
To turne her eyes from his intent away:
For he in slights and jugling feates did flow,
And of legierdemayne the mysteries did
　　know.

XIV

To which whilest she lent her intentive
　　mind,
He suddenly his net upon her threw,
That oversprad her like a puffe of wind;
And snatching her soone up, ere well she
　　knew,
Ran with her fast away unto his mew,
Crying for helpe aloud.　But when as ny
He came unto his cave, and there did vew
The armed knights stopping his passage by,
He threw his burden downe, and fast away
　　did fly.

XV

But Artegall him after did pursew,
The whiles the Prince there kept the en-
　　trance still:
Up to the rocke he ran, and thereon flew
Like a wyld gote, leaping from hill to hill,
And dauncing on the craggy cliffes at will;
That deadly daunger seem'd in all mens
　　sight,
To tempt such steps, where footing was so
　　ill:
Ne ought avayled for the armed knight
To thinke to follow him, that was so swift
　　and light.

XVI

Which when he saw, his yron man he sent
To follow him; for he was swift in chace.
He him pursewd, where ever that he went;
Both over rockes, and hilles, and every
    place,
Where so he fled, he followd him apace:
So that he shortly forst him to forsake
The hight, and downe descend unto the
    base.
There he him courst a fresh, and soone did
    make
To leave his proper forme, and other shape
    to take.

XVII

Into a foxe himselfe he first did tourne;
But he him hunted like a foxe full fast:
Then to a bush himselfe he did transforme;
But he the bush did beat, till that at last
Into a bird it chaung'd, and from him past,
Flying from tree to tree, from wand to
    wand:
But he then stones at it so long did cast,
That like a stone it fell upon the land;
But he then tooke it up, and held fast in
    his hand.

XVIII

So he it brought with him unto the knights,
And to his lord, Sir Artegall, it lent,
Warning him hold it fast, for feare of
    slights.
Who whilest in hand it gryping hard he
    hent,
Into a hedgehogge all unwares it went,
And prickt him so that he away it threw.
Then gan it runne away incontinent,
Being returned to his former hew:
But Talus soone him overtooke, and back-
    ward drew.

XIX

But when as he would to a snake againe
Have turn'd himselfe, he with his yron flayle
Gan drive at him, with so huge might and
    maine,
That all his bones as small as sandy grayle
He broke, and did his bowels disentrayle;
Crying in vaine for helpe, when helpe was
    past.
So did deceipt the selfe deceiver fayle.
There they him left a carrion outcast,
For beasts and foules to feede upon for
    their repast.

XX

Thence forth they passed with that gentle
    mayd,
To see her ladie, as they did agree.
To which when she approched, thus she
    sayd:
' Loe now, right noble knights, arriv'd ye
    bee
Nigh to the place which ye desir'd to see:
There shall ye see my soverayne Lady
    Queene,
Most sacred wight, most debonayre and
    free,
That ever yet upon this earth was seene,
Or that with diademe hath ever crowned
    beene.'

XXI

The gentle knights rejoyced much to heare
The prayses of that prince so manifold,
And passing litle further, commen were
Where they a stately pallace did behold,
Of pompous show, much more then she had
    told;
With many towres and tarras mounted hye,
And all their tops bright glistering with
    gold,
That seemed to outshine the dimmed skye,
And with their brightnesse daz'd the
    straunge beholders eye.

XXII

There they alighting, by that damzell were
Directed in, and shewed all the sight:
Whose porch, that most magnificke did ap-
    peare,
Stood open wyde to all men day and night;
Yet warded well by one of mickle might,
That sate thereby, with gyantlike resem-
    blance,
To keepe out Guyle, and Malice, and De-
    spight,
That under shew oftimes of fayned sem-
    blance
Are wont in princes courts to worke great
    scath and hindrance.

XXIII

His name was Awe; by whom they passing
    in
Went up the hall, that was a large wyde
    roome,
All full of people making troublous din,
And wondrous noyse, as if that there were
    some

Which unto them was dealing righteous
doome.
By whom they passing, through the thickest preasse,
The marshall of the hall to them did
come;
His name hight Order, who, commaunding
peace,
Them guyded through the throng, that did
their clamors ceasse.

XXIV

They ceast their clamors upon them to
gaze;
Whom seeing all in armour bright as day,
Straunge there to see, it did them much
amaze,
And with unwonted terror halfe affray:
For never saw they there the like array;
Ne ever was the name of warre there
spoken,
But joyous peace and quietnesse alway,
Dealing just judgements, that mote not be
broken
For any brybes, or threates of any to be
wroken.

XXV

There as they entred at the scriene, they
saw
Some one, whose tongue was for his tres-
passe vyle
Nayld to a post, adjudged so by law:
For that therewith he falsely did revyle
And foule blaspheme that queene for
forged guyle,
Both with bold speaches which he blazed
had,
And with lewd poems which he did com-
pyle;
For the bold title of a poet bad
He on himselfe had ta'en, and rayling
rymes had sprad.

XXVI

Thus there he stood, whylest high over his
head
There written was the purport of his sin,
In cyphers strange, that few could rightly
read,
Bon font: but *Bon*, that once had written
bin,
Was raced out, and *Mal* was now put in:
So now *Malfont* was plainely to be red;
Eyther for th' evill which he did therein,

Or that he likened was to a welhed
Of evill words, and wicked sclaunders by
him shed.

XXVII

They, passing by, were guyded by degree
Unto the presence of that gratious queene:
Who sate on high, that she might all men
see,
And might of all men royally be seene,
Upon a throne of gold full bright and
sheene,
Adorned all with gemmes of endlesse price,
As either might for wealth have gotten
bene,
Or could be fram'd by workmans rare de-
vice;
And all embost with lyons and with flour-
delice.

XXVIII

All over her a cloth of state was spred,
Not of rich tissew, nor of cloth of gold,
Nor of ought else that may be richest
red,
But like a cloud, as likest may be told,
That her brode spreading wings did wyde
unfold;
Whose skirts were bordred with bright
sunny beams,
Glistring like gold, amongst the plights en-
rold,
And here and there shooting forth silver
streames,
Mongst which crept litle angels through
the glittering gleames.

XXIX

Seemed those litle angels did uphold
The cloth of state, and on their purpled
wings
Did beare the pendants, through their nim-
blesse bold:
Besides, a thousand more of such as sings
Hymnes to High God, and carols heavenly
things,
Encompassed the throne on which she sate:
She angel-like, the heyre of ancient kings
And mightie conquerors, in royall state,
Whylest kings and kesars at her feet did
them prostrate.

XXX

Thus she did sit in soverayne majestie,
Holding a scepter in her royall hand,

The sacred pledge of peace and clemencie,
With which High God had blest her happie
    land,
Maugre so many foes which did withstand.
But at her feet her sword was likewise
    layde,
Whose long rest rusted the bright steely
    brand;
Yet when as foes enforst, or friends sought
    ayde,
She could it sternely draw, that all the
    world dismayde.

XXXI

And round about, before her feet there sate
A bevie of faire virgins clad in white,
That goodly seem'd t' adorne her royall
    state,
All lovely daughters of high Jove, that
    hight
Litæ, by him begot in loves delight
Upon the righteous Themis: those they say
Upon Joves judgement seat wayt day and
    night,
And when in wrath he threats the worlds
    decay,
They doe his anger calme, and cruell ven-
    geance stay.

XXXII

They also doe by his divine permission
Upon the thrones of mortall princes tend,
And often treat for pardon and remission
To suppliants, through frayltie which of-
    fend.
Those did upon Mercillaes throne attend:
Just Dice, wise Eunomie, myld Eirene;
And them amongst, her glorie to commend,
Sate goodly Temperance in garments clene,
And sacred Reverence, yborne of heavenly
    strene.

XXXIII

Thus did she sit in royall rich estate,
Admyr'd of many, honoured of all,
Whylest underneath her feete, there as she
    sate,
An huge great lyon lay, that mote appall
An hardie courage, like captived thrall,
With a strong yron chaine and coller bound,
That once he could not move, nor quich at
    all;
Yet did he murmure with rebellious sound,
And softly royne, when salvage choler gan
    redound.

XXXIV

So sitting high in dreaded soverayntie,
Those two strange knights were to her pre-
    sence brought;
Who, bowing low before her majestie,
Did to her myld obeysance, as they ought,
And meekest boone that they imagine
    mought.
To whom she eke inclyning her withall,
As a faire stoupe of her high soaring
    thought,
A chearefull countenance on them let fall,
Yet tempred with some majestie imperiall.

XXXV

As the bright sunne, what time his fierie
    teme
Towards the westerne brim begins to draw,
Gins to abate the brightnesse of his beme,
And fervour of his flames somewhat adaw:
So did this mightie ladie, when she saw
Those two strange knights such homage to
    her make,
Bate somewhat of that majestie and awe,
That whylome wont to doe so many quake,
And with more myld aspect those two to
    entertake.

XXXVI

Now at that instant, as occasion fell,
When these two stranger knights arriv'd in
    place,
She was about affaires of common wele,
Dealing of justice with indifferent grace,
And hearing pleas of people meane and
    base.
Mongst which, as then, there was for to be
    heard
The tryall of a great and weightie case,
Which on both sides was then debating
    hard:
But at the sight of these, those were a while
    debard.

XXXVII

But after all her princely entertayne,
To th' hearing of that former cause in
    hand
Her selfe eftsoones she gan convert againe;
Which that those knights likewise mote un-
    derstand,
And witnesse forth aright in forrain land,
Taking them up unto her stately throne,
Where they mote heare the matter
    throughly scand

On either part, she placed th' one on th'
one,
The other on the other side, and neare them
none.

XXXVIII

Then was there brought, as prisoner to the
barre,
A ladie of great countenance and place,
But that she it with foule abuse did marre;
Yet did appeare rare beautie in her face,
But blotted with condition vile and base,
That all her other honour did obscure,
And titles of nobilitie deface:
Yet in that wretched semblant, she did sure
The peoples great compassion unto her al-
lure.

XXXIX

Then up arose a person of deepe reach,
And rare in-sight, hard matters to revele;
That well could charme his tongue, and
time his speach
To all assayes; his name was called Zele:
He gan that ladie strongly to appele
Of many haynous crymes, by her enured,
And with sharpe reasons rang her such a
pele,
That those whom she to pitie had allured
He now t' abhorre and loath her person had
procured.

XL

First gan he tell, how this, that seem'd so
faire
And royally arayd, Duessa hight,
That false Duessa, which had wrought great
care
And mickle mischiefe unto many a knight,
By her beguyled and confounded quight:
But not for those she now in question came,
Though also those mote question'd be
aright,
But for vyld treasons and outrageous shame,
Which she against the dred Mercilla oft did
frame.

XLI

For she whylome (as ye mote yet right
well
Remember) had her counsels false con-
spyred
With faithlesse Blandamour and Paridell,
(Both two her paramours, both by her
hyred,

And both with hope of shadowes vaine in-
spyred,)
And with them practiz'd, how for to de-
pryve
Mercilla of her crowne, by her aspyred,
That she might it unto her selfe deryve,
And tryumph in their blood, whom she to
death did dryve.

XLII

But through high heavens grace, which fav-
our not
The wicked driftes of trayterous desynes
Gainst loiall princes, all this cursed plot,
Ere proofe it tooke, discovered was be-
tymes,
And th' actours won the meede meet for
their crymes.
Such be the meede of all that by such mene
Unto the type of kingdomes title clymes.
But false Duessa, now untitled queene,
Was brought to her sad doome, as here was
to be seene.

XLIII

Strongly did Zele her haynous fact enforce,
And many other crimes of foule defame
Against her brought, to banish all remorse,
And aggravate the horror of her blame.
And with him to make part against her,
came
Many grave persons, that against her pled:
First was a sage old syre, that had to name
The Kingdomes Care, with a white silver
hed,
That many high regards and reasons gainst
her red.

XLIV

Then gan Authority her to appose
With peremptorie powre, that made all
mute;
And then the Law of Nations gainst her
rose,
And reasons brought, that no man could
refute;
Next gan Religion gainst her to impute
High Gods beheast, and powre of holy
lawes;
Then gan the Peoples Cry and Commons
Sute
Importune care of their owne publicke
cause;
And lastly Justice charged her with breach
of lawes.

XLV

But then for her, on the contrarie part,
Rose many advocates for her to plead:
First there came Pittie, with full tender
   hart,
And with her joyn'd Regard of Woman-
   head;
And then came Daunger, threatning hid-
   den dread
And high alliance unto forren powre;
Then came Nobilitie of Birth, that bread
Great ruth through her misfortunes tra-
   gicke stowre;
And lastly Griefe did plead, and many
   teares forth powre.

XLVI

With the neare touch whereof in tender
   hart
The Briton Prince was sore empassionate,
And woxe inclined much unto her part,
Through the sad terror of so dreadfull fate,
And wretched ruine of so high estate,
That for great ruth his courage gan relent.
Which when as Zele perceived to abate,
He gan his earnest fervour to augment,
And many fearefull objects to them to pre-
   sent.

XLVII

He gan t' efforce the evidence anew,
And new accusements to produce in place:
He brought forth that old hag of hellish
   hew,
The cursed Ate, brought her face to face,
Who privie was, and partie in the case:
She, glad of spoyle and ruinous decay,
Did her appeach, and, to her more dis-
   grace,
The plot of all her practise did display,
And all her traynes and all her treasons
   forth did lay.

XLVIII

Then brought he forth, with griesly grim
   aspect,
Abhorred Murder, who with bloudie knyfe
Yet dropping fresh in hand did her detect,
And there with guiltie bloudshed charged
   ryfe:
Then brought he forth Sedition, breeding
   stryfe
In troublous wits, and mutinous uprore:
Then brought he forth Incontinence of
   Lyfe,

Even foule Adulterie her face before,
And lewd Impietie, that her accused sore.

XLIX

All which when as the Prince had heard
   and seene,
His former fancies ruth he gan repent,
And from her partie eftsoones was drawen
   cleene.
But Artegall, with constant firme intent,
For zeale of justice was against her bent.
So was she guiltie deemed of them all.
Then Zele began to urge her punishment,
And to their queene for judgement loudly
   call,
Unto Mercilla myld, for justice gainst the
   thrall.

L

But she, whose princely breast was touched
   nere
With piteous ruth of her so wretched
   plight,
Though plaine she saw, by all that she did
   heare,
That she of death was guiltie found by
   right,
Yet would not let just vengeance on her
   light;
But rather let in stead thereof to fall
Few perling drops from her faire lampes
   of light;
The which she covering with her purple
   pall
Would have the passion hid, and up arose
   withall.

CANTO X

Prince Arthur takes the enterprize
   For Belgee for to fight:
Gerioneos seneschall
   He slayes in Belges right.

I

SOME clarkes doe doubt in their devicefull
   art,
Whether this heavenly thing whereof I
   treat,
To weeten Mercie, be of Justice part,
Or drawne forth from her by divine ex-
   treate.
This well I wote, that sure she is as great,
And meriteth to have as high a place,
Sith in th' Almighties everlasting seat

She first was bred, and borne of heavenly
    race;
From thence pour'd down on men, by influ-
    ence of grace.

II

For if that vertue be of so great might,
Which from just verdict will for nothing
    start,
But, to preserve inviolated right,
Oft spilles the principall, to save the part;
So much more then is that of powre and
    art,
That seekes to save the subject of her
    skill,
Yet never doth from doome of right de-
    part:
As it is greater prayse to save then spill,
And better to reforme then to cut off the
    ill.

III

Who then can thee, Mercilla, throughly
    prayse,
That herein doest all earthly princes pas?
What heavenly muse shall thy great honour
    rayse
Up to the skies, whence first deriv'd it was,
And now on earth it selfe enlarged has
From th' utmost brinke of the Americke
    shore
Unto the margent of the Molucas?
Those nations farre thy justice doe adore:
But thine owne people do thy mercy prayse
    much more.

IV

Much more it praysed was of those two
    knights,
The noble Prince and righteous Artegall,
When they had seene and heard her doome
    a rights
Against Duessa, damned by them all;
But by her tempred without griefe or gall,
Till strong constraint did her thereto en-
    force:
And yet even then ruing her wilfull fall
With more then needfull naturall remorse,
And yeelding the last honour to her
    wretched corse.

V

During all which, those knights continu'd
    there,
Both doing and receiving curtesies

Of that great ladie, who with goodly chere
Them entertayn'd, fit for their dignities,
Approving dayly to their noble eyes
Royall examples of her mercies rare,
And worthie paterns of her clemencies;
Which till this day mongst many living
    are,
Who them to their posterities doe still
    declare.

VI

Amongst the rest, which in that space
    befell,
There came two springals of full tender
    yeares,
Farre thence from forrein land, where they
    did dwell,
To seeke for succour of her and of her
    peares,
With humble prayers and intreatfull teares;
Sent by their mother, who a widow was,
Wrapt in great dolours and in deadly feares
By a strong tyrant, who invaded has
Her land, and slaine her children ruefully,
    alas!

VII

Her name was Belgæ, who in former age
A ladie of great worth and wealth had
    beene,
And mother of a frutefull heritage,
Even seventeene goodly sonnes; which who
    had seene
In their first flowre, before this fatall teene
Them overtooke, and their faire blossomes
    blasted,
More happie mother would her surely weene
Then famous Niobe, before she tasted
Latonaes childrens wrath, that all her issue
    wasted.

VIII

But this fell tyrant, through his tortious
    powre,
Had left her now but five of all that brood:
For twelve of them he did by times de-
    voure,
And to his idole sacrifice their blood,
Whylest he of none was stopped, nor with-
    stood.
For soothly he was one of matchlesse might,
Of horrible aspect and dreadfull mood,
And had three bodies in one wast empight,
And th' armes and legs of three, to succour
    him in fight.

IX

And sooth they say that he was borne and
  bred
Of gyants race, the sonne of Geryon,
He that whylome in Spaine so sore was
  dred
For his huge powre and great oppression,
Which brought that land to his subjection
Through his three bodies powre, in one
  combynd;
And eke all strangers, in that region
Arryving, to his kyne for food assynd;
The fayrest kyne alive, but of the fiercest
  kynd.

X

For they were all, they say, of purple hew,
Kept by a cowheard, hight Eurytion,
A cruell carle, the which all strangers
  slew,
Ne day nor night did sleepe, t' attend them
  on,
But walkt about them ever and anone,
With his two headed dogge, that Orthrus
  hight;
Orthrus begotten by great Typhaon
And foule Echidna, in the house of Night;
But Hercules them all did overcome in
  fight.

XI

His sonne was this, Geryoneo hight;
Who, after that his monstrous father fell
Under Alcides club, streight tooke his flight
From that sad land, where he his syre did
  quell,
And came to this, where Belge then did
  dwell
And flourish in all wealth and happinesse,
Being then new made widow (as befell)
After her noble husbands late decesse;
Which gave beginning to her woe and
  wretchednesse.

XII

Then this bold tyrant, of her widowhed
Taking advantage, and her yet fresh woes,
Himselfe and service to her offered,
Her to defend against all forrein foes,
That should their powre against her right
  oppose.
Whereof she glad, now needing strong de-
  fence,
Him entertayn'd, and did her champion
  chose:

Which long he usd with carefull diligence,
The better to confirme her fearelesse confidence.

XIII

By meanes whereof, she did at last commit
All to his hands, and gave him soveraine
  powre
To doe what ever he thought good or fit.
Which having got, he gan forth from that
  howre
To stirre up strife, and many a tragicke
  stowre,
Giving her dearest children one by one
Unto a dreadfull monster to devoure,
And setting up an idole of his owne,
The image of his monstrous parent Geryone.

XIV

So tyrannizing, and oppressing all,
The woefull widow had no meanes now left,
But unto gratious great Mercilla call
For ayde against that cruell tyrants theft,
Ere all her children he from her had reft.
Therefore these two, her eldest sonnes, she
  sent,
To seeke for succour of this ladies gieft:
To whom their sute they humbly did pre-
  sent,
In th' hearing of full many knights and
  ladies gent.

XV

Amongst the which then fortuned to bee
The noble Briton Prince, with his brave
  peare;
Who when he none of all those knights did
  see
Hastily bent that enterprise to heare,
Nor undertake the same, for cowheard feare,
He stepped forth with courage bold and
  great,
Admyr'd of all the rest in presence there,
And humbly gan that mightie queene en-
  treat
To graunt him that adventure for his former
  feat.

XVI

She gladly graunted it: then he straight
  way
Himselfe unto his journey gan prepare,
And all his armours readie dight that day,
That nought the morrow next mote stay
  his fare.

The morrow next appear'd, with purple
　　hayre
Yet dropping fresh out of the Indian fount,
And bringing light into the heavens fayre,
When he was readie to his steede to mount,
Unto his way, which now was all his care
　　and count.

XVII

Then taking humble leave of that great
　　queene,
Who gave him roiall giftes and riches rare,
As tokens of her thankefull mind beseene,
And leaving Artegall to his owne care,
Upon his voyage forth he gan to fare,
With those two gentle youthes, which him
　　did guide,
And all his way before him still prepare.
Ne after him did Artigall abide,
But on his first adventure forward forth
　　did ride.

XVIII

It was not long till that the Prince arrived
Within the land where dwelt that ladie sad,
Whereof that tyrant had her now deprived,
And into moores and marshes banisht had,
Out of the pleasant soyle and citties glad,
In which she wont to harbour happily:
But now his cruelty so sore she drad,
That to those fennes for fastnesse she did
　　fly,
And there her selfe did hyde from his hard
　　tyranny.

XIX

There he her found in sorrow and dismay,
All solitarie without living wight;
For all her other children, through affray,
Had hid themselves, or taken further
　　flight:
And eke her selfe through sudden strange
　　affright,
When one in armes she saw, began to
　　fly;
But when her owne two sonnes she had in
　　sight,
She gan take hart, and looke up joyfully:
For well she wist this knight came succour
　　to supply:

XX

And running unto them with greedy joyes,
Fell straight about their neckes, as they did
　　kneele,

And bursting forth in teares, 'Ah! my
　　sweet boyes,'
Sayd she, ' yet now I gin new life to feele,
And feeble spirits, that gan faint and reele,
Now rise againe at this your joyous sight.
Alreadie seemes that Fortunes headlong
　　wheele
Begins to turne, and sunne to shine more
　　bright
Then it was wont, through comfort of this
　　noble knight.'

XXI

Then turning unto him, 'And you, sir
　　knight,'
Said she, 'that taken have this toylesome
　　paine
For wretched woman, miserable wight,
May you in heaven immortall guerdon gaine
For so great travell as you doe sustaine:
For other meede may hope for none of
　　mee,
To whom nought else but bare life doth re-
　　maine;
And that so wretched one, as ye do see,
Is liker lingring death then loathed life to
　　bee.'

XXII

Much was he moved with her piteous plight,
And low dismounting from his loftie steede,
Gan to recomfort her all that he might,
Seeking to drive away deepe rooted dreede,
With hope of helpe in that her greatest
　　neede.
So thence he wished her with him to wend,
Unto some place where they mote rest and
　　feede,
And she take comfort, which God now did
　　send:
Good hart in evils doth the evils much
　　amend.

XXIII

' Ay me !' sayd she, ' and whether shall I
　　goe ?
Are not all places full of forraine powres ?
My pallaces possessed of my foe,
My cities sackt, and their sky-threating
　　towres
Raced, and made smooth fields now full of
　　flowres ?
Onely these marishes and myrie bogs,
In which the fearefull ewftes do build their
　　bowres,

Yeeld me an hostry mongst the croking
    frogs,
And harbour here in safety from those
    ravenous dogs.'

XXIV

'Nathlesse,' said he, 'deare ladie, with me
    goe;
Some place shall us receive, and harbour
    yield;
If not, we will it force, maugre your foe,
And purchase it to us with speare and
    shield:
And if all fayle, yet farewell open field:
The Earth to all her creatures lodging
    lends.'
With such his chearefull speaches he doth
    wield
Her mind so well, that to his will she
    bends,
And bynding up her locks and weeds, forth
    with him wends.

XXV

They came unto a citie farre up land,
The which whylome that ladies owne had
    bene;
But now by force extort out of her hand
By her strong foe, who had defaced cleene
Her stately towres and buildings sunny
    sheene,
Shut up her haven, mard her marchants
    trade,
Robbed her people, that full rich had
    beene,
And in her necke a castle huge had made,
The which did her commaund, without
    needing perswade.

XXVI

That castle was the strength of all that
    state,
Untill that state by strength was pulled
    downe,
And that same citie, so now ruinate,
Had bene the keye of all that kingdomes
    crowne;
Both goodly castle, and both goodly towne,
Till that th' offended Heavens list to lowre
Upon their blisse, and balefull Fortune
    frowne,
When those gainst states and kingdomes
    do conjure,
Who then can thinke their hedlong ruine
    to recure?

XXVII

But he had brought it now in servile bond,
And made it beare the yoke of Inquisition,
Stryving long time in vaine it to withstond;
Yet glad at last to make most base sub-
    mission,
And life enjoy for any composition.
So now he hath new lawes and orders new
Imposd on it, with many a hard condi-
    tion,
And forced it the honour that is dew
To God to doe unto his idole most untrew.

XXVIII

To him he hath, before this castle greene,
Built a faire chappell, and an altar framed
Of costly ivory, full rich beseene,
On which that cursed idole, farre proclamed,
He hath set up, and him his god hath
    named,
Offring to him in sinfull sacrifice
The flesh of men, to Gods owne likenesse
    framed,
And powring forth their bloud in brutishe
    wize,
That any yron eyes to see it would agrize.

XXIX

And for more horror and more crueltie,
Under that cursed idols altar stone
An hideous monster doth in darknesse lie,
Whose dreadfull shape was never seene of
    none
That lives on earth, but unto those alone
The which unto him sacrificed bee.
Those he devoures, they say, both flesh and
    bone:
What else they have is all the tyrants fee;
So that no whit of them remayning one may
    see.

XXX

There eke he placed a strong garrisone,
And set a seneschall of dreaded might,
That by his powre oppressed every one,
And vanquished all ventrous knights in
    fight;
To whom he wont shew all the shame he
    might,
After that them in battell he had wonne.
To which when now they gan approch in
    sight,
The ladie counseld him the place to shonne,
Whereas so many knights had fouly bene
    fordonne.

XXXI

Her fearefull speaches nought he did regard,
But ryding streight under the castle wall,
Called aloud unto the watchfull ward,
Which there did wayte, willing them forth
    to call
Into the field their tyrants seneschall.
To whom when tydings thereof came, he
    streight
Cals for his armes, and arming him withall,
Eftsoones forth pricked proudly in his
    might,
And gan with courage fierce addresse him to
    the fight.

XXXII

They both encounter in the middle plaine,
And their sharpe speares doe both together
    smite
Amid their shields, with so huge might
    and maine,
That seem'd their soules they wold have
    ryven quight
Out of their breasts, with furious despight.
Yet could the seneschals no entrance find
Into the Princes shield, where it empight,
So pure the mettall was, and well refynd,
But shivered all about, and scattered in the
    wynd.

XXXIII

Not so the Princes, but with restlesse force
Into his shield it readie passage found,
Both through his haberjeon and eke his
    corse:
Which tombling downe upon the sense-
    lesse ground,
Gave leave unto his ghost from thraldome
    bound,
To wander in the griesly shades of night.
There did the Prince him leave in deadly
    swound,
And thence unto the castle marched right,
To see if entrance there as yet obtaine he
    might.

XXXIV

But as he nigher drew, three knights he
    spyde,
All arm'd to point, issuing forth a pace,
Which towards him with all their powre
    did ryde,
And meeting him right in the middle race,
Did all their speares attonce on him en-
    chace,

As three great culverings for battrie bent,
And leveld all against one certaine place,
Doe all attonce their thunders rage forth
    rent,
That makes the wals to stagger with aston-
    ishment.

XXXV

So all attonce they on the Prince did thon-
    der;
Who from his saddle swarved nought
    asyde,
Ne to their force gave way, that was great
    wonder,
But like a bulwarke firmely did abyde,
Rebutting him which in the midst did
    ryde,
With so huge rigour, that his mortall
    speare
Past through his shield, and pierst through
    either syde,
That downe he fell uppon his mother deare,
And powred forth his wretched life in
    deadly dreare.

XXXVI

Whom when his other fellowes saw, they
    fled
As fast as feete could carry them away;
And after them the Prince as swiftly sped,
To be aveng'd of their unknightly play.
There whilest they, entring, th' one did th'
    other stay,
The hindmost in the gate he overhent,
And as he pressed in, him there did slay:
His carkasse, tumbling on the threshold,
    sent
His groning soule unto her place of punish-
    ment.

XXXVII

The other, which was entred, laboured fast
To sperre the gate; but that same lumpe
    of clay,
Whose grudging ghost was thereout fled
    and past,
Right in the middest of the threshold lay,
That it the posterne did from closing stay:
The whiles the Prince hard preased in be-
    tweene,
And entraunce wonne. Streight th' other
    fled away,
And ran into the hall, where he did weene
Him selfe to save: but he there slew him
    at the skreene.

XXXVIII

Then all the rest which in that castle were,
Seeing that sad ensample them before,
Durst not abide, but fled away for feare,
And them convayd out at a posterne dore.
Long sought the Prince, but when he
    found no more
T' oppose against his powre, he forth is-
    sued
Unto that lady, where he her had lore,
And her gan cheare with what she there
    had vewed,
And what she had not seene within unto
    her shewed.

XXXIX

Who with right humble thankes him goodly
    greeting,
For so great prowesse as he there had
    proved,
Much greater then was ever in her weet-
    ing,
With great admiraunce inwardly was
    moved,
And honourd him with all that her be-
    hoved.
Thenceforth into that castle he her led,
With her two sonnes, right deare of her be-
    loved,
Where all that night them selves they
    cherished,
And from her balefull minde all care he
    banished.

CANTO XI

Prince Arthure overcomes the great
    Gerioneo in fight:
Doth slay the monster, and restore
    Belge unto her right.

I

IT often fals in course of common life,
That right long time is overborne of
    wrong,
Through avarice, or powre, or guile, or
    strife,
That weakens her, and makes her party
    strong:
But Justice, though her dome she doe pro-
    long,
Yet at the last she will her owne cause
    right:
As by sad Belge seemes, whose wrongs
    though long

She suffred, yet at length she did requight,
And sent redresse thereof by this brave
    Briton knight.

II

Whereof when newes was to that tyrant
    brought,
How that the Lady Belge now had found
A champion, that had with his champion
    fought,
And laid his seneschall low on the ground,
And eke him selfe did threaten to con-
    found,
He gan to burne in rage, and friese in
    feare,
Doubting sad end of principle unsound:
Yet sith he heard but one that did appeare,
He did him selfe encourage, and take bet-
    ter cheare.

III

Nathelesse him selfe he armed all in hast,
And forth he far'd with all his many bad,
Ne stayed step, till that he came at last
Unto the castle which they conquerd had.
There with huge terrour, to be more ydrad,
He sternely marcht before the castle gate,
And with bold vaunts and ydle threatning
    bad
Deliver him his owne, ere yet too late,
To which they had no right, nor any wrong-
    full state.

IV

The Prince staid not his aunswere to devize,
But opening streight the sparre, forth to
    him came,
Full nobly mounted in right warlike wize;
And asked him, if that he were the same,
Who all that wrong unto that wofull dame
So long had done, and from her native land
Exiled her, that all the world spake shame.
He boldly aunswerd him, he there did
    stand
That would his doings justifie with his owne
    hand.

V

With that so furiously at him he flew,
As if he would have overrun him streight,
And with his huge great yron axe gan hew
So hideously uppon his armour bright,
As he to peeces would have chopt it quight:
That the bold Prince was forced foote to
    give

To his first rage, and yeeld to his despight;
The whilest at him so dreadfully he drive,
That seem'd a marble rocke asunder could
　　have rive.

VI

Thereto a great advauntage eke he has
Through his three double hands thrise
　　multiplyde,
Besides the double strength which in them
　　was:
For stil when fit occasion did betyde,
He could his weapon shift from side to syde,
From hand to hand, and with such nimblesse
　　sly
Could wield about, that ere it were espide,
The wicked stroke did wound his enemy,
Behinde, beside, before, as he it list apply.

VII

Which uncouth use when as the Prince
　　perceived,
He gan to watch the wielding of his hand,
Least by such slight he were unwares de-
　　ceived;
And ever ere he saw the stroke to land,
He would it meete and warily withstand.
One time, when he his weapon faynd to
　　shift,
As he was wont, and chang'd from hand to
　　hand,
He met him with a counterstroke so swift,
That quite smit off his arme, as he it up
　　did lift.

VIII

Therewith, all fraught with fury and dis-
　　daine,
He brayd aloud for very fell despight,
And sodainely t' avenge him selfe againe,
Gan into one assemble all the might
Of all his hands, and heaved them on hight,
Thinking to pay him with that one for all:
But the sad steele seizd not, where it was
　　hight,
Uppon the childe, but somewhat short did
　　fall,
And lighting on his horses head, him quite
　　did mall.

IX

Downe streight to ground fell his astonisht
　　steed,
And eke to th' earth his burden with him
　　bare:

But he him selfe full lightly from him
　　freed,
And gan him selfe to fight on foote prepare.
Whereof when as the gyant was aware,
He wox right blyth, as he had got thereby,
And laught so loud, that all his teeth wide
　　bare
One might have seene enraung'd disorderly,
Like to a rancke of piles, that pitched are
　　awry.

X

Eftsoones againe his axe he raught on hie,
Ere he were throughly buckled to his geare,
And can let drive at him so dreadfullie,
That had he chaunced not his shield to
　　reare,
Ere that huge stroke arrived on him neare,
He had him surely cloven quite in twaine.
But th' adamantine shield which he did
　　beare
So well was tempred, that, for all his maine,
It would no passage yeeld unto his purpose
　　vaine.

XI

Yet was the stroke so forcibly applide,
That made him stagger with uncertaine
　　sway,
As if he would have tottered to one side.
Wherewith full wroth, he fiercely gan assay
That curt'sie with like kindnesse to repay;
And smote at him with so importune might,
That two more of his armes did fall away,
Like fruitlesse braunches, which the
　　hatchets slight
Hath pruned from the native tree, and
　　cropped quight.

XII

With that all mad and furious he grew,
Like a fell mastiffe through enraging heat,
And curst, and band, and blasphemies forth
　　threw
Against his gods, and fire to them did
　　threat,
And hell unto him selfe with horrour great.
Thenceforth he car'd no more which way
　　he strooke,
Nor where it light, but gan to chaufe and
　　sweat,
And gnasht his teeth, and his head at him
　　shooke,
And sternely him beheld with grim and
　　ghastly looke.

XIII

Nought fear'd the childe his lookes, ne yet
  his threats,
But onely wexed now the more aware,
To save him selfe from those his furious
  heats,
And watch advauntage, how to worke his
  care;
The which good fortune to him offred faire.
For as he in his rage him overstrooke,
He, ere he could his weapon backe repaire,
His side all bare and naked overtooke,
And with his mortal steel quite throgh
  the body strooke.

XIV

Through all three bodies he him strooke
  attonce,
That all the three attonce fell on the plaine:
Else should he thrise have needed for the
  nonce
Them to have stricken, and thrise to have
  slaine.
So now all three one sencelesse lumpe remaine,
Enwallow'd in his owne blacke bloudy
  gore,
And byting th' earth for very deaths disdaine;
Who, with a cloud of night him covering,
  bore
Downe to the house of dole, his daies there
  to deplore.

XV

Which when the lady from the castle
  saw,
Where she with her two sonnes did look-
  ing stand,
She towards him in hast her selfe did
  draw,
To greet him the good fortune of his hand:
And all the people both of towne and
  land,
Which there stood gazing from the citties
  wall
Upon these warriours, greedy t' under-
  stand
To whether should the victory befall,
Now when they saw it falne, they eke him
  greeted all.

XVI

But Belge with her sonnes prostrated low
Before his feete, in all that peoples sight,
Mongst joyes mixing some tears, mongst
  wele some wo,
Him thus bespake: 'O most redoubted
  knight,
The which hast me, of all most wretched
  wight,
That earst was dead, restor'd to life againe,
And these weake impes replanted by thy
  might;
What guerdon can I give thee for thy paine,
But even that which thou savedst, thine
  still to remaine?'

XVII

He tooke her up forby the lilly hand,
And her recomforted the best he might,
Saying: 'Deare lady, deedes ought not be
  scand
By th' authors manhood, nor the doers
  might,
But by their trueth and by the causes right:
That same is it, which fought for you this
  day.
What other meed then need me to requight,
But that which yeeldeth vertues meed
  alway?
That is the vertue selfe, which her reward
  doth pay.'

XVIII

She humbly thankt him for that wondrous
  grace,
And further sayd: 'Ah! sir, but mote ye
  please,
Sith ye thus farre have tendred my poore
  case,
As from my chiefest foe me to release,
That your victorious arme will not yet
  cease,
Till ye have rooted all the relickes out
Of that vilde race, and stablished my
  peace.'
'What is there else,' sayd he, 'left of their
  rout?
Declare it boldly, dame, and doe not stand
  in dout.'

XIX

'Then wote you, sir, that in this church
  hereby,
There stands an idole of great note and
  name,
The which this gyant reared first on hie,
And of his owne vaine fancies thought did
  frame:

To whom, for endlesse horrour of his
    shame,
He offred up for daily sacrifize
My children and my people, burnt in flame,
With all the tortures that he could devize,
The more t' aggrate his god with such his
    blouddy guize.

XX

' And underneath this idoll there doth lie
An hideous monster, that doth it defend,
And feedes on all the carkasses that die
In sacrifize unto that cursed feend:
Whose ugly shape none ever saw, nor
    kend,
That ever scap'd: for of a man they say
It has the voice, that speaches forth doth
    send,
Even blasphemous words, which she doth
    bray
Out of her poysnous entrails, fraught with
    dire decay.'

XXI

Which when the Prince heard tell, his heart
    gan earne
For great desire, that monster to assay,
And prayd the place of her abode to
    learne.
Which being shew'd, he gan him selfe
    streight way
Thereto addresse, and his bright shield
    display.
So to the church he came, where it was
    told
The monster underneath the altar lay;
There he that idoll saw of massy gold
Most richly made, but there no monster
    did behold.

XXII

Upon the image with his naked blade
Three times, as in defiance, there he strooke;
And the third time, out of an hidden shade,
There forth issewd, from under th' altars
    smooke,
A dreadfull feend, with fowle deformed
    looke,
That stretcht it selfe, as it had long lyen
    still;
And her long taile and fethers strongly
    shooke,
That all the temple did with terrour fill;
Yet him nought terrifide, that feared no-
    thing ill.

XXIII

An huge great beast it was, when it in
    length
Was stretched forth, that nigh fild all the
    place,
And seem'd to be of infinite great strength;
Horrible, hideous, and of hellish race,
Borne of the brooding of Echidna base,
Or other like infernall Furies kinde:
For of a mayd she had the outward face,
To hide the horrour which did lurke be-
    hinde,
The better to beguile whom she so fond did
    finde.

XXIV

Thereto the body of a dog she had,
Full of fell ravin and fierce greedinesse;
A lions clawes, with powre and rigour clad,
To rend and teare what so she can op-
    presse;
A dragons taile, whose sting without re-
    dresse
Full deadly wounds, where so it is em-
    pight;
And eagles wings, for scope and speedinesse,
That nothing may escape her reaching
    might,
Whereto she ever list to make her hardy
    flight.

XXV

Much like in foulnesse and deformity
Unto that monster whom the Theban
    knight,
The father of that fatall progeny,
Made kill her selfe for very hearts de-
    spight,
That he had red her riddle, which no wight
Could ever loose, but suffred deadly doole.
So also did this monster use like slight
To many a one which came unto her schoole,
Whom she did put to death, deceived like a
    foole.

XXVI

She comming forth, when as she first be-
    held
The armed Prince, with shield so blazing
    bright,
Her ready to assaile, was greatly queld,
And much dismayd with that dismayfull
    sight,
That backe she would have turnd for great
    affright.

But he gan her with courage fierce assay,
That forst her turne againe in her despight,
To save her selfe, least that he did her slay:
And sure he had her slaine, had she not
    turnd her way.

XXVII

Tho, when she saw that she was forst to
    fight,
She flew at him, like to an hellish feend,
And on his shield tooke hold with all her
    might,
As if that it she would in peeces rend,
Or reave out of the hand that did it hend.
Strongly he strove out of her greedy gripe
To loose his shield, and long while did con-
    tend:
But when he could not quite it, with one
    stripe
Her lions clawes he from her feete away
    did wipe.

XXVIII

With that aloude she gan to bray and yell,
And fowle blasphemous speaches forth did
    cast,
And bitter curses, horrible to tell,
That even the temple, wherein she was plast,
Did quake to heare, and nigh asunder brast.
Tho with her huge long taile she at him
    strooke,
That made him stagger, and stand halfe
    agast
With trembling joynts, as he for terrour
    shooke;
Who nought was terrifide, but greater
    courage tooke.

XXIX

As when the mast of some well timbred
    hulke
Is with the blast of some outragious storme
Blowne downe, it shakes the bottome of
    the bulke,
And makes her ribs to cracke, as they were
    torne,
Whilest still she stands as stonisht and
    forlorne:
So was he stound with stroke of her huge
    taile.
But ere that it she backe againe had borne,
He with his sword it strooke, that without
    faile
He joynted it, and mard the swinging of
    her flaile.

XXX

Then gan she cry much louder then afore,
That all the people there without it heard,
And Belge selfe was therewith stonied sore,
As if the onely sound thereof she feard.
But then the feend her selfe more fiercely
    reard
Uppon her wide great wings, and strongly
    flew
With all her body at his head and beard,
That had he not foreseene with heedfull
    vew,
And thrown his shield atween, she had
    him done to rew.

XXXI

But as she prest on him with heavy sway,
Under her wombe his fatall sword he thrust,
And for her entrailes made an open way
To issue forth; the which, once being brust,
Like to a great mill damb forth fiercely
    gusht,
And powred out of her infernall sinke
Most ugly filth, and poyson therewith rusht,
That him nigh choked with the deadly
    stinke:
Such loathly matter were small lust to
    speake, or thinke.

XXXII

Then downe to ground fell that deformed
    masse,
Breathing out clouds of sulphure fowle and
    blacke,
In which a puddle of contagion was,
More loathd then Lerna, or then Stygian
    lake,
That any man would nigh awhaped make.
Whom when he saw on ground, he was full
    glad,
And streight went forth his gladnesse to
    partake
With Belge, who watcht all this while full
    sad,
Wayting what end would be of that same
    daunger drad.

XXXIII

Whom when she saw so joyously come
    forth,
She gan rejoyce, and shew triumphant chere,
Lauding and praysing his renowmed worth
By all the names that honorable were.
Then in he brought her, and her shewed
    there

The present of his paines, that monsters
spoyle,
And eke that idoll deem'd so costly dere;
Whom he did all to peeces breake, and
foyle
In filthy durt, and left so in the loathely
soyle.

XXXIV

Then all the people, which beheld that day,
Gan shout aloud, that unto heaven it rong;
And all the damzels of that towne in ray
Came dauncing forth, and joyous carrols
song:
So him they led through all their streetes
along,
Crowned with girlonds of immortall baies,
And all the vulgar did about them throng,
To see the man, whose everlasting praise
They all were bound to all posterities to
raise.

XXXV

There he with Belgæ did a while remaine,
Making great feast and joyous merriment,
Untill he had her settled in her raine,
With safe assuraunce and establishment.
Then to his first emprize his mind he lent,
Full loath to Belgæ and to all the rest:
Of whom yet taking leave, thenceforth he
went
And to his former journey him addrest,
On which long way he rode, ne ever day
did rest.

XXXVI

But turne we now to noble Artegall;
Who, having left Mercilla, streight way went
On his first quest, the which him forth did
call,
To weet, to worke Irenaes franchisement,
And eke Grantortoes worthy punishment.
So forth he fared as his manner was,
With onely Talus wayting diligent,
Through many perils and much way did
pas,
Till nigh unto the place at length approcht
he has.

XXXVII

There as he traveld by the way, he met
An aged wight, wayfaring all alone,
Who through his yeares long since had set
aside
The use of armes, and battell quite forgone:

To whom as he approcht, he knew anone
That it was he which whilome did attend
On faire Irene in her affliction,
When first to Faery court he saw her
wend,
Unto his Soveraine Queene her suite for to
commend.

XXXVIII

Whom by his name saluting, thus he gan:
' Haile, good Sir Sergis, truest knight alive,
Well tride in all thy ladies troubles than
When her that tyrant did of crowne de-
prive;
What new ocasion doth thee hither drive,
Whiles she alone is left, and thou here
found ?
Or is she thrall, or doth she not survive ? '
To whom he thus : ' She liveth sure and
sound;
But by that tyrant is in wretched thral-
dome bound.

XXXIX

' For she, presuming on th' appointed tyde,
In which ye promist, as ye were a knight,
To meete her at the Salvage Ilands syde,
And then and there for triall of her right
With her unrighteous enemy to fight,
Did thither come, where she, afrayd of
nought,
By guilefull treason and by subtill slight
Surprized was, and to Grantorto brought,
Who her imprisond hath, and her life often
sought.

XL

' And now he hath to her prefixt a day,
By which if that no champion doe appeare,
Which will her cause in battailous array
Against him justifie, and prove her cleare
Of all those crimes that he gainst her doth
reare,
She death shall sure aby.' Those tidings
sad
Did much abash Sir Artegall to heare,
And grieved sore, that through his fault
she had
Fallen into that tyrants hand and usage bad.

XLI

Then thus replide: ' Now sure and by my
life,
Too much am I too blame for that faire
maide,

That have her drawne to all this troublous
  strife,
Through promise to afford her timely aide,
Which by default I have not yet defraide.
But witnesse unto me, ye heavens, that
  know
How cleare I am from blame of this up-
  braide:
For ye into like thraldome me did throw,
And kept from complishing the faith which
  I did owe.

XLII

' But now aread, Sir Sergis, how long space
Hath he her lent, a champion to provide.'
' Ten daies,' quoth he, ' he graunted hath of
  grace,
For that he weeneth well, before that tide
None can have tidings to assist her side.
For all the shores, which to the sea accoste,
He day and night doth ward both far and
  wide,
That none can there arrive without an
  hoste:
So her he deemes already but a damned
  ghoste.'

XLIII

' Now turne againe,' Sir Artegall then
  sayd;
' For if I live till those ten daies have end,
Assure your selfe, sir knight, she shall have
  ayd,
Though I this dearest life for her doe
  spend.'
So backeward he attone with him did wend.
Tho, as they rode together on their way,
A rout of people they before them kend,
Flocking together in confusde array,
As if that there were some tumultuous af-
  fray.

XLIV

To which as they approcht, the cause to
  know,
They saw a knight in daungerous distresse
Of a rude rout him chasing to and fro,
That sought with lawlesse powre him to
  oppresse,
And bring in bondage of their brutishnesse:
And farre away, amid their rakehell bands,
They spide a lady left all succourlesse,
Crying, and holding up her wretched hands
To him for aide, who long in vaine their
  rage withstands.

XLV

Yet still he strives, ne any perill spares,
To reskue her from their rude violence,
And like a lion wood amongst them fares,
Dealing his dreadfull blowes with large dis-
  pence,
Gainst which the pallid death findes no de-
  fence.
But all in vaine; their numbers are so
  great,
That naught may boot to banishe them
  from thence:
For soone as he their outrage backe doth
  beat,
They turne afresh, and oft renew their for-
  mer threat.

XLVI

And now they doe so sharpely him assay,
That they his shield in peeces battred have,
And forced him to throw it quite away,
Fro dangers dread his doubtfull life to save;
Albe that it most safety to him gave,
And much did magnifie his noble name:
For from the day that he thus did it leave,
Amongst all knights he blotted was with
  blame,
And counted but a recreant knight, with
  endles shame.

XLVII

Whom when they thus distressed did be-
  hold,
They drew unto his aide; but that rude
  rout
Them also gan assaile with outrage bold,
And forced them, how ever strong and
  stout
They were, as well approv'd in many a
  doubt,
Backe to recule; untill that yron man
With his huge flaile began to lay about,
From whose sterne presence they diffused
  ran,
Like scattred chaffe, the which the wind
  away doth fan.

XLVIII

So when that knight from perill cleare was
  freed,
He, drawing neare, began to greete them
  faire,
And yeeld great thankes for their so goodly deed,
In saving him from daungerous despaire

Of those which sought his life for to em-
    paire.
Of whom Sir Artegall gan then enquire
The whole occasion of his late misfare,
And who he was, and what those villaines
    were,
The which with mortall malice him pursu'd
    so nere.

XLIX

To whom he thus: 'My name is Burbon
    hight,
Well knowne, and far renowmed hereto-
    fore,
Untill late mischiefe did uppon me light,
That all my former praise hath blemisht
    sore;
And that faire lady, which in that uprore
Ye with those caytives saw, Flourdelis
    hight,
Is mine owne love, though me she have
    forlore,
Whether withheld from me by wrongfull
    might,
Or with her owne good will, I cannot read
    aright.

L

'But sure to me her faith she first did
    plight,
To be my love, and take me for her lord,
Till that a tyrant, which Grandtorto hight,
With golden giftes and many a guilefull
    word
Entyced her, to him for to accord.
O who may not with gifts and words be
    tempted?
Sith which she hath me ever since abhord,
And to my foe hath guilefully consented:
Ay me, that ever guyle in wemen was in-
    vented!

LI

'And now he hath this troupe of villains
    sent,
By open force to fetch her quite away:
Gainst whom my selfe I long in vaine have
    bent
To rescue her, and daily meanes assay,
Yet rescue her thence by no meanes I may:
For they doe me with multitude oppresse,
And with unequall might doe overlay,
That oft I driven am to great distresse,
And forced to forgoe th' attempt remedi-
    lesse.'

LII

'But why have ye,' said Artegall, 'forborne
Your owne good shield in daungerous dis-
    may?
That is the greatest shame and foulest
    scorne,
Which unto any knight behappen may,
To loose the badge that should his deedes
    display.'
To whom Sir Burbon, blushing halfe for
    shame,
'That shall I unto you,' quoth he, 'bewray;
Least ye therefore mote happily me blame,
And deeme it doen of will, that through
    inforcement came.

LIII

'True is, that I at first was dubbed knight
By a good knight, the Knight of the Red-
    crosse;
Who when he gave me armes, in field to
    fight,
Gave me a shield, in which he did endosse
His deare Redeemers badge upon the bosse:
The same long while I bore, and there-
    withall
Fought many battels without wound or
    losse;
Therewith Grandtorto selfe I did appall,
And made him oftentimes in field before
    me fall.

LIV

'But for that many did that shield envie,
And cruell enemies increased more;
To stint all strife and troublous enmitie,
That bloudie scutchin being battered sore,
I layd aside, and have of late forbore,
Hoping thereby to have my love obtayned:
Yet can I not my love have nathemore;
For she by force is still fro me detayned,
And with corruptfull brybes is to untruth
    mis-trayned.'

LV

To whom thus Artegall: 'Certes, sir knight,
Hard is the case the which ye doe com-
    plaine;
Yet not so hard (for nought so hard may
    light,
That it to such a streight mote you con-
    straine)
As to abandon that which doth containe
Your honours stile, that is your warlike
    shield.

All perill ought be lesse, and lesse all
    paine,
Then losse of fame in disaventrous field:
Dye rather, then doe ought that mote dis-
    honour yield.'

LVI

'Not so,' quoth he; 'for yet, when time
    doth serve,
My former shield I may resume againe:
To temporize is not from truth to swerve,
Ne for advantage terme to entertaine,
When as necessitie doth it constraine.'
'Fie on such forgerie,' said Artegall,
'Under one hood to shadow faces twaine !
Knights ought be true, and truth is one in
    all:
Of all things, to dissemble fouly may be-
    fall.'

LVII

'Yet let me you of courtesie request,'
Said Burbon, 'to assist me now at need
Against these pesants which have me op-
    prest,
And forced me to so infamous deed,
That yet my love may from their hands be
    freed.'
Sir Artegall, albe he earst did wyte
His wavering mind, yet to his aide agreed,
And buckling him eftsoones unto the fight,
Did set upon those troupes with all his
    powre and might.

LVIII

Who flocking round about them, as a
    swarme
Of flyes upon a birchen bough doth cluster,
Did them assault with terrible allarme,
And over all the fields themselves did
    muster,
With bils and glayves making a dreadfull
    luster;
That forst at first those knights backe to
    retyre:
As when the wrathfull Boreas doth bluster,
Nought may abide the tempest of his yre;
Both man and beast doe fly, and succour
    doe inquyre.

LIX

But when as overblowen was that brunt,
Those knights began a fresh them to assayle,
And all about the fields like squirrels hunt;
But chiefly Talus with his yron flayle,

Gainst which no flight nor rescue mote
    avayle,
Made cruell havocke of the baser crew,
And chaced them both over hill and dale:
The raskall manie soone they overthrew,
But the two knights themselves their cap-
    tains did subdew.

LX

At last they came whereas that ladie bode,
Whom now her keepers had forsaken
    quight,
To save themselves, and scattered were
    abrode:
Her halfe dismayd they found in doubtfull
    plight,
As neither glad nor sorie for their sight;
Yet wondrous faire she was, and richly
    clad
In roiall robes, and many jewels dight,
But that those villens through their usage
    bad
Them fouly rent and shamefully defaced
    had.

LXI

But Burbon, streight dismounting from his
    steed,
Unto her ran with greedie great desyre,
And catching her fast by her ragged weed,
Would have embraced her with hart en-
    tyre.
But she, backstarting with disdainefull yre,
Bad him avaunt, ne would unto his lore
Allured be, for prayer nor for meed.
Whom when those knights so froward and
    forlore
Beheld, they her rebuked and upbrayded
    sore.

LXII

Sayd Artegall: 'What foule disgrace is
    this
To so faire ladie as ye seeme in sight,
To blot your beautie, that unblemisht is,
With so foule blame as breach of faith once
    plight,
Or change of love for any worlds de-
    light !
Is ought on earth so pretious or deare,
As prayse and honour ? Or is ought so
    bright
And beautifull as glories beames appeare,
Whose goodly light then Phebus lampe
    doth shine more cleare ?

LXIII

'Why then will ye, fond dame, attempted
    bee
Unto a strangers love, so lightly placed,
For guiftes of gold or any worldly glee,
To leave the love that ye before embraced,
And let your fame with falshood be de-
    faced ?
Fie on the pelfe for which good name is
    sold,
And honour with indignitie debased !
Dearer is love then life, and fame then
    gold;
But dearer then them both your faith once
    plighted hold.'

LXIV

Much was the ladie in her gentle mind
Abasht at his rebuke, that bit her neare,
Ne ought to answere thereunto did find;
But hanging downe her head with heavie
    cheare,
Stood long amaz'd, as she amated weare.
Which Burbon seeing, her againe assayd,
And clasping twixt his armes, her up did
    reare
Upon his steede, whiles she no whit gaine-
    sayd;
So bore her quite away, nor well nor ill
    apayd.

LXV

Nathlesse the yron man did still pursew
That raskall many with unpittied spoyle,
Ne ceassed not, till all their scattred crew
Into the sea he drove quite from that soyle,
The which they troubled had with great
    turmoyle.
But Artegall, seeing his cruell deed,
Commaunded him from slaughter to re-
    coyle,
And to his voyage gan againe proceed:
For that the terme, approching fast, re-
    quired speed.

CANTO XII

Artegall doth Sir Burbon aide,
  And blames for changing shield :
He with the great Grantorto fights,
  And slaieth him in field.

I

O SACRED hunger of ambitious mindes,
And impotent desire of men to raine,
Whom neither dread of God, that devils
    bindes,
Nor lawes of men, that common weales
    containe,
Nor bands of nature, that wilde beastes
    restraine,
Can keepe from outrage and from doing
    wrong,
Where they may hope a kingdome to
    obtaine.
No faith so firme, no trust can be so strong,
No love so lasting then, that may enduren
    long.

II

Witnesse may Burbon be, whom all the
    bands
Which may a knight assure had surely
    bound,
Untill the love of lordship and of lands
Made him become most faithlesse and un-
    sound:
And witnesse be Gerioneo found,
Who for like cause faire Belge did oppresse,
And right and wrong most cruelly con-
    found:
And so be now Grantorto, who no lesse
Then all the rest burst out to all outragious-
    nesse.

III

Gainst whom Sir Artegall, long having
    since
Taken in hand th' exploit, being thereto
Appointed by that mightie Faerie prince,
Great Gloriane, that tyrant to fordoo,
Through other great adventures hethertoo
Had it forslackt. But now time drawing ny,
To him assynd, her high beheast to doo,
To the sea shore he gan his way apply,
To weete if shipping readie he mote there
    descry.

IV

Tho, when they came to the sea coast, they
    found
A ship all readie (as good fortune fell)
To put to sea, with whom they did com-
    pound
To passe them over, where them list to tell:
The winde and weather served them so
    well,
That in one day they with the coast did
    fall;
Whereas they readie found, them to repell,

Great hostes of men in order martiall,
Which them forbad to land, and footing
    did forstall.

V

But nathemore would they from land re-
    fraine,
But when as nigh unto the shore they drew,
That foot of man might sound the bottome
    plaine,
Talus into the sea did forth issew,
Though darts from shore and stones they
    at him threw;
And wading through the waves with sted-
    fast sway,
Maugre the might of all those troupes in
    vew,
Did win the shore, whence he them chast
    away,
And made to fly, like doves whom the eagle
    doth affray.

VI

The whyles Sir Artegall with that old
    knight
Did forth descend, there being none them
    neare,
And forward marched to a towne in sight.
By this came tydings to the tyrants eare,
By those which earst did fly away for feare,
Of their arrivall: wherewith troubled sore,
He all his forces streight to him did reare,
And forth issuing with his scouts afore,
Meant them to have incountred, ere they
    left the shore.

VII

But ere he marched farre, he with them
    met,
And fiercely charged them with all his
    force;
But Talus sternely did upon them set,
And brusht and battred them without re-
    morse,
That on the ground he left full many a corse;
Ne any able was him to withstand,
But he them overthrew both man and horse,
That they lay scattred over all the land,
As thicke as doth the seede after the sow-
    ers hand.

VIII

Till Artegall, him seeing so to rage,
Willd him to stay, and signe of truce did
    make:

To which all harkning, did a while asswage
Their forces furie, and their terror slake;
Till he an herauld cald, and to him spake,
Willing him wend unto the tyrant streight,
And tell him that not for such slaughters
    sake
He thether came, but for to trie the right
Of fayre Irenaes cause with him in single
    fight:

IX

And willed him for to reclayme with speed
His scattred people, ere they all were slaine,
And time and place convenient to areed,
In which they two the combat might dar-
    raine.
Which message when Grantorto heard, full
    fayne
And glad he was the slaughter so to stay,
And pointed for the combat twixt them
    twayne
The morrow next, ne gave him longer day:
So sounded the retraite, and drew his folke
    away.

X

That night Sir Artegall did cause his tent
There to be pitched on the open plaine;
For he had given streight commaundement,
That none should dare him once to enter-
    taine:
Which none durst breake, though many
    would right faine
For fayre Irena, whom they loved deare.
But yet old Sergis did so well him paine,
That from close friends, that dar'd not to
    appeare,
He all things did purvay, which for them
    needfull weare.

XI

The morrow next, that was the dismall day
Appointed for Irenas death before,
So soone as it did to the world display
His chearefull face, and light to men re-
    store,
The heavy mayd, to whom none tydings
    bore
Of Artegals arryvall, her to free,
Lookt up with eyes full sad and hart full
    sore;
Weening her lifes last howre then neare to
    bee,
Sith no redemption nigh she did nor heare
    nor see.

XII

Then up she rose, and on her selfe did
    dight
Most squalid garments, fit for such a day,
And with dull countenance, and with dole-
    ful spright,
She forth was brought in sorrowfull dis-
    may,
For to receive the doome of her decay.
But comming to the place, and finding
    there
Sir Artegall, in battailous array
Wayting his foe, it did her dead hart
    cheare,
And new life to her lent, in midst of deadly
    feare.

XIII

Like as a tender rose in open plaine,
That with untimely drought nigh withered
    was,
And hung the head, soone as few drops of
    raine
Thereon distill, and deaw her daintie face,
Gins to looke up, and with fresh wonted
    grace
Dispreds the glorie of her leaves gay;
Such was Irenas countenance, such her
    case,
When Artegall she saw in that array,
There wayting for the tyrant, till it was
    farre day.

XIV

Who came at length, with proud presump-
    teous gate,
Into the field, as if he fearelesse were,
All armed in a cote of yron plate,
Of great defence to ward the deadly feare,
And on his head a steele cap he did weare
Of colour rustie browne, but sure and
    strong;
And in his hand an huge polaxe did beare,
Whose steale was yron studded, but not
    long,
With which he wont to fight, to justifie his
    wrong.

XV

Of stature huge and hideous he was,
Like to a giant for his monstrous hight,
And did in strength most sorts of men sur-
    pas,
Ne ever any found his match in might;
Thereto he had great skill in single fight:

His face was ugly and his countenance
    sterne,
That could have frayd one with the very
    sight,
And gaped like a gulfe when he did gerne,
That whether man or monster one could
    scarse discerne.

XVI

Soone as he did within the listes appeare,
With dreadfull looke he Artegall beheld,
As if he would have daunted him with
    feare,
And grinning griesly, did against him weld
His deadly weapon, which in hand he held.
But th' Elfin swayne, that oft had seene
    like sight,
Was with his ghastly count'nance nothing
    queld,
But gan him streight to buckle to the fight,
And cast his shield about, to be in readie
    plight.

XVII

The trompets sound, and they together goe,
With dreadfull terror and with fell intent;
And their huge strokes full daungerously
    bestow,
To doe most dammage where as most they
    ment.
But with such force and furie violent
The tyrant thundred his thicke blowes so
    fast,
That through the yron walles their way
    they rent,
And even to the vitall parts they past,
Ne ought could them endure, but all they
    cleft or brast.

XVIII

Which cruell outrage when as Artegall
Did well avize, thenceforth with warie heed
He shund his strokes, where ever they did
    fall,
And way did give unto their gracelesse
    speed:
As when a skilfull marriner doth reed
A storme approching, that doth perill
    threat,
He will not bide the daunger of such
    dread,
But strikes his sayles, and vereth his main-
    sheat,
And lends unto it leave the emptie ayre to
    beat.

XIX

So did the Faerie knight himselfe abeare,
And stouped oft, his head from shame to
　　shield;
No shame to stoupe, ones head more high
　　to reare,
And, much to gaine, a litle for to yield;
So stoutest knights doen oftentimes in field.
But still the tyrant sternely at him layd,
And did his yron axe so nimbly wield,
That many wounds into his flesh it made,
And with his burdenous blowes him sore
　　did overlade.

XX

Yet when as fit advantage he did spy,
The whiles the cursed felon high did reare
His cruell hand, to smite him mortally,
Under his stroke he to him stepping neare,
Right in the flanke him strooke with
　　deadly dreare,
That the gore bloud, thence gushing griev-
　　ously,
Did underneath him like a pond appeare,
And all his armour did with purple dye:
Thereat he brayed loud, and yelled dread-
　　fully.

XXI

Yet the huge stroke, which he before in-
　　tended,
Kept on his course, as he did it direct,
And with such monstrous poise adowne de-
　　scended,
That seemed nought could him from death
　　protect:
But he it well did ward with wise respect,
And twixt him and the blow his shield did
　　cast,
Which thereon seizing, tooke no great
　　effect,
But byting deepe therein did sticke so fast,
That by no meanes it backe againe he forth
　　could wrast.

XXII

Long while he tug'd and strove, to get it
　　out,
And all his powre applyed thereunto,
That he therewith the knight drew all
　　about:
Nathlesse, for all that ever he could doe,
His axe he could not from his shield undoe.
Which Artegall perceiving, strooke no
　　more,

But loosing soone his shield, did it forgoe,
And whiles he combred was therewith so
　　sore,
He gan at him let drive more fiercely then
　　afore.

XXIII

So well he him pursew'd, that at the last
He stroke him with Chrysaor on the hed,
That with the souse thereof full sore
　　aghast,
He staggered to and fro in doubtfull sted.
Againe, whiles he him saw so ill bested,
He did him smite with all his might and
　　maine,
That, falling, on his mother earth he fed:
Whom when he saw prostrated on the
　　plaine,
He lightly reft his head, to ease him of his
　　paine.

XXIV

Which when the people round about him
　　saw,
They shouted all for joy of his successe,
Glad to be quit from that proud tyrants
　　awe,
Which with strong powre did them long
　　time oppresse;
And running all with greedie joyfulnesse
To faire Irena, at her feet did fall,
And her adored with due humblenesse,
As their true liege and princesse naturall;
And eke her champions glorie sounded over
　　all.

XXV

Who streight her leading with meete
　　majestie
Unto the pallace, where their kings did
　　rayne,
Did her therein establish peaceablie,
And to her kingdomes seat restore agayne;
And all such persons as did late maintayne
That tyrants part, with close or open ayde,
He sorely punished with heavie payne;
That in short space, whiles there with her
　　he stayd,
Not one was left that durst her once have
　　disobayd.

XXVI

During which time that he did there re-
　　maine,
His studie was true justice how to deale,

And day and night employ'd his busie paine
How to reforme that ragged common-weale:
And that same yron man, which could re-
veale
All hidden crimes, through all that realme
he sent,
To search out those that usd to rob and
steale,
Or did rebell gainst lawfull government;
On whom he did inflict most grievous pun-
ishment.

XXVII

But ere he could reforme it thoroughly,
He through occasion called was away
To Faerie court, that of necessity
His course of justice he was forst to stay,
And Talus to revoke from the right way,
In which he was that realme for to re-
dresse.
But envies cloud still dimmeth vertues ray.
So having freed Irena from distresse,
He tooke his leave of her, there left in
heavinesse.

XXVIII

Tho, as he backe returned from that land,
And there arriv'd againe, whence forth he
set,
He had not passed farre upon the strand,
When as two old ill favour'd hags he met,
By the way side being together set;
Two griesly creatures; and, to that their
faces
Most foule and filthie were, their garments
yet,
Being all rag'd and tatter'd, their disgraces
Did much the more augment, and made
most ugly cases.

XXIX

The one of them, that elder did appeare,
With her dull eyes did seeme to looke
askew,
That her mis-shape much helpt; and her
foule heare
Hung loose and loathsomely: thereto her
hew
Was wan and leane, that all her teeth arew
And all her bones might through her
cheekes be red;
Her lips were like raw lether, pale and blew,
And as she spake, therewith she slavered;
Yet spake she seldom, but thought more,
the lesse she sed.

XXX

Her hands were foule and durtie, never
washt
In all her life, with long nayles over raught,
Like puttocks clawes: with th' one of
which she scracht
Her cursed head, although it itched naught;
The other held a snake with venime fraught,
On which she fed and gnawed hungrily,
As if that long she had not eaten ought;
That round about her jawes one might de-
scry
The bloudie gore and poyson dropping
lothsomely.

XXXI

Her name was Envie, knowen well thereby;
Whose nature is to grieve and grudge at all
That ever she sees doen prays-worthily,
Whose sight to her is greatest crosse may
fall,
And vexeth so, that makes her eat her gall.
For when she wanteth other thing to eat,
She feedes on her owne maw unnaturall,
And of her owne foule entrayles makes her
meat;
Meat fit for such a monsters monsterous
dyeat.

XXXII

And if she hapt of any good to heare,
That had to any happily betid,
Then would she inly fret, and grieve, and
teare
Her flesh for felnesse, which she inward hid:
But if she heard of ill that any did,
Or harme that any had, then would she make
Great cheare, like one unto a banquet bid;
And in anothers losse great pleasure take,
As she had got thereby, and gayned a great
stake.

XXXIII

The other nothing better was then shee;
Agreeing in bad will and cancred kynd,
But in bad maner they did disagree:
For what so Envie good or bad did fynd
She did conceale, and murder her owne
mynd;
But this, what ever evill she conceived,
Did spred abroad, and throw in th' open
wynd.
Yet this in all her words might be perceived,
That all she sought was mens good name to
have bereaved.

XXXIV

For what soever good by any sayd
Or doen she heard, she would streight-
wayes invent
How to deprave, or slaunderously upbrayd,
Or to misconstrue of a mans intent,
And turne to ill the thing that well was ment.
Therefore she used often to resort
To common haunts, and companies fre-
quent,
To hearke what any one did good report,
To blot the same with blame, or wrest in
wicked sort.

XXXV

And if that any ill she heard of any,
She would it eeke, and make much worse
by telling,
And take great joy to publish it to many,
That every matter worse was for her
melling.
Her name was hight Detraction, and her
dwelling
Was neare to Envie, even her neighbour
next;
A wicked hag, and Envy selfe excelling
In mischiefe: for her selfe she onely vext;
But this same both her selfe and others eke
perplext.

XXXVI

Her face was ugly, and her mouth distort,
Foming with poyson round about her gils,
In which her cursed tongue full sharpe and
short
Appear'd like aspis sting, that closely kils,
Or cruelly does wound, whom so she wils:
A distaffe in her other hand she had,
Upon the which she litle spinnes, but spils,
And faynes to weave false tales and leasings
bad,
To throw amongst the good, which others
had disprad.

XXXVII

These two now had themselves combynd in
one,
And linckt together gainst Sir Artegall,
For whom they wayted as his mortall fone,
How they might make him into mischiefe
fall,
For freeing from their snares Irena thrall:
Besides, unto themselves they gotten had
A monster, which the Blatant Beast men
call,

A dreadfull feend, of gods and men ydrad,
Whom they by slights allur'd, and to their
purpose lad.

XXXVIII

Such were these hags, and so unhandsome
drest:
Who when they nigh approching had espyde
Sir Artegall, return'd from his late quest,
They both arose, and at him loudly cryde,
As it had bene two shepheards curres had
scryde
A ravenous wolfe amongst the scattered
flocks.
And Envie first, as she that first him eyde,
Towardes him runs, and with rude flaring
lockes
About her eares, does beat her brest and
forhead knockes.

XXXIX

Then from her mouth the gobbet she does
take,
The which whyleare she was so greedily
Devouring, even that halfe-gnawen snake,
And at him throwes it most despightfully.
The cursed serpent, though she hungrily
Earst chawd thereon, yet was not all so dead,
But that some life remayned secretly,
And as he past afore withouten dread,
Bit him behind, that long the marke was to
be read.

XL

Then th' other comming neare, gan him
revile
And fouly rayle, with all she could invent;
Saying that he had with unmanly guile
And foule abusion both his honour blent,
And that bright sword, the sword of Justice
lent,
Had stayned with reprochfull crueltie
In guiltlesse blood of many an innocent:
As for Grandtorto, him with treacherie
And traynes having surpriz'd, he fouly did
to die.

XLI

Thereto the Blatant Beast, by them set on,
At him began aloud to barke and bay,
With bitter rage and fell contention,
That all the woods and rockes nigh to that
way
Began to quake and tremble with dismay,
And all the aire rebellowed againe,

So dreadfully his hundred tongues did bray:
And evermore those hags them selves did
      paine
To sharpen him, and their owne cursed
      tongs did straine.

XLII

And still among, most bitter wordes they
      spake,
Most shamefull, most unrighteous, most
      untrew,
That they the mildest man alive would make
Forget his patience, and yeeld vengeaunce
      dew
To her, that so false sclaunders at him
      threw.
And more to make them pierce and wound
      more deepe,
She with the sting which in her vile tongue
      grew
Did sharpen them, and in fresh poyson
      steepe:
Yet he past on, and seem'd of them to take
      no keepe.

XLIII

But Talus, hearing her so lewdly raile,
And speake so ill of him that well deserved,
Would her have chastiz'd with his yron
      flaile,
If her Sir Artegall had not preserved,
And him forbidden, who his heast observed.
So much the more at him still did she
      scold,
And stones did cast; yet he for nought
      would swerve
From his right course, but still the way did
      hold
To Faery court, where what him fell shall
      else be told.

THE SIXTE BOOKE
OF THE FAERIE QUEENE
CONTAYNING
THE LEGEND OF SIR CALIDORE
OR
OF COURTESIE

I

THE waies, through which my weary steps
      I guyde,
In this delightfull land of Faery,

Are so exceeding spacious and wyde,
And sprinckled with such sweet variety
Of all that pleasant is to eare or eye,
That I, nigh ravisht with rare thoughts de-
      light,
My tedious travell doe forget thereby;
And when I gin to feele decay of might,
It strength to me supplies, and chears my
      dulled spright.

II

Such secret comfort and such heavenly
      pleasures,
Ye sacred imps, that on Parnasso dwell,
And there the keeping have of learnings
      threasures,
Which doe all worldly riches farre excell,
Into the mindes of mortall men doe well,
And goodly fury into them infuse;
Guyde ye my footing, and conduct me
      well
In these strange waies, where never foote
      did use,
Ne none can find, but who was taught them
      by the Muse.

III

Revele to me the sacred noursery
Of Vertue, which with you doth there re-
      maine,
Where it in silver bowre does hidden ly
From view of men, and wicked worlds dis-
      daine;
Since it at first was by the gods with paine
Planted in earth, being deriv'd at furst
From heavenly seedes of bounty soveraine,
And by them long with carefull labour
      nurst,
Till it to ripenesse grew, and forth to hon-
      our burst.

IV

Amongst them all growes not a fayrer
      flowre,
Then is the bloosme of comely Courtesie,
Which, though it on a lowly stalke doe
      bowre,
Yet brancheth forth in brave nobilitie,
And spreds it selfe through all civilitie:
Of which though present age doe plenteous
      seeme,
Yet, being matcht with plaine antiquitie,
Ye will them all but fayned showes esteeme,
Which carry colours faire, that feeble eies
      misdeeme.

V

But in the triall of true Curtesie,
Its now so farre from that which then it
    was,
That it indeed is nought but forgerie,
Fashion'd to please the eies of them that
    pas,
Which see not perfect things but in a glas:
Yet is that glasse so gay that it can blynd
The wisest sight, to thinke gold that is bras.
But Vertues seat is deepe within the mynd,
And not in outward shows, but inward
    thoughts defynd.

VI

But where shall I in all antiquity
So faire a patterne finde, where may be
    seene
The goodly praise of princely Curtesie,
As in your selfe, O soveraine Lady Queene?
In whose pure minde, as in a mirrour sheene,
It showes, and with her brightnesse doth
    inflame
The eyes of all which thereon fixed beene;
But meriteth indeede an higher name:
Yet so from low to high uplifted is your
    fame.

VII

Then pardon me, most dreaded Soveraine,
That from your selfe I doe this vertue bring,
And to your selfe doe it returne againe:
So from the ocean all rivers spring,
And tribute backe repay as to their king:
Right so from you all goodly vertues well
Into the rest which round about you ring,
Faire lords and ladies, which about you
    dwell,
And doe adorne your court, where courte-
    sies excell.

CANTO I

Calidore saves from Maleffort
A damzell used vylde:
Doth vanquish Crudor, and doth make
Briana wexe more mylde.

I

Of Court, it seemes, men Courtesie doe call,
For that it there most useth to abound;
And well beseemeth that in princes hall
That vertue should be plentifully found,
Which of all goodly manners is the ground,
And roote of civill conversation.

Right so in Faery court it did redound,
Where curteous knights and ladies most did
    won
Of all on earth, and made a matchlesse
    paragon.

II

But mongst them all was none more courte-
    ous knight
Then Calidore, beloved over all:
In whom it seemes that gentlenesse of
    spright
And manners mylde were planted naturall;
To which he adding comely guize withall,
And gracious speach, did steale mens hearts
    away.
Nathlesse thereto he was full stout and tall,
And well approv'd in batteilous affray,
That him did much renowme, and far his
    fame display.

III

Ne was there knight, ne was there lady
    found
In Faery court, but him did deare embrace
For his faire usage and conditions sound,
The which in all mens liking gayned place,
And with the greatest purchast greatest
    grace:
Which he could wisely use, and well apply,
To please the best, and th' evill to embase:
For he loathd leasing and base flattery,
And loved simple truth and stedfast hon-
    esty.

IV

And now he was in travell on his way,
Uppon an hard adventure sore bestad,
Whenas by chaunce he met upon a day
With Artegall, returning yet halfe sad
From his late conquest which he gotten
    had.
Who whenas each of other had a sight,
They knew them selves, and both their per-
    sons rad:
When Calidore thus first: 'Haile, noblest
    knight
Of all this day on ground that breathen liv-
    ing spright!

V

'Now tell, if please you, of the good suc-
    cesse
Which ye have had in your late enter-
    prize.'

To whom Sir Artegall gan to expresse
His whole exploite and valorous emprize,
In order as it did to him arize.
'Now, happy man!' sayd then Sir Cali-
    dore,
'Which have, so goodly as ye can devize,
Atchiev'd so hard a quest as few before;
That shall you most renowmed make for
    evermore.

VI

But where ye ended have, now I begin
To tread an endlesse trace, withouten
    guyde,
Or good direction how to enter in,
Or how to issue forth in waies untryde,
In perils strange, in labours long and wide,
In which although good fortune me befall,
Yet shall it not by none be testifyde.'
'What is that quest,' quoth then Sir Arte-
    gall,
'That you into such perils presently doth
    call?'

VII

'The Blattant Beast,' quoth he, 'I doe
    pursew,
And through the world incessantly doe
    chase,
Till I him overtake, or else subdew:
Yet know I not or how or in what place
To find him out, yet still I forward trace.'
'What is that Blattant Beast?' then he
    replide.
'It is a monster bred of hellishe race,'
Then answerd he, 'which often hath an-
    noyd
Good knights and ladies true, and many
    else destroyd.

VIII

'Of Cerberus whilome he was begot,
And fell Chimæra in her darkesome den,
Through fowle commixture of his filthy
    blot;
Where he was fostred long in Stygian
    fen,
Till he to perfect ripenesse grew, and then
Into this wicked world he forth was sent,
To be the plague and scourge of wretched
    men:
Whom with vile tongue and venemous in-
    tent
He sore doth wound, and bite, and cruelly
    torment.'

IX

'Then, since the Salvage Island I did
    leave,'
Sayd Artegall, 'I such a beast did see,
The which did seeme a thousand tongues to
    have,
That all in spight and malice did agree,
With which he bayd and loudly barkt at
    mee,
As if that he attonce would me devoure.
But I, that knew my selfe from perill free,
Did nought regard his malice nor his
    powre,
But he the more his wicked poyson forth
    did poure.'

X

'That surely is that beast,' saide Calidore,
'Which I pursue, of whom I am right
    glad
To heare these tidings, which of none afore
Through all my weary travell I have had:
Yet now some hope your words unto me
    add.'
'Now God you speed,' quoth then Sir
    Artegall,
'And keepe your body from the daunger
    drad:
For ye have much adoe to deale withall.'
So both tooke goodly leave, and parted
    severall.

XI

Sir Calidore thence travelled not long,
When as by chaunce a comely squire he
    found,
That thorough some more mighty enemies
    wrong
Both hand and foote unto a tree was bound:
Who, seeing him from farre, with piteous
    sound
Of his shrill cries him called to his aide.
To whom approching, in that painefull
    stound
When he him saw, for no demaunds he
    staide,
But first him losde, and afterwards thus to
    him saide:

XII

'Unhappy squire! what hard mishap thee
    brought
Into this bay of perill and disgrace?
What cruell hand thy wretched thraldome
    wrought,

And thee captyved in this shamefull
place?'
To whom he answerd thus: 'My haplesse
case
Is not occasiond through my misdesert,
But through misfortune, which did me
abase
Unto this shame, and my young hope subvert,
Ere that I in her guilefull traines was well
expert.

XIII

'Not farre from hence, uppon yond rocky
hill,
Hard by a streight there stands a castle
strong,
Which doth observe a custome lewd and
ill,
And it hath long mayntaind with mighty
wrong:
For may no knight nor lady passe along
That way, (and yet they needs must passe
that way,
By reason of the streight, and rocks
among,)
But they that ladies lockes doe shave away,
And that knights berd for toll, which they
for passage pay.'

XIV

'A shamefull use as ever I did heare,'
Sayd Calidore, 'and to be overthrowne.
But by what meanes did they at first it
reare,
And for what cause? tell, if thou have it
knowne.'
Sayd then that squire: 'The lady which
doth owne
This castle is by name Briana hight;
Then which a prouder lady liveth none:
She long time hath deare lov'd a doughty
knight,
And sought to win his love by all the
meanes she might.

XV

'His name is Crudor; who, through high
disdaine
And proud despight of his selfe pleasing
mynd,
Refused hath to yeeld her love againe,
Untill a mantle she for him doe fynd,
With beards of knights and locks of ladies
lynd.

Which to provide, she hath this castle dight,
And therein hath a seneschall assynd,
Cald Maleffort, a man of mickle might,
Who executes her wicked will, with worse
despight.

XVI

'He this same day, as I that way did come
With a faire damzell, my beloved deare,
In execution of her lawlesse doome,
Did set uppon us flying both for feare:
For little bootes against him hand to reare
Me first he tooke, unhable to withstond,
And whiles he her pursued every where,
Till his returne unto this tree he bond:
Ne wote I surely, whether her he yet have
fond.'

XVII

Thus whiles they spake, they heard a rue-
full shrieke
Of one loud crying, which they streight
way ghest
That it was she, the which for helpe did
seeke.
Tho looking up unto the cry to lest,
They saw that carle from farre, with hand
unblest
Hayling that mayden by the yellow heare,
That all her garments from her snowy brest,
And from her head her lockes he nigh did
teare,
Ne would he spare for pitty, nor refraine
for feare.

XVIII

Which haynous sight when Calidore be-
held,
Eftsoones he loosd that squire, and so him
left,
With hearts dismay and inward dolour
queld,
For to pursue that villaine, which had reft
That piteous spoile by so injurious theft.
Whom overtaking, loude to him he cryde:
'Leave, faytor, quickely that misgotten
weft
To him that hath it better justifyde,
And turne thee soone to him of whom thou
art defyde.'

XIX

Who hearkning to that voice, him selfe
upreard,
And seeing him so fiercely towardes make,

Against him stoutly ran, as nought afeard,
But rather more enrag'd for those words
 sake;
And with sterne count'naunce thus unto
 him spake:
' Art thou the caytive that defyest me,
And for this mayd, whose party thou doest
 take,
Wilt give thy beard, though it but little
 bee ?
Yet shall it not her lockes for raunsome
 fro me free.'

XX

With that he fiercely at him flew, and layd
On hideous strokes with most importune
 might,
That oft he made him stagger as unstayd,
And oft recuile to shunne his sharpe de-
 spight.
But Calidore, that was well skild in fight,
Him long forbore, and still his spirite
 spar'd,
Lying in waite, how him he damadge might.
But when he felt him shrinke, and come to
 ward,
He greater grew, and gan to drive at him
 more hard.

XXI

Like as a water streame, whose swelling
 sourse
Shall drive a mill, within strong bancks is
 pent,
And long restrayned of his ready course;
So soone as passage is unto him lent,
Breakes forth, and makes his way more
 violent:
Such was the fury of Sir Calidore,
When once he felt his foeman to relent;
He fiercely him pursu'd, and pressed sore,
Who as he still decayd, so he encreased
 more.

XXII

The heavy burden of whose dreadfull
 might
When as the carle no longer could sustaine,
His heart gan faint, and streight he tooke
 his flight
Toward the castle, where, if need constraine,
His hope of refuge used to remaine.
Whom Calidore perceiving fast to flie,
He him pursu'd and chaced through the
 plaine,

That he for dread of death gan loude to
 crie
Unto the ward, to open to him hastilie.

XXIII

They from the wall him seeing so aghast,
The gate soone opened to receive him in,
But Calidore did follow him so fast,
That even in the porch he him did win,
And cleft his head asunder to his chin.
The carkasse, tumbling downe within the
 dore,
Did choke the entraunce with a lumpe of
 sin,
That it could not be shut, whilest Calidore
Did enter in, and slew the porter on the
 flore.

XXIV

With that the rest, the which the castle
 kept,
About him flockt, and hard at him did lay;
But he them all from him full lightly swept,
As doth a steare, in heat of sommers day,
With his long taile the bryzes brush away.
Thence passing forth, into the hall he came,
Where of the lady selfe in sad dismay
He was ymett, who with uncomely shame
Gan him salute, and fowle upbrayd with
 faulty blame.

XXV

'False traytor knight,' sayd she, 'no knight
 at all,
But scorne of armes, that hast with guilty
 hand
Murdred my men, and slaine my seneschall;
Now comest thou to rob my house unmand,
And spoile my selfe, that can not thee
 withstand ?
Yet doubt thou not, but that some better
 knight
Then thou, that shall thy treason under-
 stand,
Will it avenge, and pay thee with thy right:
And if none do, yet shame shal thee with
 shame requight.'

XXVI

Much was the knight abashed at that word;
Yet answerd thus: ' Not unto me the shame,
But to the shamefull doer it afford.
Bloud is no blemish; for it is no blame
To punish those that doe deserve the same;
But they that breake bands of civilitie,

And wicked customes make, those doe de-
    fame
Both noble armes and gentle curtesie.
No greater shame to man then inhumani-
    tie.

XXVII

' Then doe your selfe, for dread of shame,
    forgoe
This evill manner which ye here maintaine,
And doe in stead thereof mild curt'sie showe
To all that passe. That shall you glory gaine
More then his love, which thus ye seeke
    t' obtaine.'
Wherewith all full of wrath, she thus re-
    plyde:
' Vile recreant ! know that I doe much dis-
    daine
Thy courteous lore, that doest my love de-
    ride,
Who scornes thy ydle scoffe, and bids thee
    be defyde.'

XXVIII

' To take defiaunce at a ladies word,'
Quoth he, ' I hold it no indignity;
But were he here, that would it with his
    sword
Abett, perhaps he mote it deare aby.'
' Cowherd,' quoth she, ' were not that thou
    wouldst fly
Ere he doe come, he should be soone in
    place.'
' If I doe so,' sayd he, ' then liberty
I leave to you, for aye me to disgrace
With all those shames that erst ye spake
    me to deface.'

XXIX

With that a dwarfe she cald to her in hast,
And taking from her hand a ring of gould,
A privy token which betweene them past,
Bad him to flie with all the speed he could
To Crudor, and desire him that he would
Vouchsafe to reskue her against a knight,
Who through strong powre had now her
    self in hould,
Having late slaine her seneschall in fight,
And all her people murdred with outragious
    might.

XXX

The dwarfe his way did hast, and went all
    night;
But Calidore did with her there abyde

The comming of that so much threatned
    knight;
Where that discourteous dame with scorn-
    full pryde
And fowle entreaty him indignifyde,
That yron heart it hardly could sustaine:
Yet he, that could his wrath full wisely
    guyde,
Did well endure her womanish disdaine,
And did him selfe from fraile impatience
    refraine.

XXXI

The morrow next, before the lampe of light
Above the earth upreard his flaming head,
The dwarfe, which bore that message to
    her knight,
Brought aunswere backe, that ere he tasted
    bread
He would her succour, and alive or dead
Her foe deliver up into her hand:
Therefore he wild her doe away all dread;
And that of him she mote assured stand,
He sent to her his basenet, as a faithfull
    band.

XXXII

Thereof full blyth the lady streight became,
And gan t' augment her bitternesse much
    more:
Yet no whit more appalled for the same,
Ne ought dismayed was Sir Calidore,
But rather did more chearefull seeme there-
    fore;
And having soone his armes about him dight,
Did issue forth, to meete his foe afore;
Where long he stayed not, when as a knight
He spide come pricking on with al his powre
    and might.

XXXIII

Well weend he streight, that he should be
    the same
Which tooke in hand her quarrell to main-
    taine;
Ne stayd to aske if it were he by name,
But coucht his speare, and ran at him
    amaine.
They bene ymett in middest of the plaine,
With so fell fury and dispiteous forse,
That neither could the others stroke sus-
    taine,
But rudely rowld to ground both man and
    horse,
Neither of other taking pitty nor remorse.

XXXIV

But Calidore uprose againe full light,
Whiles yet his foe lay fast in sencelesse
  sound;
Yet would he not him hurt, although he
  might:
For shame he weend a sleeping wight to
  wound.
But when Briana saw that drery stound,
There where she stood uppon the castle wall,
She deem'd him sure to have bene dead on
  ground,
And made such piteous mourning therewith-
  all,
That from the battlements she ready seem'd
  to fall.

XXXV

Nathlesse at length him selfe he did upreare
In lustlesse wise, as if against his will,
Ere he had slept his fill, he wakened were,
And gan to stretch his limbs; which feel-
  ing ill
Of his late fall, a while he rested still:
But when he saw his foe before in vew,
He shooke off luskishnesse, and courage
  chill
Kindling a fresh, gan battell to renew,
To prove if better foote then horsebacke
  would ensew.

XXXVI

There then began a fearefull cruell fray
Betwixt them two, for maystery of might:
For both were wondrous practicke in that
  play,
And passing well expert in single fight,
And both inflam'd with furious despight:
Which as it still encreast, so still increast
Their cruell strokes and terrible affright;
Ne once for ruth their rigour they release,
Ne once to breath a while their angers tem-
  pest ceast.

XXXVII

Thus long they trac'd and traverst to and
  fro,
And tryde all waies, how each mote en-
  trance make
Into the life of his malignant foe;
They hew'd their helmes, and plates asunder
  brake,
As they had potshares bene; for nought
  mote slake
Their greedy vengeaunces, but goary blood;

That at the last like to a purple lake
Of bloudy gore congeal'd about them stood,
Which from their riven sides forth gushed
  like a flood.

XXXVIII

At length it chaunst that both their hands
  on hie
At once did heave, with all their powre and
  might,
Thinking the utmost of their force to trie,
And prove the finall fortune of the fight:
But Calidore, that was more quicke of sight,
And nimbler handed then his enemie,
Prevented him before his stroke could
  light,
And on the helmet smote him formerlie,
That made him stoupe to ground with
  meeke humilitie.

XXXIX

And ere he could recover foot againe,
He following that faire advantage fast,
His stroke redoubled with such might and
  maine,
That him upon the ground he groveling
  cast;
And leaping to him light, would have un-
  last
His helme, to make unto his vengeance way.
Who, seeing in what daunger he was plast,
Cryde out : 'Ah mercie, sir ! doe me not
  slay,
But save my life, which lot before your
  foot doth lay.'

XL

With that his mortall hand a while he
  stayd,
And having somewhat calm'd his wrathfull
  heat
With goodly patience, thus he to him sayd:
'And is the boast of that proud ladies threat,
That menaced me from the field to beat,
Now brought to this ? By this now may
  ye learne,
Strangers no more so rudely to intreat,
But put away proud looke, and usage sterne,
The which shal nought to you but foule
  dishonor yearne.

XLI

' For nothing is more blamefull to a knight,
That court'sie doth as well as armes professe,

How ever strong and fortunate in fight,
Then the reproch of pride and cruelnesse.
In vaine he seeketh others to suppresse,
Who hath not learnd him selfe first to sub-
    dew:
All flesh is frayle, and full of ficklenesse,
Subject to fortunes chance, still chaunging
    new;
What haps to day to me to morrow may to
    you.

XLII

'Who will not mercie unto others shew,
How can he mercy ever hope to have?
To pay each with his owne is right and
    dew.
Yet since ye mercie now doe need to crave,
I will it graunt, your hopelesse life to save;
With these conditions, which I will pro-
    pound:
First, that ye better shall your selfe be-
    have
Unto all errant knights, whereso on ground;
Next, that ye ladies ayde in every stead
    and stound.'

XLIII

The wretched man, that all this while did
    dwell
In dread of death, his heasts did gladly
    heare,
And promist to performe his precept well,
And whatsoever else he would requere.
So suffring him to rise, he made him sweare
By his owne sword, and by the crosse
    thereon,
To take Briana for his loving fere,
Withouten dowre or composition;
But to release his former foule condition.

XLIV

All which accepting, and with faithfull oth
Bynding himselfe most firmely to obay,
He up arose, how ever liefe or loth,
And swore to him true fealtie for aye.
Then forth he cald from sorrowfull dismay
The sad Briana, which all this beheld:
Who comming forth yet full of late affray,
Sir Calidore upcheard, and to her teld
All this accord, to which he Crudor had
    compeld.

XLV

Whereof she now more glad then sory earst,
All overcome with infinite affect

For his exceeding courtesie, that pearst
Her stubborne hart with inward deepe
    effect,
Before his feet her selfe she did project,
And him adoring as her lives deare lord,
With all due thankes and dutifull respect,
Her selfe acknowledg'd bound for that ac-
    cord,
By which he had to her both life and love
    restord.

XLVI

So all returning to the castle glad,
Most joyfully she them did entertaine,
Where goodly glee and feast to them she
    made,
To shew her thankefull mind and meaning
    faine,
By all the meanes she mote it best explaine:
And after all, unto Sir Calidore
She freely gave that castle for his paine,
And her selfe bound to him for evermore;
So wondrously now chaung'd from that she
    was afore.

XLVII

But Calidore himselfe would not retaine
Nor land nor fee, for hyre of his good deede,
But gave them streight unto that squire
    againe,
Whom from her seneschall he lately freed,
And to his damzell, as their rightfull meed,
For recompence of all their former wrong:
There he remaind with them right well
    agreed,
Till of his wounds he wexed hole and
    strong,
And then to his first quest he passed forth
    along.

CANTO II

Calidore sees young Tristram slay
    A proud, discourteous knight:
He makes him squire, and of him learnes
    His state and present plight.

I

WHAT vertue is so fitting for a knight,
Or for a ladie whom a knight should love,
As curtesie, to beare themselves aright
To all of each degree, as doth behove?
For whether they be placed high above,
Or low beneath, yet ought they well to
    know

Their good, that none them rightly may
reprove
Of rudenesse, for not yeelding what they
owe:
Great skill it is such duties timely to bestow.

II

Thereto great helpe Dame Nature selfe
doth lend:
For some so goodly gratious are by kind,
That every action doth them much com-
mend,
And in the eyes of men great liking find;
Which others, that have greater skill in
mind,
Though they enforce themselves, cannot
attaine.
For everie thing, to which one is inclin'd,
Doth best become, and greatest grace doth
gaine:
Yet praise likewise deserve good thewes,
enforst with paine.

III

That well in courteous Calidore appeares,
Whose every deed and word that he did
say
Was like enchantment, that through both
the eares
And both the eyes did steale the hart
away.
He now againe is on his former way,
To follow his first quest, when as he
spyde
A tall young man from thence not farre
away,
Fighting on foot, as well he him descryde,
Against an armed knight, that did on
horsebacke ryde.

IV

And them beside, a ladie faire he saw,
Standing alone on foot, in foule array:
To whom himselfe he hastily did draw,
To weet the cause of so uncomely fray,
And to depart them, if so be he may.
But ere he came in place, that youth had
kild
That armed knight, that low on ground he
lay;
Which when he saw, his hart was inly
child
With great amazement, and his thought
with wonder fild.

V

Him stedfastly he markt, and saw to bee
A goodly youth of amiable grace,
Yet but a slender slip, that scarse did see
Yet seventeene yeares, but tall and faire of
face,
That sure he deem'd him borne of noble
race.
All in a woodmans jacket he was clad
Of Lincolne greene, belayd with silver
lace;
And on his head an hood with aglets sprad,
And by his side his hunters horne he hang-
ing had.

VI

Buskins he wore of costliest cordwayne,
Pinckt upon gold, and paled part per part,
As then the guize was for each gentle
swayne;
In his right hand he held a trembling dart,
Whose fellow he before had sent apart,
And in his left he held a sharpe bore-
speare,
With which he wont to launch the salvage
hart
Of many a lyon and of many a beare,
That first unto his hand in chase did hap-
pen neare.

VII

Whom Calidore a while well having vewed,
At length bespake: 'What meanes this,
gentle swaine?
Why hath thy hand too bold it selfe embrewed
In blood of knight, the which by thee is
slaine,
By thee no knight; which armes impugneth plaine?'
'Certes,' said he, 'loth were I to have broken
The law of armes; yet breake it should
againe,
Rather then let my selfe of wight be stroken,
So long as these two armes were able to be
wroken.

VIII

'For not I him, as this his ladie here
May witnesse well, did offer first to wrong,
Ne surely thus unarm'd I likely were;
But he me first, through pride and puis-
sance strong

Assayld, not knowing what to armes doth
  long.'
Perdie, great blame,' then said Sir Calidore,
'For armed knight a wight unarm'd to
  wrong.
But then aread, thou gentle chyld, wherefore
Betwixt you two began this strife and
  sterne uprore.'

IX

'That shall I sooth,' said he, 'to you de-
  clare.
I whose unryper yeares are yet unfit
For thing of weight, or worke of greater
  care,
Doe spend my dayes and bend my carelesse
  wit
To salvage chace, where I thereon may hit
In all this forrest and wyld wooddie raine:
Where, as this day I was enraunging it,
I chaunst to meete this knight, who there
  lyes slaine,
Together with this ladie, passing on the
  plaine.

X

'The knight, as ye did see, on horsebacke
  was,
And this his ladie, (that him ill became,)
On her faire feet by his horse side did pas
Through thicke and thin, unfit for any
  dame.
Yet not content, more to increase his
  shame,
When so she lagged, as she needs mote so,
He with his speare, that was to him great
  blame,
Would thumpe her forward, and inforce to
  goe,
Weeping to him in vaine, and making pit-
  eous woe.

XI

'Which when I saw, as they me passed
  by,
Much was I moved in indignant mind,
And gan to blame him for such cruelty
Towards a ladie, whom with usage kind
He rather should have taken up behind.
Wherewith he wroth, and full of proud dis-
  daine,
Tooke in foule scorne, that I such fault did
  find,

And me in lieu thereof revil'd againe,
Threatning to chastize me, as doth t' a
  chyld pertaine.

XII

'Which I no lesse disdayning, backe re-
  turned
His scornefull taunts unto his teeth againe,
That he streight way with haughtie choler
  burned,
And with his speare strooke me one stroke
  or twaine;
Which I enforst to beare, though to my
  paine,
Cast to requite, and with a slender dart,
Fellow of this I beare, throwne not in
  vaine,
Strooke him, as seemeth, underneath the
  hart,
That through the wound his spirit shortly
  did depart.'

XIII

Much did Sir Calidore admyre his speach
Tempred so well, but more admyr'd the
  stroke
That through the mayles had made so
  strong a breach
Into his hart, and had so sternely wroke
His wrath on him that first occasion broke.
Yet rested not, but further gan inquire
Of that same ladie, whether what he spoke
Were soothly so, and that th' unrighteous ire
Of her owne knight had given him his owne
  due hire.

XIV

Of all which when as she could nought deny,
But cleard that stripling of th' imputed
  blame,
Sayd then Sir Calidore : 'Neither will I
Him charge with guilt, but rather doe quite
  clame:
For what he spake, for you he spake it,
  dame;
And what he did, he did him selfe to save:
Against both which that knight wrought
  knightlesse shame.
For knights and all men this by nature have,
Towards all womenkind them kindly to be-
  have.

XV

' But sith that he is gone irrevocable,
Please it you, ladie, to us to aread,

What cause could make him so dishonour-
    able,
To drive you so on foot, unfit to tread
And lackey by him, gainst all womanhead?'
'Certes, sir knight,' sayd she, 'full loth I
    were
To rayse a lyving blame against the dead:
But since it me concernes, my selfe to clere,
I will the truth discover, as it chaunst
    whylere.

XVI

'This day, as he and I together roade
Upon our way, to which we weren bent,
We chaunst to come foreby a covert glade
Within a wood, whereas a ladie gent
Sate with a knight in joyous jolliment
Of their franke loves, free from all gealous
    spyes:
Faire was the ladie sure, that mote content
An hart not carried with too curious eyes,
And unto him did shew all lovely courtesyes.

XVII

'Whom when my knight did see so lovely
    faire,
He inly gan her lover to envy,
And wish that he part of his spoyle might
    share.
Whereto when as my presence he did spy
To be a let, he bad me by and by
For to alight: but when as I was loth
My loves owne part to leave so suddenly,
He with strong hand down from his steed
    me throw'th,
And with presumpteous powre against that
    knight streight go'th.

XVIII

'Unarm'd all was the knight, as then more
    meete
For ladies service and for loves delight,
Then fearing any foeman there to meete:
Whereof he taking oddes, streight bids him
    dight
Himselfe to yeeld his love, or else to fight.
Whereat the other starting up dismayd,
Yet boldly answer'd, as he rightly might,
To leave his love he should be ill apayd,
In which he had good right gaynst all that
    it gainesayd.

XIX

'Yet since he was not presently in plight
Her to defend, or his to justifie,

He him requested, as he was a knight,
To lend him day his better right to trie,
Or stay till he his armes, which were
    thereby,
Might lightly fetch. But he was fierce and
    whot,
Ne time would give, nor any termes aby,
But at him flew, and with his speare him
    smot;
From which to thinke to save himselfe it
    booted not.

XX

'Meane while his ladie, which this outrage
    saw,
Whilest they together for the quarrey
    strove,
Into the covert did her selfe withdraw,
And closely hid her selfe within the grove.
My knight hers soone, as seemes, to daun-
    ger drove
And left sore wounded: but when her he
    mist,
He woxe halfe mad, and in that rage gan
    rove
And range through all the wood, where so
    he wist
She hidden was, and sought her so long as
    him list.

XXI

'But when as her he by no meanes could
    find,
After long search and chauff, he turned
    backe
Unto the place where me he left behind:
There gan he me to curse and ban, for lacke
Of that faire bootie, and with bitter wracke
To wreake on me the guilt of his owne
    wrong.
Of all which I yet glad to beare the packe,
Strove to appease him, and perswaded long:
But still his passion grew more violent and
    strong.

XXII

'Then as it were t'avenge his wrath on mee,
When forward we should fare, he flat re-
    fused
To take me up (as this young man did see)
Upon his steed, for no just cause accused,
But forst to trot on foot, and foule misused,
Pounching me with the butt end of his
    speare,
In vaine complayning to be so abused;

For he regarded neither playnt nor teare,
But more enforst my paine, the more my
    plaints to heare.

XXIII

' So passed we, till this young man us met,
And being moov'd with pittie of my plight,
Spake, as was meet, for ease of my regret:
Whereof befell what now is in your sight.'
' Now sure,' then said Sir Calidore, ' and
    right
Me seemes, that him befell by his owne
    fault:
Who ever thinkes through confidence of
    might,
Or through support of count'nance proud
    and hault,
To wrong the weaker, oft falles in his owne
    assault.'

XXIV

Then turning backe unto that gentle boy,
Which had himselfe so stoutly well acquit;
Seeing his face so lovely sterne and coy,
And hearing th' answeres of his pregnant
    wit,
He praysd it much, and much admyred it;
That sure he weend him borne of noble
    blood,
With whom those graces did so goodly fit:
And when he long had him beholding stood,
He burst into these words, as to him seemed
    good:

XXV

' Faire gentle swayne, and yet as stout as
    fayre,
That in these woods amongst the nymphs
    dost wonne,
Which daily may to thy sweete lookes re-
    payre,
As they are wont unto Latonaes sonne,
After his chace on woodie Cynthus donne:
Well may I certes such an one thee read,
As by thy worth thou worthily hast wonne,
Or surely borne of some heroicke sead,
That in thy face appeares and gratious
    goodlyhead.

XXVI

' But should it not displease thee it to tell,
(Unlesse thou in these woods thy selfe con-
    ceale
For love amongst the woodie gods to dwell,)
I would thy selfe require thee to reveale,

For deare affection and unfayned zeale,
Which to thy noble personage I beare,
And wish thee grow in worship and great
    weale.
For since the day that armes I first did
    reare,
I never saw in any greater hope appeare.'

XXVII

To whom then thus the noble youth: ' May
    be,
Sir knight, that, by discovering my estate,
Harme may arise unweeting unto me;
Nathelesse, sith ye so courteous seemed
    late,
To you I will not feare it to relate.
Then wote ye that I am a Briton borne,
Sonne of a king, how ever thorough fate
Or fortune I my countrie have forlorne,
And lost the crowne which should my head
    by right adorne.

XXVIII

' And Tristram is my name, the onely heire
Of good King Meliogras, which did rayne
In Cornewale, till that he through lives
    despeire
Untimely dyde, before I did attaine
Ripe yeares of reason, my right to main-
    taine.
After whose death, his brother seeing mee
An infant, weake a kingdome to sustaine,
Upon him tooke the roiall high degree,
And sent me, where him list, instructed for
    to bee.

XXIX

' The widow queene, my mother, which then
    hight
Faire Emiline, conceiving then great feare
Of my fraile safetie, resting in the might
Of him that did the kingly scepter beare,
Whose gealous dread enduring not a peare
Is wont to cut off all that doubt may breed,
Thought best away me to remove some-
    where
Into some forrein land, where as no need
Of dreaded daunger might his doubtfull
    humor feed.

XXX

' So taking counsell of a wise man red,
She was by him adviz'd to send me quight
Out of the countrie wherein I was bred,
The which the fertile Lionesse is hight,

Into the land of Faerie, where no wight
Should weet of me, nor worke me any
    wrong.
To whose wise read she hearkning, sent me
    streight
Into this land, where I have wond thus
    long,
Since I was ten yeares old, now growen to
    stature strong.

XXXI

'All which my daies I have not lewdly
    spent,
Nor spilt the blossome of my tender yeares
In ydlesse, but, as was convenient,
Have trayned bene with many noble feres
In gentle thewes, and such like seemely
    leres.
Mongst which my most delight hath alwaies
    been,
To hunt the salvage chace amongst my
    peres,
Of all that raungeth in the forrest greene;
Of which none is to me unknowne, that ev'r
    was seene.

XXXII

'Ne is there hauke which mantleth her on
    pearch,
Whether high towring, or accoasting low,
But I the measure of her flight doe search,
And all her pray, and all her diet know.
Such be our joyes, which in these forrests
    grow:
Onely the use of armes, which most I joy,
And fitteth most for noble swayne to know,
I have not tasted yet, yet past a boy,
And being now high time these strong
    joynts to imploy.

XXXIII

'Therefore, good sir, sith now occasion fit
Doth fall, whose like hereafter seldome
    may,
Let me this crave, unworthy though of it,
That ye will make me squire without de-
    lay,
That from henceforth in batteilous array
I may beare armes, and learne to use them
    right;
The rather since that fortune hath this
    day
Given to me the spoile of this dead knight,
These goodly gilden armes, which I have
    won in fight.'

XXXIV

All which when well Sir Calidore had
    heard,
Him much more now then earst he gan ad-
    mire,
For the rare hope which in his yeares ap-
    pear'd,
And thus replide: 'Faire chyld, the high
    desire
To love of armes, which in you doth aspire,
I may not certes without blame denie;
But rather wish that some more noble hire
(Though none more noble then is chevalrie)
I had, you to reward with greater dignitie.'

XXXV

There him he causd to kneele, and made to
    sweare
Faith to his knight, and truth to ladies all,
And never to be recreant, for feare
Of perill, or of ought that might befall:
So he him dubbed, and his squire did call.
Full glad and joyous then young Tristram
    grew,
Like as a flowre, whose silken leaves small,
Long shut up in the bud from heavens vew,
At length breakes forth, and brode dis-
    playes his smyling hew.

XXXVI

Thus when they long had treated to and fro,
And Calidore betooke him to depart,
Chyld Tristram prayd that he with him
    might goe
On his adventure, vowing not to start,
But wayt on him in every place and part.
Whereat Sir Calidore did much delight,
And greatly joy'd at his so noble hart,
In hope he sure would prove a doughtie
    knight:
Yet for the time this answere he to him
    behight:

XXXVII

'Glad would I surely be, thou courteous
    squire,
To have thy presence in my present quest,
That mote thy kindled courage set on fire,
And flame forth honour in thy noble brest:
But I am bound by vow, which I profest
To my dread Soveraine, when I it assayd,
That in atchievement of her high behest
I should no creature joyne unto mine ayde;
Forthy I may not graunt that ye so
    greatly prayde.

XXXVIII

'But since this ladie is all desolate,
And needeth safegard now upon her way,
Ye may doe well in this her needfull state
To succour her from daunger of dismay;
That thankfull guerdon may to you repay.'
The noble ympe, of such new service fayne,
It gladly did accept, as he did say.
So taking courteous leave, they parted twayne,
And Calidore forth passed to his former payne.

XXXIX

But Tristram, then despoyling that dead knight
Of all those goodly implements of prayse,
Long fed his greedie eyes with the faire sight
Of the bright mettall, shyning like sunne rayes;
Handling and turning them a thousand wayes.
And after having them upon him dight,
He tooke that ladie, and her up did rayse
Upon the steed of her owne late dead knight,
So with her marched forth, as she did him behight.

XL

There to their fortune leave we them awhile,
And turne we backe to good Sir Calidore;
Who, ere he thence had traveild many a mile,
Came to the place, whereas ye heard afore
This knight, whom Tristram slew, had wounded sore
Another knight in his despiteous pryde;
There he that knight found lying on the flore,
With many wounds full perilous and wyde,
That all his garments and the grasse in vermeill dyde.

XLI

And there beside him sate upon the ground
His wofull ladie, piteously complayning
With loud laments that most unluckie stound,
And her sad selfe with carefull hand constrayning
To wype his wounds, and ease their bitter payning.

XLII

Which sorie sight when Calidore did vew
With heavie eyne, from teares uneath refrayning,
His mightie hart their mournefull case can rew,
And for their better comfort to them nigher drew.

XLII

Then speaking to the ladie, thus he sayd:
'Ye dolefull dame, let not your griefe empeach
To tell what cruell hand hath thus arayd
This knight unarm'd, with so unknightly breach
Of armes, that if I yet him nigh may reach,
I may avenge him of so foule despight.'
The ladie, hearing his so courteous speach,
Gan reare her eyes as to the chearefull light,
And from her sory hart few heavie words forth sight:

XLIII

In which she shew'd, how that discourteous knight
(Whom Tristram slew) them in that shadow found,
Joying together in unblam'd delight,
And him unarm'd, as now he lay on ground,
Charg'd with his speare and mortally did wound,
Withouten cause, but onely her to reave
From him, to whom she was for ever bound:
Yet when she fled into that covert greave,
He, her not finding, both them thus nigh dead did leave.

XLIV

When Calidore this ruefull storie had
Well understood, he gan of her demand,
What manner wight he was, and how yclad,
Which had this outrage wrought with wicked hand.
She then, like as she best could understand,
Him thus describ'd, to be of stature large,
Clad all in gilden armes, with azure band
Quartred athwart, and bearing in his targe
A ladie on rough waves row'd in a sommer barge.

XLV

Then gan Sir Calidore to ghesse streight way,
By many signes which she described had,

That this was he whom Tristram earst did
    slay,
And to her said: 'Dame, be no longer sad:
For he that hath your knight so ill bestad
Is now him selfe in much more wretched
    plight;
These eyes him saw upon the cold earth
    sprad,
The meede of his desert for that despight,
Which to your selfe he wrought, and to
    your loved knight.

XLVI

'Therefore, faire lady, lay aside this griefe,
Which ye have gathered to your gentle
    hart,
For that displeasure; and thinke what re-
    liefe
Were best devise for this your lovers smart,
And how ye may him hence, and to what
    part,
Convay to be recur'd.' She thankt him
    deare,
Both for that newes he did to her impart,
And for the courteous care which he did
    beare
Both to her love and to her selfe in that sad
    dreare.

XLVII

Yet could she not devise by any wit,
How thence she might convay him to some
    place.
For him to trouble she it thought unfit,
That was a straunger to her wretched case;
And him to beare, she thought it thing too
    base.
Which when as he perceiv'd, he thus be-
    spake:
'Faire lady, let it not you seeme disgrace,
To beare this burden on your dainty backe;
My selfe will beare a part, coportion of
    your packe.'

XLVIII

So off he did his shield, and downeward
    layd
Upon the ground, like to an hollow beare;
And powring balme, which he had long pur-
    vayd,
Into his wounds, him up thereon did reare,
And twixt them both with parted paines did
    beare,
Twixt life and death, not knowing what was
    donne.

Thence they him carried to a castle neare,
In which a worthy auncient knight did
    wonne:
Where what ensu'd shall in next canto be
    begonne.

CANTO III

Calidore brings Priscilla home;
Pursues the Blatant Beast;
Saves Serena, whilest Calepine
By Turpine is opprest.

I

TRUE is, that whilome that good poet sayd,
The gentle minde by gentle deeds is knowne:
For a man by nothing is so well bewrayd
As by his manners, in which plaine is
    showne
Of what degree and what race he is growne.
For seldome seene, a trotting stalion get
An ambling colt, that is his proper owne:
So seldome seene, that one in basenesse set
Doth noble courage shew, with curteous
    manners met.

II

But evermore contrary hath bene tryde,
That gentle bloud will gentle manners breed;
As well may be in Calidore descryde,
By late ensample of that courteous deed
Done to that wounded knight in his great
    need,
Whom on his backe he bore, till he him
    brought
Unto the castle where they had decreed.
There of the knight, the which that castle
    ought,
To make abode that night he greatly was
    besought.

III

He was to weete a man of full ripe yeares,
That in his youth had beene of mickle
    might,
And borne great sway in armes amongst his
    peares:
But now weake age had dimd his candle
    light.
Yet was he courteous still to every wight,
And loved all that did to armes incline;
And was the father of that wounded knight,
Whom Calidore thus carried on his chine;
And Aldus was his name, and his sonnes
    Aladine.

IV

Who, when he saw his sonne so ill bedight
With bleeding wounds, brought home upon
    a beare
By a faire lady and a straunger knight,
Was inly touched with compassion deare,
And deare affection of so dolefull dreare,
That he these words burst forth: 'Ah, sory
    boy !
Is this the hope that to my hoary heare
Thou brings? aie me ! is this the timely joy,
Which I expected long, now turnd to sad
    annoy ?

V

'Such is the weakenesse of all mortall hope;
So tickle is the state of earthly things,
That ere they come unto their aymed scope,
They fall too short of our fraile reckon-
    ings,
And bring us bale and bitter sorrowings,
In stead of comfort, which we should em-
    brace:
This is the state of keasars and of kings.
Let none therefore, that is in meaner place,
Too greatly grieve at any his unlucky case.'

VI

So well and wisely did that good old knight
Temper his griefe, and turned it to cheare,
To cheare his guests, whom he had stayd
    that night,
And make their welcome to them well ap-
    peare:
That to Sir Calidore was easie geare;
But that faire lady would be cheard for
    nought,
But sigh'd and sorrow'd for her lover deare,
And inly did afflict her pensive thought,
With thinking to what case her name should
    now be brought.

VII

For she was daughter to a noble lord,
Which dwelt thereby, who sought her to
    affy
To a great pere; but she did disaccord,
Ne could her liking to his love apply,
But lov'd this fresh young knight, who
    dwelt her ny,
The lusty Aladine, though meaner borne
And of lesse livelood and hability,
Yet full of valour, the which did adorne
His meanesse much, and make her th' others
    riches scorne.

VIII

So having both found fit occasion,
They met together in that luckelesse glade;
Where that proud knight in his presump-
    tion
The gentle Aladine did earst invade,
Being unarm'd and set in secret shade.
Whereof she now bethinking, gan t' advize,
How great a hazard she at earst had made
Of her good fame, and further gan devize,
How she the blame might salve with
    coloured disguize.

IX

But Calidore with all good courtesie
Fain'd her to frolicke, and to put away
The pensive fit of her melancholie;
And that old knight by all meanes did
    assay
To make them both as merry as he may.
So they the evening past, till time of rest,
When Calidore in seemly good array
Unto his bowre was brought, and, there
    undrest,
Did sleepe all night through weary travell
    of his quest.

X

But faire Priscilla (so that lady hight)
Would to no bed, nor take no kindely
    sleepe,
But by her wounded love did watch all
    night,
And all the night for bitter anguish weepe,
And with her teares his wounds did wash
    and steepe.
So well she washt them, and so well she
    wacht him,
That of the deadly swound, in which full
    deepe
He drenched was, she at the length dis-
    pacht him,
And drove away the stound which mortally
    attacht him.

XI

The morrow next, when day gan to up-
    looke,
He also gan uplooke with drery eye,
Like one that out of deadly dreame awooke:
Where when he saw his faire Priscilla by,
He deepely sigh'd, and groaned inwardly,
To thinke of this ill state in which she
    stood,
To which she for his sake had weetingly

Now brought her selfe, and blam'd her
    noble blood:
For first, next after life, he tendered her
    good.

XII

Which she perceiving, did with plenteous
    teares
His care more then her owne compassionate,
Forgetfull of her owne, to minde his feares:
So both conspiring, gan to intimate
Each others griefe with zeale affectionate,
And twixt them twaine with equall care to
    cast,
How to save hole her hazarded estate;
For which the onely helpe now left them last
Seem'd to be Calidore: all other helpes
    were past.

XIII

Him they did deeme, as sure to them he
    seemed,
A courteous knight, and full of faithfull
    trust:
Therefore to him their cause they best
    esteemed
Whole to commit, and to his dealing just.
Earely, so soone as Titans beames forth
    brust
Through the thicke clouds, in which they
    steeped lay
All night in darkenesse, duld with yron rust,
Calidore, rising up as fresh as day,
Gan freshly him addresse unto his former
    way.

XIV

But first him seemed fit, that wounded
    knight
To visite, after this nights perillous passe,
And to salute him, if he were in plight,
And eke that lady, his faire lovely lasse.
There him he found much better then he
    was,
And moved speach to him of things of
    course,
The anguish of his paine to overpasse:
Mongst which he namely did to him dis-
    course
Of former daies mishap, his sorrowes
    wicked sourse.

XV

Of which occasion Aldine taking hold,
Gan breake to him the fortunes of his love,

And all his disadventures to unfold;
That Calidore it dearly deepe did move.
In th' end, his kyndly courtesie to prove,
He him by all the bands of love besought,
And as it mote a faithfull friend behove,
To safeconduct his love, and not for ought
To leave, till to her fathers house he had
    her brought.

XVI

Sir Calidore his faith thereto did plight,
It to performe: so after little stay,
That she her selfe had to the journey dight,
He passed forth with her in faire array,
Fearelesse, who ought did thinke or ought
    did say,
Sith his own thought he knew most cleare
    from wite.
So as they past together on their way,
He can devize this counter-cast of slight,
To give faire colour to that ladies cause in
    sight.

XVII

Streight to the carkasse of that knight he
    went,
The cause of all this evill, who was slaine
The day before by just avengement
Of noble Tristram, where it did remaine:
There he the necke thereof did cut in twaine,
And tooke with him the head, the signe of
    shame.
So forth he passed thorough that daies paine,
Till to that ladies fathers house he came,
Most pensive man, through feare, what of
    his childe became.

XVIII

There he arriving boldly, did present
The fearefull lady to her father deare,
Most perfect pure, and guiltlesse innocent
Of blame, as he did on his knighthood sweare,
Since first he saw her, and did free from
    feare
Of a discourteous knight, who her had reft,
And by outragious force away did beare:
Witnesse thereof he shew'd his head there
    left,
And wretched life forlorne for vengement
    of his theft.

XIX

Most joyfull man her sire was, her to see,
And heare th' adventure of her late mis-
    chaunce;

And thousand thankes to Calidore for fee
Of his large paines in her deliveraunce
Did yeeld; ne lesse the lady did advaunce.
Thus having her restored trustily,
As he had vow'd, some small continuaunce
He there did make, and then most carefully
Unto his first exploite he did him selfe apply.

XX

So as he was pursuing of his quest,
He chaunst to come whereas a jolly knight
In covert shade him selfe did safely rest,
To solace with his lady in delight:
His warlike armes he had from him undight;
For that him selfe he thought from daunger
    free,
And far from envious eyes that mote him
    spight.
And eke the lady was full faire to see,
And courteous withall, becomming her de-
    gree.

XXI

To whom Sir Calidore approaching nye,
Ere they were well aware of living wight,
Them much abasht, but more him selfe
    thereby,
That he so rudely did uppon them light,
And troubled had their quiet loves delight.
Yet since it was his fortune, not his fault,
Him selfe thereof he labour'd to acquite,
And pardon crav'd for his so rash default,
That he gainst courtesie so fowly did de-
    fault.

XXII

With which his gentle words and goodly wit
He soone allayd that knights conceiv'd dis-
    pleasure,
That he besought him downe by him to sit,
That they mote treat of things abrode at
    leasure;
And of adventures, which had in his mea-
    sure
Of so long waies to him befallen late.
So downe he sate, and with delightfull
    pleasure
His long adventures gan to him relate,
Which he endured had through daungerous
    debate.

XXIII

Of which whilest they discoursed both to-
    gether,
The faire Serena (so his lady hight)

Allur'd with myldnesse of the gentle wether,
And pleasaunce of the place, the which was
    dight
With divers flowres distinct with rare de-
    light,
Wandred about the fields, as liking led
Her wavering lust after her wandring sight,
To make a garland to adorne her hed,
Without suspect of ill or daungers hidden
    dred.

XXIV

All sodainely out of the forrest nere
The Blatant Beast forth rushing unaware,
Caught her thus loosely wandring here and
    there,
And in his wide great mouth away her bare,
Crying aloud in vaine, to shew her sad mis-
    fare
Unto the knights, and calling oft for ayde,
Who with the horrour of her haplesse care
Hastily starting up, like men dismayde,
Ran after fast to reskue the distressed
    mayde.

XXV

The Beast, with their pursuit incited more,
Into the wood was bearing her apace
For to have spoyled her, when Calidore,
Who was more light of foote and swift in
    chace,
Him overtooke in middest of his race:
And fiercely charging him with all his
    might,
Forst to forgoe his pray there in the place,
And to betake him selfe to fearefull flight;
For he durst not abide with Calidore to
    fight.

XXVI

Who nathelesse, when he the lady saw
There left on ground, though in full evill
    plight,
Yet knowing that her knight now neare did
    draw,
Staide not to succour her in that affright,
But follow'd fast the monster in his flight:
Through woods and hils he follow'd him so
    fast,
That he nould let him breath nor gather
    spright,
But forst him gape and gaspe, with dread
    aghast,
As if his lungs and lites were nigh a sunder
    brast.

XXVII

And now by this, Sir Calepine (so hight)
Came to the place, where he his lady found
In dolorous dismay and deadly plight,
All in gore bloud there tumbled on the
    ground,
Having both sides through grypt with
    griesly wound.
His weapons soone from him he threw away,
And stouping downe to her in drery swound,
Uprear'd her from the ground, whereon she
    lay,
And in his tender armes her forced up to
    stay.

XXVIII

So well he did his busie paines apply,
That the faint sprite he did revoke againe
To her fraile mansion of mortality.
Then up he tooke her twixt his armes twaine,
And setting on his steede, her did sustaine
With carefull hands, soft footing her be-
    side,
Till to some place of rest they mote at-
    taine,
Where she in safe assuraunce mote abide,
Till she recured were of those her woundes
    wide.

XXIX

Now when as Phœbus with his fiery waine
Unto his inne began to draw apace,
Tho, wexing weary of that toylesome paine,
In travelling on foote so long a space,
Not wont on foote with heavy armes to
    trace,
Downe in a dale forby a rivers syde,
He chaunst to spie a faire and stately place,
To which he meant his weary steps to
    guyde,
In hope there for his love some succour to
    provyde.

XXX

But comming to the rivers side he found
That hardly passable on foote it was:
Therefore there still he stood as in a stound,
Ne wist which way he through the foord
    mote pas.
Thus whilest he was in this distressed case,
Devising what to doe, he nigh espyde
An armed knight approaching to the place,
With a faire lady lincked by his syde,
The which themselves prepard thorough the
    foord to ride.

XXXI

Whom Calepine saluting (as became)
Besought of courtesie, in that his neede,
For safe conducting of his sickely dame
Through that same perillous foord with
    better heede,
To take him up behinde upon his steed:
To whom that other did this taunt returne.
'Perdy, thou peasant knight, mightst
    rightly reed
Me then to be full base and evill borne,
If I would beare behinde a burden of such
    scorne.

XXXII

' But as thou hast thy steed forlorne with
    shame
So fare on foote till thou another gayne,
And let thy lady likewise doe the same,
Or beare her on thy backe with pleasing
    payne,
And prove thy manhood on the billowes
    vayne.'
With which rude speach his lady much dis-
    pleased,
Did him reprove, yet could him not re-
    strayne,
And would on her owne palfrey him have
    eased,
For pitty of his dame, whom she saw so
    diseased.

XXXIII

Sir Calepine her thanckt, yet, inly wroth
Against her knight, her gentlenesse refused,
And carelesly into the river goth,
As in despight to be so fowle abused
Of a rude churle, whom often he accused
Of fowle discourtesie, unfit for knight;
And strongly wading through the waves
    unused,
With speare in th' one hand, stayd him
    selfe upright,
With th' other staide his lady up with
    steddy might.

XXXIV

And all the while, that same discourteous
    knight
Stood on the further bancke beholding him,
At whose calamity, for more despight,
He laught, and mockt to see him like to
    swim.
But when as Calepine came to the brim,
And saw his carriage past that perill well,

Looking at that same carle with count'nance
  grim,
His heart with vengeaunce inwardly did
  swell,
And forth at last did breake in speaches
  sharpe and fell:

XXXV

'Unknightly knight, the blemish of that
  name,
And blot of all that armes uppon them take,
Which is the badge of honour and of fame,
Loe! I defie thee, and here challenge make,
That thou for ever doe those armes forsake,
And be for ever held a recreant knight,
Unlesse thou dare for thy deare ladies sake,
And for thine owne defence, on foote alight,
To justifie thy fault gainst me in equall
  fight.'

XXXVI

The dastard, that did heare him selfe
  defyde,
Seem'd not to weigh his threatfull words
  at all,
But laught them out, as if his greater pryde
Did scorne the challenge of so base a thrall:
Or had no courage, or else had no gall.
So much the more was Calepine offended,
That him to no revenge he forth could call,
But both his challenge and him selfe con-
  temned,
Ne cared as a coward so to be condemned.

XXXVII

But he, nought weighing what he sayd or
  did,
Turned his steede about another way,
And with his lady to the castle rid,
Where was his won; ne did the other stay,
But after went directly as he may,
For his sicke charge some harbour there to
  seeke;
Where he arriving with the fall of day,
Drew to the gate, and there with prayers
  meeke,
And myld entreaty, lodging did for her
  beseeke.

XXXVIII

But the rude porter, that no manners had,
Did shut the gate against him in his face,
And entraunce boldly unto him forbad.
Nathelesse the knight, now in so needy case,
Gan him entreat even with submission base,

And humbly praid to let them in that night:
Who to him aunswer'd, that there was no
  place
Of lodging fit for any errant knight,
Unlesse that with his lord he formerly did
  fight.

XXXIX

'Full loth am I,' quoth he, 'as now at earst,
When day is spent, and rest us needeth most,
And that this lady, both whose sides are
  pearst
With wounds, is ready to forgo the ghost:
Ne would I gladly combate with mine host,
That should to me such curtesie afford,
Unlesse that I were thereunto enforst.
But yet aread to me, how hight thy lord,
That doth thus strongly ward the castle of
  the ford.'

XL

'His name,' quoth he, 'if that thou list to
  learne,
Is hight Sir Turpine, one of mickle might
And manhood rare, but terrible and stearne
In all assaies to every errant knight,
Because of one that wrought him fowle
  despight.'
'Ill seemes,' sayd he, 'if he so valiaunt be,
That he should be so sterne to stranger
  wight:
For seldome yet did living creature see
That curtesie and manhood ever disagree.

XLI

'But go thy waies to him, and fro me say,
That here is at his gate an errant knight,
That house-rome craves, yet would be loth
  t' assay
The proofe of battell, now in doubtfull night,
Or curtesie with rudenesse to requite:
Yet if he needes will fight, crave leave till
  morne,
And tell with all the lamentable plight
In which this lady languisheth forlorne,
That pitty craves, as he of woman was
  yborne.'

XLII

The groome went streight way in, and to
  his lord
Declar'd the message, which that knight
  did move;
Who sitting with his lady then at bord,
Not onely did not his demaund approve,

But both himselfe revil'd, and eke his love;
Albe his lady, that Blandina hight,
Him of ungentle usage did reprove,
And earnestly entreated that they might
Finde favour to be lodged there for that
    same night.

XLIII

Yet would he not perswaded be for ought,
Ne from his currish will a whit reclame.
Which answer when the groome returning
    brought
To Calepine, his heart did inly flame
With wrathfull fury for so foule a shame,
That he could not thereof avenged bee:
But most for pitty of his dearest dame,
Whom now in deadly daunger he did see;
Yet had no meanes to comfort, nor procure
    her glee.

XLIV

But all in vaine; forwhy no remedy
He saw, the present mischiefe to redresse,
But th' utmost end perforce for to aby,
Which that nights fortune would for him
    addresse.
So downe he tooke his lady in distresse,
And layd her underneath a bush to sleepe,
Cover'd with cold, and wrapt in wretched-
    nesse,
Whiles he him selfe all night did nought
    but weepe,
And wary watch about her for her safegard
    keepe.

XLV

The morrow next, so soone as joyous day
Did shew it selfe in sunny beames bedight,
Serena full of dolorous dismay,
Twixt darkenesse dread and hope of living
    light,
Uprear'd her head to see that chearefull
    sight.
Then Calepine, how ever inly wroth,
And greedy to avenge that vile despight,
Yet for the feeble ladies sake, full loth
To make there lenger stay, forth on his
    journey goth.

XLVI

He goth on foote all armed by her side,
Upstaying still her selfe uppon her steede,
Being unhable else alone to ride;
So sore her sides, so much her wounds did
    bleede:

Till that at length, in his extreamest neede,
He chaunst far off an armed knight to spy,
Pursuing him apace with greedy speede,
Whom well he wist to be some enemy,
That meant to make advantage of his
    misery.

XLVII

Wherefore he stayd, till that he nearer
    drew,
To weet what issue would thereof betyde:
Tho, whenas he approched nigh in vew,
By certaine signes he plainely him descryde
To be the man that with such scornefull
    pryde
Had him abusde and shamed yesterday;
Therefore misdoubting, least he should
    misguyde
His former malice to some new assay,
He cast to keepe him selfe so safely as he
    may.

XLVIII

By this the other came in place likewise,
And couching close his speare and all his
    powre,
As bent to some malicious enterprise,
He bad him stand, t' abide the bitter stoure
Of his sore vengeaunce, or to make avoure
Of the lewd words and deedes which he
    had done:
With that ran at him, as he would devoure
His life attonce; who nought could do, but
    shun
The perill of his pride, or else be overrun.

XLIX

Yet he him still pursew'd from place to
    place,
With full intent him cruelly to kill,
And like a wilde goate round about did
    chace,
Flying the fury of his bloudy will.
But his best succour and refuge was still
Behinde his ladies backe, who to him cryde,
And called oft with prayers loud and shrill,
As ever he to lady was affyde,
To spare her knight, and rest with reason
    pacifyde.

L

But he the more thereby enraged was,
And with more eager felnesse him pursew'd,
So that at length, after long weary chace,
Having by chaunce a close advantage vew'd,

He over raught him, having long eschew'd
His violence in vaine, and with his spere
Strooke through his shoulder, that the blood
ensew'd
In great aboundance, as a well it were,
That forth out of an hill fresh gushing did
appere.

LI

Yet ceast he not for all that cruell wound,
But chaste him still, for all his ladies cry,
Not satisfyde till on the fatall ground
He saw his life powrd forth dispiteously:
The which was certes in great jeopardy,
Had not a wondrous chaunce his reskue
wrought,
And saved from his cruell villany:
Such chaunces oft exceed all humaine
thought:
That in another canto shall to end be
brought.

CANTO IV

Calepine by a salvage man
From Turpine reskewed is ;
And whylest an infant from a beare
He saves, his love doth misse.

I

LIKE as a ship with dreadfull storme long
tost,
Having spent all her mastes and her
ground-hold,
Now farre from harbour likely to be lost,
At last some fisher barke doth neare be-
hold,
That giveth comfort to her courage cold:
Such was the state of this most courteous
knight,
Being oppressed by that faytour bold,
That he remayned in most perilous plight,
And his sad ladie left in pitifull affright.

II

Till that by fortune, passing all foresight,
A salvage man, which in those woods did
wonne,
Drawne with that ladies loud and piteous
shright,
Toward the same incessantly did ronne,
To understand what there was to be donne.
There he this most discourteous craven
found,
As fiercely yet as when he first begonne

Chasing the gentle Calepine around,
Ne sparing him the more for all his grievous wound.

III

The salvage man, that never till this houre
Did taste of pittie, neither gentlesse knew,
Seeing his sharpe assault and cruell stoure,
Was much emmoved at his perils vew,
That even his ruder hart began to rew,
And feele compassion of his evill plight,
Against his foe that did him so pursew:
From whom he meant to free him, if he
might,
And him avenge of that so villenous de-
spight.

IV

Yet armes or weapon had he none to fight,
Ne knew the use of warlike instruments,
Save such as sudden rage him lent to smite.
But naked, without needfull vestiments
To clad his corpse with meete habiliments,
He cared not for dint of sword nor speere,
No more then for the stroke of strawes or
bents:
For from his mothers wombe, which him
did beare,
He was invulnerable made by magicke
leare.

V

He stayed not t' advize, which way were
best
His foe t' assayle, or how himselfe to gard,
But with fierce fury and with force infest
Upon him ran; who being well prepard,
His first assault full warily did ward,
And with the push of his sharp-pointed
speare
Full on the breast him strooke, so strong
and hard
That forst him backe recoyle, and reele
areare;
Yet in his bodie made no wound nor bloud
appeare.

VI

With that the wyld man more enraged
grew,
Like to a tygre that hath mist his pray,
And with mad mood againe upon him
flew,
Regarding neither speare, that mote him
slay,

Nor his fierce steed, that mote him much
dismay:
The salvage nation doth all dread despize.
Tho on his shield he griple hold did lay,
And held the same so hard, that by no wize
He could him force to loose, or leave his
enterprize.

VII

Long did he wrest and wring it to and fro,
And every way did try, but all in vaine:
For he would not his greedie grype forgoe,
But hayld and puld with all his might and
maine,
That from his steed him nigh he drew
againe.
Who having now no use of his long speare,
So nigh at hand, nor force his shield to
straine,
Both speare and shield, as things that need-
lesse were,
He quite forsooke, and fled himselfe away
for feare.

VIII

But after him the wyld man ran apace,
And him pursewed with importune speed,
(For he was swift as any bucke in chace)
And had he not in his extreamest need,
Bene helped through the swiftnesse of his
steed,
He had him overtaken in his flight.
Who ever, as he saw him nigh succeed,
Gan cry aloud with horrible affright,
And shrieked out, a thing uncomely for a
knight.

IX

But when the salvage saw his labour vaine,
In following of him that fled so fast,
He wearie woxe, and backe return'd againe
With speede unto the place whereas he last
Had left that couple, nere their utmost
cast.
There he that knight full sorely bleeding
found,
And eke the ladie fearefully aghast,
Both for the perill of the present stound,
And also for the sharpnesse of her rank-
ling wound.

X

For though she were right glad, so rid to bee
From that vile lozell which her late offended.

Yet now no lesse encombrance she did see,
And perill, by this salvage man pretended;
Gainst whom she saw no meanes to be de-
fended,
By reason that her knight was wounded
sore.
Therefore her selfe she wholy recom-
mended
To Gods sole grace, whom she did oft im-
plore
To send her succour, being of all hope for-
lore.

XI

But the wyld man, contrarie to her feare,
Came to her creeping like a fawning hound,
And by rude tokens made to her appeare
His deepe compassion of her dolefull stound,
Kissing his hands, and crouching to the
ground;
For other language had he none, nor speach,
But a soft murmure, and confused sound
Of senselesse words, which Nature did him
teach,
T' expresse his passions, which his reason
did empeach.

XII

And comming likewise to the wounded
knight,
When he beheld the streames of purple
blood
Yet flowing fresh, as moved with the sight,
He made great mone after his salvage
mood,
And running streight into the thickest wood,
A certaine herbe from thence unto him
brought,
Whose vertue he by use well understood:
The juyce whereof into his wound he
wrought,
And stopt the bleeding straight, ere he it
staunched thought.

XIII

Then taking up that recreants shield and
speare,
Which earst he left, he signes unto them
made,
With him to wend unto his wonning neare:
To which he easily did them perswade.
Farre in the forrest, by a hollow glade,
Covered with mossie shrubs, which spred-
ding brode
Did underneath them make a gloomy shade;

Where foot of living creature never trode,
Ne scarse wyld beasts durst come, there
    was this wights abode.

XIV

Thether he brought these unacquainted
    guests;
To whom faire semblance, as he could, he
    shewed
By signes, by lookes, and all his other
    gests.
But the bare ground, with hoarie mosse be-
    strowed,
Must be their bed, their pillow was unsowed,
And the frutes of the forrest was their
    feast:
For their bad stuard neither plough'd nor
    sowed,
Ne fed on flesh, ne ever of wyld beast
Did taste the bloud, obaying Natures first
    beheast.

XV

Yet howsoever base and meane it were,
They tooke it well, and thanked God for
    all,
Which had them freed from that deadly
    feare,
And sav'd from being to that caytive thrall.
Here they of force (as fortune now did fall)
Compelled were themselves a while to rest,
Glad of that easement, though it were but
    small;
That having there their wounds awhile re-
    drest,
They mote the abler be to passe unto the
    rest.

XVI

During which time, that wyld man did apply
His best endevour and his daily paine,
In seeking all the woods both farre and nye
For herbes to dresse their wounds; still
    seeming faine,
When ought he did that did their lyking
    gaine.
So as ere long he had that knightes wound
Recured well, and made him whole againe:
But that same ladies hurt no herbe he found
Which could redresse, for it was inwardly
    unsound.

XVII

Now when as Calepine was woxen strong,
Upon a day he cast abrode to wend,

To take the ayre and heare the thrushes
    song,
Unarm'd, as fearing neither foe nor frend,
And without sword his person to defend.
There him befell, unlooked for before,
An hard adventure with unhappie end,
A cruell beare, the which an infant bore
Betwixt his bloodie jawes, besprinckled all
    with gore.

XVIII

The litle babe did loudly scrike and squall,
And all the woods with piteous plaints did
    fill,
As if his cry did meane for helpe to call
To Calepine, whose eares those shrieches
    shrill,
Percing his hart, with pities point did thrill;
That after him he ran with zealous haste,
To rescue th' infant, ere he did him kill:
Whom though he saw now somewhat over-
    past,
Yet by the cry he follow'd, and pursewed
    fast.

XIX

Well then him chaunst his heavy armes to
    want,
Whose burden mote empeach his needfull
    speed,
And hinder him from libertie to pant:
For having long time, as his daily weed,
Them wont to weare, and wend on foot for
    need,
Now wanting them he felt himselfe so light,
That like an hauke, which feeling her selfe
    freed
From bels and jesses, which did let her flight,
Him seem'd his feet did fly, and in their
    speed delight.

XX

So well he sped him, that the wearie beare
Ere long he overtooke, and forst to stay,
And without weapon him assayling neare,
Compeld him soone the spoyle adowne to
    lay.
Wherewith the beast, enrag'd to loose his
    pray,
Upon him turned, and with greedie force
And furie, to be crossed in his way,
Gaping full wyde, did thinke without re-
    morse
To be aveng'd on him, and to devoure hi
    corse.

XXI

But the bold knight, no whit thereat dis-
mayd,
But catching up in hand a ragged stone,
Which lay thereby (so Fortune him did ayde)
Upon him ran, and thrust it all attone
Into his gaping throte, that made him grone
And gaspe for breath, that he nigh choked
was,
Being unable to digest that bone;
Ne could it upward come, nor downward
passe,
Ne could he brooke the coldnesse of the
stony masse.

XXII

Whom when as he thus combred did behold,
Stryving in vaine that nigh his bowels brast,
He with him closd, and laying mightie hold
Upon his throte, did gripe his gorge so fast,
That, wanting breath, him downe to ground
he cast;
And then oppressing him with urgent paine,
Ere long enforst to breath his utmost blast,
Gnashing his cruell teeth at him in vaine,
And threatning his sharpe clawes, now
wanting powre to straine.

XXIII

Then tooke he up betwixt his armes twaine
The litle babe, sweet relickes of his pray;
Whom pitying to heare so sore complaine,
From his soft eyes the teares he wypt away,
And from his face the filth that did it ray,
And every litle limbe he searcht around,
And every part that under sweathbands lay,
Least that the beasts sharpe teeth had any
wound
Made in his tender flesh; but whole them all
he found.

XXIV

So having all his bands againe uptyde,
He with him thought backe to returne
againe:
But when he lookt about on every syde,
To weet which way were best to entertaine,
To bring him to the place where he would
faine,
He could no path nor tract of foot descry,
Ne by inquirie learne, nor ghesse by ayme;
For nought but woods and forrests farre
and nye,
That all about did close the compasse of his
eye.

XXV

Much was he then encombred, ne could
tell
Which way to take: now west he went a
while,
Then north; then neither, but as fortune
fell.
So up and downe he wandred many a mile,
With wearie travell and uncertaine toile,
Yet nought the nearer to his journeys end;
And evermore his lovely litle spoile
Crying for food did greatly him offend.
So all that day in wandring vainely he did
spend.

XXVI

At last, about the setting of the sunne,
Him selfe out of the forest he did wynd,
And by good fortune the plaine champion
wonne:
Where looking all about, where he mote fynd
Some place of succour to content his mynd,
At length he heard under the forrests syde
A voice, that seemed of some woman kynd
Which to her selfe lamenting loudly cryde,
And oft complayn'd of Fate, and Fortune
oft defyde.

XXVII

To whom approching, when as she per-
ceived
A stranger wight in place, her plaint she
stayd,
As if she doubted to have bene deceived,
Or loth to let her sorrowes be bewrayd.
Whom when as Calepine saw so dismayd,
He to her drew, and with faire blandish-
ment
Her chearing up, thus gently to her sayd:
' What be you, wofull dame, which thus
lament?
And for what cause declare, so mote ye not
repent.'

XXVIII

To whom she thus: ' What need me, sir, to
tell
That which your selfe have earst ared so
right?
A wofull dame ye have me termed well;
So much more wofull, as my wofull plight
Cannot redressed be by living wight.'
' Nathlesse,' quoth he, ' if need doe not you
bynd,
Doe it disclose, to ease your grieved spright:

Oftimes it haps, that sorrowes of the mynd
Find remedie unsought, which seeking can-
      not fynd.'

XXIX

Then thus began the lamentable dame:
' Sith then ye needs will know the griefe I
      hoord,
I am th' unfortunate Matilde by name,
The wife of bold Sir Bruin, who is lord
Of all this land, late conquer'd by his sword
From a great gyant, called Cormoraunt;
Whom he did overthrow by yonder foord,
And in three battailes did so deadly daunt,
That he dare not returne for all his daily
      vaunt.

XXX

' So is my lord now seiz'd of all the land,
As in his fee, with peaceable estate,
And quietly doth hold it in his hand,
Ne any dares with him for it debate.
But to these happie fortunes cruell fate
Hath joyn'd one evill, which doth overthrow
All these our joyes, and all our blisse abate;
And like in time to further ill to grow,
And all this land with endlesse losse to over-
      flow.

XXXI

' For th' heavens, envying our prosperitie,
Have not vouchsaft to graunt unto us twaine
The gladfull blessing of posteritie,
Which we might see after our selves re-
      maine
In th' heritage of our unhappie paine:
So that for want of heires it to defend,
All is in time like to returne againe
To that foule feend, who dayly doth attend
To leape into the same after our lives end.

XXXII

' But most my lord is grieved herewithall,
And makes exceeding mone, when he does
      thinke
That all this land unto his foe shall fall,
For which he long in vaine did sweat and
      swinke,
That now the same he greatly doth for-
      thinke.
Yet was it sayd, there should to him a sonne
Be gotten, not begotten, which should drinke
And dry up all the water which doth ronne
In the next brooke, by whom that feend
      shold be fordonne.

XXXIII

' Well hop't he then, when this was prophe-
      side,
That from his sides some noble chyld should
      rize,
The which through fame should farre be
      magnifide,
And this proud gyant should with brave
      emprize
Quite overthrow, who now ginnes to de-
      spize
The good Sir Bruin, growing farre in yeares;
Who thinkes from me his sorrow all doth
      rize.
Lo! this my cause of griefe to you ap-
      peares;
For which I thus doe mourne, and poure
      forth ceaselesse teares.'

XXXIV

Which when he heard, he inly touched was
With tender ruth for her unworthy griefe,
And when he had devized of her case,
He gan in mind conceive a fit reliefe
For all her paine, if please her make the
      priefe.
And having cheared her, thus said: ' Faire
      dame,
In evils counsell is the comfort chiefe;
Which though I be not wise enough to
      frame,
Yet, as I well it meane, vouchsafe it with-
      out blame.

XXXV

' If that the cause of this your languish-
      ment
Be lacke of children to supply your place,
Lo! how good fortune doth to you present
This litle babe, of sweete and lovely face,
And spotlesse spirit, in which ye may en-
      chace
What ever formes ye list thereto apply,
Being now soft and fit them to embrace;
Whether ye list him traine in chevalry,
Or noursle up in lore of learn'd philosophy.

XXXVI

' And certes it hath oftentimes bene seene,
That of the like, whose linage was un-
      knowne,
More brave and noble knights have raysed
      beene,
As their victorious deedes have often
      showen,

Being with fame through many nations
　　blowen,
Then those which have bene dandled in the
　　lap.
Therefore some thought that those brave
　　imps were sowen
Here by the gods, and fed with heavenly sap,
That made them grow so high t' all honor-
　　able hap.'

XXXVII

The ladie, hearkning to his sensefull speach,
Found nothing that he said unmeet nor
　　geason,
Having oft seene it tryde, as he did teach.
Therefore inclyning to his goodly reason,
Agreeing well both with the place and sea-
　　son,
She gladly did of that same babe accept,
As of her owne by liverey and seisin,
And having over it a litle wept,
She bore it thence, and ever as her owne it
　　kept.

XXXVIII

Right glad was Calepine to be so rid
Of his young charge, whereof he skilled
　　nought:
Ne she lesse glad; for she so wisely did,
And with her husband under hand so
　　wrought,
That when that infant unto him she brought,
She made him thinke it surely was his owne,
And it in goodly thewes so well upbrought,
That it became a famous knight well knowne,
And did right noble deedes, the which els-
　　where are showne.

XXXIX

But Calepine now being left alone
Under the greenewoods side in sorie plight,
Withouten armes or steede to ride upon,
Or house to hide his head from heavens
　　spight,
Albe that dame, by all the meanes she might,
Him oft desired home with her to wend,
And offred him, his courtesie to requite,
Both horse and armes, and what so else to
　　lend,
Yet he them all refusd, though thankt her
　　as a frend;

XL

And for exceeding griefe which inly grew,
That he his love so lucklesse now had lost,

On the cold ground, maugre, himselfe he
　　threw,
For fell despight, to be so sorely crost;
And there all night himselfe in anguish tost,
Vowing that never he in bed againe
His limbes would rest, ne lig in ease em-
　　bost,
Till that his ladies sight he mote attaine,
Or understand that she in safetie did re-
　　maine.

CANTO V

The salvage serves Serena well
Till she Prince Arthure fynd;
Who her together with his squyre
With th' hermit leaves behynd.

I

O WHAT an easie thing is to descry
The gentle bloud, how ever it be wrapt
In sad misfortunes foule deformity,
And wretched sorrowes, which have often
　　hapt!
For howsoever it may grow mis-shapt,
Like this wyld man, being undisciplynd,
That to all vertue it may seeme unapt,
Yet will it shew some sparkes of gentle
　　mynd,
And at the last breake forth in his owne
　　proper kynd.

II

That plainely may in this wyld man be red,
Who, though he were still in this desert
　　wood,
Mongst salvage beasts, both rudely borne
　　and bred,
Ne ever saw faire guize, ne learned good,
Yet shewd some token of his gentle blood
By gentle usage of that wretched dame.
For certes he was borne of noble blood,
How ever by hard hap he hether came;
As ye may know, when time shall be to tell
　　the same.

III

Who, when as now long time he lacked had
The good Sir Calepine, that farre was
　　strayd,
Did wexe exceeding sorrowfull and sad,
As he of some misfortune were afrayd:
And leaving there this ladie all dismayd,
Went forth streightway into the forrest
　　wyde,

To seeke if he perchance a sleepe were layd,
Or what so else were unto him betyde:
He sought him farre and neare, yet him no
    where he spyde.

IV

Tho, backe returning to that sorie dame,
He shewed semblant of exceeding mone,
By speaking signes, as he them best could
    frame;
Now wringing both his wretched hands in
    one,
Now beating his hard head upon a stone,
That ruth it was to see him so lament.
By which she well perceiving what was
    done,
Gan teare her hayre, and all her garments
    rent,
And beat her breast, and piteously her selfe
    torment.

V

Upon the ground her selfe she fiercely
    threw,
Regardlesse of her wounds, yet bleeding
    rife,
That with their bloud did all the flore im-
    brew,
As if her breast new launcht with murd-
    rous knife
Would streight dislodge the wretched
    wearie life.
There she long groveling and deepe gron-
    ing lay,
As if her vitall powers were at strife
With stronger death, and feared their de-
    cay:
Such were this ladies pangs and dolorous
    assay.

VI

Whom when the salvage saw so sore dis-
    trest,
He reared her up from the bloudie ground,
And sought, by all the meanes that he
    could best,
Her to recure out of that stony swound,
And staunch the bleeding of her dreary
    wound.
Yet nould she be recomforted for nought,
Ne cease her sorrow and impatient stound,
But day and night did vexe her carefull
    thought,
And ever more and more her owne afflic-
    tion wrought.

VII

At length, when as no hope of his retourne
She saw now left, she cast to leave the
    place,
And wend abrode, though feeble and for-
    lorne,
To seeke some comfort in that sorie case.
His steede, now strong through rest so long
    a space,
Well as she could, she got, and did bedight,
And being thereon mounted, forth did
    pace,
Withouten guide, her to conduct aright,
Or gard, her to defend from bold oppres-
    sors might.

VIII

Whom when her host saw readie to de-
    part,
He would not suffer her alone to fare,
But gan himselfe address to take her part.
Those warlike armes, which Calepine whyl-
    eare
Had left behind, he gan eftsoones prepare,
And put them all about himselfe unfit,
His shield, his helmet, and his curats bare;
But without sword upon his thigh to sit:
Sir Calepine himselfe away had hidden it.

IX

So forth they traveld, an uneven payre,
That mote to all men seeme an uncouth
    sight;
A salvage man matcht with a ladie fayre,
That rather seem'd the conquest of his
    might,
Gotten by spoyle, then purchaced aright.
But he did her attend most carefully,
And faithfully did serve both day and
    night,
Withouten thought of shame or villeny,
Ne ever shewed signe of foule disloyalty.

X

Upon a day, as on their way they went,
It chaunst some furniture about her steed
To be disordred by some accident:
Which to redresse, she did th' assistance
    need
Of this her groome, which he by signes did
    reede,
And streight his combrous armes aside did
    lay
Upon the ground, withouten doubt or
    dreed,

And in his homely wize began to assay
T' amend what was amisse, and put in right
    aray.

XI

Bout which whilest he was busied thus
    hard,
Lo where a knight together with his squire,
All arm'd to point, came ryding thether-
    ward,
Which seemed by their portance and attire,
To be two errant knights, that did inquire
After adventures, where they mote them
    get.
Those were to weet (if that ye it require)
Prince Arthur and young Timias, which
    met
By straunge occasion, that here needs forth
    be set.

XII

After that Timias had againe recured
The favour of Belphebe, (as ye heard)
And of her grace did stand againe assured,
To happie blisse he was full high uprear'd,
Nether of envy nor of chaunge afeard,
Though many foes did him maligne there-
    fore,
And with unjust detraction him did beard;
Yet he himselfe so well and wisely bore,
That in her soveraine lyking he dwelt ever-
    more.

XIII

But of them all which did his ruine seeke,
Three mightie enemies did him most de-
    spight,
Three mightie ones, and cruell minded eeke,
That him not onely sought by open might
To overthrow, but to supplant by slight.
The first of them by name was cald De-
    spetto,
Exceeding all the rest in powre and hight;
The second, not so strong, but wise, De-
    cetto;
The third, nor strong nor wise, but spight-
    fullest, Defetto.

XIV

Oftimes their sundry powres they did em-
    ploy,
And severall deceipts, but all in vaine:
For neither they by force could him de-
    stroy,
Ne yet entrap in treasons subtill traine.

Therefore conspiring all together plaine,
They did their counsels now in one com-
    pound;
Where singled forces faile, conjoynd may
    gaine.
The Blatant Beast the fittest meanes they
    found,
To worke his utter shame, and throughly
    him confound.

XV

Upon a day, as they the time did waite,
When he did raunge the wood for salvage
    game,
They sent that Blatant Beast to be a baite,
To draw him from his deare beloved dame
Unwares into the daunger of defame.
For well they wist that squire to be so
    bold,
That no one beast in forrest, wylde or tame,
Met him in chase, but he it challenge would,
And plucke the pray oftimes out of their
    greedy hould.

XVI

The hardy boy, as they devised had,
Seeing the ugly monster passing by,
Upon him set, of perill nought adrad,
Ne skilfull of the uncouth jeopardy;
And charged him so fierce and furiously,
That, his great force unable to endure,
He forced was to turne from him and fly:
Yet, ere he fled, he with his tooth impure
Him heedlesse bit, the whiles he was thereof
    secure.

XVII

Securely he did after him pursew,
Thinking by speed to overtake his flight;
Who through thicke woods and brakes and
    briers him drew,
To weary him the more, and waste his
    spight,
So that he now has almost spent his spright:
Till that at length unto a woody glade
He came, whose covert stopt his further
    sight;
There his three foes, shrowded in guilefull
    shade,
Out of their ambush broke, and gan him to
    invade.

XVIII

Sharpely they all attonce did him assaile,
Burning with inward rancour and despight,

And heaped strokes did round about him
    haile
With so huge force, that seemed nothing
    might
Beare off their blowes from percing
    thorough quite.
Yet he them all so warily did ward,
That none of them in his soft flesh did bite,
And all the while his backe for best safe-
    gard
He lent against a tree, that backeward on-
    set bard.

XIX

Like a wylde bull, that, being at a bay,
Is bayted of a mastiffe and a hound
And a curre-dog, that doe him sharpe as-
    say
On every side, and beat about him round;
But most that curre, barking with bitter
    sownd,
And creeping still behinde, doth him in-
    comber,
That in his chauffe he digs the trampled
    ground,
And threats his horns, and bellowes like
    the thonder:
So did that squire his foes disperse and
    drive asonder.

XX

Him well behoved so; for his three foes
Sought to encompasse him on every side,
And dangerously did round about enclose.
But most of all Defetto him annoyde,
Creeping behinde him still to have de-
    stroyde;
So did Decetto eke him circumvent;
But stout Despetto, in his greater pryde,
Did front him face to face against him
    bent:
Yet he them all withstood, and often made
    relent.

XXI

Till that at length, nigh tyrd with former
    chace,
And weary now with carefull keeping ward,
He gan to shrinke, and somewhat to give
    place,
Full like ere long to have escaped hard;
When as unwares he in the forrest heard
A trampling steede, that with his neighing
    fast
Did warne his rider be uppon his gard;

With noise whereof the squire, now nigh
    aghast,
Revived was, and sad dispaire away did
    cast.

XXII

Eftsoones he spide a knight approching nye,
Who, seeing one in so great daunger set
Mongst many foes, him selfe did faster hye,
To reskue him, and his weake part abet,
For pitty so to see him overset.
Whom soone as his three enemies did vew,
They fled, and fast into the wood did get:
Him booted not to thinke them to pursew,
The covert was so thicke, that did no pas-
    sage shew.

XXIII

Then turning to that swaine, him well he
    knew
To be his Timias, his owne true squire:
Whereof exceeding glad, he to him drew,
And him embracing twixt his armes entire,
Him thus bespake: ' My liefe, my lifes
    desire,
Why have ye me alone thus long yleft ?
Tell me, what worlds despight, or heavens
    yre,
Hath you thus long away from me bereft ?
Where have ye all this while bin wandring,
    where bene weft ? '

XXIV

With that he sighed deepe for inward tyne:
To whom the squire nought aunswered
    againe,
But shedding few soft teares from tender
    eyne,
His deare affect with silence did restraine,
And shut up all his plaint in privy paine.
There they awhile some gracious speaches
    spent,
As to them seemed fit time to entertaine.
After all which up to their steedes they
    went,
And forth together rode, a comely couple-
    ment.

XXV

So now they be arrived both in sight
Of this wyld man, whom they full busie
    found
About the sad Serena things to dight,
With those brave armours lying on the
    ground,

That seem'd the spoile of some right well
    renownd.
Which when that squire beheld, he to them
    stept,
Thinking to take them from that hylding
    hound:
But he it seeing, lightly to him lept,
And sternely with strong hand it from his
    handling kept.

XXVI

Gnashing his grinded teeth with griesly
    looke,
And sparkling fire out of his furious eyne,
Him with his fist unwares on th' head he
    strooke,
That made him downe unto the earth en-
    cline;
Whence soone upstarting, much he gan re-
    pine,
And laying hand upon his wrathfull blade,
Thought therewithall forthwith him to have
    slaine;
Who it perceiving, hand upon him layd,
And greedily him griping, his avengement
    stayd.

XXVII

With that aloude the faire Serena cryde
Unto the knight, them to dispart in twaine:
Who to them stepping did them soone
    divide,
And did from further violence restraine,
Albe the wyld-man hardly would refraine.
Then gan the Prince of her for to de-
    mand,
What and from whence she was, and by what
    traine
She fell into that salvage villaines hand,
And whether free with him she now were,
    or in band.

XXVIII

To whom she thus: 'I am, as now ye see,
The wretchedst dame, that live this day on
    ground,
Who both in minde, the which most grieveth
    me,
And body have receiv'd a mortall wound,
That hath me driven to this drery stound.
I was erewhile the love of Calepine,
Who whether he alive be to be found,
Or by some deadly chaunce be done to
    pine,
Since I him lately lost, uneath is to define.

XXIX

'In salvage forrest I him lost of late,
Where I had surely long ere this bene dead,
Or else remained in most wretched state,
Had not this wylde man in that wofull stead
Kept and delivered me from deadly dread.
In such a salvage wight, of brutish kynd,
Amongst wilde beastes in desert forrests
    bred,
It is most straunge and wonderfull to fynd
So milde humanity and perfect gentle mynd.

XXX

'Let me therefore this favour for him finde,
That ye will not your wrath upon him
    wreake,
Sith he cannot expresse his simple minde,
Ne yours conceive, ne but by tokens speake:
Small praise to prove your powre on wight
    so weake.'
With such faire words she did their heate
    asswage,
And the strong course of their displeasure
    breake,
That they to pitty turnd their former rage,
And each sought to supply the office of her
    page.

XXXI

So having all things well about her dight,
She on her way cast forward to proceede,
And they her forth conducted, where they
    might
Finde harbour fit to comfort her great
    neede.
For now her wounds corruption gan to breed;
And eke this squire, who likewise wounded
    was
Of that same monster late, for lacke of
    heed,
Now gan to faint, and further could not pas
Through feeblenesse, which all his limbes
    oppressed has.

XXXII

So forth they rode together all in troupe,
To seeke some place, the which mote yeeld
    some ease
To these sicke twaine, that now began to
    droupe:
And all the way the Prince sought to ap-
    pease
The bitter anguish of their sharpe disease,
By all the courteous meanes he could in-
    vent;

Somewhile with merry purpose fit to please,
And otherwhile with good encouragement,
To make them to endure the pains did them
    torment.

XXXIII

Mongst which, Serena did to him relate
The foule discourt'sies and unknightly
    parts,
Which Turpine had unto her shewed late,
Without compassion of her cruell smarts,
Although Blandina did with all her arts
Him otherwise perswade, all that she
    might;
Yet he of malice, without her desarts,
Not onely her excluded late at night,
But also trayterously did wound her weary
    knight.

XXXIV

Wherewith the Prince sore moved, there
    avoud
That, soone as he returned backe againe,
He would avenge th' abuses of that proud
And shamefull knight, of whom she did
    complaine.
This wize did they each other entertaine,
To passe the tedious travell of the way;
Till towards night they came unto a plaine,
By which a little hermitage there lay,
Far from all neighbourhood, the which
    annoy it may.

XXXV

And nigh thereto a little chappell stoode,
Which being all with yvy overspred,
Deckt all the roofe and shadowing the roode,
Seem'd like a grove faire braunched over
    hed:
Therein the hermite, which his life here led
In streight observaunce of religious vow,
Was wont his howres and holy things to
    bed;
And therein he likewise was praying now,
Whenas these knights arriv'd, they wist not
    where nor how.

XXXVI

They stayd not there, but streight way in
    did pas.
Whom when the hermite present saw in
    place,
From his devotion streight he troubled was;
Which breaking of, he toward them did
    pace,
With stayed steps and grave beseeming
    grace:
For well it seem'd that whilome he had
    beene
Some goodly person, and of gentle race,
That could his good to all, and well did
    weene,
How each to entertaine with curt'sie well
    beseene.

XXXVII

And soothly it was sayd by common fame,
So long as age enabled him thereto,
That he had bene a man of mickle name,
Renowmed much in armes and derring doe:
But being aged now and weary to
Of warres delight and worlds contentious
    toyle,
The name of knighthood he did disavow,
And hanging up his armes and warlike
    spoyle,
From all this worlds incombraunce did
    himselfe assoyle.

XXXVIII

He thence them led into his hermitage,
Letting their steedes to graze upon the
    greene:
Small was his house, and like a little cage,
For his owne turne, yet inly neate and
    clene,
Deckt with greene boughes and flowers gay
    beseene.
Therein he them full faire did entertaine,
Not with such forged showes, as fitter
    beene
For courting fooles, that curtesies would
    faine,
But with entire affection and appearaunce
    plaine.

XXXIX

Yet was their fare but homely, such as hee
Did use his feeble body to sustaine;
The which full gladly they did take in gree,
Such as it was, ne did of want complaine,
But being well suffiz'd, them rested faine.
But faire Serene all night could take no
    rest,
Ne yet that gentle squire, for grievous
    paine
Of their late woundes, the which the Blat-
    ant Beast
Had given them, whose griefe through suf-
    fraunce sore increast.

614 THE FAERIE QUEENE

XL

So all that night they past in great disease,
Till that the morning, bringing earely light
To guide mens labours, brought them also
  ease,
And some asswagement of their painefull
  plight.
Then up they rose, and gan them selves to
  dight
Unto their journey; but that squire and
  dame
So faint and feeble were, that they ne
  might
Endure to travell, nor one foote to frame:
Their hearts were sicke, their sides were
  sore, their feete were lame.

XLI

Therefore the Prince, whom great affaires
  in mynd
Would not permit to make there lenger
  stay,
Was forced there to leave them both behynd,
In that good hermits charge, whom he did
  pray
To tend them well. So forth he went his
  way,
And with him eke the salvage, that whyleare,
Seeing his royall usage and array,
Was greatly growne in love of that brave
  pere,
Would needes depart, as shall declared be
  elsewhere.

CANTO VI

The hermite heales both squire and dame
Of their sore maladies;
He Turpine doth defeate, and shame
For his late villanies.

I

No wound, which warlike hand of enemy
Inflicts with dint of sword, so sore doth light
As doth the poysnous sting, which infamy
Infixeth in the name of noble wight:
For by no art, nor any leaches might,
It ever can recured be againe;
Ne all the skill, which that immortall
  spright
Of Podalyrius did in it retaine,
Can remedy such hurts; such hurts are
  hellish paine.

II

Such were the wounds the which that Blat-
  ant Beast
Made in the bodies of that squire and
  dame;
And being such, were now much more in-
  creast,
For want of taking heede unto the same,
That now corrupt and curelesse they be-
  came.
Howbe that carefull hermite did his best,
With many kindes of medicines meete, to
  tame
The poysnous humour, which did most infest
Their ranckling wounds, and every day them
  duely drest.

III

For he right well in leaches craft was seene,
And through the long experience of his
  dayes,
Which had in many fortunes tossed beene,
And past through many perillous assayes,
He knew the diverse went of mortall wayes,
And in the mindes of men had great insight
Which with sage counsell, when they went
  astray,
He could enforme, and them reduce aright
And al the passions heale, which wound the
  weaker spright.

IV

For whylome he had bene a doughty
  knight,
As any one that lived in his daies,
And proved oft in many perillous fight,
Of which he grace and glory wonne al
  waies,
And in all battels bore away the baies.
But being now attacht with timely age,
And weary of this worlds unquiet waies,
He tooke him selfe unto this hermitage,
In which he liv'd alone, like carelesse bird
  in cage.

V

One day, as he was searching of their
  wounds,
He found that they had festred privily,
And ranckling inward with unruly stounds,
The inner parts now gan to putrify,
That quite they seem'd past helpe of sur-
  gery,
And rather needed to be disciplinde
With holesome reede of sad sobriety,

To rule the stubborne rage of passion
        blinde:
Give salves to every sore, but counsell to
    the minde.

VI

So taking them apart into his cell,
He to that point fit speaches gan to frame,
As he the art of words knew wondrous
    well,
And eke could doe, as well as say, the
    same,
And thus he to them sayd: 'Faire daugh-
    ter-dame,
And you, faire sonne, which here thus long
    now lie
In piteous languor, since ye hither came,
In vaine of me ye hope for remedie,
And I likewise in vaine doe salves to you
    applie.

VII

'For in your selfe your onely helpe doth lie,
To heale your selves, and must proceed
    alone
From your owne will to cure your maladie.
Who can him cure, that will be cur'd of
    none ?
If therefore health ye seeke, observe this
    one.
First learne your outward sences to refraine
From things that stirre up fraile affection;
Your eies, your eares, your tongue, your
    talke restraine
From that they most affect, and in due
    termes containe.

VIII

'For from those outward sences, ill affected,
The seede of all this evill first doth spring,
Which at the first, before it had infected,
Mote easie be supprest with little thing:
But being growen strong, it forth doth
    bring
Sorrow, and anguish, and impatient paine
In th' inner parts, and lastly, scattering
Contagious poyson close through every
    vaine,
It never rests, till it have wrought his finall
    bane.

IX

'For that beastes teeth, which wounded you
    tofore,
Are so exceeding venemous and keene,

Made all of rusty yron, ranckling sore,
That where they bite, it booteth not to
    weene
With salve, or antidote, or other mene,
It ever to amend: ne marvaile ought;
For that same beast was bred of hellish
    strene,
And long in darksome Stygian den up-
    brought,
Begot of foule Echidna, as in bookes is
    taught.

X

'Echidna is a monster direfull dred,
Whom gods doe hate, and heavens abhor to
    see;
So hideous is her shape, so huge her hed,
That even the hellish fiends affrighted bee
At sight thereof, and from her presence
    flee:
Yet did her face and former parts professe
A faire young mayden, full of comely glee;
But all her hinder parts did plaine expresse
A monstrous dragon, full of fearefull ugli-
    nesse.

XI

'To her the gods, for her so dreadfull face,
In fearefull darkenesse, furthest from the
    skie,
And from the earth, appointed have her
    place
Mongst rocks and caves, where she enrold
    doth lie
In hideous horrour and obscurity,
Wasting the strength of her immortall age.
There did Typhaon with her company,
Cruell Typhaon, whose tempestuous rage
Make th' heavens tremble oft, and him with
    vowes asswage.

XII

'Of that commixtion they did then beget
This hellish dog, that hight the Blatant
    Beast;
A wicked monster, that his tongue doth
    whet
Gainst all, both good and bad, both most
    and least,
And poures his poysnous gall forth to infest
The noblest wights with notable defame:
Ne ever knight, that bore so lofty creast,
Ne ever lady of so honest name,
But he them spotted with reproch, or se-
    crete shame.

XIII

'In vaine therefore it were, with medicine
To goe about to salve such kynd of sore,
That rather needes wise read and disci-
    pline,
Then outward salves, that may augment it
    more.'
'Aye me!' sayd then Serena, sighing sore,
'What hope of helpe doth then for us re-
    maine,
If that no salves may us to health restore?'
'But sith we need good counsell,' sayd the
    swaine,
'Aread, good sire, some counsell, that may
    us sustaine.'

XIV

'The best,' sayd he, 'that I can you ad-
    vize,
Is to avoide the occasion of the ill:
For when the cause, whence evill doth arize,
Removed is, th' effect surceaseth still.
Abstaine from pleasure, and restraine your
    will,
Subdue desire, and bridle loose delight,
Use scanted diet, and forbeare your fill,
Shun secresie, and talke in open sight:
So shall you soone repaire your present
    evill plight.'

XV

Thus having sayd, his sickely patients
Did gladly hearken to his grave beheast,
And kept so well his wise commaunde-
    ments,
That in short space their malady was ceast,
And eke the biting of that harmefull beast
Was throughly heal'd.   Tho when they did
    perceave
Their wounds recur'd, and forces reincreast,
Of that good hermite both they tooke their
    leave,
And went both on their way, ne ech would
    other leave;

XVI

But each the other vow'd t' accompany:
The lady, for that she was much in dred,
Now left alone in great extremity;
The squire, for that he courteous was in-
    deed,
Would not her leave alone in her great need.
So both together traveld, till they met
With a faire mayden clad in mourning
    weed,

Upon a mangy jade unmeetely set,
And a lewd foole her leading thorough dry
    and wet.

XVII

But by what meanes that shame to her be-
    fell,
And how thereof her selfe she did acquite,
I must a while forbeare to you to tell;
Till that, as comes by course, I doe recite
What fortune to the Briton Prince did lite,
Pursuing that proud knight, the which
    whileare
Wrought to Sir Calepine so foule despight;
And eke his lady, though she sickely were,
So lewdly had abusde, as ye did lately heare.

XVIII

The Prince, according to the former token,
Which faire Serene to him delivered had,
Pursu'd him streight, in mynd to bene
    ywroken
Of all the vile demeane, and usage bad,
With which he had those two so ill bestad;
Ne wight with him on that adventure went,
But that wylde man, whom though he oft
    forbad,
Yet for no bidding, nor for being shent,
Would he restrayned be from his attende-
    ment.

XIX

Arriving there, as did by chaunce befall,
He found the gate wyde ope, and in he rode
Ne stayd, till that he came into the hall:
Where soft dismounting like a weary lode,
Upon the ground with feeble feete he trode
As he unable were for very neede
To move one foote, but there must make
    abode;
The whiles the salvage man did take his
    steede,
And in some stable neare did set him up to
    feede.

XX

Ere long to him a homely groome there
    came,
That in rude wise him asked, what he was
That durst so boldly, without let or shame
Into his lords forbidden hall to passe.
To whom the Prince, him fayning to embase,
Mylde answer made, he was an errant
    knight,
The which was fall'n into this feeble case

Through many wounds, which lately he in
    fight
Received had, and prayd to pitty his ill
    plight.

XXI

But he, the more outrageous and bold,
Sternely did bid him quickely thence
    avaunt,
Or deare aby, forwhy his lord of old
Did hate all errant knights, which there did
    haunt,
Ne lodging would to any of them graunt;
And therefore lightly bad him packe away,
Not sparing him with bitter words to taunt;
And therewithall rude hand on him did
    lay,
To thrust him out of dore doing his worst
    assay.

XXII

Which when the salvage, comming now in
    place,
Beheld, eftsoones he all enraged grew,
And running streight upon that villaine
    base,
Like a fell lion at him fiercely flew,
And with his teeth and nailes, in present
    vew,
Him rudely rent, and all to peeces tore:
So miserably him all helpelesse slew,
That with the noise, whilest he did loudly
    rore,
The people of the house rose forth in great
    uprore.

XXIII

Who when on ground they saw their fellow
    slaine,
And that same knight and salvage standing
    by,
Upon them two they fell with might and
    maine,
And on them layd so huge and horribly,
As if they would have slaine them presently.
But the bold Prince defended him so well,
And their assault withstood so mightily,
That, maugre all their might, he did repell
And beat them back, whilest many under-
    neath him fell.

XXIV

Yet he them still so sharpely did pursew,
That few of them he left alive, which
    fled,

Those evill tidings to their lord to shew.
Who hearing how his people badly sped,
Came forth in hast: where when as with
    the dead
He saw the ground all strow'd, and that
    same knight
And salvage with their bloud fresh steem-
    ing red,
He woxe nigh mad with wrath and fell de-
    spight,
And with reprochfull words him thus be-
    spake on hight:

XXV

'Art thou he, traytor, that with treason
    vile
Hast slaine my men in this unmanly maner,
And now triumphest in the piteous spoile
Of these poore folk, whose soules with black
    dishonor
And foule defame doe decke thy bloudy
    baner?
The meede whereof shall shortly be thy
    shame,
And wretched end, which still attendeth on
    her.'
With that him selfe to battell he did frame;
So did his forty yeomen, which there with
    him came.

XXVI

With dreadfull force they all did him as-
    saile,
And round about with boystrous strokes
    oppresse,
That on his shield did rattle like to haile
In a great tempest; that, in such distresse,
He wist not to which side him to addresse.
And evermore that craven cowherd knight
Was at his backe with heartlesse heedinesse,
Wayting if he unwares him murther might:
For cowardize doth still in villany delight.

XXVII

Whereof whenas the Prince was well aware,
He to him turnd with furious intent,
And him against his powre gan to prepare;
Like a fierce bull, that being busie bent
To fight with many foes about him ment,
Feeling some curre behinde his heeles to bite,
Turnes him about with fell avengement;
So likewise turnde the Prince upon the
    knight,
And layd at him amaine with all his will
    and might.

XXVIII

Who when he once his dreadfull strokes
    had tasted,
Durst not the furie of his force abyde,
But turn'd abacke, and to retyre him hasted
Through the thick prease, there thinking
    him to hyde.
But when the Prince had once him plainely
    eyde,
He foot by foot him followed alway,
Ne would him suffer once to shrinke asyde,
But joyning close, huge lode at him did lay:
Who flying still did ward, and warding fly
    away.

XXIX

But when his foe he still so eger saw,
Unto his heeles himselfe he did betake,
Hoping unto some refuge to withdraw:
Ne would the Prince him ever foot for-
    sake,
Where so he went, but after him did make.
He fled from roome to roome, from place to
    place,
Whylest every joynt for dread of death did
    quake,
Still looking after him that did him chace;
That made him evermore increase his
    speedie pace.

XXX

At last he up into the chamber came,
Whereas his love was sitting all alone,
Wayting what tydings of her folke became.
There did the Prince him overtake anone,
Crying in vaine to her, him to bemone;
And with his sword him on the head did
    smyte,
That to the ground he fell in senselesse
    swone:
Yet whether thwart or flatly it did lyte,
The tempred steele did not into his brayne-
    pan byte.

XXXI

Which when the ladie saw, with great
    affright
She starting up, began to shrieke aloud,
And with her garment covering him from
    sight,
Seem'd under her protection him to shroud;
And falling lowly at his feet, her bowd
Upon her knee, intreating him for grace,
And often him besought, and prayd, and
    vowd;

That, with the ruth of her so wretched
    case,
He stayd his second strooke, and did his
    hand abase.

XXXII

Her weed she then withdrawing, did him
    discover,
Who now come to himselfe, yet would not
    rize,
But still did lie as dead, and quake, and
    quiver,
That even the Prince his basenesse did de-
    spize,
And eke his dame, him seeing in such
    guize,
Gan him recomfort, and from ground to
    reare.
Who rising up at last in ghastly wize,
Like troubled ghost did dreadfully appeare,
As one that had no life him left through
    former feare.

XXXIII

Whom when the Prince so deadly saw dis-
    mayd,
He for such basenesse shamefully him shent,
And with sharpe words did bitterly up-
    brayd:
' Vile cowheard dogge, now doe I much re-
    pent,
That ever I this life unto thee lent,
Whereof thou, caytive, so unworthie art;
That both thy love, for lacke of hardiment,
And eke thy selfe, for want of manly hart,
And eke all knights hast shamed with this
    knightlesse part.

XXXIV

' Yet further hast thou heaped shame to
    shame,
And crime to crime, by this thy cowheard
    feare.
For first it was to thee reprochfull blame,
To erect this wicked custome, which I
    heare
Gainst errant knights and ladies thou dost
    reare;
Whom, when thou mayst, thou dost of arms
    despoile,
Or of their upper garment which they weare:
Yet doest thou not with manhood, but with
    guile,
Maintaine this evill use, thy foes thereby to
    foile.

XXXV

'And lastly, in approvance of thy wrong
To shew such faintnesse and foule cowardize
Is greatest shame: for oft it falles, that
　　strong
And valiant knights doe rashly enterprize,
Either for fame, or else for exercize,
A wrongfull quarrell to maintaine by fight;
Yet have, through prowesse and their brave
　　emprize,
Gotten great worship in this worldes sight:
For greater force there needs to maintaine
　　wrong then right.

XXXVI

'Yet since thy life unto this ladie fayre
I given have, live in reproch and scorne;
Ne ever armes, ne ever knighthood dare
Hence to professe: for shame is to adorne
With so brave badges one so basely borne;
But onely breath, sith that I did forgive.'
So having from his craven bodie torne
Those goodly armes, he them away did give,
And onely suffred him this wretched life to
　　live.

XXXVII

There whilest he thus was setling things
　　above,
Atwene that ladie myld and recreant knight,
To whom his life he graunted for her love,
He gan bethinke him, in what perilous
　　plight
He had behynd him left that salvage wight,
Amongst so many foes, whom sure he
　　thought
By this quite slaine in so unequall fight:
Therefore descending backe in haste, he
　　sought
If yet he were alive, or to destruction
　　brought.

XXXVIII

There he him found environed about
With slaughtred bodies, which his hand had
　　slaine,
And laying yet a fresh, with courage stout,
Upon the rest that did alive remaine;
Whom he likewise right sorely did con-
　　straine,
Like scattred sheepe, to seeke for safetie,
After he gotten had with busie paine
Some of their weapons which thereby did lie,
With which he layd about, and made them
　　fast to flie.

XXXIX

Whom when the Prince so felly saw to rage,
Approching to him neare, his hand he stayd,
And sought, by making signes, him to as-
　　swage:
Who them perceiving, streight to him
　　obayd,
As to his lord, and downe his weapons layd,
As if he long had to his heasts bene trayned.
Thence he him brought away, and up con-
　　vayd
Into the chamber, where that dame re-
　　mayned
With her unworthy knight, who ill him en-
　　tertayned.

XL

Whom when the salvage saw from daunger
　　free,
Sitting beside his ladie there at ease,
He well remembred that the same was hee
Which lately sought his lord for to dis-
　　please:
Tho all in rage, he on him streight did
　　seaze,
As if he would in peeces him have rent;
And were not that the Prince did him ap-
　　peaze,
He had not left one limbe of him unrent:
But streight he held his hand at his com-
　　maundement.

XLI

Thus having all things well in peace or-
　　dayned,
The Prince himselfe there all that night
　　did rest,
Where him Blandina fayrely entertayned,
With all the courteous glee and goodly
　　feast
The which for him she could imagine best.
For well she knew the wayes to win good
　　will
Of every wight, that were not too infest,
And how to please the minds of good and
　　ill,
Through tempering of her words and lookes
　　by wondrous skill.

XLII

Yet were her words and lookes but false
　　and fayned,
To some hid end to make more easie way,
Or to allure such fondlings, whom she
　　trayned

Into her trap unto their owne decay:
Thereto, when needed, she could weepe and
    pray,
And when her listed, she could fawne and
    flatter;
Now smyling smoothly, like to sommers
    day,
Now glooming sadly, so to cloke her mat-
    ter;
Yet were her words but wynd, and all her
    teares but water.

XLIII

Whether such grace were given her by
    kynd,
As women wont their guilefull wits to
    guyde,
Or learn'd the art to please, I doe not fynd.
This well I wote, that she so well applyde
Her pleasing tongue, that soone she paci-
    fyde
The wrathfull Prince, and wrought her hus-
    bands peace.
Who nathelesse not therewith satisfyde,
His rancorous despight did not releasse,
Ne secretly from thought of fell revenge
    surceasse.

XLIV

For all that night, the whyles the Prince
    did rest
In carelesse couch, not weeting what was
    ment,
He watcht in close awayt with weapons
    prest,
Willing to worke his villenous intent
On him that had so shamefully him shent:
Yet durst he not for very cowardize
Effect the same, whylest all the night was
    spent.
The morrow next the Prince did early rize,
And passed forth, to follow his first enter-
    prize.

CANTO VII

Turpine is baffuld ; his two knights
Doe gaine their treasons meed.
Fayre Mirabellaes punishment
For loves disdaine decreed.

I

LIKE as the gentle hart it selfe bewrayes
In doing gentle deedes with franke delight,
Even so the baser mind it selfe displayes
In cancred malice and revengefull spight.

For to maligne, t' envie, t' use shifting
    slight,
Be arguments of a vile donghill mind,
Which what it dare not doe by open might,
To worke by wicked treason wayes doth
    find,
By such discourteous deeds discovering his
    base kind.

II

That well appeares in this discourteous
    knight,
The coward Turpine, whereof now I treat;
Who notwithstanding that in former fight
He of the Prince his life received late,
Yet in his mind malitious and ingrate
He gan devize to be aveng'd anew
For all that shame, which kindled inward
    hate.
Therefore, so soone as he was out of vew,
Himselfe in hast he arm'd, and did him
    fast pursew.

III

Well did he tract his steps, as he did
    ryde,
Yet would not neare approch in daungers
    eye,
But kept aloofe for dread to be descryde,
Untill fit time and place he mote espy,
Where he mote worke him scath and vil-
    leny.
At last he met two knights to him un-
    knowne,
The which were armed both agreeably,
And both combynd, what ever chaunce
    were blowne,
Betwixt them to divide, and each to make
    his owne.

IV

To whom false Turpine comming courte-
    ously,
To cloke the mischiefe which he inly ment,
Gan to complaine of great discourtesie,
Which a straunge knight, that neare afore
    him went,
Had doen to him, and his deare ladie shent:
Which if they would afford him ayde at
    need
For to avenge, in time convenient,
They should accomplish both a knightly
    deed,
And for their paines obtaine of him a goodly
    meed.

V

The knights beleev'd that all he sayd was
    trew,
And being fresh and full of youthly spright,
Were glad to heare of that adventure new,
In which they mote make triall of their
    might,
Which never yet they had approv'd in fight;
And eke desirous of the offred meed.
Said then the one of them: ' Where is that
    wight,
The which hath doen to thee this wrongfull
    deed,
That we may it avenge, and punish him
    with speed ? '

VI

' He rides,' said Turpine, ' there not farre
    afore,
With a wyld man soft footing by his syde,
That if ye list to haste a litle more,
Ye may him overtake in timely tyde.'
Eftsoones they pricked forth with forward
    pryde,
And ere that litle while they ridden had,
The gentle Prince not farre away they
    spyde,
Ryding a softly pace with portance sad,
Devizing of his love more then of daunger
    drad.

VII

Then one of them aloud unto him cryde,
Bidding him turne againe, false traytour
    knight,
Foule womanwronger, for he him defyde.
With that they both at once with equall
    spight
Did bend their speares, and both with
    equall might
Against him ran; but th' one did misse his
    marke,
And being carried with his force forth-
    right,
Glaunst swiftly by; like to that heavenly
    sparke,
Which, glyding through the ayre, lights all
    the heavens darke.

VIII

But th' other, ayming better, did him smite
Full in the shield, with so impetuous
    powre,
That all his launce in peeces shivered quite,
And scattered all about, fell on the flowre.

But the stout Prince, with much more
    steddy stowre,
Full on his bever did him strike so sore,
That the cold steele, through piercing, did
    devowre
His vitall breath, and to the ground him
    bore,
Where still he bathed lay in his owne
    bloody gore.

IX

As when a cast of faulcons make their
    flight
At an herneshaw, that lyes aloft on wing,
The whyles they strike at him with heed-
    lesse might,
The warie foule his bill doth backward
    wring;
On which the first, whose force her first
    doth bring,
Her selfe quite through the bodie doth en-
    gore,
And falleth downe to ground like sense-
    lesse thing,
But th' other, not so swift as she before,
Fayles of her souse, and passing by doth
    hurt no more.

X

By this the other, which was passed by,
Himselfe recovering, was return'd to fight;
Where when he saw his fellow lifelesse ly,
He much was daunted with so dismall sight;
Yet nought abating of his former spight,
Let drive at him with so malitious mynd,
As if he would have passed through him
    quight:
But the steele-head no stedfast hold could
    fynd,
But glauncing by, deceiv'd him of that he
    desynd.

XI

Not so the Prince: for his well learned
    speare
Tooke surer hould, and from his horses
    backe
Above a launces length him forth did
    beare,
And gainst the cold hard earth so sore him
    strake,
That all his bones in peeces nigh he brake.
Where seeing him so lie, he left his steed,
And to him leaping, vengeance thought to
    take

Of him, for all his former follies meed,
With flaming sword in hand his terror
   more to breed.

XII

The fearefull swayne, beholding death so
   nie,
Cryde out aloud, for mercie, him to save;
In lieu whereof he would to him descrie
Great treason to him meant, his life to
   reave.
The Prince soone hearkned, and his life
   forgave.
Then thus said he: 'There is a straunger
   knight,
The which, for promise of great meed, us
   drave
To this attempt, to wreake his hid despight,
For that himselfe thereto did want suffi-
   cient might.'

XIII

The Prince much mused at such villenie,
And sayd: 'Now sure ye well have earn'd
   your meed,
For th' one is dead, and th' other soone
   shall die,
Unlesse to me thou hether bring with
   speed
The wretch that hyr'd you to this wicked
   deed.'
He glad of life, and willing eke to wreake
The guilt on him which did this mischiefe
   breed,
Swore by his sword, that neither day nor
   weeke
He would surceasse, but him, where so he
   were, would seeke.

XIV

So up he rose, and forth streight way he
   went
Backe to the place where Turpine late he
   lore:
There he him found in great astonishment,
To see him so bedight with bloodie gore
And griesly wounds that him appalled
   sore.
Yet thus at length he said: 'How now, sir
   knight?
What meaneth this which here I see be-
   fore?
How fortuneth this foule uncomely plight,
So different from that which earst ye
   seem'd in sight?'

XV

'Perdie,' said he, 'in evill houre it fell,
That ever I for meed did undertake
So hard a taske as life for hyre to sell;
The which I earst adventur'd for your sake.
Witnesse the wounds, and this wyde bloudie
   lake,
Which ye may see yet all about me steeme.
Therefore now yeeld, as ye did promise
   make,
My due reward, the which right well I
   deeme
I yearned have, that life so dearely did re-
   deeme.'

XVI

'But where then is,' quoth he halfe wroth-
   fully,
'Where is the bootie, which therefore I
   bought,
That cursed caytive, my strong enemy,
That recreant knight, whose hated life I
   sought?
And where is eke your friend, which halfe
   it ought?'
'He lyes,' said he, 'upon the cold bare
   ground,
Slayne of that errant knight, with whom he
   fought;
Whom afterwards my selfe with many a
   wound
Did slay againe, as ye may see there in the
   stound.'

XVII

Thereof false Turpin was full glad and
   faine,
And needs with him streight to the place
   would ryde,
Where he himselfe might see his foeman
   slaine;
For else his feare could not be satisfyde.
So as they rode, he saw the way all dyde
With streames of bloud; which tracting by
   the traile,
Ere long they came whereas in evill tyde
That other swayne, like ashes deadly pale,
Lay in the lap of death, rewing his wretched
   bale.

XVIII

Much did the craven seeme to mone his
   case,
That for his sake his deare life had forgone;

And him bewayling with affection base,
Did counterfeit kind pittie, where was none:
For wheres no courage, theres no ruth nor
    mone.
Thence passing forth, not farre away he
    found
Whereas the Prince himselfe lay all alone,
Loosely displayd upon the grassie ground,
Possessed of sweete sleepe, that luld him
    soft in swound.

XIX

Wearie of travell in his former fight,
He there in shade himselfe had layd to rest
Having his armes and warlike things un-
    dight,
Fearelesse of foes that mote his peace
    molest;
The whyles his salvage page, that wont be
    prest,
Was wandred in the wood another way,
To doe some thing, that seemed to him best,
The whyles his lord in silver slomber lay,
Like to the evening starre adorn'd with
    deawy ray.

XX

Whom when as Turpin saw so loosely layd,
He weened well that he in deed was dead,
Like as that other knight to him had sayd:
But when he nigh approcht, he mote aread
Plaine signes in him of life and livelihead.
Whereat much griev'd against that
    straunger knight,
That him too light of credence did mislead,
He would have backe retyred from that
    sight,
That was to him on earth the deadliest de-
    spight.

XXI

But that same knight would not once let
    him start,
But plainely gan to him declare the case
Of all his mischiefe and late lucklesse
    smart;
How both he and his fellow there in place
Were vanquished, and put to foule dis-
    grace,
And how that he, in lieu of life him lent,
Had vow'd unto the victor, him to trace
And follow through the world, where so he
    went,
Till that he him delivered to his punish-
    ment.

XXII

He, therewith much abashed and affrayd,
Began to tremble every limbe and vaine;
And softly whispering him, entyrely prayd
T' advize him better then by such a traine
Him to betray unto a straunger swaine:
Yet rather counseld him contrarywize,
Sith he likewise did wrong by him sustaine,
To joyne with him and vengeance to de-
    vize,
Whylest time did offer meanes him sleeping
    to surprize.

XXIII

Nathelesse, for all his speach, the gentle
    knight
Would not be tempted to such villenie,
Regarding more his faith which he did
    plight,
All were it to his mortall enemie,
Then to entrap him by false treacherie:
Great shame in lieges blood to be embrew'd.
Thus whylest they were debating diverslie,
The salvage forth out of the wood issew'd
Backe to the place whereas his lord he sleep-
    ing vew'd.

XXIV

There when he saw those two so neare him
    stand,
He doubted much what mote their meaning
    bee,
And throwing downe his load out of his
    hand,
To weet great store of forrest frute, which
    hee
Had for his food late gathered from the
    tree,
Himselfe unto his weapon he betooke,
That was an oaken plant, which lately hee
Rent by the root; which he so sternely
    shooke,
That like an hazell wand it quivered and
    quooke.

XXV

Whereat the Prince awaking, when he spyde
The traytour Turpin with that other knight,
He started up, and snatching neare his
    syde
His trustie sword, the servant of his might,
Like a fell lyon leaped to him light,
And his left hand upon his collar layd.
Therewith the cowheard, deaded with af-
    fright,

Fell flat to ground, ne word unto him sayd,
But holding up his hands, with silence
    mercie prayd.

XXVI

But he so full of indignation was,
That to his prayer nought he would in-
    cline,
But as he lay upon the humbled gras,
His foot he set on his vile necke, in signe
Of servile yoke, that nobler harts repine.
Then, letting him arise like abject thrall,
He gan to him object his haynous crime,
And to revile, and rate, and recreant call,
And lastly to despoyle of knightly banner-
    all.

XXVII

And after all, for greater infamie,
He by the heeles him hung upon a tree,
And baffuld so, that all which passed by
The picture of his punishment might see,
And by the like ensample warned bee,
How ever they through treason doe tres-
    passe.
But turn we now backe to that ladie free,
Whom late we left ryding upon an asse,
Led by a carle and foole, which by her side
    did passe.

XXVIII

She was a ladie of great dignitie,
And lifted up to honorable place,
Famous through all the land of Faerie,
Though of meane parentage and kindred
    base,
Yet deckt with wondrous giftes of Natures
    grace,
That all men did her person much admire,
And praise the feature of her goodly face,
The beames whereof did kindle lovely fire
In th' harts of many a knight, and many a
    gentle squire.

XXIX

But she thereof grew proud and insolent,
That none she worthie thought to be her
    fere,
But scornd them all, that love unto her
    ment:
Yet was she lov'd of many a worthy pere;
Unworthy she to be belov'd so dere,
That could not weigh of worthinesse aright:
For beautie is more glorious bright and
    clere,

The more it is admir'd of many a wight,
And noblest she that served is of noblest
    knight.

XXX

But this coy damzell thought contrariwize,
That such proud looks would make her
    praysed more;
And that the more she did all love despize,
The more would wretched lovers her adore.
What cared she, who sighed for her sore,
Or who did wayle or watch the wearie
    night?
Let them that list their lucklesse lot de-
    plore;
She was borne free, not bound to any wight,
And so would ever live, and love her owne
    delight.

XXXI

Through such her stubborne stifnesse and
    hard hart,
Many a wretch, for want of remedie,
Did languish long in lifeconsuming smart,
And at the last through dreary dolour die:
Whylest she, the ladie of her libertie,
Did boast her beautie had such soveraine
    might,
That with the onely twinckle of her eye,
She could or save or spill whom she would
    hight.
What could the gods doe more, but doe it
    more aright?

XXXII

But loe! the gods, that mortall follies vew,
Did worthily revenge this maydens pride;
And nought regarding her so goodly hew,
Did laugh at her, that many did deride,
Whilest she did weepe, of no man mercifide.
For on a day, when Cupid kept his court,
As he is wont at each Saint Valentide,
Unto the which all lovers doe resort,
That of their loves successe they there may
    make report;

XXXIII

It fortun'd then, that when the roules were
    red,
In which the names of all Loves folke were
    fyled,
That many there were missing, which were
    ded,
Or kept in bands, or from their loves ex-
    yled,

Or by some other violence despoyled.
Which when as Cupid heard, he wexed
    wroth,
And doubting to be wronged, or beguyled,
He bad his eyes to be unblindfold both,
That he might see his men, and muster
    them by oth.

XXXIV

Then found he many missing of his crew,
Which wont doe suit and service to his
    might;
Of whom what was becomen no man knew.
Therefore a jurie was impaneld streight,
T' enquire of them, whether by force, or
    sleight,
Or their owne guilt, they were away con-
    vayd.
To whom foule Infamie and fell Despight
Gave evidence, that they were all betrayd,
And murdred cruelly by a rebellious mayd.

XXXV

Fayre Mirabella was her name, whereby
Of all those crymes she there indited
    was:
All which when Cupid heard, he by and
    by,
In great displeasure, wild a capias
Should issue forth, t' attach that scornefull
    lasse.
The warrant straight was made, and there-
    withall
A baylieffe errant forth in post did passe,
Whom they by name there Portamore did
    call;
He which doth summon lovers to Loves
    judgement hall.

XXXVI

The damzell was attacht, and shortly
    brought
Unto the barre, whereas she was arrayned:
But she thereto nould plead, nor answere
    ought,
Even for stubborne pride, which her re-
    strayned.
So judgement past, as is by law ordayned
In cases like; which when at last she saw,
Her stubborne hart, which love before dis-
    dayned,
Gan stoupe, and falling downe with humble
    awe,
Cryde mercie, to abate the extremitie of
    law.

XXXVII

The sonne of Venus, who is myld by kynd,
But where he is provokt with peevishnesse,
Unto her prayers piteously enclynd,
And did the rigour of his doome represse;
Yet not so freely, but that nathelesse
He unto her a penance did impose,
Which was, that through this worlds wyde
    wildernes
She wander should in companie of those,
Till she had sav'd so many loves as she did
    lose.

XXXVIII

So now she had bene wandring two whole
    yeares
Throughout the world, in this uncomely
    case,
Wasting her goodly hew in heavie teares,
And her good dayes in dolorous disgrace:
Yet had she not in all these two yeares
    space
Saved but two, yet in two yeares before,
Throgh her dispiteous pride, whilest love
    lackt place,
She had destroyed two and twenty more.
Aie me! how could her love make half
    amends therefore?

XXXIX

And now she was uppon the weary way,
When as the gentle squire, with faire Se-
    rene,
Met her in such misseeming foule array;
The whiles that mighty man did her de-
    meane
With all the evill termes and cruell meane,
That he could make; and eeke that angry
    foole
Which follow'd her, with cursed hands un-
    cleane
Whipping her horse, did with his smarting
    toole
Oft whip her dainty selfe, and much aug-
    ment her doole.

XL

Ne ought it mote availe her to entreat
The one or th' other, better her to use:
For both so wilfull were and obstinate,
That all her piteous plaint they did refuse,
And rather did the more her beate and
    bruse.
But most the former villaine, which did
    lead

Her tyreling jade, was bent her to abuse;
Who, though she were with wearinesse nigh
    dead,
Yet would not let her lite, nor rest a little
    stead.

XLI

For he was sterne and terrible by nature,
And eeke of person huge and hideous,
Exceeding much the measure of mans
    stature,
And rather like a gyant monstruous.
For sooth he was descended of the hous
Of those old gyants, which did warres dar-
    raine
Against the heaven in order battailous,
And sib to great Orgolio, which was slaine
By Arthure, when as Unas knight he did
    maintaine.

XLII

His lookes were dreadfull, and his fiery
    eies,
Like two great beacons, glared bright and
    wyde,
Glauncing askew, as if his enemies
He scorned in his overweening pryde;
And stalking stately like a crane, did stryde
At every step uppon the tiptoes hie;
And all the way he went, on every syde
He gaz'd about, and stared horriblie,
As if he with his lookes would all men
    terrifie.

XLIII

He wore no armour, ne for none did care,
As no whit dreading any living wight;
But in a jacket, quilted richly rare
Upon checklaton, he was straungely dight;
And on his head a roll of linnen plight,
Like to the Mores of Malaber, he wore,
With which his locks, as blacke as pitchy
    night,
Were bound about, and voyded from be-
    fore;
And in his hand a mighty yron club he bore.

XLIV

This was Disdaine, who led that ladies
    horse
Through thick and thin, through mountains
    and through plains,
Compelling her, wher she would not, by
    force,
Haling her palfrey by the hempen raines.

But that same foole, which most increast
    her paines,
Was Scorne, who, having in his hand a
    whip,
Her therewith yirks, and still when she
    complaines,
The more he laughes, and does her closely
    quip,
To see her sore lament, and bite her tender
    lip.

XLV

Whose cruell handling when that squire
    beheld,
And saw those villaines her so vildely
    use,
His gentle heart with indignation sweld,
And could no lenger beare so great abuse,
As such a lady so to beate and bruse;
But to him stepping, such a stroke him
    lent,
That forst him th' halter from his hand to
    loose,
And maugre all his might, backe to re-
    lent:
Else had he surely there bene slaine, or
    fowly shent.

XLVI

The villaine, wroth for greeting him so
    sore,
Gathered him selfe together soone againe,
And with his yron batton which he bore
Let drive at him so dreadfully amaine,
That for his safety he did him constraine
To give him ground, and shift to every
    side,
Rather then once his burden to sustaine:
For bootelesse thing him seemed, to abide
So mighty blowes, or prove the puissaunce
    of his pride.

XLVII

Like as a mastiffe, having at a bay
A salvage bull, whose cruell hornes doe
    threat
Desperate daunger, if he them assay,
Traceth his ground, and round about doth
    beat,
To spy where he may some advauntage
    get,
The whiles the beast doth rage and loudly
    rore;
So did the squire, the whiles the carle did
    fret

And fume in his disdainefull mynd the
    more,
And oftentimes by Turmagant and Ma-
    hound swore.

XLVIII

Nathelesse so sharpely still he him pur-
    sewd,
That at advantage him at last he tooke,
When his foote slipt (that slip he dearely
    rewd,)
And with his yron club to ground him
    strooke;
Where still he lay, ne out of swoune
    awooke,
Till heavy hand the carle upon him layd,
And bound him fast: tho, when he up did
    looke,
And saw him selfe captiv'd, he was dis-
    mayd,
Ne powre had to withstand, ne hope of any
    ayd.

XLIX

Then up he made him rise, and forward
    fare,
Led in a rope, which both his hands did
    bynd;
Ne ought that foole for pitty did him spare,
But with his whip him following behynd,
Him often scourg'd, and forst his feete to
    fynd:
And other whiles with bitter mockes and
    mowes
He would him scorne, that to his gentle
    mynd
Was much more grievous then the others
    blowes:
Words sharpely wound, but greatest griefe
    of scorning growes.

L

The faire Serena, when she saw him fall
Under that villaines club, then surely
    thought
That slaine he was, or made a wretched
    thrall,
And fled away with all the speede she
    mought,
To seeke for safety; which long time she
    sought,
And past through many perils by the way,
Ere she againe to Calepine was brought;
The which discourse as now I must delay,
Till Mirabellaes fortunes I doe further say.

CANTO VIII

Prince Arthure overcomes Disdaine;
    Quites Mirabell from dreed;
Serena, found of salvages,
    By Calepine is freed.

I

YE gentle ladies, in whose soveraine powre
Love hath the glory of his kingdome left,
And th' hearts of men, as your eternall
    dowre,
In yron chaines, of liberty bereft,
Delivered hath into your hands by gift;
Be well aware, how ye the same doe use,
That pride doe not to tyranny you lift;
Least, if men you of cruelty accuse,
He from you take that chiefedome, which
    ye doe abuse.

II

And as ye soft and tender are by kynde,
Adornd with goodly gifts of beauties grace,
So be ye soft and tender eeke in mynde;
But cruelty and hardnesse from you chace,
That all your other praises will deface,
And from you turne the love of men to
    hate.
Ensample take of Mirabellaes case,
Who from the high degree of happy state
Fell into wretched woes, which she repented
    late.

III

Who after thraldome of the gentle squire,
Which she beheld with lamentable eye,
Was touched with compassion entire,
And much lamented his calamity,
That for her sake fell into misery:
Which booted nought for prayers, nor for
    threat
To hope for to release or mollify;
For aye the more that she did them entreat,
The more they him misust, and cruelly did
    beat.

IV

So as they forward on their way did pas,
Him still reviling and afflicting sore,
They met Prince Arthure with Sir Enias,
(That was that courteous knight, whom he
    before
Having subdew'd, yet did to life restore,)
To whom as they approcht, they gan aug-
    ment
Their cruelty, and him to punish more,

Scourging and haling him more vehement;
As if it them should grieve to see his pun-
    ishment.

V

The squire him selfe, when as he saw his
    lord,
The witnesse of his wretchednesse, in place,
Was much asham'd, that with an hempen
    cord
He like a dog was led in captive case,
And did his head for bashfulnesse abase,
As loth to see, or to be seene at all:
Shame would be hid. But whenas Enias
Beheld two such, of two such villaines thrall,
His manly mynde was much emmoved there-
    withall;

VI

And to the Prince thus sayd: ' See you, sir
    knight,
The greatest shame that ever eye yet saw,
Yond lady and her squire with foule de-
    spight
Abusde, against all reason and all law,
Without regard of pitty or of awe ?
See how they doe that squire beat and re-
    vile !
See how they doe the lady hale and draw !
But if ye please to lend me leave a while,
I will them soone acquite, and both of blame
    assoile.'

VII

The Prince assented, and then he streight
    way
Dismounting light, his shield about him
    threw,
With which approching, thus he gan to
    say:
' Abide, ye caytive treachetours untrew,
That have with treason thralled unto you
These two, unworthy of your wretched
    bands;
And now your crime with cruelty pursew.
Abide, and from them lay your loathly
    hands;
Or else abide the death that hard before you
    stands.'

VIII

The villaine stayd not aunswer to invent,
But with his yron club preparing way,
His mindes sad message backe unto him
    sent;

The which descended with such dreadfull
    sway,
That seemed nought the course thereof
    could stay,
No more then lightening from the lofty sky:
Ne list the knight the powre thereof assay,
Whose doome was death, but lightly slip-
    ping by,
Unwares defrauded his intended destiny.

IX

And to requite him with the like againe,
With his sharpe sword he fiercely at him
    flew,
And strooke so strongly, that the carle with
    paine
Saved him selfe, but that he there him slew:
Yet sav'd not so, but that the bloud it drew,
And gave his foe good hope of victory.
Who therewith flesht, upon him set anew,
And with the second stroke thought cer-
    tainely
To have supplyde the first, and paide the
    usury.

X

But Fortune aunswerd not unto his call;
For as his hand was heaved up on hight,
The villaine met him in the middle fall,
And with his club bet backe his brondyron
    bright
So forcibly, that with his owne hands might
Rebeaten backe upon him selfe againe,
He driven was to ground in selfe despight;
From whence ere he recovery could gaine,
He in his necke had set his foote with fell
    disdaine.

XI

With that the foole, which did that end
    awayte,
Came running in, and whilest on ground he
    lay,
Laide heavy hands on him, and held so
    strayte,
That downe he kept him with his scorne-
    full sway,
So as he could not weld him any way.
The whiles that other villaine went about
Him to have bound, and thrald without de-
    lay;
The whiles the foole did him revile and
    flout,
Threatning to yoke them two and tame
    their corage stout.

XII

As when a sturdy ploughman with his
    hynde
By strength have overthrowne a stubborne
    steare,
They downe him hold, and fast with cords do
    bynde,
Till they him force the buxome yoke to
    beare:
So did these two this knight oft tug and
    teare.
Which when the Prince beheld, there stand-
    ing by,
He left his lofty steede to aide him neare,
And buckling soone him selfe, gan fiercely
    fly
Uppon that carle, to save his friend from
    jeopardy.

XIII

The villaine, leaving him unto his mate,
To be captiv'd and handled as he list,
Himselfe addrest unto this new debate,
And with his club him all about so blist,
That he which way to turne him scarcely
    wist:
Sometimes aloft he layd, sometimes alow,
Now here, now there, and oft him neare he
    mist;
So doubtfully, that hardly one could know
Whether more wary were to give or ward
    the blow.

XIV

But yet the Prince so well enured was
With such huge strokes, approved oft in
    fight,
That way to them he gave forth right to
    pas;
Ne would endure the daunger of their
    might,
But wayt advantage, when they downe did
    light.
At last the caytive after long discourse,
When all his strokes he saw avoyded quite,
Resolved in one t' assemble all his force,
And make one end of him without ruth or
    remorse.

XV

His dreadfull hand he heaved up aloft,
And with his dreadfull instrument of yre
Thought sure have pownded him to powder
    soft,
Or deepe emboweld in the earth entyre:

But Fortune did not with his will conspire;
For ere his stroke attayned his intent,
The noble childe, preventing his desire,
Under his club with wary boldnesse went,
And smote him on the knee, that never yet
    was bent.

XVI

It never yet was bent, ne bent it now,
Albe the stroke so strong and puissant
    were,
That seem'd a marble pillour it could bow;
But all that leg, which did his body beare,
It crackt throughout (yet did no bloud ap-
    peare)
So as it was unable to support
So huge a burden on such broken geare,
But fell to ground, like to a lumpe of
    durt,
Whence he assayd to rise, but could not for
    his hurt.

XVII

Eftsoones the Prince to him full nimbly
    stept,
And least he should recover foote againe,
His head meant from his shoulders to have
    swept.
Which when the lady saw, she cryde amaine:
' Stay, stay, sir knight, for love of God ab-
    staine
From that unwares ye weetlesse doe intend;
Slay not that carle, though worthy to be
    slaine:
For more on him doth then him selfe de-
    pend;
My life will by his death have lamentable
    end.'

XVIII

He staide his hand according her desire,
Yet nathemore him suffred to arize;
But still suppressing, gan of her inquire,
What meaning mote those uncouth words
    comprize,
That in that villaines health her safety
    lies:
That, were no might in man, nor heart in
    knights,
Which durst her dreaded reskue enter-
    prize,
Yet heavens them selves, that favour feeble
    rights,
Would for it selfe redresse, and punish such
    despights.

XIX

Then bursting forth in teares, which gushed
        fast
Like many water streames, a while she
        stayd;
Till the sharpe passion being overpast,
Her tongue to her restord, then thus she
        sayd:
'Nor heavens, nor men can me, most
        wretched mayd,
Deliver from the doome of my desart,
The which the God of Love hath on me
        layd,
And damned to endure this direfull smart,
For penaunce of my proud and hard re-
        bellious hart.

XX

'In prime of youthly yeares, when first the
        flowre
Of beauty gan to bud, and bloosme delight,
And Nature me endu'd with plenteous
        dowre
Of all her gifts, that pleasde each living
        sight,
I was belov'd of many a gentle knight,
And sude and sought with all the service
        dew:
Full many a one for me deepe groand and
        sight,
And to the dore of death for sorrow drew,
Complayning out on me, that would not on
        them rew.

XXI

'But let them love that list, or live or die;
Me list not die for any lovers doole:
Ne list me leave my loved libertie,
To pitty him that list to play the foole:
To love my selfe I learned had in schoole.
Thus I triumphed long in lovers paine,
And sitting carelesse on the scorners stoole,
Did laugh at those that did lament and
        plaine:
But all is now repayd with interest againe.

XXII

'For loe! the winged god, that woundeth
        harts,
Causde me be called to accompt therefore,
And for revengement of those wrongfull
        smarts,
Which I to others did inflict afore,
Addeem'd me to endure this penaunce sore;
That in this wize, and this unmeete array,

With these two lewd companions, and no
        more,
Disdaine and Scorne, I through the world
        should stray,
Till I have sav'd so many, as I earst did
        slay.'

XXIII

'Certes,' sayd then the Prince, 'the god is
        just,
That taketh vengeaunce of his peoples
        spoile.
For were no law in love, but all that lust
Might them oppresse, and painefully tur-
        moile,
His kingdome would continue but a while.
But tell me, lady, wherefore doe you beare
This bottle thus before you with such toile,
And eeke this wallet at your backe arreare,
That for these carles to carry much more
        comely were?'

XXIV

'Here in this bottle,' sayd the sory mayd,
'I put the teares of my contrition,
Till to the brim I have it full defrayd:
And in this bag, which I behinde me don,
I put repentaunce for things past and gon.
Yet is the bottle leake, and bag so torne
That all which I put in fals out anon,
And is behinde me trodden downe of
        Scorne,
Who mocketh all my paine, and laughs the
        more I mourn.'

XXV

The infant hearkned wisely to her tale,
And wondred much at Cupids judg'ment
        wise,
That could so meekly make proud hearts
        avale,
And wreake him selfe on them that him
        despise.
Then suffred he Disdaine up to arise,
Who was not able up him selfe to reare,
By meanes his leg, through his late lucke-
        lesse prise,
Was crackt in twaine, but by his foolish
        feare
Was holpen up, who him supported stand-
        ing neare.

XXVI

But being up, he lookt againe aloft,
As if he never had received fall;

And with sterne eye-browes stared at him
 oft,
As if he would have daunted him with all:
And standing on his tiptoes, to seeme tall,
Downe on his golden feete he often gazed,
As if such pride the other could apall;
Who was so far from being ought amazed,
That he his lookes despised, and his boast
 dispraized.

XXVII

Then turning backe unto that captive
 thrall,
Who all this while stood there beside them
 bound,
Unwilling to be knowne, or seene at all,
He from those bands weend him to have
 unwound.
But when, approching neare, he plainely
 found
It was his owne true groome, the gentle
 squire,
He thereat wext exceedingly astound,
And him did oft embrace, and oft admire,
Ne could with seeing satisfie his great de-
 sire.

XXVIII

Meane while the salvage man, when he be-
 held
That huge great foole oppressing th' other
 knight,
Whom with his weight unweldy downe he
 held,
He flew upon him, like a greedy kight
Unto some carrion offered to his sight,
And downe him plucking, with his nayles
 and teeth
Gan him to hale, and teare, and scratch,
 and bite;
And from him taking his owne whip, there-
 with
So sore him scourgeth, that the bloud downe
 followeth.

XXIX

And sure I weene, had not the ladies cry
Procur'd the Prince his cruell hand to
 stay,
He would with whipping him have done to
 dye:
But being checkt, he did abstaine streight
 way,
And let him rise. Then thus the Prince
 gan say:

'Now, lady, sith your fortunes thus dis-
 pose,
That, if ye list have liberty, ye may,
Unto your selfe I freely leave to chose,
Whether I shall you leave, or from these
 villaines lose.'

XXX

'Ah! nay, sir knight,' sayd she, 'it may
 not be,
But that I needes must by all meanes ful-
 fill
This penaunce, which enjoyned is to me,
Least unto me betide a greater ill;
Yet no lesse thankes to you for your good
 will.'
So humbly taking leave, she turnd aside:
But Arthure with the rest went onward
 still
On his first quest, in which did him be-
 tide
A great adventure, which did him from
 them devide.

XXXI

But first it falleth me by course to tell
Of faire Serena, who, as earst you heard,
When first the gentle squire at variaunce
 fell
With those two carles, fled fast away,
 afeard
Of villany to be to her inferd:
So fresh the image of her former dread,
Yet dwelling in her eye, to her appeard,
That every foote did tremble, which did
 tread,
And every body two, and two she foure did
 read.

XXXII

Through hils and dales, through bushes and
 through breres
Long thus she fled, till that at last she
 thought
Her selfe now past the perill of her feares.
Then looking round about, and seeing
 nought
Which doubt of daunger to her offer
 mought,
She from her palfrey lighted on the plaine,
And sitting downe, her selfe a while be-
 thought
Of her long travell and turmoyling paine:
And often did of love, and oft of lucke
 complaine

XXXIII

And evermore she blamed Calepine,
The good Sir Calepine, her owne true
      knight,
As th' onely author of her wofull tine:
For being of his love to her so light,
As her to leave in such a piteous plight.
Yet never turtle truer to his make,
Then he was tride unto his lady bright:
Who all this while endured for her sake
Great perill of his life, and restlesse paines
      did take.

XXXIV

Tho when as all her plaints she had dis-
      playd,
And well disburdened her engrieved brest,
Upon the grasse her selfe adowne she layd;
Where, being tyrde with travell, and op-
      prest
With sorrow, she betooke her selfe to rest.
There whilest in Morpheus bosome safe
      she lay,
Fearelesse of ought that mote her peace
      molest,
False Fortune did her safety betray
Unto a straunge mischaunce, that menac'd
      her decay.

XXXV

In these wylde deserts, where she now
      abode,
There dwelt a salvage nation, which did
      live
Of stealth and spoile, and making nightly
      rode
Into their neighbours borders; ne did give
Them selves to any trade, as for to drive
The painefull plough, or cattell for to
      breed,
Or by adventrous marchandize to thrive;
But on the labours of poore men to feed,
And serve their owne necessities with others
      need.

XXXVI

Thereto they usde one most accursed or-
      der,
To eate the flesh of men, whom they mote
      fynde,
And straungers to devoure, which on their
      border
Were brought by errour, or by wreckfull
      wynde:
A monstrous cruelty gainst course of kynde.

They towards evening wandring every way,
To seeke for booty, came by fortune blynde
Whereas this lady, like a sheepe astray,
Now drowned in the depth of sleepe all
      fearelesse lay.

XXXVII

Soone as they spide her, lord! what glad-
      full glee
They made amongst them selves! but
      when her face
Like the faire yvory shining they did see,
Each gan his fellow solace and embrace,
For joy of such good hap by heavenly
      grace.
Then gan they to devize what course to
      take:
Whether to slay her there upon the place,
Or suffer her out of her sleepe to wake,
And then her eate attonce, or many meales
      to make.

XXXVIII

The best advizement was, of bad, to let her
Sleepe out her fill, without encomberment:
For sleepe, they sayd, would make her bat-
      till better.
Then, when she wakt, they all gave one
      consent,
That since by grace of God she there was
      sent,
Unto their god they would her sacrifize,
Whose share, her guiltlesse bloud, they
      would present;
But of her dainty flesh they did devize
To make a common feast, and feed with
      gurmandize.

XXXIX

So round about her they them selves did
      place
Upon the grasse, and diversely dispose,
As each thought best to spend the lingring
      space.
Some with their eyes the daintest morsels
      chose;
Some praise her paps, some praise her lips
      and nose;
Some whet their knives, and strip their
      elboes bare:
The priest him selfe a garland doth com-
      pose
Of finest flowres, and with full busie care
His bloudy vessels wash, and holy fire pre-
      pare.

XL

The damzell wakes; then all attonce up-
start,
And round about her flocke, like many flies,
Whooping and hallowing on every part,
As if they would have rent the brasen skies.
Which when she sees with ghastly griefful
eies,
Her heart does quake, and deadly pallid
hew
Benumbes her cheekes: then out aloud she
cries,
Where none is nigh to heare, that will her
rew,
And rends her golden locks, and snowy
brests embrew.

XLI

But all bootes not: they hands upon her
lay;
And first they spoile her of her jewels
deare,
And afterwards of all her rich array;
The which amongst them they in peeces
teare,
And of the pray each one a part doth beare.
Now being naked, to their sordid eyes
The goodly threasures of Nature appeare:
Which as they view with lustfull fantasyes,
Each wisheth to him selfe, and to the rest
envyes.

XLII

Her yvorie necke, her alablaster brest,
Her paps, which like white silken pillowes
were,
For Love in soft delight thereon to rest;
Her tender sides, her bellie white and clere,
Which like an altar did it selfe uprere,
To offer sacrifice divine thereon;
Her goodly thighes, whose glorie did ap-
peare
Like a triumphall arch, and thereupon
The spoiles of princes hang'd, which were
in battel won.

XLIII

Those daintie parts, the dearlings of delight,
Which mote not be prophan'd of common
eyes,
Those villeins vew'd with loose lascivious
sight,
And closely tempted with their craftie
spyes;

And some of them gan mongst themselves
devize,
Thereof by force to take their beastly
pleasure:
But them the priest rebuking, did advize
To dare not to pollute so sacred threasure,
Vow'd to the gods: religion held even
theeves in measure.

XLIV

So being stayd, they her from thence di-
rected
Unto a litle grove not farre asyde,
In which an altar shortly they erected,
To slay her on. And now the eventyde
His brode black wings had through the
heavens wyde
By this dispred, that was the tyme or-
dayned
For such a dismall deed, their guilt to
hyde:
Of few greene turfes an altar soone they
fayned,
And deckt it all with flowres, which they
nigh hand obtayned.

XLV

Tho, when as all things readie were aright,
The damzell was before the altar set,
Being alreadie dead with fearefull fright.
To whom the priest with naked armes full
net
Approching nigh, and murdrous knife well
whet,
Gan mutter close a certaine secret charme,
With other divelish ceremonies met:
Which doen, he gan aloft t' advance his
arme,
Whereat they shouted all, and made a loud
alarme.

XLVI

Then gan the bagpypes and the hornes to
shrill,
And shrieke aloud, that, with the peoples
voyce
Confused, did the ayre with terror fill,
And made the wood to tremble at the
noyce:
The whyles she wayld, the more they did
rejoyce.
Now mote ye understand that to this grove
Sir Calepine, by chaunce more then by
choyce,

The selfe same evening fortune hether
    drove,
As he to seeke Serena through the woods
    did rove.

XLVII

Long had he sought her, and through many
    a soyle
Had traveld still on foot in heavie armes,
Ne ought was tyred with his endlesse toyle,
Ne ought was feared of his certaine
    harmes:
And now, all weetlesse of the wretched
    stormes,
In which his love was lost, he slept full fast,
Till, being waked with these loud alarmes,
He lightly started up like one aghast,
And catching up his arms, streight to the
    noise forth past.

XLVIII

There by th' uncertaine glims of starry
    night,
And by the twinkling of their sacred fire,
He mote perceive a litle dawning sight
Of all which there was doing in that quire:
Mongst whom a woman spoyld of all attire
He spyde, lamenting her unluckie strife,
And groning sore from grieved hart en-
    tire;
Eftsoones he saw one with a naked knife
Readie to launch her brest, and let out
    loved life.

XLIX

With that he thrusts into the thickest
    throng,
And even as his right hand adowne de-
    scends,
He him preventing, layes on earth along,
And sacrifizeth to th' infernall feends.
Then to the rest his wrathfull hand he
    bends,
Of whom he makes such havocke and such
    hew,
That swarmes of damned soules to hell he
    sends:
The rest, that scape his sword and death
    eschew,
Fly like a flocke of doves before a faulcons
    vew.

L

From them returning to that ladie backe,
Whom by the altar he doth sitting find,

Yet fearing death, and next to death the
    lacke
Of clothes to cover what they ought by
    kind,
He first her hands beginneth to unbind,
And then to question of her present woe,
And afterwards to cheare with speaches
    kind.
But she, for nought that he could say or
    doe,
One word durst speake, or answere him a
    whit thereto.

LI

So inward shame of her uncomely case
She did conceive, through care of woman-
    hood,
That though the night did cover her dis-
    grace,
Yet she in so unwomanly a mood
Would not bewray the state in which she
    stood.
So all that night to him unknowen she
    past.
But day, that doth discover bad and good,
Ensewing, made her knowen to him at
    last:
The end whereof Ile keepe untill another
    cast.

CANTO IX

Calidore hostes with Meliboe
And loves fayre Pastorell;
Coridon envies him, yet he
For ill rewards him well.

I

Now turne againe my teme, thou jolly
    swayne,
Backe to the furrow which I lately left;
I lately left a furrow, one or twayne,
Unplough'd, the which my coulter hath
    not cleft:
Yet seem'd the soyle both fayre and frute-
    full eft,
As I it past, that were too great a shame,
That so rich frute should be from us be-
    reft;
Besides the great dishonour and defame,
Which should befall to Calidores immor-
    tall name.

II

Great travell hath the gentle Calidore
And toyle endured, sith I left him last

Sewing the Blatant Beast, which I forbore
To finish then, for other present hast.
Full many pathes and perils he hath past,
Through hils, through dales, throgh for-
    ests, and throgh plaines,
In that same quest which fortune on him
    cast,
Which he atchieved to his owne great
    gaines,
Reaping eternall glorie of his restlesse
    paines.

III

So sharply he the monster did pursew,
That day nor night he suffred him to rest,
Ne rested he himselfe but natures dew,
For dread of daunger, not to be redrest,
If he for slouth forslackt so famous quest.
Him first from court he to the citties
    coursed,
And from the citties to the townes him
    prest,
And from the townes into the countrie
    forsed,
And from the country back to private
    farmes he scorsed.

IV

From thence into the open fields he fled,
Whereas the heardes were keeping of their
    neat,
And shepheards singing to their flockes,
    that fed,
Layes of sweete love and youthes delight-
    full heat:
Him thether eke for all his fearefull threat
He followed fast, and chaced him so nie,
That to the folds, where sheepe at night
    doe seat,
And to the litle cots, where shepherds lie
In winters wrathfull time, he forced him
    to flie.

V

There on a day, as he pursew'd the chace,
He chaunst to spy a sort of shepheard
    groomes,
Playing on pypes, and caroling apace,
The whyles their beasts there in the
    budded broomes
Beside them fed, and nipt the tender
    bloomes:
For other worldly wealth they cared
    nought.
To whom Sir Calidore yet sweating comes,

And them to tell him courteously be-
    sought,
If such a beast they saw, which he had
    thether brought.

VI

They answer'd him that no such beast they
    saw,
Nor any wicked feend that mote offend
Their happie flockes, nor daunger to them
    draw:
But if that such there were (as none they
    kend)
They prayd High God them farre from
    them to send.
Then one of them him seeing so to sweat,
After his rusticke wise, that well he weend,
Offred him drinke, to quench his thirstie
    heat,
And if he hungry were, him offred eke to
    eat.

VII

The knight was nothing nice, where was
    no need,
And tooke their gentle offer: so adowne
They prayd him sit, and gave him for to
    feed
Such homely what as serves the simple
    clowne,
That doth despise the dainties of the towne.
Tho, having fed his fill, he there besyde
Saw a faire damzell, which did weare a
    crowne
Of sundry flowres, with silken ribbands
    tyde,
Yclad in home-made greene that her owne
    hands had dyde.

VIII

Upon a litle hillocke she was placed
Higher then all the rest, and round about
Environ'd with a girland, goodly graced,
Of lovely lasses, and them all without
The lustie shepheard swaynes sate in a rout,
The which did pype and sing her prayses
    dew,
And oft rejoyce, and oft for wonder shout,
As if some miracle of heavenly hew
Were downe to them descended in that
    earthly vew.

IX

And soothly sure she was full fayre of face,
And perfectly well shapt in every lim,

Which she did more augment with modest
grace
And comely carriage of her count'nance
trim,
That all the rest like lesser lamps did dim:
Who, her admiring as some heavenly wight,
Did for their soveraine goddesse her es-
teeme,
And caroling her name both day and night,
The fayrest Pastorella her by name did
hight.

X

Ne was there heard, ne was there shep-
heards swayne,
But her did honour, and eke many a one
Burnt in her love, and with sweet pleasing
payne
Full many a night for her did sigh and
grone:
But most of all the shepheard Coridon
For her did languish, and his deare life
spend;
Yet neither she for him nor other none
Did care a whit, ne any liking lend:
Though meane her lot, yet higher did her
mind ascend.

XI

Her whyles Sir Calidore there vewed well,
And markt her rare demeanure, which him
seemed
So farre the meane of shepheards to ex-
cell,
As that he in his mind her worthy deemed
To be a princes paragone esteemed,
He was unwares surprisd in subtile bands
Of the Blynd Boy, ne thence could be re-
deemed
By any skill out of his cruell hands,
Caught like the bird which gazing still on
others stands.

XII

So stood he still long gazing thereupon,
Ne any will had thence to move away,
Although his quest were farre afore him
gon;
But after he had fed, yet did he stay,
And sate there still, untill the flying day
Was farre forth spent, discoursing diversly
Of sundry things, as fell, to worke delay;
And evermore his speach he did apply
To th' heards, but meant them to the
damzels fantazy.

XIII

By this the moystie night approching fast,
Her deawy humour gan on th' earth to
shed,
That warn'd the shepheards to their homes
to hast
Their tender flocks, now being fully fed,
For feare of wetting them before their
bed;
Then came to them a good old aged syre,
Whose silver lockes bedeckt his beard and
hed,
With shepheards hooke in hand, and fit
attyre,
That wild the damzell rise; the day did
now expyre.

XIV

He was, to weet, by common voice es-
teemed
The father of the fayrest Pastorell,
And of her selfe in very deede so deemed;
Yet was not so, but, as old stories tell,
Found her by fortune, which to him befell,
In th' open fields an infant left alone,
And taking up brought home, and noursed
well
As his owne chyld; for other he had none;
That she in tract of time accompted was
his owne.

XV

She at his bidding meekely did arise,
And streight unto her litle flocke did fare:
Then all the rest about her rose likewise,
And each his sundrie sheepe with severall
care
Gathered together, and them homeward
bare:
Whylest everie one with helping hands did
strive
Amongst themselves, and did their labours
share,
To helpe faire Pastorella home to drive
Her fleecie flocke; but Coridon most helpe
did give.

XVI

But Meliboee (so hight that good old man)
Now seeing Calidore left all alone,
And night arrived hard at hand, began
Him to invite unto his simple home;
Which though it were a cottage clad with
lome,
And all things therein meane, yet better so

To lodge then in the salvage fields to rome.
The knight full gladly soone agreed thereto,
Being his harts owne wish, and home with
    him did go.

XVII

There he was welcom'd of that honest
    syre,
And of his aged beldame homely well;
Who him besought himselfe to disattyre,
And rest himselfe, till supper time befell;
By which home came the fayrest Pastorell,
After her flocke she in their fold had tyde;
And, supper readie dight, they to it fell
With small adoe, and nature satisfyde,
The which doth litle crave, contented to
    abyde.

XVIII

Tho when they had their hunger slaked
    well,
And the fayre mayd the table ta'ne away,
The gentle knight, as he that did excell
In courtesie, and well could doe and say,
For so great kindnesse as he found that
    day
Gan greatly thanke his host and his good
    wife;
And drawing thence his speach another
    way,
Gan highly to commend the happie life
Which shepheards lead, without debate or
    bitter strife.

XIX

'How much,' sayd he, 'more happie is the
    state,
In which ye, father, here doe dwell at ease,
Leading a life so free and fortunate
From all the tempests of these worldly
    seas,
Which tosse the rest in daungerous dis-
    ease;
Where warres, and wreckes, and wicked
    enmitie
Doe them afflict, which no man can ap-
    pease !
That certes I your happinesse envie,
And wish my lot were plast in such feli-
    citie.'

XX

'Surely, my sonne,' then answer'd he
    againe,
'If happie, then it is in this intent,

That, having small, yet doe I not com-
    plaine
Of want, ne wish for more it to augment,
But doe my selfe, with that I have, con-
    tent;
So taught of nature, which doth litle need
Of forreine helpes to lifes due nourish-
    ment:
The fields my food, my flocke my rayment
    breed;
No better doe I weare, no better doe I feed.

XXI

'Therefore I doe not any one envy,
Nor am envyde of any one therefore;
They that have much, feare much to loose
    thereby,
And store of cares doth follow riches store.
The litle that I have growes dayly more
Without my care, but onely to attend it;
My lambes doe every yeare increase their
    score,
And my flockes father daily doth amend it.
What have I, but to praise th' Almighty,
    that doth send it ?

XXII

'To them that list, the worlds gay showes I
    leave,
And to great ones such follies doe for-
    give,
Which oft through pride do their owne
    perill weave,
And through ambition downe themselves
    doe drive
To sad decay, that might contented live.
Me no such cares nor combrous thoughts
    offend,
Ne once my minds unmoved quiet grieve,
But all the night in silver sleepe I spend,
And all the day, to what I list I doe attend.

XXIII

'Sometimes I hunt the fox, the vowed foe
Unto my lambes, and him dislodge away;
Sometime the fawne I practise from the
    doe,
Or from the goat her kidde how to convay;
Another while I baytes and nets display,
The birds to catch, or fishes to beguyle:
And when I wearie am, I downe doe lay
My limbes in every shade, to rest from
    toyle,
And drinke of every brooke, when thirst
    my throte doth boyle.

XXIV

'The time was once, in my first prime of
　　yeares,
When pride of youth forth pricked my
　　desire,
That I disdain'd amongst mine equall peares
To follow sheepe, and shepheards base at-
　　tire:
For further fortune then I would inquire,
And leaving home, to roiall court I sought;
Where I did sell my selfe for yearely hire,
And in the princes gardin daily wrought:
There I beheld such vainenesse, as I never
　　thought.

XXV

'With sight whereof soone cloyd, and long
　　deluded
With idle hopes, which them doe enter-
　　taine,
After I had ten yeares my selfe excluded
From native home, and spent my youth in
　　vaine,
I gan my follies to my selfe to plaine,
And this sweet peace, whose lacke did then
　　appeare.
Tho backe returning to my sheepe againe,
I from thenceforth have learn'd to love
　　more deare
This lowly quiet life, which I inherite here.'

XXVI

Whylest thus he talkt, the knight with
　　greedy care
Hong still upon his melting mouth attent;
Whose sensefull words empierst his hart
　　so neare,
That he was rapt with double ravishment,
Both of his speach, that wrought him great
　　content,
And also of the object of his vew,
On which his hungry eye was alwayes
　　bent;
That twixt his pleasing tongue and her
　　faire hew
He lost himselfe, and like one halfe en-
　　traunced grew.

XXVII

Yet to occasion meanes to worke his mind,
And to insinuate his harts desire,
He thus replyde : ' Now surely, syre, I
　　find,
That all this worlds gay showes, which we
　　admire,

Be but vaine shadowes to this safe retyre
Of life, which here in lowlinesse ye lead,
Fearelesse of foes, or Fortunes wrackfull
　　yre,
Which tosseth states, and under foot doth
　　tread
The mightie ones, affrayd of every chaunges
　　dread.

XXVIII

'That even I, which daily doe behold
The glorie of the great, mongst whom I
　　won,
And now have prov'd what happinesse ye
　　hold
In this small plot of your dominion,
Now loath great lordship and ambition;
And wish the heavens so much had graced
　　mee,
As graunt me live in like condition;
Or that my fortunes might transposed bee
From pitch of higher place unto this low
　　degree.'

XXIX

'In vaine,' said then old Meliboe, 'doe
　　men
The heavens of their fortunes fault accuse,
Sith they know best what is the best for
　　them:
For they to each such fortune doe diffuse,
As they doe know each can most aptly use.
For not that which men covet most is
　　best,
Nor that thing worst which men do most
　　refuse;
But fittest is, that all contented rest
With that they hold: each hath his fortune
　　in his brest.

XXX

'It is the mynd that maketh good or ill,
That maketh wretch or happie, rich or
　　poore:
For some, that hath abundance at his will,
Hath not enough, but wants in greatest
　　store;
And other, that hath litle, askes no more,
But in that litle is both rich and wise;
For wisedome is most riches; fooles there-
　　fore
They are, which fortunes doe by vowes de-
　　vize,
Sith each unto himselfe his life may for-
　　tunize.'

XXXI

'Since then in each mans self,' said Calidore,
' It is, to fashion his owne lyfes estate,
Give leave awhyle, good father, in this
    shore
To rest my barcke, which hath bene beaten
    late
With stormes of fortune and tempestuous
    fate,
In seas of troubles and of toylesome paine,
That, whether quite from them for to re-
    trate
I shall resolve, or backe to turne againe,
I may here with your selfe some small
    repose obtaine.

XXXII

' Not that the burden of so bold a guest
Shall chargefull be, or chaunge to you at
    all;
For your meane food shall be my daily
    feast,
And this your cabin both my bowre and
    hall.
Besides, for recompence hereof, I shall
You well reward, and golden guerdon give,
That may perhaps you better much withall,
And in this quiet make you safer live.'
So forth he drew much gold, and toward
    him it drive.

XXXIII

But the good man, nought tempted with
    the offer
Of his rich mould, did thrust it farre away,
And thus bespake: ' Sir knight, your boun-
    teous proffer
Be farre fro me, to whom ye ill display
That mucky masse, the cause of mens
    decay,
That mote empaire my peace with daungers
    dread.
But, if ye algates covet to assay
This simple sort of life, that shepheards
    lead,
Be it your owne: our rudenesse to your
    selfe aread.'

XXXIV

So there that night Sir Calidore did dwell,
And long while after, whilest him list re-
    maine,
Dayly beholding the faire Pastorell,
And feeding on the bayt of his owne bane.
During which time he did her entertaine

With all kind courtesies he could invent;
And every day, her companie to gaine,
When to the field she went, he with her
    went:
So for to quench his fire, he did it more
    augment.

XXXV

But she, that never had acquainted beene
With such queint usage, fit for queenes and
    kings,
Ne ever had such knightly service seene,
But, being bred under base shepheards
    wings,
Had ever learn'd to love the lowly things,
Did litle whit regard his courteous guize,
But cared more for Colins carolings
Then all that he could doe, or ever devize:
His layes, his loves, his lookes she did them
    all despize.

XXXVI

Which Calidore perceiving, thought it best
To chaunge the manner of his loftie looke;
And doffing his bright armes, himselfe ad-
    drest
In shepheards weed, and in his hand he
    tooke,
In stead of steelehead speare, a shep-
    heards hooke,
That who had seene him then would have
    bethought
On Phrygian Paris by Plexippus brooke,
When he the love of fayre Oenone sought,
What time the golden apple was unto him
    brought.

XXXVII

So being clad, unto the fields he went
With the faire Pastorella every day,
And kept her sheepe with diligent attent,
Watching to drive the ravenous wolfe away,
The whylest at pleasure she mote sport and
    play;
And every evening helping them to fold:
And otherwhiles, for need, he did assay
In his strong hand their rugged teats to
    hold,
And out of them to presse the milke: love
    so much could.

XXXVIII

Which seeing Coridon, who her likewise
Long time had lov'd, and hop'd her love to
    gaine,

He much was troubled at that straungers
          guize,
And many gealous thoughts conceiv'd in
          vaine,
That this of all his labour and long paine
Should reap the harvest, ere it ripened
          were;
That made him scoule, and pout, and oft
          complaine
Of Pastorell to all the shepheards there,
That she did love a stranger swayne then
          him more dere.

XXXIX

And ever, when he came in companie
Where Calidore was present, he would
          loure
And byte his lip, and even for gealousie
Was readie oft his owne hart to devoure,
Impatient of any paramoure:
Who on the other side did seeme so farre
From malicing, or grudging his good
          houre,
That all he could, he graced him with her,
Ne ever shewed signe of rancour or of
          jarre.

XL

And oft, when Coridon unto her brought
Or litle sparrowes, stolen from their nest,
Or wanton squirrels, in the woods farre
          sought,
Or other daintie thing for her addrest,
He would commend his guift, and make
          the best.
Yet she no whit his presents did regard,
Ne him could find to fancie in her brest:
This newcome shepheard had his market
          mard.
Old love is litle worth when new is more
          prefard.

XLI

One day when as the shepheard swaynes
          together
Were met, to make their sports and merrie
          glee,
As they are wont in faire sunshynie
          weather,
The whiles their flockes in shadowes
          shrouded bee,
They fell to daunce: then did they all agree,
That Colin Clout should pipe, as one most
          fit;
And Calidore should lead the ring, as hee

That most in Pastorellaes grace did sit.
Thereat frown'd Coridon, and his lip closely
          bit.

XLII

But Calidore, of courteous inclination,
Tooke Coridon and set him in his place,
That he should lead the daunce, as was his
          fashion;
For Coridon could daunce, and trimly
          trace.
And when as Pastorella, him to grace,
Her flowry garlond tooke from her owne
          head,
And plast on his, he did it soone displace,
And did it put on Coridons in stead:
Then Coridon woxe frollicke, that earst
          seemed dead.

XLIII

Another time, when as they did dispose
To practise games, and maisteries to try,
They for their judge did Pastorella chose;
A garland was the meed of victory.
There Coridon, forth stepping openly,
Did chalenge Calidore to wrestling game:
For he, through long and perfect industry,
Therein well practisd was, and in the same
Thought sure t' avenge his grudge, and
          worke his foe great shame.

XLIV

But Calidore he greatly did mistake;
For he was strong and mightily stiffe pight,
That with one fall his necke he almost
          brake,
And had he not upon him fallen light,
His dearest joynt he sure had broken
          quight.
Then was the oaken crowne by Pastorell
Given to Calidore, as his due right;
But he, that did in courtesie excell,
Gave it to Coridon, and said he wonne it
          well.

XLV

Thus did the gentle knight himselfe abeare
Amongst that rusticke rout in all his deeds,
That even they the which his rivals were
Could not maligne him, but commend him
          needs:
For courtesie amongst the rudest breeds
Good will and favour. So it surely wrought
With this faire mayd, and in her mynde
          the seeds

Of perfect love did sow, that last forth
    brought
The fruite of joy and blisse, though long
    time dearely bought.

XLVI

Thus Calidore continu'd there long time,
To winne the love of the faire Pastorell;
Which having got, he used without crime
Or blamefull blot, but menaged so well,
That he, of all the rest which there did
    dwell,
Was favoured, and to her grace com-
    mended.
But what straunge fortunes unto him be-
    fell,
Ere he attain'd the point by him intended,
Shall more conveniently in other place be
    ended.

CANTO X

Calidore sees the Graces daunce
  To Colins melody :
    The whiles his Pastorell is led
      Into captivity.

I

WHO now does follow the foule Blatant
    Beast,
Whilest Calidore does follow that faire
    mayd,
Unmyndfull of his vow, and high beheast
Which by the Faery Queene was on him
    layd,
That he should never leave, nor be delayd
From chacing him, till he had it att-
    chieved ?
But now entrapt of Love, which him be-
    trayd,
He mindeth more how he may be relieved
With grace from her whose love his heart
    hath sore engrieved.

II

That from henceforth he meanes no more
    to sew
His former quest, so full of toile and paine;
Another quest, another game in vew
He hath, the guerdon of his love to gaine:
With whom he myndes for ever to remaine,
And set his rest amongst the rusticke sort,
Rather then hunt still after shadowes vaine
Of courtly favour, fed with light report
Of every blaste, and sayling alwaies in the
    port.

III

Ne certes mote he greatly blamed be,
From so high step to stoupe unto so low.
For who had tasted once (as oft did he)
The happy peace which there doth over-
    flow,
And prov'd the perfect pleasures which
    doe grow
Amongst poore hyndes, in hils, in woods,
    in dales,
Would never more delight in painted show
Of such false blisse, as there is set for
    stales,
T' entrap unwary fooles in their eternall
    bales.

IV

For what hath all that goodly glorious
    gaze
Like to one sight which Calidore did vew ?
The glaunce whereof their dimmed eies
    would daze,
That never more they should endure the
    shew
Of that sunne-shine, that makes them looke
    askew.
Ne ought in all that world of beauties rare,
(Save onely Glorianaes heavenly hew,
To which what can compare ?) can it com-
    pare;
The which, as commeth now by course, I
    will declare.

V

One day as he did raunge the fields abroad,
Whilest his faire Pastorella was elsewhere,
He chaunst to come, far from all peoples
    troad,
Unto a place, whose pleasaunce did appere
To passe all others on the earth which
    were:
For all that ever was by Natures skill
Devized to worke delight was gathered
    there,
And there by her were poured forth at fill,
As if, this to adorne, she all the rest did
    pill.

VI

It was an hill plaste in an open plaine,
That round about was bordered with a
    wood
Of matchlesse hight, that seem'd th' earth
    to disdaine;
In which all trees of honour stately stood,

And did all winter as in sommer bud,
Spredding pavilions for the birds to bowre,
Which in their lower braunches sung aloud;
And in their tops the soring hauke did towre,
Sitting like king of fowles in majesty and powre.

VII

And at the foote thereof, a gentle flud
His silver waves did softly tumble downe,
Unmard with ragged mosse or filthy mud;
Ne mote wylde beastes, ne mote the ruder clowne
Thereto approch, ne filth mote therein drowne:
But nymphes and faeries by the bancks did sit,
In the woods shade, which did the waters crowne,
Keeping all noysome things away from it,
And to the waters fall tuning their accents fit.

VIII

And on the top thereof a spacious plaine
Did spred it selfe, to serve to all delight,
Either to daunce, when they to daunce would faine,
Or else to course about their bases light;
Ne ought there wanted, which for pleasure might
Desired be, or thence to banish bale:
So pleasauntly the hill with equall hight
Did seeme to overlooke the lowly vale;
Therefore it rightly cleeped was Mount Acidale.

IX

They say that Venus, when she did dispose
Her selfe to pleasaunce, used to resort
Unto this place, and therein to repose
And rest her selfe, as in a gladsome port,
Or with the Graces there to play and sport;
That even her owne Cytheron, though in it
She used most to keepe her royall court,
And in her soveraine majesty to sit,
She in regard hereof refusde and thought unfit.

X

Unto this place when as the Elfin knight
Approcht, him seemed that the merry sound

Of a shrill pipe he playing heard on hight,
And many feete fast thumping th' hollow ground,
That through the woods their eccho did rebound.
He nigher drew, to weete what mote it be;
There he a troupe of ladies dauncing found
Full merrily, and making gladfull glee,
And in the midst a shepheard piping he did see.

XI

He durst not enter into th' open greene,
For dread of them unwares to be descryde,
For breaking of their daunce, if he were seene;
But in the covert of the wood did byde,
Beholding all, yet of them unespyde.
There he did see, that pleased much his sight,
That even he him selfe his eyes envyde,
An hundred naked maidens lilly white,
All raunged in a ring, and dauncing in delight.

XII

All they without were raunged in a ring,
And daunced round; but in the midst of them
Three other ladies did both daunce and sing,
The whilest the rest them round about did hemme,
And like a girlond did in compasse stemme:
And in the middest of those same three was placed
Another damzell, as a precious gemme
Amidst a ring most richly well enchaced,
That with her goodly presence all the rest much graced.

XIII

Looke how the crowne, which Ariadne wore
Upon her yvory forehead that same day
That Theseus her unto his bridale bore,
When the bold Centaures made that bloudy fray
With the fierce Lapithes, which did them dismay,
Being now placed in the firmament,
Through the bright heaven doth her beames display,
And is unto the starres an ornament,
Which round about her move in order excellent:

XIV

Such was the beauty of this goodly band,
Whose sundry parts were here too long to
    tell:
But she that in the midst of them did
    stand
Seem'd all the rest in beauty to excell,
Crownd with a rosie girlond, that right
    well
Did her beseeme. And ever, as the crew
About her daunst, sweet flowres, that far
    did smell,
And fragrant odours they uppon her threw;
But most of all, those three did her with
    gifts endew.

XV

Those were the Graces, daughters of de-
    light,
Handmaides of Venus, which are wont to
    haunt
Uppon this hill, and daunce there day and
    night:
Those three to men all gifts of grace do
    graunt,
And all that Venus in her selfe doth vaunt
Is borrowed of them. But that faire one,
That in the midst was placed paravaunt,
Was she to whom that shepheard pypt
    alone,
That made him pipe so merrily, as never
    none.

XVI

She was, to weete, that jolly shepheards
    lasse,
Which piped there unto that merry rout;
That jolly shepheard which there piped
    was
Poore Colin Clout (who knowes not Colin
    Clout?)
He pypt apace, whilest they him daunst
    about.
Pype, jolly shepheard, pype thou now
    apace
Unto thy love, that made thee low to lout;
Thy love is present there with thee in
    place,
Thy love is there advaunst to be another
    Grace.

XVII

Much wondred Calidore at this straunge
    sight,
Whose like before his eye had never seene

And standing long astonished in spright,
And rapt with pleasaunce, wist not what to
    weene;
Whether it were the traine of Beauties
    Queene,
Or nymphes, or faeries, or enchaunted
    show,
With which his eyes mote have deluded
    beene.
Therefore resolving, what it was, to know,
Out of the wood he rose, and toward them
    did go.

XVIII

But soone as he appeared to their vew,
They vanisht all away out of his sight,
And cleane were gone, which way he never
    knew;
All save the shepheard, who, for fell de-
    spight
Of that displeasure, broke his bag-pipe
    quight,
And made great mone for that unhappy
    turne.
But Calidore, though no lesse sory wight
For that mishap, yet seeing him to mourne,
Drew neare, that he the truth of all by
    him mote learne:

XIX

And first him greeting, thus unto him
    spake:
'Haile, jolly shepheard, which thy joyous
    dayes
Here leadest in this goodly merry make,
Frequented of these gentle nymphes al-
    wayes,
Which to thee flocke, to heare thy lovely
    layes !
Tell me, what mote these dainty damzels
    be,
Which here with thee doe make their
    pleasant playes ?
Right happy thou, that mayst them freely
    see:
But why, when I them saw, fled they away
    from me ? '

XX

'Not I so happy,' answerd then that
    swaine,
'As thou unhappy, which them thence
    didst chace,
Whom by no meanes thou canst recall
    againe;

For being gone, none can them bring in place,
But whom they of them selves list so to grace.'
'Right sory I,' saide then Sir Calidore,
'That my ill fortune did them hence displace.
But since things passed none may now restore,
Tell me, what were they all, whose lacke thee grieves so sore.'

XXI

Tho gan that shepheard thus for to dilate:
'Then wote thou shepheard, whatsoever thou bee,
That all those ladies which thou sawest late
Are Venus damzels, all within her fee,
But differing in honour and degree:
They all are Graces, which on her depend,
Besides a thousand more, which ready bee
Her to adorne, when so she forth doth wend:
But those three in the midst doe chiefe on her attend.

XXII

'They are the daughters of sky-ruling Jove,
By him begot of faire Eurynome,
The Oceans daughter, in this pleasant grove,
As he, this way comming from feastfull glee
Of Thetis wedding with Æacidee,
In sommers shade him selfe here rested weary.
The first of them hight mylde Euphrosyne,
Next faire Aglaia, last Thalia merry:
Sweete goddesses all three, which me in mirth do cherry.

XXIII

'These three on men all gracious gifts bestow,
Which decke the body or adorne the mynde,
To make them lovely or well favoured show,
As comely carriage, entertainement kynde,
Sweete semblaunt, friendly offices that bynde,
And all the complements of curtesie:
They teach us, how to each degree and kynde

We should our selves demeane, to low, to hie,
To friends, to foes; which skill men call civility.

XXIV

'Therefore they alwaies smoothly seeme to smile,
That we likewise should mylde and gentle be,
And also naked are, that without guile
Or false dissemblaunce all them plaine may see,
Simple and true, from covert malice free:
And eeke them selves so in their daunce they bore,
That two of them still froward seem'd to bee,
But one still towards shew'd her selfe afore;
That good should from us goe, then come, in greater store.

XXV

'Such were those goddesses which ye did see;
But that fourth mayd, which there amidst them traced,
Who can aread what creature mote she bee,
Whether a creature, or a goddesse graced
With heavenly gifts from heven first enraced?
But what so sure she was, she worthy was
To be the fourth with those three other placed:
Yet was she certes but a countrey lasse,
Yet she all other countrey lasses farre did passe.

XXVI

'So farre as doth the daughter of the day
All other lesser lights in light excell,
So farre doth she in beautyfull array
Above all other lasses beare the bell:
Ne lesse in vertue, that beseemes her well,
Doth she exceede the rest of all her race;
For which the Graces, that here wont to dwell,
Have for more honor brought her to this place,
And graced her so much to be another Grace.

XXVII

'Another Grace she well deserves to be,
In whom so many graces gathered are,

Excelling much the meane of her degree;
Divine resemblaunce, beauty soveraine
    rare,
Firme chastity, that spight ne blemish
    dare;
All which she with such courtesie doth
    grace,
That all her peres cannot with her com-
    pare,
But quite are dimmed when she is in place.
She made me often pipe, and now to pipe
    apace.

XXVIII

'Sunne of the world, great glory of the
    sky,
That all the earth doest lighten with thy
    rayes,
Great Gloriana, greatest Majesty,
Pardon thy shepheard, mongst so many
    layes
As he hath sung of thee in all his dayes,
To make one minime of thy poore hand-
    mayd,
And underneath thy feete to place her
    prayse,
That, when thy glory shall be farre dis-
    playd
To future age, of her this mention may be
    made.'

XXIX

When thus that shepherd ended had his
    speach,
Sayd Calidore: 'Now sure it yrketh mee,
That to thy blisse I made this luckelesse
    breach,
As now the author of thy bale to be,
Thus to bereave thy loves deare sight
    from thee:
But, gentle shepheard, pardon thou my
    shame,
Who rashly sought that which I mote not
    see.'
Thus did the courteous knight excuse his
    blame,
And to recomfort him all comely meanes
    did frame.

XXX

In such discourses they together spent
Long time, as fit occasion forth them led;
With which the knight him selfe did much
    content,
And with delight his greedy fancy fed,

Both of his words, which he with reason
    red,
And also of the place, whose pleasures rare
With such regard his sences ravished,
That thence he had no will away to fare,
But wisht that with that shepheard he
    mote dwelling share.

XXXI

But that envenimd sting, the which of yore
His poysnous point deepe fixed in his hart
Had left, now gan afresh to rancle sore,
And to renue the rigour of his smart:
Which to recure, no skill of leaches art
Mote him availe, but to returne againe
To his wounds worker, that with lovely dart
Dinting his brest, had bred his restlesse
    paine,
Like as the wounded whale to shore flies
    from the maine.

XXXII

So taking leave of that same gentle swaine,
He backe returned to his rusticke wonne,
Where his faire Pastorella did remaine:
To whome, in sort as he at first begonne,
He daily did apply him selfe to donne
All dewfull service, voide of thoughts im-
    pure:
Ne any paines ne perill did he shonne,
By which he might her to his love allure,
And liking in her yet untamed heart pro-
    cure.

XXXIII

And evermore the shepheard Coridon,
What ever thing he did her to aggrate,
Did strive to match with strong contention,
And all his paines did closely emulate;
Whether it were to caroll, as they sate
Keeping their sheepe, or games to exercize,
Or to present her with their labours late;
Through which if any grace chaunst to
    arize
To him, the shepheard streight with jeal-
    ousie did frize.

XXXIV

One day as they all three together went
To the greene wood, to gather strawberies,
There chaunst to them a dangerous acci-
    dent:
A tigre forth out of the wood did rise,
That with fell clawes full of fierce gour-
    mandize,

And greedy mouth, wide gaping like hell
	gate,
Did runne at Pastorell her to surprize;
Whom she beholding, now all desolate
Gan cry to them aloud, to helpe her all too
	late.

XXXV

Which Coridon first hearing, ran in hast
To reskue her, but when he saw the feend,
Through cowherd feare he fled away as
	fast,
Ne durst abide the daunger of the end;
His life he steemed dearer then his frend.
But Calidore soone comming to her ayde,
When he the beast saw ready now to rend
His loves deare spoile, in which his heart
	was prayde,
He ran at him enraged, in stead of being
	frayde.

XXXVI

He had no weapon, but his shepheards
	hooke,
To serve the vengeaunce of his wrathfull
	will;
With which so sternely he the monster
	strooke,
That to the ground astonished he fell;
Whence ere he could recov'r, he did him
	quell,
And hewing off his head, it presented
Before the feete of the faire Pastorell;
Who scarcely yet from former feare ex-
	empted,
A thousand times him thankt, that had her
	death prevented.

XXXVII

From that day forth she gan him to affect,
And daily more her favour to augment;
But Coridon for cowherdize reject,
Fit to keepe sheepe, unfit for loves content:
The gentle heart scornes base disparage-
	ment.
Yet Calidore did not despise him quight,
But usde him friendly for further intent,
That by his fellowship he colour might
Both his estate and love from skill of any
	wight.

XXXVIII

So well he wood her, and so well he
	wrought her,
With humble service, and with daily sute,

That at the last unto his will he brought
	her;
Which he so wisely well did prosecute,
That of his love he reapt the timely frute,
And joyed long in close felicity:
Till Fortune, fraught with malice, blinde
	and brute,
That envies lovers long prosperity,
Blew up a bitter storme of foule adversity.

XXXIX

It fortuned one day, when Calidore
Was hunting in the woods (as was his
	trade)
A lawlesse people, Brigants hight of yore,
That never usde to live by plough nor
	spade,
But fed on spoile and booty, which they
	made
Upon their neighbours which did nigh
	them border,
The dwelling of these shepheards did in-
	vade,
And spoyld their houses, and them selves
	did murder,
And drove away their flocks, with other
	much disorder.

XL

Amongst the rest, the which they then did
	pray,
They spoyld old Melibee of all he had,
And all his people captive led away;
Mongst which this lucklesse mayd away
	was lad,
Faire Pastorella, sorrowfull and sad,
Most sorrowfull, most sad, that ever sight,
Now made the spoile of theeves and Bri-
	gants bad,
Which was the conquest of the gentlest
	knight
That ever liv'd, and th' onely glory of his
	might.

XLI

With them also was taken Coridon,
And carried captive by those theeves away;
Who in the covert of the night, that none
Mote them descry, nor reskue from their
	pray,
Unto their dwelling did them close con-
	vay.
Their dwelling in a little island was,
Covered with shrubby woods, in which no
	way

Appeard for people in nor out to pas,
Nor any footing fynde for overgrowen gras.

XLII

For underneath the ground their way was
    made,
Through hollow caves, that no man mote
    discover
For the thicke shrubs, which did them
    alwaies shade
From view of living wight, and covered
    over:
But darkenesse dred and daily night did
    hover
Through all the inner parts, wherein they
    dwelt;
Ne lightned was with window, nor with
    lover,
But with continuall candlelight, which delt
A doubtfull sense of things, not so well
    seene as felt.

XLIII

Hither those Brigants brought their pre-
    sent pray,
And kept them with continuall watch and
    ward,
Meaning, so soone as they convenient may,
For slaves to sell them, for no small re-
    ward,
To merchants, which them kept in bond-
    age hard,
Or sold againe. Now when faire Pastorell
Into this place was brought, and kept with
    gard
Of griesly theeves, she thought her self
    in hell,
Where with such damned fiends she should
    in darkenesse dwell.

XLIV

But for to tell the dolefull dreriment,
And pittifull complaints, which there she
    made,
Where day and night she nought did but
    lament
Her wretched life, shut up in deadly shade,
And waste her goodly beauty, which did
    fade
Like to a flowre that feeles no heate of
    sunne,
Which may her feeble leaves with comfort
    glade —
But what befell her in that theevish wonne
Will in an other canto better be begonne.

CANTO XI

The theeves fall out for Pastorell,
    Whilest Mellbee is slaine:
Her Calidore from them redeemes,
    And bringeth backe againe.

I

THE joyes of love, if they should ever last,
Without affliction or disquietnesse,
That worldly chaunces doe amongst them
    cast,
Would be on earth too great a blessed-
    nesse,
Liker to heaven then mortall wretched-
    nesse.
Therefore the winged god, to let men
    weet
That here on earth is no sure happinesse,
A thousand sowres hath tempred with one
    sweet,
To make it seeme more deare and dainty,
    as is meet.

II

Like as is now befalne to this faire mayd,
Faire Pastorell, of whom is now my song,
Who being now in dreadfull darkenesse
    layd,
Amongst those theeves, which her in bond-
    age strong
Detaynd, yet Fortune, not with all this
    wrong
Contented, greater mischiefe on her threw,
And sorrowes heapt on her in greater
    throng;
That who so heares her heavinesse would
    rew
And pitty her sad plight, so chang'd from
    pleasaunt hew.

III

Whylest thus she in these hellish dens re-
    mayned,
Wrapped in wretched cares and hearts
    unrest,
It so befell (as Fortune had ordayned)
That he which was their capitaine profest,
And had the chiefe commaund of all the
    rest,
One day as he did all his prisoners vew,
With lustfull eyes beheld that lovely guest,
Faire Pastorella, whose sad mournefull
    hew
Like the faire morning clad in misty fog
    did shew.

IV

At sight whereof his barbarous heart was
    fired,
And inly burnt with flames most raging
    whot,
That her alone he for his part desired
Of all the other pray which they had got,
And her in mynde did to him selfe allot.
From that day forth he kyndnesse to her
    showed,
And sought her love by all the meanes he
    mote;
With looks, with words, with gifts he oft
    her wowed,
And mixed threats among, and much unto
    her vowed.

V

But all that ever he could doe or say
Her constant mynd could not a whit re-
    move,
Nor draw unto the lure of his lewd lay,
To graunt him favour or afford him love.
Yet ceast he not to sew, and all waies
    prove,
By which he mote accomplish his request,
Saying and doing all that mote behove;
Ne day nor night he suffred her to rest,
But her all night did watch, and all the
    day molest.

VI

At last when him she so importune saw,
Fearing least he at length the raines would
    lend
Unto his lust, and make his will his law,
Sith in his powre she was to foe or frend,
She thought it best, for shadow, to pretend
Some shew of favour, by him gracing
    small,
That she thereby mote either freely wend,
Or at more ease continue there his thrall:
A little well is lent, that gaineth more
    withall.

VII

So from thenceforth, when love he to her
    made,
With better tearmes she did him entertaine,
Which gave him hope, and did him halfe
    perswade,
That he in time her joyaunce should ob-
    taine.
But when she saw, through that small
    favours gaine,

That further then she willing was he prest,
She found no meanes to barre him, but to
    faine
A sodaine sickenesse, which her sore op-
    prest,
And made unfit to serve his lawlesse
    mindes behest.

VIII

By meanes whereof she would not him per-
    mit
Once to approch to her in privity,
But onely mongst the rest by her to sit,
Mourning the rigour of her malady,
And seeking all things meete for remedy.
But she resolv'd no remedy to fynde,
Nor better cheare to shew in misery,
Till Fortune would her captive bonds un-
    bynde:
Her sickenesse was not of the body, but
    the mynde.

IX

During which space that she thus sicke did
    lie,
It chaunst a sort of merchants, which were
    wount
To skim those coastes, for bondmen there
    to buy,
And by such trafficke after gaines to hunt,
Arrived in this isle, though bare and blunt,
T' inquire for slaves; where being readie
    met
By some of these same theeves, at the in-
    stant brunt,
Were brought unto their captaine, who was
    set
By his faire patients side with sorrowfull
    regret.

X

To whom they shewed, how those marchants
    were
Arriv'd in place, their bondslaves for to buy,
And therefore prayd that those same cap-
    tives there
Mote to them for their most commodity
Be sold, and mongst them shared equally.
This their request the captaine much ap-
    palled;
Yet could he not their just demaund deny,
And willed streight the slaves should forth
    be called,
And sold for most advantage, not to be
    forestalled.

XI

Then forth the good old Meliboe was brought,
And Coridon, with many other moe,
Whom they before in diverse spoyles had
    caught:
All which he to the marchants sale did
    showe.
Till some, which did the sundry prisoners
    knowe,
Gan to inquire for that faire shepherdesse,
Which with the rest they tooke not long
    agoe,
And gan her forme and feature to expresse,
The more t' augment her price through
    praise of comlinesse.

XII

To whom the captaine in full angry wize
Made answere, that the mayd of whom
    they spake
Was his owne purchase and his onely prize,
With which none had to doe, ne ought par-
    take,
But he himselfe, which did that conquest
    make;
Litle for him to have one silly lasse:
Besides through sicknesse now so wan and
    weake,
That nothing meet in marchandise to passe.
So shew'd them her, to prove how pale and
    weake she was.

XIII

The sight of whom, though now decayd
    and mard,
And eke but hardly seene by candle-light,
Yet like a diamond of rich regard,
In doubtfull shadow of the darkesome
    night,
With starrie beames about her shining
    bright,
These marchants fixed eyes did so amaze,
That what through wonder, and what
    through delight,
A while on her they greedily did gaze,
And did her greatly like, and did her
    greatly praize.

XIV

At last when all the rest them offred were,
And prises to them placed at their pleas-
    ure,
They all refused in regard of her,
Ne ought would buy, how ever prisd with
    measure,

Withouten her, whose worth above all
    threasure
They did esteeme, and offred store of gold.
But then the captaine, fraught with more
    displeasure,
Bad them be still, his love should not be
    sold:
The rest take if they would, he her to him
    would hold.

XV

Therewith some other of the chiefest
    theeves
Boldly him bad such injurie forbeare;
For that same mayd, how ever it him
    greeves,
Should with the rest be sold before him
    theare,
To make the prises of the rest more deare.
That with great rage he stoutly doth denay;
And fiercely drawing forth his blade, doth
    sweare,
That who so hardie hand on her doth lay,
It dearely shall aby, and death for handsell
    pay.

XVI

Thus as they words amongst them multiply,
They fall to strokes, the frute of too much
    talke,
And the mad steele about doth fiercely fly,
Not sparing wight, ne leaving any balke,
But making way for Death at large to
    walke:
Who, in the horror of the griesly night,
In thousand dreadfull shapes doth mongst
    them stalke,
And makes huge havocke, whiles the can-
    dlelight
Out quenched leaves no skill nor difference
    of wight.

XVII

Like as a sort of hungry dogs, ymet
About some carcase by the common way,
Doe fall together, stryving each to get
The greatest portion of the greedie pray;
All on confused heapes themselves assay,
And snatch, and byte, and rend, and tug,
    and teare,
That who them sees would wonder at their
    fray,
And who sees not would be affrayd to heare:
Such was the conflict of those cruell Brig-
    ants there.

XVIII

But first of all, their captives they doe kill,
Least they should joyne against the weaker
    side,
Or rise against the remnant at their will:
Old Meliboe is slaine, and him beside
His aged wife, with many others wide;
But Coridon, escaping craftily,
Creepes forth of dores, whilst darknes him
    doth hide,
And flyes away as fast as he can hye,
Ne stayeth leave to take, before his friends
    doe dye.

XIX

But Pastorella, wofull wretched elfe,
Was by the captaine all this while defended,
Who, minding more her safety then him-
    selfe,
His target alwayes over her pretended;
By meanes whereof, that mote not be
    amended,
He at the length was slaine, and layd on
    ground,
Yet holding fast twixt both his armes ex-
    tended
Fayre Pastorell, who with the selfe same
    wound
Launcht through the arme, fell down with
    him in drerie swound.

XX

There lay she covered with confused
    preasse
Of carcases, which dying on her fell.
Tho, when as he was dead, the fray gan
    ceasse,
And each to other calling, did compell
To stay their cruell hands from slaughter
    fell,
Sith they that were the cause of all were
    gone.
Thereto they all attonce agreed well,
And lighting candles new, gan search
    anone,
How many of their friends were slaine,
    how many fone.

XXI

Their captaine there they cruelly found
    kild,
And in his armes the dreary dying mayd,
Like a sweet angell twixt two clouds up-
    hild:
Her lovely light was dimmed and decayd,

With cloud of death upon her eyes dis-
    playd;
Yet did the cloud make even that dimmed
    light
Seeme much more lovely in that darknesse
    layd,
And twixt the twinckling of her eye-lids
    bright
To sparke out litle beames, like starres in
    foggie night.

XXII

But when they mov'd the carcases aside,
They found that life did yet in her re-
    maine:
Then all their helpes they busily applyde,
To call the soule backe to her home
    againe;
And wrought so well with labour and long
    paine,
That they to life recovered her at last.
Who sighing sore, as if her hart in twaine
Had riven bene, and all her hart strings
    brast,
With drearie drouping eyne lookt up like
    one aghast.

XXIII

There she beheld, that sore her griev'd to
    see,
Her father and her friends about her
    lying,
Her selfe sole left, a second spoyle to bee
Of those that, having saved her from
    dying,
Renew'd her death by timely death deny-
    ing.
What now is left her but to wayle and
    weepe,
Wringing her hands, and ruefully loud
    crying?
Ne cared she her wound in teares to
    steepe,
Albe with all their might those Brigants
    her did keepe.

XXIV

But when they saw her now reliv'd againe,
They left her so, in charge of one the best
Of many worst, who with unkind disdaine
And cruell rigour her did much molest;
Scarse yeelding her due food, or timely
    rest,
And scarsely suffring her infestred wound,
That sore her payn'd, by any to be drest.

So leave we her in wretched thraldome
bound,
And turne we backe to Calidore, where we
him found.

XXV

Who when he backe returned from the
wood,
And saw his shepheards cottage spoyled
quight,
And his love reft away, he wexed wood,
And halfe enraged at that ruefull sight,
That even his hart, for very fell despight,
And his owne flesh he readie was to teare:
He chauft, he griev'd, he fretted, and he
sight,
And fared like a furious wyld beare,
Whose whelpes are stolne away, she being
otherwhere.

XXVI

Ne wight he found, to whom he might
complaine,
Ne wight he found, of whom he might inquire;
That more increast the anguish of his
paine.
He sought the woods; but no man could
see there:
He sought the plaines; but could no tydings
heare:
The woods did nought but ecchoes vaine
rebound;
The playnes all waste and emptie did appeare:
Where wont the shepheards oft their pypes
resound,
And feed an hundred flocks, there now not
one he found.

XXVII

At last, as there he romed up and downe,
He chaunst one comming towards him to
spy,
That seem'd to be some sorie simple clowne,
With ragged weedes, and lockes upstaring
hye,
As if he did from some late daunger fly,
And yet his feare did follow him be-
hynd:
Who as he unto him approched nye,
He mote perceive by signes which he did
fynd,
That Coridon it was, the silly shepherds
hynd.

XXVIII

Tho to him running fast, he did not stay
To greet him first, but askt, where were
the rest;
Where Pastorell? Who full of fresh dis-
may,
And gushing forth in teares, was so opprest,
That he no word could speake, but smit his
brest,
And up to heaven his eyes fast streming
threw.
Whereat the knight amaz'd, yet did not rest,
But askt againe, what ment that rufull hew:
Where was his Pastorell? where all the
other crew?

XXIX

'Ah, well away!' sayd he then sighing sore,
'That ever I did live, this day to see,
This dismall day, and was not dead before,
Before I saw faire Pastorella dye!'
'Die? out alas!' then Calidore did cry,
'How could the death dare ever her to quell?
But read, thou shepheard, read what destiny
Or other dyrefull hap from heaven or hell
Hath wrought this wicked deed: doe feare
away, and tell.'

XXX

Tho, when the shepheard breathed had a
whyle,
He thus began: 'Where shall I then commence
This wofull tale? or how those Brigants
vyle,
With cruell rage and dreadfull violence
Spoyld all our cots, and caried us from
hence?
Or how faire Pastorell should have bene
sold
To marchants, but was sav'd with strong
defence?
Or how those theeves, whilest one sought
her to hold,
Fell all at ods, and fought through fury
fierce and bold?

XXXI

'In that same conflict (woe is me!) befell
This fatall chaunce, this dolefull accident,
Whose heavy tydings now I have to tell.
First all the captives, which they here had
hent,
Were by them slaine by generall consent;
Old Melibœ and his good wife withall

These eyes saw die, and dearely did la-
　　ment:
But when the lot to Pastorell did fall,
Their captaine long withstood, and did her
　　death forstall.

XXXII

' But what could he gainst all them doe
　　alone ?
It could not boot; needs mote she die at
　　last:
I onely scapt through great confusione
Of cryes and clamors, which amongst them
　　past,
In dreadfull darknesse dreadfully aghast;
That better were with them to have bene
　　dead,
Then here to see all desolate and wast,
Despoyled of those joyes and jollyhead,
Which with those gentle shepherds here I
　　wont to lead.'

XXXIII

When Calidore these ruefull newes had
　　raught,
His hart quite deaded was with anguish
　　great,
And all his wits with doole were nigh dis-
　　traught,
That he his face, his head, his brest did
　　beat,
And death it selfe unto himselfe did
　　threat;
Oft cursing th' heavens, that so cruell
　　were
To her, whose name he often did repeat;
And wishing oft, that he were present
　　there,
When she was slaine, or had bene to her
　　succour nere.

XXXIV

But after griefe awhile had had his course,
And spent it selfe in mourning, he at last
Began to mitigate his swelling sourse,
And in his mind with better reason cast,
How he might save her life, if life did
　　last;
Or if that dead, how he her death might
　　wreake,
Sith otherwise he could not mend thing
　　past;
Or if it to revenge he were too weake,
Then for to die with her, and his lives
　　threed to breake.

XXXV

Tho Coridon he prayd, sith he well knew
The readie way unto that theevish wonne,
To wend with him, and be his conduct trew
Unto the place, to see what should be
　　donne.
But he, whose hart through feare was late
　　fordonne,
Would not for ought be drawne to former
　　drede,
But by all meanes the daunger knowne did
　　shonne:
Yet Calidore so well him wrought with
　　meed,
And faire bespoke with words, that he at
　　last agreed.

XXXVI

So forth they goe together (God before)
Both clad in shepheards weeds agreeably,
And both with shepheards hookes: but Cali-
　　dore
Had, underneath, him armed privily.
Tho, to the place when they approched nye,
They chaunst, upon an hill not farre away,
Some flockes of sheepe and shepheards to
　　espy;
To whom they both agreed to take their
　　way,
In hope there newes to learne, how they
　　mote best assay.

XXXVII

There did they find, that which they did not
　　feare,
The selfe same flocks the which those theeves
　　had reft
From Meliboe and from themselves whyl-
　　eare,
And certaine of the theeves there by them
　　left,
The which for want of heards themselves
　　then kept.
Right well knew Coridon his owne late
　　sheepe,
And seeing them, for tender pittie wept:
But when he saw the theeves which did
　　them keepe,
His hart gan fayle, albe he saw them all
　　asleepe.

XXXVIII

But Calidore recomforting his griefe,
Though not his feare; for nought may feare
　　disswade;

Him hardly forward drew, whereas the
    thiefe
Lay sleeping soundly in the bushes shade;
Whom Coridon him counseld to invade
Now all unwares, and take the spoyle away;
But he, that in his mind had closely made
A further purpose, would not so them slay,
But gently waking them, gave them the
    time of day.

XXXIX

Tho sitting downe by them upon the greene,
Of sundrie things he purpose gan to faine;
That he by them might certaine tydings
    weene
Of Pastorell, were she alive or slaine.
Mongst which the theeves them questioned
    againe,
What mister men, and eke from whence
    they were.
To whom they answer'd, as did appertaine,
That they were poore heardgroomes, the
    which whylere
Had from their maisters fled, and now
    sought hyre elswhere.

XL

Whereof right glad they seem'd, and offer
    made
To hyre them well, if they their flockes
    would keepe:
For they themselves were evill groomes,
    they sayd,
Unwont with heards to watch, or pasture
    sheepe,
But to forray the land, or scoure the deepe.
Thereto they soone agreed, and earnest
    tooke,
To keepe their flockes for litle hyre and
    chepe;
For they for better hyre did shortly looke:
So there all day they bode, till light the
    sky forsooke.

XLI

Tho, when as towards darksome night it
    drew,
Unto their hellish dens those theeves them
    brought,
Where shortly they in great acquaintance
    grew,
And all the secrets of their entrayles sought.
There did they find, contrarie to their
    thought,
That Pastorell yet liv'd, but all the rest

Were dead, right so as Coridon had taught:
Whereof they both full glad and blyth did
    rest,
But chiefly Calidore, whom griefe had most
    possest.

XLII

At length, when they occasion fittest found,
In dead of night, when all the theeves did
    rest
After a late forray, and slept full sound,
Sir Calidore him arm'd, as he thought best,
Having of late by diligent inquest
Provided him a sword of meanest sort:
With which he streight went to the cap-
    taines nest.
But Coridon durst not with him consort,
Ne durst abide behind, for dread of worse
    effort.

XLIII

When to the cave they came, they found
    it fast:
But Calidore with huge resistlesse might
The dores assayled, and the locks upbrast.
With noyse whereof the theefe awaking
    light,
Unto the entrance ran: where the bold
    knight,
Encountring him, with small resistance
    slew;
The whiles faire Pastorell through great
    affright
Was almost dead, misdoubting least of new
Some uprore were like that which lately
    she did vew.

XLIV

But when as Calidore was comen in,
And gan aloud for Pastorell to call,
Knowing his voice, although not heard long
    sin,
She sudden was revived therewithall,
And wondrous joy felt in her spirits thrall:
Like him that being long in tempest tost,
Looking each houre into deathes mouth to
    fall,
At length espyes at hand the happie cost,
On which he safety hopes, that earst feard
    to be lost.

XLV

Her gentle hart, that now long season past
Had never joyance felt, nor chearefull
    thought,

Began some smacke of comfort new to tast,
Like lyfull heat to nummed senses brought,
And life to feele, that long for death had
    sought;
Ne lesse in hart rejoyced Calidore,
When he her found, but, like to one dis-
    traught
And robd of reason, towards her him bore,
A thousand times embrast, and kist a thou-
    sand more.

XLVI

But now by this, with noyse of late uprore,
The hue and cry was raysed all about;
And all the Brigants, flocking in great store,
Unto the cave gan preasse, nought having
    dout
Of that was doen, and entred in a rout.
But Calidore in th' entry close did stand,
And entertayning them with courage stout,
Still slew the formost that came first to
    hand,
So long, till all the entry was with bodies
    mand.

XLVII

Tho, when no more could nigh to him ap-
    proch,
He breath'd his sword, and rested him till
    day:
Which when he spyde upon the earth t'
    encroch,
Through the dead carcases he made his way,
Mongst which he found a sword of better
    say,
With which he forth went into th' open
    light:
Where all the rest for him did readie stay,
And fierce assayling him, with all their
    might
Gan all upon him lay: there gan a dreadfull
    fight.

XLVIII

How many flyes in whottest sommers day
Do seize upon some beast, whose flesh is
    bare,
That all the place with swarmes do overlay,
And with their litle stings right felly fare;
So many theeves about him swarming are,
All which do him assayle on every side,
And sore oppresse, ne any him doth spare:
But he doth with his raging brond divide
Their thickest troups, and round about him
    scattreth wide.

XLIX

Like as a lion mongst an heard of dere,
Disperseth them to catch his choysest pray;
So did he fly amongst them here and there,
And all that nere him came did hew and
    slay,
Till he had strowd with bodies all the way;
That none his daunger daring to abide,
Fled from his wrath, and did themselves
    convay
Into their caves, their heads from death to
    hide,
Ne any left, that victorie to him envide.

L

Then backe returning to his dearest deare,
He her gan to recomfort, all he might,
With gladfull speaches and with lovely
    cheare,
And forth her bringing to the joyous light,
Whereof she long had lackt the wishfull
    sight,
Deviz'd all goodly meanes, from her to
    drive
The sad remembrance of her wretched
    plight.
So her uneath at last he did revive,
That long had lyen dead, and made againe
    alive.

LI

This doen, into those theevish dens he went,
And thence did all the spoyles and threa-
    sures take,
Which they from many long had robd and
    rent,
But Fortune now the victors meed did make;
Of which the best he did his love betake;
And also all those flockes, which they be-
    fore
Had reft from Meliboe and from his make,
He did them all to Coridon restore:
So drove them all away, and his love with
    him bore.

CANTO XII

Fayre Pastorella by great hap
    Her parents understands.
Calidore doth the Blatant Beast
    Subdew, and bynd in bands.

I

LIKE as a ship, that through the ocean wyde
Directs her course unto one certaine cost,

Is met of many a counter winde and tyde,
With which her winged speed is let and
    crost,
And she her selfe in stormie surges tost;
Yet making many a borde, and many a bay,
Still winneth way, ne hath her compasse
    lost:
Right so it fares with me in this long way,
Whose course is often stayd, yet never is
    astray.

II

For all that hetherto hath long delayd
This gentle knight from sewing his first
    quest,
Though out of course, yet hath not bene
    mis-sayd,
To shew the courtesie by him profest
Even unto the lowest and the least.
But now I come into my course againe,
To his atchievement of the Blatant Beast;
Who all this while at will did range and
    raine,
Whilst none was him to stop, nor none him
    to restraine.

III

Sir Calidore, when thus he now had raught
Faire Pastorella from those Brigants powre,
Unto the Castle of Beigard her brought,
Whereof was lord the good Sir Bella-
    moure;
Who whylome was, in his youthes freshest
    flowre,
A lustie knight as ever wielded speare,
And had endured many a dreadfull stoure
In bloudy battell for a ladie deare,
The fayrest ladie then of all that living
    were.

IV

Her name was Claribell, whose father hight
The Lord of Many Ilands, farre renound
For his great riches and his greater might.
He, through the wealth wherein he did
    abound,
This daughter thought in wedlocke to have
    bound
Unto the Prince of Picteland bordering
    nere;
But she, whose sides before with secret
    wound
Of love to Bellamoure empierced were,
By all meanes shund to match with any
    forrein fere.

V

And Bellamour againe so well her pleased,
With dayly service and attendance dew,
That of her love he was entyrely seized,
And closely did her wed, but knowne to
    few.
Which when her father understood, he grew
In so great rage, that them in dongeon
    deepe
Without compassion cruelly he threw;
Yet did so streightly them a sunder keepe,
That neither could to company of th' other
    creepe.

VI

Nathlesse Sir Bellamour, whether through
    grace
Or secret guifts, so with his keepers
    wrought,
That to his love sometimes he came in
    place,
Whereof her wombe, unwist to wight, was
    fraught,
And in dew time a mayden child forth
    brought.
Which she streight way, for dread least, if
    her syre
Should know thereof, to slay he would
    have sought,
Delivered to her handmayd, that for hyre
She should it cause be fostred under
    straunge attyre.

VII

The trustie damzell bearing it abrode
Into the emptie fields, where living wight
Mote not bewray the secret of her lode,
She forth gan lay unto the open light
The litle babe, to take thereof a sight.
Whom whylest she did with watrie eyne
    behold,
Upon the litle brest, like christall bright,
She mote perceive a litle purple mold,
That like a rose her silken leaves did faire
    unfold.

VIII

Well she it markt, and pittied the more,
Yet could not remedie her wretched case,
But, closing it againe like as before,
Bedeaw'd with teares there left it in the
    place:
Yet left not quite, but drew a litle space
Behind the bushes, where she her did
    hyde,

To weet what mortall hand, or heavens
   grace,
Would for the wretched infants helpe pro-
   vyde,
For which it loudly cald, and pittifully
   cryde.

IX

At length a shepheard, which there by did
   keepe
His fleecie flocke upon the playnes around,
Led with the infants cry, that loud did
   weepe,
Came to the place; where when he wrapped
   found
Th' abandond spoyle, he softly it unbound;
And seeing there that did him pittie sore,
He tooke it up, and in his mantle wound;
So home unto his honest wife it bore,
Who as her owne it nurst, and named
   evermore.

X

Thus long continu'd Claribell a thrall,
And Bellamour in bands, till that her syre
Departed life, and left unto them all.
Then all the stormes of Fortunes former
   yre
Were turnd, and they to freedome did re-
   tyre.
Thenceforth they joy'd in happinesse to-
   gether,
And lived long in peace and love entyre,
Without disquiet or dislike of ether,
Till time that Calidore brought Pastorella
   thether.

XI

Both whom they goodly well did entertaine;
For Bellamour knew Calidore right well,
And loved for his prowesse, sith they twaine
Long since had fought in field: als Clari-
   bell
No lesse did tender the faire Pastorell,
Seeing her weake and wan, through durance
   long.
There they a while together thus did dwell
In much delight, and many joyes among,
Untill the damzell gan to wex more sound
   and strong.

XII

Tho gan Sir Calidore him to advize
Of his first quest, which he had long forlore.

Asham'd to thinke, how he that enter-
   prize,
The which the Faery Queene had long
   afore
Bequeath'd to him, forslacked had so sore;
That much he feared, least reprochfull
   blame
With foule dishonour him mote blot there-
   fore;
Besides the losse of so much loos and fame,
As through the world thereby should glorifie
   his name.

XIII

Therefore resolving to returne in hast
Unto so great atchievement, he bethought
To leave his love, now perill being past,
With Claribell, whylest he that monster
   sought
Throughout the world, and to destruction
   brought.
So taking leave of his faire Pastorell,
Whom to recomfort all the meanes he
   wrought,
With thanks to Bellamour and Claribell,
He went forth on his quest, and did that
   him befell.

XIV

But first, ere I doe his adventures tell
In this exploite, me needeth to declare
What did betide to the faire Pastorell,
During his absence left in heavy care,
Through daily mourning and nightly mis-
   fare:
Yet did that auncient matrone all she might,
To cherish her with all things choice and
   rare;
And her owne handmayd, that Melissa
   hight,
Appointed to attend her dewly day and
   night.

XV

Who in a morning, when this mayden faire
Was dighting her, having her snowy brest
As yet not laced, nor her golden haire
Into their comely tresses dewly drest,
Chaunst to espy upon her yvory chest
The rosie marke, which she remembred
   well
That litle infant had, which forth she kest,
The daughter of her Lady Claribell,
The which she bore the whiles in prison she
   did dwell.

XVI

Which well avizing, streight she gan to cast
In her conceiptfull mynd, that this faire
mayd
Was that same infant, which so long sith past
She in the open fields had loosely layd
To fortunes spoile, unable it to ayd.
So, full of joy, streight forth she ran in hast
Unto her mistresse, being halfe dismayd,
To tell her how the heavens had her graste,
To save her chylde, which in misfortunes
mouth was plaste.

XVII

The sober mother, seeing such her mood,
Yet knowing not what meant that sodaine
thro,
Askt her, how mote her words be under-
stood,
And what the matter was, that mov'd her so.
'My liefe,' sayd she, 'ye know that long ygo,
Whilest ye in durance dwelt, ye to me gave
A little mayde, the which ye chylded tho;
The same againe if now ye list to have,
The same is yonder lady, whom High God
did save.'

XVIII

Much was the lady troubled at that speach,
And gan to question streight how she it
knew.
'Most certaine markes,' sayd she, 'do me
it teach,
For on her brest I with these eyes did vew
The litle purple rose which thereon grew,
Whereof her name ye then to her did give.
Besides, her countenaunce and her likely
hew,
Matched with equall yeares, do surely
prieve
That yond same is your daughter sure,
which yet doth live.'

XIX

The matrone stayd no lenger to enquire,
But forth in hast ran to the straunger mayd;
Whom catching greedily for great desire,
Rent up her brest, and bosome open layd,
In which that rose she plainely saw displayd.
Then her embracing twixt her armes
twaine,
She long so held, and softly weeping sayd:
'And livest thou, my daughter, now againe?
And art thou yet alive, whom dead I long
did faine?'

XX

Tho further asking her of sundry things,
And times comparing with their accidents,
She found at last by very certaine signes,
And speaking markes of passed monu-
ments,
That this young mayd, whom chance to her
presents,
Is her owne daughter, her owne infant
deare.
Tho, wondring long at those so straunge
events,
A thousand times she her embraced nere,
With many a joyfull kisse, and many a
melting teare.

XXI

Who ever is the mother of one chylde,
Which having thought long dead, she
fyndes alive,
Let her by proofe of that which she hath
fylde
In her owne breast, this mothers joy de-
scrive:
For other none such passion can contrive
In perfect forme, as this good lady felt,
When she so faire a daughter saw survive,
As Pastorella was, that nigh she swelt
For passing joy, which did all into pitty
melt.

XXII

Thence running forth unto her loved lord,
She unto him recounted all that fell:
Who joyning joy with her in one accord,
Acknowledg'd for his owne faire Pastorell.
There leave we them in joy, and let us tell
Of Calidore, who, seeking all this while
That monstrous beast by finall force to
quell,
Through every place, with restlesse paine
and toile,
Him follow'd by the tract of his outragious
spoile.

XXIII

Through all estates he found that he had
past,
In which he many massacres had left,
And to the clergy now was come at last;
In which such spoile, such havocke, and
such theft
He wrought, that thence all goodnesse he
bereft,
That endlesse were to tell. The Elfin knight,

Who now no place besides unsought had
    left,
At length into a monastere did light,
Where he him found despoyling all with
    maine and might.

XXIV

Into their cloysters now he broken had,
Through which the monckes he chaced here
    and there,
And them pursu'd into their dortours sad,
And searched all their cels and secrets
    neare;
In which what filth and ordure did appeare
Were yrkesome to report; yet that foule
    beast,
Nought sparing them, the more did tosse
    and teare,
And ransacke all their dennes from most to
    least,
Regarding nought religion, nor their holy
    heast.

XXV

From thence into the sacred church he broke,
And robd the chancell, and the deskes
    downe threw,
And altars fouled, and blasphemy spoke,
And th' images, for all their goodly hew,
Did cast to ground, whilest none was them
    to rew;
So all confounded and disordered there.
But seeing Calidore, away he flew,
Knowing his fatall hand by former feare;
But he him fast pursuing, soone approched
    neare

XXVI

Him in a narrow place he overtooke,
And fierce assailing forst him turne againe:
Sternely he turnd againe, when he him
    strooke
With his sharpe steele, and ran at him
    amaine
With open mouth, that seemed to containe
A full good pecke within the utmost brim,
All set with yron teeth in raunges twaine,
That terrifide his foes, and armed him,
Appearing like the mouth of Orcus griesly
    grim.

XXVII

And therein were a thousand tongs em-
    pight,
Of sundry kindes, and sundry quality;

Some were of dogs, that barked day and
    night,
And some of cats, that wrawling still did cry,
And some of beares, that groynd continu-
    ally,
And some of tygres, that did seeme to gren
And snar at all that ever passed by:
But most of them were tongues of mortall
    men,
Which spake reprochfully, not caring where
    nor when.

XXVIII

And them amongst were mingled here and
    there
The tongues of serpents with three forked
    stings,
That spat out poyson and gore bloudy gere
At all that came within his ravenings,
And spake licentious words and hatefull
    things
Of good and bad alike, of low and hie;
Ne kesars spared he a whit, nor kings,
But either blotted them with infamie,
Or bit them with his banefull teeth of injury.

XXIX

But Calidore, thereof no whit afrayd,
Rencountred him with so impetuous might,
That th' outrage of his violence he stayd,
And bet abacke, threatning in vaine to bite,
And spitting forth the poyson of his spight,
That fomed all about his bloody jawes,
Tho, rearing up his former feete on hight,
He rampt upon him with his ravenous
    pawes,
As if he would have rent him with his
    cruell clawes.

XXX

But he right well aware, his rage to ward,
Did cast his shield atweene, and there-
    withall
Putting his puissaunce forth, pursu'd so
    hard,
That backeward he enforced him to fall,
And being downe, ere he new helpe could
    call,
His shield he on him threw, and fast
    downe held,
Like as a bullocke, that in bloudy stall
Of butchers balefull hand to ground is
    feld,
Is forcibly kept downe, till he be throughly
    queld.

XXXI

Full cruelly the beast did rage and rore,
To be downe held, and maystred so with
might,
That he gan fret and fome out bloudy gore,
Striving in vaine to rere him selfe upright.
For still the more he strove, the more the
knight
Did him suppresse, and forcibly subdew;
That made him almost mad for fell de-
spight.
He grind, hee bit, he scratcht, he venim
threw,
And fared like a feend, right horrible in
hew:

XXXII

Or like the hell-borne Hydra, which they
faine
That great Alcides whilome overthrew,
After that he had labourd long in vaine
To crop his thousand heads, the which still
new
Forth budded, and in greater number grew.
Such was the fury of this hellish beast,
Whilest Calidore him under him downe
threw;
Who nathemore his heavy load releast,
But aye the more he rag'd, the more his
powre increast.

XXXIII

Tho when the beast saw he mote nought
availe
By force, he gan his hundred tongues apply,
And sharpely at him to revile and raile,
With bitter termes of shamefull infamy;
Oft interlacing many a forged lie,
Whose like he never once did speake, nor
heare,
Nor ever thought thing so unworthily:
Yet did he nought, for all that, him for-
beare,
But strained him so streightly that he chokt
him neare.

XXXIV

At last, when as he found his force to
shrincke,
And rage to quaile, he tooke a muzzell strong
Of surest yron, made with many a lincke;
Therewith he mured up his mouth along,
And therein shut up his blasphemous tong,
For never more defaming gentle knight,
Or unto lovely lady doing wrong:

And thereunto a great long chaine he tight,
With which he drew him forth, even in his
own despight.

XXXV

Like as whylome that strong Tirynthian
swaine
Brought forth with him the dreadfull dog
of hell,
Against his will fast bound in yron chaine,
And roring horribly, did him compell
To see the hatefull sunne, that he might tell
To griesly Pluto what on earth was donne,
And to the other damned ghosts, which dwell
For aye in darkenesse, which day light doth
shonne:
So led this knight his captyve with like
conquest wonne.

XXXVI

Yet greatly did the beast repine at those
Straunge bands, whose like till then he
never bore,
Ne ever any durst till then impose,
And chauffed inly, seeing now no more
Him liberty was left aloud to rore:
Yet durst he not draw backe, nor once
withstand
The proved powre of noble Calidore,
But trembled underneath his mighty hand,
And like a fearefull dog him followed
through the land.

XXXVII

Him through all Faery Land he follow'd so,
As if he learned had obedience long,
That all the people, where so he did go,
Out of their townes did round about him
throng,
To see him leade that beast in bondage
strong,
And seeing it, much wondred at the sight;
And all such persons as he earst did wrong
Rejoyced much to see his captive plight,
And much admyr'd the beast, but more
admyr'd the knight.

XXXVIII

Thus was this monster, by the maystring
might
Of doughty Calidore, supprest and tamed,
That never more he mote endammadge
wight
With his vile tongue, which many had defamed.

And many causelesse caused to be blamed:
So did he eeke long after this remaine,
Untill that, whether wicked fate so framed,
Or fault of men, he broke his yron chaine,
And got into the world at liberty againe.

XXXIX

Thenceforth more mischiefe and more scath
    he wrought
To mortall men, then he had done before;
Ne ever could, by any, more be brought
Into like bands, ne maystred any more:
Albe that long time after Calidore,
The good Sir Pelleas him tooke in hand,
And after him Sir Lamoracke of yore,
And all his brethren borne in Britaine
    land;
Yet none of them could ever bring him into
    band.

XL

So now he raungeth through the world
    againe,
And rageth sore in each degree and state;

Ne any is, that may him now restraine,
He growen is so great and strong of late,
Barking and biting all that him doe bate,
Albe they worthy blame, or cleare of crime:
Ne spareth he most learned wits to rate,
Ne spareth he the gentle poets rime,
But rends without regard of person or of
    time.

XLI

Ne may this homely verse, of many meanest,
Hope to escape his venemous despite,
More then my former writs, all were they
    cleanest,
From blamefull blot, and free from all that
    wite,
With which some wicked tongues did it
    backebite,
And bring into a mighty peres displeasure,
That never so deserved to endite.
Therfore do you, my rimes, keep better
    measure,
And seeke to please, that now is counted
    wisemens threasure.

TWO CANTOS

OF

MUTABILITIE

WHICH, BOTH FOR FORME AND MATTER, APPEAR TO BE PARCELL OF SOME FOL-
LOWING BOOKE OF THE

FAERIE QUEENE

UNDER THE LEGEND

OF

CONSTANCIE

NEVER BEFORE IMPRINTED

CANTO VI

Proud Change (not pleasd in mortall things
    Beneath the moone to raigne)
Pretends, as well of gods as men,
    To be the soveraine.

I

WHAT man that sees the ever-whirling
    wheele
Of Change, the which all mortall things
    doth sway,
But that therby doth find, and plainly feele,

How Mutability in them doth play
Her cruell sports, to many mens decay?
Which that to all may better yet appeare,
I will rehearse that whylome I heard say,
How she at first her selfe began to reare
Gainst all the gods, and th' empire sought
    from them to beare.

II

But first, here falleth fittest to unfold
Her antique race and linage ancient,
As I have found it registred of old

In Faery Land mongst records permanent.
She was, to weet, a daughter by descent
Of those old Titans that did whylome
strive
With Saturnes sonne for heavens regiment;
Whom though high Jove of kingdome did
deprive,
Yet many of their stemme long after did
survive.

III

And many of them afterwards obtain'd
Great power of Jove, and high authority:
As Hecatè, in whose almighty hand
He plac't all rule and principality,
To be by her disposed diversly,
To gods and men, as she them list divide;
And drad Bellona, that doth sound on hie
Warres and allarums unto nations wide,
That makes both heaven and earth to trem-
ble at her pride.

IV

So likewise did this Titanesse aspire,
Rule and dominion to her selfe to gaine;
That as a goddesse men might her ad-
mire,
And heavenly honours yield, as to them
twaine.
And first, on earth she sought it to ob-
taine;
Where she such proofe and sad examples
shewed
Of her great power, to many ones great
paine,
That not men onely (whom she soone sub-
dewed),
But eke all other creatures, her bad dooings
rewed.

V

For she the face of earthly things so
changed,
That all which Nature had establisht first
In good estate, and in meet order ranged,
She did pervert, and all their statutes
burst:
And all the worlds faire frame (which none
yet durst
Of gods or men to alter or misguide)
She alter'd quite, and made them all ac-
curst
That God had blest, and did at first pro-
vide
In that still happy state for ever to abide.

VI

Ne shee the lawes of Nature onely brake,
But eke of Justice, and of Policie;
And wrong of right, and bad of good did
make,
And death for life exchanged foolishlie:
Since which, all living wights have learn'd
to die,
And all this world is woxen daily worse.
O pittious worke of Mutabilitie!
By which we all are subject to that curse,
And death, in stead of life, have sucked
from our nurse.

VII

And now, when all the earth she thus had
brought
To her behest, and thralled to her might,
She gan to cast in her ambitious thought
T' attempt the empire of the heavens hight,
And Jove himselfe to shoulder from his
right.
And first, she past the region of the ayre,
And of the fire, whose substance thin and
slight
Made no resistance, ne could her contraire,
But ready passage to her pleasure did pre-
paire.

VIII

Thence to the circle of the Moone she
clambe,
Where Cynthia raignes in everlasting glory,
To whose bright shining palace straight she
came,
All fairely deckt with heavens goodly story:
Whose silver gates (by which there sate an
hory
Old aged sire, with hower-glasse in hand,
Hight Tyme) she entred, were he liefe or
sory:
Ne staide till she the highest stage had
scand,
Where Cynthia did sit, that never still did
stand.

IX

Her sitting on an ivory throne shee found,
Drawne of two steeds, th' one black, the
other white,
Environd with tenne thousand starres
around,
That duly her attended day and night;
And by her side there ran her page, that
hight

Vesper, whom we the evening-starre intend:
That with his torche, still twinkling like
  twylight,
Her lightened all the way where she should
  wend,
And joy to weary wandring travailers did
  lend:

X

That when the hardy Titanesse beheld
The goodly building of her palace bright,
Made of the heavens substance, and up-held
With thousand crystall pillors of huge
  hight,
Shee gan to burne in her ambitious spright,
And t' envie her that in such glorie raigned.
Eftsoones she cast by force and tortious
  might
Her to displace, and to her selfe to have
  gained
The kingdome of the night, and waters by
  her wained.

XI

Boldly she bid the goddesse downe descend,
And let her selfe into that ivory throne;
For shee her selfe more worthy thereof
  wend,
And better able it to guide alone:
Whether to men, whose fall she did be-
  mone,
Or unto gods, whose state she did maligne,
Or to th' infernall powers, her need give lone
Of her faire light and bounty most be-
  nigne,
Her selfe of all that rule shee deemed most
  condigne.

XII

But shee that had to her that soveraigne
  seat
By highest Jove assign'd, therein to beare
Nights burning lamp, regarded not her
  threat,
Ne yielded ought for favour or for feare;
But with sterne countenaunce and disdain-
  full cheare,
Bending her horned browes, did put her
  back:
And boldly blaming her for comming there,
Bade her attonce from heavens coast to
  pack,
Or at her perill bide the wrathfull thunders
  wrack.

XIII

Yet nathemore the Giantesse forbare:
But boldly preacing-on, raught forth her
  hand
To pluck her downe perforce from off her
  chaire;
And there-with lifting up her golden wand,
Threatned to strike her if she did with-
  stand.
Where-at the starres, which round about
  her blazed,
And eke the Moones bright wagon, still did
  stand.
All beeing with so bold attempt amazed,
And on her uncouth habit and sterne looke
  still gazed.

XIV

Meane-while the lower world, which nothing
  knew
Of all that chaunced here, was darkned
  quite;
And eke the heavens, and all the heavenly
  crew
Of happy wights, now unpurvaide of light,
Were much afraid, and wondred at that
  sight;
Fearing least Chaos broken had his chaine,
And brought againe on them eternall night:
But chiefely Mercury, that next doth raigne,
Ran forth in haste, unto the king of gods to
  plaine.

XV

All ran together with a great out-cry
To Joves faire palace, fixt in heavens hight;
And beating at his gates full earnestly,
Gan call to him aloud with all their might,
To know what meant that suddaine lack of
  light.
The father of the gods, when this he heard,
Was troubled much at their so strange af-
  fright,
Doubting least Typhon were againe up-
  rear'd,
Or other his old foes, that once him sorely
  fear'd.

XVI

Eftsoones the sonne of Maia forth he sent
Downe to the circle of the Moone, to knowe
The cause of this so strange astonishment,
And why shee did her wonted course for-
  slowe;
And if that any were on earth belowe

That did with charmes or magick her
    molest,
Him to attache, and downe to hell to
    throwe:
But, if from heaven it were, then to ar-
    rest
The author, and him bring before his pre-
    sence prest.

XVII

The wingd-foot god so fast his plumes did
    beat,
That soone he came where-as the Titanesse
Was striving with faire Cynthia for her
    seat:
At whose strange sight and haughty hard-
    inesse
He wondred much, and feared her no lesse.
Yet laying feare aside to doe his charge,
At last he bade her (with bold stedfast-
    nesse)
Ceasse to molest the Moone to walke at
    large,
Or come before high Jove, her dooings to
    discharge.

XVIII

And there-with-all, he on her shoulder
    laid
His snaky-wreathed mace, whose awfull
    power
Doth make both gods and hellish fiends
    affraid:
Where-at the Titanesse did sternely lower,
And stoutly answer'd, that in evill hower
He from his Jove such message to her
    brought,
To bid her leave faire Cynthias silver bower;
Sith shee his Jove and him esteemed nought,
No more then Cynthia's selfe; but all their
    kingdoms sought.

XIX

The heavens herald staid not to reply,
But past away, his doings to relate
Unto his lord; who now, in th' highest sky,
Was placed in his principall estate,
With all the gods about him congregate:
To whom when Hermes had his message
    told,
It did them all exceedingly amate,
Save Jove; who, changing nought his coun-
    t'nance bold,
Did unto them at length these speeches
    wise unfold:

XX

' Harken to mee awhile, yee heavenly pow-
    ers:
Ye may remember since th' Earths cursed
    seed
Sought to assaile the heavens eternall tow-
    ers,
And to us all exceeding feare did breed:
But how we then defeated all their deed,
Yee all doe knowe, and them destroied
    quite;
Yet not so quite, but that there did suc-
    ceed
An off-spring of their bloud, which did alite
Upon the fruitfull earth, which doth us yet
    despite.

XXI

' Of that bad seed is this bold woman bred,
That now with bold presumption doth aspire
To thrust faire Phœbe from her silver bed,
And eke our selves from heavens high em-
    pire,
If that her might were match to her desire:
Wherefore, it now behoves us to advise
What way is best to drive her to retire;
Whether by open force or counsell wise,
Areed, ye sonnes of God, as best ye can
    devise.'

XXII

So having said, he ceast; and with his brow
(His black eye-brow, whose doomefull
    dreaded beck
Is wont to wield the world unto his vow,
And even the highest powers of heaven to
    check)
Made signe to them in their degrees to
    speake:
Who straight gan cast their counsell grave
    and wise.
Meane-while th' Earths daughter, thogh she
    nought did reck
Of Hermes message, yet gan now advise,
What course were best to take in this hot
    bold emprize.

XXIII

Eftsoones she thus resolv'd; that whil'st
    the gods
(After returne of Hermes embassie)
Were troubled, and amongst themselves at
    ods,
Before they could new counsels re-allie,
To set upon them in that extasie;

And take what fortune time and place would
    lend:
So forth she rose, and through the purest
    sky
To Joves high palace straight cast to ascend,
To prosecute her plot: good on-set boads
    good end.

XXIV

Shee there arriving, boldly in did pass;
Where all the gods she found in counsell
    close,
All quite unarm'd, as then their manner
    was.
At sight of her they suddaine all arose,
In great amaze, ne wist what way to chose.
But Jove, all fearelesse, forc't them to aby;
And in his soveraine throne, gan straight
    dispose
Himselfe more full of grace and majestie,
That mote encheare his friends, and foes
    mote terrifie.

XXV

That when the haughty Titanesse beheld,
All were she fraught with pride and impu-
    dence,
Yet with the sight thereof was almost queld;
And inly quaking, seem'd as reft of sense,
And voyd of speech in that drad audience;
Untill that Jove himselfe her selfe bespake:
'Speake, thou fraile woman, speake with
    confidence;
Whence art thou, and what doost thou here
    now make?
What idle errand hast thou, earths man-
    sion to forsake ? '

XXVI

Shee, halfe confused with his great com-
    maund,
Yet gathering spirit of her natures pride,
Him boldly answer'd thus to his demaund:
'I am a daughter, by the mothers side,
Of her that is grand-mother magnifide
Of all the gods, great Earth, great Chaos
    child:
But by the fathers (be it not envide)
I greater am in bloud (whereon I build)
Then all the gods, though wrongfully from
    heaven exil'd.

XXVII

' For Titan (as ye all acknowledge must)
Was Saturnes elder brother by birth-right;

Both, sonnes of Uranus: but by unjust
And guilefull meanes, through Corybantes
    slight,
The younger thrust the elder from his
    right:
Since which thou, Jove, injuriously hast
    held
The heavens rule from Titans sonnes by
    might;
And them to hellish dungeons downe hast
    feld:
Witnesse, ye heavens, the truth of all that
    I have teld.'

XXVIII

Whil'st she thus spake, the gods, that gave
    good eare
To her bold words, and marked well her
    grace,
Beeing of stature tall as any there
Of all the gods, and beautifull of face
As any of the goddesses in place,
Stood all astonied; like a sort of steeres,
Mongst whom some beast of strange and
    forraine race
Unwares is chaunc't, far straying from his
    peeres:
So did their ghastly gaze bewray their hid-
    den feares.

XXIX

Till, having pauz'd awhile, Jove thus be-
    spake:
' Will never mortall thoughts ceasse to as-
    pire,
In this bold sort, to heaven claime to
    make,
And touch celestiall seates with earthly
    mire ?
I would have thought that bold Procrustes
    hire,
Or Typhons fall, or proud Ixions paine,
Or great Prometheus tasting of our ire,
Would have suffiz'd the rest for to re-
    straine,
And warn'd all men, by their example, to
    refraine:

XXX

' But now this off-scum of that cursed fry
Dare to renew the like bold enterprize,
And chalenge th' heritage of this our skie;
Whom what should hinder, but that we
    likewise
Should handle as the rest of her allies,

And thunder-drive to hell?' With that,
he shooke
His nectar-deawed locks, with which the
skyes
And all the world beneath for terror quooke,
And eft his burning levin-brond in hand he
tooke.

XXXI

But, when he looked on her lovely face,
In which faire beames of beauty did ap-
peare,
That could the greatest wrath soone turne
to grace
(Such sway doth beauty even in heaven
beare)
He staide his hand: and having chang'd his
cheare,
He thus againe in milder wise began:
'But ah! if gods should strive with flesh
yfere,
Then shortly should the progeny of man
Be rooted out, if Jove should doe still what
he can.

XXXII

'But thee, faire Titans child, I rather weene,
Through some vaine errour, or inducement
light,
To see that mortall eyes have never seene;
Or through ensample of thy sisters might,
Bellona, whose great glory thou doost
spight,
Since thou hast seene her dreadfull power
belowe,
Mongst wretched men, dismaide with her
affright,
To bandie crownes, and kingdomes to be-
stowe:
And sure thy worth no lesse then hers doth
seem to showe.

XXXIII

'But wote thou this, thou hardy Titanesse,
That not the worth of any living wight
May challenge ought in heavens interesse;
Much lesse the title of old Titans right:
For we by conquest of our soveraine might,
And by eternall doome of Fates decree,
Have wonne the empire of the heavens
bright;
Which to ourselves we hold, and to whom
wee
Shall worthy deeme partakers of our blisse
to bee.

XXXIV

'Then ceasse thy idle claime, thou foolish
gerle,
And seeke by grace and goodnesse to ob-
taine
That place from which by folly Titan fell;
There-to thou maist perhaps, if so thou
faine,
Have Jove thy gratious lord and sover-
aigne.'
So having said, she thus to him replide:
'Ceasse, Saturnes sonne, to seeke by prof-
fers vaine
Of idle hopes t' allure mee to thy side,
For to betray my right, before I have it
tride.

XXXV

'But thee, O Jove, no equall judge I deeme
Of my desert, or of my dewfull right;
That in thine owne behalfe maist partiall
seeme:
But to the highest him, that is behight
Father of gods and men by equall might,
To weet, the god of Nature, I appeale.'
There-at Jove wexed wroth, and in his
spright
Did inly grudge, yet did it well conceale;
And bade Dan Phœbus scribe her appella-
tion seale.

XXXVI

Eftsoones the time and place appointed
were,
Where all, both heavenly powers and earthly
wights,
Before great Natures presence should ap-
peare,
For triall of their titles and best rights:
That was, to weet, upon the highest hights
Of Arlo-hill (Who knowes not Arlo-hill?)
That is the highest head (in all mens sights)
Of my old father Mole, whom shepheards
quill
Renowmed hath with hymnes fit for a rurall
skill.

XXXVII

And, were it not ill fitting for this file,
To sing of hilles and woods, mongst warres
and knights,
I would abate the sternenesse of my stile,
Mongst these sterne stounds to mingle soft
delights;
And tell how Arlo through Dianaes spights

(Beeing of old the best and fairest hill
That was in all this holy-islands hights)
Was made the most unpleasant and most ill.
Meane while, O Clio, lend Calliope thy quill.

XXXVIII

Whylome, when Ireland florished in fame
Of wealths and goodnesse, far above the
rest
Of all that beare the British Islands name,
The gods then us'd (for pleasure and for
rest)
Oft to resort there-to, when seem'd them
best:
But none of all there-in more pleasure
found
Then Cynthia, that is soveraine queene pro-
fest
Of woods and forrests, which therein
abound,
Sprinkled with wholsom waters more then
most on ground.

XXXIX

But mongst them all, as fittest for her
game,
Either for chace of beasts with hound or
boawe,
Or for to shroude in shade from Phœbus
flame,
Or bathe in fountaines that doe freshly
flowe,
Or from high hilles, or from the dales be-
lowe,
She chose this Arlo; where shee did resort
With all her nymphes enranged on a rowe,
With whom the woody gods did oft con-
sort:
For with the nymphes the satyres love to
play and sport.

XL

Amongst the which there was a nymph
that hight
Molanna, daughter of old Father Mole,
And sister unto Mulla, faire and bright,
Unto whose bed false Bregog whylome
stole,
That Shepheard Colin dearely did condole,
And made her lucklesse loves well knowne
to be.
But this Molanna, were she not so shole,
Were no lesse faire and beautifull then shee:
Yet as she is, a fairer flood may no man
see.

XLI

For, first, she springs out of two marble
rocks,
On which a grove of oakes high-mounted
growes,
That as a girlond seemes to deck the locks
Of som faire bride, brought forth with
pompous showes
Out of her bowre, that many flowers strowes:
So, through the flowry dales she tumbling
downe,
Through many woods and shady coverts
flowes
(That on each side her silver channell
crowne)
Till to the plaine she come, whose valleyes
shee doth drowne.

XLII

In her sweet streames Diana used oft
(After her sweatie chace and toilesome play)
To bathe her selfe; and after, on the soft
And downy grasse, her dainty limbes to lay
In covert shade, where none behold her
may:
For much she hated sight of living eye.
Foolish god Faunus, though full many a day
He saw her clad, yet longed foolishly
To see her naked mongst her nymphes in
privity.

XLIII

No way he found to compasse his desire,
But to corrupt Molanna, this her maid,
Her to discover for some secret hire:
So her with flattering words he first assaid;
And after, pleasing gifts for her purvaid,
Queene-apples, and red cherries from the
tree,
With which he her allured and betraid,
To tell what time he might her lady see
When she her selfe did bathe, that he
might secret bee.

XLIV

There-to hee promist, if shee would him
pleasure
With this small boone, to quit her with a
better;
To weet, that where-as shee had out of
measure
Long lov'd the Fanchin, who by nought did
set her,
That he would undertake for this to get her
To be his love, and of him liked well:

Besides all which, he vow'd to be her debter
For many moe good turnes then he would
    tell;
The least of which this little pleasure should
    excell.

XLV

The simple maid did yield to him anone;
And eft him placed where he close might
    view
That never any saw, save onely one,
Who, for his hire to so foole-hardy dew,
Was of his hounds devour'd in hunters hew.
Tho, as her manner was on sunny day,
Diana, with her nymphes about her, drew
To this sweet spring; where, doffing her
    array,
She bath'd her lovely limbes, for Jove a
    likely pray.

XLVI

There Faunus saw that pleased much his
    eye,
And made his hart to tickle in his brest,
That, for great joy of some-what he did
    spy,
He could him not containe in silent rest;
But breaking forth in laughter, loud pro-
    fest
His foolish thought. A foolish Faune in-
    deed,
That couldst not hold thy selfe so hidden
    blest,
But wouldest needs thine owne conceit
    areed !
Babblers unworthy been of so divine a
    meed.

XLVII

The goddesse, all abashed with that noise,
In haste forth started from the guilty
    brooke;
And running straight where-as she heard
    his voice,
Enclos'd the bush about, and there him
    tooke,
Like darred larke, not daring up to looke
On her whose sight before so much he
    sought.
Thence forth they drew him by the hornes,
    and shooke
Nigh all to peeces, that they left him
    nought;
And then into the open light they forth
    him brought.

XLVIII

Like as an huswife, that with busie care
Thinks of her dairie to make wondrous
    gaine,
Finding where-as some wicked beast un-
    ware
That breakes into her dayr' house, there
    doth draine
Her creaming pannes, and frustrate all her
    paine,
Hath, in some snare or gin set close behind,
Entrapped him, and caught into her traine,
Then thinkes what punishment were best
    assign'd,
And thousand deathes deviseth in her venge-
    full mind:

XLIX

So did Diana and her maydens all
Use silly Faunus, now within their baile:
They mocke and scorne him, and him foule
    miscall;
Some by the nose him pluckt, some by the
    taile,
And by his goatish beard some did him haile:
Yet he (poore soule!) with patience all did
    beare;
For nought against their wils might coun-
    tervaile:
Ne ought he said, what ever he did heare;
But hanging downe his head, did like a
    mome appeare.

L

At length, when they had flouted him their
    fill,
They gan to cast what penaunce him to give.
Some would have gelt him, but that same
    would spill
The wood-gods breed, which must for ever
    live:
Others would through the river him have
    drive,
And ducked deepe; but that seem'd pen-
    aunce light:
But most agreed, and did this sentence give,
Him in deares skin to clad, and in that
    plight
To hunt him with their hounds, him selfe
    save how hee might.

LI

But Cynthia's selfe, more angry then the
    rest,
Thought not enough to punish him in sport,

And of her shame to make a gamesome
jest;
But gan examine him in straighter sort,
Which of her nymphes, or other close con-
sort,
Him thither brought, and her to him be-
traid.
He, much affeard, to her confessed short
That 't was Molanna which her so bewraid.
Then all attonce their hands upon Molanna
laid.

LII

But him (according as they had decreed)
With a deeres-skin they covered, and then
chast
With all their hounds, that after him did
speed;
But he, more speedy, from them fled more
fast
Then any deere: so sore him dread aghast.
They after follow'd all with shrill out-
cry,
Shouting as they the heavens would have
brast:
That all the woods and dales, where he did
flie,
Did ring againe, and loud reeccho to the
skie.

LIII

So they him follow'd till they weary were;
When, back returning to Molann' againe,
They, by commaund'ment of Diana, there
Her whelm'd with stones. Yet Faunus
(for her paine)
Of her beloved Fanchin did obtaine,
That her he would receive unto his bed.
So now her waves passe through a pleasant
plaine,
Till with the Fanchin she her selfe doe wed,
And (both combin'd) themselves in one faire
river spred.

LIV

Nath'lesse, Diana, full of indignation,
Thence-forth abandond her delicious brooke;
In whose sweet streame, before that bad
occasion,
So much delight to bathe her limbes she
tooke:
Ne onely her, but also quite forsooke
All those faire forrests about Arlo hid,
And all that mountaine, which doth over-
looke

The richest champian that may else be rid,
And the faire Shure, in which are thousand
salmons bred.

LV

Them all, and all that she so deare did
way,
Thence-forth she left; and parting from the
place,
There-on an heavy haplesse curse did lay,
To weet, that wolves, where she was wont
to space,
Should harbour'd be, and all those woods
deface,
And thieves should rob and spoile that
coast around.
Since which, those woods, and all that
goodly chase,
Doth to this day with wolves and thieves
abound:
Which too-too true that lands in-dwellers
since have found.

CANTO VII

Pealing from Jove to Natur's bar,
Bold Alteration pleades
Large evidence: but Nature soone
Her righteous doome areads.

I

AH! whither doost thou now, thou greater
Muse,
Me from these woods and pleasing forrests
bring?
And my fraile spirit (that dooth oft refuse
This too high flight, unfit for her weake
wing)
Lift up aloft, to tell of heavens king
(Thy soveraine sire) his fortunate successe,
And victory in bigger noates to sing,
Which he obtain'd against that Titanesse,
That him of heavens empire sought to dis-
possesse?

II

Yet sith I needs must follow thy behest,
Doe thou my weaker wit with skill inspire,
Fit for this turne; and in my feeble brest
Kindle fresh sparks of that immortall fire
Which learned minds inflameth with desire
Of heavenly things: for who but thou
alone,
That art yborne of heaven and heavenly
sire,

Can tell things doen in heaven so long
  ygone,
So farre past memory of man that may be
  knowne ?

III

Now, at the time that was before agreed,
The gods assembled all on Arlo hill;
As well those that are sprung of heavenly
  seed,
As those that all the other world doe fill,
And rule both sea and land unto their will:
Onely th' infernall powers might not ap-
  peare;
Aswell for horror of their count'naunce ill,
As for th' unruly fiends which they did
  feare;
Yet Pluto and Proserpina were present
  there.

IV

And thither also came all other creatures,
What-ever life or motion doe retaine,
According to their sundry kinds of fea-
  tures;
That Arlo scarsly could them all containe;
So full they filled every hill and plaine:
And had not Natures sergeant (that is
  Order)
Them well disposed by his busie paine,
And raunged farre abroad in every border,
They would have caused much confusion
  and disorder.

V

Then forth issewed (great goddesse) great
  Dame Nature,
With goodly port and gracious majesty,
Being far greater and more tall of stature
Then any of the gods or powers on hie:
Yet certes by her face and physnomy,
Whether she man or woman inly were,
That could not any creature well descry:
For, with a veile that wimpled every
  where,
Her head and face was hid, that mote to
  none appeare.

VI

That, some doe say, was so by skill devized,
To hide the terror of her uncouth hew
From mortall eyes, that should be sore
  agrized;
For that her face did like a lion shew,
That eye of wight could not indure to view:

But others tell that it so beautious was,
And round about such beames of splendor
  threw,
That it the sunne a thousand times did
  pass,
Ne could be seene, but like an image in a
  glass.

VII

That well may seemen true: for well I
  weene
That this same day, when she on Arlo sat,
Her garment was so bright and wondrous
  sheene,
That my fraile wit cannot devize to what
It to compare, nor finde like stuffe to that:
As those three sacred saints, though else
  most wise,
Yet on Mount Thabor quite their wits for-
  gat,
When they their glorious Lord in strange
  disguise
Transfigur'd sawe; his garments so did daze
  their eyes.

VIII

In a fayre plaine upon an equall hill
She placed was in a pavilion;
Not such as craftes-men by their idle skill
Are wont for princes states to fashion:
But th' Earth her self, of her owne motion,
Out of her fruitfull bosome made to growe
Most dainty trees, that, shooting up anon,
Did seeme to bow their bloosming heads
  full lowe,
For homage unto her, and like a throne did
  shew.

IX

So hard it is for any living wight
All her array and vestiments to tell,
That old Dan Geffrey (in whose gentle
  spright,
The pure well head of poesie did dwell)
In his *Foules Parley* durst not with it mel,
But it transferd to Alane, who he thought
Had in his *Plaint of Kinde* describ'd it well:
Which who will read set forth so as it
  ought,
Go seek he out that Alane where he may
  be sought.

X

And all the earth far underneath her feete
Was dight with flowres, that voluntary grew

Out of the ground, and sent forth odours
　　sweet;
Tenne thousand mores of sundry sent and
　　hew,
That might delight the smell, or please the
　　view;
The which the nymphes from all the brooks
　　thereby
Had gathered, which they at her foot-stoole
　　threw;
That richer seem'd then any tapestry,
That princes bowres adorne with painted
　　imagery.

XI

And Mole himselfe, to honour her the
　　more,
Did deck himself in freshest faire attire,
And his high head, that seemeth alwaies
　　hore
With hardned frosts of former winters ire,
He with an oaken girlond now did tire,
As if the love of some new nymph late
　　seene
Had in him kindled youthfull fresh desire,
And made him change his gray attire to
　　greene:
Ah, gentle Mole! such joyance hath thee
　　well beseene.

XII

Was never so great joyance since the day
That all the gods whylome assembled were
On Hæmus hill in their divine array,
To celebrate the solemne bridall cheare
Twixt Peleus and Dame Thetis pointed
　　there;
Where Phœbus self, that god of poets
　　hight,
They say did sing the spousall hymne full
　　cleere,
That all the gods were ravisht with de-
　　light
Of his celestiall song, and musicks won-
　　drous might.

XIII

This great grandmother of all creatures
　　bred,
Great Nature, ever young yet full of eld,
Still mooving, yet unmoved from her sted,
Unseene of any, yet of all beheld,
Thus sitting in her throne, as I have teld,
Before her came Dame Mutabilitie;
And being lowe before her presence feld,

With meek obaysance and humilitie,
Thus gan her plaintif plea, with words to
　　amplifie:

XIV

'To thee, O greatest goddesse, onely great,
An humble suppliant loe! I lowely fly,
Seeking for right, which I of thee entreat,
Who right to all dost deale indifferently,
Damning all wrong and tortious injurie,
Which any of thy creatures doe to other
(Oppressing them with power, unequally)
Sith of them all thou art the equall mother,
And knittest each to each, as brother unto
　　brother.

XV

'To thee therefore of this same Jove I
　　plaine,
And of his fellow gods that faine to be,
That challenge to themselves the whole
　　worlds raign;
Of which the greatest part is due to me,
And heaven it selfe by heritage in fee:
For heaven and earth I both alike do
　　deeme,
Sith heaven and earth are both alike to
　　thee;
And gods no more then men thou doest
　　esteeme:
For even the gods to thee, as men to gods,
　　do seeme.

XVI

'Then weigh, O soveraigne goddesse, by
　　what right
These gods do claime the worlds whole
　　soverainty,
And that is onely dew unto thy might
Arrogate to themselves ambitiously:
As for the gods owne principality,
Which Jove usurpes unjustly, that to be
My heritage, Jove's self cannot deny,
From my great grandsire Titan unto mee
Deriv'd by dew descent; as is well knowen
　　to thee.

XVII

'Yet mauger Jove, and all his gods beside,
I doe possesse the worlds most regiment;
As, if ye please it into parts divide,
And every parts inholders to convent,
Shall to your eyes appeare incontinent,
And first, the Earth (great mother of us all)
That only seems unmov'd and permanent,

And unto Mutability not thrall,
Yet is she chang'd in part, and eeke in
generall.

XVIII

'For all that from her springs, and is
ybredde,
How-ever fayre it flourish for a time,
Yet see we soone decay; and, being dead,
To turne again unto their earthly slime:
Yet, out of their decay and mortall crime,
We daily see new creatures to arize,
And of their winter spring another prime,
Unlike in forme, and chang'd by strange
disguise;
So turne they still about, and change in
restlesse wise.

XIX

'As for her tenants, that is, man and beasts,
The beasts we daily see massacred dy,
As thralls and vassals unto mens beheasts:
And men themselves doe change continually,
From youth to eld, from wealth to poverty,
From good to bad, from bad to worst of all:
Ne doe their bodies only flit and fly;
But eeke their minds (which they immortall
call)
Still change and vary thoughts, as new oc-
casions fall.

XX

'Ne is the water in more constant case;
Whether those same on high, or these be-
lowe.
For th' ocean moveth stil from place to place;
And every river still doth ebbe and flowe:
Ne any lake, that seems most still and slowe,
Ne poole so small, that can his smoothnesse
holde,
When any winde doth under heaven blowe;
With which the clouds are also tost and
roll'd;
Now like great hills; and streight, like
sluces, them unfold.

XXI

'So likewise are all watry living wights
Still tost and turned with continuall change,
Never abyding in their stedfast plights.
The fish, still floting, doe at randon range,
And never rest, but evermore exchange
Their dwelling places, as the streames them
carrie:
Ne have the watry foules a certaine grange

Wherein to rest, ne in one stead do tarry;
But flitting still doe flie, and still their
places vary.

XXII

'Next is the ayre: which who feeles not
by sense
(For of all sense it is the middle meane)
To flit still? and, with subtill influence
Of his thin spirit, all creatures to main-
taine
In state of life? O weake life! that does
leane
On thing so tickle as th' unsteady ayre;
Which every howre is chang'd, and altred
cleane
With every blast that bloweth fowle or
faire:
The faire doth it prolong; the fowle doth
it impaire.

XXIII

'Therein the changes infinite beholde,
Which to her creatures every minute
chaunce:
Now, boyling hot: streight, friezing deadly
cold:
Now, faire sun-shine, that makes all skip
and daunce:
Streight, bitter storms and balefull countenance,
That makes them all to shiver and to
shake:
Rayne, hayle, and snowe do pay them sad
penance,
And dreadfull thunder-claps (that make
them quake)
With flames and flashing lights that thousand changes make.

XXIV

'Last is the fire: which, though it live for
ever,
Ne can be quenched quite, yet, every day,
Wee see his parts, so soone as they do
sever,
To lose their heat, and shortly to decay;
So makes himself his owne consuming
pray.
Ne any living creatures doth he breed:
But all that are of others bredd doth slay,
And with their death his cruell life dooth
feed;
Nought leaving, but their barren ashes,
without seed.

XXV

'Thus all these fower (the which the
    ground-work bee
Of all the world, and of all living wights)
To thousand sorts of change we subject
    see:
Yet are they chang'd (by other wondrous
    slights)
Into themselves, and lose their native
    mights:
The fire to aire, and th' ayre to water
    sheere,
And water into earth: yet water fights
With fire, and aire with earth, approaching
    neere:
Yet all are in one body, and as one ap-
    peare.

XXVI

'So in them all raignes Mutabilitie;
How-ever these, that gods themselves do
    call,
Of them doe claime the rule and sover-
    ainty:
As Vesta, of the fire æthereall;
Vulcan, of this, with us so usuall;
Ops, of the earth; and Juno, of the ayre;
Neptune, of seas; and nymphes, of rivers
    all:
For all those rivers to me subject are;
And all the rest, which they usurp, be all
    my share.

XXVII

'Which to approven true, as I have told,
Vouchsafe, O goddesse, to thy presence call
The rest which doe the world in being
    hold:
As times and seasons of the yeare that
    fall:
Of all the which demand in generall,
Or judge thy selfe, by verdit of thine eye,
Whether to me they are not subject all.'
Nature did yeeld thereto; and by-and-by,
Bade Order call them all before her
    majesty.

XXVIII

So forth issew'd the seasons of the yeare:
First, lusty Spring, all dight in leaves of
    flowres
That freshly budded and new bloosms did
    beare
(In which a thousand birds had built their
    bowres.

That sweetly sung, to call forth paramours):
And in his hand a javelin he did beare,
And on his head (as fit for warlike stoures)
A guilt engraven morion he did weare;
That, as some did him love, so others did
    him feare.

XXIX

Then came the jolly Sommer, being dight
In a thin silken cassock coloured greene,
That was unlyned all, to be more light:
And on his head a girlond well beseene
He wore, from which, as he had chauffed
    been,
The sweat did drop; and in his hand he bore
A boawe and shaftes, as he in forrest greene
Had hunted late the libbard or the bore,
And now would bathe his limbes, with labor
    heated sore.

XXX

Then came the Autumne, all in yellow clad,
As though he joyed in his plentious store,
Laden with fruits that made him laugh, full
    glad
That he had banisht hunger, which to-fore
Had by the belly oft him pinched sore.
Upon his head a wreath, that was enrold
With eares of corne of every sort, he bore:
And in his hand a sickle he did holde,
To reape the ripened fruits the which the
    earth had yold.

XXXI

Lastly came Winter, cloathed all in frize,
Chattering his teeth for cold that did him
    chill,
Whil'st on his hoary beard his breath did
    freese,
And the dull drops, that from his purpled
    bill
As from a limbeck did adown distill.
In his right hand a tipped staffe he held,
With which his feeble steps he stayed still:
For he was faint with cold, and weak with
    eld;
That scarse his loosed limbes he hable was
    to weld.

XXXII

These, marching softly, thus in order went,
And after them the monthes all riding
    came:
First, sturdy March, with brows full sternly
    bent,

And armed strongly, rode upon a ram,
The same which over Hellespontus swam:
Yet in his hand a spade he also hent,
And in a bag all sorts of seeds ysame,
Which on the earth he strowed as he went,
And fild her womb with fruitfull hope of
nourishment.

XXXIII

Next came fresh Aprill, full of lustyhed,
And wanton as a kid whose horne new buds:
Upon a bull he rode, the same which led
Europa floting through th' Argolick fluds:
His hornes were gilden all with golden
studs,
And garnished with garlonds goodly dight
Of all the fairest flowres and freshest buds
Which th' earth brings forth, and wet he
seem'd in sight
With waves, through which he waded for
his loves delight.

XXXIV

Then came faire May, the fayrest mayd on
ground,
Deckt all with dainties of her seasons pryde,
And throwing flowres out of her lap around:
Upon two brethrens shoulders she did ride,
The twinnes of Leda; which on eyther side
Supported her like to their soveraine queene.
Lord! how all creatures laught, when her
they spide,
And leapt and daunc't as they had ravisht
beene!
And Cupid selfe about her fluttred all in
greene.

XXXV

And after her came jolly June, arrayd
All in greene leaves, as he a player were;
Yet in his time he wrought as well as playd,
That by his plough-yrons mote right well
appeare:
Upon a crab he rode, that him did beare
With crooked crawling steps an uncouth
pase,
And backward yode, as bargemen wont to
fare
Bending their force contrary to their face,
Like that ungracious crew which faines de-
murest grace.

XXXVI

Then came hot July boyling like to fire
That all his garments he had cast away:

Upon a lyon raging yet with ire
He boldly rode, and made him to obay:
It was the beast that whylome did forray
The Nemæan forrest, till th' Amphytrionide
Him slew, and with his hide did him array:
Behinde his back a sithe, and by his side
Under his belt he bore a sickle circling wide.

XXXVII

The sixt was August, being rich arrayd
In garment all of gold downe to the ground:
Yet rode he not, but led a lovely mayd
Forth by the lilly hand, the which was
cround
With eares of corne, and full her hand was
found:
That was the righteous virgin which of old
Liv'd here on earth, and plenty made
abound;
But, after wrong was lov'd and justice solde,
She left th' unrighteous world and was to
heaven extold.

XXXVIII

Next him September marched eeke on foote;
Yet was he heavy laden with the spoyle
Of harvests riches, which he made his boot,
And him enricht with bounty of the soyle:
In his one hand, as fit for harvests toyle,
He held a knife-hook; and in th' other hand
A paire of waights, with which he did as-
soyle
Both more and lesse, where it in doubt did
stand,
And equall gave to each as justice duly
scann'd.

XXXIX

Then came October full of merry glee:
For yet his noule was totty of the must,
Which he was treading in the wine-fats
see,
And of the joyous oyle, whose gentle gust
Made him so frollick and so full of lust:
Upon a dreadfull scorpion he did ride,
The same which by Dianaes doom unjust
Slew great Orion: and eeke by his side
He had his ploughing-share and coulter
ready tyde.

XL

Next was November; he full grosse and
fat,
As fed with lard, and that right well might
seeme:

For he had been a fatting hogs of late,
That yet his browes with sweat did reek
    and steem,
And yet the season was full sharp and
    breem;
In planting eeke he took no small delight.
Whereon he rode, not easie was to deeme;
For it a dreadfull centaure was in sight,
The seed of Saturne and faire Nais, Chiron
    hight.

XLI

And after him came next the chill Decem-
    ber:
Yet he, through merry feasting which he
    made,
And great bonfires, did not the cold remem-
    ber;
His Saviours birth his mind so much did
    glad:
Upon a shaggy-bearded goat he rade,
The same wherewith Dan Jove in tender
    yeares,
They say, was nourisht by th' Idæan mayd;
And in his hand a broad deepe boawle he
    beares,
Of which he freely drinks an health to all
    his peeres.

XLII

Then came old January, wrapped well
In many weeds to keep the cold away;
Yet did he quake and quiver like to quell,
And blowe his nayles to warme them if he
    may:
For they were numbd with holding all the
    day
An hatchet keene, with which he felled
    wood,
And from the trees did lop the needlesse
    spray:
Upon an huge great earth-pot steane he
    stood,
From whose wide mouth there flowed forth
    the Romane floud.

XLIII

And lastly came cold February, sitting
In an old wagon, for he could not ride;
Drawne of two fishes for the season fitting,
Which through the flood before did softly
    slyde
And swim away: yet had he by his side
His plough and harnesse fit to till the
    ground,

And tooles to prune the trees, before the
    pride
Of hasting Prime did make them burgein
    round.
So past the twelve months forth, and their
    dew places found.

XLIV

And after these there came the Day and
    Night,
Riding together both with equall pase,
Th' one on a palfrey blacke, the other
    white:
But Night had covered her uncomely face
With a blacke veile, and held in hand a
    mace,
On top whereof the moon and stars were
    pight,
And Sleep and Darknesse round about did
    trace:
But Day did beare, upon his scepters hight,
The goodly sun, encompast all with beames
    bright.

XLV

Then came the Howres, faire daughters of
    high Jove
And timely Night, the which were all en-
    dewed
With wondrous beauty fit to kindle love;
But they were virgins all, and love es-
    chewed,
That might forslack the charge to them
    fore-shewed
By mighty Jove; who did them porters
    make
Of heavens gate (whence all the gods is-
    sued)
Which they did dayly watch, and nightly
    wake
By even turnes, ne ever did their charge
    forsake.

XLVI

And after all came Life, and lastly Death:
Death with most grim and griesly visage
    seene,
Yet is he nought but parting of the breath;
Ne ought to see, but like a shade to weene,
Unbodied, unsoul'd, unheard, unseene:
But Life was like a faire young lusty boy,
Such as they faine Dan Cupid to have beene,
Full of delightfull health and lively joy,
Deckt all with flowres, and wings of gold
    fit to employ.

XLVII

When these were past, thus gan the Titan-
   esse:
'Lo! mighty mother, now be judge, and
   say
Whether in all thy creatures more or lesse
Change doth not raign and beare the great-
   est sway:
For who sees not that Time on all doth
   pray?
But times do change and move continually:
So nothing here long standeth in one stay:
Wherefore, this lower world who can deny
But to be subject still to Mutabilitie?'

XLVIII

Then thus gan Jove: 'Right true it is, that
   these,
And all things else that under heaven dwell,
Are chaung'd of Time, who doth them all
   disseise
Of being: but who is it (to me tell)
That Time himselfe doth move and still
   compell
To keepe his course? Is not that namely
   wee,
Which poure that vertue from our heavenly
   cell
That moves them all, and makes them
   changed be?
So them we gods doe rule, and in them also
   thee.'

XLIX

To whom thus Mutability: 'The things
Which we see not how they are mov'd and
   swayd
Ye may attribute to your selves as kings,
And say they by your secret powre are
   made:
But what we see not, who shall us per-
   swade?
But were they so, as ye them faine to be,
Mov'd by your might, and ordred by your
   ayde;
Yet what if I can prove, that even yee
Your selves are likewise chang'd, and sub-
   ject unto mee?

L

'And first, concerning her that is the first,
Even you, faire Cynthia, whom so much ye
   make
Joves dearest darling; she was bred and
   nurst

On Cynthus hill, whence she her name did
   take:
Then is she mortall borne, how-so ye crake;
Besides, her face and countenance every
   day
We changed see, and sundry forms partake,
Now hornd, now round, now bright, now
   brown and gray;
So that *as changefull as the moone* men use
   to say.

LI

'Next Mercury, who though he lesse ap-
   peare
To change his hew, and alwayes seeme as
   one,
Yet he his course doth altar every yeare,
And is of late far out of order gone:
So Venus eeke, that goodly paragone,
Though faire all night, yet is she darke all
   day;
And Phœbus self, who lightsome is alone,
Yet is he oft eclipsed by the way,
And fills the darkned world with terror
   and dismay.

LII

'Now Mars, that valiant man, is changed
   most:
For he some times so far runs out of square,
That he his way doth seem quite to have
   lost,
And cleane without his usuall sphere to
   fare;
That even these star-gazers stonisht are
At sight thereof, and damne their lying
   bookes:
So likewise grim Sir Saturne oft doth spare
His sterne aspect, and calme his crabbed
   lookes:
So many turning cranks these have, so
   many crookes.

LIII

'But you, Dan Jove, that only constant are,
And king of all the rest, as ye do clame,
Are you not subject eeke to this misfare?
Then let me aske you this withouten blame:
Where were ye borne? Some say in Crete
   by name,
Others in Thebes, and others other-where;
But wheresoever they comment the same,
They all consent that ye begotten were
And borne here in this world, ne other can
   appeare.

LIV

'Then are ye mortall borne, and thrall to
    me,
Unlesse the kingdome of the sky yee make
Immortall and unchangeable to be:
Besides, that power and vertue which ye
    spake,
That ye here worke, doth many changes
    take,
And your owne natures change: for each
    of you,
That vertue have, or this or that to make,
Is checkt and changed from his nature trew,
By others opposition or obliquid view.

LV

'Besides, the sundry motions of your
    spheares,
So sundry waies and fashions as clerkes
    faine,
Some in short space, and some in longer
    yeares;
What is the same but alteration plaine?
Onely the starrie skie doth still remaine:
Yet do the starres and signes therein still
    move,
And even it self is mov'd, as wizards saine.
But all that moveth doth mutation love:
Therefore both you and them to me I sub-
    ject prove.

LVI

'Then since within this wide great uni-
    verse
Nothing doth firme and permanent appeare,
But all things tost and turned by trans-
    verse:
What then should let, but I aloft should
    reare
My trophee, and from all the triumph
    beare?
Now judge then (O thou greatest god-
    desse trew!)
According as thy selfe doest see and heare,
And unto me addoom that is my dew;
That is the rule of all, all being rul'd by
    you.'

LVII

So having ended, silence long ensewed;
Ne Nature to or fro spake for a space,
But, with firme eyes affixt, the ground still
    viewed.
Meane while, all creatures, looking in her
    face,

Expecting th' end of this so doubtfull case,
Did hang in long suspence what would en-
    sew,
To whether side should fall the soveraigne
    place:
At length, she, looking up with chearefull
    view,
The silence brake, and gave her doome in
    speeches few:

LVIII

'I well consider all that ye have sayd,
And find that all things stedfastnes doe hate
And changed be: yet being rightly wayd,
They are not changed from their first
    estate;
But by their change their being doe dilate:
And turning to themselves at length
    againe,
Doe worke their owne perfection so by fate:
Then over them Change doth not rule and
    raigne;
But they raigne over Change, and doe
    their states maintaine.

LIX

'Cease therefore, daughter, further to
    aspire,
And thee content thus to be rul'd by me:
For thy decay thou seekst by thy desire:
But time shall come that all shall changed
    bee,
And from thenceforth none no more
    change shall see.'
So was the Titaness put downe and whist,
And Jove confirm'd in his imperiall see.
Then was that whole assembly quite dis-
    mist,
And Natur's selfe did vanish, whither no
    man wist.

THE VIII. CANTO, UNPERFITE

I

When I bethinke me on that speech whyl-
    eare
Of Mutability, and well it way,
Me seemes, that though she all unworthy
    were
Of the heav'ns rule, yet, very sooth to say,
In all things else she beares the greatest
    sway:
Which makes me loath this state of life so
    tickle,

And love of things so vaine to cast away;
Whose flowring pride, so fading and so
fickle,
Short Time shall soon cut down with his
consuming sickle.

II

Then gin I thinke on that which Nature
sayd,
Of that same time when no more change
shall be,

But stedfast rest of all things, firmely
stayd
Upon the pillours of eternity,
That is contrayr to Mutabilitie:
For all that moveth doth in change de-
light:
But thence-forth all shall rest eternally
With Him that is the God of Sabbaoth
hight:
O that great Sabbaoth God graunt me that
Sabaoths sight !

DAPHNAÏDA

AN ELEGIE UPON THE DEATH OF THE NOBLE AND VERTUOUS
DOUGLAS HOWARD, DAUGHTER AND HEIRE OF HENRY
LORD HOWARD, VISCOUNT BYNDON, AND WIFE
OF ARTHURE GORGES ESQUIER

DEDICATED TO THE RIGHT HONORABLE THE LADY HELENA,
MARQUESSE OF NORTHAMPTON

BY ED. SP.

AT LONDON
PRINTED FOR WILLIAM PONSONBY, DWELLING IN PAULES CHURCHYARD AT THE
SIGNE OF THE BISHOPS HEAD
1591

TO THE RIGHT HONORABLE AND VERTUOUS LADY HELENA MAR-
QUESSE OF NORTH-HAMPTON

I HAVE the rather presumed humbly to offer unto your Honour the dedication of this little poëme, for that the noble and vertuous gentlewoman of whom it is written was by match neere alied, and in affection greatly devoted unto your Ladiship. The occasion why I wrote the same was aswell the great good fame which I heard of her deceassed, as the particular goodwill which I beare unto her husband Master Arthur Gorges, a lover of learning and vertue, whose house, as your Ladiship by mariage hath honoured, so doe I find the name of them by many notable records, to be of great antiquitie in this realme, and such as have ever borne themselves with honourable rep-utation to the world, and unspotted loyal-tie to their prince and countrey: besides,

so lineally are they descended from the Howards, as that the Lady Anne Howard, eldest daughter to John Duke of Norfolke, was wife to Sir Edmund, mother to Sir Edward, and grandmother to Sir William and Sir Thomas Gorges, Knightes. And therefore I doe assure my selfe that no due honour done to the White Lyon, but will be most gratefull to your Ladiship, whose husband and children do so neerely participate with the bloud of that noble family. So in all dutie I recommende this pamphlet, and the good acceptance thereof, to your honourable favour and protection. London, this first of Januarie, 1591.

Your Honours humbly ever,
Ed. Sp.

[According to the usage of the sixteenth century in England, ' this first of Januarie, 1591,' subscribed to the dedicatory letter of *Daphnaïda*, would read in modern style, 1592; for the civil year did not begin till March 25. The compiler of a calendar might head his list of the months with January, for that was by long tradition the leader of the astronomical year; but a writer of letters would date according to the civil year. Yet it seems most unlikely that Spenser should have been in London in January, 1592. The patent for his pension, one main cause apparently of his long abode in England, had been finally issued in the preceding February; the preface of *Complaints* refers to him as already departed over sea, and since that volume was entered upon the Stationers' Register in December, 1590, it is likely to have been issued not more than a few months later; finally, the dedication of *Colin Clout's Come Home Again* is dated from Kilcolman ' the 27 of December, 1591 ' — only five days before ' this first of Januarie,' 1592. That particular clash of dates, to be sure, has been explained by a recent critic on the supposition that *Colin Clout's Come Home Again* celebrates before the fact a merely prospective return to Ireland, that, in other words, it was written in England and dated from Kilcolman only by way of fiction. On the whole, however, one can more easily believe that in dating the dedication of *Daphnaïda* Spenser followed the Continental usage, or that he or the printer blundered, that, in either case, the date is meant for New Year's, 1591, modern style, — especially since the lady whose death the poem records died in August, 1590.

Daphnaïda cannot pretend to greatness, yet few of Spenser's poems are more thoroughly characteristic. Conventional in mode, with hardly a note of full imaginative conviction, it is quietly and unfailingly harmonious. Its stanza, in which, by mere transposition of a line, he creates out of the orthodox rhyme royal a form of haunting cadence, almost as beautiful as the stanza of ' October,' would alone raise it high above the perfunctory.]

DAPHNAÏDA

WHAT ever man he be, whose heavie minde,
With griefe of mournefull great mishap opprest,
Fit matter for his cares increase would finde:
Let reade the rufull plaint herein exprest
Of one (I weene) the wofulst man alive,
Even sad Alcyon, whose empierced brest
Sharpe sorrowe did in thousand peeces rive.

But who so else in pleasure findeth sense,
Or in this wretched life dooth take delight,
Let him be banisht farre away from hence: 10
Ne let the Sacred Sisters here be hight,
Though they of sorrowe heavilie can sing;
For even their heavie song would breede delight:
But here no tunes, save sobs and grones, shall ring.

In stead of them and their sweet harmonie,
Let those three Fatall Sisters, whose sad hands
Doo weave the direfull threds of destinie,
And in their wrath breake off the vitall bands,
Approach hereto: and let the dreadfull queene
Of darkenes deepe come from the Stygian strands, 20
And grisly ghosts, to heare this dolefull teene.

In gloomie evening, when the wearie sun
After his dayes long labour drew to rest,
And sweatie steedes, now having over-run
The compast skie, gan water in the west,
I walkt abroade to breath the freshing ayre
In open fields, whose flowring pride, opprest
With early frosts, had lost their beautie faire.

There came unto my minde a troublous thought,
Which dayly dooth my weaker wit possesse, 30
Ne lets it rest, untill it forth have brought
Her long borne infant, fruit of heavinesse,
Which she conceived hath through meditation
Of this worlds vainnesse and lifes wretchednesse,
That yet my soule it deepely doth empassion.

So as I muzed on the miserie
In which men live, and I of many most,
Most miserable man, I did espie
Where towards me a sory wight did cost,
Clad all in black, that mourning did bewray, 40
And Jaakob staffe in hand devoutly crost,
Like to some pilgrim come from farre away.

His carelesse locks, uncombed and unshorne,
Hong long adowne, and bearde all over-
    growne,
That well he seemd to be sum wight for-
    lorne:
Downe to the earth his heavie eyes were
    throwne
As loathing light; and ever as he went,
He sighed soft, and inly deepe did grone,
As if his heart in peeces would have rent.

Approaching nigh, his face I vewed nere, 50
And by the semblant of his countenance
Me seemd I had his person seene elsewhere,
Most like Alcyon seeming at a glaunce;
Alcyon he, the jollie shepheard swaine,
That wont full merrilie to pipe and daunce,
And fill with pleasance every wood and
    plaine.

Yet halfe in doubt because of his disguize,
I softlie sayd, 'Alcyon!' Therewithall
He lookt aside as in disdainefull wise,
Yet stayed not: till I againe did call. 60
Then turning back, he saide with hollow
    sound,
'Who is it that dooth name me, wofull
    thrall,
The wretchedst man that treades this day
    on ground?'

'One whome like wofulnesse, impressed
    deepe,
Hath made fit mate thy wretched case to
    heare,
And given like cause with thee to waile and
    weepe:
Griefe findes some ease by him that like
    does beare.
Then stay, Alcyon, gentle shepheard, stay,'
Quoth I, 'till thou have to my trustie eare
Committed what thee dooth so ill apay.' 70

'Cease, foolish man,' saide he halfe wroth-
    fully,
'To seeke to heare that which cannot be
    told:
For the huge anguish, which dooth multiply
My dying paines, no tongue can well unfold:
Ne doo I care that any should bemone
My hard mishap, or any weepe that would,
But seeke alone to weepe, and dye alone.'

'Then be it so,' quoth I, 'that thou art bent
To die alone, unpitied, unplained;

Yet ere thou die, it were convenient 80
To tell the cause which thee theretoo con-
    strained,
Least that the world thee dead accuse of
    guilt,
And say, when thou of none shalt be main-
    tained,
That thou for secret crime thy blood hast
    spilt.'

'Who life dooes loath, and longs to bee
    unbound
From the strong shackles of fraile flesh,'
    quoth he,
'Nought cares at all what they that live on
    ground
Deeme the occasion of his death to bee:
Rather desires to be forgotten quight,
Than question made of his calamitie; 90
For harts deep sorrow hates both life and
    light.

'Yet since so much thou seemst to rue my
    griefe,
And carest for one that for himselfe cares
    nought,
(Signe of thy love, though nought for my
    reliefe:
For my reliefe exceedeth living thought,)
I will to thee this heavie case relate.
Then harken well till it to ende be brought,
For never didst thou heare more haplesse
    fate.

'Whilome I usde (as thou right well doest
    know)
My little flocke on westerne downes to
    keepe, 100
Not far from whence Sabrinaes streame
    doth flow,
And flowrie bancks with silver liquor steepe:
Nought carde I then for worldly change or
    chaunce,
For all my joy was on my gentle sheepe,
And to my pype to caroll and to daunce.

'It there befell, as I the fields did range
Fearelesse and free, a faire young Lionesse,
White as the native rose before the chaunge
Which Venus blood did in her leaves im-
    presse,
I spied playing on the grassie playne 110
Her youthfull sports and kindlie wanton-
    nesse,
That did all other beasts in beawtie staine.

'Much was I moved at so goodly sight,
Whose like before mine eye had seldome
    seene,
And gan to cast how I her compasse might,
And bring to hand, that yet had never beene:
So well I wrought with mildnes and with
    paine,
That I her caught disporting on the grene,
And brought away fast bound with silver
    chaine.

'And afterwards I handled her so fayre, 120
That though by kind shee stout and salvage
    were,
For being borne an auncient lions haire,
And of the race that all wild beastes do feare,
Yet I her fram'd and wan so to my bent,
That shee became so meeke and milde of
    cheare
As the least lamb in all my flock that went.

'For shee in field, where ever I did wend,
Would wend with me, and waite by me all
    day:
And all the night that I in watch did spend,
If cause requir'd, or els in sleepe, if nay, 130
Shee would all night by mee or watch or
    sleepe;
And evermore when I did sleepe or play,
She of my flock would take full warie keepe.

'Safe then and safest were my sillie sheepe,
Ne fear'd the wolfe, ne fear'd the wildest
    beast,
All were I drown'd in carelesse quiet deepe:
My lovelie Lionesse without beheast
So carefull was for them and for my good,
That when I waked, neither most nor least
I found miscaried or in plaine or wood. 140

'Oft did the shepheards, which my hap did
    heare,
And oft their lasses, which my luck envide,
Daylie resort to me from farre and neare,
To see my Lyonesse, whose praises wide
Were spred abroad; and when her worth-
    inesse
Much greater than the rude report they
    tri'de,
They her did praise, and my good fortune
    blesse.

'Long thus I joyed in my happinesse,
And well did hope my joy would have no
    end:

But oh! fond man! that in worlds fickle-
    nesse 150
Reposedst hope, or weenedst her thy frend
That glories most in mortall miseries,
And daylie doth her changefull counsels
    bend,
To make new matter fit for tragedies!

'For whilest I was thus without dread or
    dout,
A cruell Satyre with his murdrous dart,
Greedie of mischiefe, ranging all about,
Gave her the fatall wound of deadly smart,
And reft fro me my sweete companion,
And reft fro me my love, my life, my hart:
My Lyonesse (ah, woe is mee!) is gon. 161

'Out of the world thus was she reft awaie,
Out of the world, unworthie such a spoyle;
And borne to heaven, for heaven a fitter pray;
Much fitter than the lyon which with toyle
Alcides slew, and fixt in firmament:
Her now I seek throughout this earthlie
    soyle,
And seeking misse, and missing doe lament.'

Therewith he gan afresh to waile and weepe,
That I for pittie of his heavie plight 170
Could not abstaine mine eyes with teares to
    steepe:
But when I saw the anguish of his spright
Some deale alaid, I him bespake againe:
'Certes, Alcyon, painfull is thy plight,
That it in me breeds almost equall paine.

'Yet doth not my dull wit well understand
The riddle of thy loved Lionesse;
For rare it seemes in reason to be skand,
That man, who doth the whole worlds rule
    possesse,
Should to a beast his noble hart embase, 180
And be the vassall of his vassalesse:
Therefore more plaine aread this doubtfull
    case.'

Then sighing sore, 'Daphne thou knewest,'
    quoth he;
'She now is dead': ne more endured to say,
But fell to ground for great extreamitie;
That I, beholding it, with deepe dismay
Was much appald, and lightly him uprear-
    ing,
Revoked life, that would have fled away,
All were my self through griefe in deadly
    drearing.

Then gan I him to comfort all my best, 190
And with milde counsaile strove to mitigate
The stormie passion of his troubled brest:
But he thereby was more empassionate;
As stubborne steed, that is with curb re-
    strained,
Becomes more fierce and fervent in his gate;
And breaking foorth at last, thus dearnelie
    plained.

I

' What man henceforth, that breatheth vi-
    tall ayre,
Will honour Heaven, or heavenlie powers
    adore,
Which so unjustlie doe their judgments
    share   199
Mongst earthly wights, as to afflict so sore
The innocent as those which do transgresse,
And do not spare the best or fairest more
Than worst or fowlest, but doe both op-
    presse ?

' If this be right, why did they then create
The world so fayre, sith fairenesse is
    neglected ?
Or whie be they themselves immaculate,
If purest things be not by them respected ?
She faire, shee pure, most faire, most pure
    she was,
Yet was by them as thing impure rejected:
Yet shee in purenesse heaven it selfe did pas.

' In pureness and in all celestiall grace, 211
That men admire in goodlie womankinde,
She did excell, and seem'd of angels race,
Living on earth like angell new divinde,
Adorn'd with wisedome and with chastitie,
And all the dowries of a noble mind,
Which did her beautie much more beautifie.

' No age hath bred (since fayre Astræa left
The sinfull world) more vertue in a wight,
And when she parted hence, with her she
    reft   220
Great hope, and robd her race of bountie
    quight:
Well may the shepheard lasses now lament,
For dubble losse by her hath on them light,
To loose both her and bounties ornament.

' Ne let Elisa, royall shepheardesse,
The praises of my parted love envy,
For she hath praises in all plenteousnesse
Powr'd upon her, like showers of Castaly.

By her own shepheard, Colin her owne
    shepherd,   229
That her with heavenly hymnes doth deifie,
Of rusticke muse full hardly to be betterd.

' She is the rose, the glorie of the day,
And mine the primrose in the lowly shade:
Mine ? ah, not mine ! amisse I mine did say:
Not mine, but His which mine awhile her
    made:
Mine to be His, with Him to live for ay.
O that so faire a flower so soone should fade,
And through untimely tempest fall away !

' She fell away in her first ages spring,
Whil'st yet her leafe was greene, and fresh
    her rinde,   240
And whil'st her braunch faire blossomes
    foorth did bring,
She fell away against all course of kinde:
For age to dye is right, but youth is wrong;
She fel away like fruit blowne downe with
    winde:
Weepe, shepheard, weepe, to make my un-
    dersong.

II

' What hart so stony hard, but that would
    weepe,
And poure foorth fountaines of incessant
    teares ?
What Timon, but would let compassion
    creepe
Into his brest, and pierce his frosen eares ?
In stead of teares, whose brackish bitter
    well   250
I wasted have, my heart blood dropping
    weares,
To thinke to ground how that faire blossome
    fell.

' Yet fell she not as one enforst to dye,
Ne dyde with dread and grudging discon-
    tent,
But as one toyld with travaile downe doth
    lye,
So lay she downe, as if to sleepe she went,
And closde her eyes with carelesse quiet-
    nesse;
The whiles soft death away her spirit hent,
And soule assoyld from sinfull fleshlinesse.

' Yet ere that life her lodging did forsake,
She, all resolv'd and ready to remove,   261
Calling to me (ay me !) this wise bespake:

" Alcyon ! ah, my first and latest love !
Ah ! why does my Alcyon weepe and
   mourne,
And grieve my ghost, that ill mote him be-
   hove,
As if to me had chanst some evill tourne ?

' " I, since the messenger is come for mee
That summons soules unto the bridale feast
Of his great Lord, must needes depart from
   thee,
And straight obay his soveraine beheast: 270
Why should Alcyon then so sore lament
That I from miserie shall be releast,
And freed from wretched long imprison-
   ment ?

' " Our daies are full of dolor and disease,
Our life afflicted with incessant paine,
That nought on earth may lessen or appease.
Why then should I desire here to remaine ?
Or why should he that loves me, sorie bee
For my deliverance, or at all complaine
My good to heare, and toward joyes to
   see ?   280

' " I goe, and long desired have to goe,
I goe with gladnesse to my wished rest,
Whereas no worlds sad care, nor wasting
   woe,
May come their happie quiet to molest,
But saints and angels in celestiall thrones
Eternally Him praise that hath them blest;
There shall I be amongst those blessed ones.

' " Yet ere I goe, a pledge I leave with thee
Of the late love, the which betwixt us
   past,
My young Ambrosia; in lieu of mee   290
Love her: so shall our love for ever last.
Thus, deare, adieu ! whom I expect ere
   long."
So having said, away she softly past;
Weepe, shepheard, weepe, to make mine
   undersong.

III

' So oft as I record those piercing words,
Which yet are deepe engraven in my brest,
And those last deadly accents, which like
   swords
Did wound my heart and rend my bleeding
   chest,
With those sweet sugred speaches doo com-
   pare

The which my soule first conquerd and
   possest,   300
The first beginners of my endlesse care;

' And when those pallid cheekes and ashy
   hew,
In which sad Death his pourtraicture had
   writ,
And when those hollow eyes and deadly
   view,
On which the clowde of ghastly night did
   sit,
I match with that sweet smile and chear-
   full brow,
Which all the world subdued unto it;
How happie was I then, and wretched now !

' How happie was I, when I saw her leade
The shepheards daughters dauncing in a
   rownd !   310
How trimly would she trace and softly
   tread
The tender grasse, with rosie garland
   crownd !
And when she list advance her heavenly
   voyce,
Both Nimphs and Muses nigh she made
   astownd,
And flocks and shepheards caused to rejoyce.

' But now, ye shepheard lasses, who shall
   lead
Your wandring troupes, or sing your vire-
   layes ?
Or who shall dight your bowres, sith she is
   dead
That was the lady of your holy dayes ?
Let now your blisse be turned into bale, 320
And into plaints convert your joyous playes,
And with the same fill every hill and dale.

' Let bagpipe never more be heard to shrill,
That may allure the senses to delight;
Ne ever shepheard sound his oaten quill
Unto the many, that provoke them might
To idle pleasance: but let ghastlinesse
And drery horror dim the chearfull light,
To make the image of true heavinesse.

' Let birds be silent on the naked spray, 330
And shady woods resound with dreadfull
   yells;
Let streaming floods their hastie courses
   stay,

And parching drought drie up the christall
    wells;
Let th' earth be barren, and bring foorth
    no flowres,
And th' ayre be fild with noyse of dolefull
    knells,
And wandring spirits walke untimely
    howres.

' And Nature, nurse of every living thing,
Let rest her selfe from her long wearinesse,
And cease henceforth things kindly forth
    to bring,
But hideous monsters full of uglinesse; 340
For she it is that hath me done this wrong;
No nurse, but stepdame cruell mercilesse.
Weepe, shepheard, weepe, to make my
    undersong.

IV

' My litle flocke, whom earst I lov'd so
    well,
And wont to feede with finest grasse that
    grew,
Feede ye hencefoorth on bitter astrofell,
And stinking smallage, and unsaverie rew;
And when your mawes are with those weeds
    corrupted,
Be ye the pray of wolves: ne will I rew
That with your carkasses wild beasts be
    glutted.   350

' Ne worse to you, my sillie sheepe, I pray,
Ne sorer vengeance wish on you to fall
Than to my selfe, for whose confusde
    decay
To carelesse heavens I doo daylie call:
But heavens refuse to heare a wretches cry;
And cruell Death doth scorne to come at
    call,
Or graunt his boone that most desires to
    dye.

' The good and righteous he away doth take,
To plague th' unrighteous which alive re-
    maine:
But the ungodly ones he doth forsake, 360
By living long to multiplie their paine:
Els surely death should be no punishment,
As the great Judge at first did it ordaine,
But rather riddance from long languish-
    ment.

' Therefore my Daphne they have tane away;
For worthie of a better place was she:

But me unworthie willed here to stay,
That with her lacke I might tormented be.
Sith then they so have ordred, I will pay
Penance to her according their decree, 370
And to her ghost doo service day by day.

' For I will walke this wandring pilgrimage,
Throughout the world from one to other
    end,
And in affliction wast my better age:
My bread shall be the anguish of my mind,
My drink the teares which fro mine eyes
    do raine,
My bed the ground that hardest I may fynd:
So will I wilfully increase my paine.

' And she, my love that was, my saint that
    is,
When she beholds from her celestiall
    throne   380
(In which shee joyeth in eternall blis)
My bitter penance, will my case bemone,
And pitie me that living thus doo die:
For heavenly spirits have compassion
On mortall men, and rue their miserie.

' So when I have with sorrowe satisfide
Th' importune Fates, which vengeance on
    me seeke,
And th' heavens with long languor paci-
    fide,
She, for pure pitie of my sufferance meeke,
Will send for me; for which I daylie long, 390
And will till then my painfull penance eeke.
Weep, shepheard, weep, to make my under
    song.

V

' Hencefoorth I hate what ever Nature
    made,
And in her workmanship no pleasure finde:
For they be all but vaine, and quickly fade,
So soone as on them blowes the northern
    winde;
They tarrie not, but flit and fall away,
Leaving behind them nought but griefe of
    minde,
And mocking such as thinke they long will
    stay.

' I hate the heaven, because it doth with-
    hold   400
Me from my love, and eke my love from
    me;
I hate the earth, because it is the mold

Of fleshly slime and fraile mortalitie;
I hate the fire, because to nought it flyes,
I hate the ayre, because sighes of it be,
I hate the sea, because it teares supplyes.

' I hate the day, because it lendeth light
To see all things, and not my love to see;
I hate the darkenesse and the drery night,
Because they breed sad balefulnesse in
      mee;   410
I hate all times, because all times doo fly
So fast away, and may not stayed bee,
But as a speedie post that passeth by.

' I hate to speake, my voyce is spent with
      crying:
I hate to heare, lowd plaints have duld
      mine eares:
I hate to tast, for food withholds my dying:
I hate to see, mine eyes are dimd with
      teares:
I hate to smell, no sweet on earth is left:
I hate to feele, my flesh is numbd with
      feares:
So all my senses from me are bereft.   420

' I hate all men, and shun all woman-
      kinde;
The one, because as I they wretched are,
The other, for because I doo not finde
My love with them, that wont to be their
      starre:
And life I hate, because it will not last,
And death I hate, because it life doth
      marre,
And all I hate, that is to come or past.

' So all the world, and all in it I hate,
Because it changeth ever too and fro,
And never standeth in one certaine state, 430
But still unstedfast round about doth goe,
Like a mill wheele, in midst of miserie,
Driven with streames of wretchednesse and
      woe,
That dying lives, and living still does dye.

' So doo I live, so doo I daylie die,
And pine away in selfe-consuming paine:
Sith she that did my vitall powres sup-
      plie,
And feeble spirits in their force maintaine,
Is fetcht fro me, why seeke I to prolong
My wearie daies in dolor and disdaine ? 440
Weep, shepheard, weep, to make my under-
      song.

VI

' Why doo I longer live in lifes despight,
And doo not dye then in despight of death ?
Why doo I longer see this loathsome light,
And doo in darkenesse not abridge my breath,
Sith all my sorrow should have end thereby,
And cares finde quiet ? Is it so uneath
To leave this life, or dolorous to dye ?

' To live I finde it deadly dolorous;
For life drawes care, and care continuall
      woe: 450
Therefore to dye must needes be joyeous,
And wishfull thing this sad life to forgoe.
But I must stay; I may it not amend;
My Daphne hence departing bad me so;
She bad me stay, till she for me did send.

' Yet, whilest I in this wretched vale doo
      stay,
My wearie feete shall ever wandring be,
That still I may be readie on my way,
When as her messenger doth come for me:
Ne will I rest my feete for feeblenesse, 460
Ne will I rest my limmes for fraïltie,
Ne will I rest mine eyes for heavinesse.

' But, as the mother of the gods, that sought
For faire Euridyce, her daughter deere,
Throghout the world, with wofull heavie
      thought,
So will I travell whilest I tarrie heere,
Ne will I lodge, ne will I ever lin,
Ne when as drouping Titan draweth neere
To loose his teeme, will I take up my inne.

' Ne sleepe (the harbenger of wearie
      wights)   470
Shall ever lodge upon mine ey-lids more,
Ne shall with rest refresh my fainting
      sprights,
Nor failing force to former strength re-
      store:
But I will wake and sorrow all the night
With Philumene, my fortune to deplore,
With Philumene, the partner of my plight.

' And ever as I see the starres to fall,
And under ground to goe, to give them
      light
Which dwell in darknes, I to minde will
      call
How my faire starre (that shinde on me so
      bright)   480
Fell sodainly and faded under ground;

Since whose departure, day is turnd to night,
And night without a Venus starre is found.

'But soone as day doth shew his deawie
    face,
And calls foorth men unto their toylsome
    trade,
I will withdraw me to some darksome place,
Or some deepe cave, or solitarie shade;
There will I sigh and sorrow all day long,
And the huge burden of my cares unlade.
Weep, shepheard, weep, to make my under-
    song.   490

VII

'Hence foorth mine eyes shall never more
    behold
Faire thing on earth, ne feed on false de-
    light
Of ought that framed is of mortall moulde,
Sith that my fairest flower is faded quight:
For all I see is vaine and transitorie,
Ne will be helde in anie stedfast plight,
But in a moment loose their grace and
    glorie.

'And ye, fond men, on Fortunes wheele that
    ride,
Or in ought under heaven repose assurance,
Be it riches, beautie, or honors pride,   500
Be sure that they shall have no long endur-
    ance,
But ere ye be aware will flit away;
For nought of them is yours, but th' onely
    usance
Of a small time, which none ascertaine may.

'And ye, true lovers, whom desastrous
    chaunce
Hath farre exiled from your ladies grace,
To mourne in sorrow and sad sufferaunce,
When ye doo heare me in that desert place
Lamenting lowde my Daphnes elegie,
Helpe me to wayle my miserable case,   510
And when life parts, vouchsafe to close mine
    eye.

'And ye, more happie lovers, which enjoy
The presence of your dearest loves delight,
When ye doo heare my sorrowfull annoy,
Yet pittie me in your empassiond spright,
And thinke that such mishap as chaunst to
    me
May happen unto the most happiest wight;
For all mens states alike unstedfast be.

'And ye, my fellow shepheards, which do
    feed
Your carelesse flocks on hils and open
    plaines,   520
With better fortune than did me succeed,
Remember yet my undeserved paines;
And when ye heare that I am dead or slaine,
Lament my lot, and tell your fellow swaines
That sad Alcyon dyde in lifes disdaine.

'And ye, faire damsels, shepheards dere
    delights,
That with your loves do their rude hearts
    possesse,
When as my hearse shall happen to your
    sightes,
Vouchsafe to deck the same with cyparesse;
And ever sprinckle brackish teares among,
In pitie of my undeserv'd distresse,   531
The which I, wretch, endured have thus long.

'And ye, poore pilgrims, that with restlesse
    toyle
Wearie your selves in wandring desert
    wayes,
Till that you come where ye your vowes
    assoyle,
When passing by ye read these wofull layes
On my grave written, rue my Daphnes
    wrong,
And mourne for me that languish out my
    dayes.
Cease, shepheard, cease, and end thy under-
    song.'

Thus when he ended had his heavie
    plaint,   540
The heaviest plaint that ever I heard sound,
His cheekes wext pale, and sprights began
    to faint,
As if againe he would have fallen to ground;
Which when I saw, I (stepping to him light)
Amooved him out of his stonie swound,
And gan him to recomfort as I might.

But he no waie recomforted would be,
Nor suffer solace to approach him nie,
But casting up a sdeinfull eie at me,
That in his traunce I would not let him
    lie,   550
Did rend his haire, and beat his blubbred
    face,
As one disposed wilfullie to die,
That I sore griev'd to see his wretched case.

Tho when the pang was somewhat overpast,
And the outragious passion nigh appeased,
I him desirde, sith daie was overcast
And darke night fast approched, to be
    pleased
To turne aside unto my cabinet,
And staie with me, till he were better eased
Of that strong stownd which him so sore
    beset.   560

But by no meanes I could him win there-
    to,
Ne longer him intreate with me to staie,
But without taking leave he foorth did goe
With staggring pace and dismall lookes
    dismay,
As if that Death he in the face had seene,
Or hellish hags had met upon the way:
But what of him became I cannot weene.

COLIN CLOUTS COME HOME AGAINE
BY ED. SPENCER

LONDON

PRINTED FOR WILLIAM PONSONBIE

1595

TO THE RIGHT WORTHY AND NOBLE KNIGHT SIR WALTER RALEIGH,
CAPTAINE OF HER MAJESTIES GUARD, LORD WARDEIN OF THE STAN-
NERIES, AND LIEUTENANT OF THE COUNTIE OF CORNWALL

Sir, that you may see that I am not
alwaies ydle as yee thinke, though not
greatly well occupied, nor altogither undu-
tifull, though not precisely officious, I make
you present of this simple pastorall, unworthie of your higher conceipt for the
meanesse of the stile, but agreeing with the
truth in circumstance and matter. The
which I humbly beseech you to accept in
part of paiment of the infinite debt in which
I acknowledge my selfe bounden unto you,
for your singular favours and sundrie good
turnes shewed to me at my late being in England, and with your good countenance protect against the malice of evill mouthes,
which are alwaies wide open to carpe at
and misconstrue my simple meaning. I
pray continually for your happinesse. From
my house of Kilcolman, the 27 of December, 1591.

Yours ever humbly,
Ed. Sp.

[Colin Clout's Come Home Again is the record
of the poet's expedition to England with Raleigh in 1589 and of what he found there at
court. It was obviously written not long after
his return to Kilcolman and sent to his friend
as soon as done. About four years later, probably by way of revision for the press, he made
changes inspired by intervening events.
In a poem of such content, it was natural
that he should adopt his old incognito of the
Shepherd's Calendar and appear as Colin Clout.
In that character, he would naturally need his
old friend and interlocutor, Hobbinol, to start
the dialogue, and when he came to the theme
of court love-making, he could hardly fail to
sing a palinode upon his old mistress Rosalind.
They were set personages of the fiction. Yet

Colin Clout's Come Home Again owes little
to the Calendar; for its art is essentially more
direct. In the earlier poem whatever facts of
personal experience and opinion are to be discerned we see dimly and ambiguously through
a kind of luminous fog: love-story and satire
are altogether baffling. In the later, the story
is almost as clear as a chronicle, the satire almost as direct and vivid as that of 'Mother
Hubberd's Tale.' Its pastoralism, indeed, is
more a point of view than a set disguise, or,
at least, the mask is worn lightly and removed
at will. From the allegorical to the literal the
style winds to and fro flexibly, according as
the poet's memories take form. It is free, not
run in moulds. Beside it the beauties of the
Calendar seem almost academic.]

COLIN CLOUTS COME HOME AGAINE

THE shepheards boy (best knowen by that
name)
That after Tityrus first sung his lay,
Laies of sweet love, without rebuke or
blame,
Sate (as his custome was) upon a day,
Charming his oaten pipe unto his peres,
The shepheard swaines that did about him
play:
Who all the while, with greedie listfull
eares,
Did stand astonisht at his curious skill,
Like hartlesse deare, dismayd with thunders
sound.
At last when as he piped had his fill,   10
He rested him: and sitting then around,
One of those groomes (a jolly groome was
he,
As ever piped on an oaten reed,
And lov'd this shepheard dearest in degree,
Hight Hobbinol) gan thus to him areed.
  'Colin, my liefe, my life, how great a
losse
Had all the shepheards nation by thy lacke !
And I, poore swaine, of many, greatest
crosse:
That, sith thy Muse first since thy turning
backe
Was heard to sound as she was wont on
hye,   20
Hast made us all so blessed and so blythe.
Whilest thou wast hence, all dead in dole
did lie:
The woods were heard to waile full many
a sythe,
And all their birds with silence to com-
plaine:
The fields with faded flowers did seem to
mourne,
And all their flocks from feeding to re-
fraine:
The running waters wept for thy returne,
And all their fish with languour did lament:
But now both woods and fields and floods
revive,
Sith thou art come, their cause of meri-
ment,   30
That us, late dead, hast made againe alive.
But were it not too painfull to repeat
The passed fortunes, which to thee befell
In thy late voyage, we thee would entreat,
Now at thy leisure them to us to tell.'

To whom the shepheard gently answered
thus:
'Hobbin, thou temptest me to that I covet:
For of good passed newly to discus,
By dubble usurie doth twise renew it.
And since I saw that Angels blessed eie,   40
Her worlds bright sun, her heavens fairest
light,
My mind, full of my thoughts satietie,
Doth feed on sweet contentment of that
sight:
Since that same day in nought I take
delight,
Ne feeling have in any earthly pleasure,
But in remembrance of that glorious bright,
My lifes sole blisse, my hearts eternall
threasure.
Wake then, my pipe ! my sleepie Muse,
awake !
Till I have told her praises lasting long:
Hobbin desires, thou maist it not forsake.   50
Harke then, ye jolly shepheards, to my song.'
  With that they all gan throng about him
neare,
With hungrie eares to heare his harmonie:
The whiles their flocks, devoyd of dangers
feare,
Did round about them feed at libertie.
  'One day,' quoth he, 'I sat (as was my
trade)
Unde the foote of Mole, that mountaine
hore,
Keeping my sheepe amongst the cooly shade
Of the greene alders by the Mullaes shore.
There a straunge shepheard chaunst to
find me out,   60
Whether allured with my pipes delight,
Whose pleasing sound yshrilled far about,
Or thither led by chaunce, I know not right:
Whom when I asked from what place he
came,
And how he hight, himselfe he did ycleepe
The Shepheard of the Ocean by name,
And said he came far from the main-sea
deepe.
He, sitting me beside in that same shade,
Provoked me to plaie some pleasant fit,
And when he heard the musicke which I
made,   70
He found himselfe full greatly pleasd at it:
Yet æmuling my pipe, he tooke in hond
My pipe, before that æmuled of many,
And plaid theron; (for well that skill he
cond)
Himselfe as skilfull in that art as any.

He pip'd, I sung, and when he sung, I piped,
By chaunge of turnes, each making other
mery,
Neither envying other, nor envied,
So piped we, untill we both were weary.'
  There interrupting him, a bonie swaine, 80
That Cuddy hight, him thus atweene be-
spake:
' And should it not thy readie course re-
straine,
I would request thee, Colin, for my sake,
To tell what thou didst sing, when he did
plaie:
For well I weene it worth recounting was,
Whether it were some hymne, or morall
laie,
Or carol made to praise thy loved lasse.'
  ' Nor of my love, nor of my lasse,' quoth
he,
' I then did sing, as then occasion fell:
For love had me forlorne, forlorne of me, 90
That made me in that desart chose to dwell.
But of my river Bregogs love I soong,
Which to the shiny Mulla he did beare,
And yet doth beare, and ever will, so long
As water doth within his bancks appeare.'
  ' Of fellowship,' said then that bony boy,
' Record to us that lovely lay againe:
The staie whereof shall nought these eares
annoy,
Who all that Colin makes do covet faine.'
  ' Heare then,' quoth he, ' the tenor of my
tale, 100
In sort as I it to that shepheard told:
No leasing new, nor grandams fable stale,
But aunoient truth confirm'd with credence
old.
  ' Old Father Mole, (Mole hight that moun-
tain gray
That walls the northside of Armulla dale)
He had a daughter fresh as floure of May,
Which gave that name unto that pleasant
vale;
Mulla, the daughter of old Mole, so hight
The nimph, which of that water course has
charge,
That, springing out of Mole, doth run downe
right 110
To Buttevant, where spreading forth at
large,
It giveth name unto that auncient cittie,
Which Kilnemullah cleped is of old:
Whose ragged ruines breed great ruth and
pittie
To travailers which it from far behold.

Full faine she lov'd, and was belov'd full
faine
Of her owne brother river, Bregog hight,
So hight because of this deceitfull traine
Which he with Mulla wrought to win de-
light.   119
But her old sire, more carefull of her good,
And meaning her much better to preferre,
Did thinke to match her with the neighbour
flood,
Which Allo hight, Broadwater called farre:
And wrought so well with his continuall
paine,
That he that river for his daughter wonne:
The dowre agreed, the day assigned plaine,
The place appointed where it should be
doone.
Nath'lesse the nymph her former liking
held;
For love will not be drawne, but must be
ledde;
And Bregog did so well her fancie weld, 130
That her good will he got her first to wedde.
But, for her father, sitting still on hie,
Did warily still watch which way she went,
And eke from far observ'd, with jealous eie,
Which way his course the wanton Bregog
bent,
Him to deceive, for all his watchfull ward,
The wily lover did devise this slight:
First into many parts his streame he shar'd,
That, whilest the one was watcht, the other
might
Passe unespide to meete her by the way; 140
And then besides, those little streames so
broken
He under ground so closely did convay,
That of their passage doth appeare no token,
Till they into the Mullaes water slide.
So secretly did he his love enjoy:
Yet not so secret, but it was deseride,
And told her father by a shepheards boy.
Who, wondrous wroth for that so foule de-
spight,
In great avenge did roll downe from his
hill
Huge mightie stones, the which encomber
might 150
His passage, and his water-courses spill.
So of a river, which he was of old,
He none was made, but scattred all to
nought,
And, lost emong those rocks into him rold,
Did lose his name: so deare his love he
bought.'

Which having said, him Thestylis bespake:
'Now by my life this was a mery lay,
Worthie of Colin selfe, that did it make.
But read now eke, of friendship I thee pray,
What dittie did that other shepheard sing?
For I do covet most the same to heare, 161
As men use most to covet forreine thing.'
    'That shall I eke,' quoth he, 'to you declare.

His song was all a lamentable lay,
Of great unkindnesse, and of usage hard,
Of Cynthia, the Ladie of the Sea,
Which from her presence faultlesse him debard.

And ever and anon, with singulfs rife,
He cryed out, to make his undersong:
"Ah! my loves queene, and goddesse of my life, 170
Who shall me pittie, when thou doest me wrong?"'

    Then gan a gentle bonylasse to speake,
That Marin hight: 'Right well he sure did plaine,
That could great Cynthiaes sore displeasure breake,
And move to take him to her grace againe.
But tell on further, Colin, as befell
Twixt him and thee, that thee did hence dissuade.'

    'When thus our pipes we both had wearied well,'
Quoth he, 'and each an end of singing made,
He gan to cast great lyking to my lore, 180
And great dislyking to my lucklesse lot,
That banisht had my selfe, like wight forlore,
Into that waste, where I was quite forgot.
The which to leave, thenceforth he counseld mee,
Unmeet for man in whom was ought regardfull,
And wend with him, his Cynthia to see,
Whose grace was great, and bounty most rewardfull:
Besides her peerlesse skill in making well,
And all the ornaments of wondrous wit,
Such as all womankynd did far excell, 190
Such as the world admyr'd and praised it:
So what with hope of good, and hate of ill,
He me perswaded forth with him to fare;
Nought tooke I with me, but mine oaten quill:
Small needments else need shepheard to prepare.

So to the sea we came; the sea? that is
A world of waters heaped up on hie,
Rolling like mountaines in wide wildernesse,
Horrible, hideous, roaring with hoarse crie.'
    'And is the sea,' quoth Coridon, 'so fearfull?'
                                                 200
    'Fearfull much more,' quoth he, 'then hart can fear:
Thousand wyld beasts with deep mouthes gaping direfull
Therin stil wait poore passengers to teare.
Who life doth loath, and longs death to behold,
Before he die, alreadie dead with feare,
And yet would live with heart halfe stonie cold,
Let him to sea, and he shall see it there.
And yet as ghastly dreadfull as it seemes,
Bold men, presuming life for gaine to sell,
Dare tempt that gulf, and in those wandring stremes 210
Seek waies unknowne, waies leading down to hell.

For as we stood there waiting on the strond,
Behold! an huge great vessell to us came,
Dauncing upon the waters back to lond,
As if it scornd the daunger of the same;
Yet was it but a wooden frame and fraile,
Glewed togither with some subtile matter,
Yet had it armes and wings, and head and taile,
And life to move it selfe upon the water.
Strange thing, how bold and swift the monster was, 220
That neither car'd for wynd, nor haile, nor raine,
Nor swelling waves, but thorough them did passe
So proudly that she made them roare againe!
The same aboord us gently did receave,
And without harme us farre away did beare,
So farre that land, our mother, us did leave,
And nought but sea and heaven to us appeare.
Then hartlesse quite and full of inward feare,
That shepheard I besought to me to tell,
Under what skie, or in what world we were, 230
In which I saw no living people dwell.
Who me recomforting all that he might,
Told me that that same was the regiment
Of a great shepheardesse, that Cynthia hight,
His liege, his ladie, and his lifes regent.

"If then," quoth I, " a shepheardesse she
  bee,
Where be the flockes and heards, which she
  doth keep?
And where may I the hills and pastures
  see,
On which she useth for to feed her sheepe?"
"These be the hills," quoth he, " the surges
  hie,   240
On which faire Cynthia her heards doth
  feed:
Her heards be thousand fishes, with their
  frie,
Which in the bosome of the billowes breed.
Of them the shepheard which hath charge
  in chief
Is Triton blowing loud his wreathed horne:
At sound whereof, they all for their relief
Wend too and fro at evening and at morne.
And Proteus eke with him does drive his
  heard
Of stinking seales and porcpisces together,
With hoary head and deawy dropping
  beard,   250
Compelling them which way he list, and
  whether.
And I among the rest, of many least,
Have in the ocean charge to me assignd:
Where I will live or die at her beheast,
And serve and honour her with faithfull
  mind.
Besides, an hundred nymphs, all heavenly
  borne,
And of immortall race, doo still attend
To wash faire Cynthiaes sheep, when they
  be shorne,
And fold them up, when they have made
  an end.
Those be the shepheards which my Cynthia
  serve   260
At sea, beside a thousand moe at land:
For land and sea my Cynthia doth deserve
To have in her commandement at hand."
Thereat I wondred much, till, wondring
  more
And more, at length we land far off de-
  scryde:
Which sight much gladed me; for much
  afore
I feard least land we never should have
  eyde:
Thereto our ship her course directly bent,
As if the way she perfectly had knowne.
We Lunday passe; by that same name is
  ment   270

An island which the first to west was
  showne.
From thence another world of land we kend,
Floting amid the sea in jeopardie,
And round about with mightie white rocks
  hemd,
Against the seas encroching crueltie.
Those same, the shepheard told me, were
  the fields
In which Dame Cynthia her landheards fed,
Faire goodly fields, then which Armulla
  yields
None fairer, nor more fruitfull to be red.
The first to which we nigh approched was 280
An high headland thrust far into the sea,
Like to an horne, whereof the name it has,
Yet seemed to be a goodly pleasant lea:
There did a loftie mount at first us greet,
Which did a stately heape of stones upreare,
That seemd amid the surges for to fleet,
Much greater then that frame which us did
  beare:
There did our ship her fruitfull wombe un-
  lade,
And put us all ashore on Cynthias land.'
  'What land is that thou meanst,' then
    Cuddy sayd,   290
'And is there other, then whereon we
  stand?'
  'Ah! Cuddy,' then quoth Colin, ' thous a
    fon,
That hast not seene least part of Natures
  worke:
Much more there is unkend then thou doest
  kon,
And much more that does from mens know-
  ledge lurke.
For that same land much larger is then this,
And other men and beasts and birds doth
  feed:
There fruitfull corne, faire trees, fresh herb-
  age is,
And all things else that living creatures
  need.
Besides most goodly rivers there appeare, 300
No whit inferiour to thy Funchins praise,
Or unto Allo or to Mulla cleare:
Nought hast thou, foolish boy, seene in thy
  daies.'
  'But if that land be there,' quoth he, ' as
    here,
And is theyr heaven likewise there all one?
And if like heaven, be heavenly graces there,
Like as in this same world where we do
  wone?'

'Both heaven and heavenly graces do
        much more,'
Quoth he, 'abound in that same land then
        this.
For there all happie peace and plenteous
        store
Conspire in one to make contented blisse: 310
No wayling there nor wretchednesse is
        heard,
No bloodie issues nor no leprosies,
No griesly famine, nor no raging sweard,
No nightly bodrags, nor no hue and cries:
The shepheards there abroad may safely lie,
On hills and downes, withouten dread or
        daunger:
No ravenous wolves the good mans hope
        destroy,
Nor outlawes fell affray the forest raunger.
There learned arts do florish in great
        honor, 320
And poets wits are had in peerlesse price:
Religion hath lay powre to rest upon her,
Advancing vertue and suppressing vice.
For end, all good, all grace there freely
        growes,
Had people grace it gratefully to use:
For God his gifts there plenteously bestowes,
But gracelesse men them greatly do abuse.'
    'But say on further,' then said Corylas,
'The rest of thine adventures, that betyded.'
    'Foorth on our voyage we by land did
        passe,'
Quoth he, 'as that same shepheard still us 330
        guyded,
Untill that we to Cynthiaes presence came:
Whose glorie, greater then my simple
        thought,
I found much greater then the former fame;
Such greatnes I cannot compare to ought:
But if I her like ought on earth might read,
I would her lyken to a crowne of lillies,
Upon a virgin brydes adorned head,
With roses dight and goolds and daffa-
        dillies;
Or like the circlet of a turtle true, 340
In which all colours of the rainbow bee;
Or like faire Phebes garlond shining new,
In which all pure perfection one may see.
But vaine it is to thinke, by paragone
Of earthly things, to judge of things divine:
Her power, her mercy, and her wisedome,
        none
Can deeme, but who the Godhead can define.
Why then do I, base shepheard bold and
        blind,

Presume the things so sacred to prophane?
More fit it is t' adore, with humble mind, 350
The image of the heavens in shape humane.'
    With that Alexis broke his tale asunder,
Saying: 'By wondring at thy Cynthiaes
        praise,
Colin, thy selfe thou mak'st us more to
        wonder,
And, her upraising, doest thy selfe upraise.
But let us heare what grace she shewed thee,
And how that shepheard strange thy cause
        advanced.'
    'The Shepheard of the Ocean,' quoth he,
'Unto that Goddesse grace me first enhanced,
And to mine oaten pipe enclin'd her eare, 360
That she thenceforth therein gan take de-
        light,
And it desir'd at timely houres to heare,
All were my notes but rude and roughly
        dight;
For not by measure of her owne great
        mynd
And wondrous worth she mott my simple
        song,
But joyd that country shepheard ought
        could fynd
Worth harkening to, emongst the learned
        throng.'
    'Why,' said Alexis then, 'what needeth
        shee,
That is so great a shepheardesse her selfe
And hath so many shepheards in her fee, 370
To heare thee sing, a simple silly elfe?
Or be the shepheards which do serve her
        laesie,
That they list not their mery pipes applie?
Or be their pipes untunable and craesie,
That they cannot her honour worthylie?'
    'Ah! nay,' said Colin, 'neither so, nor so:
For better shepheards be not under skie,
Nor better hable, when they list to blow
Their pipes aloud, when they list to blow
There is good Harpalus, now woxen aged 380
In faithfull service of faire Cynthia:
And there is Corydon, though meanly
        waged,
Yet hablest wit of most I know this day.
And there is sad Alcyon, bent to mourne,
Though fit to frame an everlasting dittie,
Whose gentle spright for Daphnes death
        doth tourn
Sweet layes of love to endlesse plaints of
        pittie.
Ah! pensive boy, pursue that brave con-
        ceipt,

In thy sweet *Eglantine of Meriflure*,
Lift up thy notes unto their wonted
    height,   390
That may thy Muse and mates to mirth
    allure.
There eke is Palin, worthie of great praise,
Albe he envie at my rustick quill:
And there is pleasing Alcon, could he raise
His tunes from laies to matter of more skill.
And there is old Palemon, free from spight,
Whose carefull pipe may make the hearer
    rew:
Yet he himselfe may rewed be more right,
That sung so long untill quite hoarse he
    grew.
And there is Alabaster, throughly taught 400
In all this skill, though knowen yet to few,
Yet, were he knowne to Cynthia as he
    ought,
His *Eliseïs* would be redde anew.
Who lives that can match that heroick song,
Which he hath of that mightie princesse
    made ?
O dreaded Dread, do not thy selfe that
    wrong,
To let thy fame lie so in hidden shade:
But call it forth, O call him forth to thee,
To end thy glorie which he hath begun:
That when he finisht hath as it should be, 410
No braver poeme can be under sun.
Nor Po nor Tyburs swans so much re-
    nowned,
Nor all the brood of Greece so highly
    praised,
Can match that Muse when it with bayes is
    crowned,
And to the pitch of her perfection raised.
And there is a new shepheard late up sprong,
The which doth all afore him far surpasse:
Appearing well in that well tuned song
Which late he sung unto a scornfull lasse.
Yet doth his trembling Muse but lowly
    flie,   420
As daring not too rashly mount on hight,
And doth her tender plumes as yet but trie
In loves soft laies and looser thoughts de-
    light.
Then rouze thy feathers quickly, Daniell,
And to what course thou please thy selfe
    advance:
But most, me seemes, thy accent will excell
In tragick plaints and passionate mischance.
And there that Shepheard of the Ocean is,
That spends his wit in loves consuming
    smart:

Full sweetly tempred is that Muse of his, 430
That can empierce a princes mightie hart.
There also is (ah ! no, he is not now)
But since I said he is, he quite is gone:
Amyntas quite is gone and lies full low,
Having his Amaryllis left to mone.
Helpe, O ye shepheards, helpe ye all in this,
Helpe Amaryllis this her losse to mourne:
Her losse is yours, your losse Amyntas is,
Amyntas, floure of shepheards pride for-
    lorne.
He, whilest he lived, was the noblest swaine
That ever piped in an oaten quill: 441
Both did he other which could pipe main-
    taine,
And eke could pipe himselfe with passing
    skill.
And there, though last not least, is Aetion;
A gentler shepheard may no where be found;
Whose Muse, full of high thoughts inven-
    tion,
Doth like himselfe heroically sound.
All these, and many others mo, remaine,
Now after Astrofell is dead and gone:
But while as Astrofell did live and raine, 450
Amongst all these was none his paragone.
All these do florish in their sundry kynd,
And do their Cynthia immortall make:
Yet found I lyking in her royall mynd,
Not for my skill, but for that shepheards
    sake.'
    Then spake a lovely lasse, hight Lucida:
' Shepheard, enough of shepheards thou hast
    told,
Which favour thee and honour Cynthia:
But of so many nymphs which she doth hold
In her retinew, thou hast nothing sayd; 460
That seems, with none of them thou favor
    foundest,
Or art ingratefull to each gentle mayd,
That none of all their due deserts resound-
    est.'
    ' Ah ! far be it,' quoth Colin Clout, ' fro
    me,
That I of gentle mayds should ill deserve:
For that my selfe I do professe to be
Vassall to one, whom all my dayes I serve;
The beame of beautie sparkled from above,
The floure of vertue and pure chastitie, 469
The blossome of sweet joy and perfect love,
The pearle of peerlesse grace and modestie:
To her my thoughts I daily dedicate,
To her my heart I nightly martyrize,
To her my love I lowly do prostrate,
To her my life I wholly sacrifice:

My thought, my heart, my love, my life is
    shee,
And I hers ever onely, ever one:
One ever I all vowed hers to bee,
One ever I, and others never none.'
Then thus Melissa said: 'Thrise happie
    mayd,   480
Whom thou doest so enforce to deifie,
That woods, and hills, and valleyes thou
    hast made
Her name to eccho unto heaven hie.
But say, who else vouchsafed thee of grace?'
  'They all,' quoth he, 'me graced goodly
    well,
That all I praise, but in the highest place,
Urania, sister unto Astrofell,
In whose brave mynd, as in a golden cofer,
All heavenly gifts and riches locked are;
More rich then pearles of Ynde, or gold of
    Opher,   490
And in her sex more wonderfull and rare.
Ne lesse praise worthie I Theana read,
Whose goodly beames, though they be over
    dight
With mourning stole of carefull wydowhead,
Yet through that darksome vale do glister
    bright.
She is the well of bountie and brave mynd,
Excelling most in glorie and great light:
She is the ornament of womankind,
And courts chief garlond with all vertues
    dight.
Therefore great Cynthia her in chiefest
    grace   500
Doth hold, and next unto her selfe advance,
Well worthie of so honourable place,
For her great worth and noble governance.
Ne lesse praise worthie is her sister deare,
Faire Marian, the Muses onely darling:
Whose beautie shyneth as the morning
    cleare,
With silver deaw upon the roses pearling.
Ne lesse praise worthie is Mansilia,
Best knowne by bearing up great Cynthiaes
    traine:
That same is she to whom *Daphnaida*   510
Upon her neeces death I did complaine.
She is the paterne of true womanhead,
And onely mirrhor of feminitie:
Worthie next after Cynthia to tread,
As she is next her in nobilitie.
Ne lesse praise worthie Galathea seemes,
Then best of all that honourable crew,
Faire Galathea, with bright shining beames
Inflaming feeble eyes that her do view.

She there then waited upon Cynthia,   520
Yet there is not her won, but here with us
About the borders of our rich Coshma,
Now made of Maa the nymph delitious.
Ne lesse praisworthie faire Neæra is,
Neæra ours, not theirs, though there she be,
For of the famous Shure the nymph she is,
For high desert advaunst to that degree.
She is the blosome of grace and curtesie,
Adorned with all honourable parts:
She is the braunch of true nobilitie,   530
Belov'd of high and low with faithfull
    harts.
Ne lesse praisworthie Stella do I read,
Though nought my praises of her needed
    arre,
Whom verse of noblest shepheard lately
    dead
Hath prais'd and rais'd above each other
    starre.
Ne lesse praisworthie are the sisters three,
The honor of the noble familie
Of which I meanest boast my selfe to be,
And most that unto them I am so nie:
Phyllis, Charillis, and sweet Amaryllis: 540
Phyllis the faire is eldest of the three;
The next to her is bountifull Charillis;
But th' youngest is the highest in degree.
Phyllis, the floure of rare perfection,
Faire spreading forth her leaves with fresh
    delight,
That, with their beauties amorous reflexion,
Bereave of sence each rash beholders sight.
But sweet Charillis is the paragone
Of peerlesse price, and ornament of praise,
Admyr'd of all, yet envied of none,   550
Through the myld temperance of her goodly
    raies.
Thrise happie do I hold thee, noble swaine,
The which art of so rich a spoile possest,
And it embracing deare without disdaine,
Hast sole possession in so chaste a brest.
Of all the shepheards daughters which there
    bee,
And yet there be the fairest under skie,
Or that elsewhere I ever yet did see,
A fairer nymph yet never saw mine eie:
She is the pride and primrose of the rest,   560
Made by the Maker selfe to be admired,
And like a goodly beacon high addrest,
That is with sparks of heavenlie beautie
    fired.
But Amaryllis, whether fortunate,
Or else unfortunate, may I aread?
That freed is from Cupids yoke by fate,

Since which she doth new bands adventure
    dread.
Shepheard, what ever thou hast heard to be
In this or that praysd diversly apart,   569
In her thou maist them all assembled see,
And seald up in the threasure of her hart.
Ne thee lesse worthie, gentle Flavia,
For thy chaste life and vertue I esteeme:
Ne thee lesse worthie, curteous Candida,
For thy true love and loyaltie I deeme.
Besides yet many mo that Cynthia serve,
Right noble nymphs, and high to be com-
    mended:
But if I all should praise as they deserve,
This sun would faile me ere I halfe had
    ended.
Therefore in closure of a thankfull mynd 580
I deeme it best to hold eternally
Their bounteous deeds and noble favours
    shrynd,
Then by discourse them to indignifie.'
   So having said, Aglaura him bespake:
' Colin, well worthie were those goodly fa-
    vours
Bestowd on thee, that so of them doest
    make,
And them requitest with thy thankfull la-
    bours.
But of great Cynthiaes goodnesse and high
    grace
Finish the storie which thou hast begunne.'
   ' More eath,' quoth he, ' it is in such a
    case   590
How to begin, then know how to have
    donne.
For everie gift and everie goodly meed,
Which she on me bestowd, demaunds a
    day;
And everie day in which she did a deed
Demaunds a yeare it duly to display.
Her words were like a streame of honny
    fleeting,
The which doth softly trickle from the hive,
Hable to melt the hearers heart unweeting,
And eke to make the dead againe alive.
Her deeds were like great clusters of ripe
    grapes,   600
Which load the braunches of the fruitfull
    vine,
Offring to fall into each mouth that gapes,
And fill the same with store of timely wine.
Her lookes were like beames of the morn-
    ing sun,
Forth looking through the windowes of the
    east,

When first the fleecie cattell have begun
Upon the perled grasse to make their feast.
Her thoughts are like the fume of franck-
    incence,
Which from a golden censer forth doth rise,
And throwing forth sweet odours mounts
    fro thence   610
In rolling globes up to the vauted skies.
There she beholds, with high aspiring
    thought,
The cradle of her owne creation,
Emongst the seats of angels heavenly
    wrought,
Much like an angell in all forme and fash-
    ion.'
   ' Colin,' said Cuddy then, ' thou hast forgot
Thy selfe, me seemes, too much, to mount
    so hie:
Such loftie flight base shepheard seemeth
    not,
From flocks and fields to angels and to skie.'
   ' True,' answered he, ' but her great ex-
    cellence   620
Lifts me above the measure of my might:
That, being fild with furious insolence,
I feele my selfe like one yrapt in spright.
For when I thinke of her, as oft I ought,
Then want I words to speake it fitly forth:
And when I speake of her what I have
    thought,
I cannot thinke according to her worth.
Yet will I thinke of her, yet will I speake,
So long as life my limbs doth hold together,
And when as death these vitall bands shall
    breake,   630
Her name recorded I will leave for ever.
Her name in every tree I will endosse,
That, as the trees do grow, her name may
    grow:
And in the ground each where will it en-
    grosse,
And fill with stones, that all men may it
    know.
The speaking woods and murmuring waters
    fall,
Her name Ile teach in knowen termes to
    frame:
And eke my lambs, when for their dams
    they call,
Ile teach to call for Cynthia by name.
And long while after I am dead and rotten,
Amongst the shepheards daughters dancing
    rownd,   641
My layes made of her shall not be forgot-
    ten.

But sung by them with flowry gyrlonds
    crownd.
And ye, who so ye be, that shall survive,
When as ye heare her memory renewed,
Be witnesse of her bountie here alive,
Which she to Colin her poore shepheard
    shewed.'
Much was the whole assembly of those
    heards
Moov'd at his speech, so feelingly he spake,
And stood awhile astonisht at his words, 650
Till Thestylis at last their silence brake,
Saying: 'Why, Colin, since thou foundst
    such grace
With Cynthia and all her noble crew,
Why didst thou ever leave that happie
    place,
In which such wealth might unto thee ac-
    crew;
And back returnedst to this barrein soyle,
Where cold and care and penury do dwell,
Here to keep sheepe, with hunger and with
    toyle?
Most wretched he, that is and cannot tell.'
    'Happie indeed,' said Colin, 'I him hold,
That may that blessed presence still en-
    joy,   661
Of fortune and of envy uncomptrold,
Which still are wont most happie states t'
    annoy:
But I, by that which little while I prooved,
Some part of those enormities did see,
The which in court continually hooved,
And followd those which happie seemd to
    bee.
Therefore I, silly man, whose former dayes
Had in rude fields bene altogether spent,
Durst not adventure such unknowen
    wayes,   670
Nor trust the guile of Fortunes blandish-
    ment,
But rather chose back to my sheep to
    tourne,
Whose utmost hardnesse I before had
    tryde,
Then, having learnd repentance late, to
    mourne
Emongst those wretches which I there de-
    scryde.'
    'Shepheard,' said Thestylis, 'it seemes of
    spight
Thou speakest thus gainst their felicitie,
Which thou enviest, rather then of right
That ought in them blameworthie thou
    doest spie.'

'Cause have I none,' quoth he, 'of can-
    cred will   680
To quite them ill, that me demeand so
    well:
But selfe-regard of private good or ill
Moves me of each, so as I found, to tell,
And eke to warne yong shepheards wan-
    dring wit,
Which, through report of that lives painted
    blisse,
Abandon quiet home, to seeke for it,
And leave their lambes to losse, misled
    amisse.
For, sooth to say, it is no sort of life
For shepheard fit to lead in that same place,
Where each one seeks with malice and with
    strife,   690
To thrust downe other into foule disgrace,
Himselfe to raise; and he doth soonest rise
That best can handle his deceitfull wit
In subtil shifts, and finest sleights devise,
Either by slaundring his well deemed name,
Through leasings lewd and fained forgerie,
Or else by breeding him some blot of blame,
By creeping close into his secrecie;
To which him needs a guilefull hollow hart,
Masked with faire dissembling curtesie, 700
A filed toung furnisht with tearmes of art,
No art of schoole, but courtiers schoolery.
For arts of schoole have there small coun-
    tenance,
Counted but toyes to busie ydle braines,
And there professours find small mainten-
    ance,
But to be instruments of others gaines.
Ne is there place for any gentle wit,
Unlesse to please, it selfe it can applie:
But shouldred is, or out of doore quite shit,
As base, or blunt, unmeet for melodie. 710
For each mans worth is measured by his
    weed,
As harts by hornes, or asses by their eares:
Yet asses been not all whose eares exceed,
Nor yet all harts, that hornes the highest
    beares.
For highest lookes have not the highest
    mynd,
Nor haughtie words most full of highest
    thoughts:
But are like bladders blowen up with wynd,
That being prickt do vanish into noughts.
Even such is all their vaunted vanitie,
Nought else but smoke, that fumeth soone
    away;   720
Such is their glorie that in simple eie

Seeme greatest, when their garments are
  most gay.
So they themselves for praise of fooles do
  sell,
And all their wealth for painting on a wall;
With price whereof they buy a golden bell,
And purchace highest rowmes in bowre and
  hall:
Whiles single Truth and simple Honestie
Do wander up and downe despys'd of all;
Their plaine attire such glorious gallantry
Disdaines so much, that none them in doth
  call.'   730
  'Ah! Colin,' then said Hobbinol, 'the
    blame
Which thou imputest is too generall,
As if not any gentle wit of name,
Nor honest mynd might there be found at
  all.
For well I wot, sith I my selfe was there,
To wait on Lobbin (Lobbin well thou knew-
  est)
Full many worthie ones then waiting were,
As ever else in princes court thou vewest.
Of which among you many yet remaine, 739
Whose names I cannot readily now ghesse:
Those that poore sutors papers do retaine,
And those that skill of medicine professe,
And those that do to Cynthia expound
The ledden of straunge languages in charge:
For Cynthia doth in sciences abound,
And gives to their professors stipends large.
Therefore unjustly thou doest wyte them
  all,
For that which thou mislikedst in a few.'
  'Blame is,' quoth he, 'more blamelesse
    generall,
Then that which private errours doth pur-
  sew: 750
For well I wot, that there amongst them
  bee
Full many persons of right worthie parts,
Both for report of spotlesse honestie,
And for profession of all learned arts,
Whose praise hereby no whit impaired is,
Though blame do light on those that faultie
  bee;
For all the rest do most-what far amis,
And yet their owne misfaring will not see:
For either they be puffed up with pride,
Or fraught with envie that their galls do
  swell,   760
Or they their dayes to ydlenesse divide,
Or drownded lie in pleasures wastefull
  well,

In which like moldwarps nousling still
  they lurke,
Unmyndfull of chiefe parts of manlinesse,
And do themselves, for want of other
  worke,
Vaine votaries of laesie Love professe,
Whose service high so basely they ensew,
That Cupid selfe of them ashamed is,
And mustring all his men in Venus vew,
Denies them quite for servitors of his.' 770
  'And is Love then,' said Corylas, 'once
    knowne
In court, and his sweet lore professed
  there?
I weened sure he was our god alone,
And only woond in fields and forests here.'
  'Not so,' quoth he, 'love most abound-
    eth there.
For all the walls and windows there are
  writ
All full of love, and love, and love my
  deare,
And all their talke and studie is of it.
Ne any there doth brave or valiant seeme,
Unlesse that some gay mistresse badge he
  beares: 780
Ne any one himselfe doth ought esteeme,
Unlesse he swim in love up to the eares.
But they of Love and of his sacred lere,
(As it should be) all otherwise devise,
Then we poore shepheards are accustomd
  here,
And him do sue and serve all otherwise.
For with lewd speeches, and licentious
  deeds,
His mightie mysteries they do prophane,
And use his ydle name to other needs,
But as a complement for courting vaine. 790
So him they do not serve as they professe,
But make him serve to them for sordid
  uses:
Ah! my dread lord, that doest liege hearts
  possesse,
Avenge thy selfe on them for their abuses!
But we poore shepheards, whether rightly
  so,
Or through our rudenesse into errour led,
Do make religion how we rashly go
To serve that god, that is so greatly dred;
For him the greatest of the gods we deeme,
Borne without syre or couples of one
  kynd,   800
For Venus selfe doth soly couples seeme,
Both male and female through commixture
  joynd.

So pure and spotlesse Cupid forth she
    brought,
And in the Gardens of Adonis nurst:
Where growing he his owne perfection
    wrought,
And shortly was of all the gods the first.
Then got he bow and shafts of gold and lead,
In which so fell and puissant he grew,
That Jove himselfe his powre began to
    dread,
And taking up to heaven, him godded
    new.   810
From thence he shooles his arrowes every
    where
Into the world, at randon as he will,
On us fraile men, his wretched vassals here,
Like as himselfe us pleaseth save or spill.
So we him worship, so we him adore
With humble hearts to heaven uplifted hie,
That to true loves he may us evermore
Preferre, and of their grace us dignifie:
Ne is there shepheard, ne yet shepheards
    swaine,
What ever feeds in forest or in field,   820
That dare with evil deed or leasing vaine
Blaspheme his powre, or termes unworthie
    yield.'
    ' Shepheard, it seemes that some celestiall
        rage
Of love,' quoth Cuddy, ' is breath'd into thy
    brest,
That powreth forth these oracles so sage
Of that high powre, wherewith thou art
    possest.
But never wist I till this present day,
Albe of Love I alwayes humbly deemed,
That he was such an one as thou doest say,
And so religiously to be esteemed.   830
Well may it seeme, by this thy deep insight,
That of that god the priest thou shouldest
    bee:
So well thou wot'st the mysterie of his
    might,
As if his godhead thou didst present see.'
    ' Of Loves perfection perfectly to speake,
Or of his nature rightly to define,
Indeed,' said Colin, ' passeth reasons reach,
And needs his priest t' expresse his powre
    divine.
For long before the world he was ybore,
And bred above in Venus bosome deare: 840
For by his powre the world was made of
    yore,
And all that therein wondrous doth ap-
    peare.

For how should else things so far from
    attone,
And so great enemies as of them bee,
Be ever drawne together into one,
And taught in such accordance to agree ?
Through him the cold began to covet heat,
And water fire; the light to mount on hie,
And th' heavie downe to peize; the hungry
    t' eat,   ·
And voydnesse to seeke full satietie.   850
So, being former foes, they wexed friends,
And gan by litle learne to love each other:
So being knit, they brought forth other
    kynds
Out of the fruitfull wombe of their great
    mother.
Then first gan heaven out of darknesse
    dread
For to appeare, and brought forth chear-
    full day:
Next gan the earth to shew her naked
    head,
Out of deep waters which her drownd
    alway.
And shortly after, everie living wight
Crept forth like wormes out of her slimie
    nature,   860
Soone as on them the suns life giving light
Had powred kindly heat and formall fea-
    ture:
Thenceforth they gan each one his like to
    love,
And like himselfe desire for to beget:
The lyon chose his mate, the turtle dove
Her deare, the dolphin his owne dolphinet;
But man, that had the sparke of reasons
    might,
More then the rest to rule his passion,
Chose for his love the fairest in his sight,
Like as himselfe was fairest by creation.
For beautie is the bayt which with de-
    light   871
Doth man allure for to enlarge his kynd,
Beautie, the burning lamp of heavens light,
Darting her beames into each feeble mynd:
Against whose powre, nor god nor man can
    fynd
Defence, ne ward the daunger of the wound,
But, being hurt, seeke to be medicynd
Of her that first did stir that mortall
    stownd.
Then do they cry and call to Love apace,
With praiers lowd importuning the skie, 880
Whence he them heares, and when he list
    shew grace,

Does graunt them grace that otherwise
    would die.
So Love is lord of all the world by right,
And rules the creatures by his powrfull saw;
All being made the vassalls of his might,
Through secret sence which therto doth
    them draw.
Thus ought all lovers of their lord to
    deeme,
And with chaste heart to honor him alway:
But who so else doth otherwise esteeme,
Are outlawes, and his lore do disobay.   890
For their desire is base, and doth not merit
The name of love, but of disloyall lust:
Ne mongst true lovers they shall place
    inherit,
But as exuls out of his court be thrust.'
So having said, Melissa spake at will:
'Colin, thou now full deeply hast divynd
Of love and beautie, and with wondrous
    skill
Hast Cupid selfe depainted in his kynd.
To thee are all true lovers greatly bound,
That doest their cause so mightily de-
    fend: 900
But most, all wemen are thy debtors found,
That doest their bountie still so much
    commend.'
'That ill,' said Hobbinol, 'they him
    requite,
For having loved ever one most deare:
He is repayd with scorne and foule de-
    spite,
That yrkes each gentle heart which it doth
    heare.'
'Indeed,' said Lucid, 'I have often heard
Faire Rosalind of divers fowly blamed,
For being to that swaine too cruell hard,
That her bright glorie else hath much
    defamed.   910
But who can tell what cause had that faire
    mayd
To use him so that used her so well ?
Or who with blame can justly her upbrayd,
For loving not ? for who can love com-
    pell ?
And sooth to say, it is foolhardie thing,
Rashly to wyten creatures so divine,
For demigods they be, and first did spring
From heaven, though graft in frailnesse
    feminine.
And well I wote that oft I heard it spoken,
How one that fairest Helene did revile, 920
Through judgement of the gods, to been
    ywroken,

Lost both his eyes, and so remaynd long
    while,
Till he recanted had his wicked rimes,
And made amends to her with treble praise:
Beware therefore, ye groomes, I read be-
    times,
How rashly blame of Rosalind ye raise.'
'Ah ! shepheards,' then said Colin, 'ye
    ne weet
How great a guilt upon your heads ye
    draw,
To make so bold a doome, with words un-
    meet,
Of thing celestiall which ye never saw. 930
For she is not like as the other crew
Of shepheards daughters which emongst
    you bee,
But of divine regard and heavenly hew,
Excelling all that ever ye did see.
Not then to her, that scorned thing so
    base,
But to my selfe the blame, that lookt so
    hie:
So hie her thoughts as she her selfe have
    place,
And loath each lowly thing with loftie
    eie.
Yet so much grace let her vouchsafe to
    grant
To simple swaine, sith her I may not love,
Yet that I may her honour paravant,   941
And praise her worth, though far my wit
    above.
Such grace shall be some guerdon for the
    griefe
And long affliction which I have endured:
Such grace sometimes shall give me some
    reliefe,
And ease of paine which cannot be re-
    cured.
And ye, my fellow shepheards, which do
    see
And heare the languours of my too long
    dying,
Unto the world for ever witnesse bee,
That hers I die, nought to the world deny-
    ing   950
This simple trophe of her great conquest.'
So having ended, he from ground did
    rise,
And after him uprose eke all the rest:
All loth to part, but that the glooming
    skies
Warnd them to draw their bleating flocks
    to rest.

ASTROPHEL

A PASTORALL ELEGIE UPON THE DEATH OF THE MOST NOBLE AND VALOROUS KNIGHT, SIR PHILIP SIDNEY

DEDICATED

TO THE MOST BEAUTIFULL AND VERTUOUS LADIE, THE COUNTESSE OF ESSEX

[*Astrophel* and the collection of obituary poems to which it serves as a kind of prologue were published in the same volume with *Colin Clout's Come Home Again*, in 1595. The dedication was to Sidney's widow, who in the spring of 1590 had become, by remarriage, the Countess of Essex. Sidney's sister, the Countess of Pembroke, presumably furnished that 'dolefull lay' which is set down to 'his sister that Clorinda hight.' The authors of the other poems, though undeclared, can, all but one, be traced by contemporary evidence — which need not be retailed here.

In 1595 most, if not all, of this poetry had been extant for several years: some of it had already seen print. The verses by the Countess of Pembroke would seem to be those referred to in 'The Ruins of Time,' which is of 1590: —

    'who can better sing
Than thine owne sister, peerles ladie bright,
Which to thee sings with deep harts sorrowing,
Sorrowing tempered with deare delight?'

The last line fits the lament of Clorinda exactly. Bryskett's poem, 'The Mourning Muse of Thestylis,' had been entered upon the Stationers' Register in August, 1587, and had perhaps in due course been published, though no copy of the issue has survived. Matthew Roydon's 'Elegy' and the two 'Epitaphs' had appeared in *The Phœnix Nest* of 1593, and are heard of earlier, Roydon's poem in 1589, Raleigh's in 1591. All the poems, except *Astro-* *phel* itself, may very well date from the twelve-month following Sidney's death in October, 1586.

Concerning *Astrophel* the only evidence is that of the dedication to 'The Ruins of Time.' 'Sithens my late cumming into England,' writes Spenser, 'some frends of mine, . . . knowing with howe straight bandes of duetie I was tied to him [i. e. Sidney] . . . have sought to revive them by upbraiding me, for that I have not shewed anie thankefull remembrance towards him or any of them [i. e. the Dudleys], but suffer their names to sleep in silence and forgetfulnesse. Whome chieflie to satisfie, or els to avoide that fowle blot of unthankefulnesse, I have conceived this small poeme.' At the time of writing thus, in 1590, Spenser cannot have already composed *Astrophel*. Yet he probably did compose it before his return to Ireland, for, once back there, he would be far removed from occasions to commemorate Sidney. What the occasion of this volume was we cannot know. Quite possibly he had little to do with originating the anthology or with dedicating it to the Countess of Essex: his part may have been only to supply a general prologue. One may note that for this he contented himself with the stanza-form of the Countess of Pembroke's elegy, a form which he had used in the *Calendar* and in such probably youthful work as 'The Tears of the Muses,' but which by 1590 his taste must surely have outgrown.]

ASTROPHEL

SHEPHEARDS, that wont on pipes of oaten reed
Oft times to plaine your loves concealed smart,
And with your piteous layes have learnd to breed
Compassion in a countrey lasses hart,
Hearken, ye gentle shepheards, to my song,
And place my dolefull plaint your plaints emong.

To you alone I sing this mournfull verse,
The mournfulst verse that ever man heard tell;
To you, whose softened hearts it may empierse
With dolours dart for death of Astrophel:
To you I sing, and to none other wight,
For well I wot my rymes bene rudely dight.

Yet as they been, if any nycer wit
Shall hap to heare, or covet them to read,

Thinke he, that such are for such ones most
    fit,
Made not to please the living but the dead.
And if in him found pity ever place,
Let him be moov'd to pity such a case.

———

A GENTLE shepheard borne in Arcady,
Of gentlest race that ever shepheard bore,
About the grassie banckes of Hæmony
Did keepe his sheep, his litle stock and store.
Full carefully he kept them day and night,
In fairest fields; and Astrophel he hight.

Young Astrophel, the pride of shepheards
    praise,
Young Astrophel, the rusticke lasses love,
Far passing all the pastors of his daies,
In all that seemly shepheard might be-
    hove: 10
In one thing onely fayling of the best,
That he was not so happie as the rest.

For from the time that first the nymph,
    his mother,
Him forth did bring, and taught her lambs
    to feed,
A sclender swaine, excelling far each other
In comely shape, like her that did him breed,
He grew up fast in goodnesse and in grace,
And doubly faire wox both in mynd and
    face.

Which daily more and more he did aug-
    ment,
With gentle usage and demeanure myld, 20
That all mens hearts with secret ravishment
He stole away, and weetingly beguyld.
Ne Spight it selfe, that all good things doth
    spill,
Found ought in him that she could say was
    ill.

His sports were faire, his joyance innocent,
Sweet without sowre, and honny without
    gall,
And he himselfe seemd made for meriment,
Merily masking both in bowre and hall:
There was no pleasure nor delightfull play,
When Astrophel so ever was away.   30

For he could pipe, and daunce, and caroll
    sweet,
Emongst the shepheards in their shearing
    feast;

As somers larke that with her song doth
    greet
The dawning day forth comming from the
    East.
And layes of love he also could compose:
Thrise happie she whom he to praise did
    chose.

Full many maydens often did him woo
Them to vouchsafe emongst his rimes to
    name,
Or make for them, as he was wont to doo
For her that did his heart with love in-
    flame.   40
For which they promised to dight for
    him
Gay chapelets of flowers and gyrlonds trim.

And many a nymph both of the wood and
    brooke,
Soone as his oaten pipe began to shrill,
Both christall wells and shadie groves for-
    sooke,
To heare the charmes of his enchanting
    skill;
And brought him presents, flowers if it were
    prime,
Or mellow fruit if it were harvest time.

But he for none of them did care a whit,
(Yet wood gods for them often sighed
    sore,)   50
Ne for their gifts, unworthie of his wit,
Yet not unworthie of the countries store.
For one alone he cared, for one he sight,
His lifes desire, and his deare loves de-
    light.

Stella the faire, the fairest star in skie,
As faire as Venus or the fairest faire,
(A fairer star saw never living eie,)
Shot her sharp pointed beames through
    purest aire.
Her he did love, her he alone did honor,
His thoughts, his rimes, his songs were all
    upon her.   60

To her he vowd the service of his daies,
On her he spent the riches of his wit:
For her he made hymnes of immortall
    praise,
Of onely her he sung, he thought, he writ.
Her, and but her, of love he worthie
    deemed;
For all the rest but litle he esteemed.

Ne her with ydle words alone he wowed,
And verses vaine, (yet verses are not vaine)
But with brave deeds, to her sole service
    vowed,
And bold atchievements, her did enter-
    taine. 70
For both in deeds and words he nourtred
    was,
Both wise and hardie (too hardie, alas !)

In wrestling nimble, and in renning swift,
In shooting steddie, and in swimming
    strong:
Well made to strike, to throw, to leape, to
    lift,
And all the sports that shepheards are
    emong:
In every one he vanquisht every one,
He vanquisht all, and vanquisht was of
    none.

Besides, in hunting such felicitie,
Or rather infelicitie, he found, 80
That every field and forest far away
He sought, where salvage beasts do most
    abound.
No beast so salvage, but he could it kill;
No chace so hard, but he therein had skill.

Such skill, matcht with such courage as he
    had,
Did prick him foorth with proud desire of
    praise,
To seek abroad, of daunger nought y'drad,
His mistresse name, and his owne fame, to
    raise.
What need perill to be sought abroad,
Since round about us it doth make abroad ? 90

It fortuned, as he that perilous game
In forreine soyle pursued far away,
Into a forest wide and waste he came,
Where store he heard to be of salvage pray.
So wide a forest and so waste as this,
Nor famous Ardeyn, nor fowle Arlo, is.

There his welwoven toyles and subtil traines
He laid the brutish nation to enwrap:
So well he wrought with practise and with
    paines,
That he of them great troups did soone
    entrap. 100
Full happie man (misweening much) was
    hee,
So rich a spoile within his power to see.

Eftsoones, all heedlesse of his dearest hale,
Full greedily into the heard he thrust,
To slaughter them, and worke their finall
    bale,
Least that his toyle should of their troups
    be brust.
Wide wounds emongst them many one he
    made,
Now with his sharp borespear, now with his
    blade.

His care was all how he them all might
    kill,
That none might scape (so partiall unto
    none):
Ill mynd, so much to mynd anothers ill, 110
As to become unmyndfull of his owne:
But pardon that unto the cruell skies,
That from himselfe to them withdrew his
    eies.

So as he rag'd emongst that beastly rout,
A cruell beast of most accursed brood
Upon him turnd (despeyre makes cowards
    stout)
And, with fell tooth accustomed to blood,
Launched his thigh with so mischievous
    might,
That it both bone and muscles ryved
    quight. 120

So deadly was the dint and deep the wound,
And so huge streames of blood thereout did
    flow,
That he endured not the direfull stound,
But on the cold deare earth himselfe did
    throw.
The whiles the captive heard his nets did
    rend,
And having none to let, to wood did wend.

Ah ! where were ye this while, his shepheard
    peares,
To whom alive was nought so deare as hee ?
And ye, faire mayds, the matches of his
    yeares,
Which in his grace did boast you most to
    bee ? 130
Ah ! where were ye, when he of you had
    need,
To stop his wound, that wondrously did
    bleed ?

Ah, wretched boy, the shape of dreryhead,
And sad ensample of mans suddein end !

Full litle faileth but thou shalt be dead,
Unpitied, unplaynd, of foe or frend;
Whilest none is nigh, thine eylids up to
  close,
And kisse thy lips like faded leaves of rose.

A sort of shepheards, sewing of the chace,
As they the forest raunged on a day,   140
By fate or fortune came unto the place,
Where as the lucklesse boy yet bleeding lay;
Yet bleeding lay, and yet would still have
  bled,
Had not good hap those shepheards thether
  led.

They stopt his wound (too late to stop it
  was)
And in their armes then softly did him
  reare:
Tho (as he wild) unto his loved lasse,
His dearest love, him dolefully did beare.
The dolefulst beare that ever man did see
Was Astrophel, but dearest unto mee.   150

She, when she saw her love in such a plight,
With crudled blood and filthie gore de-
  formed,
That wont to be with flowers and gyrlonds
  dight,
And her deare favours dearly well adorned,
Her face, the fairest face that eye mote see,
She likewise did deforme like him to bee.

Her yellow locks, that shone so bright and
  long,
As sunny beames in fairest somers day,
She fiersly tore, and with outragious wrong
From her red cheeks the roses rent away, 160
And her faire brest, the threasury of joy,
She spoyld thereof, and filled with annoy.

His palled face, impictured with death,
She bathed oft with teares and dried oft:
And with sweet kisses suckt the wasting
  breath
Out of his lips like lillies pale and soft:
And oft she cald to him, who answerd
  nought,
But onely by his lookes did tell his thought.

The rest of her impatient regret,
And piteous mone the which she for him
  made,   170
No toong can tell, nor any forth can set,
But he whose heart like sorrow did invade.

At last when paine his vitall powres had
  spent,
His wasted life her weary lodge forwent.

Which when she saw, she staied not a whit,
But after him did make untimely haste:
Forthwith her ghost out of her corps did
  flit,
And followed her make like turtle chaste;
To prove that death their hearts cannot
  divide,
Which living were in love so firmly tide.

The gods, which all things see, this same
  beheld,   181
And pittying this paire of lovers trew,
Transformed them, there lying on the field,
Into one flowre that is both red and blew:
It first growes red, and then to blew doth
  fade,
Like Astrophel, which thereinto was made.

And in the midst thereof a star appeares,
As fairly formd as any star in skyes,
Resembling Stella in her freshest yeares,
Forth darting beames of beautie from her
  eyes;   190
And all the day it standeth full of deow,
Which is the teares that from her eyes did
  flow.

That hearbe, of some, Starlight is cald by
  name,
Of others Penthia, though not so well:
But thou, where ever thou doest finde the
  same,
From this day forth do call it Astrophel:
And when so ever thou it up doest take,
Do pluck it softly for that shepheards
  sake.

Hereof when tydings far abroad did passe,
The shepheards all which loved him full
  deare,   200
And sure full deare of all he loved was,
Did thether flock to see what they did
  heare.
And when that pitteous spectacle they
  vewed,
The same with bitter teares they all be-
  dewed.

And every one did make exceeding mone,
With inward anguish and great griefe opprest:

And every one did weep and waile and
 mone,
And meanes deviz'd to shew his sorrow
 best:
That from that houre since first on grassie
 greene
Shepheards kept sheep, was not like
 mourning seen.   210

But first his sister, that Clorinda hight,
The gentlest shepheardesse that lives this
 day,
And most resembling both in shape and
 spright
Her brother deare, began this dolefull lay.
Which, least I marre the sweetnesse of
 the vearse,
In sort as she it sung I will rehearse.

[Verses presumably by the Countess of
Pembroke.]

Ay me ! to whom shall I my case complaine,
That may compassion my impatient griefe ?
Or where shall I unfold my inward paine,
That my enriven heart may find reliefe ?
Shall I unto the heavenly powres it show ?
Or unto earthly men that dwell below ?

To heavens ? Ah ! they, alas ! the authors
 were,
And workers of my unremedied wo:
For they foresee what to us happens here,
And they foresaw, yet suffred this be so. 10
From them comes good, from them comes
 also il;
That which they made, who can them warne
 to spill ?

To men ? Ah ! they, alas ! like wretched
 bee,
And subject to the heavens ordinance:
Bound to abide what ever they decree,
Their best redresse is their best suffer-
 ance.
How then can they, like wretched, comfort
 mee,
The which no lesse need comforted to bee ?

Then to my selfe will I my sorrow mourne,
Sith none alive like sorrowfull remaines: 20
And to my selfe my plaints shall back re-
 tourne,
To pay their usury with doubled paines.

The woods, the hills, the rivers shall resound
The mournfull accent of my sorrowes
 ground.

Woods, hills, and rivers now are desolate,
Sith he is gone the which them all did grace:
And all the fields do waile their widow state,
Sith death their fairest flowre did late deface.
The fairest flowre in field that ever grew
Was Astrophel; that was, we all may rew. 30

What cruell hand of cursed foe unknowne
Hath cropt the stalke which bore so faire a
 flowre ?
Untimely cropt, before it well were growne,
And cleane defaced in untimely howre.
Great losse to all that ever him did see,
Great losse to all, but greatest losse to mee !

Breake now your gyrlonds, O ye shepheards
 lasses,
Sith the faire flowre which them adornd is
 gon:
The flowre which them adornd is gone to
 ashes;
Never againe let lasse put gyrlond on. 40
In stead of gyrlond, weare sad cypres nowe,
And bitter elder, broken from the bowe.

Ne ever sing the love-layes which he made;
Who ever made such layes of love as hee ?
Ne ever read the riddles which he sayd
Unto your selves, to make you mery glee.
Your mery glee is now laid all abed,
Your mery maker now, alasse ! is dead.

Death, the devourer of all worlds delight,
Hath robbed you and reft fro me my joy: 50
Both you and me and all the world he quight
Hath robd of joyance, and left sad annoy.
Joy of the world and shepheards pride was
 hee:
Shepheards, hope never like againe to see.

Oh Death ! that hast us of such riches reft,
Tell us at least, what hast thou with it done ?
What is become of him whose flowre here
 left
Is but the shadow of his likenesse gone ?
Scarse like the shadow of that which he was,
Nought like, but that he like a shade did
 pas.   60

But that immortall spirit, which was deckt
With all the dowries of celestiall grace,

By soveraine choyce from th' hevenly quires
    select,
And lineally deriv'd from angels race,
O ! what is now of it become, aread.
Ay me ! can so divine a thing be dead ?

Ah, no ! it is not dead, ne can it die,
But lives for aie in blisfull Paradise:
Where like a new-borne babe it soft doth
    lie,
In bed of lillies wrapt in tender wise,   70
And compast all about with roses sweet,
And daintie violets from head to feet.

There thousand birds, all of celestiall brood,
To him do sweetly caroll day and night;
And with straunge notes, of him well under-
    stood,
Lull him a sleep in angelick delight;
Whilest in sweet dreame to him presented
    bee
Immortall beauties, which no eye may see.

But he them sees, and takes exceeding
    pleasure
Of their divine aspects, appearing plaine, 80
And kindling love in him above all measure,
Sweet love, still joyous, never feeling paine.
For what so goodly forme he there doth see,
He may enjoy from jealous rancor free.

There liveth he in everlasting blis,
Sweet spirit, never fearing more to die:
Ne dreading harme from any foes of his,
Ne fearing salvage beasts more crueltie:
Whilest we here, wretches, waile his private
    lack,
And with vaine vowes do often call him
    back.   90

But live thou there, still happie, happie
    spirit,
And give us leave thee here thus to la-
    ment:
Not thee that doest thy heavens joy inherit,
But our owne selves that here in dole are
    drent.
Thus do we weep and waile, and wear our
    eies,
Mourning in others our owne miseries.

———

WHICH when she ended had, another
    swaine,
Of gentle wit and daintie sweet device,

Whom Astrophel full deare did enter-
    taine,
Whilest here he liv'd, and held in passing
    price,   220
Hight Thestylis, began his mournfull
    tourne,
And made the Muses in his song to mourne.

And after him full many other moe,
As everie one in order lov'd him best,
Gan dight themselves t' expresse their in-
    ward woe,
With dolefull layes unto the time addrest.
The which I here in order will rehearse,
As fittest flowres to deck his mournfull
    hearse.

THE MOURNING MUSE OF
THESTYLIS

[By Lodowick Bryskett.]

COME forth, ye Nymphes, come forth, for-
    sake your watry bowres,
Forsake your mossy caves, and help me to
    lament:
Help me to tune my dolefull notes to gur-
    gling sound
Of Liffies tumbling streames: come, let
    salt teares of ours
Mix with his waters fresh. O come, let
    one consent
Joyne us to mourne with wailfull plaints
    the deadly wound
Which fatall clap hath made; decreed by
    higher powres;
The dreery day in which they have from
    us yrent
The noblest plant that might from East to
    West be found.
Mourne, mourn great Philips fall, mourn
    we his wofull end,   10
Whom spitefull Death hath pluct untimely
    from the tree,
Whiles yet his yeares in flowre did promise
    worthie frute.
    Ah ! dreadfull Mars, why didst thou not
    thy knight defend ?
What wrathfull mood, what fault of ours
    hath moved thee
Of such a shining light to leave us desti-
    tute ?
Thou with benigne aspect sometime didst
    us behold,

Thou hast in Britons valour tane delight
of old,
And with thy presence oft vouchsaft to
attribute
Fame and renowme to us for glorious martiall deeds.
But now thy ireful bemes have chill'd our
harts with cold;   20
Thou hast estrang'd thy self, and deignest
not our land:
Farre off to others now thy favour honour
breeds,
And high disdaine doth cause thee shun
our clime (I feare.)
For hadst thou not bene wroth, or that
time neare at hand,
Thou wouldst have heard the cry that woful England made;
Eke Zelands piteous plaints and Hollands
toren heare
Would haply have appeas'd thy divine an-
gry mynd.
Thou shouldst have seen the trees refuse
to yeeld their shade,
And wailing to let fall the honor of their
head,
And birds in mournfull tunes lamenting in
their kinde.   30
Up from his tombe the mightie Corineus rose,
Who cursing oft the Fates that this mishap
had bred,
His hoary locks he tare, calling the heavens
unkinde.
The Thames was heard to roare, the Reyne
and eke the Mose,
The Schald, the Danow selfe this great
mischance did rue,
With torment and with grief; their fountains pure and cleere
Were troubled, and with swelling flouds
declar'd their woes.
The Muses comfortles, the Nymphs with
paled hue,
The silvan gods likewise came running farre
and neere,
And all with teares bedeawd, and eyes cast
up on hie,   40
'O help, O help, ye gods!' they ghastly
gan to crie.
'O chaunge the cruell fate of this so rare
a wight,
And graunt that natures course may measure out his age!'
The beasts their foode forsooke, and trembling fearfully,

Each sought his cave or den, this cry did
them so fright.
Out from amid the waves, by storme then
stirr'd to rage,
This crie did cause to rise th' old father
Ocean hoare,
Who, grave with eld, and full of majestie
in sight,
Spake in this wise: 'Refrain,' quoth he,
'your teares and plaints,
Cease these your idle words, make vaine
requests no more.   50
No humble speech nor mone may move the
fixed stint
Of destinie or death: such is his will that
paints
The earth with colours fresh, the darkest
skies with store
Of starry lights: and though your teares
a hart of flint
Might tender make, yet nought herein they
will prevaile.'
    Whiles thus he said, the noble knight,
who gan to feele
His vitall force to faint, and Death with
cruell dint
Of direfull dart his mortall bodie to assaile,
With eyes lift up to heav'n, and courage
franke as steele,
With cheerfull face, where valour lively
was exprest,   60
But humble mynd, he said: 'O Lord, if
ought this fraile
And earthly carcasse have thy service
sought t' advaunce;
If my desire have bene still to relieve th'
opprest;
If, justice to maintaine, that valour I have
spent
Which thou me gav'st; or if henceforth I
might advaunce
Thy name, thy truth, then spare me (Lord)
if thou think best;
Forbeare these unripe yeares. But if thy
will be bent,
If that prefixed time be come which thou
hast set,
Through pure and fervent faith, I hope now
to be plast
In th' everlasting blis which with thy precious blood   70
Thou purchase didst for us.' With that a
sigh he fet,
And straight a cloudie mist his sences
overcast,

His lips waxt pale and wan, like damaske
roses bud
Cast from the stalke, or like in field to
purple flowre,
Which languisheth being shred by culter
as it past.
A trembling chilly cold ran throgh their
veines, which were
With eies brimfull of teares to see his
fatall howre;
Whose blustring sighes at first their sorrow did declare;
Next, murmuring ensude; at last they not
forbeare
Plaine outcries, all against the heav'ns that
enviously   80
Depriv'd us of a spright so perfect and so
rare.
The sun his lightsom beames did shrowd,
and hide his face
For griefe, whereby the earth feard night
eternally:
The mountaines eachwhere shooke, the
rivers turn'd their streames,
And th' aire gan winterlike to rage and
fret apace:
And grisly ghosts by night were seene, and
fierie gleames
Amid the clouds, with claps of thunder,
that did seeme
To rent the skies, and made both man and
beast afeard.
The birds of ill presage this lucklesse
chance foretold,
By dernfull noise, and dogs with howling
made man deeme   90
Some mischief was at hand: for such they
do esteeme
As tokens of mishap, and so have done of old.
  Ah! that thou hadst but heard his lovely
Stella plaine
Her greevous losse, or seene her heavie
mourning cheere,
While she, with woe opprest, her sorrowes
did unfold.
Her haire hung lose neglect, about her
shoulders twaine,
And from those two bright starres, to him
sometime so deere,
Her heart sent drops of pearle, which fell
in foyson downe
Twixt lilly and the rose. She wroong her
hands with paine,
And piteously gan say: 'My true and
faithfull pheere,   100

Alas, and woe is me! why should my fortune frowne
On me thus frowardly, to rob me of my
joy?
What cruell envious hand hath taken thee
away,
And with thee my content, my comfort,
and my stay?
Thou onelie wast the ease of trouble and
annoy,
When they did me assaile, in thee my
hopes did rest.
Alas! what now is left but grief, that
night and day
Afflicts this wofull life, and with continuall
rage
Torments ten thousand waies my miserable brest?
O greedie envious heav'n, what needed
thee to have   110
Enricht with such a jewell this unhappie age,
To take it back againe so soone? Alas!
when shall
Mine eies see ought that may content
them, since thy grave
My onely treasure hides, the joyes of my
poore hart?
As here with thee on earth I liv'd, even so
equall
Methinkes it were with thee in heav'n I did
abide:
And as our troubles all we here on earth
did part,
So reason would that there of thy most
happie state
I had my share. Alas! if thou my trustie
guide
Were wont to be, how canst thou leave me
thus alone   120
In darknesse and astray, weake, wearie,
desolate,
Plung'd in a world of woe, refusing for to
take
Me with thee to the place of rest where
thou art gone?'
This said, she held her peace, for sorrow
tide her toong;
And instead of more words, seemd that her
eies a lake
Of teares had bene, they flow'd so plen-
teously therefro:
And with her sobs and sighs th' aire round
about her roong.
  If Venus, when she waild her deare
Adonis slaine,

Ought moov'd in thy fiers hart compassion
    of her woe,
His noble sisters plaints, her sighes and
    teares emong,   130
Would sure have made thee milde, and
    inly rue her paine.
Aurora halfe so faire her selfe did never show,
When from old Tithons bed shee weeping
    did arise.
The blinded archer-boy, like larke in showre
    of raine,
Sat bathing of his wings, and glad the time
    did spend
Under those cristall drops which fell from
    her faire eies,
And at their brightest beames him proynd
    in lovely wise.
Yet sorie for her grief, which he could not
    amend,
The gentle boy gan wipe her eies, and
    clear those lights,
Those lights through which his glory and
    his conquests shine.   140
The Graces tuckt her hair, which hung like
    threds of gold,
Along her yvorie brest, the treasure of de-
    lights.
All things with her to weep, it seemed, did
    encline,
The trees, the hills, the dales, the caves,
    the stones so cold.
The aire did help them mourne, with dark
    clouds, raine, and mist,
Forbearing many a day to cleare it selfe
    againe;
Which made them eftsoones feare the daies
    of Pirrha shold
Of creatures spoile the earth, their fatall
    threds untwist.
For Phœbus gladsome raies were wished
    for in vaine,
And with her quivering light Latonas
    daughter faire,   150
And Charles-waine eke refus'd to be the
    shipmans guide.
On Neptune warre was made by Aeolus
    and his traine,
Who, letting loose the winds, tost and tor-
    mented th' aire,
So that on ev'ry coast men shipwrack did
    abide,
Or else were swallowed up in open sea with
    waves,
And such as came to shoare were beaten
    with despaire.

The Medwaies silver streames, that wont so
    still to slide,
Were troubled now and wrothe: whose
    hidden hollow caves
Along his banks, with fog then shrowded
    from mans eye,
Ay 'Phillip!' did resownd, aie 'Phillip!'
    they did crie.   160
His nimphs were seen no more (thogh
    custom stil it craves)
With haire spred to the wynd themselves
    to bath or sport,
Or with the hooke or net, barefooted wan-
    tonly,
The pleasant daintie fish to entangle or
    deceive.
The shepheards left their wonted places of
    resort;
Their bagpipes now were still; their loving
    mery layes
Were quite forgot; and now their flocks
    men might perceive
To wander and to straie, all carelesly
    neglect:
And in the stead of mirth and pleasure,
    nights and dayes
Nought els was to be heard, but woes,
    complaints, and mone.   170
    But thou (O blessed soule) doest haply
        not respect
These teares we shead, though full of loving
    pure affect,
Having affixt thine eyes on that most glo-
    rious throne,
Where full of majestie the High Creator
    reignes:
In whose bright shining face thy joyes are
    all complete;
Whose love kindles thy spright; where,
    happie alwaies one,
Thou liv'st in blis that earthly passion never
    staines;
Where from the purest spring the sacred
    nectar sweete
Is thy continuall drinke; where thou doest
    gather now
Of well emploied life th' inestimable gaines.
There Venus on thee smiles, Apollo gives
    thee place,   181
And Mars in reverent wise doth to thy
    vertue bow,
And decks his fiery sphere, to do thee hon-
    our most.
In highest part whereof, thy valour for to
    grace,

A chaire of gold he setts to thee, and there
doth tell
Thy noble acts arew, whereby even they
that boast
Themselves of auncient fame, as Pirrhus,
Hanniball,
Scipio, and Cæsar, with the rest that did
excell
In martiall prowesse, high thy glorie do
admire.
All haile, therefore, O worthie Phillip
immortall,   190
The flowre of Sydneyes race, the honour of
thy name!
Whose worthie praise to sing my Muses
not aspire,
But sorrowfull and sad these teares to thee
let fall,
Yet wish their verses might so farre and
wide thy fame
Extend, that envies rage, nor time, might
end the same.

A PASTORALL AEGLOGUE UPON THE DEATH OF SIR PHILLIP SIDNEY, KNIGHT, &c.

[By Lodowick Bryskett.]

LYCON. COLIN.

COLIN, well fits thy sad cheare this sad
stownd,
This wofull stownd, wherein all things
complaine
This great mishap, this greevous losse of
owres.
Hear'st thou the Crown? how with hollow
sownd
He slides away, and murmuring doth plaine,
And seemes to say unto the fading flowres
Along his bankes, unto the bared trees,
'Phillisides is dead'? Up, jolly swaine,
Thou that with skill canst tune a dolefull
lay,
Help him to mourn. My hart with grief
doth freese,   10
Hoarse is my voice with crying, else a part
Sure would I beare, though rude: but as I
may,
With sobs and sighes I second will thy
song,
And so expresse the sorrowes of my hart.
  Colin. Ah, Lycon, Lycon! what need
skill, to teach

A grieved mynd powre forth his plaints?
How long
Hath the pore turtle gon to schooi (ween-
est thou)
To learne to mourne her lost make? No,
no, each
Creature by nature can tell how to waile.
Seest not these flocks, how sad they wan-
der now?   20
Seemeth their leaders bell their bleating
tunes
In dolefull sound. Like him, not one doth
faile
With hanging head to shew a heavie
cheare.
What bird (I pray thee) hast thou seen
that prunes
Himselfe of late? Did any cheerfull note
Come to thine eares, or gladsome sight ap-
peare
Unto thine eies, since that same fatall
howre?
Hath not the aire put on his mourning
coat,
And testified his grief with flowing teares?
Sith, then, it seemeth each thing, to his
powre,   30
Doth us invite to make a sad consort,
Come, let us joyne our mournfull song
with theirs.
Griefe will endite, and sorrow will enforce
Thy voice, and Eccho will our words re-
port.
  Lycon. Though my rude rymes ill with
thy verses frame,
That others farre excell, yet will I force
My selfe to answere thee the best I can,
And honor my base words with his high
name.
But if my plaints annoy thee where thou
sit
In secret shade or cave, vouchsafe (O Pan)
To pardon me, and here this hard con-
straint   41
With patience while I sing, and pittie it.
And eke ye rurall Muses, that do dwell
In these wilde woods, if ever piteous plaint
We did endite, or taught a wofull minde
With words of pure affect his griefe to tell,
Instruct me now. Now, Colin, then goe on,
And I will follow thee, though farre be-
hinde.
  Colin. Phillisides is dead. O harmfull
death,
O deadly harme! Unhappie Albion,   50

When shalt thou see emong thy shepheards all,
Any so sage, so perfect ? Whom uneath
Envie could touch for vertuous life and skill;
Curteous, valiant, and liberall.
Behold the sacred Pales, where with haire
Untrust she sits, in shade of yonder hill,
And her faire face bent sadly downe, doth send
A floud of teares to bathe the earth; and there
Doth call the heav'ns despightfull, envious,
Cruell his fate, that made so short an end 60
Of that same life, well worthie to have bene
Prolongd with many yeares, happie and famous.
The Nymphs and Oreades her round about
Do sit lamenting on the grassie grene,
And with shrill cries, beating their whitest brests,
Accuse the direfull dart that Death sent out
To give the fatall stroke. The starres they blame,
That deafe or carelesse seeme at their request.
The pleasant shade of stately groves they shun;
They leave their cristall springs, where they wont frame 70
Sweet bowres of myrtel twigs and lawrel faire,
To sport themselves free from the scorching sun.
And now the hollow caves, where horror darke
Doth dwell, whence banisht is the gladsome aire,
They seeke; and there in mourning spend their time
With wailfull tunes, whiles wolves do howle and barke,
And seem to beare a bourdon to their plaint.
  Lycon. Phillisides is dead. O dolefull ryme !
Why should my toong expresse thee ? Who is left
Now to uphold thy hopes, when they do faint, 80
Lycon unfortunate ? What spitefull fate,
What lucklesse destinie, hath thee bereft

Of thy chief comfort, of thy onely stay ?
Where is become thy wonted happie state,
(Alas !) wherein through many a hill and dale,
Through pleasant woods, and many an unknowne way,
Along the bankes of many silver streames,
Thou with him yodest, and with him didst scale
The craggie rocks of th' Alpes and Appenine,
Still with the Muses sporting, while those beames 90
Of vertue kindled in his noble brest,
Which after did so gloriously forth shine ?
But (woe is me !) they now yquenched are
All suddeinly, and death hath them opprest.
Loe Father Neptune, with sad countenance,
How he sitts mourning on the strond now bare,
Yonder, where th' Ocean with his rolling waves
The white feete washeth (wailing this mischance)
Of Dover cliffes. His sacred skirt about
The sea-gods all are set; from their moist caves 100
All for his comfort gathered there they be.
The Thamis rich, the Humber rough and stout,
The fruitfull Severne with the rest are come
To helpe their lord to mourne, and eke to see
The dolefull sight, and sad pomp funerall
Of the dead corps passing through his kingdome.
And all their heads, with cypres gyrlonds crown'd,
With wofull shrikes salute him, great and small.
Eke wailfull Eccho, forgetting her deare
Narcissus, their last accents doth resownd.
  Colin. Phillisides is dead. O lucklesse age, 111
O widow world ! O brookes and fountains cleere,
O hills, O dales, O woods, that oft have rong
With his sweet caroling, which could asswage
The fiercest wrath of tygre or of beare;
Ye Silvans, Fawnes, and Satyres, that emong

These thickets oft have daunst after his pipe;
Ye Nymphs and Nayades with golden
  heare,
That oft have left your purest cristall
  springs
To harken to his layes, that coulden wipe
Away all griefe and sorrow from your
  harts: 121
Alas ! who now is left that like him sings ?
When shall you heare againe like har-
  monie ?
So sweet a sownd who to you now im-
  parts ?
Loe where engraved by his hand yet lives
The name of Stella, in yonder bay tree.
Happie name, happie tree ! faire may you
  grow,
And spred your sacred branch, which honor
  gives
To famous emperours, and poets crowne.
Unhappie flock, that wander scattred now,
What marvell if through grief ye woxen
  leane,   131
Forsake your food, and hang your heads
  adowne ?
For such a shepheard never shall you
  guide,
Whose parting hath of weale bereft you
  cleane.
  Lycon. Phillisides is dead. O happie
    sprite,
That now in heav'n with blessed soules
  doest bide,
Looke down a while from where thou sitst
  above,
And see how busie shepheards be to endite
Sad songs of grief, their sorrowes to de-
  clare,   139
And gratefull memory of their kynd love.
Behold my selfe with Colin, gentle swaine,
(Whose lerned muse thou cherisht most
  whyleare)
Where we, thy name recording, seeke to
  ease
The inward torment and tormenting paine,
That thy departure to us both hath bred;
Ne can each others sorrow yet appease.
Behold the fountains now left desolate,
And withred grasse with cypres boughes
  bespred;
Behold these floures which on thy grave
  we strew,
Which, faded, shew the givers faded state,
(Though eke they shew their fervent zeale
  and pure)   151

Whose onely comfort on thy welfare grew.
Whose praiers importune shall the heav'ns
  for ay,
That to thy ashes rest they may assure;
That learnedst shepheards honor may thy
  name
With yeerly praises, and the Nymphs al-
  way
Thy tomb may deck with fresh and sweet-
  est flowres;
And that for ever may endure thy fame.
  Colin. The sun (lo !) hastned hath his
    face to steep
In western waves; and th' aire with stormy
  showres   160
Warnes us to drive homewards our silly
  sheep.
Lycon, lett's rise, and take of them good
  keep.

  Virtute summa : cætera fortuna.

  L. B.

AN ELEGIE, OR FRIENDS PAS-
SION, FOR HIS ASTROPHILL

WRITTEN UPON THE DEATH OF THE
RIGHT HONOURABLE SIR PHILLIP SID-
NEY, KNIGHT, LORD GOVERNOUR OF
FLUSHING

[By Matthew Roydon.]

As then, no winde at all there blew,
No swelling cloude accloid the aire;
The skie, like glasse of watchet hew,
Reflected Phœbus golden haire;
  The garnisht tree no pendant stird,
  No voice was heard of anie bird.

There might you see the burly beare,
The lion king, the elephant;
The maiden unicorne was there,
So was Acteons horned plant,   10
  And what of wilde or tame are found
  Were coucht in order on the ground.

Alcides speckled poplar tree,
The palme that monarchs do obtaine,
With love juice staind, the mulberie,
The fruit that dewes the poets braine,
  And Phillis philbert there away,
  Comparde with mirtle and the bay,

The tree that coffins doth adorne,
With stately height threatning the skie,   20
And for the bed of love forlorne,
The blacke and dolefull ebonie,
  All in a circle compast were,
  Like to an amphitheater.

Upon the branches of those trees
The airie winged people sat,
Distinguished in od degrees,
One sort is this, another that.
  Here Philomell, that knowes full well
  What force and wit in love doth dwell. 30

The skiebred egle, roiall bird,
Percht there upon an oke above;
The turtle by him never stird,
Example of immortall love;
The swan that sings about to dy,
Leaving Meander, stood thereby.

And that which was of woonder most,
The phœnix left sweet Arabie,
And on a cædar in this coast
Built up her tombe of spicerie,   40
  As I conjecture by the same,
  Preparde to take her dying flame.

In midst and center of this plot,
I saw one groveling on the grasse:
A man or stone, I knew not that:
No stone; of man the figure was,
  And yet I could not count him one,
  More than the image made of stone.

At length I might perceive him reare
His bodie on his elbow end: 50
Earthly and pale with gastly cheare,
Upon his knees he upward tend,
  Seeming like one in uncouth stound,
  To be ascending out the ground.

A grievous sigh forthwith he throwes,
As might have torne the vitall strings;
Then down his cheeks the teares so flows,
As doth the streame of many springs.
  So thunder rends the cloud in twaine,
  And makes a passage for the raine.   60

Incontinent, with trembling sound
He wofully gan to complaine;
Such were the accents as might wound,
And teare a diamond rocke in twaine:
  After his throbs did somewhat stay,
  Thus heavily he gan to say.

' O sunne,' said he, seeing the sunne,
' On wretched me why dost thou shine ?
My star is falne, my comfort done,
Out is the apple of my eine: 70
  Shine upon those possesse delight,
  And let me live in endlesse night.

' O griefe that liest upon my soule,
As heavie as a mount of lead,
The remnant of my life controll,
Consort me quickly with the dead;
  Halfe of this hart, this sprite, and will,
  Di'de in the brest of Astrophill.

' And you, compassionate of my wo,
Gentle birds, beasts, and shadie trees,   80
I am assurde ye long to kno
What be the sorrowes me agreev's;
  Listen ye then to that insu'th,
  And heare a tale of teares and ruthe.

' You knew — who knew not ? — Astro-
  phill:
(That I should live to say I knew,
And have not in possession still !)
Things knowne permit me to renew;
  Of him you know his merit such,
  I cannot say, you heare, too much.   90

' Within these woods of Arcadie
He chiefe delight and pleasure tooke,
And on the mountaine Parthenie,
Upon the chrystall liquid brooke,
  The Muses met him ev'ry day,
  That taught him sing, to write, and
  say.

' When he descended downe the mount,
His personage seemed most divine,
A thousand graces one might count
Upon his lovely cheerfull eine,   100
  To heare him speake and sweetly smile,
  You were in Paradise the while.

' A sweet attractive kinde of grace,
A full assurance given by lookes,
Continuall comfort in a face,
The lineaments of Gospell bookes;
  I trowe that countenance cannot lie,
  Whose thoughts are legible in the eie.

' Was never eie, did see that face,
Was never eare, did heare that tong,   110
Was never minde, did minde his grace,
That ever thought the travell long,

But eies, and eares, and ev'ry thought,
Were with his sweete perfections
    caught.

'O God, that such a worthy man,
In whom so rare desarts did raigne,
Desired thus, must leave us than,
And we to wish for him in vaine!
    O could the stars that bred that wit
    In force no longer fixed sit?   120

'Then being fild with learned dew,
The Muses willed him to love;
That instrument can aptly shew
How finely our conceits will move:
    As Bacchus opes dissembled harts,
    So Love sets out our better parts.

'Stella, a nymph within this wood,
Most rare and rich of heavenly blis,
The highest in his fancie stood,
And she could well demerite this: 130
    Tis likely they acquainted soone;
    He was a sun, and she a moone.

'Our Astrophill did Stella love;
O Stella, vaunt of Astrophill,
Albeit thy graces gods may move,
Where wilt thou finde an Astrophill?
    The rose and lillie have their prime,
    And so hath beautie but a time.

'Although thy beautie do exceed,
In common sight of ev'ry eie,   140
Yet in his poesies when we reede,
It is apparant more thereby:
    He that hath love and judgement too
    Sees more than any other doo.

'Then Astrophill hath honord thee;
For when thy bodie is extinct,
Thy graces shall eternall be,
And live by vertue of his inke;
    For by his verses he doth give
    To short livde beautie aye to live.   150

'Above all others this is hee,
Which erst approved in his song
That love and honor might agree,
And that pure love will do no wrong.
    Sweet saints! it is no sinne nor blame,
    To love a man of vertuous name.

'Did never love so sweetly breath
In any mortall brest before;

Did never Muse inspire beneath
A poets braine with finer store: 160
    He wrote of love with high conceit,
    And beautie reard above her height.

'Then Pallas afterward attyrde
Our Astrophill with her device,
Whom in his armor heaven admyrde,
As of the nation of the skies;
    He sparkled in his armes afarrs,
    As he were dight with fierie starrs.

'The blaze whereof when Mars beheld,
(An envious eie doth see afar)   170
"Such majestie," quoth he, "is seeld,
Such majestie my mart may mar;
    Perhaps this may a suter be,
    To set Mars by his deitie."

'In this surmize he made with speede
An iron cane, wherein he put
The thunder that in cloudes do breede;
The flame and bolt togither shut
    With privie force burst out againe,
    And so our Astrophill was slaine.'   180

His word, 'was slaine,' straightway did
    move,
And Natures inward life strings twitch:
The skie immediately above
Was dimd with hideous clouds of pitch,
    The wrastling winds from out the ground
    Fild all the aire with ratling sound.

The bending trees exprest a grone,
And sigh'd the sorrow of his fall,
The forrest beasts made ruthfull mone,
The birds did tune their mourning call,   190
    And Philomell for Astrophill
    Unto her notes annext a phill.

The turtle dove with tunes of ruthe
Shewd feeling passion of his death;
Me thought she said, 'I tell thee truthe,
Was never he that drew in breath
    Unto his love more trustie found,
    Than he for whom our griefs abound.'

The swan, that was in presence heere,
Began his funerall dirge to sing: 200
'Good things,' quoth he, 'may scarce ap-
    peere,
But passe away with speedie wing:
    This mortall life as death is tride,
    And death gives life,'— and so he di'de.

The generall sorrow that was made
Among the creatures of Kinde
Fired the phœnix where she laide,
Her ashes flying with the winde,
 So as I might with reason see,
 That such a phœnix nere should bee. 210

Haply the cinders, driven about,
May breede an offspring neere that kinde,
But hardly a peere to that, I doubt;
It cannot sinke into my minde,
 That under branches ere can bee
 Of worth and value as the tree.

The egle markt with pearcing sight
The mournfull habite of the place,
And parted thence with mounting flight,
To signifie to Jove the case, 220
 What sorrow Nature doth sustaine
 For Astrophill by envie slaine.

And while I followed with mine eie
The flight the egle upward tooke,
All things did vanish by and by,
And disappeared from my looke;
 The trees, beasts, birds, and grove was
  gone,
 So was the friend that made this mone.

This spectacle had firmly wrought
A deepe compassion in my spright; 230
My molting hart issude, me thought,
In streames forth at mine eies aright:
 And here my pen is forst to shrinke,
 My teares discollors so mine inke.

AN EPITAPH UPON THE RIGHT HONOURABLE SIR PHILLIP SIDNEY, KNIGHT: LORD GOVERNOR OF FLUSHING

[By Sir Walter Raleigh.]

To praise thy life, or waile thy worthie
 death,
And want thy wit, thy wit high, pure, divine,
Is far beyond the powre of mortall line,
Nor any one hath worth that draweth
 breath.

Yet rich in zeale, though poore in learnings
 lore,
And friendly care obscurde in secret brest,

And love that envie in thy life supprest,
Thy deere life done, and death, hath doubled
 more.

And I, that in thy time and living state
Did onely praise thy vertues in my
 thought, 10
As one that seeld the rising sun hath
 sought,
With words and teares now waile thy timelesse fate.

Drawne was thy race aright from princely
 line,
Nor lesse than such, (by gifts that Nature
 gave,
The common mother that all creatures
 have,)
Doth vertue shew, and princely linage
 shine.

A king gave thee thy name; a kingly
 minde,
That God thee gave, who found it now too
 deere
For this base world, and hath resumde it
 neere,
To sit in skies, and sort with powres divine. 20

Kent thy birth daies, and Oxford held thy
 youth;
The heavens made hast, and staid nor
 yeers nor time;
The fruits of age grew ripe in thy first
 prime,
Thy will, thy words; thy words the seales
 of truth.

Great gifts and wisedom rare imployd thee
 thence,
To treat from kings with those more great
 than kings,
Such hope men had to lay the highest
 things
On thy wise youth, to be transported
 hence.

Whence to sharpe wars sweet honor did
 thee call,
Thy countries love, religion, and thy
 friends: 30
Of worthy men the marks, the lives, and
 ends,
And her defence, for whom we labor all.

There didst thou vanquish shame and tedious age,
Griefe, sorrow, sicknes, and base Fortunes
might:
Thy rising day saw never wofull night,
But past with praise from of this worldly
stage.

Back to the campe by thee that day was
brought,
First thine owne death, and after thy long
fame;
Teares to the soldiers, the proud Castilians
shame;
Vertue exprest, and honor truly taught. 40

What hath he lost, that such great grace
hath woon?
Yoong yeeres for endles yeeres, and hope
unsure
Of Fortunes gifts for wealth that still shall
dure:
Oh happie race with so great praises
run!

England doth hold thy lims, that bred the
same;
Flaunders thy valure, where it last was
tried;
The campe thy sorrow, where thy bodie
died;
Thy friends, thy want; the world, thy vertues fame.

Nations thy wit, our mindes lay up thy
love;
Letters thy learning; thy losse, yeeres long
to come; 50
In worthy harts sorrow hath made thy
tombe;
Thy soule and spright enrich the heavens
above.

Thy liberall hart imbalmd in gratefull
teares,
Yoong sighs, sweet sighes, sage sighes, bewaile thy fall:
Envie her sting, and Spite hath left her
gall;
Malice her selfe a mourning garment
weares.

That day their Hanniball died, our Scipio
fell,
Scipio, Cicero, and Petrarch of our time.

Whose vertues, wounded by my worthlesse
rime,
Let angels speake, and heaven thy praises
tell. 60

ANOTHER OF THE SAME

[Ascribed by Charles Lamb, 'from internal
testimony,' to Fulke Greville, Lord Brooke.]

SILENCE augmenteth grief, writing encreaseth rage;
Stald are my thoughts, which lov'd, and lost,
the wonder of our age;
Yet quickned now with fire, though dead
with frost ere now,
Enrag'de I write, I know not what: dead,
quick, I know not how.

Hard harted mindes relent, and Rigors
teares abound,
And Envie strangely rues his end, in whom
no fault she found;
Knowledge her light hath lost, Valor hath
slaine her knight,
Sidney is dead, dead is my friend, dead is
the worlds delight.

Place pensive wailes his fall, whose presence
was her pride;
Time crieth out, 'My ebbe is come: his life
was my spring tide;' 10
Fame mournes in that she lost the ground
of her reports;
Ech living wight laments his lacke, and all
in sundry sorts.

He was (wo worth that word!) to ech well
thinking minde,
A spotlesse friend, a matchles man, whose
vertue ever shinde,
Declaring in his thoughts, his life, and that
he writ,
Highest conceits, longest foresights, and
deepest works of wit.

He, onely like himselfe, was second unto
none,
Whose deth (though life) we rue, and
wrong, and al in vain do mone;
Their losse, not him, waile they that fill the
world with cries;
Death slue not him, but he made death his
ladder to the skies. 20

Now sinke of sorrow I, who live, the more
    the wrong,
Who wishing death, whom Deth denies,
    whose thred is al to long,
Who tied to wretched life, who lookes for
    no reliefe,
Must spend my ever dying daies in never
    ending griefe.

Harts ease and onely I like parallels run
    on,
Whose equall length keep equall bredth,
    and never meet in one;
Yet for not wronging him, my thoughts, my
    sorrowes cell,
Shall not run out, though leake they will,
    for liking him so well.

Farewell to you, my hopes, my wonted
    waking dreames,
Farewell, sometimes enjoyed joy, eclipsed
    are thy beames, 30

Farewell selfe pleasing thoughts, which
    quietnes brings foorth,
And farewel friendships sacred league,
    uniting minds of woorth.

And farewell mery hart, the gift of guilt-
    lesse mindes,
And all sports which, for lives restore,
    varietie assignes;
Let all that sweete is voyd; in me no mirth
    may dwell;
Phillip, the cause of all this woe, my lives
    content, farewell!

Now Rime, the sonne of Rage, which art
    no kin to Skill,
And endles Griefe, which deads my life,
    yet knowes not how to kill,
Go seeke that haples tombe; which if ye
    hap to finde,
Salute the stones that keep the lims that
    held so good a minde. 40

FINIS

LONDON

PRINTED BY T. C. FOR WILLIAM PONSONBIE

1595

AMORETTI AND EPITHALAMION

WRITTEN NOT LONG SINCE BY EDMUNDE SPENSER

PRINTED FOR WILLIAM PONSONBY, 1595

TO THE RIGHT WORSHIPFULL SIR ROBART NEEDHAM, KNIGHT

SIR, to gratulate your safe return from Ireland, I had nothing so readie, nor thought any thing so meete, as these sweete conceited sonets, the deede of that weldeserving gentleman, Maister Edmond Spenser: whose name sufficiently warranting the worthinesse of the work, I do more confidently presume to publish it in his absence, under your name, to whom (in my poore opinion) the patronage therof doth in some respectes properly appertaine. For, besides your judgement and delighte in learned poesie, this gentle Muse, for het former perfection long wished for in Englande, nowe at length crossing the seas in your happy companye, (though to your selfe unknowne) seemeth to make choyse of you, as meetest to give her deserved countenaunce, after her retourne: entertaine her, then, (right worshipfull) in sorte best beseeming your gentle minde, and her merite, and take in worth my good will herein, who seeke no more, but to shew my selfe yours in all dutifull affection.   W. P.

[The *Amoretti* and *Epithalamion* were entered upon the Stationers' Register, November 19, 1594, and published in 1595, perhaps somewhat earlier than *Colin Clout's Come Home Again* and *Astrophel*. The date of their composition is fixed, almost beyond dispute, by the inscription on the title page, 'written not long since;' for, according to line 267 of the *Epithalamion*, Spenser's wedding day was June 11, which the 'not long since' marks for 1594, and there being no reason to suppose any considerable gap between the *Epithalamion* and the *Amoretti*, sonnet lxvii of the latter must refer to the previous New Year's, sonnet iv to New Year's, 1593. All minor indications of time confirm this hypothetical chronology.

The record of the courtship, indeed, is singularly convincing, altogether different from the unrealities of most of the sonneteering of that day. In *Delia*, in *Idea*, in *Diana*, one may read for pages at a stretch with the sensation of being on a treeless plain : the ladies celebrated are as vague as pantheism ; there is not a hint at real human relations in a life of every-day affairs. In the *Amoretti*, on the other hand, we are constantly within sight of fact, however trivial. The poet, accustomed, it seems, to easy conquests, makes definite advances too soon, and is ignominiously beaten back ; he is chidden by a friend for not pushing on more vigorously with his *Faery Queen*, and pleads the distractions of his suit; at the close of a visit, when he should be departing, there comes up a violent storm of rain, and he knows not whether to stay or go, or he walks with his mistress upon the beach and writes her name in the sand, whereupon the waves wash it out. Behind the graceful banalities of fancy, the imitations of previous imitators of Petrarch, almost inevitable in an Elizabethan sonnet sequence, one may read the history of a genuine courtship as clearly as in a set of old letters. The suitor is a man of forty years ; in the eyes of the world, apparently, not a brilliant match, for when the lady finally accepts him, friends accuse her of a *mésalliance :* she is slow to be won (the courtship is of more than a year), yields finally with some misgivings, retains her maidenly aloofness after betrothal. 'His heroine,' writes the most recent of the critics, 'is the wayward mistress, the "sweet warrior" of every sixteenth century sonneteer. But difference of view is inevitable as to whether she owe most to Petrarch's *dolce guerrera*, or to De Baif's *belle ennemie*, or to Desportes' *douce adversaire*.' Such 'difference of view' is surely needless. Whatever fancies the poet may have borrowed, he has not borrowed the temperament of his mistress: it may please him to mention little except her pride; but her pride is clearly her own. We read it in a dozen characteristic touches, — in her fear to lose her maidenly independence (lxv), in the 'too constant stiffenesse' which denies him the perquisites of an accepted lover (lxxxiii), in her flare of anger at the tale of a busybody (lxxxv). It is, moreover, matter of general note, excites resentment (v). She goes about with her head proudly erect and her eyes as proudly (though the poet chooses to call that 'humblesse') fixed upon the ground (xiii). In all these traits as the poet sets them down, there may indeed be fanciful exaggeration, and in the great marriage song it may please him to ignore them, but to deny their essential truth is surely to read the sonnets too sceptically. Even a Petrarchist may draw from the life, and Spenser, to an unpreoccupied eye, would seem to have done just that.

One can hardly leave the *Amoretti* without mention of the rhyme-scheme. In this the disconnected quatrains of the common Elizabethan, or Shakespearean, type of sonnet are linked after the manner of Marot, like the quatrains of 'April' and 'November.' Attempt has been made to prove that Spenser took this sonnet-form direct from a contemporary Scottish poet, Alexander Montgomery, who made use of it some years the earlier; but the argument is hardly convincing. For, given the common Elizabethan type, any two poets familiar with the linked quatrains of Marot, as both Montgomery and Spenser unquestionably were, might evolve the same variant form quite independently. Their invention has not survived in the practice of later poets; perhaps because, though nearly as exacting as the regular Italian type, it is less finely proportioned, less stately.

Concerning the *Epithalamion* and its exquisite emotional tone, full and serene, a critic may best be silent. As to the four small poems, commonly entitled 'epigrams,' which divide it from the *Amoretti*, they are casual experiments in a vein then very much worked in France, imitations of that late and minor Greek poetry which clusters in and about the Anthology. The second and third have parallels in Marot (*Epigrammes* lxiv and ciii); the fourth is one of the most popular fancies of the time, derived from a poem of the pseudo-Anacreon group, and translated or imitated by no less than eight contemporary Frenchmen, Ronsard (*Odes*, IV, 14) at their head. To an epigram of Philodemus (*Anthologia Palatina*, V, 123) we owe the twenty-first strophe of the *Epithalamion* itself.]

G. W. SENIOR, TO THE AUTHOR

DARKE is the day, when Phœbus face is shrowded,
And weaker sights may wander soone astray:
But when they see his glorious raies unclowded,
With steddy steps they keepe the perfect way:
So while this Muse in forraine landes doth stay,
Invention weepes, and pens are cast aside,
The time, like night, depriv'd of chearefull day,
And few do write, but ah! too soone may slide.
Then, hie thee home, that art our perfect guide,
And with thy wit illustrate Englands fame,
Dawnting thereby our neighboures auncient pride,
That do for poesie challendge cheefest name.
So we that live, and ages that succeede,
With great applause thy learned works shall reede.

Ah! Colin, whether on the lowly plaine,
Pyping to shepherds thy sweete roundelaies,
Or whether singing, in some lofty vaine,
Heroick deedes of past or present daies,
Or whether in thy lovely mistris praise
Thou list to exercise thy learned quill,
Thy Muse hath got such grace, and power to please,
With rare invention, bewtified by skill,
As who therein can ever joy their fill?
O therefore let that happy Muse proceede
To clime the height of Vertues sacred hill,
Where endles honor shall be made thy meede:
Because no malice of succeeding daies
Can rase those records of thy lasting praise.
G. W. I.

I

HAPPY ye leaves! when as those lilly hands,
Which hold my life in their dead doing might,
Shall handle you, and hold in loves soft bands,
Lyke captives trembling at the victors sight.
And happy lines! on which, with starry light,
Those lamping eyes will deigne sometimes to look,
And reade the sorrowes of my dying spright,
Written with teares in harts close bleeding book.

And happy rymes ! bath'd in the sacred
    brooke
Of Helicon, whence she derived is,
When ye behold that angels blessed looke,
My soules long lacked foode, my heavens
    blis.
Leaves, lines, and rymes, seeke her to please
    alone,
Whom if ye please, I care for other none.

II

Unquiet thought, whom at the first I bred
Of th' inward bale of my love pined hart,
And sithens have with sighes and sorrowes
    fed,
Till greater then my wombe thou woxen
    art:
Breake forth at length out of the inner
    part,
In which thou lurkest lyke to vipers brood,
And seeke some succour, both to ease my
    smart
And also to sustayne thy selfe with food.
But if in presence of that fayrest proud
Thou chance to come, fall lowly at her
    feet;
And with meeke humblesse and afflicted
    mood
Pardon for thee, and grace for me intreat.
Which if she graunt, then live, and my love
    cherish,
If not, die soone, and I with thee will perish.

III

The soverayne beauty which I doo ad-
    myre,
Witnesse the world how worthy to be
    prayzed;
The light wherof hath kindled heavenly
    fyre
In my fraile spirit, by her from basenesse
    raysed:
That being now with her huge brightnesse
    dazed,
Base thing I can no more endure to view;
But looking still on her, I stand amazed
At wondrous sight of so celestiall hew.
So when my toung would speak her praises
    dew,
It stopped is with thoughts astonishment;
And when my pen would write her titles
    true,
It ravisht is with fancies wonderment.
Yet in my hart I then both speake and write
The wonder that my wit cannot endite.

IV

New Yeare, forth looking out of Janus
    gate,
Doth seeme to promise hope of new delight,
And bidding th' old adieu, his passed date
Bids all old thoughts to die in dumpish
    spright;
And calling forth out of sad Winters night
Fresh Love, that long hath slept in cheer-
    lesse bower,
Wils him awake, and soone about him dight
His wanton wings and darts of deadly
    power.
For lusty Spring now in his timely howre
Is ready to come forth, him to receive;
And warnes the Earth with divers colord
    flowre
To decke hir selfe, and her faire mantle
    weave.
Then you, faire flowre, in whom fresh youth
    doth raine,
Prepare your selfe new love to entertaine.

V

Rudely thou wrongest my deare harts
    desire,
In finding fault with her too portly pride:
The thing which I doo most in her admire
Is of the world unworthy most envide.
For in those lofty lookes is close implide
Scorn of base things, and sdeigne of foule
    dishonor;
Thretning rash eies which gaze on her so
    wide,
That loosely they ne dare to looke upon
    her.
Such pride is praise, such portlinesse is
    honor,
That boldned innocence beares in hir eies,
And her faire countenance, like a goodly
    banner,
Spreds in defiaunce of all enemies.
Was never in this world ought worthy tride,
Without some spark of such self-pleasing
    pride.

VI

Be nought dismayd that her unmoved mind
Doth still persist in her rebellious pride:
Such love, not lyke to lusts of baser kynd,
The harder wonne, the firmer will abide.
The durefull oake, whose sap is not yet
    dride,
Is long ere it conceive the kindling fyre:
But when it once doth burne, it doth divide

Great heat, and makes his flames to heaven
    aspire.
So hard it is to kindle new desire
In gentle brest, that shall endure for ever:
Deepe is the wound that dints the parts
    entire
With chast affects, that naught but death
    can sever.
Then thinke not long in taking litle paine
To knit the knot that ever shall remaine.

VII

Fayre eyes, the myrrour of my mazed hart,
What wondrous vertue is contaynd in you,
The which both lyfe and death forth from
    you dart
Into the object of your mighty view?
For when ye mildly looke with lovely hew,
Then is my soule with life and love in-
    spired:
But when ye lowre, or looke on me askew,
Then doe I die, as one with lightning fyred.
But since that lyfe is more then death
    desyred,
Looke ever lovely, as becomes you best,
That your bright beams, of my weak eies
    admyred,
May kindle living fire within my brest.
Such life should be the honor of your light,
Such death the sad ensample of your might.

VIII

More then most faire, full of the living
    fire
Kindled above unto the Maker neere:
No eies, but joyes, in which al powers con-
    spire,
That to the world naught else be counted
    deare:
Thrugh your bright beams doth not the
    blinded guest
Shoot out his darts to base affections wound;
But angels come, to lead fraile mindes to
    rest
In chast desires, on heavenly beauty bound.
You frame my thoughts, and fashion me
    within,
You stop my toung, and teach my hart to
    speake,
You calme the storme that passion did begin,
Strong thrugh your cause, but by your ver-
    tue weak.
Dark is the world where your light shined
    never;
Well is he borne that may behold you ever.

IX

Long-while I sought to what I might com-
    pare
Those powrefull eies which lighten my
    dark spright;
Yet find I nought on earth to which I dare
Resemble th' ymage of their goodly light.
Not to the sun; for they doo shine by night:
Nor to the moone; for they are changed
    never:
Nor to the starres; for they have purer
    sight:
Nor to the fire; for they consume not ever:
Nor to the lightning; for they still persever:
Nor to the diamond; for they are more
    tender:
Nor unto christall; for nought may them
    sever:
Nor unto glasse; such basenesse mought
    offend her.
Then to the Maker selfe they likest be,
Whose light doth lighten all that here we
    see.

X

Unrighteous Lord of Love, what law is this,
That me thou makest thus tormented be,
The whiles she lordeth in licentious blisse
Of her freewill, scorning both thee and me?
See how the tyrannesse doth joy to see
The huge massacres which her eyes do
    make,
And humbled harts brings captive unto
    thee,
That thou of them mayst mightie ven-
    geance take!
But her proud hart doe thou a little shake,
And that high look, with which she doth
    comptroll
All this worlds pride, bow to a baser make,
And al her faults in thy black booke enroll:
That I may laugh at her in equall sort
As she doth laugh at me, and makes my
    pain her sport.

XI

Dayly when I do seeke and sew for peace,
And hostages doe offer for my truth,
She, cruell warriour, doth her selfe ad-
    dresse
To battell, and the weary war renew'th:
Ne wilbe moov'd with reason or with rewth,
To graunt small respit to my restlesse toile;
But greedily her fell intent poursewth,
Of my poore life to make unpitteid spoile.

Yet my poore life, all sorrowes to assoyle,
I would her yield, her wrath to pacify:
But then she seekes, with torment and tur-
moyle,
To force me live, and will not let me dy.
All paine hath end, and every war hath
peace;
But mine no price nor prayer may surcease.

XII

One day I sought with her hart-thrilling eies
To make a truce, and termes to entertaine,
All fearlesse then of so false enimies,
Which sought me to entrap in treasons
traine.
So as I then disarmed did remaine,
A wicked ambush, which lay hidden long
In the close covert of her guilefull eyen,
Thence breaking forth, did thick about me
throng.
Too feeble I t' abide the brunt so strong,
Was forst to yeeld my selfe into their
hands:
Who me captiving streight with rigorous
wrong,
Have ever since me kept in cruell bands.
So, ladie, now to you I doo complaine,
Against your eies that justice I may gaine.

XIII

In that proud port which her so goodly
graceth,
Whiles her faire face she reares up to the
skie,
And to the ground her eie lids low embaseth,
Most goodly temperature ye may descry:
Myld humblesse mixt with awfull majesty.
For looking on the earth, whence she was
borne,
Her minde remembreth her mortalitie:
What so is fayrest shall to earth returne.
But that same lofty countenance seemes to
scorne
Base thing, and thinke how she to heaven
may clime,
Treading downe earth as lothsome and for-
lorne,
That hinders heavenly thoughts with drossy
slime.
Yet lowly still vouchsafe to looke on me;
Such lowlinesse shall make you lofty be.

XIV

Retourne agayne, my forces late dismayd,
Unto the siege by you abandon'd quite.

Great shame it is to leave, like one afrayd,
So fayre a peece for one repulse so light.
Gaynst such strong castles needeth greater
might
Then those small forts which ye were wont
belay:
Such haughty mynds, enur'd to hardy fight,
Disdayne to yield unto the first assay.
Bring therefore all the forces that ye may,
And lay incessant battery to her heart;
Playnts, prayers, vowes, ruth, sorrow, and
dismay;
Those engins can the proudest love convert.
And if those fayle, fall down and dy before
her;
So dying live, and living do adore her.

XV

Ye tradefull merchants, that with weary
toyle
Do seeke most pretious things to make your
gain,
And both the Indias of their treasures
spoile,
What needeth you to seeke so farre in
vaine?
For loe! my love doth in her selfe containe
All this worlds riches that may farre be
found:
If saphyres, loe! her eies be saphyres
plaine;
If rubies, loe! hir lips be rubies sound;
If pearles, hir teeth be pearles both pure
and round;
If yvorie, her forhead yvory weene;
If gold, her locks are finest gold on ground;
If silver, her faire hands are silver sheene:
But that which fairest is but few behold,
Her mind, adornd with vertues manifold.

XVI

One day as I unwarily did gaze
On those fayre eyes, my loves immortall
light,
The whiles my stonisht hart stood in amaze,
Through sweet illusion of her lookes de-
light,
I mote perceive how, in her glauncing sight,
Legions of loves with little wings did fly,
Darting their deadly arrowes, fyry bright,
At every rash beholder passing by.
One of those archers closely I did spy,
Ayming his arrow at my very hart:
When suddenly, with twincle of her eye,
The damzell broke his misintended dart.

Had she not so doon, sure I had bene
    slayne;
Yet as it was, I hardly scap't with paine.

XVII

The glorious pourtraict of that angels face,
Made to amaze weake mens confused skil,
And this worlds worthlesse glory to em-
    base,
What pen, what pencill, can expresse her
    fill?
For though he colours could devize at will,
And eke his learned hand at pleasure guide,
Least, trembling, it his workmanship should
    spill,
Yet many wondrous things there are be-
    side.
The sweet eye-glaunces, that like arrowes
    glide,
The charming smiles, that rob sence from
    the hart,
The lovely pleasance, and the lofty pride,
Cannot expressed be by any art.
A greater craftesmans hand thereto doth
    neede,
That can expresse the life of things indeed.

XVIII

The rolling wheele, that runneth often
    round,
The hardest steele in tract of time doth
    teare:
And drizling drops, that often doe redound,
The firmest flint doth in continuance weare:
Yet cannot I, with many a dropping teare
And long intreaty, soften her hard hart,
That she will once vouchsafe my plaint to
    heare,
Or looke with pitty on my payneful smart.
But when I pleade, she bids me play my
    part,
And when I weep, she sayes teares are but
    water,
And when I sigh, she sayes I know the art,
And when I waile, she turnes hir selfe to
    laughter.
So do I weepe, and wayle, and pleade in
    vaine,
Whiles she as steele and flint doth still
    remayne.

XIX

The merry cuckow, messenger of Spring,
His trompet shrill hath thrise already
    sounded,

That warnes al lovers wayt upon their king,
Who now is comming forth with girland
    crouned.
With noyse whereof the quyre of byrds re-
    sounded,
Their anthemes sweet, devized of Loves
    prayse,
That all the woods theyr ecchoes back re-
    bounded,
As if they knew the meaning of their layes.
But mongst them all which did Loves honor
    rayse,
No word was heard of her that most it
    ought,
But she his precept proudly disobayes,
And doth his ydle message set at nought.
Therefore, O Love, unlesse she turne to thee
Ere cuckow end, let her a rebell be.

XX

In vaine I seeke and sew to her for grace,
And doe myne humbled hart before her
    poure:
The whiles her foot she in my necke doth
    place,
And tread my life downe in the lowly floure.
And yet the lyon, that is lord of power,
And reigneth over every beast in field,
In his most pride disdeigneth to devoure
The silly lambe that to his might doth yield.
But she, more cruell and more salvage
    wylde,
Than either lyon or the lyonesse,
Shames not to be with guiltlesse bloud de-
    fylde,
But taketh glory in her cruelnesse.
Fayrer then fayrest, let none ever say
That ye were blooded in a yeelded pray.

XXI

Was it the worke of Nature or of Art,
Which tempred so the feature of her face,
That pride and meeknesse, mixt by equall
    part,
Doe both appeare t' adorne her beauties
    grace?
For with mild pleasance, which doth pride
    displace,
She to her love doth lookers eyes allure;
And with sterne countenance back again
    doth chace
Their looser lookes that stir up lustes im-
    pure.
With such strange termes her eyes she doth
    inure,

That with one looke she doth my life dis-
    may,
And with another doth it streight recure:
Her smile me drawes, her frowne me
    drives away.
Thus doth she traine and teach me with her
    lookes:
Such art of eyes I never read in bookes.

XXII

This holy season, fit to fast and pray,
Men to devotion ought to be inclynd:
Therefore, I lykewise, on so holy day,
For my sweet saynt some service fit will
    find.
Her temple fayre is built within my mind,
In which her glorious ymage placed is,
On which my thoughts doo day and night
    attend,
Lyke sacred priests that never thinke
    amisse.
There I to her, as th' author of my blisse,
Will builde an altar to appease her yre;
And on the same my hart will sacrifise,
Burning in flames of pure and chast desyre:
The which vouchsafe, O goddesse, to accept,
Amongst thy deerest relicks to be kept.

XXIII

Penelope, for her Ulisses sake,
Deviz'd a web her wooers to deceave,
In which the worke that she all day did
    make,
The same at night she did againe unreave.
Such subtile craft my damzell doth con-
    ceave,
Th' importune suit of my desire to shonne:
For all that I in many dayes doo weave
In one short houre I find by her undonne.
So when I thinke to end that I begonne,
I must begin and never bring to end:
For with one looke she spils that long I
    sponne,
And with one word my whole years work
    doth rend.
Such labour like the spyders web I fynd,
Whose fruitlesse worke is broken with least
    wynd.

XXIV

When I behold that beauties wonderment,
And rare perfection of each goodly part,
Of Natures skill the onely complement,
I honor and admire the Makers art.
But when I feele the bitter balefull smart

Which her fayre eyes unwares doe worke
    in mee,
That death out of theyr shiny beames doe
    dart,
I thinke that I a new Pandora see;
Whom all the gods in councell did agree,
Into this sinfull world from heaven to send,
That she to wicked men a scourge should
    bee,
For all their faults with which they did of-
    fend.
But since ye are my scourge, I will intreat
That for my faults ye will me gently beat.

XXV

How long shall this lyke dying lyfe endure,
And know no end of her owne mysery,
But wast and weare away in termes unsure,
Twixt feare and hope depending doubtfully?
Yet better were attonce to let me die,
And shew the last ensample of your pride,
Then to torment me thus with cruelty,
To prove your powre, which I too wel have
    tride.
But yet if in your hardned brest ye hide
A close intent at last to shew me grace,
Then all the woes and wrecks which I abide
As meanes of blisse I gladly wil embrace,
And wish that more and greater they might
    be,
That greater meede at last may turne to
    mee.

XXVI

Sweet is the rose, but growes upon a brere;
Sweet is the junipere, but sharpe his bough;
Sweet is the eglantine, but pricketh nere;
Sweet is the firbloome, but his braunches
    rough;
Sweet is the cypresse, but his rynd is tough;
Sweet is the nut, but bitter is his pill;
Sweet is the broome-flowre, but yet sowre
    enough;
And sweet is moly, but his root is ill.
So every sweet with soure is tempred still,
That maketh it be coveted the more:
For easie things, that may be got at will,
Most sorts of men doe set but little store.
Why then should I accoumpt of little paine,
That endlesse pleasure shall unto me gaine?

XXVII

Faire proud! now tell me, why should
    faire be proud,
Sith all worlds glorie is but drosse uncleane,

And in the shade of death it selfe shall
    shroud,
How ever now thereof ye little weene?
That goodly idoll, now so gay beseene,
Shall doffe her fleshes borowd fayre attyre,
And be forgot as it had never beene,
That many now much worship and admire.
Ne any then shall after it inquire,
Ne any mention shall thereof remaine,
But what this verse, that never shall expyre,
Shall to you purchas with her thankles paine.
Faire, be no lenger proud of that shall per-
    ish,
But that which shall you make immortall
    cherish.

XXVIII

The laurel leafe which you this day doe
    weare
Gives me great hope of your relenting
    mynd:
For since it is the badg which I doe beare,
Ye, bearing it, doe seeme to me inclind.
The powre thereof, which ofte in me I find,
Let it lykewise your gentle brest inspire
With sweet infusion, and put you in mind
Of that proud mayd whom now those leaves
    attyre.
Proud Daphne, scorning Phæbus lovely
    fyre,
On the Thessalian shore from him did flie:
For which the gods, in theyr revengefull
    yre,
Did her transforme into a laurell tree.
Then fly no more, fayre love, from Phebus
    chace,
But in your brest his leafe and love embrace.

XXIX

See how the stubborne damzell doth deprave
My simple meaning with disdaynfull scorne,
And by the bay which I unto her gave
Accompts my self her captive quite for-
    lorne.
The bay (quoth she) is of the victours borne,
Yielded them by the vanquisht as theyr
    meeds,
And they therewith doe poetes heads adorne,
To sing the glory of their famous deedes.
But sith she will the conquest challeng
    needs,
Let her accept me as her faithfull thrall,
That her great triumph, which my skill
    exceeds,
I may in trump of fame blaze over all.

Then would I decke her head with glorious
    bayes,
And fill the world with her victorious
    prayse.

XXX

My love is lyke to yse, and I to fyre;
How comes it then that this her cold so
    great
Is not dissolv'd through my so hot desyre,
But harder growes the more I her intreat?
Or how comes it that my exceeding heat
Is not delayd by her hart frosen cold,
But that I burne much more in boyling
    sweat,
And feele my flames augmented manifold?
What more miraculous thing may be told,
That fire, which all things melts, should
    harden yse,
And yse, which is congeald with sencelesse
    cold,
Should kindle fyre by wonderful devyse?
Such is the powre of love in gentle mind,
That it can alter all the course of kynd.

XXXI

Ah! why hath Nature to so hard a hart
Given so goodly giftes of beauties grace,
Whose pryde depraves each other better
    part,
And all those pretious ornaments deface?
Sith to all other beastes of bloody race
A dreadfull countenaunce she given hath,
That with theyr terrour al the rest may chace,
And warne to shun the daunger of theyr
    wrath.
But my proud one doth worke the greater
    scath,
Through sweet allurement of her lovely
    hew,
That she the better may in bloody bath
Of such poore thralls her cruell hands
    embrew.
But did she know how ill these two accord,
Such cruelty she would have soone abhord.

XXXII

The paynefull smith with force of fervent
    heat
The hardest yron soone doth mollify;
That with his heavy sledge he can it beat,
And fashion to what he it list apply.
Yet cannot all these flames in which I fry
Her hart, more harde then yron, soft a whit,
Ne all the playnts and prayers with which I

Doe beat on th' andvyle of her stubberne
  wit:
But still, the more she fervent sees my fit,
The more she frieseth in her wilfull pryde;
And harder growes, the harder she is smit,
With all the playnts which to her be ap-
  plyde.
What then remaines but I to ashes burne,
And she to stones at length all frosen turne?

XXXIII

Great wrong I doe, I can it not deny,
To that most sacred empresse, my dear
  dred,
Not finishing her Queene of Faëry,
That mote enlarge her living prayses, dead.
But Lodwick, this of grace to me aread:
Do ye not thinck th' accomplishment of it
Sufficient worke for one mans simple head,
All were it, as the rest, but rudely writ?
How then should I, without another wit,
Thinck ever to endure so tædious toyle,
Sins that this one is tost with troublous fit
Of a proud love, that doth my spirite spoyle?
Cease then, till she vouchsafe to grawnt me
  rest,
Or lend you me another living brest.

XXXIV

Lyke as a ship, that through the ocean wyde
By conduct of some star doth make her
  way,
Whenas a storme hath dimd her trusty
  guyde,
Out of her course doth wander far astray;
So I, whose star, that wont with her bright
  ray
Me to direct, with cloudes is overcast,
Doe wander now in darknesse and dismay,
Through hidden perils round about me plast.
Yet hope I well, that when this storme is
  past,
My Helice, the lodestar of my lyfe,
Will shine again, and looke on me at last,
With lovely light to cleare my cloudy grief.
Till then I wander carefull comfortlesse,
In secret sorrow and sad pensivenesse.

XXXV

My hungry eyes, through greedy covetize
Still to behold the object of their paine,
With no contentment can themselves suffize,
But having pine, and having not complaine.
For lacking it, they cannot lyfe sustayne,
And having it, they gaze on it the more:

In their amazement lyke Narcissus vaine,
Whose eyes him starv'd: so plenty makes
  me poore.
Yet are mine eyes so filled with the store
Of that faire sight, that nothing else they
  brooke,
But lothe the things which they did like
  before,
And can no more endure on them to looke.
All this worlds glory seemeth vayne to
  me,
And all their showes but shadowes, saving
  she.

XXXVI

Tell me, when shall these wearie woes have
  end,
Or shall their ruthlesse torment never cease,
But al my dayes in pining languor spend,
Without hope of aswagement or release?
Is there no meanes for me to purchace peace,
Or make agreement with her thrilling eyes:
But that their cruelty doth still increace,
And dayly more augment my miseryes?
But when ye have shewed all extremityes,
Then thinke how litle glory ye have gayned
By slaying him, whose lyfe though ye de-
  spyse,
Mote have your life in honour long main-
  tayned.
But by his death, which some perhaps will
  mone,
Ye shall condemned be of many a one.

XXXVII

What guyle is this, that those her golden
  tresses
She doth attyre under a net of gold,
And with sly skill so cunningly them dresses,
That which is gold or heare may scarse be
  told?
Is it that mens frayle eyes, which gaze too
  bold,
She may entangle in that golden snare,
And being caught, may craftily enfold
Theyr weaker harts, which are not wel
  aware?
Take heed therefore, myne eyes, how ye
  doe stare
Henceforth too rashly on that guilefull
  net,
In which if ever ye entrapped are,
Out of her bands ye by no meanes shall get.
Fondnesse it were for any, being free,
To covet fetters, though they golden bee.

XXXVIII

Arion, when, through tempests cruel wracke,
He forth was thrown into the greedy seas,
Through the sweet musick which his harp did make
Allur'd a dolphin him from death to ease.
But my rude musick, which was wont to please
Some dainty eares, cannot, with any skill,
The dreadfull tempest of her wrath appease,
Nor move the dolphin from her stubborne will;
But in her pride she dooth persever still,
All carelesse how my life for her decayse:
Yet with one word she can it save or spill.
To spill were pitty, but to save were prayse.
Chose rather to be praysd for dooing good,
Then to be blam'd for spilling guiltlesse blood.

XXXIX

Sweet smile, the daughter of the Queene of Love,
Expressing all thy mothers powrefull art,
With which she wonts to temper angry Jove,
When all the gods he threats with thundring dart:
Sweet is thy vertue, as thy selfe sweet art.
For when on me thou shinedst late in sadnesse,
A melting pleasance ran through every part,
And me revived with hart robbing gladnesse:
Whylest rapt with joy resembling heavenly madnes,
My soule was ravisht quite, as in a traunce,
And feeling thence no more her sorowes sadnesse,
Fed on the fulnesse of that chearefull glaunce.
More sweet than nectar, or ambrosiall meat,
Seem'd every bit which thenceforth I did eat.

XL

Mark when she smiles with amiable cheare,
And tell me whereto can ye lyken it;
When on each eyelid sweetly doe appeare
An hundred Graces as in shade to sit.
Lykest it seemeth, in my simple wit,
Unto the fayre sunshine in somers day,
That, when a dreadfull storme away is flit,
Thrugh the broad world doth spred his goodly ray:
At sight whereof, each bird that sits on spray,
And every beast that to his den was fled,
Comes forth afresh out of their late dismay,
And to the light lift up theyr drouping hed.
So my storme beaten hart likewise is cheared
With that sunshine, when cloudy looks are cleared.

XLI

Is it her nature, or is it her will,
To be so cruell to an humbled foe?
If nature, then she may it mend with skill,
If will, then she at will may will forgoe.
But if her nature and her wil be so,
That she will plague the man that loves her most,
And take delight t'encrease a wretches woe,
Then all her natures goodly guifts are lost;
And that same glorious beauties ydle boast
Is but a bayt such wretches to beguile,
As, being long in her loves tempest tost,
She meanes at last to make her piteous spoyle.
O fayrest fayre, let never it be named,
That so fayre beauty was so fowly shamed.

XLII

The love which me so cruelly tormenteth
So pleasing is in my extreamest paine,
That all the more my sorrow it augmenteth,
The more I love and doe embrace my bane.
Ne doe I wish (for wishing were but vaine)
To be acquit fro my continuall smart,
But joy, her thrall for ever to remayne,
And yield for pledge my poore captyved hart;
The which, that it from her may never start,
Let her, yf please her, bynd with adamant chayne,
And from all wandring loves, which mote pervart
His safe assurance, strongly it restrayne.
Onely let her abstaine from cruelty,
And doe me not before my time to dy.

XLIII

Shall I then silent be, or shall I speake?
And if I speake, her wrath renew I shall:
And if I silent be, my hart will breake,
Or choked be with overflowing gall.

What tyranny is this, both my hart to
thrall,
And eke my toung with proud restraint to
tie;
That nether I may speake nor thinke at all,
But like a stupid stock in silence die !
Yet I my hart with silence secretly
Will teach to speak, and my just cause to
plead,
And eke mine eies, with meek humility,
Love-learned letters to her eyes to read:
Which her deep wit, that true harts thought
can spel,
Wil soone conceive, and learne to construe
well.

XLIV

When those renoumed noble peres of Greece
Thrugh stubborn pride amongst themselves
did jar,
Forgetfull of the famous golden fleece,
Then Orpheus with his harp theyr strife did
bar.
But this continuall cruell civill warre,
The which my selfe against my selfe doe
make,
Whilest my weak powres of passions war-
reid arre,
No skill can stint, nor reason can aslake.
But when in hand my tunelesse harp I take,
Then doe I more augment my foes despight,
And griefe renew, and passions doe awake
To battaile, fresh against my selfe to fight.
Mongst whome the more I seeke to settle
peace,
The more I fynd their malice to increace.

XLV

Leave, lady, in your glasse of christall
clene
Your goodly selfe for evermore to vew,
And in my selfe, my inward selfe I meane,
Most lively lyke behold your semblant
trew.
Within my hart, though hardly it can shew
Thing so divine to vew of earthly eye,
The fayre idea of your celestiall hew
And every part remaines immortally:
And were it not that through your cruelty
With sorrow dimmed and deformd it were,
The goodly ymage of your visnomy
Clearer then christall would therein appere.
But if your selfe in me ye playne will see,
Remove the cause by which your fayre
beames darkned be.

XLVI

When my abodes prefixed time is spent,
My cruell fayre streight bids me wend my
way:
But then from heaven most hideous stormes
are sent,
As willing me against her will to stay.
Whom then shall I, or heaven or her, obay ?
The heavens know best what is the best for
me:
But as she will, whose will my life doth
sway,
My lower heaven, so it perforce must bee.
But ye high hevens, that all this sorowe
see,
Sith all your tempests cannot hold me backe,
Aswage your stormes, or else both you and
she
Will both together me too sorely wrack.
Enough it is for one man to sustaine
The stormes which she alone on me doth
raine.

XLVII

Trust not the treason of those smyling
lookes,
Untill ye have theyr guylefull traynes well
tryde:
For they are lyke but unto golden hookes,
That from the foolish fish theyr bayts do
hyde:
So she with flattring smyles weake harts
doth guyde
Unto her love, and tempte to theyr decay;
Whome being caught, she kills with cruell
pryde,
And feeds at pleasure on the wretched pray.
Yet even whylst her bloody hands them
slay,
Her eyes looke lovely, and upon them
smyle,
That they take pleasure in her cruell play;
And, dying, doe them selves of payne be-
guyle.
O mighty charm ! which makes men love
theyr bane,
And thinck they dy with pleasure, live with
payne.

XLVIII

Innocent paper, whom too cruell hand
Did make the matter to avenge her yre,
And ere she could thy cause wel under-
stand,
Did sacrifize unto the greedy fyre:

Well worthy thou to have found better
    hyre
Then so bad end, for hereticks ordayned:
Yet heresy nor treason didst conspire,
But plead thy maisters cause, unjustly
    payned:
Whom she, all carelesse of his griefe, con-
    strayned
To utter forth the anguish of his hart:
And would not heare, when he to her com-
    playned
The piteous passion of his dying smart.
Yet live for ever, though against her will,
And speake her good, though she requite it
    ill.

XLIX

Fayre cruell, why are ye so fierce and
    cruell ?
Is it because your eyes have powre to kill ?
Then know, that mercy is the Mighties
    jewell,
And greater glory thinke to save then spill.
But if it be your pleasure and proud will
To shew the powre of your imperious eyes,
Then not on him that never thought you ill,
But bend your force against your enemyes.
Let them feele th' utmost of your crueltyes,
And kill with looks, as cockatrices doo:
But him that at your footstoole humbled
    lies,
With mercifull regard, give mercy too.
Such mercy shal you make admyred to be;
So shall you live by giving life to me.

L

Long languishing in double malady,
Of my harts wound and of my bodies greife,
There came to me a leach, that would apply
Fit medicines for my bodies best reliefe.
Vayne man ! (quod I) that hast but little
    priefe
In deep discovery of the mynds disease,
Is not the hart of all the body chiefe,
And rules the members as it selfe doth
    please ?
Then with some cordialls seeke first to ap-
    pease
The inward languour of my wounded hart,
And then my body shall have shortly ease:
But such sweet cordialls passe physitions art.
Then, my lyfes leach, doe you your skill re-
    veale,
And with one salve both hart and body
    heale.

LI

Doe I not see that fayrest ymages
Of hardest marble are of purpose made,
For that they should endure through many
    ages,
Ne let theyr famous moniments to fade ?
Why then doe I, untrainde in lovers trade,
Her hardnes blame, which I should more
    commend ?
Sith never ought was excellent assayde,
Which was not hard t' atchive and bring to
    end:
Ne ought so hard, but he that would attend
Mote soften it and to his will allure:
So doe I hope her stubborne hart to bend,
And that it then more stedfast will en-
    dure.
Onely my paines wil be the more to get her:
But having her, my joy wil be the greater.

LII

So oft as homeward I from her depart,
I go lyke one that, having lost the field,
Is prisoner led away with heavy hart,
Despoyld of warlike armes and knowen
    shield.
So doe I now my selfe a prisoner yeeld
To sorrow and to solitary paine:
From presence of my dearest deare exylde,
Longwhile alone in languor to remaine.
There let no thought of joy, or pleasure
    vaine,
Dare to approch, that may my solace breed;
But sudden dumps, and drery sad disdayne
Of all worlds gladnesse, more my torment
    feed.
So I her absens will my penaunce make,
That of her presens I my meed may take.

LIII

The panther, knowing that his spotted hyde
Doth please all beasts, but that his looks
    them fray,
Within a bush his dreadfull head doth hide,
To let them gaze, whylest he on them may
    pray.
Right so my cruell fayre with me doth
    play:
For with the goodly semblant of her hew
She doth allure me to mine owne decay,
And then no mercy will unto me shew.
Great shame it is, thing so divine in view,
Made for to be the worlds most ornament,
To make the bayte her gazers to embrew:
Good shames to be to ill an instrument:

But mercy doth with beautie best agree,
As in theyr Maker ye them best may see.

LIV

Of this worlds theatre in which we stay,
My love, lyke the spectator, ydly sits,
Beholding me, that all the pageants play,
Disguysing diversly my troubled wits.
Sometimes I joy, when glad occasion fits,
And mask in myrth lyke to a comedy:
Soone after, when my joy to sorrow flits,
I waile, and make my woes a tragedy.
Yet she, beholding me with constant eye,
Delights not in my merth, nor rues my
   smart:
But when I laugh, she mocks, and when I
   cry,
She laughes, and hardens evermore her hart.
What then can move her ? If nor merth
   nor mone,
She is no woman, but a sencelesse stone.

LV

So oft as I her beauty doe behold,
And therewith doe her cruelty compare,
I marvaile of what substance was the mould
The which her made attonce so cruell faire.
Not earth; for her high thoghts more
   heavenly are:
Not water; for her love doth burne like
   fyre:
Not ayre; for she is not so light or rare:
Not fyre; for she doth friese with faint
   desire.
Then needs another element inquire,
Whereof she mote be made; that is the
   skye.
For to the heaven her haughty looks aspire,
And eke her mind is pure immortall hye.
Then sith to heaven ye lykened are the best,
Be lyke in mercy as in all the rest.

LVI

Fayre ye be sure, but cruell and unkind,
As is a tygre, that with greedinesse
Hunts after bloud, when he by chance doth
   find
A feeble beast, doth felly him oppresse.
Fayre be ye sure, but proud and pittilesse,
As is a storme, that all things doth pros-
   trate,
Finding a tree alone all comfortlesse,
Beats on it strongly, it to ruinate.
Fayre be ye sure, but hard and obstinate,
As is a rocke amidst the raging floods.

Gaynst which a ship, of succour desolate,
Doth suffer wreck both of her selfe and
   goods.
That ship, that tree, and that same beast
   am I,
Whom ye doe wreck, doe ruine, and destroy.

LVII

Sweet warriour, when shall I have peace
   with you ?
High time it is this warre now ended were:
Which I no lenger can endure to sue,
Ne your incessant battry more to beare.
So weake my powres, so sore my wounds
   appeare,
That wonder is how I should live a jot,
Seeing my hart through launced every
   where
With thousand arrowes which your eies
   have shot:
Yet shoot ye sharpely still, and spare me
   not,
But glory thinke to make these cruel
   stoures.
Ye cruell one ! what glory can be got,
In slaying him that would live gladly
   yours ?
Make peace therefore, and graunt me timely
   grace,
That al my wounds wil heale in little space.

LVIII

By her that is most assured to her selfe
Weake is th' assurance that weake flesh re-
   poseth
In her owne powre, and scorneth others
   ayde;
That soonest fals, when as she most sup-
   poseth
Her selfe assurd, and is of nought affrayd.
All flesh is frayle, and all her strength un-
   stayd,
Like a vaine bubble blowen up with ayre:
Devouring tyme and changeful chance have
   prayd
Her glories pride, that none may it repayre.
Ne none so rich or wise, so strong or fayre,
But fayleth, trusting on his owne assurance:
And he that standeth on the hyghest stayre
Fals lowest: for on earth nought hath en-
   duraunce.
Why then doe ye, proud fayre, misdeeme
   so farre,
That to your selfe ye most assured arre ?

LIX

Thrise happie she that is so well assured
Unto her selfe, and setled so in hart,
That nether will for better be allured,
Ne feard with worse to any chaunce to
    start:
But, like a steddy ship, doth strongly part
The raging waves, and keepes her course
    aright,
Ne ought for tempest doth from it depart,
Ne ought for fayrer weathers false delight.
Such selfe assurance need not feare the
    spight
Of grudging foes, ne favour seek of friends:
But in the stay of her owne stedfast might,
Nether to one her selfe nor other bends.
Most happy she that most assured doth
    rest;
But he most happy who such one loves best.

LX

They that in course of heavenly spheares
    are skild
To every planet point his sundry yeare,
In which her circles voyage is fulfild:
As Mars in three score yeares doth run his
    spheare.
So since the winged god his planet cleare
Began in me to move, one yeare is spent:
The which doth longer unto me appeare,
Then al those fourty which my life outwent.
Then, by that count which lovers books in-
    vent,
The spheare of Cupid fourty yeares con-
    taines:
Which I have wasted in long languishment,
That seemd the longer for my greater
    paines.
But let my loves fayre planet short her
    wayes
This yeare ensuing, or else short my dayes.

LXI

The glorious image of the Makers beautie,
My soverayne saynt, the idoll of my thought,
Dare not henceforth, above the bounds of
    dewtie,
T' accuse of pride, or rashly blame for
    ought.
For being, as she is, divinely wrought,
And of the brood of angels hevenly borne,
And with the crew of blessed saynts up-
    brought,
Each of which did her with theyr guifts
    adorne,

The bud of joy, the blossome of the morne,
The beame of light, whom mortal eyes
    admyre,
What reason is it then but she should scorne
Base things, that to her love too bold aspire ?
Such heavenly formes ought rather wor-
    shipt be,
Then dare be lov'd by men of meane degree.

LXII

The weary yeare his race now having run,
The new begins his compast course anew:
With shew of morning mylde he hath begun,
Betokening peace and plenty to ensew.
So let us, which this chaunge of weather
    vew,
Chaunge eeke our mynds, and former lives
    amend;
The old yeares sinnes forepast let us eschew,
And fly the faults with which we did offend.
Then shall the new yeares joy forth freshly
    send
Into the glooming world his gladsome ray:
And all these stormes, which now his beauty
    blend,
Shall turne to caulmes, and tymely cleare
    away.
So likewise, love, cheare you your heavy
    spright,
And chaunge old yeares annoy to new de-
    light.

LXIII

After long stormes and tempests sad assay,
Which hardly I endured heretofore,
In dread of death, and daungerous dismay,
With which my silly barke was tossed sore,
I doe at length descry the happy shore,
In which I hope ere long for to arryve:
Fayre soyle it seemes from far, and fraught
    with store
Of all that deare and daynty is alyve.
Most happy he that can at last atchyve
The joyous safety of so sweet a rest;
Whose least delight sufficeth to deprive
Remembrance of all paines which him op-
    prest.
All paines are nothing in respect of this,
All sorrowes short that gaine eternall blisse,

LXIV

Comming to kisse her lyps, (such grace I
    found)
Me seemd I smelt a gardin of sweet
    flowres,

That dainty odours from them threw
	around,
For damzels fit to decke their lovers bowres.
Her lips did smell lyke unto gillyflowers;
Her ruddy cheekes lyke unto roses red;
Her snowy browes lyke budded bellamoures;
Her lovely eyes lyke pincks but newly
	spred;
Her goodly bosome lyke a strawberry bed;
Her neck lyke to a bounch of cullambynes;
Her brest lyke lillyes, ere theyr leaves be
	shed;
Her nipples lyke yong blossomd jessemynes.
Such fragrant flowres doe give most odor-
	ous smell,
But her sweet odour did them all excell.

LXV

The doubt which ye misdeeme, fayre love,
	is vaine,
That fondly feare to loose your liberty,
When loosing one, two liberties ye gayne,
And make him bond that bondage earst dyd
	fly.
Sweet be the bands the which true love doth
	tye,
Without constraynt or dread of any ill:
The gentle birde feeles no captivity
Within her cage, but singes and feeds her
	fill.
There Pride dare not approch, nor Discord
	spill
The league twixt them that loyal love hath
	bound:
But simple Truth and mutuall Good Will
Seekes with sweet peace to salve each
	others wound:
There Fayth doth fearlesse dwell in brasen
	towre,
And spotlesse Pleasure builds her sacred
	bowre.

LXVI

To all those happy blessings which ye have,
With plenteous hand by heaven upon you
	thrown,
This one disparagement they to you gave,
That ye your love lent to so meane a one.
Yee, whose high worths surpassing paragon
Could not on earth have found one fit for
	mate,
Ne but in heaven matchable to none,
Why did ye stoup unto so lowly state?
But ye thereby much greater glory gate,
Then had ye sorted with a princes pere:

For now your light doth more it selfe dilate,
And in my darknesse greater doth appeare.
Yet since your light hath once enlumind me,
With my reflex yours shall encreased be.

LXVII

Lyke as a huntsman, after weary chace,
Seeing the game from him escapt away,
Sits downe to rest him in some shady place,
With panting hounds beguiled of their pray:
So, after long pursuit and vaine assay,
When I all weary had the chace forsooke,
The gentle deare returnd the selfe-same
	way,
Thinking to quench her thirst at the next
	brooke.
There she, beholding me with mylder looke,
Sought not to fly, but fearlesse still did
	bide:
Till I in hand her yet halfe trembling tooke,
And with her owne goodwill hir fyrmely
	tyde.
Strange thing, me seemd, to see a beast
	so wyld,
So goodly wonne, with her owne will beguyld.

LXVIII

Most glorious Lord of lyfe, that on this
	day
Didst make thy triumph over death and sin,
And having harrowd hell, didst bring away
Captivity thence captive, us to win:
This joyous day, deare Lord, with joy begin,
And grant that we, for whom thou diddest
	dye,
Being with thy deare blood clene washt
	from sin,
May live for ever in felicity:
And that thy love we weighing worthily,
May likewise love thee for the same againe;
And for thy sake, that all lyke deare didst
	buy,
With love may one another entertayne.
So let us love, deare love, lyke as we ought:
Love is the lesson which the Lord us taught.

LXIX

The famous warriors of the anticke world
Used trophees to erect in stately wize,
In which they would the records have enrold
Of theyr great deeds and valarous emprize.
What trophee then shall I most fit devize,
In which I may record the memory
Of my loves conquest, peerelesse beauties
	prise,

Adorn'd with honour, love, and chastity?
Even this verse, vowd to eternity,
Shall be thereof immortall moniment,
And tell her prayse to all posterity,
That may admire such worlds rare wonderment;
The happy purchase of my glorious spoile,
Gotten at last with labour and long toyle.

LXX

Fresh Spring, the herald of loves mighty king,
In whose cote-armour richly are displayd
All sorts of flowers the which on earth do spring,
In goodly colours gloriously arrayd,
Goe to my love, where she is carelesse layd,
Yet in her winters bowre, not well awake;
Tell her the joyous time wil not be staid,
Unlesse she doe him by the forelock take:
Bid her therefore her selfe soone ready make,
To wayt on Love amongst his lovely crew,
Where every one that misseth then her make
Shall be by him amearst with penance dew.
Make hast therefore, sweet love, whilest it is prime;
For none can call againe the passed time.

LXXI

I joy to see how, in your drawen work,
Your selfe unto the bee ye doe compare,
And me unto the spyder, that doth lurke
In close awayt to catch her unaware.
Right so your selfe were caught in cunning snare
Of a deare foe, and thralled to his love:
In whose streight bands ye now captived are
So firmely, that ye never may remove.
But as your worke is woven all about
With woodbynd flowers and fragrant eglantine,
So sweet your prison you in time shall prove,
With many deare delights bedecked fyne:
And all thensforth eternall peace shall see
Betweene the spyder and the gentle bee.

LXXII

Oft when my spirit doth spred her bolder winges,
In mind to mount up to the purest sky,
It down is weighd with thoght of earthly things,
And clogd with burden of mortality:

Where, when that soverayne beauty it doth spy,
Resembling heavens glory in her light,
Drawne with sweet pleasures bayt, it back doth fly,
And unto heaven forgets her former flight.
There my fraile fancy, fed with full delight,
Doth bath in blisse, and mantleth most at ease;
Ne thinks of other heaven, but how it might
Her harts desire with most contentment please.
Hart need not wish none other happinesse,
But here on earth to have such hevens blisse.

LXXIII

Being my selfe captyved here in care,
My hart, whom none with servile bands can tye,
But the fayre tresses of your golden hayre,
Breaking his prison, forth to you doth fly.
Like as a byrd, that in ones hand doth spy
Desired food, to it doth make his flight,
Even so my hart, that wont on your fayre eye
To feed his fill, flyes backe unto your sight.
Doe you him take, and in your bosome bright
Gently encage, that he may be your thrall:
Perhaps he there may learne, with rare delight,
To sing your name and prayses over all,
That it hereafter may you not repent,
Him lodging in your bosome to have lent.

LXXIV

Most happy letters! fram'd by skilfull trade,
With which that happy name was first desynd,
The which three times thrise happy hath me made,
With guifts of body, fortune, and of mind.
The first my being to me gave by kind,
From mothers womb deriv'd by dew descent:
The second is my sovereigne Queene most kind,
That honour and large richesse to me lent:
The third, my love, my lives last ornament,
By whom my spirit out of dust was raysed,
To speake her prayse and glory excellent,
Of all alive most worthy to be praysed.
Ye three Elizabeths, for ever live,
That three such graces did unto me give.

LXXV

One day I wrote her name upon the strand,
But came the waves and washed it away:
Agayne I wrote it with a second hand,
But came the tyde, and made my paynes
    his pray.
Vayne man, sayd she, that doest in vaine
    assay
A mortall thing so to immortalize !
For I my selve shall lyke to this decay,
And eek my name bee wyped out lykewize.
Not so (quod I) let baser things devize
To dy in dust, but you shall live by fame:
My verse your vertues rare shall eternize,
And in the hevens wryte your glorious
    name;
Where, whenas death shall all the world
    subdew,
Our love shall live, and later life renew.

LXXVI

Fayre bosome, fraught with vertues richest
    tresure,
The neast of love, the lodging of delight,
The bowre of blisse, the paradice of plea-
    sure,
The sacred harbour of that hevenly spright;
How was I ravisht with your lovely sight,
And my frayle thoughts too rashly led
    astray !
Whiles diving deepe through amorous in-
    sight,
On the sweet spoyle of beautie they did
    pray,
And twixt her paps, like early fruit in May,
Whose harvest seemd to hasten now apace,
They loosely did theyr wanton winges dis-
    play,
And there to rest themselves did boldly
    place.
Sweet thoughts, I envy your so happy
    rest,
Which oft I wisht, yet never was so blest.

LXXVII

Was it a dreame, or did I see it playne ?
A goodly table of pure yvory,
All spred with juncats fit to entertayne
The greatest prince with pompous roialty:
Mongst which, there in a silver dish did ly
Twoo golden apples of unvalewd price,
Far passing those which Hercules came by,
Or those which Atalanta did entice;
Exceeding sweet, yet voyd of sinfull vice;
That many sought, yet none could ever taste;

Sweet fruit of pleasure, brought from Para-
    dice
By Love himselfe, and in his garden plaste.
Her brest that table was, so richly spredd;
My thoughts the guests, which would there-
    on have fedd.

LXXVIII

Lackyng my love, I go from place to place,
Lyke a young fawne that late hath lost the
    hynd,
And seeke each where, where last I sawe
    her face,
Whose ymage yet I carry fresh in mynd.
I seeke the fields with her late footing synd,
I seeke her bowre with her late presence
    deckt,
Yet nor in field nor bowre I her can fynd;
Yet field and bowre are full of her aspect.
But when myne eyes I therunto direct,
They ydly back returne to me agayne,
And when I hope to see theyr trew object,
I fynd my selfe but fed with fancies vayne.
Ceasse then, myne eyes, to seeke her selfe
    to see,
And let my thoughts behold her selfe in
    mee.

LXXIX

Men call you fayre, and you doe credit it,
For that your selfe ye dayly such doe see:
But the trew fayre, that is the gentle wit
And vertuous mind, is much more praysd
    of me.
For all the rest, how ever fayre it be,
Shall turne to nought and loose that glori-
    ous hew:
But onely that is permanent, and free
From frayle corruption, that doth flesh
    ensew.
That is true beautie: that doth argue you
To be divine, and borne of heavenly seed,
Deriv'd from that fayre Spirit from whom
    al true
And perfect beauty did at first proceed.
He onely fayre, and what he fayre hath
    made;
All other fayre, lyke flowres, untymely
    fade.

LXXX

After so long a race as I have run
Through Faery Land, which those six books
    compile,
Give leave to rest me, being halfe fordonne,

And gather to my selfe new breath awhile.
Then, as a steed refreshed after toyle,
Out of my prison I will breake anew:
And stoutly will that second worke assoyle,
With strong endevour and attention dew.
Till then give leave to me, in pleasant mew
To sport my muse, and sing my loves sweet
     praise:
The contemplation of whose heavenly hew
My spirit to an higher pitch will rayse.
But let her prayses yet be low and meane,
Fit for the handmayd of the Faery Queene.

LXXXI

Fayre is my love, when her fayre golden
     heares
With the loose wynd ye waving chance to
     marke:
Fayre, when the rose in her red cheekes ap-
     peares,
Or in her eyes the fyre of love does sparke:
Fayre, when her brest, lyke a rich laden
     barke
With pretious merchandize, she forth doth
     lay:
Fayre, when that cloud of pryde, which oft
     doth dark
Her goodly light, with smiles she drives
     away.
But fayrest she, when so she doth display
The gate with pearles and rubyes richly
     dight,
Throgh which her words so wise do make
     their way,
To beare the message of her gentle spright.
The rest be works of Natures wonderment,
But this the worke of harts astonishment.

LXXXII

Joy of my life, full oft for loving you
I blesse my lot, that was so lucky placed:
But then the more your owne mishap I rew,
That are so much by so meane love embased.
For had the equall hevens so much you
     graced
In this as in the rest, ye mote invent
Som hevenly wit, whose verse could have en-
     chased
Your glorious name in golden moniment.
But since ye deignd so goodly to relent
To me your thrall, in whom is little worth,
That little that I am shall all be spent
In setting your immortall prayses forth:
Whose lofty argument, uplifting me,
Shall lift you up unto an high degree.

LXXXIII

Let not one sparke of filthy lustfull fyre
Breake out, that may her sacred peace
     molest;
Ne one light glance of sensuall desyre
Attempt to work her gentle mindes unrest:
But pure affections bred in spotlesse brest,
And modest thoughts breathd from wel
     tempred sprites,
Goe visit her in her chast bowre of rest,
Accompanyde with angelick delightes.
There fill your selfe with those most joyous
     sights,
The which my selfe could never yet attayne:
But speake no word to her of these sad
     plights,
Which her too constant stiffenesse doth con-
     strayn.
Onely behold her rare perfection,
And blesse your fortunes fayre election.

LXXXIV

The world, that cannot deeme of worthy
     things,
When I doe praise her, say I doe but flatter:
So does the cuckow, when the mavis sings,
Begin his witlesse note apace to clatter.
But they that skill not of so heavenly mat-
     ter,
All that they know not, envy or admyre:
Rather then envy, let them wonder at her,
But not to deeme of her desert aspyre.
Deepe in the closet of my parts entyre,
Her worth is written with a golden quill:
That me with heavenly fury doth inspire,
And my glad mouth with her sweet prayses
     fill:
Which when as Fame in her shrill trump
     shal thunder,
Let the world chose to envy or to wonder.

LXXXV

Venemous toung, tipt with vile adders sting,
Of that selfe kynd with which the Furies
     fell
Theyr snaky heads doe combe, from which
     a spring
Of poysoned words and spitefull speeches
     well,
Let all the plagues and horrid paines of
     hell
Upon thee fall for thine accursed hyre,
That with false forged lyes, which thou didst
     tel,
In my true love did stirre up coles of yre;

The sparkes whereof let kindle thine own
   fyre,
And catching hold on thine own wicked hed,
Consume thee quite, that didst with guile
   conspire
In my sweet peace such breaches to have
   bred.
Shame be thy meed, and mischiefe thy re-
   ward,
Due to thy selfe, that it for me prepard.

LXXXVI

Since I did leave the presence of my love,
Many long weary dayes I have outworne,
And many nights, that slowly seemd to move
Theyr sad protract from evening untill
   morne.
For when as day the heaven doth adorne,
I wish that night the noyous day would end:
And when as night hath us of light forlorne,
I wish that day would shortly reascend.
Thus I the time with expectation spend,
And faine my griefe with chaunges to be-
   guile,
That further seemes his terme still to extend,
And maketh every minute seem a myle.
So sorrow still doth seeme too long to last;
But joyous houres doo fly away too fast.

LXXXVII

Since I have lackt the comfort of that light,
The which was wont to lead my thoughts
   astray,
I wander as in darknesse of the night,
Affrayd of every dangers least dismay.
Ne ought I see, though in the clearest day,
When others gaze upon theyr shadowes
   vayne,
But th' onely image of that heavenly ray,
Whereof some glance doth in mine eie re-
   mayne.
Of which beholding the idæa playne,
Through contemplation of my purest part,
With light thereof I doe my selfe sustayne,
And thereon feed my love-affamisht hart.
But with such brightnesse whylest I fill my
   mind,
I starve my body, and mine eyes doe blynd.

LXXXVIII

Lyke as the culver on the bared bough
Sits mourning for the absence of her mate,
And in her songs sends many a wishfull vow
For his returne, that seemes to linger late:
So I alone, now left disconsolate,

Mourne to my selfe the absence of my love,
And wandring here and there all desolate,
Seek with my playnts to match that mourn-
   ful dove:
Ne joy of ought that under heaven doth
   hove
Can comfort me, but her owne joyous sight,
Whose sweet aspect both god and man can
   move,
In her unspotted pleasauns to delight.
Dark is my day, whyles her fayre light I
   mis,
And dead my life that wants such lively blis.

I

In youth, before I waxed old,
The blynd boy, Venus baby,
For want of cunning made me bold,
In bitter hyve to grope for honny:
   But when he saw me stung and cry,
   He tooke his wings and away did fly.

II

As Diane hunted on a day,
She chaunst to come where Cupid lay,
   His quiver by his head:
One of his shafts she stole away,
And one of hers did close convay
   Into the others stead:
With that Love wounded my loves hart,
But Diane beasts with Cupids dart.

III

I saw, in secret to my dame
How little Cupid humbly came,
   And sayd to her 'All hayle, my mother!'
But when he saw me laugh, for shame
His face with bashfull blood did flame,
   Not knowing Venus from the other.
'Then, never blush, Cupid,' quoth I,
'For many have err'd in this beauty.'

IV

Upon a day, as Love lay sweetly slumbring,
   All in his mothers lap,
A gentle bee, with his loud trumpet
   murm'ring,
   About him flew by hap.
Whereof when he was wakened with the
   noyse,
   And saw the beast so small:
'Whats this,' quoth he, 'that gives so great
   a voyce,
   That wakens men withall?'

In angry wize he flyes about,
And threatens all with corage stout. 10

To whom his mother closely smiling sayd,
  Twixt earnest and twixt game:
'See, thou thy selfe likewise art lyttle made,
  If thou regard the same.
And yet thou suffrest neyther gods in sky,
  Nor men in earth to rest;
But when thou art disposed cruelly,
  Theyr sleepe thou doost molest.
    Then eyther change thy cruelty,
    Or give lyke leave unto the fly.' 20

Nathlesse, the cruell boy, not so content,
  Would needs the fly pursue,
And in his hand, with heedlesse hardiment,
  Him caught for to subdue.
But when on it he hasty hand did lay,
  The bee him stung therefore:
'Now out, alasse,' he cryde, 'and welaway!
  I wounded am full sore:
    The fly, that I so much did scorne,
    Hath hurt me with his little horne.' 30

Unto his mother straight he weeping came,
  And of his griefe complayned:
Who could not chose but laugh at his fond game,
  Though sad to see him pained.
'Think now,' quod she, 'my sonne, how great the smart
  Of those whom thou dost wound:
Full many thou hast pricked to the hart,
  That pitty never found:
    Therefore, henceforth some pitty take,
    When thou doest spoyle of lovers make.' 40

She tooke him streight full pitiously lamenting,
  And wrapt him in her smock:
She wrapt him softly, all the while repenting
  That he the fly did mock.
She drest his wound, and it embaulmed wel
  With salve of soveraigne might:
And then she bath'd him in a dainty well,
  The well of deare delight.
    Who would not oft be stung as this,
    To be so bath'd in Venus blis? 50

The wanton boy was shortly wel recured
  Of that his malady:

But he, soone after, fresh againe enured
  His former cruelty.
And since that time he wounded hath my selfe
  With his sharpe dart of love:
And now forgets the cruell carelesse elfe
  His mothers heast to prove.
    So now I languish, till he please
    My pining anguish to appease. 60

EPITHALAMION

YE learned sisters, which have oftentimes
Beene to me ayding, others to adorne,
Whom ye thought worthy of your gracefull rymes,
That even the greatest did not greatly scorne
To heare theyr names sung in your simple layes,
But joyed in theyr praise;
And when ye list your owne mishaps to mourne,
Which death, or love, or fortunes wreck did rayse,
Your string could soone to sadder tenor turne,
And teach the woods and waters to lament
Your dolefull dreriment: 11
Now lay those sorrowfull complaints aside,
And having all your heads with girland crownd,
Helpe me mine owne loves prayses to resound;
Ne let the same of any be envide:
So Orpheus did for his owne bride:
So I unto my selfe alone will sing;
The woods shall to me answer, and my eccho ring.

Early, before the worlds light giving lampe
His golden beame upon the hils doth spred,
Having disperst the nights unchearefull dampe, 21
Doe ye awake, and, with fresh lustyhed,
Go to the bowre of my beloved love,
My truest turtle dove:
Bid her awake; for Hymen is awake,
And long since ready forth his maske to move,
With his bright tead that flames with many a flake,
And many a bachelor to waite on him,
In theyr fresh garments trim.

Bid her awake therefore, and soone her
dight,   30
For lo ! the wished day is come at last,
That shall, for al the paynes and sorrowes
past,
Pay to her usury of long delight:
And whylest she doth her dight,
Doe ye to her of joy and solace sing,
That all the woods may answer, and your
eccho ring.

Bring with you all the nymphes that you
can heare,
Both of the rivers and the forrests greene,
And of the sea that neighbours to her neare,
Al with gay girlands goodly wel beseene. 40
And let them also with them bring in hand
Another gay girland,
For my fayre love, of lillyes and of roses,
Bound truelove wize with a blew silke
riband.
And let them make great store of bridale
poses,
And let them eeke bring store of other
flowers,
To deck the bridale bowers.
And let the ground whereas her foot shall
tread,
For feare the stones her tender foot should
wrong,
Be strewed with fragrant flowers all along,
And diapred lyke the discolored mead. 51
Which done, doe at her chamber dore awayt,
For she will waken strayt;
The whiles doe ye this song unto her sing,
The woods shall to you answer, and your
eccho ring.

Ye nymphes of Mulla, which with carefull
heed
The silver scaly trouts doe tend full well,
And greedy pikes which use therein to feed,
(Those trouts and pikes all others doo excell)
And ye likewise which keepe the rushy lake,
Where none doo fishes take,   61
Bynd up the locks the which hang scatterd
light,
And in his waters, which your mirror make,
Behold your faces as the christall bright,
That when you come whereas my love doth
lie,
No blemish she may spie.
And eke ye lightfoot mayds which keepe the
dere
That on the hoary mountayne use to towre,

And the wylde wolves, which seeke them
to devoure,
With your steele darts doo chace from
comming neer,   70
Be also present heere,
To helpe to decke her, and to help to sing,
That all the woods may answer, and your
eccho ring.

Wake now, my love, awake ! for it is time:
The rosy Morne long since left Tithones bed,
All ready to her silver coche to clyme,
And Phœbus gins to shew his glorious hed.
Hark how the cheerefull birds do chaunt
theyr laies,
And carroll of loves praise !
The merry larke hir mattins sings aloft, 80
The thrush replyes, the mavis descant
playes,
The ouzell shrills, the ruddock warbles soft,
So goodly all agree, with sweet consent,
To this dayes merriment.
Ah ! my deere love, why doe ye sleepe thus
long,
When meeter were that ye should now
awake,
T' awayt the comming of your joyous make,
And hearken to the birds love-learned song,
The deawy leaves among ?
For they of joy and pleasance to you sing,
That all the woods them answer, and theyr
eccho ring.   91

My love is now awake out of her dreame,
And her fayre eyes, like stars that dimmed
were
With darksome cloud, now shew theyr good-
ly beams
More bright then Hesperus his head doth
rere.
Come now, ye damzels, daughters of delight,
Helpe quickly her to dight.
But first come ye, fayre Houres, which
were begot,
In Joves sweet paradice, of Day and Night,
Which doe the seasons of the year allot, 100
And al that ever in this world is fayre
Do make and still repayre.
And ye three handmayds of the Cyprian
Queene,
The which doe still adorne her beauties
pride,
Helpe to addorne my beautifullest bride:
And as ye her array, still throw betweene
Some graces to be seene:

And as ye use to Venus, to her sing,
The whiles the woods shal answer, and your
 eccho ring.

Now is my love all ready forth to come: 110
Let all the virgins therefore well awayt,
And ye fresh boyes, that tend upon her
 groome,
Prepare your selves, for he is comming
 strayt.
Set all your things in seemely good aray,
Fit for so joyfull day,
The joyfulst day that ever sunne did see.
Faire Sun, shew forth thy favourable ray,
And let thy lifull heat not fervent be,
For feare of burning her sunshyny face,
Her beauty to disgrace. 120
O fayrest Phœbus, father of the Muse,
If ever I did honour thee aright,
Or sing the thing that mote thy mind delight,
Doe not thy servants simple boone refuse,
But let this day, let this one day be myne,
Let all the rest be thine.
Then I thy soverayne prayses loud wil sing,
That all the woods shal answer, and theyr
 eccho ring.

Harke how the minstrels gin to shrill aloud
Their merry musick that resounds from far,
The pipe, the tabor, and the trembling croud,
That well agree withouten breach or jar. 132
But most of all the damzels doe delite,
When they their tymbrels smyte,
And thereunto doe daunce and carrol sweet,
That all the sences they doe ravish quite,
The whyles the boyes run up and downe the
 street,
Crying aloud with strong confused noyce,
As if it were one voyce.
'Hymen, Iö Hymen, Hymen,' they do shout,
That even to the heavens theyr shouting
 shrill 141
Doth reach, and all the firmament doth fill;
To which the people, standing all about,
As in approvance doe thereto applaud,
And loud advaunce her laud,
And evermore they 'Hymen, Hymen' sing,
That al the woods them answer, and theyr
 eccho ring.

Loe! where she comes along with portly
 pace,
Lyke Phœbe, from her chamber of the east,
Arysing forth to run her mighty race, 150
Clad all in white, that seemes a virgin best.

So well it her beseemes, that ye would weene
Some angell she had beene.
Her long loose yellow locks lyke golden
 wyre,
Sprinckled with perle, and perling flowres
 atweene,
Doe lyke a golden mantle her attyre,
And being crowned with a girland greene,
Seeme lyke some mayden queene.
Her modest eyes, abashed to behold
So many gazers as on her do stare, 160
Upon the lowly ground affixed are;
Ne dare lift up her countenance too bold,
But blush to heare her prayses sung so loud,
So farre from being proud.
Nathlesse doe ye still loud her prayses sing,
That all the woods may answer, and your
 eccho ring.

Tell me, ye merchants daughters, did ye see
So fayre a creature in your towne before,
So sweet, so lovely, and so mild as she,
Adornd with beautyes grace and vertues
 store? 170
Her goodly eyes lyke saphyres shining
 bright,
Her forehead yvory white,
Her cheekes lyke apples which the sun hath
 rudded,
Her lips lyke cherryes charming men to
 byte,
Her brest like to a bowle of creame uncrud-
 ded,
Her paps lyke lyllies budded,
Her snowie necke lyke to a marble towre,
And all her body like a pallace fayre,
Ascending uppe, with many a stately stayre,
To honors seat and chastities sweet bowre.
Why stand ye still, ye virgins, in amaze, 181
Upon her so to gaze,
Whiles ye forget your former lay to sing,
To which the woods did answer, and your
 eccho ring?

But if ye saw that which no eyes can see,
The inward beauty of her lively spright,
Garnisht with heavenly guifts of high de-
 gree,
Much more then would ye wonder at that
 sight,
And stand astonisht lyke to those which
 red
Medusaes mazeful hed. 190
There dwels sweet Love, and constant Chas-
 tity,

Unspotted Fayth, and comely Womanhood,
Regard of Honour, and mild Modesty;
There Vertue raynes as queene in royal
    throne,
And giveth lawes alone,
The which the base affections doe obay,
And yeeld theyr services unto her will;
Ne thought of thing uncomely ever may
Thereto approch to tempt her mind to ill.
Had ye once seene these her celestial threa-
    sures,   200
And unrevealed pleasures,
Then would ye wonder, and her prayses sing,
That al the woods should answer, and your
    echo ring.

Open the temple gates unto my love,
Open them wide that she may enter in,
And all the postes adorne as doth behove,
And all the pillours deck with girlands trim,
For to receyve this saynt with honour dew,
That commeth in to you.   209
With trembling steps and humble reverence,
She commeth in before th' Almighties vew:
Of her, ye virgins, learne obedience,
When so ye come into those holy places,
To humble your proud faces.
Bring her up to th' high altar, that she may
The sacred ceremonies there partake,
The which do endlesse matrimony make;
And let the roring organs loudly play
The praises of the Lord in lively notes,
The whiles with hollow throates   220
The choristers the joyous antheme sing,
That al the woods may answere, and their
    eccho ring.

Behold, whiles she before the altar stands,
Hearing the holy priest that to her speakes,
And blesseth her with his two happy hands,
How the red roses flush up in her cheekes,
And the pure snow with goodly vermill
    stayne,
Like crimsin dyde in grayne:
That even th' angels, which continually
About the sacred altare doe remaine,   230
Forget their service and about her fly,
Ofte peeping in her face, that seemes more
    fayre,
The more they on it stare.
But her sad eyes, still fastened on the
    ground,
Are governed with goodly modesty,
That suffers not one looke to glaunce awry,
Which may let in a little thought unsownd.

Why blush ye, love, to give to me your hand,
The pledge of all our band ?
Sing, ye sweet angels, Alleluya sing,   240
That all the woods may answere, and your
    eccho ring.

Now al is done; bring home the bride againe,
Bring home the triumph of our victory,
Bring home with you the glory of her gaine,
With joyance bring her and with jollity.
Never had man more joyfull day then this,
Whom heaven would heape with blis.
Make feast therefore now all this live long
    day;
This day for ever to me holy is;
Poure out the wine without restraint or stay,
Poure not by cups, but by the belly full,   251
Poure out to all that wull,
And sprinkle all the postes and wals with
    wine,
That they may sweat, and drunken be with-
    all.
Crowne ye God Bacchus with a coronall,
And Hymen also crowne with wreathes of
    vine;
And let the Graces daunce unto the rest,
For they can doo it best:
The whiles the maydens doe theyr carroll
    sing,
To which the woods shal answer, and theyr
    eccho ring.   260

Ring ye the bels, ye yong men of the towne,
And leave your wonted labors for this day:
This day is holy; doe ye write it downe,
That ye for ever it remember may.
This day the sunne is in his chiefest hight,
With Barnaby the bright,
From whence declining daily by degrees,
He somewhat loseth of his heat and light,
When once the Crab behind his back he sees.
But for this time it ill ordained was,   270
To chose the longest day in all the yeare,
And shortest night, when longest fitter
    weare:
Yet never day so long, but late would passe.
Ring ye the bels, to make it weare away,
And bonefiers make all day,
And daunce about them, and about them
    sing:
That all the woods may answer, and your
    eccho ring.

Ah ! when will this long weary day have end,
And lende me leave to come unto my love ?

How slowly do the houres theyr numbers
spend !
How slowly does sad Time his feathers
move !
Hast thee, O fayrest planet, to thy home
Within the westerne fome:
Thy tyred steedes long since have need of
rest.
Long though it be, at last I see it gloome,
And the bright evening star with golden
creast
Appeare out of the east.
Fayre childe of beauty, glorious lampe of
love,
That all the host of heaven in rankes doost
lead,
And guydest lovers through the nightes
dread,
How chearefully thou lookest from above,
And seemst to laugh atweene thy twin-
kling light,
As joying in the sight
Of these glad many, which for joy doe sing,
That all the woods them answer, and their
echo ring !

Now ceasse, ye damsels, your delights fore-
past;
Enough is it that all the day was youres:
Now day is doen, and night is nighing fast:
Now bring the bryde into the brydall
boures.
The night is come, now soone her disaray,
And in her bed her lay;
Lay her in lillies and in violets,
And silken courteins over her display,
And odourd sheetes, and Arras coverlets.
Behold how goodly my faire love does ly,
In proud humility !
Like unto Maia, when as Jove her tooke
In Tempe, lying on the flowry gras,
Twixt sleepe and wake, after she weary was
With bathing in the Acidalian brooke.
Now it is night, ye damsels may be gon,
And leave my love alone,
And leave likewise your former lay to sing:
The woods no more shal answere, nor your
echo ring.

Now welcome, night ! thou night so long
expected,
That long daies labour doest at last defray,
And all my cares, which cruell Love col-
lected,
Hast sumd in one, and cancelled for aye:

Spread thy broad wing over my love and me,
That no man may us see,
And in thy sable mantle us enwrap,
From feare of perrill and foule horror free.
Let no false treason seeke us to entrap,
Nor any dread disquiet once annoy
The safety of our joy:
But let the night be calme and quietsome,
Without tempestuous storms or sad afray:
Lyke as when Jove with fayre Alcmena lay,
When he begot the great Tirynthian groome:
Or lyke as when he with thy selfe did lie,
And begot Majesty.
And let the mayds and yongmen cease to
sing:
Ne let the woods them answer, nor theyr
eccho ring.

Let no lamenting cryes, nor dolefull teares,
Be heard all night within, nor yet without:
Ne let false whispers, breeding hidden
feares,
Breake gentle sleepe with misconceived
dout.
Let no deluding dreames, nor dreadful
sights,
Make sudden sad affrights;
Ne let house-fyres, nor lightnings helplesse
harmes,
Ne let the Pouke, nor other evill sprights,
Ne let mischivous witches with theyr
charmes,
Ne let hob goblins, names whose sense we
see not,
Fray us with things that be not.
Let not the shriech oule, nor the storke be
heard,
Nor the night raven that still deadly yels,
Nor damned ghosts cald up with mighty
spels,
Nor griesly vultures make us once affeard:
Ne let th' unpleasant quyre of frogs still
croking
Make us to wish theyr choking.
Let none of these theyr drery accents sing;
Ne let the woods them answer, nor theyr
eccho ring.

But let stil Silence trew night watches
keepe,
That sacred Peace may in assurance rayne,
And tymely Sleep, when it is tyme to
sleepe,
May poure his limbs forth on your pleasant
playne,

The whiles an hundred little winged loves,
Like divers fethered doves,
Shall fly and flutter round about our bed,
And in the secret darke, that none reproves,
Their prety stealthes shall worke, and
    snares shal spread   361
To filch away sweet snatches of delight,
Conceald through covert night.
Ye sonnes of Venus, play your sports at will:
For greedy Pleasure, carelesse of your toyes,
Thinks more upon her paradise of joyes,
Then what ye do, albe it good or ill.
All night therefore attend your merry play,
For it will soone be day:
Now none doth hinder you, that say or sing,
Ne will the woods now answer, nor your
    eccho ring.   371

Who is the same which at my window
    peepes ?
Or whose is that faire face that shines so
    bright ?
Is it not Cinthia, she that never sleepes,
But walkes about high heaven al the night ?
O fayrest goddesse, do thou not envy
My love with me to spy:
For thou likewise didst love, though now
    unthought,
And for a fleece of woll, which privily
The Latmian shephard once unto thee
    brought,   380
His pleasures with thee wrought.
Therefore to us be favorable now;
And sith of wemens labours thou hast
    charge,
And generation goodly dost enlarge,
Encline thy will t' effect our wishfull vow,
And the chast wombe informe with timely
    seed,
That may our comfort breed:
Till which we cease our hopefull hap to sing,
Ne let the woods us answere, nor our eccho
    ring.

And thou, great Juno, which with awful
    might   390
The lawes of wedlock still dost patronize,
And the religion of the faith first plight
With sacred rites hast taught to solemnize,
And eeke for comfort often called art

Of women in their smart,
Eternally bind thou this lovely band,
And all thy blessings unto us impart.
And thou, glad Genius, in whose gentle hand
The bridale bowre and geniall bed remaine,
Without blemish or staine,   400
And the sweet pleasures of theyr loves
    delight
With secret ayde doest succour and supply,
Till they bring forth the fruitfull progeny,
Send us the timely fruit of this same night.
And thou, fayre Hebe, and thou, Hymen
    free,
Grant that it may so be.
Til which we cease your further prayse to
    sing,
Ne any woods shal answer, nor your eccho
    ring.

And ye high heavens, the temple of the
    gods,   409
In which a thousand torches flaming bright
Doe burne, that to us wretched earthly clods
In dreadfull darknesse lend desired light,
And all ye powers which in the same re-
    mayne,
More then we men can fayne,
Poure out your blessing on us plentiously,
And happy influence upon us raine,
That we may raise a large posterity,
Which from the earth, which they may
    long possesse
With lasting happinesse,   419
Up to your haughty pallaces may mount,
And for the guerdon of theyr glorious merit,
May heavenly tabernacles there inherit,
Of blessed saints for to increase the count.
So let us rest, sweet love, in hope of this,
And cease till then our tymely joyes to sing:
The woods no more us answer, nor our eccho
    ring.

Song, made in lieu of many ornaments
With which my love should duly have bene
    dect,
Which cutting off through hasty accidents,
Ye would not stay your dew time to expect,
But promist both to recompens,   431
Be unto her a goodly ornament,
And for short time an endlesse moniment.

FINIS

IMPRINTED BY P. S. FOR WILLIAM PONSONBY

FOWRE HYMNES

MADE BY

EDM. SPENSER

LONDON

PRINTED FOR WILLIAM PONSONBY

1596

TO THE RIGHT HONORABLE AND MOST VERTUOUS LADIES, THE LADIE MARGARET COUNTESSE OF CUMBERLAND, AND THE LADIE MARIE COUNTESSE OF WARWICKE

HAVING, in the greener times of my youth, composed these former two hymnes in the praise of love and beautie, and finding that the same too much pleased those of like age and disposition, which, being too vehemently caried with that kind of affection, do rather sucke out poyson to their strong passion, then hony to their honest delight, I was moved by the one of you two most excellent Ladies, to call in the same. But being unable so to doe, by reason that many copies thereof were formerly scattered abroad, I resolved at least to amend, and by way of retractation to reforme them, making in stead of those two hymnes of earthly or naturall love and beautie, two others of heavenly and celestiall. The which I doe dedicate joyntly unto you two honorable sisters, as to the most excellent and rare ornaments of all true love and beautie, both in the one and the other kinde, humbly beseeching you to vouchsafe the patronage of them, and to accept this my humble service, in lieu of the great graces and honourable favours which ye dayly shew unto me, untill such time as I may by better meanes yeeld you some more notable testimonie of my thankfull mind and dutifull devotion.

And even so I pray for your happinesse.

Greenwich, this first of September, 1596.

Your Honors most bounden ever
in all humble service,
Ed. Sp.

[The noblewomen to whom this volume is dedicated were sisters, of the great Russell family. The Lady Margaret was that Countess of Cumberland to whom Daniel, a few years later, addressed the most noble of his poems. The Countess of Warwick (whose name was Anne, not Mary) was the widow of Leicester's brother, 'the good earl,' and, as such, had found mention in 'The Ruins of Time.'

The words of the dedication have been variously interpreted. The first pair of hymns, composed, we read, 'in the greener times of my youth,' (by which we are to understand, probably, the period of the *Calendar* and of ' Mother Hubberd's Tale') having ' too much pleased those of like age and disposition,' were apparently, in 1596, still popular: but one of the noble sisters, disapproving of them, would have them ' called in ; ' whereupon, ' being unable so to doe,' the poet ' resolved at least to amend and by way of retractation to reforme them, making, in stead of those two hymns of earthly or naturall love and beautie, two others of heavenly and celestiall.' The difficulty is in the final clauses. Did the poet, besides composing the two later hymns, also reduce the earlier to inoffensiveness ? or did he let these stand as originally written, and atone for them merely by composing their substitutes ? At first, it would seem as if the second interpretation, though more in accord with the words of the letter, were impossible. For in the earlier hymns, as they are printed, there could surely be nothing to shock the most extravagant of prudes : besides, if the lady objected to them in their early form, why should the poet publish them in that form ? Yet if, on the other hand, these hymns, as they are printed, be the result of expurgation, one does not see what the poet can have expurgated. Both are organically Platonic : there would seem to be no place in them, at any point, for matter even faintly licentious. Perhaps, however, it has been assumed too readily that the fault of these early hymns was of that kind. Dr. Grosart thinks that the sister who protested was the Countess of Warwick, for she is known to have inclined to Puritanism. If it was she, her protest may very well have been, not against immodesty, but against the very subject matter of these hymns, 'earthly or naturall love and beautie.' She may have reprobated them for sinful vanities, just as her nephew, Sidney, being on his death-bed, reprobated his own *Arcadia* and gave earnest orders for its destruction. In atonement for such a fault, Spenser might well issue the early hymns as they had been written, and let their vanity be foil to the earnestness of the later, composed to replace them. His repentance would then be that of the December eclogue : —

'I, that whilome wont to frame my pype
Unto the shifting of the shepheards foote,
Sike follies nowe have gathered as too ripe,
And cast hem out as rotten and unsoote.
The loser lasse [Rosalind] I cast to please nomore :
One if I please [i. e. God], enough is me therefore.'

The later repentance certainly need not be taken as at all more serious than the earlier, need not be read as an example of 'the sensitive purity of the poet's nature.' In composing his first two hymns he had aimed to embody in verse some of those Neo-Platonic doctrines which were then so popular in Italy, best known to Englishmen, perhaps, in the fourth book of Castiglione's *Courtier*. His success had been the more brilliant in that he was first in England to occupy the field. Later, when the Countess of Warwick would have persuaded him that such vanities were unworthy of a 'sage and serious' poet, one can understand how he might acquiesce, and, without very real contrition for these youthful hymns, gratify her by others more in consonance with her convictions. For the Neo-Platonic modes of thought were as applicable to Christian doctrine as to theories of 'earthly or naturall love and beautie,' and a poet might be sincere in both uses, since neither would be understood literally and since both embodied the spirit of his most serious thought.]

AN HYMNE IN HONOUR OF LOVE

LOVE, that long since hast to thy mighty powre
Perforce subdude my poore captived hart,
And raging now therein with restlesse stowre,
Doest tyrannize in everie weaker part,
Faine would I seeke to ease my bitter smart
By any service I might do to thee,
Or ought that else might to thee pleasing bee.

And now t' asswage the force of this new flame,
And make thee more propitious in my need,
I meane to sing the praises of thy name, 10
And thy victorious conquests to areed;
By which thou madest many harts to bleed
Of mighty victors, with wyde wounds embrewed,
And by thy cruell darts to thee subdewed.

Onely I feare my wits, enfeebled late
Through the sharpe sorrowes which thou hast me bred,
Should faint, and words should faile me to relate
The wondrous triumphs of thy great godhed.

But, if thou wouldst vouchsafe to overspred
Me with the shadow of thy gentle wing, 20
I should enabled be thy actes to sing.

Come then, O come, thou mightie God of Love,
Out of thy silver bowres and secret blisse,
Where thou doest sit in Venus lap above,
Bathing thy wings in her ambrosiall kisse,
That sweeter farre then any nectar is;
Come softly, and my feeble breast inspire
With gentle furie, kindled of thy fire.

And ye, sweet Muses, which have often proved
The piercing points of his avengefull darts,
And ye, faire nimphs, which oftentimes have loved 31
The cruell worker of your kindly smarts,
Prepare your selves, and open wide your harts,
For to receive the triumph of your glorie,
That made you merie oft, when ye were sorie.

And ye, faire blossomes of youths wanton breed,
Which in the conquests of your beautie bost,

Wherewith your lovers feeble eyes you feed,
But sterve their harts, that needeth nour-
    ture most,
Prepare your selves to march amongst his
    host,
And all the way this sacred hymne do sing, 40
Made in the honor of your soveraigne king.

GREAT God of might, that reignest in the
    mynd,
And all the bodie to thy hest doest frame,
Victor of gods, subduer of mankynd,
That doest the lions and fell tigers tame,
Making their cruell rage thy scornefull
    game,
And in their roring taking great delight,
Who can expresse the glorie of thy might?

Or who alive can perfectly declare   50
The wondrous cradle of thine infancie,
When thy great mother Venus first thee
    bare,
Begot of Plentie and of Penurie,
Though elder then thine owne nativitie;
And yet a chyld, renewing still thy yeares,
And yet the eldest of the heavenly peares?

For ere this worlds still moving mightie
    masse
Out of great Chaos ugly prison crept,
In which his goodly face long hidden was
From heavens view, and in deepe darknesse
    kept,   60
Love, that had now long time securely slept
In Venus lap, unarmed then and naked,
Gan reare his head, by Clotho being waked.

And taking to him wings of his owne heate,
Kindled at first from heavens life-giving
    fyre,
He gan to move out of his idle seate,
Weakely at first, but after with desyre
Lifted aloft, he gan to mount up hyre,
And like fresh eagle, make his hardie flight
Through all that great wide wast, yet want-
    ing light.   70

Yet wanting light to guide his wandring
    way,
His owne faire mother, for all creatures sake,
Did lend him light from her owne goodly
    ray:
Then through the world his way he gan to
    take,
The world, that was not till he did it make,

Whose sundrie parts he from them selves
    did sever,
The which before had lyen confused ever.

The earth, the ayre, the water, and the fyre,
Then gan to raunge them selves in huge
    array,
And with contrary forces to conspyre   80
Each against other, by all meanes they may,
Threatning their owne confusion and decay:
Ayre hated earth, and water hated fyre,
Till Love relented their rebellious yre.

He then them tooke, and tempering goodly
    well
Their contrary dislikes with loved meanes,
Did place them all in order, and compell
To keepe them selves within their sundrie
    raines,
Together linkt with adamantine chaines;
Yet so as that in every living wight   90
They mixe themselves, and shew their
    kindly might.

So ever since they firmely have remained,
And duly well observed his beheast;
Through which now all these things that are
    contained
Within this goodly cope, both most and
    least,
Their being have, and dayly are increast
Through secret sparks of his infused fyre,
Which in the barraine cold he doth inspyre.

Thereby they all do live, and moved are
To multiply the likenesse of their kynd, 100
Whilest they seeke onely, without further
    care,
To quench the flame which they in burning
    fynd:
But man, that breathes a more immortall
    mynd,
Not for lusts sake, but for eternitie,
Seekes to enlarge his lasting progenie.

For having yet in his deducted spright
Some sparks remaining of that heavenly
    fyre,
He is enlumind with that goodly light,
Unto like goodly semblant to aspyre:
Therefore in choice of love, he doth desyre
That seemes on earth most heavenly, to
    embrace;   111
That same is Beautie, borne of heavenly
    race.

For sure, of all that in this mortall frame
Contained is, nought more divine doth seeme,
Or that resembleth more th' immortall
　　flame
Of heavenly light, then Beauties glorious
　　beame.
What wonder then, if with such rage
　　extreme
Fraile men, whose eyes seek heavenly things
　　to see,
At sight thereof so much enravisht bee ?

Which well perceiving, that imperious boy
Doth therwith tip his sharp empoisned
　　darts;　　　　　　　　　　　　　121
Which, glancing through the eyes with coun-
　　tenance coy,
Rest not till they have pierst the trembling
　　harts,
And kindled flame in all their inner parts,
Which suckes the blood, and drinketh up
　　the lyfe
Of carefull wretches with consuming griefe.

Thenceforth they playne, and make ful pit-
　　eous mone
Unto the author of their balefull bane;
The daies they waste, the nights they grieve
　　and grone,
Their lives they loath, and heavens light
　　disdaine;　　　　　　　　　　　130
No light but that whose lampe doth yet
　　remaine
Fresh burning in the image of their eye,
They deigne to see, and seeing it still dye.

The whylst thou, tyrant Love, doest laugh
　　and scorne
At their complaints, making their paine thy
　　play;
Whylest they lye languishing like thrals
　　forlorne,
The whyles thou doest triumph in their
　　decay,
And otherwhyles, their dying to delay,
Thou doest emmarble the proud hart of her,
Whose love before their life they doe pre-
　　fer.　　　　　　　　　　　　　140

So hast thou often done (ay me the more !)
To me thy vassall, whose yet bleeding hart
With thousand wounds thou mangled hast
　　so sore
That whole remaines scarse any little part;
Yet to augment the anguish of my smart,

Thou hast enfrosen her disdainefull brest,
That no one drop of pitie there doth rest.

Why then do I this honor unto thee,
Thus to ennoble thy victorious name,　149
Since thou doest shew no favour unto mee,
Ne once move ruth in that rebellious dame,
Somewhat to slacke the rigour of my flame?
Certes small glory doest thou winne hereby,
To let her live thus free, and me to dy.

But if thou be indeede, as men thee call,
The worlds great parent, the most kind
　　preserver
Of living wights, the soveraine lord of all,
How falles it then that with thy furious
　　fervour
Thou doest afflict as well the not deserver,
As him that doeth thy lovely heasts de-
　　spize,　　　　　　　　　　　160
And on thy subjects most doest tyrannize ?

Yet herein eke thy glory seemeth more,
By so hard handling those which best thee
　　serve,
That ere thou doest them unto grace restore,
Thou mayest well trie if they will ever
　　swerve,
And mayest them make it better to deserve,
And having got it, may it more esteeme;
For things hard gotten men more dearely
　　deeme.　　　　　　　　　　　168

So hard those heavenly beauties be enfyred,
As things divine least passions doe impresse,
The more of stedfast mynds to be admyred,
The more they stayed be on stedfastnesse:
But baseborne mynds such lamps regard
　　the lesse,
Which at first blowing take not hastie fyre;
Such fancies feele no love, but loose desyre.

For Love is lord of truth and loialtie,
Lifting himselfe out of the lowly dust
On golden plumes up to the purest skie,
Above the reach of loathly sinfull lust,
Whose base affect, through cowardly dis-
　　trust　　　　　　　　　　　180
Of his weake wings, dare not to heaven fly,
But like a moldwarpe in the earth doth ly,

His dunghill thoughts, which do themselves
　　enure
To dirtie drosse, no higher dare aspyre,
Ne can his feeble earthly eyes endure

The flaming light of that celestiall fyre,
Which kindleth love in generous desyre,
And makes him mount above the native
    might
Of heavie earth, up to the heavens hight.

Such is the powre of that sweet passion, 190
That it all sordid basenesse doth expell,
And the refyned mynd doth newly fashion
Unto a fairer forme, which now doth dwell
In his high thought, that would it selfe ex-
    cell;
Which he beholding still with constant
    sight,
Admires the mirrour of so heavenly light.

Whose image printing in his deepest wit,
He thereon feeds his hungrie fantasy,
Still full, yet never satisfyde with it;
Like Tantale, that in store doth sterved ly,
So doth he pine in most satiety; 201
For nought may quench his infinite desyre,
Once kindled through that first conceived
    fyre.

Thereon his mynd affixed wholly is,
Ne thinks on ought, but how it to attaine;
His care, his joy, his hope is all on this,
That seemes in it all blisses to containe,
In sight whereof all other blisse seemes
    vaine.
Thrise happie man, might he the same
    possesse,
He faines himselfe, and doth his fortune
    blesse. 210

And though he do not win his wish to end,
Yet thus farre happie he him selfe doth
    weene,
That heavens such happie grace did to him
    lend,
As thing on earth so heavenly to have seene,
His harts enshrined saint, his heavens
    queene,
Fairer then fairest, in his fayning eye,
Whose sole aspect he counts felicitye.

Then forth he casts in his unquiet thought,
What he may do, her favour to obtaine;
What brave exploit, what perill hardly
    wrought, 220
What puissant conquest, what adventurous
    paine,
May please her best, and grace unto him
    gaine:

He dreads no danger, nor misfortune feares;
His faith, his fortune, in his breast he beares.

Thou art his god, thou art his mightie guyde,
Thou, being blind, letst him not see his
    feares,
But cariest him to that which he hath eyde,
Through seas, through flames, through thou-
    sand swords and speares:
Ne ought so strong that may his force with-
    stand,
With which thou armest his resistlesse hand.

Witnesse Leander in the Euxine waves, 231
And stout Æneas in the Trojane fyre,
Achilles preassing through the Phrygian
    glaives,
And Orpheus daring to provoke the yre
Of damned fiends, to get his love retyre·
For both through heaven and hell thou
    makest way,
To win them worship which to thee obay.

And if by all these perils and these paynes
He may but purchase lyking in her eye,
What heavens of joy then to himselfe he
    faynes ! 240
Eftsoones he wypes quite out of memory
What ever ill before he did aby;
Had it bene death, yet would he die againe,
To live thus happie as her grace to gaine.

Yet when he hath found favour to his will,
He nathemore can so contented rest,
But forceth further on, and striveth still
T' approch more neare, till in her inmost
    brest
He may embosomd bee, and loved best;
And yet not best, but to be lov'd alone; 250
For love can not endure a paragone.

The feare whereof, O how doth it torment
His troubled mynd with more then hellish
    paine !
And to his fayning fansie represent
Sights never seene, and thousand shadowes
    vaine,
To breake his sleepe and waste his ydle
    braine;
Thou that hast never lov'd canst not beleeve
Least part of th' evils which poore lovers
    greeve.

The gnawing envie, the hart-fretting feare,
The vaine surmizes, the distrustfull showes,

The false reports that flying tales doe beare,
The doubts, the daungers, the delayes, the woes,   262
The fayned friends, the unassured foes,
With thousands more then any tongue can tell,
Doe make a lovers life a wretches hell.

Yet is there one more cursed then they all,
That cancker worme, that monster Gelosie,
Which eates the hart, and feedes upon the gall,
Turning all loves delight to miserie,
Through feare of loosing his felicitie.   270
Ah, gods ! that ever ye that monster placed
In gentle love, that all his joyes defaced !

By these, O Love, thou doest thy entrance make
Unto thy heaven, and doest the more endeere
Thy pleasures unto those which them partake,
As after stormes, when clouds begin to cleare,
The sunne more bright and glorious doth appeare;
So thou thy folke, through paines of Purgatorie,
Dost beare unto thy blisse, and heavens glorie.

There thou them placest in a paradize   280
Of all delight and joyous happie rest,
Where they doe feede on nectar heavenly wize,
With Hercules and Hebe, and the rest
Of Venus dearlings, through her bountie blest,
And lie like gods in yvorie beds arayd,
With rose and lillies over them displayd.

There with thy daughter Pleasure they doe play
Their hurtlesse sports, without rebuke or blame,
And in her snowy bosome boldly lay
Their quiet heads, devoyd of guilty shame,
After full joyance of their gentle game;   291
Then her they crowne their goddesse and their queene,
And decke with floures thy altars well beseene.

Ay me ! deare lord, that ever I might hope,
For all the paines and woes that I endure,
To come at length unto the wished scope

Of my desire, or might my selfe assure,
That happie port for ever to recure !
Then would I thinke these paines no paines at all,   299
And all my woes to be but penance small.

Then would I sing of thine immortall praise
An heavenly hymne, such as the angels sing,
And thy triumphant name then would I raise
Bove all the gods, thee onely honoring,
My guide, my god, my victor, and my king:
Till then, dread lord, vouchsafe to take of me
This simple song, thus fram'd in praise of thee.

AN HYMNE IN HONOUR OF BEAUTIE

Ah ! whither, Love, wilt thou now carrie mee ?
What wontlesse fury dost thou now inspire
Into my feeble breast, too full of thee ?
Whylest seeking to aslake thy raging fyre,
Thou in me kindlest much more great desyre,
And up aloft above my strength doest rayse
The wondrous matter of my fyre to prayse.

That as I earst in praise of thine owne name,
So now in honour of thy mother deare,
An honourable hymne I eke should frame,
And with the brightnesse of her beautie cleare,   11
The ravisht harts of gazefull men might reare
To admiration of that heavenly light,
From whence proceeds such soule enchaunting might.

Therto do thou, great goddesse, Queene of Beauty,
Mother of Love, and of all worlds delight,
Without whose soverayne grace and kindly dewty
Nothing on earth seemes fayre to fleshly sight,
Doe thou vouchsafe with thy love-kindling light
T' illuminate my dim and dulled eyne,   20
And beautifie this sacred hymne of thyne.

That both to thee, to whom I meane it most,
And eke to her, whose faire immortall beame
Hath darted fyre into my feeble ghost,

That now it wasted is with woes extreame,
It may so please that she at length will
    streame
Some deaw of grace into my withered hart,
After long sorrow and consuming smart.

WHAT time this worlds great workmaister
        did cast
To make al things such as we now behold, 30
It seemes that he before his eyes had plast
A goodly paterne, to whose perfect mould
He fashiond them as comely as he could,
That now so faire and seemely they ap-
    peare
As nought may be amended any wheare.

That wondrous paterne, wheresoere it bee,
Whether in earth layd up in secret store,
Or else in heaven, that no man may it see
With sinfull eyes, for feare it to deflore,
Is perfect Beautie, which all men adore; 40
Whose face and feature doth so much excell
All mortall sence, that none the same may
    tell.

Thereof as every earthly thing partakes
Or more or lesse, by influence divine,
So it more faire accordingly it makes,
And the grosse matter of this earthly myne,
Which clotheth it, thereafter doth refyne,
Doing away the drosse which dims the
    light
Of that faire beame which therein is em-
    pight.

For through infusion of celestiall powre 50
The duller earth it quickneth with delight,
And life-full spirits privily doth powre
Through all the parts, that to the lookers
    sight
They seeme to please. That is thy soveraine
    might,
O Cyprian queene, which, flowing from the
    beame
Of thy bright starre, thou into them doest
    streame.

That is the thing which giveth pleasant
    grace
To all things faire, that kindleth lively
    fyre,
Light of thy lampe, which, shyning in the
    face, 59
Thence to the soule darts amorous desyre,
And robs the harts of those which it admyre;

Therewith thou pointest thy sons poysned
    arrow,
That wounds the life, and wastes the inmost
    marrow.

How vainely then doe ydle wits invent
That Beautie is nought else but mixture
    made
Of colours faire, and goodly temp'rament
Of pure complexions, that shall quickly
    fade
And passe away, like to a sommers shade,
Or that it is but comely composition
Of parts well measurd, with meet dispo-
    sition !
                        70

Hath white and red in it such wondrous
    powre,
That it can pierce through th' eyes unto the
    hart,
And therein stirre such rage and restlesse
    stowre,
As nought but death can stint his dolours
    smart ?
Or can proportion of the outward part
Move such affection in the inward mynd,
That it can rob both sense, and reason
    blynd ?

Why doe not then the blossomes of the field,
Which are arayd with much more orient
    hew,
And to the sense most daintie odours yield, 79
Worke like impression in the lookers vew ?
Or why doe not faire pictures like powre
    shew,
In which oftimes we Nature see of Art
Exceld, in perfect limming every part ?

But ah ! beleeve me, there is more then so,
That workes such wonders in the minds of
    men.
I, that have often prov'd, too well it know;
And who so list the like assayes to ken
Shall find by tryall, and confesse it then, 89
That Beautie is not, as fond men misdeeme,
An outward shew of things that onely seeme.

For that same goodly hew of white and red,
With which the cheekes are sprinckled, shal
    decay,
And those sweete rosy leaves, so fairely
    spred
Upon the lips, shall fade and fall away
To that they were, even to corrupted clay.

That golden wyre, those sparckling stars so
    bright
Shall turne to dust, and loose their goodly
    light.

But that faire lampe, from whose celestiall
    ray
That light proceedes which kindleth lovers
    fire,   100
Shall never be extinguisht nor decay;
But when the vitall spirits doe expyre,
Unto her native planet shall retyre;
For it is heavenly borne, and can not die,
Being a parcell of the purest skie.

For when the soule, the which derived was,
At first, out of that great immortall Spright,
By whom all live to love, whilome did pas
Downe from the top of purest heavens hight,
To be embodied here, it then tooke light 110
And lively spirits from that fayrest starre,
Which lights the world forth from his firie
    carre.

Which powre retayning still, or more or
    lesse,
When she in fleshly seede is eft enraced,
Through every part she doth the same im-
    presse,
According as the heavens have her graced,
And frames her house, in which she will be
    placed,
Fit for her selfe, adorning it with spoyle
Of th' heavenly riches which she robd ere-
    whyle.

Thereof it comes that these faire soules,
    which have   120
The most resemblance of that heavenly
    light,
Frame to themselves most beautifull and
    brave
Their fleshly bowre, most fit for their de-
    light,
And the grosse matter by a soveraine might
Tempers so trim, that it may well be seene
A pallace fit for such a virgin queene.

So every spirit, as it is most pure,
And hath in it the more of heavenly light,
So it the fairer bodie doth procure
To habit in, and it more fairely dight   130
With chearefull grace and amiable sight.
For of the soule the bodie forme doth take:
For soule is forme, and doth the bodie make.

Therefore, where ever that thou doest be-
    hold
A comely corpse, with beautie faire en-
    dewed,
Know this for certaine, that the same doth
    hold
A beauteous soule, with faire conditions
    thewed,
Fit to receive the seede of vertue strewed.
For all that faire is, is by nature good; 139
That is a signe to know the gentle blood.

Yet oft it falles that many a gentle mynde
Dwels in deformed tabernacle drownd,
Either by chaunce, against the course of
    kynd,
Or through unaptnesse in the substance
    fownd,
Which it assumed of some stubborne
    grownd,
That will not yield unto her formes direc-
    tion,
But is deform'd with some foule imper-
    fection.

And oft it falles (ay me, the more to rew!)
That goodly Beautie, albe heavenly borne,
Is foule abusd, and that celestiall hew, 150
Which doth the world with her delight
    adorne,
Made but the bait of sinne, and sinners
    scorne;
Whilest every one doth seeke and sew to
    have it,
But every one doth seeke but to deprave it.

Yet nathemore is that faire Beauties blame,
But theirs that do abuse it unto ill:
Nothing so good, but that through guilty
    shame
May be corrupt, and wrested unto will.
Nathelesse the soule is faire and beauteous
    still,
How ever fleshes fault it filthy make: 160
For things immortall no corruption take.

But ye, faire dames, the worlds deare orna-
    ments,
And lively images of heavens light,
Let not your beames with such disparage-
    ments
Be dimd, and your bright glorie darkned
    quight,
But mindfull still of your first countries
    sight,

Doe still preserve your first informed
grace,
Whose shadow yet shynes in your beauteous
face.

Loath that foule blot, that hellish fierbrand,
Disloiall lust, faire Beauties foulest blame,
That base affections, which your eares
would bland, 171
Commend to you by loves abused name;
But is indeede the bondslave of defame;
Which will the garland of your glorie marre,
And quench the light of your bright shyning
starre.

But gentle love, that loiall is and trew,
Will more illumine your resplendent ray,
And adde more brightnesse to your goodly
hew,
From light of his pure fire, which, by like
way
Kindled of yours, your likenesse doth dis-
play, 180
Like as two mirrours, by opposd reflexion,
Doe both expresse the faces first impression.

Therefore, to make your beautie more ap-
peare,
It you behoves to love, and forth to lay
That heavenly riches which in you ye beare,
That men the more admyre their fountaine
may;
For else what booteth that celestiall ray,
If it in darknesse be enshrined ever,
That it of loving eyes be vewed never?

But in your choice of loves, this well advize,
That likest to your selves ye them select, 191
The which your forms first sourse may sym-
pathize,
And with like beauties parts be inly deckt:
For if you loosely love without respect,
It is no love, but a discordant warre,
Whose unlike parts amongst themselves do
jarre.

For love is a celestiall harmonie
Of likely harts composd of starres concent,
Which joyne together in sweete sympathie,
To worke ech others joy and true content,
Which they have harbourd since their first
descent 201
Out of their heavenly bowres, where they
did see
And know ech other here belov'd to bee.

Then wrong it were that any other twaine
Should in loves gentle band combyned bee,
But those whom Heaven did at first ordaine,
And made out of one mould the more t'
agree:
For all that like the beautie which they see
Streight do not love: for love is not so light,
As streight to burne at first beholders sight.

But they which love indeede looke otherwise,
With pure regard and spotlesse true intent,
Drawing out of the object of their eyes 213
A more refyned forme, which they present
Unto their mind, voide of all blemishment;
Which it reducing to her first perfection,
Beholdeth free from fleshes frayle infection.

And then conforming it unto the light,
Which in it selfe it hath remaining still,
Of that first sunne, yet sparckling in his sight,
Thereof he fashions in his higher skill 221
An heavenly beautie to his fancies will,
And it embracing in his mind entyre,
The mirrour of his owne thought doth ad-
myre.

Which seeing now so inly faire to be,
As outward it appeareth to the eye,
And with his spirits proportion to agree,
He thereon fixeth all his fantasie,
And fully setteth his felicitie,
Counting it fairer then it is indeede, 230
And yet indeede her fairenesse doth ex-
ceede.

For lovers eyes more sharply sighted bee
Then other mens, and in deare loves delight
See more then any other eyes can see,
Through mutuall receipt of beames bright,
Which carrie privie message to the spright,
And to their eyes that inmost faire display,
As plaine as light discovers dawning day.

Therein they see, through amorous eye-
glaunces,
Armies of Loves still flying too and fro, 240
Which dart at them their litle fierie launces:
Whom having wounded, backe againe they go,
Carrying compassion to their lovely foe;
Who, seeing her faire eyes so sharpe effect,
Cures all their sorrowes with one sweete
aspect.

In which how many wonders doe they reede
To their conceipt, that others never see!

Now of her smiles, with which their soules
they feede,
Like gods with nectar in their bankets free,
Now of her lookes, which like to cordials
bee;   250
But when her words embassade forth she
sends,
Lord, how sweete musicke that unto them
lends !

Sometimes upon her forhead they behold
A thousand graces masking in delight;
Sometimes within her eye-lids they unfold
Ten thousand sweet belgards, which to their
sight
Doe seeme like twinckling starres in frostie
night;
But on her lips, like rosy buds in May,
So many millions of chaste pleasures play.

All those, O Cytherea, and thousands more
Thy handmaides be, which do on thee at-
tend,   261
To decke thy beautie with their dainties
store,
That may it more to mortall eyes commend,
And make it more admyr'd of foe and frend;
That in mens harts thou mayst thy throne
enstall,
And spred thy lovely kingdome over all.

Then Iö, tryumph! O great Beauties Queene,
Advance the banner of thy conquest hie,
That all this world, the which thy vassals
beene,
May draw to thee, and with dew fealtie 270
Adore the powre of thy great majestie,
Singing this hymne in honour of thy name,
Compyld by me, which thy poore liegeman
am.

In lieu whereof graunt, O great soveraine,
That she, whose conquering beautie doth
captive
My trembling hart in her eternall chaine,
One drop of grace at length will to me give,
That I her bounden thrall by her may live,
And this same life, which first fro me she
reaved,
May owe to her, of whom I it receaved. 280

And you, faire Venus dearling, my deare
dread,
Fresh flowre of grace, great goddesse of my
life,

When your faire eyes these fearefull lines
shal read,
Deigne to let fall one drop of dew reliefe,
That may recure my harts long pyning
griefe,
And shew what wondrous powre your beauty
hath,
That can restore a damned wight from death.

AN HYMNE OF HEAVENLY LOVE

Love, lift me up upon thy golden wings,
From this base world unto thy heavens
hight,
Where I may see those admirable things
Which there thou workest by thy soveraine
might,
Farre above feeble reach of earthly sight,
That I thereof an heavenly hymne may sing
Unto the God of Love, high heavens king.

Many lewd layes (ah, woe is me the more !)
In praise of that mad fit which fooles call
love,   9
I have in th' heat of youth made heretofore,
That in light wits did loose affection move.
But all those follies now I do reprove,
And turned have the tenor of my string,
The heavenly prayses of true love to sing.

And ye that wont with greedy vaine desire
To reade my fault, and wondring at my
flame,
To warme your selves at my wide sparckling
fire,
Sith now that heat is quenched, quench my
blame,
And in her ashes shrowd my dying shame:
For who my passed follies now pursewes, 20
Beginnes his owne, and my old fault re-
newes.

Before this worlds great frame, in which
al things
Are now containd, found any being place,
Ere flitting Time could wag his eyas wings
About that mightie bound, which doth em-
brace
The rolling spheres, and parts their houres
by space,
That high eternall Powre, which now doth
move
In all these things, mov'd in it selfe by love

It lov'd it selfe, because it selfe was faire;
(For faire is lov'd;) and of it selfe begot 30
Like to it selfe his eldest Sonne and Heire,
Eternall, pure, and voide of sinfull blot,
The firstling of his joy, in whom no jot
Of loves dislike or pride was to be found,
Whom he therefore with equall honour
    crownd.

With him he raignd, before all time pre-
    scribed,
In endlesse glorie and immortall might,
Together with that third from them derived,
Most wise, most holy, most almightie
    Spright,
Whose kingdomes throne no thought of
    earthly wight   40
Can comprehend, much lesse my trembling
    verse
With equall words can hope it to reherse.

Yet, O most blessed Spirit, pure lampe of
    light,
Eternall spring of grace and wisedome trew,
Vouchsafe to shed into my barren spright
Some little drop of thy celestiall dew,
That may my rymes with sweet infuse em-
    brew,
And give me words equall unto my thought,
To tell the marveiles by thy mercie wrought.

Yet being pregnant still with powrefull
    grace,   50
And full of fruitfull love, that loves to get
Things like himselfe, and to enlarge his
    race,
His second brood, though not in powre so
    great,
Yet full of beautie, next he did beget,
An infinite increase of angels bright,
All glistring glorious in their Makers light.

To them the heavens illimitable hight
(Not this round heaven, which we from
    hence behold,
Adornd with thousand lamps of burning
    light,
And with ten thousand gemmes of shyning
    gold)   60
He gave as their inheritance to hold,
That they might serve him in eternall blis,
And be partakers of those joyes of his.

There they in their trinall triplicities
About him wait, and on his will depend,

Either with nimble wings to cut the skies,
When he them on his messages doth send,
Or on his owne dread presence to attend,
Where they behold the glorie of his light,
And caroll hymnes of love both day and
    night.   70

Both day and night is unto them all one,
For he his beames doth still to them extend,
That darknesse there appeareth never none;
Ne hath their day, ne hath their blisse an
    end,
But there their termelesse time in pleasure
    spend;
Ne ever should their happinesse decay,
Had not they dar'd their Lord to disobay.

But pride, impatient of long resting peace,
Did puffe them up with greedy bold ambition,
That they gan cast their state how to in-
    crease   80
Above the fortune of their first condition,
And sit in Gods owne seat without com-
    mission:
The brightest angell, even the Child of
    Light,
Drew millions more against their God to
    fight.

Th' Almighty, seeing their so bold assay,
Kindled the flame of his consuming yre,
And with his onely breath them blew away
From heavens hight, to which they did
    aspyre,
To deepest hell, and lake of damned fyre;
Where they in darknesse and dread horror
    dwell,
Hating the happie light from which they 90
    fell.

So that next off-spring of the Makers love,
Next to himselfe in glorious degree,
Degendering to hate, fell from above
Through pride; (for pride and love may ill
    agree)
And now of sinne to all ensample bee:
How then can sinfull flesh it selfe assure,
Sith purest angels fell to be impure?

But that Eternall Fount of love and grace,
Still flowing forth his goodnesse unto all,
Now seeing left a waste and emptie place
In his wyde pallace, through those angels
    fall,   100
Cast to supply the same, and to enstall

A new unknowen colony therein,
Whose root from earths base groundworke
  shold begin.

Therefore of clay, base, vile, and next to
  nought,
Yet form'd by wondrous skill, and by his
  might,
According to an heavenly patterne wrought,
Which he had fashiond in his wise fore-
  sight,
He man did make, and breathd a living
  spright   110
Into his face most beautifull and fayre,
Endewd with wisedomes riches, heavenly,
  rare.

Such he him made, that he resemble might
Himselfe, as mortall thing immortall could;
Him to be lord of every living wight
He made by love out of his owne like mould,
In whom he might his mightie selfe be-
  hould:
For love doth love the thing belov'd to see,
That like it selfe in lovely shape may bee.

But man, forgetfull of his Makers grace, 120
No lesse then angels, whom he did ensew,
Fell from the hope of promist heavenly
  place,
Into the mouth of death, to sinners dew,
And all his off-spring into thraldome
  threw:
Where they for ever should in bonds re-
  maine
Of never dead, yet ever dying paine.

Till that great Lord of Love, which him at
  first
Made of meere love, and after liked well,
Seeing him lie like creature long accurst
In that deepe horror of despeyred hell, 130
Him, wretch, in doole would let no lenger
  dwell,
But cast out of that bondage to redeeme,
And pay the price, all were his debt extreeme.

Out of the bosome of eternall blisse,
In which he reigned with his glorious Syre,
He downe descended, like a most demisse
And abject thrall, in fleshes fraile attyre,
That he for him might pay sinnes deadly
  hyre,
And him restore unto that happie state 139
In which he stood before his haplesse fate.

In flesh at first the guilt committed was,
Therefore in flesh it must be satisfyde:
Nor spirit, nor angell, though they man
  surpas,
Could make amends to God for mans mis-
  guyde,
But onely man himselfe, who selfe did slyde.
So, taking flesh of sacred virgins wombe,
For mans deare sake he did a man become.

And that most blessed bodie, which was
  borne
Without all blemish or reprochfull blame,
He freely gave to be both rent and torne 150
Of cruell hands, who with despightfull
  shame
Revyling him, that them most vile became,
At length him nayled on a gallow tree,
And slew the just by most unjust decree.

O huge and most unspeakeable impression
Of loves deepe wound, that pierst the piteous
  hart
Of that deare Lord with so entyre affection,
And sharply launching every inner part,
Dolours of death into his soule did dart; 160
Doing him die, that never it deserved,
To free his foes, that from his heast had
  swerved!

What hart can feele least touch of so sore
  launch,
Or thought can think the depth of so deare
  wound,
Whose bleeding sourse their streames yet
  never staunch,
But stil do flow, and freshly still redound,
To heale the sores of sinfull soules unsound,
And clense the guilt of that infected cryme,
Which was enrooted in all fleshly slyme?

O blessed Well of Love! O Floure of Grace!
O glorious Morning Starre! O Lampe of
  Light!   170
Most lively image of thy Fathers face,
Eternall King of Glorie, Lord of Might,
Meeke Lambe of God, before all worlds
  behight,
How can we thee requite for all this good?
Or what can prize that thy most precious
  blood?

Yet nought thou ask'st in lieu of all this
  love,
But love of us, for guerdon of thy paine.

Ay me! what can us lesse then that behove?
Had he required life of us againe,
Had it beene wrong to aske his owne with
 gaine?   180
He gave us life, he it restored lost;
Then life were least, that us so litle cost.

But he our life hath left unto us free,
Free that was thrall, and blessed that was
 band;
Ne ought demaunds, but that we loving bee,
As he himselfe hath lov'd us afore hand,
And bound therto with an eternall band,
Him first to love, that us so dearely bought,
And next, our brethren, to his image
 wrought.

Him first to love, great right and reason is,
Who first to us our life and being gave; 191
And after, when we fared had amisse,
Us wretches from the second death did save;
And last, the food of life, which now we
 have,
Even himselfe in his deare sacrament,
To feede our hungry soules, unto us lent.

Then next, to love our brethren, that were
 made
Of that selfe mould and that selfe Makers
 hand
That we, and to the same againe shall fade,
Where they shall have like heritage of land,
How ever here on higher steps we stand;
Which also were with selfe same price re-
 deemed   202
That we, how ever of us light esteemed.

And were they not, yet since that loving
 Lord
Commaunded us to love them for his sake,
Even for his sake, and for his sacred word,
Which in his last bequest he to us spake,
We should them love, and with their needs
 partake;
Knowing that whatsoere to them we give,
We give to him, by whom we all doe live.

Such mercy he by his most holy reede 211
Unto us taught, and to approve it trew,
Ensampled it by his most righteous deede,
Shewing us mercie, miserable crew!
That we the like should to the wretches
 shew,
And love our brethren; thereby to approve
How much himselfe, that loved us, we love.

Then rouze thy selfe, O Earth, out of thy
 soyle,
In which thou wallowest like to filthy swyne,
And doest thy mynd in durty pleasures
 moyle,   220
Unmindfull of that dearest Lord of thyne;
Lift up to him thy heavie clouded eyne,
That thou his soveraine bountie mayst be-
 hold,
And read through love his mercies manifold.

Beginne from first, where he encradled was
In simple cratch, wrapt in a wad of hay,
Betweene the toylefull oxe and humble asse,
And in what rags, and in how base aray,
The glory of our heavenly riches lay,
When him the silly shepheards came to see,
Whom greatest princes sought on lowest
 knee.   231

From thence reade on the storie of his life,
His humble carriage, his unfaulty wayes,
His cancred foes, his fights, his toyle, his
 strife,
His paines, his povertie, his sharpe assayes
Through which he past his miserable dayes,
Offending none, and doing good to all,
Yet being malist both of great and small.

And looke at last, how of most wretched
 wights
He taken was, betrayd, and false accused;
How with most scornefull taunts, and fell
 despights,   241
He was revyld, disgrast, and foule abused;
How scourgd, how crownd, how buffeted,
 how brused;
And lastly, how twixt robbers crucifyde,
With bitter wounds through hands, through
 feet, and syde.

Then let thy flinty hart, that feeles no paine,
Empierced be with pittifull remorse,
And let thy bowels bleede in every vaine,
At sight of his most sacred heavenly corse,
So torne and mangled with malicious forse,
And let thy soule, whose sins his sorrows
 wrought,   251
Melt into teares, and grone in grieved
 thought.

With sence whereof whilest so thy softened
 spirit
Is inly toucht, and humbled with meeke
 zeale.

Through meditation of his endlesse merit,
Lift up thy mind to th' author of thy weale,
And to his soveraine mercie doe appeale;
Learne him to love, that loved thee so
deare,
And in thy brest his blessed image beare.

With all thy hart, with all thy soule and
mind,   260
Thou must him love, and his beheasts em-
brace;
All other loves, with which the world doth
blind
Weake fancies, and stirre up affections
base,
Thou must renounce, and utterly displace,
And give thy selfe unto him full and free,
That full and freely gave himselfe to
thee.

Then shalt thou feele thy spirit so possest,
And ravisht with devouring great desire
Of his deare selfe, that shall thy feeble
brest
Inflame with love, and set thee all on fire 270
With burning zeale, through every part
entire,
That in no earthly thing thou shalt de-
light,
But in his sweet and amiable sight.

Thenceforth all worlds desire will in thee
dye,
And all earthes glorie, on which men do
gaze,
Seeme durt and drosse in thy pure sighted
eye,
Compar'd to that celestiall beauties blaze,
Whose glorious beames all fleshly sense
doth daze
With admiration of their passing light,
Blinding the eyes and lumining the spright.

Then shall thy ravisht soule inspired bee 281
With heavenly thoughts, farre above hu-
mane skil,
And thy bright radiant eyes shall plainely
see
Th' idee of his pure glorie present still
Before thy face, that all thy spirits shall
fill
With sweete enragement of celestiall
love,
Kindled through sight of those faire things
above.

AN HYMNE OF HEAVENLY BEAUTIE

RAPT with the rage of mine own ravisht
thought,
Through contemplation of those goodly
sights,
And glorious images in heaven wrought,
Whose wondrous beauty, breathing sweet
delights,
Do kindle love in high conceipted sprights,
I faine to tell the things that I behold,
But feele my wits to faile, and tongue to
fold.

Vouchsafe then, O Thou most Almightie
Spright,
From whom all guifts of wit and knowledge
flow,
To shed into my breast some sparkling light
Of thine eternall truth, that I may show 11
Some litle beames to mortall eyes below
Of that immortall Beautie, there with
Thee,
Which in my weake distraughted mynd I
see.

That with the glorie of so goodly sight,
The hearts of men, which fondly here ad-
myre
Faire seeming shewes, and feed on vaine
delight,
Transported with celestiall desyre
Of those faire formes, may lift themselves
up hyer,
And learne to love with zealous humble
dewty   20
Th' Eternall Fountaine of that heavenly
Beauty.

Beginning then below, with th' easie vew
Of this base world, subject to fleshly eye,
From thence to mount aloft by order dew
To contemplation of th' immortall sky,
Of the soare faulcon so I learne to fly,
That flags awhile her fluttering wings be-
neath,
Till she her selfe for stronger flight can
breath.

Then looke, who list thy gazefull eyes to
feed
With sight of that is faire, looke on the
frame   30
Of this wyde universe, and therein reed

The endlesse kinds of creatures, which by
    name
Thou canst not count, much lesse their na-
    tures aime:
All which are made with wondrous wise
    respect,
And all with admirable beautie deckt.

First th' earth, on adamantine pillers
    founded,
Amid the sea, engirt with brasen bands;
Then th' aire, still flitting, but yet firmely
    bounded
On everie side with pyles of flaming brands,
Never consum'd, nor quencht with mortall
    hands;   40
And last, that mightie shining christall wall,
Wherewith he hath encompassed this All.

By view whereof, it plainly may appeare,
That still as every thing doth upward
    tend,
And further is from earth, so still more
    cleare
And faire it growes, till to his perfect end
Of purest Beautie it at last ascend:
Ayre more then water, fire much more then
    ayre,
And heaven then fire appeares more pure
    and fayre.

Looke thou no further, but affixe thine eye
On that bright shynie round still moving
    masse,   51
The house of blessed gods, which men call
    skye,
All sowd with glistring stars more thicke
    then grasse,
Whereof each other doth in brightnesse
    passe;
But those two most, which, ruling night
    and day,
As king and queene, the heavens empire
    sway.

And tell me then, what hast thou ever seene
That to their beautie may compared bee?
Or can the sight that is most sharpe and
    keene
Endure their captains flaming head to see?
How much lesse those, much higher in de-
    gree,   61
And so much fairer, and much more then
    these,
As these are fairer then the land and seas?

For farre above these heavens which here
    we see,
Be others farre exceeding these in light,
Not bounded, not corrupt, as these same bee,
But infinite in largenesse and in hight,
Unmoving, uncorrupt, and spotlesse bright,
That need no sunne t' illuminate their
    spheres,
But their owne native light farre passing
    theirs.   70

And as these heavens still by degrees arize,
Untill they come to their first movers bound,
That in his mightie compasse doth comprize
And carrie all the rest with him around,
So those likewise doe by degrees redound,
And rise more faire, till they at last arive
To the most faire, whereto they all do strive.

Faire is the heaven where happy soules have
    place,
In full enjoyment of felicitie,
Whence they doe still behold the glorious
    face   80
Of the Divine Eternall Majestie;
More faire is that where those Idees on hie
Enraunged be, which Plato so admyred,
And pure Intelligences from God inspyred.

Yet fairer is that heaven in which doe raine
The soveraine Powres and mightie Poten-
    tates,
Which in their high protections doe containe
All mortall princes and imperiall states;
And fayrer yet whereas the royall Seates
And heavenly Dominations are set,   90
From whom all earthly governance is fet.

Yet farre more faire be those bright Cher-
    ubins,
Which all with golden wings are overdight,
And those eternall burning Seraphins,
Which from their faces dart out fierie light;
Yet fairer then they both, and much more
    bright,
Be th' Angels and Archangels, which attend
On Gods owne person, without rest or end.

These thus in faire each other farre excelling,
As to the Highest they approch more
    neare,   100
Yet is that Highest farre beyond all telling,
Fairer then all the rest which there appeare,
Though all their beauties joynd together
    were:

How then can mortall tongue hope to ex-
    presse
The image of such endlesse perfectnesse ?

Cease then, my tongue, and lend unto my
    mynd
Leave to bethinke how great that Beautie is,
Whose utmost parts so beautifull I fynd;
How much more those essentiall parts of
    His,
His truth, his love, his wisedome, and his
    blis,   110
His grace, his doome, his mercy, and his
    might,
By which he lends us of himselfe a sight !

Those unto all he daily doth display,
And shew himselfe in th' image of his grace,
As in a looking glasse, through which he
    may
Be seene of all his creatures vile and base,
That are unable else to see his face,
His glorious face, which glistereth else so
    bright,
That th' angels selves can not endure his
    sight.

But we fraile wights, whose sight cannot
    sustaine   120
The suns bright beames, when he on us doth
    shyne,
But that their points rebutted backe againe
Are duld, how can we see with feeble eyne
The glory of that Majestie Divine,
In sight of whom both sun and moone are
    darke,
Compared to his least resplendent sparke ?

The meanes, therefore, which unto us is lent,
Him to behold, is on his workes to looke,
Which he hath made in beauty excellent,
And in the same, as in a brasen booke,   130
To reade enregistred in every nooke
His goodnesse, which his beautie doth de-
    clare,
For all thats good is beautifull and faire.

Thence gathering plumes of perfect specu-
    lation,
To impe the wings of thy high flying mynd,
Mount up aloft, through heavenly contem-
    plation,
From this darke world, whose damps the
    soule do blynd,
And like the native brood of eagles kynd,

On that bright Sunne of Glorie fixe thine
    eyes,
Clear'd from grosse mists of fraile infirmi-
    ties.   140

Humbled with feare and awfull reverence,
Before the footestoole of his Majestie,
Throw thy selfe downe with trembling in-
    nocence,
Ne dare looke up with corruptible eye
On the dred face of that great Deity,
For feare lest, if he chaunce to looke on
    thee,
Thou turne to nought, and quite confounded
    be.

But lowly fall before his mercie seate,
Close covered with the Lambes integrity
From the just wrath of his avengefull
    threate   150
That sits upon the righteous throne on hy:
His throne is built upon Eternity,
More firme and durable then steele or brasse
Or the hard diamond, which them both doth
    passe.

His scepter is the rod of Righteousnesse,
With which he bruseth all his foes to dust,
And the great Dragon strongly doth re-
    presse,
Under the rigour of his judgement just;
His seate is Truth, to which the faithfull
    trust;
From whence proceed her beames so pure
    and bright,   160
That all about him sheddeth glorious light.

Light farre exceeding that bright blazing
    sparke,
Which darted is from Titans flaming head,
That with his beames enlumineth the darke
And dampish air, wherby al things are red:
Whose nature yet so much is marvelled
Of mortall wits, that it doth much amaze
The greatest wisards which thereon do gaze.

But that immortall light which there doth.
    shine
Is many thousand times more bright, more
    cleare,   170
More excellent, more glorious, more divine;
Through which to God all mortall actions
    here,
And even the thoughts of men, do plaine
    appeare:

For from th' Eternall Truth it doth proceed,
Through heavenly vertue, which her beames
   doe breed.

With the great glorie of that wondrous light
His throne is all encompassed around,
And hid in his owne brightnesse from the
   sight
Of all that looke thereon with eyes unsound:
And underneath his feet are to be found 180
Thunder, and lightning, and tempestuous
   fyre,
The instruments of his avenging yre.

There in his bosome Sapience doth sit,
The soveraine dearling of the Deity,
Clad like a queene in royall robes, most fit
For so great powre and peerelesse majesty,
And all with gemmes and jewels gorgeously
Adornd, that brighter then the starres ap-
   peare,
And make her native brightnes seem more
   cleare.

And on her head a crowne of purest gold
Is set, in signe of highest soveraignty; 191
And in her hand a scepter she doth hold,
With which she rules the house of God on
   hy,
And menageth the ever-moving sky,
And in the same these lower creatures all,
Subjected to her powre imperiall.

Both heaven and earth obey unto her will,
And all the creatures which they both con-
   taine:
For of her fulnesse, which the world doth
   fill,
They all partake, and do in state remaine,
As their great Maker did at first ordaine, 201
Through observation of her high beheast,
By which they first were made, and still
   increast.

The fairenesse of her face no tongue can
   tell;
For she the daughters of all wemens race,
And angels eke, in beautie doth excell,
Sparkled on her from Gods owne glorious
   face,
And more increast by her owne goodly
   grace,
That it doth farre exceed all humane
   thought,
Ne can on earth compared be to ought. 210

Ne could that painter (had he lived yet)
Which pictured Venus with so curious quill
That all posteritie admyred it,
Have purtrayd this, for all his maistring
   skill;
Ne she her selfe, had she remained still,
And were as faire as fabling wits do fayne,
Could once come neare this Beauty sover-
   ayne.

But had those wits, the wonders of their
   dayes,
Or that sweete Teian poet which did spend
His plenteous vaine in setting forth her
   prayse,
Seene but a glims of this which I pretend, 220
How wondrously would he her face com-
   mend,
Above that idole of his fayning thought,
That all the world shold with his rimes be
   fraught !

How then dare I, the novice of his art,
Presume to picture so divine a wight,
Or hope t' expresse her least perfections
   part,
Whose beautie filles the heavens with her
   light,
And darkes the earth with shadow of her
   sight ?
Ah ! gentle Muse, thou art too weake and
   faint, 230
The pourtraict of so heavenly hew to paint.

Let angels, which her goodly face behold
And see at will, her soveraigne praises
   sing,
And those most sacred mysteries unfold
Of that faire love of mightie Heavens King.
Enough is me t' admyre so heavenly thing,
And being thus with her huge love possest,
In th' only wonder of her selfe to rest.

But who so may, thrise happie man him hold
Of all on earth, whom God so much doth
   grace, 240
And lets his owne Beloved to behold:
For in the view of her celestiall face
All joy, all blisse, all happinesse have place,
Ne ought on earth can want unto the wight
Who of her selfe can win the wishfull sight.

For she out of her secret threasury
Plentie of riches forth on him will powre,
Even heavenly riches, which there hidden ly

Within the closet of her chastest bowre, 249
Th' eternall portion of her precious dowre,
Which Mighty God hath given to her free,
And to all those which thereof worthy
    bee.

None thereof worthy be, but those whom
    shee
Vouchsafeth to her presence to receave,
And letteth them her lovely face to see,
Wherof such wondrous pleasures they con-
    ceave,
And sweete contentment, that it doth be-
    reave
Their soule of sense, through infinite
    delight,
And them transport from flesh into the
    spright.

In which they see such admirable things,
As carries them into an extasy, 261
And heare such heavenly notes, and carol-
    ings
Of Gods high praise, that filles the brasen
    sky,
And feele such joy and pleasure inwardly,
That maketh them all worldly cares for-
    get,
And onely thinke on that before them
    set.

Ne from thenceforth doth any fleshly sense,
Or idle thought of earthly things remaine;
But all that earst seemd sweet seemes now
    offense,
And all that pleased earst now seemes to
    paine: 270
Their joy, their comfort, their desire, their
    gaine,
Is fixed all on that which now they see;
All other sights but fayned shadowes bee.

And that faire lampe, which useth to
    enflame
The hearts of men with selfe consuming
    fyre,

Thenceforth seemes fowle, and full of sin-
    full blame;
And all that pompe, to which proud minds
    aspyre
By name of honor, and so much desyre,
Seemes to them basenesse, and all riches
    drosse, 279
And all mirth sadnesse, and all lucre losse.

So full their eyes are of that glorious sight,
And senses fraught with such satietie,
That in nought else on earth they can
    delight,
But in th' aspect of that felicitie,
Which they have written in their inward
    ey;
On which they feed, and in their fastened
    mynd
All happie joy and full contentment fynd.

Ah! then, my hungry soule, which long hast
    fed
On idle fancies of thy foolish thought,
And, with false Beauties flattring bait
    misled, 290
Hast after vaine deceiptfull shadowes
    sought,
Which all are fled, and now have left thee
    nought
But late repentance, through thy follies
    prief;
Ah! ceasse to gaze on matter of thy grief.

And looke at last up to that Soveraine
    Light,
From whose pure beams al perfect Beauty
    springs,
That kindleth love in every godly spright,
Even the love of God, which loathing
    brings
Of this vile world and these gay seeming
    things;
With whose sweete pleasures being so
    possest, 300
Thy straying thoughts henceforth for ever
    rest.

PROTHALAMION

OR

A SPOUSALL VERSE MADE BY

EDM. SPENSER

IN HONOUR OF THE DOUBLE MARIAGE OF THE TWO HONORABLE & VERTUOUS
LADIES, THE LADIE ELIZABETH AND THE LADIE KATHERINE SOMERSET,
DAUGHTERS TO THE RIGHT HONOURABLE THE EARLE OF WORCES-
TER AND ESPOUSED TO THE TWO WORTHIE GENTLEMEN
MASTER HENRY GILFORD, AND MASTER WILLIAM
PETER, ESQUYERS

AT LONDON

PRINTED FOR WILLIAM PONSONBY

1596

[The event celebrated in the *Prothalamion* must have occurred some time after the return of Essex from Cadiz in mid-August, 1596. It would seem to have been a ceremonial visit of the two prospective brides to Essex House, not long before their wedding. They evidently proceeded in barges by the river, probably up-stream with the tide from the court at Green-wich, accompanied in the latter part of their route by swarms of those smaller craft which then thronged the main highway of London. In this poem Spenser has refined upon the stanza-form which he invented for the *Epithalamion*. He has brought it to virtual uniformity of structure by discarding most of those small diversities of detail between strophe and strophe which, in the earlier poem, mark his first inven-tion. To the late Professor Palgrave this re-vised form seemed the more delightfully and delicately cadenced. There will probably be those, however, for whom the frank irregu-larities of the first ode, more felt than dis-tinctly observed, will have the greater charm, will seem not unlike those irregularities that enrich, without disturbing, the orderliness of certain great mediæval façades.

Unlike the stanza of the *Faery Queen*, these strophes have not found imitators, perhaps because few later poets have united fecundity and elaborateness of art so perfectly as Spen-ser. One may detect their influence upon *Lyc-idas*, but hardly more at large. Other poets of the time contented themselves with shorter or easier forms; and then came the bastard Pindaric ode, which for over a hundred years remained the type specially appropriated to larger lyric themes. In the later 'revivals' they were passed by.]

CALME was the day, and through the trem-
    bling ayre
Sweete breathing Zephyrus did softly
    play,
A gentle spirit, that lightly did delay
Hot Titans beames, which then did glyster
    fayre:
When I, whom sullein care,
Through discontent of my long fruitlesse
    stay
In princes court, and expectation vayne
Of idle hopes, which still doe fly away,
Like empty shaddowes, did afflict my
    brayne,
Walkt forth to ease my payne   10
Along the shoare of silver streaming
    Themmes;
Whose rutty bancke, the which his river
    hemmes,
Was paynted all with variable flowers,
And all the meades adornd with daintie
    gemmes,
Fit to decke maydens bowres,
And crowne their paramours,

Against the brydale day, which is not
    long:
    Sweete Themmes, runne softly, till I
    end my song.

There, in a meadow, by the rivers side,
A flocke of nymphes I chaunced to espy, 20
All lovely daughters of the flood thereby,
With goodly greenish locks all loose untyde,
As each had bene a bryde:
And each one had a little wicker basket,
Made of fine twigs entrayled curiously,
In which they gathered flowers to fill their
    flasket;
And with fine fingers cropt full feateously
The tender stalkes on hye.
Of every sort, which in that meadow grew,
They gathered some; the violet pallid blew,
The little dazie, that at evening closes, 31
The virgin lillie, and the primrose trew,
With store of vermeil roses,
To decke their bridegromes posies
Against the brydale day, which was not
    long:
    Sweete Themmes, runne softly, till I
    end my song.

With that I saw two swannes of goodly
    hewe
Come softly swimming downe along the
    lee;
Two fairer birds I yet did never see:
The snow which doth the top of Pindus
    strew   40
Did never whiter shew,
Nor Jove himselfe, when he a swan would
    be
For love of Leda, whiter did appear:
Yet Leda was, they say, as white as he,
Yet not so white as these, nor nothing neare:
So purely white they were,
That even the gentle streame, the which
    them bare,
Seem'd foule to them, and bad his billowes
    spare
To wet their silken feathers, least they
    might
Soyle their fayre plumes with water not so
    fayre,   50
And marre their beauties bright,
That shone as heavens light,
Against their brydale day, which was not
    long:
    Sweete Themmes, runne softly, till I end
    my song.

Eftsoones the nymphes, which now had
    flowers their fill,
Ran all in haste to see that silver brood,
As they came floating on the christal flood;
Whom when they sawe, they stood amazed
    still,
Their wondring eyes to fill.
Them seem'd they never saw a sight so
    fayre,   60
Of fowles so lovely, that they sure did
    deeme
Them heavenly borne, or to be that same
    payre
Which through the skie draw Venus silver
    teeme;
For sure they did not seeme
To be begot of any earthly seede,
But rather angels or of angels breede:
Yet were they bred of Somers-heat, they
    say,
In sweetest season, when each flower and
    weede
The earth did fresh aray;
So fresh they seem'd as day,   70
Even as their brydale day, which was not
    long:
    Sweete Themmes, runne softly, till I end
    my song.

Then forth they all out of their baskets
    drew
Great store of flowers, the honour of the
    field,
That to the sense did fragrant odours yeild,
All which upon those goodly birds they
    threw,
And all the waves did strew,
That like old Peneus waters they did
    seeme,
When downe along by pleasant Tempes
    shore,
Scattred with flowres, through Thessaly
    they streeme,   80
That they appeare, through lillies plenteous
    store,
Like a brydes chamber flore.
Two of those nymphes, meane while, two
    garlands bound
Of freshest flowres which in that mead
    they found,
The which presenting all in trim array,
Their snowie foreheads therewithall they
    crownd,
Whil'st one did sing this lay,
Prepar'd against that day,

Against their brydale day, which was not
long:
   Sweete Themmes, runne softly, till I end
   my song.   90

'Ye gentle birdes, the worlds faire orna-
ment,
And heavens glorie, whom this happie
hower
Doth leade unto your lovers blissfull bower,
Joy may you have and gentle hearts con-
tent
Of your loves couplement:
And let faire Venus, that is Queene of
Love,
With her heart-quelling sonne upon you
smile,
Whose smile, they say, hath vertue to
remove
All loves dislike, and friendships faultie
guile
For ever to assoile.   100
Let endlesse peace your steadfast hearts
accord,
And blessed plentie wait upon your bord;
And let your bed with pleasures chast
abound,
That fruitfull issue may to you afford,
Which may your foes confound,
And make your joyes redound,
Upon your brydale day, which is not long:
   Sweete Themmes, run softlie, till I end
   my song.'

So ended she; and all the rest around
To her redoubled that her undersong,   110
Which said, their bridale daye should not
be long.
And gentle Eccho from the neighbour
ground
Their accents did resound.
So forth those joyous birdes did passe along,
Adowne the lee, that to them murmurde
low,
As he would speake, but that he lackt a tong,
Yeat did by signes his glad affection show,
Making his streame run slow.
And all the foule which in his flood did
dwell
Gan flock about these twaine, that did ex-
cell   120
The rest so far as Cynthia doth shend
The lesser starres. So they, enranged well,
Did on those two attend,
And their best service lend,

Against their wedding day, which was not
long:
   Sweete Themmes, run softly, till I end
   my song.

At length they all to mery London came,
To mery London, my most kyndly nurse,
That to me gave this lifes first native sourse,
Though from another place I take my name,
An house of auncient fame.   131
There when they came, whereas those
bricky towres,
The which on Themmes brode aged backe
doe ryde,
Where now the studious lawyers have their
bowers,
There whylome wont the Templer Knights
to byde,
Till they decayd through pride:
Next whereunto there standes a stately
place,
Where oft I gayned giftes and goodly grace
Of that great lord which therein wont to
dwell,
Whose want too well now feeles my
freendles case: 140
But ah! here fits not well
Olde woes, but joyes to tell,
Against the bridale daye, which is not long:
   Sweete Themmes, runne softly, till I end
   my song.

Yet therein now doth lodge a noble peer,
Great Englands glory and the worlds wide
wonder,
Whose dreadfull name late through all
Spaine did thunder,
And Hercules two pillors standing neere
Did make to quake and feare.
Faire branch of honor, flower of cheval-
rie,   150
That fillest England with thy triumphes
fame,
Joy have thou of thy noble victorie,
And endlesse happinesse of thine owne
name
That promiseth the same:
That through thy prowesse and victorious
armes
Thy country may be freed from forraine
harmes;
And great Elisaes glorious name may ring
Through al the world, fil'd with thy wide
alarmes,
Which some brave Muse may sing

To ages following,   160
Upon the brydale day, which is not long:
  Sweete Themmes, runne softly, till I end
    my song.

From those high towers this noble lord
    issuing,
Like radiant Hesper when his golden hayre
In th' ocean billowes he hath bathed fayre,
Descended to the rivers open vewing,
With a great traine ensuing.
Above the rest were goodly to bee seene
Two gentle knights of lovely face and
    feature,
Beseeming well the bower of anie queene, 170

With gifts of wit and ornaments of nature,
Fit for so goodly stature:
That like the twins of Jove they seem'd in
    sight,
Which decke the bauldricke of the heavens
    bright.
They two, forth pacing to the rivers side,
Received those two faire brides, their
    loves delight,
Which, at th' appointed tyde,
Each one did make his bryde,
Against their brydale day, which is not
    long:
  Sweete Themmes, runne softly, till I end
    my song.   180

FINIS

COMMENDATORY SONNETS

[The first of these sonnets was probably no more than a friendly address, not meant for publication. The others were contributed, by way of compliment, to various books of the time.
I. Appended by Harvey to 'Foure Letters, and certaine Sonnets, especially touching Robert Greene, and other parties by him abused, etc.' 1592.
II. The first of four sonnets prefixed to 'Nennio, or A Treatise of Nobility, etc. Written in Italian by that famous Doctor and worthy Knight, Sir John Baptista Nenna of

Bari. Done into English by William Jones, Gent.' 1595.
III. The first of three sonnets prefixed to the 'Historie of George Castriot, surnamed Scanderbeg, King of Albanie: Containing his famous actes, etc. Newly translated out of French into English by Z. I. Gentleman.' 1596.
IV. The first of three sonnets and a *huitain* prefixed to 'The Commonwealth and Government of Venice. Written by the Cardinall Gaspar Contareno, and translated out of Italian into English by Lewes Lewkenor, Esquire.' 1599.]

I

To the right worshipfull, my singular good frend,
Master Gabriell Harvey, Doctor of the Lawes.

HARVEY, the happy above happiest men
I read: that, sitting like a looker-on
Of this worldes stage, doest note with
    critique pen
The sharpe dislikes of each condition:
And, as one carelesse of suspition,
Ne fawnest for the favour of the great;
Ne fearest foolish reprehension
Of faulty men, which daunger to thee
    threat;
But freely doest of what thee list en-
    treat,
Like a great lord of peerelesse liberty;
Lifting the good up to high Honours
    seat,
And the evill damning evermore to dy.

For life and death is in thy doomeful
    writing:
So thy renowme lives ever by endighting.

Dublin, this xviij. of July, 1586.

Your devoted friend, during life,

EDMUND SPENCER.

II

WHO so wil seeke by right deserts t' attaine
Unto the type of true nobility,
And not by painted shewes, and titles vaine
Derived farre from famous auncestrie,
Behold them both in their right visnomy
Here truly pourtray'd as they ought to be,
And striving both for termes of dignitie,
To be advanced highest in degree.
And when thou doost with equall insight
    see

The ods twixt both, of both then deem
    aright,
And chuse the better of them both to thee:
But thanks to him that it deserves behight;
    To Nenna first, that first this worke
        created,
    And next to Jones, that truely it trans-
        lated.

ED. SPENSER.

III

*Upon the Historie of George Castriot, alias
Scanderbeg, King of the Epirots, translated
into English.*

WHEREFORE doth vaine Antiquitie so vaunt
Her ancient monuments of mightie peeres,
And old heröes, which their world did
    daunt
With their great deedes, and fild their
    childrens eares ?
Who, rapt with wonder of their famous
    praise,
Admire their statues, their colossoes great,
Their rich triumphall arcks which they did
    raise,
Their huge pyramids, which do heaven
    threat.
Lo ! one, whom later age hath brought to
    light,
Matchable to the greatest of those great:

Great both by name, and great in power
    and might,
And meriting a meere triumphant seate.
    The scourge of Turkes, and plague of
        infidels,
    Thy acts, O Scanderbeg, this volume tels.

ED. SPENSER.

IV

THE antique Babel, empresse of the East,
Upreard her buildinges to the threatned
    skie:
And second Babell, tyrant of the West,
Her ayry towers upraised much more high.
But, with the weight of their own surque-
    dry,
They both are fallen, that all the earth did
    feare,
And buried now in their own ashes ly;
Yet shewing by their heapes how great
    they were.
But in their place doth now a third appeare,
Fayre Venice, flower of the last worlds
    delight;
And next to them in beauty draweth neare,
But farre exceedes in policie of right.
    Yet not so fayre her buildinges to behold
    As Lewkenors stile, that hath her beau-
        tie told.

EDM. SPENCER.

I

VERSES FROM THE *THEATRE* OF 1569

[IT is only within the last decade that the history of Van der Noot's *Theatre* has been known in full. Since the accounts of it in the various standard biographies of Spenser, therefore, are more or less misleading, it may be given here in some detail. The facts are set forth at length in a Flemish monograph, published at Antwerp in 1899, 'Leven en Werken van Jonker Jan Van der Noot, door Aug. Vermeylen.' The author of this excellent study is not, however, to be held responsible for all the conclusions that are set down here.

In 1569 there was published in London a small book with a big title, which ran: 'A Theatre, wherein be represented as wel the miseries and calamities that follow the voluptuous worldlings as also the greate joyes and plesures which the faithfull do enjoy. An argument both profitable and delectable to all that sincerely love the Word of God. Devised by S. John vander Noodt.' The dedication bore the date of May 25. Its author was a Flemish refugee,—a wealthy patrician of Antwerp, who, becoming disastrously prominent among the Calvinists of his native city, had in 1567 fled from the Spanish authorities into England. There, in 1568, he had composed a bitter pamphlet against Rome, which he had put forth, first in Flemish, and then, toward the close of that year, in what was to all the more cultivated of his compatriots a second mother tongue, French. Some seven months later, desirous probably of securing the widest possible audience, he arranged for the translation of his book from French into English, a tongue of which he had no literary control. The title given above is that of this third edition.

The kernel of the book was poetry: first, a translation by Clément Marot of one of Petrarch's *canzoni* ('Standomi un giorno solo alla finestra') under the title of 'Des Visions de Pétrarque'; second, the *Songe* of Joachim Du Bellay, with the omission of sonnets vi, viii, xiii, and xiv; third, four sonnets of his own composition (for he was a poet of distinguished abilities) the matter of which was drawn from the Apocalypse. For the first edition of his book he had translated the French of Marot and Du Bellay into Flemish; for the second, he had, of course, let the French stand. Of his own sonnets he had made two versions, one Flemish and one French. Then there was a long prose commentary upon these various 'visions,' likewise of his own composition in the two tongues.

In the 1569 volume this commentary is given as 'translated out of French into Englishe by Theodore Roest.' In that part of it which refers to the visions of Petrarch we read, 'I [by implication, Roest] have out of the Brabants speache turned them into the Englishe tongue;' in that part which refers to the visions of Du Bellay, 'I have translated them out of Dutch into English:' concerning the translation of the Apocalypse sonnets, we are left to make our own inferences. Comparison of texts, however, shows clearly that the translator of all this poetry, rendered it, as the prose was rendered, direct from the French: what is said about 'the Brabants speache' and 'Dutch' is pure mystification. Furthermore, if these translations from Du Bellay and Petrarch be compared with 'The Visions of Bellay' (p. 125) and 'The Visions of Petrarch, formerly translated' (p. 128), which were published under Spenser's name in 1591, it becomes clear that the latter are not independent renderings of the same French originals, but a mere literary recast of the English verses of 1569. The irregular stanzas of the Petrarch series are reduced to formal sonnets, and so are the blank verse poems of the Bellay series. Such changes as have been made are purely with a view to this transformation. Since it is improbable that even in youth Spenser should thus carefully have made over the work of another man, a mere translator, and that, having done so, his recast should have survived to be published years later in his name, the inference seems to be clear that the verses in the *Theatre* of 1569 are his.

By way of counter-argument, it has been pointed out that, whereas the translation of 1569 is sound and accurate, the acknowledged work of Spenser in this field ('The Ruins of Rome' and the four sonnets that were omitted in the *Theatre*, but rendered in the later 'Visions of Bellay') is very loose, and reveals at times exceedingly imperfect acquaintance with French, acquaintance so imperfect that he cannot be thought capable of the excellent versions in the *Theatre*. To argue thus, however, is to forget, among other things, the conditions under which, in 1569, he may be presumed to have done his work. For the prose of the *Theatre*, Van der Noot had found a capable translator in Roest; but, he being apparently no versifier, it was necessary to find some one else for the poetry. If this assistant knew French well, so much the better; if he did not, he could be helped by his

chief; in any case, his work would be super-
vised, to secure accuracy. What was chiefly
necessary was that he should be able to turn
good English verse. For this 'job' whoever
had charge of the book employed Spenser, then
no more than a bright schoolboy, about to go

up to the university. He was in no way a principal in the main undertaking; when the volume came out, therefore, it nowhere gave his
name. He had done his work and received his
pay: there was no need to acknowledge his
services.]

EPIGRAMS

I

BEING one day at my window all alone,
So many strange things hapned me to see,
As much it grieveth me to thinke thereon.
At my right hande, a hinde appearde to me,
So faire as mought the greatest god delite:
Two egre dogs dyd hir pursue in chace,
Of whiche the one was black, the other white.
With deadly force, so in their cruell race
They pinchte the haunches of this gentle beast,
That at the last, and in shorte time, I spied,
Under a rocke, where she (alas!) opprest,
Fell to the grounde, and there untimely dide.
Cruell death vanquishing so noble beautie
Oft makes me waile so harde a destinie.

II

AFTER at sea a tall ship dyd appere,
Made all of heben and white ivorie;
The sailes of golde, of silke the tackle were.
Milde was the winde, calme seemed the sea to
be:
The skie eche where did shew full bright and
faire.
With riche treasures this gay ship fraighted
was.
But sodaine storme did so turmoyle the aire,
And tombled up the sea, that she, alas!
Strake on a rocke that under water lay.
O great misfortune! O great griefe! I say,
Thus in one moment to see lost and drownde
So great riches, as lyke can not be founde.

III

THEN heavenly branches did I see arise,
Out of a fresh and lusty laurell tree
Amidde the yong grene wood. Of Paradise
Some noble plant I thought my selfe to see,
Suche store of birdes therein yshrouded were,
Chaunting in shade their sundry melodie.
My sprites were ravisht with these pleasures
there.
While on this laurell fixed was mine eye,
The skie gan every where to overcast,
And darkned was the welkin all aboute;
When sodaine flash of heavens fire outbrast,
And rent this royall tree quite by the roote.
Which makes me much and ever to complaine,
For no such shadow shal be had againe.

IV

WITHIN this wood, out of the rocke did rise
A spring of water mildely romblyng downe,
Whereto approched not in any wise
The homely shepherde, nor the ruder clowne,
But many Muses, and the Nymphes withall,
That sweetely in accorde did tune their voice

Unto the gentle sounding of the waters fall:
The sight wherof dyd make my heart re-
joyce.
But while I toke herein my chiefe delight,
I sawe (alas!) the gaping earth devoure
The spring, the place, and all cleane out of sight.
Whiche yet agreves my heart even to this houre.

V

I SAW a phœnix in the wood alone,
With purple wings and crest of golden hew;
Straunge birde he was; wherby I thought anone,
That of some heavenly wight I had the vew:
Untill he came unto the broken tree
And to the spring that late devoured was.
What say I more? Eche thing at length we
see
Doth passe away: the phœnix there, alas!
Spying the tree destroyde, the water dride,
Himselfe smote with his beake, as in dis-
daine,
And so forthwith in great despite he dide.
For pitie and love my heart yet burnes in paine.

VI

AT last, so faire a ladie did I spie,
That in thinking on hir I burne and quake.
On herbes and floures she walked pensively,
Milde, but yet love she proudely did forsake.
White seemed hir robes, yet woven so they
were,
As snowe and golde together had bene wrought.
Above the waste a darke cloude shrouded
hir,
A stinging serpent by the heele hir caught;
Wherewith she languisht as the gathered floure;
And well assurde she mounted up to joy.
Alas! in earth so nothing doth endure,
But bitter griefe, that dothe our hearts anoy.

VII

MY song, thus now in thy conclusions,
Say boldly that these same six visions
Do yelde unto thy lorde a sweete request,
Ere it be long within the earth to rest.

SONETS

I

IT was the time when rest, the gift of gods,
Sweetely sliding into the eyes of men,
Doth drowne in the forgetfulnesse of slepe
The carefull travailes of the painefull day:
Then did a ghost appeare before mine eyes
On that great rivers banke that runnes by
Rome,
And calling me then by my propre name,
He bade me upwarde unto heaven looke.
He cride to me, and 'Loe! (quod he) beholde

What under this great temple is containde,
Loe! all is nought but flying vanitie.'
So I, knowing the worldes unstedfastnesse,
Sith onely God surmountes the force of tyme,
In God alone do stay my confidence.

II

On hill, a frame an hundred cubites hie
I sawe, an hundred pillers eke about,
All of fine diamant decking the front,
And fashiond were they all in Dorike wise.
Of bricke, ne yet of marble was the wall,
But shining christall, which from top to base
Out of deepe vaute threw forth a thousand rayes
Upon an hundred steps of purest golde.
Golde was the parget : and the sielyng eke
Did shine all scaly with fine golden plates.
The floor was jaspis, and of emeraude.
O worldes vainenesse! A sodein earthquake,
loe!
Shaking the hill even from the bottome deepe,
Threwe downe this building to the lowest stone.

III

Then did appeare to me a sharped spire
Of diamant, ten feete eche way in square,
Justly proportionde up unto his height,
So hie as mought an archer reache with sight.
Upon the top therof was set a pot
Made of the mettall that we honour most.
And in this golden vessell couched were
The ashes of a mightie emperour.
Upon foure corners of the base there lay,
To beare the frame, foure great lions of golde :
A worthie tombe for such a worthie corps.
Alas! nought in this worlde but griefe endures.
A sodaine tempest from the heaven, I saw,
With flashe stroke downe this noble monument.

IV

I saw raisde up on pillers of ivorie,
Whereof the bases were of richest golde,
The chapters alabaster, christall frises,
The double front of a triumphall arke.
On eche side portraide was a victorie,
With golden wings in habite of a nymph,
And set on hie upon triumphing chaire
The auncient glorie of the Romane lordes.
The worke did shewe it selfe not wrought by
man,
But rather made by his owne skilfull hande
That forgeth thunder dartes for Jove his sire.
Let me no more see faire thing under heaven,
Sith I have seene so faire a thing as this,
With sodaine falling broken all to dust.

V

Then I behelde the faire Dodonian tree,
Upon seven hilles throw forth his gladsome
shade,
And conquerers bedecked with his leaves
Along the bankes of the Italian streame.
There many auncient trophees were erect,
Many a spoile, and many goodly signes,
To shewe the greatnesse of the stately race,
That erst descended from the Trojan bloud.
Ravisht I was to see so rare a thing,

When barbarous villaines, in disorded heape,
Outraged the honour of these noble bowes.
I hearde the tronke to grone under the wedge.
And since I saw the roote in hie disdaine
Sende forth againe a twinne of forked trees.

VI

I saw the birde that dares beholde the sunne,
With feeble flight venture to mount to heaven:
By more and more she gan to trust hir wings;
Still folowing th' example of hir damme.
I saw hir rise, and with a larger flight
Surmount the toppes even of the hiest hilles,
And pierce the cloudes, and with hir wings to
reache
The place where is the temple of the gods.
There was she lost, and sodenly I saw
Where tombling through the aire in lompe of
fire,
All flaming downe she fell upon the plaine.
I saw hir bodie turned all to dust,
And saw the foule that shunnes the cherefull
light
Out of hir ashes as a worme arise.

VII

Then all astonned with this nightly ghost,
I saw an hideous body big and strong :
Long was his beard, and side did hang his hair,
A grisly forehed and Saturnelike face.
Leaning against the belly of a pot,
He shed a water, whose outgushing streame
Ran flowing all along the creekie shoare
Where once the Troyan duke with Turnus
fought.
And at his feete a bitch wolfe did give sucke
To two yong babes. In his right hand he bare
The tree of peace, in left the conquering palme,
His head was garnisht with the laurel bow.
Then sodenly the palme and olive fell,
And faire greene laurel witherd up and dide.

VIII

Hard by a rivers side, a wailing nimphe,
Folding hir armes with thousand sighs to
heaven,
Did tune hir plaint to falling rivers sound,
Renting hir faire visage and golden haire.
' Where is (quod she) this whilome honored
face?
Where is thy glory and the auncient praise,
Where all worldes hap was reposed,
When erst of gods and man I worshipt was?
Alas! suffisde it not that civile bate
Made me the spoile and bootie of the world,
But this new Hydra, mete to be assailde
Even by an hundred such as Hercules,
With seven springing heds of monstrous crimes,
So many Neroes and Caligulaes
Must still bring forth to rule this croked shore?'

IX

Upon a hill I saw a kindled flame,
Mounting like waves with triple point to heaven,
Which of incense of precious ceder tree
With balmelike odor did perfume the aire.
A bird all white, well fetherd on hir winges,

Hereout did flie up to the throne of gods,
And singing with most plesant melodie
She climbed up to heaven in the smoke.
Of this faire fire the faire dispersed rayes
Threw forth abrode a thousand shining leames;
When sodain dropping of a golden shoure
Gan quench the glystering flame. O grevous
  chaunge!
That which erstwhile so pleasaunt scent did
  yelde
Of sulphure now did breathe corrupted smel.

X

I saw a fresh spring rise out of a rocke,
Clere as christall against the sunny beames,
The bottome yellow like the shining land,
That golden Pactol drives upon the plaine.
It seemed that arte and nature strived to joyne
There in one place all pleasures of the eye.
There was to heare a noise alluring slepe
Of many accordes more swete than mermaids
  song.
The seates and benches shone as ivorie;
An hundred nymphes sate side by side about;
When from nie hilles a naked rout of faunes
With hideous cry assembled on the place,
Which with their feete uncleane the water
  fouled,
Threw down the seats, and drove the nimphs to
  flight.

XI

At length, even at the time when Morpheus
Most truely doth appeare unto our eyes,
Wearie to see th' inconstance of the heavens,
I saw the great Typhæus sister come.
Hir head full bravely with a morian armed,
In majestie she seemde to matche the gods.
And on the shore, harde by a violent streame,
She raisde a trophee over all the worlde.
An hundred vanquisht kings gronde at hir feete,
Their armes in shamefull wise bounde at their
  backes.
While I was with so dreadfull sight afrayde,
I saw the heavens warre against hir tho;
And seing hir striken fall with clap of thunder,
With so great noyse I start in sodaine wonder.

I

I saw an ugly beast come from the sea,
That seven heads, ten crounes, ten hornes did
  beare,
Having theron the vile blaspheming name.
The cruell leopard she resembled much:
Feete of a beare, a lions throte she had.
The mightie Dragon gave to hir his power.
One of hir heads yet there I did espie,
Still freshly bleeding of a grievous wounde.
One cride aloude. 'What one is like (quod he)
This honoured Dragon, or may him withstande?'
And then came from the sea a savage beast,
With Dragons speche, and shewde his force by
  fire,
With wondrous signes to make all wights adore
The beast, in setting of hir image up.

II

I saw a woman sitting on a beast
Before mine eyes, of orenge colour hew:
Horrour and dreadfull name of blasphemie
Filde hir with pride. And seven heads I saw;
Ten hornes also the stately beast did beare.
She seemde with glorie of the scarlet faire,
And with fine perle and golde puft up in heart.
The wine of hooredome in a cup she bare.
The name of mysterie writ in hir face;
The bloud of martyrs dere were hir delite.
Most fierce and fell this woman seemde to me.
An angell then descending downe from Heaven
With thondring voice cride out aloude, and
  sayd,
'Now for a truth great Babylon is fallen.'

III

Then might I see upon a white horse set
The faithfull man with flaming countenaunce:
His head did shine with crounes set therupon;
The Worde of God made him a noble name.
His precious robe I saw embrued with bloud.
Then saw I from the heaven on horses white,
A puissant armie come the selfe same way.
Then cried a shining angell, as me thought,
That birdes from aire descending downe on
  earth
Should warre upon the kings, and eate their
  flesh.
Then did I see the beast and kings also
Joinyng their force to slea the faithfull man.
But this fierce hatefull beast and all hir traine
Is pitilesse throwne downe in pit of fire.

IV

I saw new Earth, new Heaven, sayde Saint
  John.
And loe! the sea (quod he) is now no more.
The holy citie of the Lorde from hye
Descendeth, garnisht as a loved spouse.
A voice then sayde, 'Beholde the bright abode
Of God and men. For he shall be their God,
And all their teares he shall wipe cleane away.'
Hir brightnesse greater was than can be founde
Square was this citie, and twelve gates it had.
Eche gate was of an orient perfect pearle,
The houses golde, the pavement precious stone.
A lively streame, more cleere than christall is,
Ranne through the mid, sprong from triumphant seat.
There growes lifes fruite unto the Churches
  good.

II

THE ORIGINAL CONCLUSION TO BOOK III
OF *THE FAERY QUEEN*

[The following stanzas are the original conclusion to Book III of the *Faery Queen*, as published in 1590. When Spenser came to push on with his tale, he decided that, for the sake of continuity, the reunion of Scudamour and Amoret had better be postponed. He therefore substituted the three stanzas that now conclude the book, and laid his first ending by, with the purpose, probably, of using it when the lovers should at last be brought together. This event falls at the close of canto ix of Book IV. There there is both room and need for some account of the meeting. It is more than likely that the poet meant to fit his stanzas to this new context, but, with typical carelessness, in the end left the gap unfilled.]

XLIII

At last she came unto the place, where late
She left Sir Scudamour in great distresse,
Twixt dolour and despight halfe desperate
Of his loves succour, of his owne redresse,
And of the hardie Britomarts successe:
There on the cold earth him now thrown she found,
In wilfull anguish, and dead heavinesse,
And to him cald; whose voices knowen sound
Soone as he heard, himself he reared light from ground.

XLIV

There did he see, that most on earth him joyd,
His dearest love, the comfort of his dayes,
Whose too long absence him had sore annoyd,
And wearied his life with dull delayes:
Straight he upstarted from the loathed layes,
And to her ran with hasty egernesse,
Like as a deare, that greedily embayes
In the coole soile, after long thirstinesse,
Which he in chace endured hath, now nigh breathlesse.

XLV

Lightly he clipt her twixt his armes twaine,
And streightly did embrace her body bright,
Her body, late the prison of sad paine,
Now the sweet lodge of love and deare delight:
But she, faire lady, overcommen quight
Of huge affection, did in pleasure melt,
And in sweete ravishment pourd out her spright:
No word they spake, nor earthly thing they felt,
But like two senceles stocks in long embracement dwelt.

XLVI

Had ye them seene, ye would have surely thought,
That they had beene that faire hermaphrodite,
Which that rich Romane of white marble wrought,
And in his costly bath causd to bee site:
So seemd those two, as growne together quite,
That Britomart, halfe envying their blesse,
Was much empassiond in her gentle sprite,
And to her selfe oft wisht like happinesse:
In vaine she wisht, that fate n'ould let her yet possesse.

XLVII

Thus doe those lovers with sweet countervayle
Each other of loves bitter fruit despoile.
But now my teme begins to faint and fayle,
All woxen weary of their journall toyle:
Therefore I will their sweatie yokes assoyle,
At this same furrowes end, till a new day:

And ye, faire swayns, after your long turmoyle,
Now cease your worke, and at your pleasure play:
Now cease your worke; tomorrow is an holy day.

III

LETTERS FROM SPENSER TO GABRIEL HARVEY

[The following letters were printed in 1580, with others from Harvey to Spenser, in two independent volumes, each bearing the imprint of Bynneman. (1) 'Three proper and wittie familiar Letters: lately passed betwene two Universitie men: touching the earthquake in Aprill last, and our English refourmed versifying.' (2) 'Two other very commendable Letters, of these same mens writing: both touching the foresaid artificiall versifying, and certain other particulars. More lately delivered unto the Printer.' The first of Spenser's letters appeared in the later volume; the second, together with the letter of Harvey from which an extract is here given, in the earlier.]

To the Worshipfull his very singular good friend, Maister G. H., Fellow of Trinitie Hall in Cambridge.

Good Master G.: I perceive by your most curteous and frendly letters your good will to be no lesse in deed than I alwayes esteemed. In recompence wherof, think, I beseech you, that I wil spare neither speech, nor wryting, nor aught else, whensoever and wheresoever occasion shal be offred me: yea, I will not stay till it be offred, but will seeke it, in al that possibly I may. And that you may perceive how much your counsel in al things prevaileth 10 with me, and how altogither I am ruled and over-ruled thereby, I am now determined to alter mine owne former purpose, and to subscribe to your advizement: being notwithstanding resolved stil to abide your farther resolution. My principal doubts are these. First, I was minded for a while to have intermitted the uttering of my writings; leaste by over-much cloying their noble eares, I should gather a contempt of my self, or else seeme rather for 20 gaine and commoditie to doe it, for some sweetnesse that I have already tasted. Then also me seemeth the work too base for his excellent lordship, being made in honour of a private personage unknowne, which of some yl-willers might be upbraided, not to be so worthie as you knowe she is; or the matter not so weightie that it should be offred to so weightie a personage; or the like. The selfe former title stil liketh me well ynough, and your fine addi- 30 tion no lesse. If these and the like doubtes maye be of importaunce in your seeming, to frustrate any parte of your advice, I beseeche you without the leaste selfe love of your own purpose, councell me for the beste: and the rather doe it faithfullye and carefully, for that, in all things, I attribute so muche to your judgement that I am evermore content to adnihilate mine owne determinations, in respecte thereof. And indeede, for your selfe to, it sitteth with you 40 now to call your wits and senses togither (which are alwaies at call) when occasion is so fairely offered of estimation and preferment. For, whiles the yron is hote, it is good striking, and minds of nobles varie, as their estates. *Verum ne quid durius.*

I pray you bethinke you well hereof, good Maister G., and forthwith write me those two or three special points and caveats for the nonce, *De quibus in superioribus illis mellitissimis* 50 *longissimisque litteris tuis.* Your desire to heare of my late beeing with hir Majestie muste dye in it selfe. As for the twoo worthy gentlemen, Master Sidney and Master Dyer, they have me, I thanke them, in some use of familiarity: of whom and to whome what speache passeth for youre credite and estimation I leave your selfe to conceive, having alwayes so well conceived of my unfained affection and zeale towardes you. And nowe they have 60 proclaimed in their ἀρειωπάγῳ a generall surceasing and silence of balde rymers, and also of the verie beste to: in steade whereof, they have, by authoritie of their whole senate, prescribed certaine lawes and rules of quantities of English sillables for English verse: having had thereof already great practise and drawen mee to their faction. Newe bookes I heare of none, but only of one, that writing a certaine booke called *The Schoole of Abuse*, and dedicating it to Maister 70 Sidney, was for hys labor scorned: if at leaste it be in the goodnesse of that nature to scorne. Suche follie is it, not to regarde aforehande the inclination and qualitie of him to whome wee dedicate oure bookes. Suche mighte I happily incurre, entituling *My Slomber*, and the other pamphlets, unto his honor. I meant them rather to Maister Dyer. But I am, of late, more in love wyth my Englishe versifying than with ryming: whyche I should have done long since, 80 if I would then have followed your coun- 81 cell. *Sed te solum jam tum suspicabar cum Aschamo sapere: nunc aulam video egregios alere poetas Anglicos.* Maister E. K. hartily desireth to be commended unto your worshippe: of whome what accompte he maketh, youre selfe shall hereafter perceive by hys paynefull and dutifull verses of your selfe.

Thus muche was written at Westminster yesternight: but comming this morning, beeying the sixteenth of October, to Mystresse Kerkes, to have it delivered to the carrier, I re- 92 ceyved youre letter, sente me the laste weeke: whereby I perceive you otherwhiles continue your old exercise of versifying in English: whych glorie I had now thought shoulde have bene onely ours heere at London and the court.

Truste me, your verses I like passingly well, and envye your hidden paines in this kinde, or rather maligne and grudge at your selfe, that woulde not once imparte so muche to me. But once or twice, you make a breache in Mais- 103 ter Drants rules: *quod tamen condonabimus*

tanto poëtæ, tuæque ipsius maximæ in his rebus autoritati. You shall see, when we meete in London, (whiche when it shall be, certifye us,) howe fast I have followed after you in that course: beware, leaste in time I overtake you. *Veruntamen te solum sequar, (ut sæpenumero sum professus,) nunquam sane assequar, dum* 113 *vivam.* And nowe requite I you with the like, not with the verye beste, but with the 113 verye shortest, namely with a few *Iambickes.* I dare warrant, they be precisely perfect for the feete (as you can easily judge) and varie not one inch from the rule. I will imparte yours to Maister Sidney and Maister Dyer, at my nexte going to the courte. I praye you, keepe mine close to your selfe, or your verie entire friendes, Maister Preston, Maister Still, and the reste. 121

Iambicum Trimetrum.

Unhappie Verse, the witnesse of my unhappie state,
  Make thy selfe fluttring wings of thy fast flying
  Thought, and fly forth unto my love, whersoever she be:

Whether lying reastlesse in heavy bedde, or else
  Sitting so cheerelesse at the cheerfull boorde, or else
  Playing alone carelesse on hir heavenlie virginals.

If in bed, tell hir, that my eyes can take no reste:
  If at boorde, tell hir, that my mouth can eate no meate:
  If at hir virginals, tel hir, I can heare no mirth. 130

Asked why? say: Waking love suffereth no sleepe:
  Say, that raging love dothe appall the weake stomacke:
  Say, that lamenting love marreth the musicall.

Tell hir, that hir pleasures were wonte to lull me asleepe:
  Tell hir, that hir beautie was wonte to feede mine eyes:
  Tell hir, that hir sweete tongue was wonte to make me mirth.

Nowe doe I nightly waste, wanting my kindely reste:
  Nowe doe I dayly starve, wanting my lively foode:
  Nowe doe I alwayes dye, wanting thy timely mirth.

And if I waste, who will bewaile my heavy chaunce? 140
  And if I starve, who will record my cursed end?
  And if I dye, who will saye: *This was Immerito?*

I thought once agayne here to have made an ende, with a heartie *Vale*, of the best fashion: but loe! an ylfavoured myschaunce. My last farewell, whereof I made great accompt, and muche marvelled you shoulde make no mention thereof, I am nowe tolde, (in the Divel's name,) was thorough one mans negligence quite forgotten, but shoulde nowe undoubtedly have 150 beene sent, whether I hadde come or no. Seing it can now be no otherwise, I pray you take all togither, wyth all their faultes: and nowe I hope you will vouchsafe mee an answeare of the largest size, or else I tell you true, you shall bee verye deepe in my debte: notwythstandyng thys other sweete, but shorte letter, and fine, but fewe verses. But I woulde rather I might yet see youre owne good selfe, and receive a reciprocall farewell from your owne sweete 160 mouth.

Ad ornatissimum virum, multis jamdiu nominibus clarissimum, G. H., Immerito sui, mox in Gallias navigaturi, Εὐτυχεῖν.

Sic malus egregium, sic non inimicus amicum,
Sicque novus veterem jubet ipse poëta poëtam
Salvere, ac cælo post secula multa secundo,
Jam reducem, cælo mage quam nunc ipse secundo,
Utier. Ecce deus, (modo sit deus ille, renixum
Qui vocet in scelus, et juratos perdat amores)
Ecce deus mihi clara dedit modo signa marinus,
Et sua veligero lenis parat æquora ligno,
Mox sulcanda; suas etiam pater Æolus iras 170
Ponit, et ingentes animos Aquilonis —
Cuncta vijs sic apta meis: ego solus ineptus.
Nam mihi nescio quo mens saucia vulnere, dudum
Fluctuat ancipiti pelago, dum navita proram
Invalidam validus rapit huc Amor, et rapit illuc.
Consilijs Ratio melioribus usa, decusque
Immortale levi diffessa Cupidinis arcu.
Angimur hoc dubio, et portu vexamur in ipso.
Magne pharetrati nunc tu contemptor Amoris,
(Id tibi Dij nomen precor haud impune remittant) 180
Hos nodos exsolve, et eris mihi magnus Apollo.
Spiritus ad summos, scio, te generosus honores
Exstimulat, majusque docet spirare poëtam.
Quam levis est Amor, et tamen haud levis est
Amor omnis.
Ergo nihil laudi reputas æquale perenni,
Præque sacrosancta splendoris imagine tanti,
Cætera, quæ vecors, uti numina, vulgus adorat,
Prædia, amicitias, urbana peculia, nummos,
Quæque placent oculis, formas, spectacula, amores,
Conculcare soles, ut humum, et ludibria sensus.
Digna meo certe Harvejo sententia, digna 191
Oratore amplo, et generoso pectore, quam non
Stoica formidet veterum sapientia vinclis
Sancire æternis: sapor haud tamen omnibus idem.
Dicitur effæti proles facunda Laërtæ,
Quamlibet ignoti jactata per æquora cæli,
Inque procelloso longum exsul gurgite ponto,
Præ tamen amplexu lachrymosæ conjugis, ortus

Cælestes, Divûmque thoros sprevisse beatos.
Tantum amor, et mulier, vel amore potentior.
Illum 200
Tu tamen illudis: tua magnificentia tanta est:
Præque subumbrata splendoris imagine tanti,
Præque illo meritis famosis nomine parto,
Cætera, quæ vecors, uti numina, vulgus adorat,
Prædia, amicitias, armenta, peculia, nummos,
Quæque placent oculis, formas, spectacula, amores,
Quæque placent ori, quæque auribus, omnia temnis.
Næ tu grande sapis! sapor at sapientia non est:
Omnis et in parvis bene qui scit desipuisse,
Sæpe supercilijs palmam sapientibus aufert. 210
Ludit Aristippum modo tetrica turba sophorum,
Mitia purpureo moderantem verba tyranno:
Ludit Aristippus dictamina vana sophorum,
Quos levis emensi male torquet culicis umbra:
Et quisquis placuisse studet heroibus altis,
Desipuisse studet; sic gratia crescit ineptis.
Denique laurigeris quisquis sua tempora vittis
Insignire volet, populoque placere faventi,
Desipere insanus discit, turpemque pudendæ
Stultitiæ laudem quærit. Pater Ennius unus
Dictus in innumeris sapiens: laudatur at ipse
Carmina vesano fudisse liquentia vino. 222
Nec tu, pace tua, nostri Cato Maxime sæcli,
Nomen honorati sacrum mereare poëtæ,
Quantumvis illustre canas, et nobile carmen,
Ni *stultire* velis, sic stultorum omnia plena.
Tuta sed in medio superest via gurgite, nam qui
Nec reliquis nimium vult desipuisse videri,
Nec sapuisse nimis, sapientem dixeris unum:
Hinc te merserit unda, illinc combusserit ignis.
Nec tu delicias nimis aspernare fluentes, 231
Nec sero dominam venientem in vota, nec aurum,
Si sapis, oblatum, (Curijs ea, Fabricijsque
Linque viris miseris miseranda sophismata: quondam
Grande sui decus ij, nostri sed dedecus ævi :)
Nec sectare nimis. Res utraque crimine plena.
Hoc bene qui callet, (si quis tamen hoc bene callet)
Scribe, vel invito sapientem hunc Socrate solum.
Vis facit una pios: justos facit altera: et altra
Egregie cordata ac fortia pectora: verum 240
Omne tulit punctum, *qui miscuit utile dulci.*
Dij mihi dulce diu dederant: verum utile nunquam:
Utile nunc etiam, O utinam quoque dulce dedissent.
Dij mihi, (quippe Dijs æquivalia maxima parvis,)
Ni nimis invideant mortalibus esse beatis,
Dulce simul tribuisse queant, simul utile: tanta
Sed fortuna tua est: pariter quæque utile, quæque
Dulce dat ad placitum: sævo nos sydere nati
Quæsitum imus eam per inhospita Caucasa longe, 249
Perque Pyrenæos montes, Babilonaque turpem.
Quod si quæsitum nec ibi invenerimus, ingens
Æquor inexhaustis permensi erroribus, ultra
Fluctibus in medijs socij quæremus Vlyssis.
Passibus inde deam fessis comitabimur ægram,

Nobile cui furtum quærenti defuit orbis.
Namque sinu pudet in patrio, tenebrisque puden-
  dis,
Non nimis ingenio juvenem infœlice virentes
Officijs frustra deperdere vilibus annos,
Frugibus et vacuas speratis cernere spicas.
Ibimus ergo statim, (quis eunti fausta precetur ?)
Et pede clivosas fesso calcabimus Alpes.   261
Quis dabit interea, conditas rore Britanno,
Quis tibi litterulas ? quis carmen amore petul-
  cum ?
Musa sub Oebalij desueta cacumine montis,
Flebit inexhausto tam longa silentia planctu,
Lugebitque sacrum lacrymis Helicona tacen-
  tem.
Harveiusque bonus, (charus licet omnibus idem,
Idque suo merito, prope suavior omnibus unus)
Angelus et Gabriel, (quamvis comitatus amicis
Innumeris, geniûmque choro stipatus amæno)
Immerito tamen unum absentem sæpe requiret,
Optabitque, Utinam meus hic Edmundus ades-
  set,   272
Qui nova scripsisset, nec amores conticuisset,
Ipse suos, et sæpe animo verbisque benignis
Fausta precaretur : Deus illum aliquando redu-
  cat. &c.

  Plura vellem per Charites, sed non licet per
Musas.
  Vale, Vale plurimum, Mi amabilissime Har-
veie, meo cordi, meorum omnium longe charis-
sime.

  I was minded also to have sent you some English verses, or rymes, for a farewell ; but, by   282
my troth, I have no spare time in the world to
thinke on such toyes, that, you knowe, will demaund a freer head than mine is presently. I
beseeche you by all your curtesies and graces,
let me be answered ere I goe ; which will be (I
hope, I feare, I thinke) the next weeke, if I can
be dispatched of my Lorde. I goe thither, as
sent by him, and maintained most what of   290
him : and there am to employ my time, my body,
my minde, to his Honours service. Thus, with
many superhartie commendations and recom-
mendations to your selfe, and all my friendes
with you, I ende my last farewell, not thinking
any more to write unto you before I goe : and
withall committing to your faithfull credence
the eternall memorie of our everlasting friendship, the inviolable memorie of our unspotted
friendshippe, the sacred memorie of our   300
vowed friendship : which I beseech you continue
with usuall writings, as you may, and of all things
let me heare some newes from you : as gentle
Master Sidney, I thanke his good worship, hath
required of me, and so promised to doe againe.
Qui monet, ut facias, quod jam facis, you knowe
the rest. You may alwayes send them most
safely to me by Mistresse Kerke, and by none
other. So once againe, and yet once more,
farewell most hartily, mine owne good Mas-   310
ter H., and love me, as I love you, and thinke
upon poore Immerito, as he thinketh uppon you.
  Leycester House, this 5 [16 ?] of October,
1579.

Per mare, per terras,
        Vivus mortuusque,
        Tuus Immerito.

*To my long approoved and singular good frende,
        Master G. H.*

  GOOD MASTER H.: I doubt not but you have
some great important matter in hande, which
al this while restraineth your penne, and wonted
readinesse in provoking me unto that wherein
your selfe nowe faulte. If there bee any such
thing in hatching, I pray you hartily, lette us
knowe, before al the worlde see it. But if
happly you dwell altogither in Justinians courte,
and give your selfe to be devoured of secreate
studies, as of all likelyhood you doe, yet at   10
least imparte some your olde or newe, Latine or
Englishe, eloquent and gallant poesies to us, from
whose eyes, you saye, you keepe in a manner
nothing hidden. Little newes is here stirred:
but that olde greate matter still depending.
His Honoure never better. I thinke the earthquake was also there wyth you (which I would
gladly learne) as it was here with us; over-
throwing divers old buildings and peeces of
churches. Sure verye straunge to be hearde   20
of in these countries, and yet I heare some saye (I
knowe not howe truely) that they have knowne
the like before in their dayes. *Sed quid vobis
videtur magnis philosophis ?* I like your late
Englishe hexameters so exceedingly well, that
I also enure my penne sometime in that kinde :
whyche I fynd, indeede, as I have heard you
often defende in worde, neither so harde, nor so
harshe, that it will easily and fairely yeelde it
selfe to oure moother tongue. For the onely   30
or chiefest hardnesse, whych seemeth, is in the
accente : whyche sometime gapeth, and as it were
yawneth ilfavouredly, comming shorte of that
it should, and sometime exceeding the measure
of the number : as in *carpenter*, the middle sillable being used shorte in speache, when it
shall be read long in verse, seemeth like a lame
gosling, that draweth one legge after hir : and
heaven, beeing used shorte as one sillable, when
it is in verse, stretched out with a *diastole*,   40
is like a lame dogge that holdes up one legge.
But it is to be wonne with custome, and rough
words must be subdued with use. For why, a
Gods name, may not we, as else the Greekes,
have the kingdome of oure owne language,
and measure our accentes by the sounde, reserv-
ing the quantitie to the verse ? Loe ! here I let
you see my olde use of toying in rymes, turned
into your artificiall straightnesse of verse by
this *tetrasticon*. I beseech you tell me your   50
fancie, without parcialitie.

See yee the blindefoulded pretie god, that feath-
    ered archer,
  Of lovers miseries which maketh his bloodie
    game ?
Wote ye why his moother with a veale hath
    coovered his face ?
  Trust me, least he my loove happely chaunce
    to beholde.

Seeme they comparable to those two which I translated you *ex tempore* in bed, the last time we lay togither in Westminster?

That which I eate, did I joy, and that which I
    greedily gorged :
As for those many goodly matters leaft I for
    others.   60

I would hartily wish, you would either send me the rules and precepts of arte which you observe in quantities, or else followe mine, that Master Philip Sidney gave me, being the very same which Master Drant devised, but enlarged with Master Sidneys own judgement, and augmented with my observations, that we might both accorde and agree in one: leaste we overthrowe one an other, and be overthrown of the rest. Truste me, you will hardly beleeve what 70 greate good liking and estimation Maister Dyer had of your *Satyricall Verses*, and I, since the viewe thereof, having before of my selfe had speciall liking of Englishe versifying, am even nowe aboute to give you some token, what and howe well therein I am able to doe: for, to tell you trueth, I minde shortely, at convenient leysure, to sette forth a booke in this kinde, whyche I entitle *Epithalamion Thamesis*, whyche booke I dare undertake wil be very 80 profitable for the knowledge, and rare for the invention and manner of handling. For in setting forth the marriage of the Thames, I shewe his first beginning, and offspring, and all the countrey that he passeth thorough, and also describe all the rivers throughout Englande, whyche came to this wedding, and their righte names, and right passage, &c. A worke, beleeve me, of much labour: wherein, notwithstanding, Master Holinshed hath muche furthered and 90 advantaged me, who therein hath bestowed singular paines, in searching oute their firste heades and sourses, and also in tracing and dogging oute all their course, til they fall into the sea.

O Tite, siquid ego,
Ecquid erit pretij ?

But of that more hereafter. Nowe, my *Dreames* and *Dying Pellicane* being fully fin- 99 ished (as I partelye signified in my laste letters) and presentlye to bee imprinted, I wil in hande forthwith with my *Faery Queene*, whyche I praye you hartily send me with al expedition, and your frendly letters, and long expected judgement wythal, whyche let not be shorte, but in all pointes suche as you ordinarilye use and I extraordinarily desire. *Multum vale. Westminster. Quarto Nonas Aprilis, 1580. Sed, amabo te, meum Corculum tibi se ex animo commendat plurimum : jamdiu mirata, te nihil* 110 *ad literas suas responsi dedisse. Vide, quæso, ne id tibi capitale sit : mihi certe quidem erit, ꝫeque tibi hercle impune, ut opinor. Iterum vale, et quam voles sæpe.*

        Yours alwayes to commaunde,
                      IMMERITO.

Postscripte.

I take best my *Dreames* shoulde come forth alone, being growen by meanes of the Glosse (running continually in maner of a paraphrase) full as great as my *Calendar*. Therin be some 120 things excellently, and many things wittily, discoursed of E. K. and the pictures so singularly set forth and purtrayed, as if Michael Angelo were there, he could (I think) nor amende the beste, nor reprehende the worst. I knowe you woulde lyke them passing wel. Of my *Stemmata Dudleiana*, and especially of the sundry apostrophes therein, addressed you knowe to whome, muste more advisement be had, 129 than so lightly to sende them abroade: howbeit, trust me (though I doe never very well,) yet in my owne fancie, I never dyd better: *Veruntamen te sequor solum: nunquam vero assequar.*

Extract from Harvey's Reply.

But ever and ever, me thinkes your great Catoes *Ecquid erit pretij*, and our little Catoes *Res age quæ prosunt*, make suche a buzzing and ringing in my head, that I have little joy to animate and encourage either you or him [his small brother] to goe forward, unlesse ye might make account of some certaine ordinarie wages, or at the leastwise have your meate and drinke for your dayes workes. As for my selfe, howsoever I have toyed and trifled heretofore, I 10 am now taught, and I trust I shall shortly learne (no remedie, I must of meere necessitie give you over in the playne fielde) to employ my travayle and tyme wholly or chiefely on those studies and practizes that carrie, as they saye, meate in their mouth, having evermore their eye uppon the title *De pane lucrando*, and their hand upon their halfpenny. For, I pray now, what saith Master Cuddie, *alias* you know who, in the tenth Æglogue of the foresaid famous new *Cal-* 20 *ender?*

Piers, I have piped earst so long with payne,
That all myne oten reedes been rent and wore,
And my poore Muse hath spent her spared
    store,
Yet little good hath got, and much lesse gayne.
Such pleasaunce makes the grashopper so poore,
And ligge so layde, when winter doth her
    strayne.

The dapper ditties, that I woont devize,
To feede youthes fancie, and the flocking fry,
Delighten much : what I the bett forthy ?   30
They han the pleasure, I a selender prize.
I beate the bushe, the birdes to them doe flye,
What good thereof to Cuddy can arise ?

But Master Collin Cloute is not every body, and albeit his olde companions, Master Cuddie and Master Hobbinoll, be as little beholding to their Mistresse Poetrie, as ever you wist, yet he peradventure, by the meanes of hir speciall favour, and some personall priviledge, may happely live by *Dying Pellicanes*, and purchase great 40 landes and lordshippes with the money, which his *Calendar* and *Dreames* have, and will affourde him. *Extra jocum*, I like your *Dreames* passingly well : and the rather, bicause they savour of that singular extraordinarie veine and invention, whiche I ever fancied moste, and in a manner admired onelye in Lucian, Petrarche, Aretine, Pasquill, and all the most delicate and fine conceited Grecians and Italians : (for the Romanes to speake of are but verye ciphars in 50 this kinde :) whose chiefest endevour and drifte was, to have nothing vulgare, but, in some respecte or other, and especially in lively hyperbolicall amplifications, rare, queint, and odde in every pointe, and, as a man woulde saye, a degree or two, at the leaste, above the reache and compasse of a common schollers capacitie. In whiche respecte notwithstanding, as well for the singularitie of the manner as the divinitie of the matter, I hearde once a divine preferre 60 Saint Johns Revelation before al the veriest metaphysicall visions and jollyest conceited dreames or extasies that ever were devised by one or other, howe admirable or superexcellent soever they seemed otherwise to the worlde. And truely I am so confirmed in this opinion, that when I bethinke me of the verie notablest and moste wonderful propheticall or poeticall vision that ever I read, or hearde, me seemeth the proportion is so unequall, that there hardly appeareth anye semblaunce of comparison : no 71 more in a manner (specially for poets) than doth betweene the incomprehensible wisedome of God and the sensible wit of man. But what needeth this digression betweene you and me ? I dare saye you wyll holde your selfe reasonably wel satisfied, if youre *Dreames* be but as well esteemed of in Englande as Petrarches *Visions* be in Italy : whiche, I assure you, is the very 79

worst I wish you. But see how I have the arte memorative at commaundement. In good faith, I had once again nigh forgotten your *Faerie Queene :* howbeit, by good chaunce, I have nowe sent hir home at the laste, neither in better nor worse case than I founde hir. And must you of necessitie have my judgement of hir in deede? To be plaine, I am voyde of al judgement, if your *Nine Comœdies*, wherunto, in imitation of Herodotus, you give the names of the nine Muses, (and in one mans fansie not unworthily), 90 come not neerer Ariostoes comœdies, eyther for the finenesse of plausible elocution, or the rarenesse of poetical invention, than that *Elvish Queene* doth to his *Orlando Furioso*, which, notwithstanding, you wil needes seeme to emulate, and hope to overgo, as you flatly professed your self in one of your last letters. Besides that you know, it hath bene the usual practise of the most exquisite and odde wittes in all nations, and specially in Italie, rather to shewe 100 and advaunce themselves that way, than any other : as namely, those three notorious dyscoursing heads, Bibiena, Machiavel, and Aretine did, (to let Bembo and Ariosto passe,) with the great admiration and wonderment of the whole countrey : being, in deede, reputed matchable in all points, both for conceyt of witte, and eloquent decyphering of matters, either with Aristophanes and Menander in Greek, or with Plautus and Terence in Latin, or with any 110 other in any other tong. But I wil not stand greatly with you in your owne matters. If so be the Faerye Queene be fairer in your eie than the Nine Muses, and Hobgoblin runne away with the garland from Apollo, marke what I saye : and yet I will not say that I thought, but there an end for this once, and fare you well, till God or some good aungell putte you in a better minde.

A LIST OF REJECTED READINGS

For the various publications of Spenser the following texts have been adopted as standard:—

The Shepheardes Calender, 1579.
Complaints, 1591.
The Faerie Queene, I–III, 1596 (but with the spelling of 1590).
The Faerie Queene, IV–VI, 1596.
The Faerie Queene, VII (Cantos on Mutability), 1609.
Daphnaïda, 1591.

Colin Clouts Come Home Again and *Astrophel*, 1595.
Amoretti and Epithalamion, 1595.
Fowre Hymnes, 1596.
Prothalamion, 1596.
Van der Noot's Theatre, 1569.
Letters, 1580.

Whenever a reading given by these texts has been departed from, it is recorded in the following list, together with the substitute adopted. Other variants are ignored, except for incidental purposes ; as are evident misprints (unless these have some glimmering of sense or the support of another editor) and (except occasionally) changes in punctuation. In each case, the first reading given is that which has been adopted, the second is that which has been rejected.

It should be remembered that different copies of the same edition not infrequently give different readings. It may well be, therefore, that the present list will be found to conflict here and there with others more authoritative. Such differences will hardly be of importance, except for bibliographical controversy.

THE SHEPHEARDES CALENDER
[Quartos of 1581 & 1586 not collated.]

PAGE

6 *Epistle* 157. *it* (1591, 1597). Omitted 1579.

7 235. *sc.* Substituted here and elsewhere for obsolete *s.* of old editions.

8 *Generall Argument* 13. *more shepherds then* (1597) : 1579 = *most shepheards and.*

8 42. *containe* (1597) : 1579 = *conceive.*

8 96. *Abib.* Old editions = *Abil.*

16 *March* 4. *nigheth* (1611) : 1579, 1591, 1597 = *nighest.*

25 *Maye* 150. *saye* (1597) : 1579 = *sayd.*

34 *Julye* 230. *bett* (v. *Glosse* 162). Old editions = *better.*

34 Emblems. *Thomalins.* Old editions = *Palinodes.*

34 *Glosse* 38. *a Dane.* Old editions = *the Dane*, by confusion with next line.

37 *August* 84. *thy* (1597) : 1579 = *my.*

37 104. *curelesse.* Collier's emendation for *carelesse* of old editions.

41 *September* 145. *yeed.* 1579, 1591, 1597 = *yeeld ;* 1611 = *yead.*

43 *Glosse* 59. The dates are omitted in old editions ; 1579 leaves a space for them.

45 *October* 79. *thy* (1591, 1597) : 1579 = *the.*

45 97. *Cud.* (1591, 1597). In 1579 there is no indication of change in speaker.

46 *October Glosse* 68. *Arcadian.* 1579 = *Aradian ;* 1591, 1597, 1611 = *Arabian.*

49 *November* 98. *heame* (v. *Glosse* 58). 1579 = *heme.*

52 *November Glosse* 89. *signe* (1591, 1597). Omitted in 1579.

53 *December* 29. *recked* (1611) : 1579 = *wreaked.*

53 43. *derring doe* (v. *Glosse* 13). 1579 = *derring to.*

55 Emblem. *Vivitur, etc.* Not in any of the early editions. First given by Hughes (1715).

55 *Glosse* 51. Reading of 1591, 1597. 1579 inserts *as* before *Theocritus.*

56 113. *edax.* Omitted in old editions.

COMPLAINTS

67 *Ruines of Time* 551. *which* (1611) : 1591 = *with.*

69 675. *worldes.* Old editions = *worlds.* Cf. *Mother Hubberds Tale* 87, *Epithalamion* 290.

78 *Teares of the Muses* 600. *living* (1611) : 1591 = *loving.*

85 *Virgils Gnat* 406. *fluttering* (1611) : 1591 = *flattering*, which is contradicted by *fowlie them upbraydes.*

86 511. *Rhœtean* (1611) : 1591 = *Rhetœan.* The Latin is ' Rhœtei litoris ora.'

87 575. *billowes.* Old editions = *billowe*, but the next line gives *them.*

91 *Mother Hubberds Tale* 87. *worldes* (1611) : 1591 = *worlds.* Cf. *Ruines of Time* 675, *Epithalamion* 290.

94 308. *winges.* Old editions = *wings.* Cf. l. 87.

98 648. *at all.* 1591 drops *at.*

103 1025. *lord.* Old editions = *lords.*

108 *Ruines of Rome* IV, 6. *The old giants.* 1591 = *Th'old giants ;* 1611 = *The giants old.* In Spenser's text, *the* is often, before a vowel, contracted to *th'*, when the metre unmistakably demands the full form. Cf. F. Q. Bk. V, c. iii, st. 11.

111 xv, 14. *To have become.* 1591 = *To become ;* 1611 (in attempted emendation of metre) *Now to become.* The French ' N'estre plus rien ' suggests the reading adopted.

111 XVIII, 5. *ornaments*. Old editions = *ornament*. The French has ' ornements.'

114 XXX, 8. *stackes* (1611): 1591 = *stalkes*.

118 *Muiopotmos* 196. *Dull* (1611). Not in 1591.

121 370. *framde craftilie* (1611): 1591 = *did slily frame*.

124 *Visions of the Worlds Vanitie* VIII, 12. *native* (1611) : 1591 = *natures*.

125 *The Visions of Bellay* II, 8. *On*. 1591 & 1611 = *One*.

125 IV, 1. *pillours*. 1591 & 1611 = *pillowes*. 1569 = *pillers*.

128 *The Visions of Petrarch* III, 1. *Then* (1569): 1591 = *The*. The French original begins *Après*.

129 VII, 1. *behold*. 1591, 1611 = *beheld*.

THE FAERIE QUEENE

136 *A Letter of the Authors*. Together with the Commendatory Verses and the Dedicatory Sonnets, this letter is placed, in 1590, at the close of the volume, for the reason that it was written while the work was in press, as the date 'January, 1589' (modern style 1590) denotes. In 1596, when the enlarged poem appeared in two volumes, the letter and the verses were left where they had been, at the close of the first. It has seemed better to follow modern usage by placing them at the outset.

137 162. *vi. Ephes*. Old editions = *v. Ephes*.

145 Bk. I, c. i, st. 4, l. 5 f. For the colon after *throw* the early editions give a comma, and for the comma after *mournd* a colon. The interchange adopted makes better sense. For the use of a colon between strictly correlative clauses, see c. iv, st. 16, where the early editions give one after *call* (l. 5).

148 st. 28. *passed* (1590): 1596 = *passeth*.

156 c. ii, st. 29. *him thither* (1590): 1596 drops *him*.

157 st. 40. *unweeting* (1590): 1596 = *unweening*.

163 c. iii, st. 34. *spurd* (1590): 1596 = *spurnd*.

166 c. iv, st. 12. *a queene* (1590): 1596 drops *a*. *realme* (1590): 1596 = *realmes*.

166 st. 16. *glitterand* (1590): 1596 = *glitter and*.

167 st. 20, l. 3. *From* (1590): 1596 = *For*.

171 c. v, st. 1. *did he* (1590): 1596 drops *he*.

176 st. 41. *nigh weary* (1590): 1596 = *high weary*.

180 c. vi, st. 15. *Or Bacchus* (1590): 1596 = *Of Bacchus*.

191 c. vii, st. 48. *yee* (1590): 1596 = *you*. A typical example of numerous variants in 1596. It is simply inconceivable that, having once written *yee*, Spenser should have substituted, deliberately, *you*, which half spoils the line.

195 c. viii, st. 21. *his forces* (Church). Old editions = *their forces*.

196 st. 27. *equall eye* (1590): 1596 = *equall eyes*. Cf. c. ix, st. 47.

198 st. 41. *and helmets* (1590): 1596 drops *and*.

198 st. 44. *dislike*. Old editions = *delight*, which spoils the obvious sense of the passage, and which was obviously caught from the preceding line. The substitute was suggested by Daniel's *Delia* liv : —
'Like as the lute delights or else dislikes,
As is his art that plays upon the same, etc.'

201 c. ix, st. 18. *as pledges* (1590): 1596 = *the pledges*.

206 st. 53. *feeble* (1590): 1596 = *seely*.

209 c. x, st. 20. *Dry-shod . . . tway*. This line first appears in the folio of 1609.

211 st. 36. *Their gates* (1609): 1590, 1596 = *There gates*.
call in commers by. 1590, 1596 = *call in commers by*.

213 st. 50. *quoth she* (1590): 1596 = *quoth he*.

214 st. 52. *Brings* (1609): 1590, 1596 = *Bring*.

215 st. 61. *peaceably thy* (1590): 1596 = *peaceably to thy*.

215 st. 62. *they' are* (1590): 1596 drops *they'*.

215 st. 64. *doen nominate* (1590): 1596 = *doen then nominate*.

217 c. xi, st. 8. *vaste* (1590): 1596 = *wast*.

220 st. 27. *vaunt* (1590): 1596 = *daunt*.

221 st. 37. *yelled* (1609): 1590, 1596 = *yelded*. This and several other misprints have been recorded only because they are deliberately adopted by Dr. Grosart.

223 st. 51. *the deawy* (1590): 1596 = *her deawy*.

226 c. xii, st. 16. *pleasure* (1590): 1596 = *pleasures*.

227 st. 21. *that dawning day is drawing* (1590): 1596 = *the dawning day is dawning*.

227 st. 28. *her* (1590): 1596 = *his*.

229 st. 40. *His heart* (1590): 1596 = *Her heart*.

231 Bk. II, c. i, st. 8. *with faire* (1590): 1596 = *with a faire*.

234 st. 31. *handling* (1590): 1596 = *handing*.

236 st. 39. *dolour* (1590): 1596 = *labour*.

236 st. 40. *gore* (1590): 1596 = *gold*.

236 st. 44. *avenging* (1590): 1596 = *revenging*, a change that clogs the verse.

238 st. 59. *equall* (1590): 1596 = *evill*.

240 c. ii, st. 7. *pray* (Collier). Old editions = *chace*, caught from the line below.

240 st. 9. *whose* (1590): 1596 = *those*.

242 st. 21. *cald* (1590): 1596 = *calth*.

242 st. 23. *boldly* (1590): 1596 = *bloudy*.

243 st. 28. *their champions*. 1590 = *her champions*; 1596 = *their champion*.

244 st. 34. *thought her*. 1590 = *though ther*; 1596 = *thought their*.

244 st. 40. *peaceably* (1590): 1596 = *peaceable*.

245 st. 42. *hold*. For rhyme. Old editions = *make*.

245 st. 44. *enrold*. 1590 = *entrold*; 1596 = *introld*.

246 c. iii, st. 4. *glory he* (1590): 1596 = *glory vaine*.

246 st. 9. *From that* (1590): 1596 = *For that*.

249 st. 28. *sport*. For rhyme. Old editions = *play*.

257 c. iv, st. 36. *Falne into* (1590): 1596 = *Falne unto*.

259 c. v, st. 8. *hurtle* (1590): 1596 = *hurtle*.

261 st. 19. *said shee* (1609): 1590, 1596 = *said hee*.

262 st. 27. *her Bowre* (1590): 1596 = *his Bowre.*
262 st. 29. *prickling* (1590): 1596 = *pricking.*
263 st. 34. *So' he* (Child). 1590, 1596 = *So, he.*
The apostrophe is an ordinary mark of
elision.
264 c. vi, st. 1. *her victories* (1590): 1596 =
their victories.
265 st. 14. *love lay* (1590): 1596 = *loud lay.*
266 st. 18. *griesy* (1590): 1596 = *griesly.* Cf. st.
20, 46.
267 st. 27. *there passage* (1609): 1590, 1596 =
their passage.
268 st. 35. *shend* (1590): 1596 = *shent.*
270 st. 45. *Burning* (1590): 1596 = *But.*
270 st. 50. *liver.* Old editions = *livers.*
271 c. vii, st. 4. *Well yet* (1590): 1596 = *Well it.*
And covetous (1590): 1596 = *A covetous.*
272 st. 11. *and throw* (1590): 1596 drops *and.*
273 st. 18. *that antique* (1590): 1596 drops *that.*
276 st. 37. *when an* (1590): 1596 = *when as.*
276 st. 40. *As if that.* 1590, 1596 = *As if the ;* but
in the list of errata appended to both, we
are directed to change *the* to *that* on p. 283,
which begins with this line and ends with
the last of st. 43. The only other *the's*
that could be changed are those of st. 42,
l. 8 and st. 43, l. 2.
276 st. 41. *his looke* (1590): 1596 = *to looke.*
278 st. 52. *With which.* Old editions = *Which
with.*
279 st. 64. *his pray* (1590): 1596 = *the pray.*
284 c. viii, st. 29. *upheave* (Morris). For rhyme.
Old editions = *upreare.* Cf. Bk. VI, c.
viii, st. 10, l. 2.
285 st. 40. *well as he it* (1590): 1596 = *wisely as
it.* The later reading seems too flat and
inexpressive to be attributed to revision
by the poet.
287 st. 48. *Prince Arthur* (1609): 1590, 1596 =
Sir Guyon.
288 c. ix, arg. *flight* (1590): 1596 = *fight.*
289 st. 9. *weete.* Old editions = *wote.*
290 st. 16. *with blustring* (1590): 1596 drops *with.*
291 st. 21. *fensible* (1590): 1596 = *sensible.*
297 st. 7. *liveden* (1590): 1596 = *lived then.*
297 st. 9. *Assaracs* (1590): 1596 = *Assaraos.*
299 st. 20. *to sway* (1590): 1596 = *of sway.*
301 st. 34. *Then his* (1590): 1596 = *Till his. Till*
probably caught from previous line.
301 st. 37. *stird with* (1590): 1596 = *stird up.*
302 st. 43. *sonne* (1590): 1596 = *sonnes.*
Sisillus. Old editions = *Sifillus.*
302 st. 49. *defrayd* (1590): 1596 = *did defray.*
303 st. 51. *his armes* (1590): 1596 drops *his.*
304 st. 65. *have forst* (1590): 1596 = *enforst.*
305 st. 68. *seemed* (1590): 1596 = *seemeth.*
306 c. xi, st. 2. *and for* (1590): 1596 drops *for.*
307 st. 4. *And he* (1590): 1596 drops *he.*
308 st. 13. *is dreadfull* (1590): 1596 = *was
dreadfull.*
308 st. 18. *therewithall* (1590): 1596 = *therewith
all,* which may be a mere variant in word-
division.
309 st. 23. *support* (1590): 1596 = *disport.*
315 c. xii, st. 20. *their bote* (1590): 1596 = *the
bote.*

317 st. 32. *That art* (1590): 1596 = *Thou art.*
320 st. 52. *Or Eden selfe* (1590): 1596 = *Of
Eden.*
320 st. 54. *hyacine* (1611): 1590, 1596, 1609 =
hyacint.
320 st. 57. *nought* (1590): 1596 = *not.*
323 st. 81. *that same* (1590): 1596 = *the same.*
324 st. 83. *spoyle* (1590): 1596 = *spoyld.*
327 Bk. III, c. i, st. 14. *creature* (1590): 1596 =
creatures.
329 st. 31. *and of many* (1590): 1596 drops *of.*
331 st. 41. *lightly* (1609): 1590, 1596 = *highly.*
332 st. 48. *loathly* (1590): 1596 = *loathy.*
332 st. 54. *be guiled.* 1590 = *be-guiled ;* 1596 =
beguiled ; 1609 = *be 'guiled.*
333 st. 60. *wary* (1609): 1590, 1596 = *weary.*
339 c. ii, st. 36. *other* (1590): 1596 = *others.*
344 c. iii, st. 22. *Greeke* (1590): 1596 = *Greece.*
345 st. 29. *With thee* (1590): 1596 = *Where thee.*
346 st. 35. *thy Britons* (1590): 1596 = *the Britons.*
346 st. 37. *their fatall* (1590): 1596 = *the fatall.*
347 st. 46. *outronne* (1590): 1596 = *overoune.*
348 st. 50. *as earst* (1609). Not in 1590 or 1596.
348 st. 51. *disguise* (1590): 1596 = *devise.*
349 st. 57. *unveeting* (1590): 1596 = *unmeeting.*
351 st. 13. *did into* (1590): 1596 drops *did.*
353 st. 33. *raynes* (1590): 1596 = *traines.*
359 c. v, st. 5. *A fayrer* (1590): 1596 = *And
fairer. And* is caught from the following line.
359 st. 11. *may ye* (1590): 1596 = *may you.*
363 st. 37. *followd* (1590): 1596 = *follow.*
364 st. 44. *revew* (1590): 1596 = *renew.*
369 c. vi, st. 28. *thence* (1590): 1596 = *hence.*
371 st. 40. *saw.* For rhyme. Old editions =
spyde.
372 st. 45. *And dearest love* (1609). Not in 1590,
1596.
374 c. vii, st. 9. *like to.* Old editions = *like two.*
375 st. 13. *hath gaz'd* (1590): 1596 = *had gazed.*
375 st. 18. *Might be by the witch or that.* 1590
= *Might by the witch or by ;* 1596 = *Might
be the witch or that.*
377 st. 34. *containe.* For rhyme. Old editions =
enclose. Cf. Bk. V, c. xii, st. 1, Bk. III,
c. ix, st. 46.
382 c. viii, st. 9. *whom* (1609): 1590, 1596 = *who.*
382 st. 11. *he was* (1590): 1596 drops *he.*
384 st. 23. *this same* (1590): 1596 = *the same.*
390 c. ix, st. 13. *And so defyde* (1590): 1596
drops *so.*
390 st. 14. *in kenell* (1590): 1596 = *to kenell.*
391 st. 22. *her speare* (1590): 1596 = *the speare.*
391 st. 24. *But most* (1590): 1596 drops *most.*
394 st. 48. *to sea* (1590): 1596 = *to the sea.*
397 c. x, st. 13. *did beare* (1590): 1596 = *would
beare.*
399 st. 30. *rownded* (1590): 1596 = *grounded.*
399 st. 31. *vertues pay* (1609): 1590 = *vertuous
pray ;* 1596 = *vertues pray.*
402 st. 52. *day spring* (1590): 1596 = *day springs.*
404 c. xi, st. 4. *all that I ever* (1590): 1596 =
that I did ever.
did him (1590): 1596 = *him did.*
407 st. 27. *formost.* Old editions = *formest.*

PAGE

408 st. 39. *stag* (Jortin). Old editions =*hag.*
409 st. 47. *hevens hight* (Upton). Old editions=
   heven bright.
412 c. xii, st. 12. *too or froe* (1590) : 1596 = *to*
   and fro.
413 st. 18. *hony-laden.* Old editions= *hony-*
   lady.
417 Bk. IV, Title. *Triamond* (1611) : 1596,
   1609= *Telamond.*
439 c. iii, st. 43. *quietage.* Old editions =
   quiet age.
441 c. iv, st. 2. *Blandamour* (1679). Earlier editions = *Scudamour.* Here and in Bk. II,
   c. viii, st. 48, also in Bk. VI, c. vi, st. 17,
   the mistake can be corrected without injury to the verse. In Bk. III, c. ii, st. 4,
   the mistake must stand. All are due,
   probably, to some carelessness of the
   poet.
444 c. iv, st. 24. *beamlike* (1609) : 1596 = *brave-*
   like.
444 st. 29. *cuffing* (1611) : 1596, 1609 = *cuffling.*
446 st. 39. *queynt.* 1596 = *quyent.*
447 st. 45. *avenge* (1609) : 1596 = *evenge.*
450 c. v, st. 25. *one* (1609) : 1596 = *once.*
457 c. vi, st. 24. *turning feare* (1609) : 1596 =
   turning his feare.
457 st. 28. *Him thus* (Upton and Church).
   1596 = *Her thus ;* 1609 = *He thus.*
460 c. vii, st. 1. *darts* (1609) : 1596 = *dart.*
465 st. 34. *sad* (1609) : 1596 = *said.*
468 c. viii, st. 12. *made her* (Church). Old editions = *made him.*
476 c. ix, st. 1. *vertuous* (1609) : 1596 = *vertues.*
477 st. 11. *them did see* (Church). Old editions
   = *him did see.*
478 st. 17. *quest.* Old editions = *guest.*
479 st. 26. *Then* (Church). 1596 = *Their ;* 1609 =
   There.
480 st. 30. *repayed* (1609) : 1596 = *repayred.*
481 st. 37. *sir knights* (Upton). Old editions =
   Sir knight.
481 st. 39, l. 8. 1596 inserts, between *wretch*
   and *and I,* which may = *aye.* This is
   dropped by 1609.
484 c. x, st. 19. *meanest* (1609) : 1596 = *nearest.*
492 c. xi, st. 17. *age.* For rhyme. Old editions = *times.*
494 st. 34. *Grant.* Old editions = *Guant.*
496 st. 48. *Eudore.* 1596, 1609 = *Endore.*
503 Bk. V, Prologue, st. 11. *stead* (1609):
   1596 = *place.*
517 c. iii, st. 11, l. 7. *The other.* 1596 = *Th'*
   other.
   l. 9. *the other.* 1596, 1609 = *th' other.*
526 c. iv, st. 36. *watchman* (1609) : 1596 =
   watchmen.
529 c. v, st. 12, l. 2. 1596 has no comma after
   saw.
538 c. vi, st. 16. *thinge* (Collier). Old editions =
   things.
538 st. 19. *the even-tide* (1609) : 1596 = *th' even-*
   tide.
540 st. 29. *armed,* 1596 = *arm'd.*
542 c. vii, st. 6, l. 9. *his.* Old editions = *her ;*
   but v. st. 15, 16.

PAGE

553 c. viii, st. 40. *well knowen* (1609) : 1596 =
   well knowne.
557 c. ix, st. 18. *hard* (1609) : 1596 = *hart.*
558 st. 26. *Bon font* (Church). 1596, 1609 =
   Bon fons.
559 st. 33. *rebellious* (1609) : 1596 = *rebellions.*
562 c. x, st. 3. *Americke* (Todd). Old editions =
   Armericke, which may be meant for Ar
   morica ; but, in such a passage, Spensei
   would hardly ignore Guiana and Vir
   ginia.
562 st. 8. *idole.* Old editions= *idols.*
572 c. xi, st. 40. *shall sure aby* (1611) : 1596, 1609
   = *shall by.*
573 st. 41. *know* (Upton). Old editions= *knew.*
575 st. 61. *froward* (1609) : 1596 = *forward.*
577 c. xii, st. 1. *enduren* (1609) : 1596 = *endure.*
577 st. 6, l. 5. 1596 has no comma after *feare.*
578 st. 16. *sight.* 1596 = *fight.*
583 Bk. VI, Prologue, st. 6. *fame* (Jortin). 1596,
   1609 = *name.*
590 c. ii, st. 3. *deed and word* (1609) : 1596 =
   act and deed. In this stanza *eares* and
   eyes are, in the old editions, transposed.
600 c. iii, st. 30. *thorough* (1609) : 1596 = *through.*
   Perhaps Spenser wrote *prepared through.*
605 c. iv, st. 13. *Where* (i609) : 1596 = *There.*
608 c. v, arg. *Serena* (Hughes). Old editions =
   Matilda, probably by confusion with c.
   iv, st. 29.
613 st. 39. *gree* (1609) : 1596 = *glee.*
616 c. vi, st. 16. *the other* (1609) : 1596 = *th' other.*
616 st. 17. *Calepine* (Hughes). Old editions =
   Calidore.
619 st. 35. *fight* (1609) : 1596 = *right.*
620 c. vii, st. 3. *armed* (1609) : 1596 = *arm'd.*
634 c. viii, st. 47. *toyle* (1609) : 1596 = *toyles.*
638 c. ix, st. 28. *the heavens.* 1596, 1609 = *th'*
   heavens.
641 st. 46. *did dwell* (1611) : 1596, 1609 = *did*
   well.
641 c. x, st. 2, l. 9. *in* (1609) : 1596 = *on.*
644 st. 24. *froward* (1611) : 1596, 1609 = *forward.*
660 c. xii, st. 41. *cleanest.* Old editions = *clear-*
   est, but the following *From* supports the
   emendation suggested by rhyme.
660 Bk. VII. For convenience of reference
   these cantos have been headed ' Book
   VII.'
661 c. vi, st. 7. *the empire.* 1609 = *th' empire.*
668 c. vii, st. 2. *feeble* (Hughes). Old editions =
   sable. Cf. Bk. I, c. xi, st. 6, *Hymn Love.*
   27, *Hymn Beautie,* 3.
669 st. 9. *Kinde.* Old editions = *Kindes,* but
   Spenser probably knew Chaucer's verse
   well enough.
674 st. 41. *rade.* For rhyme. Old editions =
   rode. Cf. Bk. V, c. ii, st. 13.

DAPHNAÏDA

Since the British Museum copy of the edition
of 1591 lacks the letter of dedication, I have
been obliged, for this letter, to follow the text
of Morris.
683 391. *till.* Old editions = *tell.*

COLIN CLOUTS COME HOME AGAINE

ASTROPHEL, ETC.

AMORETTI AND EPITHALAMION

FOWRE HYMNES

COMMENDATORY SONNETS

VAN DER NOOT'S THEATRE

LETTERS

NOTES

The system of reference is that used in the Glossary. The numbers go in pairs, in which the first (of heavier type) stands for the page, the second for the line, stanza, or sonnet number on that page. Thus, **97**, 570 = p. 97, line 570 (in *Mother Hubberds Tale*); **326**, 6 = p. 326, stanza VI (in *The Faerie Queene*, Bk. III, c. I); **730**, 67 = p. 730, sonnet LXVII (in the *Amoretti*). Occasionally, where there is no number, the title is given in brief. Thus, **141**, *Grey* = the sonnet to Lord Grey prefixed to *The Faerie Queene* (on p. 141). One exception is to be remarked: in notes upon *The Faerie Queene* or any of the sonnet series, the number of the stanza or sonnet which contains the word or passage commented upon is given in Roman numerals, instead of Arabic.

The following abbreviations are used : —

arg. = argument.	*lit.* = literally.
Bk. = Book.	*M. E.* = Middle English.
c. = canto.	*N. E. D.* = New English Dictionary.
cent. = century.	*p.* = page.
cf. = compare.	*plur.* = plural.
cst. = construction.	*pp.* = past participle.
f. = and the following.	*pres.* = present tense.
fig. = figuratively.	*pret.* = preterite or past tense.
Fr. = French.	*Prol.* = the prologue or introductory stanzas to
imper. = imperative.	each book of *The Faerie Queene*.
impers. = impersonal.	*pron.* = pronoun.
infin. = infinitive.	*q. v.* = which see.
intrans. = intransitive.	*reflex.* = reflexive.
Ital. = Italian.	*st.* = stanza.
l. = line.	*v.* = see.
Lat. = Latin.	*v. n.* = see note on.

1, THE SHEPHEARDES CALENDER. Title. *Proportionable :* corresponding.

4, TO HIS BOOKE. 3. *president :* precedent, pattern. Cf. **521,** 2.

    10. *All as :* the use of *all* for a mere intensive is of the commonest in Spenser. Cf. **188,** 28, **37,** 81.

5, EPISTLE. 1. *Uncouthe, unkiste :* v. *Troilus & Criseyde,* I, 809.

    35. *the knitting . . . intricate :* the composition so compact and periodic.

6, 110. *the compasse of hys bent :* the extent of his purpose.

    130. *other some :* some others. Cf. **292,** 35.

    158. *conne them thanke :* know, feel gratitude to them.

    166. *leaste :* i. e. least educated.

    174. *hunt the letter :* alliterate; the stock Elizabethan term.

7, 222. *wel sented :* gifted with keen scent.

    224. *principals :* large wing feathers.

    237. *be proportioned :* correspond.

    240. *an olde name :* ' The Calendar of Shepherds,' an almanac enriched with doctrine on the health of the soul and of the body, astronomical data, etc. It was very popular in the first half of the sixteenth century.

    259. *furre estraunged :* absent far abroad.

    273. *voued :* devoted. Cf. **29** *arg.*

    300. *envie of :* indignation at.

8, GENERALL ARGUMENT. 30. *sentence :* meaning.

9, 119. *minded.* v. n. **257,** 40.

    JANUARYE. 9. *some care he tooke :* he was suffering some affliction. Cf. **342,** 5.

10, 28. *wast :* wasted.

    33. *hoary frost.* Cf. ' sunny beames,' **208,** 12.

    58. *cracknelles :* thin, crisp biscuits.

    63. *deignes :* accepts, views with favor. Cf. **705,** 21; also ' vouchsafe,' **607,** 34.

    65. *devise :* invention. Cf. **12,** 95.

    66. *laughes :* derides.

    71. *the while abye :* expiate (the time of) their failure.

    77. *sonned :* i. e. sunned.

11, JANUARYE GLOSSE. 10. *unlikelyhoode, etc. :* i. e. Latin names would be incongruous in rustic English verse.

    48. *Unico Aretino :* E. K. obviously means the infamous Pietro Aretino. The epithet *unico*, however, was properly the badge of another Aretine, Bernardo Accolti, famous for improvisation in verse.

    78. *leaning on hope :* Cf. **208,** 14. *Anchòra speme,* ' he still hopes,' gives a typical pun.

    FEBRUARIE *arg.* 6. *unhappy :* ill conditioned. v. n. **90,** 49.

    FEBRUARIE. 4. *All as :* just as if.

    8. *it avales :* each tail droops.

    9. *Lewdly :* ignorantly. Cf. **14,** 245.

12, 14. *fall :* course of decline.

    17. *Selfe :* myself. v. n. **53,** 76.

    30. *like Good Fryday :* i. e. ruefully.

    43. *chamfred :* a ' chamfer ' is a groove or fluting cut in stone or wood.

    52. *wouldest :* wouldst desire.

    57. *lopp and top :* ' exuberant growth, that which is cut off in trimming a tree or bush ' (Herford).

75. *venteth :* snuffeth.
85. *kenst little good :* knowest little of proper behavior. Cf. **16,** 56.
90. *greevaunce :* suffering. Cf. **125,** 3.
95. *novells :* stories (Ital. *novelle*).
13, 110. *larded :* fattened.
114. *honor :* foliage.
116. *thelement :* the air. Though earth, water and fire were equally elements, air was regarded as the element *par excellence.* When the others are mentioned, it is commonly with a distinguishing adjective, as in **390,** 15, **271,** 5.
131. *lusty :* pleasant, handsome.
133. *wast :* useless. Cf. **150,** 42.
151. *Pleaseth you :* may it please you.
160. *painted :* false, plausible.
162. *colowred crime :* false accusation.
166. *primrose.* v. n. **693,** 560.
14, 208. *sacred with :* consecrated by.
245. *lewd :* foolish.
FEBRUARIE GLOSSE. 16. *Chaucers verse :* v. *Hous of Fame,* III, 135 f.
15, 111. *startuppe :* 'a kind of rustic shoes with high tops, or half gaiters' (Nares).
129. *counterbuff :* counter (as in boxing).
16, MARCH. 2. *As weren overwent :* as if we were overcome.
13. *studde :* stem, stock. Cf. **80,** 84.
30. *Or made :* or hast thou been made.
34. *utter :* put forth.
46. *sithens, etc. :* This is but the third morning since the time.
51. *dell :* a pit.
53. *Mought her . . . attones :* If only her neck might have been dislocated at the same time.
54. *neede :* needed.
55. *Thelf :* the elf, imp.
56. *can better good :* knows better what good conduct is. Cf. **12,** 85.
74. *some quicke :* some living thing.
81. *lope :* leaped.
85. The comma after 'I' is the punctuation of the original. To place it, in accordance with modern usage, after 'seeing' is to destroy the cadence of the line. In Spenser the subject is very commonly connected with a preceding participial clause rather than with the main verb. Cf. **238,** 56, **260,** 12, **303,** 54, **335,** 5.
17, 92. *lepped :* i. e. leaped.
111. *peeretree :* pear tree.
MARCH GLOSS. 1. *This Æglogue . . . Theocritus :* It is after the second idyl of Bion.
18, APRILL. 10. *for :* because. Cf. **13,** 126, **299,** 1.
17. *What is he for a ladde :* what sort of a lad is he?
21. *the southerne shephearde :* commonly taken for Sidney, but perhaps more probably Leicester (v. **62,** 225 ff.) or Bishop Young.
19, 25. *is starte :* has broken away. Cf. **594,** 36.
67. *compare :* find a match for. Cf. **211,** 30.
97. *plaine :* absolutely.
20, 126. *principall :* princely.
135. *tawdrie lace :* a band of lace-work bought at the fair of St. Audrey.
138 ff. *coronations :* carnations. *sops in wine :* a carnation mottled red and white. *pawnce :*

pansy. *chevisaunce :* an unknown flower. *flowre delice :* the iris. Cf. **265,** 16.
152. *damsines :* damsons, plums.
156. *taking :* a seizure, throe.
157. *naught caren . . . bent :* they who are so foolishly inclined heed nothing.
APRILL GLOSSE. 25. *glenne :* E. K.'s definition of *glen* is impossible. He evidently guesses at the poet's meaning.
122. *principall.* v. n. **20,** 126.
22, 253. *poesye :* posy, motto.
23, MAYE. 4. *gawdy greene :* a yellowish green.
38. *fondnesse :* foolishness. Cf. **724,** 37. *inly :* heartily.
48. *Of other :* by others. Cf. **19,** 90, **426,** 2.
49. *What fallen :* what troubles befall.
63. *What . . . tend :* wherefore should shepherds attend to, etc.
24, 69. *spent in cost :* expended.
75. *Algrind :* Grindal, Archbishop of Canterbury, 1575–83, friendly to the Puritans.
78. *impaire :* deteriorate. Cf. **522,** 8.
80. *countenaunce :* social appearances. Cf. **101,** 846.
83. *regard :* have care for.
99. *straight.* v. n. **731,** 71.
102. *entent :* the particular endeavor as distinguished from the general end.
106. *fee in sufferaunce :* revenues allowed them.
131. *baile nor borrowe :* surety nor pledge.
146. *right :* absolutely.
25, 157. *beare of :* fend off.
158. *seemeth :* is seemly.
164. *none accordaunce :* no terms of agreement.
175. *too very :* too absolutely.
177. *dame :* i. e. dam.
184. *favour :* comeliness.
191. *as he mought me :* as may he (bless) me. Cf. **36,** 13.
192. *jollitee :* prettiness.
196. *displaie :* spread out.
219. *collusion :* craft.
231. *amazed :* 'threw into confusion' (Herford).
26, 237. *be kend :* been recognized.
240. *babes :* dolls, puppets.
241. *biggen :* a close-fitting cap or hood.
251. *clinck :* keyhole, latch (?).
264. *lack of dead :* short of death.
265. *your beastlyhead :* your beasthood.
266. *donne :* dun.
299. *Of which . . . prise :* which her son had rated too high (i. e. at the price of his life).
309. *Sir John :* a stock term for a Roman Catholic priest.
312. *and if :* if, indeed. Cf. **36,** 21.
29, JUNE arg. 1. *vowed :* devoted. Cf. **7,** 273.
JUNE. 13. *boste :* display. Cf. **270,** 50.
20. *winding :* either pliable, or bending, drooping. *witche :* probably a variety of ash.
24. *elvish :* malicious.
27. *heydeguyes :* hays. The hay was 'a country dance having a winding or serpentine movement' (N. E. D.).
38. *stayed :* staid, sober. Cf. **258,** 1, **317,** 29.
39. *above :* on the surface.
43. *queene apples :* quinces.
30, 53. *lower spring :* undergrowth.

65. *conne no skill :* know (have) no understanding. Cf. **32**, 45.

76. *falls hem best :* it best befalls them.

78. *frame :* express.

82. *homely as I can :* in such homely style as I am capable of.

95. *learne :* for similar use cf. **180**, 12, **182**, 25, **378**, 36.

31, JUNE GLOSSE. 93. *staffe :* stave, stanza.

32, 123. *suggestion :* temptation.

JULYE *arg.* 4. *Morrell :* perhaps Elmer or Aylmer, Bishop of London, 1577–94, a leader of the High Church party.

JULYE. 5. *swayne :* hired servant.

9. *God shield :* God forbid.

13. *fast :* sure.

28. *overture :* open or exposed place.

29. *thee lust :* it please thee.

31. *what :* thing, things. Cf. **635**, 7.

34. *rekes, etc.* v. E. K. glosse (**34**, 47).

36. *blere myne eyes :* deceive, hoodwink me.

45. *con of Muses skill.* v. n. **30**, 65.

33, 72. *hilles :* Final *es*, for the modern *s*, particularly in the genitive, is not infrequently used by Spenser as a distinct syllable. Cf. **63**, 286, **94**, 308; v. n. **77**, 508.

74. *Our Ladyes Bowre :* the Holy House of Loreto. E. K. here manifestly misunderstands the poet.

78. *haunten rathe :* resort early.

85. *melampode :* black hellebore.

86. *teribinth :* the turpentine-tree.

119. *sample :* example.

131. *in eche degree :* in every point.

140. *shepheards kynd :* class of shepherds.

160. *in place :* in his very presence.

162. *first of all his cote :* chief in the fold, in care of the sheep.

171. *so nighly wore :* worn so nearly out.

173. *pall :* rich cloth.

34, 184. *misusage :* abuse, corrupt practice.

188. *chippes :* parings of bread-crust.

193. *thriftye :* abundant.

195. *What neede hem :* Wherefore is it necessary for them to.

199. *kernes.* v. **35**, 158. *knaves :* menials.

215 ff. This seems to be an allegory of Grindal's (v. n. **24**, 75) disgrace with the Queen for refusing to repress the Puritans. The Queen hoped to break them by him; the result was his own disaster. The name appears as both Algrind and Algrin, with inconsistency perhaps intentional.

35, JULY GLOSSE. 151. *Goore :* i. e. Gower.

166. *alludeth :* ascribeth.

36, AUGUST *arg.* 7. *proper :* comely. Cf. **52**, 123.

AUGUST. 1. *game :* stake.

7. What the devil has brought you to this state ?

13. *mischief mought :* may mischief, etc. Cf. **25**, 191.

24. *was dared :* was challenged (in vain).

37, 41. *in the playne field :* in open contest.

67. *saye.* v. n. **412**, 8.

38, 130. *uprightly :* justly, truly. Cf. **39**, 26.

134. *wroughten :* worked, carved.

148. *matter of his deede :* i. e. verse of his making, composition.

149. *listneth :* listen.

164. *voyd :* depart. Cf. **715**, 35.

178. *yrksome :* grievous. v. n. **698**, 906.

39, AUGUST GLOSSE. 26. *uprightly :* justly, exactly.

49. *Willye not yeelding :* ' vinto non vitto' may be rendered ' vanquished not subdued.'

SEPTEMBER. 10. *at mischiefe :* by misfortune.

40, 24. *astate :* condition.

41. *carven :* cut. Cf. **283**, 22.

44. *bate :* baited.

45. *state :* stately.

58. *Wel-away the while :* alas the time. Cf. **9**, 8.

63. *here by there :* here and there.

84. *the more :* the greater number.

93. *balk :* miss. v. n. **649**, 16.

41, 103. *to mirke :* too, very obscure.

109. *blont :* blunt, rude.

113. *graseth :* makes ravage.

120. *in theyr steads :* ' in their abodes, among themselves' (Herford).

122. *pricke :* the peg that fastened the clout, or bull's eye, to the target.

124. *brace hem about :* encompass them.

130. *wagmoires overgrast :* quagmires overgrown with grass.

146. *they had be better :* A confusion of two cst. : they had better, it would have been better for them to have.

169. *mayntenaunce :* decorum.

171. *Roffynn :* Dr. John Young, Master of Pembroke Hall during Spenser's residence; created Bishop of Rochester (Roffensis) in 1578. He then made Spenser his secretary.

175. *convenable :* consistent.

176. *selje :* own. Cf. **53**, 46.

42, 198. *weanell wast.* v. **143**, 112.

232. *with shepheard sittes not :* (it) becomes not shepherd to. Cf. **149**, 30.

240. *chaungeable rest :* intervals of rest.

246. *mought I thee praye Of :* let me beg you for.

43, SEPTEMBER GLOSSE. 16. *usurped of :* used by.

72. *christened :* Christian.

44, OCTOBER. 14. *fry :* young folk.

24. *trayned :* allured.

35. *sheddeth :* is shed, disperseth.

41. *doubted :* redoubted, feared. Cf. **53**, 22.

45, 49 f. : i. e. When vigorous playing of more martial themes has relaxed the strings of your lyre, lowered its pitch. Cf. **217**, 7.

68. *brought a bedde of :* was delivered of, as in childbirth, or, was brought to the couch of.

70. *put in preace :* to set forth for competition.

75. *fayne :* i. e. depict imaginatively.

78. *Tom Piper :* the piper who played for the morris-dancers.

87 f. *Her peeced . . . scanne :* Her patched feathers are not in condition for such an attempt : to mount to such a famous flight pertains to Colin.

105. *Let powre :* let him pour. *thriftie :* plenteous. Cf. **34**, 193.

114. *queint :* i. e. elegantly accoutred. *in her equipage :* in her retinue (cf. **104**, 1118), or 'her' may mean Bellona's, and 'equipage' array.

46, 119. *shall han their bellies layd :* shall have been delivered of their young.

OCTOBER GLOSSE. 23. *conspyre :* agree.

48, NOVEMBER arg. 3. *Dido :* apparently some lady of Leicester's family.

5. *required :* requested. v. **213,** 50.

NOVEMBER. 16. *in Fishes haske :* The sun enters the constellation Pisces, not in November, but in February. v. **674,** 43.

23. *sike Poetes prayse :* praise as a poet of such verse.

24. *Relieve :* take up again.

26. *Before him, etc. :* in his presence it befits the hedge sparrow to be silent. Cf. **42, 232.**

39. *went :* walked. Cf. **167,** 23.

43. *rownde :* well turned.

49, 52. *as I conne, etc. :* as well as I know how, I will exert my knowledge or skill.

91. *quaile :* perish.

96. *cracknells.* v. n. **10,** 58.

113. *Lobbin :* probably Leicester.

50, 131. *without remorse :* without relenting, intermission ; also l. 167.

155. *marked scope :* target aimed at. Cf. **597,** 5.

171. *cease thy sorrowes sourse :* check the spring, or flow, of thy grief.

183. *Unwise . . . to weete :* Lacking wisdom to know, and therefore wretched.

52, NOVEMBER GLOSSE. 79. *Gaskin :* George Gascoigne.

DECEMBER arg. 3. *proportioneth :* compareth.

DECEMBER. 15. *sonet :* a little poem or song. In the original of Marot, *chansonettes.*

53, 17. *cabinet :* bower. v. **324,** 83.

22. *doubted.* v. n. **44,** 41.

23. *went :* walked, ranged. Cf. **48,** 39.

27. *pricket :* a buck in his second year.

46. *Pan his owne selfe pype :* Pan's own pipe. Cf. **41,** 176.

68. *formall rowmes :* symmetrical compartments.

75. *also :* even so.

76. *selfe :* itself. Used as equivalent to the Latin *ipse* in various persons. Cf. **326,** 6, **316,** 23, 12, 17, **355,** 38, **347,** 46.

78. *shame :* disaster.

54, 81. *sale :* sallow, a net of sallow withes.

87. *soothe :* augury.

98. *harvest :* autumn; also l. 129.

119. *loser :* too loose, fickle. The reference is, of course, to Rosalind.

120. *One :* i. e. God.

55, DECEMBER GLOSSE. 25. *hath alwayes aspect to :* in strict astrological language, only a heavenly body can have aspect to a heavenly body. E. K. means that Venus governs and implies beauty.

56, EPILOGUE. 10. *the Pilgrim, etc. :* The author of the *Plowman's Tale,* a satire on the clergy, written nominally as one of the *Canterbury Tales* and, in sixteenth-century editions of Chaucer, added to the series. Spenser evidently did not accept the tale as Chaucer's. He may have thought it Langland's, as did Dryden (*Preface to Fables*).

59, THE RUINES OF TIME. *Letter* 1. *bountifull :* full of goodness, excellent. Cf. **115,** *Letter.*

13. *disdeigned the world of :* deemed the world unworthy of.

THE RUINES OF TIME. 1. *on :* one.

3. *Verlame :* Verulamium, near St. Albans, one of the chief towns of Roman Britain.

61, 102. *Troynovant :* London.

116. *prizde with :* rated at.

62, 163. *lamentable :* lamenting.

169. *Cambden :* William Camden, the antiquarian. His *Britannia* appeared in 1586.

184. *A mightie Prince :* Leicester, died 1588.

189. *Right and loyall :* Leicester's motto, *Droit et loyal.*

190. *I saw him die :* Leicester having died at Cornbury Lodge in Oxfordshire, commentators have been puzzled by these words; but Verlame (chosen, as a type of vanished greatness, to set forth the tragedy of the great house) is using no more than ordinary imaginative freedom.

204. *oaker :* ochre.

216. *the foxe :* probably Burghley, as in ' Mother Hubberd's Tale.'

63, 233. *trie :* experience. v. **460,** 2.

239. *his brother :* Ambrose Dudley, Earl of Warwick, died 1589.

245. *His noble spouse :* Anne Russell.

260. *his sister :* Mary Dudley, wife of Sir Henry Sidney, mother of Sir Philip, died 1586. *thy father :* Francis, 2d Earl of Bedford, died 1585.

267. *He, noble bud :* Edward Russell, grandson of the 2d Earl of Bedford, and himself the 3d Earl. ' His sonne' (l. 266) either is a slip or means his heir, descendant.

274. *thy husbands sister.* v. n. l. 260.

278–315. Sir Philip Sidney, died 1586.

279. *brood :* offspring, child, as in l. 379.

286. *worldes.* v. n. **33,** 72. Cf. l. 620, 675.

64, 317. *thine owne sister :* Mary Sidney, Countess of Pembroke.

328. *Arcadian pipe :* an allusion to the *Arcadia,* Sidney's pastoral romance.

341. *heroes :* here and elsewhere, with few exceptions, pronounced he-ró-es. v. n. **33,** 72.

344. *of themselves :* themselves.

370. *repose :* place, set.

65, 388. One of the abbreviated articles here was meant to count for a full syllable, *the,* not *th'.* Some editors fill out the line by making *dies* dissyllabic — an impossibility.

408. *aspired :* raised up.

429. *from to die :* Cf. ' from to wreak,' **284,** 28.

436. *Melibœ :* Sir Francis Walsingham, died April 6, 1590. His poet is Thomas Watson; who in the same year published a Latin eclogue in his memory, entitled *Melibœus.*

442–444. *Those two, etc. :* ' There be two things that grieve my heart . . . a man of war that suffereth poverty ; and men of understanding that are not set by.' Ecclesiasticus, **26,** 28. In the sixteenth century this book was sometimes reckoned among the ' Books of Solomon.' *indignities :* stirrings of resentment. Cf. **465,** 36.

447–455. The allusion is to Burghley.

66, 490. *pageants :* tableaux, usually allegorical,

exhibited on stages or moving cars as part of a public celebration.

491 ff.: The first group of six sonnets is concerning Leicester; the second group concerning Sidney.

67, 523–525. Apparently some unexecuted device for the *Faery Queen*. v. Bk. III, c. v. *staine*. v. n. **679**, 112.

561. *two beares :* Leicester and his brother, the Earl of Warwick. v. **44**, 48.

567. *compast*. v. n. **445**, 30.

572. *oppresse :* crush, smother.

68, 609. *Philisides :* Phili(p) Sid(ney), 'lover of the star.' A name invented by Sidney for himself. 'Astrophel' and 'Stella' (his mistress) are derivatives.

611. *divin'd*. v. n. **681**, 214.

616. *the Northern Beare :* Leicester.

69, 665. *Whether*. v. n. **157**, 37.

70, THE TEARES OF THE MUSES. 9. *traversing :* turning aside.

22. *rebound :* reverberate. Cf. **179**, 8, **411**, 6, **651**, 26.

71, 36. *like :* in like manner, likewise. *heavily :* grievously. v. n. **678**, 12.

53. *crew :* used by Spenser without derogatory implication. Cf. **199**, 50, **293**, 40.

70. *type*. v. n. **560**, 42.

72, 143. *event :* fate. Cf. **86**, 534.

73, 204. *laughing game :* laughing stock.

207. *counter :* encounter.

208. *Willy :* The main question is whether or not ' that same gentle spirit ' (l. 217) refers to ' our pleasant Willy.' It would certainly seem to, except that Willy is said (l. 208) to be ' dead of late ' and the ' gentle spirit ' (l. 221) to ' sit in idle cell.' If the two are different, Willy may be Richard Tarleton, the comic actor, died 1588. The ' gentle spirit ' is almost certainly John Lyly, the author of court comedies, who from 1584 to about 1590 produced no plays.

232. *breaches of her singulfs :* the intervals of her sobbing. Cf. **354**, 35.

74, 265. *stout :* arrogant. Cf. **494**, 30.

76, 386. *devicefull :* full of imaginative possibilities.

436. *degenerate :* degrade.

77, 462. *the starris seaven :* the Great Bear, otherwise known as Charles' Wain.

466. *prize of value :* excellence of valor. Cf. **267**, 29, **405**, 14.

508. Apparently, *movement* is here of three syllables. Cf. *safety*, **315**, 17, *avengement*, **119**, 240.

512, 514. *viewe, vew :* For such repetition of a word in rhyme, with slightly different spelling to disguise the repetition, cf. *saints, sayncts* (**33**, 113, 115), *vade, fade* (**112**, 20); the converse of the old rule that words of like form might be rhymed, if of different sense.

519. *case :* chance, fortune.

78, 549. *diapase :* diapason.

585. *worldes*. v. n. **33**, 72.

591. *savour :* relish.

79, VIRGILS GNAT. 16, *strong :* i. e. strung.

21. *brood :* brooding place, as in **272**, 8.

80, 57. *roome :* place, station. Cf. **205**, 41, **359**, 11.

72. *befalls :* falls in their way, is to be found.

84. *stud*. v. n. **16**, 13.

105. *whelky :* shelly (?).

81, 119. *neate :* clear.

141. *resolv'd :* relaxed.

149. *Ascræan bard :* Hesiod.

154. *batt :* staff, crook. v. **93**, 217.

82, 196. *taking to hoste :* entertaining. ' hoste ' = a place of entertainment.

197. *those trees :* poplars.

201. *that same tree :* the almond-tree.

220. *her brothers strokes :* the hot beams of the sun. *whose boughes she, etc. :* i. e. the ivy enfolds the poplar's boughs. The translation is considerably confused.

223. The myrtle tree is Myrrha. Cf. **340**, 41.

83, 284. *rare :* with an interval, apart.

308. *tyre :* deck or gird. Cf. **670**, 11.

84, 333. *in lieu of :* in return for.

353. *thankes :* service.

362. *safetie*. v. n. **77**, 508. *tender*. v. n. **372**, 51.

85, 396. *unkinde*. v. n. **340**, 43.

417. *waladay :* welladay.

444. *Tartar :* Tartarus. v. l. 543.

448. *trespassed :* committed wrongfully.

86, 494. *coy :* disdainful.

497. *divorces :* i. e. deaths.

511. *Rhœtean shore :* from Rhesus, one of the rivers flowing from Ida into the sea.

514. *thwarting :* interposing.

534. *event :* success. Cf. **72**, 143.

87, 542. *gulphing :* eddying, swirling.

543. *Tartarie :* Tartarus. Cf. **191**, 44.

557. *type*. v. n. **560**, 42.

568. *clave :* i. e. cleft.

600. *vertue*. v. n. **109**, 8.

88, 615. *vow'd :* devoted (to ruin), doomed.

616. *Trembling :* trembling at.

639. *heavily :* sorrowfully.

673. *Sabine flowre :* the savine.

90, MOTHER HUBBERDS TALE. 1–8. 'The righteous Maide' is Astræa, who, after leaving earth at the close of the Golden Age, became the constellation Virgo. The sun enters the sign of Virgo in August, in which month Sirius, the dog star, (' the hot Syrian dog ') is near him. The sign of July is Leo, during part of which month Sirius has been with the sun; hence, when the sun enters Virgo, Sirius, attending him, leaves 'baiting the chafed Lion.' The sickness of the dog days was, of course, ascribed to Sirius. v. **32**, 17–24 and E. K.'s note thereon. *upbraide*. v. n. **479**, 28.

35. *seem'd :* beseemed. Cf. **25**, 158.

45. *civill :* civilized. Cf. **583**, 1.

48. *lyeke :* like.

49. *unhappie :* mischievous.

53. *goship :* gossip, crony.

91, 60. *regard :* repute. Cf. l. 685.

85. *lymiter :* ' a friar licensed to beg within a certain district ' (Tyrwhitt).

87. *worldes*. v. n. **33**, 72.

106. *did neede :* was needful.

111. *a Gods name :* of, in God's name. Cf. **41**, 100.

92, 188. *for . . . bruted :* be reported as branded cattle astray.

93, 217. *bat :* quarter-staff.
  268. *that . . . balke :* which lay out of the way of his liking (N. E. D.) or (by reverse phrasing) which his taste balked at.
  269. *handsomely :* dexterously.
94, 297. *meanly :* moderately.
  308. *winges.* v. n. **33,** 72.
  309. *Expired.* v. n. **425,** 54.
  323. *acquite themselves unto :* clear themselves in the eyes of.
95, 361. *formall :* i. e. regularly ordained.
  371. *squib :* flashy, pretentious fellow.
  390. *Sir.* v. n. **26,** 309.
  394. *attend.* v. n. **235,** 35. *playes :* sports, play. Cf. **682,** 321.
  400. *bootles boad :* abode, dwelt unprofitably.
96, 453. *trentals :* services of thirty masses for the dead.
  454. *memories :* services for the dead.
  486. *beneficiall :* a benefice, or, a letter presenting to a benefice.
  501. *or :* ere.
  502. *throng :* press, push. The *pret.* of M. E. 'thringen' used as *infin.* Cf. **372,** 44.
  505 f. After the rhymes in Ascham's *Schoolmaster* (ed. Arber, p. 54).
    'To laughe, to lie, to flatter, to face:
    Foure waies in court to win men grace.'
  'Face' = assume a lying countenance.
  506. *companie :* play the good fellow.
  507. *beetle stock :* the handle of a beetle, or large rammer, hence, fig., a tool.
  511. *cast a figure :* make astrological calculations.
  518. *primitias :* first year's revenue.
97, 520. *in privitie :* secretly. Cf. **648,** 8.
  523. *compound a better penie :* make a cheaper bargain.
  527. *cope :* bargain.
  531. *franke :* free.
  547. *discipline :* instruction.
  552. *them sped :* succeeded.
  579. *occasion for their tourne :* opportunity that they could make use of.
98, 620–624. 'The Queen was so much pleased with the results of the Portugal expedition of 1589, that she honored the commanders, and Sir Walter Raleigh among the rest, with a gold chain' (Child).
  Enchaste : encircled or adorned.
  625–630. A sudden break in the sense, due to the revision of 1590. In the text of 1579, the question 'Who now in court doth beare the greatest sway' (l. 616) was probably answered by an allusion to Leicester. In 1590 this was made over into the allusion to the commanders of the Portugal expedition (l. 620 ff.); yet not so carefully but that the original intent still showed (l. 625 ff.). *So wilde a beast* is Leicester; *his late chayne* is his marriage to the Countess of Essex, the revelation of which in 1579 brought him into deepest disgrace with the Queen.
  631. *if fortune thee :* if it befall thee. Cf. **231,** 5.
99, 685. *regard :* worth. Cf. **698,** 933, **649,** 13.
  717. *the brave courtier :* commonly supposed to be modelled on Sidney.

  742. *nigh aymed ring, etc. :* practice for steadiness in directing the spear. A ring was hung up, and the horseman, charging at it, endeavored to carry it off on his spear.
  749. *gowned beast :* horses were sometimes decorated with drapery that nearly swept the ground.
100, 778. *In whatso, etc. :* in whatsoever affair it may please him (the prince) to employ his (the courtier's) person.
  783. *policie.* v. n. **140,** *Hatton.*
  784. *courting :* attendance at court.
  785. *strange :* foreign. Cf. l. 1121, **304,** 64, **117,** 78.
  802. *mumming and masking :* masquerading.
  803. *balliards :* i. e. billiards.
  830. *kindly wise desire :* natural desire of wisdom.
  840. *reach :* launch, aim.
101, 846. *countenaunce.* v. n. **24,** 80.
  857. *coosinage :* i. e. cozenage. *cleanly :* dexterous.
  862. *cleanly coosined :* dexterously cozened.
  883. *abuse :* beguile.
  893. *had ywist :* 'had I known!' an ejaculation of repentance. 'A wise man saith not, had I wist' (*Tottel's Misc.* ed. Arber, p. 244).
  901 f. Spenser felt that what favor he had won with the Queen was rendered nugatory by the opposition of Burghley. The old story has it that Burghley delayed the grant of the pension as long as possible.
  908. *tendance :* waiting.
  910. *assurance :* security.
  913. *himselfe will a daw trie :* will find himself by experience to be a fool. v. n. **517,** 17.
102, 930. *uncased :* i. e. exposed.
  939. *copesmate :* confederate.
  944. *hardnesse :* hardship. Cf. **470,** 27.
  997. *whither :* which of the two. v. n. **157,** 37.
103, 1010. *For making :* lest he should make. Cf. **317,** 35, **368,** 18, **659,** 34.
  1015. *cleanly.* v. n. l. 857.
  1036. *pollicie :* cunning. v. n. **166,** 12.
104, 1086. *Thenceforth.* v. n. **465,** 33.
  1090. *corpse.* v. n. **748,** 135. *invasion :* assault. v. n. **610,** 17.
  1124. *Beavers :* introduced solely as being of 'two kindes,' half fish, half flesh — for so our ancestors believed.
  1137 ff. Apparently directed at Burghley.
  1140. *counterpoint :* artifice. Cf. **23,** *arg.*
  1144. *fiaunt :* fiat, warrant.
  1160. *ferme :* farm, lease (as of the taxes).
105, 1188. *in place :* into the presence of the prince.
106, 1245. *stal'd :* 'Stalling' a debt was forbearing for a time to exact payment. The Fox's penalty should not be remitted or postponed.
  1294. *tempereth :* controls.
  1306. *rackt :* extorted.
107, 1334. *grating :* fretting, consuming. Cf. **390,** 14, **238,** 56, also **526,** 37.
  1380. *uncase :* strip.
108, RUINES OF ROME. Most of the obscurities

in this series are due to misunderstanding or bungling of Du Bellay's French.

II. *Olympus.* v. n. **378, 41.**

IV. *the More :* the Moor.

stomacke : i. e. breast. 16th cent. Fr. *estomac.*

109, VIII. *vertue :* manly worth, valor. Cf. **87, 600, 155,** 19.

vertuous : manly, valorous. Cf. **171,** 1.

nephewes : descendants. Cf. **284,** 29.

111, XVIII. *yearely presidents :* the consuls.

and sixe months greater : and the rule of six months (i. e. the dictatorship) grew still greater.

112, XVIII. *opposing :* making opposition.

XX. *compas :* a circle or sphere.

vade, fade : different forms of the same word, for nominal rhyme. Cf. **513,** 40.

XXII. *Byze :* Byzantium.

113, XXIII. *forborne :* spared.

cancring : cankering, corrupting.

humours superfluitie : Health was supposed to depend on the right proportion and distribution of the four bodily humors: blood, phlegm, yellow bile, black bile. The excess of any one would cause disease.

XXIV. *equall :* of the same kind.

114, XXX. *by degree :* by degrees.

XXXI. *Aemathian fields :* The reference is to the battle of Pharsalus.

115, MUIOPOTMOS. *Letter.* 7. *abandoned from my selfe :* put out of my own jurisdiction, i. e. as having renounced my independence.

8. *vowed.* v. n. **7,** 273.

29. *take in worth :* accept indulgently. Cf. **141,** *Ormond,* **143,** *Penbroke.*

116, MUIOPOTMOS. 13. *detect :* reveal. Cf. **561,** 48.

17. *flies.* v. n. **735,** 20.

117, 78. *oricalche :* brass or some similar metal.

strange. v. n. **100, 785.**

118, 148. *franke :* vigorous.

159. *choicefull :* fickle.

187. *saulge :* sage.

196. *setuale :* valerian.

199. *colworts :* plants of the cabbage kind. *perseline :* purslain; 'comforting,' because it 'doth mitigate the great heat in al the inward parts of the bodye, semblably of the head and eyes' (Sir Thos. Elyot).

119, 229. *all and some :* one and all. Cf. **415,** 30.

240. *avengement.* v. n. **77,** 508.

271. *compare :* vie.

120, 292. *spring :* youth.

297. *empale :* inclose.

121, 380. *principall.* v. n. **20,** 126.

414. *throw :* i. e. throe.

420. *on hed :* headlong.

428. *winges.* v. n. **33,** 72.

124, VISIONS OF THE WORLDS VANITIE. IX.

wring : compel, master.

X. *dreadles :* secure from danger.

125, THE VISIONS OF BELLAY. II. *of Afrike golds enchase :* enchased with, etc.

parget : a facing of ornamental plaster work, for walls or ceiling.

jasp : jasper.

III. *level :* mark.

grievance. v. n. **12, 90.**

IV. *chapters :* capitals.

126, V. *A twinne of forked trees :* the Papacy and the Holy Roman Empire.

VI. *nones :* i. e. nonce.

soyle : the mire caused by her blood.

spoyle : hide. Cf. **117,** 68 ; also **435, 16.**

VII. *haughtie :* lofty.

127, IX. *creakie :* indented with creeks.

X. *this Hydra :* the Papacy.

XI. This sonnet allegorizes the corruption of Christianity by the donation of Constantine.

XII. *rout :* crowd and jostle.

XIII. *sad Florentine :* Petrarch. See *Visions of Petrarch* II, p. 128.

128, XIII. *raisd' againe :* the revival of the Empire by Charlemagne.

XIV. *that same :* the new Jerusalem, Revelation **21.** *Which saw :* The Fr. original makes 'which' the object of the verb.

the messenger, etc. : the Evangelist (St. John).

XV. *Typhœus sister :* Du Bellay means Bellona. The genealogy might be explained from **379,** 47 and **661,** 2 and 3.

136, THE FAERIE QUEENE. *Letter.* 13. *by accidents :* side issues.

17. *plausible :* acceptable.

18. *coloured :* embellished.

39. *coloured :* depicted.

58. *accounted by :* valued according to.

60. *commune sence :* the senses as opposed to the reason.

137, 99. *deedes . . . applyable :* those deeds that are pertinent to, that illustrate.

154. *Presently :* immediately.

172. *The second day :* This account is at odds with **235,** 35 ff.

197. *intendments :* things designed.

138 ff. COMMENDATORY VERSES. Of these poems the first two are by Raleigh, the third by Harvey, the others of unknown authorship.

A VISION. *accesse :* coming.

ANOTHER OF THE SAME. *of the same :* by the same author.

Philumena : Philomel, the nightingale. Cf. **684,** 475.

TO THE LEARNED SHEPEHEARD. *gave thee the bell :* awarded the prize, the supremacy. Cf. **644,** 26.

Alow : praise.

139, ibid. *warres :* makes war on.

Let not conceipt, etc. : let not fancy deceive your sober judgment.

empyring : ruling absolutely, flaming — a characteristic pun.

R. S. *Ludds . . . towne :* London.

H. B. *Desertes findes dew :* merits find due recognition.

140, IGNOTO. *Would raise . . . tend :* would raise a suspicion that the praiser felt some doubt as to the merit of the work, which doubt his elaborate praise would tend to manifest.

set it forth : praise it.

140 ff. DEDICATORY SONNETS.

HATTON. *Policy :* statecraft.

OXENFORD. *vele.* v. n. **145,** 4.

141, ibid. *Heliconian ymps :* the Muses.
That : him that.
NORTHUMBERLAND. *patronize :* protect.
ORMOND. *salvage soyl :* Ireland.
thy brave mansione : at Kilkenny.
Receive . . . in worth. v. n. **115,** *Letter.*
HOWARD. *heroes.* v. n. **64,** 341.
huge castles : the galleons of the Armada.
GREY. *your endlesse debt :* my endless debt to you.
account : render account of.
142, RALEIGH. *To tast :* If one taste.
thy poeme : One canto of this has survived, *The 21st and Last Book of the Ocean to Cynthia,* published by Archdeacon Hannah in 1870. Cf. **325,** 4 and 5.
BURLEIGH. *censure :* judgment.
CUMBERLAND. Cumberland had recently been appointed (1589) Queen's champion. *late assaies :* probably the naval expedition to the Azores, from which he returned in the last days of 1589.
HUNSDON. Henry Carey, Lord Hunsdon, was son of Anne Boleyn's sister. His victory against odds at the battle of the Gelt in Cumberland (1570) ended the rebellion of the northern earls.
BUCKHURST. v. n. **691,** 380.
143, ibid. *unadvised :* unperceived.
COUNTESSE OF PENBROKE. Mary Sidney, sister of Sir Philip, 'that most heroicke spirit.'
in good worth to take. v. n. **115,** *Letter.*
144, LADIES IN THE COURT. *The Chian peincter :* Spenser seems to have in mind Apelles and his Venus of Cos, for which various courtesans of the city served as models. Perhaps he confused this painting with Zeuxis' Helen of Croton, in the painting of which the artist had for models the five most beautiful maidens of the city.
THE FIRST BOOKE, Prologue, I. *in lowly shephards weeds :* in the *Shepherd's Calendar.*
II. *O holy virgin :* Clio.
weaker : too weak ; a very common use of the comparative in Spenser.
III. *Mart :* Mars.
IV. *vile :* lowly.
that . . . type : Gloriana, the Faery Queen.
afflicted : lowly. Cf. **718,** 2.
145, Canto I, III. *bond :* bound.
worshippe : honor. Cf. **231,** 6, **335,** 8.
IV. *vele :* i. e. veil. Cf. **448,** 10, **693,** 495.
wimpled : pleated.
Seemed : it seemed. The omission of the impersonal subject is very common.
in a line : by a cord.
V. *compeld :* summoned (Lat. *compellare*).
146, x. *diverse.* v. n. **239,** 3.
XI. *about :* out of.
by tract : by following the track.
XII. *wade :* go, move.
XIV. *disdaine :* all that would excite disdain or loathing.
XV. *bred :* were born.
147, XVI. *upstart :* started up.
XIX. *grate :* chafe. Cf. **526,** 37, **107,** 1334.
griefe : anger.

XXI. *his later . . . avale :* his flood begins later to subside. . .
148, XXIII. *cumbrous :* harassing. Cf. **290, 17.**
XXIV. *manly :* human.
XXVI. *unkindly :* unnatural.
needeth him : it is necessary for him. For omission of the impers. pron. v. **154,** 12, **161,** 20.
XXVII. *like succeed it may :* similar (i. e. successful adventures) may follow it.
XXVIII. *to frend :* as a friend, on his side, or perhaps, to befriend him. Cf. **343,** 14, **648, 6.**
149, XXX. *as that :* as one who. Cf. **7,** 224.
With holy father sits not : it befits not a hermit. Cf. **42,** 232.
XXXIV. *wyde.* v. n. **539,** 22.
XXXV. *and all things :* and (rest is equivalent to having) all things.
XXXVI. *sad humor :* heavy moisture. For the connection between moistness of the brain and sleep, v. n. **150,** 42.
riddes : sends off.
150, XLI. *ever . . . loft :* Spenser surely has in mind the sound of rain on the roof.
XLII. *waste.* v. n. **13,** 133.
dryer braine : too dry brain. It was believed that what made old folk sleep lightly and little was deficiency of moisture in the brain. That is the reason given by Boccaccio in his *Ameto* for the wakefulness of the old husband of Agapas. Any condition of light, troubled sleep, disturbed by dreams, seems to have been ascribed to deficiency of moisture.
all : altogether. Cf. **237,** 46.
XLIII. *sent :* sense.
XLIV. *diverse :* perverse.
the yvorie dore : that by which false dreams go out.
151, XLVI. *borne without her dew :* brought into being unduly, unnaturally.
L. *halfe enraged.* v. n. **651,** 25.
despight : indignation (not malicious).
152, LIV. *beguiled of :* disappointed in.
LV. *irkesome :* troubled.
Canto II, arg. ruth : misery.
I. *northerne wagoner :* Boötes.
sevenfold teme : Charles' Wain (i. e. the Great Bear).
stedfast starre : the pole star.
153, III. *misdeeming :* causing misconception, misleading. Cf. 'misconceyving night,' **401,** 47.
IV. *repast :* refreshment, repose. Cf. **199,** 2, **520,** 40.
V. *enbracement.* v. n. **77,** 508.
And would : 'he' omitted. Such omission of pron., especially ' it,' is very common. Cf. **159,** 6, l. 9.
hardly : with difficulty. Cf. **160,** 14, **188,** 21, **681,** 231.
VI. *Yrkesome :* weary.
VII. *Titan :* the sun ; the common Elizabethan name.
baser : too humble.
X. *in seeming wise :* in the way of mere appearance.
154, XII. *him chaunst :* it befell him. Cf. ' Him booteth,' **161,** 20.

XIII. *like a Persian mitre :* something like (or, as it were) a Persian mitre. Cf. **185**, 4.

XV. *amazed :* bewildered, stupefied. Cf. **25**, 231, **161**, 22.

XVII. *Each others . . . envies :* each envies the other's. v. Glossary.

spies : i. e. the eyes. Cf. **330**, 36, **633**, 43.

repining : indignant. Cf. **612**, 26.

155, XVIII. *bitter fitt :* the throes of death.

assured : secure, firm.

rigor : violence. Cf. **194**, 18, **361**, 23.

share : slice. Cf. **456**, 19.

from blame . . . blest : lit., preserved him from harm. Spenser means, failed to harm him. Cf. **455**, 13.

XIX. *vertue.* v. n. **109**, 8.

haughty : lofty. Cf. **126**, 7, **296**, 1, **740**, 420.

156, XXVII. *dainty . . . maketh derth :* apparently a proverb = fastidiousness brings scarcity, poverty ; turned by play on words to mean, coyness makes dearness, preciousness.

XXX. *purposes.* v. n. **335**, 4.

gory bloud : gore blood, clotted blood.

XXXI. *that happened :* that which happened.

XXXI. *dreadfull passion :* passion of dread. Cf. 'revenging will,' **161**, 22.

Limbo lake : Limbo was properly a sort of outer room to Hell, for virtuous heathen, unbaptized infants, etc., a place, according to Dante, of 'grief without tortures,' where 'without hope we live in desire.' 'Limbo lake' was taken by Spenser from the *Mirror for Magistrates* as meaning the shores of the Styx, Hell generally. Cf. **261**, 22, **402**, 54.

mistake : mislead.

rare : thin, faint.

157, XXXVI. *take in hand :* maintain.

dye : hazard, chance. Cf. **260**, 13.

XXXVII. *Whether :* which (of the two). Cf. **422**, 32, **476**, 1, **69**, 665.

won. v. n. **245**, 44.

XXXVIII. *when . . . in place :* when none present was fair. v. n. **105**, 1188.

XXXIX. *treen mould :* the form of a tree. Cf. **188**, 26.

158, XLIII. *well :* well being.

suffised : satisfied.

XLV. *careless :* uncared for. Cf. **446**, 38.

Canto III, I. *her brightnes :* i. e. beauty's. The reference may be to audiences with the Queen in 1579 (v. **769**, 52). It may be to Rosalind.

159, II. *touch :* the touchstone, by which gold was tested.

deryv'd : diverted. v. n. **560**, 41.

VI. *As he :* as if he.

160, XI. *her cast in deadly hew :* made her pale as death. 'Hew' in Spenser rarely means color ; but v. **493**, 27.

XIV. *hardly :* with difficulty. She had difficulty in dispelling their fear. Cf. **153**, 5.

XVI. *deadly :* deathlike. Cf. **149**, 36.

nightly . . . severall : thefts by night and pillage in various places. v. n. **301**, 39.

161, XIX. *disdainfull :* indignant.

supprest : For this sense of physical pressing or keeping down cf. **183**. 40, **629**, 18.

XXI. *that . . . Greeke :* Ulysses.

XXII. *parted :* departed. Cf. **681**, 226.

amazed : bewildered, frantic.

revenging will : desire of revenge.

XXIII. *dishonesty :* unchastity.

XXIV. *prevaile :* avail. Cf. **164**, 43.

162, XXVI. *wyde :* to one side. v. n. **539**, 22.

by name : especially, and no other. Cf 'namely,' **675**, 48.

XXVII. *unto . . . light :* befall my sore heart.

XXIX. *that mote . . . accept :* which may it please you to accept.

XXXI. *Orions hound :* Sirius, the dog star.

crownes with cups : salutes with bumpers, cups crowned, filled to the brim.

163, XXXII. *her all that fell :* all that befell her.

XXXIV. *bent :* levelled and aimed.

XXXVII. *in place :* who art present. For a similar purely expletive use v. **185**, 5.

XXXVIII. *in field . . . in round lists :* The distinction is between the open field, wherever foes may meet, and the *champ clos*, or enclosed ground, for set combats.

164, XL. *misfeigning :* feigning with evil intent.

XLIII. *will or nill.* v. n. **462**, 16.

XLIV. *in beastly kind :* in the nature of a beast, as a beast by nature.

165, *Canto IV,* III. *degree and place :* order and rank. Cf. **323**, 79, **468**, 14.

scaped hard : escaped with difficulty. Cf. **611**, 21.

bend his pace : direct his steps.

IV. *timely :* measured. Cf. **171**, 3.

VIII. *Titans.* v. n. **153**, 7.

As envying : The subject is 'throne.'

X. *was layne :* was laid, lay.

166, XII. *pollicie :* in the sense of Macchiavellism.

six wizards : six wise men ; the other deadly sins, of which pride is leader.

XIV. *prancke :* adjust for display. Cf. **246**, 6.

XVI. *hurtlen :* hurtle, rush jostling.

167, XVII. *dispredden :* spread out. Cf. **244**, 40.

XVIII. *Taught . . . applyde :* The beasts were taught to obey the counsellors' beast-like orders, which were accommodated ('applyde'), by reason of like qualities, to the beasts' natures ('kindes') : i. e. each counsellor was of like nature to the beast that he rode.

amis : amice, a priestly vestment.

XXI. *like a crane :* Alciati so represents Gluttony in his 90th emblem.

gorge : what he had swallowed.

XXII. *bouzing can :* a drinking-can.

XXIII. *dry :* thirsty.

go : walk. Cf. **48**, 39.

168, XXVIII. *compare :* gather.

XXX. *chaw :* chew. Cf. **80**, 86, **256**, 29.

chaw : jaw.

XXXI. *say.* v. n. **412**, 8.

169, XXXIV. *car'd for :* was heedful of, shrank from. Cf. **650**, 23. *avengement.* v. n. **77**, 508.

XXXV. *unthrifty scath :* wicked harm.

Saint Fraunces fire : probably St. Anthony's fire, or erysipelas.

XXXIX. *envious* : which he begrudged him.
which ought : who owned.
wage : gage, stake.
XL. *hurtlen* : hurtle, clash.
171, XLIX. *helplesse hap* : unavoidable chance.
dewties : dues.
LI. *that I* : when I. Cf. **221,** 33.
Canto V, I. *vertuous.* v. n. **109,** 8.
III. *timely* : measured. Cf. **165,** 4.
172, V. *a paled greene* : a green enclosed by pal-
ings ; the *champ clos.* v. n. **163,** 38.
173, XVI. *on hight* : on high, loudly. Cf. **617,** 24,
642, 10, **527,** 45.
XVII. *woundes.* v. n. **33,** 72.
embalme : anoint. Cf. **466,** 40.
divide : to run a series of notes into many
shorter ones to the same ground bass or harmony.
174, XIX. *as she . . . plight* : in the same condition in which she had left him.
XXI. *unacquainted* : unwonted, strange.
XXIII. *so evill heare* : are held in such ill repute,
i. e. brought to such open disgrace.
Nightes : a dissyllable. v. n. **33,** 72.
XXV. *excheat* : i. e. gain.
175, XXVIII. *the fine element* : the air. v. n. **13,**
116.
176, XXXV. *reele* : roll.
gin : engine of torture, rack.
XXXVI. *forth* : on. Cf. **350,** 62.
redresse : set to rights, heal. Cf. **344,** 18,
364, 41, **453,** 39.
XXXIX. *smart* : agony.
177, XLIII. *els* : already.
XLIV. *cure* : i. e. care.
XLV. *to ryde* : for riding.
XLVII. *king of Babylon* : Nebuchadnezzar.
178, XLVIII. *That name . . . upbrayd* : Alexander, by posing as son of Jupiter Ammon,
dishonored the name of his real father Philip.
Canto VI, I. *bewaile* : ' The suggestion that it
was meant as a derivative of *wale,* to choose,
is worthless ' (N. E. D.).
foolhappie : blindly lucky.
II. *dreed* : object of reverence. Cf. **144,** 4, **469,**
17.
179, ibid. *one to other Ynd* : the East to the West
Indies.
III. *treatie* : diplomacy. Cf. **327,** 11.
IV. *diamond* : adamant, a more or less fictitious
mineral or metal, supposed of supreme hard-
ness. Cf. **201,** 19.
VI. *comfortlesse* : helpless. Cf. **336,** 14.
VIII. *rebownded.* v. n. **70,** 22.
IX. *blubbred* : used several times by Spenser,
always seriously, **232,** 13, **505,** 13, **685,** 551.
180, XI. *fearfull fit* : fit of fear   v. n. **156,** 32.
horror : roughness. Cf. ' horrid,' **182,** 25.
feare . . . obey : to allay her fear, they
teach their backward-bent knees to obey her
humbly, i. e. kneel to her.
XIII. *suspect of crime* : suspicion (i. e. fear) of
reproach.
XIV. *horned* : horny.
XV. *intent* : attention, gaze.
XVI. *bethinkes not* : cannot determine.
181, XVII. *pourtraiture* : image.

XXIII. *aspyre* : grow up.
XXIV. *bastard.* v. n. **251,** 42.
182, XXV. *horrid vew* : savage appearance.
XXX. *repaire* : return.
ofspring : family, i. e. the Satyrs. Cf. **305,**
69.
XXXI. *compare* : gather, learn (?). Cf. **168,** 28.
XXXII. *thence arise* : rise and depart, get away
thence. Cf. ' thence amounted,' **206,** 54.
183, XXXV. *Jacobs staffe* : a pilgrim's staff. In
religious art, St. James is distinguished by a
pilgrim's staff and a scallop shell. Cf. **678,** 41.
XXXVII. *the further processe, etc.* : i. e. what remained to be known of the tragedy.
XL. *supprest.* v. n. **161,** 19.
184, XLII, ll. 7–9. Sansloy refers to the events
of **163,** 33–39. ' Had the knight been with
his arms, Archimago, who foolishly bore
them, would not now be regretting the mistake he made in venturing to fight me. Your
own experience, I hope, will soon confirm
his mistake.' The last line is obscured by
the word play of ' errour' and ' proven true.'
XLIII. *plate* : armor made of plates of metal,
which encased the body like a shell.
maile : armor made of interlinked rings of
metal, which fitted the body like a garment.
Mail was sometimes worn beneath plate. Cf.
259, 9.
pitty. v. n. **656,** 9.
XLIV. *entire* : with full vigor.
XLV. *drery* : horrible.
XLVII. *lovers token, etc.* : In tournaments a
knight often bore his lady's token, a sleeve,
a glove, upon his helmet. Sansloy is speaking
of the blow that he aims at Satyrane's head.
185, XLVIII. *this battels end* : The outcome of
the battle is never told. Sansloy reappears in
241, 18 ff. ; Satyrane in **377,** 29 ff. Spenser
did not follow the movements of his minor
characters with the scrupulous care of Ariosto.
Canto VII, II. *plate.* v. n. **184,** 43.
IV. *like a girlond* : as it were, a garland. Cf.
154, 13.
V. *in place.* v. n. **163,** 37.
186, IX. *expyre* : come to the end of their term.
Cf. **283,** 24.
XI. *That when* : 'That' (= who) is redundant.
Cf. **187,** 20, **583,** 4, **541,** 37, **509,** 11.
praunce : stalk.
XII. *so maynly mercilesse* : with such merciless
might.
187, XIII. *th'onely breath* : the mere breath.
188, XXI. *hardly.* v. n. **153,** 5.
XXIII. *seeled up* : To tame a hawk, the fal-
coner ' seeled' its eyes, i. e. stitched the lids
together.
deadly : mortal, of death. Cf. **436,** 20.
XXVI, l. 9. The dwarf was in doubt whether
the knight, having been made captive, were
alive or dead.
XXVII. *sorrowfull assay* : the assault of sorrow.
v. n. **156,** 32.
XXVIII. *assynd* : pointed out.
189, XXXI. *horrid.* v. n. **409,** 44.
couched on the bever : The bever was the movable visor of a helmet. Except in fight, when

it was lowered to protect the face, its position was on top of the helmet in front of the crest.

190, XXXVII. *rowels :* ' the *rolling* part of the canon-bit ' (Child).

XXXIX. *helplesse.* v. n. **739,** 340.

XLI. *paire :* impair, weaken.

XLII. *That her perswaded. . . . And said :* The omission of 'they' and 'she' exemplifies a cst. common in Spenser.

191, XLIII. *equal destinies Did ronne about :* The destinies moved equably in their spheres. The reference seems to be to the influence of the stars.

XLIV. *Tartary :* Tartarus. Cf. **85,** 444.

XLV. *coast :* region. Cf. **342,** 6.

XLVIII. *disaventurous deare :* unfortunate injury.

XLIX. *despight :* contumelious treatment.

L. *he himselfe betooke.* v. n. **325,** 2.

192, ibid. *onely foe :* especial, chief foe. Cf. **230,** 2.

LI. *dissolute :* unstrung, enfeebled.

194, *Canto VIII,* XV. *lightly :* at once.

XVI. *scalpe :* i. e. skull.

XVII. *grieved :* injured, hurt.

XVIII. *rigor.* v. n. **155,** 18.

195, XXII. *drift :* impetus.

XXIII. *ruine :* fall.

196, XXVII. *And you :* the Squire.

equall : impartial, just. Cf. **205,** 47, **237,** 50.

restore : make return for, reward.

quite : requite.

XXIX. *car'd :* took pains.

XXX. *unused rust :* the rust of disuse.

197, XXXIV. *doted :* imbecile.

without any breach : without need of breaking or forcing it.

XL. *nicer :* too dainty.

198, XLI. *deceived of.* v. n. **423,** 36.

XLV. *avenge :* take vengeance on.

XLVI. *tire :* head-dress. Cf. **290,** 19.

call : caul, a close-fitting, net-work cap, part of a woman's head-dress.

199, XLVII. *loathd :* disgusted.

Canto IX, I. The 'chayne' is the quality which Arthur embodies, ' magnificence ' (magnanimity) the virtue which ' is the perfection of all the rest, and conteineth in it them all.' *safety.* Cf. **315,** 17 ; v. n. **77,** 508.

I. *repast :* repose. Cf. **153,** 4.

Them list : it pleased them. Cf. **32,** 29.

200, V. *tutors nouriture to oversee :* to supervise the training given me by my tutor.

in her just term : in its due course. Cf. ' just time,' **201,** 14.

VII. *fatal :* prophetic.

Whilome : ever. v. n. **327,** 14.

forced fury : violence of compulsion.

his : its, i. e. the wound's.

find : find heart to, choose to. Cf. **376,** 26, **381,** 1.

X. *government :* self-control.

201, XII. *prouder :* over proud.

XIV. *when . . . expired :* in due course of time.

XV. *devoyd :* empty.

XVI. *hew :* expression.

on grownd : on earth.

XVIII. *voyage :* journey. Cf. **235,** 34.

XIX. *sure :* genuine.

Embowd : arched, rounded ; or perhaps, set with bosses.

203, XXXI. *worldes.* v. n. **33,** 72.

mealt'h melteth. Cf. ' dealth,' **419,** 6.

XXXII. *deadly :* deathlike. Cf. **160,** 16.

204, XXXVI. *wallowd :* rolled. Commonly used by Spenser for the modern ' wallowing.' Cf. **362,** 26, **404,** 7.

205, XLI. *centonell :* i. e. sentinel.

roome. v. n. **80,** 57.

XLIII. *I wote :* in the sense of ' I trow.'

avengement. v. n. **77,** 508.

XLVI. *sinfull hire :* service to sin.

XLVII. *equall.* v. n. **196,** 27.

206, XLVIII. *inchaunted rimes :* incantations.

XLIX. *amazement :* perplexity, distraction. Cf. **724,** 35, **154,** 15.

table : picture.

LIV. *thence amounted :* mounted and departed, departed thence. Cf. ' thence arise,' **182,** 32.

unbid : i. e. unprayed for.

drest : i. e. treated.

207, *Canto X,* II. *raw :* unstrung.

chearen : refresh himself.

IV. *spousd :* betrothed.

VI. *francklin :* freeholder, ' a class of landowners of free, but not noble, birth and ranking next below the gentry ' (N. E. D.).

VII. *knew his good to, etc. :* knew how to bear himself toward men of all classes, to show proper discrimination of rank. Cf. **589,** 1, **613,** 36, **608,** 2.

courting nicetee : courtier-like exquisiteness.

208, IX. *ever-dying dread :* perpetual fear of death. Cf. **248,** 21.

long a day : a long time, many a day.

XII. *in place :* to the spot.

Like sunny beames : as it were, sunbeams. Cf. **185,** 4. ' Sunny beams' for ' sunbeams' is common in Spenser. Cf. **321,** 63, **391,** 20 ; also ' starry light,' **323,** 78.

XIV. *as befell :* as it fell out — merely expletive. Cf. **290,** 17.

XV. *encounters :* goes to meet.

209, XIX. *documents :* lessons.

210, XXIV. *intreat :* persuade.

passion : suffering. Cf. **467,** 3.

XXV. *infected :* ingrained (like a dye).

211, XXX. *bounty.* v. n. **332,** 49.

compare. v. n. **19,** 67.

XXXI. *that joyd her to :* which it delighted her to.

XXXII. *seeming meet :* seemly.

XXXIII. *well to donne :* well-doing.

XXXIV. *descryde :* declared, revealed. Cf. **622,** 12.

worldes. v. n. **33,** 72.

XXXVI. *bead-men :* men of prayer.

wayting : watching. Cf. **406,** 21.

212, XL. *bras :* Lat. *aes,* money.

He, that harrowd hell : Christ, who ' despoiled ' Hell, on his descent thither after his death, by breaking down its gates and leading out the souls of the patriarchs and prophets

who till then had been, as it were, in captivity
there. Cf. **730**, 68.

XLI. *throw :* i. e. throe.

XLII. *engrave :* i. e. bury. Cf. **239**, 60.
feare : make afraid. Cf. **662**, 15.

213, XLVIII. *car'd :* took care of.

XLIX. *more :* greatly.
clomb : climbed. Cf. ' clambe,' **661**, 8.

L. *require :* request. Cf. **481**, 41, **48**, *arg.*

214, LIV. *each where :* in every place. Cf. **694**, 634.

LV. *ditty :* theme. Cf. **303**, 50.

LVI. *commonly :* sociably, familiarly.
empeopled : settled.

215, LXI. *presage :* point out beforehand.
signe : signal cry, watchword.

LXIII. *bequeathed :* entrusted.

LXIV. *nominate :* i. e. call, set down for.

LXV. *in place :* purely expletive, as in **163**, 37,
185, 5.

216, LXVI. *Georgos :* Greek γεωργός, a husbandman.

217, *Canto XI,* v. *wyde.* v. n. **162**, 26.
Muse : Clio, child (' ympe ') of Phœbus and
Mnemosyne (memory, hence 'aged ').

VII. *Till I of warres, etc. :* Spenser was apparently planning for his later books, or for his
second part, some celebration of the war with
Philip II. 'Bryton fieldes with Sarazin blood
bedyde' suggests imitation of the war of the
Saracens in France, as narrated in the *Orlando
Furioso.*
haughtie : high pitched.
second tenor : melody of lower pitch. Cf. **45**,
50.
his : The possessive *'s.*

IX. *rouze :* raise, erect. Cf. **250**, 35.

218, XIII, l. 1. *that :* that which, what.
seare : searing.

XV. *pas :* pace.
drest. v. n. **411**, 55.

XVI. *rigorous :* violent. v. n. **155**, 18.

XIX. *subject :* underlying.

219, ibid. *flightes.* v. n. **33**, 72.
hagard hauke : an untamed hawk.
hable might : the capacity of its strength. Cf.
373, 3.
pounces : talons. Cf. **526**, 42.

XX. *disseized of his gryping grosse :* dispossessed
of his great gripful.

XXI. *each other to avenge :* to take vengeance
each on the other. Cf. **198**, 45.

XXII. *gory blood.* v. n. **156**, 30.

XXIV. *forsake :* shun. Cf. **687**, 50, **266**, 21.

XXV. *pight in :* struck against.

220, XXVI. *cace :* condition, plight. Cf. **273**, 16.

XXX. *Silo :* the pool of Siloam.

221, XXXIII. *That :* when. Cf. **171**, 51.
safety. v. n. **77**, 508.

XXXIV. *As eagle :* Every ten years the eagle
mounts to the circle of fire and thence plunges
into the ocean, from which it emerges with
fresh plumage.

XXXVIII. *intended :* stretched forth.
would . . . behott : would have promised
him life, expected him to live, believed he
was alive. Cf. **446**, 40.
griefe : pain.

XL. *outrage :* clamor.

222, XLI. *For harder was, etc. :* The posthumous
edition of 1609 changes *For* to *Nor*, which has
been generally adopted by modern editors.
The style of Spenser being above all continu-
ous, *For*, though it confuses the sense, seems
to me the more characteristic reading.

XLIII. *minisht :* i. e. diminished.

XLIV. *stew :* lit. a hot room for vapor baths.

XLVI. *the crime . . . fall :* the standing reproach to Adam for having sinned.

223, XLVIII. *dainty deare :* exceedingly precious.
Cf. **353**, 23.
appointed : made ready.

L. *vertuous :* having peculiar qualities or ex-
cellences, efficacious. Cf. **283**, 22.

LI. *for hast :* through haste.

LII. *woundes.* v. n. **33**, 72.

LIII. *retyrd :* withdrawn.

LIV. *false :* treacherous, insecure.

224, *Canto XII,* v. *armes to sownd :* to clash
arms (as in **169**, 40), hence to wage battle.

225, VII. *song :* i. e. sung.

VIII. *her self-resemblance :* i. e. being crowned,
she now resembled her real self, a king's
daughter.

XIII. *shaumes.* v. n. **528**, 4.

226, ibid. *of great name :* noted, hence valuable.
Cf. **182**, 29.

XVI. *passionate :* express.

XVII. *seised :* got possession of, reached.

XVIII. *that proud Paynim King.* v. n. **217**, 7.

XX. *In sort as :* according as.

227, XXII. *wimple :* the veil ' that wimpled was
full low' (**145**, 4).
woven neare : close-woven.

XXIII. *enchace :* serve as setting to. v. n. **449**,
12.

XXIV. *pretence :* importance.

XXV. *unwary :* unexpected.
passage right : going straight on.
fast : close.
disclosing : unfolding. Cf. **449**, 16, **351**,
13.

XXVII. *guilty heavens of :* heavens polluted by.

228, XXVIII. *well to fare :* farewell.

XXXIII. *pardon me :* give me leave.

XXXIV. *practicke paine :* artful pains.

229, XXXVI. *bains :* i. e. banns.

XXXVII. *bushy teade :* a torch of white-thorn;
used in Roman bridal processions.

XXXIX. *trinall triplicities.* v. n. **751**, 64.

XLII. *spent :* worn out.

230, THE SECOND BOOKE, Prologue, IV. *inquyre :*
seek information.
admyre : wonder.

v. *beames.* v. n. **33**, 72.
Canto I, II. *onely :* especial. Cf. **192**, 50,
474, 57, **484**, 21, **646**, 40.

231, ibid. *late ygoe :* a short time since.

III. *of all . . . end :* the object at which his
whole purpose aimed. Cf. **153**, 9, **322**, 69.
fayre fyled : smooth. Cf. **149**, 35.

IV. *stales :* decoys, snares. Cf. **641**, 3.

v. *him fortuned :* it befell him. Cf. **98**, 631.
337, 22.

VI. *demure :* sober (without affectation).

worship. v. n. **145,** 3.
Sir Huon : Huon of Bordeaux, hero of a romance in which King Oberon of the Fairies is a main figure.

VIII. *misers :* wretch's.

IX. *languorous constraynt :* distressful affliction.
in place : purely expletive. Cf. **429,** 22. v. n. **163,** 37.

232, XI. *looser :* too loose, dishevelled. Cf. **54,** 119. v. n. **144,** 2.

XII. *chaleng :* track.

233, XVIII. *make :* devise. Cf. **153,** 9.

XX. *abyde :* pay the penalty (by confusion with *abye*).

XXI. *semblant plaine :* honest appearance.

234, XXIV. *overplast :* placed, raised above.

XXVI. *embrace :* brace, secure.
in the rest : The rest was a projecting support, riveted to the cuirass, which served to steady the spear when levelled for the charge.
pace : move. Cf. **218,** 15.
abace : lower. Cf. **618,** 31, **628,** 5.

XXIX. *bevers.* v. n. **189,** 31.
mote I weet : I should like to know.

XXXI. *of him . . . cognizaunce :* recognized him perfectly.

235, XXXIII. *pageant.* v. n. **66,** 490.
mote yee thee : may you prosper.

XXXIV. *voyage :* journey. Cf. **201,** 18.
steedy : i. e. steady.

XXXV. *attend :* give heed to. Cf. **95,** 394.

XXXVI. *pageaunts.* v. n. **66,** 490.
in lives despight : hating life. Cf. **684,** 442.
warne : keep off.

236, XXXVIII. *seele.* v. n. **188,** 23.

XLIII. *hop :* 'formerly a general synonym for *leap*' (N. E. D.).

237, XLVII. *which :* that which. Cf. ' that,' **218,** 13, l. 1.

L. *equall.* v. n. **196,** 27.

238, LIII. *forbeare :* part with.

LV. *him that death does give :* Mort-dant.
her that loves to live : Ama-vi[t]a.
Bacchus . . . lincke : this wine is mixed with water.

LVI. *grate.* v. n. **107,** 1334.
wreath : turn away.

LVIII. *squire :* the carpenter's square.
in the meane : meanwhile.

LIX. *doth buriall teene :* Child suggests 'do obsequious sorrow' (*Hamlet*, I, ii, 92). The sense requires 'doth grant burial.' There being no authority for ' teen ' = grant or give or appoint, Mayhew suggests ' leene ' = lend, give.

239, ibid. *For . . . beene :* ' For I think it as great a calamity to remain dishonorably unburied, as to die dishonorably ' (Child).

LX. *engrave.* v. n. **212,** 42.
obsequy : obsequies.
affection : deep feeling (that may issue in revenge).
Canto II, arg. face : appearance.

II. *scattered :* let drop at random.

III. *guiltie :* ' stained with the color of guilt ' (Child).
diverse : distracting.

240, V. *To proofe of :* To the effecting of.

VII. *Dan.* v. n. **669,** 9.

IX. *tryde.* v. n. **517,** 17.

X. *mind :* put him in mind of.
revengement. v. n. **77,** 508.

XI. *barbes :* protective or ornamental trappings for the breast and flanks of a war-horse.

241, XV. *breaded tramels :* braided plaits. Cf. **391,** 20.

XVI. *fest :* festivity.
countenaunce : make a show of.

242, XXII. *Lybicke ocean :* the Lybian desert.

XXV. *forcing to invade :* putting forth his strength to attack. Cf. **277,** 51, **610,** 17.

243, XXVII. *heare :* listen.

XXXIII. *grace to reconcile :* ' gratiam conciliare, to regain each other's favor ' (Church).

244, XXXIV. *utter :* outer. Cf. **483,** 11.

XXXV. *solace :* pleasure, mirth. Cf. **264,** 3.
court : due regard to his attentions, his court.

XXXVII. *mineon :* darling, wanton.

XXXVIII. *extremities of their outrage :* extremes of their (opposite) excesses.

XXXIX. *attempered :* regulated.

XL. *dispredden :* spread out.

245, XLIV. *wonne :* overcome. Cf. **157,** 37, **565,** 30.

XLV. *purpose.* v. n. **335,** 4.
Canto III, I. *Titan :* the sun. Cf. **153,** 7.

246, III. *Patience perforce :* a common proverbial phrasing of submission to circumstances. Cf. **395,** 3.

IV. *bountie :* manly virtue, valor. Cf. **336,** 10, **332,** 49.
kestrell : ' a hawk of a base, unserviceable breed ' (Nares).
kynd : nature.

V. *selfe-loved personage :* love of his own personal appearance. Cf. **338,** 26.
But for : But because. Cf. **18,** 10.

VI. *bravery :* bravado.

VIII. *dead-doing :* death-dealing.
miser. v. n. **231,** 8.
to hold of him in fee : i. e. to be his vassal.

247, XIII. *gin :* craft.

XIV. *gagd :* left as pledges.

XV, ll. 5, 8. *of :* with.

248, XVII. *on even coast :* on even terms (*c.* = ground ?). Cf. **436,** 24.

XVIII. *that monster make :* effect that miracle.

XXI. *dying dreed :* dread of death.
worth : dignity, rank.

249, XXVI. *aygulets :* ' an ornament consisting properly of a gold or silver tag or pendant attached to a fringe, whence . . . any metallic stud, plate, or spangle worn on the dress ' (N. E. D.).

XXVII. *antickes :* fantastic, grotesque figures. Cf. **410,** 51.

XXX. *inspyre :* breathe.
rude : disordered.

250, XXXIV. *marke :* make a mark of.

XXXV. *rowze.* v. n. **217,** 9.

XXXVII. *himselfe to vaunt :* to advance ? or to swagger ? or to exult ?

251, XXXVIII. *praise :* excellence, virtue. Cf. **323,** 80, **366,** 55.

XL. *Behaves :* disciplines. Cf. **531,** 23.
   mis : err. Cf. **388,** 2.
XLII. *bastard :* mongrel, ignoble. Cf. **181,** 24.
XLIII. *pesaunt :* peasant, low fellow.
   vayne : useless (to him).
XLIV. *with such ghastlinesse :* so terrifyingly.
252, XLV. *on foote :* one foot. Cf. **59,** 1.
XLVI. *in dew degree :* i. e. in regulated gait. Cf.
   413, 18.
   Canto IV , I. *pretence :* design. Cf. **549,** 10.
   native influence : influence of the stars at
   birth.
III. *agree :* compose. Cf. **433,** *arg.*
IV. *Her other leg :* one of her legs. Cf. **530,** 15,
   581, 36.
v. *walke :* go, move. Cf. **413,** 15.
VI. *remorse :* compassion. Cf. **159,** 5, **379,** 43.
253, ibid. *avengement.* v. n. **77, 508.**
VII, l. 9. *nought :* not at all.
VIII. *goodly menaging :* i. e. according to ' good
   form.'
254, XIV. *quaild :* overcome. Cf. **386,** 34.
XX. *partake :* make partaker of.
   privitie : secret.
255, XXVI. *staynd :* dimmed. v. n. **679,** 12.
256, XXVIII. *Her proper face :* her own face, who
   she really was.
   deathes. v. n. **33, 72.**
XXXII. *enforst :* added vigor to.
257, XXXVI. *advaunce :* boast.
XXXVII. *varlet :* a manservant to a knight.
XXXVIII. *word :* motto. Cf. **446,** 39.
   beseemed : seemed, or perhaps, was fit. Cf.
   291, 26.
   dight : prepared, dipped.
XXXIX. *to purpose : à propos,* fittingly.
XL. *mindes :* is minded. Cf. **641,** 2.
258, XLIII. *streight :* strictly. Cf. **613,** 35.
XLVI. *intended.* v. n. **422,** 27.
   Canto V , I. *staied.* v. n. **29,** 38.
259, v. *ment :* i. e. directed.
IX. *plate . . . male.* v. n. **184,** 43.
   falsed . . . blowes : feinted.
260, XI. *the saint :* i. e. the image of the Faery
   Queen. Cf. **288,** 2-4.
XII. *hye :* forcibly.
   Ne deeme, etc. : Nor estimate thy force by
   what is only an unjust award of Fortune.
   maugre : curse on.
XIII. *maistring might on :* restraining the exercise of his power on.
   die : chance. Cf. **157,** 36.
XIV. *wondered :* wondered at.
XV, l. 5. *that :* that which.
   Vaine : In vain.
261, XXIII. *disdeignd :* was indignant at. Cf.
   ' dis**d**ainfull,' **161,** 19.
262, XXVII. *sightes :* looks, appearance. Cf.
   293, 36, **208,** 14.
XXXI. *the stately tree :* the poplar.
XXXII. *meriment :* Spenser probably wrote
   meriments, as in **322,** 68.
263, XXXV. *In which :* into which.
XXXVI. *utmost grudging spright :* ' last reluc-
   tant breath ' (Child).
264, *Canto VI ,* I. *maysteries :* achievements.
II. *gondelay :* a gondola, shallop.

III. *solace :* recreation. Cf. **169,** 37, **244,** 35.
VI. *purpose.* v. n. **335,** 4.
VII. *leaves.* v. n. **33,** 72.
265, X. *by ayme :* direct.
   bourne : stream.
XI. *waste and voyd :* solitary and uninhabited.
   Cf. **394,** 49.
XV. *nothing envious : nihil invida,* in no way
   hostile.
266, XVI. *boure :* i. e. bower.
   letts : leaves. Cf. **435,** 11.
XIX. *to hond :* close up. Cf. **217,** 18.
XXI. *bonds :* bounds. Cf. **145,** 3.
   forsake : refuse to have anything to do with.
267, XXVI. *part :* treatment. Cf. **613,** 33.
   impart : accord.
XXVI. *time the tide renewd :* time brought back
   the proper moment.
XXIX. *valew :* worth, valor. Cf. **77, 466.**
   haberjeons dismayld : cut asunder the links
   of their chain-armor coats.
   giambeux : steel leggings.
268, XXXII. *Wo worth :* woeful become, woe befall.
   his owne : i. e. human.
XXXIV. *alarmes :* onsets. Cf. **445,** 35.
269, XXXIX. *beastes.* v. n. **33,** 72.
XL. *fayrely :* peaceably.
XLII. *stept :* steeped.
XLIII. *Harrow :* ' a cry of distress or alarm, a
   call for succour ' (N. E. D.). *Out* and *wellaway* are much the same. Cf. **286,** 46, **40,**
   58.
XLIV. *After pursewing :* a compound adjective.
   requyre : call for.
270, XLVI. *Engrost.* v. n. **351,** 13.
XLVII. *arming sword :* a sword made for battle,
   as distinguished from a ceremonial or a
   tournament sword.
L. *boste :* undertake boastfully. Cf. **29,** 13.
   thunder light : lightning.
271, LI. *qualifyde :* assuaged.
   Canto VII , I. *experiment :* experience.
III. *uncivile :* uncivilized.
v. *driven :* beaten (thin).
   distent : distended.
   ingowes : ingots.
VI. *doubtfull :* fearful, afraid (qualifies *him*).
272, VIII. *brood.* v. n. **79,** 21.
X. *worldly mucke.* Cf. **388,** 4, **511,** 27.
XIV. *Adrian gulf :* the Adriatic Sea.
273, XVI. *unreproved :* blameless.
   cacs. v. n. **220,** 26.
XVIII. *wage :* let out on hire.
XIX. *by unrighteous lott :* by the injustice of
   fate.
274, XXV. *spoile :* take as booty, plunder. Cf.
   118, 186.
   next to Death, etc. : Sleep is to be likened most
   closely to Death.
XXVI. *dismall day :* the Day of Doom. Cf. **287,**
   51, **524,** 26.
XXVIII. *breaches :* projections.
   guifte : quality.
276, XLIII. *deare :* preciously. Cf. **223,** 48.
277, L. *causelesse :* without cause.
278, LII. *tetra mad :* perhaps *tetrum solanum;*

deadly nightshade ; 'mad,' as causing madness.

Mortall samnitis : possibly the savin-tree, supposed to produce abortion.

cicuta : hemlock.

Socrates . . . Critias : Spenser seems to be confusing Socrates and Crito with Theramenes and Critias.

LIII. *entreat :* occupy herself in.

LIV. *but they, etc. :* unless they, etc.

LVIII. *liquour :* liquid. Cf. **292,** 32.

279, LIX. *Of grace :* as a favor, for kindness' sake.

LXII. *in purity :* in disculpation.

280, *Canto VIII,* I. *serve to :* For this Latinism cf. **364,** 47, **119,** 230.

281, XII. *brutenesse :* unintelligence, stupidity.

stile : cognizance.

282, XVIII. *impresse :* make an impression, sink.

XX. *medæwart :* meadow-sweet.

283, XXII. *vertuous.* v. n. **223,** 50.

XXIV. *his life her, etc. :* his life's destined term ; (*her,* for genitive of feminine *vita.*)

XXV. *Mote I beseech :* I would beseech. Cf. **234,** 29.

cace. v. n. **220,** 26.

XXVI. *ghost :* soul, being.

XXVII. *debate the chalenge :* dispute the claim. Cf. **420,** 12.

284, XXVIII. *prolong.* v. n. **442,** 12.

XXIX. *nephewes :* grandson's. Cf. **174,** 22, **353,** 22, **109,** 8.

XXX. *Termagaunt :* according to the romances, one of the gods of the Saracens. Mahoune (i. e. Mahomet) was another. Cf. **284,** 33, **627,** 47.

285, XXXIV. *His single speare :* his spear alone.

doe him . . . redresse : help him. Cf. **526,** 41.

XXXV. *his ground to traverse wyde :* to shift his ground repeatedly (like side-stepping in boxing). Cf. **456,** 18.

XXXVI. *wyde :* out of position. Cf. **539,** 22.

XXXVIII. *hacqueton :* a quilted jacket worn under armor.

XL. *as he it ought :* as he that owned it.

286, XLVI. *Harrow, etc.* v. n. **69,** 43.

287, L. *bittur :* bittern.

LI. *dismall day.* v. n. **274,** 26.

LII. *in despight of.* v. n. **684,** 443.

288, LVI. *done my dew in place :* done my duty on the spot, here.

Canto IX, II. *gentle court :* courteous address.

mote I . . . read : may I understand, by your courtesy, why, etc.

289, XIII. *villeins :* in the earlier sense of serfs or of base-born country rabble.

290, XV. *orders :* ranks.

idle : empty.

XVI. *fennes of Allan :* the great bog of Allen, a little west of Dublin.

XVII. *combrous.* v. n. **148,** 23.

XIX. *Braunched :* embroidered in sprigged patterns.

sweete rosiere : perhaps sweetbriar. (*r.* = rose-bush.)

291, XXII. The circle is the head ; the triangle, the legs (the ground forming the base). The circle includes the greatest, the triangle the least space, among plane figures ; hence 'first and last.' The circle has, of course, been always used as a symbol of perfection, immortality, etc. ; the triangle is here interpreted as the antithesis ; the masculine, the nobler quality, is of the former, against the feminine of the latter. The ' quadrate,' or rectangle, is the body, in proportion nine long by seven broad. This length, nine, is equal to the circumference of the circle, the head.

diapase : diapason. Cf. **78,** 549.

XXIV. *from Ireland :* ' Ireland yields excellent marble near Dublin, Kilkenny, and Cork ' (Fynes Moryson).

compasse : proportion.

compacture : union of parts.

XXVI. *as beseemed right :* as was right seemly. Cf. **196,** 32.

XXVII. *Against :* in preparation for the time when.

XXVIII. *yeoman :* a gentleman attendant in a royal or noble household.

292, ibid. *bestow :* dispose. Cf. **541,** 40.

XXIX. *Mongiball :* Ital. *Mongibello,* another name for Ætna.

XXIX, XXX. ' The air introduced by breathing served to regulate, to maintain, and at the same time to temper, to refrigerate the innate heat of the heart, that fire which, placed in the heart at the beginning, continued there all life and was the one source of the warmth of the body.' (Of the Galenic doctrine, in Foster's *Hist. of Physiology.*)

inspyre : breathe in. Cf. **743,** 98.

XXXII. *nought :* valueless.

Port Esquiline : The Campus Esquilinus, near this gate of Rome, was where criminals were executed, the poor buried, refuse of all kinds dumped. It was notoriously unsanitary. Cf. **108,** 4.

avoided : ejected.

XXXV. *other some.* v. n. **6,** 130.

293, XXXVIII. *this word :* Collier suggests *mood.* Perhaps *this w.* = what you have just called attention to.

XLI. *castory :* a color (red ?) derived from castoreum.

294, XLIII. *embrace :* cherish. Cf. **385,** 29.

XLIV. *oversee :* overlook.

sought : invited.

XLVI. *sly :* subtile, thin.

XLVII. The three chief rooms are the three ventricles into which mediæval physiology divided the brain. The front ventricle receives sensations ; these are passed on to the second, in the middle, where they become material for imagination, reason, etc. ; the third, at the back, is that of memory. Spenser modifies the plan somewhat, to accommodate the three master faculties, imagination, judgment, memory.

XLVIII. *he, whom Greece :* Socrates.

by many parts : by many times.

that sage Pylian syre : Nestor.

contrive : wear away.

XLIX. *comprize :* understand.

295, L. *hippodames :* sea-horses. Cf. **408,** 40.

LII. *house of agonyes :* 'The twelfth house is that of affliction, misery, and suffering, distress of every kind, grief, persecution, malice, secret enmity, anxiety, envy, imprisonment, treason, sedition, assassination, and suicide. . . . It is said to be the joy of Saturn, because he is the parent of malignity. . . . Saturn, being here, gives every evil, except death, that can afflict mankind' (Wilson, *Dict. of Astrology*).

LIII. *wittily :* intelligently, wisely.

296, LIX. *governements :* plural forced by rhyme. Cf. 'auncestryes,' **296,** 1.

Canto X, I. *haughty.* v. n. **155,** 19.

needes me : is needful to me.

III. *Mæonian quill :* the pen or the pipe of Homer. These two meanings of 'quill' cannot always be distinguished. In **48,** 35, and **682,** 325, as generally in pastoral verse, 'quill'= pipe. Elsewhere it may = pen, as in **733,** 84. *rote.* v. n. **476,** 6.

297, v. *unmannurd :* untilled.

VI. *invade :* enter, penetrate. Cf. **371,** 37.

VII. *liveden :* lived.

VIII. *companing :* companying, cohabiting. Cf. **615,** 11.

IX. *fatall error :* fated wandering. Cf. **342,** 2, **343,** 15, **393,** 41.

X. *The westerne Hogh :* the Hoe at Plymouth.

298, XII. *inquyre :* call. Sense forced by rhyme.

XIII. *Britany :* Britain. Cf. **61,** 100, **346,** 32, **348,** 52.

XIV. *Albania . . . Logris :* according to the chronicles, separated by the Humber; but in **495,** 36, used of modern Scotland and England, separated by the Tweed.

XV. *a nation straung :* the Huns.

Noyes : Noah's.

display : spread out.

XVIII. *ordaind :* set in order.

299, XX, l. 1. *for :* forasmuch as.

XXIII. *semblaunce :* resemblance.

XXIV. *Scaldis :* the Scheldt.

Hania : Hainault.

Esthambruges : Bruges.

Henalois : men of Hainault.

scuith guiridh : Welsh for 'green shield.'

y scuith gogh : the red shield.

XXV. *Cairleill :* ('cair' = city) Carlisle.

Cairleon : Chester.

XXVI. *Cairbadon :* Bath.

quick : live.

300, ibid. *through flight :* He imitated Icarus, and was dashed in pieces.

XXVII. *parentage :* parents, parent.

XXIX. *Celtica :* France.

XXX. *weeke :* i. e. wick.

XXXI. *leav'd :* levied.

301, XXXV. *oppresse :* fall upon, surprise. Cf. **324,** 81, **536,** 4.

XXXVII. *stressed :* distressed. Cf. **405,** 18.

loose : disunited.

XXXVIII. *miscreate :* i. e. unlawful ruler.

Cambry : Wales.

XXXIX. *stealth :* robbery, rapine.

XL. *That sacked Rome, etc. :* The Romans, hav-

ing sworn allegiance, treacherously attempted to destroy their conquerors, who thereupon sacked the city.

XLI. *Easterland :* vaguely, the country to the east.

foy : money paid as a mark of fealty.

302, XLII. *found :* devised. Cf. **691,** 366.

layes : laws.

XLIII. *carcas :* often used by Spenser for the human body, alive or dead, without implication of contempt. Cf. **284,** 27, **311,** 38, **312,** 42.

XLV. *reseized :* reinstated.

successe : succession.

XLVI. *Troynovant :* London.

303, L. *ditty.* v. n. **214,** 55.

LI. *draught :* device, stratagem.

LIII. *Evangely :* gospel.

LIV. *Bunduca :* Boadicea.

besides : by the side of.

LV. *on . . . serv'd :* delivered, hurled at.

LVII. *proper :* own.

304, LIX. *agreement.* v. n. **77,** 508.

LXI. *with easy hand :* easily, quickly.

LXIII. *Easterlings :* men from the east, the pirates of the North Sea.

scatterlings : rovers.

LXIV. *gathering to feare :* deeming reason for alarm.

305, LXVIII. *Uther :* the father of Arthur.

cesure : formal stop.

attend : stay. Cf. **607,** 31.

LXIX. *ofspring :* pedigree. Cf. **182,** 30.

LXXI. *the gardins of Adonis.* v. Bk. III, c. vi.

306, LXXV. *Elficleos :* Henry VII.

Elferon : Arthur.

Oberon : Henry VIII.

LXXVI. *memoriall :* memory.

Tanaquill : Elizabeth.

Canto XI, I. *sinfull vellenage :* bondage to sin.

307, VIII. *beckes :* beaks.

lynces : lynx's.

308, XI. *puttockes :* kites.

XII. *oystriges :* ostriches.

faste : i. e. faced.

XIII. *urchins :* hedgehogs.

XV. *pretend :* attempt. Cf. **549,** 10.

309, XXII. *Thereto :* in addition to this, besides. Cf. **319,** 51, **419,** 7.

XXIII. *her other legge.* v. n. **252,** 4.

XXIV. *quarrell :* properly, the square-headed, short, heavy arrow of a cross-bow.

expell : send forth.

310, XXVIII. *strew :* scattered.

XXIX. *lode upon him layd :* belabored him with blows. Cf. **618,** 28.

bane : death, destruction.

XXX. *on ground :* on earth. Cf. **373,** 52.

nearely drive : push hard.

XXXI. *invade.* v. n. **610,** 17.

XXXII. *his native seat :* the region of fire between the air and the sphere of the moon. The rising of fire was explained by its effort to return to its proper place, this region.

XXXIII. *quar'le.* v. n. **309,** 24.

311, XXXIV. *fild his place :* i. e. 'measured his length.'

XXXV. *sundry way :* the parting of ways.

312, XLII. *wrest :* wrench, twist.

XLVI. *taking his full course :* to reckon the full distance.

313, *Canto XII,* I. *pricke :* point.

III. *worldes.* v. n. **33,** 72.

up . . . lay : The common term for the modern ' throw up.'

IV. *magnes stone :* loadstone.

rift : riven mass.

VI. *Tartare.* v. n. **85,** 444.

314, XI. *seeming now and than :* that appear here and there.

315, XVI. *purpose diversly :* talk of this and that. v. n. **335,** 4.

XVII. *safety.* v. n. **77,** 508.

XXI. *utmost sandy breach :* the broken water, mixed with sand, at the edge of the sandbank.

fetch : reach.

316, XXIII, XXIV. These sea monsters are of the natural history of Spenser's day. The recorded descriptions of them need not be given here.

XXIII. *Spring-headed :* ' with heads springing or budding forth from their bodies ' (Upton).

monoceros : emended by some editors to ' monoceroses,' for the sake of the plural. But the word, as it stands, is plural. Cf. Puttenham's *Art of English Poesie* (ed. Arber, p. 52) : ' wild beasts, as elephants, rhinoceros, tigers, leopards, and others.'

XXVII. *seemely :* comely. Cf. **468,** 14.

317, XXIX. *embosome :* implant.

bayt : refresh with rest.

XXX. *like :* as it were.

an halfe theatre : a semi-circular theatre as distinguished from an amphitheatre.

XXXI. *fondly :* foolishly. Cf. **381,** 61.

Heliconian maides : the Muses.

XXXIII. *meane :* tenor or alto.

XXXIV. *leveled :* directed, aimed. Cf. **125,** 3.

XXXVI. *unfortunate :* ill-omened.

fatall : boding ruin.

strich : the screech-owl.

318, XXXVII. *sacred :* cursed. Cf. **576,** 1.

XLIII. *Nought feard, etc. :* Their physical force (that of the knight and his guide) roused no fear (in the inmates) that they would capture that fortalice ; what did rouse such fear was wisdom's power, etc., spiritual qualities.

319, XLIV. *wondred :* wonderful.

XLVII. *Genius.* Cf. **370,** 31 ff.

XLIX. *charmed semblants sly :* raised by magic immaterial phantasms. Cf. **294,** 46.

L. *and goodly :* Possibly *and* is a slip for *was.*

LI. *Thereto.* v. n. **309,** 22.

joviall : propitious.

spirit : breath.

320, LIII. *forward right :* straight ahead. ` Cf. **350,** 61.

LIV. *hyacine :* hyacinth, probably the sapphire.

LVI. *with daintie breach :* crushing them daintily.

322, LXIX. *drift :* design. Cf. **231,** 3.

LXXI. *discreet :* distinct.

323, LXXVI. *display :* descry.

LXXXI. *for that same :* ' occasion ' understood.

formally. Cf. **53,** 68.

324, ibid. *opprest.* v. n. **301,** 35.

wrest : twist, or wrestle

LXXXIII. *cabinets :* summer-houses. Cf. **53,** 17, **686,** 558.

LXXXV. *like monstruous :* similarly monstrous.

325, THE THIRDE BOOKE, Prologue, I. *It falls me :* It falls to me.

Neede but behold : It is necessary only that they should behold.

IV. *that sweete verse.* v. n. **142,** *Raleigh.*

beames. v. n. **33,** 72.

V. *If ought . . . abuse :* if any fault may chance to offend her taste.

Canto I, I. *procur'd :* entreated.

II. *he him selfe betooke, etc. :* either ' he betook himself to ' or ' he himself took,' as in **91,** 69. Cf. **191,** 50.

326, IV. *couch :* crouch, stoop.

V. *spurne :* spur.

VI. *crouper :* i. e. crupper.

VIII. *Venus looking glas :* Cf. **337,** 18 ff. One of the very many minor inconsistencies of the poem, due perhaps to change of plan.

327, XI. *like treaty handeled :* used similar diplomacy. Cf. **179,** 3.

XIV. *whylome :* at times.

XV. *whales bone :* the tusks of the walrus, a common form of ivory in the Middle Ages. ' Whales' is a dissyllable. v. n. **33,** 72.

328, XVIII. *envy . . . gealosy :* indignation . . . anger. Cf. **356,** 47, **7,** 300.

XIX. *pace :* pass.

XXI. *before . . . assay :* durst attack him in front.

329, XXV. *maistery :* superior force. Cf. **424,** 46.

XXX. *swords . . . mard :* marred the honor of, debased.

330, XXXIII. *meane degree :* medium rank.

XXXIV. *Toure :* Tours.

XXXVII. *Dreadfull :* fearful, afraid.

XXXVIII. *lively :* in real life, actually. Cf. **407,** 30.

XXXIX. *worldes.* v. n. **33,** 72.

331, XL. *looser :* over lax.

XLI. *bed :* i. e. couch.

XLII. *vented up her umbriere :* raised, as for air, the face-guard of her helmet.

XLIII. *Breakes forth :* breaks a way for.

discomfited : dejected.

XLIV. *tilt and turnament.* v. n. **548,** 7.

332, XLVIII. *outrage :* intemperance. Cf. **244,** 38.

XLIX. *bounty :* goodness, virtue. Cf. **582,** 3, **211,** 30.

bounteous : good, virtuous. Cf. **336,** 10, **404,** 10.

L. *dissembled it with ignoraunce :* i. e. feigned not to understand her meaning.

LI. *Lyæus :* Bacchus.

spight or spare : grudging or stint.

LII. *loose :* i. e. relax.

purport : disguise.

LIV. *perplexe :* torment. Cf. **581,** 35.

333, LV. *rebuke :* reproach, shame.

LVI. *basciomani :* hand-kissing.

LVII. *moist daughters :* the Hyades.

LVIII. *Avoided :* departed.
despoile : disrobe.
LXI. *with easy shifte :* moving softly.
LXII. *leachour :* i. e. lecher.
ghastly : terrified.
334, LXVII. *ungentle trade :* conduct, practice unbecoming gentlefolk.
Canto II, I. *proper :* own. Cf. **303,** 57.
indifferent : impartial. Cf. **559,** 36.
memoree : record. Cf. **140,** *Essex.*
335, IV. *Guyon :* not Guyon, but the Redcross Knight.
purpose : Fr. *propos,* discourse. Cf. **419,** 7, **264,** 6, **245,** 45, **156,** 30.
inquest : quest. Cf. **653,** 42.
V. *flake :* flash. Cf. **220,** 26.
VII. *The Greater Brytayne :* 'To distinguish it from the Lesser Brittany in France. The reader will please to remember that, throughout this poem, the Britons (the people of Wales) are all along distinguished from the English and the Scotch; and that England alone (as divided from Scotland and Wales) is the scene of Faerie Land' (Church). Faery Land, however, has no geographical relations to existing lands. In the chronicle passages of the poem (Bk. II, c. x, Bk. III, c. iii, c. ix, st. 33–51) no attention is paid to Faery Land at all. In Bk. II, c. x, st. 70–76, it is treated as separate.
VIII. *worth and worship :* dignity and honor. Cf. **248,** 21.
336, IX. *borne the name :* been most famous.
X. *bounteous :* virtuous, manly. Cf. **332,** 49, **246,** 4.
aware : on your guard. Cf. **536,** 1, **569,** 13.
XII. *occasion :* induce.
balke : bandy words.
XIII. *Whose prowesse paragone :* the equal of whose prowess.
XIV. *comfortlesse :* helpless.
XVI. *vaunt :* probably, put forward, present to view. Cf. **441,** 7.
337, XVIII. *solemniz'd :* celebrated.
XXI. *convince :* convict, expose.
XXII. *it fortuned, etc.* v. n. **231,** 5.
XXIII. *buxome . . . prone :* pliant . . . submissive.
XXIV. *ventayle :* the movable face-guard of a helmet.
338, XXV. *ermilin :* ermine.
XXVI. *personage :* personal appearance.
339, XXXII. *gryefe :* i. e. grief.
XXXIV. *armes.* v. n. **33,** 72.
streightly. v. n. **731,** 71.
340, XLII. *welfare.* Cf. 'farewell,' **565,** 24.
XLIII. *Beldame :* good mother (not yet a term of reproach). Cf. **344,** 17, **374,** 8.
unkinde : unnatural. Cf. **85,** 396.
XLV. *howre.* v. n. **640,** 39.
No shadow . . . powre : There is no shadow that is not governed by a body.
cyphers : astrological signs or figures.
341, XLVII. *displayd :* spread. Cf. **298,** 15.
lamp . . . steepe : She extinguished the lamp by submerging the wick in the oil. To blow it out would be unlucky.

XLVIII. *appele :* address by way of appeal.
verse : i. e. incantation, spell. Cf. **238,** 55, **149,** 37, **220,** 27. Cf. also 'rimes,' **206,** 48.
XLIX. *colt wood :* coltsfoot.
342, *Canto III,* II. *fatall.* v. n. **297,** 9.
descents : lines of descent.
heroes. v. n. **64,** 341.
V. *great care she tooke :* she endured great grief. Cf. **9,** 9.
VI. *coast.* v. n. **191,** 45.
the Africk Ismael : the Saracens or Moors, supposed descendants of Ishmael.
VII. *counseld :* took counsel.
343, XIII. *coosen :* kinsman. Cf. **345,** 29.
XIV. *love to frend.* v. n. **148,** **28.**
XV. *fatall end :* 'some purpose of the Fates' (Child).
344, XVIII. *redrest.* v. n. **176,** 36.
XXI. *of grace.* v. n. **279,** 59.
345, XXV. *pertake :* to carry through? to impart? *constant terme :* fixed limit or end, outcome.
XXVII. *closure :* bound, limit.
346, XXXII. *heroes.* v. n. **64,** 341.
the six islands : Ireland, Iceland, Gothland, the Orkneys, Norway, Dacia (Denmark).
XXXIII. *Norveyses :* Norwegians.
347, XLIV. *notifide.* v. n. **416,** 39.
XLVI. *a Raven :* the Danes.
348, ibid. *faithlesse chickens :* the Danes being heathen.
XLVII. *a Lion :* William the Conqueror.
XLVIII. *a sparke, etc. :* In 1278 Llewellyn, the last British prince, gave up Wales and retired to Anglesey (Mona). Henry VII was born in Anglesey.
XLIX. *a royall Virgin :* Elizabeth.
the great Castle : the king of Castile. Cf. **141,** Howard.
LI. *Of all that . . . inquird :* Concerning everything about which they needed to make inquiry.
possesse : i. e. achieve.
LII. *armes.* v. n. **33,** 72.
350, LXI. *forward right.* v. n. **320,** 53.
LXII. *affectionate :* disposed.
diverst : turned aside.
forth : straight on.
351, *Canto IV,* VI. *her blinded guest :* Love.
X. *continent :* land. Cf. **354,** 30.
table : votive tablet. Cf. **249,** 24.
XII. *coosen :* kindred. v. n. **343,** 13.
XIII. *engroste :* thickened. Cf. **270,** 46.
disclo'ste, etc. : set free, let loose her affliction in a storm of anger.
352, XVI. *againe :* on her part. Cf. **655,** 5.
scuchin : i. e. scutcheon, shield.
mayled : made of chain armor. v. n. **184,** 43. Cf. **362,** 31, **528,** 2.
on an heape : in a heap.
353, XXI. *perswade :* entreat.
XXIV. *deare :* dearly.
knife : a stock term of the old romances for 'sword.' Cf. **183,** 38.
XXVIII. *vainely :* erroneously.
354, XXX. *continent :* ground. Cf. **351,** 10.
XXXI. *pensife :* used by Spenser only with the implication of sorrow. Cf. **10,** 76.

XXXII. *abid :* abode, became.
XXXIII. *commaundement.* v. n. **77**, 508.
rowndell : a globule.
XXXIV. *temed :* harnessed teamwise.
XXXV. *her sobbing breaches :* the intervals of her sobbing. Cf. **73**, 232.
355, XXXVIII. *the grave self to engrosse :* to fill the grave oneself.
XXXIX. *maligne :* view with malice. Cf. **662**, 11.
XLI. *lore :* teaching.
XLII. *clim :* i. e. climb.
356, XLIV. *th' ensample, etc. :* ' i. e. who had given this specimen of her power ' (Child).
brooke : ply.
XLV. Here and in the argument of c. i we find traces of an early plan abandoned, according to which Archimago and Duessa were to be main agents of evil in Bk. III, as they had been in Bk. I and, to a lesser degree, in Bk. II. Archimago is here mentioned for the last time.
XLVI. *howndes.* v. n. **33**, 72.
XLIX. *tassell gent :* the male goshawk.
357, LII. *scope :* a mark, i. e. object of desire.
LVI. *from Stygian . . . handmaide :* calls (i. e. summons) from Stygian deep thee, whom in his blind error he holds his goddess, and calls (i. e. names) thee great Dame Nature's handmaid.
358, LX. *beames.* v. n. **33**, 72.
LXI. *intent :* mood. Cf. **201**, 12
Canto V, I. *pageaunts :* rôles, parts.
variable kindes : various natures.
II. *ungentlenesse :* conduct unbecoming a gentleman.
359, XI. *rowme.* v. n. **80**, 57.
abide : be in store for.
361, XIX. *mayles :* the rings of which chain armor was composed. Cf. **528**, 3.
XXII. *load upon him layd.* v. n. **310**, 29.
XXIII. *rigor.* v. n. **155**, 18.
ferme : The sense lies in the idea of holding on lease, not absolutely.
XXV. *continent :* land. Cf. **351**, 10.
362, XXVIII. *persue :* perhaps some technical term of the chase = means of pursuing, trail. Perhaps a printer's slip for ' issue,' the *per* being caught from ' perceav'd.'
XXX. *Besides all hope :* contrary to all expectation.
XXXI. *light :* i. e. she relieved his head of, etc. Cf. **229**, 42.
XXXII. *divine tobacco :* supposed by the early users of it to have medicinal properties.
363, XXXIII. *marbles plaine :* smooth stones.
handes. v. n. **33**, 72.
XXXIV. *hopelesse :* unhoped for.
XXXVI. *safety.* v. n. **77**, 508.
XXXVIII. *case.* v. n. **220**, 26.
364, XLI. *redrest.* v. n. **176**, 36.
reduced : brought back. Cf. **346**, 32, **614**, 3.
XLII. *rebownd :* apparently no more than ' dart out.' Forced by rhyme.
XLIII. *releast :* i. e. saved.
XLVI. *deathes.* v. n. **33**, 72.
XLVII, l. 2. Suspected to be a reference to the scattering of the Armada by storms.

365, XLVIII. *by art :* after its manner (?). Cf. **539**, 24. Such phrases as this, forced by rhyme, usually carry some vague sense, not easily expressed.
366, *Canto VI*, VI. *beames.* v. n. **33**, 72.
367, VIII. *Informed :* formed.
XII. *her heavenly hous, etc.* Cf. **747**, 29-59.
368, XVIII. *lanck :* Used by Spenser where we should use ' slender.' Cf. **391**, 21.
for hindring : lest they should hinder. Cf. **103**, 1010.
XIX. *compriz'd :* gathered together.
XXI. *ill . . . apayd :* you must be afflicted.
369, XXIII. *let . . . envide :* ' do not grudge him that praise ' (Child).
370, XXX. *account :* enumerate or recount.
weeds : i. e. plants. Cf. **237**, 52.
counted : recounted.
XXXV. *sondry :* separate.
371, XXXVIII. *conditioned :* bound (as by a contract).
XLII. *harvest :* autumn. Cf. **54**, 98.
they clyme : Who climb (unless the indwellers, after fruit) is not clear.
372, XLIV. *caprifole :* honeysuckle or woodbine.
XLV. *Amintas :* probably Sir Philip Sidney, mortally wounded at Zutphen.
LI. *tendered :* cared for. Cf. **84**, 362, **569**, 18.
373, LII, LIII. This account of Scudamour's wooing of Amoret does not agree with that in Bk. IV, c. x.
worldes. v. n. **33**, 72.
Canto VII, III. *hable puissaunce :* strength sufficient for his need. Cf. **219**, 19.
IV. *subject to :* lying beneath. Cf. **218**, 19.
overcame : overspread.
374, VII. *gin :* scheme.
VIII. *while :* until. Cf. **727**, 53.
XII. *for . . . donne :* good for doing nothing.
375, ibid. *lewd :* ignorant.
XIII. *at undertime :* in the latter part of the day.
XVI. *lovely semblaunces :* shows of love.
resemblaunces : Todd quotes Barret's Dict., 1580, ' To resemble : to smile upon, to favour.'
XVIII. *compast :* plotted.
XIX. *kent :* kenned, became aware.
376, XXI. *to plight :* to good condition. Cf. **390**, 19.
XXII. *mishapt :* misshapen.
XXIII. *sent :* scent. Cf. **670**, 10.
XXIV. *wex areare :* fall behind, slacken.
XXVI. *fond.* v. n. **200**, 7.
377, XXX. *unfilde :* unburnished. ' Filing ' is a common term with Spenser for polishing. Cf. **149**, 35.
XXXIV. *containe :* to confine. In the old editions, ' enclose.' *Containe* is the nearest equivalent that rhymes. Cf. **576**, 1.
XXXV. *implacable :* irremediable.
378, XXXIX. *stare :* glitter.
High God in peeces tare. Cf. *Canterbury Tales*, C. 474.
' It is grisly for to here hem swere ;
Our blissed lordes body they to-tere ; '
i. e. they swear by all the parts of God's body; a form of blasphemy long surviving in ' zounds,' ' sblood,' etc.

XLI. *Mount Olympus :* In confusing Olympus and Olympia Spenser is accompanied by Sidney, who makes the same, to us almost inconceivable, blunder in his *Defence of Poesy.* Cf. **108**, 2.

379, XLIII. *remorse.* v. n. **252**, 6.

XLVI. *along the lands :* a convenient expletive. Cf. **464**, 25.

381, LVIII. *jane :* a small silver coin of Genoa.
to chose : ' if you please.'

LIX. *maintenaunce :* condition of life.

LX. *handsome :* convenient.

LXI. *fondly.* v. n. **317**, 31.
land : place. Cf. **379**, 46.
Canto VIII, I. *causelesse . . . accord:* without having consented to any action that might deserve such a fate.
finde. v. n. **200**, 7.

II. *fate :* i. e. her fated term of life.

III. *riv'd . . . brest :* split his breast and torn his heart out. Cf. **436**, 18, **566**, 32.

382, v. *In hand . . . tooke:* undertook. Cf. **397**, 19.

VII. *thryse :* a third part.

VIII. *Him needed not instruct :* it was not necessary to instruct him.

X. *armes.* v. n. **33**, 72.

383, XIII. *next to :* second to.

XVI. *as he mote on high :* as loudly as he could.
bide him batteill : endure, undergo battle with him.
treat : parley. Cf. **594**, 36.

XVII. *els.* v. n. **451**, 28.

384, XIX. *without abode :* without delay.

XX. *queene :* i. e. Fortune.

XXII. *drover :* a fishing boat.

385, XXVII. *it may behove :* it behooves you to be active in her behalf.

XXVIII. *presage :* have an inkling of.

XXIX. *embrace :* to esteem. Cf. **583**, 3.

XXXI. *card :* compass-card or chart. Cf. **271**, 1.
yrkesome : loathsome. v. n. **698**, 906.
frayle : melting.

XXXIII. *attached neare :* nearly seized or caught.

XXXIV. *recomfort, and accourage :* cheer and encourage.

386, ibid. *quayld.* v. n. **254**, 14.

XL. *exprest :* manifested, showed. Cf. **302**, 13, **615**, 10.
leman : sweetheart.

387, XLIII. *yrkes.* v. n. **698**, 906.

XLVII, l. 7. *That :* which.
repent : grieve for.

XLVIII. *That ye :* that which ye.
of report : from hearsay knowledge. Cf. ' depend of,' and ' proceed of,' **440**, 1.

388, LI. *Mote not mislike you :* may it not displease you.
relate : bring back.
Canto IX, II. *mis :* err. Cf. **251**, 40.

III. *privitie :* seclusion.

IV. *bounty.* v. n. **332**, 49.

389, v. *his other blincked eye.* v. n. **252**, 4. One of his eyes is quite blind (**392**, 27), the other is blinking, dim.

VI. *misdeeme :* entertain to his discredit.

VII. *misdonne :* misbehave.

containe : keep within bounds, restrain. Cf. **541**, 1, **543**, 11, **615**, 7.

XI. *ordered :* prepared.

XII. *of courtesie :* i. e. of want of courtesy. The defect is implied in the verb.

390, XIII. *whyleare :* goes with ' full.' The shed was full since a while before.

XIV. *grate.* v. n. **107**, 1334.

XVI. *counterchaunge to scorse :* give the return blow.

XVIII. *him to beave with all :* to bear with him.

XIX. *dissembled what they did not see :* feigned not to notice his want of hospitality.
in plight. v. n. **376**, 21.

391, XX. *tramells :* plaits. Cf. **241**, 15.

XXVI. *late recourse :* recent retirement.

392, XXVII. *he him selfe :* Malbecco.
sided : was on the side towards.

XXX. *Bacchus fruit . . . plate :* wine out of the silver *patera* or cup.

XXXI, ll. 1-3. He pledges her in a cup of wine ; she reaches to take the cup out of his hand, to pledge him in return, feigns to ' mistake' it, i. e. to grasp it carelessly, and spills, etc.
the ape . . . cape : ' Fools used formerly to carry apes on their shoulders ; and to put the ape upon a man was a phrase equivalent to "make a fool of him"' (Upton).

XXXII. *Purpose was moved :* proposition was made.

XXXIII, l. 8 f. ' since the stain which has come upon thine ancient renown has disgraced the offspring of thy great ancestors, and sullied thy glory in later times ' (Child).

393, XXXVIII. *extract :* descended.
Troynovant : London.

XLI. *safegard :* safety.
fatall errour : destined wandering. Cf. **297**, 9.

XLII. *contract :* ally himself by.
contract : contracted, a common form of the pp.

394, XLIII. *Into . . . convart :* each to have the title of sovereignty stand in its own name.
remoud : remov'd. One of the most ingenious of Spenser's distortions in rhyme, to be appreciated only in the old editions, in which *u* and *v,* in any but the initial position, are represented alike by *u.* The word could thus be pronounced so as to rhyme with *bloud,* and yet to the eye preserve its normal form. Cf. *recoure,* **479**, 25.

XLV. *Upon whose stubborne neck . . . her foot :* The reference is to London Bridge, between the close-set piers of which the water ran in rapids that were avoided by smaller boats.

XLVI. *scope :* tract.

XLIX. *Which . . . abrode :* ' Which' is the object of ' seeking,' i. e. exploring.

395, LI. *Your countrey kin :* your kinsman by country, your countryman.
Canto X, III. *patience perforce.* v. n. **246**, 3. Here the phrase may possibly be used half adverbially, for in neither 1590 nor 1596 is it separated from what follows by punctuation.

396, VI. *bord :* table.
fortun'd : chanced.
ungentlenesse. v. n. **358**, 2.

VIII. *Bransles :* songs to be danced to.
purposes : the conversational game of cross-purposes, questions and answers.
x. *dispurvayaunce :* lack of provisions.
reskewes : attempts, by friends on the outside, to bring relief.
397, XIX. *takes in hond :* undertakes. Cf. **382,** 5.
399, XXVIII. *albee I simple such :* though I be so simple.
XXIX. *bouget :* budget, wallet.
war-monger : a mercenary soldier.
XXX. *stoupt . . . winde :* an image from falconry. He did not swoop on the prey, but remained poised above it.
XXXIII. *jollity :* gallant appearance.
400, XXXV. *having filcht her bells.* v. n. **605,** 19.
401, XLII. *safety.* v. n. **77,** 508.
XLIV. *redd :* declared, bestowed.
XLV. *brouzes :* young shoots.
XLVI. *shed :* besprinkle.
XLVII. *his faire hornes :* the metaphorical horns of the cuckold are here suddenly become real.
misconceyving. v. n. **153,** 3.
402, LIV. *staring eyes dismay :* the dismay of staring eyes, eyes staring in dismay.
403, LIX. *pasture :* food.
404, *Canto XI,* IV. *all that I ever finde :* all (of his sex) that I ever heard of.
VIII. *invade :* intrude on.
x. *bounteous.* v. n. **332,** 49.
day : i. e. time.
405, XII. *drerinesse :* anguish.
XIII. *Whereas . . . mistooke :* where he wrongly supposed there was, etc.
XIV. *values :* valor's. Cf. **77,** 466.
XVIII. *stresse :* distress. Cf. **301,** 37.
406, XIX. *that more . . . sought :* that is to be sought more than death is to be avoided.
XX. *disprofesse :* renounce the profession of.
dresse : adjust.
XXI. *wait.* v. n. **211,** 36.
XXIV. *praise :* praiseworthy action.
XXV. *with equall space :* equally.
revolt : turn back.
407, XXVII. *utmost :* outermost. Cf. **658,** 26, **756,** 108.
XXX. *lively :* really. Cf. **330,** 38.
408, XXXV. *Thracian mayd :* Proserpina.
XXXVII. *lusty :* handsome. Cf. **13,** 131.
XXXIX. *cowheard . . . cowheard :* a characteristic pun — herder of cows and coward.
XL. *hippodames :* sea-horses.
409, XLIV. *horrid :* rough. Cf. **189,** 31, **182,** 25.
410, LI. *by many partes :* by a considerable proportion, by much.
LIV. *intend :* signify. Cf. **28,** 232.
411, LV. *welpointed :* well-appointed, in good condition.
dresse : set in order. Cf. **218,** 15.
Canto XII, arg. decayd : wasted. Cf. **522,** 8, **382,** 4.
II. *atwixt :* i. e. mingled with, accompanying the wind.
persevered : the Elizabethan form of the word was ' persever.'
IV. *cyphered :* charactered, written.

VI. *report :* response, echo.
rebound. v. n. **70,** 22.
412, VIII. *say :* a fine, thin woollen stuff. Cf. **168,** 31, **37,** 67.
IX. *disguysed :* fashioned fantastically.
x. *disguyse :* fantastic fashion.
Albanese-wyse : in Albanian fashion.
XIII. *sprinckle :* a brush for sprinkling holy water.
413, XV. *walkte.* v. n. **252,** 5.
lattis : ' The allusion is to the Italian name *Gelosia:* such blinds and lattices as they may see through, yet not be seen; such as suspicious and jealous persons use' (Upton).
XVIII. *degree :* order. Cf. **252,** 46.
XX. *honour :* adornment, covering.
414, XXII. *in perfect kinde :* in perfect condition, i. e. with perfect clearness.
XV. *winges.* v. n. **33,** 72.
XXIV. *each :* each other.
XXVII. *rigorous.* v. n. **218,** 16.
415, XXX. *all and some :* one and all. Cf. **113,** 229.
XXXII. *Not caring.* v. n. **109,** 34.
XXXIII. *ment :* intended, directed. Cf. **247,** 11.
rashly he did wrest : he quickly turned aside.
416, XXXVII. *Abode :* waited.
XXXVIII. *safety.* v. n. **77,** 508.
XXXIX. *notifyde :* proclaimed, or perhaps, known. Cf. **347,** 44.
XLI, l. 7. The edition of 1590 contains a number of alexandrines out of place, i. e. in other positions than at the close of stanzas. In the edition of 1596 these are mostly reduced to ten syllable lines. In the poem as a whole there remain three: here, in **257,** 41, and in **599,** 24.
XLIII. *fained :* sham. Cf. **695, 696, 758,** 273.
417, THE FOURTH BOOKE, Prologue, I. *The rugged forhead :* Burghley.
418, III. *heroes.* v. n. **64,** 341.
v. *feare :* formidableness.
Canto I, I. *unworthie :* undeserved. Cf. **499,** 17, **607,** 34.
419, VI. *health :* welfare. Cf. **121,** 378.
dealth : dealeth, bestoweth. Cf. ' mealt'h,' **203,** 31.
stealth. v. n. **301,** 39.
VII. *Thereto.* v. n. **309,** 22.
doubtfull to be wayd : doubtful to be weighed, judged, of doubtful significance.
purpos. v. n. **335,** 4.
other whiles . . . otherwhiles : now . . . again.
XI. *so far in dout :* of such doubtful consistency.
420, XII. *chalenge :* claim. Cf. **283,** 27, **450,** 25.
quitted : freed, reft.
of . . . fitted : furnished with.
XIII. *prodigious :* portentous.
XVIII. *each degree :* people of all classes. Cf. **433,** 2.
421, XXI. *Disshivered :* shivered into fragments.
XXII. *signe :* memorial ?
his princes five : Cassander, Lysimachus, Ptolemy, Seleucus, and perhaps Antigonus.
to them : among themselves.
422, XXVII. *intended :* directed. Cf. **258,** 46.
comprehended : contained.

XXVIII. *matchlesse :* i. e. not alike.
odde : diverse. Cf. **711,** 27.
XXIX. *handes.* v. n. **33,** 72.
XXXII. *descrie :* denote, express.
whether. v. n. **157,** 37.
423, XXXVI. *Him selfe . . . deceave :* He cheated himself out of, etc. Cf. **198,** 41.
XXXVII. *his other companie :* the rest of his party.
424, XLVI. *maisterdome :* masterfulness. Cf. **329,** 25.
XLVII. *a willow bough :* the badge of forlorn lovers.
425, XLIX. *shivering :* i. e. quivering. Cf. **427,** 14, **435,** 10.
L. *got :* gained. Cf. **568,** 9, **580,** 32.
LII. *thine avenge :* vengeance on thee.
LIV. *expyred :* brought to an end. Cf. **460,** 43, **94,** 309.
426, *Canto II,* I. *ympes of Greece :* the Argonauts. Cf. **421,** 23.
II. *that prudent Romane :* Menenius Agrippa.
VI. *scoffed :* spoken in derision.
torne : i. e. turn.
427, X. *draft :* attraction.
beraft : bereft, despoiled.
XII. *way'd :* journeyed.
XV. *remorse :* ' biting or cutting force' (N. E. D.).
428, XVI. *stemme ech other :* collide, prow on.
XIX. *unfitting :* i. e. to their true natures.
429, XXVII. *prefard :* preferred, recommended.
430, XXX. *partake :* to share.
XXXII. *Whylome, etc. :* With the change of 'oldë' to ' antique,' this is the opening verse of the Knight's Tale. The story that Spenser revives is, of course, the unfinished tale of the Squire. He chooses to regard this, not as ' left half told,' but as defaced by Time, i. e. in good part lost.
Dan. v. n. **669,** 9.
XXXIV. *Ne dare I like :* nor do I dare attempt the same.
431, XXXVII. *bethought :* took thought. Cf. **756,** 107.
XLII. *curtaxe :* properly a kind of short sword or cutlass, but used by Spenser for a battle-ax (short-handled ?). v. **436,** 17.
432, XLVII, l. 5. *went :* going, travel. Cf. **453,** 46, **614,** 3.
433, LI. *free :* do away with.
Canto III, I. *Deathes.* v. n. **33,** 72.
II. *each degree.* v. n. **420,** 18.
434, III. *define :* decide. Cf. **612,** 28.
VII. *harder :* hardier, tougher.
IX. *arresting :* stopping.
not : i. e. ' note,' could not.
435, XI. *thy mischalenge and abet :* thy wrongful challenge and thy maintaining of it.
let. v. n. **266,** 16.
XII. *gorget :* a piece of armor for the throat.
XIII. *traduction :* transmission.
derived : transferred. v. n. **560,** 41.
other brethren : Church emends to ' second brother,' in accordance with **433,** 52, and **436,** 21 f., but Spenser, in such matters, is often unprecise.

XVI. *spoyle :* dead body. Cf. **572,** 33, **646,** 35; v. n. **126,** 6
436, XVIII. *stinted :* put an end to. Cf. **104,** 1092, **351,** 8.
gave way unto : gave way before.
XX. *deadly :* dead, in death. Cf. **188,** 23.
XXIV. *on equall cost :* on even terms. v. n. **248,** 17.
437, XXV. *water-sprinkles :* sprinkled drops of water.
XXVII. *the Shenan :* the river Shannon.
439, XLII. *in lovely lore :* in amorous fashion.
XLV. Rinaldo was cured of his mad passion for Angelica by drinking of a fountain in the forest of Ardennes. v. *Orlando Furioso,* I, 78, XLII, 60–67. Ariosto is referred to as Tuscan (he was a Lombard) because the literary language of Italy sprang from the dialect of Tuscany.
XLVI. *listes.* v. n. **33,** 72.
440, L. *Too weet . . . befeld :* This curious locution, the ' happening' of ' news,' is to be found also in **183,** 34.
441, *Canto IV,* II. *descride :* examined.
IV. *Disgracing :* reviling.
bore : borne.
V. *brode :* widely.
VI. *folke-mote :* a meeting of people.
VII. *vaunted :* thrust forward.
442, XII. *long :* distant.
prolong : defer. Cf. **567,** 1.
443, XVII. *maiden-headed :* He bore on his shield the cognizance of the Order of Maidenhead. Cf. **288,** 2–6. On other occasions he bears his own cognizance, a Satyr's head. Cf. **377,** 30.
XVIII. *wag :* For serious use v. **506,** 22, **750,** 24.
444, XXIII. *glode :* glided.
XXV. *part :* party.
XXVII. *misdid :* did aught amiss.
XXIX. *cuffing close :* dealing blows at close quarters. Cf. **154,** 17.
445, XXX. *compast :* rounded. Cf. **67,** 567.
XXXI. *out of his pray :* from his preying, clutch. Cf. **646,** 41.
XXXIII. *There as :* There where.
XXXV. *allarme :* onset. Cf. **268,** 34.
husband farme : tilled farm.
all : any.
XXXVI. *relest :* released, surrendered.
446, XXXVII. *some while :* at times.
XXXVIII. *carelesse :* uncared for. Cf. **158,** 45.
XXXIX. *describe :* i. e. interpreted.
word. v. n. **257,** 38.
Salvagesse sans finesse : ' wildness without art' (Church).
XL. *charg'd :* levelled, aimed.
him life behote. v. n. **221,** 38.
XLI. *ere his hand he reard :* So long as his spear held, his hand would be down, aiming it.
447, XLVIII. *beauties prize :* excellence of beauty. Cf. **77,** 466.
Canto V, arg. Doth sleepe, etc. : One must supply Care as subject.
I. *for reasons speciall privitie :* ' Because reason has to do with the special connection (between chivalry and beauty)' (Warren).
448, III, l. 9. *usd :* practiced. Cf. **168,** 32.

449, XII. *enchace :* give fitting expression to. Cf. **227,** 23.

he that thought, etc. v. n. **144,** *Ladies.*

XVI. *disclos'd :* unfastened. Cf. **227,** 25.

450, XVIII. *invest :* put on.

XXV. *chalenge.* v. n. **420,** 12.

451, ibid. *alone :* without being compelled.

XXVI. *befall :* fall.

alone. v. n. **451,** 25.

XXXVIII. *else :* elsewhere. Cf. **582,** 43, **383,** 17.

453, XXXIX. *redrest :* refreshed. v. n. **176,** 36.

needed much . . . to desire : must necessarily much desire.

XLIII. *dayly :* of the daytime.

XLVI. *a went.* Cf. **432,** 47.

454, *Canto VI,* III. *voide :* swerve from.

IV. *time yet serves :* time yet favors, it is yet desirable.

v. *have ye . . . shonne :* have you come to this forest for some special purpose? which seems more probable, seeing that you have shunned encounter with one whose arms you have recognized.

455, VII. *that many . . . dread :* which makes many dread him.

IX. *when they :* It would seem as if 'they' should be 'he,' accidentally confused by the printer with the second 'they' of the line.

XIII. *blest.* v. n. **155,** 18.

456, XIX. *ventayle.* v. n. **337,** 24.

shard : shared, cut. Cf. **428,** 17, **529,** 9.

457, XXII. *of his . . . religion :* 'turned his wonder into devotion' (Church).

458, XXXII. *empart :* assign.

460, XLIII. *expire.* v. n. **425,** 54.

XLIV. *Ne wight him to attend :* He reappears in Bk. V, however, attended by Talus.

XLVI. *by her did set :* esteemed her. Cf. **666,** 44.

Canto VII, II. *tride :* experienced. Cf. **468,** 9, 63, 233.

461, V. *rape :* robbery.

VII. *was . . . seene :* seemed (Lat. *videri*).

462, XII. *into darkenesse drive :* i. e. will not suffer to be practiced in the light of day.

XV. *irkes.* v. n. **698,** 906.

XVI. *willed or nilled :* was willing or was unwilling. Cf. *will or nill,* **164,** 43.

463, XXII. *staies :* stays for.

Thracian Nimphes : the Amazons.

464, XXV. *on the land :* on the ground, on his feet. Cf. **542,** 7.

XXVII. *hazard neare :* put in great danger of being hurt. Cf. **121,** 378.

XXX. *tynde :* kindled.

XXXI. *draught :* drawing (of the bow).

distraught : lit. drawn asunder. Cf. **528,** 2.

465, XXXII. *admir'd :* wondered at, gazed at with astonishment. Cf. **631,** 27.

XXXIII. *Thenceforth :* From that place onward. Cf. **104,** 1086, **572,** 35.

XXXVI. *indignity :* indignation. Cf. **65,** 444.

466, XL. *embaulm'd :* anointed. Cf. **173,** 17.

unshed : unparted.

XLIV. *aunswere mum :* say nothing.

XLV. *usage.* v. n. **583,** 3.

467, *Canto VIII,* I. *Well said the wiseman :* 'The king's displeasure is a messenger of death.' Proverbs 16, 14, Coverdale's version.

III. *passion :* suffering. Cf. **210,** 24.

IV. *sensibly compyld :* feelingly composed.

468, IX. *tride.* v. n. **460,** 2.

pertake : partake of, endure.

XII. *glib :* 'a thick curled bush of haire, hanging downe over theyr eyes, and monstrously disguising them.' (Of Irish customs, in Spenser's *View of the Present State of Ireland*.)

XIV. *man of place :* man of rank.

469, XIX. *evill rate :* bad, poor supply.

470, XXV. *causelesse :* without foundation of truth.

XXVII. *hardnesse.* v. n. **102,** 944.

endur'd : hardened.

471, XXVIII. *all onely lent :* entirely gave up.

Regardlesse, of that, etc. : The *of* must do double duty — regardless of being by that.

XXIX. *misregard :* distorted vision.

XXXI. *the stronger pride :* the pride of greater strength.

warre old : 'That is, *worse old*, the older form of *world* being *woruld* or *weorold*. This cynical derivation resembles that of *man* from the Saxon *mán*, sin, and is only a little more fantastic' (Child).

XXXIV. *on footpace :* a combination, apparently, of *on foot* and *at a footpace.*

472, XXXVII. *spare :* restrain.

XLI. *unredrest :* unsuccored, or past help.

473, XLIV. *Mahoune :* Mahomet.

XLV. *his god :* 'Mahoune,' as above. In the old romances, he is a god of the Saracens. v. n. **284,** 30.

XLVI. *accident :* i. e. occurrence.

XLVIII. *brought Unto his bay :* brought to bay before him.

474, LI. *mercilesse :* without hope of mercy.

LIII. *freely set :* set free. Cf. 'freely wend,' **648,** 6.

LIV. *restore . . . reserve :* apparently, let cut . . . keep in.

LV. *reveale :* discover, find out.

LVII. *onely :* especial. Cf. **230** (c. i), 2.

475, LVIII. *to me agree :* assent to my proposal.

LXIII. *streight.* v. n. **731,** 71.

LXIV. *mercilesse :* obtaining no mercy.

476, *Canto IX, arg.* The only marriage specifically mentioned is that of Poeana, but she marries the 'trusty squire,' Placidas, not Amyas, the squire of low degree. Most editors change *Poeana* to *Æmylia,* which indeed assorts the lovers properly, but none the less misrepresents Spenser's meaning. He had in mind to indicate the marriage of Poeana, and simply mistook her lover.

I. *Whether :* which (properly, of two). v. n. **157,** 37.

III. *refraine :* restrain. Cf. **486,** 36.

VI. *rote :* 'There appear to have been two kinds of *rotes,* one a sort of psaltery or harp played with a plectrum or quill, the other much the same as the fiddle' (Mayhew). Cf. **296,** 3.

477, XI. *mazd :* marvelled.

XIV. *corsive :* i. e. corrosive.

478. ibid. *goodly dyde :* of goodly color, complexion.
xx. *beseemed :* graced.
479, xxiv. *upbraide :* scolding.
successe : outcome.
xxviii. *upbraide :* disgrace. Cf. **573,** 41, 90, 2.
480, xxx. *laid :* struck. Cf. **629,** 13.
xxxii. *would them faine :* desired them.
xxxiii. *coast :* quarter, direction. Cf. **537,** 7.
xxxiv. *hartned :* encouraged.
xxxv. *instantly :* urgently.
481, xxxvi. *challenge :* accusation.
xxxviii, l. 7. *sorrow :* afflict.
waide : weighed, valued. Cf. **668,** 55.
xxxix. Scudamour has not yet perceived Amoret. In st. iv of the next canto he speaks of beholding her. Upton suggests that after the present stanza (481, 39) Spenser intended to make use of the original conclusion to Bk. III (v. Appendix II).
xli. *require :* solicit. Cf. **213,** 50.
Canto X, i. *redound :* preponderate.
482, v. *spilt :* inlaid.
vi. *fare :* passage. Cf. **563,** 16.
prepare : provide.
vii. *would it faine to force :* would desire to force it.
483, xi. *utter.* v. n. 244, 34.
xiii. *occasions :* pretexts.
484, xviii. *litle count did hold :* were held in light esteem.
xxi. *onely :* one absolutely. Cf. **230,** 2.
xxiii. *to ghesse :* to the conception, one might think.
485, xxv. *balkt :* i. e. ceased.
xxvi. *aspire :* inspire.
xxvii. *Hyllus :* i. e. Hylas.
Titus and Gesippus : v. Boccaccio, *Decameron,* X, 8.
486, xxxi. *Danisk :* Danish.
xxxv. *hell them quight :* hell requite them, all end in a hell of discord.
xxxvi. *refrayned.* v. n. **476,** 3.
487, xxxix. *masse :* substance. Cf. **388, 4.**
to esteeme : to be reckoned.
xl. *Phidias, etc. :* It was with the Aphrodite of the Cnidians, by Praxiteles, that the youth fell in love.
xliii. *paragons disdayning :* the disdain of their mistresses.
488, xlv. *dœdale :* fertile in creations of beauty.
489, lii. *rate :* manner.
liii. *wade :* Cf. use in **146,** 12.
liv. *drest :* ordered, performed.
lv. *warie :* Upton suggests *wearie.*
lvi. *like astonisht :* as it were confounded. Cf. **185, 4.**
490, *Canto XI,* iii. *begor'd :* smeared with gore.
iv. *descride :* distinguished.
491, ix. *most and least.* v. n. **615,** 12.
x. *O thou :* Clio.
492, xxi. *Oranochy :* Orinoco.
Of warlike Amazons : The discoverer of the Amazon, Orellana, seeing some armed women on the banks, called it the river of the Amazons.
493, xxii. *this to you, O Britons :* evidently in-

spired by Raleigh's ambitions concerning Guiana. His first expedition thither was of 1595.
xxiii. *spouse :* bridegroom.
xxviii. *Troynovant :* London.
494, xxx. *stout :* haughty. Cf. **74,** 265.
xxxi. *chockt :* choked.
adamants : Bristol diamonds.
xxxv. *Holland :* The southeastern part of Lincolnshire, where the Welland enters the sea, is called Holland.
495, xxxvi. *Gualsever :* Wall of Severus.
Logris land : England.
Albany : Scotland.
xl. *the Irishe rivers :* See the delightful paper by P. W. Joyce in *Fraser's* for March, 1878.
496, xliv. *late staind with English blood :* in Glendalough, in Wicklow, where Lord Grey was defeated by the Irish, August, 1580.
xlv. *water chamelot :* watered camlet.
l. *hight of many heastes :* Spenser evidently takes the latter part of the name as coming from νόμος, law.
497, lii, l. 7. The sense seems to be that these 'floods and fountaines' are indeed born of the ocean, but through the agency of sun and air.
499, *Canto XII,* xvii. *unworthy.* v. n. **418, 1.**
her bereaved cares : her woeful bereavement.
xviii. *short :* near at hand.
500, xx. *raw :* prominent ('rawboned').
xxiii. *lent :* given. v. n. **557,** 18.
xxvi. *shrieve :* i. e. shrive.
501, xxxi. *replevie :* bail out.
502, xxxiv. *perfec-ti-ón . . . inspéc-tion :* Such very archaic rhymes persist in Spenser's work to the end. Cf. **92,** 213, 214 ; **119,** 242, 244 ; **693,** 544, 546.
THE FIFTH BOOKE, Prologue, iii. *outhyred :* let out to hire.
iv. *the heavens revolution :* 'In this and the succeeding stanza, the effects of the precession of the equinoxes are correctly stated. The points where the ecliptic cuts the equator have a retrograde motion from east to west of about fifty seconds in a year. The equinoctial points were first fixed in the time of Hipparchus, since which time they have gone back nearly thirty degrees, which is the space occupied by each sign in the zodiac, so that the sun is now in the constellation Aries at the period of the year when he was formerly in Taurus, and in Taurus when he was formerly in Gemini, etc.' (Hillard).
503, vii. *He is declyned :* 'This refers to the diminution of the obliquity of the ecliptic, by which the sun recedes from the pole, and approaches the equator' (Hillard). Spenser or his printer has substituted thirty for thirteen.
the southerne lake : the Southern Sea of Herodotus, bordering the country of the ' long-lived ' Ethiopians.
viii. *star-read :* interpretation, lore of the stars. The record is from Herodotus, II, 142.
ix. *divide :* dispense. Cf. **718,** 6, 526, 39.
x. *his cause to end :* to fulfil justice (which is His cause). Cf. **745,** 211.
505, *Canto I,* xi. *The heavens . . . baudricke :* the

Zodiac, set with constellations as a baldric might be with jewels, and slung diagonally, like a baldric. Cf. **762**, 1 74.

sixt in her degree : Virgo is the sign of August, which, the year beginning with March, was the sixth month.

her righteous ballance : the constellation Libra, the sign of September.

xv. *pranke :* act of malice.

506, ibid. *thanke :* cause for thankfulness.

xxi. *stones.* v. n. **33**, 72.

507, xxiii. *his love :* i. e. the squire's.

good : property.

xxiv. *yield :* concede.

xxv. *by sacrament . . . fight :* The three early modes of determining guilt. (1) The accused took oath that he was not guilty, and brought twelve compurgators, who swore that his oath was true. (2) Failing to secure compurgators, he submitted to the ordeal of fire or water, or (3) in Norman times, to trial by combat. *condiscend :* assent.

xxvii. *cald in dread :* put in danger.

508, Canto II, i. *heroes.* v. n. **64**, 341.

vi. *whose scalp is bare :* 'Most of the northern nations thought wearing the hair long *a sign of freedom ;* the contrary *bewrayed bondage*' (Upton).

509, xi. *Who as they . . . A villaine to them came :* Church suggests (for *Who*) *Tho* = Then; Morris prints *When.* But the construction with pleonastic *who* is very common in the poem. Cf. **541**, 37 (l. 2), **583**, 4 (l. 6), **187**, 20 (l. 5), **186**, 11 (l. 1).

xiii. *bestrad :* bestrode.

510, xvi. *handy :* i. e. by hand.

xvii. *experiment :* art.

512, xxix. *coasted.* v. n. **678**, 39.

xxxi. *containe :* be contained.

xxxiii. *peoples traine :* people who followed him.

xxxiv. *equall :* equality.

so much . . . to trow : so much is to be held more than what is right. Cf. 'pretious to esteeme,' **487**, 39.

xxxvi. *new in pound :* anew in the scales.

514, xlv. *weight :* scale.

xlvii. *For they doe nought but :* Church suggests (for *but*) *'bout.* Spenser seems to mean, however, that though the scales indicate what is right or what is wrong, the mind alone can *weigh* (estimate) the value of the right. The thought, at best, is difficult.

l. *timbered :* massive.

515, liv. *turn'd :* returned. Cf. **395**, *arg.*

516, Canto III, vii. *morrow :* morning. Cf. **16**, 3, 46.

517, xiv. *greet :* offer congratulations on. Cf. st. 15, also **569**, 15.

xvi. *undertake :* maintain.

xvii. *tride :* proved, found to be. Cf. **240**, 9, **680**, 146, **101**, 913.

519, xxix. *defame :* inflict disgrace on.

xxx. *deceaved :* taken fraudulently.

520, xxxiv. *undertake :* take in, become aware of.

xxxv. *displayd :* exposed.

xxxvii. *and fowly shent :* i. e. to shave his beard was to disgrace it as a badge of dignity.

baffuld : to 'baffle' was to inflict open infamy upon a perjured knight. One set part of the punishment was hanging him up by the heels. Cf. Bk. VI, c. vii, *arg.* and st. 27.

unherst : lit., took off the 'herse,' or frame, on which they were hung. But Braggadochio was wearing his armor.

xl. *repast.* v. n. **153**, 4.

521, Canto IV, ii. *impugne :* fight against, resist. *president :* precedent, pattern. Cf. **4**, *To his Booke.*

vi. *thereby :* upon that point.

522, vii. *ere many yeares :* not many years ago.

viii. *empaire.* v. n. **24**, 78.

xiii. *ordained :* selected.

523, xv. *espiall :* identification.

524, xxi. *then :* a blunder for *them ?*

xxvi. *dismall day.* v. n. **274**, 26.

525, xxix. *hold of :* acknowledge allegiance to the order of.

Maidenhead. v. **289**, 6.

xxxii. *observaunce :* ordinance.

in lives despight : in scorn of life. Cf. **684**, 442.

xxxv. *deathes.* v. n. **33**, 72.

526, xxxvi. *to harnesse :* to arms.

xxxvii. *neare . . . few :* The only blunder in rhyme which does not correct itself. In other cases, the word which the poet had in mind is evident on the face of the context. Church proposes *new.*

grate : chafe. Cf. **147**, 19, **107**, 1334.

xxxix. *doale :* dole, alms.

divide : dispense.

xl. *plaintiffe :* plaintive, as in **405**, 12, but with legal sense involved.

xli. *redresse :* succor. Cf. **285**, 34.

distraught : i. e. deprived.

xlii. *pounce :* talon. Cf. **219**, 19.

527, xlv. *on hight :* on high. v. n. **173**, 16.

xlvi. *voided :* cleared. Cf. **626**, 43.

safety. v. n. **77**, 508.

528, li. *could weete :* knew how. By itself, *could* = knew how, as in **542**, 5.

Canto V, arg. wrought : worked, practiced on.

ii. *Trayled :* Trimmed.

diversly distraught : drawn apart in divers directions.

iii. *Basted with bends :* Trimmed with bands, sewn on.

mailes : chain mail.

cemitare : scimetar.

iv. *shaumes :* a wind instrument consisting of a double reed-pipe set in a round mouthpiece. Cf. **225**, 13.

530, xv. *Whose other wing :* One of whose wings. Cf. **252**, 4.

xviii. *lucklesse :* shedding disastrous influence. *crooke :* gibbet (Lat. *crux*).

xx. *curiets :* cuirass.

bases : a skirt of mail worn by knights on horseback.

531, xxiii. *behave :* regulate. Cf. **251**, 40.

532, xxix. *looser :* too free.

XXXIII. *streight* : rigorous. Cf. **613**, 35.
pretence. v. n. **549**, 10.
XXXV. *conceiving* : grasping, understanding.
533, ibid. *markewhite* : The bull's eye of the old
target was white.
XXXVIII. *And, though unlike, they, etc.* : And
although (though that is unlikely) they, etc.
So 1596, making *though* do double service.
1609 reads *And though (unlike) they, etc.* : i. e.
and though (which is unlikely) they, etc.
This later reading looks like an editor's attempt to emend a loose but characteristic
construction.
XL. *worne* : spent. Cf. **149**, 31.
XLI. *Chiefely* : especially.
534, **XLIII.** *causelesse* : undeserved. Cf. **534**, 43.
535, **XLIX.** *invade* : make an impression on. Cf.
297, 6.
LVI. *find.* v. n. **200**, 7.
536, *Canto VI*, I. *aware.* v. n. **336**, 10.
II. *character* : image.
III. In those passages of the *Orlando Furioso*
(xxx, 84 ff., xxxii, 10 ff.) which Spenser imi-
tates in this canto, Bradamante is awaiting
Ruggiero at her home in the castle of Montal-
bano. It would be difficult to say where Spenser imagines Britomart to be. When she parts
from Arthegall (Bk. IV, c. vi, st. 46) she joins
Scudamour in his search for Amoret. She is
present at their reunion (Bk. IV, c. ix), the
last we hear of her till now. Now she is waiting for Arthegall — somewhere, in a castle,
alone. It is part of the charm of Faery Land
that we should not much care where she may
be.
IV. *opprest.* v. n. **301**, 35.
V. *For houres, etc.* : The confusion of this passage has been ascribed to the printer, but it
may well be no more than careless writing.
Cf. **222**, 41, l. 4 ff. The simplest and most
natural of the emendations suggested is to interchange *houres* with *dayes*, *weekes* with
moneths.
537, **VII.** *coast.* v. n. **480**, 33.
IX. *conscience* : consciousness.
X. *intent* : meaning. Cf. **637**, 20.
538, **XVI.** *compacte* : concerted.
XIX. *shot* : shot up, advanced.
539, **XXII.** *wide* : distant, out of the way. Cf.
149, 34, **162**, 26, **217**, 5, **285**, 36.
XXIV. *by that art* : in that manner.
540, **XXXI.** *practise* : conspiracy.
XXXIII. *like fathers sonnes* : sons of a like father,
sons like their father.
541, **XXXVI.** *mountenance of a flight* : extent of
an arrow-flight.
lidge : ledge, edge.
XL. *bestow* : dispose of. Cf. **292**, 28.
Canto VII, I. *containes* : controls, governs.
Cf. **389**, 7.
542, **III.** *shade* : represent figuratively. Cf. st. 2.
IV. *portend* : signify.
VII. *land* : ground. Cf. **464**, 25.
IX. *bake* : harden.
543, **XI.** *containe.* v. n. **389**, 7.
XIII. *priestes.* v. n. **33**, 72.
544, **XIX.** *adjur'd* : sworn.

XXI. *hood* : i. e. mask.
brood : extraction, as in **159**, 8.
XXII. *clemence* : clemency.
545, **XXV.** *them forth to hold* : to keep them
(Talus and Britomart) out.
XXVII. *whilome* : some time before.
546, **XXXII.** *depravest* : defamest.
XXXVIII. *And then too well beleev'd, etc.* : This
can hardly mean more than that she now perceived how untrue her former jealous fears
had been.
XXXIX. *his favours likelynesse* : the likeness of
his countenance ; i. e. she did not recognize
him.
548, *Canto VIII*, **VII.** *tilt and turnament* : The
tilt was the combat of two knights charging
each other with spears. The tournament was
the contest of many knights with both spear
and sword.
VIII. *mistooke* : seized disastrously.
549, **X.** *pretence* : purpose. Cf. **532**, 33, **252**, 1.
XIV. *shade* : veil. Cf. **556**, 12.
550, **XVIII.** *maligne.* v. n. **662**, 11.
551, **XXX.** *sublime* : haughty.
avengement. v. n. **77**, 508.
552, **XXXIV.** *lesse or more* : smaller or greater.
th'ayrie wyde : 'Wyde' is a noun, as 'vast' in
the 'vast of night,' *Tempest*, I, ii, 327.
XXXV. *throe* : i. e. throw.
553, **XXXVIII.** *feare.* Cf. **202**, 21, **651**, 27.
mazed : terrified. Cf. **161**, 22.
XXXIX. *resty* : stubborn.
554, **XLIX.** *scath* : harmfulness.
555, *Canto IX*, v. *face.* v. n. **96**, 506.
556, **X.** *breech* : i. e. breeches.
XI. *in the compasse . . . tooke* : caught within
reach of his clutch.
XII. *Sardonian* : sardonic.
XIII. *flow* : abound.
557, **XVI.** *the base* : low ground.
XVII. *wand* : bough.
XVIII. *lent* : gave, committed. Cf. **296**, 58,
483, 12.
XIX. *the selfe deceiver* : the deceiver himself.
558, **XXV.** *scriene* : 'In some mediæval . . . halls
a partition extending across the lower end,
forming a lobby within the main entrance
doors and having a gallery above ' (Century
Dict.).
XXVI. *Eyther for th' evill, etc.* : Spenser plays
upon the double sense of *font*, (1) Fr. 'they
do,' (2) a spring or 'welhed.'
559, **XXXVI.** *indifferent* : impartial. Cf. **334**, 1.
XXXVII. *Her selfe . . . convert* : She immediately turned.
560, **XXXIX.** *charme* : tune. Cf. **46**, 118.
To all assayes : to every crisis, occasion.
appele : accuse.
XLI. *aspyred* : ambitioned, coveted.
deryve : transfer. Cf. **159**, 3, **435**, 13.
XLII. *Ere proofe it tooke* : Ere it was put to
trial, executed.
type : mark, rank, dignity. Cf. **71**, 70, **87**,
557.
XLIV. *impute* : bring to bear as an argument.
561, **XLVIII.** *detect* : expose. Cf. **116**, 13.
L. *guiltie* : deserving.

562, *Canto X,* IV. *doome a rights :* give judgment rightfully.

VIII. *by times :* at various times.

563, XV. *for his former feat :* i. e. for having rescued Samient and slain the Soudan.

XVI. *armours :* warlike accoutrements. For a similar specific use v. **349,** 58.

fare : going. Cf. **482,** 6.

564, ibid. *count :* consideration. Cf. **484,** 18.

XVIII. *fastnesse :* security. Cf. **555,** 5.

XXI. *may hope for none of mee :* none may hope for of me.

565, XXIV. *farewell open field :* may it fare well with us in the open field. Cf. 'welfare,' **340,** 42.

XXV. *without needing perswade :* 'without the necessity of persuasion ; by force or violence ' (Upton).

XXVI. *conjure :* conspire.

XXVIII. *castle greene :* castle's green.

XXIX, l. 7. *he :* In c. xi this monster is described as female.

XXX. *wonne.* v. n. **245,** 44.

566, XXXIII. *restlesse :* unresting, not to be checked. Cf. **635,** 2.

XXXIV. *enchace :* set, fix.

culverings : i. e. culverins ; in the sixteenth century the largest cannon in ordinary use.

XXXVII. *skreene.* v. n. **558,** 25.

567, *Canto XI,* I. *party :* adversary (Fr. *partie*).

dome : decree.

prolong : defer. Cf. **284,** 28, **442,** 12.

II. *principle :* beginning.

III. *state :* estate, title.

568, V. *rive :* riven.

VIII. *mall :* disable.

X. *buckled to his geare :* ready for the business.

XII. *it light :* the blow alighted. Cf. **681,** 223.

569, XIII. *aware :* wary. Cf. **536,** 1, **336,** 10.

him overstrooke : struck too far.

repaire : draw back. Cf. **182,** 30.

XV. *greet him :* offer him congratulations on. Cf. **517,** 14.

land : country.

XVIII. *tendred.* v. n. **372,** 51.

570, 25. *that monster :* the Sphinx.

the Theban knight : Œdipus.

loose : solve.

deadly doole : the pangs of death.

571, XXVII. *stripe :* stroke.

XXXI. *wombe :* belly.

572, XXXIII. *spoyle.* v. n. **435,** 16.

XXXV. *thenceforth.* v. n. **465,** 33.

XL. *prefixt.* v. n. **726,** 46.

XLI. *too blame :* perhaps *blame* = blameworthy ; more probably *too* = to.

573, ibid. *defraide :* made good.

upbraide. v. n. **479,** 28.

complishing : fulfilling.

XLII. *lent :* granted. v. n. **557,** 18.

XLVII. *diffused :* dispersed.

574, XLVIII. *enquire :* One might expect *inquere.*

L. *to him for to accord :* to come to terms with, accept him.

LI. *remedilesse :* hopeless. Cf. **192,** 51.

LIII. *bosse :* The centre of the shield often bulged out in a rounded prominence, or was adorned with a smaller knob.

LIV. *mis-trayned :* led astray.

LV. *light :* happen.

stile. v. n. **281,** 12.

575, LVI. *terme :* misprinted for *terms ?* Cf. *idols* for *idole,* c. x, st. 8.

Of all things . . . befall : 'May shame attend particularly on those who dissemble ' (Church). Cf. 'faire befall' = good luck to, **139,** *Hobynoll.*

LVIII. *allarme :* tumult, din.

inquyre : seek. Cf. **610,** 11, **230,** 4.

LXI. *meed :* Church suggests, for rhyme, *hyre.* This rhyme-emendation is not as convincing as the others, adopted, since the rhyme to *meed* exists in ll. 1 and 3. Spenser, looking for the rhyme-sound, may well have slipped.

576, LXIII. *indignitie :* dishonorable action.

Canto XII, arg. The first two lines, it will be observed, concern events of the preceding canto.

I. *sacred :* cursed. Cf. **318,** 37.

impotent : uncontrollable.

IV. *with the coast did fall :* reached the coast.

577, X. *streight :* strict.

commaundement. v. n. **77,** 508.

578, XIII. *farre day :* far on in the day.

XV. *sorts :* troops (?).

579, XXII. *loosing soone his shield :* That Arthegall, so soon after condemning Burbon sternly for abandoning his shield (c. xi, sts. 52–56), should abandon his own, is one of the grosser inconsistencies of the poem, due to the allegory. Burbon's shield has a meaning, Arthegall's not.

XXIII. *on his mother earth he fed :* i. e. he bit the dust.

580, XXVIII. *to that :* besides that.

disgraces : ugliness.

XXX. *over raught :* reaching beyond the tips of her fingers.

581, XXXV. *perplext.* v. n. **332,** 54.

XXXVI. *her other hand :* one of her hands. Cf. **252,** 4.

disprad : spread abroad.

582, XLIII. *else.* v. n. **451,** 28.

THE SIXTE BOOKE, Prologue, II. *doe well :* cause to well up or flow.

fury : inspiration. Cf. **138,** *Learned Sh.*

use : resort habitually.

III. *bounty.* v. n. **332,** 49.

IV. *civilitie :* civilized life. Cf. **586,** 26.

583, *Canto I,* III. *embrace :* have regard for. Cf. **385,** 29.

usage : behavior. Cf. **466,** 45.

584, X. *severall :* asunder, each to his own way.

585, XIII. *streight :* pass.

XVIII. *hath it better justifyde :* 'has established a better claim to it ' (Child).

586, XX. *shrinke, and come to ward :* relax his assault and take to defensive fighting.

XXIII. *win :* overtake.

587, XXX. *entreaty :* treatment.

XXXI. *basenet :* a small, light steel headpiece.

band : pledge.

588, XXXVI. *affright :* fearsomeness, terribleness.

589, *Canto II*, I. *know Their good.* v. n. **207,** 7.
590, II. *enforce themselves :* strive hard. Cf. **693,** 481.
  enforst : achieved by effort.
  v. *aglets.* v. n. 'aygulets,' **249,** 26.
  VI. *cordwayne :* Spanish leather (of Cordova). *Pinckt upon gold :* decorated with a punctured design, backed by gold.
  paled part per part : In heraldry, 'party per pale' means that the shield is divided by a vertical line into two equal parts of different color.
  VII. *impugneth plaine :* is in plain violation of.
591, XIII. *occasion broke :* broke the peace and thereby occasioned the combat.
  XIV. *quite clame :* declare free, acquit.
592, XVIII. *taking oddes :* taking advantage.
593, XXIX. *where as no need, etc. :* where I should not necessarily give him occasion to feed his suspicious ('doubtfull,') humor on fears of danger.
  XXX. *a wise man red :* a man reputed wise.
594, XXXI. *convenient :* fitting.
  chace : beasts of the chase, game.
  XXXII. *mantleth :* To 'mantle' was to stretch wings and legs, for ease. Used of hawks at rest on the perch.
  XXXV. *leaves.* v. n. **33,** 72.
  XXXVI. *treated :* conversed. Cf. **383,** 16.
  start. v. n. **19,** 25.
596, XLVII. *coportion :* an equal share.
  Canto III, I. *that good poet :* Chaucer, in the Wife of Bath's Tale, l. 253 ff., especially l. 314,
    'he is gentil that doth gentil dedis.'
  basenesse : low station of life.
597, v. *aymed scope :* mark aimed at. Cf. 'marked scope,' **50,** 55. That passage is the original one of which this is a replica.
  VIII. *invade :* attack.
  bethinking. v. n. **431,** 37.
  IX. *Fain'd her to frolicke :* Tried to cheer her.
  X. *dispacht :* relieved.
598, XI. *tendered :* held dear. Cf. **372,** 51.
  XIV. *overpasse :* enable him to ignore.
599, XXIV. *unaware :* i. e. unawares.
600, XXXIII. *unused :* i. e. he was unaccustomed to such a mode of fording.
  XXXIV. *carriage :* burden.
601, XXXIX. *as now at earst :* now immediately.
  XLII. *move :* present, submit.
602, XLVIII. *and all :* a blunder for *with all ?*
603, L. *eschew'd :* evaded. Cf. **634,** 49.
  Canto IV, I. *ground-hold :* ground-tackle ; cables and anchor.
  II. *incessantly :* immediately.
604, VII. *straine :* i. e. grip. Cf. **274,** 21.
  VIII. *nigh succeed :* get close in pursuit.
  IX. *nere their utmost cast :* in extremities.
  X. *pretended :* presented. Cf. **757,** 221.
605, XVI. *knightes.* v. n. **33,** 72.
  XIX. *bels and jesses :* 'Jesses' were short straps, one on each leg of the hawk, to which was attached the leash that held her in restraint on the fist. The bells were also attached to the legs. Both jesses and bells were left on the hawk when the leash was slipped, as part of her constant harness. Hence the appro-

priateness of the comparison : she ordinarily flies with this weight on her.
606, XXIII. *armes.* v. n. **33,** 72.
  sweathbands : swaddling bands.
  XXIV. *inquirie :* search.
  ayme : conjecture.
  XXVI. *woman kynd :* i. e. womankind = woman ; as in the old ballad :
    ' That every womankind should have
    Their right breast cut away.'
                   [Dyce's Peele.]
607, XXXI. *In th' heritage . . . paine :* 'To inherit our *unsuccessful labor*, the fruits of exertions which have been to no purpose since we are without children ' (Child).
  attend : wait. Cf. **305,** 68.
  XXXIV. *unworthy.* v. n. **418,** 1.
  vouchsafe it : vouchsafe to accept it. Cf. 'deignes,' **10,** 63.
608, XXXVII. *liverey and seisin :* delivery and possession.
  Canto V, II. *good :* proper behavior. Cf. **207,** 7.
609, IX. *uneven :* ill assorted.
610, XI. *inquire.* v. n. **575,** 58.
  XIV. *singled :* isolated.
  XVI. *skilfull of :* aware of.
  secure : heedless.
  XVII. *Securely :* heedlessly.
  invade : assault. Cf. **242,** 25, **310,** 31.
611, XX. *circumvent :* go round about.
  XXI. *escaped hard.* v. n. **165,** 3.
  XXII. *overset :* overmatched.
612, XXVI. *repine :* be indignant. Cf. **154,** 17.
  XXVII. *traine :* series of occurrences.
  XXVIII. *define :* decide, be sure. Cf. **434,** 3.
  XXX. *tokens :* signs, gestures.
613, XXXIII. *parts :* acts. Cf. **267,** 26.
  XXXV. *streight :* i. e. strait, strict. Cf. **577,** 10, **535,** 50, **42,** 236.
  howres . . . to bed : to say (lit. pray) his prayers, i. e. those appointed for the seven set times of prayer.
  XXXVI. *could his good.* v. n. **207,** 7.
  weene : for 'weet,' know.
  XXXVIII. *For his owne turne :* Adapted to his needs.
  XXXIX. *suffraunce :* neglect.
614, XL. *one foote to frame :* to direct, take, one step. Cf. **196,** 30.
  Canto VI, arg. *He :* i. e. Arthur.
  III. *went :* course. Cf. **453,** 46.
  enforme : instruct.
  reduce : lead back. Cf. **364,** 41.
615, VII. *in due termes containe :* restrain within proper bounds.
  X. *professe :* present the appearance of.
  expresse : make manifest.
  XI. *company.* v. n. **297,** 8.
  XII. *most and least :* highest and lowest in rank. Cf. **491,** 9.
616, XVIII. *token :* indication (for finding).
  his attendement : attendance on him. v. n. **77, 508.**
617, XXI. *doing his worst assay :* exerting his utmost efforts.
  XXIV. *on hight.* v. n. **173,** 16.
  XXVII. *avengement.* v. n. **77, 508.**

618, XXVIII. *lode at him did lay.* v. n. **310,** 29.
XXX. *him to bemone :* perhaps, to plead with or for him (Arthur or Turpine) with moans. *thwart :* athwart. Cf. **378,** 43.
XXXI. *abase.* v. n. **234,** 26.
619, XXXVI. *Hence :* Henceforward.
XLII. *fondlings :* simpletons.
620, XLIV. *whylest.* v. n. **727,** 53.
Canto VII, III. *agreeably :* similarly. Cf. **652,** 36.
621, VI. *in timely tyde :* in seasonable time.
IX. *cast :* couple.
622, XII. *In lieu whereof :* In return for which.
descrie. v. n. **211,** 34.
XVI. *againe :* in return.
624, XXVI. *repine :* repine at, disdain. Cf. **612,** 26.
to him object : to lay before him.
bannerall : a small streamer or pennon on the spear of a knight.
XXVII. *baffuld.* v. n. **520,** 37.
upon an asse : Elsewhere, with characteristic looseness, her beast is imaged as a 'mangy jade,' a 'horse,' and a 'palfrey.'
XXIX. *weigh of :* estimate.
XXXII. *Saint Valentide :* St. Valentine's season.
XXXIII. *roules :* i. e. rolls.
626, XLIII. *checklaton :* a 'kind of guilded leather with which they [the Anglo-Irish] embroder theyr Irish jackes [i. e. jackets]' (Spenser's *View of the Present State of Ireland*).
voyded : cleared. Cf. **527,** 46.
627, XLVII. *by Turmagant and Mahound swore.* v. n. **284,** 30.
XLIX. *in a rope.* v. n. 'in a line,' **145,** 4.
628, *Canto VIII,* V. *bashfulnesse :* sense of shame, mortification.
abase. v. n. **234,** 26.
VI. *of blame assoile :* deliver from their shameful plight.
VII. *Abide* (ll. 4 and 8) : stop.
abide (l. 9) : await.
X. *in the middle fall :* in the middle of his stroke, as his sword came down. Cf. 'in the middle plaine,' **566,** 32.
in selfe despight : in spite of himself.
XI. *strayte :* tight. Cf. **731,** 71.
629, XII. *the buxome yoke to beare :* to bear the yoke submissively.
XIII. *layd :* laid on, struck. Cf. **480,** 30.
XIV. *discourse :* holding forth, fighting.
630, XX. *out on me :* probably an ejaculation of complaint. In most modern editions, it is italicized.
XXIV. *it full defrayd :* fully discharged the account.
XXV. *wisely :* considerately.
By meanes : Because.
631, XXVI. *dispraized :* held in contempt.
XXVII. *admire.* v. n. **465,** 32.
XXX. *A great adventure :* The poet never reached this part of his plan. Arthur now disappears finally.
XXXI. *to her inferd :* inflicted on her.
632, XXXIV. *safety.* v. n. **77,** 508.
XXXV. *stealth.* v. n. **301,** 39.
rode : inroad.

XXXVI. *order :* custom.
XXXVIII. *encomberment :* molestation.
633, XLIII. *tempted :* made trial of.
craftie spyes : the eyes. Cf. **154,** 17.
in measure : within bounds.
XLIV. *nigh hand :* near at hand.
XLV. *met :* joined, united. Cf. **596,** 1, **322,** 71.
634, XLVII. *feared of :* alarmed by.
XLIX. *hew :* hewing.
eschew. v. n. **603,** 50.
LI. *mood :* mode, manner.
635, *Canto IX,* II. *restlesse :* unresting. Cf. **566,** 33.
IV. *heardes :* herdsmen.
seat : i. e. rest, lie.
VII. *what.* v. n. **32,** 31.
636, XI. *the bird.* v. n. **667,** 47.
XVI. *clad with lome :* plastered with clay.
637, XVII. *himselfe to disattyre :* to doff his arms, take to dishabille.
XX. *intent :* sense. Cf. **537,** 10.
638, XXIV. *to . . . sought :* proceeded to.
XXX. *doe by vowes devize :* plan to obtain by vows and prayers.
fortunize : control the fortunes of, or make fortunate.
639, XXXVI. *bethought On :* thought of. Cf. **597,** 8.
640, XXXIX. *paramoure :* rival lover (by analogy to *paragone*).
houre : perhaps from 16th century Fr. *heur* = fortune (good or bad). Cf. **340,** 45.
XLIII. *maisteries :* contests of strength.
XLIV. *stiffe pight :* solidly put together, firmly knit.
His dearest joynt : i. e. his neck.
XLV. *needs :* must needs.
641, ibid. *last :* at last.
Canto X, II. *myndes :* purposes. Cf. **257,** 40.
set his rest : make his abode. A punning use (as in *Romeo and Juliet,* V. iii. 110) of the gaming phrase, 'to set up one's rest,' i. e. make one's wager.
sayling . . . port : waiting for favorable winds, kept by head-winds from getting under way.
III. *stales.* v. n. **231,** 4.
IV. *can it compare :* can rival it. Cf. **19,** 67.
642, VI. *towre :* perch high. Cf. **736,** 68.
VIII. *bases :* in the game of prisoner's base.
X. *on hight.* v. n. **173,** 16.
XII. *in compasse stemme :* stay, confine within bounds.
644, XXIII. *entertainement :* manners.
XXIV. *That two of them, etc.* Cf. **22,** 165 ff.
XXVI. *beare the bell :* take first place (as the leader in the flock of sheep carries a bell). Cf. 'give the bell,' **138,** *Learned Sh.*
645, XXVII. *meane :* middle point, hence norm. Cf. **636,** 11, **273,** 16.
Divine resemblaunce : likeness to the divine.
blemish : asperse.
XXVIII. *minime :* in early music, the shortest note used.
XXIX. *yrketh.* v. n. **698,** 906.
XXXIII. *frize :* i. e. freeze.

646, xxxiv. *surprize :* seize.

   helpe her all too late : For *her* Collier suggests *ere,* but the phrase, as it stands, is more characteristic.

   xxxv. *spoile :* body. Cf. **435,** 16.

   in which . . . prayde : in which his own heart was the prey, i. e. to rend her body would be to rend his heart.

   xxxvii. *colour :* conceal.

   xl. *onely :* especial. Cf. **230** (c. i.), 2.

   xli. *from their pray.* v. n. **445,** 31.

647, xlii. *daily night :* night even by day. Cf. **453,** 43.

   xliv. *glade :* gladden. Cf. **401,** 44.

648, *Canto XI,* vi. *to foe or frend :* to treat as foe or friend. Cf. **148,** 28.

   shadow : subterfuge.

   small : slightly.

   freely wend : get free. Cf. **474,** 53.

   vii. *her joyaunce :* the enjoyment of her.

   viii. *in privity :* privately. Cf. **97,** 520.

   ix. *blunt :* uncultivated, wild.

   at the instant brunt : at the very outset, immediately.

   x. *commodity :* profit.

   not to be forestalled : without reserve.

649, xii. *marchandise :* traffic.

   xiv. *prisd with measure :* offered at a moderate price.

   xvi. *balke :* a small ridge or strip of ground in ploughed field, which, through carelessness in ploughing, has escaped the share ; hence, fig., an omission, exception. Cf. **40,** 93.

   xvii. *themselves assay :* attack each other.

650, xviii. *wide :* extensively, in great numbers.

   xix. *pretended :* stretched out.

   xxiii. *Ne cared she.* v. n. **169,** 34.

   xxiv. *infestred :* festered.

651, xxv. *halfe enraged :* became half frantic. Cf. **151,** 50.

   xxvi. *rebound.* v. n. **70,** 22.

652, xxxv. *conduct :* guide.

   xxxvi. *agreeably.* v. n. **620,** 3.

   xxxvii. *heards :* herdsmen, here shepherds. Cf. **635,** 4.

653, xxxviii. *the thiefe :* i. e. the thieves.

   gave them the time of day : 'gave them the salutation appropriate to the time of day ' (Child).

   xxxix. *as did appertaine :* as was appropriate (to their disguise).

   xl. *evill :* bad, i. e. poor, inefficient.

   xliii. *of new :* anew.

654, xlvi. *mand :* i. e. manned.

655, *Canto XII,* i. *borde :* tack.

   bay : bend.

   v. *againe :* on his part. Cf. **352,** 16.

656, ix. *pittie :* fill with pity. Cf. **184,** 43.

657, xvii. *thro :* emotion.

   chylded : gave birth to.

   xviii. *likely hew :* similar complexion.

   Matched with equall yeares : 'corresponding with the distance of time ' (Church).

   xix. *armes.* v. n. **33,** 72.

   xx. *monuments :* i. e. records, relics.

   xxi. *fylde :* i. e. recorded.

   contrive : i. e. imagine.

   xxiii. *estates :* classes of society.

658, xxiv. *dortours :* bed-chambers.

   yrkesome : loathsome. v. n. **698, 906.**

   xxvi. *utmost.* v. n. **407,** 27.

   xxix. *former :* fore.

   on hight : aloft. Cf. **379,** 47.

659, xxxiv. *For never more defaming :* that it might never more defame. Cf. **715,** 27, **103,** 1010.

660, xl. *bate :* i. e. bait, worry.

   xli. *a mighty peres :* Burghley's. It is noticeable that this second part of the *Faery Queen* begins and ends with reference to the poet's being out of favor with the great minister. The change in tone from the sonnet to Burghley which accompanies the first part is unmistakable. In the interval had occurred the delay over the pension and the publication of the satiric references in the 'Ruins of Time' and 'Mother Hubberd's Tale.'

   That never . . . endite : which (i. e. my former writs) never deserved to be indicted, accused, of such offence.

   Two CANTOS OF MUTABILITIE. To facilitate reference, this incomplete book has commonly been numbered continuously with the preceding.

661, *Canto VI,* viii. *clambe :* climbed.

   stage : floor.

662, ix. *intend :* designate as.

   xi. *wend :* weened.

   maligne : envy. Cf. **550,** 18, **355,** 39.

   her need : she must.

   condigne : deserving.

   xiv. *unpurvaide of :* unprovided with.

   xv. *fear'd :* made afraid.

663, xvii. *discharge :* exonerate, justify.

   xix. *estate :* pavilion of state. Cf. ' states; **669,** 8.

   xx. *since :* the time (past) when.

   which doth us yet despite : which (the earth) still bears us a grudge.

   xxii. *beck :* a gesture of command with hand or head.

   xxiii. *extasie :* bewilderment.

664, xxv. *what . . . make ? :* what is your present business here ?

665, xxxiii. *challenge . . . interesse :* claim any interest (i. e. title, right) in heaven.

   xxxvi. *Arlo-hill . . . old father Mole :* North of Kilcolman lie the Ballahoura Mountains ; east of these, with a lower stretch between, the Galties, of which the highest peak is Galtymore. Both ranges are included by Spenser in the name 'old father Mole.' Galtymore rises directly above the forest valley of Aherlo or Arlo, whence the name that Spenser gives it, 'Arlo-hill.'

   xxxvii. *this file :* the course of this story.

666, xl. *Molanna :* A small stream, the Behanna, which, flowing from a double source high up in the Galties, runs a precipitous course to join the Funsheon, a larger stream, about sixteen miles east of Kilcolman. The lower course of the Behanna is cumbered with rocks carried down by winter floods (st. 53).

   That Shepheard Colin, etc. v. **688,** 104 ff.

   condole : bewail.

XLIV. *by nought did set her* : cared nought for her. Cf. **460**, 46.

667, XLV. *for his hire . . . dew* : for his reward, well deserved by one so foolhardy.

XLVII. *darred larke* : Larks were caught by being terrified or fascinated into quiescence. ' Like unto men that dare larks, which hold up an hoby [small hawk] that the larks' eyes, being ever on the hoby, should not see the net that is laid on their heads ' (Cranmer, 1556). On sunshiny days larks were sometimes 'dared' with small mirrors.

XLIX. *baile* : custody, power.

668, LI. *close consort* : secret associate.

short : shortly, soon.

LIV. *may else be rid* : may be read, i. e. seen, elsewhere, i. e. anywhere.

LV. *way* : i. e. weigh, esteem.

Canto VII, I. *thou greater Muse* : Clio, who, in st. 37 of the previous canto, 'lent Calliope her quill,' and who now resumes it.

669, III. *feare* : keep in awe.

v. *wimpled every where* : covered every part as with a wimple.

VIII. *equall* : symmetrical.

states. v. n. **663**, 19.

IX. *Dan* : Master. Cf. **240**, 7, **430**, 32. The reference is to Chaucer's *Parlement of Foules*, ll. 316-318.

'And right as Aleyn, in the Pleynt of Kinde,
Devyseth Nature of aray and face,
In swich aray men mighten hir ther finde.'

The author to whom the task of describing Nature is thus 'transferd' is a certain Alanus de Insulis, of the 12th century ; his book bears the title, *De Planctu Naturæ*.

670, x, l. 7. Most modern editions reject *which* (the reading of both 1609 and 1611) as superfluous. It does indeed confuse the thought, but no more than is characteristic of Spenser's occasional haste. v. n. **536**, 5. To omit it, and begin a fresh sentence or division with l. 3, seems merely to substitute the difficulty of unnaturalness for that of confusion.

XIV. *indifferently* : impartially.

unequally : unjustly.

XVII. *most regiment* : chief government.

inholders : tenants.

convent : convene.

672, xxv. *themselves* : each other. Cf. **649**, 17.

XXVIII. *morion* : a helmet without face-guard.

XXXI. *bill* : beak, nose.

673, xxxv. *that ungracious crew* : Warton thinks this a slur on the Puritans ; Child, on an 'affected manner of retiring from a room without turning the back.'

XXXVII. *the righteous virgin* : Astræa. Cf. **504**, 5 ff.

extold : carried up.

XXXVIII. *A paire of waights* : Libra, the zodiacal sign of September.

XXXIX. *wine-fats* : wine-vat's. *see* : sea ?

XL. *lard* : bacon.

674, XLII. *earth-pot steane* : large earthen jar. ' Stean ' was first a stone jar ; then a jar of either stone or earth. The constellation Aquarius.

XLIII. *harnesse* : gear.

burgein : burgeon, bud.

XLIV. *beames*. v. n. **33**, 72.

675, XLVII. *namely wee* : we and no other. Cf. 'by name,' **162**, 26.

XLIX. *perswade* : convince of.

LIII. *comment* : devise, feign.

676, LVII. *affixt* : fixed, set. Cf. **336**, 11.

677, *Canto VIII*, II. *that Sabaoths sight* : 'Spenser confounds *Sabaoth* (hosts) with *Sabbath* (rest). He obviously means the latter only : all things are to "rest eternally with him that is the God of Rest "' (Child).

DAPHNAÏDA, Letter. *the White Lyon* : the badge of the Howards.

678, 12. *heavilie* : sorrowfully. Cf. **88**, 639, **71**, 36.

30. *weaker* : too weak. v. n. **144**, 2.

39. *cost* : coast, approach, move. Cf. **12**, 29.

41. *Jaakob staffe*. v. n. **183**, 35.

679, 108. *the chaunge, etc.* : Natalis Comes relates that Venus, hastening to help Adonis, was wounded in the foot by the thorn of a rose, from which time the rose, till then white, was red with her blood.

112. *staine* : eclipse, excel. Cf. **67**, 525, **255**, 26.

680, 116. *bring to hand* : capture.

146. *tri'de*. v. n. **517**, 17.

156. *A crueR Satyre* : an adaptation of Death to the pastoral mode.

178. *rare it seemes . . . skand* : it seems strange in the eye of reason.

681, 214. *new divinde* : newly made divine. Cf. **68**, 610.

226. *parted* : departed. Cf. **161**, 22.

231. *full hardly*. v. n. **153**, 5.

682, 265. *that ill mote him behove* : which should become him ill.

321. *playes*. v. n. **95**, 394.

683, 346. *astrofell*. v. n. **702**, 196.

684, 442. *in lifes despight* : in scorn of, hating, life. Cf. **525**, 32, **235**, 36.

443. *in despight of* : in scorn of. Cf. **287**, 52.

470. *harbenger* : one who goes before to provide lodging.

475. *Philumene* : Philomel, the nightingale.

685, 521. *succeed* : befall.

529. *cyparesse* : cypress.

686, 558. *cabinet* : little cabin.

564. *dismall lookes dismay*. v. n. 'staring eyes dismay,' **402**, 54.

687, COLIN CLOUTS COME HOME AGAINE, 2. *Tityrus* : Chaucer, as in the *Calendar*.

19. *turning backe* : return.

32. *painfull* : troublesome.

40. *that Angels* : Elizabeth's.

50. *forsake* : evade, shun. Cf. **219**, 24.

66. *The Shepheard of the Ocean*. v. n. **142**, Raleigh.

69. *fit* : air.

74. *that skill he cond* : he knew that art.

688, 80. *bonie* : i. e. bonny, as in l. 96.

96. *Of fellowship* : for good fellowship' sake.

104. *Old Father Mole*. v. n. **665**, 36.

108 ff. *Mulla* : the Awbeg, a stream which, rising to the north of Kilcolman in the Balla-

houra Mountains, sweeps a wide course to the west and south and east past Buttevant (whose old name was Kilnemullah), till, to the south of Kilcolman, it joins the Bregoge, which flows down from the same mountains, in the north-east, to meet it. Between them they almost describe a rough circle about Kilcolman. After the junction, the Awbeg turns south and empties into the Blackwater, in Spenser's day commonly called Broadwater.

118. *So hight, etc.* : 'Bregog' is Irish for 'false, deceitful.'

689. 156. *Thestylis :* Spenser's friend in the Irish civil service, Lodowick Bryskett.

159. *of friendship.* v. n. **688,** 96.

690, 245. *Triton :* This line supplied the conclusion to Wordsworth's famous sonnet 'The world is too much with us.' Craik suggests that Triton is meant for Howard of Effingham, Proteus (l. 248) for Hawkins.

274. *mightie white rocks :* Spenser attributes to the west coast the more celebrated cliffs of the south and east.

282. *Like to an horne, etc. :* Cornwall. Spenser and Raleigh sailed, probably from Cork, around Land's End, to Penzance or perhaps Plymouth.

284. *a loftie mount :* probably St. Michael's Mount near Penzance ; possibly the Hoe at Plymouth.

301. *thy Funchins.* v. n. **666,** 40.

691, 322. *to rest upon her :* to rest herself upon.

339. *goolds :* marigolds.

340. *the circlet of a turtle :* the iridescent band about a dove's neck.

342. *Phebes garlond :* the moon-rainbow.

351. *humane :* human.

366. *fynd :* invent. Cf. **302,** 42.

380. *There is, etc. :* The reference of almost every pastoral name in this list has been disputed.

Harpalus : perhaps Thomas Sackville, Lord Buckhurst, author of the noble *Induction* to the *Mirror for Magistrates.* After the sonnet prefixed to the *Faery Queen* (p. 142), Spenser would hardly omit Buckhurst from the list, and his social eminence would naturally entitle him to first place. In 1591 he was fifty-five years old (for poetical purposes age began earlier in those days), and had served the Queen most actively in various distinguished offices for over twenty years.

382. *Corydon :* Fleay suggests Sir Edward Dyer, founder, with Sidney, of the Areopagus. Spenser could hardly omit him, and his eminence might well place him next to Buckhurst. 'Meanly waged,' then, would signify 'indifferently rewarded' — as by not being yet knighted, an honor which he did not receive till 1596.

384. *Alcyon :* Sir Arthur Gorges, for whom *Daphnaïda* was written. His verse, for the most part, has remained in manuscript.

692, 392. *Palin :* Thomas Challoner, a writer of pastorals (?).

394. *Alcon :* Thomas Watson, the Petrarchist (?).

396. *old Palemon :* Thomas Churchyard, born about 1520, a voluminous and dull poet of the pre-Spenserian era.

400. *Alabaster :* William Alabaster. His *Elisets* was a Latin poem meant to extend to twelve books, but never finished. The manuscript is extant at Emmanuel College, Cambridge.

416. *a new shepheard :* Samuel Daniel, who about 1590 became tutor to the son of the Countess of Pembroke, Spenser's friend and patroness. 'That well tuned song' is *Delia,* of which some sonnets appeared surreptitiously in 1591, the authorized edition in 1592. In 1592 appeared also *The Complaint of Rosamond,* alluded to in l. 427.

434. *Amyntas :* Ferdinando Stanley, Lord Strange, who in 1593 became fifth Earl of Derby and who died early in 1594. v. *Amaryllis,* l. 564 ff. and note.

444. *Aetion :* Formerly accepted as Shakespeare, but now more commonly as Michael Drayton, who in 1593 published *Idea, Rowland's Sacrifice to the Nine Muses,* inspired largely by the *Shepherd's Calendar,* also the *Legend of Pierce Gaveston.* Line 447 would then refer to his heroic pseudonym, Rowland.

449. *Astrofell :* Sidney.

473. *martyrize :* devote as martyr.

693, 481. *enforce :* strive. Cf. **590,** 2.

487. *Urania :* the Countess of Pembroke.

492. *Theana :* Anne Russell, widow of Ambrose Dudley, Earl of Warwick, who died in 1589.

495. *vale :* i. e. veil.

505. *Faire Marian :* Margaret, Countess of Cumberland.

508. *Mansilia :* the Marchioness of Northampton.

516. *Galathea :* not yet identified.

524. *Neæra :* also unidentified.

532. *Stella :* Lady Rich, celebrated by Sidney in *Astrophel and Stella.*

540. *Phyllis, Charillis, . . . Amaryllis:* Elizabeth, Anne, and Alice Spencer, daughters of Sir John Spencer of Althorpe. To them respectively the poet dedicated 'Muiopotmos,' 'Mother Hubberd's Tale,' and 'The Tears of the Muses.'

560. *primrose :* the first or chief rose, the paragon.

564 ff. The husband of Alice Spencer (v. n. *Amyntas,* l. 434) died in 1594. She remained a widow till 1600, when she married Sir Thomas Egerton, the patron of Donne. It was in her honor that Milton composed his *Arcades,* about 1633.

694, 572. *Flavia :* not yet identified.

574. *Candida :* also unidentified.

580. *closure :* enclosure.

622. *furious insolence :* inspired ecstasy.

634. *each where :* everywhere. Cf. **214,** 54.

695, 696. *fained forgerie :* false invention.

702. *schoolery :* school-learning.

705. *there :* probably a blunder for *their ;* 'those who profess them.' Cf. l. 746.

718. *noughts :* to match *bladders.*

696, 724. *painting on a wall :* Cf. 'Painting thy outward walls so costly gay.' Shakespeare, Sonnet 146.

736. *Lobbin :* Leicester, as in **49,** 113.

745. *sciences :* branches of knowledge.

797. *make religion :* feel conscientious scruples.

800. *couples :* coupling, union.

801. *soly couples :* individually a couple.

697, 818. *dignifie :* make worthy.

836. *of . . . define :* determine.

844. *of them :* among them. The enemies are 'hot, cold, moist and dry, four champions fierce,' the four elements.

862. *formall feature :* the mould of form.

866. *dolphinet :* female dolphin.

698, 884. *saw :* decree.

906. *yrkes :* pains, grieves (stronger than the modern sense). Cf. **387,** 43, **462,** 15, **645,** 29.

910. *her bright glorie else :* her glory else bright.

933. *regard.* v. n. **99,** 685.

700, ASTROPHEL, 1. *borne in Arcady :* in allusion to Sidney's pastoral romance, the *Arcadia.*

22. *weetingly :* i. e. those who were beguiled were aware of the beguilement, and yet were beguiled.

55. *Stella :* Sidney's titular mistress, Lady Rich.

701, 91. From this point on, the reference is to Sidney's service in the Netherlands.

96. *Ardeyn :* the forest of Ardennes, famous in romance. Cf. **439,** 45.

Arlo. v. n. **665,** 36.

119. *his thigh :* Sidney's wound was in the thigh.

702, 196. *Astrophel :* perhaps the sea starwort, *aster tripolium.* Cf. **683,** 346.

703 (Verses by the Countess of Pembroke), 12. *warne :* prevent or forbid.

704, THE MOURNING MUSE OF THESTYLIS, 4. *Liffies :* the river Liffey, at whose mouth is Dublin.

7. *clap :* stroke of ill fortune.

705, 21. *deignest not :* deignest not to favor, viewest with disfavor. Cf. **10,** 63.

34. *Reyne :* Rhene or Rhine.

Mose : Meuse.

35. *Danow :* Danube.

706, 75. *shred :* lopped.

707, 171. *respect :* heed. Cf. **21,** 53.

176. *one :* unchangingly.

708, A PASTORALL AEGLOGUE, 4. *the Orown :* presumably some Irish river.

8. *Phillisides.* v. n. **68,** 609.

709, 77. *bourdon :* burden, accompaniment.

84 ff. Bryskett was Sidney's companion upon his Continental tour of 1572–75.

710, AN ELEGIE, 9. *maiden unicorne :* 'The unicorn was the symbol of chivalry in the Middle Ages, and it was fabled that the creature became tame in presence of a virgin' (Child).

711, 27. *od :* different. Cf. **422,** 28.

52. *tend :* stretched.

712, 131. *acquainted :* became acquainted.

174. *set Mars by :* oust Mars from.

713, 206. *creatures :* a trisyllable.

Kinde : Nature.

AN EPITAPH, 5–8. This stanza defies grammatical analysis and interpretation. The original has no comma after *death.*

12. *timelesse :* untimely.

715, ANOTHER, 25. *onely I :* I left alone.

27. *for not wronging :* lest I wrong.

35. *Let all . . . voyd :* a quotation from **38,** 164.

716, AMORETTI, Letter. *sweete conceited :* sweetly conceived. Cf. **773,** 62.

718, II, 11. *afflicted.* v. n. **144,** 4.

VI, 7. *divide :* dispense. Cf. **503,** 9.

720, XIII, 4. *temperature :* mixture.

721, XVIII, 3. *redound :* overflow. Cf. **159,** 8, **182,** 30.

XXI, 9. *termes :* extremes (?).

722, XXII, 1. *This holy season :* not Lent but some saint's day.

XXVI, 13. *accompt of :* take into account.

723, XXVIII, 3. *the badg which I doe beare :* as a poet. The office of poet laureate was not yet in existence.

XXIX, 1. *deprave :* misinterpret.

3. *bay :* laurel.

XXXII, 4. *to what . . . apply :* to whatever he chooses to use it for.

724, XXXIII, 5. *Lodwick :* Bryskett, his friend in the Irish civil service. From its position in the series one would judge this sonnet to be of 1593.

XXXIV, 10. *Helice :* the Great Bear ; but perhaps Spenser means 'Cynosure,' the Lesser Bear, in which constellation is the pole star.

XXXV, 7. *amazement :* stupefaction, hence infatuation. Cf. **206,** 49 ; v. n. **154,** 15.

XXXVII, 13. *Fondnesse :* Foolishness. Cf. **23,** 38.

726, XLVI, 1. *prefixed :* fixed, settled beforehand. Cf. **572,** 40.

727, LII, 11. *dumps :* a word common in the poetry of the mid-sixteenth century, but soon to pass out of serious use.

LIII, 4. *whylest :* until (Lat. *dum*). Cf. **620,** 44, **374,** 8.

728, LVIII. *By her, etc. :* This heading probably belongs to LIX, which is a retort to LVIII.

729, LX, 1–4. The planetary 'yeare' to which Spenser refers is apparently the period of 'restitution,' that during which a planet, leaving a given position with regard to the sun, will return to that same position ; the period, in other words, during which the revolutions of the planet in its epicycle and of the sun in its orbit will bring both back to the same relative position (of course, only approximate). For Mars, Ptolemy reckons this period at 79 years. Had Spenser, then, written '*four* score,' he would have been exact enough for his purpose ; but at Kilcolman he was not likely to have access to astronomical tables.

730, LXIV, 7. *bellamoures :* a flower unidentified.

LXV, 1. *misdeeme :* conceive amiss. Cf. **224,** 55.

LXVIII, 1. *this day :* Easter.

3, *having harrowd hell.* v. n. **212,** 40.

731, LXX, 2. *cote-armour* : a herald's tabard.
12. *amearst* : amerced, punished.
LXXI, 7. *streight* : close, firm. Cf. **24, 99, 475,** **63, 628,** 11.
9. *is woven all about* : Most modern editions change *about* (the reading of all the early texts) to *above*, for the sake of rhyme ; but the sense requires *about*. Morris conjectures 'is all about ywove.'
LXXII, 10. *mantleth.* v. n. **594,** 32.
732, LXXV, 1. *the strand :* the beach at Youghal (?)
9. *quod* : the older form of 'quoth.' Cf. **735,** 35.
LXXVII, 6. *unvalewd* : invaluable.
LXXVIII, 5. *synd* : signed, marked.
LXXX. From its position in the series, this sonnet would seem to be of the late spring of 1594, not long before his marriage.
733, ibid. 9. *mew* : retreat ; lit., the cage in which hawks were put for the moulting season.
LXXXIV, 3. *mavis.* v. n. **736,** 81.
LXXXV, 2. *selfe* : same, very. Cf. **753, 198.**
734, LXXXVIII, 14. *lively* : vital. Cf. **74, 254.** (Epigrams) II, 5. *close convay* : secretly transfer.
735, IV, 20. *fly* : used of any winged insect. Cf. **116,** 17.
EPITHALAMION, 8. *wreck* : violence.
736, 39. *that neighbours* : Her home was at Kilcoran, on the bay of Youghal.
68. *towre* : a term of falconry = to soar in a spiral, or to sail far aloft in circles (cf. **594,** 32). Here applied somewhat fantastically to deer far up on the mountain. Cf. **642, 6.**
81. *mavis* : song thrush.
descant : the melody or counterpoint sung to the *cantus* or plainsong.
82. *ouzell* : blackbird.
ruddock : redbreast.
83 f. *agree . . . To :* accord with. *consent :* harmony.
737, 131. *croud* : viol.
738, 239. *band* : i. e. tie.
265 ff. *This day, etc.* : June 11, St. Barnabas' day, which (the old calendar being at that time ten days out) was also the day of the summer solstice.
739, 290. *nightes* : For this word as a dissyllable cf. **174,** 23.
340. *helplesse* : irremediable. Cf. **171,** 49, **190,** 39.
341. *the Pouke* : Robin Goodfellow.
740, 376. *envy* : be indignant, or begrudge.
420. *haughty.* v. n. **155,** 19.
429. *hasty accidents* : the accidents of haste ; i. e. the marriage day was probably changed at short notice to a date earlier than that originally set.
430. *expect* : await.
431. *both* : both us lovers.
433. *for* : instead of.
743, HYMNE IN HONOUR OF LOVE, 53. *Begot of, etc.* : According to Diotima's account (in the *Symposium*), Love is born of Poros (Plenty) and Penia (Poverty). How Spenser adapted this fancy to the common myth, which he

gives in the previous line, is not clear, perhaps is not meant to be.
106. *deducted* : derived. Cf. **748,** 106 ff.
744, 122. *with countenance coy* : Warton suggests, for *with, from ;* but perhaps Spenser means that the darts of love enter in at the eyes simultaneously with the image of the fair one.
149. *ennoble* : exalt.
169. *enfyred* : hardened in the fire.
170. *As things, etc.* : a parenthesis ; as things divine are least impressed by passion.
745, 211. *win his wish to end* : succeed in achieving his wish. Cf. **503,** 10.
217. *Whose sole aspect* : The mere sight of whom.
746, 263. *unassured foes* : foes not to be trusted, or foes who he is not sure are foes.
285. *arayd* : ranged.
HYMNE IN HONOUR OF BEAUTIE, 23. *her* : Rosalind.
747, 88. *the like assayes to ken* : to make the same tests.
748, 97. *That golden wyre, etc.* Cf. **382,** 7.
135. *corpse* : Frequent in Spenser for the living body. Cf. **104,** 1090, **117,** 60, **159,** 5, **164,** 42, **198,** 40, **232,** 10.
749, 167. *informed* : imparted.
192. *sympathize* : be in accord with.
194. *respect* : heed. Cf. **579,** 21.
198. *Of likely . . . concent* : Of similar hearts combined by harmony of the stars.
235. *beames.* v. n. **33,** 72.
750, 251. *embissade* : on embassy.
252. *lends* : affords. v. n. **557,** 18.
HYMNE OF HEAVENLY LOVE, 13. *tenor.* v. n. 45, 50.
751, 39. *Spright* : Spirit. Cf. **197,** 36.
47. *with . . . embrew* : saturate with sweet infusion.
64. *trinall triplicities* : Cf. **229,** 39. The hierarchy of the nine heavenly orders, grouped in three trines, first systematized by Dionysius the Areopagite. v. Dante, *Paradiso* XXVIII. In the order of nearness to God they stand : I, 1. Seraphim ; 2. Cherubim ; 3. Thrones. II, 1. Dominations ; 2. Virtues ; 3. Powers. III, 1. Princedoms ; 2. Archangels ; 3. Angels. In **755,** 85 ff. Spenser gives an imperfect and confused list of them, a list purely fanciful.
83. *Child of Light* : Lucifer.
100. *flowing* : pouring.
752, 130. *despeyred* : hopeless.
138. *sinnes deadly hyre* : 'The wages of sin is death.'
753, 192. *fared had amisse* : had gone astray.
198. *selfe.* v. n. **733,** 85.
754, 264. *displace* : banish.
284. *idee* : idea. Cf. **755,** 82.
286. *enragement* : madness, rapture.
HYMNE OF HEAVENLY BEAUTIE, 5. *high conceipted* : high minded.
26. *soare faulcon* : a young falcon yet in its first plumage, which is sorrel.
755, 34. *respect* : consideration. Cf. **749,** 194.
52. *gods* : Most modern editions change this reading of the oldest texts to *God*. Spenser is

contrasting the material heavens, which he chooses to call the house of the gods, with the immaterial heavens of the empyrean (l. 64 ff.), the peculiar abode of God. Such mingling of pagan and Christian elements is surely natural enough in a neo-Platonic poem.

72. *first movers :* the *primum mobile*, which, in the Ptolemaic system, is the outermost of the heavenly spheres and imparts motion to each.

75. *redound :* transcend. Cf. **481,** 1.

99. *faire :* beauty.

756, 107. *bethinke.* v. n. **431,** 37.

108. *utmost.* v. n. **407,** 27.

134. *speculation :* sight.

166. *marvelled :* wondered at.

757, 211. *that painter.* v. n. **144,** *Ladies.*

212. *quill :* i. e. brush.

214. *maistring :* superior.

219. *Teian poet :* Anacreon.

221. *pretend :* present. Cf. **604,** 10.

758, 273. *fayned :* unreal.

759, PROTHALAMION, 12. *rutty :* rooty.

13. *variable :* various. Cf. **358,** 1.

760, 17. *long :* distant. Cf. **442,** 12.

23. It was the custom of weddings that the bride should let her hair hang free.

67. *Somers-heat :* i. e. Somerset.

761, 110. *redoubled :* re-echoed.

132. *those bricky towres :* the Temple. Formerly the abode of the Knights Templar ; after the dissolution of their order, granted to the Knights of St. John, and by them leased to the students of the Common Law, who have remained there ever since.

137. *a stately place :* Leicester House, where, in the poet's London days of 1578–80, dwelt his chief patron, the Earl of Leicester. In 1596 it was in occupation of the Earl of Essex and called Essex House.

147 ff. The reference is to the brilliant exploit

of 1596, when the Spanish fleet was burned in Cadiz harbor and the town captured and sacked. Essex commanded the land forces. *Hercules two pillors :* the rocks on either side the strait of Gibraltar.

153 f. This seems to be a pun on *Devereux,* the Earl's family name, as = *devenir heureux* or simply *heureux.*

762, 173 f. *the twins of Jove :* Castor and Pollux, who were made the constellation Gemini. *bauldricke.* v. n. **505,** 11.

COMMENDATORY SONNETS. I, 4. *dislikes :* grievances.

12. *damning :* sentencing. Cf. **530,** 17.

763, III, 12. *meere :* absolute.

IV, 3. *second Babell :* Rome.

766 (The *Theatre* of 1569), VII, 1. *nightly :* nocturnal.

767, XI, 14. *start :* awoke with a start.

768 (Letters) 18. *uttering :* publishing, not necessarily in print.

23. *the work :* evidently the *Calendar.*

his excellent lordship : Leicester, to whom apparently, at this time, the *Calendar* was meant to be dedicated.

769, 69. *one, that :* Stephen Gosson.

82. *cum Aschamo :* It was Roger Ascham who, in his *Schoolmaster,* began the crusade for the recovery of classic measures.

103. *Maister Drants rules :* Archdeacon Thomas Drant (died 1578) would have subjected English prosody strictly to classic law.

771, 285. *presently :* at present.

313. *this* 5 [16 ?] *of October.* v. **769,** 90 f.

773, 62. *jollyest conceited :* most finely conceived. v. n. **716,** Letter.

78. *Petrarches Visions :* presumably the *canzone* (*Standomi un giorno solo alla finestra*) translated by Marot as *Des Visions de Pétrarque,* and from him by Spenser.

A CATALOGUE OF
PERSONS, PLACES, ANIMALS, AND THINGS
CONCERNED IN OR CONNECTED WITH
THE ACTION OF THE *FAERY QUEEN*
ACCOMPANIED BY BRIEF ALLEGORICAL EXPLANATIONS

[This catalogue is not meant to include all heralds, men-at-arms, attendants, etc., who merely fill the back stage of the poem, nor all romance ' properties ' used in the staging. Neither does it take account of the ' chronicle of Briton kings ' in canto x of Book II, and similar passages. It is meant to include whoever and whatever in the story proper has a name, function, or definite meaning.

The allegorical explanations are necessarily short, scattering, and more or less incomplete. They cannot pretend to vie with connected and systematic schemes of interpretation.

The system of reference is as follows: Roman numbers in capitals (e. g. VI) refer to book ; Roman numbers in small letters (e. g. vi) refer to canto ; Arabic numbers refer to stanza.]

Abessa. Superstition, child of blindness of heart. I, iii, 10 ff.

Acheron. I, v, 33.

Acidale, Mount. VI, x, 5–9; IV, v, 5.

Acrasia. Self-indulgence in the pleasures of the senses. In II, i, *arg.* and xii, 1 termed 'pleasure.' II, i, 51–55, v, 27, xii, 72 ff.; III, i, 2.

Acrates v. Pyrochles.

Actea. IV, xi, 50.

Adicia. Injustice, 'wrong.' V, viii, 20 ff., ix, 1.

Adonis. III, vi, 46–49. **Garden of —.** III, vi, 29 ff.

Adulterie. V, ix, 48.

Æmylia. IV, vii, viii, 19 ff., ix, 1–16.

Aesculapius. I, v, 36 ff.

Aeternitie. II, iv, 41.

Agape. The name means 'love.' IV, ii, 41 ff.

Agave. IV, xi, 49.

Agdistes v. Genius.

Agenor. IV, xi, 15.

Aglaia. VI, x, 12–15, 22–24.

Aladine, Aldine. VI, ii, 16–21, iii, 1–16.

Albion. IV, xi, 15 f.

Aldus. VI, iii, 2–9.

Alebius. IV, xi, 14.

Alimeda. IV, xi, 51.

Allo. IV, xi, 41.

Alma. The soul. II, ix, xi; III, i, 1. **v. Temperance, House of.**

Alpheus. IV, xi, 21.

Amavia. She 'that loves to live.' II, i, *arg.*, 35 ff.

Amazons. V, iv, 21 ff., v, vii, 24 ff. **River of the —.** IV, xi, 21.

Ambition. II, vii, 46.

Amendment. I, x, 26.

Amidas. V, iv, 4 ff.

Amoret. III, vi, xi, xii; IV, i, v, 13, 19, 20, 29, vi, 34–38, 46 f., vii, viii, 19 ff., ix, 17 ff., x. **v. Timias.**

Amphisa. III, vi, 4.

Amphitrite. IV, xi, 11, 49.

Amyas. The Squire of Low Degree. IV, vii, 15–18, viii, 50 ff., ix, 1 ff.

Anamnestes. The faculty of summoning up memories. II, ix, 58.

Angel. II, viii, 1–8.

Angela. III, iii, 55–58.

Anger. III, xii, 25.

Antiquitee of Faery Lond. II, ix, 60, x, 70 ff.

Aon. IV, xi, 15.

Apollo. III, iv, 41; IV, xii, 25 f.

Appetite. II, ix, 28.

Aprill. VII, vii, 33.

Archimago. Designated as 'hypocrisy' (I, i, *arg.*), but, in his miscellaneous activities as enchanter and agent of deceit, not to be fully described by any one label. In Bk. I, a type of the Jesuits. I, i, 29 ff., ii, 1–11, iii, 24 ff., vi, 34 ff., xii, 24 ff.; II, i, 1–25, iii, 11–19, vi, 47 ff., viii, 10, 11, 19–22, 56; III, iv, 45.

Argante. III, vii, 37, xi, 3 f.

Arion. IV, xi, 23.

Arlo Hill. v. Notes. VII, vi, 36 ff., vii, 3 ff.

Armeddan. VI, iii, 5.

Arras. III, i, 34–38, xi, 28–46.

Artegall, Arthegall. The champion of Justice; Arthur, Lord Grey of Wilton. III, ii, iii; **IV,** iv, 39 ff., v, 9, 21, vi; **V;** VI, i, 4–10.

Arthur. Magnificence (or magnanimity), the virtue which is the perfection of and contains all the rest. As the deliverer in Bk. I and perhaps also in Bk. II, Heavenly Grace (I, viii, 1). Perhaps intended originally to represent the Earl of Leicester. In V, x and xi, Leicester. I, vii, 29 ff., viii, ix, 1–20; II, viii, ix, x, xi; III, i, 1–18, iv, 45 ff., v, 1–12; IV, vii, 42 ff., viii, ix; V, viii, ix, x, xi, 1–35; VI, v, 11 ff., vi, 17 ff., vii, 1–27, viii, 4–30. His shield, I, vii, 33–36, viii, 19–21; V, viii, 37 ff., xi, 10. His horn, I, viii, 3–5; II, ix, 11. His sword, **v. Morddure.** His horse, **v. Spumador.**

Asopus. IV, xi, 14.

Astræa. V. i, 5–12.

Astræus. IV, xi, 13.

Ate. The goddess of mischief. IV, i, 17 ff., ii, iv. 3, 9–12, v, 22 f., ix, 24; V, ix, 47.

Humiltâ. Humility. I, x, 5.
Huon. II, i, 6.
Hyllus. Hylas. IV, x, 27.
Hyponeo. IV, xi, 51.

Idle Lake. The approach to sensual excess is by way of idleness. II, vi, xii.
Idleness. I, iv, 18–20, 36, 43.
Ignaro. Ignorance. I, viii, 30–34.
Impatience. II, xi, 23 ff.
Impietie. V, ix, 48.
Impotence. II, xi, 23 ff.
Inachus. IV, xi, 15.
Incontinence of Lyfe. V, ix, 48.
Indus. IV, xi, 21.
Infamie. VI, vii, 34.
Infant. VI, iv, 17–38. v. also **Ruddymane.**
Infirmity. III, xii, 25.
Ino. IV, xi, 13.
Irena, Eirena. Ireland. V, i, 3 f., xi, 38–43, xii.
Isis Church. V, vii, 1–24.
Ister. IV, xi, 20.
Ixion. I, v, 35.

January. VII, vii, 42.
Jarre v. Pyrochles.
Jocante. Jesting. III, i, 45.
Jonathan. IV, x, 27.
Jove. VII, vi, vii.
Joyeous v. Castle.
July. VII, vii, 36.
June. VII, vii, 35.
Justice. V, ix, 44.

Kenet. IV, xi, 29.
Kingdomes Care, The. Lord Burghley. V, ix, 43.
Kirkrapine. Plunder of the Church by the upper clergy, who amassed benefices and who inclined to the superstitions of Rome. Cf. the *Shepherd's Calendar*. Or perhaps, the wealthy monastic clergy, suppressed by Henry VIII. I, iii, 16–20.
Knight. Unhorsed by Britomart, IV, i, 9–15 ; slain by Tristram, VI, ii, iii, 17 f.; companion of Enias, VI, vii, 3–8.
Knights. Adicia's, V, viii, 4–23; Geryoneo's, V, x, 34–37; in Radegund's prison, V, v, 22 f., vii, 43.

Labryde v. Satyrane.
Lachesis. IV, ii, 47 ff.
Lady. Slain by Sangliere, V, i, 14 ff.; carried off by Sangliere, V, i, 16 ff.; rescued by Tristram, VI, ii. v. also **Temperance, House of.**
Lamb v. Una.
Lamoracke. VI, xii, 39.
Lansack. V, iii, 5.
Laomedia. IV, xi, 51.
Law of Nations, The. V, ix, 44.
Lechery. I, iv, 24–26.
Lee. IV, xi, 29; IV, xi, 44.
Liagore. III, iv, 41; IV, xi, 51.
Life. VII, vii, 46. **Well of** — and **Tree of** —, the two sacraments, 'as generally necessary to salvation,' baptism and the supper of the Lord. I, xi, 29–36, 46–50.
Liffar. IV, xi, 41.
Liffy. IV, xi, 41.

Lindus. IV, xi, 39.
Lion. Reason (?). The killing of Kirkrapine, perhaps, the suppression of the monasteries by Henry VIII. I, iii. Another, of even more doubtful significance, V, ix, 33.
Lionesse. VI, ii, 30.
Lisianassa. IV, xi, 50.
Litæ. Prayers, petitions. V, ix, 31 f.
Lone. IV, xi, 39.
Losse of Time. III, xii, 25.
Love. IV, x, 32–36.
Lucida. IV, v, 11.
Lucifera. Pride, chief of the seven deadly sins. The other six counsel and serve Pride. Her house, then, is, in the larger sense, the life of sin, to which a false religion naturally leads. I, iv, v.
Lucy. V, iv, 4–20.
Lust. IV, vii.

Mæander. IV, xi, 21.
Maidens. I, xii, 6–8; II, xii, 27–29. v. **Damsel.**
Maidenhead, Order of. II, ii, 42, ix, 2–6; IV, iv, 17, 22, 38, 48; V, iv, 29.
Malbecco. 'The cuckold;' in the end a mere embodiment of Jealousy. III, ix, x.
Malecasta. Unchastity. III, i, 20 ff.
Maleffort. VI, i.
Maleger. The life of the evil desires and passions. His twelve troops, the seven deadly sins and the sins of the five senses. II, xi.
Malengin. 'Evil ingenuity,' guile. V, ix, *arg.*, 4–19.
Malfont. v. Notes. V, ix, 25 f.
Malvenù. 'Ill come.' I, iv, 6.
Mammon. 'The care of this world and the deceitfulness of riches.' II, vii.
Many Ilands, Lord of. VI, xii, 4 ff.
March. VII, vii, 32.
Maridunum. III, iii, 7.
Marinell. III, iv; IV, xi, xii; V, ii, 2–4, iii.
Mars. VII, vii, 52.
Matilda. III, iii, 13.
Matilde. VI, iv, 26 ff.
May. VII, vii, 34.
Mayre. IV, xi, 44.
Medina. The 'golden mean' of Aristotelian ethics, virtue conceived as a mean between extremes of defect and excess. The 'mothers three,' perhaps, the three elements of the soul, (according to Plato,) the reasonable, the appetitive, the passionate. II, ii, iii, 1 f. v. **Elissa.**
Medway. IV, xi.
Meliboe. Sir Francis Walsingham, father-in-law of Sidney. V, ix, x, 40 ff., xi, 11, 18, xii, 9. His wife. VI, ix, 17, xi, 18, xii, 9.
Meliogras. VI, ii, 28.
Melissa. VI, xii.
Melite. IV, xi, 49.
Menevia. III, iii, 55.
Menippe. IV, xi, 51.
Merchants. VI, xi, 9 ff.
Mercilla. Queen Elizabeth, as an exponent of mercy and also (V, viii, 20, x, 1) of justice. V, viii, 16–23, ix, 20 ff., x, 1–17.
Mercury. VII, vi, 14 ff., vii, 51.
Mercy. I, x, 34 f, 45–50.

Shure. IV, xi, 42 f.; VII, vi, 54.
Silence. IV, x, 51.
Sisyphus. I, v, 35.
Skell. IV, xi, 37.
Slane. IV, xi, 41.
Sleep. VII, vii, 44. **House of —.** II, vii, 25. **v. Morpheus.**
Slowth v. Idleness.
Sophy. II, ix, 6.
Sorrow. II, vii, 22; III, xii, 25.
Souldan, The. Spain. His overthrow on 'the greene' by the power of the magic shield, the defeat of the Armada at sea by interposition of God, in storms. V, viii.
Speranza. Hope. I, x, 4, 12, 14, 22.
Spio. IV, xi, 48.
Sprights. I, i, 38 ff., ii, 2–5; II, vii. 32; III, viii, 4 f.
Spring. VII, vii, 28.
Spumador. 'The foamer.' II, viii, 17, xi, 19; III, iv, 61; IV, viii, 22, 37; V, viii, 36, xi, 8 f.; VI, v, 21.
Squire. Righted by Artegall, V, i, 13–30 ; righted by Calidore, VI, i ; Arthur's squire **v. Timias;** Squire of Low Degree **v. Amyas.**
Squire of Dames. III, vii, 37 ff., viii, 44 ff., ix; IV, ii, 20–31, iv, 2 f., v, 18.
Stoure. IV, xi, 32.
Strife. II, vii, 21; III, xii, 25.
Strond v. Castle.
Sture. IV, xi, 33.
Summer. VII, vii, 29.
Suspect. III, xii, 14 f.
Swale. IV, xi, 37.
Sylvanus. I, vi, 14–17, 33.

Talus. Power, as the servant and executor of Justice. V, i, 12 ff., ii, iii, 37 ff., iv, v, 19, vi, vii, 26, 35 f., viii, 29, ix, xi, 47 ff., xii.
Tamar. IV, xi, 31.
Tanaquill. II, x, 76. **v. Gloriana.**
Tantalus. I, v, 35; II, vii, 57–60.
Temperance. V, ix, 32. **House of —.** 'Man's body,' the habitation of the soul (Alma). The anatomical details hardly need elucidation. See, however, the Notes. The ladies and their paramours (ix, 34 ff.) are the tastes, sentiments, etc. II, ix, xi.
Terpin. V, iv, 21 ff., v, 18.
Terwin. I, ix, 27 ff.
Tethys. IV, xi, 18.
Thalia. The Nereid, IV, xi, 49; the Grace, VI, x, 12–15, 22–24.
Thame. IV, xi, 24–26.
Thamis. IV, xi.
Theise. IV, xi, 47.
Themiste. IV, xi, 51.
Therion v. Satyrane.
Theseus. I, v, 35; IV, x, 27.
Thetis. The river, IV, xi, 29; the Nereid, IV, xi, 48.
Thyamis v. Satyrane.
Tiger. II, xi, 20–33; VI, x, 34–36.
Time. III, vi, 39–41; VII, vi, 8, vii, 47 f.
Timias. In his relations with Belphœbe, taken by most critics to represent Raleigh, and the Amoret episode (IV. vii. viii). Raleigh's affair with

Elizabeth Throgmorton, the Queen's maid of honor, whom he seduced and then married, to the Queen's exceeding wrath. Others see a reference to Leicester and his secret marriage with the Countess of Essex ; but when Bk. IV was written, that affair was ancient history. I, vii, 37, viii; II, viii, 17, ix, 11, xi, 17, 29–31, 48; III, i, 18, iv, 47, v; IV, vii, 23 ff., viii, 1–18; VI, v, 11 ff., vi, 1–16, vii, 39 ff., viii, 1–30.
Timon. I, ix, 4.
Titan. VII, vi, 27.
Titus. IV, x, 27.
Tityus. I, v, 35.
Treason. II, vii, 22; IV, x, 20.
Tree of Life v. Life.
Trent. IV, xi, 35.
Trevisan. I, ix, 21 ff.
Triamond. One of the two champions of Friendship. IV, ii, 30 ff., iii, iv, v.
Tristram. VI, ii.
Triton. III, iv, 33; IV, xi, 12.
Trompart. 'The deceiver.' Perhaps Simier, Alençon's envoy. II, iii; III, viii, 13, 19, x, 20–43, 54; V, iii, 38.
Trowis. IV, xi, 41.
Tryphon. III, iv, 43; IV, xi, 6 f., xii, 22–24.
Turpine. VI, iii, 30 ff., iv, 1–9, v, 33 f., vi, 17 ff., vii, 1–27. v. also **Terpin.**
Twede. IV, xi, 36.
Tybris. IV, xi, 21.
Tygris. IV, xi, 20.
Tyne. IV, xi, 36.
Typhaon. V, x, 10; VI, vi, 11 f.
Typhœus. I, v, 35; III, vii, 47.

Ulfin. III, iii, 55.
Una. Truth. I, i, ii, 1–8, iii, vi, vii, 20 ff., viii, ix, x, xi, xii; II, i, 19; III, i, 24. Her ass, at first a symbol of humility, then a mere beast. I, i, 4, iii, 4, 44, vi, 19, etc. Her lamb (which, being inconvenient to the action, at once disappears), a symbol of innocence. I, i, 4. Her parents, variously interpreted : the Old and New Testaments, denied by the Roman Church to the laity, or Adam and Eve, as representatives of the human race. I, i, 5, vii, 43 ff., xi, 3, xii.
Unthriftyhead. III, xii, 25. **Quicksand of —.** II, xii, 18 f.
Ure. IV, xi, 37.
Uther Pendragon. II, x, 68; III, iii, 52.

Vanitie. I, iv, 13.
Venus. III, vi; VII, vii, 51. Her girdle, IV, v. 2–6. Her temple and image, IV, x.
Verdant. II, xii, 72 ff.
Vesper. VII, vi, 9.
Villeins. (Maleger's) II, ix, 12–17, xi. **(Grantorto's)** V, xi, 44 ff.

Wandring Islands. II, xii, 10–14.
Warders. The teeth. II, ix, 26.
Watchman. I, xii, 2; II, ix, 11 f.; IV, ix, 5; V, iv, 36.
Well v. Fountain.
Well of Life v. Life.
Welland. IV, xi, 35.
Werfe. IV, xi, 37.

Winter. VII, vii, 31.
Witch. III, vii, 6-23, viii, 2-9. Her son. III, vii, 12-21, viii, 2-13. v. also **Duessa, Acrasia.**
Womanhood. IV, x, 49 ff.
Wrath. I, iv, 33-35.
Wylibourne. IV, xi, 32

Yar. IV, xi, 33.
Yeomen. VI, vi, 25 ff.
Young men. I, xii, 5 f.

Zele. In two distinct forms. I, x, 6; V, ix, 39 ff.

GLOSSARY

[For the system of reference, etc., see the heading of *Notes*.]

Aband: to abandon, 304, 65.

Abashment: dismay, panic, 383, 16, 386, 34.

Abeare: to comport (oneself), 579, 19, 640, 45.

Able v. Abye.

Abject: to cast down, 556, 9.

Aboord, abord: adrift (for **abroad**?), 111, 14, 94, 324; on or along the surface of, 80, 46; **lay a.**, to bring one's ship alongside of, for fight, 396, 6.

Abouts: about, 204, 36.

Abrade, abrayd: to arouse, startle out of sleep, 333, 61, 404, 8.

Abray (*pret.* **abraid, abrayd**): to start out of sleep or a swoon, to awake, 459, 36, 443, 22.

Abusion: abuse, 581, 40; deception, fraud, 419, 7, 107, 1363; **turne to a.**, to abuse, 93, 220.

Abye: to pay the penalty for, 284, 33, 369, 24; to suffer, endure, 745, 242; to endure, last, 373, 3; to abide, face, 257, 40.

Accloy: to clog, 273, 15; to cumber, 13, 135.

Accoast v. Accoste.

Accompt: to account, 636, 14.

Accorage: to encourage, 244, 38, 385, 34.

According: according to, in accordance with, 683, 370, 629, 18; accordingly, 305, 71.

Accoste: to be adjacent, 573, 42; to move close to the ground, 594, 32.

Accourage v. Accorage.

Accourt: to pay court to, 241, 16.

Accoy: to soothe, 475, 59; to daunt, 12, 47.

Accoyl: to gather together, 292, 30.

Accrewe: to increase, 111, 15; to collect, 456, 18.

Accustom: to be wont, 327, 13.

Achates: provisions bought, 292, 31.

Acquight, acquite (*pp.* **acquit**): to deliver, release, 192, 1, 313, 3, 526, 39.

Adaw: to subdue, daunt, appall, 559, 35, 375, 13, 544, 20; to lose vigor, wane, 457, 26.

Adayes: daily, 16, 42.

Addeeme: to adjudge, 517, 15.

Addoome: to adjudge, 676, 56.

Address: to prepare, make ready, adjust, 435, 14, 195, 22, 193, 6, 326, 4; to set up, erect, 126, 5, 693, 562; to equip, attire, 154, 11, 639, 36; to direct, 234, 25, 218, 17, 208, 11; (*reflex.*) to direct one's course, 351, 6, 539, 22, 400, 40.

Admiraunce: admiration, 567, 39.

Adore: to adorn, 496, 46.

Adorne: adornment, 413, 20.

Adrad, adred: terrified, afraid, 506, 22, 334, 62, 437, 25, 83, 304.

Advance (*pret.*, *pp.* **advaunst**): to lift up, 311, 34, 737, 145; to extol, 44, 47, 387, 43; to stimulate, impel, 232, 10.

Advengement: revenge, 434, 8.

Adventer: to adventure; take the chance of, 528, 5, 103, 1005.

Adventure: hap, chance, 117, 67, 181, 21, 428, 20; opportunity, 436, 20; venture, risk, 327, 10, 694, 567.

Advew: to view, 518, 20.

Advise, avise: to look at, examine, perceive, observe, consider, reflect on, 384, 23, 429, 22, 296, 59, 476, 4, 293, 38, 176, 40, 749, 190; to recognize, 466, 43; to purpose, resolve, 310, 27; (*reflex.*) to bethink (oneself), take thought, consider, resolve, 93, 281, 270, 46, 342, 6, 400, 40, 414, 28; **well avisd, ill avisd** (of persons), discreet, indiscreet, 316, 26, 321, 61, 380, 57.

Advizement: reflection, 260, 13; counsel, 289, 9.

Adward: an award, 484, 17; to award, 501, 30.

Aemuling, -ed: emulating, -ed, 687, 72, 73.

Afarrs: afar, 712, 167.

Afeard v. Affeard.

Affamisht: famished, 734, 87.

Affeard: frightened, afraid, 252, 45, 402, 52.

Affect: feeling, affection, appetite, passion, 589, 45, 611, 24, 719, 6, 744, 180.

Affection: emotion, 124, 12, 597, 4; passion, appetite, 615, 7, 256, 34, 375, 15; inclination, bias, 458, 33.

Affide v. Affy.

Affoord, afford: to yield, grant, consent, 282, 19, 266, 19; to attribute, 586, 26.

Affrap: to strike, 234, 26, 335, 6.

Affray: to alarm, terrify, scare away, 172, 8, 287, 48, 484, 16 — assault, 583, 2; rout, panic, 443, 22; fear, terror, 564, 19, 160, 12.

Affrended: made friends, 440, 50.

Affret: impetuous onset, 390, 16, 428, 15.

Affright: frightened, 263, 37.

Affront: to confront, oppose, attack, 436, 22, 351, 7, 261, 20.

Affy: to confide, 535, 53; to betroth, 597, 7, 515, 2.

Aflot: afloat, overflowed, 127, 9.

Aggrace: to favor, 209, 18; to give or add grace to, 320, 58 — goodwill, graciousness, 288, 56.

Aggrate: to please, gratify, 263, 33, 76, 406; to thank, pay acknowledgments, 429, 23.

Aggreeve v. Agreeve.

Aghast (*pret.*): frightened, terrified, 280, 4, 358, 3, 668, 52.

Agone: ago, 84, 359.

Agraste: *pret.* of **aggrace**, q. v.

Agreeve, agrieve: to afflict, grieve, vex, 129, 4, 60, 91, 465, 37, 213, 49.

Agrise, agrize: to horrify, terrify, 337, 24, 565, 28, 669, 6; to make horrible or terrible (?), 270, 46, 468, 12.

Aguise: to attire, array, 98, 656, 264, 7, 335, 31; to fashion, 337, 18.

Alablaster: alabaster, 633, 42.

Albe, albee: although, 10, 67, 748, 149; despite, 548, 3. Albe is a contraction of albeit = although it be (that). In the phrases, albe, albe he, albe it, etc., with a following verb, albe is resolved into its elements (al + be), and the phrases = although (or whether) he be, etc., 26, 266, 508, 6, 660, 40. [Cf. All were.]

Alegge, allegge: to alleviate, 16, 5, 336, 15.

Aleggeaunce: alleviation, 364, 42.

Alew: halloo, howling, 537, 13.

Algate, algates: in any way, in any case, by all means, at all events, 639, 33, 519, 30, 261, 20; altogether, 230, 2, 332, 53; for all that, nevertheless, 240, 12, 460, 44, 48, 21.

Alienate (pp.): estranged, 18 arg.

Alight (pp.): lighted, fallen, 161, 20.

All were: in phrases, a. w. he, a. w. it, etc. Here all = although: the phrases = although he were, etc., 240, 12, 325, Prol., 2, 40, 64. [Cf. Albe.]

Allegge v. Alegge.

Als, alls: also, 140, Ignoto, 201, 18; als . . . as, so . . . as, 202, 21; als . . . and, both . . . and, 32, 8.

Also: even so, 53, 75.

Alsoone: as soon, 33, 101.

Amate: to dishearten, dismay, subdue, 205, 45, 231, 6, 377, 35 — to bear company, 292, 34.

Amenage: to domesticate, tame, or to manage, handle, 253, 11.

Amenance: bearing, conduct, 434, 5, 288, 5.

Amend (pp.): amended, 33, 170.

Amiddes: amid, 149, 36.

Among: here and there, 685, 530; betweenwhiles, every now and then, 582, 42, 54, 112.

Amove, amoove: to stir, stir up, excite, rouse, 405, 13, 232, 12, 170, 45, 201, 18, 218, 16, 685, 545; to remove, 268, 37, 395, 1; a. of, to question about, 391, 24.

Annoy: vexation, grief, anguish, 293, 35, 181, 17, 597, 4; anger, 369, 24; annoyes, mischievous, injurious acts, 245, 43 — to afflict, grieve, 768, 44.

Anon, anone: immediately, forthwith, 329, 25, 572, 37.

Apall v. Appall.

Apay: always with well or ill and usually as pp. (apayd). Two root meanings: — (1) to satisfy, please (well or ill), 576, 64, 341, 47, 453, 42. Ill a. sometimes = to afflict, 679, 70, 316, 28. (2) to repay, requite, 532, 33, 481, 40, 363, 36. [v. Ypaid.]

Appall, apall: to fade, languish, decay, 457, 26; to cause to fade or decay, to enfeeble, to quell, 243, 32, 331, 46.

Apparaunce: appearance, 332, 52.

Appeach: to impeach, accuse, inform against, 286, 44, 311, 40, 396, 6, 533, 37, 561, 47.

Appellation: appeal, 665, 35.

Apply: to join (to), 331, 40, 63, 236; to prosecute, ply, 213, 46, 307, 7, 404, 6; to accommodate, adapt, 358, 61, 376, 24, 46, 9; to direct (one's course), 264, 5, 524, 21; to address, 317, 32.

Appose: to confront with questions, examine, 560, 44.

Approvance: approval, 737, 144; maintenance, 619, 35.

Approve: to prove, demonstrate, 255, 24, 329;

27, 672, 27; to put to proof, test, 621, 5, 247, 15; to experience, feel, 391, 24, 182, 26.

Arayd v. Array.

Arborett: a little tree, a shrub, 265, 12.

Arck, arke: an arch, 113, 27, 125, 4.

Aread, arede, areed (pp. aredd): to declare, make known, utter, tell, speak, 196, 31, 200, 6, 203, 28, 209, 17, 247, 14, 71, 52, 687, 15; to guess, conjecture, perceive, 375, 16, 520, 35, 537, 8; to interpret, unriddle, 231, 7, 449, 15; to counsel, 144, 1, 227, 28, 383, 17; to decree, appoint, adjudge, 577, 9, 639, 33.

Arear, arrear, arere: backward, 311, 36, 86, 468; behind, 630, 23, wex a., to fall off, slacken, 376, 24.

Aredd, arede, areed v. Aread.

Arere v. Arear.

Arew: in a row, 580, 29; in succession, 708, 186.

Arights: in accordance with right, 562, 4.

Arive: to come to shore, 112, 21.

Arke: a coffer, chest, 442, 15. [v. also Arck.]

Armory: armor, a suit of armor, 148, 27, 349, 59.

Arraught: seized, snatched, 301, 34.

Array: to put in (sorry) plight, treat (ill), 202, 23, 511, 25, 595, 42.

Arrear v. Arear.

Arret: to commit, entrust, assign, 281, 8, 307, 7, 382, 7; to adjudge, 450, 21.

As: as if, 159, 6, 220, 31, 223, 48; as then, at that time, 17, 113, 559, 36.

Aslake: to assuage, appease, 726, 44, 163, 36.

Aspy: to espy, 403, 3.

Assay: proof, test, trial, 425, 50, 275, 34, 747, 88, 142, Cumberland, 235, 35, 247, 12; attempt, endeavor, 617, 21; hostile attempt, assault, 524, 23, 193, 8, 285, 36; approved quality, value, 154, 13, 352, 18, 552, 37 — to put to proof, try, examine, 192, 2, 221, 34, 527, 47, 225, 9; to experience, 301, 40; to afflict, 36, 5; to assail, 253, 6, 328, 21; to endeavor, 165, 8.

Assieged: besieged, 308, 15.

Assize: measurement, 125, 2.

Assoile: to set free, deliver, 681, 259, 435, 13, 261, 19, 385, 32; to solve, determine, 673, 38; to acquit oneself of, 481, 36, 685, 535, 733, 80; to remove, put away, 768, 47, 761, 100, 720, 11, 333, 58, 457, 25.

Assott (pp. assotted, assott): to infatuate, befool, 297, 8, 384, 22, 16, 25.

Astart, astert: to start up, 338, 29; to disturb, 51, 187.

Astoined: confounded, 127, 9.

Astond v. Astound.

Astonied v. Astony.

Astonish: to stun, 473, 43, 568, 9, 268, 31; to bewilder, 524, 27.

Astonishment: stupor, 386, 35; loss of wits, frenzy, 270, 49; consternation, 383, 12.

Astony: to stun, 34, 227, 154, 15, 16; to confound, 515, 54.

Astound, astond: stunned, 204, 35, 352, 17; confounded, appalled, 156, 31, 193, 5, 469, 19.

Aswage: to grow less violent, 159, 5.

Attach: to seize, 385, 33, 310, 28, 597, 10, 614, 4.

Attaint: to taint; sully, dim, 419, 5, 189, 34.

Attempt: to tempt, **576**, 63.

Attent: attention, **395**, 52, **639**, 37 — attentive, **638**, 26.

Attone, at one: in a body, together, **236**, 42, **292**, 28, **388**, 2, **76**, 418; at once, once for all, **498**, 9, **514**, 48 — agreement, **697**, 843.

Attonement: concord, **550**, 21.

Attones, attons: at once, **16**, 53, **334**, 63.

Attrapt: furnished with trappings, **446**, 39.

Aumayld: enamelled, **249**, 27.

Avale, availe: to descend, **289**, 10, **439**, 46; to subside, droop, **147**, 21, **338**, 27, **11**, 8; to lower, bring down, **484**, 19, **10**, 73.

Avaunt: to advance, **246**, 6; to depart, **617**, 21.

Avenge: vengeance, **348**, 46, **427**, 15.

Aventer: used only of spears: to level or set in rest (?), **455**, 11; to thrust (?), **329**, 28, **434**, 9.

Avise, avize v. **Advise.**

Avizefull: observing, **457**, 26.

Avoud: *pret.* of avow, q. v.

Avoure: avowal, **602**, 48.

Avow: to vow, **269**, 40, **341**, 46, **359**, 11, **613**, 34; to vow to, swear by, **289**, 7.

Avyse v. **Advise.**

Awaite: ambush, **360**, 17, **483**, 14.

Awarned: warned, **401**, 46.

Awayes: away, **85**, 430.

Awhape: to dismay, terrify, **91**, 72, **461**, 5, **571**, 32.

Bace v. **Base.**

Bancket v. **Banket.**

Band: to banish, interdict, **340**, 41.

Banket: a banquet, **306**, 2, **369**, 22.

Base: the game of prisoner's base, **548**, 5; one of the bases or 'homes,' **642**, 8; **bid b.**, to challenge a player to leave his base or 'home' and come out into the field for a race, **44**, 5; hence, fig., to challenge, or to pursue, **404**, 5 — low, **175**, 31, **322**, 71, **341**, 50; lowly, humble, **240**, 6, **90**, 44, 4, *To His Booke*, **143**, *Buckhurst*, **531**, 25, **601**, 38.

Basen: extended, staring, **98**, 670.

Bash: to flinch, quail, **257**, 37.

Bate: strife, discord, **766**, 8 — (*pret.*): bit, **259**, 7.

Battailous: warlike, **171**, 2, **283**, 22.

Battellant: engaged in battle, **124**, 8.

Battill: to grow fat, **632**, 38.

Batton: a club, **626**, 46.

Bayes: bathes, **185**, 3.

Be, bee: been, **26**, **237**, 41, 146, **436**, 21; are, **751**, 96.

Beades: prayers (with or without the use of the rosary), **149**, 30, **207**, 3, **208**, 8; a rosary, **160**, 13. [v. **Bid.**]

Beare, bere: a stretcher, a bier, **596**, 48, **317**, 36; a funeral monument, **343**, 11 — a burden, **702**, 149.

Beath: to heat green wood for straightening or hardening, **461**, 7.

Beauperes: companions, **330**, 35.

Become: to go to, **209**, 16, **350**, 1; happen, **392**, 32; as became, as was fitting, **292**, 28, **391**, 26, **208**, 11.

Bed: bid, **205**, 41, **355**, 39. [v. further **Bid.**]

Bedes v. **Beades.**

Bedight (*infin.* and *pp.*): to equip, dress, adorn;

609, 7, **309**, 22, **371**, 43, **227**, 21; to order, dispose, **503**, 10; to treat, to maltreat, **270**, 50, **45**, 89; ill b., disfigured, marred, **232**, 14, **271**, 3.

Bee v. **Be.**

Beene, bene, bin: be, **237**, 52, **239**, 59; are, **39**, 10, **239**, 3, 5, **138**, *Another, etc.*

Befeld: befallen, **440**, 50.

Beforne: before (of place), **25**, 160, **243**, 27.

Beginne: beginning, **344**, 21.

Behalve: behalf, **444**, 27.

Behappen: to happen, **574**, 52.

Beheast: behest, e. g. **167**, 18.

Behight (*pret., pp.* **behight** or **behote, behott**): to vow, promise, **245**, 1, **490**, 6, **221**, 38; to deliver, entrust, grant, adjudge, **213**, 50, **281**, 9, **448**, 7, **763**, 2; to command, ordain, **307**, 4, **308**, 17, **119**, 241; to name, pronounce, deem, **53**, 54, **379**, 47, **665**, 35, **215**, 64, **437**, 31, **424**, 44; to speak, address, **429**, 23, **544**, 20.

Belaccoyle: fair greeting, **457**, 25.

Belamoure: a sweetheart, **266**, 16.

Belamy: a fair friend, **278**, 52.

Belay: to trim, **590**, 5; to beleaguer, **720**, 14.

Belgardes: amorous or lovely looks, **395**, 52, **750**, 256.

Belive, bilive, bylive, blive: in lively manner, quickly, promptly, eagerly, **42**, 227, **175**, 32, **328**, 18, **360**, 16, **248**, 18.

Bellibone: *belle et bonne*, a fair maid, **19**, 92.

Belove: to love, **11**, 31.

Belyde: counterfeited, **396**, 7.

Bend: a band, fillet, stripe, **275**, 30, **249**, 27; a troop, **23**, 32.

Bene v. **Beene.**

Bent: compliant, **41**, 149.

Bereave: to take away, as by force, **77**, 489, 67, **577**, 645, 29, **536**, 2, **533**, 37, **284**, 29, **152**, 52.

Beseeke: to beseech, **440**, 47, **601**, 37.

Beseen: provided, **564**, 17; equipped, arrayed, **670**, 11; as adjective with **well, gay, rich**, etc., well ordered, well arrayed, comely, accomplished, gay to look upon, etc., **88**, 651, 73, 180, **331**, 45, **224**, 5, **565**, 28, **723**, 27.

Besit: to befit, become, **272**, 10, **428**, 19.

Bespeak: to utter, **12**, 97; to speak, say, **340**, 42, **283**, 27; to address, **231**, 8.

Besprent, besprint: besprinkled, **54**, 135, **49**, 111.

Bested, bestad: beset, **361**, 22, **437**, 25; with **ill, sorely, strangely**, etc., brought to evil plight, in sorry, strange plight, sorely put to it, etc., **616**, 18, **234**, 30, **237**, 52, **402**, 54, 148, 24, **501**, 33.

Bestedded: assisted, **418**, 3.

Bet v. **Bett.**

Betake: to commit, deliver, deliver to, **376**, 25, **369**, 28, **227**, 25, **654**, 51; to betake oneself, take (to), **175**, 28, **205**, 44; to take, **91**, 69.

Beteeme: to grant, **282**, 19.

Betid, betide: betided, happened, **360**, 13, **498**, 4, **234**, 26, **609**, 3.

Betight (*pp.* **betight**): to betide, **41**, 73, **50**, 174.

Bett: beat, beaten, **321**, 63, **242**, 22, **179**, 5, **189**, 28 — better, **34**, 230, 44, 15.

Bewray: to betray, reveal, tell, **169**, 39, **175**, 30, **337**, 21, **341**, *arg.*, **518**, 25, **38**, 176; to discover, **479**, 28.

Bickerment: altercation, 521, 6.
Bid, bed: (always with **beads, howres,** etc.), to pray, to perform rites, 149, 30, **207,** 3, **613,** 35.
Bilive v. Belive.
Bin v. Beene.
Bit: bite, 554, 49, 80, 83, 117, 62.
Blame: to bring reproach upon, to disgrace, 282, 16, 598, 11, 487, 41 — blemish, harm, 248, 22, 388, 1, 326, 9, 155, 18.
Bland: to cajole, 749, 171.
Blaze: to depict heraldically, 517, 14; to depict, 5, 87.
Blend (*pp.* blent): to blind, daze, 253, 7, 323, 80, 438, 35, 83, 311 — to disturb, dim, stain, pollute, 729, 62, 388, 1, 392, 33, 259, 5, 537, 13, 107, 1330.
Blesse: bliss, 207, *arg.*, 484, 23 — to protect, preserve, 155, 18, 186, 12, 203, 28, 310, 30, 455, 13 — to brandish, 172, 6, 195, 22.
Blin: to cease from, 361, 22.
Blist: blessed, 466, 46, 33, 174 — brandished, 629, 13. [v. Blesse.]
Blive v. Belive.
Bloncket: gray, gray-blue, light blue, 23, 5.
Blont v. Blunt.
Bloosme: blossom, 582, 4 — to blossom, 630, 20, 669, 8.
Bodrags: forays, 691, 315. [v. Bordragings.]
Bonibell: same as bellibone, q. v., 37, 62.
Bonilasse: a bonny lass, 37, 77, 689, 172.
Boone: a prayer, 377, 34.
Boord v. Bord.
Boot: profit, 406, 19; booty, 556, 10, 673, 38.
Bord, boord: to accost, address, 239, 5, 255, 24, 315, 16; to border on, skirt, 495, 43 — jesting, 442, 13; a flam, fib, 344, 19.
Bordragings: forays, 304, 63. [v. Bodrags.]
Borrell: of the laity, unlearned, 33, 95.
Borrowe, borowe: a pledge, surety, 24, 131, 25, 150, 40, 96; borrowing, 101, 852.
Boughtes: coils, 146, 15, 217, 11, 83, 255.
Bounce, bounse: to beat, knock, 407, 27, 510, 21.
Bountiest: most virtuous, 359, 8.
Bountyhed: virtue, goodness, worth, 313, 1, 366, 3, 331, 41; generosity, 348, 47; excellence, 296, 2.
Bownd: to go, lead, 216, 67.
Bowre: to lodge, dwell, 642, 6, 582, 4.
Bowrs: muscles, 198, 41.
Boystrous: massive, 193, 10.
Brag, -ly: ostentatious, -ly, finely, 12, 71, 16, 14.
Brame: longing, 341, 52.
Brast: burst, 192, 4, 202, 21.
Brave: fine, handsome, splendid, 189, 32, 202, 19, 212, 42, 325, 83, 748, 122; admirable, excellent, 342, 3, 246, 4, 249, 24, 692, 411, 115, *Letter;* finely, 165, 8 — to brag, swagger, 546, 32, 111, 14 — -ly: finely, gallantly, 249, 27, 265, 13.
Brawned: brawny, 198, 41.
Bray: a harsh cry, 475, 62 — to cry out, or sound, harshly or shrilly, 147, 17, 161, 23, 179, 7, 411, 6.
Breare v. Brere.
Breme, breem: fierce, bitter, 12, 43, 674, 40.
Bren (*pret., pp.* brent): to burn, 346, 34, 439, 45, 200, 10, 220, 28.

Brere: a briar, 13, 115, 211, 35.
Brickle: brittle, fragile, 487, 39, 66, 499.
Brize: a gadfly, 123, 2, 586, 24.
Brocage: pandering, 5, 13, 101, 851.
Brondiron: a sword, 445, 32, 628, 10.
Brust: to burst, 22, 261, 344, 19, 332, 48, 446, 41.
Bryze v. Brize.
Buegle: bead-work, 12, 66.
Buffe: a blow, 154, 17, 219, 24.
Bug: a bugbear, 248, 20, 316, 25.
Bugle: wild ox, 192, 3.
Burdenous: heavy, grievous, 579, 19, 24, 132.
Buskets: bushes, 23, 10.
But: unless, 337, 17, 388, 50.
But if: unless, 332, 53, 383, 17, 463, 23, 41, 143; if only, 37, 112.
Buxome: yielding, compliant, submissive, 221, 37, 354, 32, 337, 23, 41, 149, 98, 626.
By and by: immediately, forthwith, 192, 2, 264, 5, 500, 25, 104, 1108.
Bylive v. Belive.
Bynempt: uttered (a vow), 239, 60; promised, 48, 46; named, 34, 214.

Cærule: azure, 81, 163.
Caitive v. Caytive.
Camis, camus: a light, loose robe or tunic (Fr. *chemise*), 528, 2, 249, 26.
Can: know, knows, 12, 77, 16, 56; could, knew, knew how, 613, 36, 542, 5. [v. Con.] — (*aux.*) did, 156, 29, 170, 46, 315, 15, 568, 10; do, does, 29, 26, 173, 17.
Cancred: cankered, malignant, 695, 680, 230, 1.
Cantion: a song, 46, 13.
Capitaine: captain, 290, 15, 647, 3.
Captivaunce: captivity, 379, 45, 538, 17.
Capuccio: a hood, 412, 10.
Care: grief, distress, 467, 5, 498, 12, 599, 24; take c., feel grief, be afflicted, 342, 5, 9, 9.
Carefull: sorrowful, afflicted, 201, 15, 179, 6; careworn, anxious, 140, *Hatton*, 270, 47; painful, 190, 39, 54, 133 — -ly: woefully, 382, 4.
Carle: used rather miscellaneously for a man of unchivalrous, rude, villainous or mean nature and manners, 600, 34, 381, *arg.*, 453, 44, 276, 43, 206, 54, 388, 3.
Cast: to deliberate, 680, 115, 41, 114; to plan, 237, 48, 157, 38; to resolve, 173, 12, 201, 15, 375, 15, 591, 12; to arrange, 185, 1; (*reflex.*) to resolve, 13, 125, 189 — a bout, 400, 35; occasion, 634, 51.
Causen: to give reasons, 391, 26.
Caytive: captive, 177, 45, 196, 32, 200, 11; mean, ignoble, 250, 35, 289, 13, 375, 16, 397, 17 — a menial, wretch, villain, 230, 1, 254, 16, 285, 37, 586, 19.
Cesse: to cease, 476, 2.
Chaire v. Chayre.
Champian, champion: level open country, a plain, 510, 15, 606, 26, 114, 31.
Charet: a chariot, 174, 20, 438, 38.
Charme: to tune, play, 46, 118, 687, 5, 556, 13 — a song, 74, 244, 700, 46.
Chaufe, chauff: to heat, 163, 33; to chafe, rub, vex, fume, 188, 21, 218, 15, 514, 46 — chafe, 592, 21.

Chayre: a chariot, car, **166**, 17, **169**, 37, **126**, 4
— chary, 365, 51.

Cherry: to cheer, **644**, 22.

Chevisaunce: enterprise, achievement, **289**, 8, **379**, 45, **406**, 24; a bargain, **24**, 92.

Chiefe: a head, **50**, 115.

Childe: a youth of gentle birth, not yet knighted, **594**, 36; a knight in the prime of manhood, **473**, 44, **568**, 8; a 'faire young man,' **281**, 7. [Cf. Infant.]

Chose: to choose, **64**, 371, **563**, 12.

Chusd: chosen, **240**, 5.

Chyld v. **Childe.**

Clad: to clothe, **603**, 4.

Clame: a shout, **483**, 11 — to declare, **591**, 14, **486**, 30.

Clarkes v. **Clerkes.**

Cleeped, cleped: called, named, **246**, 8, **296**, 58, **642**, 8, **688**, 113.

Clerkes: men of learning, scholars, **561**, 1, **676**, **65**, 75, 335.

Clift: a cliff, **195**, 22, **351**, 7; a cleft, **479**, 27.

Clink: a latch (?), **26**, 251.

Clip: to clasp, embrace, **768**, 45, **382**, 10.

Close, -ly: secret, -ly, 263, 34, **292**, 32, **333**, 57, **338**, 28.

Clouted: clotted, 49, 99 — bandaged, **16**, 50.

Cloyd: 'a term used among farriers when a horse is pricked by a nail' (Church), **372**, 48.

Common, commen: to commune, **293**, 41, **555**, 4.

Commune: common, **366**, 5.

Compile v. **Compyle.**

Complement: completion, completeness, **94**, 338 366, 55; a crowning work, **722**, 24; proficiency, **99**, 692; an embellishment, **78**, 542, **696**, 790; an accomplishment, **644**, 23.

Complexion: physical constitution, or temperament, 367, 8, **371**, 38, **403**, 59; (plur.) colors (of the complexion), 248, 22, **747**, 67.

Complot: a scheme, **551**, 25, **92**, 178.

Comportaunce: behavior, **234**, 29.

Compyle: to compose, indite, 558, 25, **467**, 4, **76**, 432; to heap up, **336**, 12, **366**, 1; to construct, frame, 113, 25, **343**, 10, **377**, 30; to constitute, **732**, 80; to settle, **478**, 17.

Con, kon: to know, 41, 90, **687**, 74, **690**, 294, **541**, 35; to know how, be able, 49, 52 [v. **Can, Couth.**] — to learn, **12**, 92, **42**, 215.

Conceipt, conceit: a conception, idea, device, fancy, 136, 5, 91, **138**, 205, **100**, 827; understanding, imagination, judgment, **89**, Letter, **686**, Letter.

Conceiptfull: clever, quick, **657**, 16.

Concent: harmony, concord, 411, 5, **82**, 225, **736**, 83, 749, 198.

Concented: harmonized, **426**, 2.

Concrew: to become matted, **466**, 40.

Cond v. **Con.**

Condition: quality, temper (generally in plur.), **495**, 38, 470, 24, 388, 4, **308**, 11, **167**, 18.

Confound (pp.): confounded, **30**, 63.

Congregate (pp.): congregated, **663**, 19.

Conne v. **Con.**

Conqueresse: a woman conqueror, **546**, 36.

Consent v. **Concent.**

Consort: a company, fellowship, **274**, 22; accord, **224**, 4: the musical accord of instruments

or voices, a concert, **292**, 35, **262**, 31 **331**, 40, 71, 28.

Constraine: to reduce to straits, distress, **530**, 15, **293**, 36, **91**, 56; to strive, **402**, 49.

Constraint: distress, affliction, 152, 53, **231**, **9**, 393, 40, **466**, 45.

Contecke: strife, discord, **334**, 64, **25**, 163.

Contempt (pp.): contemned, 49, 48.

Contract (pp.): contracted, 393, 42.

Contraire: opposed, **677**, 2 — the contrary, **96**, 494 — to withstand, **661**, 7.

Controverse: a controversy, **447**, 2.

Convay: to carry off, to steal, 155, 24, **240**, 11, 292, 32, **460**, 47, **475**, 61.

Conveyance: theft, **101**, 856.

Corage, courage: heart, spirit, nature, mind, 178, 1, 360, 15, **336**, 10, **327**, 11, **252**, 46, **318**, 40, 317, 29; lustiness, **157**, 35; appetite, **322**, **68**; anger, 399, 30.

Corbe: crooked, **12**, 56 — a corbel, **482**, 6.

Corrupt (pp.): corrupted, **748**, 158.

Coste: side, 94, 294.

Cott: a little boat, **265**, 9.

Countercast: a counterplot, **598**, 16.

Counterchaunge: repayment in kind, **390**, **16.**

Counterfesaunce: counterfeiting, imposture, 199, 49, **382**, 8; mimicry, **73**, 197.

Counterfet, -fetted, -fect: counterfeited, counterfeit, 477, 11, 277, 45, **42**, 206.

Counterpeise: to counterbalance, **514**, **46.**

Countervayle: compensation, **768**, 47.

Courage v. **Corage.**

Coure: to cherish, brood on (as a hen her **eggs** or chickens), **126**, 8, **281**, 9.

Courteise, courtesly: courteous, courteously, **375**, 15, **405**, 13.

Couth: knew how to, could, 9, 10, 13, 190, **29**, 41, **279**, 58 [v. **Con, Can**]; (aux.) did, 33, 138. [v. **Can.**]

Coverture: shelter, **32**, 26; deceit, **99**, 683.

Covetise : covetousness, 40, 82, **168**, 29, **272**, 12.

Cowardree: cowardice, **102**, 986.

Cowheard, cowherd: a coward, cowardly, **587**, 28, **563**, 15.

Cowherdize, cowardize: cowardice, **646**, 37, **442**, 11.

Crag: the neck, 40, 45, **12**, 82.

Crake: to utter arrogantly, **517**, 16; to **brag**, 675, 50 — a brag, 307, 10.

Cranck: vaingloriously, **40**, 46.

Cranks: windings, **675**, 52.

Craples: grapples, claws, **553**, 40.

Crased: weak, infirm, **391**, 26.

Cratch: the manger (at Bethlehem), **753**, 226.

Cremosin, cremsin: crimson, 19, 59, 13, 130.

Crewe: a pot, 14, 209.

Crime: an accusation, matter of accusation, **13**, 162, **451**, 31, **470**, 25; reproach, blame, **223**, **46**, 180, 13.

Croupe: crupper, **352**, 16.

Cruddle: to curdle, congeal, **12**, **46**, 11, **ary**, 206, 52.

Cruddy: clotted, 175, 29, **348**, 47.

Crudle v. **Cruddle.**

Crumenall: a purse, **41**, 119.

Culver: a dove, **378**, 39, **734**, 88.
Curat, curats, curiets: a cuirass, **609**, 8, **552**, **34**, **530**, 20.
Custom: to be wont, **509**, 7.

Daint: dainty, **207**, 2, **318**, 42, **325**. *Prol.*, 2.
Damnify: to injure, hurt, **223**, 52, **269**, 43.
Darrayne: to order, manage, **476**, 4; **d. battle**, **d. war**, to maintain battle, wage war, to fight, **169**, 40, **242**, 26, **328**, 20, **444**, 26.
Darre: to dare, **527**, 44, **325**, *Prol.*, 2.
Date: duration, **372**, 45; term of life, **205**, 45, **283**, 24, **415**, 35; the limit or end of life, death, **236**, 44; decree, doom, **495**, 38.
Daunt: to discomfit, overthrow, vanquish, **17**, 114, **285**, 34, **336**, 16; to daze, stun, **147**, 18, **154**, 15, **195**, 21.
Dayes-man: an umpire, **284**, 28.
Daynt v. Daint.
Dead: to die, die away, **500**, 20; to kill, paralyze, **623**, 25, **652**, 33.
Deare: loving, **162**, 27, **417**, 1; heartfelt, earnest, **353**, 22, **124**, 12; earnestly, **240**, 8, **244**, 39, **326**, 5 — grievous, sore, **310**, 34, **731**, 71; grievously, **263**, 38, **353**, 24 — injury, **191**, 48.
Dearly: earnestly, **353**, 21; grievously, sorely, **66**, 504.
Dearnly, dearnelie v. Dernly.
Debate: contention, **417**, 1; fighting, a combat, **172**, 12, **287**, 54 — to fight, contend, **231**, 6, **390**, 14, **607**, 30.
Debatefull: contentious, **268**, 35.
Debatement: contention, **269**, 39.
Decay: destruction, ruin, death, **158**, 41, **185**, 48, **247**, 15, **287**, 51; (*plur.*) ruins, **115**, *Envoy.*
Decesse: decease, **563**, 11.
Decrew: to decrease, **456**, 18.
Deeme (*pret.* **dempt**): to judge, sit in judgment on, **38**, 137, **419**, 12, **434**, 4, **448**, 6; to decide, determine, **38**, 131, **278**, 55, **498**, 11; to adjudge, award, **498**, 9, **428**, 17; to estimate, appraise, **260**, 12, **505**, 8, **744**, 168.
Deene: din, **142**, *Hunsdon.*
Deface: to lay waste, destroy, **76**, 399, **254**, 14, **415**, 32; to violate (a law), **284**, 31; to disgrace, put to shame, **141**, *Howard*, **162**, 29, **174**, 24; to defame, disparage, **441**, 4, **124**, 11; to abash, **283**, 25; to eclipse, **255**, 25.
Defaicted: defeated, **31**, 66.
Defame: disgrace, infamy, **262**, 26, **329**, 27, **507**, 28, **610**, 15.
Defaste v. Deface.
Defeasaunce: defeat, **225**, 12.
Defeature: defeat, undoing, **456**, 17.
Defend: to fend off, repel, **321**, 63, **438**, 32, **550**, 19, **86**, 523.
Deffly: deftly, daintily, **20**, 111.
Deflore: to deflower, desecrate, **747**, 39.
Deforme: misshapen, ugly, **226**, 20, **316**, 24.
Defould, defowled: defiled, **212**, 42, **363**, 38.
Degendered, -ing: degenerated, -ing, **502**, 2, **751**, 94.
Delay: to soften, smooth, **140**, *Hatton ;* to allay, mitigate, quench, **467**, 1, **269**, 40, **292**, 30, **416**, 42, 20, 7; to get rid of, **257**, 35.
Delices: delights, **262**, 28, **482**, 6.
Deliver: nimble, **17**, 76.

Delve: a cavern, **342**, 7, **421**, 20; a dell, ravine, **271**, *arg.*, **280**, 4.
Demeane, demayne: to treat, **695**, 681, **625**, 39 — demeanor, behavior, **293**, 40, **283**, 23, **535**, 51; treatment, **616**, 18.
Demerite: to deserve, **712**, 130.
Demisse: humble, **752**, 136.
Dempt v. Deeme.
Denay: to deny, disown, **404**, 11; to refuse, 380, 57, **649**, 15.
Dent: a stroke, **399**, 32, **456**, 15. [v. **Dint.**]
Depaint, depeinct: to depict, **260**, 11, **404**, 7; to indicate, **19**, 69.
Depart: to separate, **590**, 4, **298**, 14; to remove, do away with, **351**, 6 — departure, **375**, 20.
Depasture: to devour, **322**, 73.
Depeinct v. Depaint.
Deprive: to take away, **729**, 63.
Derdoing: doing daring deeds, **272**, 10. [Cf. **Derring doe.**]
Dernfull: dismal, **706**, 90.
Dernly, dearnly: dismally, grievously, **235**, 35, 327, 14, 415, 34, **681**, 196.
Derring doe: daring deeds, daring, intrepidity, 45, 65, 53, 43, **257**, 42.
Derring dooers: doers of daring deeds, **431**, 38.
Descrive: to describe, **657**, 21.
Desine: to denote, express, **438**, 37, **542**, 8, **731**, 74; to point, aim, **464**, 30.
Despiteous, dispitous: malicious, pitiless, **279**, 62, 154, 15, **385**, 28; piteous, **548**, 8 — -ly, pitilessly, **267**, 29.
Desse: a desk, **488**, 50.
Dessignment: undertaking, **307**, 10.
Desynde v. Desine.
Detaine: detention, **538**, 15.
Devise: to depict, **235**, 31; to resolve, **267**, 30; to conjecture, guess, **294**, 42, **330**, 33, **398**, 21; to think, deliberate, **226**, 18, **621**, 6, **607**, 34; to describe, recount, to tell (of), **25**, 174, **137**, 126, **331**, 42, **467**, 3, **226**, 14, **296**, 59; to discourse, converse, **266**, 21.
Devoyr: duty, **42**, 227.
Devyse v. Devise.
Dewfull: due, fitting, **665**, 35, **496**, 44.
Dight (*pret.*, *pp.*, **dight**): to deal with, treat, **39**, 7, **505**, 14; to dispose, **338**, 30; to compose (poetry), **19**, 29; to frame, **29**, 45; to do, **510**, 18; to set in order, arrange, **166**, 14; to dress, array, deck, **656**, 15, **308**, 17, **233**, 18, **165**, 6; to put on (armor, etc.), **186**, 8, **595**, 39; 'fowly d.,' to defile, **199**, 48, **259**, 4; to prepare, make ready, **280**, 6, 276, 42, **201**, 13, **93**, 233; to betake (oneself to), to direct (oneself towards), **420**, 16, **527**, 43; to proffer, **306**, 2; to raise, **194**, 18.
Dilate: to spread out, **320**, 53.
Dint: a stroke, **147**, 18, **191**, 47, **285**, 38, **49**, 104. [Cf. **Dent**] — to wound, **645**, 31.
Dirke: dark, darkly, **39**, 6, **41**, 102 — to darken, obscure, **13**, 134.
Disadvaunce, disavaunce: to draw back, **441**, 7, **434**, 8; to stop short in, retreat from, **406**, 24.
Disaventure, dissaventure: misfortune, **205**, 45, 315, 19; at d., at random, blindly, **357**, 53.
Disaventurous, disaventerous, disadventrous: unfortunate, unhappy, **191**, 48, **200**, 11, **527**, 47, **91**, **100**.

Discided: cut in two, **422,** 27.

Discipled: trained, **417,** 1.

Discolourd: many-colored, **168,** 31, **398,** 21, **407,** 28, **409,** 47, **736,** 51.

Discounsel: to dissuade, **317,** 34, **327,** 11.

Discoure, discure: to discover, find out, **337,** 20; to reveal, **294,** 42, **348,** 50.

Discourteise: discourteous, **333,** 55.

Discure v. Discoure.

Discust: shaken off, **332,** 48.

Disease: uneasiness, discomfort, distress, **539,** 26, **614,** 40, **361,** 19, **423,** 38 — to disturb, incommode, distress, **33,** 124, **240,** 12, **242,** 24, **221,** 38, **600,** 32.

Disentrayle: to beat out, draw forth, **557,** 19, **456,** 16, **437,** 28.

Dishable: to disparage, **261,** 21.

Disherit: to disinherit, **6,** 117.

Disleall: disloyal, **259,** 5.

Dislikefull: distasteful, **481,** 40.

Disloignd: remote, **485,** 24.

Dismay: assault (?), **734,** 87; disaster, overthrow, **440,** 50, **514,** 50, **729,** 63 — to stagger, discomfit, overthrow, defeat (in fight), **259,** 7, **509,** 8, **530,** 19, **353,** 25, **418,** 2, **642,** 13; to overpower, vanquish, **251,** 42, **364,** 43, **449,** 13; (*reflex.*) to be distressed, **423,** 40; dismayd, dejected, afflicted, **293,** 37, **369,** 28, **423,** 37 — mismade, deformed (?), **307,** 11.

Dispace: (*intrans.* and *reflex.*) to roam about, **83,** 265, **119,** 250.

Dispainted: painted diversely, **295,** 50.

Disparage: an unequal match, **474,** 50 — to discourage, **296,** 2.

Disparagement: an unequal match, inequality in marriage, **383,** 12, **462,** 16, **646,** 37.

Dispence: expenditure, liberality, **292,** 29, **318,** 42, **573,** 45 — to make amends (for), **162,** 30.

Dispiteous v. Despiteous.

Disple: to discipline, **210,** 27.

Displeasaunce: displeasure, **300,** 28.

Dispost: regulated, **283,** 26.

Disthronize: to dethrone, **302,** 44.

Distort: distorted, **422,** 28, **581,** 36.

Distraicte: torn asunder, **31,** 50.

Distraine: to distress, **190,** 38; to rend, **324,** 82.

Distraughted: distracted, **754,** 14.

Distroubled: greatly troubled, **351,** 12

Dite v. Dight.

Ditt: a ditty, **265,** 13.

Do, doe, dooe, doen, done, donne, doon: (*a*) to put: do on, do off, **103,** 1062, **596,** 48; do away, **164,** 39, **339,** 33, **356,** 48, **651,** 29; (*b*) to make, cause to: do him rew, do him fall, etc., **234,** 25, **279,** 64, **247,** 12; do to die, done be dead, etc., **90,** 10, **187,** 14, **197,** 36, **198,** 45, **206,** 54, **525,** 29; to cause, or procure, **365,** 50; (*c*) to act, **383,** 13.

Dolour: physical pain, **364,** 41, **377,** 35.

Dome v. Doome.

Done, donne, dooe, doon v. Do.

Doole: pain, grief, lamentation, **405,** 17, **397,** 17, **467,** 3 — -full: doleful, **268,** 34.

Doome, dome: judgment, opinion, **139,** *Hobynoll,* **139,** *H. B.,* **141,** *Gray,* **484,** 21 — to give judgment, **562,** 4.

Doubt, dout: to hesitate, **374,** 11, **424,** 48, **27,** 42; to be afraid, fear, **387,** 47, 48; to fear for, **432,** 46 — hesitation (to act), **34,** 232; apprehension, fear, **419,** 8, **416,** 37, **403,** 59, **360,** 12, **569,** 18; danger, **573,** 47; **make d.,** to hesitate, **343,** 14; **be out of d.,** to be convinced, **51,** 22.

Doucepere: (i. e. one of the twelve peers of Charlemagne) a champion, **399,** 31.

Doure: a dower, **522,** 8.

Dout v. Doubt.

Drad: dreaded, dread, **413,** 18, **571,** 32; feared for, **38,** 50.

Drapets: cloths, **291,** 27.

Dreare, drere: gloom, sadness, sorrow, **198,** 40, **566,** 35, **596,** 46, **597,** 4; horribleness (?), **472,** 42.

Drearing: sorrowing, **680,** 189.

Drearyhead, drerihedd, dryrihedd: sorrow, horror, dismalness, **327,** 16, **333,** 62, **338,** 30, **121,** 347.

Dreed: dread, **238,** 52.

Dreeriment v. Dreriment.

Drenched, drent: submerged, **221,** 34, **279,** 61; drowned, **495,** 38, **48,** 37.

Drere, drerihedd v. Dreare, drearyhead.

Dreriment: gloom, **193,** 9, **271,** 1; torpor (?), **267,** 27; anguish, **48,** 36, **220,** 32, **232,** 15; horror, terror, **158,** 44, **256,** 31, **464,** 29.

Drevill: a sloven, **426,** 3.

Drive, driv'd: drove, struck, pushed, **204,** 38, **355,** 37, **378,** 40, **568,** 5, **639,** 32; driven. **667,** 50; hastened, **238,** 55.

Drousyhed: drowsiness, **153,** 7.

Droyle: to drudge, **92,** 157.

Dryrihed v. Drearyhead.

Duefull v. Dewfull.

Dumpish: heavy, spiritless, **718,** 4, **426,** 5.

Durefull: enduring, durable, **487,** 39, **718,** 6.

Each: each other, **414,** 24; **e. other, e. others,** each the other, each the other's, **172,** 6, **219,** 21, **154,** 17, **166,** 14.

Earne, erne: to yearn, **145,** 3, **201,** 18, **252,** 46, **398,** 21.

Earst, erst: first, **33,** 164, **250,** 33; previously, formerly, a while before or ago, **183,** 40, **184,** 42, **194,** 18, **230,** 2, **250,** 32 — **at earst,** at first, **234,** 29; at length, already, **254,** 14, **502,** 2, **39,** 6, **54,** 105; instantly, suddenly, **257,** 39, **270,** 49.

Eath, ethe: easy, **40,** 17, **33,** 90, **251,** 40, **253,** 11; ready, apt, **459,** 40.

Edify: to build, **67,** 551, **149,** 34, **328,** 20; settle (a country), **327,** 14.

Eeke, eke: to increase, **40,** 30, **177,** 42, **339,** 35, **581,** 35.

Effierce: to make fierce, **407,** 27. [Cf. **Enfierce.**]

Efforce: to force, force open, carry by force, **275,** 30, **389,** 9; to violate, **179,** 4; to constrain, compel, **318,** 43, **416,** 43; to intensify, emphasize, **336,** 15, **561,** 47 — **efforced:** strained, **280,** 4.

Effray: to frighten, scare, **147,** 16.

Eft: again, **436,** 21; **now . . . eft, now . . . then, 286,** 41; (as frequent connective in narration) then, forthwith, **202,** 25, **248,** 21, **311,** 36, **460,** 45, **506,** 21, **519,** 27; moreover, likewise, **634,** 1, **665,** 30, **42,** 191; afterwards, **254,** 18.

Eftsoone, eftsoones: soon after, presently, forthwith, **233,** 17, **137,** 167, **152,** 3, **210,** 24, **216,** 4.

Eine v. Eyen.

Elles: else, **387**, 48.
Embace v. **Embase.**
Embar: to confine, imprison, **156**, 31, **191**, 44, **405**, 16.
Embase: to lower, **720**, 13; to humble, degrade, **733**, 82, **375**, 15, **583**, 3, **616**, 20, **99**, 732; to discredit, disgrace, **327**, 12, **392**, 33.
Embatteiled: armed for battle, **258**, 2.
Embay: to bathe, steep, imbrue, **768**, 44, **367**, 7, **210**, 27, **236**, 40, **321**, 60, **413**, 21, **119**, 206; to pervade, suffuse, **287**, 55, **201**, 13.
Embayld: enclosed, **249**, 27.
Embleme: a motto, e. g. **10**.
Embosse: to encase, sheathe, **161**, 24, **334**, 64, **608**, 40, **219**, 20.
Embost: (of a hunted animal) driven to extremity, exhausted, **328**, 22, **413**, 17, **203**, 29.
Emboyl: to boil, **220**, 28, **253**, 9.
Embrave: to beautify, adorn, **114**, 29, **49**, 109, **239**, 60.
Embreaded: braided, **368**, 18.
Embrew, imbrew: to stain, to stain with blood, **742**, 13, **727**, 53, **633**, 40, **368**, 17; (of a weapon) to shed blood, to stain itself (in blood), **183**, 38, **221**, 36; to steep, plunge (a weapon in), **415**, 32, **113**, 24; to saturate (with), **751**, 47; to shed (blood, etc.), **346**, 38, **504**, *arg.*, **263**, 33.
Embusied: busied, **464**, 29.
Eme: uncle, **302**, 47.
Emeraudes: emeralds, **320**, 54.
Emmove, enmove: to affect, agitate, stir up, **155**, 21, **190**, 38, **205**, 48, **237**, 50; to be moved, **467**, 3.
Emong, emongst: among, amongst, **315**, 10, **295**, 52.
Empare: to impair, **215**, 63.
Emparlaunce: parley, **480**, 31, **528**, 50.
Empassionate (*pp.*): impassioned, **681**, 193, **561**, 46.
Empeach, impeach: to hinder, impede, **87**, 576, **197**, 34, **305**, 68, **405**, 12, **486**, 36; to impair, mar, **273**, 15 — obstruction or impairment, **320**, 56.
Emperished: enfeebled, ruined, **12**, 53, **376**, 20.
Emperce, empierce: to pierce, transfix, **239**, 1, **286**, 45, **361**, 19, **393**, 39.
Empight: implanted, **361**, 20, **562**, 8; fixed itself (in), **258**, 46, **434**, 10.
Emplonged: plunged (into), **397**, 17.
-en: a very frequent termination to verbal forms, e. g. **184**, 42, **215**, 64, **555**, 4, **41**, 114.
Enaunter: lest, **14**, 200, **24**, 78.
Encheare: to cheer, **664**, 24.
Encheason: cause, reason, motive, **24**, **147**, **41**, 116, **234**, 30.
Endevourment: endeavor, **94**, 298.
Endew, indew: to take in, 'inwardly digest,' **396**, 9; to endow, **171**, 51.
Endlong: from end to end, continuously, **395**, 51, **397**, 19.
Endosse: to inscribe, **694**, 632, **574**, 53.
Ene: any, **54**, 93.
Enfelon'd: made furious, **554**, 48.
Enfested: embittered, **121**, 354.
Enfierce: to make fierce, **253**, 8. [Cf. **Effierce.**]
Enfouldred: thunderous, **221**, 40.
Enfrosen: congealed, **744**, 146.
Enfyred: hardened as by fire, **744**, 169.

Engine: a device, plot, wiles, **233**, 23, **255**, 27, **195**, 23, **333**, 57, **396**, 7.
Engore: to gore, wound, **330**, 38, **621**, 9, **362**, 28; to goad, **286**, 42; to shed (blood), **387**, 48.
Engraffed, engraft: ingrafted, implanted, **337**, 17, **344**, 18, **427**, 10.
Engrained: dyed in grain, **13**, 131, **88**, 666.
Engrieved, engreeved: grieved, afflicted, **255**, 23, **333**, 59, **369**, 21, **632**, 34.
Enhance: to raise, exalt, **147**, 17, **177**, 47, **268**, 31, **277**, 44, **691**, 359.
Enlumine: to illuminate, give light to, **288**, 4, **503**, 7, **730**, 66, 5, 98.
Enmove v. **Emmove.**
Enrace: to implant, **365**, 52, **644**, 25, **748**, 114.
Enrange: to dispose, draw up, **761**, 122, **411**, 5, **218**, 13, **242**, 21; to rove, **591**, 9.
Enranckle: to envenom, **381**, 2.
Enriven: riven, **552**, 34.
Ensample: to give an example of, **136**, 30, **753**, 213.
Enseame: to bring together (in), **494**, 35.
Ensew, ensewen, ensue: to follow, pursue, **63**, 266, **476**, 5, **404**, 5, **143**, *Norris*, **174**, 25; to persecute, afflict, **205**, 44, **732**, 79; to imitate, **320**, 59; to follow after, succeed, **752**, 121; to result from, **169**, 34; to appertain to, **245**, 2.
Ensnarle: to ensnare, **556**, 9.
Entayld: carved, cut, **249**, 27, **267**, 29.
Entayle: carving, **271**, 4.
Enterdeale: mutual dealing, negotiation, **100**, 785, **550**, 21.
Enterpris, enterprize: to undertake, **191**, 45, **233**, 19, **400**, 40, **406**, 24, **501**, 28 — to receive as guest, **241**, 14.
Entertaine: to maintain, **95**, 398; to treat (well or ill), **144**, 43; to engage the attention of, hence, to hoodwink, **483**, 13, **638**, 25, **181**, 1; to receive, welcome, accept, **388**, 3, **393**, 42, **382**, 4, **211**, 32, **225**, 12, **289**, 6, **563**, 12; to encounter, **87**, 563; to take, enter upon, **606**, 24, **720**, 12 — entertainment, reception, **470**, 27, **559**, 37, **104**, 1085.
Entertake: to receive, **559**, 35
Entertayne v. **Entertaine.**
Entire: pure, absolute, **340**, 44; sincere, **477**, 13; inner, inward, secret, **719**, 6, **470**, 23, **473**, 48, **332**, 47, **375**, 16 — wholly, completely, **282**, 15; heart and soul, **259**, 8 — -ly: earnestly, **220**, 32, **395**, 51, **623**, 22.
Entitle, entitule: to dedicate (a book), **1**, *title*, **769**, 76.
Entraile: coiling, a coil, **147**, 16.
Entrall: entrails, **313**, 6, **316**, 25.
Entrayld, entrailed: entwined, interlaced, **249**, 27, **409**, 46, **36**, 30, **760**, 25.
Entreat, intreat: to treat (a person well or ill), **207**, 7, **483**, 10, **588**, 40; to treat (of a subject), **407**, 29, **504**, 1, **762**, 1; to persuade, **210**, 24.
Entyre v. **Entire.**
Enure, inure: to put in practice, to use, exercise, **735**, 53, **721**, 21, **771**, 26, **430**, 29; to commit (a crime), **560**, 39; **enured with**, accustomed to, **629**, 14.
Envy: hatred, indignation, **393**, 38, **356**, 47, **328**, 18, **7**, 300 — to be indignant, **740**, 376; to begrudge, **199**, 1, **272**, 8, **289**, 7, **365**, 50 — to vie with, emulate, **154**, 17, **327**, 13.

Enwallowed (*pp*.): rolled or tumbled (in), **354**, 34, **569**, 14.

Equalize: to be equal to, to rival, **113**, 26, **394**, 44.

Erne v. Earne.

Erst v. Earst.

Esloyne: (*reflex.*) to keep aloof (from), **167**, 20.

Essoyne: excuse, **167**, 20.

Eugh: yew, **146**, 9.

Eughen: yewen, of yew, **99**, **747**, **218**, 19.

Every: any, **637**, 23; every one, **262**, 32, **263**, 33.

Ewftes: efts, newts, **564**, 23.

Ewghen v. Eughen.

Expert: to experience, **50**, 186.

Extent (*pp*.): extended, **279**, 61.

Extinct (*pp*.): cut off, killed, **408**, 37.

Extirpe: to root out, **210**, 25.

Extort (*pp*.): extorted, **508**, 5, **519**, 30.

Extreate: extraction, **561**, 1.

Exul: an exile, **698**, 894.

Eyas: (of hawks) newly fledged, **221**, 34, **750**, 24.

Eyen, eyne, eine: eyes, **138**, *Another*, **165**, 204.

Eyght: eighth, **46**, 12.

Fact: a deed, especially an evil deed, **169**, 34, **204**, 37, **385**, 32, **393**, 38.

Fade, vade: to decay, fall off, etc., **727**, 51, **112**, 20 (*bis*), **513**, 40 (*bis*), **185**, 4; to attenuate, **391**, 20.

Faine, fayne: glad, **12**, 67, **180**, 12; eager, **458**, 33; well-disposed, **589**, 46 — gladly, **470**, 27; eagerly, heartily, **99**, 116; of necessity, perforce, **85**, 419 — to take pleasure, to delight, **581**, 36, **322**, 74; to desire, **754**, 6, **391**, 24, **447**, 47, **535**, 53; to attempt, **506**, 22, **597**, 9 — [= feign] to fashion, **633**, 44; to pain, **551**, 24; to imagine, to imagine falsely, to err, **740**, 414, **745**, 210, 216, **657**, 19, **462**, 15; to conceal, dissemble, **225**, 10, **248**, 20, **337**, 17.

Faitour v. Faytour.

Fall: fallen, **41**, 147.

False: to forge, **230**, 1; to break (faith), **29**, 241, **205**, 46, **319**, 44; to deceive, **156**, 30, **332**, 47; **f. blows**, to feint, **259**, 9.

Falser: a deceiver, a cheat, **26**, 305, **56**, *Epilogue*.

Falshedd: treachery, **83**, 246.

Farforth: to a great extent, **395**, 53.

Fault: to sin, **307**, 9; to be in error, **8**, 58; to be deficient, **6**, 205.

Favourlesse: unpropitious, **289**, 7.

Fay: faith, **41**, 107, **550**, 19.

Fayl: to default in (a trust), **500**, 23; to deceive, **260**, 11, **409**, 46.

Fayne v. Faine.

Faytour, faytor: a fortune-telling vagabond, an impostor, cheat, villain, **23**, 39, **228**, 35, **234**, 30, **336**, 13, **424**, 44, **603**, 1.

Feare: to make afraid, **212**, 42, **316**, 25, **352**, 15, **662**, 15; to impel by fear, **729**, 59. [v. also **Fere.**]

Feateously: deftly, **760**, 27.

Feature: make, form, character, **199**, 49, **391**, 21, **529**, 12, **432**, 44.

Fee: property, revenue, **24**, 106, **547**, 43, **477**, 13, **212**, 43; employment, service, **691**, 370, **644**, 21; a prize, a reward, **272**, 9, **278**, 56, **423**, 35, **482**, 3.

Feebled: weakened, **195**, 23.

Feeblesse: feebleness, **472**, 37.

Fell: to prostrate (oneself), **268**, 32; **be feld**, to prostrate oneself, to let fall, to fall, **670**, 13, **318**, 40, **199**, 47 — gall, rancor, **403**, 2.

Felon: a villain, **162**, 29, **284**, 30.

Felonous: fierce, cruel, wicked, **13**, 156, **83**, 295, **334**, 65, **486**, 33.

Fensible: capable of being defended, strong, **291**, 21, **396**, 10.

Ferce, -ly: fierce, fiercely, **163**, 35, **241**, 19.

Fere, feare, pheere: a companion, a mate, **139**, 6, **630**, 25, **440**, 52, **207**, 4, **706**, 100.

Fett (*pret.*, *pp*. **fet**): to fetch, **326**, 8, **517**, 11, **117**, 77.

Fewter, feuter: to put (a spear) in rest, **455**, 10, **447**, 45.

Fifte: fifth, **168**, 32.

Fine: end, **438**, 37; result, **321**, 59.

Finesse: fineness, **20**, 135.

Firme: to fix, **271**, 1.

Fit: a seizure, throe, impulse, **68**, 598, **183**, 37, **220**, 27, **342**, 1, **371**, 41, **458**, 30; furious **f.**, merry **f.**, an access of fury, of mirth, etc., **169**, 34, **180**, 11, **254**, 14, **266**, 21; a mood, **170**, 45, **217**, 7 — to be suitable, **728**, 54, **45**, 88, **240**, 11; **f. with**, to harmonize with, be becoming to, **593**, 24, **197**, 33.

Flag: (of wings) to beat weakly, **140**, *Essex*, **754**, 27.

Flaggy: sagging, perhaps also pliant, **217**, 10, **371**, 39, **354**, 33, **123**, 5.

Flame: to set on fire, inflame, **390**, 18, **505**, 14, **264**, 8.

Flasket: a long, shallow basket, **760**, 26.

Fleet: to float, **272**, 14, **315**, 14, **480**, 33, **690**, 286; to flow, **694**, 596; to run away, **389**, 7.

Flex: flax, **332**, 47.

Flit: fleet, **140**, *Essex*, **257**, 38, **266**, 20; light, unsubstantial, **333**, 56, **403**, 57 — to shift, **728**, 54, **165**, 5 — flitted, departed, **725**, 40, **319**, 44.

Flitting: fleeting, moving, **750**, 24, **280**, 2; shifting, unstable, **218**, 18.

Flore, floure, flowre: a floor, **292**, 34; the ground, **286**, 42, **297**, 10, **609**, 5, **621**, 8, **721**, 20.

Flourdelice: the heraldic fleur-de-lis, **558**, 27.

Floure: to flower, **393**, 39. [v. also **Flore.**]

Flowre v. Flore.

Foen v. Fone.

Foltring: faltering, **237**, 47, **405**, 12.

Fon: a foolish fellow, **12**, 69, 40, 68, **690**, 292.

Fond: found, e. g. **288**, 56.

Fone, foen: foes, **155**, 23, **247**, 13, **283**, 8, **297**, 10.

Fonly: foolishly, **23**, 58.

Food: feud, enmity, **193**, 9, **231**, 3.

Foolhardize: foolhardiness, **241**, 17, **258**, 42, **346**, 35.

Forby v. Foreby.

Force: to strive, **242**, 25, **277**, 51, **384**, 26, **19** 24.

Fordo: to overthrow, ruin, **576**, 3, **237**, 51, **211**, 33.

Fordonne: reduced to extremes, exhausted, **177**, 41, **346**, 34, **732**, 80 — ruin, **448**, 7.

Foreby, forby: beside, hard by, **183**, 39, **211**, 36, **515**, 54; past, **327**, 15; by, **569**, 17.

Forelend v. Forlend.

Forelie: to lie before, **249**, 29.

Forelift: to raise in front, **218**, 15.

Forepast: gone by, by-gone, **67**, 576, **72**, 104, **137**, 121, **550**, 21.

Foreread: to presage, **116**, 29.

Foresay: to renounce, **24**, 82; to exclude, **32**, 69.

Foreshew: to prescribe, **674**, 45.

Forespent: already spent, past, **205**, 43.

Forestall v. Forstall.

Foretaught: taught aforetime, **187**, 18.

Forewent: gone before, **33**, 117.

Forgery: deceit, fraud, **317**, 28, **332**, 53, **520**, 39, **575**, 56.

Forgive: to grant, **619**, 36, **622**, 12; to give over (to), **637**, 22.

Forgo: to forsake, **702**, 174, **90**, 22, **359**, 10, **553**, 40; to fall away from, **421**, 24; to lose, let slip, 247, 12, **455**, 11, **601**, 39.

Forhaile: to harass, **42**, 243.

Forhent: overtaken, **356**, 49.

Forlend, forelend: to relinquish, give over (to), **356**, 47, **434**, 6.

Forlore: lost, **250**, 31; abandoned, deserted, **320**, 52, **373**, 53, **395**, 52, **487**, 40; perverse, depraved, **575**, 61, **209**, 21; undone, **197**, 39.

Forlorne: brought to naught, undone, ruined, **245**, *arg.*, **263**, 35, **174**, 23, **469**, 15, **123**, 6.

Former: fore, front, **484**, 20, **615**, 10, **658**, 29, **625**, 40.

Formerly: first, beforehand, **313**, 1, **588**, 38, **601**, 38.

Forpass: to pass along, pass by, **398**, 20, **97**, 519.

Forpined: wasted away, **403**, 57.

Forslack: to neglect, **576**, 3, **635**, 3, **656**, 12; to cause neglect of, **674**, 45.

Forslow: to delay, impede, **483**, 15, **662**, 16, **31**, 119.

Forspent: wasted, **452**, 34.

Forstall, forestall: to beset (a way), bar (entrance), **289**, 11, **331**, 46, **484**, 17; to obstruct, hinder, prevent, **478**, 19, **652**, 31, **26**, 273; f. of, to deprive of, hinder in, **448**, 9, **534**, 47, **42**, 231; to pre-occupy, pre-engage, **577**, 4, **257**, 39.

Forswatt: covered with sweat, **19**, 99.

Forswonck: exhausted with labor, **19**, 99.

Forthinke: to think better of, **499**, 14; to deplore, **607**, 32.

Forthy: therefore, **25**, 221, **329**, 30, **279**, 65; therefor, because of that, **16**, 37, **33**, 71, **378**, 38.

Fortilage: a fortalice, **318**, 43.

Fortunelesse: unlucky, **470**, 27, **91**, 100.

Forwander: to wander aimlessly or astray, **183**, 34, **406**, 20.

Forwarn: to forfend, **155**, 18, **359**, 9.

Forwaste: to lay utterly waste, **145**, 5, **216**, 1, **303**, 52.

Forwearied: exhausted with fatigue, **149**, 32, **201**, 13, **209**, 17.

Forwhy: for the reason that, because, **341**, 49, **499**, 15, **512**, 32, **602**, 44, **617**, 21.

Forworne: worn out, **183**, 35.

Foster: a forester, **327**, 17, **358**, *arg.*, **360**, 13.

Fouldring: thunderous, **242**, 20.

Fowle: ugly, hideous, **180**, 15, **175**, 30, **307**, 5; shamefully, **178**, 48.

Fowly: foully, severely, **185**, 5, **698**, 908.

Foyle: to trample, **572**, 33.

Foyn: to thrust or lunge, **259**, 9, **286**, 47, **437**, 25.

Foyson: abundance, **706**, 98.

Fraight: fraught, **40**, 84, **228**, 35.

Frame: to train, discipline, **680**, 124, **213**, 45; to direct, steady (one's steps), **328**, 20, **196**, 30; (*reflex.*) to apply oneself, **241**, 16; to be in harmony (with), **708**, 35 — order, condition, 44, 25, **36**, 3.

Franchisement: liberation, **572**, 36.

Franion: a free-living gallant, **244**, 37; a quean, **518**, 22.

Fray: to make afraid, **343**, 12, **150**, 38, **152**, 52, **161**, 19, **318**, 40.

Free: of gentle birth and breeding, noble, generous, gracious, **331**, 44, **482**, 3.

Frenne: a stranger, **19**, 28.

Fresh: to refresh, **534**, 45, **678**, 26.

Frett: to gnaw, to rend, **244**, 34, **184**, 44.

Fro: from, **237**, 48.

Fromwarde: turned away, **22**, 169.

Frorne: frozen, **14**, 243.

Frory: frosty, **386**, 35.

Froward: turned away, **644**, 24.

Frowy: 'musty or mossy' (E. K.), **33**, 111, **385**, 30.

Fry: to burn, be tormented (in fire, or in passion), **176**, 33, **238**, 58, **723**, 32; to boil, foam, **319**, 45, **510**, 15.

Funerall: death, **155**, 20, **262**, 25; a monument, **108**, 3.

Furniment: equipment, **438**, 38.

Furnitures: accoutrements, trappings, **116**, 56, **137**, 164, **327**, 11, **375**, 18.

Furre: far, 7, 259.

Fyne: to sift out, **54**, 125.

Gainstrive: to resist, **254**, 14, **462**, 12.

Galage: a wooden shoe, **14**, 244, **41**, 131.

Gallimaufray: an utter jumble, 6, 129.

Gan v. Gin.

Gang: to walk, go, **16**, 57, **41**. 100.

Garre: to make, cause to, **18**, 1, **41**, 106.

Gastfull: ghastly, **38**, 170.

Gate: a way, path, **146**, 13, **315**, 17, 56, *Epilogue*; a going, course, steps, **354**, 32, **196**, 30, **97**, 600, **388**, 51; gait, manner of walking, **194**, 12, **103**, 1084 — a goat, **25**, 177 — got, **730**, 66.

Gazefull: absorbed in gazing, **485**, 28, **746**, 12.

Geare, gere: material, matter, **496**, 45, **658**, 28; business, an affair, **597**, 6, **568**, 10, **551**, 30.

Geason: uncommon, **90**, 12; extravagant, **608**, 37.

Gelly blood: clotted blood, **355**, 40.

Gelt: a lunatic, **463**, 21 — gold or gilt metal, **12**, 65.

Gemmes: buds, **759**, 14.

Gent: of gentle or high birth; hence, of knights, brave, courteous, etc., of ladies, gracious, gentle, etc., **203**, 27, **356**, 45, **331**, 44, **308**, 17, **200**, 6, **234**, 30, **303**, 52.

Gentlesse: gentleness, **603**, 3.

Gere v. Geare.

German: a brother, **172**, 10, **173**, 13, **286**, 46.

Gerne: to bare the teeth, snarl, **578**, 15.

Gest: a deed, exploit, **102**, 978, **482**, 4, **334**, 1 — bearing, carriage, **338**, 24, 27, **382**, 8; a gesture, **291**, 26, **605**, 14.

Gether: to gather, **20**, 152.

Ghost: spirit, soul, **172**, 11, **236**, 42, **286**, 45, 682, 265, 84, 337 — -ly: spiritual, **93**, 280, **96**, 479.

Gieft: gift, giving, **563**, 14.

Gilden: golden, **16**, 82; gilded, **673**, 33, **594**, 33, 595, 44.

Gin, ginne, gynne (*pret.* **gan**): to begin (usually followed by *infin.* with or without *to*), **11**, 2, **12**, 39, **44**, 25, **10**, 73, 75, **179**, 9, **227**, 24, **429**, 24. **gan** (auxiliary followed by *infin.* without *to*) = did, **208**, 12, **202**, 21, 154, 15, **282**, 15. **gin** = do (?), **219**, 21. [Cf. **Can.**]

Gipsen: a gipsy, **91**, 86.

Girland, girlond: a garland, e.g. **167**, 22, **172**, 5.

Giust: a joust, tilt, **145**, 1, **44**, 39 — to joust, 419, 11.

Glaive, glave: a kind of halbert, a blade fixed to a staff, **575**, 58; a spear, a sword, used also of a club, **745**, 233, **484**, 19, **464**, 28.

Glee: cheer, welcome, **209**, 15, **602**, 43, **619**, 41, **26**, 282.

Glims: a glimpse, **757**, 221; gleams, glimmering, **540**, 29, **634**, 48.

Glitterand: glittering, **33**, 177, **166**, 16, **189**, 29.

Gnarre: to snarl, **176**, 34.

Goe: gone, **33**, 118.

Goodlihead: goodliness, comeliness, **593**, 25, 339, 38; (as a form of address,) **250**, 33, **13**, 184, 26, 270.

Gore blood: clotted blood, **236**, 39, **600**, 27; **gore bloudy, 658**, 28.

Gored: bloodied, **284**, 32.

Gourmandize: gluttony, **632**, 38, **645**, 34.

Governall: management, **319**, 48.

Governaunce: order, **301**, 38; self-control, behavior, **253**, 7, **234**, 29, 63, 270, **121**, 384.

Grace: to be gracious to, **215**, 64, **638**, 28, **644**, 26, **657**, 16, **748**, 116.

Gracelesse: lacking favor, **37**, 113; merciless, cruel, **434**, 8, **578**, 18.

Graffed: grafted, **14**, 242.

Graft: grafted, **698**, 918.

Graile: gravel, **185**, 6, **557**, 19, **127**, 12.

Gramercy: many thanks, **277**, 50, **289**, 9.

Graplement: grappling, **310**, 29.

Graste: *pret.* of **Grace**, q. v.

Grayle v. Graile.

Greave: a thicket, **595**, 43; a tree, **401**, 42.

Gree: rank, 34, 215 — favor, **173**, 16, **246**, 5; **take (or receive) in gree**, to accept with good will, take in good part, **140**, *Oxenford*, **613**, 39, **539**, 21.

Greete: to weep, mourn, **18**, 1 — mourning, weeping, **37**, 66.

Greisly v. Griesly.

Gren: to grin, show the teeth, **180**, 1K, **463**, 24, 658, 27.

Gride v. Gryde.

Griefull: sorrowful, **420**, 16.

Griesly, greisly, grisely, gryesly: grisly, horrible, grim, **202**, 21, **310**, 29, **313**, 6, **317**, 35, **73**, 185, 84, 326.

Griesy, grysie, gryesy: horrible, hideous, grim, **204**, 35, **266**, 18, **308**, 12, **334**, 67, **413**, 19.

Griple: griping, grasping, **604**, 6, **168**, 31 — a grip, **509**, 14.

Grisely v. Griesly.

Gronefull: lugubrious, **312**, 42.

Groome: a stock term for shepherds and their men, **687**, 12, **16**, 62, **653**, 40; a serving-man, retainer, **209**, 17, **229**, 37, **505**, 12.

Groyn: to growl, **658**, 27.

Grudge: to murmur, be discontented, chafe, 155, 19, **236**, 42, **665**, 35; to chafe at, **267**, 30 — resentment, **480**, 32, **358**, 61.

Grudgefull: resentful, **470**, 28.

Grutch: to murmur, repine, **244**, 34.

Gryde (*pp.* **gryde**): to pierce, transfix, **285**, 36, 333, 62, **339**, 37, **392**, 29, **11**, 4.

Gryesly v. Griesly.

Gryesy, grysie v. Griesy.

Guarish: to cure, **364**, 41, **437**, 29.

Guile, guylen: to deceive, **332**, 54, **389**, 7.

Guiler: a deceiver, **400**, 37, **279**, 64.

Guise: style, **482**, 6, **538**, 20; custom, habit, 590, 6, **316**, 21; mode of life, conduct, comportment, **330**, 33, **570**, 19, **167**, 20, **182**, 25, **226**, 14, 608, 2; external appearance, **321**, 66.

Gulfe: maw, **41**, 185.

Gurmandize v. Gourmandize.

Guylen, guyler v. Guile, guiler.

Gyeld: a guild-hall, **276**, 43.

Gylden v. Gilden.

Gynne, gynst v. Gin.

Habergeon: a sleeveless jacket of mail armor, 267, 29, **349**, 57, **361**, 19, **362**, 31, **427**, 15, **528**, 2.

Hability: wealth, means, **597**, 7.

Habitaunce: dwelling-place, **271**, 7.

Haile v. Hayle.

Hale: health, welfare, **701**, 103.

Halfen: half, imperfect, **396**, 5.

Halfendeale: half, **395**, 53.

Han: have, 46, 119, 23, 49.

Happely, happily: by chance, haply, **16**, 31, 523, 21, **230**, 3, 138, 207.

Harbrough: a place of shelter, **29**, 19.

Hard: heard, 93, 267, **291**, 25.

Hardyhed: hardihood, 4, *To His Booke*, **116**, 27.

Haske: a wicker basket for fish, **48**, 16.

Hastly, hastely: hastily, **156**, 29, **398**, 23.

Hauberk, haubergh, hauberque: a long coat of chain mail, **286**, 44, 352, 16, **437**, 30.

Haught, hault: lofty, **182**, 29; haughty, **593**, 23.

Haulst: embraced, **440**, 49.

Hault v. Haught.

Haviour, haveour: ¦the whole deportment of a man, physical and moral, as controlled by the mind' (Herford), **19**, 66, **41**, 106, **373**, 52; bearing, **241**, 15, **411**, 3.

Hayle: to hale, drag, **253**, 8, **385**, 31, **553**, 39.

Haynous: odious, **585**, 18.

Hazardize: peril, **315**, 19.

Hazardry: dicing, gaming, **333**, 57; rashness, 260, 13.

Headlessehood: heedlessness, **12**, 86.
Heame: home, **49**, 98.
Heard: a herdsman, keeper of cattle or sheep, **635**, 4, **636**, 10, **652**, 37.
Heardgroome: a keeper of cattle or sheep, **12**, 35, **653**, 39.
Heare: hair, **161**, 22, **154**, 11, **189**, 32.
Hearie: hairy, **327**, 16.
Hearse v. Herse.
Heast: a hest, command, **187**, 18; a vow, **658**, 24.
Heavinesse: animosity, **172**, 6; grief, misery, **272**, 12, **547**, 44, **75**, 366, **678**, 32.
Heben: ebony, **128**, 2; of ebony, ebon, **144**, 3, **190**, 37, **454**, 6.
Heedinesse: heedfulness, **540**, 34, **617**, 26.
Heedy: heedful, **41**, 167, **556**, 13.
Hefte (*pret.* of **heave**): lifted, **221**, 39; hurled, **435**, 12.
Hem: them, **24**, 147, **26**, 304.
Hend: to grasp, **571**, 27.
Henge: a hinge, **219**, 21.
Hent: took, seized, held, **308**, 17, **253**, 12, **270**, 49, **673**, 32, **14**, 195; lifted (up), borne away (into), **239**, 1, **50**, 169; h. **in hand**, undertook, undertaken, **32**, 37, **381**, 61.
Hept: heaped, **377**, 33.
Her: their, **25**, 160, **41**, 112; he, him, **39**, 1, 2, 3, 4; its, **240**, 7; for genitive *'s* of a noun whose gender in Lat. is feminine, **283**, 24.
Herbars: shrubs trained on trellises, **294**, 46.
Herce v. Herse.
Herehence: from this, **17**, 53.
Herneshaw: a heron, **621**, 9.
Herry v. Hery.
Hersall: rehearsal, **405**, 18.
Herse, herce, hearse: a bier, (vaguely) a tomb, **282**, 16, **350**, 1, **69**, 679, **685**, 528 — rehearsal, ceremonial, **341**, 48; refrain, **49**, 60.
Hery, herry: to praise, worship, honor, **12**, 62, **48**, 10, **331**, 43, **314**, 13.
Hether: hither, e. g. **463**, 18.
Hetherward: hitherward, **37**, 46.
Hew: form, shape, feature, appearance, aspect, **667**, 45, **317**, 31, **262**, 27, **189**, 35, **197**, 38, **157**, **40**, 183, 38, **647**, 2, **117**, 120.
Hidder and shidder: male and female sheep, **42**, 211.
Hight (*pret.* **hote, hot,** *pp.* **hight**): to decree, determine, appoint, **624**, 31, **463**, 17; to direct (a blow), **568**, 8; to summon, **678**, 11; to assign, grant, **165**, 6, **487**, 38, **474**, 54; to call (by name), to name, **636**, 9, **448**, 6, **454**, 4, **191**, 46, **207**, 5; to be called (**hight =** is called, **hote =** was called), **233**, 18, **214**, 55, **220**, 29, **446**, 40, **42**, 194; to mention by name, **33**, 164; to purport, **41**, 172.
Hild: held, **439**, 42, **492**, 17.
His: its, **194**, 19, **349**, 60; for genitive *'s*, **202**, **21**, 369, 24, **391**, 27, **668**, 1, **53**, 46.
Holpen: helped, **630**, 25.
Hoord: to hoard, heap up, **388**, 4, **88**, 657.
Hoove v. Hove.
Hospitage: the duties of the guest, **396**, 6.
Hospitale: a lodging-place, **289**, 10.
Host: to entertain as guest, **388**, *arg.*, **470**, 27; to be a guest, lodge (with), **634**, *arg.;* take to h., to entertain, **82**, 196.

Hostlesse: inhospitable, **403**, 3.
Hostry: an inn, lodging-place, **565**, 23.
Hot, hote v. Hight.
Housling: sacramental, **229**, 37.
Hove, hoove: to be poised, to float, **376**, 27; to hover about, wait, abide, **398**, 20, **695**, **666**, **734**, 88 — to rise, **156**, 31.
Howbe: howbeit, **614**, 2.
Hububs: confused cries or noise, **401**, 43.
Hugger mugger: secrecy, **92**, 139.
Humblesse: humbleness, humility, **155**, 21, 162, 26, **225**, 8, **227**, 25.
Humour: moisture, **367**, 9; according to the older physiology, any fluid or vapor of the body, **72**, 112, **362**, 29, **403**, 59, **149**, 36, **201**, 13, **113**, 23.
Hundreth: a hundred, **125**, 2.
Hurtle: to brandish, **276**, 42; h. **round**, to skirmish about, **259**, 8, **444**, 29.
Husband: a husbandman, **437**, 29, **93**, 266.
Hylding: vile, worthless, **612**, 25.

Idole, idoll: an image, **109**, 5, **723**, 27, **244**, 41; a counterfeit, **382**, 11, **449**, 15.
Imbrew v. Embrew.
Imp v. Impe.
Impacable: unappeasable, **65**, 395, **479**, 22.
Impe: a young shoot of a tree, hence a scion of a noble house, child, young man, etc., **493**, 26, **144**, 3, **181**, 24, **200**, 6, **217**, 5, **365**, 53 — to graft, to strengthen or repair a hawk's wings by engrafting feathers, **476**, 4, **756**, 135.
Impeach v. Empeach.
Imperceable: unpierceable, **218**, 17.
Implore: supplication, **263**, 37.
Imply: to enfold, involve, envelope, **168**, 31, **179**, 6, **219**, 23, **543**, 12, **370**, 34.
Importable: unbearable, **285**, 35.
Importune: grievous, **226**, 16, **347**, 44; vehement, impetuous, **223**, 53, **267**, 29, **298**, 15; importunate, **648**, 6 — to portend, **327**, 16.
Importunely: importunately, **280**, 4.
Improvided: unforeseen, **228**, 34.
In, inne, ynne: an abode, quarters, resting place, **149**, 33, **48**, 16, **53**, 72, **345**, 30, **600**, 29, **317**, 32.
Incompared: peerless, **143**, *Walsingham.*
Incontinent: immediately, **179**, 8, **288**, 1, **436**, 18.
Indew v. Endew.
Indignaunce: indignation, **405**, 13.
Indigne: unworthy, **422**, 30.
Indignify: to treat with indignity, to disgrace, **587**, 30, **694**, 583.
Infant: a youth of gentle or high birth, a knight in the prime of manhood (Arthur), **418**, *Prol.*, 5, **630**, 25, **288**, 56, **309**, 25; applied to Britomart, **341**, 49, **349**, 56. [Cf. **Childe.**]
Infest: hostile, **603**, 5, **619**, 41 — to assail, afflict, **66**, 460, **615**, 12; to infect, **217**, 6.
Ingate: entrance, **483**, 12, **60**, 47.
Inne v. In.
Inquere (*pret.* **inquerd**): to inquire, **149**, 31, 161, 25, **183**, 36.
Intendiment: understanding, **72**, 144, **362**, 32; intention, purpose, **411**, 5; attentive consideration, **228**, 31.
Intentive: attentive, **556**, 14.

Interesse: interest, title, **665**, 33,
Intermedle: to intermingle, **137**, 196.
Intreat v. Entreat.
Intuse: a contusion, **363**, 33.
Inure v. Enure.
Invent: to find, to find out, **733**, 82, **180**, 15, **359**, 10, **510**, 20, **574**, 50; to compose, **70**, 12.
Irrenowmed: inglorious, **233**, 23.

Javel: a low rascal, **94**, 309.
Jolliment: merriment, joyfulness, **264**, 3, **491**, **12**, **592**, 16.
Jolly: courageous, **145**, 1, **154**, 11; comely, goodly, gallant, **292**, 34, **331**, 45, **49**, 47, **139**, *Hobynoll;* 'fine,' 'nice,' etc., **41**, 165.
Jollyhead: mirth, gaiety, **652**, 32.
Jouisaunce: joyousness, festivity, **48**, 2, **23**, 25.
Journall: daily, **220**, 31.
Juncates: sweetmeats, delicacies, **527**, 49, **732**, 77.

Kales: keys, **484**, 18.
Keasars v. Kesars.
Keep: a charge, **33**, 133. take k., take k. of, to pay heed, take notice of, give thought to, **556**, 13, **150**, 40, **82**, 241; to take care of, take charge of, concern oneself with, **52**, 8, **93**, 290, **680**, 133, **400**, 38.
Keight: caught, **338**, 30, **540**, 29.
Kemd: combed, **540**, 4.
Kerve: to cut, **418**, 4.
Kesars, keasars: kaisers, emperors, **271**, 5, **460**, 1.
Kest: cast, **312**, 42, **220**, 31.
Ketch: to catch, **371**, 37.
Kilt: killed, **175**, 26, **214**, 57.
Kind, kynd: nature, **713**, 206, **158**, 43, **164**, 44, **358**, 1, **370**, 30, **669**, 9; sex, **335**, 4; race, kin, 142, *Cumberland*, **497**, 52, **181**, 18.
Kindly: natural, **193**, 11, **200**, 9; innate, native, **162**, 28, **76**, 383; characteristically, **104**, 1137.
Kinred: kindred, kinship, **301**, 35, **26**, 271.
Knightlesse: unknightly, **184**, 41, **591**, 14.
Knowe: known, **41**, 161.
Kon v. Con.
Kydst: knewest, **54**, 92, 93.
Kynd v. Kind.
Kynded: sprung, begotten, **533**, 40.

Labourous: toilsome, **93**, 266.
Lad: led, **145**, 4, **467**, 2.
Laire, lare: pasture, **471**, 29; ground, **474**, 51.
Latch: to catch, **17**, 93.
Launce: a scale, balance, **373**, 4.
Launch: to pierce, transfix, **188**, 25, **236**, 38; to inflict (a wound), **339**, 37, **50**, 139 — a piercing, **752**, 162.
Lay v. Laye.
Layd: prostrated, faint, **44**, 12.
Laye, lay: laity, **24**, 76 — a lea, meadow, field, 51, **188**, **80**, 110; the ground, **398**, 23, **383**, 15 — a stall (?), **48**, 15.
Layes: laws, **302**, 42 — the ground, **768**, **44**.
Lazar: a leper, **165**, 3.
Leake, leke: leaky, **176**, 35, **630**, **24**.

Leames: gleams, **767**, 9.
Leany: lean, **34**, 199.
Leape: a kind of basket-like net to catch fish in, **55**, 41.
Leare v. Lere.
Leasing, lesinge: lying, a lie, **688**, 102, **36**; 285, **99**, 699, **185**, 48, **295**, 51.
Least: lest, e. g. **156**, 31, **231**, 7.
Ledden: language, form of speech, **492**, 19; **696**, 744.
Lee: lea, plain, **61**, 135; hence often the surface of a river, the stream (cf. **428**, 16), **68**, 603; 760, 38, **761**, 115, **510**, 19.
Leefe v. Liefe.
Leese: to lose, **41**, 135.
Leke v. Leake.
Lengd: longed, **26**, 250.
Lenger: longer, e. g. **174**, 19, **203**, 30, **23**, 19.
Lere, leare: to learn, **52**, 4 — learning, lore; 696, 783, **405**, 16, **439**, 40; a lesson, **26**, 262, **594**; 31, **376**, 21.
Lesinge v. Leasing.
Lest: to listen, **585**, 17.
Let: to hinder, impede, **187**, 20, **284**, 28, **360**, 17, **555**, 7, **605**, 19, **655**, 1 — hindrance, an impediment, **194**, 13, **592**, 17, **310**, 31.
Lever v. Liefe.
Levin: lightning, **37**, 87, **365**, 48, **541**, 40.
Levin-brond: the thunderbolt, **665**, 30.
Lewd: ignorant, unskillful, foolish, **375**, 12; 351, 9, 14, 245; vile, base, **471**, 35, **520**, 36 — -ly: ignorantly, foolishly, **11**, 9; ill, vilely, **594**, 31; 616, 17, **546**, 32, **470**, 24 — -nesse: baseness; wickedness, **520**, 38, **358**, 58.
Libbard: a leopard, **60**, 68, **463**, 23.
Lich: like, **377**, 29.
Lidge: a ledge, edge, **541**, 36.
Liefe, leefe: (*a*) dear, dearly, **40**, 11, **243**, 30, 440, 52, **478**, 15. (*b*) more liefe, liefer, lever (than), more precious, acceptable (than), **386**, 42, 328, 24, **359**, 7, 256, 28; me lever were, I had lever, I had rather, **335**, 6, **203**, 32, **25**, 167. (*c*) willing, desirous, **390**, 13, 14, **661**, 8; devoted, **33**, 165 — a love, **201**, 17, **328**, 24.
Lifull, lyfull: lifeful, vitalizing, **737**, 119, **654**; 45.
Lig, liggen: to lie, **608**, 40, 24, 125, **42**, **234**.
Lignage, linage: lineage, **305**, 71, **544**, 21, **145**; 5.
Like: to please, **768**, 30, **91**, 94, 95, **274**, 27; **528**, 1.
Lill: to loll, **176**, 34.
Lin: to cease, cease from, **148**, 24, **176**, 35, **344**, **22**, 345, 30, **384**, 24, **684**, 467.
Linage v. Lignage.
Line: linen, **542**, 6, **121**, 364.
List (*pres.* and *pret.*): is, are, was, were pleased, 389, 7, **155**, 22, **209**, 20, **305**, 66, **630**, 21; me list, him list, us listeth, etc., it pleases, pleased me, etc., **273**, 19, **630**, 21, **189**, 35, **199**, 2, **92**, 169.
Live: life, **419**, 6, **434**, 4.
Livelod, livelood: livelihood, **522**, 9, **597**, 7.
Livelyhed: living form, **288**, 3; life, **623**, 20; livelihood, **239**, 2.
Loast v. Lose.
Loft: a roof (?), **150**, 41; a ceiling (or floor); **539**, 27.

Long: to belong, **170**, 48, **349, 58.**
Loord: a lubber, **32**, 33, **374,** 12.
Loos: praise, **656,** 12.
Lore: left, **417,** 44, **567,** 38.
Loring: teaching, **547,** 42.
Lorne: lost, **53,** 52; deserted, **40,** 57, **10,** 62, **164,** 2.
Lorrell: a worthless fellow, **33,** 93.
Lose, losen (*pp.* **loast, lo'ste**): to loosen, release, etc., **127,** 9, **321,** 67, **411,** 2, **388,** 51, **372, 48, 631,** 29; to dissolve, **351,** 13; to become loose, **519,** 28 — wanton, inconstant, **323,** 76, **54,** 119.
Losel: a worthless fellow, a scoundrel, **75,** 324, **246,** 4, **604,** 10.
Lo'ste v. Lose.
Lovely: affectionate, **162,** 30 ; of love, amatory, amorous, **459,** 40, **516,** 5, **407,** 32, **723,** 28 — amorously, **179,** 4.
Lover: a louver, a lantern-like opening in the roof, **647,** 42.
Lowe: lowly, **33,** 165.
Lozell v. Losel.
Lug: a rod, **297,** 11.
Lumine: to give light to, **754,** 280.
Luskishnesse: sluggishness, **588,** 35.
Lust: pleasure, delight, **673,** 39, **571,** 31; inclination, appetite, **423,** 34, **497,** 51, **279,** 64 — to desire, choose, **48,** 21, **32,** 29, **272,** 11, **277,** 49; (*pret.*) lust, **516,** 6, **550,** 22.
Lustfull: lusty, **10,** 37, **116,** 34.
Lustihede v. Lustyhed.
Lustlesse: feeble, languid, **167,** 20, **357,** 56, **588,** 35.
Lustyhed: pleasure, enjoyment, gay living, **401,** 45, **152,** 3, **23,** 42; lustiness, vigor, **25,** 204, **116,** 54, **236,** 41.
Lyfull v. Lifull.
Lynage v. Lignage.
Lyne v. Line.

Maine: strength, force, **186,** 11, **193,** 7, **290,** 14, **308,** 15, **568,** 10 — -ly: mightily, violently, **328,** 21, **186,** 12.
Maister: a master, **269,** 38; to master, **253,** 10, **260,** 14. [Also in compounds.]
Maistresse: a mistress, **185,** 1.
Make: a mate, companion, **186,** 7, **187,** 15, **403,** 2, **702,** 178 — to compose poetry, compose, **18,** 19, **30,** 82, **73,** 215, **688,** 99, **689,** 188; **maked,** made, **409,** 44.
Making: the composition of poetry, **5, 3.**
Malefice: an evil deed, **104,** 1154.
Malengine: guile, **332,** 53.
Malice: to envy, hate, **640,** 39, **119,** 257, **753,** 238.
Maltalent: resentment, **358,** 61.
Many: a retinue, **414,** 23, **499,** 18; a band, company, **389,** 11, **23,** 23.
Mart: trade, traffic, **158,** *arg.,* **40,** 37, **712,** 172.
Martelled: hammered, **378,** 42.
Maske: to masquerade, to go disguised (in gay or strange attire), **9,** 24, **348,** 51, **144,** 1, **185,** 1.
Masking: masquerading, **100,** 802.
Mate: to confound, overcome, **200,** 12, **469,** 17.
Maugre, mauger, maulgre: in spite of, despite, **352,** 15, **855,** 39, **425,** 48, **670,** 17 — in spite of oneself, against one's will, **407,** 26, **507,**

29; resentfully, **608,** 40 — curse on, **360,** 12; curse on it, **359,** 7.
May: a maid, **48,** 39.
Mayne, -ly v. Maine.
Mayster v. Maister.
Mazeful: confounding, **737,** 190.
Mazer, mazer-bowle: a large drinking bowl, **36,** 26, **319,** 49.
Meane, mene: means, **416,** 40, **514,** 45, **560,** 42, **625,** 39.
Mear: to bound, **112,** 22.
Medle: to mingle, mix, **19,** 68, **26,** 263, **239,** 61.
Meint, ment: mixed, mingled, **51,** 203, **33,** 84, **80,** 75, **153,** 5, **408,** 36, **529,** 12, **617,** 27.
Mell: to meddle, have to do (with), **34,** 208, **581,** 35, **149,** 30, **669,** 9, **555,** 1.
Memorize: to preserve or perpetuate or celebrate the memory of, **64,** 364, **142,** *Buckhurst,* **76,** 440.
Menage: management, **142,** *Burleigh,* **414,** 22 — to control, wield, **190,** 37, **241,** 18, **291,** 27; to husband, **641,** 46; m. **arms,** to fight, **139,** *W. L.*
Mendes: amends, **233,** 20.
Mene v. Meane.
Ment v. Meint.
Merciable: merciful, **41,** 174.
Mercify: to pity, **624,** 32.
Merimake, merrymake: merry-making, sport, **23,** 15, **48,** 9, **266,** 21, **643,** 19.
Merveil: to marvel, **383,** 12.
Merveilous: marvelous, **343,** 13.
Mesprise, misprize: a blunder, **315,** 19, **480,** 35 — contempt, **276,** 39, **389,** 9, **442,** 11, **534,** 48.
Mew: a cage or cell, **262,** 27; a hiding-place or retreat, **273,** 19, **382,** 4, **174,** 20, **556,** 14, **733,** 80.
Meynt v. Meint.
Mickle, mickell: great, much, **231,** 6, **253,** 7, **528,** 3, **511,** 29. [v. **Muchell.**]
Mid: middle, **432,** 48.
Middest: midmost, **166,** 15 — the midst, **447,** 44; the middle one (of three), **241,** 13.
Mieve: to move, **501,** 26.
Miniments: memorials, **467,** 6.
Mirkesome: murky, dark, **175,** 28.
Misavised: ill-advised, **336,** 9.
Miscall: to revile, **324,** 86, **470,** 24.
Misconceipt: misconception, **454,** 2.
Miscreaunce: misbelief, **24,** 91, **287,** 51.
Miscreaunt: a misbeliever, infidel, **173,** 13, **184,** 41, **284,** 31.
Misdempt: misdeemed, misjudged, **399,** 29.
Misdesert: ill desert, **585,** 12.
Misdight: ill clad, **546,** 37.
Misdoubt: to suspect, fear, **483,** 12, **429,** 23, **602,** 47.
Misfall: to befall unluckily, **529,** 10.
Misfare: deviation, **675,** 53; misfortune, **574,** 48; affliction, sorrow, **451,** 30, **454,** 2, **467,** 5, **498,** 12, **656,** 14.
Misfaring: misbehavior, **696,** 758.
Misget: to obtain wrongfully, **585,** 18.
Misgo: to go wrong, **34,** 201. [Cf. **Miswend.**]
Misgovernaunce: misgovernment, **48, 4.**
Misguyde: trespass, sin, **752,** 144.
Mishappen: to happen disastrously, **161,** 20.
Mislike, misleek: to displease, **388,** 51; m. of, to dislike, take exception to, **514,** 49, **25,** 162.

Misprize v. Mesprise.

Misregard: heedlessness, **471,** 29.

Missay: to say needlessly, **655,** 2; to speak falsely, **39,** 2; to scold, **457,** 27; to speak ill (of), **41,** 106.

Misseeme: to misbecome, **100,** 804, **348,** 53, **384,** 26.

Misseeming: unseemly, **202,** 23, **243,** 31 — simulation, **192,** 50.

Mis-shape: deformity, **580,** 29.

Mister: kind of, **41,** 103, **202,** 23, **359,** 5, **500,** 22.

Misthought: misperception, **475,** 58.

Mistreth: is necessary, **380,** 51.

Misweene: to misjudge, mistake, **701,** 101, **230,** 3, **554,** 46.

Misweening: misjudgment, **164,** 1.

Miswend (*pp.* **miswent**): to go astray, go wrong, come to grief, **451,** 30, **36,** 16, **91,** 128. [Cf. **Misgo.**]

Mizzle: to drizzle, **51,** 208.

Mo, moe: more, **23,** 68, **205,** 44.

Mochell v. Muchell.

Mold: a mole, **655,** 7.

Moldwarpe: a mole, **696,** 763, **744,** 182.

Molt: melted, **259,** 8.

Molting: melting, **713,** 231.

Mome: a buffoon, blockhead, **667,** 49.

Monastere: a monastery, **658,** 23.

Monefull: mournful, **537,** 12.

Moniment, monument: a relic, record, **553,** 43, **323,** 80, **296,** 59, **657,** 20; a distinctive mark, stamp, **271,** 5.

Monstruous: monstrous, **324,** 85, **626,** 41.

More: a plant, **670,** 10.

Morish: marshy, **493,** 29.

Most-what: for the most part, generally, **32,** **46,** **41,** 104, **696,** 757.

Mote, mot: must, **40,** 14, **240,** 12, **267,** 24, **284,** 33; may, **235,** 33, **201,** 17; might, **427,** 8, **156,** 29, **157,** 37, **195,** 19 — moten, **370,** 31. [Cf. **Mought.**]

Mott: measured, **691,** 365.

Mought: might, could, **150,** 42, **397,** 18, **559,** 34, **627,** 50, **631,** 32; may, **138,** *Hobynoll,* **25,** 191, **36,** 13; must, **12,** 24, **25,** 157, **42,** 241. [Used interchangeably with **mote,** q. v., another word.]

Mountenaunce: amount, extent, **383,** 18, **406,** 20, **541,** 36.

Mowes: grimaces, **627,** 49.

Moyity: a half, **317,** 31.

Muchell: great, much, **170,** 46, **181,** 20, **377,** 32, 13, 109; greatly, much, **399,** 31, **36,** 23.

Mumming: masquerading, **100,** 802.

Munificence: fortification, **298,** 15.

Mure: to wall, close, **659,** 34.

Muse: to wonder, **233,** 19, **450,** 21, **622,** 13.

Musicall: music, **23,** 28.

Mutine: to mutiny, **514,** 51.

Myster v. Mister.

Napron: an apron, **530,** 20.

Narre: nearer, **33,** 97, **111,** 16.

Nas: has not, **23,** 61.

Nathelesse, nathlesse, nath'lesse, nethelesse: nevertheless, none the less, **206,** 54, **233,** 20, **333,** 55, **450,** 20, **583,** 2, **6,** 186.

Nathemore, nathemoe: none the more, **202,** 25, **253,** 8, **450,** 20.

Ne: nor, **12,** 21, **143,** *Carew,* **174,** 19, **179,** 2 — not, **25,** 152, **178,** 1, **336,** 14.

Neglect (*pp.*): neglected, **706,** 96.

Nempt: named, **399,** 29.

Net: pure, clean, **413,** 20, **633,** 45.

Nethelesse v. Nathelesse.

Newell: a novelty, **26,** 276.

Nigardise: niggardliness, **469,** 15.

Nigh, nye: to draw near, **16,** 4, **26,** 316, **39,** 195.

Nill, n'ill: will not, **359,** 11, **201,** 15, **164,** 43; desire not, **275,** 33 — nilled, was unwilling, **463,** 16.

Nimblesse: nimbleness, **558,** 29, **568,** 6.

Nis: is not, **29,** 19, **24,** 144.

Noblesse, nobilesse: nobleness, **4,** *To His Booke,* **196,** 26, **282,** 18.

Noriture v. Nouriture.

Nosethril, nosthril: nostril, **219,** 22, **391,** 22, **124,** 8.

Note, no'te, not: (*ne wot*) know not, **41,** 110, **226,** 17; know or knows not how to, cannot, **230,** 4, **384,** 23, **414,** 26; (*ne mote ?*) might not, could not, **348,** 50, **252,** 4, **254,** 13, **434,** 9.

Nould, n'ould: would not, **625,** 36, **284,** 30.

Noule: noddle, **673,** 39.

Nourice: a nurse, **62,** 169.

Nouriture, noriture, nourture: nourishment, **743,** 39, **535,** 53; bringing up, training, **200,** 5, **245,** 2, **305,** 69.

Noursle v. Nousle.

Nourtred: nurtured, **701,** 71.

Nousle, nousell, noursle: to foster, train, rear, **181,** 23, **504,** 6, **607,** 35, **31,** 45; to burrow, **494,** 32, **696,** 763.

Noy: to vex, afflict, **210,** 24, **222,** 45.

Noyance: annoyance, grievousness, **148,** 23, **411,** 2.

Noyous: vexatious, tedious, **734,** 86, **223,** 50; grievous, harmful, **290,** 16, **292,** 32, **197,** 40, **177,** 45.

Nye v. Nigh.

Nys v. Nis.

Obeysaunce: obedience, **24,** 120, **532,** 28.

Obliquid: directed obliquely, **676,** 54.

Offend: to assail, **307,** 6, **224,** 1; to harm, **231,** 3, **281,** 8; to incommode, **321,** 63, **606,** 25.

Ordinaunce: arrangement, device, **292,** 30, **434,** 5, **92,** 173; ordnance, **308,** 14.

Ought: owned, **169,** 39, **285,** 40, **596,** 2, **622,** 16; owed, **331,** 44, **721,** 19.

Our: ours, **33,** 76.

Outgo: to go out, **23,** 20; to pass through, complete, **729,** 60, **367,** 9.

Outlaunce: to thrust out, **117,** 82.

Outlearne: to find out, **470,** 22.

Outward: to keep out, **505,** 10.

Outwell: to pour out, **147,** 21, **86,** 502.

Outwin: to get out from, **421,** 20.

Outwind: to extricate, **516,** 9.

Outwrest: to extort, **255,** 23.

Outwrought: completed, **279,** 65.

Over all: everywhere, **211,** 34, **222,** 46; all over, **251,** 44.

Overcatch: to overtake, **464,** 31.

Overcraw: to triumph over, **206**, 50.
Overdight: overspread, covered, **278**, 53, **471**, 34, **693**, 493.
Overgive: to give over, abandon, **93**, 249.
Overgo: to overcome, overwhelm, **508**, 7, **118**, 134; (*pp.*) **overwent**, overcome, **16**, 2, **548**, 7.
Overhaile: to draw over, **10**, 75.
Overhent: overtook, overtaken, **298**, 18, **361**, 25, **375**, 19, **548**, 4.
Overkest: overcast, **367**, 10, **66**, 457.
Overlay: to overmatch, overpower, **574**, 51, **33**, 151, **120**, 337.
Overraught: extended beyond, **580**, 30; overtook, **603**, 50.
Overren: to overrun, oppress, **510**, 19.
Overthwart: opposite, **489**, 51.
Owch: a brooch, **154**, 13, **211**, 31, **353**, 23.
Owre: ore, **271**, 5, **352**, 18.

Paddock: a toad, **53**, 70.
Paine: punishment, penalty, **498**, 11, **103**, 1072, **273**, 21; pains taken, care, labor, **261**, 24, **364**, 42, **582**, 3, **183**, 33, **188**, 24, **228**, 34, **595**, 38; difficulty, **628**, 9; **with easie p.**, at one's ease, **106**, 1264 — (*reflex.*) to take pains, exert oneself, **38**, 133, **166**, 15, **459**, 40, **493**, 25, **577**, 10, **582**, 41.
Paire: to impair, **190**, 41.
Pall: to make pale, **702**, 163; to enfeeble, **521**, 5.
Pannikell: the brain pan, **361**, 23.
Paragon, paragone: a match, an equal, **477**, 11, **141**, *Ormond*, **336**, 13; a mate, mistress, **400**, **35**, **422**, 33, **426**, 8, **636**, 11; a rival, **745**, 251; a contest, **448**, 9, **119**, 274; excellence, **730**, 66; comparison, **691**, 344, **388**, 2, **518**, 24; rivalry, **349**, 54, **103**, 1026.
Paravant, paravaunt: face to face, **336**, 16; preëminently, **643**, 15, **698**, 941.
Pardale: a pard, **182**, 26.
Parture: departure, **387**, 46.
Pas, passe: to surpass, exceed, excel, **241**, 17, **267**, 25, **426**, 2, **427**, 10; to care, **104**, 1150; **p. by, p. of**, to care for, esteem, **475**, 63, **268**, 37.
Pastor: a shepherd, **700**, 9, **139**, *Hobynoll*.
Patrone: a pattern, **145**, *arg*.
Paunce, pawnce: pansy, **330**, 36, **408**, 37, **20**, 142.
Pavone: peacock, **409**, 47.
Payne v. Paine.
Payse v. Peise.
Peal: to appeal, **668**, *arg*.
Peare, peere, pere: [besides modern senses] a companion, **563**, 15, **504**, 6, **254**, 18, **176**, 37; a champion, **193**, 7, **344**, 22, **398**, 26; a prince, **226**, 17.
Peaze v. Poyse.
Peece: a structure, **214**, 59; a castle, **308**, 14, **396**, 10, **510**, 21, **720**, 14; a ship, **319**, 44.
Peere v. Peare.
Peinct: to paint, **13**, 121.
Peise, peize, payse: to weigh down, to sink, **514**, 46, **697**, 849; to poise, **297**, 5.
Penne: a quill, **217**, 10.
Perce, percen: to pierce, **154**, 17, **189**, 33, **205**, 48, **158**, 1, **451**, 31.
Perceable: pierceable, **145**, 7.
Perdy, perdie, perdee: Fr. *pardieu*, literally 'by God,' **184**, 42, **266**, 22, **398**, 27.

Pere v. Peare.
Peregall: quite equal, **36**, 8.
Perlous: perilous, **266**, 19.
Persant: piercing, **213**, 47, **248**, 23.
Perse v. Perce.
Persever: to persevere, **411**, 2.
Perst v. Perce.
Perswade: persuasion, **565**, 25.
Pert: open, plain, **41**, 162.
Pheere v. Fere.
Phocas: seals, **385**, 30.
Physnomy, visnomy: physiognomy, visage, **120**, 310, **522**, 11, **669**, 5.
Pictural: a picture, **295**, 53.
Pight: pitched, set, placed, **364**, 40, **485**, 25, **158**, 42, **197**, 37; hurled, struck, **219**, 25; plunged, **548**, 8.
Pill: peel, rind, **722**, 26 — to plunder, **105**, 1198, **508**, 6, **641**, 5.
Pine: pain, wasting, **40**, 65, **204**, 35, **531**, 22; death, **612**, 28 — to afflict, waste, **341**, 52, **213**, 48, **198**, 40.
Pinneed: pinioned, **524**, 22.
Place: rank, **165**, 3, **323**, 79, **468**, 14 — **in p.** on the spot, present, **157**, 38, **176**, 36, **227**, 23; to the spot, into presence, **208**, 12, **376**, 23, **100**, 834.
P'lace: palace, **78**, 580.
Pleasaunce, pleasauns, plesaunce: complaisance, **156**, 30, **100**, 799, **721**, 21; pleasantness, **734**, 88, **319**, 50, **23**, 7; pleasure, **16**, *arg.*, **725**, 39, **321**, 65.
Plesh: a plash, pool, **285**, 36.
Plight: a plait, fold, **249**, 26, **293**, 40, **558**, 28 — to plait, fold, **264**, 7, **626**, 43, **391**, 21.
Poëtresse: a poetess, **78**, 576.
Point: to appoint, **205**, 41, **498**, 11, **70**, 10 — **to p.**, completely, exactly, **147**, 16, **154**, 12, **336**, 16.
Poise, peaze: weight, force, momentum, **512**, 34, **579**, 21, **223**, 54, **111**, 16; a blow, **337**, 20.
Pol: to plunder, **508**, 6.
Porcpisces: porpoises, **690**, 249.
Portance: bearing, **246**, 5, **248**, 21, **338**, 27, **610**, 11.
Portesse: a breviary, **167**, 19.
Portracture: a picture, **98**, 611.
Potshare: a potsherd, **588**, 37.
Pouldred: pulverized, **186**, 12, **114**, 27; sprinkled or whitened, **338**, 25.
Pourtrahed: portrayed, **197**, 33, **292**, 33, **330**, 34.
Pourtraict, pourtract: a portrait, picture, **236**, 39, **248**, 22, **286**, 43 — to portray, picture, **144**, *Ladies*, **136**, 42.
Pousse: pulse, **37**, 46.
Poynant: piercing, keen, **187**, 19, **285**, 36, **326**, 5.
Poyse v. Poise.
Practicke: practiced, skillful, **114**, 29, **588**, 36, **545**, 29, **434**, 7, **246**, 9, **231**, 3, **228**, 34.
Practise, practize: to plot, conspire, **637**, 23, **412**, 11, **560**, 41 — knavery, treachery, conspiracy, **42**, 202, **345**, 28, **561**, 47.
Pray: to make prey of, ravage, **523**, 14, **646**, 40, **202**, 20, **728**, 58 — **prayes:** plunder, spoils, **410**, 52.

Preace, preasse: to press, throng, **277**, 44, **540**, 29; to insist, **226**, 19 — thronging, **159**, 3; a press, crowd, **328**, 23, **277**, 46.

Preeve v. Prieve.

Preife v. Priefe.

Prejudize: forejudgment, **295**, 49.

Prepense: to consider beforehand, **405**, 14.

Prest: ready, **284**, 28, **472**, 41, **545**, 27, **620**, 44; assiduous, **452**, 36, **623**, 19; promptly, **663**, 16 — ready p., fully prepared, **436**, 22, **548**, 9.

Prevent: to outstrip, anticipate, **423**, 41, **588**, 38, **101**, 881, 94, 332; to frustrate, **484**, 20.

Previe: privy, 16, 35 — prevelie, privily, 26, 252.

Price: to pay the price of, **175**, 26, **204**, 37. [v. also **Prise.**]

Priefe, preife: trial, examination, demonstration, **95**, 408, **547**, 44, **270**, 51, **201**, 17; experience, **198**, 43, **237**, 48, **727**, 50; efficacy, **210**, 24.

Prieve, preeve: to prove, **525**, 33, **657**, 18, **107**, 1366.

Prise, prize: a contest (?), **630**, 25 — price, estimation, excellence, **480**, 35, **95**, 420, **77**, **466** — to pay the price of, **752**, 175, **490**, 5; to rate, **649**, 14, **61**, 116.

Prive: privy, 41, 162.

Prize v. Prise.

Proll: to prowl, 41, 160.

Prostrate (*pp.*): prostrated, **87**, 558.

Protense: extension, 342, 4.

Protract: protraction, **734**, 86.

Provokement: provocation, 441, 4.

Prow: hardy, valiant, **345**, 28, **247**, 15, **263**, 36.

Proyne: to preen, **707**, 137.

Pryse v. Prise.

Pumy: pumice (?), **16**, 89, **262**, 30, **363**, 39.

Purchase: to acquire, win, **104**, 1148, **37**, 41, **551**, 25, **554**, 51, **248**, 18 — acquisition, **160**, 16, **475**, 62; booty, plunder, **649**, 12, **87**, 591.

Purfled: embroidered or decorated along the edge, **154**, 13, **249**, 26.

Puttocke: a kite, **308**, 11, **530**, 15.

Pyne v. Pine.

Pyoning: digging of intrenchments, **304**, 63.

Quaint v. Queint.

Quart: a quarter, **298**, 14.

Quayd: subdued, 194, 14.

Queint, quaint: elaborate, elegant, **639**, 35, **484**, 22, 45, 114; strange, **544**, 21; fastidious, prim, 374, 10, **419**, 5 — skillfully, **376**, 22 — quenched, 260, 11.

Quell: to kill, destroy, **646**, 36, **651**, 29, **377**, 35, **242**, 20; to fail, perish, **16**, 8, **674**, 42.

Queme: to please, **23**, 15.

Quich: to stir, **559**, 33.

Quietage: quiet, 439, 43.

Quight, quite: free, clear, **109**, 8, **591**, 14. [v. also **Quit.**]

Quire: a company, **634**, 48.

Quit, quitten, quite, quight: to free, rescue, redeem, **215**, 63, **179**, 6, **193**, 10, **571**, 27. **627**, *arg.*, **14**, 213; to rid (oneself of), to get rid of, 62, 230, 24, 131; to clear or acquit, **233**, 20; to requite, repay, to make a return for, **695**, 681, **666**, 44, **212**, 37, **216**, 67, **154**, 17; to salute in return, 149, 30, **209**, 15. [v. also **Quight.**]

Quod: quoth, **732**, 75, **735**, 35.

Quooke: quaked, **398**, 24, **623**, 24.

Race (raced, ra'st, rast, raste): to scratch, 323, 80; to erase, **558**, 26, **347**, 43; to raze, **324**, 83, 346, 34, **511**, 28, **74**, 268; to cut off, **529**, 11.

Rad, rade: rode, **509**, 13, **674**, 41. [v. also **Read.**]

Raft: reft, **148**, 24.

Raile: to gush, flow, **184**, 43, **285**, 37, **409**, 46, **59**. 12, **127**, 12.

Raine: realm, region, **273**, 21, **356**, 49, **591**, 9, 743, 88.

Rancke, ranke: proud, froward, **11**, 1, **254**, 15; abundant, **34**, 211 — violently, **452**, 33, **246**, 6.

Randon, at: impetuously, with headlong force, 253, 7; at liberty, uncontrolled, **400**, 36, **23**, 46; at random, **75**, 321.

Rase: to scratch, **334**, 65. [v. also **Race.**]

Rash: to cut, slash, **428**, 17; to tear (off), **516**, 8 — swiftly, hastily, **249**, 30, **105**, 1214 — ly: swiftly, hastily, **415**, 33, **334**, 62.

Raskall: of the rabble, vulgar, base (r. routes, r. many), **189**, 35, **225**, 9, **290**, 15, **515**, 54, **575**, 59.

Ra'st, rast, raste v. Race.

Rathe: quickly, soon, early, **345**, 28, **54**, 98, **33**, 78; **rather**, earlier, sooner, **12**, 83, **537**, 9, 430, 34.

Raught: reached, **245**, 2, **182**, 29, **187**, 18, **568**, 10; took in hand, seized, **326**, 5; took or snatched (away), **443**, 20; **to him r.**, took, taken in hand, **206**, 51, **309**, 25, **96**, 441.

Raunch: to pull, **37**, 97.

Ray: array, **572**, 34, **514**, 50, **68**, 640 — to soil, defile, **385**, 32, **606**, 23, **236**, 40.

Rayle: railing, **424**, 43. [v. also **Raile.**]

Rayne v. Raine.

Rayon: a ray, **125**, 2.

Read, reede (*pret. pp.* **rad, red, rid**) : to declare, make known, tell, **36**, 15, **230**, *Prol.*, 2, **233**, 18, **234**, 30, **537**, 10; to name, call, **191**, 46, **265**, 9; to guess, recognize, perceive, see, **322**, 70, **583**, 4, **195**, 21, **196**, 33, **147**, 21, **668**, 54, **737**, 189; to deem, consider, regard, **600**, 31, **233**, 17, **271**, 2, **272**, 7, **272**, 12; to advise, **146**, 13, **209**, 17 — language, **486**, 34; a declaration or saying, **483**, 10, **501**, 27, **32**, 11; a precept, **753**, 211; a decision, **507**, 26; advice, **594**, 30; a theme, **503**, 11.

Ræædifye: to rebuild, **302**, 46.

Re-allie: to rally, recompose, **663**, 23.

Reame: a realm, **365**, 53, **473**, 45.

Reare: to lift, raise, bring up **240**, 11, **446**, 41, **595**, 42, **593**, 26, **266**, 21, **308**, 17, **304**, 64, **577**, 6; to establish, **585**, 14; to carry off, take away, tear away, **402**, 53, **384**, 19, **454**, 6, **472**, 42; to get rid of, **367**, 10; to rouse, bring on, **334**, 64, **322**, 68, **423**, 34, **326**, 9.

Rebut: to drive back, repel, **223**, 53, **242**, 23, **382**, 10, **756**, 122; to recoil, **154**, 15.

Rechlesse: reckless, **102**, 950.

Reclame, reclayme: to call back, **577**, 9; to retreat, **602**, 43 — recall, **397**, 16.

Recomfortlesse: comfortless, **539**, 24.

Record: to remember, **499**, 19, **114**, 28, **682**, 295; to recite, **19**, 30, **688**, 97.

Recoure, recower: to recover, regain, **436**, 20, **479**, 25, **489**, 58. [v. **Recure.**]

Recourse: return, retirement, **458**, 29, **508**, 2, **544**, 20, **391**, 26 — to return, **137**, 120.

Recower v. Recoure.

Recoyle, recuile, recule: to retreat, retire, **586**, 20, **556**, 9, **573**, 47, **576**, 65, **209**, 17, **99**, 754; to push or drag back, **315**, 19.

Recure: to remedy, reinvigorate, restore, **13**, **154**, 214, 52, **199**, 2, **177**, 44, **210**, 24, **238**, 54 — to recover, regain, **314**, 12, **315**, 19, **363**, 34; to attain, **746**, 298. [v. **Recoure.**]

Redd, Reede v. Read.

Regiment: government, rule, control, **347**, 40, **471**, 30, **551**, 30, **661**, 2, **670**, 17; a kingdom, **296**, 59, **508**, 30, **689**, 233.

Release: to relax, **588**, 36, **226**, 19; to remit, **239**, 60; to abandon, **428**, 19, **589**, 43.

Relent: to abate, slacken, **426**, 2, **310**, 27, **356**, 49; to relax effort, **428**, 18; to give way, **611**, 20, **437**, 26; to soften, qualify, **371**, 39, 40, 84, **368**, 743, 84; to repent, **369**, 25 — slackening of speed, **544**, 24.

Relide: rallied, joined forces, **479**, 26.

Relive: to bring back to life, revive, **650**, 24, **354**, 35, **206**, 52; to cheer, **381**, 3.

Remercy: to thank, **308**, 16.

Remoud: removed, **394**, 43.

Renfierce: to make more fierce, **286**, 45.

Renforce, re'nforce: to make fresh efforts, **254**, 14; to compel again, **302**, 48.

Renne: to run, **20**, 118, **30**, 61, **36**, 3; (*pp.*) 42, 224.

Renowme: renown, **359**, 11.

Renowmed: renowned, e. g. **216**, 2, **207**, 3.

Rent: to rend, **706**, 88; to hurl, **566**, 34.

Renverse: to turn upside down, **170**, 41, **520**, 37.

Repent: repentance, **414**, 24.

Repriefe: reproof, reproach, **381**, 1, **342**, 5, **256**, 28, **203**, 29.

Reprieve: to reprove, **539**, 24.

Reprive: to reprieve, rescue, **521**, *arg.*, **525**, 35, **501**, 31, **238**, 55.

Reprize: to take again, **312**, 44, **442**, 8.

Repryve v. Reprive.

Requere: to request, **160**, 12; to demand, **182**, 27, **551**, 27.

Requite, requight (*pret.* **requit**): to salute in return, **97**, 587, **213**, 49, **440**, 47, **454**, 4, **538**, 20.

Resiant: resident, **493**, 28.

Respire: to take breath, enjoy a respite, **184**, 44, **200**, 8, **220**, 28, **269**, 44.

Restore: restitution, **360**, 18; refreshment, **715**, 34.

Retraite, retrate: retreat, **577**, 9, **489**, 57 — to retreat, **146**, 13, **194**, 12.

Retraitt, retrate: a portrait, **288**, 4; expression, **249**, 25.

Retyre: retirement, retreat, **638**, 27, **745**, 235.

Revengement: revenge, **445**, 35.

Reverse: to drive away, get rid of, **341**, 48, **451**, 31; to bring back, **206**, 48; to return, **350**, 1, **112**, 22.

Revoke: to call back, withdraw, **580**, 27, **182**, 28, **146**, 12, **406**, 21; to restrain, **243**, 28.

Rew: a row, order, **368**, 17, **370**, 35, **531**, 22, 73, 173.

Rew, rue: to afflict, **155**, 21; to pity, compassionate, **151**, 51, **156**, 26, **469**, 20, **562**, 4, **647**, 2; to grieve, **692**, 397.

Rewardfull: liberal in rewards, **689**, 187.

Richesse: wealth, **165**, 7, **177**, 47.

Rid v. Read.

Ridd: rode, **360**, 13.

Rifte: riven, **274**, 23, **223**, 54.

Rine: rind, bark, **13**, 111.

Riotise: riotous, extravagant living, **167**, 20, **330**, 33, **414**, 25.

Rocke: a distaff, **432**, 48.

Rontes: young bullocks, **11**, 5.

Rove: to shoot an arrow with an elevation, not point blank, **144**, 3, **332**, 50, **533**, 35, 37, 79.

Rowme: room, e. g. **407**, 27.

Rownd: to whisper to, **399**, 30.

Royne: to growl, **559**, 33.

Rubine: a ruby, **249**, 24, **320**, 54.

Rudded: made ruddy, **737**, 173.

Rue v. Rew.

Ruff: to ruffle, **338**, 27, **407**, 32, 76, 402.

Ruffin: disordered, **169**, 34.

Ruinate (*pp.* **ruinate**): to throw down, bring to ruin, **314**, 7, **385**, 28, **565**, 26, **728**, 56, **103**, 1040.

Rulesse: lawless, **85**, 431.

Rybaudrye: ribaldry, **45**, 76.

Sacrify: to sacrifice, **319**, 49.

Sad: heavy, **284**, 30, **236**, 45, **149**, 36; firm, steady, **160**, 10; sober, grave, sedate, **226**, 15, **224**, 5, **207**, 7, **148**, 29, **145**, 2, **738**, 234, 23, 5 — -ly: heavily, **352**, 16.

Safe: save, **381**, 60.

Saine v. Sayne.

Salewd v. Salued.

Saliaunce: onslaught, **234**, 29.

Salued: saluted, **283**, 23, **457**, 25.

Salvage: savage, wild, **159**, 5, **180**, 11, **286**, 42.

Salve: to heal, remedy, help, **299**, 21, **444**, 27, **534**, 43, **597**, 8, 6, 122; to bring about (by way of help), **419**, 11.

Sam: together, **25**, 168, **214**, 57. [v. **Ysame.**]

Saufgard: safeguard, **259**, 8.

Say: proof, quality, **654**, 47.

Sayne: say, **32**, 32, **394**, 48, **393**, 40, **676**, 55.

Scan: to climb, mount to, **661**, 8, **45**, 88.

Scarmoges: skirmishes, **268**, 34.

Scerne: to discern, **398**, 22.

Sclaunder: slander, **467**, *arg.*, **558**, 26.

Sclave: a slave, **275**, 33.

Sclender: slender, fine, **511**, 27, **332**, 47.

Scorse: exchange, **295**, 55 — to exchange, **390**, 16 — to chase (?), **635**, 3.

Scrike: to screech, **605**, 18.

Scrine: a chest for papers, **144**, 2, **295**, 56.

Scruze: to crush, squeeze, **312**, 46, **320**, 56, **363**, 33.

Scry: to descry, **581**, 38.

Scryne v. Scrine.

Sdaine, sdeigne: disdain, **535**, 51, **718**, 5 — to disdain, **140**, *Essex*, **331**, 40, **333**, 55, **534**, 44.

Sdeignfull: disdainful, **527**, 43, **374**, 10 — -ly: disdainfully, **105**, 1234.

Sease v. Seize.

See: a seat (of dignity, or authority), **102**, **980**, **366**, 2, **486**, 30, **676**, 59.

Seeld: seldom, **713**, 11 — rare, **712**, 171.

Seely v. Silly.

Seemelesse: unseemly, **511**, 25.

Seemlyhed: comeliness, **468**, 14.

Seen: skilled, experienced, **6**, 131, **54**, 82, **430**, 35, **516**, 5.

Seew v. Sew.

Seize: to fasten, fix, **161**, 19, **194**, 15, **519**, 29, **526**, 40; to fix itself (in), **221**, 38.

Selcouth: strange, **468**, 14.

Sell: a saddle, **240**, 11, **349**, 60.

Selve: self, **732**, 75.

Semblably: in like manner, **141**, *Howard*.

Semblant: appearance, aspect, mien, **154**, 12, **339**, 38, **288**, 2, **293**, 39, **486**, 31, **644**, 23, **80**, 93; a phantasm, **319**, 49, **357**, 54.

Sens: since, **450**, 23.

Sensefull: reasonable, **608**, 37, **638**, 26.

Sew: to follow, pursue, **357**, 50, **393**, 37, **241**, 17, **272**, 9, **479**, 26, **641**, 2; **s. to**, to entreat, woo, **501**, 29, **364**, 47, **533**, 41.

Shamefast: modest, bashful, **531**, 25, **156**, 27, **208**, 15 — -nesse: modesty, **518**, 23.

Shard: a boundary, **269**, 38.

Sheare v. Sheere.

Sheave: a sheaf, **54**, 123.

Sheene: bright, fair, **244**, 40, **48**, 38, **297**, 8, **232**, 10.

Sheere: pure, clear, **672**, 25, **456**, 20, **340**, 44, **404**, 7.

Shend (*pret. pp.* **shent**): to put to shame, disgrace, **33**, 172, **761**, 121, **232**, 11, **234**, 27, **268**, 35, **388**, 1; to reproach, revile, **152**, 53, **259**, 5.

Shene v. Sheene.

Shere v. Sheere.

Shidder v. Hidder.

Shine: shining, **434**, 3.

Shit: shut, **695**, 709.

Shoke: shook, **218**, 15.

Shope: shaped, **533**, 39.

Short: to shorten, **729**, 60.

Shriech: a screech, **605**, 18.

Shriech-owle, shriek-o: the screech-owl, **739**, 345, **61**, 130, **74**, 283.

Shright: a shriek, **278**, 57, **603**, 2 — shrieked, **385**, 32.

Sib: a kinsman, or of kin (to), **626**, 41, **345**, 26, 26, 269.

Sich: such, **377**, 29, **40**, 79, **41**, 178.

Sicker, syker: assured, **95**, 430 — surely, **12**, 55, 32, **33**, **33**, 93 — -nesse: safety, **376**, 25; self-reliance, **411**, 55.

Side: loose, trailing, **127**, 9, **766**, 7.

Siege: a seat, **244**, 39.

Sield: hung (with), **531**, 21.

Sient: a scion, **504**, 1.

Sight: sighed, **595**, 42, **700**, 53.

Sike: such, **14**, 211, **24**, 82, **44**, 35.

Silly, seely: simple, harmless, helpless, ' poor,' **149**, 30, **155**, 21, **180**, 10, **183**, 35, **246**, 6, **374**, 8, **32**, 30, 34, 190, **729**, 63.

Simplesse: simplicity, foolishness, **33**, 172.

Sin: since, **653**, 44.

Singulf: a sob, **405**, 12, **537**, 13, **73**, 232, **689**, 168.

Sit, sit with: (*impers.*) to befit, to be incumbent on, 48, 26, **149**, 30, **42**, 232, **769**, 40.

Site, sited: placed, situated, **768**, 46, **370**, 31.

Sith: since the time when, **326**, 7, **344**, 16; since, because, for, **177**, 43, **337**, 17.

Sithe, sith: time, times, **687**, 23, **399**, 33, **10**, 49.

Sithence, sithens: since that time, 16, 46, **32**, 69, **335**, 6, **339**, 39; afterwards, **522**, 13 — since, because, **171**, 51, **200**, 8.

Sixt: sixth, **212**, 42, **411**, 2.

Skill: to understand, **95**, 381; s. of, to be versed in, to understand, **733**, 84, **608**, 38, **332**, 50; (*impers.*) to matter, **523**, 14 — power of discernment, understanding, knowledge, **238**, 54, **347**, 45, **353**, 25, **372**, 46, **388**, 3, **432**, 44, **646**, 37, **30**, 65.

Skippet: a skiff, **315**, 14.

Slake: to slacken, **172**, 10, **343**, 10, **548**, 5.

Slight: craft, cunning, **598**, 16, **610**, 13; a device, **189**, 30.

Slipper: slippery, **50**, 153.

Slombred: stunned, insensible, **187**, 15, **281**, 11.

Slombry: drowsy, **369**, 26.

Slug: to dawdle, vegetate, **375**, 12, **233**, 23.

Smirke: smart, **12**, 72.

Smit: smote, **155**, 18, **568**, 7.

Smot: smote, smitten, **195**, 24, **219**, 25, **340**, 46.

Smouldring, smouldry: suffocating, **187**, 13, **259**, 3, **406**, 21.

Snar: to snarl, **658**, 27.

Snebbe, snib: to chide, snub, **13**, 126, **95**, 372.

Snubbe: a snag, **193**, 7.

Soft: to soften, **723**, 32.

Softly: easy, quiet, **621**, 6.

Soile v. Soyle.

Sold: pay, **289**, 6.

Solein, sollein: sullen, gloomy, 48, 17, **25**, 213.

Solemnize: solemnization, **207**, 4.

Soly: solely, singly, **696**, 801, **478**, 18.

Somd: fledged, **7**, 217.

Somedele: somewhat, **23**, 56.

Soote: sweetly, **20**, 111, **45**, 90.

Soothlich, soothly: truly, in truth, **336**, 14, **591**, 13, **613**, 37.

Soothsay: a prediction, **295**, 51, **430**, 35, **491**, 13; an omen, **388**, 50.

Sort: a company, band, swarm, etc., **702**, 139, **635**, 5, **487**, 43, **331**, 40, **526**, 36 — to consort (with), **713**, 20.

Souce v. Souse.

Sound: a swoon, **588**, 34, **444**, 24, **358**, *arg.* [Cf. **Swound.**]

Souse: to swoop, **172**, 8; to fall violently, **352**, 16; to deal sweeping blows, **437**, 25; to strike violently, **445**, 30; to cast to ground, **461**, 9 — the swoop of a bird of prey, **311**, 36, **436**, 19; sweeping blows, **524**, 24.

Southsaye v. Soothsay.

Sovenaunce: remembrance, **264**, 8, **287**, 51, 24, 82, **48**, 5.

Sowce v. Souse.

Sownd v. Sound.

Sowne: a sound, **139**, *R. S.*, **150**, 41, **270**, 47, **354**, 30.

Sowse v. Souse.

Soyle: the slough in which a wild boar has wallowed, or the marshy ground or water to which a hunted boar or deer takes for refuge, **753**, 218, **126**, 6, **768**, 44, **489**, 55; the prey, **435**, 16.

Space: to roam, **432**, 44, **474**, 54, **505**, 11, **668**, 55.

Spalles: shoulders, **267**, 29.

Spangs: spangles, **496**, 45.

Sparke: to sparkle, **733**, 81.

Sparre: a bar or bolt, **567**, 4 — to bar, bolt, **566**, 37, 25, 224.

Spend (*pp.*): spent, **24**, 71.

Sperre v. Sparre.

Sperse: to scatter, diffuse, **520**, 37, **170**, 48, **150**, 39.

Spight: injury, shame, **335**, 8; grudging, stinting, **332**, 51 — to begrudge, envy, **25**, 198, **77**, **523**, 166, 14, **359**, 7, **532**, 29, **536**, 6, **665**, 32.

Spill: to destroy, **380**, 54, **164**, 43 ; to mar, ruin, 293, 37, **384**, 26, **536**, 1, **12**, 52, **32**, 68; to perish, **37**, 60.

Spire: to shoot or put forth, **365**, 52, **59**, *Letter*.

Sprad: spread, **558**. 25.

Sprent: sprinkled, **319**, 45, **428**, 18, **119**, 239.

Spright: breath, spirits, **599**, 26, **610**, 17, **263**, 36, **174**, 19; the mind, **253**, 7, **665**, 35.

Springal: a youth, **562**, 6.

Spyal: a spy, **231**, 4.

Spyre v. Spire.

Stadle: a support, staff, **180**, 14.

Stanck: weary, **40**, 47.

Stead, sted, steed: place, a place, **138**, *Vision*, 205, 41, **242**, 21, **258**, 42; a space of time, **626**, 40; a steading, farm (?), **23**, 43; an abode, **41**, 120; a situation, condition, plight, **101**, 861, **612**, 29, **579**, 23, **444**, 22, **336**, 16.

Steale: a handle, **578**, 14.

Steane: a large jar, **674**, 42.

Sted, steed, v. Stead.

Steem: to esteem, **448**, 3, **646**, 35.

Stent: to stint, stop, **253**, 12.

Sterve: to die, perish, **268**, 34, **418**, 4; to starve, **745**, 200.

Steven: a sound, **42**, 224.

Stie v. Sty.

Still: to fall in drops, **338**, 29, **465**, 35.

Stire: to steer, govern, **231**, 7 — to move, stir, incite, **379**, 45, **292**, 30, **258**, 2.

Stomachous: haughty or resentful, **283**, 23.

Stomacke: arrogance, **104**, 1103, **276**, 41.

Stonied: confounded, dismayed, **571**, 30.

Stonishment: insensibility, swoon, **352**, 19.

Stonisht: dismayed, **417**, 44.

Stoond, stound: stunned, **186**, 12, **571**, 29.

Stound, stownd: [apparently several distinct words.] (1) the state of being stunned, **600**, 30; a stunning effect, **459**, 37; a stunning blow, **444**, 24; a disconcerting sight, **374**, 7; a loud sound, **343**, 9, **334**, 63. (2) a throe, pang, pain, **538**, 17, **75**, 373, **26**, 257. (3) a moment, a time, **40**, 56, **90**, 26, **197**, 38, **221**, 36; a crisis, peril, calamity, harm, **193**, 12, **195**, 25, **309**, 25, **368**, 38, **518**, 22; a period of effort, **55**, 140.

Stoup: to swoop down, **106**, 1262, **218**, 18, **378**, 39, **399**, 30 — a swoop, **530**, 15.

Stowre, stoure: [the most flexible of Spenser's words: most examples can be interpreted vari-

ously.] turmoil, disturbance, strife, **747**, 73, **193**, 5, **518**, 21, **142**, *Raleigh*, **266**, 16; a combat, encounter, an assault, onset, force or violence (in attack), **655**, 3, **191**, 48, **186**, 12, **285**, 35, **286**, 43, 259, 10, **603**, 3, **621**, 8; distress, an affliction, a misfortune, **561**, 45, **153**, 7, **162**, 30, **170**, 46, **178**, 51; a paroxysm, **348**, 50; a storm, the blast or violence of a storm, **390**, 13, **287**, 48, **10**, 27; a moment, a crisis, **10**, 51, **250**, 34.

Straint: gripe, **509**, 14.

Strake: a streak, **254**, 15. [v. also **Stroke**.]

Strene: strain, race, **559**, 32, **615**, 9.

Strifull v. Stryfull.

Stroke, strooke, strake (*pret.*): struck, **155**, 19, **172**, 11, **173**, 12, **250**, 32, **253**, 7 ; **stroken** (*pp.*), **590**, 7.

Strond: a stream, **266**, 19.

Strooke v. Stroke.

Stryfull: full of strife, contentious, **241**, 13, **336**, 12, **450**, 24, **103**, 1021.

Sty: to mount, ascend, soar, **140**, *Essex*, **219**, 25, **277**, 46, **116**, 42; to float in the air, **480**, 33.

Submisse: humble, **489**, 51.

Subverse: to subvert, destroy, **105**, 1234, **416**, 42.

Suffisaunce: contentment, **119**, 207.

Suit: following, pursuit, **548**, 3, **215**, 60, **357**, 52, **404**, 5.

Surbate (*pp.* **surbet**): to bruise or chafe (the feet), **354**, 34, **242**, 22.

Surcease: to desist, **105**, 1221, **428**, 19; to come to an end, **616**, 14, **20**, 125; to desist from, 328, 23, **354**, 31, **357**, 52; to put an end to, **513**, 37, **720**, 11.

Surquedry: presumption, arrogance, **512**, 30, **327**, 13, **317**, 31, **318**, 39.

Survew: to view from above, **294**, 45, **82**, 221; to look over, **13**, 145.

Suspect: suspicion, **180**, 13, **412**, 14, **546**, 38.

Suspence: suspended, **458**, 34.

Swarve: to swerve, **208**, 14, **251**, 42.

Swat (*pret.*): sweat, **358**, 3, **514**, 46.

Swelt: fainted, died, **657**, 21, **461**, 9; burned, **186**, 6, **407**, 27.

Swerd, sweard: a sword, **217**, 9, **437**, 31.

Swinck, swinke: to toil, **272**, 8, **607**, 32, **41**, 132 — toil, **23**, 36, **32**, 34.

Swinge: to singe, **220**, 26.

Swinke v. Swinck.

Swound, swowne, swone: a swoon, **609**, 6, 618, 30, **424**, 43, **150**, 41, **206**, 52. [Cf. **Sound**.]

Sybbe v. Sib.

Syker v. Sicker.

Syrlye: 'stately and prowde' (E. K.), **34**, 203.

Sythe v. Sithe.

Tabrere: a tabor-player, **23**, 22.

Talants: talons, **199**, 48, **222**, 41.

Tapet: a piece of tapestry, **119**, 276, **407**, 29.

Tarras: terraces, **557**, 21.

Teade: a torch, **229**, 37, **120**, 293, **735**, 27.

Teene: grief, woe, 48, 41, **204**, 34, **232**, 15, **233**, 21, 364, 40; harm, **226**, 18, **562**, 7.]v. **Tine**.]

Teld: told, **589**, 44, **664**, 27.

Tene v. Teene.

Thee: to prosper, **235**, 33, **308**, 17.

Then: than, e. g. **23**, 64, **695**, 674, 156, 26.

Thetch: to thatch, **93**, 264.
Thether: thither, e. g. **165**, 2, **469**, 21.
Thewed: mannered, conditioned (well or ill), **267**, 26, **12**, 96, **748**, 137.
Thewes: mental and moral qualities, manners, behavior, **594**, 31, **199**, 3, **207**, 4, **478**, 14.
Thick: a thicket, **236**, 39, **248**, 21.
Thilke: this same, that same, this, that, **10**, 61, **16**, 13, **16**, 49, **23**, 1.
Tho, thoe: then, e. g. **147**, 18, **151**, 50, **24**, 109 — those, **40**, 32.
Thorough: through, e. g. **149**, 32, **168**, 28.
Threasury: treasure, **280**, 4.
Threttie: thirty, **12**, 17.
Thrid: a thread, **432**, 48.
Thrill: to pierce, **209**, 19, **183**, 37, **464**, 31.
Thrillant, thrilling: piercing, keen, **219**, 20, **164**, 42, **258**, 46.
Thrist: thirst, **266**, 17 — to thirst, **183**, 38. [v. Thrust.]
Thristy: thirsty, **18**, 8, **212**, 38.
Thrive: thriven, **42**, 226.
Throughly: thoroughly, **177**, 45, **206**, 50; through, **505**, 10.
Throw: to strike, **390**, 16 — a stroke, a thrust, **259**, 9, **286**, 41, **361**, 21, **392**, 29, **72**, 134 — a while, **357**, 53.
Thrust: thirst, **379**, 50 — to thirst, **243**, 29. [v. Thrist.]
Tickle: unstable, uncertain, **353**, 28, **597**, 5, **671**, 22, **129**, 7.
Tide: a time, season, **156**, 29, **369**, 21, **392**, 32, **460**, 47, **46**, 117.
Tight: tied, **524**, 22, **659**, 34.
Tine: grief, **201**, 15, **438**, 37, **70**, 3; wrath, malice, **502**, 34, **403**, 1; harm, **505**, 13 [v. Teene] — to kindle, **84**, 394, **281**, 11, **349**, 57, **375**, 15; to inflame, **309**, 21.
Tire: a train or series, **169**, 35.
To-: a prefix to verbs which intensifies their meaning. v. To-brusd, etc.
To-brusd: battered exceedingly, **553**, 44.
Tofore: formerly, **441**, 7, **672**, 30.
Toot: to look about, **16**, 66.
To-perishe: to perish utterly, **64**, 361.
Toren: torn, **705**, 26.
To-rent: tattered, torn to pieces, **461**, 8, **548**, 4, **553**, 43.
Tort: wrong (inflicted), **224**, 4, **336**, 12, **471**, 31, **62**, 167.
Tortious: unjust, wrongfully injurious, **477**, 12, **241**, 18.
To-torne: tattered, **556**, 10.
Totty: unsteady, **12**, 55, **673**, 39.
Tour: a tower, **393**, 35 — to tower, **317**, 30.
Touze: to harass, worry, **310**, 33.
Toward: approaching, imminent, **682**, 280, **255**, 22, **326**, 9; promising, **116**, 26.
To-worne: worn out, **556**, 10.
Trace: to tread, **143**, *Walsingham ;* to walk, go, **196**, 31, **281**, 10, **471**, 34, **600**, 29; to move about, **456**, 18; to step (in dance), **640**, 42; (of a road) to ' go,' **273**, 21; to rush, **420**, 13 — a step, pace, **29**, 27.
Tract: to trace, track, **232**, 12, **269**, 39, **620**, 3, **622**, 17 — a track, trace, **83**, 279, 95, 406, 657,

22, **606**, 24, **159**, 10; the course, lapse (of time), **636**, 14, **522**, 8.
Trade: tread, trail, **74**, 275, **269**, 39; conduct, a practice, dealings, **334**, 67, **646**, 39, **29**, 45, **407**, 32; sojourn, abode, **317**, 30 — to dwell, **491**, 9.
Traine: the tail, **26**, 281, **147**, 18, **221**, 37; proceedings, **510**, 15; a draw-net, **147**, 18; guile, an artifice, **343**, 11, **203**, 31, **184**, 41, **179**, 3, **471**, 31, **688**, 118.
Transfard: transformed, **407**, 31.
Transmew: to transform, change, **189**, 35, **330**, 38, **250**, 37.
Transmove: to transform, **409**, 43.
Trasforme: to transform, **262**, 27.
Travel: travail, labor, **94**, 310, **312**, 44.
Traveled, traveiled: tormented, harassed, **9**, *arg.*, **6**, 183.
Trayne v. Traine.
Treachetour: a traitor, **303**, 51, **628**, 7.
Treachour: a traitor, **170**, 41, **203**, 32.
Treague: a truce, **243**, 33.
Trenchand: cutting, keen, **219**, 24.
Trode, troad: tread, footing, **394**, 49, **641**, 5, **32**, 14; a path, **40**, 92, 95, 406.
Truncked: truncated, **193**, 10, **259**, 4.
Trye: tried, proved, **511**, 26.
Turribant: a turban, **493**, 28.
Tway: two, **33**, 152, **23**, 18, **525**, 35, **404**, 11.
Twayne: atwain, asunder, **595**, 38.
Twight: to twit, upbraid, **537**, 12.
Twyfold: twofold, **175**, 28.
Tyne: to perish, **495**, 36. [v. also Tine.]
Tyran: a tyrant, **208**, 9, **45**, 98.
Tyrannesse: a female tyrant, **177**, 46.
Tyranning: tyrannizing, **460**, 1.
Tyreling: tired, jaded or mean, meagre (?), **327**, 17, **626**, 40.

Uncouth: unknown, **5**, 1, **40**, 60; unusual, strange, **147**, 15, **179**, 9.
Uncrudded: uncurdled, **737**, 175.
Underfong: to get, **48**, 22; to entrap, beguile, **30**, 103, **509**, 7.
Underkeep: to keep under, **71**, 77, **377**, 33.
Underlay: to surpass, **80**, 99.
Underminde: to undermine, **540**, 32, **32**, 122.
Undersaye: to assert in contradiction, **40**, 91.
Undersong: a burden, refrain, **38**, 128, **681**, 245, **689**, 169, **761**, 110.
Undight: to doff, **547**, 41, **390**, 19, **159**, 4 — (*pp.*) undressed, **315**, 15.
Uneath, uneth, uneathes, unnethes: difficult, **360**, 17, **211**, 31 — with difficulty, scarcely, **234**, 27, **237**, 49, **263**, 1, 9, 6, **40**, 48; almost (?), **216**, 4; in distress, **204**, 38.
Unheedily: by heedlessness, **483**, 13.
Unhele, unheale: to uncover, **321**, 64, **449**, 10.
Unkend, unkent: unknown, **491**, 13, 4, *To His Booke.*
Unlich: unlike, **175**, 28.
Unnethes v. Uneath.
Unperfite: imperfect, **676**, *Title.*
Unreave: to unravel, **722**, 23.
Unred: untold of, **497**, 2.
Unruliment: unruliness, **479**, 23.
Unsoote: unsweet, **54**, 118.
Unthriftyhead: unthriftiness, **414**, 25.

Until: unto, **50**, 185, **216**, 4.

Unware: unaware, **254**, 17 — -ly: unawares, **434**, 8.

Unwares: unawares, **182**, 27, **231**, 4, **628**, 8; unknown (to), **444**, 27; unsuspiciously, **26**. 275.

Unweeting: ignorant, unconscious, **185**, 6, **215**, 65, **254**, 17 — by accident, **208**, 9; unknown (to), **349**, 57, **463**, 17; unawares, **694**, 598, **98**, 606 — -ly: by accident, **549**, 15.

Unweldy: unwieldy, **290**, 13.

Unwist: unknown, **338**, 26 — without knowing how, **506**, 22.

Upbrast: burst open, **653**, 43.

Upbray: to chide, **424**, 42; to disgrace, **258**, 45 — a rebuke, an invective, **372**, 50.

Upcheare: to comfort, **589**, 44.

Uphild: upheld, **650**, 21.

Uphoord: to heap up, **78**, 553.

Uplean: to lean (on), **81**, 154.

Upryst: uprisen, **16**, 18.

Upstay: to support, **413**, 21.

Usaunce: use, **271**, 7.

Vade v. Fade.

Vail: to lower, **391**, 20.

Vainesse: vanity, **125**, 2.

Valiance: worth, 64, 324; valor, **247**, 14.

Vantage: to profit, avail, **171**, 49.

Vaunce: to advance, **443**, 17.

Vaute, vawte: a vault, **292**, 29, **85**, **444** — to vault, 99, 693.

Vellet: velvet, **25**, 185.

Vengeable: deserving, revenge, or revengeful, **256**, 30, **258**, 46.

Vengement: avengement, **598**, 18.

Venger: an avenger, **161**, 20.

Ventre: to venture, 464, 31.

Ventrous: venturous, **429**, 27, **454**, 4.

Verdit: a verdict, **672**, 27.

Vermeill, vermell, vermill, vermily: vermilion, **248**, 22, **299**, 24, **382**, 6, **738**, 227.

Vestiment: a garment, clothing, **415**, 29, **538**, 19.

Vild: vile, **158**, arg., **205**, 46, **569**, 18; low, vulgar, **375**, 15; lowly, **375**, 17 — vilely, **583**, arg. — -ly: vilely, 164, 43.

Visnomy v. Physnomy.

Vylde v. Vild.

Wae: woe, **40**, 25.

Wagmoire: a quagmire, **41**, 130.

Waide v. Way.

Waift: a waif, **501**, 31.

Wailefull: lamenting, mournful, lamentable, **12**, 82, **38**, 162, **355**, 38.

Waine: to draw, sway (?), **662**, 10. [v. also **Wayne**.]

Wake: awake, **30**, 87.

Wan: won, **241**, 17, **247**, 16.

War v. Warre.

Ware: wary, cautious, **185**, 1, **198**, 44.

Warelesse: heedless, **484**, 20, **530**, 17; unaware, **426**, 3; unfelt, unconscious, **506**, 22.

Warely: warily, **207**, 5.

War-hable: fit for war, **304**, 62.

Wariment: wariness, **435**, 17.

Warke, werk: work, **24** 145. **235**. 32, **95**, 416.

Warray, warrey: to harry with war, wage war on, **726**, 44, **177**, 48, **303**, 50; to wage war, **365**, 48.

Warre: worse, **471**, 31, **41**, 108 — a ware, **36**, 26.

Wast: waste, **743**, 70; waist, **562**, 8.

Wastefull, wastfull: devastating, **9**, 2; uninhabited, desolate, **38**, 151, **149**, 32, **271**, 2.

Wastnes: desolation, waste places, **159**, 3.

Watchet: pale blue, **355**, 40, **493**, 27, **710**, 3.

Wawes: waves, **313**, 4.

Way: to weigh, judge, value, **419**, 7, **668**, 55, **29**, 47; to experience (?), **481**, 38.

Waylefull v. Wailefull.

Wayment: to lament, wail, **75**, 355, **232**, 16 — lamentation, 354, 35, **65**, 390.

Wayne: a chariot, **165**, 9, **176**, 41, **358**, 60.

Weanell: a weanling, **42**, 198.

Wearish: wizened, **452**, 34.

Weave (pret. pp. **weft**): to toss, waft, **611**, 23; to be wafted, float, **522**, 10, **266**, 18.

Weeldlesse: unwieldy, **436**, 19.

Weet, weeten: to know, learn, understand, **50**, 183, **159**, 6, **160**, 11, **183**, 34, **335**, 6, **359**, 7; to know how, be able, **528**, 51 — **to w.**, to wit, that is, to be specific, etc., **305**, 71, **561**, 1, **452**, 34, **506**, 3. [v. **Wist, Wot**.] — to wet, 480, 33.

Weeting: knowledge, **567**, 39.

Weetingly: deliberately, **597**, 11.

Weetlesse: ignorant, **263**, 36; unperceived, 338, 26; senseless, **32**, 35 — ignorantly, **629**, 17; at random, **393**, 41.

Weft: a waif, **400**, 36, **426**, 4 — (pp.): waived; shunned, **355**, 36. [v. also **Weave**.]

Weld: to govern, manage, 105, 1232, **417**, 1, **556**, 11; to move, swing, wave, **423**, 37, **628**, 11. 672, 31, **220**, 28, **59**, 14; to wear, bear, **44**, 40, **25**, 206.

Welke: to fade, grow dim, **148**, 23; to make dim, 48, 13, **10**, 73.

Weren, werne: were, **254**, 14, **431**, 41.

Wex: wax, **382**, 6 — to wax, grow, become, **299**, 20, **236**, 42, **168**, 30; to make greater, **433**, 52 — **wexen:** waxen, **53**, 68; grown, become, **66**, 472. [v. **Woxe**.]

Whally: discolored (as in wall-eyes), **167**, 24.

Wheare v. Where.

When as: when, **156**, 32, **204**, 37, **206**, 51, **254**, 16.

Whenceforth: forth from which place, **120**, 316.

When so: whenever, when, **342**, 7.

Where, wheare: a place, spot, part, **352**, 19, **396**, 9, **669**, 5, **23**, 9.

Whereas: where, e. g. **682**, 283, **160**, 12, **175**, 29.

Where so: wheresoever, **233**, 18, **442**, 13.

Whether: whither, **690**, 251, **53**, 63, **458**, 35.

Whilere v. Whyleare.

Whiles: while, **200**, 9, **206**, 49, **256**, 34 — **the whiles:** while, **200**, 8; meanwhile, **252**, 2, 293, 40, **328**, 19, **411**, 6; the w. . . . the w., while . . . at the same time, **279**, 62.

Whist: silenced, **676**, 59.

Whither: whether, 44, 45; which one, **102**, 997.

Whott: hot, e. g. **210**, 26.

Whyleare, whilere: some time ago or before, lately, **367**, 13, **369**, 26, **280**, 3, **240**, 11, **203**, 28.
Whyles v. Whiles.
Widder: wider, **42**, 210.
Widowhead: widowhood, **74**, 240.
Wight: active, nimble, **17**, 91 — **-ly:** quickly, **39**, 5. [v. also **Wite.**]
Wimble: nimble, **17**, 91.
Wisard: a wise man, a sage, **295**, 53, **497**, 2, **676**, 55.
Wist (*pret.* of **Weet**): knew, **175**, 27, **253**, 6; supposed, **592**, 20.
Wite, witen, wight: to blame, chide, **315**, 16, **357**, 52, **698**, **916**, 25, 159 — censure, blame, **30**, 100, **598**, 16.
Witelesse: blameless, **38**, 136.
Withhault: withheld, **307**, 9.
Withouten: without, **182**, 27, **511**, 25.
Wivehood: wifehood, **448**, 3.
Wively: wifely, **448**, 3.
Wizard v. Wisard.
Woe: sorrowful, **287**, 53, **423**, 38.
Womanhed: womanhood, **369**, 28.
Won v. Wonne.
Wonderous: wondrous, **117**, 74.
Wonne, wone, woon: a dwelling, **273**, 20, **470**, 22 — to dwell, abide, **690**, 307, **696**, 774, **79**, 18, **277**, 49, **549**, 16, **394**, 48 — to be wont, **391**, 21, **13**, 119.
Wont: was wont, wert wont, **149**, 34, **194**, 18, **44**, 4; are wont, **11**, 7, **157**, 40; **wonts**, is wont, **251**, 41, **245**, 42 — wonted, customary, **24**, 80, **515**, 1; made use of, **527**, 44.
Wontlesse: unwonted, **746**, 2.
Wood: mad, frantic, **169**, 34, **174**, 20, **253**, 11, **651**, 25 — **-nes:** madness, **407**, 27.
Woon: won, **714**, 41. [v. also **Wonne.**]
Wot, wote (*pres.* of **Weet**)**:** know, **146**, 13, **149**, 32, **203**, 31, **247**, 16, **389**, 7.
Wowe: to woo, **648**, 4, **701**, 67.
Woxe: waxed, grew, became, **104**, 1103, **281**, 9; woxen, grown, become, **141**, *Howard*, **169**, 34. [v. **Wex.**]
Wrack: violence, **456**, 21, **592**, 21, **11**, 10, **725**, 38 — to wreck, **726**, 46.
Wrackfull: destructive, **638**, 27.
Wrast: to wrest, **579**, 21.
Wrate: wrote, **415**, 31.
Wrath: wroth, **473**, 43.
Wrawl: to waul (as a cat), **658**, 27.
Wreake: malicious injury, an act of malice, **379**, 48, **198**, 43, **226**, 16, **65**, 397; wreck, a wreck, **108**, 3, **72**, 124.
Wreakfull: avenging, **505**, 8.
Wrecke: to wreak, **524**, 24.
Wrest: the wrist, **242**, 21, **497**, 51.
Wrigle: wriggling, ' wiggling,' **11**, 7.
Wrizled: wrinkled, **199**, 47.
Wroke, wroken: wreaked, **428**, 21, **464**, 26, **514**, 47, **591**, 13.
Wroth: wrath, **260**, 13.

Wull: will, **738**, 252.
Wyte v. Wite.

Y-: a common prefix to the *pp.* of verbs, sometimes to the *pret.* (as **yglaunst**, **268**, 31) and to the *infin.* (as **yshend**, **38**, 139).
Yate: a gate, **25**, 224.
Ybet: beaten, **442**, 9.
Yblent: blinded, obscured, **20**, 155, **153**, 5, **271**, 1. [v. **Blend**].
Ybore: born, **353**, 21.
Ycled: clad, **169**, 38.
Ycleepe: to call, name, **687**, 65; **ycleped**, called, **359**, 8. [v. **Cleeped.**]
Ycond: learned, **26**, 262. [v. **Con.**]
Ydlesse: idleness, **594**, 31.
Ydrad: dreaded, **145**, 2; afraid, **701**, 87.
Ydred: afraid, **318**, 38, **411**, 2.
Yearne: to earn, **588**, 40, **622**, 15.
Yede, yeed (*pret.* **yode, yod**): to go, **214**, 53, **216**, 5, **252**, 2, **422**, 28, **33**, 109, **709**, 88.
Yeld: to yield, **127**, 11.
Yeven: given, **20**, 114.
Yfere: in company, together, **19**, 68, **199**, 1; **235**, 35, **327**, 12.
Yfostered: brought up, **372**, 51.
Ygoe: gone, **23**, 67 — ago, e. g. **41**, 171, **359**, 9.
Ygone: ago, **495**, 39, **669**, 2.
Yirk: to lash, **626**, 44.
Yit: yet, e: g. **295**, 50.
Ylike: alike, **53**, 36, **16**, 39, **168**, 27.
Ylke: the same, **38**, 142.
Ymolt: melted, **406**, 25.
Ymp v. Impe.
Ynne v. In.
Yod, yode v. Yede.
Yold: yielded, **406**, 25, **405**, 17, **672**, 30.
Yond: mad, furious, outrageous, **285**, 40, **376**, 26.
Yongth, youngth: youth, **116**, 34, **12**, 87, **48**, 20.
Yougthly, youngthly, youthly: of youth; youthful, **53**, 75, **122**, 431, **200**, 9 — youthfully, **221**, 34.
Ypaid: satisfied, pleased (well or ill), **398**, 25. [v. **Apay.**]
Ypent: pent up, **9**, 4.
Ypight: placed, situated, **203**, 33. [v. **Pight.**]
Yplight: plighted, **245**, 1, **277**, 50.
Yrent (*pret.*): rent, **354**, 30.
Ysame: together, **673**, 32. [v. **Sam.**]
Yshend: to disgrace, **38**, 139. [v. **Shend.**]
Yshrilled (*pret.*): sounded shrilly, **687**, 62.
Ytake: taken, **30**, 84.
Ythundered: smitten with the thunderbolt, **70**, 8.
Ytost: harassed, **29**, 12.
Ywis: surely, certainly, etc., **233**, 19, **355**, 37, **380**, 53.
Ywrake, ywroke, ywroken: wreaked, **469**, 14, **457**, 23, **698**, 921.

INDEX OF FIRST LINES

INDEX OF TITLES